# Cities of the United States

**SIXTH EDITION**

# Cities of the United States

**SIXTH EDITION**

VOLUME 3

**THE MIDWEST**

GALE
CENGAGE Learning™

Detroit • New York • San Francisco • New Haven, Conn • Waterville, Maine • London

**Cities of the United States, 6th edition**

Product Management: Leigh Ann Cusack

Project Editor: Kristy A. Harper

Imaging and Multimedia: Lezlie Light

Rights and Acquisitions: Jermaine Bobbitt, Dean Dauphinais

Product Design: Pamela A. E. Galbreath

Composition and Electronic Prepress: Evi Seoud

Manufacturing: Rita Wimberley

*Gale*
27500 Drake Rd.
Farmington Hills, MI 48331-3535

ISBN-13: 978-0-7876-9629-0 (4-vol. set)   ISBN-10: 0-7876-9629-3 (4-vol. set)
ISBN-13: 978-0-7876-9630-6 (vol. 1)   ISBN-10: 0-7876-9630-7 (vol. 1)
ISBN-13: 978-0-7876-9631-3 (vol. 2)   ISBN-10: 0-7876-9631-5 (vol. 2)
ISBN-13: 978-0-7876-9632-0 (vol. 3)   ISBN-10: 0-7876-9632-3 (vol. 3)
ISBN-13: 978-0-7876-9633-7 (vol. 4)   ISBN-10: 0-7876-9633-1 (vol. 4)

ISSN 0899-6075

This title is also available as an e-book.
ISBN-13: 978-1-4144-3759-0    ISBN-10: 1-4144-3759-5
Contact your Gale sales representative for ordering information.

Printed in the United States of America
1 2 3 4 5 6 7 12 11 10 09 08

# Contents

## VOLUME 2—THE WEST

# VOLUME 3—THE MIDWEST

# VOLUME 4—THE NORTHEAST

# Introduction

*Cities of the United States (CUS)* provides a one-stop source for all the vital information you need on 199 of America's top cities—those fastest-growing, as well as those with a particular historical, political, industrial, and/or commercial significance. Spanning the entire country, from Anaheim to Virginia Beach, each geographically-arranged volume of *CUS* brings together a wide range of comprehensive data. The volumes include: *The South; The West; The Midwest;* and *The Northeast.*

Within each volume, the city-specific profiles organize pertinent facts, data, and figures related to demographic, economic, cultural, geographic, social, and recreational conditions. Assembling a myriad of sources, *CUS* offers researchers, travelers, students, and media professionals a convenient resource for discovering each city's past, present, and future.

For this completely updated sixth edition, ten new cities have been added, providing even greater access to the country's growing urban centers. The new city profiles include:

- Aberdeen, SD
- Aurora, CO
- Cambridge, MA
- Chesapeake, VA
- Huntsville, AL
- Missoula, MT
- Shreveport, LA
- Sioux City, IA
- Vancouver, WA
- Winston-Salem, NC

# Key Features Unlock Vital Information

*Cities of the United States* offers a range of key features, allowing easy access to targeted information. Features include:

- Section headings—Comprehensive categories, which include **History, Geography and Climate, Population Profile, Municipal Government, Economy, Education, Research, Health Care, Recreation, Convention Facilities, Transportation,** and **Communications** (including city web sites), make it easy for you to locate answers to your specific questions.

- Combined facts and analysis—Fact-packed charts and detailed descriptions bring you the statistics and the rest of the story.

- "In Brief" fact sheets—One-page "at a glance" overviews provide the essential facts for each state and each city profiled.

- Economic information—Detailed updates about such topics as incentive programs, development projects, and largest employers help you rate the business climate using criteria that matter to you.

- Directory information—Contact information at the end of many entry sections provides addresses, phone numbers, and email addresses for organizations, agencies, and institutions you may need to contact.

- Selected bibliography listings—Historical accounts, biographical works, and other print resources suggest titles to read if you wish to learn more about a particular city.

- Web sites for vital city resources—Access points to URLs for information-rich sources, such as city government, visitors and convention bureaus, economic development agencies, libraries, schools, and newspapers provide researchers an opportunity to explore cities in more detail.

- Enlightening illustrations—Numerous photographs highlight points of interest to you.

- Handy indexing—A referencing guide not only to main city entries, but also to the hundreds of people and place names that fall within those main entries, leading you directly to the information you seek.

# Designed for a Variety of Users

Whether you are a researcher, traveler, or executive on the move, *CUS* serves your needs. This is the reference long sought by a variety of users:

- Business people, market researchers, and other decision-makers will find the current data that helps them stay informed.

- People vacationing, conventioneering, or relocating will consult this source for questions they have about what's new, unique, or significant about where they are going.

- Students, media professionals, and researchers will discover their background work already completed.

# Definitions of Key Statistical Resources

Following are explanations of key resources used for statistical data:

*ACCRA (The Council for Community Economic Research; formerly the American Chamber of Commerce Researchers Association):* The Cost of Living Index, produced quarterly, provides a useful and reasonably accurate measure of living cost differences among urban areas. Items on which the Index is based have been carefully chosen to reflect the different categories of consumer expenditures, such as groceries, housing, utilities, transportation, health care, and miscellaneous goods and services; taxes are excluded. Weights assigned to relative costs are based on government survey data on expenditure patterns for mid-management households (typically the average professional worker's home, new construction with 2,400 square feet of living space). All items are priced in each place at a specified time and according to standardized specifications. Information regarding ACCRA and the Cost of Living Index can be found at www.accra.org. Please note that the ACCRA Cost of Living Index and ACCRA housing price information are reprinted by permission of ACCRA.

*Metropolitan Statistical Area (MSA):* The U.S. Office of Management and Budget (OMB) provides that each Metropolitan Statistical Area must include (a) at least one city with 50,000 or more inhabitants, or (b) a U.S. Census Bureau-defined urbanized area (of at least 50,000 inhabitants) and a total metropolitan population of at least 100,000 (75,000 in New England). The term was adopted in 1983. The term "metropolitan area" (MA) became effective in 1990. During the 2000 Census, the MSA standards were revised, establishing Core Based Statistical Areas (CBSAs). CBSAs may be either Metropolitan Statistical Areas or Micropolitan Statistical Areas. It is important to note that standards, and therefore content of 1990 Census MSAs, are not identical to 2000 Census MSA standards. Additional information regarding MSAs can be found at http://census.state.nc.us/glossary/msa.html.

*FBI Crime Index Total:* The total number of index offenses reported to the FBI during the year through its Uniform Crime Reporting Program. The FBI receives monthly and annual reports from law enforcement agencies throughout the country. City police, sheriffs, and state police file reports on the number of index offenses that become known to them. The FBI Crime Index offenses are: murder and non-negligent manslaughter; forcible rape; robbery; aggravated assault; burglary; larceny; motor vehicle theft; and arson.

*Estimates of population:* Between decennial censuses, the U.S. Bureau of the Census publishes estimates of the population using the decennial census data as benchmarks and data available from various agencies, both state and federal, including births and deaths, and school statistics, among other data.

## Method of Compilation

The editors of *Cities of the United States* consulted numerous sources to secure the kinds of data most valuable to you. Each entry gathers together economic information culled in part from the U.S. Department of Labor/Bureau of Labor Statistics and state departments of labor and commerce, population figures derived from the U.S. Department of Commerce/ Bureau of the Census and from city and state agencies, educational and municipal government data supplied by local authorities, historical narrative based on a variety of accounts, and geographical and climatic profiles from the National Oceanic and Atmospheric Administration. Along with material supplied by chambers of commerce, convention and visitors bureaus, and other local sources, background information was drawn from periodicals and books chosen for their timeliness and accuracy. Through print resources, web sites, email contact, and/or phone calls with agency representatives, the information contained reflects current conditions.

## Acknowledgments

The editors are grateful for the assistance provided by dozens of helpful chambers of commerce and convention and visitors bureau professionals, as well as municipal, library, and school employees for their invaluable generosity and expertise.

## Comments and Suggestions Welcome

If you have questions, concerns, or comments about *Cities of the United States*, please contact the Project Editors:

> *Cities of the United States*
> Gale
> 27500 Drake Road
> Farmington Hills, MI 48331
> Phone: (248)699-4253
> Toll-free: (800)347-GALE
> Fax: (248)699-8075
> URL: gale.cengage.com

# Cities of the United States

**SIXTH EDITION**

# Illinois

# The State in Brief

**Nickname:** Prairie State

**Motto:** State sovereignty—national union

**Flower:** Native violet

**Bird:** Cardinal

**Area:** 57,914 square miles (2000; U.S. rank 25th)

**Elevation:** Ranges from 279 feet to 1,235 feet above sea level

**Climate:** Temperate, with hot summers and cold, snowy winters

**Admitted to Union:** December 3, 1818

**Capital:** Springfield

**Head Official:** Governor Rod R. Blagojevich (D) (until 2010)

**Population**

    **1980:** 11,427,000
    **1990:** 11,543,000
    **2000:** 12,419,647
    **2006 estimate:** 12,831,970
    **Percent change, 1990–2000:** 8.6%
    **U.S. rank in 2006:** 5th
    **Percent of residents born in state:** 66.86% (2006)
    **Density:** 229.6 people per square mile (2006)
    **2006 FBI Crime Index Total:** 456,976

**Racial and Ethnic Characteristics (2006)**

    **White:** 9,074,653
    **Black or African American:** 1,898,346
    **American Indian and Alaska Native:** 23,310
    **Asian:** 536,992
    **Native Hawaiian and Pacific Islander:** 3,201
    **Hispanic or Latino (may be of any race):** 1,888,439
    **Other:** 1,095,611

**Age Characteristics (2006)**

    **Population under 5 years old:** 889,338
    **Population 5 to 19 years old:** 2,711,265
    **Percent of population 65 years and over:** 11.9%
    **Median age:** 35.7

**Vital Statistics**

    **Total number of births (2006):** 178,985
    **Total number of deaths (2006):** 105,407
    **AIDS cases reported through 2005:** 32,595

**Economy**

    **Major industries:** Manufacturing; mining; agriculture; oil; trade; finance, insurance, and real estate; services
    **Unemployment rate (2006):** 7.2%
    **Per capita income (2006):** $26,514
    **Median household income (2006):** $52,006
    **Percentage of persons below poverty level (2006):** 12.3%
    **Income tax rate:** 3.0%
    **Sales tax rate:** 6.25%

# Aurora

## ■ The City in Brief

**Founded:** 1834 (incorporated 1845)

**Head Official:** Mayor Tom Wesiner (D) (since 2005)

**City Population**

    1980: 81,293
    1990: 100,279
    2000: 142,990
    2006 estimate: 170,617
    Percent change, 1990–2000: 42.6%
    U.S. rank in 1980: Not available
    U.S. rank in 1990: 201st (State rank: 3rd)
    U.S. rank in 2000: 147th (State rank: 3rd)

**Metropolitan Area Population**

    1980: 7,937,000
    1990: 8,066,000
    2000: 9,157,540
    2006 estimate: Not available
    Percent change, 1990–2000: 11.1%
    U.S. rank in 1980: Not available
    U.S. rank in 1990: 3rd
    U.S. rank in 2000: 3rd

**Area:** 38.5 square miles (2000)

**Elevation:** Average 676 feet above sea level

**Average Annual Temperature:** 47.9° F

**Average Annual Precipitation:** 38.4 inches

**Major Economic Sectors:** Manufacturing, retail, entertainment

**Unemployment Rate:** 3.9% (June 2007)

**Per Capita Income:** $23,454 (2005)

**2005 FBI Crime Index Property:** 4,832

**2005 FBI Crime Index Violent:** Not available

**Major Colleges and Universities:** Aurora University, Waubonsee Community College

**Daily Newspaper:** *The Beacon News*

## ■ Introduction

About 35 miles west of Chicago, Aurora is the largest city in the Fox River Valley. Aurora developed as an independent city and still sees itself as such, but suburban sprawl has reached westwards from Chicago and Aurora is now considered part of the broader "Chicagoland" area. While residents escape the rush and the housing prices of nearby Chicago, they're also finding Aurora has much to offer in terms of economical advantages, education, recreation, and overall quality of life—all the while still being close enough to a major city for a day trip or workday commute.

## ■ Geography and Climate

Aurora is located in northeastern Illinois, straddling both the east and west sides of the Fox River. The Fox River Valley runs fairly north-south around the river. The area is part of the Great Lakes Plains, which are mainly flat except for some small hills in the west near the start of the Till Plains, the flat fertile area covering most of the state. Aurora is situated far enough away from Lake Michigan to not receive any lake effect snow, but still averages about 38 inches of snow a year, with January being the snowiest month. Temperatures in the summer months average in the low 80s, with about 4 inches of rainfall per month.

**Area:** 38.5 square miles (2000)

**Elevation:** Average 676 feet above sea level

**Average Temperature:** 47.9° F

**Average Annual Precipitation:** 38.4 inches

# ■ History

Originally, Aurora was home to a village of 500 Potawatomi Native Americans who traded peacefully with white settlers in the area. In 1834 Joseph and Samuel McCarty came west from New York to look for a site to build a sawmill and found the Fox River. An island at a bend in the river provided a great location to establish mills and factories where water power could be harnessed. At first there were two separate settlements on either side of the river, but they merged in 1857 to form the town of Aurora. Aurora quickly developed into a manufacturing town, first known for textiles and later for heavy machinery, foundries, and machine shops. The Chicago, Burlington & Quincy Railroad extended its line to Aurora in 1849. Soon after, the railroad became the area's largest employer, locating its repair and railcar construction shops there. The repair shop necessitated the building of a roundhouse, the largest stone roundhouse constructed in the country. The railroad was the largest employer until the 1960s.

Socially the town was very progressive from the start. The first free public school district in Illinois was started in Aurora in 1851. The town experienced an influx of European immigrants in the latter half of the nineteenth century, drawn by its industrial jobs. Abolitionist organizations appeared in Aurora before the start of the Civil War, and out of 20 congregations in 1887, two African American churches thrived. By 1870, the city had more than 10,000 residents, and by 1890 there were approximately 20,000 residents—a testament to the city's industrial development.

In 1881 Aurora was the first town in Illinois to light its streets with electric lights, which gave the city its nickname, "The City of Lights." On May 26, 1909, one of the strongest earthquakes to hit Illinois knocked over chimneys in Aurora and was felt over 500,000 square miles. In the 1910s, Aurora was home for a time to six different automobile companies, all of which were eventually unsuccessful.

Aurora continued to be a manufacturing powerhouse through both world wars and the Great Depression. The railroad shops, which once employed 2,500 and covered 70 acres, closed in 1974, and all but three of the buildings were demolished. In the 1980s many factories started to close, and unemployment jumped to more than 15 percent. Aurora responded to this by welcoming a riverboat casino to its downtown, developing the area around the casino, developing nearby residential communities, and, most importantly, creating multiple business parks on the outer edges of the city.

Today Aurora is enjoying a population resurgence, having increased more than 40 percent between 1990 and 2000. Businesses continue to move and expand into the area. As real estate prices go up in Chicagoland, the Fox Valley is being seen as a market waiting to be tapped, and more and more Chicago workers are finding homes in Aurora.

***Historical Information:*** Aurora Historical Society, PO Box 905, Aurora, IL 60507; telephone (630)906-0650; www.aurorahistoricalsociety.org

# ■ Population Profile

**Metropolitan Area Residents**
    1980: 7,937,000
    1990: 8,066,000
    2000: 9,157,540
    2006 estimate: Not available
    Percent change, 1990–2000: 11.1%
    U.S. rank in 1980: Not available
    U.S. rank in 1990: 3rd
    U.S. rank in 2000: 3rd

**City Residents**
    1980: 81,293
    1990: 100,279
    2000: 142,990
    2006 estimate: 170,617
    Percent change, 1990–2000: 42.6%
    U.S. rank in 1980: Not available
    U.S. rank in 1990: 201st (State rank: 3rd)
    U.S. rank in 2000: 147th (State rank: 3rd)

**Density:** 3,711.5 people per square mile (2000)

**Racial and ethnic characteristics (2005)**
    White: 122,200
    Black: 17,465
    American Indian and Alaska Native: 0
    Asian: 10,945
    Native Hawaiian and Pacific Islander: 0
    Hispanic or Latino (may be of any race): 67,715
    Other: 16,921

**Percent of residents born in state:** 56.0% (2000)

**Age characteristics (2005)**
    Population under 5 years old: 18,529
    Population 5 to 9 years old: 15,107
    Population 10 to 14 years old: 12,228
    Population 15 to 19 years old: 10,960
    Population 20 to 24 years old: 13,120

©Kim Karpeles/Alamy

Population 25 to 34 years old: 32,654
Population 35 to 44 years old: 29,410
Population 45 to 54 years old: 18,295
Population 55 to 59 years old: 6,623
Population 60 to 64 years old: 4,043
Population 65 to 74 years old: 5,965
Population 75 to 84 years old: 2,734
Population 85 years and older: 822
Median age: 29.5 years

**Births (2006, MSA)**

Total number: 37,672

**Deaths (2006, MSA)**

Total number: 14,824

**Money income (2005)**

Per capita income: $23,454
Median household income: $55,950
Total households: 54,416

**Number of households with income of ...**

less than $10,000: 3,259
$10,000 to $14,999: 1,900
$15,000 to $24,999: 4,637

$25,000 to $34,999: 5,178
$35,000 to $49,999: 8,953
$50,000 to $74,999: 11,081
$75,000 to $99,999: 9,505
$100,000 to $149,999: 6,953
$150,000 to $199,999: 1,571
$200,000 or more: 1,379

**Percent of families below poverty level:** 9.9% (2005)

**2005 FBI Crime Index Property:** 4,832

**2005 FBI Crime Index Violent:** Not available

# ■ Municipal Government

Aurora has a mayor-council form of government. The mayor is elected at large every four years and maintains a full-time position. Of the 12 aldermen composing the council, 10 are elected from each of the 10 wards, with 2 elected city-wide as aldermen-at-large. Aldermen are elected for four-year terms, with half the council running for office on odd-numbered years. The position of alderman is part-time. The council has four standing committees: planning and development; finance; government operations; and buildings, grounds, and infrastructure.

**Head Official:** Mayor Tom Wesiner (D) (since 2005; current term expires 2009)

**Total Number of City Employees:** 1,280 (2007)

*City Information:* City of Aurora, City Hall, 44 East Downer Place, Aurora, IL 60507; telephone (630)264-4636; www.aurora-il.org

# ■ Economy

## Major Industries and Commercial Activity

Heavy industry helped build Aurora, with the Fox River being used for power to run saw and textile mills. As the Industrial Revolution progressed and the railroad came to town, Aurora became a manufacturer of railroad cars, including some of the first dining cars built in the United States. While manufacturing has declined somewhat in the past decades, it is still an important sector of the economy. In 2007 Caterpillar Inc., one of the nation's largest construction machinery designers and manufacturers, was one of the area's largest employers.

Service industries have gained important roles in the local economy. Educational services offer a large number of jobs through six area public school districts, Aurora University, and Waubonsee Community College. Health care and social assistance services are also solid contributors to the economy, with Rush-Copley Medical Center, Provena Mercy Medical Center, and Dryer Medical Clinics being major employers.

Financial and insurance services are beginning to expand into the area, with local major employers being Farmer's Insurance Group, Metlife, Hartford Financial Services, and Old Second National Bank.

**Items and goods produced:** construction machinery, steel products, fabricated metals, tools, office and retail shelving, valves, electronics, health and beauty products

## Incentive Programs—New and Existing Companies

*Local programs:* The Aurora Economic Development Commission (AEDC) was created in 1981 to attract and keep companies in Aurora and the Fox River Valley. It offers a number of services to businesses such as training and education, permit reviews, planning, financing, utilities and infrastructure. Aurora Downtown is an organization created to facilitate projects in the Special Service Tax Area in order to improve and develop the historic downtown area.

The City of Aurora, through Aurora Downtown, provides grants for exterior restoration to renew original architectural features, and interior rehabilitation for HVAC, plumbing, structural and electrical work in the historic downtown area. The AEDC, with Waubonsee Community College, has a Small Business Center to help companies with business financing and preparation of business plans. AEDC helps businesses secure financing with tax exempt Industrial Revenue Bonds for qualified applicants.

In 1977 the Illinois legislature adopted the Tax Increment Allocation Redevelopment Act to provide municipalities with a unique tool to finance and stimulate urban redevelopment. Through the use of Tax Increment Financing (TIF), cities can stimulate private investment by offering incentives to attract and retain businesses, improve their community areas, and maintain a well-educated and highly trained labor force. The City of Aurora has several TIF districts.

*State programs:* The Illinois Development Finance Authority's mission is to issue taxable and tax-exempt bonds and make loans for businesses and non-profit groups in Illinois. They have bond and loan programs for industry and small businesses, as well as for agriculture, health care, education and local governments. The Illinois State Treasurer's Office has many economic programs for businesses, such as below-rate business loans under the Economic Recovery program, low cost financing for development of tourist and historic building restoration through the Experience Illinois Program, and the State Treasurer's Economic Program (STEP). STEP and STEP Small Business provide loans to bring in or expand businesses, and create and retain jobs. The Economic Development for Growing Economy Tax Credit Program (EDGE) is a statewide program to benefit companies that relocate or expand operations within the state. Qualifying companies must make an investment of at least $5 million in capital improvements and create a minimum of 25 new full-time jobs in the state. Companies with 100 or fewer employees must make a capital investment of $1 million and create at least five full-time jobs to qualify. The High Impact Business program is designed to encourage large-scale economic development initiatives. Business projects that involve at least $12 million in investments and the creation of 500 full-time jobs may qualify for investment tax credits and state sales tax exemptions on building materials, utilities, and the purchase, repair, or replacement of manufacturing equipment. Other state sponsored tax credits include a Research and Development Tax Credit of 6.5 percent and a Manufacturer's Purchase Credit of 6.25 percent for qualified businesses. A number of loan programs are available.

*Job training programs:* The Aurora Economic Development Commission brings together prospective employers and job training providers through Waubonsee

Community College and the College of Du Page. Grants are available for assistance with employee training through AEDC. Waubonsee has many programs in manufacturing and technical skills, computer skills, management training, and health and safety issues. The college also works with the Department of Labor's Bureau of Apprenticeship Training (BAT) to create apprenticeship programs with companies and organizations around the area. The Illinois Department of Employment Security and the Bureau of Workforce Development combine federal and state money to help with job seekers' training, job search and placement services, and development of core job skills.

## Development Projects

More than 3.2 million square feet of commercial and industrial space was developed and $290 million spent in new city investments in 2004. In that year, Chicago Premium Outlets opened, a shopping center with 120 outlet stores that added approximately 1,000 jobs to the community. Aurora University began a five-year, $50 million plan of new construction and renovation on its campus. Hyundai Motor America expanded its operations in Aurora by opening a $17 million office and parts distribution center. A multiple-year project during the mid-2000s is a plan to upgrade Aurora Airport by building 120 new hangars, spending $7.2 million on refurbishing its runway, and building a new $3.2 million taxiway for the secondary runway.

In 2005 Provena Mercy Medical Center added a 100,000-square-foot Surgery Center to its campus. The $33 million addition was the largest project in the almost 100-year history of the hospital. In 2006 Waubonsee Community College received a $35,300 innovative technology grant from the state to open a Community Technology Center designed to provide computer training skills for Aurora citizens and students. In 2007 the City of Aurora was certified as the first River Edge Redevelopment Zone in the state. The River Edge Redevelopment Initiative is a pilot program designed to offer incentives and assistance in revitalizing riverfront areas. The Aurora River Edge Redevelopment zone includes former industrial lands along the east and west riverfronts. Developers and businesses working within the zone are eligible for a variety of tax exemptions and credits. Also in 2007 the city received a $27,000 Recycling Expansion and Modernization Program grant from the state to develop and implement a total waste management plan for the riverfront area.

*Economic Development Information:* Aurora Economic Development Commission, 43 West Galena Blvd., Aurora, IL 60506; telephone (630)897-5500; www.aurora-il.org/aedc. Downtown Aurora, One South Broadway, Aurora, IL 60505; telephone (630)844-3670; www.auroradowntown.org. Kane County Board, 719 Batavia Avenue Building A, Geneva, IL 60134; telephone (630)232-5930; www.countyofkane.org.

## Commercial Shipping

Created as a railroad town, Aurora is still traversed by the Burlington Northern Santa Fe and the Elgin, Joliet & Eastern railroads, which connect to the nation's largest train gateway, Chicago. Both railroads support industrial development departments. For air freight, Chicago's O'Hare and Midway airports are major cargo hubs, with national and international routes. O'Hare International Airport, about 35 miles away from Aurora, hosts 23 cargo carriers serving over 210 global destinations. O'Hare is one of the top ten busiest cargo-moving airports in North America. O'Hare is part of a designated Foreign Trade Zone and all major railroads provide service throughout the Chicago area.

There is one line-haul motor freight carrier with a terminal in Aurora and seven line-haul carriers providing daily service to the area, with one specializing in heavy machinery transport. I-88 runs close by. Other easily accessible interstates are I-55, 40, I-80, I-90, I-94, and I-355.

## Labor Force and Employment Outlook

As Chicagoland expands its influence westward, the commuter rail link makes Aurora a viable destination for workers in Chicago to afford new and vintage homes and condominiums. As the population of the Fox Valley increases, Aurora's long history of development and fairly stable economy serves as an anchor for this growth, along with Naperville to the east. The basic employment trends for the city in the past decade have shown that manufacturing jobs are decreasing in number while service jobs, particularly in education, health care, and financial services, are increasing.

For the Chicago-Naperville-Joliet MSA, the top five occupations in 2007 were office and administrative support, sales, service, management, and professional occupations. Long-term employment projections for 2004-2014 predict a decline in manufacturing jobs. Professional and business services are projected to show the greatest increase in available jobs, followed by health care and social assistance, and educational services. The leisure and hospitality sectors are likely to show an increase as well.

The following is a summary of data regarding the Aurora City metropolitan area labor force, 2005 annual averages.

**Size of nonagricultural labor force:** 84,349

**Number of workers employed in ...**

    construction and mining: 6,212
    manufacturing: 13,953
    trade, transportation and utilities: 14,236

information: 2,535
financial activities: 7,087
professional and business services: 11,155
educational and health services: 15,379
leisure and hospitality: 7,331
other services: 4,278
government: 7,732

**Average hourly earnings of production workers employed in manufacturing:** Not available

**Unemployment rate:** 3.9% (June 2007)

| Largest employers (2007) | Number of employees |
|---|---|
| Caterpillar Inc. | 3,000 |
| Farmers Insurance Group | 1,700 |
| Waubonsee Community College | 1,571 |
| Aurora School District #129 | 1,500 |
| Aurora School District #131 | 1,320 |
| Rush-Copley Medical Center | 1,300 |
| City of Aurora | 1,280 |
| LTD Commodities | 1,200 |
| Provena Medical Center | 1,200 |
| Dreyer Medical Clinic | 1,145 |
| Fox Valley Park District | 1,072 |
| Hollywood Casino—Aurora | 1,009 |

## Cost of Living

Aurora's cost of living, as well as its housing prices, are slightly below the national average. According to Coldwell Banker's annual Home Price Comparison Index (HPCI), the median price for a 2,200-square-foot house with 4 bedrooms and 2.5 bathrooms in Aurora in 2005 was $291,700.

The following is a summary of data regarding several key cost of living factors for the Aurora area.

**2007 (1st quarter) ACCRA Average House Price:** Not available

**2007 (1st quarter) ACCRA Cost of Living Index:** Not available

**State income tax rate:** 3.0% of Federal Adjusted Gross Income, with modifications

**State sales tax rate:** 6.25%

**Local income tax rate:** None

**Local sales tax rate:** 0.75%

**Property tax rate:** $7.94 per $100 assessed valuation (2002)

***Economic Information:*** Illinois Department of Commerce and Economic Opportunity, 620 E. Adams, Springfield, IL 62701; telephone (217)782-7500; www.illinoisbiz.biz/dceo. Kane County Board, 719 Batavia Avenue Building A, Geneva, IL 60134; telephone (630) 232-5930; www.countyofkane.org

# ■ Education and Research

## Elementary and Secondary Schools

There are six public school districts serving Aurora. The primary districts are the West Aurora District 129 (WAD), East Aurora District 131 (EAD), and Indian Prairie District 204 (IPD). Special education classes are offered in the WAD through the Hope D. Wall School in Aurora. Indian Plains High School, in the IPD, offers an alternative education program for high school seniors who have fallen behind in their graduation requirements. Aurora is also home to the Illinois Mathematics and Science Academy, a public residential high school for grades 10-12. It is internationally known as a school whose students reach the highest levels of achievement in the sciences, technology, and mathematics, by partnering with scientists at state research facilities.

The following is a summary of data regarding School District 129 as of the 2005–2006 school year.

**Total enrollment:** 12,500

**Number of facilities**
elementary schools: 12
junior high/middle schools: 4
senior high schools: 1
other: 2

**Student/teacher ratio:** 18.1:1

**Teacher salaries (2005–06)**
elementary median: $46,070
junior high/middle median: $47,040
secondary median: $47,990

**Funding per pupil:** $6,385

There are also about 20 private and parochial schools in the city.

***Public School Information:*** West Aurora School District 129, 80 S. River St., Aurora, IL 60506; telephone (630)301-5000; www.sd129.org. East Aurora District 131, McKnight Service Center, 417 Fifth Street, Aurora, IL 60505; telephone (630)299-5550; www.d131.kane.k12.il.us. Indian Prairie School District 204, Crouse Education Center, 780 Shoreline Drive, Aurora,

IL 60504; telephone (630)375-3000; http://ipsdweb.
ipsd.org

## Colleges and Universities

Aurora University, with about 4,000 students, is a private, independent university that offers 40 undergraduate degrees, 8 master's degrees, and one doctorate (in education) through three colleges: the College of Arts and Science, the College of Education, and the College of Professional Studies. The university has an additional campus in Williams Bay, Wisconsin.

The Aurora campus of Waubonsee Community College has two-year degree programs in areas such as communications, humanities, fine arts, health and life sciences, science and technology, social sciences, and business, intended for easy transfer to four-year schools. The college has certificate programs, continuing professional education classes, distance learning, and online courses available. Extension sites for Aurora University and Northern Illinois University are based on the Aurora campus. A number of vocational and workforce development programs are available at the college as well.

Chicago area colleges and universities include the University of Chicago, DePaul University, Loyola University Chicago, Saint Xavier University, the University of Illinois at Chicago, Northeastern Illinois University, the Illinois Institute of Technology, and Chicago State University.

## Libraries and Research Centers

The Aurora Public Library has been in existence since 1881 and moved into its current residence in 1904. It was refurbished and expanded in 1969 and again in 1980. Beside the main branch, there is the Eola Road Branch on the east side of the city and the West Branch, both built in the 1990s. A bookmobile also serves the city. In 2002 a computer training facility was installed at the library. The library system offers genealogy research services and travel planning services for card holders.

The Charles B. Phillips Library at Aurora University has more than 99,000 books, 518 periodical subscriptions, a multitude of research materials (including full-text online journals) and access to dozens of databases. Aurora University is home to the Schingoethe Center for Native American Cultures, a museum and research center for studies into Native American cultural artifacts. Waubonsee Community College has the Todd Library to help with its students' research needs.

The Institute for Collaboration at Aurora University serves as a resource for students and professionals in the fields of education, health and human services, and business and government. The Institute supports programs in collaborative leadership research.

There are two major national research centers in the area. The Argonne National Laboratory is run by the University of Chicago for the U.S. Department of

Energy. Its focus is on energy resources, high energy physics, materials sciences and nanotechnology, environmental management, and national security. The Fermi National Accelerator Laboratory is home to the country's largest particle accelerator and conducts research on energy and matter.

***Public Library Information:*** Aurora Public Library, Main Library, 1 E. Benton Street, Aurora, IL 60505; telephone (630)264-4100; www.aurora.lib.il.us

# ■ Health Care

Aurora is home to two major hospitals: Provena Mercy Medical Center and Rush-Copley Medical Center. Provena, a 356-bed facility, has a family birthing center, an emergency medicine center, behavioral treatment, the area's first Diabetic Wellness Center, a sleep disorders clinic, and orthopedic services. Provena supports a Level II Trauma Center and a special Chest Pain Center as well. The Sister Rita Heart Center at Provena Mercy has a clinic, surgical suites, rehabilitation services, and a pediatric cardiology unit. The Provena Fox Knoll Retirement Community, Provena McAuley Manor (rehabilitation and long-term care), and Provena Home Care are all located in Aurora.

Rush-Copley Medical Center offers 150 private rooms on a 98-acre campus. Among Rush-Copley's special services are centers for cancer care, heart and vascular care, women's health, and neuroscience. Emergency services are provided in a Level II Trauma Center, with a special designation for pediatric emergency care. Rush-Copley sponsors HealthPlex, a 166,000-square-foot athletic and tennis club.

Dreyer Medical Clinics, owned by Advocate Health Care, provide doctors to communities throughout the Fox River Valley, including five clinics in Aurora.

# ■ Recreation

## Sightseeing

Aurora is home to many historic buildings and residences. A self-guided walking tour of the architecture of the downtown area is available, with historic facts sent to your cell phone, at the Aurora Area Visitor and Convention Bureau. The Stolp Island National Register Historic District in the middle of the Fox River has buildings dating from the 1850s, and has many fine examples of architectural terra cotta. The William Tanner House, an Italianate mansion, is open for tours May through December and is part of the Aurora History Center. The Sri Venkateswara Swami Temple of Greater Chicago is a beautiful Hindu Temple blending ancient design and modern architectural technology. The oldest limestone railroad roundhouse in the country has been restored and converted into Walter Payton's Round-house, a brew pub, museum, and live entertainment venue.

The Red Oak Nature Center, on the banks of the Fox River, is in North Aurora. It has many trails to explore, a cave (a rarity in Illinois), and a natural history museum, with an observation deck and picnic areas. The Phillips Park Zoo is free of charge and features animals from the Americas. The African American Heritage Museum and Black Veterans Archives has an amazing display of sculptures created by a self-taught artist, Dr. Charles Smith. Memorials and hundreds of figures from African American history are displayed outdoors in the yard of Dr. Smith's former home.

The riverboat Hollywood Casino Aurora has a 53,000-square-foot casino with more than a thousand slot machines and table games, three restaurants, and a theater with live entertainment.

## Arts and Culture

The Art Deco Paramount Arts Centre originally opened in 1931 and was the first air-conditioned theater outside of Chicago. Magnificently restored in 1978, it now presents touring musicians, theatrical performances, improvisation, comedians, and a free film series in the summer. The Riverfront Playhouse has been producing plays since 1978, and also provides a theater series for children. The Borealis Theater Company is the professional theater in residence at Aurora University.

Music venues include Fermilab, which plays host to an eclectic range of concerts, and Walter Payton's Roundhouse, host to music and comedy performers. The Fox Valley Concert Band performs free in Aurora and surrounding communities year round. Aurora University has its Music by the Lake concert series in the summer months at the Allyn Pavilion for the Performing Arts.

The David L. Pierce Art and History Center has rotating art exhibits, as well as displays of military memorabilia from the Grand Army of the Republic. At Aurora University, the Downstairs Dunham Gallery features shows by students and local artists. Gallery 44 is a gallery for local artists showcasing many different media.

The museums and attractions of the Aurora area show great diversity in subject matter, ranging from cutting-edge science to appreciation for its prairie and frontier roots. Blackberry Farms Pioneer Village, run by the Fox Valley Park District, is a living history museum featuring the Farm Museum and its collection of nineteenth century farm implements, the Streets Museum with 11 turn-of-the-century stores, the Discovery Barn, a carousel, pony rides, and a miniature train. Pioneer craft demonstrations, a one-room schoolhouse, and buildings from the 1840s delight school groups and families May through October. The Aurora Historical Society has a collection of artifacts from Aurora's past, including three mastodon skulls unearthed in the 1930s. The Aurora Regional Fire Museum has fire fighting vehicles dating back to 1850, along with thousands of photos and artifacts. The Schingoethe Center for Native American Cultures at Aurora University contains archaeological exhibits, examples of historical and contemporary Native American art, and a research library.

Sci-Tech Hands-On Museum has dozens of exhibits exploring electricity, magnetism, chemistry, life sciences, light, and physics, making scientific concepts understandable and fun for visitors. Traveling exhibits and an outdoor science park make the museum a destination for families, schools, and scouting groups. In nearby Batavia is the Fermi National Accelerator Laboratory (Fermilab), a high energy physics lab conducting research into the mysteries of matter and energy. Visitors are welcome for tours of the facility and to enjoy recreational and nature activities on its restored prairie land, including visiting the lab's own herd of bison. The Air Classics Museum of Aviation located at Aurora Municipal Airport has a collection of military jets, prop aircraft, and helicopters from World War II through the 1990s. Visitors are able to sit in some of the aircraft's cockpits and view aviation uniforms and memorabilia.

## Festivals and Holidays

Aurora celebrates the cold winters every February during the Phillips Park Winterfest, with dog sled rides, ice carving, skating, sledding, snowshoeing, nature hikes, and a snowman building contest. Spring brings not only flowers, but myriad events to the Fox River Valley. The Fox River Valley Park District holds an Easter Egg Hunt in April at the Prisco Community Center. In May comes the Taste of Downtown Aurora, featuring booths from area restaurants; the North Aurora Pet Parade; the Memorial Day Parade; and the Aurora Pow-Wow, with dancing, crafts and food from many different Native American tribes. In summer time, Downtown Alive! events include themed dance parties and lunchtime concerts. Blues on the Fox in June is a festival that brings national blues acts to Aurora's downtown. Fourth of July celebrations include a parade, a concert, and fireworks. Also in July is Chase the Moon, a midnight bike ride looping from Aurora to Batavia; the Puerto Rican Cultural Festival; and the Kane County Fair. In August, Soul Fest, featuring home cooked food, games, music, and the Black Business Expo, comes to May Street Park. The Midwest Literary Festival is in September, as is the Fall Harvest Festival at Blackberry Farm's Pioneer Village, and the Downtown Arts Festival. A Veterans Day parade and ceremony runs through downtown Aurora in November. Holiday Magic at the end of November welcomes Santa and Mrs. Claus with the Parade of Lights, fireworks, and a tree lighting ceremony. Through December, the paths at Phillips Park Zoo are lit with holiday lights for strolling at night.

## Sports for the Spectator

Since 1991, The Kane County Cougars baseball team has played in Philip B. Elfstrom Field in nearby Geneva, Illinois. Currently a class A affiliate of the Oakland Athletics, the Cougars are part of the Midwest League. Extremely popular in the area, they routinely have more than 500,000 attendees each season. Aurora's sports fans also root for teams in Chicago, like baseball's Cubs and White Sox, football's Bears, basketball's Bulls, hockey's Blackhawks and Wolves, arena football's Rush, and soccer's Fire. Aurora University Spartan athletics is a Division III program, with men's and women's teams in basketball, soccer, tennis, track and field, and men's baseball and football.

## Sports for the Participant

Aurora's parks are run by the Fox Valley Park District, which has 110 parks in all the communities it serves. Eight parks are located directly in the city. The Eola Community Center and Fitness Club has gymnasiums, a track, dance studios, an indoor playground, baseball fields and two sand volleyball courts. The Prisco Community Center is in Aurora's McCullough Park and was renovated in 2003. The Vaughn Athletic Center features a huge field house for team sports, a 10,000-square-foot fitness center, nine tennis courts and two swimming pools. For bicyclists and runners, there are more than 30 miles on four paved trails, two of which run through Aurora. The Aurora Tennis Club is an indoor facility with year-round court times and lessons for kids and adults. The district runs two 18-hole golf courses, Fox Bend and Orchard Valley, which was rated four-stars by Golf Digest magazine. The Aurora City Golf Course, the Aurora Country Club, and six other courses are in the immediate vicinity. The Fox Valley Trail runs along the Fox River from Aurora north to Crystal Lake. The district runs Splash Country Water Park, containing a zero-depth pool, water slides, a kid's water play area, and a 1,100-foot-long lazy river. The Phillips Park Aquatic Center also offers several water slides, a zero-depth pool, and kid-friendly areas.

The Sport Zone Park is a multi-sport center for the whole family. Outdoors, it features mini-golf, batting cages, and a go-cart track. The main feature is its 72,000-square-foot dome, which is a driving range during the day and is converted to soccer, baseball, or softball fields in the evening. The Aurora Archery Range hosts the annual National Field Archery Association Tournament.

## Shopping and Dining

Three large shopping centers are big draws to Aurora. The recently completed Chicago Premium Outlet center has 120 stores, including Ann Taylor, Brooks Brothers, Giorgio Armani, and Kate Spade, and offers discount shopping every day. Westfield Shoppingtown Fox Valley is anchored by four large department stores and has 180 other shops. Northgate Shopping Center has several big-box retailers and other smaller stores. The Route 59 Corridor and the Randall/Orchard Road corridor are main shopping districts for Aurora, North Aurora, and Batavia. The Aurora Farmer's Market is held on Saturday mornings June through October and is one of several in surrounding communities.

Aurora has a wide variety of family, ethnic and fine dining choices. Steakhouses, Italian, Mexican, and Chinese restaurants abound. Notable is Savannah's Restaurant and Tea Room, at the Fox Valley Mall, featuring Southern cuisine and afternoon teas.

*Visitor Information:* Aurora Area Convention and Visitors Bureau, 43 W. Galena Blvd., Aurora, IL 60506; telephone (630)897-5581 or (800)477-4369; www. emjoyaurora.com. City of Aurora, Customer Service, 910B N. Farnsworth Ave., Aurora, IL 60505; telephone (630)264-4636; http://www.aurora-il.org

# ■ Convention Facilities

In nearby St. Charles, Illinois, the Pheasant Run Resort & Spa is the area's largest conference facility. With a 320-seat auditorium, 100,000 square feet of meeting space, four ballrooms, and a 38,000-square-foot Exposition Center, it can handle most types of functions. Accommodations and amenities include 473 rooms, an 18-hole golf course, a day spa, and live entertainment. The DuPage County Expo Center, also in St. Charles, has 25,000 square feet of column-free trade show space. The Hilton Garden Inn in St. Charles has 120 rooms and 26,000 square feet of meeting and conference space. The Kane County Fairgrounds are rentable for concerts, exhibitions, auctions, and trade shows.

Aurora has 10 hotels and motels for visitors staying in the city. The Comfort Suites City Center has 82 suites and 3 meeting rooms, and the adjacent Walter Payton's Roundhouse has banquet and catering facilities for up to 600. The Hampton Inn and Suites has a 5,000-square-foot conference and meeting center, and has a 6,000-square-foot indoor water park. The Fox Valley Park District also rents out their facilities and community centers. The Fox Valley Country Club in North Aurora has banquet and event space available.

*Convention Information:* Aurora Area Convention and Visitors Bureau, 43 W. Galena Blvd., Aurora, IL 60506; telephone (630)897-5581 or (800)477-4369; www.emjoyaurora.com

# ■ Transportation

## Approaching the City

Aurora Municipal Airport serves private and corporate aircraft with about 450 flights daily. Helicopter services are also supported. Chicago's Midway and O'Hare

International airports are the major commercial airports of the area. O'Hare International Airport, about 35 miles away from Aurora, hosts 41 major domestic and international commercial carriers scheduling more than 880,000 flights annually. One of the busiest air facilities in the world, O'Hare accommodates more than 5.8 million passengers each month, with a total of over 76 million in 2006.

The primary interstate highway into the Aurora area is I-88, which runs east-west to the north of the city center. I-55 runs south and east of the city. U.S. routes 30 and 34 and state routes 59 and 47 also lead into the city. Amtrak provides service to Naperville (about eight miles away) and Plano (13 miles away). METRA, a commuter rail system, connects Aurora with Chicago and its suburbs. Greyhound provides long-distance bus service from a stop at the Aurora Transportation Center.

### Traveling in the City

Aurora straddles the Fox River in a mainly north-south direction, with several bridges crossing it at intervals. Public transportation is handled by the PACE bus system, which operates 23 shuttle buses on 15 fixed routes in Aurora and surrounding communities. Paratransit service and Dial-A-Ride are available for the disabled and the elderly.

## ■ Communications

### Newspapers and Magazines

*The Beacon News* is Aurora's daily newspaper, with a daily circulation of over 27,000. It is published by the Suburban Chicago Newspaper group of papers, owned by Sun-Times News Group.

### Television and Radio

Aurora is home to Telefuture, a Spanish language UHF television station. Broadcasts from all major commercial networks and several independent and PBS stations in the Chicagoland area are received in Aurora. Four radio stations broadcast talk, rock, and Spanish language programming from the city and are supplemented by broadcasts from Chicago and closer Kane and DuPage county stations.

***Media Information:*** *The Beacon News* 101 South River Street, Aurora, Illinois 60506; telephone (630)844-5844; www.suburbanchicagonews.com/beaconnews

### Aurora Online

Aurora Area Convention and Visitors Bureau. Available www.enjoyaurora.com

Aurora Downtown. Available www.auroradowntown.org

Aurora Economic Development Commission. Available www.aurora-il.org/aedc

Aurora Hispanic Chamber of Commerce. Available www.ahcc-il.com

Aurora Public Library. Available www.aurora.lib.il.us

Aurora University. Available www.aurora.edu

*The Beacon News.* Available www.suburbanchicagonews.com/beaconnews

City of Aurora Home Page. Available www.aurora-il.org

East Aurora School District. Available www.d131.kane.k12.il.us

Fox Valley Park District. Available www.foxvalleyparkdistrict.org

Greater Aurora Chamber of Commerce. Available www.aurorachamber.com

West Aurora School District. Available www.sd129.org

BIBLIOGRAPHY

Edwards, Jim and Wynette, *Aurora: A Diverse People Build Their City* (Charleston, SC: Arcadia Publishers, 1998)

Keiser, John H., *Building for the Centuries: Illinois, 1865 to 1898* (Chicago, IL: University of Illinois Press, 1997)

# Chicago

## ■ The City in Brief

**Founded:** 1830 (incorporated 1837)

**Head Official:** Mayor Richard M. Daley (D) (since 1989)

**City Population**

    1980: 3,005,000
    1990: 2,783,726
    2000: 2,896,016
    2006 estimate: 2,833,321
    Percent change, 1990–2000: 4%
    U.S. rank in 1980: 2nd
    U.S. rank in 1990: 3rd (State rank: 1st)
    U.S. rank in 2000: 3rd (State rank: 1st)

**Metropolitan Area Population**

    1980: 7,937,290
    1990: 7,410,858 (PMSA)
    2000: 8,272,768
    2006 estimate: 9,505,748
    Percent change, 1990–2000: 23.6%
    U.S. rank in 1980: 3rd
    U.S. rank in 1990: 3rd
    U.S. rank in 2000: 3rd

**Area:** 228.4 square miles (2000)

**Elevation:** 578.5 feet above sea level

**Average Annual Temperatures:** January, 22.0° F; July, 73.3° F; annual average, 49.1° F

**Average Annual Precipitation:** 36.27 inches of rain; 38.5 inches of snow

**Major Economic Sectors:** Services, wholesale and retail trade, manufacturing, government

**Unemployment Rate:** 5.5% (June 2007)

**Per Capita Income:** $23,449 (2005)

**2005 FBI Crime Index Property:** 131,183

**2005 FBI Crime Index Violent:** Not available

**Major Colleges and Universities:** University of Chicago; University of Illinois at Chicago; DePaul University; Loyola University Chicago; Illinois Institute of Technology

**Daily Newspaper:** *Chicago Tribune; Chicago Sun-Times*

## ■ Introduction

Chicago, the seat of Illinois's Cook County and the third largest city in the country, is the focus of a consolidated metropolitan statistical area that covers the primary metropolitan statistical areas of Gary, Indiana; Kankakee, Illinois; and Kenosha, Wisconsin. "Brawling" was the word Carl Sandburg applied to Chicago in his poem about the city. No longer the "Hog Butcher for the World," at the dawn of the twenty-first century Chicago is still an enthusiastically combative city with a lively political life. A railroad hub in the latter half of the nineteenth century, when its population had already reached 300,000 people, Chicago became a major force in the nation's development. Today, it is a national transportation, industrial, telecommunications, and financial leader, as well as a city of great architectural significance, ethnic diversity, and cultural wealth. The only inland urban area to rank with major East and West Coast metropolises, Chicago has achieved international status through the quality of its cultural institutions and its position as a world financial center.

## ■ Geography and Climate

Chicago rests along the southwest shore of Lake Michigan and extends westward on an inland plain. The Chicago River, which cuts through downtown Chicago, once flowed into Lake Michigan. However, due to severe problems with public sanitation in the late 1800s, the course of the river was reversed, primarily by the Chicago Sanitary and Ship Canal. Today the river is probably best known for the green dye poured into it every St. Patrick's Day.

The climate of Chicago is continental, with frequently changing weather bringing temperatures that range from relatively warm in the summer to relatively cold in the winter. Temperatures of 96 degrees or higher occur during summers; winters can register a low of minus 15 degrees. Snowfall near the lakeshore is usually heavy because of cold air movement off Lake Michigan. Summer thunderstorms are frequently heavy but variable, as parts of the city may receive substantial rainfall while other sectors will have none. Strong wind gusts in the central business district are caused by the channeling of winds between tall buildings; however, the nickname "windy city" that is often applied to Chicago does not refer to the average wind speed, which is no greater than in many other parts of the country. Chicagoans instead attribute the nickname to their reputed penchant for talking proudly about their city.

**Area:** 228.4 square miles (2000)

**Elevation:** 578.5 feet above sea level

**Average Temperatures:** January, 22.0° F; July, 73.3° F; annual average, 49.1° F

**Average Annual Precipitation:** 36.27 inches of rain; 38.5 inches of snow

# ■ History

### Lakeshore Site Begins With Trading Post, Fort

The earliest known inhabitants of the area they called "Chicaugou" were Native Americans of the Illinois tribe. The meaning of the word "Chicaugou" is variously interpreted to mean great, powerful, or strong, depending on the dialect. In the Chippewa dialect the word "shegahg" meant "wild onion"; it is said that an abundance of wild onions grew in the region.

The first people of European descent to reach Chicago were the explorers Father Jacques Marquette and Louis Joliet, who encamped on the Lake Michigan shore at the mouth of the Chicago River in 1673. A century later, in 1783, Jean-Baptiste Du Sable, the son of a French merchant from Quebec and a Haitian slave, left New Orleans and established a fur-trading post in the same area. The site was advantageous for transportation, because it afforded a short portage between the Chicago River, part of the Great Lakes waterway, and the Des Plaines River, connected to the Mississippi waterway via the Illinois River. Sable mysteriously vanished in 1800, and John Kinzie, the region's first English civilian settler,

took over the trading post. Soon a United States garrison, Fort Dearborn, was built to defend the post. In 1812 angry Potawatomi killed most of the traders, except for the Kinzie family, and destroyed Fort Dearborn, which was rebuilt in 1816.

A survey and plat of the growing settlement were filed in 1830, at which time the area numbered 350 inhabitants. Chicago was chartered as a town in 1833 and rechartered as a city in 1837. The completion of the Illinois-Michigan Canal in 1848 turned the city into a marketing center for grain and food products. The first railroad arrived the same year the canal was opened, and within a decade Chicago was the focal point for 3,000 miles of track. The productive grain industry fed cattle and hogs, and Chicago emerged as the site of a major livestock market and meatpacking industry, surpassing Cincinnati as the nation's pork packer. Cattle merchants formed the Union Stock Yards and Transit Company.

Cyrus McCormick opened a factory in the city in 1847 to manufacture his reaper, leading the way for Chicago to become a farm implements hub. The city also became a leader in the processing of lumber for furniture, buildings, and fencing. Chicago industries outfitted Union troops during the Civil War, when the grain and farm machinery industries also experienced wartime growth. George Pullman began to produce railroad sleeping cars in Chicago in 1867. The next year the city's first blast furnace was built. At this time merchants Potter Palmer, Marshall Field, and Levi Leter began shipping consumer goods to general stores in the Midwest.

### Growth Creates Challenges, Opportunities

Chicago's rapid growth resulted in congested residential sectors where the poor were relegated to shabby housing without proper sanitation. Chicago was radically changed, however, on October 8, 1871, by a cataclysmic fire that burned for 27 hours. At that time two-thirds of the city's buildings were made of wood and the summer had been especially dry; high winds spread the fire quickly. Although the stockyards, freight yards, and factory district were spared, Chicago's commercial area was completely destroyed; 8,000 buildings and property valued at just under $200 million were lost. More than 90,000 people were left homeless and 300 people lost their lives.

Since the city's industrial infrastructure was unscathed by the fire, rebuilding progressed rapidly, and Chicago was essentially rebuilt within a year. When the economic panic of 1873 swept the rest of the nation, Chicago was relatively protected from the ensuing depression. The city's prosperity in the post-fire era was founded on an expansion of its industrial and marketing base. Assembly-line techniques were introduced in the meat packing industry, and technological improvements benefited the steel and farm machinery makers. The United States Steel South Works, based in Chicago, became one of the largest such operations in the world. At that time George Pullman established his Palace Car Company in a nearby town he owned and named after himself, which was later annexed to Chicago.

Chicago celebrated its two decades of growth by sponsoring the World's Columbian Exposition of 1893, which also marked the 400th anniversary of Christopher Columbus's discovery of America, and which attracted more than 21 million visitors to the city. Chicago at this time was at the forefront of architectural innovation and became known as the birthplace of the skyscraper. Of particular architectural importance is the Chicago Board of Trade, where commodity futures are bought and sold. A politically active city, Chicago underwent a period of reform in the late 1890s. A civil service was inaugurated in 1895, and numerous reform organizations attempted to influence public opinion.

## Political Trends Shape City's Future

Five-term Mayor Carter H. Harrison Jr. brought the reform spirit to a high point, but weak law enforcement and other factors allowed gangsters such as Alphonse "Scarface" Capone and John Dillinger to rise to power in the 1920s and 1930s. Chicago was characterized the world over as a gangster headquarters long after Democratic reform Mayor Anton J. Cermak initiated cleanup efforts. He also introduced a style of ward and district politics copied after the New York City Tammany Hall political machine. Cermak was killed by an assassin's bullet intended for President-elect Franklin D. Roosevelt, but Cermak's political organization continued under Mayor Edward J. Kelly.

In 1933 Chicago gained world attention once again when it hosted A Century of Progress, a world exposition that celebrated the city's incorporation as a municipality; Chicago's industrial and financial advances and prosperity were on display despite the era's economic depression. In 1942 scientists working in Chicago produced the first nuclear chain reaction and thus advanced the creation of atomic weaponry and energy. During its history, Chicago has frequently been the site of national political meetings, including the Republican Party gathering to nominate Abraham Lincoln in 1860 and the Democratic Party convention that nominated Hubert H. Humphrey in 1968. The latter brought protestors against the Vietnam War to Chicago's streets and drew national attention to Mayor Richard J. Daley's handling of the demonstrators.

## The Mayors Daley

The most powerful symbol of Chicago politics, Richard J. Daley served as mayor from 1955 until his death in 1976. Daley was a major force in the national

Democratic Party and was considered the last "big city boss." His son, Richard M. Daley, ran for Chicago's mayoral office in 1989 in an election that *Time* magazine characterized as "an ethnic power struggle" that divided the city along racial lines. Chicago's first African American mayor, Harold Washington, had been elected in 1983 and reelected in 1987, but after his death the coalition of African Americans and white liberals that had elected him broke down; African American voter participation was down from previous elections while, according to *Time,* Daley's "richly financed campaign produced a large turnout among whites. Result: Daley, by 55% to 41%." Daley won 58 percent of the vote in 1995. As mayor of a city known for its widely diverse neighborhoods of Germans, Scandinavians, Irish, Jews, Italians, Poles, Eastern Europeans, Asians, Hispanics, and African Americans, Daley has faced the challenge of uniting the spirit of a divided city entering the twenty-first century as an internationally important urban center. With a national reputation as a skilled and astute negotiator, with powerful political supporters at the national level, Mayor Daley received another vote of confidence when the Democratic Party selected Chicago as the site of the 1996 National Convention. Mayor Daley has privatized a number of city government operations and by 1996 had passed balanced budgets seven years in a row; this and other successes accounted for his selection as national spokesperson for the U.S. Conference of Mayors in 1996. In 2005 Mayor Daley outlined his goals for the city in his annual City of Chicago address. These goals included a city in which every family could afford housing in a safe neighborhood, a city in which every child receives a quality education, and a city where good jobs are available to those who want to work.

Work on these goals had an almost immediate effect. In 2007 Chicago was named as "City of the Future" by *fDi Magazine* (a publication of the *Financial Times*). In the magazine's survey, Chicago was the only city to rank in the top five of all seven selection categories. The city was ranked first in the NAFTA region (USA, Canada, and Mexico) for Best Economic Potential, Best Infrastructure, and Best Development and Investment Promotion; second for Most Cost Effective; third for Best Human Resources and Best Quality of Life; and fifth for Most Business Friendly.

Today's Chicago exists as a cultural mecca, with world-class museums, restaurants, theater, and arts. Still, the "other side" of Chicago is not as shiny, in terms of blighted housing projects and crime—a stigma hard for any large city to overcome, yet continually addressed by the mayor and city leaders.

***Historical Information:*** Chicago Historical Society, 1629 North Clark Street at North Avenue, Chicago, IL 60614; telephone (312)642-4600; www.encyclopedia. chicagohistory.org

Image copyright pmphoto, 2007. Used under license from Shutterstock.com.

## ■ Population Profile

### Metropolitan Area Residents

1980: 7,937,290
1990: 7,410,858 (PMSA)
2000: 8,272,768
2006 estimate: 9,505,748
Percent change, 1990–2000: 23.6%
U.S. rank in 1980: 3rd
U.S. rank in 1990: 3rd
U.S. rank in 2000: 3rd

### City Residents

1980: 3,005,000
1990: 2,783,726
2000: 2,896,016
2006 estimate: 2,833,321
Percent change, 1990–2000: 4%
U.S. rank in 1980: 2nd
U.S. rank in 1990: 3rd (State rank: 1st)
U.S. rank in 2000: 3rd (State rank: 1st)

**Density:** 12,750.3 people per square mile (2000)

### Racial and ethnic characteristics (2005)

White: 1,042,025
Black: 943,752
American Indian and Alaska Native: 4,583
Asian: 128,650
Native Hawaiian and Pacific Islander: 1,940
Hispanic or Latino (may be of any race): 778,234
Other: 537,199

**Percent of residents born in state:** 57.7% (2000)

### Age characteristics (2005)

Population under 5 years old: 215,448
Population 5 to 9 years old: 192,010
Population 10 to 14 years old: 192,047
Population 15 to 19 years old: 173,662
Population 20 to 24 years old: 200,989
Population 25 to 34 years old: 463,236
Population 35 to 44 years old: 401,679
Population 45 to 54 years old: 343,098
Population 55 to 59 years old: 137,742
Population 60 to 64 years old: 105,930
Population 65 to 74 years old: 143,922
Population 75 to 84 years old: 97,850
Population 85 years and older: 34,313
Median age: 33.1 years

**Births (2006, Metropolitan Division)**

Total number: 116,444

**Deaths (2006, Metropolitan Division)**

Total number: 58,016

**Money income (2005)**

Per capita income: $23,449

Median household income: $41,015

Total households: 1,020,605

**Number of households with income of . . .**

less than $10,000: 133,257

$10,000 to $14,999: 73,223

$15,000 to $24,999: 123,892

$25,000 to $34,999: 121,258

$35,000 to $49,999: 142,230

$50,000 to $74,999: 173,114

$75,000 to $99,999: 98,598

$100,000 to $149,999: 91,842

$150,000 to $199,999: 31,506

$200,000 or more: 31,685

**Percent of families below poverty level:** 12% (2005)

**2005 FBI Crime Index Property:** 131,183

**2005 FBI Crime Index Violent:** Not available

# ■ Municipal Government

The Chicago city government is headed by a strong mayor and a nonpartisan, 50-member council; the mayor and council members (called aldermen) are elected to four-year terms. Aldermen are elected from 50 wards.

**Head Official:** Mayor Richard M. Daley (D) (since 1989; current term expires 2011)

**Total Number of City Employees:** more than 39,675 (2005)

*City Information:* Mayor's Office, City of Chicago, 121 N. Lasalle Street, Room 507, Chicago, IL 60602; telephone (312)744-3300; http://egov.cityofchicago.org

# ■ Economy

## Major Industries and Commercial Activity

The Chicago-Naperville-Joliet MSA has a diverse economy with primary industries (in terms of number of jobs) being trade, transportation, and utilities; professional and business services; educational and health services; leisure and hospitality; and financial services. The government sector is also significant.

Several major manufacturing companies have facilities in Chicago. One of the largest is Boeing Co., which was the largest manufacturing firm in the state in 2007 and was ranked as 28th nationally in the *Fortune* 500 the same year. O'Brien Recycling Corp., STARCON International, Inc., FreightCar America Inc., and United Scrap Metal were among the 50 fastest growing companies in Chicago in 2007, according to *Chicago Business*. The source of nationally distributed magazines, catalogs, educational materials, encyclopedias, and specialized publications, Chicago ranks second only to New York in the publishing industry. R.R. Donnelley & Sons is one of the largest publishing and printing firms in the nation. It also was ranked among the *Fortune* 500 in 2007. Two *Fortune* 500 utilities are based in Chicago: Exelon and Integrys Energy Group. Other Chicago companies in the *Fortune* 500 for 2007 included Smurfit-Stone Container, Ryerson, USG Corp, Wm. Wrigley Jr., and Northern Trust Corp. Manufacturing companies with headquarters in Chicago include Abbott Laboratories, CF Industries, Akzo Nobel, TAP Pharmaceuticals, Materials Science Corp., Kraft Foods, and Toshiba Machine.

A substantial industrial base and a major inland port contribute to the city's position as a national transportation and distribution center. Concert Group Logistics LLC was ranked as the city's second-fastest growing company in 2007 by *Chicago Business*. Phoenix International Freight was also among the top 50.

Health cares services have a solid base in the economy. The hospitals, clinics, laboratories, and schools of the Illinois Medical District generate about $3.3 billion in economic activity each year with an estimated 50,000 direct and indirect jobs and $24 million in annual local taxes. The Chicago Technology Park within the district continues to attract new tech and research firms to its state-of-the art facilities. Technology-based industries have grown rapidly within the city, particularly in information technology. In 2006 over 345,000 info-tech employees were at work in Chicago. Motorola, VTech Electronics, and Telular all have headquarters in the city. AT&T, MCI, Sprint Nextel, and Verizon all have offices in the city as well. Scientific research and development service organizations have also been drawn to the area. Argonne National Laboratory is managed and operated, in part, by a team from the University of Chicago. Underwriters Laboratories and Essential Group have headquarters in the Chicago area.

Retail sales are quite high in the Chicago area. In 2007 the Chicago metropolitan area was ranked as third in the nation, with retail sales larger than those of 28 states. Business and financial services have a major role in the city's economy. In 2007 the Chicago Board of Trade and the Chicago Mercantile Exchange completed a merger that resulted in the establishment of the largest and most diverse exchange in the world. Chicago is also home to the Federal Reserve Bank. In 2007 optionsXpress, Advanced Equities Financial Corp, Acquity Group, and Calamos Asset Management Inc. were in the top 50 fastest growing companies according to *Crain's Chicago Business*. Some of the top names in securities and commodities contracts brokerage have offices in Chicago, including Charles Schwab, Merrill Lynch, Wachovia Securities, Goldman Sachs, and E*Trade Capital Markets. In the June/July 2007 issue of *Trader Monthly* magazine, Chicago was named number one among the Top 50 Trading Cities in the World. The magazine, which is aimed at professional traders and hedge fund managers, ranked 50 cities worldwide in an effort to find the ultimate place to live and trade. Chicago serves as headquarters to several national insurance companies, including Allstate, Blue Cross and Blue Shield Association, CNA Financial, UnitedHealthcare of Illinois, and Trustmark Insurance.

**Items and goods produced:** paper, newspapers, magazines, books, food products, concrete products, clay, glass, primary metals, machinery, packaging materials, pharmaceuticals, paint, adhesives, coatings, fabricated metals, plastics, electrical equipment, communications equipment, medical devices, agricultural feedstock and chemicals

## Incentive Programs—New and Existing Companies

*Local programs:* The City of Chicago Department of Planning and Development (DPD) actively promotes growth and development in Chicago's diverse neighborhoods with a focus on the continued economic development of the city. The department works with the existing business community and also works to attract new business to Chicago. All of this is done in the context of holistic, community-based planning, closely coordinating activities with residents and community organizations. The department's Technology Development Division works with the Chicago Partnership for Economic Development to strengthen the city's information technology sector.

DPD promotes effective neighborhood planning by coordinating the strategic allocation of public funds to maximize private investment—and the attraction of new companies—by providing a menu of financial resources, neighborhood improvements, site location assistance, and the expediting of permits and licenses. DPD also has the primary responsibility for preserving city landmarks and protecting the Chicago River and the Lake Michigan shoreline.

In 1977 the Illinois legislature adopted the Tax Increment Allocation Redevelopment Act to provide municipalities with a unique tool to finance and stimulate urban redevelopment. Through the use of Tax Increment Financing (TIF), cities can stimulate private investment by offering incentives to attract and retain

businesses, improve their community areas, and maintain a well-educated and highly trained labor force. TIF is by far the most popular incentive program in Chicago; by the end of 2003, Chicago had invested $870 million in TIF funds and benefited from $5.4 billion in private investment. Cook County Property Tax Incentives are also available.

*State and federal programs:* Chicago has six state-designated Enterprise Zones. Businesses located in an Enterprise Zone are eligible for an Investment Tax Credit, a Building and Materials Sales Tax Exemption (6.25 percent), and a Machinery and Equipment/Pollution Control Facilities Sales Tax Exemption (6.25 percent). A Jobs Tax Credit of $500 is also available for jobs, created in the zones, for certified dislocated or economically disadvantaged workers. Three areas within the city are U.S.-designated Empowerment Zones. Incentives within an Empowerment Zone include employer wage credits of up to $3,000 for wages and training expenses for qualified zone residents employed within the zone, tax-exempt bond financing for business expansions, and certain property tax deductions. Foreign Trade Zone incentives apply for city businesses as well. The Economic Development for Growing Economy Tax Credit Program (EDGE) is a statewide program to benefit companies that relocate or expand operations within the state. Qualifying companies must make an investment of at least $5 million in capital improvements and create a minimum of 25 new full-time jobs in the state. Companies with 100 or fewer employees must make a capital investment of $1 million and create at least five full-time jobs to qualify. The High Impact Business program is designed to encourage large-scale economic development initiatives. Business projects that involve at least $12 million in investments and the creation of 500 full-time jobs may qualify for investment tax credits and state sales tax exemptions on building materials, utilities, and the purchase, repair, or replacement of manufacturing equipment. Other state sponsored tax credits include a Research and development Tax Credit of 6.5 percent and a Manufacturer's Purchase Credit of 6.25 percent for qualified businesses. A number of loan programs are available.

*Job training programs:* The Mayor's Office of Workforce Development (MOWD) assists job seekers—including those who have been laid off—in finding and keeping jobs. The Mayor's Office also sponsors Workforce Solutions, a program to help Chicago businesses find, train, and retain employees. The five Chicago Workforce Centers located throughout the city, as well as 30 community-based affiliate organizations, offer services such as basic job skills courses, access to job listings, seminars in resume writing and interviewing, and veterans services. Through the Employer Training and Investment Program, qualified employers may receive grants for up to 50 percent of costs in training new employees.

## Development Projects

In the summer of 2004, the long-anticipated Millennium Park opened. Conceived in the late 1990s with the goal of creating more usable space in Grant Park, the $475 million park is a state-of-the-art example of modern city green space. The Jay Pritzker Pavilion, designed by world-renowned architect Frank Gehry, is an outdoor concert venue that seats 4,000 people. The Cloud Gate, sculpted by Anish Kapoor, is a 110-ton elliptical sculpture made of stainless steel. Visitors can walk under and around the sculpture, which resembles a giant bean and reflects Chicago's skyline. Another popular attraction is the Jarume Plensa-designed Crown Fountain, two 50-foot high towers made of glass blocks and situated in a reflecting pool. The towers feature changing video images of the faces of Chicagoans, from which jets of water appear to descend.

In 2005 groundbreaking began on the Art Institute of Chicago's new museum wing on the museum's northeast corner. The Modern Wing, expected to be completed in 2009, is designed by architect Renzo Piano and is expected to add approximately 264,000 square feet of space to the museum. The Wing will include a new Ryan Education Center. The $198 million addition will add a contemporary appeal to the museum's 19th century building.

The O'Hare Modernization Program, announced in 1999, is Chicago's O'Hare International Airport's 20-year master plan for modernization and capital improvement. The plan outlines possible projects and funding sources without a clear expectation that all of the improvements or additions will be made. As of 2007 a $6.6 billion portion of the program was under construction that would add a new western terminal facility and reconfigure existing runways. The entire plan would require over $13 billion in funding through passenger facility charges, general airport revenue bonds, and federal Airport Improvement Program funds. No state or local taxes will be used in these projects.

The year 2007 marked the grand opening of McCormick Place West, the $882 million expansion of the McCormick Place convention facility. The expansion added 470,000 square feet of exhibition space and 250,000 square feet of meeting space to the existing McCormick Place campus. The new facility is expected to generate about 25,000 new jobs and an additional $1.3 billion in annual local spending. As of 2007 construction was still underway on this project.

Also in 2007, the Chicago Housing Authority gained city council approval for its Roosevelt Square Redevelopment Project. The project calls for redevelopment and construction of 255 mixed-income for-sale residential units on 38 parcels of city-owned land. Seventy-six units will be sold at affordable prices while the remaining 179 residential units will be offered at market rates. The total cost of the development project is $99

million. Previous redevelopment projects at Roosevelt Square resulted in 233 mixed-income for-sale units and 3,000 square feet of retail space.

The same year the city approved a project to redevelop an old city fire station on Hamlin Avenue into the Firehouse Community Arts Center. The three-story building will be converted into a community arts center for people between the ages of 12 to 21 and offer a wide variety of programs including educational tutoring, computer training, graphic arts and music classes, and culinary instruction. The total cost of the project is $548,905.

In February of 2007 the mayor announced the opening of the Chicago China Development Corporation in Shanghai, China. This public-private, not-for-profit corporation is chaired by the mayor with oversight by a board of directors of Chicago business leaders who have been appointed by the mayor. The city hopes the new office will encourage Chinese investment in Chicago and develop new markets in China for products and services produced by Chicago companies.

***Economic Development Information:*** Chicago Department of Planning and Development, 121 N. LaSalle Street, #1000, Chicago, IL 60602; telephone (312)744-9476; www.cityofchicago.org/plananddevelop. World Business Chicago, 177 North State St., Ste. 500, Chicago, IL 60601; telephone (312)553-0500; www.worldbusinesschicago.com

## Commercial Shipping

Since its founding, Chicago has been an important transportation and distribution point. The city became a world port in 1959 with the opening of the St. Lawrence Seaway, which provides a direct link from the Great Lakes to the Atlantic Ocean. The Port of Chicago handles marine, rail, and overland freight. The city is the site of the nation's busiest rail hub, where all six class one North American railroads interchange. The state of Illinois maintains the third-highest combined mileage of railroads and paved highways in the country. Hundreds of motor freight carriers serve the metropolitan area and trucking companies ship more than 50 million tons of freight each year; railroads average more than 40 million tons. O'Hare International Airport hosts 23 cargo carriers serving over 210 global destinations. O'Hare is one of the top ten busiest cargo-moving airports in North America. The port and airport are part of a designated Foreign Trade Zone.

## Labor Force and Employment Outlook

In 2006 the annual unemployment rate for Chicago-Naperville-Joliet MSA was about 4.4 percent. That number went up to about 5.5 percent in July of 2007. The loss of jobs for both unskilled and college-educated workers can be attributed to the Internet bust of the early 2000s, an ailing economy, plant closings, and the relocation of companies once headquartered in Chicago. However, the unemployment rate seems now to be on a decline. In 2007 the top five occupations were office and administrative support, sales, service, management, and professional occupations. Long-term employment projections for 2004-2014 predict a decline in manufacturing jobs. Professional and business services are projected to show the greatest increase in available jobs, followed by health care and social assistance, and educational services. The leisure and hospitality sectors are likely to show an increase as well.

Like many large cities, Chicago has a large immigrant population. The immigrants come from all over the world, including Poland, Mexico, India, the former Soviet Union, the Philippines, and China. Despite fears that low-skilled immigrants would not be assimilated into an increasingly high-tech economy, local analysts say the newcomers are following the success track of earlier groups, working their way into the middle class after performing service and laboring jobs.

The following is a summary of data regarding the Chicago-Naperville-Joliet IL-IN-WI metropolitan area labor force, 2006 annual averages.

**Size of nonagricultural labor force:** 3,845,800

**Number of workers employed in . . .**

construction and mining: 180,300
manufacturing: 390,200
trade, transportation and utilities: 921,600
information: 91,100
financial activities: 332,100
professional and business services: 729,000
educational and health services: 575,100
leisure and hospitality: 398,700
other services: 197,600
government: 565,200

**Average hourly earnings of production workers employed in manufacturing:** $15.77

**Unemployment rate:** 5.5% (June 2007)

| Largest employers (2005) | Number of employees |
|---|---|
| U.S. Government | 78,000 |
| Chicago Public Schools | 43,783 |
| City of Chicago | 39,675 |
| Jewel-Osco | 34,037 |
| Cook County | 25,482 |
| Advocate Health Care | 25,279 |
| United Parcel Service of America Inc. | 19,346 |
| State of Illinois | 17,056 |
| SBC Communications Inc. | 16,500 |
| Wal-Mart Stores | 16,350 |

## Cost of Living

The cost of living in Chicago is higher than the national average. The following is a summary of data regarding several key cost of living factors in the Chicago area.

**2007 (1st quarter) ACCRA Average House Price:** $368,027

**2007 (1st quarter) ACCRA Cost of Living Index:** 113.7

**State income tax rate:** 3.0% of Federal Adjusted Gross Income, with modifications

**State sales tax rate:** 6.25%

**Local income tax rate:** None

**Local sales tax rate:** 2.75%

**Property tax rate:** 7.247 mills (2002)

***Economic Information:*** World Business Chicago, 177 North State St., Ste. 500, Chicago, IL 60601; telephone (312)553-0500; www.worldbusinesschicago.com

# ■ Education and Research

## Elementary and Secondary Schools

The Chicago Public Schools (CPS) system is the largest public elementary and secondary educational system in Illinois. Several initiatives, such as the Chicago Reading Initiative and the Chicago Math and Science Initiative are programs that have been implemented district-wide to ensure students meet minimum achievement standards in basic subjects. The After School Matters program is a partnership between CPS, the Chicago Park District, the Chicago Public Library, and the City of Chicago. Apprenticeships and club activities offer teens exposure to and on-the-job training in the arts, sports technology, and communications. Special two-year secondary school programs called Achievement Academies have been developed for students who do not meet the promotion criteria to enter high school. The achievement academy programs, located within existing high schools, are a collaborative effort between Chicago Public Schools and Johns Hopkins University of Baltimore Maryland.

Charter schools have taken root in the city. In 1997 the Illinois General Assembly approved 60 charter schools for the state. Chicago itself started 49 charter schools between 1997 and 2007. In 2004 the city announced a program called the Renaissance 2010 initiative. Renaissance 2010 calls for 100 new schools to be established by 2010. Through the plan, a competitive, community-based selection process will determine the best school operators for each site.

In 2007 the system included 4 military academies (high school), 51 magnet schools, 12 vocational and career schools, 9 achievement academies, and 9 special education sites.

Because of the city's large foreign-born population, the school system employs bilingual teachers in 20 languages. Special schools include Chicago High School for Agricultural Sciences, situated on the last farm in the city of Chicago, which prepares students for jobs in agriculture, and Curie Metropolitan High School, with magnet programs in the performing and creative arts and electronic repair and maintenance.

The following is a summary of data regarding the Chicago Public Schools as of the 2005–2006 school year.

**Total enrollment:** 429,982

**Number of facilities**

    elementary schools: 465
    junior high/middle schools: 16
    senior high schools: 115
    other: 27

**Student/teacher ratio:** 16.8:1

**Teacher salaries (2005–06)**

    elementary median: $52,950
    junior high/middle median: $49,870
    secondary median: $59,930

**Funding per pupil:** $8,157

The Archdiocese of Chicago operates over 240 schools in Cook and Lake counties, with an enrollment in excess of 107,000 students. There are several independent or other religious-affiliated private schools in the city.

***Public Schools Information:*** Chicago Public Schools, 125 South Clark Street, Chicago, IL 60603; telephone (773)553-1000; www.cps.k12.il.us

## Colleges and Universities

There are three major public universities in the city. The University of Illinois at Chicago (UIC) was established in 1982 by the consolidation of the University of Illinois Medical Center campus, the Chicago Circle campus, and the Navy Pier campus. UIC is a public research university that enrolls approximately 25,125 students earning bachelor's, master's, and doctoral degrees and first professional degrees in dentistry, medicine, and pharmacy.

Chicago State University offers bachelor's degrees through the Colleges of Arts and Sciences, Business, Education, and Health Sciences. Master's degrees are available through the College of Arts and Sciences and the College of Education. Enrollment is about 7,000 students. Northeastern Illinois University offers over 70 undergraduate and graduate programs. In addition to the main campus, the school has two Chicago satellite sites:

NEIU-El Centro and the Carruthers Center for Inner City Studies.

The private University of Chicago (UC), founded with an endowment by John D. Rockefeller in 1891, enjoys an international reputation for pioneering science research and the "Chicago plan" in undergraduate education. The university claims more than 80 Nobel laureates—far more than any other university in the country. The university administers advanced scholarship and research centers, including the Enrico Fermi Institute, the Enrico Fermi National Accelerator Laboratory, and the Argonne National Laboratory, among others. Enrollment is over 13,400 students. In 2008 *U.S. News & World Report* ranked the University of Chicago as ninth among the top national universities.

The city's three leading Catholic institutions are DePaul University, offering undergraduate, master's and doctorate and law programs to more than 23,000 students; Loyola University Chicago, which awards bachelor's, master's, and doctoral degrees, first-professional degrees in dentistry, law, and medicine, and a master's degree in divinity to its more than 15,500 students; and Saint Xavier University, where popular recent majors among its 5,678 students were business, nursing, and education.

North Park University, a liberal arts university affiliated with the Evangelical Covenant Church, has an enrollment of over 3,100 students. The school offers 50 undergraduate majors and graduate programs in the fields of music, education, nursing, and business and nonprofit management. The North Park Theological Seminary shares the campus. Moody Bible Institute, a private Christian college known primarily for its worldwide broadcast ministries, offers bachelor's and master's degrees, primarily in ministry-related fields.

The Illinois Institute of Technology (IIT) enrolls more than 6,000 students and offers professional programs in the sciences, engineering, law, art, and architecture. In 2008 *U.S. News & World Report* ranked IIT among the Top 100 National Universities. The School of the Art Institute of Chicago, with more than 2,588 students, holds national stature in art instruction. Rush University, part of the Rush University Medical Center campus, includes the Rush Medical College, the College of Nursing, the College of Health Sciences, and the Graduate College. Enrollment is over 1,300 students.

City Colleges of Chicago is a network of seven main colleges in the city, each of which has its own satellite departments as well. The main City College campus sponsors the French Pastry School; Daley College sponsors the West Side Technical Institute; Harold Washington College offers an adult education program; Kennedy-King College sponsors Dawson Technical Institute and the Washburne Culinary Institute; Malcolm X College offers a special West Side Learning Center; Olive-Harvey College has the South Chicago Learning Center; Truman College sponsors the Truman Technical Center; and Wright College sponsors the Humboldt Park Vocational Education Center. Each of the colleges offers associate's degrees, certificate programs, and continuing education classes.

Other colleges in the area include Columbia College, DeVry University, the Harrington Institute of Interior Design, the Illinois College of Optometry, Lexington College, Westwood College, Northwestern Business College, Fox College, and Vandercook College of Music.

## Libraries and Research Centers

The Chicago Public Library encompasses 77 neighborhood branches, 2 regional libraries, and the central Harold Washington Library Center, which opened in 1991 and is one of the foremost educational and cultural resources in the city of Chicago. At 756,000 square feet, the library center is one of the largest municipal buildings in the world. The library's collection consists of about 6.5 million books, 14,500 periodicals and serials, 90,000 audiovisual titles, and 3 million microfiche. A special collection of books and materials in 90 foreign languages is maintained and the library center is the repository for the Chicago Theater Collection, the Civil War Collection, and the Chicago Blues Archives. The library center also boasts an 18,000-square-foot children's library, a bustling business/science/technology division, and a Teacher Resource Center offering print and online resources to assist educators. On display throughout the building is an extensive public art collection.

Staff members in each library of the public library system build their own collections and tailor services to meet the needs of their local communities. Since 1989, the city has built or renovated more than 40 branch libraries. Currently, new construction projects, renovations, expansions, and consolidation projects are underway. All of Chicago's public libraries offer free Internet access and free access to research databases.

The approximately 275 other libraries located in Chicago are affiliated with such entities as government agencies, colleges and universities, cultural and historical societies, professional organizations, research institutes, religious organizations, hospitals and medical associations, private corporations, and law firms.

The University of Chicago, internationally recognized for excellence in education and research, maintains a central library facility with more than 7 million printed works and 30 million manuscripts and archival pieces. Special collections are maintained in American and British literature, American history, theology and biblical criticism, American and British drama, and Continental literature. The University of Chicago operates seven separate library facilities, including the D'Angelo Law Library and the Social Service Administration Library.

The Newberry Library, an independent research library, was founded in 1887. Free to the public, the library's non-circulating research materials number more

than 1.5 million volumes, 5 million manuscript pages, and 300,000 historic maps; among the special collections are the Edward E. Ayer Collection (American Indian history), the Prince Louis-Lucien Bonaparte Collection (historical linguistics), the Everett D. Graff Collection (western Americana), and the John M. Wing Foundation (printing, book arts, and the history of the book).

One of the largest research libraries in Chicago is the Center for Research Libraries, an international not-for-profit consortium of colleges, universities, and libraries that makes available scholarly research resources to users everywhere. It houses more than 5 million books and periodicals; fields of study include Africa, South Asia, South East Asia, Latin America, and war crime trials. The Chicago Academy of Sciences' International Center for the Advancement of Scientific Literacy (ICASL) is the leading research organization in the world studying and measuring the impact of science and technology on public awareness. The National Opinion Research Center collects current opinion poll reports conducted for commercial television networks, newspapers, state governments, and professional pollsters such as Gallup and Harris. The Chicago Historical Society maintains research collections on Chicago, the Civil War, Abraham Lincoln, Illinois, and United States history.

The University of Chicago is a major research university with numerous institutes and centers devoted to a wide range of studies. These include the Kavli Institute for Cosmological Physics, the Institute for Biophysical Dynamics, the Asthma Center, the Great Lakes Regional Center of Excellence for Biodefense and Emerging Infectious Diseases, the Pew Forum on Religion and Public Life, the Climate Systems Center, and the Center for Decision Research. The University of Chicago served as the primary manager and operator of Argonne National Laboratory until 2006, when management came under UChicago Argonne, LLC, a partnership between the University, Jacobs Engineering Group Inc., and BWX Technologies Inc. Argonne National Laboratory is known for its research in support of the U.S. Department of Energy.

The University of Illinois at Chicago also serves as a major research university with centers and institutes that include the Energy Resources Center, the Institute for Juvenile Research, the Center for Pharmoeconomic Research, the Institute for Tuberculosis Research, and the WHO Collaborating Center for Traditional Medicine. Research centers at Illinois Institute of Technology include the Center of Excellence in Polymer Science and Engineering, the Center for Complex Systems and Dynamics, the Center for Work Zone Safety and Mobility, the Fluid Dynamics Research Center, the National Center for Food Safety and Technology, and the Center for the Study of Ethics in Professions.

The Chicago Technology Park (CTP) is a 56-acre area within the Illinois Medical District (IMD) that supports companies in the fields of drug discovery and delivery, medical devices and testing, genomics, nano-technology and more. The CTP Research Center is home to about 30 biotech firms including Charles River Laboratories, Euclid Diagnostics, Novadrug, and Integrated Genomics, Inc.

Other research centers in the Chicago area include those maintained by Bell Labs, Nalco Chemical, the Institute of Gas Technology, the Illinois State Psychiatric Institute, the Institute for Psychoanalysis, and the Institute on the Church in Urban-Industrial Society.

***Public Library Information:*** Chicago Public Library, 400 South State Street, Chicago, IL 60605. Information Center, telephone (312)747-4300; www.chipublib.org

# ■ Health Care

Chicago ranks among the country's leading centers for health care and referral as well as for medical training and research, generally due to the university hospitals, teaching centers, and medical facilities. Hospital facilities in Chicago have undergone major changes in the past 25 years, however. Between 1980 and 2004, the number of hospitals in Chicago has shrunk by nearly 35 percent, from 64 hospitals in 1980 to 42 in 2004, representing a decrease in hospital beds by nearly 50 percent.

The University of Chicago Medical Center, nationally recognized for training and research, is associated with the University of Chicago colleges of medicine, dentistry, nursing, and pharmacy; individual facilities are Bernard Mitchell Hospital, The UC Corner Children's Hospital, the Duchossois Center for Advanced Medicine, and Chicago Lying-in Hospital. A full range of general and specialized services are available as well as a chemical dependence program, corporate health services, an eating disorders program, geriatric and health evaluation services, and centers for treatment of kidney stones and sexually transmitted diseases. In 2007 the University of Chicago Medical Center was listed on the "Honor Roll of Best Hospitals" by *U.S. News & World Report.*

The Illinois Medical District covers 560 acres in the heart of Chicago. Encompassing 4 major medical centers, 4 medical institutions, 5 health clinics, 12 public safety institutes, and the Chicago Technology Park, it is the largest urban medical district in the country. The University of Illinois Medical Center is part of the district. It offers a full range of medical services with specialties in islet transplants and small bowel transplants. The 464-bed John H. Stroger, Jr. Hospital of Cook County features a Level I Trauma Center and specialty services for chronic diseases and burn care. The privately-run Rush University Medical Center, also in the district, encompasses the 613-bed main hospital (Rush-Presbyterian-St. Luke's Medical Center), the 61-bed Johnston R. Bowman health Center, and the Rush University Medical College and Rush

School of Nursing. The hospital operates centers for treatment of cancer, multiple sclerosis, cardiac ailments, sleep disorders, alcohol and substance abuse, Alzheimer's disease, epilepsy, and arthritis. The complex also houses organ and bone marrow transplant units as well as the Chicago and Northeastern Regional Poison Control Center. The Jesse Brown VA Medical Center is also part of the district.

# ■ Recreation

## Sightseeing

Chicago is an ethnically diverse, architecturally important, and culturally rich city. It can be appreciated from the observation floor of the Sears Tower, at 110 stories the third-tallest manmade structure in the world. In fact, three of the world's 10 tallest buildings are located in Chicago, along with the tallest apartment building, the largest hotel, the largest commercial structure, and the largest post office. Guided sightseeing tours are available for viewing the city's architecture, finance and business districts, ethnic neighborhoods, cultural institutions, and even gangland sites from the Prohibition Era.

The distinctive Chicago School of Architecture, with its aesthetic credo, "form follows function," was shaped by such masters as Louis Sullivan, Frank Lloyd Wright, and a later functionalist architect, Ludwig Mies van der Rohe—all of whom designed buildings in the city and produced in Chicago a veritable living architectural museum. Also important are the city's outdoor sculptures and art works. Pablo Picasso's gift to Chicago, a 50-foot-tall sculpture of rusted steel at the Civic Center Plaza, has become a symbol of the city's modernity. Other works include Claes Oldenburg's *Batcolumn,* Alexander Calder's 53-foot-high red Flamingo stabile, Marc Chagall's *Four Seasons* mosaic, Louise Nevelson's *Dawn Shadow,* Joan Miro's *Chicago,* and Jean Dubuffet's *Monument with Standing Beast.*

The Shedd Aquarium, the world's largest indoor aquarium, cares for more than 21,000 aquatic mammals, reptiles, amphibians, invertebrates, and fishes. A major attraction is the Oceanarium, the world's largest indoor marine mammal pavilion, featuring beluga whales, dolphins, Alaskan sea otters, seals, and penguins. In 2003 the aquarium unveiled its Wild Reef shark exhibit. Next to the Shedd Aquarium, the Adler Planetarium and Astronomy Museum sits on a peninsula that juts a half mile into Lake Michigan. The Museum of Science and Industry, founded in 1933, houses thousands of exhibits, including the Idea Factory and Omnimax Theatre; a full-scale, working coal mine; a WWII captured German submarine; a Boeing 727 airplane that visitors can walk through; and a walk-though model of a human heart. It was the first museum in North America to feature the concept of hands-on exhibits. The Chicago area's two zoos are the Brookfield Zoo and the Lincoln Park Zoo. Just north of the city, the Chicago Botanic Garden features an international collection of flora on 385 acres.

## Arts and Culture

Chicago's major cultural institutions rank with the best in the world. The Chicago Symphony Orchestra plays a season of more than 150 concerts, with programs at Symphony Center from September to June and summer concerts at Ravinia Park in Highland Park. Equally prestigious is the Lyric Opera of Chicago, which stages classical and innovative operas at the recently renovated Civic Opera House.

Other musical offerings range from Dixieland jazz imported by the late Louis Armstrong to the electrified urban blues sound pioneered by Muddy Waters, frequently referred to as Chicago Blues. All-night jazz and blues clubs are a Chicago tradition. The Ravinia Festival is a summer season of outstanding classical, popular, and jazz concerts performed by well-known artists.

More than 50 producing theaters delight Chicago audiences with fare ranging from serious to satirical. The Goodman Theatre, Chicago's oldest and largest non-profit professional theater, presents a season of classical and modern dramatic productions. Chicago theater is perhaps best represented by Steppenwolf Theatre Company, a Tony Award-winning repertory company that focuses on new plays, neglected works, and re-interpretations of masterpieces. Since 1959, The Second City, a resident comedy company that produces biting satires, has had a direct influence on American comedy as its members have gone on to star on the "Saturday Night Live" and "SCTV" television programs and in Hollywood movies. Chicago's historic and architecturally significant theater houses include the restored 1920s Chicago Theatre, Shubert Theatre and Auditorium Theatre, built by Dankmar Adler and Louis Sullivan in 1889. Chicago's active theater scene includes young companies such as the Lookingglass Theatre Company and dinner theater groups. There are also several dance companies in the city, including the Joffrey Ballet of Chicago.

The Art Institute of Chicago is another local institution with an international reputation. Its collection is recognized for French Impressionist and Post-Impressionist paintings and for comprehensive holdings of American art and photographs. The Mexican Fine Arts Center Museum is the first Mexican museum in the United States and the only Latino museum accredited by the American Association of Museums; galleries of Polish, Swedish, Chinese, Japanese, and Korean art have opened in the city as well. The National Vietnam Veterans Art Museum houses a permanent collection of more than 500 pieces focusing on war from the soldiers' perspective. Chicago's love of art is even evidenced in the Loop's parking garage, where famous paintings are reproduced.

The Field Museum of Natural History, founded in 1893, is rated among the top museums in the world; its holdings number more than 16 million artifacts and specimens from the fields of anthropology, botany, geology, and zoology. A scientific research institution, the Field Museum examines life and culture from pre-history to the present time.

The Chicago Academy of Sciences, founded in 1857, was Chicago's first museum and features natural science exhibits as well as timely scientific displays. Among the special attractions are life-size dioramas on natural areas of the Great Lakes and the children's gallery with its lifelike animated dinosaurs and prehistoric creatures. The Academy's Peggy Notebaert Nature Museum features 73,000 square feet of interactive, environmental education. The city's oldest cultural institution is the Chicago Historical Society; its galleries are filled with folk art, furniture, costumes, and manuscripts and a unique audiovisual presentation of the Great Chicago Fire. The DuSable Museum is the nation's first museum dedicated to preserving, displaying, and interpreting the culture, history, and achievements of African Americans.

The Museum of Contemporary Art, one of the largest of its kind in the country at 151,000 square feet, focuses on contemporary works that are often risk-taking and controversial. Its permanent collection includes works by Christo, Rene Magritte, and Andy Warhol. The Chicago Cultural Center presents hundreds of free programs, concerts, and exhibitions annually. Visitors to the center can see the world's largest Tiffany stained-glass dome.

***Arts and Culture Information:*** Chicago Cultural Center, 78 E. Washington Street, Chicago, IL 60602; telephone (312)744-6630; www.chicagoculturalcenter .org

## Festivals and Holidays

The Chicago Park District and the city's major cultural institutions sponsor events throughout the year, but special summer programming is designed to tap into Chicago's heritage and to attract tourists. The Chicago Blues Festival takes place the second weekend in June at the Petrillo Music Shell and brings the best blues musicians to one of the world's blues capitals for concerts, food, and exchange of memorabilia. The Printers Row Book Fair, in June, is the largest free literary event in the Midwest. Taste of Chicago, held over two weeks in late June and early July, features food sampling from Chicago restaurants as well as entertainment in Grant Park. Viva Chicago, held in August-September, is a festival celebrating Latino music, food, and arts and crafts at the Petrillo Music Shell. Other music festivals held annually in Chicago include Chicago Gospel Festival (June), Chicago Country Music Festival (June-July), Chicago Jazz Festival (August-September), Celtic Festival Chicago (September), and World Music Fest Chicago (September-October). Mayor Daley's Holiday Sports

Festival is held in December. October's Chicago International Film Festival is one of the largest in the country.

Chicago's city parks offer a wealth of free activities in the summer, such as the Grant Park Symphony Orchestra's four weekly concerts at the nation's largest free symphonic music festival.

***Visitor Information:*** Chicago Convention and Tourism Bureau, 2301 S. Lake Shore Drive, Chicago, IL 60616; telephone (312)567-8500; www.choosechicago.com

## Sports for the Spectator

Chicago fields at least one team in each of the major professional sports and is one of the only cities in the United States with two professional baseball teams in the Major League Baseball Association. The Chicago Cubs compete in the central division of the National League and play their home games at Wrigley Field, a turn-of-the-century steel and concrete structure where seats are close to the field. The Chicago White Sox of the American League's central division play their home games at U.S. Cellular Field on the city's South Side. The teams—and their fans—enjoy a fierce rivalry. The Chicago Bears of the National Football League's National Conference compete in central division home games at the recently renovated Soldier Field. The Chicago Fire, Chicago's Major League Soccer franchise, also play at Soldier Field. The Chicago Blackhawks of the National Hockey League and the Chicago Bulls of the National Basketball Association play their home schedules at the United Center.

The American Hockey League's Chicago Wolves and the Chicago Rush of the Arena Football League play at the Allstate Arena in nearby Rosemont.

Auto racing fans can view competition at Chicago Motor Speedway in Cicero, while horse racing action takes place from July to November at Hawthorne Race Course in Stickney/Cicero.

## Sports for the Participant

The Chicago Park District maintains some 552 parks spread out over 7,300 acres, including Lincoln Park, Grant Park, Jackson Park, and Washington Park. Chicago's paved lakefront pathway stretches along the shore from the south side of the city to the north side; thousands of Chicago residents and visitors use the path daily for cycling, strolling, running, in-line skating, and even commuting from one end of the city to the other. Located in the metropolitan area are forest preserves, 6 golf courses, tennis courts, swimming pools and lagoons, spraypool and water playgrounds, 33 beaches, and numerous athletic fields. In the summertime Chicago becomes the country's largest beach town as sun fanciers flock to 29 miles of lakefront beaches and yacht clubs to enjoy watersports. Lake Michigan, once one of the most industrially abused regions of the Great Lakes, has experienced a remarkable environmental recovery. The fishing season on Lake Michigan runs year round, while the lake's boating season generally extends from May 15 to October 15; the Park District maintains jurisdiction over the city's nine harbors.

A major attraction is the annual Chicago to Mackinac Island (Michigan) sailboat race, during which participants sail the length of Lake Michigan. Chicago also boasts two golf courses built atop a former solid-waste dump. The prize-winning environmental engineering project, called Harborside International Golf Center, is only 16 minutes from downtown Chicago.

The LaSalle Bank Chicago Marathon, started in 1977 as the Mayor Daley Marathon, has become one of the most prestigious—and largest—marathon events in the world. Held each October, nearly 40,000 elite and recreational runners complete the 26.2-mile race that begins and ends at Grant Park. Hundreds of thousands of spectators line the course, which passes through the downtown Loop and many of the city's ethnic neighborhoods. Due to its fast, flat course, several world records have been set at the Chicago Marathon.

## Shopping and Dining

Chicago's commercial district, formerly confined to the area known as The Loop, which was defined by a circuit of elevated trains, now pushes north of the Chicago River to Oak Street. Known as the "Magnificent Mile," the shopping area is considered the Rodeo Drive of the Midwest. Here, in and around buildings of architectural interest, are located some of the world's finest specialty stores. Water Tower Place on North Michigan is a seven-level modern shopping emporium with Chicago-based Marshall Field's and Lord & Taylor. A block away, Chicago Place, an eight-level mall, is anchored by Saks Fifth Avenue and houses Talbots, Ann Taylor, and Chiaroscuro. American Girl Place is a popular destination for young girls and their parents, where they can purchase American Girl dolls and accessories, have tea in the café, or view a show in the American Girl Theater. At 900 North Michigan shops are Bloomingdale's, Coach, Gucci, and Teuscher Chocolates of Switzerland. On nearby Oak Street one can find designs from Paris, Milan, and New York. North of the bustling Michigan Avenue shopping area is the Armitage-Halsted-Webster shopping area, with upscale restaurants and shops. Newly refurbished State Street, located downtown, offers a seven-block shopping experience at such landmarks as Carson Pirie Scott & Company and the flagship Marshall Field's.

Downtown Chicago features a remarkable diversity of bookstores, ranging from the Afrocentric Bookstore to The Savvy Traveler. Book lovers might like to pick up a copy of the Greater Loop Book District's pamphlet, showing the location of more than 20 bookstores in the Loop. It is available at airports, bookstores, and all visitor information centers.

On the waterfront, Navy Pier offers more than 50 acres of parks, promenades, gardens, shops, restaurants, and entertainment in a renovated warehouse. On North Orleans Street are the Merchandise Mart, the world's largest wholesale center, and the Chicago Apparel Center.

Chicago is served by some of the nation's finest restaurants. Every type of cuisine, from ethnic to traditional American fare, is available at restaurants in metropolitan Chicago. The city's eateries, housed in elegant turn-of-the century hotels, modern chrome and glass structures, and neighborhood cafes, are recognized for consistently high quality. Among Chicago's most renowned restaurants are Ambria, Benkay, Charlie Trotter's, The Dining Room (Ritz-Carlton Hotel), Entre Nous (Fairmont Hotel), Frontera Grill, Gordon, Jackie's, La Tour (Park Hyatt), Nick's Fish Market, Restaurant Suntory, Seasons (Four Seasons Hotel), and Yoshi's Cafe. Once known as the city of steak houses by the dozens, Chicago's superior steak restaurants now include Morton's of Chicago, Gibsons Steakhouse, the Palm Restaurant, Eli's The Place for Steak, Chicago Chop House, and The Saloon. The deep-dish style of pizza originated in Chicago.

***Visitor Information:*** Chicago Convention and Tourism Bureau, 2301 S. Lake Shore Drive, Chicago, IL 60616; telephone (312)567-8500; www.choosechicago .com

# ■ Convention Facilities

Chicago, one of the most popular convention cities in the United States, is home to McCormick Place, the largest exhibition center in North America. Set on the edge of Lake Michigan, McCormick Place contains more than 2.2 million square feet of exhibit space. The complex also features the 4,249-seat Arie Crown Theater, three 345-seat theaters, 112 meeting rooms, assembly seating for 10,000 people, and 8,000 parking spaces. The addition of the adjoining McCormick Place West, expected to be completed in 2008, will add approximately 470,000 square feet of exhibition space and 250,000 square feet of meeting room space to the facility. Chicago is known for its mix of gracious dowager hotels and modern glass towers with spectacular views of Lake Michigan.

Navy Pier offers space for mid-size events, with 170,000 square feet of exhibit space and 36 meeting rooms. The Chicago Cultural Center and University Center have event and meeting spaces available. Other special meeting facilities are available at museums, theaters, stadiums, corporations, and colleges and universities in the Chicago area.

***Convention Information:*** Chicago Convention and Tourism Bureau, 2301 S. Lake Shore Drive, Chicago, IL 60616; telephone (312)567-8500; www.choosechicago .com

# ■ Transportation

## Approaching the City

The destination of the majority of air traffic into Chicago is O'Hare International Airport, located 17 miles northwest of downtown, where 41 major domestic and international commercial carriers schedule more than 880,000 flights annually. One of the busiest air facilities in the world, O'Hare accommodates more than 5.8 million passengers each month, with a total of over 76 million in 2006. Continental Airport Express provides van service between O'Hare and all downtown hotels, the North Shore, and Oak Brook suburbs; Chicago Transit Authority (CTA) provides rapid transit train service between O'Hare and downtown. Taxis are available at the lower level curbfront of all terminals.

Several other commuter and general aviation airports are located throughout the Chicago metropolitan area; among them is Midway Airport, ten miles from downtown, which is served by 10 major airlines and known as the "premier point-to-point airport in the nation." Midway serves over 1.4 million passengers each month, with a total of over 18 million in 2006.

Passenger rail service into Chicago is provided by Amtrak from cities in all regions of the United States. The Northern Indiana Commuter Transportation District operates the South Shore Line, a 90-mile electric railway that can speed commuters to Millennium Station in Chicago from the South Bend Airport. The Regional Transit Authority (RTA) operates bus and rapid-transit service into the city from the distant suburbs. Regional rail transportation is available through Metropolitan Rail (Metra).

A somewhat complex network of interstate highways facilitates access into the metropolitan area as well as the Loop district. Approaching from the northwest is I-94, which merges with the John F. Kennedy Expressway leading downtown. I-294 (the Tri-State Tollway), an outerbelt on the west side, joins I-80 to the south. Other westerly approaches are: State Road 5, the East-West Tollway, which becomes I-290; I-90, the North-West Tollway, which intersects I-290; and I-55, the Adlai Stevenson Expressway. Approaches from the south include I-94, the Calumet Expressway; I-57; and I-90, the Chicago Skyway; all of these merge with the Dan Ryan Expressway leading into the city. Running south of Chicago is I-80, which connects with I-55, I-57, I-90, and I-94; near the Indiana border I-80 joins I-90 to become the Northern Indiana Toll Road.

## Traveling in the City

Chicago streets conform to a consistent grid pattern; major thoroughfares include east-west State Street and north-south Madison Street, which intersect downtown and provide the numerical orientation for all addresses.

Lake Shore Drive, affording a scenic view of Lake Michigan and the skyline, extends along the lake from the northern to the southern city limits.

Metra runs commuter trains and buses between the city and suburbs. The Chicago Transit Authority (CTA) operates bus, subway, and elevated train (the "El") routes between the Loop and the nearby suburbs. Cabs are readily available in the downtown area. Parking in Chicago can be problematic; for this reason several city-run parking garages are available.

# ■ Communications

## Newspapers and Magazines

Chicago's major daily newspapers are the *Chicago Tribune* and the *Chicago Sun-Times*, both of which are distributed in morning and Sunday editions and maintain an Internet presence. In 2007 the *Chicago Tribune* was the eighth largest newspaper in the nation with an estimated daily circulation of 566,827. The Sun-Times Media Group, which is the publisher of the *Chicago Sun-Times*, publishes several weekly local newspapers for the Chicago area. These include *Edison-Norwood Times Review*, the *Harlem-Irving Times,* the *Wicker Park/Bucktown Booster*, and *Skyline Chicago*. Other weeklies in Chicago include the *Chicago Independent Bulletin, Journal, Reporter,* and the *Southwest News Herald*.

*The Chicago Reader,* an alternative weekly, covers entertainment, social, and cultural issues.

A number of African American and ethnic newspapers circulate regularly, including *Chicago Crusader, Chicago Daily Defender, Chicago Weekend,*and *Hyde Park Citizen*. Several ethnic language papers are published in the city, such as *Greek Press, Chicago Shimpo* (Japanese), *Korea Times,* and *Draugas* (Lithuanian).

Chicago is a national leader in publishing and printing of journals and magazines. Nationally known titles include *American Libraries, Ebony, Jet,* and *Poetry*. Specialized trade magazines cover a comprehensive range of subjects such as health care, international trade, consumer issues, industry and trade, agriculture, politics, business, and professional information. The University of Chicago is the source of several scholarly journals; among the areas covered are philology, literature, the sciences, ethics, business, labor, history, library science, medicine, and law.

Moody Publishers, a Christian publishing house affiliated with the Moody Bible Institute, is based in Chicago.

## Television and Radio

Chicago is a broadcast media center for a wide region of the Midwest. Television viewers receive programming from 12 commercial, public, and independent stations based in the Chicago metropolitan area. Television programs filmed in Chicago for a national audience include *The Oprah Winfrey Show* and the movie review program *Ebert and Roeper.*There are 37 AM and 11 FM radio stations in the city broadcasting a complete selection of formats, including all major types of music, news, talk shows, public interest features, and market reports. The Moody Broadcasting Network, affiliated with the Moody Bible Institute, is headquartered in Chicago.

*Media Information:* *Chicago Tribune*, Chicago Tribune Company, 435 North Michigan, Chicago, IL 60611; telephone (312)222-3232; www.chicagotribune. com. *Chicago Sun-Times*, 350 North Orleans St., Chicago, IL 60654; telephone (312)321-3000; www.sun-times.com. *Chicago Reader*, 11 East Illinois, Chicago, IL 60611; telephone (312)828-0350; www.chicagoreader. com

## Chicago Online

Chicago Convention and Tourism Bureau. Available www.choosechicago.com

Chicago History Museum. Available www .chicagohs.org

Chicago Public Library. Available www.chipublib .org

Chicago Public Schools. Available www.cps.k12.il.us *Chicago Tribune.*Available www.chicagotribune .com

Illinois Department of Commerce and Community Affairs. Available www.illinois.gov

McCormick Place Complex. Available www .mccormickplace.com

BIBLIOGRAPHY

Bellow, Saul, *The Adventures of Augie March* (New York: Avon, 1977, 1953)

Miller, Donald L., *City of the Century: The Epic of Chicago and the Making of America* (New York: Simon & Schuster, 1996)

Sinclair, Upton, *The Jungle* (Urbana, IL: University of Illinois Press, 1988)

# Peoria

## ■ The City in Brief

**Founded:** 1819 (incorporated 1835)

**Head Official:** Mayor Jim Ardis (since 2005)

**City Population**
> 1980: 124,600
> 1990: 113,508
> 2000: 112,936
> 2006 estimate: 113,107
> Percent change, 1990–2000: −0.5%
> U.S. rank in 1980: 126th
> U.S. rank in 1990: 157th (State rank: 3rd)
> U.S. rank in 2000: 223rd

**Metropolitan Area Population**
> 1980: 366,000
> 1990: 339,172
> 2000: 347,387
> 2006 estimate: 370,194
> Percent change, 1990–2000: 2.4%
> U.S. rank in 1980: 90th
> U.S. rank in 1990: Not available
> U.S. rank in 2000: 116th

**Area:** 40.9 square miles (2000)

**Elevation:** 652 feet above sea level

**Average Annual Temperatures:** January, 22.5° F; July, 75.1° F; annual average, 50.8° F

**Average Annual Precipitation:** 36.03 inches of rain; 24.9 inches of snow

**Major Economic Sectors:** Agriculture, manufacturing, information technologies

**Unemployment Rate:** 4.4% (June 2007)

**Per Capita Income:** $25,791 (2005)

**2005 FBI Crime Index Property:** 7,470

**2005 FBI Crime Index Violent:** Not available

**Major Colleges and Universities:** Bradley University; Eureka College; Illinois Central College

**Daily Newspaper:** *Journal Star*

## ■ Introduction

Peoria is the seat of Peoria County and the center of the Peoria-Pekin MSA that includes Marshall, Peoria, Stark, Tazewell, and Woodford counties. The city is considered the oldest continuously inhabited American community west of the Allegheny Mountains. Another of Peoria's distinctions is its typicality: in terms of such demographic characteristics as median age and purchasing patterns, the city's general makeup is almost identical to that of the United States as a whole, thus making it an ideal test market for consumer researchers. The city has also gained attention for both its social and business friendliness. In 2006 Peoria was named as one of the top ten best mannered cities in the country by etiquette expert Marjabelle Young Stewart. In 2005 the city was named among the top 40 best cities for "Most Balanced Economy and Growth" by *Inc.* magazine; in the same survey Peoria ranked at number 55 for "Best Places–Medium Sized Cities."

## ■ Geography and Climate

Peoria is set in a level tableland surrounded by gently rolling terrain on the Illinois River. The continental climate produces changeable weather and a wide range of temperature extremes. June and September are generally the most pleasant months; an extended period of warm, dry weather occurs during Indian summer in late October and early November. Precipitation is heaviest during the growing season and lowest in midwinter.

**Area:** 40.9 square miles (2000)

**Elevation:** 652 feet above sea level

**Average Temperatures:** January, 22.5° F; July, 75.1° F; annual average, 50.8° F

**Average Annual Precipitation:** 36.03 inches of rain; 24.9 inches of snow

# ■ History

## French Explore Peoria Tribe Territory

Native Americans lived in the area surrounding present-day Peoria for 12,000 years before the coming of Europeans. They took fish from the fresh waters of Peoria Lake and hunted for game in the surrounding valley. They called the river valley *Pimiteoui* (pronounced Pee-Mee-Twee), meaning "land of great abundance" or "fat lake." The valley was known far and wide among Native Americans as a great winter hunting ground.

Peoria was the first European settlement in Illinois and one of the earliest in the middle of America. French explorers Louis Joliet and Pere Marquette canoed into the river valley in 1673 during their exploration of the Mississippi River. Six years later another French explorer, Robert Cavelier, sieur de La Salle, ventured down the Illinois River with a party of 30 men to establish forts and trading posts in order to strengthen France's hold on the middle of America. Because it was winter and the weather inclement, the party was forced to land; LaSalle built a small fort on the east bluff of the Peoria river valley and called it Fort Crevecoeur ("broken heart"). The fort was the first European building to be built in the middle of America. It was mysteriously abandoned after four months and these words were found burned into the side of an unfinished boat found on the site: "Nous sommes tous sauvages" (We are all savages).

With the help of the tribes of the Illini nation, in 1691 the French military, under the charge of Henri de Tonti, built a massive fortification, called Fort Pimiteoui, on Peoria's shores, near the site of present-day Detweiller Marina on the popular Pimiteoui Trail that winds along the riverfront. Outside the walls of the fort, a French settlement grew among the Illini villages, becoming the first European settlement in the state of Illinois.

By 1763 the British flag was being flown over Illinois, but the French Peorians persevered and enjoyed life much as they would have done in the rural countryside of France. One of the villagers, Jean Baptiste Maillet, moved the core of the French village to the site of present-day Downtown Riverfront Park in 1778. Another villager, Jean-Baptiste Du Sable, left in 1784 and became the founder of Chicago.

Following the American Revolution, a number of Peorians received land grants from the U.S. Congress in gratitude for their support during the war. In October 1812, the area felt the pressure of thousands of American settlers heading west; Native American Potawatomi villages in the region were destroyed by troops under the command of the Illinois Territory Governor Ninian Edwards. A month later, American soldiers overran the French village and deported its inhabitants to a wilderness around Alton, Illinois. After 120 years French Peoria was gone forever.

American soldiers built Fort Clark in 1813. Today the fort is commemorated in the riverfront Liberty Park Pavilion. The first American settlers began farming there in 1819. Soon the small village experienced a great economic and population boom.

## Economic Growth Paired with Historic Events

With its abundance of natural resources, Peoria industries grew up. They included meat-packing, casting foundries, pottery making, wholesale warehousing, distilleries, and earth-moving and farm machinery manufacturing. Ancient Indian trails were turned into solid roads, and steamboats and ferries replaced canoes. The city became a massive railroad hub. The area's fresh, clear water, abundance of corn, and ease of transportation contributed to making the city the "Whiskey Capital of the World" by 1900. Distilleries and their related industries brought tremendous wealth, and Peoria became one of the largest tax-paying districts in the country. Prosperity enabled city leaders to strive to develop a model city.

State-of-the-art municipal buildings were erected, such as the red sandstone City Hall (1889). Models of Peoria's innovative schools, such as the Grail School (1892), were exhibited across the nation. Massive churches such as St. Mary's Cathedral (1889) were built. Beautiful parks such as Glen Oak Park (1896) and Laura Bradley Park (1897) were laid out. Present-day historic districts such as High Street-Moss Avenue, Roanoke-Randolph Street, and Glen Oak Avenue evoke an era that Peoria endeavors to preserve.

The city of Peoria has been the site of historic events and the home of famous Americans. In 1854 Abraham Lincoln, rebutting a speech by Stephen Douglas, for the first time publicly denounced slavery as incompatible with American institutions; this clash predated the famous Lincoln-Douglas debates by four years. The original mold strain for penicillin was discovered by scientists in Peoria. The first African American person to vote in the United States did so in Peoria on April 4, 1870. Peorian Herb Jamison was a medalist in the first modern Olympics in Greece in 1896. The Caterpillar Tractor Company was established in Peoria in 1925 through the merger of Benjamin Holt Co. and the C. L. Best Tractor Co. In 2007 the Caterpillar, Inc. was the largest employer in the city and county.

In the second half of the twentieth century Peoria was awarded an All-America City designation three times (1953, 1966, and 1989). Into the early 2000s the city has

©James Blank.

continued to build on its all-American reputation in promoting itself as a city with "big city assets" and "smaller town" lifestyle. A vaudeville-era phrase "to play in Peoria" is still used to characterize the thoughts and habits of a "typical" American. In 2004 *Forbes* ranked Peoria the most affordable U.S. metropolitan area in which to live. In 2005 the city was named among the top 40 best cities for "Most Balanced Economy and Growth" by *Inc.* magazine; in the same survey Peoria ranked at number 55 for "Best Places–Medium Sized Cities." A short list of native Peorians include the late Senator Everett Dirksen; Betty Friedan, author of *The Feminine Mystique*; and comedian and actor Richard Pryor.

***Historical Information:*** Peoria Historical Society, 611 SW Washington Street, Peoria, IL 61602; telephone (309)674-1921; www.peoriahistoricalsociety.org

## ■ Population Profile

### Metropolitan Area Residents

1980: 366,000
1990: 339,172
2000: 347,387

2006 estimate: 370,194
Percent change, 1990–2000: 2.4%
U.S. rank in 1980: 90th
U.S. rank in 1990: Not available
U.S. rank in 2000: 116th

### City Residents

1980: 124,600
1990: 113,508
2000: 112,936
2006 estimate: 113,107
Percent change, 1990–2000: −0.5%
U.S. rank in 1980: 126th
U.S. rank in 1990: 157th (State rank: 3rd)
U.S. rank in 2000: 223rd

**Density:** 2,543.4 people per square mile (2000)

### Racial and ethnic characteristics (2000)

White: 78,254
Black: 27,992
American Indian and Alaska Native: 229
Asian: 2,629
Native Hawaiian and Pacific Islander: 42
Hispanic or Latino (may be of any race): 2,839

Other: 1,355

**Percent of residents born in state:** 72.3% (2000)

**Age characteristics (2005)**

Population under 5 years old: 8,950
Population 5 to 9 years old: 6,959
Population 10 to 14 years old: 7,040
Population 15 to 19 years old: 6,441
Population 20 to 24 years old: 8,373
Population 25 to 34 years old: 14,015
Population 35 to 44 years old: 12,707
Population 45 to 54 years old: 13,573
Population 55 to 59 years old: 5,560
Population 60 to 64 years old: 4,501
Population 65 to 74 years old: 7,060
Population 75 to 84 years old: 5,605
Population 85 years and older: 1,352
Median age: 34.4 years

**Births (2006, County)**

Total number: 2,679

**Deaths (2006, County)**

Total number: 1,840

**Money income (2005)**

Per capita income: $25,791
Median household income: $40,276
Total households: 45,053

**Number of households with income of . . .**

less than $10,000: 4,102
$10,000 to $14,999: 3,663
$15,000 to $24,999: 6,502
$25,000 to $34,999: 5,223
$35,000 to $49,999: 6,979
$50,000 to $74,999: 8,616
$75,000 to $99,999: 4,596
$100,000 to $149,999: 3,432
$150,000 to $199,999: 839
$200,000 or more: 1,101

**Percent of families below poverty level:** 10% (2005)

**2005 FBI Crime Index Property:** 7,470

**2005 FBI Crime Index Violent:** Not available

# ■ Municipal Government

The city of Peoria operates under a council-manager form of government. One council member is elected from each of five districts and five members are elected at large. The mayor is the official head of the city; he heads the council and is elected by the total electorate.

**Head Official:** Mayor Jim Ardis (since 2005; current term expires 2009)

**Total Number of City Employees:** about 800 (2007)

*City Information:*   City of Peoria, 419 Fulton, Peoria, IL 61602; telephone (309)494-8524; www.ci.peoria.il.us

# ■ Economy

## Major Industries and Commercial Activity

Located at the center of a fertile agricultural region, with corn and soybeans as principal crops, Peoria is an important livestock and grain exporting market. Farm production and livestock sales in the three-county area are among the highest in the nation. Peoria is surrounded by rich bituminous coal fields that hold reserves estimated to last for 150 years and slated for worldwide distribution.

In 2007 the largest number of jobs in Peoria were found in the trade, transportation, and manufacturing sectors. Peoria is the headquarters of Caterpillar Inc., one of the nation's largest companies for the design, manufacturing, and marketing of mining, agricultural, and forestry machinery. Caterpillar was the city's largest employer in 2007. Keystone Steel and Wire Co. and L.R. Nelson Corporation are also headquartered in the city. Other top manufacturing employers include SC2, Komatsu Mining Systems, and Interstate Brands. The city is also the base for several distilleries and breweries.

Educational and health services also account for a large number of local jobs. In health care, Methodist Medical Center, Proctor Hospital, and OSF Saint Francis Medical Center are top employers. In education the Peoria School District 150 and Bradley University are top employers. The government sector includes the Peoria Air Guard 182nd Airlift Wing, as well as county and city government offices.

Professional and business services are becoming increasingly more important to the local economy. AFFINA Corp. (market research), Clifton Gunderson LLP (accounting and bookkeeping services), and CEFCU (financial services) all maintain headquarters in Peoria. Illinois Mutual Life Insurance and RLI Corp. are also headquartered in the city. Peoria is a main test market for several national consumer research firms such as Nielsen Data Markets, Inc., which has established one of its six facilities in the city.

The city is taking steps to increase the number of high tech and research businesses that call Peoria home. The National Center for Agriculture Research is operated in Peoria by the United States Department of Agriculture; there, soil testing and chemical development are important areas of research. Peoria has formed the Biotechnical Research and Development Consortium to allow private development and marketing of the products developed at the center's Agricultural Research Lab and to expand the use of patents into the private sector. In 2007 the city opened the Peoria NEXT Innovation Center as a business incubator to attract similar employers.

**Items and goods produced:** fences, nails, steel and wire products, construction machinery, chemical additives, mining and agricultural machinery, sprinklers, valves, hoses, video movies systems

## Incentive Programs—New and Existing Companies

*Local programs:* Business is encouraged in Peoria through a variety of local programs. Among economic incentives are sales and property tax credits and exemptions, and industrial revenue bonds. The Economic Development Council for Central Illinois (EDC) assists Peoria-area businesses in start-up, growth, or expansion. Bradley University offers assistance to new businesses through the Asia Trade Center, the Business Technology Incubator, and the Small Business Development Center.

The City of Peoria has a low interest loan program known as the Business Development Fund (BDF). This program provides low interest loans as secondary or "gap" financing. Its use is tied to job creation or retention. Other financing programs are offered through the Heartland Capital Network.

In 1977 the Illinois legislature adopted the Tax Increment Allocation Redevelopment Act to provide municipalities with a unique tool to finance and stimulate urban redevelopment. Through the use of Tax Increment Financing (TIF), cities can stimulate private investment by offering incentives to attract and retain businesses, improve their community areas, and maintain a well-educated and highly trained labor force. In 2007 there were seven TIF districts in the city.

*State programs:* Peoria has nine areas that are state-designated Enterprise Zones. Businesses located in an Enterprise Zone are eligible for an Investment Tax Credit, a Building and Materials Sales Tax Exemption (6.25 percent), and a Machinery and Equipment/Pollution Control Facilities Sales Tax Exemption (6.25 percent). A Jobs Tax Credit of $500 is also available for jobs, created in the zones, for certified dislocated or economically disadvantaged workers. Foreign Trade Zone incentives apply for city businesses as well.

The Economic Development for Growing Economy Tax Credit Program (EDGE) is a statewide program to benefit companies that relocate or expand operations within the state. Qualifying companies must make an investment of at least $5 million in capital improvements and create a minimum of 25 new full-time jobs in the state. Companies with 100 or fewer employees must make a capital investment of $1 million and create at least five full-time jobs to qualify. The High Impact Business program is designed to encourage large-scale economic development initiatives. Business projects that involve at least $12 million in investments and the creation of 500 full-time jobs may qualify for investment tax credits and state sales tax exemptions on building materials, utilities, and the purchase, repair, or replacement of manufacturing equipment. Other state sponsored tax credits include a Research and Development Tax Credit of 6.5 percent and a Manufacturer's Purchase Credit of 6.25 percent for qualified businesses. A number of loan programs are available.

*Job training programs:* Job training is available through state agencies and educational institutions. The Workforce Network is a partnership between local and state workforce organizations that enables them to coordinate their services and offer them through a one-stop system. Their Career Resource Center offers job search, education, and career-training information in a user-friendly environment. Through the Employer Training and Investment Program, qualified employers may receive grants for up to 50 percent of costs in training new employees. Federally funded workforce development programs are administered through the Peoria Workforce Development Department.

## Development Projects

In 2001 several local community and businesses leaders joined with organizations such as the Methodist Medical Center, Bradley University, and the National Center for Agriculture Research to form Peoria NEXT, a not-for-profit foundation dedicated to creating a more diverse economy for the city through growth in the technology and research and development sectors. In 2007 the city celebrated the opening of the Peoria NEXT Innovation Center. The $13.5-million center will serve as a business incubator under the management of the Technology Commercialization Center of Bradley University. The 48,000-square-foot building can house up to 22 companies. Bradley University and the Caterpillar Technical Services Division will serve as anchor tenants.

In 2003 Governor Blagojevich signed an act to create the six-county Heart of Illinois Regional Port District currently known as TransPORT. The district covers 60 miles of the Illinois River as it cuts through Fulton, Marshall, Mason, Peoria, Tazewell, and Woodford counties. Governed by a nine-member board, TransPORT hopes to serve as a job generator and an economic growth engine for the entire region as members encourage and promote the use of the waterway and the transportation and distribution companies available in the area. As of 2007 companies partnered with TransPORT included Genesee & Wyoming, Caterpillar, G&D Integrated, and Diamond Vogel.

In 2005 Governor Blagojevich announced the Turner Center for Entrepreneurship at Bradley University would receive $250,000 in funding from the Illinois

Department of Commerce and Economic Opportunity to further expand its programs. As of 2007 those programs included a financial award program of up to $5,000 designed to help small business owners and entrepreneurs obtain professional services for business plan assistance, evaluation of startup and expansion plans, and other approved support services.

***Economic Development Information:*** The Economic Development Council for Central Illinois, 124 SW Adams Street, Suite 300, Peoria, IL 61602-1388; telephone (309)676-7500; www.edc.centralillinois.org. Illinois Department of Commerce and Economic Opportunity, 620 E. Adams, Springfield, IL 62701; telephone (217)782-7500; www.illinoisbiz.biz/dceo

## Commercial Shipping

With access to several interstate and federal highways, the entire tri-county area is linked to markets nationwide by 60 trucking firms and 4 transportation brokers. Air cargo transfer facilities are available at Greater Peoria Regional Airport, with over 50 million tons of cargo and mail handled there each year. The primary air cargo carriers are Fed Ex, DHL, Emery and UPS; however, some passenger flights carry cargo as well. The airport is a U.S. Customs point of entry and part of the Peoria Foreign Trade Zone.

The Peoria Barge terminal on the Illinois River is a major multi-modal terminal for the state. Two main barge lines (American Commercial Barge and ARTCO) transport more than 48 million tons during a year-round navigation season through the Peoria Lock and Dam, a major link from the Gulf of Mexico to the St. Lawrence Seaway. Four Class I railroads serve the tri-county area: Burlington Northern Santa Fe, Canadian National, Norfolk Southern, and Union Pacific. There are five regional railroads as well.

## Labor Force and Employment Outlook

As of 2006 nearly 88 percent of workers in the city had a high school degree or higher and 32 percent had a bachelor's degree or higher; both figures were above the national average. Manufacturers and agribusinesses are said to have been successful in retraining and modernizing the work force through the strong training networks between the private and education sectors. Peoria has always been a strong retail market; further retail development in the downtown area and more strip malls are expected. Employment projections for 2004 through 2014 indicate that the greatest increase in job availability will be in the professional and business services sector, particularly in scientific and technology services and management and computer systems design-related services. Health care and educational services are also expected to show increased job levels. The manufacturing sector is only expected to lose a small number of jobs.

The following is a summary of data regarding the Peoria metropolitan area labor force, 2006 annual averages.

**Size of nonagricultural labor force: 184,000**

**Number of workers employed in . . .**

construction and mining: 9,000
manufacturing: 31,500
trade, transportation and utilities: 34,900
information: 3,100
financial activities: 8,600
professional and business services: 20,300
educational and health services: 31,300
leisure and hospitality: 16,900
other services: 7,400
government: 20,900

**Average hourly earnings of production workers employed in manufacturing: $17.69**

**Unemployment rate: 4.4% (June 2007)**

| *Largest employers 2007* | *Number of employees* |
| --- | --- |
| Caterpillar, Inc. | 17,000 |
| OSF Saint Francis Medical Center | 5,100 |
| Peoria School District 150 | 3,000 |
| Methodist Medical Center | 2,500 |
| XPAC | 1,700 |
| Peoria Air Guard 182nd Airlift Wing | 1,248 |
| Keystone Steel and Wire Co. | 1,200 |
| G & D Intergrated Peoria School District 150 | 1,200 |
| Peoria County | 1,033 |
| Morton Metalcraft Company | 1,000 |

## Cost of Living

The following is a summary of data regarding several key cost of living factors in the Peoria area.

**2007 (1st quarter) ACCRA Average House Price:** $271,817

**2007 (1st quarter) ACCRA Cost of Living Index:** 97.2

**State income tax rate:** 3.0% of Federal Adjusted Gross Income, with modifications

**State sales tax rate:** 6.25%

**Local income tax rate:** None

**Local sales tax rate:** 1.5% (2005)

**Property tax rate:** 7.9419% per $100 assessed valuation (2002)

***Economic Information:*** Peoria Area Chamber of Commerce, 124 SW Adams, Suite 300, Peoria, IL 61602-1388; telephone (309)676-0755; www.peoriachamber.org

## ■ Education and Research

### Elementary and Secondary Schools

The Peoria Public Schools District 150 is the fifth-largest public elementary and secondary school system in the state of Illinois. A seven-member, nonpartisan board of education appoints a superintendent by majority vote. In 2007 about 43.5 percent of all teachers in the district had a master's degree or above.

In 2007 each of the comprehensive high schools in the district supported a specialized academy program. These included the Business Academy at Peoria High School, Health Science Academy at Richwoods High School, Industrial Technology Academy at Manual High School, and Technology Pathways Academy at Woodruff High School. Roosevelt Magnet School is a fine arts magnet for students in fifth through eighth grade. Programs for gifted students are available through most schools. Washington Gift School accepts the top students from the gifted programs in grades five through eight. Special education and alternative education programs are available. The Peoria Adult Education and Family Literacy Center is sponsored in part by the district.

The following is a summary of data regarding the Peoria Public Schools as of the 2005–2006 school year.

**Total enrollment:** 14,600

**Number of facilities**

elementary schools: 15
junior high/middle schools: 10
senior high schools: 5
other: 7

**Student/teacher ratio:** 15.8:1

**Teacher salaries (2005–06)**

elementary median: $41,360
junior high/middle median: $42,650
secondary median: $47,530

**Funding per pupil:** $8,556

Offering private educations are the Peoria Catholic Diocese, Concordia Lutheran, the Hebrew Day School, Peoria Academy, and Peoria Christian.

***Public Schools Information:*** Peoria Public Schools, 3202 N. Wisconsin Avenue, Peoria, IL 61603; telephone (309)672-6512; www.psd150.org

### Colleges and Universities

Bradley University, founded in 1897, enrolls about 6,127 students and offers more than 100 undergraduate programs and 14 graduate degrees. Fields include business and accounting, all major engineering specialties, music, nursing, and teacher education.

Eureka College, located in Eureka, is a four-year liberal arts college. It was the first college in the state to admit men and women on an equal basis. It is also known as the alma mater of former president Ronald Reagan. The school offers 30 undergraduate majors. Enrollment is about 520 students.

The University of Illinois College of Medicine (UICM) at Peoria serves students in their second through fourth year of medical school. There are about 150 students at the Peoria campus. The school houses the College of Nursing and the School of Public Health as well as the Library of Health Sciences.

The Saint Francis College of Nursing, part of the OSF Saint Francis Medical Center, offers bachelor's and master's degrees. The medical center has nine residency programs through the University of Illinois College of Medicine at Peoria. OSF Saint Francis is also the clinical site for a variety of area colleges including Bradley University, Illinois Central College, and the University of Illinois.

Illinois Central College is a two-year institution that schedules courses in university transfer curricula and vocational and continuing education programs on three local campuses for more than 20,000 students. Associate degrees are offered in 152 programs of study; certificates are offered in more 95 subjects. Midstate College offers a wide variety of associate and certificate programs as well as bachelor's degrees in accounting, management information systems, and business administration. The Peoria campus of Robert Morris College (based in Chicago) offers bachelor's degrees in business administration, computer networking, and medical assisting. Associate's degrees are also available in business administration, computer networking, graphic arts, and medical assisting.

Among colleges and universities within commuting distance of Peoria are Illinois State University in Normal, Western Illinois University in Macomb, and Carl Sandburg College and Knox College in Galesburg.

### Libraries and Research Centers

The Peoria Public Library maintains a central facility with more than 800,000 volumes and more than 1,300 periodical titles as well as music recordings, videos, and DVDs; subject interests include business, census materials, early government documents, genealogy, and local history. The library's comprehensive Internet website allows patrons to access the card catalog and research databases. In addition to the main library facility, the library operates five branches and a bookmobile. The library has an interlibrary loan program through the Alliance Library System.

The Cullom-Davis Library on the Bradley University campus has holdings of more than 536,000 volumes. Special collections include federal and state documents as well as material pertaining to industrial arts history, Abraham Lincoln, and oral history; the library also houses the Harry L. Spooner Library of the Peoria Historical Society. The Library of Health Sciences at the University of Illinois College of Medicine in Peoria is open to the public for research. Special borrowing privileges may be obtained through application.

Bradley University supports several research programs, including the Institute for Urban Affairs and Business Research, the Center for Business and Economic Research, and the Business and Technology Data Center. Other centers for special studies include the C. C. Wheeler Institute for the Holistic Study of Family Well-Being and the Center for Emerging Technologies in Infrastructure. Work done at Peoria's National Center for Agricultural Utilization Research, one of four USDA Agricultural Research Service labs, made possible the mass production of penicillin and the early and economical production of dextran as a blood-volume expander.

***Public Library Information:*** Peoria Public Library, 107 NE Monroe Street, Peoria, IL 61602-1070; (309) 497-2000; www.peoriapubliclibrary.org

# ■ Health Care

OSF Saint Francis Medical Center is home to the only Level I Trauma Center in Central Illinois. The center is also home to the Illinois Neurological Institute/OSF Stroke Network, the OSF Saint Francis Heart Hospital/ OSF Cardiac Network, and the 127-bed Children's Hospital of Illinois. The Medical Center supports six outpatient clinics and three PromptCare sites.

Methodist Medical Center of Illinois includes a 330-bed hospital and several primary care and walk-in clinics. Specialized care centers within the hospital include the Pain Management Clinic, the Parkinson's Center, the Sleep Center, Diabetes Care Center, Epilepsy Center and Home Health Services.

Proctor Hospital features an all-private room facility with specialized care centers for cardiac services, women's health, a Wound Care Clinic, and senior care. The hospital also hosts the Illinois Institute for Addiction Recovery. First Care sites offer primary care for illnesses and minor injuries.

Specialized treatment is available at St. Jude Children's Research Hospital, the Midwest affiliate of St. Jude Children's Research Hospital in Tennessee; the Institute for Physical Medicine and Rehabilitation; and the Allied Agencies Center, which provides research, therapy, and education and training for handicapped patients. Also located in the city are the American Red Cross Peoria Regional Blood Center and Marvin Hult Health Education Center.

# ■ Recreation

## Sightseeing

Visitors can get the best experience of the city during the months of May through October, when CityLink provides a two-hour historic trolley tour with narration provided by the Peoria Historical Society.

Glen Oak Park is a 100-acre park that serves as home to the Glen Oak Zoo. Zoo animals range from large cats and marsupials to reptiles and amphibians. The Luthy Memorial Botanical Garden is also part of Glen Oak Park. The Wildlife Prairie State Park is a 2,000-acre zoological park that provides a habitat for animals native to Illinois, including bison, elk, wolves, cougars, bears, waterfowl, and American bald eagles. The park also contains a country store, pioneer farmstead, walking trails, and a miniature railroad that runs through the grounds. Parks along the riverfront host concerts, festivals, and outdoor sports activities.

Aspects of Peoria's agricultural heritage are the focus of tours of the National Center for Agricultural Utilization Research, Linden Hills Farms, Tanners Orchard, Caterpillar Inc., McGlothlin Farm Park, and Wildlife Prairie Park.

## Arts and Culture

The Lakeview Museum of Arts and Sciences houses permanent collections of Illinois folk art and African art, a planetarium, and a children's Discovery Center. The African American Hall of Fame Museum at the Proctor Center is devoted to the collection, study, and exhibition of African American life and culture.

Peoria performing arts organizations include the Peoria Symphony Orchestra, Peoria Ballet Company, Opera Illinois, and Peoria Area Civic Chorale, all of which perform at the Peoria Civic Center Theater. Theater in Peoria is represented by such organizations as Corn Stock Theatre, Peoria Players, Eastlight Theatre, One World Theatre Company, and Barn II Dinner Theater. The Peoria Civic Center also serves as a venue for touring concerts and family events.

ArtsPartners, based in Peoria, serves as an umbrella organization for the arts in central Illinois.

## Festivals and Holidays

Eureka College hosts an annual Eureka Lilac Festival and Fine Arts Fair in April. The Steamboat Sports festival takes place in June, offering activities and entertainment for the entire family. The celebration of Independence

Day is capped by the Fourth of July fireworks display on the riverfront. Peoria's largest annual event is the Heart of Illinois Fair in July at the Exposition Gardens, which attracts nearly 250,000 people. August features the Taste of Peoria Festival at Riverfront Festival Park. Oktoberfest, held in September, is a festival that celebrates German culture and food. The century-old Santa Claus Parade, the country's longest running event of its kind, takes place each year on Thanksgiving Day.

## Sports for the Spectator
The Peoria Chiefs, a Class A affiliate of the Chicago Cubs, are league leaders each year in home game attendance at O'Brien Field. The Peoria Rivermen compete in the American Hockey League and play home games in the modern indoor facility, the Peoria Civic Center. The Peoria Rough Riders play for the United Indoor Football Association. Both Bradley University and Illinois Central College field competitive basketball teams. The annual Steamboat Classic attracts world-class, international middle-distance runners. Racing fans enjoy the Grand National TT Motorcycle Race in August.

## Sports for the Participant
The Peoria Pleasure Driveway and Park District consists of nearly 9,000 acres providing facilities for outdoor and indoor sports. Included are 7 golf courses, indoor and outdoor swimming pools, and 39 public tennis courts. Also available are two artificial ice-skating rinks, an archery range, a BMX bicycle racing course, horseshoe pits, shuffleboard courts, and a shooting range. Peoria Lake offers fishing and boating. The Par-A-Dice Riverboat Casino, docked in East Peoria, offers high-stakes gambling on the scenic Illinois River. The Glen Oak Park Fishing Lagoon serves fishermen during warmer months and ice skaters in the winter.

## Shopping and Dining
Peoria shoppers can choose from 60 shopping centers and malls located throughout the greater metropolitan area. The Shoppes at Grand Prairie is an open air mall with retail tenants such as Bergner's, Eddie Bauer, Borders, Dick's Sporting Goods, and Old Navy. The Metro Centre offers a wide variety of shopping and dining establishments. Northwoods Mall is anchored by department stores Famous Barr, JCPenney, and Sears. Unique, one-of-a-kind shops can be found along the Peoria Riverfront District. Duryea Center-Northwestern Place is an upscale shopping center. Peoria is also home to the Illinois Antique Center, with more than 100 booth spaces. Other Peoria locations include the Westlake Shopping Center and Sterling Plaza.

The dining choices in Peoria feature ethnic food as well as gourmet cuisine and a variety of well known fast food chains and family-style restaurants. Sushi Popo serves fine-dining Chinese and Japanese cuisine. Irish Fare can be had at Kelleher's Irish Pub and Eatery. Italian choices include Old Chicago Restaurant, Ponte Vecchio, and Rizzi's Italian Ristorante. German American food and European beers are enjoyed at the Peoria Hofbrau. Regional specialties include barbecued ribs and pork tenderloin sandwiches.

*Visitor Information:* Peoria Area Convention and Visitors Bureau, 456 Fulton Street, Suite 300, Peoria, IL 61602; telephone (800)747-0302; www.peoria.org

# ■ Convention Facilities

Peoria's principal meeting site is the Peoria Civic Center, located in the revitalized downtown district. It features a 12,145-seat arena, 63,668 square feet of exhibit space, and a theater with seating for 2,244 people. Concerts, sporting events, rodeos, ice shows, and operas are among the events held at the Civic Center. The Exposition Gardens offers an alternative venue for events and meetings. The Youth Building contains 14,000 square feet of unobstructed exhibit space. Peoria area hotels and motels offer more than 3,000 lodging rooms and also have convention and meeting room facilities.

*Convention Information:* Peoria Area Convention and Visitors Bureau, 456 Fulton Street, Suite 300, Peoria, IL 61602; telephone (800)747-0302; www.peoria.org

# ■ Transportation

## Approaching the City
The Greater Peoria Regional Airport has scheduled daily flights to and from 11 major hub cities through 5 major airline carriers. Interstate 74 passes directly through the city while I-74 circles around it to the southwest. I-155, I-39, and I-55 all connect to I-474. I-80 (north of the city) connects to I-39. Amtrak stations are located in Bloomington and Lincoln, both about 35 to 40 miles away. Greyhound maintains a bus station at the airport.

## Traveling in the City
Peoria is compact but not crowded. The average commute is 10 minutes. CityLink, sponsored by the Greater Peoria Mass Transit District, offers mass public transportation around the greater metropolitan area. Trolley Express serves the downtown area.

# ■ Communications

## Newspapers and Magazines
The major newspaper in Peoria is the *Journal Star,* which is published every morning. Content and archives of past stories are available on the paper's website. Other neigh-

borhood and suburban newspapers circulate weekly, including the *Morton Times News* and the *Peoria Times Observer.The Community Word* is an independently owned weekly paper on local interest. Central Illinois Business Publishers, based in Peoria, publish the monthly community-interest magazines *InterBusiness Issues, The Peoria Woman, Art & Society,* and *Peoria Progress. The Catholic Post* is the weekly paper of the Diocese of Peoria.

## Television and Radio

Six television stations are based in Peoria; cable service is available through four services. Ten radio stations furnish diversified programming.

*Media Information:* *Journal Star,* 1 News Plaza, Peoria, IL 61643; telephone (309)686-3000; www .pjstar.com

### Peoria Online

City of Peoria home page. Available www.ci.peoria .il.us

Economic Development Council for Central Illinois. Available www.edc.centralillinois.org

Illinois Department of Commerce and Community Affairs. Available www.commerce.state.il.us

*Journal Star.* Available www.pjstar.com

Peoria Area Chamber of Commerce. Available www .peoriachamber.org

Peoria Area Convention and Visitors Bureau home page. Available www.peoria.org

Peoria Historical Society. Available www .peoriahistoricalsociety.org

Peoria Park District. Available www.peoriaparks.org

Peoria Public Library. Available www.peoria.lib.il.us

BIBLIOGRAPHY

Farmer, Philip Jose, *Nothing Burns in Hell* (New York: Forge, 1998)

# Springfield

## ■ The City in Brief

**Founded:** 1821 (incorporated 1832)

**Head Official:** Mayor Timothy J. Davlin (since 2003)

**City Population**

    1980: 99,637
    1990: 105,227
    2000: 111,454
    2006 estimate: 116,482
    Percent change, 1990–2000: 3.9%
    U.S. rank in 1980: 171st
    U.S. rank in 1990: 183rd (State rank: 4th)
    U.S. rank in 2000: 225th (State rank: 6th)

**Metropolitan Area Population**

    1980: 187,770
    1990: 189,550
    2000: 188,951
    2006 estimate: 206,112
    Percent change, 1990–2000: −.3%
    U.S. rank in 1980: Not available
    U.S. rank in 1990: Not available
    U.S. rank in 2000: 165th

**Area:** 54 square miles (2000)

**Elevation:** 588 feet above sea level

**Average Annual Temperatures:** January, 25.1° F; July, 76.3° F; annual average, 52.7° F

**Average Annual Precipitation:** 35.56 inches of rain; 23.1 inches of snow

**Major Economic Sectors:** Government, services, wholesale and retail trade

**Unemployment Rate:** 4.6% (June 2007)

**Per Capita Income:** $27,052 (2005)

**2005 FBI Crime Index Property:** 7,345

**2005 FBI Crime Index Violent:** Not available

**Major Colleges and Universities:** University of Illinois at Springfield; Southern Illinois University School of Medicine; Lincoln Land Community College; Springfield College in Illinois

**Daily Newspaper:** *State Journal-Register*

## ■ Introduction

Springfield is the capital of Illinois and the seat of Sangamon County, which is included in the Springfield metropolitan area. The city is the commercial, health care, financial, and cultural center for a wide agricultural region. Springfield bills itself as "The City Lincoln Loved," since it served as the home, workplace, and political base of Abraham Lincoln for nearly twenty-four years prior to his election as President of the United States. Springfield is also a popular tourist destination.

## ■ Geography and Climate

Springfield is located south of the Sangamon River on level to gently sloping terrain in a fertile agricultural region in central Illinois. The city is 190 miles southwest of Chicago, 95 miles northeast of St. Louis, and 193 miles west of Indianapolis. Springfield's climate consists of four seasons, with warm summers and cold winters.

**Area:** 54 square miles (2000)

**Elevation:** 588 feet above sea level

**Average Temperatures:** January, 25.1° F; July, 76.3° F; annual average, 52.7° F

**Average Annual Precipitation:** 35.56 inches of rain; 23.1 inches of snow

# ■ History

## Sangamon River Valley Attracts Settlers

At the time Illinois was admitted to the Union in 1818, the city of Springfield did not exist. In that same year Elisha Kelly of North Carolina, attracted to the fertile Sangamon River valley, built the first homestead at a location that is now the northwest corner of Springfield's Second and Jefferson streets. Other settlers soon arrived and a small settlement began to take shape around the Kelly cabin. When Sangamon County was created in 1821, the Kelly colony was the only one large enough to house county officials. The town was named Springfield in April 1821, the name being derived from Spring Creek and one of the Kelly family's fields. Springfield became the county seat in 1825 and received its incorporation in 1832.

Through the leadership of young Abraham Lincoln, one of the "Long Nine"—seven representatives and two senators whose total height measured 54 feet—the state capital of Illinois was transferred from Vandalia to Springfield. Lincoln, who lived in the village of New Salem, 20 miles northwest of the city, moved to the new capital on April 15, 1837; he remained there until he left for Washington, D.C., on February 11, 1861, as the sixteenth president-elect of the United States on the eve of the American Civil War. During Lincoln's twenty-five years in Springfield as a lawyer and politician, the city experienced prosperity and growth, becoming a city in 1840 and recording a population of 9,400 people by 1860.

## Monuments Memorialize Lincoln in Springfield

The city of Springfield is a tribute to Lincoln, rivaling Washington, D.C., in the grandeur and significance of its public monuments, shrines, and historic buildings. The Old State Capitol, a Greek Revival style building constructed in 1837, is one of the most historically significant structures west of the Alleghenies. Lincoln delivered his "House Divided" speech on June 16, 1858, and maintained an office as president-elect there. His body lay in state in the Capitol's House of Representatives on May 5, 1865. The Lincoln Tomb and memorial in Oak Ridge Cemetery was dedicated in 1874. The marble burial chamber holds the bodies of Lincoln, his wife Mary, and sons Edward Baker, William Wallace, and Thomas ("Tad"). The Lincoln Memorial Garden and Nature Center, designed by Jens Jensen, reflects the Illinois landscape of Lincoln's time. The Lincoln Home National Historic Site, the Lincoln-Herndon Law Offices, the Lincoln Depot (formerly Great Western depot, where he gave his farewell speech to Springfield), and the Lincoln Family Pew at the First Presbyterian Church complete the sites memorializing Lincoln's life in Springfield.

At the center of Springfield's history and daily life is state politics. After the Civil War, to prevent the removal of the capital to Peoria, Springfield citizens bought the old capitol building for $200,000, which was then used to finance a new structure. Begun in 1868 and finished 20 years later at a cost of $4.5 million, the capitol rises 461 feet above the city and is in the form of a Latin cross with a vast dome in the center, capped with stained glass. The building was renovated in 1958.

## Springfield Emerges as Regional Center

In 1914 the Russell Sage Foundation picked Springfield for one of its sociological surveys to aid social welfare organizations. The creation of man-made Lake Springfield, the largest civic project in the city's history, was approved in 1930 and financed by a bond issue and federal funds. The city became a wholesale and retail center for the thriving agricultural region.

Throughout the 1900s the city became a regional center for education through the addition of Springfield College (1929), Lincoln Land Community College (1967), Sangamon State University (1969), and the Southern Illinois University (SIU) School of Medicine (1970). Sangamon State became the University of Illinois at Springfield in 1995. In 2004, Springfield College entered into a joint partnership with Benedictine University to create Benedictine University Springfield College in Illinois. The development of the city's health care industry began to take shape during about the same time, in part through the presence of the SIU School of Medicine. St. John's Hospital and the Memorial Medical Center have grown to become major employers for the city. The impact of the health care industry for the city and the region was recognized through the creation of the Illinois Medical District at Springfield in 2003. The district is a state-designated zone that is expected to attract and encourage the growth of health care service organizations as well as related tech and research firms. In 2007, the district was renamed as the Mid-Illinois Medical District. It is the second such district in the state, the first being in Chicago. As of 2007 the educational and health care services sectors were considered to be major industries in the city, with expectations for major growth into 2014.

Today, Springfield continues to serve as a center of government, culture, and business for central Illinois. With the addition of the multi-million-dollar Abraham Lincoln Presidential Library and Museum, the city also continues to be an attraction for national and international visitors interested in presidential and American history.

***Historical Information:*** Sangamon County Historical Society, 308 E. Adams St., Springfield, IL 62701; telephone (217)753-4900; www.sancohis.org. Illinois State Historical Society, 210 1/2 S. 6th St., Springfield, IL 62701; telephone (217)525-2781; www.history illinois.org

*Courtesy of the Springfield Convention & Visitors Bureau. Reproduced by permission.*

# ■ Population Profile

## Metropolitan Area Residents

1980: 187,770
1990: 189,550
2000: 188,951
2006 estimate: 206,112
Percent change, 1990–2000: −.3%
U.S. rank in 1980: Not available
U.S. rank in 1990: Not available
U.S. rank in 2000: 165th

## City Residents

1980: 99,637
1990: 105,227
2000: 111,454
2006 estimate: 116,482
Percent change, 1990–2000: 3.9%
U.S. rank in 1980: 171st
U.S. rank in 1990: 183rd (State rank: 4th)
U.S. rank in 2000: 225th (State rank: 6th)

**Density:** 2,063.9 people per square mile (2000)

**Racial and ethnic characteristics (2005)**

White: 88,300
Black: 16,894
American Indian and Alaska Native: 34
Asian: 1,613
Native Hawaiian and Pacific Islander: 0
Hispanic or Latino (may be of any race): 1,303
Other: 530

**Percent of residents born in state:** 78.2% (2000)

**Age characteristics (2005)**

Population under 5 years old: 7,396
Population 5 to 9 years old: 7,018
Population 10 to 14 years old: 7,025
Population 15 to 19 years old: 6,957
Population 20 to 24 years old: 6,904
Population 25 to 34 years old: 17,042
Population 35 to 44 years old: 14,624
Population 45 to 54 years old: 16,218
Population 55 to 59 years old: 8,765
Population 60 to 64 years old: 4,003
Population 65 to 74 years old: 7,443
Population 75 to 84 years old: 5,225
Population 85 years and older: 1,642
Median age: 37 years

**Births (2006, MSA)**

Total number: 2,703

**Deaths (2006, MSA)**

Total number: 2,004

**Money income (2005)**

Per capita income: $27,052
Median household income: $43,054
Total households: 49,056

**Number of households with income of**...

less than $10,000: 4,390
$10,000 to $14,999: 3,447
$15,000 to $24,999: 7,105
$25,000 to $34,999: 5,364
$35,000 to $49,999: 8,022
$50,000 to $74,999: 9,059
$75,000 to $99,999: 5,401
$100,000 to $149,999: 3,979
$150,000 to $199,999: 1,175
$200,000 or more: 1,114

**Percent of families below poverty level:** 11.1% (2005)

**2005 FBI Crime Index Property:** 7,345

**2005 FBI Crime Index Violent:** Not available

# ■ Municipal Government

Springfield operates under an aldermanic form of municipal government. The 10 aldermen, each representing one of 10 wards, and the mayor, who is the head official and a member of council, serve four-year terms.

**Head Official:** Mayor Timothy J. Davlin (since April 2003; current term expires 2011)

**Total Number of City Employees:** 1,707 (2007)

*City Information:* City of Springfield, 800 E. Monroe, Springfield, IL 62701; telephone (217)789-2000; www.springfield.il.us

# ■ Economy

## Major Industries and Commercial Activity

Springfield's diversified economic base is balanced between the public and private sectors; government, professional and health services, and wholesale and retail trade are the principal industries.

The government sector has the largest number of jobs with state and local officials and organizations both based in the city. The Illinois National Guard maintains a headquarters at Camp Lincoln in Springfield. These three

entities, the State of Illinois, the City of Springfield, and the Illinois National Guard, are among the top ten employers in the city.

Health care is the largest private sector industry. Memorial Health System, St. John's Hospital, and Springfield Clinic are among the largest employers in both the city and the county. The creation of the Mid-Illinois Medical District in Springfield, which encompasses the area surrounding all of these major medical institutions, is expected to serve as a catalyst for the growth of new and existing businesses dedicated to health care services and research and development in health or biotech fields.

Educational services are also an important part of the economy. Springfield School District 186, Southern Illinois University School of Medicine, and University of Illinois at Springfield are all major employers.

The city is a central trade area for 23 communities within a 50-mile radius. Retail sales in Sangamon county are over $5 billion each year. A central location and a highly developed transportation and communications network contribute to the city's position as a center of trade and business. Manufacturing firms in Sangamon County produce goods for national distribution and international export. In 2005 there were about 143 manufacturing firms in the county with 3,280 employees. The number of construction firms that year was at about 578 with 3,754 employees.

Tourism is beginning to find a more substantial role in the local economy as the city continues to build on its status as the Land of Lincoln.

**Items and goods produced:** tractors, electric meters, radio parts, flour, cereal products, automatic coffee makers, mattresses, plastic pipe, farm implements, livestock and poultry feeds, yeast, power plant boiler installations, printed circuits, steel storage tanks

## Incentive Programs—New and Existing Companies

*Local programs:* The city of Springfield offers a special Business Loan Program that provides funding up to $50,000 for non-manufacturing businesses and up to $100,000 for manufacturing businesses. The loans are granted based on job creation and gap financing.

In 1977 the Illinois legislature adopted the Tax Increment Allocation Redevelopment Act to provide municipalities with a unique tool to finance and stimulate urban redevelopment. Through the use of Tax Increment Financing (TIF), cities can stimulate private investment by offering incentives to attract and retain businesses, improve their community areas, and maintain a well-educated and highly trained labor force. Springfield has seven TIF districts.

*State programs:* Businesses located in the state-designated Springfield Enterprise Zone are eligible for an Investment Tax Credit, a Building and Materials Sales Tax Exemption (6.25 percent), and a Machinery and Equipment/Pollution Control Facilities Sales Tax Exemption (6.25 percent). A Jobs Tax Credit of $500 is also available for jobs, created in the zones, for certified dislocated or economically disadvantaged workers. The Economic Development for Growing Economy Tax Credit Program (EDGE) is a statewide program to benefit companies that relocate or expand operations within the state. Qualifying companies must make an investment of at least $5 million in capital improvements and create a minimum of 25 new full-time jobs in the state. Companies with 100 or fewer employees must make a capital investment of $1 million and create at least five full-time jobs to qualify. The High Impact Business program is designed to encourage large-scale economic development initiatives. Business projects that involve at least $12 million in investments and the creation of 500 full-time jobs may qualify for investment tax credits and state sales tax exemptions on building materials, utilities, and the purchase, repair, or replacement of manufacturing equipment. Other state sponsored tax credits include a Research and Development Tax Credit of 6.5 percent and a Manufacturer's Purchase Credit of 6.25 percent for qualified businesses. A number of loan programs are available.

*Job training programs:* The Capital Area Career Center is a vocational center operated through a partnership of local school districts to prepare students to enter particular occupations and to offer continuing education to employees. The Business Education Partnership, a collaborative effort between the Springfield Public Schools, the Illinois Association of School Boards, and the University of Illinois at Springfield, works to provide appropriate vocational education programs for students and adults. Lincoln Land Community College offers professional development training. Through the Illinois Employer Training and Investment Program, qualified employers may receive grants for up to 50 percent of costs in training new employees.

## Development Projects

Springfield has recently undergone a spurt of intense economic development with many companies and organizations building in or relocating to the area. In 2004 Wells Fargo Home Mortgage opened a new, $41 million, 185,000-square-foot facility, giving the company the capacity to accommodate 750 employees. Later that year a new, 43,000-square-foot Illinois Supreme Court Building opened. In 2005 the Illinois Air National Guard received $10 million in federal funding for the construction of a new facility to be located at Springfield Capital Airport. The new facility will have more than 45,000 square feet of space to be used as a dining area, medical clinic, and administrative offices.

In 2005 Springfield opened the Abraham Lincoln Presidential Library and Museum, an event that drew local and national media attention. The 160,000-square-foot, $115 million library and museum serve as the center for research and study of the life and times of Abraham Lincoln and the American Civil War. It is the nation's largest presidential library. In 2007 the Illinois Professional Land Surveyors Association (IPLSA) was still at work renovating the former Roberts Bros. building on Old Capitol Plaza into a new National Museum of Surveying. The project will take an investment of about $1 million. The city has agreed to offer $200,000 through a downtown tax increment financing program. IPLSA hopes to complete construction in 2008.

In 2007 M. J. Kellner Foodservice, the only locally owned food distributor in Springfield, announced plans to expand its operation and invest $8.7 million into a new state-of-the-art facility. The same year H. D. Smith, a national drug wholesaler, announced a $50 million facility expansion project that will create a new campus for the company's corporate headquarters in Springfield. Federal Express also announced plans to build a new distribution center in the city.

In February of 2007 Governor Rod R. Blagojevich announced a $413,750 International Tourism Grant to the Springfield Convention and Visitors Bureau (CVB). The grant, which is administered by the Illinois Department of Commerce and Economic Opportunity's (DCEO) Bureau of Tourism, will be used to develop, coordinate and promote additional international tourism to Springfield. Since 2003 over $1.7 million dollars has been given to the region through the International Tourism Grant Program.

*Economic Development Information:* City of Springfield Office of Planning and Economic Development, 800 E. Monroe, Room 107, Springfield, IL 62701; telephone (217)789-2377; www.springfield.il.us/oped. Illinois Department of Commerce and Economic Opportunity, 620 E. Adams, Springfield, IL 62701; telephone (217)782-7500; www.illinoisbiz.biz/dceo

## Commercial Shipping

A transportation hub for markets throughout the United States, the Springfield metropolitan area is served by 35 intrastate and 75 interstate motor freight carriers. Forty-one truck terminals are located in the community. Springfield and Sangamon County are linked with major national rail networks via five railroads, two of which operate facilities in the city, and a local rail company that maintains a switchyard. Abraham Lincoln Capital Airport provides daily commercial flights, as well as complete charter, aircraft repair and maintenance, and fuel services.

## Labor Force and Employment Outlook

The Springfield-Sangamon County labor force is one of the largest in central Illinois, with the highest commuting-in rate of any central Illinois community. The labor pool in the Springfield area is extensive and includes unemployed, under-employed, and re-entering retirees.

In an audit conducted by The Center for Governmental Studies at Northern Illinois University, researchers found that the overall labor quality in Springfield is considered among the best in the nation by local employers. Employers rated employees good or very good on job performance as it relates to trainability, basic skills, productivity, and attitudes. The presence of two major public universities, community colleges, and several schools offering vocational training provide for a fairly well-educated and well-prepared workforce. Employees also showed low rates of turnover and absenteeism.

Long term projections calculated for 2004-2014 indicate that the city will see a decrease in the number of jobs available in government and manufacturing sectors. Increases are most likely in professional and business services, educational services, health care services, and leisure and hospitality.

The following is a summary of data regarding the Springfield metropolitan area labor force, 2006 annual averages.

**Size of nonagricultural labor force:** 111,800

**Number of workers employed in ...**

> construction and mining: 4,800
> manufacturing: 3,300
> trade, transportation and utilities: 18,000
> information: 2,900
> financial activities: 7,600
> professional and business services: 10,400
> educational and health services: 16,800
> leisure and hospitality: 11,300
> other services: 6,600
> government: 30,100

**Average hourly earnings of production workers employed in manufacturing:** Not available

**Unemployment rate:** 4.6% (June 2007)

| *Largest employers (2007)* | *Number of employees* |
|---|---|
| State of Illinois | 17,000 |
| Memorial Health System | 3,400 |
| St. John's Hospital | 2,839 |
| Illinois National Guard | 2,700 |
| Springfield School District no. 186 | 2,019 |
| City of Springfield | 1,707 |

| Horace Mann Insurance Company | 1,280 |
|---|---|
| SIU School of Medicine | 1,200 |
| Springfield Clinic, LLP | 900 |
| SBC | 900 |
| U.S. Postal Service | 900 |

## Cost of Living

With a cost of living level below the national average, Springfield residents are reported to have higher disposable incomes for recreation, savings, and other discretionary expenditures.

The following is a summary of data regarding several key cost of living factors in the Springfield area.

**2007 (1st quarter) ACCRA Average House Price:** $274,357

**2007 (1st quarter) ACCRA Cost of Living Index:** 92.5

**State income tax rate:** 3.0% of Federal Adjusted Gross Income, with modifications

**State sales tax rate:** 6.25%

**Local income tax rate:** None

**Local sales tax rate:** 2.5% (plus a county tax of 0.25%)

**Property tax rate:** 7.87% (valuation is 33.3% of real property)

***Economic Information:*** Greater Springfield Chamber of Commerce, 3 S. Old State Capitol Plaza, Springfield, IL 62701; telephone (217)525-1173; www.gscc.org

# ■ Education and Research

## Elementary and Secondary Schools

Springfield Public School District 186 is one of the largest districts in the state. It is administered by a seven-member, nonpartisan board of education that appoints a superintendent. In 2007 about 49 percent of the district's teachers had bachelor's degrees and 51 percent held master's degrees or above. There were 23 National Board Certified Teachers. Special education services are available for students from ages 3 through 21. The AVID program (Advancement Via Individual Determination) is offered district-wide to assist underachieving students in gaining the extra help they need to complete their college preparatory courses. The Douglas Alternative Program and Lawrence Education Center offer alternative educational programming for high school students and young adults seeking to obtain basic education and vocational education goals. The Capital Area Career Center offers

21 vocational programs for high school juniors and seniors. Students of Capital attend a half-day program on-site and complete other coursework as part of a home schooling program. Magnet schools are available for gifted students at the elementary and middle school levels. The Springfield Ball Charter School serves children from preschool through eighth grade.

The following is a summary of data regarding the Springfield Public School District 186 as of the 2005–2006 school year.

**Total enrollment:** 14,240

**Number of facilities**

elementary schools: 25
junior high/middle schools: 5
senior high schools: 3
other: 2

**Student/teacher ratio:** 15.6:1

**Teacher salaries (2005–06)**

elementary median: $47,810
junior high/middle median: $40,970
secondary median: $45,460

**Funding per pupil:** $7,450

Springfield is also served by several private and parochial elementary and secondary schools.

*Public Schools Information:* Springfield Public School District 186, 1900 W. Monroe St., Springfield, IL 62704; telephone (217)525-3006; www.springfield.k12.il.us

## Colleges and Universities

The University of Illinois at Springfield (UIS), one of three University of Illinois campuses, is a four-year institution with an enrollment of over 4,900 students. The school offers 21 bachelor's degree programs, 20 master's programs, and 1 doctoral program through 4 colleges: Business and Management, Education and Human Services, Liberal Arts and Sciences, and Public Affairs and Administration. Popular majors are in accounting and public affairs.

The Southern Illinois University School of Medicine is a state-assisted school established in 1970 to train physicians and develop new models for providing health care in rural areas. With a four-year program, there are only 72 students in each class. First year students study in Carbondale then transfer to Springfield. Residency training programs are offered in 14 specialty areas.

Founded in 1967, Lincoln Land Community College is a community-based two-year institution with an enrollment of over 12,000 students. The school offers vocational education, programs for returning students, and a transfer curriculum. Robert Morris College is a private, not-for-profit school specializing in applied and professional education. The school has seven campuses throughout the state. The Springfield campus offers associate's and bachelor's degrees and professional diplomas in business, health studies, information technology, and art and design. Accelerated programs are offered so that students may complete a bachelor's degree in three years or an associate's degree in 15 months.

Benedictine University Springfield College (BUSC) in Illinois is a four-year institution offering both associate's and bachelor's degrees in seven fields and a master's in education. The school was founded as Springfield College in 1929 by Catholic Ursuline Sisters and was the city's first institution of higher learning. The partnership with Benedictine University took place in 2004. Through the partnership, bachelor's and master's degrees are awarded by Benedictine University and students who earn associate's degrees are automatically accepted into Benedictine's programs. In 2008 BUSC was ranked by *U.S. News & World Report* as being among the top 30 percent best schools in the Midwest.

St. John's College, a part of St. John's Hospital, offers last two years of study required for students to earn a bachelor's degree in nursing. St. John's Hospital has educational programs offering certificates in electro-neurodiagnostic technology and an associate's degree in respiratory care. Its School of Clinical Laboratory Science has a partnership with several area colleges to provide programs leading to a bachelor's degree.

## Libraries and Research Centers

The Lincoln Library, Springfield's public library, holds more than 400,000 books, about 1,000 periodical titles, plus microfilm, films, audio and videotapes, compact discs, maps, charts, and art reproductions. There are two branch locations as well as the Main Library. A special delivery service is available for the home bound. The Main Library holds a special Sangamon Valley Collection containing historic documents and resources on local history. The Southeast branch contains a special Black Culture Collection.

Springfield is also home to the Illinois State Library, which houses five million volumes. The library is a U.S. Patent and Trademark Depository Library. The library hosts a Talking Book and Braille Service and a special Illinois Author Reading Room featuring the works of Illinois natives such as Jane Addams, Ernest Hemingway, Saul Bellow, and Upton Sinclair.

Opened in 2004, the Abraham Lincoln Presidential Library and Museum (formerly the Illinois State Historical Library) is a 200,000-square-foot complex located in downtown Springfield. The facility was created to foster Abraham Lincoln scholarship and promote a greater appreciation of Illinois history. The library's archives contain more than 12 million documents, books, and artifacts relating to all areas of Illinois history. It also holds more than 5,000 newspaper titles on 89,000 microfilm reels; many date from the early nineteenth century.

Campus library facilities are maintained by Lincoln Land Community College, University of Illinois at Springfield, and Southern Illinois University School of Medicine. The Norris L. Brookens Library of the University of Illinois at Springfield has more than 540,000 volumes, 2,600 periodical subscriptions, 4,000 films and video items, and 200,000 government documents (local and state archives). The Illinois State Museum disseminates knowledge of natural history, anthropology, and art to the general public and scientists. Other libraries in the city are affiliated principally with hospitals and with government agencies such as the Illinois State Department of Energy and Natural Resources, the Illinois Environmental Protection Agency, and the Illinois Supreme Court.

The SimmonsCooper Cancer Institute at SIU has facilities for research and physician and public education. The Springfield Combines Laboratory Facility serves as a research site for SIU and the Illinois Environmental Protection Agency and Department of Public Health.

***Public Library Information:*** Lincoln Library, 326 S. 7th St., Springfield, IL 62701; telephone (217)753-4900; www.linolnlibrary.info; Illinois State Library, Gwendolyn Brooks Building, 300 S. 2nd Street, Springfield, IL 62701; telephone (217)785-5600; www.cyberdriveillinois.com

# ■ Health Care

Springfield is a primary health care center for the central Illinois region. St. John's Hospital has more than 700 beds. It has been in operation for more than 125 years and is one of the largest Catholic hospitals in the United States. Specialty services include an AthleticCare program in sports medicine, which is part of the larger Bone and Joint Services Center at St. John's. The Prairie Heart Institute, another specialty center of St. John's Hospital, has the largest heart program in Illinois. It performs more diagnostic catheterization angioplasties and heart surgeries than any single hospital in the state. St. John's also hosts the Carol Jo Vecchie Women and Children's Clinic and St. John's Children's Hospital.

Memorial Medical Center, operated by Memorial Health System, is a 600-bed acute care facility. Memorial maintains several specialty Centers of Excellence, including the Regional Burn Center, Regional Cancer Center, Regional Kidney Center, and the Center of Neuromuscular Services. Other specialized programs include the Hearing Center at Memorial, bariatric surgery, food and nutrition counseling, hospice and home health programs, and the SpineWorks Pain Center.

The Southern Illinois Trauma Center (SITC) is designated a Level I trauma center operated through a partnership of Memorial Medical Center, St. John's Hospital, and Southern Illinois University School of Medicine. The Level I trauma center host site alternates between Memorial and St. John's every year. When one hospital is not hosting the Level I trauma center, it continues to provide Level II services.

Another valuable resource to the Springfield medical community is Southern Illinois University School of Medicine. Physicians and residents from SIU provide services through most local hospitals. The SIU Springfield Center for Family Medicine Clinic is one of the largest clinics in the area. SIU Sponsors a special Rural Health Initiative program to find ways to offer adequate health care to rural communities of central and southern Illinois.

All of these medical institutions are part of the Mid-Illinois Medical District of Springfield. The second of its kind in the state (the first is in Chicago), the district is designed to support and encourage the growth of medical centers, schools, and related medical technology and research firms in the city.

***Health Care Information:*** St. John's Hospital, 800 E. Carpenter St., Springfield, IL 62769; telephone (217) 544-6464; www.st-johns.org. Memorial Health System, 701 N. 1st St., Springfield, IL 62781; telephone (217) 788-3000; www.memorialmedical.com

# ■ Recreation

## Sightseeing

Historic sites associated with Abraham Lincoln memorialize his presidency and his life in Springfield. The Old State Capitol Hall of Representatives, where Lincoln tried several hundred cases prior to the Civil War, has been reconstructed and completely furnished to re-create Lincoln's Illinois legislative years. The Lincoln Home, the only house Lincoln ever owned, is located in a four-block national historic area administered by the National Park Service. The Quaker-brown residence was home to the Lincoln family for 17 years, from 1844 to 1861. It now contains many authentic household furnishings and has been restored as closely as possible to its original condition. Neighboring 1850s-era residences have been similarly restored.

The Lincoln Depot marks the spot where Lincoln bade farewell to the city and contains restored waiting rooms, exhibits, and a video presentation recreating the 12-day journey to his inauguration. The Lincoln-Herndon Law Offices are in the only surviving structure where Lincoln maintained working law offices. At nearby Oak Ridge Cemetery, the Lincoln Tomb is marked with a sculpture honoring the 16th president. It is the final resting place of Abraham, Mary Todd, Tad, Eddie, and Willie Lincoln. In nearby New Salem 23 buildings have been restored to depict Lincoln's life here from 1831 to

1837. Costumed interpreters can be heard throughout the community's timber houses, shops, and stores.

The newest addition to Springfield's Lincoln sites is the Abraham Lincoln Presidential Library and Museum, which opened in 2004. The 200,000-square-foot complex houses the world's largest collection of documentary material on Lincoln and features high-tech exhibits, interactive displays, multimedia programs, and a reproduction of the 1861 White House. Visitors can also witness the 1860 presidential election as if it were happening today, with news coverage and campaign commercials.

There are other popular tourist attractions in the Springfield area. Designed by Frank Lloyd Wright in 1902 for socialite Susan Lawrence Dana, the Dana-Thomas House is an example of one of the architect's best-preserved prairie-style homes, with original furniture, art glass doors, windows, and light fixtures. The Washington Park Botanical Gardens and the Thomas Rees Memorial Carillon in Washington Park are other popular sights in Springfield; the carillon is the third-largest in the world and one of the few open to the public. Animal lovers will enjoy a day spent at the Henson Robinson Zoo, which houses more than 300 animals from five continents.

Visitors to Springfield might consider a trip to nearby Dickson Mounds Museum, a branch of the Illinois State Museum and one of the major on-site archaeological museums in the U.S. It contains more than 15,000 square feet of exhibits focusing on Native Americans, including art and artifact displays, hands-on activities, and multimedia presentations.

## Arts and Culture

Sponsoring a season of plays, the Springfield Theatre Centre is a community theater group performing musicals, comedies, and drama from September until June. The group generally performs at the Hoogland Center for the Arts, which houses four major performance spaces and several smaller gathering areas. The Springfield Muni Opera presents four Broadway musicals during the summer season at the 750-seat open-air theater near Lake Springfield. Each performance is accompanied by a full orchestra. The Illinois Symphony Orchestra and the Ballet Company perform at Sangamon Auditorium (University of Illinois) and other sites throughout the city and state. During the summer months, Theatre in the Park presents a variety of entertainment in a natural outdoor amphitheater at New Salem State Historic Site; the productions include a play about Lincoln's life at New Salem.

The Illinois State Museum preserves natural, anthropological, and art histories of Illinois with changing and permanent exhibits. The new natural history hall, "Changes: Dynamic Illinois Environments," demonstrates the changes in Illinois environments over the last 500 million years. The Vachel Lindsay Home is a museum and cultural center that pays tribute to one of the state's most famous artist-poets, who was known as "the prairie troubadour." The home was Lindsay's birthplace and remained his only home until his death there in 1931. The Edwards Place, built in 1833 for Benjamin and Helen Edwards, is an Italianate mansion that has been converted into an art gallery, school of art, and art library.

The Museum of Funeral Customs features exhibits that explain the customs of mourning and funeral practices among many cultures of the world. Special exhibits include a recreation of a 1920s operating (embalming) room, embalming equipment and instruments, coffins and caskets from different eras, religious items relating to funerals, and personal articles of mourning, such as clothing and jewelry.

## Festivals and Holidays

The Springfield Old Capitol Art Fair is considered one of the best art events in the United States, attracting more than 200 artists who display their work downtown near the Old State Capitol Building on the third weekend in May. The two-day event has been held for more than 40 years, and also features food vendors and live entertainment. A Children's Art Fair accompanies the main attraction. The International Carillon Festival, held seven evenings in June, is one of only a few of its kind in the country; international performers play carillon music on the bronze bells in the Thomas Rees Memorial Carillon and fireworks cap off the festival.

The Illinois State Fair, held each August over a 10-day period, draws hundreds of thousands of people each year. It hosts one of the nation's largest livestock shows, as well as farm contests and one-mile harness racing on a recognized fast track. For more than 20 years, the springtime Springfield Air Rendezvous has attracted a mix of airshow acts, from internationally known aerobatics entertainment to warbirds and ultralights. In June the city's Taste of Downtown offers visitors a variety of regional and ethnic foods from many Springfield restaurants; festivities include live music, children's activities, and a pitching booth. The International Route 66 Mother Road Festival held in Springfield in September includes a free car show and street festival with live music and activities for all ages. A Festival of Trees in late November and a Christmas Parade in December inaugurate the winter holiday season, which culminates with First Night Springfield on New Year's Eve, featuring varied musical entertainment, arts events, and a midnight fireworks display.

## Sports for the Spectator

Springfield is home to the national champion Springfield Junior Blues hockey team, a member of the North American Hockey League. Sports fans also follow several collegiate teams, including the nationally ranked University of Illinois at Springfield Prairie Stars soccer team. The annual Ladies Professional Golf Association/State

Farm Golf Classic attracts more than 100 professional golfers to compete for $500,000 in prizes.

## Sports for the Participant

The Springfield Recreation Department and the Springfield Park District maintain more than 30 parks in the city, offering facilities for fishing, hiking, jogging, picnicking, tennis, ice skating, swimming, and softball. Springfield's wildlife sanctuaries provide year-round opportunities to enjoy the countryside of Sangamon County and golfers will enjoy the city's nine golf courses. Lake Springfield, a 4,235-acre, artificially constructed reservoir, is surrounded by 57 miles of shoreline. The area around the lake supports eight parks and recreational outlets, including boat launches for canoes, motorboats, pontoons, rowboats, and sailboats, and a marina offering boat, water ski, and jet ski rentals.

*Recreation Information:* Springfield Park District, 2500 S. 11th St., Springfield, IL 62703; telephone (217) 544-1751; www.springfieldparks.org

## Shopping and Dining

Springfield is the commercial center for central Illinois, with a thriving downtown area full of shops in restored historic buildings offering unique gifts and clothing. Simon White Oaks Mall has the largest selection of merchandise in the region, with 115 stores, restaurants, and movie theaters. Illinois Artisans Shop at the Illinois State Museum features works by state artists. The Old Capitol Farmers' Market occupies two city blocks of downtown and offers fresh produce, flowers, and food from more than 60 vendors.

Restaurants in the city offer a selection of American, Continental, Mediterranean, Chinese, Thai, and Korean menus. The "horseshoe sandwich," a local staple created in Springfield in 1928, consists of a ham slice topped with an English cheddar cheese sauce, and crowned with french fries representing the nails of a horseshoe. Another regional favorite is a special "chilli" recipe served by a local parlor that has spelled chili with an extra "l" since 1909.

*Visitor Information:* Springfield Convention and Visitors Bureau, 109 North Seventh Street, Springfield, Illinois 62701; telephone (800)545-7300; www.visit-springfieldillinois.com

## ■ Convention Facilities

The Prairie Capital Convention Center, conveniently located in downtown Springfield, is the city's principal meeting and convention facility. It contains 66,000 square feet of space, and includes 44,000 square feet of column-free exhibit space. Springfield's many hotels, motels, and inns offer more than 4,000 rooms. Major hotels, such as the Hilton and Crowne Plaza also operate meeting and conference facilities. The Illinois State Fairgrounds has a 366-acre facility with 29 major buildings available for large events. And for those looking for a unique setting, the Old State Capitol, Dana-Thomas House, the Abraham Lincoln Presidential Library and Museum, and New Salem have facilities available.

*Convention Information:* Springfield Convention and Visitors Bureau, 109 North Seventh Street, Springfield, Illinois 62701; telephone (800)545-7300; www.visit-springfieldillinois.com

## ■ Transportation

### Approaching the City

The Abraham Lincoln Capital Airport is the major air transportation facility in the Springfield metropolitan area. The airport is served by three commercial carriers, United Airlines, American Airlines, and Allegiant Air, which make over 20 daily commercial flights to and from airports in St. Louis, Washington, D.C., Las Vegas, and Chicago. Charter service is also available.

The highway system in Springfield/Sangamon County includes three interstate freeways, a limited-access highway, and several state routes. Intersecting Sangamon County, I-55 (aka Route 66) runs north to south along the eastern boundary of Springfield; I-72 links the city with Champaign-Urbana, Illinois, to the east. U.S. 36 connects with I-55 south of Springfield and continues west to Jacksonville, Illinois. State routes include 4 (north-south), 29 (east-west), 54 (east-west), and 97 (east-west).

Amtrak schedules daily trains that provide service from Springfield to Chicago, Illinois, and to St. Louis, Missouri. Greyhound Bus Lines also serve the city. There are over a dozen firms offering charter bus service to and from the city.

### Traveling in the City

Streets in Springfield are laid out on a grid pattern. Washington Street, bisecting the city from east to west, and Fifth Street and Sixth Street, running parallel north to south, intersect in the center of downtown. The Springfield Mass Transit District (SMTD) operates public bus transportation on nine regularly scheduled fixed-routes Monday through Saturday. SMTD has special Historic Site Buses to direct tourists to local attractions. The Springfield trolley also offers services to major sites within the downtown area.

## ■ Communications

### Newspapers and Magazines

The *State Journal-Register* is Springfield's major daily (morning) newspaper and Illinois' oldest newspaper. The *Illinois Times* is an alternative press publication that appears weekly and is available for free at hundreds of locations in the area. The *Catholic Times* is a weekly publication of the Diocese of Springfield. *Illinois Issues* is a magazine on public affairs published 10 times a year by the University of Illinois at Springfield. *Outdoor Illinois* is a monthly magazine published by the Illinois Department of Natural Resources.

## Television and Radio

Three television stations are based in Springfield, through the NBC, FOX, and PBS networks. Cable television is also available. Radio programming is provided in Springfield by 12 AM and FM stations, broadcasting rock, contemporary, country, and classical music as well as sports, news, and talk radio.

*Media Information:* *State Journal-Register,* PO Box 219, Springfield, IL 62705-0219; telephone (217)788-1300; www.sj-r.com

## Springfield Online

Abraham Lincoln Presidential Library and Museum. Available www.alplm.org

City of Springfield home page. Available www .springfield.il.us

Downtown Springfield Inc. Available www .downtownspringfield.org

Greater Springfield Chamber of Commerce. Available www.gscc.org

Illinois State Museum. Available www.museum.state .il.us

Lincoln Home National Historic Site. Available www.nps.gov/liho

Springfield Convention and Visitors Bureau. Available www.visit-springfieldillinois.com

State of Illinois home page. Available www.state.il.us

*State Journal-Register.* Available www.sj-r.com

BIBLIOGRAPHY

Lindsay, Vachel, *The Golden Book of Springfield* (Charles H. Kerr, 2000)

Portwood, Shirley Motley, *Tell Us a Story: An African American Family in the Heartland* (Southern Illinois University Press, 2000)

# Indiana

# The State in Brief

**Nickname:** Hoosier State

**Motto:** Crossroads of America

**Flower:** Peony

**Bird:** Cardinal

**Area:** 36,417 square miles (2000; U.S. rank 38th)

**Elevation:** Ranges from 320 feet to 1,257 feet above sea level

**Climate:** Temperate, with four distinct seasons

**Admitted to Union:** December 11, 1816

**Capital:** Indianapolis

**Head Official:** Governor Mitch Daniels (R) (until 2008)

## Population

1980: 5,490,000
1990: 5,610,000
2000: 6,080,517
2006 estimate: 6,313,520
Percent change, 1990–2000: 9.7%
U.S. rank in 2006: 15th
Percent of residents born in state: 68.58% (2006)
Density: 174.9 people per square mile (2006)
2006 FBI Crime Index Total: 241,003

## Racial and Ethnic Characteristics (2006)

White: 5,427,561
Black or African American: 551,864
American Indian and Alaska Native: 10,964
Asian: 81,054
Native Hawaiian and Pacific Islander: 1,278
Hispanic or Latino (may be of any race): 299,398
Other: 151,563

## Age Characteristics (2006)

Population under 5 years old: 433,580
Population 5 to 19 years old: 1,329,442
Percent of population 65 years and over: 12.4%
Median age: 36.3

## Vital Statistics

Total number of births (2006): 86,790
Total number of deaths (2006): 55,482
AIDS cases reported through 2005: 7,963

## Economy

Major industries: Manufacturing, agriculture, mining
Unemployment rate (2006): 6.9%
Per capita income (2006): $22,781
Median household income (2006): $45,394
Percentage of persons below poverty level (2006): 12.7%
Income tax rate: 3.4%
Sales tax rate: 6.0%

# Evansville

## ■ The City in Brief

**Founded:** 1812 (incorporated 1847)

**Head Official:** Mayor Jonathan Weinzapfel (since January 2004)

**City Population**

    1980: 130,496
    1990: 126,272
    2000: 121,582
    2006 estimate: 115,738
    Percent change, 1990–2000: −3.6%
    U.S. rank in 1980: 121st
    U.S. rank in 1990: Not available
    U.S. rank in 2000: 199th (State rank: 4th)

**Metropolitan Area Population**

    1980: 276,000
    1990: 278,990
    2000: 296,195
    2006 estimate: 350,356
    Percent change, 1990–2000: 6.2%
    U.S. rank in 1980: 114th
    U.S. rank in 1990: Not available
    U.S. rank in 2000: 133rd

**Area:** 41 square miles (2000)

**Elevation:** 385.5 feet above sea level

**Average Annual Temperatures:** January, 31.0° F; July, 78.6° F; annual average, 56.0° F

**Average Annual Precipitation:** 44.27 inches of rain, 14.1 inches of snow

**Major Economic Sectors:** services, wholesale and retail trade, government

**Unemployment Rate:** 4.8% (June 2007)

**Per Capita Income:** $19,247 (2005)

**2005 FBI Crime Index Property:** 6,008

**2005 FBI Crime Index Violent:** 478

**Major Colleges and Universities:** University of Evansville; University of Southern Indiana; Ivy Tech Community College

**Daily Newspaper:** *The Evansville Courier & Press*

## ■ Introduction

The seat of Vanderburgh County, Evansville is the center of a greater metropolitan area that includes Henderson, Kentucky. Well-positioned in the days of the steamboat, the city occupies a unique prospect on a U-bend of the Ohio River where the Port of Evansville serves as a U.S. Port of Entry. While supporting a strong manufacturing economy, the city has begun to diversify its economy through financial and business services and the creation of new high-tech facilities and business incentives. In 2007 *Entrepreneur Magazine* ranked Evansville as the 29th best small city in the country for entrepreneurs and *Expansion Magazine* listed the Evansville-Henderson metropolitan area as one of the "Most Logistic Friendly Metros." Today modern architecture mixes with historic structures to make Evansville an effective blend of the present with the past.

## ■ Geography and Climate

Evansville lies along the north bank of the Ohio River in a shallow valley at the southwestern tip of Indiana. Low hills surround flat, rolling land to the north, east, and west; the valley opens onto the river to the south. The city's climate is determined by moisture-bearing low pressure formations that move across the area from the western Gulf of Mexico region northeastward over the Mississippi and Ohio valleys to the Great Lakes and northern Atlantic Coast. These storm systems, which produce considerable variation in seasonal temperatures and precipitation, are especially prevalent during the winter and spring months. The growing season lasts approximately 199 days. Evansville is the seat of Vanderburgh County.

**Area:** 41 square miles (2000)

**Elevation:** 385.5 feet above sea level

**Average Temperatures:** January, 31.0° F; July, 78.6° F; annual average, 56.0° F

**Average Annual Precipitation:** 44.27 inches of rain, 14.1 inches of snow

# ■ History

### River Location Draws Flatboat Commerce

The identity of the city of Evansville evolved from its location on the Ohio River at the spot where the river makes a dramatic U-bend. Evansville's founder was Colonel Hugh McGary, who purchased 200 acres from the federal government and built a cabin at the foot of present-day Main Street, where he started a ferry boat service. Hoping the site would become the county seat, McGary sought the advice of General Robert Evans, a member of the territorial legislature. In 1818 McGary sold a section of land above Main Street to General Evans, who replanted the town, which was made the seat of Vanderburgh County and named in honor of Evans.

Evansville prospered from the commerce of Ohio River flatboats that were piloted by colorful frontiersmen who served as both guides and navigators. Theatrical troupes wandering on the rivers in Ohio played engagements in Evansville even during its early history, establishing a local theatrical tradition that continues today. But it was the age of the steamboat that brought Evansville economic prosperity.

During the first few decades of the nineteenth century, Evansville experienced a difficult period that jeopardized the physical health of the citizens and the economic stability of the town. First the depression of 1824–1829 hit the city hard and then an epidemic of milk sickness swept through, further weakening an already vulnerable populace. Dr. William Trafton, an Evansville physician, found a cure for the ailment that brought the struggling community national recognition. In the winter of 1831–1832 additional hardship came with the freezing of the Ohio River, which paralyzed river trade, followed by floods that covered the town during the spring thaw. In the summer almost 400 people died of cholera. Then Colonel McGary was charged with horse stealing. Although he explained he had traded horses with a relative, rumors forced him to leave town in disgrace.

### Business Growth Brings New Residents

In 1836 Evansville was made the southern terminus of the Wabash & Erie Canal, which was completed in 1853 at the same time the first railroad train arrived in town. Although the canal proved not to be a financial success, it stimulated population growth and business development. European craftsmen immigrated to Evansville to work in the local factories and foundries. By 1890 more than 50,000 people lived in Evansville, which had a population of only 4,000 people when it was incorporated as a city in 1847. Serious floods in 1884, 1913, and 1937 finally led to the construction of a giant levee to protect the city, which was later known as "Plastics Valley" for the many plastics-related companies there.

Evansville continued to grow and thrive, cultivating a community rich in business opportunities, cultural events, educational outlets, and recreational activities. In 2004 the city was named an "All-America City" by the National Civic League. The award, the nation's most respected civic recognition award, was given to Evansville because of the city's progressive economic, educational, and community development initiatives. In the early 2000s the city has taken steps to encourage a more diverse economy and recruit new businesses, particularly in the areas of financial and business services, hospitality, and high-tech industries. In 2006 the Indiana Chamber of Commerce named Evansville as its Community of the Year. In 2007 *Entrepreneur Magazine* ranked Evansville as the 29th best small city in the country for entrepreneurs and *Expansion Magazine* listed the Evansville-Henderson metropolitan area as one of the "Most Logistic Friendly Metros." Worldwide ERC, a Florida-based association for global employee relocation, named Evansville as the best medium-sized metropolitan area in the nation for relocating families.

***Historical Information:*** Willard Library, 21 First Avenue, Evansville, IN 47710; telephone (812)425-4309; www.willard.lib.in.us. Indiana State Library, 140 North Senate Ave., Indianapolis, IN 46204; telephone (866)683-0008; www.statelib.lib.in.us

# ■ Population Profile

### Metropolitan Area Residents

    1980: 276,000
    1990: 278,990
    2000: 296,195
    2006 estimate: 350,356
    Percent change, 1990–2000: 6.2%
    U.S. rank in 1980: 114th
    U.S. rank in 1990: Not available
    U.S. rank in 2000: 133rd

### City Residents

    1980: 130,496

*Airphoto-Jim Wark*

1990: 126,272
2000: 121,582
2006 estimate: 115,738
Percent change, 1990–2000: −3.6%
U.S. rank in 1980: 121st
U.S. rank in 1990: Not available
U.S. rank in 2000: 199th (State rank: 4th)

**Density:** 2,987 people per square mile (2000)

**Racial and ethnic characteristics (2005)**

White: 93,260
Black: 12,197
American Indian and Alaska Native: 245
Asian: 1,287
Native Hawaiian and Pacific Islander: 0
Hispanic or Latino (may be of any race): 1,665
Other: 1,396

**Percent of residents born in state:** 69.7% (2000)

**Age characteristics (2005)**

Population under 5 years old: 8,438
Population 5 to 9 years old: 7,289
Population 10 to 14 years old: 6,972
Population 15 to 19 years old: 6,974
Population 20 to 24 years old: 7,902

Population 25 to 34 years old: 15,988
Population 35 to 44 years old: 15,005
Population 45 to 54 years old: 15,103
Population 55 to 59 years old: 6,216
Population 60 to 64 years old: 4,638
Population 65 to 74 years old: 7,326
Population 75 to 84 years old: 6,484
Population 85 years and older: 2,373
Median age: 36.4 years

**Births (2006, MSA)**

Total number: 4,551

**Deaths (2006, MSA)**

Total number: 3,470

**Money income (2005)**

Per capita income: $19,247
Median household income: $34,362
Total households: 49,215

**Number of households with income of...**

less than $10,000: 6,128
$10,000 to $14,999: 4,018
$15,000 to $24,999: 7,477
$25,000 to $34,999: 7,510
$35,000 to $49,999: 7,815

$50,000 to $74,999: 9,215
$75,000 to $99,999: 3,827
$100,000 to $149,999: 2,347
$150,000 to $199,999: 439
$200,000 or more: 439

**Percent of families below poverty level:** 10.6% (2005)

**2005 FBI Crime Index Property:** 6,008

**2005 FBI Crime Index Violent:** 478

# ■ Municipal Government

The city of Evansville is governed by a mayor and nine-member common council, all of whom are elected to four-year terms. Six council members are elected as ward representatives and three members are elected at large. The mayor, who is not a member of the council, and appointive boards oversee all municipal operations; the council approves city appropriations.

**Head Official:** Mayor Jonathan Weinzapfel (since January 2004; term expires December 31, 2008)

**Total Number of City Employees:** 1,500 (2007)

*Municipal Information:* City of Evansville, Office of the Mayor, Civic Center Complex, 1 N.W. Martin Luther King, Jr. Boulevard, Evansville, IN 47708; telephone (812)436-4962; www.evansvillegov.org

# ■ Economy

## Major Industries and Commercial Activity

Evansville is the industrial, agricultural, retail, and transportation center for the Tri-State region of Indiana, Illinois, and Kentucky and the largest city in the Evansville, IN–Henderson, KY metropolitan statistical area. The city is situated in the heart of rich coal fields. Major corporations have established regional operations and corporate headquarters in Evansville, primarily because of the area's rich natural resources, diverse transportation routes, and productive workforce. The strong manufacturing base includes such major corporations as Toyota, Whirlpool, ALCOA, AK Steel, GE Plastics, and Bristol-Myers Squibb.

Economic diversity has come in the form of health care services and financial and business services. Deaconess Health System (with four major facilities in Evansville) and St. Mary's Medical Center are major employers in the city. American General Finance, Old National Bancorp, and Fifth Third Bank are also top employers.

A fertile farming region surrounds Evansville. Regional farms yield corn, soybeans, wheat, oats, barley, melons, apples, peaches, pears, small fruits, potatoes, and various other vegetables. Meat, fruit, and vegetable packing plants operate in the city.

**Items and goods produced:** motor vehicles, prepared foods, nutritional products, refrigerators, pharmaceuticals, cold rolled steel, paints, plastic compounds and plastics products, auto glass, coal

## Incentive Programs—New and Existing Companies

*Local programs:* Vision-e, the nickname for the Economic Development Coalition of Southwest Indiana, works with the Metropolitan Evansville Chamber of Commerce for the economic well-being of the community and is the regional coordinator for economic development. The nonprofit organization assists companies with location studies, building and site searches, and feasibility studies, working closely with state and local economic development groups. One of these programs, the Strategic Development Fund, teams up two or more state businesses in similar markets, offering grants or loans to spur cooperation and creativity between industrial sectors or regions of the state.

Two square miles in Evansville are a designated Urban Enterprise Zone, offering inventory tax credits and other tax credits to eligible businesses. More than 400 companies operate within the zone. The nonprofit Evansville Industrial Foundation develops industrial sites to stimulate economic growth in the area, using a revolving fund to purchase land and develop infrastructure. Through the Tax Incremental Financing program, local municipalities are able to fund infrastructure improvements and new construction in areas needing growth or rehabilitation. The increased tax revenues from the valuator increase are used for repayment of the bond issue.

The city also has a Certified Tech Park, which is an area designated by local and state officials for high-technology business development. Certain state and local tax revenues can by recaptured for investment in continued development of the park.

*State programs:* The State of Indiana provides many programs to help Evansville area businesses. Grants and loans are available for community infrastructure improvements that would add value to company grounds, including funding for roads, rail spurs, water lines, and sewer lines. EDGE (Economic Development for Growing Economy) is a state sponsored refundable tax credit, based on payroll, which allows Indiana individual income tax withholdings from company employees to be credited against the company's state corporate income tax liability. Excess withholdings would be refunded to the company. The credits can be awarded for up to 10 years. The Hoosier Business Investment Tax Credit encourages capital investment in the state by providing a credit against a company's state tax liability. A Venture Capital

Investment Tax Credit and a Headquarters Relocation Tax Credit are also available.

*Job training programs:* The Indiana Economic Development Corporation provides two major grant programs for training and skill development: the Skills Enhancement Fund and the TECH Fund (Technology Enhancement Certification for Hoosiers). The Indiana Department of Commerce also provides grants to support skills training programs for local businesses. The funds can be used in a variety of ways, including customized training programs in specific skill areas for new employees and skills development training for existing employees. The Indiana Department of Workforce Development provides labor force recruitment services, including help with the application process, testing, and the assessment and screening of qualified applicants. Ivy Tech Community College offers workforce development programs that include customized industrial training, either on campus or at the job site, as well as a variety of technical certificate programs.

## Development Projects

The Economic Development Coalition of Southwest Indiana is one of the major forces in economic development for the region. In 2007 the city also established a new development agency, the Growth Alliance for Greater Evansville (GAGE), in order to further promote development in the downtown area.

In 2007 American General began a $35 million expansion of their downtown Evansville headquarters, which is projected to have an economic impact of over $400 million before 2009. Also in 2007, Shoe Carnival chose Evansville as a site for their $40 million corporate headquarters and distribution center. The same year, Berry Plastics announced plans to invest $20 million in the construction of a new distribution center at the Evansville Regional Airport.

Evansville received a $280,000 state grant to develop a new downtown Certified Technology Park, Innovation Pointe. Through state designation as a Certified Tech Park, certain state and local tax revenues may be recaptured locally for investment in tech park development. In 2007 Innovation Pointe was home to a small business incubator, the Arts Council of Southwestern Indiana, and GAGE.

Front Door Pride is a city program devoted to the revitalization of the near-downtown neighborhoods. Through the program, the city has established the Haynie's Corner Arts District as a site for local artists and art organizations. The city intends to renovate the Alhambra Theater as the focal point of the new district. As of 2007 the city had acquired a total of 80 parcels of land for the Front Door Pride program. Houses on these lands will either be renovated or cleared for new home construction.

As of 2007 the city continued to work with other county and state authorities on promoting the construction of Interstate 69 and the Fulton/Lloyd interchange, both of which would ease travel to and from the city. The city's River Commercializing Advisory Committee was also working with the Army Corps of Engineers on plans to develop a harbor and transportation facility near the CSX Rail Yard. The facility would expand the current port services by providing a larger area for international container shipments.

*Economic Development Information:* Metropolitan Evansville Chamber of Commerce, 100 N.W. 2nd Street, Suite 100, Evansville, IN 47706; telephone (812)425-8147; www.evansvillechamber.com. Economic Development Coalition of Southwest Indiana, 100 N.W. Second Street, Ste. 208, Evansville, IN 47708; telephone (812) 423-2020; www.southwestindiana.org

## Commercial Shipping

The Port of Evansville is located at mile 793 on the Ohio River. It is a public general cargo facility with 150,000 square feet of warehouse space. The river connects Evansville with all river markets in the central United States and on the Great Lakes and with international markets through the port of New Orleans. Evansville has been a U.S. Customs Port of Entry for more than 125 years. Because of this, it is possible to have international cargo shipped to Evansville in bond. The international cargo can then clear U.S. Customs in Evansville rather than a coastal port. Intermodal ground transportation is provided by CSX rail and several trucking companies. The Evansville Regional Airport has three airlines offering cargo service. Evansville is in the process of developing a 76-acre Foreign Trade Zone with warehouse services.

Norfolk Southern and Indiana Southern Railroad also provided service in Evansville along with 40 motor freight companies that maintain terminals in Evansville. There are also six major highway systems providing access to and from the Evansville area.

## Labor Force and Employment Outlook

Evansville boasts a highly productive labor force with a Midwestern work ethic and low absentee rates. Indiana's workers' compensation insurance rates and unemployment compensation costs are among the lowest in the country. The city has one of the highest percentages of skilled and semiskilled production workers relative to the total workforce, compared to surrounding states. In addition, the employee turnover rate is less than five percent per year. Because of the close proximity to surrounding counties, and ease of access to the Evansville area, companies regularly draw from a labor force that lies within a 30-mile radius of their work site.

In 2006 the greatest number of new jobs were found in the professional and business services and leisure and hospitality sectors. An increase in tourist and convention related activities has boosted the hospitality and leisure job markets. While manufacturing still holds a large number of employees, the city has been taking steps to increase the number of high-tech firms, and jobs, in the area.

The following is a summary of data regarding the Evansville IN-KY metropolitan area labor force, 2006 annual averages.

**Size of nonagricultural labor force:** 179,700

**Number of workers employed in . . .**

construction and mining: 13,300
manufacturing: 34,100
trade, transportation and utilities: 36,600
information: 2,900
financial activities: 6,300
professional and business services: 17,400
educational and health services: 27,400
leisure and hospitality: 16,700
other services: 7,400
government: 17,800

**Average hourly earnings of production workers employed in manufacturing:** $21.34

**Unemployment rate:** 4.8% (June 2007)

| *Largest employers (2007)* | *Number of employees* |
|---|---|
| Toyota Motor Mfg. Indiana | 4,700 |
| Deaconess Health System | 4,200 |
| St. Mary's Medical Center | 3,317 |
| Koch Enterprises | 3,300 |
| Evansville-Vanderburgh School Corporation | 3,043 |
| Industrial Contractors, Inc. | 2,500 |
| Alcoa Warrick Operations | 2,150 |
| Whirlpool Corporation | 2,083 |
| Bristol Myers Squibb/ Mead Johnson | 2,000 |
| University of Southern Indiana | 929 |

**Cost of Living**

The following is a summary of data regarding several key cost of living factors for the Evansville area.

**2007 (1st quarter) ACCRA Average House Price:** $260,603

**2007 (1st quarter) ACCRA Cost of Living Index:** 95.1

**State income tax rate:** 3.4% of Adjusted Gross Income

**State sales tax rate:** 6.0%

**Local income tax rate:** County optional income tax rate: up to 1.0%

**Local sales tax rate:** None

**Property tax rate:** up to 10.4% of assessed value

***Economic Information:*** Metropolitan Evansville Chamber of Commerce, 100 N.W. 2nd Street, Suite 100, Evansville, IN 47706; telephone (812)425-8147; www.evansvillechamber.com. Indiana Department of Workforce Development, Indiana Government Center South, 10 North Senate Ave., Indianapolis, IN 46204; telephone (800)891-6499; www.in.gov.dwd

# ■ Education and Research

## Elementary and Secondary Schools

Students from the Evansville-Vanderburgh School Corporation typically score above the national average in basic skills and above all Indiana urban school corporations on the proficiency tests. The graduation rate is about 89 percent, with about 65 percent of these students going on to pursue higher education. About 83 percent of the teaching staff have a master's degree or higher.

Bosse High School offers an International Baccalaureate program. High school students within the city schools may also qualify for dual-credit courses with University of Evansville, University of Southern Indiana, Ivy Tech and Vincennes University. The Southern Indiana Career and Technical Center (SITCT) offers two-year career and technical programs for high school juniors and seniors. Basic adult education is also available at SITCT. Signature School, a charter school, was ranked as 54th in *Newsweek* magazine's "Top 100 High Schools for 2006."

The following is a summary of data regarding the Evansville Vanderburgh School Corporation as of the 2005–2006 school year.

**Total enrollment:** 22,300

**Number of facilities**

elementary schools: 20
junior high/middle schools: 10
senior high schools: 5
other: 5

**Student/teacher ratio:** 16.2:1

**Teacher salaries (2005–06)**

elementary median: $45,770

junior high/middle median: $42,280
secondary median: $40,530

**Funding per pupil:** $7,729

In 1997, the Southern Indiana Japanese School opened at the request of Japanese companies locating in southwestern Indiana. The school serves the children of Japanese employees with an academic and cultural curriculum designed to keep students in pace with their peers in Japan, enabling a smooth transition back into the Japanese school systems once they return to their native country. The school accepts local students who have adequate Japanese language skills for classroom participation.

The area also offers a system of private, parochial, and charter school opportunities. Evansville Day School is a privately-operated school on the east side of Evansville offering classes from pre-kindergarten through grade 12 to 325 students. The Catholic Diocese of Evansville operates about 21 schools in the area. A number of other church-affiliated private schools are also available. A Montessori Academy offers educational programs for students in kindergarten through eighth grade.

*Public Schools Information:* Evansville Vanderburgh School Corporation, 1 S.E. Ninth Street, Evansville, IN 47708; telephone (812)435-8453; www.evsc.k12.in.us

## Colleges and Universities

Evansville is home to two universities and a technical college. The University of Evansville (UE), founded in 1854, is a private liberal arts and sciences university affiliated with the United Methodist Church. Total enrollment is about 2,647 students. The university also maintains a campus in Grantham, England, which is called Harlexton College. UE offers undergraduate programs in 80 areas of study in 4 academic divisions. Five graduate programs are also available. In 2008 UE was ranked as tenth in the nation of the best master's universities in the Midwest by *US News and World Report*.

The University of Southern Indiana (USI) began as a regional campus of Indiana State University in 1965 and became a separate state university in 1985. USI offers 11 master's degrees, 6 bachelor's degrees, and 4 associate's degrees in 7 academic divisions. Enrollment is over 10,000 students.

Ivy Tech Community College is a public, community college that offers associate's degree programs and certificate programs in a wide variety of fields. The main campus is in Evansville and serves over 5,700 students. There are 22 other locations throughout the state.

## Libraries and Research Centers

The Evansville Vanderburgh Public Library, founded in 1911, holds over 948,350 books, periodicals, CD-ROMs, CDs, audiovisual and audiotapes, films, slides, maps, and federal and state documents. The library operates seven branches and a bookmobile in addition to the central library, which maintains special collections on subjects including agriculture, business and management, economics, education, and religious studies. The Marcus and Mina Ravdin Memorial Collection is devoted to Judaica. The Talking Books Service, at the central branch, offers Braille books as well as recorded books and magazines.

The Willard Library of Evansville, founded in 1885, is the oldest operating library in the state of Indiana. It specializes in local history and genealogy as well as nineteenth-century periodical literature. Native Americans and Mississippi Indians are the focus at Angel Mounds State Historic Site Library. Other libraries in the city are operated by colleges and universities, corporations, the Evansville Museum of Arts and Science, churches, hospitals, and government agencies.

The University of Evansville Libraries, including the Clifford Memorial Library and the Bower-Suhrheinrich Library, hold 286,163 bound volumes and 11,396 audiovisual materials. The library also maintains over 970 print journal subscriptions and 13,000 electronic journals. The David L. Rice Library at the University of Southern Indiana is a selective depository for federal documents. Special collections include a Communal Studies Collection, which presents historic and current information on intentional communities, and the photograph collections of John Waring Doane and Paul Mueller.

The Center for Applied Research and Economic Development at the University of Southern Indiana works with local businesses and organizations on projects that include economic impact studies and new product development. The University of Southern Indiana also works with local businesses and agencies to conduct a variety of studies related to small business development.

*Public Library Information:* Evansville Vanderburgh Public Library, 200 S.E. Martin Luther King Jr. Blvd., Evansville, IN 47713; telephone (812)428-8200; www.evpl.org

## ■ Health Care

Deaconess Health System (DHS) is the primary source of care in the region. Deaconess Hospital in Evansville is a 365-bed acute care teaching hospital. It is one of the largest hospitals in the region, serving a 26-county area of southwestern Indiana, southeastern Illinois, and northwestern Kentucky. It features a Level II Trauma Center and a broad range of inpatient and outpatient medical, surgical and diagnostic services. The hospital sponsors a special Diabetes Center, a Pain Management Center, and a Sleep Center. Home and hospice care programs are provided. Primary care is available through the Family Medicine Clinic. A DHS Urgent Care Center is also located in

Evansville. The DHS Women's Hospital is dedicated solely to the needs of women and infants. This facility features 21 labor and delivery rooms, 5 surgical suites, and a 21-bed neonatal intensive care unit. Educational programs and groups for new mothers are available through the outreach programs of the hospital. Deaconess Cross Pointe is a full-service psychiatric and substance abuse/dependency hospital with 60 inpatient beds. HealthSouth Deaconess Rehabilitation Hospital offers specialized rehabilitation programs for patients recovering from stroke, brain injuries, orthopedic problems and surgeries, spinal cord injuries, amputations, pulmonary conditions, and congestive heart failure. The facility also offers a variety of occupational and recreational therapies.

St. Mary's Medical Center is a 520-bed acute care facility operated by the Daughters of Charity. The hospital also features a 32-bed extended care unit and a special care nursery. Services include a laser center, a chemical dependence center, women's health services, a long-term care program for senior citizens, and a heliport for air transportation. The St. Mary's Center for Advanced Medicine houses the outpatient laboratory and imaging services, the St. Mary's Heart Institute, the Joslin Diabetes Center, and Ohio Valley HeartCare.

# ■ Recreation

## Sightseeing

A visit to Evansville might begin at the Old Vanderburgh County Courthouse, a fine example of Beaux-Arts architecture. Completed in 1891, the courthouse exterior features statuary groups, bas-relief limestone carvings, and a giant clock housed in a bell tower; interior touches include marble floors, wainscoting, oak woodwork, brass handrails, and silverplated hardware. Another building of historic interest is the John Augustus Reitz house and museum, a 17-room French Second Empire style home built in 1871. It gives visitors an intimate look into how one of Indiana's wealthiest families lived. Also in downtown Evansville, the Old Post Office and Customs House, built in 1869, is a classic example of the Richardsonian Romanesque architectural style, featuring round arches over window and door openings and extensive use of stone masonry and towers.

Locals can test their luck at Casino Aztar, the state's first gaming riverboat. Named the *City of Evansville,* the riverboat is a 310-foot-long replica of the racing side wheel steamboat *Robert E. Lee,* and can accommodate 2,700 passengers. It offers three levels of casino action, including 1,250 slot machines and more than 70 gaming tables, including blackjack, craps, roulette, Caribbean stud, and a big six wheel. The boat is also home to five restaurants and two sports lounges. Adjacent to the boat is the Aztar hotel, with 250 guest rooms, suites, and meeting and convention facilities.

Angel Mounds State Historic Site, one of the best preserved prehistoric Native American towns in the eastern United States, dates from a period as early as 1200 A.D. when the Mississippians—as the inhabitants have been named by archaeologists—lived on the Ohio River. The site features reconstructed houses, a temple, and partial reconstruction of the original stockade wall that surrounded the settlement. An interpretive center has videos and exhibits on Indian culture and excavation at the site. Angel Mounds also features a burial mound, one of the largest prehistoric structures in the eastern United States.

New Harmony, west of Evansville, was founded by the Harmony Society in 1814 as a utopian religious community and sold in 1824 to Robert Owen, who attracted scholars, scientists, and educators to participate in communal living. The 30,000-acre community still has a population of 850 people, and visitors can take self-guided tours through the tree-lined streets of modest clapboard houses and quaint Victorian-style shops. The Athenaeum, the visitors' center designed by architect Richard Meier in 1979, is the starting point in learning about the importance of New Harmony. Nearby, the Workingmen's Institute, established by William Maclure in 1838, stands today as Indiana's oldest continuously open public lending library. The town also houses two labyrinths. A traditional shrubbery maze, based on Harmonist design, was reconstructed by the Indiana Department of Conservation in the late 1930s. The Cathedral Labyrinth is a recreation of the floor labyrinth at Chartres Cathedral located outside of Paris, France.

Mesker Park Zoo and Botanical Garden, a 67-acre zoological park containing lakes, ponds, and wooded hills, houses more than 500 exotic and domestic animals from 200 species. Many animals are free to roam in open areas surrounded by moats. The zoo also features a petting zoo, the Children's Enchanted Forest, paddle boats, bumper boats, a tram, and the Discovery Center, which focuses on the world's vanishing rainforests and animals. The Wesselman Woods Nature Preserve is comprised of 200 acres of virgin hardwood forest within the city limits, offering a wide variety of trees, shrubs, and wildflower species. Many trees reach 100 feet tall, and some are estimated to be nearly 300 years old. A Nature Center offers hands-on educational exhibits, a wildlife observation area, gift shop, and special events throughout the year.

## Arts and Culture

The Repertory People of Evansville, a local theater group, stages five productions per year, ranging from classical works to one-act shows. Established in 1925, the Evansville Civic Theatre specializes in musicals and comedy and features local performers in all of its productions. Among other local arts organizations are the Evansville Philharmonic Chorus, Ballet Evansville, Evansville Symphonic Band, Repertory People of Evansville, Evansville Dance Theatre, and Evansville Children's Theatre. The Evansville Philharmonic Orchestra is recognized as one of the finest orchestras in the Midwest. It offers several programs throughout the year in classical and pops music. The orchestra performs at the renovated Victory Theatre, a 1921 movie house reopened as a performing arts center. Theater performances are sponsored at The University Theatre (University of Southern Indiana) and the Shanklin Theatre and May Studio Theatre (University of Evansville).

The Evansville Museum of Arts and Science, located on the Ohio riverfront, offers more than 30 changing artwork exhibits dating from the sixteenth to the twentieth centuries. Its Main Street exhibit is a re-creation of a 1900 American community. The Koch Planetarium and Science Center, located within the museum, presents changing and permanent exhibits on science and technology; a steam locomotive, tavern car, and caboose are displayed on the grounds. The planetarium offers regular sky shows in its domed theater. At the Lincoln Boyhood National Memorial and State Park, visitors can see the Young Abe Lincoln Outdoor Drama, a living pioneer farm, and the grave of Lincoln's mother. The site is where Abraham Lincoln lived from age 7 to 21. Robert Municipal Stadium is a popular venue for concerts and sporting events.

## Festivals and Holidays

The Evansville Freedom Festival, lasting from mid-June to the Fourth of July, is Evansville's biggest celebration. It features a variety of activities for the family, including hydroplane racing, concerts, parades, carnival rides, food, and a fireworks display. The Germania Maennerchor Volksfest in August celebrates the food, folk music, and beer of Germany. Evansville's week-long Fall Festival, sponsored by the West Side Nut Club, is one of the largest street festivals in the country. It features free entertainment, carnival attractions, unique foods, selling booths, amateur talent competitions, and a parade. The Shrine Circus takes place every year over Thanksgiving Weekend at the Roberts Municipal Stadium. The annual Ohio River Arts Festival combines art appreciation, food, and family entertainment during the summer and the First Night Celebration throughout downtown Evansville welcomes in the New Year alcohol-free.

## Sports for the Spectator

One of the premier hydroplane races in the Midwest is Thunder on the Ohio, which attracts the fastest unlimited hydroplanes for the main event of Evansville's Freedom Festival celebration. Ellis Park Horse Track, in operation for more than 75 years, sponsors weekly thoroughbred horse racing July through Labor Day. The park offers both dirt and turf racing, and several top training stables base part of their summer season there. The Evansville Otters, a Frontier League baseball team, plays its home games at Evansville's Bosse Field.

The University of Evansville and the University of Southern Indiana field several sports teams, including the University of Evansville Aces, a Division I basketball team, and the University of Southern Indiana Eagles, a NCAA Division II basketball team.

## Sports for the Participant

Evansville offers a wealth of recreational activities for active residents and visitors. Activities include camping, fishing, boating, water skiing, hiking, swimming, tennis, and youth and adult sports programs. The city maintains 65 parks and 21 special facilities. There are also more than 40 golf courses within an hour's drive of Evansville. The city itself operates four public golf courses. Burdette Park and Aquatic Center features 145 acres of land dedicated to picnic areas, camping facilities, sports facilities, and vacation cottages. It is also home to an aquatic center with water slides, three pools, and a snack bar. A BMX racing track is available there as well. Swonder Ice Arena is a year-round ice skating facility that also offers indoor/outdoor inline skating and a skateboard park.

## Shopping and Dining

Evansville's shopping options range from unique specialty stores to malls filled with national chains. The city's downtown area, or Main Street, has more than 36 shops and restaurants. Antique and gift shops are especially popular, as are the restaurants featuring Italian, Mediterranean, Korean, Chinese, and local cuisine. The area also houses a number of bars and pubs. Shoppers looking for locally grown and fresh produce head to the Evansville Municipal Market. Built in 1918, the open-air market still offers flowers, local produce, and handmade crafts. Eastland Mall features over 37 stores and restaurants. The Franklin Street Shopping Area and Lloyd Crossing are also popular shopping spots.

Evansville's dining scene is equally as diverse. Options include everything from fine dining to fast food, and restaurants offer ethnic dishes as well as regional cuisine. Locally-owned favorites, Italian bistros, authentic Mexican, Chinese and Japanese fare, homemade Amish cooking, tasty Indian selections, traditional German restaurants, all-American delis, corner pubs, and terrific barbeque are all available options.

*Visitor Information:* Evansville Convention and Visitors Bureau, 410 S.E. Riverside Drive, Evansville, IN 47713; telephone (812)421-2200; toll-free (800)433-3025; www.evansvillecvb.org

## ■ Convention Facilities

The convention and tourism industry, which brings in millions of dollars annually, is an integral part of the Evansville economy. The Casino Aztar Executive Conference Center offers more than 11,000 square feet of meeting space, with many high-tech amenities. For those looking for larger facilities, the Executive Inn Evansville Hotel and Convention Center provides 33,000 square feet of meeting and banquet space in the heart of Evansville. It also houses 470 guest rooms and suites, and offers full-service catering.

Unique and unusual facilities are also available. The Mesker Amphitheatre offers outdoor seating for 8,500 people, with lush grounds and ample parking. Roberts Municipal Stadium features 44,000 square feet of exhibit space and 4,000 square feet of meeting room space. The arena has 12,500 seats and regularly hosts concerts, family shows, sporting events, and trade show exhibits. The Victory Theatre in downtown Evansville has nearly 2,000 seats. It is ideal for concerts, shows, and children's programs. It also offers three meeting rooms and a banquet room. More than 3,800 rooms are available as lodging throughout metropolitan Evansville at 40 hotels and motels.

*Convention Information:* Evansville Convention and Visitors Bureau, 410 S.E. Riverside Drive, Evansville, IN 47713; telephone (812)421-2200; toll-free (800) 433-3025; www.evansvillecvb.org

# ■ Transportation

## Approaching the City

The Evansville Regional Airport is served by American Eagle, Delta Connection, and Northwest Airlink, providing nonstop service to international hubs like Chicago, Detroit, Memphis, Dallas, Cincinnati, and Atlanta. The airport handles 46 daily flights and has the capabilities for further expansion and advancement. General aviation facilities are maintained at Evansville Regional Airport and at two smaller area airports.

A system of interstate, federal, state, and local highways provides easy access into the city within the Evansville vicinity and from points throughout the nation. North of the city, Interstate 64 runs east to west connecting with the north-south U.S. 41 for access into town. I-164, running north-south, connects with State Routes 57, 62, and 66 for routes into the city. Interstate 69, the planned new NAFTA interstate highway, will extend from Indianapolis to Evansville and connect with several gateways to Mexico. Interstate passenger service is provided by Greyhound Bus Lines.

## Traveling in the City

The Metropolitan Evansville Transit System (METS) schedules regular city and suburban buses on 17 fixed routes. A motorized trolley also provides transportation along the Downtown Walkway and in the downtown district. METS Mobility offers paratransit services for senior or disabled riders needing special assistance.

# ■ Communications

## Newspapers and Magazines

Evansville's major daily newspaper is the *Evansville Courier & Press,* which has an average daily circulation of 65,900 and a Sunday circulation of 89,900. The *Evansville Business Journal* is a monthly paper published by the *Evansville Courier & Press. Evansville Living* is a bimonthly city magazine showcasing the people, businesses, and community of Evansville.

## Television and Radio

Television programming is available from four stations based in Evansville, including a public broadcasting channel. Radio listeners tune in to 10 local AM and FM stations that schedule, among other formats, classical, jazz, rock, and contemporary music, religious programs, and news and special interest features. One station (WPSR–90.7FM) is hosted by students of Central High School.

*Media Information:* *Evansville Courier & Press,* 300 E. Walnut St., PO Box 268, Evansville, IN 47702; telephone (812)424-7711; www.courierpress.com

## Evansville Online

City of Evansville home page. Available www .evansvillegov.org

Economic Development Coalition of Southwest Indiana. Available www.southwestindiana.org

Evansville Chamber of Commerce. Available www .evansvillechamber.com

Evansville Convention and Visitors Bureau. Available www.evansvillecvb.org

*Evansville Courier & Press.* Available www .courierpress.com

BIBLIOGRAPHY

Bigham, Darrel E., *We Ask Only a Fair Trial: A History of the Black Community of Evansville, Indiana* (Bloomington, IN: Indiana University Press, 1987)

Patry, Robert P., *City of the Four Freedoms: A History of Evansville, Indiana* (Evansville, IN: Friends of Willard Library, 1996)

# Fort Wayne

## ■ The City in Brief

**Founded:** 1794 (incorporated 1829)

**Head Official:** Mayor Tom Henry (D) (since 2008)

**City Population**

    1980: 172,196
    1990: 195,680
    2000: 205,727
    2006 estimate: 248,637
    Percent change, 1990–2000: 1.3%
    U.S. rank in 1980: 80th
    U.S. rank in 1990: 99th
    U.S. rank in 2000: 97th

**Metropolitan Area Population**

    1980: 354,000
    1990: 456,281
    2000: 502,141
    2006 estimate: 408,071
    Percent change, 1990–2000: 10.1%
    U.S. rank in 1980: 93rd
    U.S. rank in 1990: Not available
    U.S. rank in 2000: 81st

**Area:** 78.95 square miles (2000)

**Elevation:** 790 feet above sea level

**Average Annual Temperatures:** January, 23.6° F; July, 73.4° F; annual average, 49.9° F

**Average Annual Precipitation:** 36.55 inches of rain; 32.4 inches of snow

**Major Economic Sectors:** services, wholesale and retail trade, government

**Unemployment Rate:** 4.7% (June 2007)

**Per Capita Income:** $19,565 (2005)

**2005 FBI Crime Index Property:** 10,732

**2005 FBI Crime Index Violent:** 732

**Major Colleges and Universities:** Indiana University-Purdue University Fort Wayne; Ivy Tech Community College; Indiana Institute of Technology

**Daily Newspaper:** *The Journal Gazette; The News-Sentinel*

## ■ Introduction

Because of its location at the confluence of three rivers and near the geographic center of the United States, Fort Wayne has from its earliest days been an important marketplace—first as a fur-trading post and now as the headquarters of major corporations. The outpost for "Mad" Anthony Wayne during the Indian struggles after the Revolutionary War and later the resting place of John Chapman, known also as Johnny Appleseed, the city figures prominently in the history of the settling of the western frontier. Fort Wayne, three times honored as an All-American City, is Indiana's second-largest city and the seat of Allen County.

## ■ Geography and Climate

Fort Wayne, located at the junction of the St. Mary's, St. Joseph, and Maumee rivers in northeastern Indiana, is set in level to rolling terrain. The climate is representative of the Midwestern region, with daily high and low temperature differences averaging about 20 degrees. Annual precipitation is well distributed and the freeze-free period is usually 173 days. Hailstorms occur about once a year; flooding also occurs. Snow covers the ground for about 30 days each winter, but heavy snowstorms are infrequent. Fort Wayne is the seat of Allen County.

**Area:** 78.95 square miles (2000)

**Elevation:** 790 feet above sea level

**Average Temperatures:** January, 23.6° F; July, 73.4° F; annual average, 49.9° F

**Average Annual Precipitation:** 36.55 inches of rain; 32.4 inches of snow

# ■ History

## Miami Territory Opened as Frontier

In ancient times, North American natives hunted the mastodon and other wildlife in a hostile environment after the retreat of the glaciers in the area where Fort Wayne now stands. Later, the Moundbuilders constructed an advanced civilization before mysteriously dying out around the time of the European Middle Ages. The Miami Native Americans ruled the lower peninsula region, fighting against the Iroquois who were armed by English colonists. In time the Miami reestablished themselves in the Wabash Valley and built their principal village at the Lakeside district in Fort Wayne, which they named Kekionga, meaning "blackberry patch." Kekionga evolved into Miamitown, a large settlement of Native Americans who sided with the British during the American Revolution.

Auguste Mottin de LaBalme, a French soldier fighting for the colonists, captured Miamitown in 1780 only to be defeated in his first major victory by Chief Little Turtle, one of the most feared and respected Miami leaders. After the revolution the British encouraged the Miami to attack the new nation and war parties were sent eastward from Miamitown, prompting President Washington to order armies into the center of Miami territory. Little Turtle defeated the army of General Arthur St. Clair and President Washington turned to General "Mad" Anthony Wayne, the Revolutionary War hero, to quell the rebellious tribes. General Wayne defeated the Miami at Fort Recovery in Ohio and at Fallen Timbers. Wayne marched on Miamitown and built the first American fort there. Wayne turned the fort over to Colonel John Hamtramck on October 21, 1794, and Hamtramck named it Fort Wayne the next day, which is considered the city's founding date.

Two key figures in Fort Wayne's early history were Chief Little Turtle and Williams Wells. Wells and Little Turtle signed the Treaty of Greenville, opening up the frontier, and Wells was appointed Indian agent. The two men provided leadership and stability until their deaths in 1812. Potawatomi and Miami factions then invaded Fort Wayne and General William Henry Harrison's army was sent in to regain control of the city. At the conclusion of the War of 1812 British influence on Native Americans came to a close.

## County Seat Becomes Industrial Center

Fort Wayne entered a new stage in its history with the arrival of Judge Samuel Hanna in 1819. Hanna built a trading post and a grist mill, earning himself the name "builder of the city." He was instrumental in realizing the Wabash & Erie Canal and securing Fort Wayne's first railroad. Hanna participated in organizing Allen County in 1824 and helped designate Fort Wayne as the county seat. In 1829 Fort Wayne was incorporated as a town.

Fort Wayne's growth as a Midwestern industrial center was helped along by the number of inventions conceived and developed there. In 1871 Dr. Theodore Horton introduced a hand-operated washing machine and later manufactured the first electrically powered domestic washing machine. Joseph and Cornelius Hoagland and Thomas Biddle developed a baking powder formula that proved successful. The Foster Shirtwaist Factory, capitalizing on the popularity of a boy's size-fourteen shirt among women, made the famous Gibson Girl shirtwaist. Other prominent inventions originating in Fort Wayne were the self-measuring pump designed by Silvanus Freelove Bowser and the "arc light" developed by James Jenney.

## Electronics and Lincolniana

The first nighttime professional baseball game took place in Fort Wayne in 1883 under Jenney Arc Lights. George Jacobs' discovery of an economical means of coating electrical wiring, which gave rise to the magnet wire industry, made possible modern electrical-powered products such as radios, telephones, automobiles, computers, and appliances. Homer Capehart's company of engineers invented the jukebox, which was sold to the Wurlitzer Company. Philo T. Farnsworth, a pioneer in the invention of television, bought the Capehart Company in 1938 and in time began the mass production of televisions.

Fort Wayne gained a reputation as a city receptive to innovative companies. The Magnavox Company relocated in Fort Wayne in 1930 and became a world leader in acoustical engineering. During the 1920s the Lincoln National Life Insurance Company emerged as an innovative insurance company. The company established and endowed the Lincoln Library and Museum, which houses the largest collection of materials on one man other than a biblical personage.

In subsequent decades the city's economy continued to diversify. In 1998 *Industry Week Magazine* ranked Fort Wayne as one of the top 25 world-class manufacturing communities in the nation. Fort Wayne has seen major growth in the service sector, especially in the health care field. Through its hospitals, Fort Wayne has become a medical center for the tri-state area. Tourism has grown, as visitors are drawn to the city's attractions, historical sites, festivals, and renowned dining options. The city has also continued to encourage high-tech industry. In 2003 the Center for Digital Governments ranked Fort Wayne as first in the nation in its Digital Cities Survey. In 2006 the city launched a free downtown WiFi program and initiatives to make fiber optic broadband services available at all businesses, schools, and residences.

Fort Wayne prides itself as a community with big city amenities and small town charm. The city was ranked as an All-America City by the National Civic League for 1983 and 1998. In 1998 *Money* magazine placed the city as fourth in the nation in its annual survey of "Best Places to Live" and in 1999 the city was one of five in the nation to receive the "City Livability Outstanding Achievement Award" from the U.S. Conference of Mayors.

***Historical Information:*** Allen County–Fort Wayne Historical Society, 302 East Berry Street, Fort Wayne, IN 46802; telephone (260)426-2882; www.fwhistorycenter .com

## ■ Population Profile

### Metropolitan Area Residents

> 1980: 354,000
> 1990: 456,281
> 2000: 502,141
> 2006 estimate: 408,071
> Percent change, 1990–2000: 10.1%
> U.S. rank in 1980: 93rd
> U.S. rank in 1990: Not available
> U.S. rank in 2000: 81st

### City Residents

> 1980: 172,196
> 1990: 195,680
> 2000: 205,727
> 2006 estimate: 248,637
> Percent change, 1990–2000: 1.3%
> U.S. rank in 1980: 80th
> U.S. rank in 1990: 99th
> U.S. rank in 2000: 97th

**Density:** 2,605.7 people per square mile

### Racial and ethnic characteristics (2005)

> White: 161,971
> Black: 35,858
> American Indian and Alaska Native: 404
> Asian: 4,798
> Native Hawaiian and Pacific Islander: 481
> Hispanic or Latino (may be of any race): 16,438
> Other: 8,689

**Percent of residents born in state:** 66.5% (2000)

### Age characteristics (2005)

> Population under 5 years old: 18,920

> Population 5 to 9 years old: 15,897
> Population 10 to 14 years old: 18,240
> Population 15 to 19 years old: 14,238
> Population 20 to 24 years old: 16,003
> Population 25 to 34 years old: 31,738
> Population 35 to 44 years old: 31,698
> Population 45 to 54 years old: 28,173
> Population 55 to 59 years old: 11,214
> Population 60 to 64 years old: 8,856
> Population 65 to 74 years old: 11,815
> Population 75 to 84 years old: 9,659
> Population 85 years and older: 2,895
> Median age: 33.2 years

### Births (2006, MSA)

> Total number: 6,051

### Deaths (2006, MSA)

> Total number: 3,116

### Money income (2005)

> Per capita income: $19,565
> Median household income: $38,063
> Total households: 91,447

### Number of households with income of...

> less than $10,000: 8,560
> $10,000 to $14,999: 6,635
> $15,000 to $24,999: 12,337
> $25,000 to $34,999: 14,477
> $35,000 to $49,999: 15,385
> $50,000 to $74,999: 19,441
> $75,000 to $99,999: 8,527
> $100,000 to $149,999: 4,207
> $150,000 to $199,999: 1,190
> $200,000 or more: 688

**Percent of families below poverty level:** 11.1% (2005)

**2005 FBI Crime Index Property:** 10,732

**2005 FBI Crime Index Violent:** 732

## ■ Municipal Government

The head official of the city of Fort Wayne is a strong mayor who administers the government with a nine-member council. The mayor and council members—six elected by district and three elected at large—all serve four-year terms; the mayor is not a member of the council.

**Head Official:** Mayor Tom Henry (D) (since 2008; term expires December 31, 2011)

**Total Number of City Employees:** 1,905 (2007)

*City Information:* City of Fort Wayne, 1 Main St., Fort Wayne, IN 46802; telephone (219)427-6957; www.cityoffortwayne.org

# ■ Economy

## Major Industries and Commercial Activity

Health care, manufacturing, and business and financial services have become primary industries in Fort Wayne. The city's hospitals form a regional medical center that serves the tri-state area. Demand for health care services has continued to increase alongside the area's population, particularly that of older citizens. The city's two health care networks—Parkview Health System and Lutheran Health Network—are among the city's top five employers.

Dozens of manufacturing companies in the Fort Wayne area employ 100 people or more. Notable among these is General Motors's Fort Wayne Assembly plant, which is one of the top employers in the city. The 2.5 million-square-foot plant, which built its first pickup truck in 1986, is home of the world's first full-size hybrid pickup truck. The Uniroyal Goodrich Tire Manufacturing is another major employer in the manufacturing sector.

The home offices of several insurance companies are located in Fort Wayne, including Lincoln Financial Group, which opened for business in 1905 as Lincoln National Life Insurance Company in a small rented space above a telegraph office in Fort Wayne. The company grew to become one of the largest insurance companies in the country.

The city has begun attracting new employers in the high-tech and research industries. Leading-edge communication service is available thanks to initiatives that made broadband service available throughout the city. Verizon Communications was one of the top 25 employers in 2007. The Northeast Indiana Innovation Center, a non-profit certified technology park established in 1999, is home to a research and development center for American Axle and Manufacturing, BioPoly RS, Cirrus ABS, Forward Engineering, the headquarters of ITT Aerospace Communications Division, Schwartz Biomedical, and OrthoPediatrics.

Tourism in Fort Wayne has grown in recent years, following the expansion and the building of new museums, hotels, festival parks, and meeting facilities.

**Items and goods produced:** electric motors and supplies, motion and control technologies, auto parts, trucks, tires, electronic equipment, metal processing, aircraft engines, ice cream, baked goods, baby carriages, children's riding vehicles, construction equipment, bagged ice

## Incentive Programs—New and Existing Companies

*Local programs:* The Fort Wayne–Allen County Economic Development Alliance—founded by the City of Fort Wayne, Allen County, and the Greater Fort Wayne Chamber of Commerce—supports business location, expansion, and retention in Allen County. The Alliance is a one-stop-shop for business development, serving as a coordinator of information and resources. It assists companies in many areas, including the development of long-term labor supply strategies, tax abatement on personal and real property, tax incremental financing, employee relocation assistance, site or building options and selection, and community participation. The city has a Certified Tech Park, the Northeast Indiana Innovation Center, which is an area designated by local and state officials for high-technology business development. Certain state and local tax revenues can by recaptured for investment in continued development of the park and special incentives are available for new or relocating businesses in the park.

*State programs:* EDGE (Economic Development for Growing Economy) is a state sponsored refundable tax credit, based on payroll, which allows Indiana individual income tax withholdings from company employees to be credited against the company's state corporate income tax liability. Excess withholdings would be refunded to the company. The credits can be awarded for up to 10 years. The Hoosier Business Investment Tax Credit encourages capital investment in the state by providing a credit against a company's state tax liability. A Venture Capital Investment Tax Credit and a Headquarters Relocation Tax Credit are also available.

*Job training programs:* The Indiana Economic Development Corporation provides two major grant programs for training and skill development: the Skills Enhancement Fund and the TECH Fund (Technology Enhancement Certification for Hoosiers). The Indiana Department of Commerce also provides grants to support skills training programs for local businesses. The funds can be used in a variety of ways, including customized training programs in specific skill areas for new employees and skills development training for existing employees. The Indiana Department of Workforce Development provides labor force recruitment services, including help with the application process, testing, and the assessment and screening of qualified applicants. Ivy Tech Community College offers workforce development programs that include customized industrial training, either on campus or at the job site, as well as a variety of technical certificate programs.

## Development Projects

Numerous major development projects are underway or recently completed in Fort Wayne. Among them is the plan that has created a fiber optic communications

*Advantage Aerial Inc.*

network—the only one of its kind in the Great Lakes region—bringing leading edge communication service and nearly 900 new jobs to the Fort Wayne area. In January 2005 General Motors confirmed a plan to invest approximately $175 million to upgrade its Fort Wayne Assembly plant. A $38 million expansion of Dupont Hospital was completed in 2007 and a $25 million expansion of Lutheran Hospital was completed in 2006.

In 2007 UPS announced an $11 million expansion of its Fort Wayne Package Hub that will add 17,500 square feet to its existing 58,875-square-foot facility. The expanded facility is expected to add at least 25 new jobs. Benco Dental also announced a $762,000 expansion of its Fort Wayne dental products distribution center. Pro Seal and Plastics pledged an investment of $1.3 million for a new facility that will expand its current supply business (seal, gasket, and wear rings) and add a new research and development center. Babicz Guitars USA, based in Poughkeepsie, New York, announced that it would expand its operations with a new facility in Fort Wayne to include product assembly, order fulfillment, and research and development. The defense contractor Sierra Nevada Corporation agreed to establish a new programming and engineering operation center in Fort Wayne. Edy's Ice Cream was considering expansion of its existing Fort Wayne production facility.

Since its inception in 2000, the Fort Wayne–Allen County Economic Development Alliance, generally referred to as The Alliance, has developed seven target industry clusters in its efforts to promote economic growth and diversity in the Fort Wayne metropolitan area. These clusters are: advanced manufacturing; agri-processing; aerospace and non-aerospace airport development; communications and defense; financial services; life and material science; and transportation, distributions, and logistics.

Ongoing development efforts to boost the high-tech and research sector of the economy have resulted in new and expanded businesses at the Northeast Indiana Innovation Park. This state-certified technology park began as a private and public partnership between the City of Fort Wayne, Indiana-Purdue University Fort Wayne, Allen County, the Greater Fort Wayne Chamber of Commerce, and local community stakeholders. The Innovation Center covers a 55-acre campus and has the distinction of being one of only a few non-profit research and technology centers that are ISO 9001:2000 certified. In 2007 Innovation Center tenant American Axle and Manufacturing announced that it would open a new product development and engineering center at the site.

In 2007 city officials were also beginning to take action on a new plan for sustainable growth called Reconnecting Fort Wayne. The plan focuses on finding ways to improve local transportation systems, to encourage a knowledge-based economy, and to develop more efficient energy use policies.

***Economic Development Information:*** Fort Wayne–Allen County Economic Development Alliance, 110 West Berry Street, Ste. 102, Fort Wayne, IN 46802; telephone (260)426-5568; www.thenallianceonline.com

## Commercial Shipping

Fort Wayne International Airport is the national and international air transportation center for northeastern Indiana. The airport is the headquarters and primary hub for Kitty Hawk Aircargo, which offers scheduled freights connections to over 45 domestic and international destinations. The airport is also the headquarters for Triple Crown, an intermodal rail and trucking venture of Conrail and Norfolk Southern. There are over 40 trucking companies based in Fort Wayne and Allen County. Fort Wayne is part of Foreign Trade Zone 182.

## Labor Force and Employment Outlook

The number of jobs in the health care and social assistance sector has increased significantly since the early 2000s and is considered to have continued potential for job growth. Manufacturing, in contrast, has experienced some decline, but still remains an essential part of the Fort Wayne economy, comprising a large percentage of Fort Wayne employment. Education, through the local public schools and higher education, is also a major employment sector. Service employment, which grew steadily in Fort Wayne during the early 2000s, is expected to continue its climb in upcoming years.

The following is a summary of data regarding the Fort Wayne metropolitan area labor force, 2006 annual averages.

**Size of nonagricultural labor force: 217,400**

**Number of workers employed in** . . .

> construction and mining: 11,500
> manufacturing: 38,000
> trade, transportation and utilities: 46,800
> information: 3,600
> financial activities: 12,000
> professional and business services: 21,400
> educational and health services: 34,900
> leisure and hospitality: 19,500
> other services: 8,100
> government: 21,600

**Average hourly earnings of production workers employed in manufacturing: $17.69**

**Unemployment rate: 4.7% (June 2007)**

| *Largest employers (2007)* | *Number of employees* |
|---|---|
| Fort Wayne Community Schools | 4,201 |
| Parkview Health Systems | 3,844 |
| Lutheran Health Network | 3,432 |
| General Motors Truck Group | 2,981 |
| Allen County Government | 1,964 |
| ITT Aerospace-Communications Div. | 1,910 |
| City of Fort Wayne | 1,905 |
| Lincoln Financial Group | 1,700 |
| Uniroyal Goodrich Tire Manufacturing (Michelin) | 1,502 |
| Scott's Food Stores, Inc. | 1,500 |

## Cost of Living

The following is a summary of data regarding several key cost of living factors for the Fort Wayne area.

**2007 (1st quarter) ACCRA Average House Price:** $259,213

**2007 (1st quarter) ACCRA Cost of Living Index:** 91.1

**State income tax rate:** 3.4% of Adjusted Gross Income

**State sales tax rate:** 6.0%

**Local income tax rate:** 0.8% (county tax)

**Local sales tax rate:** None

**Property tax rate:** 0.8353 per $100 assessed valuation (2000)

***Economic Information:*** Fort Wayne–Allen County Economic Development Alliance, 110 West Berry Street, Ste. 102, Fort Wayne, IN 46802; telephone (260)426-5568; www.thenallianceonline.com

# ■ Education and Research

## Elementary and Secondary Schools

Fort Wayne Community Schools is one of the largest districts in the state of Indiana and the largest in Allen County. About 84 percent of students graduate from high school and about 73 percent continue on to college. Children may attend any school in the district, with some restrictions based on space availability and racial balance.

The Bunche Early Childhood Center is the first public school in the nation to receive accreditation from the American Montessori Society. Towles Intermediate School is the only 1-8 Montessori program in the state.

South Side High School offers an International Baccalaureate program. Franke Park Elementary School is one of 50 schools in the nation to be designated as a NASA Explorer School with programs that focus on biological science and space. There are magnet schools at all levels.

Vocational programs are available through the Anthis Career Center.

The following is a summary of data regarding the Fort Wayne Community Schools as of the 2005–2006 school year.

**Total enrollment: 31,884**

**Number of facilities**

elementary schools: 34
junior high/middle schools: 10
senior high schools: 6
other: 2

**Student/teacher ratio: 17.7:1**

**Teacher salaries (2005–06)**

elementary median: $48,100
junior high/middle median: $48,280
secondary median: $48,110

**Funding per pupil: $9,316**

Additionally, Fort Wayne has several parochial and private schools offering elementary, high school, and special education opportunities.

***Public Schools Information:*** Fort Wayne Community Schools, 1200 S. Clinton St., Fort Wayne, IN; telephone (260)467-1000; www.fwcs.k12.in.us

## Colleges and Universities

Indiana University–Purdue University at Fort Wayne (IPFW) offers a complete range of undergraduate and graduate programs. The largest university in northeast Indiana, IPFW is a joint venture of two Big Ten schools and grants both Indiana University and Purdue University degrees. The main campus of Purdue is in West Lafayette, IN, and that of Indiana University is in Bloomington. Long a commuter college, IPFW opened its first student housing in 2004. Enrollment is over 10,500.

The Fort Wayne campus of the Indiana Institute of Technology, known simply as Indiana Tech, offers bachelor's degree programs in business, criminal science, and engineering and computer studies, and master's degrees in Business Administration (MBA), Science in Management (MSM), and Science in Engineering (MSE). Enrollment is over 3,000.

The University of Saint Francis is a Catholic liberal arts university with about 2,000 students, including about 250 graduate students. The school offers associate's, bachelor's, and master's degrees in a full range of majors, with additional special programs in ministry, pastoral counseling, social justice in the Franciscan tradition, and Franciscan studies.

Ivy Tech Community College is a public, community college that offers associate's degree programs and certificate programs in a wide variety of fields. There are 23 campus sites across the state. The Fort Wayne campus is the central campus for the northeast region. Associate's degrees and certificate programs are available in the fields of business, education, health sciences, liberal arts and sciences, technology, and public and social services. Enrollment is about 4,350.

Indiana Wesleyan University–Fort Wayne serves as a community education center for the Marion-based university. Students take classes that lead to the completion of an associate's, bachelor's, or master's degree. Most classes are offered on flexible schedules, including evenings and weekends, to accommodate working adults. Taylor University–Fort Wayne, an interdenominational liberal arts college with campuses in Fort Wayne and Upland, IN, also offers a full range of degree programs. Concordia University Wisconsin–Fort Wayne Center offers a Bachelor of Arts degree program with majors in human resource management, management of criminal justice, liberal arts, and business management. Concordia Theological Seminary provides pastoral training for students of the Lutheran Church–Missouri Synod.

Fort Wayne is also home to the International Business College, offering business, health care, and technology programs, and ITT Technical Institute, offering technology, drafting and design, and business programs. Post-secondary education and technical training are provided by two-year Ivy Tech State College. Other two-year colleges include Brown Mackie College, Tri-State University, and Indiana Business College-Fort Wayne.

## Libraries and Research Centers

The main facility of the Allen County Public Library is one of the busiest in the nation, with an annual circulation of well over 4.4 million books and other items. Special collections are available in such fields as local history, genealogy, heraldry, fine arts, business and technology, and federal and state documents. Its Genealogy Research Department, with more than 300,000 printed volumes and 314,000 items of microfilm and microfiche, is considered the most extensive public genealogy research library in the country. The library operates 13 branches.

The Helmke Library of Indiana University–Purdue University Fort Wayne has a collection of over 356,500 books and bound serials and over 540,000 microforms and microfilm reels. The library serves as a federal depository library and holds about 114,864 government documents. Special collections include the Historical Music Score Collection, which contains about 8,000 scores published between 1890 and 1930.

Indiana University–Purdue University at Fort Wayne sponsors 11 Centers of Excellence that focus on encouraging research and experiential learning for students and faculty alike. These include the Behavioral Health and Family Studies Institute, the Center for Reptile and Amphibian Conservation and Management, the Community Research Institute, the Institute for Decision Sciences and Theory, and Institute for Human Rights.

The research library at The Lincoln Museum has a large collection of Lincoln and Lincoln-era images in photographs, paintings, sculptures, and art prints. Several rare titles related to Lincoln are available through the library which is open by appointment only.

***Public Library Information:*** Allen County Public Library, 900 Library Plaza, Fort Wayne, IN 46802; telephone (260)421-1200; www. www.acpl.lib.in.us

# ■ Health Care

Parkview Health System (PHS) operates four main facilities in Fort Wayne. Parkview Hospital, the PHS flagship hospital, is a 575-bed acute care hospital with a Level II Adult and Pediatric Trauma Center. Parkview is the only trauma center to be verified by the American College of Surgeons in northern Indiana. The trauma center is comprised of 18 components, including a full-service emergency department, a surgical-trauma intensive care unit, a surgical care center, and a flight program with two medical helicopters. The hospital also houses a cardiac-medical intensive care unit; a continuing care skilled nursing facility; a new life center and neonatal intensive care unit; a children's center; cancer, heart, stroke, and rehabilitation centers; and a sleep disorders lab. Parkview North Hospital has 42-inpatient beds and houses an emergency department, a Family Birthing Center with a neonatal intensive care unit, ambulatory and general surgery departments, and diagnostic imaging services. An attached medical office building offers primary care services, including the Parkview Women's Health Center. The Orthopaedic Hospital at Parkview North is the only specialty hospital of its kind in northeastern Indiana. Parkview Behavioral Health Hospital is an acute care psychiatric hospital with 107 beds. Outpatient services are also available.

The Lutheran Health Network also sponsors four main facilities in Fort Wayne. Lutheran Hospital, the flagship hospital of Lutheran Health Network with 343 beds, is the region's only heart transplant facility. Other key services of the hospital include emergency services, inpatient and outpatient surgery, cardiac services, obstetrics, pediatrics, a diabetes treatment center, ortho-

pedics, occupational medicine, and a sleep lab. Lutheran Children's Hospital, located within Lutheran Hospital, supports a special outpatient cancer clinic for children, a pediatric emergency room, and a pediatric sleep disorders clinic. The Lutheran Rehabilitation Hospital is a 36-bed comprehensive medical rehabilitation hospital with inpatient and outpatient services available for patients recovering from orthopedic ailments (fractures, joint replacements, amputations), stroke, neurological disorders (spinal cord injury, Guillain Barre, multiple sclerosis), multiple trauma, and brain injury. The Dupont Hospital is a joint venture between the Lutheran Health Network and over 220 area physicians who share in the ownership and governance of the hospital. The 122-bed hospital has 13 operating rooms, emergency services, and an extensive women's health service program. St Joseph's Hospital is a 191-bed facility offering a full range of services including emergency services, inpatient and outpatient surgery, wound care, a burn center, rehabilitation programs, behavioral health, a skilled nursing unit, and home care programs.

# ■ Recreation

## Sightseeing

American history, exotic animals, and beautiful botanical gardens highlight sightseeing in Fort Wayne. Eleven museums and historical sites are within walking distance in the downtown area. A historic old fort from the War of 1812 is preserved in a park downtown where the St. Mary's and St. Joseph rivers merge to become the Maumee. The Allen County Courthouse, listed on the National Historic Register, was constructed between 1897 and 1902. It combines Greek and Roman architectural themes and is capped with a rotunda, and its ornately designed interior features Italian marble, granite columns, bright tiles, and murals.

The Fort Wayne Children's Zoo is home to more than 1,500 animals from around the world. The central area of the zoo features penguins, macaws, capuchin monkeys, sea lions, giant turtles, and the Indiana Family Farm, where visitors can pet farm animals. At the 22-acre African Veldt area, Jeep safari rides provide views of antelope, giraffes, wildebeest, zebras, and exotic birds. At the zoo's Australian Adventure, visitors can go on walkabouts or take canoe rides to view kangaroos, echidnas, lorikeets, parakeets, and dingoes. The Indonesian Rainforest area features a rare Komodo Dragon, orangutans, and Sumatran tigers. The zoo also contains a 20,000-gallon marine aquarium.

The Foellinger-Freimann Botanical Conservatory preserves rare and exotic tropical plants from around the world in its three gardens under glass: the Floral Showcase has lush, colorful seasonal displays; in the Tropical Garden, orchids, palms, and other exotic plants surround a waterfall; and the Desert House has cacti and other desert plants from the Sonoran Desert of southern Arizona and northern Mexico. Lakeside Rose Garden in northeast Fort Wayne, with 2,500 labeled plants, is recognized as one of the largest rose gardens in the country.

Science Central offers more than 30 hands-on exhibits to make learning fun. Visitors can dance on giant piano keys, create earthquakes, experience weightlessness over a moonscape, bend rainbows, and ride a high-rail bicycle.

## Arts and Culture

At the center of the performing arts in Fort Wayne is the restored Embassy Theater. Built in 1928, it is considered one of the country's most lavish architectural masterpieces. The Embassy Theatre features national touring productions from the Broadway stage, musical concerts of formats, and cinema presentations. Educational programming is also available for youth.

The Arts United Center, built in 1973 by the famous architect Louis Kahn, serves as the main performance stage for the Civic Theatre, the Youtheatre, Fort Wayne Ballet, Fort Wayne Dance Collective and the Fort Wayne Philharmonic. Arts United is the third oldest united nonprofit arts fund in the United States and the second largest arts council in the State of Indiana. The Fort Wayne Philharmonic, which performs a nine-month season of symphony, pops, and chamber music concerts, also performs at the Embassy Theatre. The Fort Wayne Civic Theatre, regarded by many as one of the outstanding regional civic theaters in the country, coordinates more than 600 volunteers a year to produce Broadway-style shows. The Fort Wayne Ballet presents two major productions in addition to the annual *Nutcracker* ballet in December. The Fort Wayne Dance Collective is northeast Indiana's only modern dance organization.

The Lincoln Museum, endowed by the Lincoln National Life Insurance Company, is the world's largest private museum and research library for Lincolniana. Housed in a 30,000-square-foot, state-of-the-art facility, the museum has interactive, hands-on exhibits for all age groups. The museum's highlights include a collection of personal possessions of Lincoln and his family; original photographs and paintings; and a rare edition of The Emancipation Proclamation, signed by Lincoln in 1864 (one of eight in the world in public collections and the only one on permanent public display); and the inkwell Lincoln used to sign the proclamation.

The Fort Wayne Museum of Art is devoted to American and European artwork from the 19th century to the present. The museum houses more than 1,300 pieces in permanent collections of paintings, prints, and sculpture in three self-contained modern buildings. The History Center, operated by the Allen County-Fort Wayne Historical Society, is located in the Old City Hall, a local architectural landmark; the museum displays

artifacts from the Stone Age to the Space Age. Highlights include law enforcement exhibits within the dank cells of the old city jail, a fully-equipped blacksmith shop, a detailed model of an American Indian village, antebellum women's dresses, and a dollhouse from 1886. At the Diehm Museum of Natural History, displays of mounted animals, birds, and fish from North America are featured in reproductions of natural habitats. The museum also has a collection of gems and minerals, as well as Far East artifacts. The Fort Wayne Firefighters Museum exhibits antique firefighting equipment and vehicles. In nearby Auburn, the Auburn Cord Duesenberg Museum, a national historic landmark, houses more than 100 examples of the world's grandest automobiles in a 1930 Art Deco factory showroom.

***Arts and Culture Information:*** Arts United of Greater Fort Wayne, 114 East Superior Street, Fort Wayne, IN 46802; telephone (260)424-0646; www.artsunited.org

## Festivals and Holidays

June brings three ethnic events to Fort Wayne: the Indiana Highland Games honors Scottish heritage with athletic competitions, bagpipes and dancing, and food; Germanfest recognizes Fort Wayne's largest ethnic group with music, dance, sports, art, and German food; and the Greek Festival brings Greek food, beverages, music, dancing, jewelry, art, clothing, and literature. Three Rivers Festival, held in mid-July for nine days, features more than 200 events that include a Festival of the Arts, Children's Fest, senior's events, a parade, races, and fireworks displays. At the Auburn Cord Deusenberg festival on Labor Day weekend in nearby Auburn, the world's largest classic automobiles are auctioned in a festive atmosphere; the festival also includes a quilt show and an antique sale. The Johnny Appleseed Festival, held in September, brings the early 1800s to life by honoring John Chapman, who introduced apple trees to the Midwest; the festival features re-enactments of pioneer life, period entertainers, and crafts. Holiday festivals from late November through December celebrate the Christmas season with a Festival of Trees, Festival of Gingerbread, a Wonderland of Wreaths at the Botanical Conservatory, and downtown lighting displays.

## Sports for the Spectator

In 2007 Street & Smith's *SportsBusiness Journal* named Fort Wayne "America's Number One Minor Sports League City." The Fort Wayne Komets, a United Hockey League team, plays a home schedule at Memorial Coliseum. The Komets captured the UHL Colonial Cup in the 2002–03 season. The Wizards, a Class A baseball team, play at Harrison Square Stadium. The Fever is the name for both the men's PDL (Premier Development League) and the women's W-League semi-pro soccer teams of the United Soccer League. Both teams play at the Hefner Soccer Fields of Indiana University–Purdue University Fort Wayne. The Fort Wayne Freedom is affiliated with United Indoor Football. Indiana-Purdue Fort Wayne Athletics is home to 16 Division I sports; the Mastodons host more than 100 athletic competitions each year.

### Sports for the Participant

Fort Wayne's public recreational facilities include 87 parks covering 2,200 acres. Amenities include tennis courts, soccer fields, softball diamonds, regulation baseball diamonds, four swimming pools, and three municipal golf courses. In 2005 *Golf Digest* listed Fort Wayne as one of the "Best Golf Towns in America." Within the county there are over 30 golf courses. The Rivergreenway Trail, a 15-mile-long trail along the banks of the city's three rivers, is ideal for bicycling, hiking, jogging, or rollerblading. The McMillen Ice Arena is a favorite spot for ice hockey, figure skating, and recreational skating. LAZER-X offers the largest laser tag arena in the Midwest at 9,000 square feet.

### Shopping and Dining

Fort Wayne supports one of the Midwest's largest enclosed malls—Glenbrook Mall—that contains 4 anchor department stores and more than 175 specialty shops and stores. Fort Wayne's Jefferson Pointe Mall offers 50 shops and restaurants and an 18-screen movie theater in an open-air setting with Mediterranean-style architecture and tree-lined courtyards.

Fort Wayne has long billed itself as "The City of Restaurants," and the 600 eating and drinking establishments in and around the city bolster that claim. For fine dining, visitors may want to try Don Hall's Old Gas House or Club Soda. Casa D'Angelo and Casa Grille Ristorante Italiano are popular spots for Italian food. On the lighter side, Cindy's Diner offers an authentic 1950s diner experience. Some Fort Wayne restaurants offer such regional favorites as hearty farm-style meals and desserts.

*Visitor Information:* Fort Wayne/Allen County Convention and Visitors Bureau, 1021 S. Calhoun St., Fort Wayne, IN 46802; telephone (800)767-7752; www.visitfortwayne.com

## ■ Convention Facilities

The Grand Wayne Convention Center hosts over 500 events each year. The 225,000-square-foot facility features 80,000 square feet of meeting space and 30,000 square feet of public areas. State-of-the-art audio and visual systems and in-house technology services are available. The 12,000-square-foot kitchen is equipped to prepare banquets for up to 6,000 people. The Grand Wayne is the second largest convention facility in the state.

The Allen County War Memorial Coliseum and Exposition Center, a city landmark, provides versatile facilities for trade shows, concerts, sporting events, stage shows, ice shows, the circus, meetings, and conventions. The facility is a memorial to the armed forces who died in World Wars I and II, and the Korean War. The arena offers a seating capacity from 10,000 to 12,500 and is ideal for spectator events; the Expo Center provides 108,000 square feet of display area and has meeting rooms accommodating 250 individuals. The Appleseed Room—designed to hold banquets, receptions, and meetings—accommodates up to 540 guests.

*Convention Information:* Fort Wayne/Allen County Convention and Visitors Bureau, 1021 S. Calhoun St., Fort Wayne, IN 46802; telephone (800)767-7752; www.visitfortwayne.com

## ■ Transportation

### Approaching the City

Fort Wayne International Airport is the destination for most air traffic into Fort Wayne. It is one of only a handful of airports in the Midwest with a 12,000-foot runway. Six commercial carriers provide flights from major cities throughout the United States, with over 100 nonstop flights daily. Connecting flights for international travel are also available. One of the top three revenue sources for the city of Fort Wayne, the Fort Wayne International Airport accommodates more than one million passengers annually. Smith Field, located north of the city, is a secondary airport for private air traffic.

Highway travel into Fort Wayne is via Interstate 69, which runs north from Indianapolis into Michigan, and Interstate 469, which encircles the city. U.S. Highways 30, 33, 27, and 24 converge in Allen County. Interstate 80, which runs east/west, is located 45 miles north of Fort Wayne via Interstate 69. Amtrak makes a stop at Waterloo, about 25 miles north of the city. Greyhound makes a stop at the South Lafayette station.

### Traveling in the City

The Fort Wayne Citilink provides intracity bus service to downtown, urban shopping centers, and area employment locations with 12 fixed routes. Citilink Access provides van service for the disabled.

## ■ Communications

### Newspapers and Magazines

The principal daily newspapers in Fort Wayne are *The Journal Gazette,* published mornings and Sundays, and the Pulitzer Prize-winning *The News-Sentinel,* published Monday through Saturday evenings. Weekly newspapers include *Frost Illustrated,* serving the African American community, and the *Macedonian Tribune,* serving the Macedonian community. *Fort Wayne Magazine* is a bimonthly publication focusing on the city. Special-interest magazines and journals published in Fort Wayne include *Business People Magazine* and *Today's Catholic,* a publication of the Diocese of Fort Wayne.

*CLIO: A Journal of Literature, History, and the Philosophy of History* is published at Indiana University–Purdue University Fort Wayne. *Concordia Theological Quarterly* is a publication of the Concordia Theological Seminary. The *Chicago Tribune* has named *Lincoln Lore,* the quarterly magazine published by The Lincoln Museum in Fort Wayne, as one of the top 50 magazines in the United States for 2007.

## Television and Radio

Four commercial television stations broadcast from Fort Wayne; cable service is available through six cable companies. Diverse radio programming, covering easy listening, top 40, rock, and country and western music as well as religious features and news and information, is provided by 16 stations in the city.

*Media Information:*  The Journal Gazette, P.O. Box 88, 600 W. Main St., Fort Wayne, IN 46801; telephone (260)461-8200; www.journalgazette.net

**Fort Wayne Online**

Allen County Public Library home page. Available www.acpl.lib.in.us

City of Fort Wayne, Indiana. Available www.cityoffortwayne.org

Fort Wayne-Allen County Convention and Visitors Bureau. Available www.visitfortwayne.com

Fort Wayne–Allen County Economic Development Alliance. Available www.theallianceonline.com

Greater Fort Wayne Chamber of Commerce. Available www.fwchamber.org

*The Journal-Gazette.* Available www.journalgazette.com

*The News-Sentinel.* Available www.news-sentinel.com

BIBLIOGRAPHY

Kavanaugh, Karen B., *A Genealogist's Guide to the Allen County Public Library, Fort Wayne, Indiana* (Fort Wayne, IN: The Author, 1981)

# Gary

## ■ The City in Brief

**Founded:** 1906 (designated a city in 1909)

**Head Official:** Mayor Rudolph Clay (D) (since 2006)

**City Population**

    1980: 151,968
    1990: 116,646
    2000: 102,746
    2006 estimate: 97,715
    Percent change, 1990–2000: −11.9
    U.S. rank in 1980: 104th
    U.S. rank in 1990: 163rd
    U.S. rank in 2000: 251st

**Metropolitan Area Population**

    1980: 643,000
    1990: 604,526
    2000: 675,971
    2006 estimate: 700,896
    Percent change, 1990–2000: 11.8%
    U.S. rank in 1980: Not available
    U.S. rank in 1990: 3rd (CMSA)
    U.S. rank in 2000: 3rd (CMSA)

**Area:** 50 square miles (2000)

**Elevation:** 590 feet above sea level

**Average Annual Temperature:** 48.9° F

**Average Annual Precipitation:** 34.66 inches of rain, 39.2 inches of snowfall

**Major Economic Sectors:** services, wholesale and retail trade, government

**Unemployment Rate:** 6.7% (June 2007)

**Per Capita Income:** $13,797 (2005)

**2005 FBI Crime Index Property:** 5,310

**2005 FBI Crime Index Violent:** 718

**Major Colleges and Universities:** Indiana University Northwest, Ivy Tech Community College

**Daily Newspaper:** *Post-Tribune*

## ■ Introduction

Once a leading steel producing center that was often called "Steel City," Gary's beautiful Lake Michigan beaches are now host to a growing tourist industry drawn to the new multi-million dollar redevelopment project featuring casino boats and marinas. Water and air pollution have been vastly improved in order to help implement this economic shift. The geographical placement of Gary in the Calumet region provides visitors with a huge variety of natural attractions, from the lakeshore to protected inland prairies, nature preserves, numerous parks, and rare wildlife. Gary exists as a port of entry with enough resources to guarantee energy for industrial expansion.

## ■ Geography and Climate

The city of Gary is located in an area known as the Calumet region at the southern tip of Lake Michigan. The Calumet region includes the northern portions of Lake and Porter counties. The city lies approximately 28 miles southeast of Chicago. Toledo is 210 miles east, Indianapolis is 153 miles southeast, Detroit is 237 miles northeast, and St. Louis is 287 miles southwest of Gary. Gary is in a region of frequently changing weather. The climate is predominantly temperate, ranging from relatively warm in the summer to relatively cold in the winter. However, this is partly modified by Lake Michigan. Very low temperatures usually develop in air that flows southward to the west of Lake Superior before reaching Gary. In summer the higher temperatures result from a south or southwest flow and therefore are not modified by the lake.

**Area:** 50 square miles (2000)

**Elevation:** 590 feet above sea level

**Average Annual Temperature:** 48.9° F

**Average Annual Precipitation:** 34.66 inches of rain, 39.2 inches of snowfall

# ■ History

### Early History

Prehistoric studies indicate that the swamps and sand dunes of the Calumet region presented hostile conditions which discouraged any permanent settlers. Migrant tribes of Miami, Ottawa, Wea, and Potawatomi hunted, fished, trapped, and sometimes farmed the area. Even these indigenous people didn't build permanent villages until the 1600s. (There were perhaps 50 Potawatomi villages left in northwest Indiana by the early 1800s, most of whom were moved to reservations by the 1850s.) Father Jacques Marquette, great French explorer of the Mississippi River Valley, led a group of fur traders and missionaries through the area using the Calumet River. The story goes that Marquette camped near the mouth of the Grand Calumet, the present site of Gary's Marquette Park. In 1822 Joseph Bailly was the first European to settle in these Indiana Dunes, which would later become southeastern Illinois and northwestern Indiana.

### Creation of City as Major Steel Center

Still, there were not many settlers until the 1900s, although post-Civil War homesteaders flocked to the more fertile farmlands in the southern part of the state. However, as the country's industrial economy grew, land once deemed inhospitable for farming was eyed for factory use. In the late 1880s large amounts of sand were removed from the dunes and shipped to Chicago for building and industrial uses. Swamps, woodlands, and dunes were leveled in order to support enormous factory structures. Gary finally became Gary when, in 1906, work was begun on a site envisioned by its namesake, Elbert H. Gary. Gary had been a judge from 1882 to 1890 and became chairman of U.S. Steel. Realizing that economic growth was moving to the Midwest, he chose the spot for its proximity to Chicago, Great Lakes shipping, and railroad access to bring in ore from Minnesota and coal from the south and east. The enormity of this undertaking necessitated U.S. Steel's forming of two new companies—the Gary Land Company to build housing and the Indiana Steel Company to construct the plant, which would

contain 12 blast furnaces and 47 steel furnaces. In addition, the harbor had to be excavated to accommodate the largest steam ships of the day and an enormous breakwater and lighthouse were built as well. Three and a half years later a mill opened. Immigrants attracted by thousands of new jobs poured in, both from eastern and southern Europe and from other parts of the United States, filling Gary with more than 16,000 inhabitants for its official designation as a city in 1909.

In one of the few historical footnotes about Gary that isn't directly involved with steel, Octave Chanute first took flight in a glider in 1896 off the windswept dunes that in a decade would become Gary. It was the world's first sustained flight in a heavier than air structure. The Wright brothers later credited Chanute's design with helping them build their first plane.

### City Attracts Workers; Growth Continues

In the next 10 years Gary more than tripled its population, with more than 55,000 residents by 1920. The city became a great ethnic melting pot as jobs in the mills continued to attract immigrants from various foreign countries, especially from Eastern Europe. Prior to World War I, organized labor failed to gain a foothold among the area's steel workers. Although Judge Gary held the same anti-labor sentiments as his contemporary and rival, Andrew Carnegie, he was somewhat less heavy handed in his approach, seeking to avoid strikes through employee relations programs and an emphasis on job safety. U.S. Steel actually pioneered job safety programs and originated the phrase "Safety First." The corporation adopted a sort of old fashioned, paternalistic relationship with its laborers similar to that of coal or textile mill "company towns." Social events and much of life outside the workplace revolved around the company; on the downside this meant blacklists kept track of any employee with the wrong political affiliations.

The post-WWI period was one of growth for Gary, which had almost instantly become the largest city in the Calumet region. Construction included many apartment buildings and houses, three ten-story buildings, the Hotel Gary, The Gary State Bank, the imposing Knights of Columbus hall, and the massive City Methodist Church. Public structures included Gary City Hall, the courthouse, a 10-acre esplanade (Gateway Park), as well as Marquette Park and Gleason Park. Gary became known as "Magic City" and "City of the Century" because of its rapid growth. Although large numbers of African Americans were drawn to the city in search of unskilled labor jobs, a quota system kept their work force at no more than 15 percent. Most of the region had segregated public facilities, and housing was racially segregated as well. African Americans were relegated to live in "the Patch", the most undesirable housing in the city. Later, Mexican workers, who ironically were brought in as strike breakers, were also forced to reside in the Patch.

## City Becomes Model for Public Education

Gary was the center of pivotal early twentieth century development in public education when William A. Wirth established a work/study/play school, popularly known as the "platoon school." It was designed to attract underprivileged children, many of whom were from non-English speaking immigrant families. The curriculum focused on preparing them to function in American society. By 1913 the school had enrolled 4,000 children.

## The Great Depression, World War II, and Beyond

Until only very recently, the history of Gary remained intertwined with the fortune or folly of the steel industry. The Great Depression of the 1930s had a devastating effect on Gary's economy, with U.S. Steel dropping from 100 percent capacity in 1929 to 15 percent in 1932. The depression also brought unionization of Gary's industries, with U. S. Steel recognizing the Steelworkers Organizing Committee as the bargaining agent for its workers in 1937. Between 1935 and 1939 the steel worker's wages rose nationally 27 percent, benefiting Gary's workers as well.

During World War II, steel production soared and the tide of prosperity continued for the next two decades. U.S. Steel production peaked in 1953 at more than 35 million tons. The Steelworkers Union held a series of long strikes in 1946 and 1952. These strikes were mostly nonviolent conflicts over wages and benefits rather than the bloody struggles over union recognition that happened elsewhere, but a 116-day long strike in 1959 had the world-changing effect of shutting down 90 percent of production of not only U.S. Steel, but also its competitors. This opened the door to competition from foreign steel, which had had negligible effect before. The long decline of American steel thus began.

Manufacturing in general declined in the region and in the whole country. Between 1979 and 1986 northwest Indiana's loss in manufacturing totaled 42.5 percent, largely in the areas of oil and steel. The world market changed again and the American steel industry rebounded a bit from the late 1980s to the early 1990s. The steel industry is still important to the local economy in Gary, although it is not the world leader it once was.

## Changing Demographics Brings African American Majority

Beginning in the 1960s, Gary's population decreased through "white flight" to the suburbs. By 1990 the population was made up of 80 percent African Americans. Voters elected Gary's first African American mayor, Richard G. Hatcher, in 1967 and for four subsequent terms. Hatcher's administration improved housing conditions in the city and helped obtain federal job training programs. In 1982 the Genesis Convention Center was built in the heart of Gary's downtown to help in the revitalization of the business district.

Gary made great progress during the 1960s and 1970s in reducing its air pollution caused by smoke from factories and steel mills. The amount of impurities in the air dropped nearly 60 percent from 1966 to 1976. The city issued nearly $180 million in revenue bonds to help U.S. Steel reduce its pollution at local facilities.

The loss of population in Gary during the 1980s, almost 25 percent, was larger than that of any other U.S. city. By 1995, the city's population was 85 percent African American. That year, Scott L. King, who is white, confounded observers when he won an upset victory in the mayoral election. He resigned from office in 2006 and was replaced by the election of Rudolph Clay.

Still battling poverty, unemployment, a shrinking population, and a less-than-stellar reputation, in the dawn of the twenty-first century the focus of community leaders and businesses in Gary has been to revitalize Gary's downtown and make the city attractive to visitors.

*Historical Information:* Indiana University Northwest Library, Calumet Regional Archives, 3400 Broadway, Gary, IN 46408; telephone (219)980-6628

# ■ Population Profile

**Metropolitan Area Residents**

1980: 643,000
1990: 604,526
2000: 675,971
2006 estimate: 700,896
Percent change, 1990–2000: 11.8%
U.S. rank in 1980: Not available
U.S. rank in 1990: 3rd (CMSA)
U.S. rank in 2000: 3rd (CMSA)

**City Residents**

1980: 151,968
1990: 116,646
2000: 102,746
2006 estimate: 97,715
Percent change, 1990–2000: −11.9
U.S. rank in 1980: 104th
U.S. rank in 1990: 163rd
U.S. rank in 2000: 251st

**Density:** 1,795 people per square mile (2000)

**Racial and ethnic characteristics (2005)**

White: 9,864
Black: 80,205
American Indian and Alaska Native: 0
Asian: 142
Native Hawaiian and Pacific Islander: 0

Hispanic or Latino (may be of any race): Not available
Other: 3,645

**Percent of residents born in state:** 63.0% (2000)

**Age characteristics (2005)**

Population under 5 years old: 9,690
Population 5 to 9 years old: 7,743
Population 10 to 14 years old: 9,488
Population 15 to 19 years old: 6,557
Population 20 to 24 years old: 5,315
Population 25 to 34 years old: 11,552
Population 35 to 44 years old: 12,073
Population 45 to 54 years old: 13,518
Population 55 to 59 years old: 5,269
Population 60 to 64 years old: 4,036
Population 65 to 74 years old: 6,406
Population 75 to 84 years old: 4,475
Population 85 years and older: 935
Median age: 32.9 years

**Births (2006, Metropolitan Division)**

Total number: 9,151

**Deaths (2006, Metropolitan Division)**

Total number: 6,266

**Money income (2005)**

Per capita income: $13,797
Median household income: $25,496
Total households: 36,702

**Number of households with income of...**

less than $10,000: 8,243
$10,000 to $14,999: 4,543
$15,000 to $24,999: 5,360
$25,000 to $34,999: 4,239
$35,000 to $49,999: 4,996
$50,000 to $74,999: 5,196
$75,000 to $99,999: 2,674
$100,000 to $149,999: 1,278
$150,000 to $199,999: 112
$200,000 or more: 61

**Percent of families below poverty level:** 14.1% (2005)

**2005 FBI Crime Index Property:** 5,310

**2005 FBI Crime Index Violent:** 718

# ■ Municipal Government

Gary's city government consists of a mayor and nine council members, six of whom are elected by district, the other three at large. Terms for all are four years.

**Head Official:** Mayor Rudolph Clay (since 2006; term expires 2010)

**Total Number of City Employees:** approximately 2,319 (2007)

*City Information:* City of Gary, City Hall, 401 Broadway, Gary, IN 46402; telephone (219)881-1301; www.gary.in.us

# ■ Economy

## Major Industries and Commercial Activity

Manufacturing, especially of steel, has been the heart of Gary and northwest Indiana. Although hard hit by decline of employment in the steel mills, primarily due to automation, the steel industry is still an integral part of Gary's economy with U.S. Steel Corporation (USS Gary Works) being the largest employer in the city in 2007. The factory scene has expanded to more light manufacturing, such as paper products, plastics, chemicals, rubber, and even food processing. The wholesale and retail trade sectors also account for a large number of jobs. The newest industry to jolt the local economy is tourism, with Majestic Star Casino boats, restaurants, and entertainment venues available at the newly renovated Buffington Harbor at the lakefront. A 20 percent gaming tax is levied on the casino boats.

Gary and Lake County are becoming increasingly popular for people from Chicago and other urban centers who seek weekend recreational getaways. City government and the Gary Community School Corporation are major employers in the city. Other major employers in 2007 included Methodist Hospital and the U.S. Postal Service.

**Items and goods produced:** steel and steel finished products including sheet metal, tin plate, tubing, and bridges; hardware, springs, windshield wipers, light fixtures, apparel and bed linens, processed foods.

## Incentive Programs—New and Existing Companies

*Local programs:* The Gary Department of Planning and Development assists businesses in several ways: through commercial development and redevelopment; infrastructure planning and development; job training initiatives'; image promotion and public relations; land, buildings, and community tours; liaison between businesses and individuals; tax abatement; and research. The Gary Business Empowerment Center offers technical support services for small businesses. Business incentive programs in Gary revolve around the Gary Urban Enterprise Association (GUEA) which manages Gary's Urban Enterprise Zone program. Urban Enterprise

Zones are low income neighborhoods which are designated for special state tax credits to businesses that employ people in the zones. Businesses in the zones are encouraged in several ways: companies may receive full forgiveness of personal property taxes paid for raw materials or finished products; employers can get up to $1,500 per employee for "employment expense credit" when they live in the zone; a loan interest credit lowers the taxes that lending institutions pay on interest earned on loans to businesses in the zone; and an equity investment credit for individual investors who pay into job training programs.

*State Programs:* EDGE (Economic Development for Growing Economy) is a state sponsored refundable tax credit, based on payroll, which allows Indiana individual income tax withholdings from company employees to be credited against the company's state corporate income tax liability. Excess withholdings would be refunded to the company. The credits can be awarded for up to 10 years. The Hoosier Business Investment Tax Credit encourages capital investment in the state by providing a credit against a company's state tax liability. A Venture Capital Investment Tax Credit and a Headquarters Relocation Tax Credit are also available.

*Job Training Programs:* The Indiana Economic Development Corporation provides two major grant programs for training and skill development: the Skills Enhancement Fund and the TECH Fund (Technology Enhancement Certification for Hoosiers). The Indiana Department of Commerce also provides grants to support skills training programs for local businesses. The funds can be used in a variety of ways, including customized training programs in specific skills areas for new employees and skills development training for existing employees. The Indiana Department of Workforce Development provides labor force recruitment services, including help with the application process, testing, and the assessment and screening of qualified applicants. Ivy Tech Community College offers workforce development programs that include customized industrial training, either on campus or at the job site, as well as a variety of technical certificate programs.

## Development Projects

One major redevelopment project in Gary has been the Buffington Harbor Lakeshore Redevelopment. The marinas for the Majestic Star Casino boats are there and much of the surrounding 25 square miles has been revamped to make it more attractive to the new tourist trade.

In 2007 several redevelopment projects were in the works at the Gary/Chicago International Airport. Airport authorities approved an agreement with the Army National Guard for the use of two hangers. The Guard has also begun construction of a 55,000-square-foot Limited

Army Aviation Support Facility. A new Instrument Landing System was installed and a runway expansion project was underway. Groundbreaking took place for the Gary Jet Center's new 38,000-square-foot hanger that will house Gulf stream type aircraft. Also at the end of 2007, the airport authority was negotiating with Cape Air to serve as a primary air service provider for the airport.

In 2007 Grainger, a nationwide distributor of facilities maintenance products, opened its newly expanded showroom on Cline Avenue. The 33,000-square-foot building has a 2,500-square-foot showroom, which is more than double the size of the original showroom. Grainger stocks over 23,000 types of industrial supplies.

Gary South Shore Development (GSSD) LLC (based in Merrillville) had requested support from the Northwest Indiana Regional Development Authority for a $56 million central South Shore Railroad depot to be built on a 12-acre site at I-65 and U.S. 20. While GSSD claims that such a development will benefit the area both in ease of travel and in new business growth, it would mean the closing of the two existing South Shore depots in Gary. Local residents and commuters argue that these closings would be detrimental to their own community growth and would waste an already existing infrastructure.

*Economic Development Information:* Department of Planning and Economic Development, 504 Broadway, Suite 625, Gary, IN 46402; telephone (219)881-5235; fax (219)881-1092. Gary Chamber of Commerce, 839 Broadway, Ste. S103, Gary, IN 46402; telephone (219) 885-7497; www.garychamber.com

## Commercial Shipping

As of late 2007 Gary/Chicago International had begun a variety of expansion and construction projects to give the airport a better advantage as a cargo shipment site. Gary has six truck terminals serving more than 100 local and international trucking lines, most of which can provide overnight shipping within a 300-mile radius. Eight railways have service into Gary.

Four major interstate highways offer easy connections to both coasts, the Gulf of Mexico, and Canada.

## Labor Force and Employment Outlook

While a large number of employment opportunities are still available in manufacturing, wholesale and retail trades have been gaining in available jobs. Educational and health services have also showed a modest increase in jobs. In 2005 it was estimated that about 80 percent of the adult population had obtained a high school diploma or higher.

The following is a summary of data regarding the Gary Metropolitan Division metropolitan area labor force, 2006 annual averages.

**Size of nonagricultural labor force:** 279,000

©Jim West/Alamy

**Number of workers employed in** ...

    construction and mining: 19,600

    manufacturing: 38,100

    trade, transportation and utilities: 60,200

    information: 2,400

    financial activities: 10,100

    professional and business services: 21,900

    educational and health services: 42,800

    leisure and hospitality: 30,700

    other services: 12,800

    government: 40,300

**Average hourly earnings of production workers employed in manufacturing:** $22.25

**Unemployment rate:** 6.7% (June 2007)

| Largest employers (2007) | Number of employees |
|---|---|
| USS-USX Corp/Gary Works | 6,800 |
| Gary Community School Corporation | 3,163 |
| Methodist Hospital Northlake | 3,081 |
| City of Gary | 2,319 |
| Majestic Star Casino | 1,050 |
| NIPSCO | 808 |
| U.S. Postal Service | 730 |
| Indiana University Northwest | 400 |
| Post-Tribune Publishing | 300 |

## Cost of Living

The cost of housing in northwest Indiana tends to be lower than many other parts of the country, with property taxes as much as 25 percent lower.

The following is a summary of data regarding several key cost of living factors for the Gary area.

**2007 (1st quarter) ACCRA Average House Price:** Not available

**2007 (1st quarter) ACCRA Cost of Living Index:** Not available

**State income tax rate:** 3.4% of Adjusted Gross Income

**State sales tax rate:** 6.0%

**Local income tax rate:** None

**Local sales tax rate:** None

**Property tax rate:** $23.42 per $100 of assessed value, assessment ratio = 33.33% for residential (2005)

*Economic Information:* Gary Chamber of Commerce, 839 Broadway, Suite S103, Gary, IN 46402; telephone (219)885-7407; www.garychamber.com

# ■ Education and Research

## Elementary and Secondary Schools

The Gary Community School Corporation serves the city's students with conventional schools, three special education facilities, one career center, and special academies that include Martin Luther King, Jr. Academy; Glen Park Academy for Excellence in Learning; and Emerson Visual and Performing Arts Center. The Benjamin Banneker Elementary School has been repeatedly singled out by the state Department of Education for meeting high standards of attendance and aptitude scores.

The following is a summary of data regarding the Gary Community School Corporation as of the 2005–2006 school year.

**Total enrollment:** 16,979

**Number of facilities**

elementary schools: 18
junior high/middle schools: 3
senior high schools: 8
other: 0

**Student/teacher ratio:** Not available

**Teacher salaries (2005–06)**

elementary median: $45,700
junior high/middle median: $47,340
secondary median: $48,200

**Funding per pupil:** $10,396

There are several private schools in the area including those affiliated with Roman Catholic, Baptist, and Seventh-day Adventist churches.

*Public Schools Information:* Gary Community School Corporation, Public Information, 620 East 10th Place, Gary, IN 46402; telephone (219)886-6400; www.garycsc.k12.in.us

## Colleges and Universities

Indiana University (IU) Northwest, one of eight IU campuses in the state, had 4,790 students enrolled for the fall of 2007. Programs at IU Northwest can lead to an associate's, bachelor's, or master's degrees. There are also certificate and pre-professional programs available. Sixty-eight majors are offered through seven academic divisions: the College of Arts and Sciences, School of Business and Economics, School of Continuing Studies, School of Education, School of Nursing and Health Professions, School of Public and Environmental Affairs, and Division of Social Work.

The Gary campus of Ivy Tech Community College offers programs in business, education, health and human services, liberal arts, and technical training. Students may work toward an associate's degree or choose a certificate program. It is one of 23 branches of Ivy Tech statewide and serves as the administrative center for Ivy Tech Northwest.

Nearby Hammond is home to prestigious Purdue University Calumet. Purdue Calumet has more than 9,300 students enrolled and over 100 fields of study in which one can earn a variety of degrees from quick certifications to master's degrees.

## Libraries and Research Centers

The Gary Public Library has over 570,000 volumes plus CDs, nearly 15,000 items of graphic materials, and more than 13,300 films and audiovisuals. The library serves as a U.S. government depository. The library consists of the main library, five branches, and one bookmobile. Its special collections focus on city and state history. The system also features free internet access, programs for children and seniors, and an African American history month program.

Lake County has its own library system with a central library and 11 branches, including 2 in Gary: the Black Oak Branch and the Forty-First Avenue Branch. It provides home service, programs for children and adults, special service to businesses, the Carol A. Derner Art Gallery, and literacy programs, among other services.

The Indiana University Northwest Library contains a collection of more than 500,000 books and periodicals. Special collection areas include the Calumet Regional Archives, the Northwest Indiana Center for Data and Analysis, the Northwest Indiana Environmental Justice Resource Center, the Northwest Indiana Geographic Information System, Lake County Central Law Library, the Educational Resources Room, and services for the visually impaired. An interlibrary loan program is in place between all libraries of the Indiana University system. Special Collections include an acclaimed series of photographs of U.S. Steel. At the IU Laboratories for Environmental Research, focus is on recycling of byproduct materials for basic industries. The Great Lakes Center for Public Affairs and Administration at IU conducts research and provides technical services for government and other institutions.

*Public Library Information:* Gary Public Library, 220 West Fifth Avenue, Gary, IN 46402-1270; telephone (219)886-2484; fax (219)886-6829; www.gary. lib.in.us

# ■ Health Care

The major health care organization serving Gary is the not-for-profit community-based Methodist Hospitals, which operates two main facilities in Gary. The Northlake Campus is an acute care hospital offering a full-range of services. Special facilities provided through Methodist Hospitals include a Rehabilitation Institute, Center for Interventional Cardiology, Child and Adolescent Program, Women's Health Resource Center, Healthy Start prenatal program, and a sleep disorder center. Other specialties are extracorporeal shock wave lithotripsy (an alternative to surgery which breaks up kidney stones with sound waves), an alcoholism institute, neuroscience institute, gerontology center, and a regional cancer treatment center. The Midlife Campus provides outpatient services, including a Diabetes Center, a rehabilitation Center, and offices for the Methodist Physician Group. Methodist Home Health Care is also based in Gary.

Edgewater Systems for Balanced Living offers behavioral health care services, including outpatient services for substance abuse and dependency. The Gary Community Health Center offers primary care and testing services for all ages.

# ■ Recreation

## Sightseeing

For those interested in architecture, there is plenty to see in Gary, including two Frank Lloyd Wright houses. The Genesis Convention Center, designed by Wendell Campbell, is a modern structure featuring an imposing glass wall across the front. St. Timothy's Church, also designed by Wendell Campbell, features two-story stained glass windows created by local artist, Tom Floyd. The Gary Bathing Beach Aquatorium is one of the first examples of modular block construction in the world. The bathhouse, designed by George W. Mahrer, was renovated in 1991 to include a museum for Octave Chanute and the Tuskegee Airmen. Another notable site is the Gothic, limestone City Methodist Church, built in 1926. The old west side historic district neighborhood was part of the original company town built by U. S. Steel in 1906.

Tours of the Gary Works, one of the largest steel plants in the world, are available by appointment. The Chanute Glider, which made the first sustained flight off the Indiana dunes in 1896, is on display at Gary Regional Airport. Orville Wright credited Octave Chanute with building the prototype of the plane that the Wright Brothers flew four years later, under power for the first time at Kitty Hawk, NC.

The Indiana Dunes National Lakeshore stretches across 15,000 acres along the shore of Lake Michigan from Gary to Michigan City, IN. Poet Carl Sandberg-described the dunes as being "to the Midwest what the Grand Canyon is to Arizona and Yosemite is to California. They constitute a signature of time and eternity." The dunes offer miles of trails for woodland hikers. The Paul H. Douglas Center for Environmental Education educates people in the fields of ecology and environmental science. The Bailly Homestead and Chellberg Farm, located along the dunes, offer glimpses of pioneer and Native American life and a brief farming history of the early 1900s. The Brunswick Park Savanna is a 49-acre park on Gary's west side. It features rare plants such as black oak, bluejoint grass, and prairie sunflowers. Brunswick Park also has tennis courts and picnic areas.

Two casino gambling boats depart from Buffington Harbor: The Majestic Star I and Majestic Star II. The dock is home to several restaurants and shops.

## Arts and Culture

Gary Art Works was established in 2001 as a community-based non-profit organization to support and encourage art and cultural activities in the city. The Gary Theater Ensemble is a multi-disciplinary guild of semi-professional actors, sponsored in part by Gary Art Works and offering performances and educational programs for students of all ages. The Octave Chanute and Tuskegee Airmen Museum at the Aquatorium is a tribute to the man considered to be the grandfather of flight and the famous group of airmen who were pioneers in the integration of the armed forces. Plays and other entertainment events are offered at Tamarack Hall at Indiana University Northwest.

## Festivals and Holidays

In June the U.S. Steelyard Stadium hosts a gospel festival with plenty of food, activities for children, and top gospel singers and groups. The Fourth of July is one of the biggest festivities of the year in Gary, with an Independence Day parade, fireworks in most parks, and a two-day Independence Day Music Festival which always features a nationally known recording artist. In mid-July everyone is treated to the Gary Air Show. The free show is held in Marquette Park, where about 20 acts including every branch of the military plus civilians perform acrobatics in the air. In August there's a Jazz Festival and in September the Labor Day Blues Festival is held.

## Sports for the Spectator

Minor league and semi-pro teams have recently come to Gary. The United States Basketball League includes the Gary Steelheads, who play in the revamped Genesis

Convention Center. The Gary Southshore Railcats are a Northern League of Professional Baseball expansion team who began playing in 2002. The following year the Railcats' home stadium was completed and named the U.S. Steel Yard. The Steel Yard seats about 6,000 and is used for concerts and conventions in the off season.

### Sports for the Participant

There are over 50 parks in Gary, including Lake Etta, which is a Lake County park whose waters are stocked with a variety of fish. Tolleston Park features an outdoor summing pool and water slide park. The city sponsors three recreational beaches along Lake Michigan: Lake Street, Marquette Park, and Wells Street. Marquette Park also features a lagoon, playground, pavilion, and a picnic area. Opportunities abound for swimming, hiking, biking, tennis, hayrides, basketball, horseback riding, running, cross country skiing, softball, and golf. Glen Park is home to the 18-hole Gleason Golf Course. Lake County also offers 20 public golf courses. For those who wish to enjoy 12,000 acres of carefully preserved nature, there is the Indiana Dunes National Lakeshore Park, which stretches across both Lake and Porter counties. The Hudson Campbell Fitness Center offers walking and jogging tracks, and courts for tennis, basketball, volleyball, and racquetball.

### Shopping and Dining

Gary and Lake County offer a wide variety of shopping venues, from quaint antique shops and specialty stores particular to the Miller beach neighborhood, to strip malls with national chain stores. The Lake Street gallery offers unique gifts of art and crafts.

Restaurants abound, from casual "soul food" places and fast food chains to new upscale establishments popping up all around the gaming and marina spots at Buffington Harbor.

*Visitor Information:* Lake County Convention and Visitors Bureau, 7770 Corinne Dr., Hammond, IN 46323; telephone (219)989-7770; toll-free (800)ALL-Lake; www.alllake.org

## ■ Convention Facilities

The strikingly designed Genesis Convention Center is the largest convention facility in Northwest Indiana and can accommodate up to 7,000 people, with 11 separate meeting rooms for 40 to 400 participants. Besides being home to the Steelheads basketball team, Genesis Center is a multi-function venue for weddings, seminars, conferences and the like. The luxurious new Trump Hotel Casino at Buffington harbor features conference facilities and many amenities such as in-room fax machines, a modern exercise facility, and

gaming, entertainment, and dining. The Marquette Park Pavilion is available for meetings, banquets, and other events.

*Convention Information:* Lake County Convention and Visitors Bureau, 7770 Corinne Dr., Hammond, IN 46323; telephone (219)989-7770; toll-free (800)ALL-Lake; www.alllake.org

## ■ Transportation

### Approaching the City

Located about 28 miles southeast of Chicago, Gary is accessible from Interstate 65 which runs north and south, and I-94/80, which runs east and west. The Indiana Toll Road I-90 connects to the Chicago Skyway to the west and the Ohio Turnpike to the east. Greyhound bus service is available into Gary. The Northern Indiana Commuter Transportation District operates the South Shore Line, a 90 mile electric railway that can speed commuters through Gary from Millennium Station in Chicago or the South Bend Airport.

As of late 2007 there was no commercial airline service available to the Gary/Chicago International Airport due to construction and expansion projects that were underway. Aircraft charter services are provided by Jet Select. The Chicago Midway Airport is about 30 minutes away by car. Midway is served by 10 commercial airlines. O'Hare International Airport, about one hour away by car, is served by over 30 commercial airlines.

### Traveling in the City

Local bus transportation is provided by Gary Public Transit Corporation, which operates 13 fixed routes throughout the city. Paratransit services are available.

## ■ Communications

### Newspapers and Magazines

The city's daily newspaper is the *Post-Tribune,* which is published in Merrillville. The *Gary Crusader* is a weekly serving the African American community.

### Television and Radio

Gary receives all major commercial television broadcasts from other cities. Cable is also available. There are only a few radio stations broadcasting directly from the city, but listeners can enjoy virtually any style of music or talk radio from other local broadcasting stations.

*Media Information:* *Post-Tribune,* 1433 E. 83rd. Ave, Merrillville, IN 46410; telephone (800)753-5533; www.post-trib.com

**Gary Online**

Calumet Regional Archives. Available www.iun
.edu/~cra/

City of Gary home page. Available www.gary.in.us

Gary Chamber of Commerce. Available www
.garychamber.com

Gary Community School Corporation. Available
www.garycsc.k12.in.us

Lake County Convention and Visitors Bureau.
Available www.alllake.org

*Post-Tribune*. Available www.post-trib.com

BIBLIOGRAPHY

Catlin, Robert A., *Racial Politics and Urban Planning:
Gary Indiana 1981-1989* (University of Kentucky,
1993)

# Indianapolis

## ■ The City in Brief

**Founded:** 1821 (incorporated 1847)

**Head Official:** Mayor Greg Ballard (R) (since 2008)

**City Population**
1980: 701,000
1990: 731,278
2000: 781,870
2006 estimate: 785,597
Percent change, 1990–2000: 6.9%
U.S. rank in 1980: 12th
U.S. rank in 1990: 13th
U.S. rank in 2000: 17th (State rank: 1st)

**Metropolitan Area Population**
1980: 1,167,000
1990: 1,380,491
2000: 1,607,486
2006 estimate: 1,666,032
Percent change, 1990–2000: 16.4%
U.S. rank in 1980: 30th
U.S. rank in 1990: Not available
U.S. rank in 2000: 29th

**Area:** 361 square miles (2000)

**Elevation:** Ranges from 645 to 910 feet above sea level

**Average Annual Temperatures:** January, 26.5° F; July, 75.4° F; annual average, 52.5° F

**Average Annual Precipitation:** 40.95 inches of rain; 23.6 inches of snow

**Major Economic Sectors:** services, wholesale and retail trade, government

**Unemployment Rate:** 4.1% (June 2007)

**Per Capita Income:** $22,566 (2005)

**2005 FBI Crime Index Property:** 50,081

**2005 FBI Crime Index Violent:** 7,948

**Major Colleges and Universities:** Indiana University-Purdue University Indianapolis; Butler University; University of Indianapolis; Ivy Tech Community College; Marian College

**Daily Newspaper:** *The Indianapolis Star*

## ■ Introduction

Indianapolis is the capital of Indiana and the seat of Marion County; the Indianapolis metropolitan statistical area includes Boone, Hamilton, Hancock, Hendricks, Johnson, Madison, Marion, Morgan, and Shelby counties. Decreed by proclamation in the nineteenth century as the state capital and carved out of the wilderness where only a settlers' camp had previously stood, Indianapolis redefined itself by the end of the twentieth century. The city is undergoing a renaissance of far-ranging proportions through development and improvement projects that are transforming both the image and the character of the downtown area. Building on the fame of the annual Indianapolis 500 automobile race, the city has become a national center for amateur sports and athletics; it is also a major financial, industrial, commercial, and transportation center for the Midwest. Education and the arts flourish in Indianapolis, and Circle Centre, an entertainment and shopping complex, has sparked renewed commercial and economic development in the city center.

## ■ Geography and Climate

Situated on level or slightly rolling terrain in central Indiana east of the White River, Indianapolis has a temperate climate; because of even distribution of precipitation throughout the year, there are no pronounced wet or dry seasons. Summers are very warm, and the invasion of polar air from the north often produces frigid winter temperatures with low humidity. Two to three times each winter, snowfalls average three inches or more.

**Area:** 361 square miles (2000)

**Elevation:** Ranges from 645 to 910 feet above sea level

**Average Temperatures:** January, 26.5° F; July, 75.4° F; annual average, 52.5° F

**Average Annual Precipitation:** 40.95 inches of rain; 23.6 inches of snow

# ■ History

## Site Chosen for Central Location

The city of Indianapolis was established not by settlers but by proclamation when Indiana was granted statehood in 1816. The United States Congress set aside four sections of public land for the site of the capital of the Union's nineteenth state. In January 1820, the Indiana legislature picked 10 commissioners and charged them with the mandate to locate the new capital as near as possible to the center of the state, the purpose being to take advantage of western migration. The following February, George Pogue and John McCormick settled with their families on land that was to become the site of Indianapolis. Other settlers soon arrived and by the summer of 1820 a dozen families had built cabins along the riverbank in a settlement named Fall Creek. In June 1820, the commissioners selected for the capital a location that was close to the exact center of the state; on that spot was the cabin of John McCormick.

After the legislature approved the site in 1821, the name Indianapolis, a combination of Indiana plus the Greek word *polis* for city, was chosen. Four square miles were allotted for the city, but the chief surveyor, E. P. Fordham, plotted an area of only one square mile because it seemed inconceivable that the capital would ever be any larger. Alexander Ralston, who previously had helped plot the District of Columbia, was hired to design the future city. He decided to model it on the nation's capital, with four broad avenues branching out diagonally to the north, south, east and west from a central circle.

In 1821 Indianapolis became the county seat of the newly configured Marion County, and four years later, when the state legislature met for the first time, Indianapolis boasted one street and a population of 600 people. By the time the town was incorporated in 1832 the population had reached only 1,000 people. Growth was slow because Indianapolis—which now holds the distinction of being one of the world's most populous cities not situated near navigable waters—lay on the banks of the White River, which was too shallow for commerce.

## Road/Rail Transport Create a Regional Center

The construction of the Central Canal from Broad Ripple to Indianapolis seemed to solve the problem temporarily, but the canal turned out to be useless when water volume decreased. The routing of the national highway through the center of Indianapolis in 1831 provided a more permanent solution, fulfilling the original purpose of the city's location. In 1847, the year Indianapolis was incorporated as a city, the Madison & Indianapolis Railroad arrived, soon to be followed by seven additional major rail lines, which gave the city access to the Ohio River.

On the eve of the Civil War the population, aided by an influx of German immigrants, had increased to 18,611 people; the city now provided modern services and supported a stable, manufacturing-based economy. With 24 army camps and a large ammunition plant, Indianapolis became a major wartime center for Union campaigns on the western front. Progress continued into the postwar period only to be set back by the inflationary recession of 1873. During the last two decades of the nineteenth century, Indianapolis experienced a period of growth known as the "golden age." It became, in 1881, one of the first American cities to install electric street lighting. Many downtown landmarks were erected in an explosion of public architecture that helped establish the city's identity. A new market, a new statehouse, and Union Station were completed in the late 1880s. The neglected Circle Park had deteriorated and was revived when the Soldiers' and Sailors' Monument was constructed in honor of the people who served in the Civil War. During this period, wealthy citizens built palatial Victorian homes on North Meridian Street, and as the result of the growth of new neighborhoods and suburbs along tree-lined avenues, Indianapolis became known as the "city of homes."

At the turn of the century, Indianapolis was a leader in the burgeoning automobile industry. Local inventor Charles H. Black is credited with building in 1891 the first internal combustion gasoline engine automobile, which eventually proved to be impractical because its ignition required a kerosene torch. Sixty-five different kinds of automobiles were in production before World War I, including Stutz, Coasts, Duesenberg, and Cole. Other Indianapolis industrialists originated many innovations and improvements in automotive manufacturing, including four-wheel brakes and the six-cylinder engine.

## Sporting Events Attract International Attention

The most significant development was the Indianapolis Motor Speedway, a 2.5-mile oval track, which was inaugurated in 1911 when an Indianapolis-made car named the Marmon won the first race. The Indianapolis 500, held on Memorial Day weekend each year, has since become one of the premier international sporting events, drawing world-wide attention. Indianapolis was a major industrial center by 1920, with a population of more than 300,000 people, yet retained much of its small-town ambience.

A pivotal event in the total transformation of Indianapolis from a manufacturing to a sporting town occurred in 1969, when a change in federal tax laws required charitable foundations to spend more money. The Lilly Endowment, a local foundation based on the Eli Lilly drug fortune decided to concentrate on Indianapolis. The result was a massive capital infusion promoting sport business in the city and leading to the conversion of the city's convention center into a 61,000-seat football stadium.

In 1970 the creation of UniGov combined city government with Marion County government, immediately making Indianapolis the eleventh largest city in the nation. The city made dramatic strides in its national reputation through initiatives implemented by the UniGov structure. Indianapolis renovated its core historical structures, built new sports facilities, and invested in the arts and entertainment. The city positioned itself as an international amateur sports capital when, in 1987, it invested in athletic facilities and hosted both the World Indoor Track and Field Championships and the Pan American Games, second in importance only to the summer Olympics.

## Indianapolis 2000 and Beyond

In January 2000 Bart Peterson, a Democrat, took office as mayor of Indianapolis. During his 1999 campaign for mayor, Peterson introduced "The Peterson Plan," a bold and detailed vision for Indianapolis in the new millennium. He focused on fighting crime more aggressively, improving public education in Marion County, and delivering better services to neighborhoods. In his first month as mayor, Mayor Peterson convened the nation's first citywide summit on race relations, bringing people together to discuss ways to bridge the gaps that sometimes exist between people of different races, religions and backgrounds. He also appointed the most diverse administration in the city's 180-year history.

Indianapolis today is a cosmopolitan blend of arts, education, culture, and sports—a city with plenty of vision for its future. Building on momentum gained in the last decade of the twentieth century, the city is in the midst of a cultural and quality-of-life resurgence. World-class sports, a diverse economy, and the presence of healthy and successful businesses round out the story of Indianapolis in the twenty-first century.

*Historical Information:* Indiana State Library, 140 N. Senate Ave., Indianapolis, IN 46204-2296; telephone (317)232-3675. Indiana Historical Society, Willard Henry Smith Memorial Library, 315 W. Ohio St. Indianapolis, IN 46202-3299; telephone (317)232-1879; fax (317)233-3109

## ■ Population Profile

### Metropolitan Area Residents

1980: 1,167,000
1990: 1,380,491
2000: 1,607,486
2006 estimate: 1,666,032
Percent change, 1990–2000: 16.4%
U.S. rank in 1980: 30th
U.S. rank in 1990: Not available
U.S. rank in 2000: 29th

### City Residents

1980: 701,000
1990: 731,278
2000: 781,870
2006 estimate: 785,597
Percent change, 1990–2000: 6.9%
U.S. rank in 1980: 12th
U.S. rank in 1990: 13th
U.S. rank in 2000: 17th (State rank: 1st)

**Density:** 2,163 people per square mile (2000)

### Racial and ethnic characteristics (2005)

White: 507,520
Black: 195,044
American Indian and Alaska Native: 2,514
Asian: 12,557
Native Hawaiian and Pacific Islander: 279
Hispanic or Latino (may be of any race): 47,764
Other: 29,218

**Percent of residents born in state:** 67.5% (2000)

### Age characteristics (2005)

Population under 5 years old: 65,812
Population 5 to 9 years old: 55,329
Population 10 to 14 years old: 57,487
Population 15 to 19 years old: 47,368
Population 20 to 24 years old: 45,007
Population 25 to 34 years old: 114,532
Population 35 to 44 years old: 119,898
Population 45 to 54 years old: 110,253
Population 55 to 59 years old: 41,538
Population 60 to 64 years old: 27,372
Population 65 to 74 years old: 42,498
Population 75 to 84 years old: 29,516
Population 85 years and older: 8,700
Median age: 34.8 years

### Births (2006, MSA)

Total number: 25,278

### Deaths (2006, MSA)

Total number: 12,827

**Money income (2005)**

Per capita income: $22,566
Median household income: $41,578
Total households: 326,261

**Number of households with income of...**

less than $10,000: 30,405
$10,000 to $14,999: 21,499
$15,000 to $24,999: 42,234
$25,000 to $34,999: 44,864
$35,000 to $49,999: 52,230
$50,000 to $74,999: 61,845
$75,000 to $99,999: 34,300
$100,000 to $149,999: 27,109
$150,000 to $199,999: 6,916
$200,000 or more: 4,859

**Percent of families below poverty level:** 10.5% (2005)

**2005 FBI Crime Index Property:** 50,081

**2005 FBI Crime Index Violent:** 7,948

# ■ Municipal Government

Since 1970 Indianapolis and Marion County have operated as a consolidated government called UniGov, with jurisdiction including all of Marion County except the town of Speedway and the cities of Beech Grove, Lawrence, and Southport. The mayor, who serves a four-year term, holds executive powers; the 29 members of city-county council are elected to four-year terms by district and at large. A six-department city government administers UniGov programs.

**Head Official:** Mayor Greg Ballard (R) (since 2008; term expires December 2011)

**Total Number of City-County Employees:** approx. 3,800 (2007)

*City Information:* Indianapolis and Marion County Government, 200 East Washington Street, City-County Building, Indianapolis, IN 46204; telephone (317)327-3601; www.indygov.org

# ■ Economy

## Major Industries and Commercial Activity

Indianapolis is a primary industrial, commercial, and transportation center for the Midwest. Situated in proximity to the vast agricultural region known as the corn belt and to the industrialized cities of the upper Midwest and the East, Indianapolis is supported by a diversified economic base. Prior to the 1980s, the city's principal industry was manufacturing, which has been displaced by education, health, and social services, and by retail trade.

As a major regional health care center, the health industry is strong and continues to grow. Major employers include Clarian Health Partners, Community Health Network, St. Vincent Hospital and Health Services, St. Francis Hospital and Health Centers, and Wishard Health Services, all of which have hospitals and clinics in the city. Indiana University–Purdue University Indianapolis is one of the cities largest employers.

Advanced manufacturing companies that are headquarters in Indianapolis include Eli Lilly and Company, Dow AgroSciences, Wabash National Corp., Subaru of Indiana Automotive Inc., and Cook Inc. Other major employers include Rolls-Royce, Allison Transmission (GMC), Roche Diagnostics, and the GM Indianapolis Metal Center.

Several distribution and logistics companies have played an important roll in the local economy as well. FedEx operates its second-largest worldwide hub in Indianapolis. The region is also home to FedEx Ground and FedEx Freight facilities, DHL Freight Service Centers, and UPS Freight Service Centers. Other large distribution companies in the region include Caterpillar Logistics Services, Quaker Sales and Distribution, United Natural Foods, and Ditan Distribution.

Having made a conscious decision to achieve prosperity through sports, Indianapolis quadrupled its tourism trade and doubled its hotel space during the period 1984–1991, largely by hosting amateur sporting events. Since that period, Indianapolis' role in the sports arena has magnified. Each major sporting event pumps tens of millions of dollars into the economy and leads to expanded business opportunities, more jobs, and increasing tax payments to the city. Besides jobs directly related to the presentation of races, the industry supports local jobs through companies producing engines, brakes, and other automotive parts; retail and marketing firms specializing in racing; radio and media; and charities that are associated with racing. In 2007 there were an estimated 400 motorsports-related firms in the Indianapolis region. Tourism and conventions, including the hotel industry, are major economic factors.

The insurance industry has long been established in Indianapolis; several insurance companies have located their headquarters and regional offices in the city. Wellpoint, Inc. and OneAmerica are major employers in the city.

**Items and goods produced:** pharmaceuticals, truck trailers, gas turbine engines, transmissions, surgical and medical instruments, motor vehicles, auto parts, heating and air conditioning units, electronics, petroleum products, fabricated metal products, food products, chemicals, paperboard

*The Indianapolis Project. Reproduced by permission of Banayote Photography Inc.*

## Incentive Programs—New and Existing Companies

***Local programs:*** The City of Indianapolis offers a maximum $20,000 grant for remediation of brownfields in its Brownfields Grant Program. The Facade Grant Program offers rebates of up to 50 percent of total cost (or a maximum of $10,000) for facade improvements. Other programs include the Neighborhood Action Grant, tax abatements for Economic Revitalization Area designation, procurement opportunities, and Community Development Block Grants. The city has a Certified Tech Park, INTECH Park, which is an area designated by local and state officials for high-technology business development. Certain state and local tax revenues can by recaptured for investment in continued development of the park and special incentives are available for new or relocating businesses in the park.

***State programs:*** EDGE (Economic Development for Growing Economy) is a state sponsored refundable tax credit, based on payroll, which allows Indiana individual income tax withholdings from company employees to be credited against the company's state corporate income tax liability. Excess withholdings would be refunded to the company. The credits can be awarded for up to 10 years.

The Hoosier Business Investment Tax Credit encourages capital investment in the state by providing a credit against a company's state tax liability. A Venture Capital Investment Tax Credit and a Headquarters Relocation Tax Credit are also available. Indianapolis is part of a federal Foreign Trade Zone. A Foreign Trade Zone offers a tax-free business environment through which businesses may delay or reduce their duty payments and avoid time consuming customs entry procedures.

***Job training programs:*** The Indiana Economic Development Corporation provides two major grant programs for training and skill development: the Skills Enhancement Fund and the TECH Fund (Technology Enhancement Certification for Hoosiers). The Indiana Department of Commerce also provides grants to support skills training programs for local businesses. The funds can be used in a variety of ways, including customized training programs in specific skill areas for new employees and skills development training for existing employees. The Indiana Department of Workforce Development provides labor force recruitment services, including help with the application process, testing, and the assessment and screening of qualified applicants. Ivy Tech Community College offers workforce development programs that include customized industrial training, either on campus or at the job site, as well as a variety of technical certificate programs.

## Development Projects

As of 2007 a $1 billion terminal building was under construction at the Indianapolis airport with a scheduled completion date in 2008. Designed by the international firm Hellmuth, Obata and Kassabaum, the new terminal will represent a small city-within-a-city. A large main space at the center of the terminal will contain security offices, retail spaces, and restaurants. The area is meant to be offered as a civic space for public events. The general design of the terminal is also meant to provide travelers with a more efficient processing and boarding experience.

In 2007 the Purdue Research Foundation announced plans to establish yet another technology park in Indianapolis. The Purdue Accelerator Park at AmeriPlex-Indianapolis is being developed in partnership with Holladay Properties Inc. and will accommodate up to 75 businesses, creating about 1,500 jobs with an average annual salary of $54,000. The park will be located along the I-70 corridor and near the midfield terminal of the Indianapolis International Airport. Designed as a multi-use facility, the site will include a 100,000- to 150,000-square-foot industrial flex building; a 50,000- to 70,000-square-foot multistory office building; a 300-bed, six-story hotel with a 30,000-square-foot conference center; and three sites for restaurants or retail shops.

The same year, the Indiana Convention Center announced a $275 million expansion project to begin in 2008 and be completed in 2010. The new center will offer 747,000 square feet of exhibition space, 129,000 square feet of meeting space, 67,000 square feet of ballroom space, and 296,000 square feet of pre-function space. A pedestrian walk-way will connect the Convention Center expansion with the new Lucas Oil Stadium. The new stadium will replace the RCA Dome, which is slated for demolition.

In 2007 ANGEL Learning, an international developer and marketer of online learning systems, announced plans to relocate its headquarters to INTECH Park, a move that will add 120 jobs for programmers, analysts, and marketers. Veolia Water also announced that it would move its North American headquarters to Indianapolis from Houston. This move will bring in 100 new jobs with an average annual wage of about $70,000. Vertex Data Science, an international provider of outsourced business services and technology solutions, will move its North American headquarters to the city as well, a move that is expected to create 400 new jobs in the city.

***Economic Development Information:*** The Indy Partnership, 111 Monument Circle, Ste. 1800, Indianapolis, IN 46204; telephone (877)236-4332; www.indy-partnership.com

## Commercial Shipping

Nicknamed the "Crossroads of America," Indianapolis is a major transportation and distribution hub for the Midwest. As the most centrally located of the largest 100 cities in the United States, Indianapolis is within 650 miles of 55 percent of all Americans, or more than 50 million households. The city is served by four interstate highways, five railroads, an international airport, and a foreign trade zone. Indianapolis International Airport is one of the top ten largest cargo airports in the country. There are over 100 motor freight carriers serving the area. Three ports serve the entire state and are all within a three hour drive of Indianapolis; Burns Harbor is located on Lake Michigan and the Ports of Indiana-Jeffersonville and Indiana-Mount Vernon are located on the Ohio River.

The hub of an extensive rail network, Indianapolis has a total of 26 rail corridors in operation and five key freight facilities. CSX and Norfolk Southern are the two Class 1 operations, and the three shortlines consist of Indiana Railroad Co., Indiana Southern, and Louisville & Indiana Rail.

## Labor Force and Employment Outlook

Indianapolis employers draw from a workforce of about one million skilled and educated regional workers. An estimated 40,000 students graduate from the region's 22 universities and colleges each year. The region also boasts a higher than national average worker productivity rate. The economic diversity of the region contributes to its success, as does its attractiveness to companies due to the transportation infrastructure, skilled workforce, business incentives, and quality of life.

With central Indiana becoming less dependent on the automobile industry, manufacturing continues to be the strongest economic sector in Indianapolis. At the end of 2006, Indianapolis manufacturing firms employed about 13.6 percent of the labor force. The retail trade employed just over 12 percent and health care industries supported about 12 percent of the area's jobs. Long term projections suggest that health care and retail jobs will be most likely to increase into 2014, particularly for registered nurses and retail salespersons. As the city has begun to focus on attracting more high-tech and research companies, there is a hope to significantly increase the number of jobs in information technology, advanced manufacturing, and life sciences.

The following is a summary of data regarding the Indianapolis-Carmel metropolitan area labor force, 2006 annual averages.

**Size of nonagricultural labor force: 900,700**

**Number of workers employed in ...**

    construction and mining: 53,200
    manufacturing: 100,300

trade, transportation and utilities: 195,500

information: 16,100

financial activities: 63,200

professional and business services: 122,700

educational and health services: 109,900

leisure and hospitality: 89,500

other services: 35,400

government: 115,000

**Average hourly earnings of production workers employed in manufacturing:** $20.82

**Unemployment rate:** 4.1% (June 2007)

| Largest employers (2005) | Number of employees |
|---|---|
| U.S. Government | 36,279 |
| State of Indiana | 35,335 |
| Eli Lilly and Co. | 17,000 |
| Indiana University | 16,497 |
| Purdue University | 13,610 |
| St.Vincent Health | 11,605 |
| General Motors Corp. | 10,442 |
| Marsh Supermarkets Inc. | 9,540 |
| Clarian Health Partners | 7,503 |
| Delphi Corp. | 7,035 |

## Cost of Living

State taxes are consistently rated among the lowest in the country in terms of total state and local tax collections per capita. Utility costs are also relatively low. Overall cost of living consistently ranks at or below the national average.

The following is a summary of data regarding several key cost of living factors in the Indianapolis area.

**2007 (1st quarter) ACCRA Average House Price:** $298,854

**2007 (1st quarter) ACCRA Cost of Living Index:** 96.1

**State income tax rate:** 3.4% of Adjusted Gross Income

**State sales tax rate:** 6.0%

**Local income tax rate:** 0.7%

**Local sales tax rate:** None

**Property tax rate:** 1.53 per $100 assessed valuation

*Economic Information:* The Indy Partnership, 111 Monument Circle, Ste. 1800, Indianapolis, IN 46204; telephone (877)236-4332; www.indypartnership.com. Indiana Economic Development Corporation, One North Capitol, Ste. 700, Indianapolis, IN 46204; telephone (800)463-8081; www.in.gov/iedc

## ■ Education and Research

### Elementary and Secondary Schools

There are 11 school districts serving the city of Indianapolis and Marion County. In most districts, parents are offered several choices of schools that their children may attend. Indianapolis Public Schools (IPS) is the largest in the city and the state. High school students in IPS are divided into Small Schools, each of which has a maximum enrollment of 400 students. In 2007 there were 24 small schools located on 5 campuses. Schools on the same campus share a cafeteria, gymnasium, and media center. IPS offers vocational education through Day Adult High School and Arsenal Technical High School. Magnet and option programs are available in 17 different fields, including performing and visual arts, health professions, environmental studies, and telecommunications. IPS offers over 60 alternative education programs. These include Pacers Academy for grades six through twelve (the first school sponsored by an NBA franchise) and Horizons, an alternative middle school.

The following is a summary of data regarding the Indianapolis Public Schools as of the 2005–2006 school year.

**Total enrollment:** 36,957

**Number of facilities**

elementary schools: 50

junior high/middle schools: 11

senior high schools: 5 (broken up into 24 "Small Schools")

other: 14

**Student/teacher ratio:** 17.4:1

**Teacher salaries (2005–06)**

elementary median: $40,980

junior high/middle median: $46,810

secondary median: $48,240

**Funding per pupil:** $9,643

There are over 50 private and parochial schools in Indianapolis. These include International School, which offers full immersion Spanish and French programs, and Park Tudor, a college preparatory school.

*Public Schools Information:* Indianapolis Public Schools, 120 East Walnut Street, Indianapolis, IN 46204; telephone (317)226-4000; www.ips.k12.in.us

### Colleges and Universities

Several public and private institutions of higher learning are located in Indianapolis. Indiana University–Purdue University Indianapolis has more than 29,000 students enrolled in associate's, baccalaureate, master's, and doctorate programs. Through 22 schools and 200 academic programs offered, areas of specialization include art, engineering technologies, dentistry, law, medical technology, nursing, occupational therapy, and social work.

Butler University, a private liberal-arts university, has an enrollment of about 4,415 students. Bachelor's and master's degrees are available in a wide variety of majors offered through five colleges. A Doctor of Pharmacy degree is also available. The University of Indianapolis, founded in 1902 by what is now the United Methodist Church, offers 70 undergraduate academic programs, 22 master's programs, and 5 doctoral programs. Enrollment is about 4,300 students.

Marian College is a Franciscan liberal-arts college that offers majors in 34 academic programs. Associate's, bachelor's, and master's degrees are available. Enrollment is about 1,800 students.

Ivy Tech Community College is a public, community college that offers associate's degree programs and certificate programs in a wide variety of fields. The main campus for the Central Indiana region is in Indianapolis. There are 22 other locations throughout the state.

## Libraries and Research Centers

In addition to its Central Branch downtown, the Indianapolis-Marion County Public Library operates 22 branches throughout the city and a bookmobile. The library, with holdings of more than 2.1 million items, has an annual circulation of more than 12 million items. The Indianapolis Special Collections Room at the Central Library includes a wide variety of historic materials, from old city directories and high school yearbooks to information on the Indianapolis 500. The library also maintains special collections on several Indianapolis authors, including the Kurt Vonnegut Collection, James Whitcomb Riley Collection, Meredith Nicholson Collection, and Booth Tarkington Collection. Other special collections include the Wright Marble Cookbook Collection and the Arthur H. Rumpf Menu Collection. The Central Library is an official U.S. Patent and Trademark Depository Library.

The Indiana State Library in downtown Indianapolis houses more than 2 million printed items plus millions of manuscripts, photographs, microfilms, and federal and state documents. Special collections include the Indiana Academy of Science Library; an Indiana Collection; a large assortment of books on tape; Braille and large print books; and a Manuscript Section housing almost three million items including war letters and eighteenth century fur traders' papers. The Indiana Historical Society Library specializes in the Civil War, early North American travel accounts, and the history of Indiana and the Northwest Territory.

The University Library at Indiana University–Purdue University Indianapolis (IUPUI) houses more than 650,000 volumes and more than 4,000 peri-

odical subscriptions; other libraries within the IUPUI system include the Herron School of Art Library, the Payton Philanthropic Studies Library, the Ruth Lilly Medical Library, the School of Dentistry Library, and the Ruth Lilly Law Library. Holdings in all the IUPUI libraries combined total more than 2.5 million items.

Butler University has two libraries: the Irwin Library and the Ruth Lilly Science Library. The libraries have a combined stock of over 250,000 volumes, 110,000 government documents, and 1,500 journal subscriptions. The Irwin Library houses a special collection of about 17,000 musical scores. The Krannert Memorial Library of the University of Indianapolis houses over 150,000 books and 1,000 periodical subscriptions.

Indianapolis is home to a variety of special libraries and research centers, many of them related to the universities. Among them is the Hudson Institute, the internationally renowned policy research organization. State agencies, such as the Indiana Department of Commerce, the Indiana Department of Education, and the Indiana Department of Environmental Management also operate libraries. Other specialized libraries are affiliated with law firms, hospitals, newspapers, publishing houses, museums, and churches and synagogues. Of unique interest are the Indianapolis Zoo Library and the Children's Museum of Indianapolis Library.

Indiana University–Purdue University Indianapolis sponsors 19 Signature Centers, which are interdisciplinary research centers. These include Center for Earth and Environmental Science; the Center for Assessing, Understanding and Managing Pain; the Center for Regenerative Biology and Medicine; the Center for the Study of Religion and American Culture; the Cellular Therapy, Hematopoietic Stem Cell Transplant Center; the Center for Family Violence Prevention, Education and Research; and the Institute for Research on Social Issues. The Indiana University School of Medicine has several research sites in Indianapolis, including the Center for Aging Research, the AIDS Clinical Research group, Biomechanics and Biomaterials Research Center, the Center for Law and Health, and the Midwest Sexually Transmitted Infections and Topical Microbicides Cooperative Research Center. Butler University is home to the Institute for Research and Scholarship and the Center for Global Education. The University of Indianapolis is home to the Institute for the Study of War and Diplomacy. Clarian Health Partners sponsor the Methodist Research Institute, Indiana University General Clinical Research Center, and an Outpatient Clinical Research Facility.

***Public Library Information:*** Indianapolis-Marion County Public Library, 40 E. St. Clair Street, Indianapolis, IN 46204; telephone (317)275-4100; www.imcpl.org

# Health Care

With 23 hospitals, Indianapolis is a Midwestern health care hub. Community Health Network has five hospitals with a total of 867 beds and over 70 primary care facilities. The network sponsors the Indiana Heart Hospital and the Indiana Surgery Centers. Clarian Health Partners includes three hospitals: Methodist Hospital, Indiana University Hospital, and Riley Hospital for Children. Methodist Hospital houses a Level 1 trauma Center and a special Neuroscience Center of Excellence. Indiana University Hospital has an extensive transplant center. In 2007 *U.S. News & World Report* ranked Clarian Health Partners as one of the top 40 Best Heart Hospitals in the nation. Clarian also has two major primary care facilities: Clarian West and Clarian North.

St. Francis Hospital features special services in cancer care, neurosurgery, massage therapy, women's and children's services, speech and hearing, and occupational therapy. St. Francis is also home to the Heart Center and the Center of Hope (for sexual assault victims). The hospital has a Level 3 neonatal intensive care unit.

St. Vincent Hospitals and Health Services has five major facilities in the city. St. Vincent Indianapolis Hospital offers special services in cardiopulmonary care, sports medicine, and bariatric weight loss services. The Peyton Manning Children's Hospital at St. Vincent's has a Level 3 neonatal intensive care unit and a pediatric emergency room. St. Vincent New Hope serves patients with developmental disabilities. The St. Vincent Pediatric Rehabilitation Center has both inpatient and outpatient services. The St. Vincent Women's Hospital Indianapolis offers a full range of services for women and infants.

Wishard Memorial Hospital is home to the IU National Center of Excellence for Women's Health, the Richard M. Fairbanks Burn Center, and a Level 1 Trauma Center. Affiliated centers include the Midtown Community Mental Health Center and the Lockenfield Village Rehabilitation and Healthcare Center.

A significant force in the regional medical community is the Indiana University School of Medicine. With a faculty of more than 1,100, research is conducted in a variety of areas, including cancer, diabetes, Alzheimer's disease, genetics, and others. IU has partnerships with all of the Clarian Health Partners locations and Wishard Memorial Hospital.

Based in Indianapolis is the national headquarters of a major physical fitness organization, the American College of Sports Medicine, which conducts studies on and aims to increase awareness about physical activity.

# Recreation

## Sightseeing

Easily within driving distance for more than half of the country's population, Indianapolis has set out to make itself an attractive tourist destination by combining diverse cultural opportunities with first-class hotels and fine shopping and dining. Revitalization of the downtown core, where modernized nineteenth-century buildings stand adjacent to futuristic structures, has made Indianapolis an architecturally interesting city.

The street grid, modeled after Washington, D.C., makes the center-city Mile Square a compact and convenient area for walking tours. In Monument Circle the Soldiers' and Sailors' Monument observation platform offers a panoramic view of the city and the surrounding countryside. The Indiana War Memorial Plaza, a five-block downtown mall providing urban green space, contains a 100-foot granite monolith, flags from all 50 states, and a fountain at University Square. The plaza houses the national headquarters of the American Legion; a museum of martial history is located in the Memorial Shrine building.

Indianapolis has turned its attention back toward the city's most prominent natural feature—the White River. Ignored for generations, the river is now the centerpiece of the Canal and White River State Park, a 250-acre urban greenspace just blocks from the city's commercial heart. The park is home to the Indianapolis Zoo, the White River Gardens, the NCAA Headquarters and Hall of Fame, the Congressional Medal of Honor Memorial, Victory Field, the Eiteljorg Museum of American Indian and Western Art, the Indiana State Museum, and an IMAX movie theater. Common spaces in the park attract personal events, such as weddings, family reunions, and picnics, to large festivals, concerts, and even conferences. The Lawn, opened in 2003, features a waterfront bandstand and space for 5,000 people.

The Indianapolis Zoo, the first urban zoo to be built in several decades, houses more than 2,000 animals. The zoo is located on 64 acres in the urban White River State Park. The whale and dolphin pavilion presents shows with bottlenose dolphins, beluga whales, and false killer whales. Piranha and giant snakes live in a simulated Amazon forest; the desert conservatory, covered by an acrylic dome, features plant and animal life from the world's arid regions.

Capitol Commons contains the Indiana Statehouse, which houses the governor's office and the General Assembly. Garfield Park, home of Garfield Park Conservatory, features more than 500 examples of tropical flora, rare carnivorous plants, and tropical birds; the park contains formal gardens, fountains and limestone bridges. The Scottish Rite Cathedral, built of Indiana limestone, is the largest Masonic temple in the world; its 54-bell carillon can be heard city wide.

Victorian architecture enthusiasts can visit the well-preserved James Whitcomb Riley Home; built in 1872, it was the residence—during the last 23 years of his life—of the Hoosier dialect poet who created Little Orphan Annie. The President Benjamin Harrison Home is a 16-room Italianate mansion, completed in 1875, where much of the original Harrison family furniture is displayed. The Massachusetts Avenue Historic Fire Station was restored in 1988 as a museum equipped with a children's fire safety laboratory.

## Arts and Culture

The Indianapolis Art Center is a not-for-profit community arts organization whose mission is to make art accessible to all residents of Indianapolis. The center consists of the Marilyn K. Glick School of Art, designed by architect Michael Graves and comprising 13 art studios, a 224-seat auditorium, a library, and a gift shop; the Cultural Complex, which features a Fiber Studio and individual artist's studios, as well as the Writers' Center of Indiana; and ARTSPARK. The 12-acre campus sits on the edge of White River and features a riverfront deck, outdoor stage, and sculpture gardens.

The Indianapolis renaissance is most evident in the city's dedication to the renewal of its cultural life. Artsgarden features an eight-story, 12,500-square-foot glass dome suspended over a downtown intersection. The $12 million Artsgarden is linked by skywalks to the RCA Dome, convention center, hotels, and Circle Centre. The Artsgarden serves as a performance, exhibition, and marketing space for the Indianapolis arts community, hosting 350 events annually. A number of historically significant nineteenth-century buildings have also been refurbished in order to present local arts organizations in the best possible environment.

The Indianapolis Symphony Orchestra, founded in 1930, performs year-round in the restored historic Hilbert Circle Theatre and at parks and elsewhere throughout the city and state. Indianapolis Opera presents four full-scale operas per season. The Indianapolis Children's Choir has received international acclaim and has been performing since 1986. The Madame Walker Theatre Center, honoring the country's first female self-made millionaire, houses the Walker Theatre, where "Jazz on the Avenue" concerts are held on Fridays.

Ballet Internationale is a professional resident troupe that performs at Murat Center. Clowes Memorial Hall on the campus of Butler University is home to the Indianapolis Opera and the Indianapolis Chamber Orchestra. Dance Kaleidoscope is the city's contemporary dance troupe.

An active theater community contributes to the city's cultural life. The Indianapolis Civic Theatre, the nation's oldest continuously active civic theater group, performs at Marian Hall Auditorium at Marian College—the groups' interim home while plans are being made to build a new, multi-purpose community theatre facility. The Indiana Repertory Theatre, the state's largest equity theater, presents more than 300 performances annually and is housed in the restored Indiana Theatre. European-style performances are the specialty of American Cabaret Theatre, formerly of New York City. Beef and Boards

Dinner Theatre presents Broadway shows, concerts, and dinner. Off-Broadway plays are staged by Phoenix Theatre, presenting 16 shows annually in a restored church in the Chatham Arch Historic District.

The Indianapolis Museum of Art (IMA) is located in a wooded cultural park. The Museum of Art holds the largest American collection of works by the nineteenth-century British landscape artist J. M. W. Turner. The J. W. Holliday Collection of Neo-Impressionist art, an extensive collection of Japanese Edo-period paintings, and the Robert Indiana *Love* painting, with a matching outdoor sculpture in large rusted letters, round out one of the most impressive collections in the Midwest.

On the grounds of the IMA is the Oldfields-Lilly House & Gardens, featuring an eighteenth-century French-style chateau, formerly the residence of J. K. Lilly Jr. and now open for tours. The Virginia B. Fairbanks Art & Nature Park offers 100 acres of natural, wooded landscape, with paths, waterways, and opportunities for visitors to experience "interaction of art and nature."

The Children's Museum is the world's largest museum of its type and one of the 20 most-visited museums in the country. The 400,000-square-foot facility features a variety of hands-on exhibits and touchable scientific experiments as well as a planetarium. Favorite exhibits include an Egyptian mummy, a Victorian carousel, and the largest public collection of toy trains. In "Passport to the World," children learn about foreign cultures through toys from around the world. Each year more than 1.1 million people visit the Children's Museum. The Eli Lilly Center for Exploration at the museum allows children to explore and experiment with current issues. A $50 million renovation was completed in 2004, opening the new Dinosphere exhibit, an immersive dinosaur experience that allows visitors a close-up look at how dinosaurs may have lived.

The award-winning Conner Prairie Pioneer Settlement, a living history museum, presents an authentic recreation of Hoosier life in the 1800s. The Indiana State Museum chronicles the history and culture of the state and features a collection of more than 400,000 artifacts and an IMAX theater. The National Art Museum of Sports is housed in the Indiana University–Purdue University Indianapolis campus' University Place and contains ancient and modern art depicting sports motifs; 40 sports are represented in 800 paintings, sculptures, and paper works. Other museums in the city are Indiana Medical History Museum, Hook's Discovery & Learning Center, and Indianapolis Motor Speedway and Hall of Fame Museum.

## Festivals and Holidays

Each year Indianapolis presents a host of festivals and fairs that celebrate the city's history, traditions, and ethnic heritage. The most elaborate is the month-long annual 500 Festival in May, which combines events associated with the Indianapolis 500 race as well as other activities, like the Mini Marathon and 5K races, a parade, Mayor's Breakfast, a Kids' Day, and others. The St. Benno Fest in March celebrates the city's German heritage. The Indiana International Film Festival, held in April, is one of two film festivals in the city. Midwestern artists present their crafts and art work in June at the Talbot Street Art Fair. The Indiana Black Expo Summer Celebration celebrates African American heritage over 10 days in July at the Indiana Convention Center.

Oktoberfest takes place in early September, followed by Penrod Arts Fair, a commemorative celebration of Indianapolis author Booth Tarkington's most famous character, with art exhibits and entertainment at the Indianapolis Museum of Art. A three-day International Festival is held in late October; the Heartland Film Festival in October celebrates independent and theatrically-released films. The Madrigal Dinners ring in the year-end holiday season on the campus of Indiana University-Purdue University at Indianapolis with a grand banquet that recreates the customs, dress, and songs of medieval England. Other festivals and events are hosted throughout the year as part of the universities and museums event schedules; others are held throughout the warmer months as part of the park district's event schedule.

## Sports for the Spectator

Best known for the Indianapolis 500 and the Allstate 400 at the Brickyard (formerly the Brickyard 400), Indianapolis made a conscious and successful effort in the 1980s to become an amateur sports capital and a major league city, a distinction that is undisputed today.

Motor sports abound at the Indianapolis Motor Speedway, with three major events and a multitude of smaller ones. The Formula One U.S. Grand Prix began there in 2000; the celebrated event happens annually in mid-July. Since 1911, the Indianapolis 500 has fielded international race car drivers testing their mettle at speeds above 200 miles per hour for 200 laps around the track; the "Indy 500" attracts more than 350,000 spectators and is held each Memorial Day weekend. The Allstate 400 at the Brickyard features NASCAR racing in August.

The 57,890-seat RCA Dome is home to the Indianapolis Colts of the National Football League (NFL). The RCA Dome also houses the National Track & Field Hall of Fame.

The Indiana Pacers of the National Basketball Association (NBA) moved to the 15-story, $183 million arena, Conseco Fieldhouse, in 1999; the structure blends old-style grace with modern conveniences. The Women's National Basketball Association expansion team, the Indiana Fever, also call Conseco Fieldhouse home. The Indianapolis Ice, a minor-league affiliate of the Chicago Blackhawks, play hockey at the Pepsi Coliseum at the Indiana State Fairgrounds. Professional tennis takes place at the Indianapolis Tennis Center.

The Triple-A Indianapolis Indians play baseball at Victory Field in White River State Park, an open-air, 13,500-seat stadium.

## Sports for the Participant

Indianapolis's commitment to sponsor world-class amateur athletic competition has made available excellent facilities to the public. The Major Taylor Velodrome—named for the first African American to win a world championship in any sport—is a state-of-the-art oval bicycle track with a 28-degree banked concrete surface; it is open to the public from March to October. Joggers can try out the track at the Indiana University Track & Soccer Stadium; the university's natatorium offers public facilities, including swimming pools, weight rooms, and a gymnasium. The Indianapolis Tennis Center makes 24 tennis courts available for public use.

The Indy Parks and Recreation Department maintains more than 10,600 acres of land comprising 173 parks; among them is the 4,395-acre Eagle Creek Park, the country's largest municipally owned and operated park, which features a competition-quality rowing course. The park system includes 26 recreation, family, and nature centers; basketball, tennis, and sand volleyball courts; 13 golf courses; softball and baseball diamonds; football and soccer fields; and 22 swimming pools/aquatic centers. Indy Greenways is a series of paved pathways throughout the city; residents walk, run, bike, and skate on the paths.

## Shopping and Dining

Circle Centre Mall, covering two city blocks in the Warehouse District at the heart of downtown Indianapolis, provides tourists and residents with many shopping, dining, and entertainment options. In addition to anchor stores Nordstrom and Parisian, Circle Centre has more than 100 specialty shops, restaurants, and nightclubs, plus a nine-screen cinema, a virtual-reality theme park, and the Indianapolis Artsgarden. Skywalks link Circle Center to seven hotels, the Indiana Convention Center, the RCA Dome, the Indiana Government Center, and offices, shops, and restaurants. Circle Centre has spurred a development boom in adjacent blocks, including the addition of a Hard Rock Cafe and several upscale restaurants.

The Indianapolis City Market, housed in an imposing nineteenth-century building, opened in 1886. Known for its fresh vegetables and meats, the year-round farmer's market is a favorite spot for downtown workers who lunch at small specialty shops. Broad Ripple Village, known as the "Greenwich Village of Indianapolis," is a renovated neighborhood of antique and other shops, art galleries, and nightclubs; a canal and paved walking trail run through it. Recent years have seen a revitalization of Massachusetts Avenue, a Soho-like downtown area of art galleries, dining establishments, and coffee houses that is most commonly referred to as Mass Ave. The Fountain

Square neighborhood, which boasts both classic and trendy eateries, 1950s-style diners, dance and jazz clubs, antique shops, and bookstores, also attracts regular patrons and visitors.

Indianapolis enjoys its share of good restaurants serving a variety of ethnic and traditional food, ranging from Nouvelle American cuisine with a Hoosier touch to authentic German and French specialties. Health food restaurants are popular, as are Japanese, Middle Eastern, coffeehouses, Italian, and Mexican. Mystery Cafe gives patrons a chance to dine and solve a "Who Dunnit."

***Visitor Information:*** Indianapolis Convention & Visitors Association, One RCA Dome, Suite 100, Indianapolis, IN 46225; telephone (800)323- INDY; www .indy.org

## ■ Convention Facilities

Indianapolis is gaining in prominence as a convention destination. The number of convention delegates is well over 1 million annually. The principal meeting facility is the Indiana Convention Center & RCA Dome. The complex, consisting of five exhibit halls and the multiuse RCA Dome, is the site of trade shows, banquets, sporting events, and concerts. Skywalks connect the convention center with the RCA Dome, Circle Centre Mall, and seven major hotels. In 2000 the Indiana Convention Center and RCA Dome underwent its third expansion/ renovation. An additional 100,000 square feet of exhibit space was added, to make a total amount of exhibit space of 403,700 square feet. The RCA Dome features 95,000 square feet of floor space.

The Indiana State Fairgrounds has 15 buildings for event use. These include the Blue Ribbon Pavilion, offering 69,000 square feet of exhibit space; the 139,000-square-foot multipurpose South Pavilion; and the 171,000-square-foot West Pavilion. The Pepsi Coliseum seats 8,000 people.

More than 120 hotels in Indianapolis offer 28,000 rooms throughout the city. Most of the downtown hotels feature meeting space and ample facilities. University Place Conference Center & Hotel, on the campus of Indiana University-Purdue University at Indianapolis, offers 28 meeting rooms (among them several banquet rooms), a 340-seat auditorium, and 278 guest rooms. The five-star Conrad Hilton hotel, with 10,000 square feet of meeting space, opened in 2006 in downtown Indianapolis.

Unique facilities for meetings and special events include the Indianapolis Artsgarden, linked to Circle Centre Mall, Union Station (a Romanesque Revival-style train station built in 1887), and the historic Murat Centre. Following an $11 million renovation, the Murat Centre features a 2,700-seat theater and the Egyptian Room, modeled after King Tut's tomb. The Indianapolis

Museum of Art's new Deer-Zink Pavilion offers seating for 500 people in the main dining room and can accommodate 300 in its reception lobby. Other unique meeting spaces include the Indianapolis Zoo, the Indianapolis Motor Speedway, and the NCAA Hall of Champions.

***Convention Information:*** Indianapolis Convention & Visitors Association, One RCA Dome, Suite 100, Indianapolis, IN 46225; telephone (800)323-INDY; www.indy.org

## ■ Transportation

### Approaching the City

The Indianapolis International Airport is located eight miles southwest of downtown and is accessible to the city via the Airport Expressway and I-70. Eleven airlines schedule about 280 daily departures, including 39 daily non-stop flights; more than 8.5 million passengers are served by the airport each year. Eagle Creek Airpark handles smaller aircraft.

Indianapolis is linked with points throughout the nation by a network of interstate highways. Intersecting the city from east to west is I-70; I-65 passes through the downtown area from the northwest to the southeast. I-69 approaches from the northeast. All of these routes connect with I-465, which encircles the metropolitan area. U.S. 40 and U.S. 36 also cross the city east-west. Amtrak offers both bus and rail service. Greyhound also serves the city.

### Traveling in the City

Streets in Indianapolis are laid out on a grid pattern. The main north-south thoroughfare is Meridian Street, which is intersected in the center of downtown by Washington Street.

Public transportation is provided by IndyGo (Indiana Public Transportation Corp.), with 28 fixed routes and special services like Dial-A-Ride, Open Door Paratransit Service, and Late Night Service. The Blue Line Circulator is an inexpensive way to visit several downtown attractions.

## ■ Communications

### Newspapers and Magazines

The major daily newspaper in Indianapolis is the morning *The Indianapolis Star.* With an average daily circulation of about 261,405, *The Indianapolis Star* was ranked as one of the top 30 newspapers in the nation in 2007. The *Indianapolis Business Journal;* the *Indianapolis Recorder,* a newspaper with an African American focus; and several neighborhood and suburban newspapers are published weekly. *Indianapolis Monthly* is a magazine featuring articles on local and state topics.

A number of magazines and special-interest journals are published in the city. Among the nationally-known magazines are *The Saturday Evening Post, Jack and Jill, Humpty Dumpty's Magazine,* and *Children's Digest. Quill,* a magazine for journalists and journalism students, is published nine times per year. Topics covered by other Indianapolis-based publications include art, religion, medicine, nursing, law, education, pets, and gymnastics.

## Television and Radio

Eight television and four cable stations broadcast from Indianapolis. The city is served by 20 AM and FM radio stations providing a variety of formats such as classical, jazz, public radio, adult contemporary, country, and talk.

*Media Information:* The *Indianapolis Star,* 307 North Pennsylvania Street, Indianapolis, IN 46204; telephone (317)444-4000; toll-free (800)669-7827; www.indystar.com

## Indianapolis Online

City of Indianapolis and Marion County home page. Available www.indygov.org

Greater Indianapolis Chamber of Commerce. Available www.indychamber.com

Indiana Historical Society. Available www.indianahistory.org

Indiana State Library. Available www.statelib.lib.in.us

Indianapolis Convention & Visitors Association. Available www.indy.org

Indianapolis Downtown. Available www.indydt.com

Indianapolis Economic Development. Available www.indianapoliseconomicdevelopment.com

*The Indianapolis Star.* Available www.indystar.com

Indy Partnership Regional Economic Development Corporation. Available www.iedc.com

BIBLIOGRAPHY

Berry, S.L., *Indianapolis* (Minneapolis, MN: Dillon Press, 1990)

Nye, Charlie, and Joe Young, eds., *Hoosier Century: 100 Years of Photography from the Indianapolis Star and News* (Sports Publishing, Inc., 1999)

# South Bend

## ■ The City in Brief

**Founded:** 1820 (incorporated 1835)

**Head Official:** Mayor Stephen J. Luecke (D) (since 1997)

**City Population**

    1980: 109,727
    1990: 105,511
    2000: 107,789
    2006 estimate: 104,905
    Percent change, 1990–2000: 1.6%
    U.S. rank in 1980: 143rd
    U.S. rank in 1990: 182nd (State rank: 5th)
    U.S. rank in 2000: 236th (State rank: 5th)

**Metropolitan Area Population**

    1980: 241,617
    1990: 247,052
    2000: 265,559
    2006 estimate: 318,007
    Percent change, 1990–2000: 7.5%
    U.S. rank in 1980: Not available
    U.S. rank in 1990: Not available
    U.S. rank in 2000: 137th

**Area:** 38.7 square miles (2000)

**Elevation:** 773 feet above sea level

**Average Annual Temperatures:** January, 23.4° F; July, 73.0° F; annual average, 49.5° F

**Average Annual Precipitation:** 39.70 inches of rain, 70.8 inches of snow

**Major Economic Sectors:** services, wholesale and retail trade, government

**Unemployment Rate:** 4.9% (June 2007)

**Per Capita Income:** $18,381 (2005)

**2005 FBI Crime Index Property:** 6,612

**2005 FBI Crime Index Violent:** 794

**Major Colleges and Universities:** University of Notre Dame; Indiana University South Bend; Ivy Tech Community College

**Daily Newspaper:** *South Bend Tribune*

## ■ Introduction

South Bend is the seat of St. Joseph County and the focus of a region known as "Michiana" that extends over five counties in Indiana and two counties in Michigan. Mishawaka lies to the east of South Bend; the two cities comprise a metropolitan statistical area and are in the heart of the nation's industrial belt. With a location on the beautiful St. Joseph River, South Bend is home to the University of Notre Dame, which is nationally recognized for its academic excellence and for "The Fighting Irish," its football team. But the city has much more to offer as well. South Bend has become a regional center for education, health care, business, and arts and entertainment, and continues to grow on the strength of communities in becoming a prime destination for businesses, residents, and visitors.

## ■ Geography and Climate

South Bend is located on the Saint Joseph River on mostly level to gently rolling terrain and some former marshlands. The proximity of Lake Michigan—the city is within 20 miles of the nearest shore—produces a moderating effect on South Bend's climate. Temperatures of 100 degrees or higher are rare and cold waves are less severe than at other locations at the same latitude.

Distribution of precipitation is relatively even throughout the year; the greatest amounts occur during the growing season, May to October. Winter is characterized by cloudiness and high humidity, with frequent periods of snow. Heavier snowfalls are often borne into the area by a cold northwest wind passing over Lake Michigan.

The area known as Michiana covers the Indiana counties of St. Joseph, LaPorte, Starke, Marshall, and Elkhart, and the Michigan counties of Berrien and Cass. For statistical purposes the Chamber of Commerce of St. Joseph County defines Michiana as counties that contribute at least 500 inbound commuting workers to St. Joseph County each day. South Bend is the seat of St. Joseph County.

**Area:** 38.7 square miles (2000)

**Elevation:** 773 feet above sea level

**Average Temperatures:** January, 23.4° F; July, 73.0° F; annual average, 49.5° F

**Average Annual Precipitation:** 39.70 inches of rain; 70.8 inches of snow

# ■ History

## French Exploration Establishes South Bend

The first European explorer to reach the region surrounding present-day South Bend was Robert Cavelier, sieur de La Salle, who in 1679 passed near the spot where today the University of Notre Dame's administration building is located. Two years later La Salle met with Miami and Illinois chiefs under a tree named Council Oak in what was then the heart of the Miami nation. They signed a peace treaty that involved a pledge from the Miami and the Illinois to fight the Iroquois. LaSalle, protected by the treaty, was free to explore the Mississippi River region in which present-day South Bend is included. He then claimed the territory for France, naming it Louisiana.

Pierre Freischutz Navarre, a Frenchman married to a Potawatomi woman, established the first trading post for the American Fur Company in 1820 near South Bend's future site. But Alexis Coquillard is credited with founding South Bend. The town's name was derived from his trading post, which was called "The Bend," and noted its southerly location on the St. Joseph River. Coquillard's business rival and friend, Colonel Lathrop M. Taylor, renamed the settlement St. Joseph in 1827 and then Southold. The U.S. Post Office officially named it South Bend. Coquillard and Taylor worked together to develop the settlement and encouraged settlers with gifts of land and money. The city was platted and named the county seat in 1831, incorporated in 1835, and chartered in 1865.

## Industry and Scholarship Enhance the City

The most significant event in the city's history was the arrival of Father Edward Sorin, the founder of the University of Notre Dame, who reached the future site of the university on November 26, 1842 with seven Brothers of the Congregation of the Holy Cross. Bishop Hailandiere of the diocese of Vincennes had given Father Sorin 600 acres to found a college for seminary and secular students as well as to start a mission for the Potawatomi Native Americans. The college's first student was Alexis Coquillard. Enrollment picked up with the arrival of the Lake Shore Railroad in 1851. A fire destroyed the campus in 1879 and the Neo-Gothic Administration Building, with its golden dome topped by a figure of the Virgin Mary, was opened later that year. The golden dome, a tradition of academic excellence, and winning football teams have become familiar symbols of this famous university, which remains a significant part of life in South Bend in the twenty-first century.

The first steam locomotive came into South Bend in 1851. In 1852 Henry and Clement Studebaker arrived in South Bend and opened a blacksmith and wagon shop. They built farm wagons, carriages, prairie schooners, and then a gasoline engine automobile in 1904, transforming the company into an automobile plant that remained in business until 1966. James Oliver came to South Bend in 1855, founding the Oliver Chilled Plow Works, which manufactured a superior farm plow that revolutionized farming and introduced a manufacturing process that replaced iron with chilled and hardened steel. The Singer Cabinet Works began production in 1868 in South Bend to take advantage of the proximity of Indiana hardwood forests, emerging as the world's largest cabinet factory by 1901. The South Bend Toy Manufacturing Company came to town in 1882. The company grew from producing simple croquet sets and small wooden toys to making doll carriages and wagons and then on to a wider variety. The South Bend Toy Works, as it was called, continued to expand until about 1973. As an increase in domestic and foreign competition took hold, the company was sold to Milton Bradley in 1981, but was still forced to close its doors in 1985.

The growth of industry and the transportation network in the late 1800s inspired rapid growth in population. The population in 1870 was 7,206. In 1880 the total jumped to 13,280 and in 1900 the total was 35,999. The population of the city reached a peak of 132,445 in 1960. Like many cities, a decline in manufacturing and the growth of suburban areas may have attributed to a decline in population. By 1980 the population was down to 109,727 and the 2000 census ranked the city's population at 107,789.

Beginning in the late 1990s, the city took measures to redevelop both the business and residential areas of the city to inspire new growth. From 1997 to 2006 the city invested over $20 million in housing programs, resulting in 1,372 new single family homes and 500 apartment units. An emphasis on improvements in public safety made the city more attractive to newcomers. With programs such as the Project Disarm Task Force, designed to get weapons off the streets; Gang Resistance and Education Training in cooperation with public schools; and the creation of over 220 neighborhood watch programs, South Bend saw a 24 percent drop in reported crimes from 1997 to 2006. Several retail and office developments were initiated in the early 2000s. In 2007 city officials were considering plans to develop a new light industry park and a certified tech park, both of which would invite new and diverse businesses to the city. These plans were part of the Greater South Bend City Plan, a community-driven 20-year development plan adopted in 2006. City Plan is designed to build on the strengths of the city and its people to position South Bend as a strong and vital regional center for business and commerce, arts, and culture and to make the city more attractive for prospective new businesses, residents, and tourists.

***Historical Information:*** Northern Indiana Center for History, 808 W. Washington Street, South Bend, IN 46601; telephone (574)235-9664; www.centerfor history.org

## ■ Population Profile

### Metropolitan Area Residents

1980: 241,617
1990: 247,052
2000: 265,559
2006 estimate: 318,007
Percent change, 1990–2000: 7.5%
U.S. rank in 1980: Not available
U.S. rank in 1990: Not available
U.S. rank in 2000: 137th

### City Residents

1980: 109,727
1990: 105,511
2000: 107,789
2006 estimate: 104,905
Percent change, 1990–2000: 1.6%
U.S. rank in 1980: 143rd
U.S. rank in 1990: 182nd (State rank: 5th)
U.S. rank in 2000: 236th (State rank: 5th)

**Density:** 2,786.4 people per square mile

### Racial and ethnic characteristics (2005)

White: 61,762
Black: 22,974
American Indian and Alaska Native: 1,117
Asian: 843

Native Hawaiian and Pacific Islander: 0
Hispanic or Latino (may be of any race): 10,617
Other: 7,713

**Percent of residents born in state:** 63.9% (2006)

### Age characteristics (2005)

Population under 5 years old: 7,197
Population 5 to 9 years old: 6,099
Population 10 to 14 years old: 8,027
Population 15 to 19 years old: 6,922
Population 20 to 24 years old: 9,146
Population 25 to 34 years old: 11,579
Population 35 to 44 years old: 13,336
Population 45 to 54 years old: 13,709
Population 55 to 59 years old: 5,026
Population 60 to 64 years old: 3,068
Population 65 to 74 years old: 4,751
Population 75 to 84 years old: 6,927
Population 85 years and older: 1,283
Median age: 34.5 years

### Births (2006, MSA)

Total number: 4,231

### Deaths (2006, MSA)

Total number: 3,012

### Money income (2005)

Per capita income: $18,381
Median household income: $31,867
Total households: 41,409

### Number of households with income of...

less than $10,000: 5,780
$10,000 to $14,999: 3,234
$15,000 to $24,999: 6,093
$25,000 to $34,999: 7,916
$35,000 to $49,999: 6,951
$50,000 to $74,999: 6,549
$75,000 to $99,999: 2,689
$100,000 to $149,999: 1,510
$150,000 to $199,999: 354
$200,000 or more: 333

**Percent of families below poverty level:** 12.8% (2005)

**2005 FBI Crime Index Property:** 6,612

**2005 FBI Crime Index Violent:** 794

## ■ Municipal Government

The city of South Bend operates under a mayor-council form of government. The mayor and nine council members are elected to four-year terms; the mayor is not

©Andre Jenny/Alamy

a member of council. Six members of the common council are elected to represent city districts and three are elected at large.

**Head Official:** Mayor Stephen J. Luecke (since 1997; current term expires 2011)

**Total Number of City Employees:** 1,261 (2007)

*City Information:* Office of the Mayor, 227 West Jefferson Blvd., Ste. 1400 N, South Bend, IN 46601; telephone (574)235-9261; www.southbendin.gov

## ■ Economy

### Major Industries and Commercial Activity

South Bend's diversified economic base consists principally of educational and health services, wholesale and retail trade, manufacturing, and government. In 2004 *Expansion Management* magazine ranked South Bend— for the first time—among the 40 hottest real estate markets for business. South Bend made the list based on available land, office and industrial space inventory, along with redevelopment opportunities for new and expanding companies.

The city benefits greatly from being a college town; in particular, Notre Dame University has a considerable impact on the economy of South Bend. The university is the largest employer for both the city and the county. The university further contributes to the area economy by partnering with area businesses for research and development projects, and providing strong job market candidates. The South Bend Community School Corporation and the South Bend chapter of the Diocese of Fort Wayne parochial schools also serve as major employers.

Health services have also boomed in South Bend in recent years. Memorial Health System has grown to become the largest health system employer in the county. Memorial's success has been linked to its central location, medical research conducted through Notre Dame, and a recent proliferation of medical-related business startups in the area. Saint Joseph Regional Medical Center follows as a top health care employer.

St. Joseph County is the second-largest retail market area in the state next to Indianapolis, with nationally recognized retailers including Martin's Supermarkets, Wal-Mart, Meijer Inc., Kroger, JCPenney, Sears Roebuck and Company, and Old Navy, to name a few. Manufacturing industries in the area include electrical equipment, automotive parts, transportation equipment, and various plastic products. AM General, producer of HMMWV (a.k.a. HUMMER) military and special purpose vehicles, is headquartered in South Bend and is one of the city's largest employers. The company's corporate offices are in South Bend and its production facilities are in nearby Mishawaka. Other manufacturing companies in South Bend include Honeywell, Robert Bosch Company, Steel Warehouse Company, Curtis Products, PEI-Genesis, and New Energy Corporation.

Another important industry in the county is tourism, which generates a significant number of jobs and revenue. Aside from the Indianapolis Motor Speedway, Notre Dame University attracts the most visitors in Indiana—nearly 700,000 visitors annually—and the county gains nearly $40 million in visitor expenditures through the university's football games alone.

**Items and goods produced:** airplanes, auto parts and accessories, automobiles, plastics, steel, electrical equipment, doors, metal works

## Incentive Programs—New and Existing Companies

*Local programs:* The city's Division of Economic Development actively promotes the retention and expansion of existing businesses and the development of new business in the city. Their offerings include financing programs, relocation incentives, land/building availability assistance, industrial revenue bonds for manufacturing facilities, tax abatement, and technical assistance through local partnerships.

*State programs:* EDGE (Economic Development for Growing Economy) is a state sponsored refundable tax credit, based on payroll, which allows Indiana individual income tax withholdings from company employees to be credited against the company's state corporate income tax liability. Excess withholdings would be refunded to the company. The credits can be awarded for up to 10 years. The Hoosier Business Investment Tax Credit encourages capital investment in the state by providing a credit against a company's state tax liability. A Venture Capital Investment Tax Credit and a Headquarters Relocation Tax Credit are also available. South Bend is part of federal Foreign Trade Zone 125. A Foreign Trade Zone offers a tax-free business environment through which businesses may delay or reduce their duty payments and avoid time consuming customs entry procedures.

*Job training programs:* The Indiana Economic Development Corporation provides two major grant programs for training and skill development: the Skills Enhancement Fund and the TECH Fund (Technology Enhancement Certification for Hoosiers). The Indiana Department of Commerce also provides grants to support skills training programs for local businesses. The

funds can be used in a variety of ways, including customized training programs in specific skills areas for new employees and skills development training for existing employees. The Indiana Department of Workforce Development provides labor force recruitment services, including help with the application process, testing, and the assessment and screening of qualified applicants. Ivy Tech Community College offers workforce development programs that include customized industrial training, either on campus or at the job site, as well as a variety of technical certificate programs.

## Development Projects

In 2006 the city adopted a community-driven, 20-year strategic development initiative called the South Bend City Plan. City Plan focuses on 10 main goals for the city's future that would expand and encourage new businesses, retail establishments, and arts and cultural organizations while also considering sustainable growth factors and the growing need for quality city services and utilities.

As of 2007 the city was working with the University of Notre Dame on development plans for a new state Certified Technology Park. A Certified Tech Park is an area designated by local and state officials for high-technology business development. Certain state and local tax revenues can by recaptured for investment in continued development of the park. The South Bend Tech Park will provide about 250,000 square feet of office and laboratory space.

Also in 2007 the South Bend Clinic was in the process of building a $40 million expansion that will double the size of the existing main facility. The same year the Salvation Army of St. Joseph County announced that it would build a new Ray and Joan Kroc Corp Community Center at Alonzo Watson Park in South Bend. The $40 million Salvation Army Kroc Center will include world-class recreational and educational facilities for a wide range of sports, arts, and educational programs. The center will include the standard fitness and sports areas, such as a gymnasium, exercise equipment, and an aquatic center. There will also be performance and rehearsal areas for music and dance groups and special studios for fine arts and digital arts, such as a state-of-the art recording studio. The classrooms at the center will serve as sites for art, music, and dance classes; computer training for all ages; a math and science academy for school aged children; and community outreach programs such as parenting skills and health education classes.

The Erskine Village and Erskine Commons shopping areas, the result of an over $60 million investment, continue to attract new businesses and have served as a catalyst for other business ventures in the immediate area.

In 2007 the Holladay Corporation began work on Phase I of Portage Prairie, a 500-acre development to include residential units, neighborhood retail, and a light industrial and distribution park. The Portage Prairie project is expected to require an investment of about $300 million.

***Economic Development Information:*** Chamber of Commerce of St. Joseph County, 401 E. Colfax Ave., Ste. 310, South Bend, IN 46617; telephone (574)234-0051; www.sjchamber.org

## Commercial Shipping

South Bend Regional Airport is the only tri-modal airport in the county serving as a stop for air, rail, and bus line travel. Designated a Foreign Trade Zone (125), South Bend is a center for manufacturers, suppliers, and vendors throughout the United States and abroad. Air freight services are offered by Federal Express, Circle Air Freight, Purolator Courier, Emery, Towne Air Freight, and Airborne. A network of interstate highways, including I-80/90, the nation's major east-west axis route, provides access to more than 70 motor freight carriers. Rail freight service is provided by Canadian National, Norfolk Southern, CSX, and Chicago Southshore South Bend Railroad.

## Labor Force and Employment Outlook

South Bend and its environs boast one of the highest concentrations of educational institutions per capita in the Midwest. About 82 percent of county residents have obtained a high school diploma and nearly 24 percent have a bachelor's degree or higher. South Bend has a large pool of skilled and semi-skilled laborers that are reported to be available, affordable, and reliable. The wage structure is competitive with other industrial communities. The greatest number of jobs have been in education, health care services, retail trade, and manufacturing. Jobs in arts, entertainment, and recreation increased countrywide by about 11 percent from 2002 to 2006.

The following is a summary of data regarding the South Bend-Mishawaka IN-MI metropolitan area labor force, 2006 annual averages.

**Size of nonagricultural labor force:** 144,800

**Number of workers employed in . . .**

> construction and mining: 6,400
> manufacturing: 20,700
> trade, transportation and utilities: 28,600
> information: 2,200
> financial activities: 7,300
> professional and business services: 12,900
> educational and health services: 31,500
> leisure and hospitality: 12,300
> other services: 5,700
> government: 17,300

**Average hourly earnings of production workers employed in manufacturing:** Not available

**Unemployment rate:** 4.9% (June 2007)

| *Largest employers (2007)* | *Number of employees* |
|---|---|
| University of Notre Dame | 4,459 |
| South Bend Community School Corporation | 3,295 |
| Memorial Health System | 3,008 |
| AM General | 2,400 |
| Saint Joseph Regional Medical Center, Inc. | 2,291 |
| City of South Bend | 1,300 |
| St. Joseph County | 900 |
| Madison Center | 780 |
| Honeywell | 777 |
| Indiana University South Bend | 714 |

## Cost of Living

The following is a summary of data regarding several key cost of living factors in the South Bend area.

**2007 (1st quarter) ACCRA Average House Price:** $245,725

**2007 (1st quarter) ACCRA Cost of Living Index:** 92.4

**State income tax rate:** 3.4% of Adjusted Gross Income

**State sales tax rate:** 6.0%

**Local income tax rate:** None

**Local sales tax rate:** None

**Property tax rate:** Averages 2.0 percent annually (2006)

***Economic Information:*** Chamber of Commerce of St. Joseph County, 401 E. Colfax Ave., Ste. 310, South Bend, IN 46617; telephone (574)234-0051; www.sjchamber.org. Indiana Department of Workforce Development, Indiana Government Center South, 10 North Senate Ave., Indianapolis, IN 46204; telephone (800) 891-6499; www.in.gov.dwd

# ■ Education and Research

## Elementary and Secondary Schools

The South Bend Community School Corporation is one of the largest school districts in the state. The district has a strong technology program with computers available to every student. Career and technical programs are available for high school students. The INTERN Program offers work-based learning opportunities for students with special needs. Through the Twenty-first Century Scholars Program, Indiana high school graduates are eligible for scholarships of up to eight semesters of tuition at participating public colleges, universities, and technical schools in the state. To be eligible, the students must maintain a 2.0 average and agree not to use drugs or alcohol and have no criminal record. Students may enroll in the program in seventh or eighth grade. Adult basic education programs are also available. The Dream Team Mentoring Program serves elementary students who are having academic or social difficulties.

The following is a summary of data regarding the South Bend Community School Corporation as of the 2005–2006 school year.

**Total enrollment:** 21,824

**Number of facilities**

elementary schools: 18
junior high/middle schools: 10
senior high schools: 4
other: 0

**Student/teacher ratio:** 18.3:1

**Teacher salaries (2005–06)**

elementary median: $48,170
junior high/middle median: $49,430
secondary median: Not available

**Funding per pupil:** $8,957

There are about 33 private and parochial schools in the greater South Bend area. Among them are a Roman Catholic elementary and high school system with an enrollment of nearly 5,000 students, as well as Hebrew schools and the Stanley Clark School, a private institution with a limited enrollment.

*Public Schools Information:* South Bend Community School Corporation, 215 South St. Joseph Street, South Bend, IN 46601; telephone (574)283-8000; www.sbcsc.k12.in.us

## Colleges and Universities

The University of Notre Dame, a top university affiliated with the Roman Catholic Church, is located in Notre Dame, IN, adjacent to South Bend. Founded in 1842 as a college for men, it became coeducational in 1972 and has an enrollment of more than 11,000 students. The university offers graduate and undergraduate degrees in arts and letters, sciences, engineering, business administration, architecture, and law. A unique feature of the curriculum is the "Executive M.B.A." program for working professionals. Notre Dame's graduation rate—95 percent—is exceeded only by Harvard, Yale, and Princeton. Community involvement is highly valued at Notre Dame; approximately 80 percent of its students engage in

volunteer work while attending the university. In 2008 Notre Dame was ranked as 19th in the nation among top universities by *U.S. World & News Report.*

Saint Mary's College, sister school of Notre Dame sponsored by the Sister of the Holy Cross, was founded in 1844 and is a women's college with an enrollment of approximately 1,527. Saint Mary's offers undergraduate degrees in 30 major areas of study and has a cooperative engineering degree program with Notre Dame. In 2008 *U.S. News and World Report* ranked Saint Mary's as one of the Top 100 National Liberal Arts Colleges in the country.

Holy Cross College is adjacent to Notre Dame. Holy Cross opened in 1966 as a two-year college; its baccalaureate program debuted in 2003. The college offers two degree programs: Associate of Arts (liberal studies) and Bachelor of Arts. Bachelor's degrees are available in liberal studies, education and theology.

Indiana University South Bend (IUSB), the third largest in the state's eight-university system, enrolls more than 7,500 students and grants associate through master's degrees in more than 100 fields. Certificate programs are also available. IUSB operates a continuing education division that provides evening, weekend, and off-campus instruction. Purdue University Statewide Technology Program at IUSB offers associate degrees in engineering technology and computer technology as well as associate and bachelor degrees in organizational leadership and supervision.

Bethel College, in nearby Mishawaka, is a liberal arts college affiliated with the United Missionary Church; Bethel grants undergraduate and graduate degrees in a wide range of programs including nursing, business administration, education, theology, international studies, and a variety of church ministry related programs.

The South Bend campus of Ivy Tech Community College is one of 23 branches of Ivy Tech statewide. Enrollment is about 5,000. Associate's degrees and certificate programs are available through over 25 academic programs in seven schools. Brown Mackie College South Bend offers bachelor's degrees in business administration, criminal justice, and legal studies. The college also offers associate's degrees in 12 programs and 6 certificate programs.

## Libraries and Research Centers

The St. Joseph County Public Library consists of a main library and eight branches housing nearly 640,000 items, including books, periodical subscriptions, computer software, microfiche, audio- and videotapes, CDs, and art reproductions. Special collections include large type books, genealogical materials, and state documents. The library also maintains a collection of Braille games (including Scrabble and Uno) and a computer with a Braille printer is available for public use. A renovation of the main library's first floor, adding two meeting rooms and a computer training room, was completed in 2003; an expansion of the second floor was completed in 2007. Local colleges and universities maintain campus libraries. Other specialized libraries in the city are associated with hospitals, government agencies, and the Studebaker National Museum.

The 11 libraries of the University of Notre Dame contain a total of about 3 million volumes, over 3 million microform units, 5,850 electronic titles, 25,200 audiovisual items, and 12,100 serial titles. The Hesburgh Library serves as the main campus library. Rare book and special collections include the Edward Gorey Collection, the Rene Descartes Collection, the Pope Paul VI Collection, a Hispanic Caribbean Literature Collection, and rare books on history and liturgy of the Roman Catholic Church. The Schurz Library at Indiana University South Bend is a member of the federal depository library system, with selective materials relating to the second Congressional district. This library also maintains archives relating to the history of the region. Other special collections include the James Lewis Cassaday Theatre Collection and the Annie Belle Boss Papers.

The University of Notre Dame supports dozens of centers conducting research in a wide variety of areas. These include The Center for Research Computing, The W. M. Keck Center for Transgene Research, The Radiation Laboratory, Walther Cancer Research Center, The Interdisciplinary Center for the Study of Biocomplexity, and The Center for Nano Science and Technology, to name a few. Indiana University-South Bend maintains a bureau of business and economic research, and an institute for applied community research.

***Public Library Information:*** St. Joseph County Public Library, 304 S. Main St., South Bend, IN 46601; telephone (574)282-4630; www.sjcpl.lib.in.us

# ■ Health Care

The three major hospitals are Memorial Hospital, St. Joseph Regional Medical Center-South Bend, and St. Joseph Regional Medical Center-Mishawaka. South Bend's first hospital, established by the Sisters of the Holy Cross in 1882, is now known as St. Joseph Regional Medical Center. Some of the features of the South Bend campus are the Women's Center, the Family Birthplace, nationally recognized cancer treatments through its Cancer Institute, accredited pain and rehabilitation programs, and a Mind/Body Medical Institute offering an innovative mind-body approach to medical treatment. The Mishawaka campus has been providing health care since 1910; its features include the Genesis Birth Center, a cardiac catheterization lab which was the first in the area to implement all-digital technology, a Wound Healing Center, an in-house laboratory, and a state-of-the-art radiology department with a new CT scanner and one of only three high-tech X-Ray machines in the United States and the only one in the Midwest. The Mishawaka campus is one of only 20 or so hospitals in the county to follow the Planetree philosophy, a holistic medical approach focusing on patients' mental, emotional, spiritual, as well as physical, well-being.

Memorial Hospital is the region's largest hospital and primary referral center, serving as a 526-bed regional referral center for cardiac, cancer, childbirth, emergency medicine, and rehabilitation services. The Leighton Trauma Center at Memorial is the only Level II trauma center in the region. Features of the hospital's clinical services include a Weight Loss and Bariatric Surgery Center; a Sleep Disorders Center; the innovative Memorial Lighthouse Medical Imaging Center; and the Leighton Heart and Vascular Center. Memorial's parent company, Memorial Health System, consisting of four affiliates—Memorial Hospital, Memorial Health Foundation, Memorial Home Care, and Memorial Medical Group—offers care and service at all levels, including inpatient and home care, medical equipment and supplies, pharmacy services, and occupational health services, as well as primary care physicians and specialists. South Bend's Madison Center provides behavioral and mental health care.

The South Bend Clinic was established in 1916 and based on the model of excellence presented by the Mayo Clinic. South Bend Clinic offers primary and specialized care through 14 locations in northern Indiana, with the main campus in downtown South Bend. The main campus offers a wide array of specialty services, including internal medicine, pediatrics, radiology, allergies, cardiology, dermatology, endocrinology, gastroenterology, general and vascular surgery, rheumatology, oncology, ophthalmology, and physical rehabilitation.

# ■ Recreation

## Sightseeing

South Bend is noted for the University of Notre Dame, for its industrial heritage, and for its municipal parks. A good place to begin a campus tour is at Notre Dame's Eck Visitors' Center, which has historical displays and a 20-minute movie about the university. Notre Dame's golden-domed Main Building is the campus's central symbol; inside, the walls are lined with murals depicting the life of Christopher Columbus by Vatican artist Luigi Gregori. The five-story Victorian building recently received a $58 million renovation, restoring its woodwork, lighting fixtures, and walls. Also on the campus are a reproduction of France's Grotto of Lourdes; the ornate Basilica of the Sacred Heart; the Log Chapel, hand-built by Father Stephen Badin—the first Catholic priest ordained in the U.S.—in 1830; the Snite Museum of Art; and an 11-story library.

Young sports fans will enjoy passing and kicking a football at the College Football Hall of Fame, a 58,000-square-foot museum devoted to every aspect of football—its players, fans, cheerleaders, and bands. The museum features interactive exhibits as well as artifacts, mementos, and photographs. Studebaker Museum traces the history of the Studebaker Company from its days as a maker of horse-drawn carriages to its innovations in the manufacture of automobiles. Among the exhibits is the carriage in which President Lincoln rode to Ford's Theater on the night he was assassinated. The Northern Indiana Center for History includes Copshaholm (The Oliver Mansion), a 38-room stone mansion built in 1895; Worker House, a cottage reflecting working-class homes of the 1930s; History Center, which charts local history through industry, individuals, clothing, and even toys; and *kidsfirst* Children's Museum. The Potawatomi Park Zoo, founded in 1902, is the oldest zoo in the state. The 23-acre zoo is home to 400 animals, including several rare and endangered species such as tigers, red pandas, cotton-top tamarins, snow leopards, and lemurs. Visitors to the South Bend Chocolate Company can tour its factory and explore its chocolate museum. Amish Acres, in nearby Nappanee, IN, is an 80-acre, 19th-century farm that showcases the customs, beliefs, and work habits of the Amish people; featured are 18 restored buildings, craft demonstrations, farm animals, musical theatre, restaurants, and quaint shops.

## Arts and Culture

The South Bend Symphony Orchestra, the Broadway Theater League, Southold Dance, and other community arts groups perform at the Morris Performing Arts Center, Indiana's oldest historic theater, built in 1922. The center also hosts a variety of national concert tours. The Symphony's concert season includes Masterworks, pops, chamber music, and a holiday concert. Special family concerts are offered as well. Broadway Theatre League presents nationally-touring Broadway shows in a season that runs between June and September. Southold Dance offers performances ranging from classic ballet to modern dance; the Nutcracker is a yearly favorite. The South Bend Civic Theatre is the largest community theatre in the state, as measured by operating budget, yearly productions, and membership; it presents a 16-play season, primarily at The Firehouse, a historic landmark.

The Snite Museum of Art, on the Notre Dame campus, holds more than 21,000 pieces in its permanent collection, featuring Rembrandt etchings, 19th-century French art, Old Master and 19th-century drawings, 19th-century European photographs, Mestrovic sculpture and drawings, Olmec and Preclassic Mesoamerican art, 20th-century art, Northern Native American art, and decorative and design arts. The South Bend Regional Museum of Art features a permanent collection focusing on American—especially Indiana—art, from the 19th

century through the present. The Hannah Lindahl Children's museum gives young people a close-up, hands-on look at how life was lived long ago.

There are several art galleries and studios in the city, including Circa Arts gallery, the Notre Dame Downtown Crossroads Gallery, and The Spurious Fugitive.

## Festivals and Holidays

South Bend's parks are the location for many of the city's festivals and special events. A major event at Leeper Park is an art fair the last weekend in June. Rum Village Park hosts Old Fashioned Summer, featuring an antique car show, entertainment, a Native American program and activities, square dancing, trail activities, and more. South Bend's Summer in the City Festival, formerly known as the Ethnic Festival, features entertainment, food, rides, and a parade. Also in June, Merrifield Park, in nearby Mishawaka, hosts Summerfest, which features food, music, craft booths, and a free evening concert. St. Patrick's Park presents a number of events, including the Firefly Festival, an outdoor music, theater, and dance program on weekends from mid-June through early August; the Blues and Ribs Fest in August; and Kee-Boon-Mein-Kaa, a traditional Indian pow wow featuring food, dancing, demonstrations, and crafts, in September. The College Football Hall of Fame Enshrinement Festival takes place in July.

***Arts and Culture Information:*** ArtsEverywhere. com, Community Foundation of St. Joseph County, P.O. Box 837, 205 W. Jefferson Blvd., Ste. 400, South Bend, IN 46624; telephone (574)232-0041; www.artsevery-where.com

## Sports for the Spectator

The University of Notre Dame Fighting Irish football team is among the most famous college teams in the world. Legendary coach Knute Rockne began the school's success in the 1920s with the "Four Horsemen" and "Seven Mules." Throughout Notre Dame's history, the Fighting Irish have been known for great players, outstanding coaches, and a schedule of games against the nation's best football teams. The home schedule is played on Saturday afternoons in the fall in Notre Dame Stadium. The Fighting Irish also field competitive teams in basketball and other sports.

The Stanley Coveleski Regional Stadium is the home field of South Bend's Class A minor league franchise baseball team, the Silver Hawks, who compete in the Midwest League in a season that runs from April to September.

## Sports for the Participant

St. Joseph County offers numerous parks and a nature preserve for year-round outdoor fun. Rum Village Park features a nature center and hiking and nature trails, while George Wilson Park offers a disc golf course considered among the best in the country. St. Patrick's Park and Bendix Woods offer cross-country skiing. The South

Bend-Mishawaka area boasts ten highly regarded golf courses, such as Blackthorn, which has been highly ranked by *Golf Digest*. The city itself sponsors three golf courses. South Bend's biggest recreational attraction is East Race Waterway, which offers kayaking and white-water rafting in the heart of downtown. The East Race Waterway is the first artificial whitewater course in North America and one of six in the world. It hosts world-class whitewater slaloms and United States Olympic Trials.

An exercise trail borders the waterway and is part of a five-mile trail that runs through the city's downtown parks and along the St. Joseph River. The South Bend Parks and Recreation Department maintain 75 local parks. The Sunburst Marathon in June offers a course from the College Football Hall of Fame to the 50-yard line of the Notre Dame Stadium.

### Shopping and Dining

South Bend-Mishawaka offers shopping opportunities ranging from enclosed malls to many small independent specialty shops. A popular stop is the Farmer's Market in South Bend, which features wares ranging from fresh produce and baked goods to flowers, pottery, hand-crafted jewelry, and antiques. Town and Country Shopping Plaza offers eclectic shops. One unique downtown spot is Sit and Knit, a Yarn Café that offers free lattes and cappuccinos to knitters. Saigon Market on west Colfax offers a variety of specialty Asian and African foods. Nearby Mishawaka boasts the second-largest retail area in the state, with its large University Park Mall, as well as numerous shops and strip malls along the Grape Road/Main Street corridor.

Northern Indiana is known for such regional food specialties as frog legs, pan-fried perch, and relishes that include bean salad, cabbage salad, and pickled beets. Other popular dining options include sushi, barbeque, pasta, prime rib, and deli sandwiches. South Bend features unique fine dining options in atmospheric settings, including Tippecanoe Place, in the restored 1888 Studebaker Mansion, resembling a feudal castle; and the Carriage House, in a converted 1850s church. Amish Acres in nearby Nappanee and Das Dutchman Essenhaus in Middlebury offer home-style Amish cooking. For a quick afternoon snack, Howard Park General Store on East Jefferson has an old-fashioned soda fountain.

*Visitor Information:* South Bend/Mishawaka Convention and Visitors Bureau, Commerce Center, 401 E. Colfax Ave., Ste. 310, South Bend, IN 46634; telephone (800)519-0577; www.livethelegends.org

## ■ Convention Facilities

South Bend/Mishawaka offers excellent meeting facilities and the community has nearly 4,000 hotel rooms. The principal meeting site in South Bend is the Century Center, situated on an 11-acre downtown riverfront park with direct access to major hotels and five miles from South Bend Regional Airport. Integrated with theaters, parks, art galleries, and a museum, the Century Center complex consists of three convention and exhibition halls, a great hall, a ballroom, a thrust-stage theater, a recital hall, and suites. Its convention and exhibition halls offer a total of 37,000 square feet of unobstructed meeting and exhibit space. The great hall, a multipurpose courtyard overlooking the white water rapids, is suitable for banquets, receptions, dinner dances, and exhibitions. The ballroom offers nearly 6,600 square feet of space suitable for meetings and banquets. Bendix Theatre has seating for 718 and is suitable for meetings, shows, and performances. The recital hall, with seating for 166, is suitable for breakout sessions and performances. The suites consist of up to 11 variable-sized rooms.

The Morris Performing Arts Center, the oldest theater in Indiana, features an auditorium, restored and renovated in 2000, that can accommodate more than 2,500 attendees for lectures, meetings, and conferences. Morris also houses the lavish Palais Royale ballroom which, restored to its 1923 grandeur in 2002, is considered the city's premier banquet facility. Additional convention facilities can be found on the University of Notre Dame campus at the Athletic and Convocation Center and the Center for Continuing Education.

*Convention Information:* South Bend/Mishawaka Convention and Visitors Bureau, Commerce Center, 401 E. Colfax Ave., Ste. 310, South Bend, IN 46634; telephone (800)519-0577; www.livethelegends.org

## ■ Transportation

### Approaching the City

Six commercial airlines schedule direct and connecting flights into South Bend at the South Bend Regional Airport from all major United States cities and points abroad. The airport, which is the second-busiest in Indiana, is the only one in the nation to have developed a multimodal transportation center offering air, intercity rail, and interstate bus service at one convenient location. The closest major airports are Chicago Midway Airport, about 97 miles away; Ft. Wayne International Airport, about 100 miles away; and Chicago O'Hare International in Chicago, about 115 miles away.

Passenger rail transportation is available by Amtrak from Boston, New York, and Chicago. Greyhound offers daily service to South Bend Regional Airport from Chicago, Detroit, Indianapolis, and Toledo. The Northern Indiana Commuter Transportation District operates the South Shore Line, a 90 mile electric railway that can speed commuters through from South Bend Regional Airport to Millennium Station in Chicago.

An efficient highway system—including Interstate 80/90 (the Indiana Toll Road) running east/west; U.S. 6, U.S. 20, and U.S. 31; and State Routes 2, 4, 23, 104, 331, and 933—affords access into the South Bend metropolitan area.

## Traveling in the City

South Bend is laid out on a grid system, the main thoroughfares within the city being north-south Main Street and Michigan Street (U.S. 31) and east-west Colfax Avenue (U.S. 20).

Transpo, the municipal bus service, schedules regular routes in both South Bend and Mishawaka. The Transpo Trolley offers special service downtown. Transpo Access is available for the elderly and handicapped.

# ■ Communications

## Newspapers

The major South Bend daily newspaper is the *South Bend Tribune,* which has a circulation of more than 63,000. Other South Bend publications include the weekly *Tri-County News, Tribune Business Weekly,* and the monthly magazine *Culture Wars,* which explores issues from the point of view of the Catholic Church. *Michiana Woman* is a bimonthly newspaper published in South Bend. The *Irish Sports Report* is a specialty weekly. *Scholastics,* published at the University of Notre Dame, is the oldest college publication in the country. Other South Bend magazines include *About Business Magazine, IN Michiana,* and *Inside Granger.*

## Television and Radio

South Bend, Mishawaka, and neighboring communities receive broadcasts from five area-based television stations and have access to several Chicago and Elkhart stations, as well as cable. There are 13 AM and FM radio stations broadcasting from South Bend, serving area listeners with music, news and information, and religious programming. The University of Notre Dame has its own radio station.

*Media Information:* *South Bend Tribune,* 225 W. Colfax Ave., South Bend, IN 46626; telephone (574) 235-6161; www.southbendtribune.com

## South Bend Online

Chamber of Commerce of St. Joseph County. Available www.sjchamber.org

South Bend Government. Available www .southbendin.gov

South Bend/Mishawaka Convention and Visitors Bureau. Available www.livethelegends.org

*South Bend Tribune.* Available www .southbendtribune.com

St. Joseph County Public Library. Available www .sjcpl.lib.in.us

BIBLIOGRAPHY

Danielson, Kay Marnon, *South Bend Indiana* (Arcadia Publishing, 2001)

Szymarek, Gene, *Cedar Grove Cemetery Inscriptions So. Bend Indiana* (Heritage Books, 1987)

# Iowa

# The State in Brief

**Nickname:** Hawkeye State

**Motto:** Our liberties we prize and our rights we will maintain

**Flower:** Wild rose

**Bird:** Eastern goldfinch

**Area:** 56,271 square miles (2000; U.S. rank 26th)

**Elevation:** Ranges from 480 feet to 1,670 feet above sea level

**Climate:** Continental, with extremes in temperature (30 degrees in winter, 100 degrees in summer)

**Admitted to Union:** December 28, 1846

**Capital:** Des Moines

**Head Official:** Governor Chet Culver (D) (until 2010)

**Population**

    **1980:** 2,914,000
    **1990:** 2,795,000
    **2000:** 2,926,382
    **2006 estimate:** 2,982,085
    **Percent change, 1990–2000:** 5.4%
    **U.S. rank in 2006:** 30th
    **Percent of residents born in state:** 72.31% (2006)
    **Density:** 53.1 people per square mile (2006)
    **2006 FBI Crime Index Total:** 92,034

**Racial and Ethnic Characteristics (2006)**

    **White:** 2,772,535
    **Black or African American:** 67,297
    **American Indian and Alaska Native:** 8,424
    **Asian:** 45,647
    **Native Hawaiian and Pacific Islander:** 370
    **Hispanic or Latino (may be of any race):** 112,987
    **Other:** 46,605

**Age Characteristics (2006)**

    **Population under 5 years old:** 191,127
    **Population 5 to 19 years old:** 617,280
    **Percent of population 65 years and over:** 14.6%
    **Median age:** 37.8

**Vital Statistics**

    **Total number of births (2006):** 39,228
    **Total number of deaths (2006):** 28,627
    **AIDS cases reported through 2005:** 1,656

**Economy**

    **Major industries:** Manufacturing; agriculture; finance, insurance, and real estate; trade; services
    **Unemployment rate (2006):** 6.9%
    **Per capita income (2006):** $23,115
    **Median household income (2006):** $44,491
    **Percentage of persons below poverty level (2006):** 11.0%
    **Income tax rate:** 0.36% to 8.98%
    **Sales tax rate:** 5.0%

# Cedar Rapids

## ■ The City in Brief

**Founded:** 1841 (incorporated 1849)

**Head Official:** Mayor Kay Halloran (since 2006)

**City Population**
>   1980: 110,243
>   1990: 108,772
>   2000: 120,758
>   2006 estimate: 124,417
>   Percent change, 1990–2000: 10.9%
>   U.S. rank in 1980: 141st
>   U.S. rank in 1990: 174th
>   U.S. rank in 2000: 181st (State rank: 2nd)

**Metropolitan Area Population**
>   1980: 169,775
>   1990: 168,767
>   2000: 191,701
>   2006 estimate: 249,320
>   Percent change, 1990–2000: 13.6%
>   U.S. rank in 1980: Not available
>   U.S. rank in 1990: Not available
>   U.S. rank in 2000: 173rd

**Area:** 63 square miles (2000)

**Elevation:** 733 feet above sea level

**Average Annual Temperature:** 49.6° F

**Average Annual Precipitation:** 36.39 inches of rain, 34.4 inches of snow

**Major Economic Sectors:** services, wholesale and retail trade, government

**Unemployment Rate:** 3.6% (June 2007)

**Per Capita Income:** $25,029 (2005)

**2005 FBI Crime Index Property:** 6,391

**2005 FBI Crime Index Violent:** 417

**Major Colleges and Universities:** Coe College; Mount Mercy College

**Daily Newspaper:** *Cedar Rapids Gazette*

## ■ Introduction

Cedar Rapids preserves a small-town atmosphere in a metropolitan setting. The industrial and cultural center of eastern Iowa, the city has undergone growth and development as it gains prominence in high-technology industries and in export trade. Expansion has been carefully monitored by civic leaders, however, so that international business may be conducted at an unhurried pace and residents may maintain their midwestern traditions. Cedar Rapids is the seat of Linn County and adjoins the city of Marion.

## ■ Geography and Climate

Cedar Rapids is situated on the Cedar River, which flows through the city, on rolling terrain in eastern Iowa. The surrounding area is laced with rivers and lakes and dotted with limestone bluffs. The climate consists of four distinct seasons, with warm days and cool nights in spring and autumn.

**Area:** 63 square miles (2000)

**Elevation:** 733 feet above sea level

**Average Temperature:** 49.6° F

**Average Annual Precipitation:** 36.39 inches of rain; 34.4 inches of snow

# ■ History

## Cedar River Supports Settlement

The Sac and the Fox, Native American tribes, hunted and trapped along the Cedar River before the arrival of Osgood Shepherd, the area's first permanent settler of European descent. Shepherd lived in a cabin on the river's east side in 1838 at what is now the location of First Avenue and First Street. A survey was made in 1841 and the newly formed town was named Rapids City after the rapids on the Cedar River; the name was changed to Cedar Rapids in 1848. In the early 1840s a dam was built across the river to provide power for the grist and lumber industries. Cedar Rapids was incorporated as a city in 1849; the town of Kingston, located on the west side of the river, was annexed to Cedar Rapids in 1870.

The early history of Cedar Rapids was highlighted by colorful characters and events. An island—now named Municipal Island—in the channel of the Cedar River was until 1851 the headquarters of the Shepherd gang, notorious horse thieves. Local residents built the steamer *The Cedar Rapids* in 1858 and used it for round trips to St. Louis; however, a collision on the Mississippi River and the arrival of the railroad ended river transportation.

Czechoslovakians, known as Bohemians, have made lasting contributions to the Cedar Rapids community. Czechs began arriving in 1852 to work in local packing plants, and soon a "Little Bohemia" was established in the southwest sector of the city (it is now known as "Czech Village"). Josef Sosel, the first Czech lawyer in the United States, was smuggled out of his native country in a barrel after he was accused of revolutionary activities; Sosel settled in Cedar Rapids, where he played a prominent role in the Czech community. In 1869 Czechs established The Reading Society, which evolved into a Little Theater movement, as well as the Light Guard Band. The Czech-language *Cedar Rapids Listy* began publication in 1906.

## Industry and Arts Flourish

The economic growth of Cedar Rapids was spurred in 1871 with the arrival, from Ireland, of T. M. Sinclair, who established one of the nation's largest meatpacking companies, T. M. Sinclair Company. Some other major local industries that date from the same era are Cherry-Burrell and the world's largest cereal mill, Quaker Oats. Cultural development was simultaneous with economic expansion, as many Cedar Rapids arts and educational institutions were formed during this period. Greene's Opera House was dedicated in 1880, the same year the Cedar Rapids Business College opened its doors. Among the school's first faculty members was Austin Palmer, the inventor of the Palmer Method of Penmanship.

For more than 60 years, city fathers challenged nearby Marion for designation as the county seat; in 1919, voters endorsed a move to Cedar Rapids. The county courthouse and the Memorial Building, dedicated in 1928 to Americans who have fought in the nation's wars, were built on Municipal Island. Grant Wood, the Iowa artist, designed the 20-foot by 24-foot stained glass window in the Memorial Building and supervised its construction in Munich, Germany.

The artistry of Wood, one of the leading practitioners of Midwestern regionalism, is felt throughout the city. Wood grew up in Cedar Rapids and taught in the community junior high school; after studying in France he returned to the city and, supported by a local patron, set up a studio. Wood's "American Gothic" caused a sensation in the art world for its uncompromising realism when it was unveiled in 1930. Wood's daring work led to success and he was hired in 1934 to teach art at the University of Iowa.

## Telecommunications Help Shape City's Future

Private enterprise, a principal force in the city's economic history, continued to be important during the first half of the twentieth century. Another Cedar Rapids native, Arthur Collins, started Collins Radio Company with eight employees during the Great Depression; the small electronics firm soon established a reputation as a leader in the industrial radio business. The company supplied electronic equipment to all branches of the armed services during World War II. Collins Radio, a major employer in the Cedar Rapids area, became a part of Rockwell Collins in 1973. Today the Cedar Rapids metropolitan area is a telecommunications and transportation center, performing an important role in the nation's economy. The Cedar Rapids "Technology Corridor" is one of the leading centers in the country for the defense electronics industry. The city has also developed a reputation as a cultural and artistic hub, with a thriving theater community and a wealth of sports and recreational activities for all. Known as the "City of Five Seasons," Cedar Rapids residents profess to have a quality of life that allows for the addition of a fifth season—one to enjoy the community and the other four seasons.

***Historical Information:*** The Carl and Mary Koehler History Center, 615 1st Avenue SE, Cedar Rapids, IA 52401; telephone (319)362-1501

# ■ Population Profile

## Metropolitan Area Residents

    1980: 169,775
    1990: 168,767

*Courtesy of the Cedar Rapids Area Convention & Visitors Bureau. Reproduced by permission.*

2000: 191,701
2006 estimate: 249,320
Percent change, 1990–2000: 13.6%
U.S. rank in 1980: Not available
U.S. rank in 1990: Not available
U.S. rank in 2000: 173rd

**City Residents**

1980: 110,243
1990: 108,772
2000: 120,758
2006 estimate: 124,417
Percent change, 1990–2000: 10.9%
U.S. rank in 1980: 141st
U.S. rank in 1990: 174th
U.S. rank in 2000: 181st (State rank: 2nd)

**Density:** 1,912.6 people per square mile (2000)

**Racial and ethnic characteristics (2005)**

White: 108,961
Black: 5,917
American Indian and Alaska Native: 0
Asian: 2,068
Native Hawaiian and Pacific Islander: 0

Hispanic or Latino (may be of any race):
2,694
Other: 912

**Percent of residents born in state:** 73.7%
(2000)

**Age characteristics (2005)**

Population under 5 years old: 8,722
Population 5 to 9 years old: 7,179
Population 10 to 14 years old: 8,499
Population 15 to 19 years old: 7,279
Population 20 to 24 years old: 7,816
Population 25 to 34 years old: 18,729
Population 35 to 44 years old: 17,554
Population 45 to 54 years old: 17,507
Population 55 to 59 years old: 6,990
Population 60 to 64 years old: 4,729
Population 65 to 74 years old: 7,169
Population 75 to 84 years old: 6,157
Population 85 years and older: 1,340
Median age: 36.1 years

**Births (2006, MSA)**

Total number: 3,341

**Deaths (2006, MSA)**

Total number: 2,015

**Money income (2005)**

Per capita income: $25,029
Median household income: $47,357
Total households: 51,850

**Number of households with income of . . .**

less than $10,000: 4,979
$10,000 to $14,999: 3,396
$15,000 to $24,999: 6,048
$25,000 to $34,999: 5,978
$35,000 to $49,999: 7,038
$50,000 to $74,999: 12,019
$75,000 to $99,999: 5,765
$100,000 to $149,999: 4,838
$150,000 to $199,999: 794
$200,000 or more: 995

**Percent of families below poverty level:** 11.8% (2005)

**2005 FBI Crime Index Property:** 6,391

**2005 FBI Crime Index Violent:** 417

# ■ Municipal Government

In 2005 Cedar Rapids switched to a Home Rule form of government. Under Home Rule, the city is governed by a part-time City Council and the City's daily affairs are run by the City Manager. The council consists of eight members plus a mayor who is elected at-large.

**Head Official:** Mayor Kay Halloran (since 2006; current term expires 2009)

**Total Number of City Employees:** 1,248 full-time (2007)

*City Information:* City of Cedar Rapids, 51 First Avenue Bridge, Cedar Rapids, IA 52401; telephone (319)286-5000

# ■ Economy

## Major Industries and Commercial Activity

In 2006 Iowa was named number one in the Midwest for the fastest growing economy by the Bureau of Economic Analysis and number three in the nation for lowest cost of doing business by the Milken Institute. The economy of Cedar Rapids has traditionally been based on the manufacture and processing of agricultural and food products, steel fabricating, tool and die making, and radios and electronics. Manufacturing, which continues to be an important economic sector, has been augmented by high-technology industries and transportation. The Cedar Rapids-Iowa City "Technology Corridor" is one of the leading centers in the country for the defense electronics industry; the fastest-growing segment of the metropolitan area economy is telecommunications and telemarketing. Advanced research and development laboratories, an educated and productive labor force, and a mid-continent location are increasingly attracting new business and industry to Cedar Rapids.

The city's association with high technology dates to the early years of Collins Radio Company. Today, Collins is part of Rockwell Collins, ranked as the largest private employer in the Cedar Rapids-Iowa City region. The company provides aviation electronic and communication technology for government, aircraft manufacturers, and hundreds of airline customers. In fact, the company's aircraft electronics are used in almost every airline in the world. Additionally, Rockwell Collins' communication systems transmit almost 70 percent of all U.S. and allied military airborne communication.

In recent years, a number of local public and private organizations joined together to help develop the "Technology Corridor." This hub for technology, life science, biotechnology, and medical supply companies is located throughout 12 communities in Johnson and Linn Counties. Its location near a number of colleges and universities enables Corridor companies to easily access education, training, research, and development. Local firms provide a variety of services such as electronic design and consultation, systems planning, equipment manufacturing, and telemarketing.

While Cedar Rapids has seen tremendous growth in technology, the city continues to succeed in attracting agricultural and food processing manufacturers. It is home to more than 275 different manufacturing plants, including Quaker Food and Beverages, which runs the world's largest cereal milling plant. Other top manufacturing employers include Rockwell Collins, Inc., Whirlpool Corporation, General Mills, Inc., and H.J. Heinz Company.

**Items and goods produced:** cereal, syrup, sugar, dairy, mining, road machinery, boxboard and containers, automotive tools and machinery, radio electronics and avionics equipment, oil burners, furniture, pumps, gravel crushers, cranes, snow plows, electric-powered shovels, trailer parts, candy, office and drainage equipment, rubber goods, plastic bags, recycled corrugated cardboard, copper alloy and plastic molding, medical and chemical products, plumbing supplies, auto parts and toys, furnaces, livestock feed, structural steel, compressed gas, pharmaceuticals, avionics and earth-moving equipment, telecommunications equipment, home appliances

## Incentive Programs—New and Existing Companies

*Local programs:* The Cedar Rapids Area Chamber of Commerce and its divisions are active in implementing growth plans, helping existing businesses, and recruiting companies from throughout the world. Its economic development division, Priority One, provides businesses with demographics and trade figures, site location assistance, and workforce development.

*State programs:* Part of the private-public partnership Cedar Rapids fosters is evident in such state programs as certain property tax exemptions, job training, low-interest loans and forgivable loans for business development, tax abatements on new research and manufacturing facilities, and state tax credits for new job creation. In addition, no sales or use taxes are assessed on equipment or computers and open port warehousing is available. The Iowa Values Fund, established in 2006, offers concentrated assistance to businesses operating in the following sectors: the life sciences, advanced manufacturing, and information solutions.

*Job training programs:* Cedar Rapids area businesses can take advantage of the Iowa Industrial New Jobs Training Program administered by Kirkwood Community College, which provides education and training for new employees of new and expanding companies at little or no cost. The Community Economic Betterment Account (CEBA) program provides financial assistance to companies that create new employment opportunities, keep existing jobs, and make new capital investment in Iowa.

## Development Projects

In 2007 the Priority One and the Iowa City Area Development Group had helped bring 6,000 new jobs and $1.464 billion in capital investment to the Technology Corridor since 2003. Projects either underway or completed in this expansion include: a U.S. Cellular expansion of its engineering and customer call center, adding 15,000 square feet and 100 new jobs; a new $10 million corporate headquarters and distribution center for Iowa Glass Co., and a dietary fiber production facility in the city built by German fiber manufacturer J. Rettenmaier & Söhne

In 2007 city planners were at work on the "Downtown Shared Vision Plan," a comprehensive, long term improvement plan for downtown Cedar Rapids. The project includes a proposed Intermodal Transportation Facility at Second Street and Seventh Avenue SE and a riverfront trail near Mays Island. Also in 2007 Legends Sport Bar and Entertainment Center opened as the first sidewalk cafe in downtown Cedar Rapids.

*Economic Development Information:* Priority One, Economic Development Division, Cedar Rapids Area Chamber of Commerce, 424 First Avenue NE, Cedar Rapids, IA 52401; telephone (319)398-5317; email infodesk@priority1.com

## Commercial Shipping

A central location, efficient access, and low supply and distribution costs have contributed to the development of Cedar Rapids as a primary transportation hub in the Midwest. The city is at the center of the NAFTA corridor, and international connections are readily accessible. Additionally, Eastern Iowa Airport is a designated Foreign Trade Zone. There are several air cargo carriers operating out of the airport: Airborne Express, Ameriflight (DHL), Federal Express, and United Parcel Service. The airport shipped 23,853 tons of mail, freight and baggage in 2006. A leader in exporting goods, Cedar Rapids works closely with top importers in Canada, Japan, Mexico, Germany and France. Iowa is the only state bordered by two navigable rivers, and many area exports leave via water.

Cedar Rapids's rail system also provides transportation services to many businesses. The Union Pacific East-West mainline travels through the city, as well as the Canadian National Railway and the Cedar Rapids and Iowa City Railway. The lines interchange with a number of major national airlines serving all of North America. In addition, Cedar Rapids is the only area able to serve Minneapolis, Chicago, St. Louis, and Omaha by freight carrier within a one-day round trip. More than 34 motor freight carriers with terminals located in the area provide interstate, intrastate and local freight services.

## Labor Force and Employment Outlook

With an educated, available, and skilled workforce, Cedar Rapids maintains a productivity rate that is substantially above the national average. Absenteeism is less than 1 percent and industrial turnover is less than 1.5 percent. Area workers produce 20 percent more than the average American worker and score high in rankings of annual value added per production worker. With approximately 70 percent of the workforce having education beyond high school, and nearly half boasting an undergraduate degree or higher, local businesses have a large pool of educated workers to choose from. And in order to further train those workers, Cedar Rapids area businesses can take advantage of the Iowa Industrial New Jobs Training Program, which provides education and training for new employees of new and expanding companies at little or no cost. The program is administered by Kirkwood Community College.

In recent years Cedar Rapids's workforce has come to reflect its increasingly diversified economy. Non-manufacturing employment in the area increased from 65,460 in 1984 to 130,000 in 2004. In 2007 the unemployment rate stood at 3.8 percent, below the national average and down from ten year highs nearing 6 percent in 2003.

The following is a summary of data regarding the Cedar Rapids metropolitan area labor force, 2006 annual averages.

**Size of nonagricultural labor force:** 134,400

**Number of workers employed in** ...

    construction and mining: 7,700
    manufacturing: 21,000
    trade, transportation and utilities: 29,700
    information: 5,100
    financial activities: 9,900
    professional and business services: 12,200
    educational and health services: 16,500
    leisure and hospitality: 11,200
    other services: 5,300
    government: 15,700

**Average hourly earnings of production workers employed in manufacturing:** Not available

**Unemployment rate:** 3.6% (June 2007)

| *Largest employers (2007)* | *Number of employees* |
|---|---|
| University of Iowa | 16,495 |
| Rockwell Collins, Inc. | 7,300 |
| University of Iowa Hospitals and Clinics | 7,113 |
| Hy-Vee Food Stores | 2,971 |
| Cedar Rapids Community School District | 2,800 |
| AEGON USA, Inc. | 2,600 |
| St. Luke's Hospital | 2,400 |
| Maytag Appliances | 2,200 |
| Mercy Medical Center | 2,060 |
| MCI | 1,528 |

## Cost of Living

Cedar Rapids's property taxes are the second-lowest of the state's eight largest cities with more than 50,000 people.

The following is a summary of data regarding several key cost of living factors in the Cedar Rapids area.

**2007 (1st quarter) ACCRA Average House Price:** $251,900

**2007 (1st quarter) ACCRA Cost of Living Index:** 92.9

**State income tax rate:** 0.36% to 8.98%

**State sales tax rate:** 5.0%

**Local income tax rate:** None

**Local sales tax rate:** None

**Property tax rate:** $34.50 per $1,000 of assessed valuation for properties within the Cedar Rapids Community School District; 51.6676% of the assessed value is subject to the property tax rate; therefore, a $100,000 house would be taxed as if it were valued at $51,667

***Economic Information:*** Cedar Rapids Area Chamber of Commerce, 424 First Avenue NE, Cedar Rapids, IA 52401; telephone (319)398-5317.

# ■ Education and Research

### Elementary and Secondary Schools

The Cedar Rapids Community School District is the second-largest of Iowa's public school systems, with an enrollment of 17,840 students. The average composite ACT score for Iowa high school students is 22.0, ranking Iowa second in the nation; Cedar Rapids's average score is 23.5. Kennedy High School is the only public high school in Iowa to offer a Chinese Language Program. In 2007 the city began a program to partner education with local businesses, called The Corridor STEM (science, technology, engineering, and math) Initiative. That same year, the district was working through a multi-year, $52 million facilities improvement plan.

The following is a summary of data regarding the Cedar Rapids Community Schools as of the 2005–2006 school year.

**Total enrollment:** 17,837

**Number of facilities**

    elementary schools: 23
    junior high/middle schools: 6
    senior high schools: 3
    other: 1

**Student/teacher ratio:** 14.3:1

**Teacher salaries (2005–06)**

    elementary median: $33,120
    junior high/middle median: $38,100
    secondary median: $34,370

**Funding per pupil:** $7,478

There are a number of private schools in greater Cedar Rapids. Catholic schools in the metropolitan area enroll nearly 3,000 students.

***Public Schools Information:*** Cedar Rapids Community Schools, Community Relations, 346 Second Avenue SW, Cedar Rapids, IA 52404; telephone (319)558-2124

### Colleges and Universities

Six institutions of higher learning are located in the Cedar Rapids area. Coe College, Mount Mercy College, and Cornell College are all four-year, private, liberal arts colleges. Coe College, founded in 1851, offers 40 degree choices and small class size, with an enrollment of 1,300 students from 33 states and 15 countries. Mount Mercy College was founded by the Sisters of Mercy and offers 35 majors, with 1,482 students in 2007. All new full-time freshmen receive some form of institutionally-funded financial aid, and in 2006-2007 nearly $6 million in scholarships were awarded. Cornell College, founded in 1853, has an enrollment of just over 1,200 students, and is ranked in the top 7 percent of the nation's colleges and universities. The student faculty ratio is 11:1. It was featured in the book *40 Colleges that Change Lives.*

In nearby Iowa City, the University of Iowa offers 100 undergraduate degree programs, 110 graduate degree programs and 74 doctorate degree programs. Its medical, dental, law, pharmacy, and business colleges are nationally recognized. The school is composed of eleven colleges and has an annual enrollment of approximately 29,000. The University of Iowa Education and Conference Center is located in downtown Cedar Rapids.

Kirkwood Community College provides around one hundred vocational/technical, arts and sciences, and adult continuing education programs. Full-time enrollment tops 15,000 students. Hamilton Business College is the oldest business college in Iowa, offering one year diplomas and two year associate degree programs.

### Libraries and Research Centers

The Cedar Rapids Public Library operates an architecturally impressive main facility as well as another branch on the west side of the city. It houses an up-to-date collection and a diverse array of services in comfortable surroundings. The library computer system, CD-ROM and Internet stations make information retrieval easy and convenient. The library offers programs for all ages, including story times, crafts, puppet and magic shows, author lectures, readings, demonstrations, and discussions. In 2005, 1,086,882 items were circulated and 576,797 people visited the libraries.

Cedar Rapids is also served by the Coe College and Kirkwood Community College libraries. Among special libraries are the National Czech and Slovak Museum and Library, which collects published and unpublished resources by and about the Czech and Slovak peoples, and the Iowa Masonic Library, which contains 100,000 volumes of reference materials and a collection of colonial, Native American, and foreign exhibits.

The University of Iowa Libraries house more than 4 million volumes and more than 40,000 serials, making it the 18th largest research collection in the country and the largest in Iowa. The university's law library has been ranked one of the top five law libraries in the nation.

***Public Library Information:*** Cedar Rapids Public Library, 500 First Street SE, Cedar Rapids, IA 52401; telephone (319)398-5123

## ■ Health Care

Two major medical centers serve Cedar Rapids: Mercy Medical Center and St. Luke's Hospital, both of which have been recognized to be among the 100 top orthopedic hospitals in the United States. St. Luke's Hospital, with its 560 beds, specializes in cardiac care, behavioral health, obstetrics, rehabilitation, pediatrics, and surgery. In both 2004 and 2005, the hospital received Solucient's "100 Top Hospitals" award. It is the only facility in the area that performs open-heart procedures. In 2000, St. Luke's opened the area's largest ambulatory surgery unit in an effort to make outpatient procedures more convenient for patients and medical staff.

Mercy Medical Center's facilities include the Mercy Cancer Center, which participates in National Cancer Institute clinical research programs. In 2007 Mount Mercy College and Mercy Medical Center celebrated the one hundreth anniversary of their joint nursing program, "Mercy Nursing." In 2002 Mercy built the J. Edward Lundy Pavilion, a 170,000-square-foot facility which houses the Katz Cardiovascular Center, Mercy Surgical Services, Women's Center, and Birthplace obstetrical unit. The health care needs of area residents are also attended to at the University of Iowa Hospital and Clinics, one of the nation's largest teaching hospitals, located approximately 25 minutes away.

***Health Care Information:*** St. Luke's Hospital, 1026 A Avenue NE, Cedar Rapids, IA 52406; telephone (319) 369-7211. Mercy Medical Center, 710 Tenth Street SE, Cedar Rapids, IA 52403; telephone (319)398-6011

## ■ Recreation

### Sightseeing

A trip to Cedar Rapids might include a visit to Brucemore Mansion and Gardens, which is a National Trust Historic Site. A 21-room Queen Anne-style mansion on a 26-acre estate, Brucemore is the ancestral home of three prominent families who used it as a center for culture and arts. Built in 1884, it is now used for a variety of cultural events, including dance and drama performance, historical tours, garden walks, lectures, workshops, and educational programs.

The National Czech & Slovak Museum & Library preserve the city's ethnic heritage; they offer two exhibit galleries that focus on Czech and Slovak history and culture. In the area downtown along the Cedar River known as The Czech Village, shops, bakeries, and stores feature authentic crafts and foods. The Science Station, housed in a refurbished brick 1917 fire station, offers hands-on science and technology exhibits for children and adults. In 2001 the McLeod/Busse IMAX Dome Theatre was added to the property, offering science and nature themed movies on a six-story wraparound screen.

The Iowa Equestrian Center at Kirkwood Community College is one of Cedar Rapids's newest attractions, and the state's most comprehensive facilities for horse shows, workshops, programs, and equestrian events. It has indoor and outdoor arenas and facilities for over 200 horses.

Several points of interest are within driving distance of Cedar Rapids. The Amana Colonies, 20 minutes south of the city, is one of Iowa's most popular tourist attractions. It is composed of seven villages first settled in 1855 by German immigrants searching for religious freedom. Today, the Colonies are home to furniture stores, wineries, bakeries, and German restaurants run by the settlers' descendents. The Herbert Hoover Presidential Library and National Historic Site is in West Branch, 25 miles from Cedar Rapids. Attractions there include the presidential library and museum, a Quaker meeting house, a blacksmith shop, Hoover's birthplace, and Hoover's grave site.

## Arts and Culture

An important part of cultural life in Cedar Rapids is the Museum of Art, with 5,000 works of art under its roof. The museum houses the world's largest collection of works by Grant Wood, Marvin Cone, and Mauricio Lasansky. They also have strong collections of early twentieth century paintings, Malvina Hoffman sculptures, and Regionalist art from the 1930s and 1940s. In 2003 Cedar Rapids also became home to the African American Historical Museum and Cultural Center of Iowa. This building features exhibits on Africa, the nation, and Iowa, and holds community and educational programs.

The city's cultural community presents a variety of concerts and shows and hosts visiting international performance groups. The renovated Paramount Theatre for the Performing Arts, with a hall of mirrors and Broadway-style marquee, is the home of the Cedar Rapids Symphony Orchestra. The symphony performs four concert series: Classics, Pops, Chamber, and Discovery Family. The Cedar Rapids Opera Theatre performs two to three operas per season. Past performances have included *Pirates of Penzance* and *La Traviata*. Its Young Artists Program allows pre-professional singers the opportunity to perform in mainstage productions.

Theatre Cedar Rapids presents eight mainstage shows in a repertoire ranging from musicals to drama, and is one of the 20 largest community theatres in the country. It is housed in the Iowa Theatre Building, first opened in 1928 and extensively renovated in 1980. Off-season the building is busy hosting a variety of other performances, including comedy shows and concerts. The Old Creamery Theatre Company performs an April-to-December season at the Amana Colonies. Area colleges sponsor a host of cultural programs. Among them is the Summer Rep series at the University of Iowa

University Theatres, which features works each season by a single modern playwright. The university's Hancher Auditorium hosts more than 40 major international cultural events each year in its 2,500-seat auditorium.

For a taste of small-town Iowa during the turn of the century, visitors can walk through the Ushers Ferry Historic Village. Composed of more than 30 authentic buildings and homes over 10 acres of land, the facility gives tours, workshops, and historical reenactments. Turn-of-the-century farm life can be relived at Seminole Valley Farm, where the restored family farm and outbuildings are now home to tours and history exhibits. In nearby Marion, the nineteenth-century Granger House is open for tours of the Victorian home and carriage house.

## Festivals and Holidays

A festival, parade, or show is scheduled nearly every weekend of the year in Cedar Rapids. The Cedar Rapids Freedom Festival, a city staple for more than 20 years, is an 11-day festival encompassing more than 75 events for all ages during the month of July. Also in July, nearby Hiawatha hosts its Hog Wild Days, a week-long festival that raises money for community programs. During the spring, the Marion Arts Festival brings together 50 artists from across the country, displaying and selling a wide variety of art. Live music, food vendors, and family-friendly activities are also featured. In January, the Amana Colonies is home to WinterFest, a day of Winter fun including a 5K run/walk, wagon rides, cross-country skiing, ice skating, and winery tours.

## Sports for the Spectator

The Cedar Rapids Kernels, a Class A farm club of the National League Anaheim Angels professional baseball club, play a full home schedule in the Midwest League at Veterans Memorial Park, which seats 5,300 people. For automobile-racing enthusiasts, Hawkeye Downs Speedway hosts a number of sanctioned racing events in modern facilities. Visiting regional and national series have included the NASCAR REMAX Series and American IndyCar Series. Hockey enthusiasts are crowding games of the new RoughRiders junior hockey team at the Cedar Rapids Ice Arena.

The full range of major college sports is presented at the University of Iowa in nearby Iowa City, where the Hawkeyes engage in Big Ten competition. Coe College, Mount Mercy College, and Kirkwood Community College in Cedar Rapids, and Cornell College in Mount Vernon compete in a number of sports.

## Sports for the Participant

Cedar Rapids boasts 73 named parks on over 4,000 acres of land. Recreation facilities include all weather basketball courts, splash pads, sand volleyball courts, a BMX dirt track at Cheyenne Park, rugby field, an off-leash dog exercise area, 23 pavilions, baseball and softball fields, picnic areas, and two frisbee golf courses. For the golfing enthusiast, the city also has 4 municipal golf courses, 4 privately owned golf courses, and 3 country clubs. The area is also home to many miles of nature trails. The Cedar Valley Nature Trail, once a railroad bed, offers 52 miles of trails for biking, hiking, and skiing through recreation areas, along riverbanks, and through small towns. The Sac and Fox National Recreational Trail follows Indian Creek through wooded areas and is used for hiking, horseback riding, bicycling, skiing, and dog sledding.

***Recreation Information:*** Cedar Rapids Parks and Recreation Department, 3601 42nd St. NE, Cedar Rapids, IA 52401; telephone (319)286-5080

## Shopping and Dining

The Cedar Rapids area offers a wide range of shopping and dining attractions. The city is home to two enclosed malls (the Lindale Mall and Westdale Mall) with a combined total of more than 170 shops. Downtown, more than 100 individual stores are woven through the city streets. In nearby Williamsburg, shoppers can find the Tanger Factory Outlet Center, with more than 70 outlet stores. Additionally, Czech Village and the Amana Colonies offer an assortment of specialty shops. Dining choices consist of a mix of ethnic and traditional cuisines, with an abundance of regional and national chains as well as unique locally owned restaurants. Three farmer's markets operate in the warm-weather months, offering locally grown fruits, vegetables, flowers, and baked goods.

***Visitor Information:*** Cedar Rapids Area Convention and Visitors Bureau, 119 First Avenue SE, Cedar Rapids, IA 52406; toll-free (800)735-5557

# ■ Convention Facilities

Cedar Rapids offers a variety of convention facilities depending on one's needs. The multipurpose Cedar Rapids Education and Conference Center, in downtown Cedar Rapids, houses different sized rooms with up-to-date multimedia equipment. The facility partners with a number of local hotels and restaurants. Coe College, Kirkwood Community College, and Mount Mercy College also offer smaller conference facilities, and for those groups looking for an abundance of space, the Hawkeye Downs Speedway, U.S. Cellular Center, and Veterans Memorial Coliseum have facilities available.

Hotels and motels in metropolitan Cedar Rapids offer accommodations for a range of meeting and convention needs. There are four area hotels specializing in conventions that can accommodate up to one thousand people: Best Western Longbranch Hotel & Convention Center, Cedar Rapids Marriott, Clarion Hotel & Convention Center, and Crowne Plaza Five Seasons Hotel.

***Convention Information:*** Cedar Rapids Convention and Visitors Bureau, 119 First Avenue SE, Cedar Rapids, IA 52406; toll-free (800)735-5557

# ■ Transportation

## Approaching the City

The Cedar Rapids Airport, just south of the center of the city off of I-380, handles an average of 80 commercial flights daily. Seven different airlines offer commercial flights out of the airport. One third of the country's population is within an hour's flight from Cedar Rapids. All passengers have access to the airport's Information Center and Business Center. In 2006, 507,724 passengers took off from the Cedar Rapids Airport.

Cedar Rapids is linked with points throughout the nation by two interstate highways, I-380 (north-south) and I-80 (east-west). Federal highways are 30/218, which runs east to west through the south sector Cedar Rapids, and 151, which intersects the city diagonally northeast to southwest. State routes include 150, running parallel with I-380, and east-west 94. Cedar Rapids is located mid-point on the newly designated "Avenue of the Saints" that connects St. Louis, Missouri and St. Paul, Minnesota. The area is also served by a number of commuter rail lines.

## Traveling in the City

The Cedar River divides Cedar Rapids into east and west sectors; for address purposes, streets are designated according to quadrants: northeast, northwest, southeast, and southwest. The City Bus Department and taxis are headquartered in the Ground Transportation Center on Fourth Avenue. Linn County LIFTS provides service to the elderly and handicapped in the metropolitan area with specially-equipped buses.

# ■ Communications

## Newspapers and Magazines

The major daily newspaper in Cedar Rapids is the *Cedar Rapids Gazette,* a locally owned morning paper. Also published in the city is *Iowa Farmer Today,* a weekly agricultural newspaper, and *Buildings,* a monthly magazine about facilities construction and management. The *Fraternal Herald (Bratrsky Vestnik)* is a monthly benefit society magazine.

## Television and Radio

Television affiliates broadcasting from Cedar Rapids include CBS and NBC, and cable service is available. A dozen AM and FM radio stations schedule musical, special interest, nostalgia, news, and public affairs programming.

***Media Information:*** *Cedar Rapids Gazette,* 500 Third Avenue SE, Cedar Rapids, IA 52406; telephone (319)398-8333

## Cedar Rapids Online

Cedar Rapids Community Schools. Available www.cr.k12.ia.us

Cedar Rapids Downtown District. Available www.downtowncr.org

*Cedar Rapids Gazette* online. Available www.gazetteonline.com

Cedar Rapids Public Library. Available www.crlibrary.org

Chamber of Commerce. Available www.cedarrapids.org

City and area information. Available www.fyiowa.com

Convention and Visitor Information. Available www.cedar-rapids.com

Priority One Economic Development Department. Available www.priority1.com

BIBLIOGRAPHY

Engle, Paul, *A Lucky American Childhood (Singular Lives)* (University of Iowa Press, 1996)

# Davenport

## ■ The City in Brief

**Founded:** 1808 (incorporated 1836)

**Head Official:** Mayor Edwin G. Winborn (since 2006)

**City Population**

    1980: 103,264
    1990: 95,333
    2000: 98,359
    2006 estimate: 99,514
    Percent change, 1990–2000: 2.8%
    U.S. rank in 1980: Not available
    U.S. rank in 1990: 212th
    U.S. rank in 2000: 267th

**Metropolitan Area Population**

    1980: 384,000
    1990: 350,861
    2000: 359,062
    2006 estimate: 377,291
    Percent change, 1990–2000: 2.3%
    U.S. rank in 1980: Not available
    U.S. rank in 1990: Not available
    U.S. rank in 2000: 114th

**Area:** 63 square miles (2000)

**Elevation:** Ranges from 579 to 700 feet above sea level

**Average Annual Temperature:** 48.1° F

**Average Annual Precipitation:** 35.1 inches

**Major Economic Sectors:** services, wholesale and retail trade, government

**Unemployment Rate:** 4.1% (June 2007)

**Per Capita Income:** $22,297 (2005)

**2005 FBI Crime Index Property:** 7,080

**2005 FBI Crime Index Violent:** 1,323

**Major Colleges and Universities:** St. Ambrose University; Marycrest International University

**Daily Newspaper:** *Quad-City Times*

## ■ Introduction

Davenport is the seat of Scott County and the largest of four cities in Iowa and Illinois that comprise the Quad Cities metropolitan area; the other three cities are Bettendorf, Iowa; Rock Island, Illinois; and Moline, Illinois. Because of its location on the Mississippi River, Davenport played an important role in western expansion during the nineteenth century; along with the other Quad Cities, Davenport continues to be a world leader in the production of farm equipment. With the introduction of riverboat gambling in the 1990s, Davenport began to emerge as a top Midwestern tourist destination. Davenport's economic resurgence, beginning in 2001, has brought millions of dollars of additional development to the city.

## ■ Geography and Climate

Davenport is set on a plain on the north bank of the Mississippi River, where the river forms the boundary between Iowa and Illinois. Davenport's section of the generally north-to-south-flowing river flows from east to west. Unlike every other major city bordering the Mississippi, Davenport has no permanent floodwall or levee, as the city prefers to retain open access to the water. Occasionally, flooding occurs and millions of dollars of property damage results. Located in the heart of an agricultural region, the city is within 300 miles of most other major Midwestern cities. Davenport's position near the geographic center of the country produces a temperate, continental climate that is characterized by a wide range in temperatures. Summers are short and hot;

winters are usually severe, with an average annual snowfall of just over 30 inches.

**Area:** 63 square miles (2000)

**Elevation:** Ranges from 579 to 700 feet above sea level

**Average Temperature:** 48.1° F

**Average Annual Precipitation:** 35.1 inches

# ■ History

### Westward Expansion Targets Davenport Townsite

In the early 1800s the land now occupied by the city of Davenport was the site of bloody fighting between Native Americans and settlers from the eastern United States. This location was valuable in the westward expansion beyond the Mississippi River, serving as a trading center of the American Fur Company. Early treaties specified that the Sac tribe could remain in their villages until the land was surveyed and sold to settlers; warfare resulted, however, after Chief Black Hawk and his followers refused to leave the land on the order of the United States Government agent at Fort Armstrong. In the fall of 1832, Black Hawk was captured and returned to Fort Armstrong, where he signed a treaty, known as the Black Hawk Purchase, that conveyed to the United States six million acres of land west of the Mississippi River.

Two figures stand out in the period that predates the formation of Davenport. The city was named for Colonel George Davenport, an Englishman who had served in the United States Army and then established a fur trading post in the vicinity. Antoine LeClaire, an interpreter who was fluent in three languages and several Native American dialects, served as interpreter for the Black Hawk Purchase. For his efforts the federal government, at the request of Chief Keokuk, awarded him a section of land opposite Rock Island and another section at the head of the rapids above Rock Island where the treaty was negotiated. In 1833, in a claim dispute over land he owned, LeClaire settled for a quarter-section bounded by Davenport's present-day Harrison Street, Warren Street, and Seventh Street. In 1835 Colonel Davenport and six other men formed a company to survey a townsite; they purchased this section from LeClaire, who succeeded in having the new town named after his good friend Davenport. The town was incorporated in 1836.

The initial sale of lots attracted few buyers and in the first year only a half dozen families relocated to the new town. LeClaire and Davenport erected a hotel on the corner of Ripley and First Streets, naming it the Hotel Davenport. By the spring of 1837, the population was growing; a town retailer, for instance, served customers who traveled hundreds of miles to buy goods from his

inventory, valued at $5,000. In December of that year, the Wisconsin Territorial Legislature authorized the creation of Scott County, named after General Winfield Scott. A dispute subsequently broke out between Davenport and neighboring Rockingham for the right to be the county seat. The matter was decided, after three elections, in favor of Davenport; in time, Rockingham was absorbed by the larger city. Davenport received its first city charter in 1839.

### Industry and Culture Establish Traditions

During the decade before the Civil War, Davenport increased its population more than fivefold, with an influx of immigrants from Germany that continued unabated into the 1890s. These new residents imported music and other cultural interests to Davenport, creating institutions such as the Davenport Public Museum and the Municipal Art Gallery. The first railroad bridge to span the Mississippi River was completed in 1856 between Davenport and Rock Island, contributing to the development of the western frontier. The Rock Island Arsenal opened in 1861 to help Union war efforts; the arsenal eventually grew to become one of the largest in the world. In the post-Civil War era Davenport prospered as a riverboat town and as a burgeoning industrial center for the manufacture of cement, steel and iron products, and leather goods.

By the turn of the twentieth century, Davenport was considered the "Washing Machine Capital of the World"—the revolutionary home appliance was invented in the city—and the "Cigar Making Capital of the Midwest." The cigar industry flourished in Davenport until World War II. Davenport counts among its former citizens a number of prominent Americans. B. J. Palmer, the inventor of chiropractics, and his son, D. D. Palmer, were lifelong residents; the younger Palmer used his radio station to introduce Americans to his new medical practice and to Davenport. Buffalo Bill Cody grew up in the rural Davenport area; Dixieland jazz great Bix Beiderbecke was born in the city; and two Pulitzer Prize winners, Charles Edward Russell and Susan Glaspell, once lived there.

Davenport and the Quad Cities region, having invested tens of millions of dollars in the 1990s on lavish riverboat casinos, provide "Midwest Magic on the Mississippi River," with a cost of living that's well below the national average.

***Historical Information:*** Putnam Museum of History and Natural Science Library, 1717 W. 12th Street, Davenport, IA 52804; telephone (319)324-1933

# ■ Population Profile

### Metropolitan Area Residents
    1980: 384,000
    1990: 350,861

©*James Blank.*

2000: 359,062
2006 estimate: 377,291
Percent change, 1990–2000: 2.3%
U.S. rank in 1980: Not available
U.S. rank in 1990: Not available
U.S. rank in 2000: 114th

**City Residents**

1980: 103,264
1990: 95,333
2000: 98,359
2006 estimate: 99,514
Percent change, 1990–2000: 2.8%
U.S. rank in 1980: Not available
U.S. rank in 1990: 212th
U.S. rank in 2000: 267th

**Density:** 1,566 people per square mile
(2000)

**Racial and ethnic characteristics (2005)**

White: 77,267
Black: 9,794
American Indian and Alaska Native: 280
Asian: 2,856

Native Hawaiian and Pacific Islander: 0
Hispanic or Latino (may be of any race): 5,929
Other: 3,782

**Percent of residents born in state:** 61.9%
(2000)

**Age characteristics (2005)**

Population under 5 years old: 7,948
Population 5 to 9 years old: 6,371
Population 10 to 14 years old: 6,724
Population 15 to 19 years old: 6,206
Population 20 to 24 years old: 6,372
Population 25 to 34 years old: 14,770
Population 35 to 44 years old: 14,368
Population 45 to 54 years old: 11,993
Population 55 to 59 years old: 6,059
Population 60 to 64 years old: 3,926
Population 65 to 74 years old: 5,496
Population 75 to 84 years old: 3,361
Population 85 years and older: 1,788
Median age: 34.7 years

**Births (2006, MSA)**

Total number: 5,132

**Deaths (2006, MSA)**

Total number: 3,487

**Money income (2005)**

Per capita income: $22,297
Median household income: $42,801
Total households: 38,541

**Number of households with income of...**

less than $10,000: 3,206
$10,000 to $14,999: 2,994
$15,000 to $24,999: 5,207
$25,000 to $34,999: 3,982
$35,000 to $49,999: 6,842
$50,000 to $74,999: 8,194
$75,000 to $99,999: 3,769
$100,000 to $149,999: 2,555
$150,000 to $199,999: 1,244
$200,000 or more: 548

**Percent of families below poverty level:** 12.4% (2005)

**2005 FBI Crime Index Property:** 7,080

**2005 FBI Crime Index Violent:** 1,323

# ■ Municipal Government

Davenport, the seat of Scott County, is administered by a council-mayor form of government. Ten city council members—eight chosen by ward and elected at large—and the mayor serve two-year terms; the mayor appoints a city administrator. Davenport, once the only city in Iowa to hold partisan political elections, has elected its mayor on a non-partisan basis since 1997.

**Head Official:** Mayor Edwin G. Winborn (since 2006; current term expires 2008)

**Total Number of City Employees:** 815 full-time (2007)

*City Information:* City Hall, 226 West 4th Street, Davenport, IA 52801; telephone (563)326-7701

# ■ Economy

## Major Industries and Commercial Activity

The Davenport economic base is diversified, with a relatively equal distribution among the manufacturing, wholesale and retail, and services sectors. Manufacturing has traditionally been a principal industry in the city; major corporations who maintain a presence in the Quad Cities include Alcoa, John Deere, Kraft, Tyson, Modern Woodmen of America, and Honda. The total value of industrial output in the area tops $40 billion. There is also a defense manufacturing presence in the region, with over 6,000 workers employed by the United States Department of Defense at the Rock Island Arsenal. Davenport is also a primary retail and wholesale trade center, drawing from a market area encompassing a radius of up to 100 miles. Business and industry in Davenport benefit from the Quad City financial community. More than 40 area banks and lending institutions, in conjunction with the state of Iowa, have established a fiscal atmosphere favorable to new business and the expansion of existing firms through progressive and conventional financing procedures. Other important regional economic sectors include food processing and packaging, information technology, warehousing, and distribution.

**Items and goods produced:** agricultural implements, construction machinery, military equipment, airplane parts, chemicals, meat and food products, lumber and timber, sheet aluminum, metal products, cement and foundry products, electronic parts, clothing, printing and publishing products

## Incentive Programs—New and Existing Companies

*Local programs:* City programs include loans and tax abatement programs for job creation and investment in real estate. The city of Davenport currently qualifies to offer the advantages of operating in an Enterprise Zone.

*State programs:* State programs include certain property tax exemptions, job training, low-interest loans and forgivable loans for business development, tax abatements on new research and manufacturing facilities, and state tax credits for new job creation. In addition, no sales or use taxes are assessed on equipment or computers and open port warehousing is available. The Iowa Values Fund, established in 2006, offers concentrated assistance to businesses operating in the following sectors: the life sciences, advanced manufacturing, and information solutions. The Revitalize Iowa's Sound Economy (RISE) provides funds to cover costs of transportation directly related to economic development projects.

*Job training programs:* Job training programs are available that offset wages and training costs of employees. These programs are paid for through the diversion of payroll and property taxes that would normally accrue to the state/community. They also provide Iowa income tax credits. The Iowa Industrial New Jobs Training Program operates in the Quad Cities through Eastern Iowa Community College.

## Development Projects

A significant development in Davenport and environs was the introduction of riverboat casino gambling in the 1990s. Tens of millions of dollars have been poured into these ventures and tourists have been responding.

Davenport's Downtown Partnership has focused on developing the city's central business district by retaining existing businesses, developing opportunities for new businesses, and providing housing for those employed in the urban area. Since 2001, the River Renaissance program has revitalized Davenport's historic downtown through more than $100 million worth of community investment.

In 2007 Davenport received a major developmental boon when it was awarded one of Iowa's "Great Places" grants. The initiative doles out state assistance to cities that present a comprehensive, workable plan for the revitilization of certain areas in order to attract new residents and business. Program requirements call for recipients to create a plan based on creating "engaging experiences; rich, diverse populations and cultures; a vital, creative economy; clean and accessible natural and built environments; well-designed infrastructure; and a shared attitude of optimism that welcomes new ideas." The Davenport plan stipulated improvements to Centennial Park, LeClaire Park and the River Drive corridor. No completion dates had been announced in 2007.

***Economic Development Information:*** Quad City Development Group, 1830 Second Avenue, Suite 200, Rock Island, IL 61201; telephone (563)326-1005; toll-free (800)747-7436

## Commercial Shipping

Davenport's mid-continent location is favorable to freight distribution, with one-day delivery by highway and rail to points throughout the Midwest. As a U.S. Customs Port of Entry and a Foreign Trade Zone (FTZ), Davenport is also a center for national and international commerce. Its Quad Cities Container Terminal works with the FTZ to permit materials to be shipped around the world without being unpacked or passing through customs until they reach their final destination. A regional headquarters of United Parcel Service is located in Davenport; in all, three cargo carriers ship through the Quad City Airport. More than 100 motor freight companies maintain warehouses in the Quad Cities. Four rail carriers provide local switching services. Of the region's nearly 50 private and public barge terminals, more than half offer access by rail and/or highway. More than 60 truck terminals and more than 70 motor freight carriers serve the Quad Cities. Bulk commodity shippers find the Quad Cities barge service to be a highly cost-efficient shipping option.

## Labor Force and Employment Outlook

Davenport claims a productive, skilled labor force that can be employed at a lower cost than the national average. Because of the area's long history as a manufacturing center, the work force possesses many of the traditional skills associated with equipment manufacturing and metal fabricating. The service sector is the fastest-growing, led

by the proliferation of gambling casinos and attendant industries catering to tourists.

In September 2007 the Quad Cities unemployment rate was 4.3 percent, down from ten-year highs of 6.6 percent in 2001, but fairly consistent with the average rate over the same time period. Between 1997 and 2007, the area work force grew by over 15,000 workers. In 2007 analysts projected that the area population would grow to over 370,000 by 2025.

The following is a summary of data regarding the Davenport city metropolitan area labor force, 2005 annual averages.

**Size of nonagricultural labor force:** 46,300

**Number of workers employed in** ...

construction and mining: 2,082
manufacturing: 7,652
trade, transportation and utilities: 8,758
information: 587
financial activities: 2,064
professional and business services: 4,424
educational and health services: 10,048
leisure and hospitality: 5,923
other services: 2,481
government: 5,901

**Average hourly earnings of production workers employed in manufacturing:** Not available

**Unemployment rate:** 4.1% (June 2007)

| *Largest Quad City employers (2003)* | *Number of employees* |
|---|---|
| Deere & Co. | 7,550 |
| Aluminum Company of America | 2,500 |
| IBP | 2,200 |
| Rock Island Arsenal | 1,814 |
| Oscar Mayer Food Corp. | 1,800 |
| Eagle Food Centers | 1,622 |
| Case Corp. | 1,600 |
| Genesis Medical Center | 1,294 |
| Trinity Medical Center | 1,203 |
| John Deere Davenport Works | 802 |
| MidAmerican Energy | 757 |

## Cost of Living

The following is a summary of data regarding several key cost of living factors in the Davenport area.

**2007 (1st quarter) ACCRA Average House Price:** $287,004

**2007 (1st quarter) ACCRA Cost of Living Index:** 96.1

**State income tax rate:** 0.36% to 8.98%

**State sales tax rate:** 5.0%

**Local income tax rate:** None

**Local sales tax rate:** 1.0%

**Property tax rate:** $32.49 per $1,000 assessed valuation

*Economic Information:* Davenport Chamber of Commerce, 102 S. Harrison Street, Davenport, IA 52801; telephone (563)322-1706

# ■ Education and Research

## Elementary and Secondary Schools

Public elementary and secondary schools in Davenport are part of the Davenport Community School District, which also serves the communities of Buffalo, Blue Grass, and Walcott. Iowa consistently ranks among the top states in the country for average ACT composite scores. The district boasts a ratio of one computer for every 3.5 students. The Davenport School Museum seeks to preserve records and memorabilia commemorating the history of the Davenport Community Schools. Nearly a thousand students graduate each year in the district.

The following is a summary of data regarding the Davenport Community Schools as of the 2005–2006 school year.

**Total enrollment:** 15,921

**Number of facilities**

elementary schools: 24
junior high/middle schools: 6
senior high schools: 3
other: 1

**Student/teacher ratio:** 15.2:1

**Teacher salaries (2005–06)**

elementary median: $39,460
junior high/middle median: $40,620
secondary median: $39,940

**Funding per pupil:** $7,645

Several private and parochial schools offer education alternatives in the Davenport metropolitan region, including Assumption High School and Trinity Lutheran School.

*Public Schools Information:* Davenport Community School District, 1606 Brady Street, Davenport, IA 52803; telephone (563)336-5000

## Colleges and Universities

The Quad Cities are home to a private, four-year liberal arts college; a state university regional center; two community colleges; a world-famous chiropractic college; and a graduate-level consortium. Among the institutions of higher learning located in Davenport is St. Ambrose University, a coeducational liberal arts college affiliated with the Catholic Church. St. Ambrose grants a master's degree in addition to baccalaureate degrees, and in 2007 there were 3870 students. Programs at St. Ambrose include music education, industrial engineering, nursing, pastoral theology, and criminal justice degrees. The Palmer College of Chiropractic, the country's oldest chiropractic institute, provides a five-year course of study toward the doctor of chiropractic degree, as well as bachelor and master of science degrees. The school has a 12:1 student-teacher ratio, and boasts that its alumni comprise nearly a third of the certified practicing chiropractors worldwide. Eastern Iowa Community College, which awards associate degrees, offers continuing education and vocational and technical training. The Quad Cities Graduate Study Center represents a consortium of eight Iowa and Illinois institutions; the center coordinates course offerings and applies credit toward advanced degrees, including 87 master's degree programs and 45 certificates.

Among colleges and universities within commuting distance of Davenport are Augustana College in Rock Island, Illinois; the University of Iowa in Iowa City; and Knox College in Galesburg, Illinois.

## Libraries and Research Centers

The Davenport Public Library operates one branch, a coffeeshop, and a bookstore in addition to its main facility, which holds approximately 300,000 volumes, including periodical subscriptions, CD-ROMs, and audio- and videotapes. In 2007 renovations were completed on the Main Library, which also houses the Richardson-Sloane Special Collections Center. Library patrons can also search for materials through the Quad-LINC library catalog, which provides access to more than 30 area libraries. The library, a depository for state and federal documents, maintains special collections on chess and Iowa authors. Also based in Davenport is Southeastern Library Services, which provides libraries in the region with reference back-up, continuing education classes, and library development and support services. Libraries Together, a group comprised of the directors of the four public libraries in Scott County, Iowa, meets monthly.

Specialized libraries and research centers in Davenport are affiliated with colleges, museums, corporations, the Scott County Genealogical Society, and the Scott County Bar Association.

*Public Library Information:* Davenport Public Library, 321 Main Street, Davenport, IA 52801-1490; telephone (563)326-7832; fax (319)326-7809

# ■ Health Care

Davenport is a health care center for the Quad City metropolitan area. Genesis Medical Center is a 502-bed facility in two campuses; the West Central Park and East Rusholme Street facilities offer more than 450 physicians and 3,100 staff members. In 2005 Genesis earned "Magnet Designation," nursing's highest honor. Palmer College operates four chiropractic clinics in the city. Other medical facilities accessible from Davenport include Trinity Medical Center in Rock Island (with over 350 beds on two campuses) and Moline, Illinois, and Genesis Medical Center Illini Campus in Silvis (which features a birth center and Emergency Room/trauma facility). Davenport residents have access to the University of Iowa Medical Center, one of the world's largest university-owned research hospitals.

# ■ Recreation

## Sightseeing

The Village of East Davenport was founded in 1851 and prospered from the logging industry along the Mississippi River, playing a significant role in western migration. Today, the village is 60 square blocks of more than 500 preserved and redeveloped homes and businesses; small shops, new businesses, and one-family residential homes are combined in a variety of historical styles. An elaborate recreation of nineteenth-century America at Christmas time takes place in the village each year on the first Friday and Saturday of December.

Among other historic sites are the Buffalo Bill Cody homestead in nearby McCausland, the Buffalo Bill Museum in LeClaire, and the Rock Island Arsenal, where Colonel George Davenport's home is located. The Davenport House is open for sightseeing from May to October on Thursday through Saturday. Attractions on Arsenal Island include the National Cemetery and the Confederate Cemetery, both dating back to the Civil War. The Vander Veer Botanical Garden, listed on the National Register of Historic Places, is a 33-acre park with annual and perennial beds, a formal rose garden, and a conservatory. The Conservatory is renowned for its floral shows and tropical plants. Another sightseeing attraction near Davenport is located on a 1,000-acre site that overlooks the Rock River Valley in Moline, Illinois, where the Deere & Company Administrative Center—the company's world headquarters—was designed by Eero Saarinen, the celebrated Finnish architect.

## Arts and Culture

The Quad City Symphony Orchestra, founded in 1914, is housed in the Adler Theatre, a restored Art Deco movie palace; the orchestra performs a six-concert season with international guest artists. The Adler is also the home of the Broadway Theatre League, which hosts touring shows. Other organizations that sponsor musical events are the Friends of Chamber Music, the Handel Oratorio Society, and the American Guild of Organists. New to Davenport's performing arts scene are the Cassandra Manning Ballet Theatre and Ballet Quad Cities. Additional restorations to the 2,400-seat Adler were completed in 2006 with funding from the River Renaissance initiative.

The Putnam Museum of History and Natural Science, situated on a bluff overlooking the Mississippi River, houses exhibits on natural science, tribal cultures, ancient civilizations, and the Mississippi River valley. The permanent exhibit, "River, Prairie and People," illustrates the history of the Quad Cities from prehistoric times to the present. The museum also houses an IMAX theater and the Heritage Theatre. The Figge Art Museum, formerly the Davenport Museum of Art, is Iowa's first municipal art museum. It is located next door to the Putnam at the entrance to Fejervary Park and contains more than 13,000 square feet of gallery space, as well as five fully equipped art-making studios and an auditorium. The Winter Garden, a glass-walled structure on the top level of the museum, provides a beautiful view of the Mississippi River. The museum's Regionalist Collection includes the Grant Wood Display, a permanent collection of the works of Iowas most famous artist. Other collections include European Old Masters, Mexican Colonial Art, and Haitian Art.

The Hauberg Indian Museum, part of Blackhawk State Historic Site in Rock Island, Illinois, preserves the heritage of the Sac and Fox tribes. Local history can be explored at the Family Museum of Arts & Science in Bettendorf. River Music Experience, a museum dedicated to American roots music, opened its doors in 2004. More than a museum, River Music Experience is also an entertainment center, as interactive exhibits expose visitors to the sounds of traditional American music.

## Festivals and Holidays

The Mississippi River in the summertime is the focal point for many of Davenport's annual events. The Fourth of July holiday features the Mississippi Valley Blues Festival. The week-long Great Mississippi Valley Fair, featuring a carnival and entertainment, begins in late July. Top Dixieland bands from around the world flock to the Bix Beiderbecke Memorial Jazz Festival in July. During the festival, a nationally known seven-mile race called the Bix Seven is run. On Mother's Day weekend and the weekend after Labor Day, Midwestern artists and craftspeople display their works on the streets of downtown Davenport. Annually in late July or early August the Quad Cities host the Great River Tug Fest, where 10-member teams from Iowa and Illinois play tug-of-war across the Mississippi River.

## Sports for the Spectator

The Quad-City Swing, a Midwest League Class A professional baseball affiliate of the St. Louis Cardinals of the National League, play a home schedule of 70 baseball games at the newly-renovated John O'Donnell Stadium in Davenport. The Quad-City Downs in East Moline sponsors televised harness racing year-round. The *Quad-City Times* Bix 7 Run is held in late July; more than 17,000 runners—including nationally known competitors—challenge the hills of Davenport. The John Deere Classic, a Professional Golfers Association event, is also held locally. The Quad City Flames, who compete in the American Hockey League, played their inaugural season at the iWireless Center in Moline in 2007-2008. Cordova Dragway Park offers drag-racing events throughout the summer, and stock car racing is available at several area tracks.

## Sports for the Participant

The Davenport Parks and Recreation Department manages 22 recreation parks on 2,200 acres of public facilities for golf, tennis, swimming, jogging, and softball. Scott County Park, 6 miles north of Davenport on more than 1,000 acres of land, features picnic grounds, an Olympic-size pool, and an 18-hole golf course. Davenport's proximity to the Mississippi River provides easy access for boating and various other water sports; riverboat casino gambling out of Davenport and Bettendorf is offered November through March. Skiing is possible from December to March in Taylor Ridge.

## Shopping and Dining

Davenport's Northpark Mall is Iowa's largest mall; anchored by five major stores, it houses more than 165 specialty shops. A variety of specialty and gift shops, clothing stores, restaurants, and taverns are located in the historic Village of East Davenport. American and family dining is the focus of the majority of local restaurants, with a sampling of Chinese cuisine, pubs, and delis also offered.

*Visitor Information:* Quad Cities Convention and Visitors Bureau, 102 S. Harrison St., Davenport, IA 52801; telephone (563)322-3911; toll-free (800)747-7800; email cvb@quadcities.com

## ■ Convention Facilities

The RiverCenter, located in downtown Davenport and accessible to the airport and interstate highways, is a complex consisting of an exhibition hall, a theater, and a luxury hotel, with a total square footage of 100,000. The exhibition hall contains 13,500 square feet of multipurpose space to accommodate up to 1,800 participants in convention, trade show, banquet, and concert settings. Separate meeting rooms, with customizing features, are designed for groups ranging from 20 to 250 people. Attached to RiverCenter are the 2,500-seat Art Deco-style Adler Theatre, President Casino Hotel, and Radisson Quad City Plaza Hotel.

Hotels and motels in Davenport offer meeting facilities; among them is the Clarion Hotel Davenport, with six meeting rooms, a ballroom, and two conference halls; 35,228 square feet of space accommodates up to 1,500 participants. Accommodations are available at traditional hotels and motels as well as bed-and-breakfasts located in historic riverfront homes, mansions, and farmhouses.

*Convention Information:* Quad Cities Convention and Visitors Bureau, 102 S. Harrison St., Davenport, IA 52801; telephone (563)322-3911 or (800)747-7800

## ■ Transportation

### Approaching the City

The Quad City International Airport, 15 minutes from downtown Davenport in Moline, Illinois, is served by 5 airlines offering daily direct flights to and from Chicago, Detroit, Atlanta, Las Vegas, Orlando, Memphis and Minneapolis-Saint Paul. In 2006 the airport served 913,522 passengers. Davenport Municipal Airport handles corporate aircraft and acts as a reliever airport for Quad City International Airport.

Four interstate, four U.S. highways, and five state highways connect Davenport with points throughout the Midwest and across the United States. I-280 is an outerbelt around the Quad City region. I-80 passes through the city from New York to San Francisco; I-74 links Davenport with Indianapolis and Cincinnati to the east. U.S. 61 runs north-south, from Minneapolis-St. Paul; U.S. 67 extends south to St. Louis; and U.S. 6 connects Davenport with the East and West Coasts.

### Traveling in the City

Corresponding to a grid pattern, Davenport's north-south streets are named and east-west streets are numbered. River Drive follows the waterfront of the Mississippi River.

Citibus, which has a fleet of about twenty buses, operates regularly scheduled bus routes in Davenport on weekdays and Saturday. Special bus service is available for the elderly and handicapped.

## ■ Communications

### Newspapers and Magazines

The Davenport daily newspaper is the morning *Quad-City Times*. Weekly newspapers are *The Catholic Messenger* and *The Davenport Leader*.

## Television and Radio

Nine commercial television stations are based in Davenport; viewers receive broadcasts from several other stations in Rock Island and Moline, Illinois; cable television service is available. Radio listeners can tune to nearly a dozen AM and FM stations broadcasting from Davenport that offer sports plus country, light, oldies, classic hits, and rock music.

***Media Information:*** *Quad-City Times,* 500 E. Third St., Davenport IA 52801 telephone (563)383-2200

## Davenport Online

City and area information. Available www.fyiowa .com

Quad Cities Convention and Visitors Bureau. Available quadcities.com

Quad Cities online. Available www.quadcities.com

Quad City Development Group. Available www .quadcities.org

BIBLIOGRAPHY

McKusick, Marshall Bassford, *The Davenport Conspiracy Revisted* (Iowa State University Press, 1991)

Renkes, Jim, *The Quad Cities and Their People* (American World Geographic, 1994)

# Des Moines

## ■ The City in Brief

**Founded:** 1843 (incorporated 1851; chartered 1857)

**Head Official:** Mayor Frank Cownie (since 2004)

**City Population**
1980: 368,000
1990: 392,928
2000: 198,682
2006 estimate: 193,886
Percent change, 1990–2000: −49.4%
U.S. rank in 1980: 74th
U.S. rank in 1990: 80th
U.S. rank in 2000: 106th (State rank: 1st)

**Metropolitan Area Population**
1980: Not available
1990: Not available
2000: 481,394
2006 estimate: 534,230
Percent change, 1990–2000: Not available
U.S. rank in 1980: 74th
U.S. rank in 1990: 80th
U.S. rank in 2000: 106th (State rank: 1st)

**Area:** 76 square miles (2000)

**Elevation:** 838 feet above sea level

**Average Annual Temperature:** 49.7° F

**Average Annual Precipitation:** 33.12 inches of rain, 33.3 inches of snow

**Major Economic Sectors:** services, wholesale and retail trade, government

**Unemployment Rate:** 3.4% (June 2007)

**Per Capita Income:** $23,262 (2005)

**2005 FBI Crime Index Property:** 13,799

**2005 FBI Crime Index Violent:** 1,228

**Major Colleges and Universities:** Drake University, Grand View College, Des Moines University

**Daily Newspaper:** *The Des Moines Register*

## ■ Introduction

Des Moines is the capital of Iowa, the seat of Polk County, and the center of a metropolitan area consisting of West Des Moines, Urbandale, Ankeny, Johnston, Clive, Windsor Heights, Altoona, and Pleasant Hill. Des Moines is fixed in the national consciousness as the place where the Presidential race begins every four years. It is also acquiring a new identity as a "post-industrial urban center," a term used by experts to describe midwestern communities that, like Des Moines, have acquired the characteristics of East and West Coast cities—impressive skylines, bustling commercial centers, suburban growth—but have at the same time retained their rural, agrarian roots.

## ■ Geography and Climate

Des Moines is situated on rolling terrain in south-central Iowa along the banks of the Des Moines River, the longest river in the state and an important tributary of the Mississippi River. Good drainage to the southwest produces fertile farmland, which is surrounded by coal fields. Marked seasonal changes occur in both temperature and precipitation. During winter, snowfall averages more than 30 inches; drifting snow often impedes transportation and sub-zero temperatures are common. Des Moines sits in a tornado zone. The growing season extends from early May to early October; approximately 60 percent of the annual precipitation occurs during this time, with maximum rainfall in late May and June. Autumn is generally sunny and dry, producing favorable conditions for drying and harvesting crops.

**Area:** 76 square miles (2000)

**Elevation:** 838 feet above sea level

**Average Temperature:** 49.7° F

**Average Annual Precipitation:** 33.12 inches of rain, 33.3 inches of snow

# ■ History

### River Fort Becomes State Capital

The city of Des Moines originated with the building of Fort Des Moines in 1843, at the confluence of the Raccoon and Des Moines rivers, as a military garrison to protect the rights of Sak and Fox tribes. Debate surrounds the correct origin of the name of Iowa's largest city. The Moingona, a native group, had located a village on the river and it appeared on the map of Jacques Marquette, the French explorer. The French expression "la riviere des moines" translates to "the river of the monks," but may approximate the name of the Moingona, who inhabited the riverbank. "De Moyen," meaning "middle," was understood as a reference to the Des Moines River being the middle distance between the Mississippi and Missouri rivers.

The Iowa River Valley was opened to new settlers in 1845; a year later, when Iowa gained statehood, the population of Fort Des Moines numbered 127 residents. After the city charter was adopted in 1857, the word Fort was dropped from the name. Des Moines officially became the state capital—and its future growth was guaranteed—in January 1858 when two oxen-driven bobsleds hauled the state's archives into the city from Iowa City.

Des Moines played an active role in the Civil War. In May 1864 Des Moines women signed a petition pledging to replace working men to free them to fight for the Union cause, but enough male recruits were found to fill the quotas. After the Civil War, in 1875, Des Moines was the site of a nationally significant speech by President Ulysses S. Grant to a reunion of the Army of Tennessee, wherein he reiterated a commitment to universal equality.

During the last quarter of the nineteenth century, wood-frame buildings in Des Moines underwent extensive construction and renovation. The impressive state capitol building, situated on an 80-acre park and featuring a gold-gilded central dome of the revived classical Roman style, was completed in 1884. In the 1880s and 1890s, local businessmen built mansions and the city's cultural life continued to flourish.

### Hospitality and Development Shape Des Moines

The history of Des Moines is filled with colorful events such as the arrival in the spring of 1894 of Kelly's Army, 1,000 unemployed men on their way to Washington, D. C., led by Charles T. Kelly, "King of the Commons." Citizens greeted them with hospitality to prevent trouble. When Kelly's Army seemed reluctant to leave, however, the townspeople bought lumber to construct an "industrial fleet" of 150 flatboats, under local union direction, to transport the men out of the city. Each man was issued a small American flag, and the waving of the flags was the last sight of Kelly's Army. Among them was the American writer Jack London.

Des Moines has distinguished itself in various ways throughout its history. The Des Moines Plan, one of the first of its kind in the nation, streamlined municipal government and charted development, taking into consideration the city's natural setting. Fort Des Moines, dedicated as a calvary post in 1903, became the first training center for the Women's Army Corps, which gained national attention. The economic base of Des Moines was substantially expanded when the city became a national insurance and publishing center. In 1949, Des Moines was named an All-America City by the National Municipal League. The honor was repeated in 1971, then again in 1981 after Des Moines had addressed urban renewal issues by committing $313 million to the restoration of the historic districts of Court Avenue and Sherman Hills.

The city of Des Moines was immobilized in the summer of 1993 by flooding of the Des Moines and Raccoon rivers. The state of Iowa was declared a national disaster area, and preliminary estimates indicated the city alone suffered more than $253 million in damages. By the year 2000 Des Moines was humming with construction activity.

At the dawn of the twenty-first century, residents were enjoying a changing landscape in downtown Des Moines as new buildings were erected or underway, including a new science museum, new main library branch, and new conference venues. In 2003 Des Moines was again named an All-America City by the National Municipal League, an honor it has received four times. Residents today appreciate the small-town atmosphere with big-city amenities afforded them in Des Moines in addition to the city's educational and cultural amenities and well-recognized quality of life.

***Historical Information:*** State Historical Society of Iowa, 600 East Locust Street, Des Moines, IA 50319; telephone (515)281-6200.

# ■ Population Profile

### Metropolitan Area Residents

1980: Not available
1990: Not available

Walter Bibikow/The Image Bank/Getty Images

2000: 481,394
2006 estimate: 534,230
Percent change, 1990–2000: Not available
U.S. rank in 1980: 74th
U.S. rank in 1990: 80th
U.S. rank in 2000: 106th (State rank: 1st)

**City Residents**

1980: 368,000
1990: 392,928
2000: 198,682
2006 estimate: 193,886
Percent change, 1990–2000: −49.4%
U.S. rank in 1980: 74th
U.S. rank in 1990: 80th
U.S. rank in 2000: 106th (State rank: 1st)

**Density:** 2,621.3 people per square mile (2000)

**Racial and ethnic characteristics (2005)**

White: 160,212
Black: 16,709
American Indian and Alaska Native: 564
Asian: 9,071
Native Hawaiian and Pacific Islander: 44

Hispanic or Latino (may be of any race): 18,952
Other: 7,701

**Percent of residents born in state:** 70.7% (2000)

**Age characteristics (2005)**

Population under 5 years old: 15,927
Population 5 to 9 years old: 13,138
Population 10 to 14 years old: 12,772
Population 15 to 19 years old: 12,209
Population 20 to 24 years old: 10,981
Population 25 to 34 years old: 32,640
Population 35 to 44 years old: 31,929
Population 45 to 54 years old: 27,014
Population 55 to 59 years old: 11,872
Population 60 to 64 years old: 8,399
Population 65 to 74 years old: 9,933
Population 75 to 84 years old: 7,360
Population 85 years and older: 2,743
Median age: 35.2 years

**Births (2006, County)**

Total number: 506

**Deaths (2006, County)**

Total number: 470

**Money income (2005)**

Per capita income: $23,262
Median household income: $42,690
Total households: 84,463

**Number of households with income of...**

less than $10,000: 5,049
$10,000 to $14,999: 5,583
$15,000 to $24,999: 11,722
$25,000 to $34,999: 11,911
$35,000 to $49,999: 12,977
$50,000 to $74,999: 20,234
$75,000 to $99,999: 9,712
$100,000 to $149,999: 4,101
$150,000 to $199,999: 1,080
$200,000 or more: 2,094

**Percent of families below poverty level:** 6.1% (2005)

**2005 FBI Crime Index Property:** 13,799

**2005 FBI Crime Index Violent:** 1,228

# ■ Municipal Government

Des Moines operates under a mayor/council form of government. The seven-member council is comprised of six council persons and a manager, who are elected to staggered terms in non-partisan elections. The manager serves a term of indefinite length at the pleasure of the council.

**Head Official:** Mayor Frank Cownie (since 2004; current term expires January 1, 2012)

**Total Number of City Employees:** 1,900 (2007)

*City Information:* Des Moines City Hall, Mayor and City Council Office, 400 Robert D. Ray Drive, Des Moines, IA 50309; telephone (515)283-4944

# ■ Economy

## Major Industries and Commercial Activity

In 2006 Iowa was named the fastest growing economy in the Midwest by the Bureau of Economic Analysis and number three in the nation for lowest cost of doing business by the Milken Institute. The Des Moines economy consists of a balance among the manufacturing, services, government, wholesale and retail trade, medical, insurance and financial services, printing, publishing, and agribusiness sectors. Manufacturing, while comprising a relatively small percentage of the city's total employment base, has a significant impact on the area economy. Manufacturing firms buy many of their supplies locally, generating more secondary jobs than any other industry. In addition, most of the goods produced are shipped outside the metropolitan area, and approximately 10 percent of manufacturing production is exported, thus contributing to the development of the local shipping industry. Some of the area's best-known manufacturers are Pella windows, Maytag and Amana appliances, and Rockwell Collins avionics equipment.

With the headquarters of approximately 70 insurance companies and the regional offices of 100 other firms located in the metropolitan area, Des Moines is a major insurance center. Betweem 1990 and 2005, employment in the insurance industry approximately doubled in Des Moines. Other service businesses, including the health care industry, employ nearly one fourth of the work force. Many area firms are active in biotechnology, conducting research in such fields as human, plant, and animal disease cures; safer pesticides and herbicides; and new, higher crop yields. In 2006 over 14,600 people were employed in the bioscience sector in Greater Des Moines.

A statewide employer based in Des Moines is Meredith Corporation, a diversified communications company specializing in printing, publishing, broadcasting, and real estate. The information technology sector, a growth area for Des Moines, employed 8,673 people in 2006. Government employs a substantial portion of the city's work force, with the state of Iowa being among the largest employers.

**Items and goods produced:** flour, cosmetics, furnaces, stove and furnace parts, agricultural implements, automotive and creamery equipment, leather products, medicine, brick, food items, paint, electric switches, and elevators

## Incentive Programs—New and Existing Businesses

The Greater Des Moines Partnership assists firms with an interest in applying for economic development financial assistance programs. Other public and private sector groups offer a variety of business assistance programs to businesses expanding in or relocating to Des Moines.

*Local programs:* A corporation intending to create 100 jobs may be eligible to receive a $400,000 low-interest or forgivable loan to help reduce its relocation cost. The City of Des Moines Office of Economic Development assists businesses in a variety of ways, including project management; identification of land, financing and other resources to facilitate projects; liaison with other city departments; referrals for business licenses; job training and recruitment; and redevelopment assistance. Qualifying Des Moines businesses are able to take advantage of several helpful tax policies, including single factor corporate income tax; tax abatement for new construction; and no property tax on machinery and equipment. Several small business loan programs and funds are available to assist qualifying small businesses in building improvements, equipment purchases, and operating costs.

*State programs:* Two areas within the City of Des Moines are designated as Iowa Enterprise Zones. New commercial and industrial businesses making a capital investment of at least $500,000 and creating 10 new jobs meeting wage and benefit targets within these designated areas may be eligible for a package of tax credits and exemptions. State programs include certain property tax exemptions, job training, low-interest loans and forgivable loans for business development, tax abatements on new research and manufacturing facilities, and state tax credits for new job creation. In addition, no sales or use taxes are assessed on equipment or computers and open port warehousing is available. The Iowa Values Fund, established in 2006, offers concentrated assistance to businesses operating in the following sectors: the life sciences, advanced manufacturing, and information solutions. The Revitalize Iowa's Sound Economy (RISE) provides funds to cover costs of transportation directly related to economic development projects.

*Job training programs:* Des Moines Area Community College (DMACC) provides a variety of business training programs. A portion of the training dollars may be used for salary reimbursement.

## Development Projects

The city of Des Moines has nine areas designated for urban renewal: Central Place Industrial Park, Guthrie Avenue Business Park, Hiatt Square, Metro Center, the ACCENT neighborhood, Airport Business Park, Airport Commerce Park South, Airport Commerce Park West, and Southeast AgriBusiness. These areas are given special consideration for public and private development.

In June 2007 DuPont and Pioneer Hi-Bred announced a $42 million plan to expand and renovate five area seed genetics plants in the greater Des Moines area. The capital investments were expected to create over 165 new jobs; no completion date had been announced.

In 2007 major renovations were underway on Hillis Elementary School, Lincoln High School, Samuelson Elementary School, and Stowe Elementary School. The New Central Library was completed in 2006, and was featured in the June 2006 issue of *The Architectural Review*.

*Economic Development Information:* Greater Des Moines Partnership, 700 Locust Street, Suite 100, Des Moines, IA 50309; telephone (515)286-4950; email info@desmoinesmetro.com. City of Des Moines, Office of Economic Development, 400 E. First Street, Des Moines, IA 50309; telephone (515)283-4004; email oed@ci.des-moines.ia.us

## Commercial Shipping

Des Moines is served by four major railroads that provide full-time switching and piggyback ramp service. Fifty-eight motor freight carriers provide overnight and one–to five–day shipping to points throughout the United States; more than 50 terminals are maintained in the community. The Des Moines airport serves as a regional hub for UPS's second-day air service, and the airport ships over 6,000 tons of freight per month. Approximately 100 companies in the Des Moines area engage in export or import activity.

## Labor Force and Employment Outlook

Local analysts contend that the best measurement of the quality of the work force is the site location decisions made by businesses. They say the greatest testimony to the quality of the Des Moines work force is that once a company locates in Des Moines, it continues to expand. Beyond a higher-quality work force, a low crime rate, short commute times in metro Des Moines, affordable housing, a broad array of education options, and attractive quality of life help local businesses recruit employees.

The major employment industries in Des Moines are financial services, insurance, government, manufacturing, trade, and services. Des Moines businesses draw employees from a five-county area consisting of more than 500,000 residents; in addition, Iowa's work force, with approximately an 86 percent high school graduation rate, ranks among the top five states. Wages are somewhat lower— about five percent—than the national average in Des Moines. Vocational and technical skills training programs are widely available. Iowa is a Right to Work state.

In September 2007 the Des Moines unemployment rate stood at 3.4 percent, slightly below the national average, but up from ten year lows below one percent around the turn of the century. The unemployment rate peaked above five percent in 2004 and 2005; between 1997 and 2007, over 40,000 net jobs were added in the area economy, while the labor force increased proportionately.

The following is a summary of data regarding the Des Moines-West Des Moines metropolitan area labor force, 2006 annual averages.

**Size of nonagricultural labor force:** 313,500

**Number of workers employed in . . .**

    construction and mining: 17,900
    manufacturing: 19,900
    trade, transportation and utilities: 65,300
    information: 9,100
    financial activities: 49,100
    professional and business services: 34,800
    educational and health services: 36,800
    leisure and hospitality: 29,000
    other services: 12,300
    government: 39,400

**Average hourly earnings of production workers employed in manufacturing:** $18.29

**Unemployment rate:** 3.4% (June 2007)

| *Largest employers (2007)* | *Number of employees* |
|---|---|
| Wells Fargo & Co. | 11,000 |
| Principal Financial Group | 7,600 |
| Mercy Medical Center | 6,200 |
| Iowa Health–Des Moines | 4,018 |
| MidAmerican Energy Company Inc. | 3,500 |
| Pioneer Hi Bred International Inc. | 2,000 |
| Hy-Vee Inc. | 1,672 |
| UPS | 1,600 |
| Allied Insurance | 1,541 |
| Qwest Communications | 1,500 |
| Wellmark Blue Cross and Blue Shield of IA | 1,480 |
| Communications Data Services Inc. | 1,200 |
| EMC Insurance Companies | 1,191 |
| Meredith Corp. | 1,020 |

## Cost of Living

Des Moines is often ranked in the top metro areas for housing affordability and a favorable cost of living. State and local taxes are lower than the U.S. average.

The following is a summary of data regarding several key cost of living factors in the Des Moines area.

**2007 (1st quarter) ACCRA Average House Price:** $275,700

**2007 (1st quarter) ACCRA Cost of Living Index:** 92.0

**State income tax rate:** 0.36% to 8.98%

**State sales tax rate:** 5.0%

**Local income tax rate:** None

**Local sales tax rate:** None

**Property tax rate:** $17.04857 per 1,000 of assessed valuation (2005)

***Economic Information:*** Greater Des Moines Partnership, 700 Locust Street, Suite 100, Des Moines, IA 50309; telephone (515)286-4950; email info@desmoinesmetro.com

## ■ Education and Research

### Elementary and Secondary Schools

The Des Moines Public School District, the largest in the state, is governed by a seven-member board of directors who are elected at large to three-year staggered terms.

The head administrator is the superintendent of schools. The district has an annual operating budget of more than $300 million.

The Des Moines public schools implement a variety of curriculum options for students at all levels. In 2006 the graduation rate was 82 percent, the highest it had been in five years. The district's Central Academy, established in 1985 for gifted students in grades 8 through 12, brings students together for half of the school day to learn among other gifted students; the other half is spent at their home school. The district's Advanced Placement program based at Central Academy is ranked in the top 1 percent in the nation, and since 1991, all of the Iowa AP State Scholars have attended Des Moines Public Schools. At the middle and secondary levels, several school-to-work programs bring students into the real world of health care, agriculture, and business. The unique Downtown School offers small classes, a year-round calendar with a six-week summer break and week-long breaks throughout the year, in three downtown locations accessible by skywalk to many downtown businesses. The Downtown School utilizes local businesses and the surrounding neighborhood as opportunities for learning; its locations are accessible to parents working downtown as well. Students in the Downtown School program are ages 5 to 11. These and other innovative programs are possible because of the cooperative spirit between the school district and business community in the greater Des Moines area.

In 2007 a "Schools First" plan was underway, utilizing some $317 million in funds to renovate or replace all schools in the district over a period of 10 years. More than $180 million of work had been completed by fall 2007, with 22 projects complete and an additional 4 under construction and 5 in the design stage.

The following is a summary of data regarding the Des Moines Public Schools as of the 2005–2006 school year.

**Total enrollment:** 30,856

**Number of facilities**
elementary schools: 38
junior high/middle schools: 14
senior high schools: 10
other: 0

**Student/teacher ratio:** 14.2:1

**Teacher salaries (2005–06)**
elementary median: $37,030
junior high/middle median: $44,930
secondary median: $37,990

**Funding per pupil:** $8,516

Among the private institutions providing the Des Moines metropolitan area with educational alternatives are Des Moines Christian, Diocese of Des Moines

Catholic Schools, Des Moines Jewish Academy, Grandview Park Baptist, and Mount Olive Lutheran. Over 5,000 students are educated privately in the city of Des Moines.

***Public Schools Information:*** Des Moines Public Schools, 1801 16th Street, Des Moines, IA 50314; telephone (515)242-7911; fax (515)242-7579

## Colleges and Universities

Drake University, a private institution founded in 1881, enrolls over 5,600 students and grants undergraduate and graduate degrees in more than seventy programs through the College of Arts and Sciences, the College of Business Administration, the School of Journalism and Mass Communication, the School of Education, the College of Pharmacy and Health Sciences, and the Law School. Drake operates a work experience program that includes cooperative education and internships. The school boasts a student-faculty ratio of 14:1, and has been ranked among "Barron's 300 Best Buys in College Education."

Grand View College, a private, Lutheran-affiliated liberal arts school, educates approximately 1,750 students and awards associate and baccalaureate degrees in several fields of study; cross-registration with Drake University and Des Moines Area Community College is available. Grand View prides itself on small classes, with an average of just fourteen students per class. It has 85 full time and 95 part time faculty members. The Des Moines University College of Osteopathic Medicine offers baccalaureate, master's, and first-professional degrees in a variety of health care areas such as osteopathic medicine and surgery, podiatric medicine and surgery, health care administration, and physical therapy. It has an annual enrollment of around 800 students.

Vocational, technical, and pre-professional education in Des Moines is provided by Des Moines Area Community College and AIB College of Business. Within commuting distance of the city are Iowa State University, an internationally renowned research university in Ames, Iowa, and Simpson College, a four-year liberal arts college in Indianola, Iowa.

## Libraries and Research Centers

The Public Library of Des Moines houses more than 500,000 volumes and nearly a thousand periodical subscriptions in addition to audiotapes, videotapes, audio CDs, and CD-ROMs. The library system includes five branches in addition to its main building. As part of a $48 million renovation, building, and expansion project, construction of a New Central Library was completed in 2006. In 2007 renovations were also underway at the North Side Library, South Side Library, and Forest Avenue Library. The library system is a depository for federal and state documents and government publications. The State Library of Iowa is also located in downtown Des Moines in the State Capitol Building; holdings include more than 450,000 volumes as well as a complete range of audio-visual materials and special collections on state of Iowa publications, law, medicine, public policy, and patents and trademarks. The library is a depository for state and patent documents.

The Iowa Library for the Blind and Physically Handicapped provides Braille books, large print books, and cassettes and disks. The Cowles Library at Drake University houses extensive holdings in all major department areas; the law library maintains an Iowa legal history collection. The Iowa Genealogical Society Library and the Grand View College Library also serve the community. The State Historical Society of Iowa Library maintains several collections, some of which reside in Des Moines.

A variety of specialized libraries and research centers located in the city are affiliated with hospitals, corporations, government agencies, law firms, the Blank Park Zoo and the Des Moines Art Center.

***Public Library Information:*** Public Library of Des Moines, 100 Locust Street, Des Moines, IA 50309; telephone (515)283-4152

# ■ Health Care

Providing all levels of care in more than 50 specialty fields, the health care network in metropolitan Des Moines consists of 8 hospitals with more than 3,000 beds. A regional trauma center and a helicopter ambulance service are also based in Des Moines.

Iowa Health Des Moines, with 3 hospitals and a total of 1,139 beds, is the city's largest medical group. The complex includes Blank Children's Hospital (which had 3,332 admissions in 2006), Iowa Methodist Medical Center (with 373 beds), and Iowa Lutheran (234 beds and 12,000 annual admissions). There are 200 additional physicians in clinics throughout the city affiliated with Iowa Health Des Moines. Mercy Medical Center, an acute care, not-for-profit Catholic-affiliated hospital with 917 beds, provides general care through its 3 Des Moines clinic and hospital campuses. Mercy employs more than 800 physicians and medical staff, and admits more than 34,000 patients per year. It was listed among the best hospitals for cardiac care in 2006 by *U.S. News and World Report*. The Des Moines Division of the Veterans Administration Central Iowa provides care to veterans. Broadlawns Medical Center consists of an acute care hospital. Mercy Capitol offers emergency, diagnostic, and surgical services and is a teaching hospital affiliated with Des Moines University's medical program.

# ■ Recreation

## Sightseeing

The starting point for a tour of Des Moines is the State Capitol, one of the nation's most beautiful public buildings and one of the largest of its kind. The 275-foot main dome is covered with 23-karat gold leaf and is flanked by four smaller domes. The capitol's interior features more than 10 different wood grains mixed with 29 types of marble in detailed stone and wood carvings, ornately painted ceilings, and mosaics and murals. Another popular site is Terrace Hill, the present residence of Iowa's governor; considered to be one of the finest examples of Second Empire architecture in the country, Terrace Hill was designed by W.W. Boyington, architect of the Chicago Water Tower. Donated to the state by the Frederick M. Hubbell family, the mansion has been refurbished to its original Victorian elegance.

In both the Courthouse and Sherman Hill districts of Des Moines, residential and commercial buildings dating to 1850 reflect changing tastes and styles in architecture; especially interesting are doorway and entrance designs. The Hoyt Sherman Place, home of one of Des Moines' most successful businessmen and an example of ornate Victorian design, is now owned by the city and open for tours. It also doubles as a music and performing arts center. The Iowa State Historical Building, completed in 1987 and housing the State Historical Library, is dedicated to Iowa's past with exhibits on natural history, Indian lore, and pioneer life. A large outdoor neon sculpture named *Plains Aurora* is displayed on top of the building.

The Des Moines Botanical Center cultivates plants and flowers under one of the biggest geodesic domes in the nation. The Center preserves a permanent collection of more than 1,000 different species of tropical and subtropical plants and cultivars, growing in their natural cycle; six thematic displays are presented each year. Living History Farms in nearby Urbandale is a 600-acre agricultural museum focusing on the history and future of farming in the Midwest; buildings, planting methods, and livestock are authentic to the five time periods represented. At Adventureland Park, more than 100 theme park rides and activities combine with permanent exhibits germane to Iowa. Salisbury House, a 42-room country manor, patterns itself after King's House of Salisbury, England, duplicating Renaissance luxury and splendor; it is owned by the Iowa State Education Association, which arranges tours. The Science Center of Iowa covers all fields of science; the center's new facility opened to the public in May 2005, featuring a 226-seat IMAX Dome Theater, a 175-seat theater for live performances, and a 50-foot Star Theater, in addition to six "experience platforms" and a changing exhibition platform. At Blank Park Zoo, where more than 1,400 animals from 104 different species inhabit 49 acres, special attractions include the Myron and Jackie Blank Discovery Center, featuring a butterfly garden and a bat cave. The Zoo celebrated its fortieth anniversary in 2006.

## Arts and Culture

One beneficiary of the city's development has been its cultural life. Funds have been invested to house the city's cultural institutions in architecturally significant facilities. The most impressive is the Des Moines Art Center, designed by international architects Eliel Saarinen, I. M. Pei, and Richard Meier. Housing art of the nineteenth and twentieth centuries in a permanent collection, the Center also sponsors international exhibits, educational programs, and film and music series. Nollen Plaza, adjacent to the Civic Center of Greater Des Moines, is a block-square amphitheater and park with a tree-lined "peace garden," a waterfall, and a reflecting pool; Claes Oldenburg's sculpture *The Crusoe Umbrella* is on view in the plaza.

The Des Moines Symphony performs at the Civic Center. The Des Moines Playhouse produces a main stage season of drama, musicals, and light drama as well as Theatre for Young People. The Ingersoll Dinner Theater features local and guest artists in Broadway musicals and plays, in addition to special attractions.

## Festivals and Holidays

In February the downtown skywalk is transformed into a 54-par putt-putt golf course for the world's largest indoor miniature golf tournament. The Drake Relays Downtown Festival, a week-long celebration in April, pits city corporations against one another in the "Fake Relays;" other festival events include a whimsical "most beautiful bulldog" contest, mascot relays, and musical entertainment. The Des Moines Arts Festival features three days of art, entertainment, and children's activities in late June. July's Taste of Des Moines offers visitors a taste of local fare. Summer ends with the Iowa State Fair in August. The Festival of Trees & Lights raises money for a local hospital with the decorating of 100 downtown trees in November during Thanksgiving week.

## Sports for the Spectator

For nearly 100 years, the Drake Relays have held the distinction of being the country's largest such event, with more than 200 colleges and universities participating from nearly every state and more than 60 countries. The relays, held in Drake Stadium at Drake University the last weekend in April, sell out each year; the competition also includes track and field events. A variety of other events are held throughout the city, making the Relays the focal point for an entire festival.

In addition to the Drake Relays, Drake University offers sporting events, including basketball, football, soccer, tennis, track, crew, softball, and golf.

The Iowa Cubs, the National League Chicago Cubs's top farm team, compete in baseball's Triple A international professional baseball league at Principal Park. The Des Moines Menace offer soccer action at Waukee Stadium, and the Des Moines Buccaneers, part of the United States Hockey League, play at 95 KGGO Arena.

### Sports for the Participant

The Des Moines Parks and Recreation Department maintains 72 city parks with a variety of facilities on 3,221 acres, including softball fields, horseshoe pits, volleyball courts, tennis courts, fitness and bicycle trails, golf courses, trails, soccer fields, play equipment, swimming pools, community centers, gardens, and an amphitheater. The city offers swimming and tennis lessons and arts and crafts programs; softball, volleyball, and tennis leagues are also sponsored by the recreation department. The Des Moines metro area offers nearly 100 public tennis courts, and many golf courses, swimming pools, and country clubs. Both indoor and outdoor sports can be enjoyed during the winter at community center gyms and ice rinks. Swimming, water skiing, fishing, and boating are popular at local rivers and lakes.

### Shopping and Dining

The Des Moines downtown shopping district is 20 square blocks connected by a second-level skywalk system that encompasses 150 shops. Altogether, more than 40 shopping squares and plazas serve shoppers throughout the metropolitan area, including five major enclosed malls, one of which is located downtown. The Downtown Farmers Market runs May through October on Saturday mornings and offers shoppers fresh fruits and vegetables, home-baked breads and pastries, hand-made clothing and jewelry, specialty cheeses and wines, and music and entertainment.

Des Moines restaurants offer choices ranging from American and Midwestern fare to ethnic and continental cuisine. Prime rib and steak entrees are specialties at a number of the better restaurants. Chinese cuisine is another local favorite; barbeque, sandwich shops, cafes, vegetarian eateries, and other ethnic restaurants are popular as well. A local seafood restaurant is considered to have one of the largest selections of fresh seafood in the Midwest. Imported Italian pasta is the specialty at one of the city's oldest and most popular eateries.

*Visitor Information:* Greater Des Moines Convention and Visitors Bureau, 400 Locust Street, Suite 265, Des Moines, IA 50309; toll-free (800)451-2625; email info@desmoinescvb.com

# ■ Convention Facilities

Several meeting and convention facilities serve Des Moines. The Iowa Events Center offers the Hy-Vee Hall, Wells Fargo Arena, Polk County Convention Complex and Veterans Memorial Auditorium. Two levels furnish space for trade shows, conventions, meetings, banquets, and other activities at the Polk County Convention Complex, including a 47,000-square-foot exhibit hall with up to 27 meeting rooms. The new Hy-Vee Hall offers 100,000 square feet of expo hall space, up to 150,000 square feet of contiguous expo space, 14,000 square feet of meeting room space, and 23,700 square feet of pre-function space. Veterans Memorial Auditorium provides seating for 7,200 to 14,000 people; a total of 98,000 square feet of space can be used for exhibitions, sporting events, and entertainment. Two other principal meeting places in the city are the Civic Center, located downtown, and the Iowa State Fairgrounds. Area hotels and motels maintain banquet and meeting facilities for large and small groups. Nearly 9,000 rooms (1,200 near convention facilities) in over 80 hotels and motels are available for lodging in metropolitan Des Moines.

*Convention Information:* Greater Des Moines Convention and Visitors Bureau, 400 Locust Street, Suite 265, Des Moines, IA 50309; toll-free (800)451-2625; email info@desmoinescvb.com

# ■ Transportation

### Approaching the City

Des Moines International Airport, 10 minutes from downtown, is served by 15 commercial airlines with daily flights handling nearly 2 million passengers annually. It offers nonstop flights to nineteen destinations.

Principal highways that intersect northeast of the city are I-80, running east to west, and I-35, extending north to south. Federal highways include east-west U.S. 6 and north-south U.S. 69.

### Traveling in the City

Downtown Des Moines is laid out on a grid pattern; in the northeast sector, streets near the Des Moines River, still conforming to a grid, follow the configuration of the river. North-south streets are numbered and east-west streets are named.

Des Moines is noted for its four-mile skywalk system, which makes the city virtually "weatherproof." It is the largest per-capita skywalk system in the world.

Public transportation is provided by the Des Moines Metropolitan Transit Authority, locally known as The Metro; special service for the handicapped is available.

# ■ Communications

## Newspapers and Magazines

The daily newspaper in Des Moines is the morning *The Des Moines Register,* many times a Pulitzer Prize winner. *Des Moines Business Record,* a weekly newspaper, covers local business news and banking and financial information. *Cityview,* an alternative newspaper featuring investigative journalism, is distributed free throughout the metro area.

Home to the Meredith Corporation and other printing and publishing firms, Des Moines is a major center for the publication of nationally-circulated magazines. Among the popular magazines produced in the city are *Better Homes and Gardens, Ladies' Home Journal, Country Home, Midwest Living,* and *Successful Farming.* A wide range of special-interest publications based in Des Moines are directed toward readers with interests in such subjects as religion, agriculture, hunting, education, and crafts.

## Television and Radio

Five commercial television stations are based in Des Moines. Cable service is available. Radio listeners receive programming from over 15 AM and FM stations.

*Media Information:* *The Des Moines Register,* PO Box 957, Des Moines, IA 50304; telephone (515)284-8000

### Des Moines Online

City of Des Moines home page. Available www .dmgov.org

City of Des Moines Office of Economic Development. Available www.dmoed.org

Des Moines Public Library. Available www .pldminfo.org

Des Moines Public Schools. Available www.dmps .k12.ia.us

*The Des Moines Register* online. Available www .dmregister.com

Greater Des Moines Convention and Visitors Bureau. Available www.seedesmoines.com

Greater Des Moines Partnership. Available www .desmoinesmetro.com

Public Library of Des Moines. Available www .pldminfo.org

BIBLIOGRAPHY

Friedricks, William B., *Covering Iowa: The History of the Des Moines Register and Tribune Company, 1849-1985* (Iowa State University Press, 2000)

# Sioux City

## ■ The City in Brief

**Founded:** 1854 (incorporated 1857)

**Head Official:** Mayor Mike Hobart (since 2007)

**City Population**

    1980: Not available
    1990: 80,505
    2000: 85,013
    2006 estimate: 83,262
    Percent change, 1990–2000: 5.59%
    U.S. rank in 1980: Not available
    U.S. rank in 1990: Not available
    U.S. rank in 2000: Not available

**Metropolitan Area Population**

    1980: Not available
    1990: 115,018
    2000: 124,130
    2006 estimate: 143,474
    Percent change, 1990–2000: 7.9%
    U.S. rank in 1980: Not available
    U.S. rank in 1990: Not available
    U.S. rank in 2000: 236th (MSA)

**Area:** 54.8 square miles (2000)

**Elevation:** 1,117 feet above sea level

**Average Annual Temperature:** 51.3° F

**Average Annual Precipitation:** 26.03 inches

**Major Economic Sectors:** services, wholesale and retail trade, government

**Unemployment Rate:** 4.0% (June 2007)

**Per Capita Income:** $18,944 (2005)

**2005 FBI Crime Index Property:** 3,590

**2005 FBI Crime Index Violent:** 400

**Major Colleges and Universities:** Briar Cliff University, Morningside College, Tri-State Graduate Center, Western Iowa Tech Community College

**Daily Newspaper:** *Sioux City Journal*

## ■ Introduction

Sioux City has always been an important center for agriculture and manufacturing, and its unique location where the Missouri River joins the Big Sioux River at the meeting of three states—Iowa, Nebraska, and South Dakota—has made it an important center for trade as well. Though the history of the city has always been entwined with the progress of commerce, Sioux City prides itself on the quality of life enjoyed by its residents. Extensive recreation programs, a low cost of living, ample outdoors offerings, and a vibrant music scene all contribute to a strong sense of community in the region. The city motto is "Successful, Surprising Sioux City" and community leaders continue to work to bring that motto into the twenty-first century.

## ■ Geography and Climate

Sioux City is located in northwest Iowa, near the state's borders with Nebraska and South Dakota. Situated in the Loess Hills near the navigational head of the Missouri River, it is the hub of the greater "Siouxland" area, which covers the border region of all three states and also includes nearby Sergeant Bluff, South Sioux City, Dakota City, Dakota Dunes, and North Sioux City. The area has a temperate, four-season climate.

**Area:** 54.8 square miles (2000)

**Elevation:** 1,117 feet above sea level

**Average Temperature:** 51.3° F

**Average Annual Precipitation:** 26.03 inches

# ■ History

The history of Siouxland stretches back at least 15,000 years, when indigenous North Americans began to settle the region. In the 1700s, these Native Americans began to interact with European settlers through the fur trade along the wide artery of the Missouri River. The famous Lewis & Clark expedition, which set out to explore the land acquired by Thomas Jefferson in the Louisiana Purchase, stopped at a spot that is now Woodbury County. The spot was an important one on the journey, since it marked the only death of a member of the expedition to occur during the entire two-year trip. The officer, Sergeant Charles Floyd, was buried on a bluff over the Missouri River, and Captain Merriweather Lewis recorded a description of the area in his journal. Forty-five years after Floyd's death, the first non-native settlers moved into the area and the Siouxland community began to grow.

Farming dominated the early Sioux City area, with its wide prairies providing perfect grazing areas for livestock. The flourishing of the steamboat industry in the late nineteenth and early twentieth centuries made Sioux City, with its unique location at the navigational head of the Missouri River, a vital trading center, and helped its manufacturing and livestock sectors grow even further. The meatpacking industry, centered around the Stock Yards downtown, grew into one of the largest livestock markets in the United States during the 20th century. In 1887, the first Sioux City "Corn Palace" was built, representing an unprecedented community effort and the city's first large tourist draw. A decade later, President Grover Cleveland came to see the famous Sioux City "Corn Palace" festival.

An 1892 flood on the Floyd River briefly decimated the meatpacking industry, but it regrouped in a safer location, stronger than ever. Local residents loved to jokingly refer to the pungent smell of the stock pens as "the smell of money." As the stockyards grew, so did the transportation industry, with railroads and trucking companies following in the wake of the steamships. The iconic local institution—The American Popcorn Company—was begun in 1914, marking the beginning of the expansion of the Sioux City food production industry. The city continued to grow in the twentieth century, despite several industrial disasters and labor unrest in the meatpacking industry in the 1920s. In the early 1930s a farmer's strike nearly shut down the city and stopped almost all food shipments for a short time.

In 1951 Sioux City garnered national attention when officials at Memorial Park Cemetery refused to bury Sergeant John R. Rice, a decorated World War II veteran and Korean War casualty, because he was Native American. The city was tarnished by accusations of racism and there was a rift between city officials and local Native Americans until nearly fifty years after the incident, when the city finally made amends with the family of Sergeant Rice. However, by the early 1960s the stigma appeared to have gone away, and Sioux City was named an "All-American City" by the National Civic League (an honor it would achieve again in 1990). The 1970s were tumultuous for Sioux City, with a troubled manufacturing sector bringing about more labor unrest. Meanwhile, city leaders attempted to bring about urban revitalization downtown, with mixed results.

Despite the decline of some of its traditional industries, including manufacturing and food processing, in the early twenty-first century, Sioux City remains an important trading hub for the Midwest. The city is proactively trying to diversify its economy and revitalize the downtown area. Local residents continue to praise Siouxland for its strong sense of tradition and community involvement.

***Historical Information:*** Sioux City Public Museum's Pearl Street Research Center, 407 Pearl St., Sioux City, IA 51101; telephone (712)224-5001

# ■ Population Profile

**Metropolitan Area Residents**

1980: Not available
1990: 115,018
2000: 124,130
2006 estimate: 143,474
Percent change, 1990–2000: 7.9%
U.S. rank in 1980: Not available
U.S. rank in 1990: Not available
U.S. rank in 2000: 236th (MSA)

**City Residents**

1980: Not available
1990: 80,505
2000: 85,013
2006 estimate: 83,262
Percent change, 1990–2000: 5.59%
U.S. rank in 1980: Not available
U.S. rank in 1990: Not available
U.S. rank in 2000: Not available

**Density:** 1,551.3 people per square mile (2000)

**Racial and ethnic characteristics (2005)**

White: 66,234
Black: 1,968
American Indian and Alaska Native: 1,065

*Airphoto-Jim Wark*

Asian: 1,881
Native Hawaiian and Pacific Islander: 0
Hispanic or Latino (may be of any race): 11,230
Other: 5,770

**Percent of residents born in state:** 66.1% (2000)

**Age characteristics (2005)**

Population under 5 years old: 5,914
Population 5 to 9 years old: 4,138
Population 10 to 14 years old: 5,536
Population 15 to 19 years old: 5,001
Population 20 to 24 years old: 6,342
Population 25 to 34 years old: 9,506
Population 35 to 44 years old: 12,009
Population 45 to 54 years old: 11,248
Population 55 to 59 years old: 3,950
Population 60 to 64 years old: 4,495
Population 65 to 74 years old: 4,948
Population 75 to 84 years old: 3,758
Population 85 years and older: 1,550
Median age: 37.5 years

**Births (2006, MSA)**

Total number: 2,218

**Deaths (2006, MSA)**

Total number: 1,272

**Money income (2005)**

Per capita income: $18,944
Median household income: $39,037
Total households: 31,797

**Number of households with income of...**

less than $10,000: 2,620
$10,000 to $14,999: 2,888
$15,000 to $24,999: 5,750
$25,000 to $34,999: 3,146
$35,000 to $49,999: 5,646
$50,000 to $74,999: 6,822
$75,000 to $99,999: 2,634
$100,000 to $149,999: 1,828
$150,000 to $199,999: 378
$200,000 or more: 85

**Percent of families below poverty level:** 14.4% (2005)

**2005 FBI Crime Index Property:** 3,590

**2005 FBI Crime Index Violent:** 400

# ■ Municipal Government

Sioux City operates under the council-manager form of government. Four city councilors and the mayor (also part of city council) all serve staggered four-year terms. City elections are held every other year, and after each election the mayor appoints another councilmember to serve as mayor pro-tem. In 2007 Sioux City citizens elected the mayor directly for the first time in 50 years.

**Head Official:** Mayor Mike Hobart (since 2007; current term expires 2011)

**Total Number of City Employees:** 726 (2007)

*City Information:* City of Sioux City Iowa, 405 6th Street, Sioux City, Iowa 51102; telephone (712)279-6109

# ■ Economy

## Major Industries and Commercial Activity

In 2006 Iowa was named the fastest-growing economy in the Midwest by the Bureau of Economic Analysis and number three in the nation for lowest cost of doing business by the Milken Institute.

Thanks to the confluence of rivers and railways, Sioux City is a major center for warehousing and distribution in the Midwest. It can easily ship to Canada, Mexico, and a number of Midwestern industrial hubs. Agriculture is also an important part of the Siouxland's economic picture. Crops grown within a 200-mile radius include corn and soybeans. Hogs, cattle, poultry, and eggs are also raised in the region.

Manufacturing, particularly of food products, is key to the Siouxland's economy. Thirteen manufacturers have their corporate headquarters in Siouxland. The area is also home to one *Fortune* 500 company, Tyson Foods. Other agricultural processing companies in the area include Cargill, John Morrell, Ag Processing, ADM, ConAgra, Beef Products, Inc., M.G. Waldbaum, and Wells's Dairy. In 2007 manufacturing accounted for 12,000 area jobs; however, this represented a loss of 5,000 jobs since 2000, indicative of a general downward trend in the industry. Between September 2006 and September 2007, the manufacturing sector in Sioux City experienced a decline of 7.7 percent. There were a few bright spots for the economy; in the same time period, professional and business jobs increased by 6 percent and government employment increased by a percentage.

However, the rapid decline of manufacturing in the early 2000s was problematic for the city's economy, and city leaders were seeking ways to diversify the economy. In 2007 Sioux City was pushing for biotechnology firms to move into the area; other targeted industries included insurance companies (already a strong presence in Iowa) and the fast-growing organic foods sector. The city received a major economic jolt in spring 2007, when Northwest Airlines announced the creation of a new corporate reservations call center in downtown Sioux City. The project was expected to bring over 330 new jobs to the area and to help boost the city's telecommunications sector.

**Items and goods produced:** meat, dairy, popcorn, candy, baked goods, brick, tile, soda pop, pipe machinery, gelatin, denim, aluminum and steel goods, trailers

## Incentive Programs—New and Existing Companies

*Local programs:* Sioux City provides incentives for business that will contribute jobs or taxable property to the community. These include tax breaks, tax increment financing in designated urban renewal areas, industrial revenue bonds for some economic development programs, and micro-loans given by the Siouxland Economic Development Corporation.

*State programs:* State programs include certain property tax exemptions, job training, low-interest loans and forgivable loans for business development, tax abatements on new research and manufacturing facilities, and state tax credits for new job creation. In addition, no sales or use taxes are assessed on equipment or computers and open port warehousing is available. The Iowa Values Fund, established in 2006, offers concentrated assistance to businesses operating in the following sectors: the life sciences, advanced manufacturing, and information solutions. The Revitalize Iowa's Sound Economy (RISE) provides funds to cover costs of transportation directly related to economic development projects.

*Job training programs:* The Community Economic Betterment Account (CEBA) program provides financial assistance to companies that create new employment opportunities, keep existing jobs, and make new capital investment in Iowa. Western Iowa Tech Community College, in conjunction with the Iowa Industrial New Jobs Training Program, helps individual companies design training programs to fit their needs. The Iowa Retraining Program, also in partnership with Western Iowa Tech, helps retrain workers to cope with technological change.

## Development Projects

In October 2005 Sioux City was named as an inaugural "Great Place" in Iowa, one of three selected from a pool of over 140 applicants. The honor meant that state resources and existing programs would be dedicated to achieving Sioux City's "Great City" proposal, which called for an expanded urban core and a diversified economy. There are five major prongs to the plan: Fourth Street Place, Front Door/Riverfront Access, the Yards, the Floyd Boulevard Food Market, and the Sioux City School of Architecture. The Fourth Street Place portion of the plan called for a new building to house the Sioux City Public Museum and Regents Center, a new connection between Nebraska and Jones Streets, rehabilitation of the Badgerow Building, and the replacement of the Heritage Parking Ramp. The plan's call for increased development of the Riverfront area incorporated the reconstruction of Interstate 29 by the Riverfront, the connection of recreational trails throughout the downtown area, and new signs throughout the area. The Yards area, a stockyard in former times, was slated for the transformation of the Yards Channel into a landscaped historical park, the restoration of the old Hose House exterior, the demolition of the KD Station, and the addition of historical architectural elements into the Gordon Drive Bridge. Improvements to the Floyd Boulevard Market were to include seminars on food issues, agricultural production and marketing, marketing space for local vendors, and the installation of a restaurant serving local foods. Planners also called for all renovations to be rendered in the Sioux City School of Architecture, a style that connotes a terra cotta branding of downtown buildings that owes much to both Art Deco and the Prairie School of Architecture. To facilitate that vision, the plan also detailed the establishment of Regents School of Design. As of 2007, no timetable had been given for the completion of the "Great Place" plan.

A "boundless playground" was scheduled to be completed in Leif Erikson Park by fall 2007. The project was a joint venture by the City of Sioux City, Opportunities Unlimited, and the Siouxland Chamber Foundation. The 200-acre Expedition Business Park, near the Sioux Gateway Park, is a joint initiative of the City and The Siouxland Initiative. The site is intended for economic development; early tenants included warehousing and distribution centers.

*Economic Development Information:* Siouxland Chamber of Commerce, 101 Pierce Street, Sioux City, IA 51101; telephone (712)255-7903

## Commercial Shipping

Iowa is the only state bordered by two navigable rivers, and many area exports leave via water. Big Soo Terminal, by the Mississippi River, is one of the largest terminals on the inland waterway system. It can service up to 250 tons of product per hour by barge, rail or truck. Big Soo has space for 115,000 tons of dry bulk storage, liquid product storage for 6,000,000 gallons, a 200,000-bushel elevator for grains, and unlimited ground storage.

Sioux City is served by the merged Burlington Northern/Santa Fe Railroads, which ships anywhere throughout the Midwest south to the Gulf, throughout the southwest to San Diego and Los Angeles, and to northwest ports in Seattle, Tacoma and Portland. It is also served by the Chicago Northwestern and Union Pacific rail lines. Sioux City is less than 600 miles from Chicago, Milwaukee, Minneapolis, Kansas City, St. Louis, Oklahoma City, Denver, and Winnipeg.

## Labor Force and Employment Outlook

Iowa is a Right-to-Work state. The labor force in Sioux City is somewhat stagnant and experienced virtually no net growth between 1997 and 2007. However, in 2006 local analysts predicted moderate population growth in greater Siouxland by 2010. The best-represented age group in Sioux City is the under age ten demographic (which comprises over 15 percent of the population), a statistic that points to a growing long-term work force.

The average manufacturing wage in Siouxland is 16 percent below the national average. Workers in Iowa, Nebraska, and South Dakota (the states that make up greater Siouxland) are ranked among the most productive in the nation. The three states also boast high standardized test averages and college graduation rates, creating an attractive work force for employers.

The following is a summary of data regarding the Sioux City IA-NE-SD metropolitan area labor force, 2006 annual averages.

**Size of nonagricultural labor force:** 72,600

**Number of workers employed in . . .**

> construction and mining: Not available
> manufacturing: 13,000
> trade, transportation and utilities: 15,700
> information: Not available
> financial activities: Not available
> professional and business services: 6,900
> educational and health services: Not available
> leisure and hospitality: 6,900
> other services: Not available
> government: 9,200

**Average hourly earnings of production workers employed in manufacturing:** Not available

**Unemployment rate:** 4.0% (June 2007)

| *Largest employers (2007)* | *Number of employees* |
|---|---|
| Tyson Foods | 4,400 |
| Mercy Medical Center | 2,000 |
| Sioux City Schools | 1,500 |
| John Morrell & Co. | 1,300 |
| St. Luke's Regional Medical Center | 1,300 |
| City of Sioux City | 770 |
| 185th Air Refueling Wing IA ANG | 690 |
| MidAmerican Energy | 659 |

| Largest employers (2007) | Number of employees |
|---|---|
| Tur-Pak Foods | 500 |
| Qwest Communications | 468 |

## Cost of Living

The following is a summary of data regarding key cost of living factors for the Sioux City area.

**2007 (1st quarter) ACCRA Average House Price:** Not available

**2007 (1st quarter) ACCRA Cost of Living Index:** Not available

**State income tax rate:** 0.36% to 8.98%

**State sales tax rate:** 5.0%

**Local income tax rate:** 1.5%

**Local sales tax rate:** 7.0%

**Property tax rate:** 1.6%

*Economic Information:* Siouxland Chamber of Commerce, 101 Pierce Street, Sioux City, IA, 51101; telephone (712)255-7903

# ■ Education and Research

## Elementary and Secondary Schools

Sioux City Community Schools served 13,898 students during the 2007-2008 school year. Nearly 60 percent of teachers in the district have a master's degree or higher. The district offers four alternative learning centers and boasts a 94 percent daily attendance rate, with standardized test score averages at or above the national rate. The school district has made state-of-the art technology a priority in all its schools, including at the elementary level, and uses PLATO Learning Resource technology to augment its emphasis on high-tech skills.

The following is a summary of data regarding the Sioux City Community School District as of the 2005–2006 school year.

**Total enrollment:** 14,048

**Number of facilities**

    elementary schools: 21
    junior high/middle schools: 3
    senior high schools: 4
    other: 0

**Student/teacher ratio:** 14.3:1

**Teacher salaries (2005–06)**

    elementary median: $36,540
    junior high/middle median: $39,660
    secondary median: $35,830

**Funding per pupil:** $5,128

Private schools in the area include Bishop Heelan Catholic Schools, Siouxland Community Christian School, and St. Paul's Lutheran School.

*Public Schools Information:* Sioux City Community Schools, 1221 Pierce Street, Sioux City, IA 51105; telephone (712)224-4663

## Colleges and Universities

Within the boundaries of Sioux City, there are a number of institutions of higher learning: Briar Cliff University, Morningside College, St. Luke's College of Nursing and Health Sciences, Tri-State Graduate Center and Western Iowa Tech Community College. University of Iowa extension classes can also be taken in Sioux City, and there are five more colleges and one university within a 65-mile drive of the city.

Briar Cliff University is a four-year, private, Franciscan college that enrolls approximately 1,100 students from 24 states. Morningside College, a four-year liberal arts institution, was founded in 1894 by the Methodist Episcopal Church and has an enrollment of 1,150 students. Morningside was selected as one of the Midwest's "Best Comprehensive Colleges's" for bachelor's degrees by *U.S. News & World Report* each year between 2005 and 2008. It has also been ranked among the "Best Midwestern Colleges" by *The Princeton Review* since 2003. St. Luke's College awards associate of science degrees in nursing, radiologic technology, and respiratory care, and offers certificate programs in computerized tomography, magnetic resonance imaging mammography, and ultrasound. The Tri-State Graduate Center is a consortium of local universities that makes graduate coursework available through online and distance-learning classes.

## Libraries and Research Centers

The Sioux City Public Library has over 47,000 active cardholders, or more than half the city's population. The library has a main library and two branches: The Wilbur Aalfs (Main) Library, the Morningside Branch Library, and the Perry Creek Branch Library. Together they house a collection of more than 200,000 volumes, and annual circulation tops half a million books and magazines. Special programs include weekly storytime sessions and a summer reading competition.

Siouxland is also home to several smaller community libraries, including the brand new South Sioux City Public Library and Dakota City Public Library. The area is also home to the Bishop Mueller Library at Briar Cliff University and the Hickman Johnson Furrow Learning Center at Morningside College.

*Public Library Information:* Wilbur Aalfs Main Library, 529 Pierce St., Sioux City, IA 51101; telephone (712)255-2933

# ■ Health Care

Sioux City is served by two major health centers, the Mercy Medical Center and St. Luke's Regional Medical Center, which have a combined 832 beds. In total, the Siouxland area has 300 physicians and surgeons and 53 dentists. Mercy Medical Center-Sioux City is a tertiary facility that is the designated Level II trauma center for the area. In 2007 Health Grades ranked the Medical Center first in Iowa for vascular surgery and cardiac interventional procedures. The hospital also ranks among the top 10 percent of the nation's 5,000 hospitals for overall cardiac services. The St. Luke's Regional Medical Center's services include a Center for Preventive Medicine, a Center for Digestive Disorders, the Bomgaars Center for Cancer Care, and the Neonatal Intensive Care Unit. St. Luke's also sponsors a number of educational medical programs for the community, including 24-hour health information hotline and free health seminars.

Sioux City is also home to the June E. Nylen Cancer Center, which houses both clinical trials and cancer treatment facilities, and the Center for Neurosciences, Orthopaedics & Spine (CNOS). There are four area assisted living centers.

*Health Care Information:* Mercy Medical Center - Sioux City, 801 5th St, Sioux City, IA 51102; telephone (712)279-2010

# ■ Recreation

## Sightseeing

Greater Siouxland (where Iowa, Nebraska and South Dakota meet) is full of things to see and do. At the Lewis & Clark Interpretive Center visitors can experience a day of reenacted soldiering as members of the Lewis & Clark's Corps of Discovery. The Sergeant Floyd Monument commemorates the only member of the Lewis & Clark expedition to die on the journey. The Chief War Eagle Monument, which overlooks the tri-state area and memorializes a local Native American leader, is a popular destination for picnics. The Flight 232 Memorial, a statue of Colonel Dennis Nielsen carrying a child to safety, commemorates the rescue efforts of the Sioux City community after the crash of United Flight 232 in 1989. The Dorothy Pecaut Nature center is home to a "walk-under" prairie, 400-gallon aquarium of native fish, and natural history dioramas. The center also has a resource library and walking trails.

For the gambler, there's Argosy Casino, housed on a riverboat on the Missouri River, which boasts 659 slots and 28 table games that include Blackjack, Roulette, Craps, Pai Gow Poker and Live Action Poker. Other casinos in the greater Siouxland area include the North Sioux "Strip, " WinnaVegas Casino, Keno Casino, and Casino Omaha.

The Historic Fourth Street area, listed on the National Register of Historic Places, is full of nineteenth century commercial buildings now home to Sioux City's finest shopping and dining. The Mid-America Air Museum, a popular local destination, is a collection of military, commercial and general aviation artifacts stretching back to the time of the Wright brothers' flight. The Sioux City Public Museum, housed in the 1893 John Peirce Mansion, has exhibits on regional and Native American history, as well as natural history.

A 30-foot statue of the Immaculate Heart of Mary Queen of Peace in Trinity Heights is surrounded by 53 acres of landscaping and prayer stations. Near the popular destination is a life-sized, hand-carved wood sculpture of the Last Supper and a 33-foot statue of the Sacred Heart of Jesus.

## Arts and Culture

Greater Siouxland is home to a remarkably vibrant local arts scene. The three-story Sioux City Art Center houses both traditional and contemporary art and features several annual exhibitions. The Center also hosts art classes for adults and children. LAMB Productions Theater puts on five shows per year, and also is home to the Lamb School of Theatre and Music.

The Orpheum Theatre, built in 1927, hosts the "Broadway Series" of musicals, as well as touring dance and theatre shows. Past performers have included Bill Cosby, Sheryl Crow, The Oak Ridge Boys, Willie Nelson, and Tony Bennett. The Orpheum is also the home of the Sioux City Symphony Orchestra, an area staple for over ninety years. The Sioux City Community Theatre stages three to four amateur productions a year. The Sioux City Concert Course, held in Eppley Auditorium, is an occasional series of classical and light opera performances. Tyson's Event Center, which holds a 10,000-seat arena, is the site for big-name musical acts and other performers who come to the area. Grandview Park is the city's only public garden, and features an ampitheater and band shell for music festivals and concerts.

## Festivals and Holidays

The Sioux City festival year begins with "First on Fourth," the city's annual New Year's Celebration held in the Historic Fourth Street District, which highlights local restaurants and features a fireworks display. Spring brings the Cornstalk music festival. June Jam, celebrating regional musicians, draws crowds topping 10,000. Awesome Biker Nights, a popular Siouxland tradition for motorcycle enthusiasts, closes the Historic Fourth Street area for automobiles to make room for cyclists. The event, a "Sturgis-style rally," is usually held in late June. Saturday in the Park, held each year over Fourth of July weekend, features a parade and musical performers. The previous evening, "The Big Parade" is held along the Missouri River. The event, which draws over 30,000 partipants, has featured past performances by such artists as Santana, Ziggy Marley, The Allman Brothers Band, and Buddy Guy. The Winnebago tribe holds an annual powwow in July in commemoration of Chief Little Priest, twenty miles outside of Sioux City. The Chili Cook-Off, held in late summer, features contests for best chili, best salsa, and best booths. In August the city hosts Freedom Fest, a free, day-long annual Christian music festival. Also held in August, the Greater Siouxland Fair & Rodeo features food, livestock exhibitions, and music. Fridays on the Promenade, held all summer long, features an eclectic program of live music. ArtSplash, held annually on the banks of the Missouri River over Labor Day Weekend, features food, crafts, live entertainment, and a fifty-ton painted sand sculpture.

## Sports for the Spectator

There are several professional sports teams in Siouxland. The Sioux City Bandits play football in the National Indoor Football League. The Sioux City Explorers are members of the Northern Baseball League and play in the 3,200-seat Lewis and Clark Stadium. The Sioux City Musketeers, who play at the Tyson Events Center, compete in the United States Hockey League, a developmental juniors league.

Every Saturday between late April and Labor Day, racing enthusiasts can attend NASCAR-Winston Racing Series races at the Park Jefferson International Speedway in Jefferson, South Dakota.

Local college fans can watch Briar Cliff University and Morningside College men's and women's athletic teams in sports that include football, baseball, softball, soccer, and basketball. Game-day trips to University of Iowa, Iowa State University, the University of South Dakota and the University of Nebraska are not unusual for Siouxland fans and alumni of the schools.

## Sports for the Participant

For the fishing enthusiast, the annual Missouri River Open Bass Tournament brings in bass fishers from wide-flung places. A plethora of fishing opportunities exist on the many local waterways, which include the Missouri River, Big Sioux River, Little Sioux River, Missouri River Oxbow Lakes, Brown's Lake, Blue Lake, and Snyders Bend Lake. Siouxland hunters find plenty of ring-necked pheasant, wild turkey, white-tailed deer, fox squirrel, duck, geese and bobwhite quail.

Each October, amateur and competitve runners participate in the Siouxland Lewis & Clark Marathon. The Long Lines Family Recreational Center features a batting cage, basketball courts, and the area's only climbing wall. The IBP Ice Rink is open year-round for skaters. Youth and adult recreational sports leagues are popular. Siouxland has over fifty park sites, trails and pools. The popular Riverfront Trail spans 1.85 miles through Chris Larsen Park, while the Gateway/River's Edge Trail runs 3 miles along the riverfront. The area also has 22 public tennis courts, a 44,000-square-foot golf dome, and 14 public golf courses.

*Recreation Information:* Siouxland Chamber of Commerce, 101 Pierce Street, Sioux City, IA 51101; telephone (712)255-7903

## Shopping and Dining

Siouxland is home to several large malls: Southern Hills Malls (anchored by Sears and JCPenney), the new Lakeport Commons, and Marketplace Shopping Center. Downtown Sioux City is also home to a cluster of free-standing shops, many of them concentrated in the Historic Fourth Street Area.

There are over 100 restaurants in greater Siouxland. A number are chain restaurants, but locally-owned favorites have cuisines that include Mexican, American, and Italian.

*Visitor Information:* Sioux City Tourism Bureau, 801 4th Street, Sioux City, IA 51101; telephone (712) 279-4800; toll-free (800)593-2228; fax (712)279-4900

# ■ Convention Facilities

The Sioux City Convention Center features a 50,000-square-foot exhibit space, with an additional 10 rooms and 10,000 square feet of meeting space. The center also features a gourmet in-house catering service. The Siouxland Convention Center was built in 1983 as an ice arena, then converted two years later into a convention facility. It has two buildings, with a total of 35,800 square feet of space, and can accommodate groups of up to 3,500 people.

There are more than twenty hotels in the Siouxland area.

*Convention Information:* Sioux City Convention Center, 801 4th Street, Sioux City, IA 51101; telephone (712)279-4800

# ■ Transportation

## Approaching the City

The Sioux Gateway Airport has the longest runway in the state of Iowa, at over 9,000 feet. Direct service is provided by Northwest to Minneapolis; Frontier Airlines also flies commercially to Denver. Eppley Airfield, in Omaha, Nebraska, offers international air service.

Interstate 29, part of the NAFTA Corridor, passes through Sioux City on its north-south route linking Winnipeg Canada with the Mexican border. I-29, about ninety minutes from downtown Sioux City, connects with two major east-west highways, I-90 and I-80. Several highways pass through Siouxland directly: U.S. 20, 75, and 77.

### Traveling in the City

Sioux City Transit System provides public transportation for Sioux City, South Sioux City, and North Sioux City. All routes are run on a pulse system, with service every thirty minutes during peak times.

There are two taxi companies in the area.

# ■ Communications

### Newspapers and Magazines

The *Sioux City Journal* is the region's daily newspaper of record. *The Globe* is the newspaper for the local Catholic community. Other periodicals published in the area include *Shoppers Guide*, *Siouxland Lifestyle Magazine*, *Local Sports Source*, and *Variety/Variedad Magazine*.

### Television and Radio

There are thirteen AM and FM radio stations broadcasting from Sioux City, in formats that include country, Christian, and easy listening. Sioux City has five television stations, including CBS and FOX affiliates, and the local station Cable One.

***Media Information:*** *Sioux City Journal*, PO Box 118, Sioux City, IA 51102; telephone (712)293-4250

### Sioux City Online

Sioux City Chamber of Commerce. Available www .siouxlandchamber.com

Sioux City Economic Development Department. Available sioux

*Sioux City Journal*. Available www.siouxcityjournal. com

Sioux City Public Library. Available www .siouxcitylibrary.org

Sioux City Public Schools. Available www .siouxcityschools.org

Sioux City Tourism. Available www .siouxcitytourism.com

BIBLIOGRAPHY

Engle, Paul, *A Lucky American Childhood* (Iowa City, IA: University of Iowa Press, 1996)

# Kansas

# The State in Brief

**Nickname:** Sunflower State

**Motto:** Ad astra per aspera (To the stars through difficulties)

**Flower:** Native sunflower

**Bird:** Western meadowlark

**Area:** 82,276 square miles (2000; U.S. rank 15th)

**Elevation:** Ranges from 680 feet to 4,039 feet above sea level

**Climate:** Temperate, but with seasonal extremes of temperature as well as blizzards, tornadoes, and severe thunderstorms; semi-arid in the west

**Admitted to Union:** January 29, 1861

**Capital:** Topeka

**Head Official:** Governor Kathleen Sebelius (D) (until 2010)

**Population**

1980: 2,364,000
1990: 2,495,000
2000: 2,688,824
2006 estimate: 2,764,075
Percent change, 1990–2000: 8.5%
U.S. rank in 2006: 33rd
Percent of residents born in state: 59.10% (2006)
Density: 33.5 people per square mile (2006)
2006 FBI Crime Index Total: 115,406

**Racial and Ethnic Characteristics (2006)**

White: 2,361,047
Black or African American: 153,560
American Indian and Alaska Native: 23,749
Asian: 60,646
Native Hawaiian and Pacific Islander: 1,145
Hispanic or Latino (may be of any race): 236,351
Other: 93,803

**Age Characteristics (2006)**

Population under 5 years old: 194,702
Population 5 to 19 years old: 585,457
Percent of population 65 years and over: 12.9%
Median age: 36.3

**Vital Statistics**

Total number of births (2006): 39,904
Total number of deaths (2006): 24,351
AIDS cases reported through 2005: 2,680

**Economy**

Major industries: Agriculture, oil production, mining, manufacturing
Unemployment rate (2006): 5.3%
Per capita income (2006): $23,818
Median household income (2006): $45,478
Percentage of persons below poverty level (2006): 12.4%
Income tax rate: 3.5% to 6.45%
Sales tax rate: 5.3%

# Kansas City

## ■ The City in Brief

**Founded:** 1843 (incorporated 1859)

**Head Official:** CEO/Mayor Joe Reardon (since 2005)

**City Population**
    1980: 161,148
    1990: 151,521
    2000: 146,866
    2006 estimate: 143,801
    Percent change, 1990–2000: −3.0%
    U.S. rank in 1980: 93rd
    U.S. rank in 1990: 115th
    U.S. rank in 2000: 161st

**Metropolitan Area Population**
    1980: 1,433,000
    1990: 1,582,875
    2000: 1,776,062
    2006 estimate: Not available
    Percent change, 1990–2000: 12.2%
    U.S. rank in 1980: 25th
    U.S. rank in 1990: Not available
    U.S. rank in 2000: 25th

**Area:** 124 square miles (2000)

**Elevation:** 740 feet above sea level

**Average Annual Temperature:** 54.7° F

**Average Annual Precipitation:** 37.98 inches of rain; 19.9 inches of snow

**Major Economic Sectors:** Services, trade, government, manufacturing

**Unemployment Rate:** 5.6% (June 2007)

**Per Capita Income:** $16,977 (2005)

**2005 FBI Crime Index Property:** 10,678

**2005 FBI Crime Index Violent:** 1,166

**Major Colleges and Universities:** Kansas City Kansas Community College; University of Kansas Medical Center

**Daily Newspaper:** *Kansas City Kansan*

## ■ Introduction

Kansas City, Kansas, is the seat of Wyandotte County and the center of a metropolitan statistical area that covers the counties of Johnson, Leavenworth, Miami, and Wyandotte in Kansas, plus several Missouri counties. Established by Wyandot Native Americans, Kansas City was the site of the drafting of the state constitution and played a crucial role in the slavery issue in the Civil War. While the economy has been strongly based in the transportation and trade industries, the city has begun to recruit new business health care, education, finance, and other professional services. The Kansas City area is recognized as one of the fastest-growing labor markets in the country and was ranked by *Entrepreneur* magazine in 2006 as one of the top U.S. cities for small business. Kansas City's cultural and recreational attractions also make it a popular Midwest tourist destination.

## ■ Geography and Climate

Gently sloping terrain and forested hills surround Kansas City, which is located on the Kansas-Missouri border at the confluence of the Kansas and Missouri Rivers. The area is laced with lakes, streams, and small rivers. A four-season climate prevails, with a substantial range in temperatures; the average annual snowfall is nearly 20 inches.

**Area:** 124 square miles (2000)

**Elevation:** 740 feet above sea level

**Average Temperature:** 54.7° F

**Average Annual Precipitation:** 37.98 inches of rain; 19.9 inches of snow

# ■ History

## Wyandot Tribe Establishes Townsite

Kansa Native Americans were the first inhabitants to occupy land near both banks of the Kansas (Kaw) River at its confluence with the Missouri River, the site of Kansas City. The explorers Meriwether Lewis and William Clark camped on Kaw Point, the land between the two rivers and now part of Kansas City, in 1804 during their exploration of the Louisiana Purchase. The land became part of the Delaware Indian reservation in 1829, and the Delaware sold the land in 1843 to the Wyandot.

The Wyandot, an integrated tribe of Native Americans and whites from western Lake Erie and the last of the migrating tribes, founded a town called Wyandott in the eastern part of the Wyandott Purchase. An educated and cultured agrarian society, they built the first free school in Kansas and reestablished their Ohio church; they also opened a community-owned store. The Wyandot, knowing their land would be highly prized by white settlers, decided to approach Congress on the issue of establishing a Territory, and elected Abelard Guthrie, a white member of the tribe by marriage, as a delegate to the Thirty-Second Congress. Guthrie was not admitted but Wyandot leaders decided to organize Kansas-Nebraska into a provisional territory on July 26, 1853, thus focusing national attention on their community.

## Slavery Issue Dominates Territory

The next year Congress passed the Kansas-Nebraska Act, which inflamed sectional sentiments on the issue of slavery in the territories and helped to contribute to the outbreak of the Civil War. The Wyandot petitioned for and received the rights of citizenship, which enabled them to divide their land among the individual members of the tribe and open the reserve to settlement. The Wyandott City Town Company was formed in 1856 to plan and develop the town, which was incorporated as a town in 1858 and as a city the next year. In July 1859 members of a convention at Wyandott wrote the constitution by which Kansas would enter the Union as a free state; however Senate politics delayed the signing of the bill until January 29, 1861. The state was known as Bleeding Kansas in the decade before the Civil War, as settlers on both sides of the slavery controversy populated the area. Wyandott citizens became active in antislavery efforts and African Americans began moving to the region after the Civil War, their migration reaching a peak between 1878 and 1882.

Beginning in 1860, when James McGrew opened the first slaughter house, and continuing when eight years later Edward Patterson and J. W. Slavens started a packing house, the city was a meat processing center. This industry received its biggest boost when Charles Francis Adams, descendant of two former presidents, built the first stockyards in the city and convinced Plankington and Armour to relocate their meat packing business from Missouri in 1871.

## Stockyards, Consolidation Contribute to Growth

Small towns around Wyandotte such as old Kansas City, Armstrong, and Armourdale sprouted up near the rail lines and packing houses. Through consolidation and legislative annexation, the city of Kansas City was created in 1886 when these towns combined with the larger Wyandotte, which vied for the naming of the new city after itself. The name Kansas City was picked, however, because it would be a more attractive inducement for the selling of municipal bonds. Argentine became part of Kansas City via petition in 1909, and Rosedale followed suit by legislative enactment in 1922. Quindaro Township, once a town named after Guthrie's Wyandot wife, was absorbed through expansion. Turner was added in 1966, thus continuing the expansion of Kansas City's borders. In 1992, the city annexed part of Wyandotte County.

Kansas City was one of the nation's first cities to locate a model industrial park away from residential areas—the Fairfax Industrial District. The city completed a two-decade urban renewal project in 1980. Still, like many other aging, working-class cities, Kansas City was plagued by a loss of population to the suburbs. Seeking to reverse that trend, a group called the Citizens for Consolidation, backed in part by Kansas City, Missouri, businesses, spearheaded a movement to consolidate city and county governments. In 1997 Kansas City voters overwhelmingly approved the consolidation into a system called the Unified Government of Wyandotte County/Kansas City, Kansas. Former schoolteacher Carol Marinovich was elected the first mayor/CEO of the new government. By 2000, the consolidation had resulted in a considerable increase in government efficiency. With city and county officials on the same team, the city was able to lure the $283 million Kansas International Speedway to Kansas City; the project was completed in 2001.

Today, the Kansas City area is recognized as one of the fastest-growing labor markets in the country. *Entrepreneur* magazine ranks it among top U.S. cities for small business and *Expansion Management* magazine identifies it as one of the best places in the U.S. to locate a company. Kansas City's cultural and recreational attractions also make it a popular Midwest tourist destination.

***Historical Information:*** Wyandotte County Historical Society and Museum, 631 N. 126th St., Bonner Springs, KS 66012; telephone (913)721-1078. Kansas

*©2008 Michael Mihalevich*

City Kansas Public Library Kansas Collection, 625 Minnesota Avenue, Kansas City, KS 66101; telephone (913) 551-3280; fax (913)279-2032

# ■ Population Profile

## Metropolitan Area Residents

1980: 1,433,000
1990: 1,582,875
2000: 1,776,062
2006 estimate: Not available
Percent change, 1990–2000: 12.2%
U.S. rank in 1980: 25th
U.S. rank in 1990: Not available
U.S. rank in 2000: 25th

## City Residents

1980: 161,148
1990: 151,521
2000: 146,866
2006 estimate: 143,801
Percent change, 1990–2000: −3.0%
U.S. rank in 1980: 93rd

U.S. rank in 1990: 115th
U.S. rank in 2000: 161st

**Density:** 1,181.9 people per square mile (2000)

**Racial and ethnic characteristics (2005)**

White: 79,060
Black: 44,620
American Indian and Alaska Native: 1,064
Asian: 2,446
Native Hawaiian and Pacific Islander: 0
Hispanic or Latino (may be of any race): 32,328
Other: 13,261

**Percent of residents born in state:** 55.0% (2000)

**Age characteristics (2005)**

Population under 5 years old: 12,080
Population 5 to 9 years old: 9,711
Population 10 to 14 years old: 11,980
Population 15 to 19 years old: 9,595
Population 20 to 24 years old: 9,425
Population 25 to 34 years old: 22,047
Population 35 to 44 years old: 20,162
Population 45 to 54 years old: 19,445

Population 55 to 59 years old: 8,039
Population 60 to 64 years old: 5,102
Population 65 to 74 years old: 7,263
Population 75 to 84 years old: 5,691
Population 85 years and older: 1,801
Median age: 33.7 years

**Births (2006)**

Total number: 2,736

**Deaths (2006)**

Total number: 1,325

**Money income (2005)**

Per capita income: $16,977
Median household income: $33,157
Total households: 53,597

**Number of households with income of ...**

less than $10,000: 6,495
$10,000 to $14,999: 4,937
$15,000 to $24,999: 7,744
$25,000 to $34,999: 8,723
$35,000 to $49,999: 8,475
$50,000 to $74,999: 9,103
$75,000 to $99,999: 5,286
$100,000 to $149,999: 2,446
$150,000 to $199,999: 257
$200,000 or more: 131

**Percent of families below poverty level:** 13.0% (2000)

**2005 FBI Crime Index Property:** 10,678

**2005 FBI Crime Index Violent:** 1,166

# ■ Municipal Government

The Unified Government of Wyandotte County/Kansas City, Kansas serves as the local government for Kansas City, Kansas, while also providing county services for the cities of Bonner Springs and Edwardsville. The mayor/CEO is elected to serve a four-year term. The mayor/CEO is the presiding member of the 11-member Board of Commissioners. Eight commissioners are elected to represent districts and two commissioners are elected at large.

**Head Official:** CEO/Mayor Joe Reardon (since 2005; term expires 2009)

**Total Number of Local Government Employees:** approximately 2,300 (2007)

*City Information:* Unified Government of Wyandotte County/Kansas City, Kansas, 701 North 7th Street, Kansas City, KS 66101; telephone (913)573-5000; www.wycokck.org

# ■ Economy

## Major Industries and Commercial Activity

The Kansas City KS-MO Metropolitan Statistical Area (KC MSA) includes the adjoining Lawrence, KS, and St. Joseph, MO, MSAs, as well as the Atchison, KS, Chillicothe, MO, Ottawa, KS, and Warrensburg, MO areas. The KC MSA supports a major trade and transportation center for the nation. It is one of the largest rail centers in the nation based on the amount of freight carried through the area. Along the Missouri River there are 41 docks and terminal facilities in the KC MSA with 7 barge lines operating from the area. The Kansas City International Airport serves as a major hub for Kansas, Missouri, Iowa, and Nebraska with 15 airlines handling cargo. Air, rail, and river transportation are supplemented by the presence of over 300 motor freight carriers in the area. It is no wonder then that the transportation, trade, distribution, and warehousing industries serve a major role in the economy of the KC MSA. Burlington Northern Santa Fe and UPS have base offices in Kansas City, Kansas.

Education and health care services have a strong role in the local economy as well. In the Kansas side of the MSA, major employers include the local public school districts, Kansas City Kansas Community College, and the University of Kansas Medical Center and Hospital. Education and health services accounted for approximately 10,177 jobs in Kansas City, Kansas, in 2006. Professional and business services have also become important with over 5,500 professional, scientific, and technical services established in the KC MSA area. The Unified Government of Wyandotte County supports about 2,300 jobs.

The KC MSA has ranked consistently as one of the best regions in the U.S. for small businesses, according to the annual listing in *Entrepreneur* magazine. In 2006 the KC MSA ranked as 11th on the national list for large cities.

While the number of manufacturing jobs in the area has declined over the last decade, there are still a significant number of jobs available in the sector. The Ford Motor Company, General Motors, Honeywell International, and Gamin International all have facilities in the KC MSA.

**Items and goods produced:** automobiles, aircraft equipment, defense systems, ammunition, global positioning systems, newspapers, greeting cards, tires, motorcycles, food products

## Incentive Programs—New and Existing Businesses

*Local programs:* The mission of Wyandotte Development Inc. is to foster, encourage, and assist new and existing businesses in Wyandotte County. Its Economic

Development Team consists of the State of Kansas, municipal governments and utilities, and other entities as needed. The Economic Development Division of the Unified Government of Wyandotte County/Kansas City, Kansas assists new businesses through tax increment financing programs and a Neighborhood Revitalization Tax Rebate Incentive Program. The Kansas City Kansas Area Chamber of Commerce offers networking opportunities, legislative efforts, community development and business/education partnerships to member companies.

*State programs:* The entire state of Kansas is designated as an Enterprise Zone. Businesses located in an Enterprise Zone are eligible for special credits such as an investment tax credit (1 percent), a building and materials sales tax exemption, and inventory tax exemption, and certain property tax exemptions and credits. A job creation tax credit of $1,500 per new job is also available for jobs created in the zone for certified dislocated or economically disadvantaged workers. A research tax credit of 6.5 percent is also available for qualified research and development investments. Businesses that are not eligible for the Enterprise Zone programs may apply for job expansion and investment tax credits. Foreign Trade Zone (FTZ) incentives are available in several zones throughout the KC MSA. Goods entering FTZs are not subject to customs tariffs until the goods leave the zone and are formally entered into U.S. customs territory. The High Performance Incentive Program offers a 10 percent corporate income tax credit on qualified capital investments for eligible companies. There is no state income tax for either personal or corporate income.

The Kansas Department of Commerce is the state's leading economic development agency. Its Business Development Division offers customized proposals for prospective companies to outline available incentives and financing programs. Financing programs include the Kansas Economic Opportunity Initiatives Fund, the Partnership Fund, and Industrial Revenue Bonds. The Kansas Bioscience Authority offers several incentive programs for relocating, expanding, and start-up companies in the bioscience industry.

*Job training programs:* Kansas 1st is a statewide program through which local colleges and universities provide job-related training through individual courses of study and businesses training programs. Through Kansas 1st, companies may create specialized programs for their employees. Companies creating new jobs may qualify for training funds through Investments in Major Projects and Comprehensive Training (IMPACT), Kansas Industrial Training (KIT), and Kansas Industrial Retraining (KIR). Programs are custom designed to meet a company's specific training needs and can involve pre-employment or on-the-job training. Skill training programs are available through the Kansas City, Kansas Area Technical School.

## Development Projects

Adjacent to the Kansas Speedway, the 400-acre Village West project has become one of the largest tourist attractions in the state and continues to develop with the addition of restaurants, shops, and entertainment establishments. The Legends Shopping Center at Village West opened in 2006. As of 2007 the total investment in the area, which includes the Kansas Speedway, Cabela's, and Nebraska Furniture Mart, was about $573 million. In competition for tourist dollars will be Schlitterbahn Vacation Village, a $750 million project that is scheduled for completion in 2011. The Village is an expansion site of the Texas based company known for its waterpark resorts. Several restaurants and retail establishments have already been completed in the resort. The tubing waterpark and one-mile riverwalk trail are scheduled for completion in 2008. An indoor skydiving experience, SkyVenture, is scheduled for completion in 2009.

In September 2007 the city was considering proposals for six destination casino resorts that could be built throughout the city.

*Economic Development Information:* Kansas City Area Development Council, 2600 Commerce Tower, 911 Main Street, Kansas City, MO 64105; telephone (816)842-2865 or (800)99KCADC; www.thinkkc.com

## Commercial Shipping

The Kansas City Metropolitan Area is one of the largest transportation hubs in the nation. Local firms provide a complete range of intermodal services, including rail, air, truck, and water, for the receiving and shipping of goods. The Greater Kansas City area is served by four Class I rail carriers: Burlington Northern Santa Fe, Kansas City Southern, Norfolk Southern, and Union Pacific. Regional rail service is provided through the Iowa, Chicago, & Eastern line, and Missouri & Northern Arkansas. Kansas City International Airport in Missouri has 4 all-cargo carriers and 11-passenger combination carriers.

There are 225 motor freight carriers serving the city, with several more available throughout the metropolitan area. Kansas City is part of the Kansas City Commercial Zone, where exemption from Interstate Commerce Commission tariff supervision is granted to shipments originating from and received within this region. Shippers and motor carriers independently negotiate rates. A number of warehouses are maintained in the area.

Seven barge lines offer shipping from the Kansas City area of the Missouri River. There are 41 docks and terminals in the metropolitan area. The shipping season runs from March through November.

## Labor Force and Employment Outlook

In 2006 an estimated 77.3 percent of the Kansas City, Kansas, population 25 years and over had obtained a high school diploma or higher level of education. About 14.8

percent of the population had a bachelor's degree or higher. The counties of Johnson, Leavenworth, and Wyandotte together represent the largest civilian labor force in the state. According to the 2002 economic survey, the largest major occupational group for Kansas City, Kansas, was office and administrative support. This group is projected to continue to increase and remain the largest through 2012. The greatest number of new jobs is projected for the sales and related occupations group. Significant increases are also projected for jobs in the health care industry. For the Kansas City KC–MO MSA the largest occupational group was in trade, transportation, and utilities, followed by professional and business services.

The following is a summary of data regarding the Kansas City metropolitan area labor force, 2006 annual averages.

**Size of nonagricultural labor force:** 433,700

**Number of workers employed in** . . .

    construction and mining: 23,000
    manufacturing: 36,800
    trade, transportation and utilities: 94,600
    information: 22,300
    financial activities: 32,200
    professional and business services: 67,500
    educational and health services: 49,000
    leisure and hospitality: 37,400
    other services: 15,100
    government: 56,000

**Average hourly earnings of production workers employed in manufacturing:** Not available

**Unemployment rate:** 5.6% (June 2007)

| *Largest employers, Wyandotte County (2003)* | *Number of employees* |
|---|---|
| University of Kansas Medical Center | 4,900 |
| Kansas City, Kansas Public Schools, USD No. 500 | 3,500 |
| General Motors | 3,350 |
| Unified Government of Wyandotte County | 2,300 |
| Associated Wholesale Grocers | 1,300 |
| Burlington Northern-Santa Fe Railroad | 1,200 |
| United Parcel Service | 907 |
| Teletech | 825 |
| Kansas City Kansas Community College | 750 |
| U.S. Bulk Mail Center | 600 |
| Swift Transportation | 600 |

Keebler Foods    550

## Cost of Living

The following is a summary of data regarding several key cost of living factors in the Kansas City area.

**2007 (1st quarter) ACCRA Average House Price:** $271,279

**2007 (1st quarter) ACCRA Cost of Living Index:** 81.6

**State income tax rate:** 3.50% to 6.45%

**State sales tax rate:** 5.3%

**Local income tax rate:** None

**Local sales tax rate:** city, 1.25%; county, 1.0%

**Property tax rate:** 1.83% per $1,000 assessed value

***Economic Information:*** Kansas City Area Development Council, 2600 Commerce Tower, 911 Main Street, Kansas City, MO 64105; telephone (816)842-2865 or (800)99KCADC; www.thinkkc.com. Kansas Department of Labor, 401 SW Topeka Blvd., Topeka, KS 66603; telephone (785)296-5000; www.dol.ks.gov

## ■ Education and Research

### Elementary and Secondary Schools

Most students in Kansas City attend schools in the Kansas City, Kansas Public Schools District. In 2003 the district was one of three in the state to be recognized by the Academic Development Institute for significant increases in student achievement. Summer High School has been listed by *Newsweek* as one of the top schools in the state. Adult education programs are offered through Area Technical School and Fairfax Learning Center. Two other districts serve students from Kansas City: Piper USD 203 and Turner USD 202. The Wyandotte Comprehensive Special Education Cooperative offers a full-range of special education services for students in the Kansas City, Piper, and Bonner Springs-Edwardsville school districts. The Kansas State School for the Blind is a day and residential school offering individualized programs for students ages 3 through 21.

The following is a summary of data regarding the Kansas City, Kansas Public Schools as of the 2005–2006 school year.

**Total enrollment:** 19,561

**Number of facilities**

    elementary schools: 30
    junior high/middle schools: 8

senior high schools: 5
other: 3

**Student/teacher ratio:** 13.1:1

**Teacher salaries (2005–06)**

elementary median: $43,511 (2004)
junior high/middle median: Not available
secondary median: Not available

**Funding per pupil:** $7,259

There are over a dozen private Christian and parochial schools in Kansas City.

***Public Schools Information:*** Kansas City, Kansas Public Schools, 625 Minnesota Avenue, Kansas City, KS 66101; telephone (913)551-3200; www.kckps.k12.ks.us. Piper USD 203, 12036 Leavenworth Rd., Kansas City, KS 66109; telephone (913)721-2088; www.piperschools.com. Turner USD 202, 800 S. 55th Street, Kansas City, KS 66106; telephone (913)288-4100; www.turnerusd202.org

### Colleges and Universities

The University of Kansas Medical Center offers degree programs through its Allied Health, Medicine, Pharmacy, Nursing, and Graduate Studies programs. The UK Medical Center maintains a prestigious biomedical research facility and provides medical care to the community.

Kansas City Kansas Community College provides two-year associate's degree programs in professional or general studies as well as transfer programs leading to baccalaureate degrees. Academic divisions include business and continuing education, humanities and fine arts, nursing and allied health, social sciences, and math, science and technology. Enrollment is over 5,500.

Donnelly College is a Catholic liberal arts and professional college offering three associate's degrees and three bachelor's degrees. Health care certificate programs are also offered. Enrollment is over 500. The University of St. Mary Western Wyandotte is a satellite campus in Kansas City at the Providence Medical Center. The main campus of the University of Saint Mary is in Leavenworth. The Kansas City site offers MBA and degree completion programs in business and psychology.

### Libraries and Research Centers

The main facility of the Kansas City Kansas Public Library is located downtown; three branches and a bookmobile are operated within the system. The Mr. and Mrs. F.L. Schlagle Library is located in Wyandotte County Lake Park as an environmental learning center. Holdings for all branches total nearly 500,000 items, including books, periodicals and newspapers, microfiche, films, records, tapes, and art reproductions. Special collections include The Kansas Collection, comprised of local historical and genealogical resources; and a Spanish Language Collection. The library also maintains a small permanent collection of art and sponsors temporary exhibits as well.

The Dykes Library, one of the largest health sciences libraries in the Midwest, is open to the public as well as staff and students of the University of Kansas Medical Center. The library of Kansas City Kansas Community College features a special collection called The Morgue, which is a collection of journals relating to the fields of mortuary science and funeral services.

Research centers at the University of Kansas Medical Center include the Center for Reproductive Biology, the Mental Retardation Research Center, the Kansas Masonic Cancer Research Institute, and the Kidney Institute.

***Public Library Information:*** Kansas City Kansas Public Library, 625 Minnesota Avenue, Kansas City, KS 66101; telephone (913)551-3280; www.kckpl.lib.ks.us

## ■ Health Care

With two major hospitals and a county health department, Kansas City is a regional leader in health care. The 508-bed University of Kansas Hospital is a teaching hospital for the University of Kansas Medical School. A Carnegie Research I institution, it receives at least $40 million in annual federal research funding. Specialty areas include ophthalmology, neuroscience and stroke, heart care, infectious diseases, pain management, and allergy, immunology, and rheumatology. A cancer consultation service is available 24 hours a day, 7 days a week through the Cancer Care and Medical Pavilion. Emergency medicine includes a Level I Trauma Center. The hospital also sponsors the Burnett Burn Center and a transplant program that includes kidney, liver, and pancreas transplants. In 2007 the University of Kansas Hospital was ranked as one of the top 30 heart care hospitals in the nation by *U.S. News & World Report.*

Providence Medical Center is a 400-bed, not-for-profit community hospital affiliated with the Sisters of Charity of Leavenworth Health System. It offers an extensive array of services including cancer and cardiac care; neurosurgery; a Family Care Center for obstetrical, pediatric and gynecological services; a Diabetes Center; Anticoagulation Clinic; Pain Clinic; and an outpatient Rehabilitation Center.

The Wyandotte County Public Health Department provides clinics for adults and children as well as immunization and family planning information. Most services are available for a nominal or sliding-scale fee.

## ■ Recreation

### Sightseeing

The National Agricultural Center and Hall of Fame in Bonner Springs was chartered by Congress in 1960 to honor the nation's farmers. Funded by private contributions, the 172-acre facility traces the history of agriculture in the United States with exhibits on rural life, customs, and material culture. Its many attractions include the Museum of Farming, the National Farmer's Memorial, a gallery of rural art, and a restored nineteenth century farming village.

The Huron Indian Cemetery located in the heart of downtown is the burial ground of the Wyandot Nation, founders of the first town in the evolution of Kansas City. Established in 1832, White Church Christian Church is the oldest church in the state that is still in use. The John Brown Statue at 27th Avenue and Sewell pays tribute to the Brown-led antislavery movement from Quindaro, Kansas. In council chambers at City Hall the history of Kansas City is told through stained-glass windows and a large mural. The Rosedale Memorial Arch, dedicated in 1923 as a memorial to World War I soldiers, replicates the Arc de Triomphe in Paris. In 1993 a monument was added underneath the arch in memory of soldiers who served in World War II, Korea and Vietnam. Grinter House, built in 1857 and furnished with authentic period furniture, is the restored home of one of the first white settlers in Kansas City, Moses Grinter, who operated a ferry across the Kaw (Kansas) River.

The Children's Museum of Kansas City features interactive discovery-based exhibits. Nearby Kansas City, Missouri, is home to the Kansas City Zoo; Worlds of Fun, a theme park with more than 50 rides and shows; and Oceans of Fun, a tropical-theme water park.

## Arts and Culture

The centerpiece for the performing arts in Kansas City is Memorial Hall, a 3,300-seat venue that hosts cultural, religious, and entertainment events year-round. The Wyandotte Players perform live family-oriented theatre at the Kansas City Kansas Community College Performing Arts Center. Commedia Sans Arte is an improvisational comedy troupe performing at the historic Alcott Arts Center (formerly the Louise May Alcott Grade School). Open-air concerts take place at the Verizon Wireless Amphitheatre in Bonner Springs.

Kansas City, Kansas's Granada Theatre is home to the Grand Barton Theatre pipe organ. One of the most impressive instruments of its kind, it weighs more than 20 tons and rises more than two stories in height. Built in 1928–1929 by Boller Brothers in a Spanish-Mediterranean style, the Granada Theatre was restored in 1986 and operated as a non-profit performing arts center during the 1980s and 1990s.

The stone and brick foundations of the Quindaro Ruins and Underground Railroad, called "the largest known archeological shrine to freedom," offer a rare glimpse into Kansas's abolitionist past. The Harry S. Truman Library and Museum in nearby Independence, Missouri contains documents and memorabilia from the Truman presidency, including a popular White House in Miniature exhibit.

The Wyandotte County Historical Museum in Bonner Springs displays local and regional artifacts, including Native American relics and other items from the county's early history. The Strawberry Hill Museum and Cultural Center is dedicated to Kansas City's Eastern European heritage. It is located in Kansas City, Kansas, in the former St. John the Baptist Children's Home, an original Queen Anne-style building constructed in 1887. Neighboring Kansas City, Missouri, is the home of the nationally renowned Nelson-Atkins Museum of Art and a number of other museums of note.

## Festivals and Holidays

Kansas City is nicknamed the "City of Festivals." The city and Wyandotte County celebrate history, culture, tradition, and ethnic heritage with annual events in which crafts, foods, and music play an important part. Recognized as one of the top 100 attractions in North America, the Renaissance Festival spans six fall weekends beginning on Labor Day weekend. Several ethnic festivals are scheduled throughout the year including Polski Days, the Croatian Festival, the Kansas City Scottish Highland Games, and Oktoberfest. The Wyandotte County Fair takes place the last weekend in July. The Great American Barbecue takes place in May, featuring barbecue contests and a Barbecue Ball. Grinter House is the location of a number of special events, including the Applefest in autumn.

## Sports for the Spectator

Greyhound, thoroughbred, and quarter horse racing take place at the dual-track Woodlands complex. The privately funded racetrack includes two separate enclosed spectator facilities, a one-mile horse track with a straightaway for thoroughbreds and quarter horses, and a greyhound track suitable for year-round racing. Lakeside Speedway has a half-mile asphalt oval track and is part of the NASCAR Winston Racing Series. The Speedway hosts many national touring series; racing takes place every Friday night from March through September. The recently completed Kansas Speedway is a state-of-the-art facility featuring a 1.5-mile racing track, 80,000 spectator seats, driving schools, custom car shows and more. In addition to NASCAR, IRL and ARCA races, the Kansas Speedway also hosts community events.

The Kansas City T-Bones play ball at CommunityAmerica Ballpark as part of the Northern League of baseball. The Wizards of Major League Soccer (outdoors) also play at CommunityAmerica Ballpark.

Nearby Kansas City, Missouri, has much to offer the sports enthusiast. The American Royal, the world's largest combined livestock show, horse show, and rodeo, takes place in autumn at the American Royal Complex in the stockyard district. The Kansas City Chiefs play in the

National Football League at Arrowhead Stadium, part of the Harry S. Truman Sports Complex. Major League Baseball's Kansas City Royals compete in the American League Central Division at Kauffman Stadium. The Kansas City Comets play indoor soccer and the Kansas City Knights play ABA basketball, both at Kemper Arena.

### Sports for the Participant

The Unified Government Parks and Recreation Department manages 44 parks and 6 recreational centers in the city with facilities for tennis, golf, swimming and picnicking. Wyandotte County Lake Park offers a 400-acre lake with marina, 1,500 acres of wooded land, a model railroad, picnic shelters and excellent fishing. Private facilities can be reserved for small and large groups. Pierson Park offers a 12-acre fishing lake, shelter houses, a children's playground, tennis courts, and a softball field.

Wyandotte County has four first-rate golf courses. Painted Hills, a public course in Kansas City, offers rolling fairways and a panoramic view of the city. Dub's Dread, a semi-private course also in Kansas City, is a challenging 18-hole course. The newly-remodeled public Sunflower Hills in Bonner Springs is considered the premier public course in the metropolitan area, with an 18-hole championship design and PGA management staff. Lake Quirva is a private course.

### Shopping and Dining

Village West, a major retail and entertainment destination, is located on a 400-acre site near the intersections of I-435 and I-70. Legends Shopping Center at Village West is an open-air shopping center that includes restaurants and a 14-screen movie theater. Village West is home to the 180,000-square-foot Cabela's show room. More than just a sport and fishing store, Cabela's in Kansas City features the largest display of life-sized mule deer in their natural surroundings and an enclosed aquarium. Nebraska Furniture Mart has a 712,000-square-foot showroom at Village West that includes the Courtyard Café, for those who want to take a break from shopping. Indian Springs Marketplace is home to the Children's Museum of Kansas City as well as a range of shops and services. Country Club Plaza and Crown Center are located in Kansas City, Missouri. City Market, also in Missouri, is a colorful farmers' market open seven days a week. Union Station is a fully refurbished 1914 landmark, now featuring unique shops and restaurants, an interactive science centre and theatre facilities. Kansas City restaurants are known for their barbecue, steaks, chicken, and ethnic cuisine, including Mexican, Greek, Asian, and Italian.

***Visitor Information:*** Kansas City, Kansas-Wyandotte County Convention and Visitors Bureau, 727 Minnesota Ave., PO Box 171517, Kansas City, KS 66101; telephone (913)321-5800; toll-free (800)264-1563; www.visitthedot.com

## ■ Convention Facilities

The Jack Reardon Convention Centre in downtown Kansas City is the site of conferences, meetings, banquets, and conventions. The facility contains 20,000 square feet of exhibit space with 12 meeting rooms and 60 booth spaces. Seating is available for up to 1,800 participants. Next door, the Hilton Garden Inn offers 147 rooms and meeting space ranging from 300 to 5,000 square feet. The Best Western Inn and Conference Center has 113 rooms and meeting space for groups of 15 to 225. Great Wolf Lodge offers 3,000 square feet of meeting space and 281 rooms. Meeting and event space may also be rented at Cabela's, the Children's Museum of Kansas, and Memorial Hall. The Sanctuary of Hope Retreat Center offers a place for small group gatherings. Some hotels, motels, and bed-and-breakfasts in the area also maintain meeting and banquet rooms.

***Convention Information:*** Kansas City, Kansas-Wyandotte County Convention and Visitors Bureau, 727 Minnesota Ave., PO Box 171517, Kansas City, KS 66101; telephone (913)321-5800; toll-free (800)264-1563; www.visitthedot.com

## ■ Transportation

### Approaching the City

Kansas City International Airport is just 16 miles north of downtown in Kansas City, Missouri. Its 13 major commercial airlines offer about 230 daily departures with nonstop service to 70 destinations. The Charles B. Wheeler Downtown Airport in Kansas City, Missouri, serves charter, corporate, and other fixed-based operator flights.

A network of interstate highways links Kansas City with points throughout the nation. I-35 runs from Duluth, Minnesota, southward through Kansas City to Laredo, Texas. I-29, originating in North Dakota, terminates in Kansas City; the Kansas Turnpike, I-70, bisects the city and extends to St. Louis and Denver, Colorado. I-435, an outerbelt, spans western Wyandotte County and connects Kansas City with the airport to the north. Amtrak and Greyhound offer service to Kansas City, Missouri.

### Traveling in the City

North-south streets in Kansas City are numbered and labeled "street;" east-west streets are named and designated "avenue." Public bus transportation is operated by the Kansas City Area Transit Authority and Unified Government Transit. These two bus systems provide integrated service Monday through Saturday. Dial-A-Ride offers public transit service for persons with disabilities. Senior Group Transportation is also available. Johnson County Transit (The JO), operates bus services throughout Johnson County Kansas and to points in both Kansas City, Kansas, and Kansas City, Missouri.

# ■ Communications

## Newspapers

The Kansas City, Kansas, daily newspaper is the *Kansas City Kansan,* published Tuesday through Saturday. Several neighborhood, ethnic, and suburban newspapers are distributed weekly and monthly, including *Wyandotte West* and the *Kansas City Record.* The *Kansas State Globe* serves the African American community. The weekly *Kansas City Jewish Chronicle* is published in Overland Park and distributed on Fridays.

## Television and Radio

There is only one network television station broadcasting directly from Kansas City; others are received from Missouri. Cable service is available locally. Five AM and FM radio stations broadcast from Kansas City, with others received from Missouri.

***Media Information:*** *Kansas City Kansan,* 7815 Parallel Parkway, Kansas City, KS 66112; telephone (913)371-4300; www.kansascitykansan.com

## Kansas City Online

Kansas City Area Development Council. Available www.smartkc.com

Kansas City Kansas Area Chamber of Commerce. Available www.kckchamber.com

Kansas City Kansas Public Library System. Available www.kckpl.lib.ks.us

Kansas City, Kansas Public Schools. Available www .kckps.k12.ks.us

Kansas City Kansas-Wyandotte County Convention and Visitors Bureau. Available www.kckcvb.org

Kansas Department of Commerce and Housing. Available www.kansascommerce.com

Unified Government of Wyandotte County and Kansas City, Kansas. Available www.wycokck.org

BIBLIOGRAPHY

Cutler, William G., *History of the State of Kansas* (Chicago, IL: A.T. Andreas, 1883)

Hemingway, Ernest, *Ernest Hemingway, Cub Reporter; Kansas City Star Stories* (Pittsburgh, PA: University of Pittsburgh Press, 1970)

Schulz, Constance B., ed., *Bust to Boom: Documentary Photographs of Kansas, 1936–1949* (University Press of Kansas, 1996)

# Overland Park

## ■ The City in Brief

**Founded:** 1905 (incorporated 1960)

**Head Official:** Carl R. Gerlach (R) (since April 2005)

**City Population**

    1980: 81,784
    1990: 111,790
    2000: 149,080
    2006 estimate: 166,722
    Percent change, 1990–2000: 33.4%
    U.S. rank in 1980: Not available
    U.S. rank in 1990: 168th (2nd in state)
    U.S. rank in 2000: 143rd (2nd in state)

**Metropolitan Area Population**

    1980: 1,449,374
    1990: 1,582,875
    2000: 1,776,062
    2006 estimate: Not available
    Percent change, 1990–2000: 12.2%
    U.S. rank in 1980: Not available
    U.S. rank in 1990: Not available
    U.S. rank in 2000: 44th

**Area:** 56.85 square miles

**Elevation:** 1,000 feet above sea level

**Average Annual Temperature:** 56.75° F

**Average Annual Precipitation:** Not available

**Major Economic Sectors:** Professional services, retail trade, manufacturing

**Unemployment Rate:** 4.4% (June 2007)

**Per Capita Income:** $35,211 (2005)

**2005 FBI Crime Index Property:** 4,559

**2005 FBI Crime Index Violent:** 494

**Major Colleges and Universities:** University of Kansas-Edwards Campus, Johnson County Community College, Baker University-School of Professional and Graduate Studies, National American University, Ottawa University-Greater Kansas City Campus, University of St. Mary Overland Park

**Daily Newspaper:** *The Kansas City Star*

## ■ Introduction

Growing up in the shadow of the two Kansas Cities (Kansas and Missouri), Overland Park has found myriad ways to distinguish itself as an affordable community populated by well-educated professionals. In 2003 Overland Park was ranked 3rd in *Money* magazine's "Hottest Towns" with more than 100,000 people in the central region. The honor was upgraded in 2006 when *Money* named the city as sixth in the nation of the "Best Places to Live." Other national honors indicate that Overland Park is a community that is child-friendly, welcoming and safe for women, and open for business. Overland Park is an urbane and thriving city in Kansas in the twenty-first century.

## ■ Geography and Climate

Located in the sub-basin of the Missouri River, Overland Park exists in the transition area between rolling green hills and the eastern edge of the Great Plains. Ice Age glaciers scoured the land and left silt deposits that have contributed to the rich agricultural history of Kansas. The meandering Missouri further softened the surface of one of the more geologically stable areas in the United States. Overland Park itself is perched on a bluff above Kansas City, protecting it from periodic floods.

Eastern Kansas experiences warm, slightly humid summers that can border on hot; winters can feel quite chilly thanks to the humidity level, but precipitation is relatively moderate. Spring ushers in a season of towering thunderstorms moving across the Plains, along with twisters that frequent the edge of Tornado Alley in which Overland Park resides. In 2007 *National Geographic Adventure* magazine named Overland Park as one of the top 50 cities to live and play.

**Area:** 56.85 square miles

**Elevation:** 1,000 feet above sea level

**Average Temperature:** 56.75° F

**Average Annual Precipitation:** Not available

# ■ History

### Early Kansas: Lying Low

The Kansas of long ago was wide open—plains scoured by a series of Ice Age glaciers and wandering rivers had become vast, level expanses under a limitless sky. Prior to the 1700s the area was sparsely populated; gradually, a growing number of native tribes discovered the richness of the glacial silt soil and the abundance of bison. The eastern portion of the state was home to many tribes that maintained individual languages and customs: Plains, Wyandotte, Sioux, Osage, Kickapoo, Shawnee, Kanza, Arkansas, Otto, Dahcotah and Ogillahah tribes all called the region home and helped establish the natural passage that would come to be known as the Santa Fe Trail .

A European presence extended into eastern Kansas in the early 1500s with the explorations of Francisco Vasquez de Coronado. The land was first claimed by France, then ceded to Spain as a sop after the country's loss in the French and Indian War. The area was contested until Spain ceded it back to France in 1800; the next year, France sold eastern Kansas to the United States as part of the Louisiana Purchase, and the region was fair game for the Manifest Destiny of the U.S. government.

### Born Free: A Matter of Perspective

Kansas didn't have to wait long. In 1802 hunter and trapper James Pursley followed a well-traveled trail to New Mexico to do some trading, following a route that travelers started to call the Santa Fe Trail. As trade heated up between merchants in Missouri and trappers in New Mexico, the trail evolved into the Santa Fe Road. Increased traffic and commerce in the area resulted in friction with native tribes still attempting to live on the land's resources. As a solution, the U.S. government negotiated a treaty in 1825 with the Shawnee Indians in Missouri; in exchange for surrendered land in Missouri, the tribe received an equivalent amount of land on a reservation in what is now Johnson County, Kansas.

A new era began for the formerly nomadic tribe that had up until then lived in eastern woodlands; the move to the plains necessitated much adaptation as the Shawnees became farmers. In 1829 the Rev. Thomas Johnson (for whom the county is named) moved to the reservation, where an Indian Manual Labor School was created. Native American children were tutored in English, manual arts, agriculture, and Christianity.

Kansas Territory became official in 1854, populated by a curious mix of passionate abolitionists and independent pioneers who supported Kansas as a "free state" because it was economically advantageous to keep slave owners out of the territory. On the front edge of the Civil War, Kansas became a state in 1861 and joined the Union. Even prior to the advent of the Civil War, proslavery factions warred with abolitionists and free soil advocates in Kansas. Ironically, a number of the free soil advocates were less interested in abolishing slavery and more interested in keeping African Americans out of Kansas altogether. Soon after a "free state" and Union victory, the U.S. government also recommended getting the Indians out, moving whole tribes south to what was being termed Indian Territory.

### Overland Park Takes Shape

Since 1821 a large city just over the Kansas-Missouri state line had begun to evolve into a major stop on the trail, railroad, and road systems. By the early 1900s, Kansas City was a burgeoning metropolitan center and had changed from trading post to destination. In 1905 William B. Strang, Jr., was staying in Kansas City with a relative when he explored the area to the west of the city and recognized its potential as a bedroom community for the metro area. Strang was particularly intrigued by a plot of land owned by several farm families and situated on a bluff; the combination of high ground and proximity to the city led him to purchase the land and start laying out a series of new communities. Thus Overland Park was created—the name is reputed to be a combination of the vision of a "park-like" city crossed with the alternate name for the Santa Fe Trail (Overland Trail).

In support of his newly-created bedroom community, Strang went on to develop an interurban train line with trolley service to Kansas City. The Strang Land Company grew busy selling off individual lots of land in business and residential segments of the new town. The city founder also had his hand in the development of Airfield Park in 1909, which combined a landing strip, aviation school, hangars and a grandstand for the locals who were fascinated with flying. Many renowned aviators made Overland Park a stop, including the Wright Brothers; an airplane industry grew up around the airfield that has continued to present day.

Thanks to Strang and other early residents of the area, Overland Park was gradually becoming a viable entity on its own merits. As an attempt to manage the swift growth in Overland Park, Mission, and Prairie Village, these collective communities were organized into an urban township form of government under a law passed by the Kansas legislature in 1940. The reborn entity, Mission Urban Township, was able to form a governmental body but lacked the right to zone or plan independently. In combination with the repercussions of the Dust Bowl days and World War II, Mission Urban Township experienced a time of stasis in the late 1930s and early 1940s, followed by a boom in residential development. In 1951 the Kaw River flooded Kansas City while the community on the bluff stayed nice and dry, and Mission Township began to see an influx of slightly damp folks. The current system of government was insufficient to deal with the resultant growth and development, leading to separation of the township communities into municipalities and the incorporation of Overland Park in 1960.

## Out of the Shadow of Kansas City

The 1960s and 1970s ushered in a period of individuation, as Overland Park established its own infrastructure of schools, businesses, and city services. Very early in its formal existence, Overland Park government initiated the practice of citizen surveys to target key concerns of the populace and to measure satisfaction with quality of life. This proactive approach led to a balanced approach to development and growth, as well as innovative juvenile delinquency and learning disability programs created in the 1970s.

Since the 1980s Overland Park has experienced a fairly consistent boom pattern, with growth in population, industry and reputation. While continuing to look forward, the city administration has also appreciated its past by supporting extensive renovations of the historic downtown area during the early 1990s. Present day Overland Park has been a regular on national ratings for quality of life, education, affordable housing, appeal to businesses, and population growth. It's a young community in many ways, with a mature approach to living and contributing. In 2006 *Money* magazine named Overland Park as one of the top ten "Best Places to Live."

***Historical Information:*** Kansas State Historical Society, 6425 SW Sixth Avenue, Topeka, KS 66615; telephone (785)272-8681; www.kshs.org

## ■ Population Profile

### Metropolitan Area Residents

1980: 1,449,374
1990: 1,582,875
2000: 1,776,062
2006 estimate: Not available
Percent change, 1990–2000: 12.2%
U.S. rank in 1980: Not available
U.S. rank in 1990: Not available
U.S. rank in 2000: 44th

### City Residents

1980: 81,784
1990: 111,790
2000: 149,080
2006 estimate: 166,722
Percent change, 1990–2000: 33.4%
U.S. rank in 1980: Not available
U.S. rank in 1990: 168th (2nd in state)
U.S. rank in 2000: 143rd (2nd in state)

**Density:** 2,627 people per square mile (2000)

### Racial and ethnic characteristics (2005)

White: 139,556
Black: 5,347
American Indian and Alaska Native: 155
Asian: 11,080
Native Hawaiian and Pacific Islander: 95
Hispanic or Latino (may be of any race): 8,116
Other: 2,218

**Percent of residents born in state:** 35.1% (2006)

### Age characteristics (2005)

Population under 5 years old: 10,478
Population 5 to 9 years old: 12,548
Population 10 to 14 years old: 10,680
Population 15 to 19 years old: 10,416
Population 20 to 24 years old: 9,858
Population 25 to 34 years old: 18,985
Population 35 to 44 years old: 28,998
Population 45 to 54 years old: 23,535
Population 55 to 59 years old: 9,515
Population 60 to 64 years old: 7,061
Population 65 to 74 years old: 10,562
Population 75 to 84 years old: 6,958
Population 85 years and older: 2,307
Median age: 37.9 years

### Births (2006)

Total number: 2,177

### Deaths (2006)

Total number: 1,108

### Money income (2005)

Per capita income: $35,211
Median household income: $64,804
Total households: 64,666

*City of Overland Park*

**Number of households with income of . . .**

less than $10,000: 2,104
$10,000 to $14,999: 2,192
$15,000 to $24,999: 5,445
$25,000 to $34,999: 5,916
$35,000 to $49,999: 9,058
$50,000 to $74,999: 11,653
$75,000 to $99,999: 8,123
$100,000 to $149,999: 11,573
$150,000 to $199,999: 5,092
$200,000 or more: 3,510

**Percent of families below poverty level:** 2.1% (2000)

**2005 FBI Crime Index Property:** 4,559

**2005 FBI Crime Index Violent:** 494

## ■ Municipal Government

Overland Park operates through the mayor-council-city manager form of government, with the mayor and 12 council members forming the governing body for the municipality. The city is divided into six districts, each of which elects two council members who serve four-year

terms with staggered elections. The mayor is elected by the general populace and also serves a four-year term in office. In April 2005 the city of Overland Park elected its first new mayor in 24 years. The governing body hires a city manager to enforce established policies and to oversee the daily operations of the city.

**Head Official:** Carl R. Gerlach (R) (since April 2005; current term expires 2009)

**Total Number of City Employees:** 1,383 (2007)

***City Information:*** City of Overland Park, City Hall, 8500 Santa Fe Drive, Overland Park, KS 66212; telephone (913)895-6000; www.opkansas.org

## ■ Economy

### Major Industries and Commercial Activity

Service-oriented businesses have taken a leading role in the city's economy, particularly in educational, health care, professional, and technical services. This may be attributed to the fact that Overland Park has one of the most well-educated workforces in the nation. In 2006 over 96 percent of the population 25 years and older had obtained a high school diploma or higher level of education. About 56 percent had a bachelor's degree or higher. As of 2006, professional, technical, and scientific services accounted for nearly 12 percent of employment, while the finance and insurance industry held a little over 11 percent of employment. With six major office parks, the city has become a dynamic corporate center. YRC Worldwide and Ferrelgas Partners are two *Fortune* 1000 companies with headquarters in Overland Park. Black and Veatch, a major engineering service firm, also maintains headquarters in the city. Sprint/Nextel, the largest employer in the city, has its operational headquarters there as well. Other major telecommunications employers include Embarq, AT&T, Alexander Open Systems, and Verizon Wireless. Leading financial services, banking, and insurance employers include Zurich North America Commercial, Wadell & Reed Financial, Swiss Re, Wells Fargo, Capital One Home Loans, Valley View Bancshares, and Accenture.

Health care and social assistance organizations accounted for about 9 percent of employment in 2006. Leading health care employers include Overland Park Regional Medical Center, Menorah Medical Center, Physicians Reference Laboratories, and St. Luke's South Hospital. The three local school districts and Johnson County Community College are among major employers in education.

Hospitality and food service jobs are a significant source of employment for the city, in part due to its easy distance from the two Kansas Cities. From 1997 to 2007 retail sales grew by over 50 percent with over 2,000 retailers in the city.

**Items and goods produced:** telecommunication technology, transportation equipment, lumber, heating and air conditioning units, promotional products

## Incentive Programs—New and Existing Companies

*Local programs:* The city of Overland Park encourages new building by allowing for abatement of up to 50 percent of property tax liability for as long as 10 years, dependent upon the size and use of construction projects. The Chamber of Commerce in Overland Park acts as a bridge for businesses negotiating the local and state systems in expanding or creating a new project. Potential business owners might also contact the Downtown Overland Park Partnership and the Overland Park Economic Development Council for assistance in establishing or expanding a business in the city.

*State programs:* The entire state of Kansas is designated as an Enterprise Zone. Businesses located in an Enterprise Zone are eligible for special credits such as an investment tax credit (1 percent), a building and materials sales tax exemption, and inventory tax exemption, and certain property tax exemptions and credits. A job creation tax credit of $1,500 per new job is also available for jobs created in the zone for certified dislocated or economically disadvantaged workers. A research tax credit of 6.5 percent is also available for qualified research and development investments. Businesses that are not eligible for the Enterprise Zone programs may apply for job expansion and investment tax credits. The High Performance Incentive Program offers a 10 percent corporate income tax credit on qualified capital investments for eligible companies. There is no state income tax for either personal or corporate income.

The Kansas Department of Commerce is the state's leading economic development agency. Its Business Development Division offers customized proposals for prospective companies to outline available incentives and financing programs. Financing programs include the Kansas Economic Opportunity Initiatives Fund, the Partnership Fund, and Industrial Revenue Bonds. The Kansas Bioscience Authority offers several incentive programs for relocating, expanding, and start-up companies in the bioscience industry.

*Job training programs:* The Overland Park Chamber of Commerce schedules two professional development seminars per month and can additionally act as a referral agent for employers looking for advanced training for their employees. Kansas 1st is a statewide program through which local colleges and universities provide job-related training through individual courses of study and business training programs. Through Kansas 1st, companies may create specialized programs for their employees. Companies creating new jobs may qualify for training funds through Investments in Major Projects and Comprehensive Training (IMPACT), Kansas Industrial Training (KIT), and Kansas Industrial Retraining (KIR). Programs are custom designed to meet a company's specific training needs and can involve pre-employment or on-the-job training. The Neighborhood Improvement and Youth Employment Act has provided funding for community enhancement projects for which high school students are hired. The Center for Business and Technology at Johnson County Community College offers about 400 on-site contract training opportunities at local area businesses. The Overland Park campus of Baker University provides educational programs tailored to specific employer needs and brings them directly to the workplace.

## Development Projects

The city's first major business park, Corporate Woods, was opened in Overland Park in the 1970s. Since then five other parks have opened: Southcreek, Executive Hills, Lighton Development, Foxhill Office Park, and Bryan Office Park. All six parks continue to expand and renovate their available properties as they attract new tenants. In 2007 Software Engineering Services announced that it would open a new regional office at

Corporate Woods. The company, which has primarily focused on government and defense projects, plans to use this site to expand its commercial consulting business to include more private-sector clients.

Also in 2007 Baker University moved into a new 30,000-square-foot facility on the corner of College and Metcalf Avenue in Overland Park. The new Baker University facility has 25 classrooms and will introduce new programs in conflict management, dispute resolution and an online MBA.

That same year Allied National, one of the nation's most respected administrators of small business employer benefit plans, announced that it would build headquarters in Overland Park. The company plans to invest over $12 million in refurbishing a property on W. 107th Street. By 2010 the company expects to have over 100 employees with an average annual salary of $56,666.

## Commercial Shipping

The neighboring Kansas City Metropolitan Area is one of the largest transportation hubs in the nation and the primary site for commercial trade in the area. Local firms provide a complete range of intermodal services, including rail, air, truck, and water, for the receiving and shipping of goods. The Greater Kansas City area is served by four Class I rail carriers: Burlington Northern Santa Fe, Kansas City Southern, Norfolk Southern, and Union Pacific. Regional rail service is provided through the Iowa, Chicago & Eastern line and Missouri & Northern Arkansas. Kansas City International Airport in Missouri has 4 all-cargo carriers and 11-passenger combination carriers.

There are 225 motor freight carriers serving the city, with several more available throughout the metropolitan area. Kansas City is part of the Kansas City Commercial Zone, where exemption from Interstate Commerce Commission tariff supervision is granted to shipments originating from and received within this region. Shippers and motor carriers independently negotiate rates. A number of warehouses are maintained in the area. The headquarters for Yellow Roadway Corporation are in Overland Park, allowing easy access to a major cargo shipping and transportation resource. Yellow transports cargo to all 50 states, Canada, the Virgin Islands, and several other international destinations.

Seven barge lines offer shipping from the Kansas City area of the Missouri River. There are 41 docks and terminals in the metropolitan area. The shipping season runs from March through November.

## Labor Force and Employment Outlook

In 2006 over 96 percent of the population 25 years and older had obtained a high school diploma or higher level of education. About 56 percent had a bachelor's degree or higher. There appears to be a slight shift in philosophy regarding higher education, starting at the K-12 level, with more emphasis on real-world experiences through technical programs and vocational institutions prior to a four-year degree being earned.

Private-sector service-oriented businesses are expected to show the greatest increase in job growth over the next decade. These include professional, scientific, technology, health care, and educational services. Retail trade may also see a significant increase.

The following is a summary of data regarding the Overland Park city metropolitan area labor force, 2005 annual averages.

**Size of nonagricultural labor force:** 85,244

**Number of workers employed in . . .**

    construction and mining: 3,858
    manufacturing: 6,458
    trade, transportation and utilities: 4,575
    information: 5,740
    financial activities: 9,260
    professional and business services: 12,709
    educational and health services: 16,450
    leisure and hospitality: 6,351
    other services: 4,013
    government: 8,690

**Average hourly earnings of production workers employed in manufacturing:** Not available

**Unemployment rate:** 4.4% (June 2007)

| *Largest employers (2007)* | *Number of employees* |
| --- | --- |
| Sprint/Nextel | 9,600 |
| Embarq | 5,000 |
| Shawnee Mission School District | 3,620 |
| Blue Valley School District | 2,700 |
| Black & Veatch | 2,250 |
| Overland Park Regional Medical Center | 2,000 |
| City of Overland Park | 1,383 |
| YRC Worldwide | 1,000 |
| Johnson County Community College | 950 |
| Zurich North America Commercial | 900 |

## Cost of Living

The following is a summary of data regarding several key cost of living factors in the Overland Park area.

**2007 (1st quarter) ACCRA Average House Price:** Not available

**2007 (1st quarter) ACCRA Cost of Living Index:** Not available

State income tax rate: 3.50% to 6.45%

State sales tax rate: 5.3%

Local income tax rate: None

Local sales tax rate: 7.525%

Property tax rate: 8.889 mills; one mill = $1 for every $1000 of assessed property value

*Economic information:* Overland Park Economic Development Council, 9001 W. 110th Street, Suite 150, Overland Park, KS 66210; telephone (913)491-3600; www.opedc.org

# ■ Education and Research

## Elementary and Secondary Schools

In a 2001 report by Population Connection, Overland Park was chosen the number one "Kid Friendly City" in the nation, based on factors such as education, health, and public safety, which all impact overall achievement in the K-12 population. Overland Park has three public school districts: Blue Valley, Shawnee Mission, and Olathe. All three districts have consistently been ranked within the top 10 percent for best public school systems by *Expansion Management* magazine.

The Blue Valley School District covers 91 square miles in south Overland Park. One of its innovative programs is the Wilderness Science Center; this outdoor laboratory encompasses 30 acres of prairie, forest, river, and wetland ecosystems. Students at the WSC put their classroom science theories to work along the trails and learning stations sprinkled throughout the open space. Several Advanced Placement courses are available for high school students.

The Shawnee Mission School District covers 72 square miles of northeast Johnson County. The school system offers over 50 honors and Advanced Placement courses for high school students. Juniors and seniors may also participate in the International Baccalaureate program at Shawnee Mission East High School. The district also sponsors the Center for International Studies at Shawnee Mission South High School. There, students may attend an all-day program which includes electives in Arabic, Chinese, and Japanese language and cultural studies as well as international law and economics. The Broadmoor Technical Center offers courses leading to careers in such fields as culinary arts, graphic design, commercial banking, computer service and networking, and fashion design. Homeschoolers in elementary and middle school are offered support through the Shawnee Mission eSchool program, which offers an online district-approved curriculum. High school students may access eSchool for independent study courses.

The Olathe Unified School District (OUSD) was formerly five separate districts. The OUSD provides the Heartland and Prairie Learning Centers for children with special needs and a Head Start program for pre-kindergartners. Approximately 10.5 percent of OUSD students reside in Overland Park, while the majority of the students are from Olathe. The student/teacher ratio in OUSD is about 16:1, allowing for more individualized attention. Advanced Placement and online education programs are available for high school students. The district offers special 21st Century High School Programs through which students take advanced courses in studies such as communications and engineering, and gain real-world experience through internships with partner organizations.

The following is a summary of data regarding the Olathe Unified School District as of the 2005–2006 school year.

Total enrollment: 23,604

Number of facilities
    elementary schools: 31
    junior high/middle schools: 8
    senior high schools: 4
    other: 4

Student/teacher ratio: 13:1

Teacher salaries (2005–06)
    elementary median: $34,725–$70,662
    junior high/middle median: Not available
    secondary median: Not available

Funding per pupil: $11,749

*Public Schools Information:* Blue Valley School District, 15020 Metcalf, PO Box 23901, Overland Park, KS 66283-0901; telephone (913)239-4000; www. bluevalleyk12.org. Olathe Unified School District, 14160 Black Bob Road, PO Box 2000, Olathe, KS 66063-2000; telephone (913)780-7000; www. olatheschools.com. Shawnee Mission School District, 7235 Antioch Road, Shawnee Mission, KS 66204; telephone (913)993-6200; www.smsd.org

## Colleges and Universities

Johnson County Community College (JCCC) offers its students a range of undergraduate courses in a two-year post-secondary education program that further develops the local workforce and prepares students for transfer to four-year universities or colleges. JCCC offers over 50 associate's degree and certificate programs. Enrollment is over 34,000. The college encourages academic, career, and personal growth through programs such as Student Life and Leadership, the Gallaudet University Regional Center (hearing impairment technical assistance and seminars), International Student Services, the Writing Center, and the Math Resource Center. The Center for Business and Technology offers about 400 on-site contract training opportunities at local area businesses.

The University of Kansas Edwards Campus opened in Overland Park in 1993. The school offers over 20 undergraduate and graduate degree completion programs with flexible scheduling for evening and weekend classes. The main campus of the University of Kansas is in Lawrence.

The Overland Park campus of Baker University (BU), a private college affiliated with the United Methodist Church, hosts a branch of the BU School of Professional and Graduate Studies. The school offers associate's and bachelor's degrees, a master's degree in business administration and a variety of certificate programs. The main campus of BU is in Baldwin City.

Overland Park is also home to one of 19 national campus locations of National American University. The campus, which opened in 2001, offers master's degree programs in business administration and management and bachelor's degrees in applied management and business administration, with concentrations in accounting, information systems, financial management, international business, and health care management.

The University of St. Mary Overland Park Campus offers accelerated degree completion programs and several master's degree programs. The main campus of the University of Saint Mary is in Leavenworth. The Ottawa University–Greater Kansas City campus is located in Overland Park. The school offers bachelor's degrees in business, education, human resources, and psychology. A Master of Business Administration as well as Master of Arts in Human Resources are also available.

### Libraries and Research Centers

The Johnson County Library system's main location is the Central Resource Library. There are an additional 12 branch libraries serving the entire county. Library patrons can access more than 1.1 million items in formats such as audio books, video and DVD movies, magazines, newspapers, and hard and soft cover books. Computer services at the library allow visitors to tap into more than 70 databases and online services to search full-text articles and reference books. The Johnson County Library is a repository for federal government documents, available both in hard copy and online. Assistive technology is available for community members with disabilities, and the library serves homebound populations with outreach and delivery programs. Various special events for children and teens are offered throughout the year.

The Billington Library on the campus of Johnson County Community College contains more than 107,000 titles in book or audiovisual format, along with a collection of more than 400,000 microforms and 600 current periodicals.

The Dykes Library, the Clendening History of Medicine Library, and the Farha Medical Library, all located at the Medical Center at the nearby University of Kansas in Kansas City, contain a wealth of health-related books, periodicals, digital collections and databases. The Medical Center also houses several research institutes conducting investigations into life processes, functions of the human body, disease processes, and health care models.

***Public Library Information:*** Johnson County Libraries, 9875 W. 87th Street, Overland Park, KS 66212; telephone (913)495-2400; www.jocolibrary.org

## ■ Health Care

The Overland Park Regional Medical Center, part of the HCA Midwest Health System, is licensed for 343 beds, serving southern Johnson County and surrounding areas with emergency services, a diabetes center, a neonatal intensive care unit, a cardiac rehabilitation program, outpatient pharmacies, and a sleep disorder clinic. The emergency department features a Level II Trauma Center and a special program for victims of sexual assault. The center also has a Level III B Neonatal Intensive Care Unit. The medical center is home to the Human Motion Institute, a clinic that houses several physician specialists in the fields of orthopedics and neurosurgery. An outpatient rehabilitation clinic is also part of the institute.

The Menorah Medical Center, also a part of the HCA Midwest Health System, moved to Johnson County in 1996 and now occupies a medical campus that includes an acute care hospital licensed for 158 beds, a doctors' building, and a number of outpatient clinics. Menorah Medical is one of 20 facilities in the country to provide access to cutting edge treatment of previously inoperable tumors and lesions. Other specialties include radiation therapy, a sleep lab, audiology services, cancer diagnostics, pain management, and a full range of neurological services.

Saint Luke's South Hospital offers emergency services, cardiac diagnostics, surgical intensive care, radiology, pain management, physical and occupational therapies, and the latest in birthing suites. The facility is licensed for 105 beds and is supported by a range of outpatient programs.

Children's Mercy South is affiliated with Children's Mercy Hospitals and Clinics based in Kansas City. This Overland Park site includes a 24-hour urgent care center, a pediatric surgicenter, imaging and laboratory services, and about 25 specialty services including developmental and behavioral sciences, neurology, and ophthalmology.

Specialized care is provided at Mid-America Rehabilitation Hospital (physical rehabilitation treatment) and Select Specialty Hospital (acute long-term care). The Med-Act emergency service is operated by the county.

# ■ Recreation

## Sightseeing

Peace and tranquility are a bargain at the Overland Park Arboretum and Botanical Gardens located on 179th Street about a mile west of U.S. Highway 69. Three hundred acres of land have been dedicated to environmental initiatives that preserve and restore ecosystems while providing educational opportunities for children and adults. Wood chip hiking trails lead through the various gardens, including the Erickson Water Garden, a Xeriscape Garden, a Rotary Children's Garden, a Native American Medicine Wheel, and the Legacy Garden. Concrete paths extending from parking areas allow visitors with physical disabilities to enjoy the rare plant species and varied biodomes that can be viewed on the grounds. An interpretive Environmental Education and Visitors Center at the Gardens offers a peek into the biology of the facility while modeling environmentally-sustainable energy systems in use at the Center.

Families with younger children will enjoy a visit to the Deanna Rose Children's Farmstead, located within the boundaries of the Overland Park Community Park. Named for a local police officer who was killed in the line of duty, the Farmstead is comprised of a petting zoo, farmhouse, a silo with slides, and picture-box gardens. Demonstration gardens depict methods of growing produce such as wheat, corn, and vegetables. The Farmstead is a seasonal operation, opening April 1st and closing for the year at the end of October.

Downtown Overland Park is a great place to wander amid centralized, locally-owned art galleries and interesting shops. The Strang Carriage House in downtown conveys visitors back to the town's beginnings, and the Farmers Market is a feast for the eyes as well as the belly.

Kansas City, Missouri, is just a few minutes away, with attractions as diverse as the Hallmark Visitors Center (the past and present of Hallmark cards), the Harley-Davidson Final Assembly Plant, the Federal Reserve Bank Visitors Center, and the Kansas City Market (an open-air farmers market). The 18th and Vine Historic Jazz District in Kansas City offers a concentrated selection of entertainment venues and museums such as the American Jazz Museum and the Negro Leagues Baseball Museum.

## Arts and Culture

The City of Overland Park has created a gallery space at the Overland Park Convention Center; six art exhibitions are presented each year to supplement the permanent displays onsite. Art at the Center focuses on works of local and regional artists. The city also coordinates a new Sculpture Exhibition at the Arboretum and Botanical Gardens; the juried sculpture show features works distributed throughout the natural beauty of the trees and flowers.

The city is committed to an ambitious public art project incorporating sculpture, lighting design, and landform alteration in accessible spots around the community. Projects on deck include landscape art and sculptures at all gateways to Overland Park, beautification projects at parks that are near high-traffic areas, murals and sculpture along a major transport corridor, and landscape sculpture at St. Andrew's Golf Course.

The Nerman Museum of Contemporary Art is located on the campus of Johnson County Community College. The museum maintains a permanent collection of paintings, photography, clay, sculptures, works on paper, and new media. Traveling exhibits are also presented and the museum galleries sponsor shows of local artists.

Local origins can be plumbed at the Johnson County Museum of History located in Shawnee and housed in a historic school. The museum contains archives documenting the development of Johnson County communities, a research library and an education center.

The greater Kansas City area puts on a great show in the performing arts; Overland Park proper touts its New Theatre Restaurant as one of the best dinner theaters in the country. The cuisine is five-star and the productions frequently feature recognizable stage, film, and television personalities. Martin City Melodrama and Vaudeville Company is a professional theater company in Overland Park, keeping audiences giggling with comedy productions and children's workshops. The Carlsen Center at Johnson County Community College offers a wide variety of programs and events year-round. Internationally-known performers are intermingled with college performing artists in an eclectic mix of opera, jazz, and classical numbers. Educational programs and classes are also available to the community.

Dance and music aficionados can rely on Kansas City, Missouri, to round out the repertoire—the Kansas City Ballet, Kansas City Symphony, Lyric Opera of Kansas City, Folly Theatre, and the Music Hall host performances all along the spectrum of the arts. Community-based theater productions are held by the Theatre League in Kansas City and professional theater performances are offered by the Kansas City Repertory Theatre. Outdoor theater can be experienced in Kansas City at the Starlight Theater and in Shawnee at the Theatre in the Park. The Wyandotte Players perform live family-oriented theatre at the Kansas City Kansas Community College Performing Arts Center.

The Kemper Museum of Contemporary Art in Kansas City, Missouri, features an international roster of artists who work in all media. A superb Asian collection crowns the exhibits at the Nelson-Atkins Museum of Art in Kansas City, which also boasts nationally-recognized collections of African, American, Native American, European, and ancient art.

*Arts and Culture Information:* Overland Park Convention and Visitors Bureau, 9001 W. 110 Street, Suite 100, Corporate Woods Building 29, Overland Park, KS 66210; toll-free (800)262-7275; www.opcvb.org

## Festivals and Holidays

Comfortable spring temperatures allow for a variety of outdoor celebrations and events, including the farmers market that operates from early April until late September. Vendors of produce, crafts, and art items set up booths near the Clock Tower, attracting hordes of locals and visitors. The Clock Tower is also the scene for a concert series that begins in early April and ends in late September, running in tandem with the farmers market. Spring showers bring more than May flowers at the Arboretum in Overland Park—from mid-May through late October, the botanical gardens and arboretum are the site of a juried Sculpture Exhibition.

Jazz in the Woods is a three-day music festival held in June on the grounds of Corporate Woods office park. Local and national jazz artists perform in Overland Park, with the proceeds going to several charities. The Downtown Overland Park Days and Art Festival in late June revolves around the resumption of an outdoor farmers market. The Fourth of July is celebrated with a bang at SpiritFest, a three-day party featuring local cuisine, three entertainment stages, and a midway.

Cooler fall temperatures bring street fairs and celebrations all around the area. The Kansas City Renaissance Festival in nearby Bonner Springs starts in early September and runs for seven weeks. Overland Park's Annual Fall Festival also occurs in late September and features art and craft booths, food vendors, and street entertainment in downtown Overland Park.

The winter holidays are kicked off in November with the Annual Holiday Market in the Farmer's Pavilion downtown. Vendors offer seasonal arts, crafts, produce, and holiday gifts on Saturdays throughout the month. The Mayor's Lighting Ceremony in mid-November features carolers, cookies, and Santa Claus as the city's communal tree is lit.

## Sports for the Spectator

Overland Park's proximity to Kansas City, Missouri, allows sports fans to immerse themselves in professional and amateur sports all year long. The Kansas City Chiefs play in the Western Division of the National Football League American Conference, with home games taking place in the Arrowhead Stadium off I-70, part of the Harry S. Truman Sports Complex. Major League Baseball's Kansas City Royals compete in the American League Central Division at Kauffman Stadium. The Kansas City Knights were a founding franchise in the American Basketball Association; home games are played in Kemper Arena from mid-November through mid-April. For the Kansas City Outlaws, the floor of the Kemper Arena is converted to an ice rink to accommodate United League Hockey play. Indoor soccer rounds out the winter season, with the Comets competing in the Major Indoor Soccer League from October through March.

Soccer heads outdoors for the Wizards' season—the team plays home games at CommunityAmerica Park in Kansas City, Kansas, and competes in the Major Soccer League. The Kansas City T-Bones play also ball at CommunityAmerica Ballpark as part of the Northern League of baseball.

The newest spectator sport in the area takes place at the Kansas Speedway in Kansas City, Kansas. This state-of-the-art facility features a 1.5-mile racing track, 80,000 spectator seats, driving schools, custom car shows and more. In addition to NASCAR, IRL and ARCA races, the Kansas Speedway also hosts community events. Greyhound, thoroughbred, and quarter horse racing take place at the dual-track Woodlands complex. The privately funded racetrack includes two separate enclosed spectator facilities, a one-mile horse track with a straightaway for thoroughbreds and quarter horses, and a greyhound track suitable for year-round racing. Lakeside Speedway (Kansas City, KS) has a half-mile asphalt oval track and is part of the NASCAR Winston Racing Series. The Speedway hosts many national touring series; racing takes place every Friday night from March through September.

## Sports for the Participant

The city has 78 parks and over 60 miles of hiking and biking trails. Classes in tai chi, yoga, aerobics, and weight training are offered through the Parks and Recreation Department of the City of Overland Park, which also coordinates youth and adult team sports in season. The city maintains the Indian Creek Trail for bikers and hikers, which winds for almost 17 miles along Indian Creek as it passes through Overland Park on its way to a convergence with the Tomahawk Creek Trail system.

The Overland Park Skate Park was created in 1997 through the efforts of an Overland Park Community Resource Officer who saw the need for a safe place for youth to skate. The park challenges users with jumps, ramps, and rails based on the urban landscape often frequented by skaters.

The city operates two public golf courses. St. Andrew's Golf Club is an 18-hole course that underwent a renovation in 1997 that was guided by LPGA player Carol Mann. The front nine holes feature wide fairways with some water hazards, while the back nine are characterized by tighter fairways, doglegs and bunkers. The Overland Park Golf Club offers 27 regulation holes that form three 18-hole courses. Putting greens, chipping greens, a grill and a pro shop round out the amenities at the Overland Park Golf Club. Both public clubs provide adult and youth instruction and leagues.

Johnson County coordinates a wide variety of sports and recreation programs, ranging from nature centers, to golf courses, to stables. The Ernie Miller Park and Nature

Center in Olathe contains 114 acres of diverse habitats, trails, a wildlife viewing room, and an aquarium. Outdoor Discovery Camps are offered for younger naturalists. Also located in Olathe is the TimberRidge Adventure Center; in addition to a professionally-facilitated challenge (ropes) course, the center provides opportunities to hike, fish, and practice archery skills. Anglers can also cast lines at Regency Park Lake in Overland Park; three acres of surface area shelters channel catfish, bluegill, hybrid sunfish, green sunfish, and largemouth bass.

### Shopping and Dining

The primary shopping mall is Oak Park Mall with more than 190 stores and restaurants. Metcalf South Shopping Center has several national chain stores. The Hawthorne Plaza contains a collection of upscale shops. A walk in downtown Overland Park will take shoppers by unique locally-owned antique stores, art galleries, and specialty stores. Overland Park's proximity to the two Kansas Cities means that locals and visitors are within easy reach of hundreds of other shopping centers and restaurants.

Barbecue figures largely on the menu of local eateries in Overland Park. Over 45 restaurants offer barbecue in one form or another. Mexican-American cuisine is also well-represented, with more than 50 establishments. The New Theatre Restaurant offers fine dining as well as fine theatrical entertainment. Asian restaurants are almost 80 in number, and Italian food is served at 32 eating places. Other culinary offerings include French, Cajun, Greek, Indian, Irish, and Jewish fare. Coffee houses run the gamut from chain franchises to locally-owned espresso bars.

## ■ Convention Facilities

The Overland Park Convention Center hosts trade shows, corporate meetings, conferences, and social events. The facility has a total of 237,000 square feet of meeting and exhibit space. Audio-visual connections and high-speed wireless service comprise only a portion of the state-of-the-art technology available to presenters and exhibitors. The center is decorated with works from local and regional artisans, including a blown-glass chandelier.

Many of the local hotels in Overland Park, Shawnee, Olathe, and the two Kansas Cities offer convention areas, banquet halls, meeting rooms, and ballrooms. The Jack Reardon Convention Centre in downtown Kansas City, Kansas, is the site of conferences, meetings, banquets, and conventions. The facility contains 20,000 square feet of exhibit space with 12 meeting rooms and 60 booth spaces. Seating is available for up to 1,800 participants. Next door, the Hilton Garden Inn offers 147 rooms and meeting space ranging from 300 to 5,000 square feet.

## ■ Transportation

### Approaching the City

Most airline passengers will arrive at Kansas City International Airport located 25 miles north of Overland Park in Kansas City, Missouri. Its 13 major commercial airlines offer about 230 daily departures with nonstop service to 70 destinations. The Johnson County Executive Airport is located between Overland Park and Olathe; originally created as a Naval auxiliary field during the second World War, the airport now provides general aviation services for corporations and other users. Air charters, aircraft sales, and flight instruction are all available onsite. The New Century AirCenter also offers general aviation services and can accommodate cargo and passenger jets.

The north-south Interstate 35 passes along the western edge of Overland Park and the east-west Interstate 70 runs just to the north. The city is further accessible via a network of bypasses that include U.S. highways (56, 69 and 71) and state highways (150 and 350). Amtrak and Greyhound offer service to Kansas City, Missouri.

### Traveling in the City

The major streets in Overland Park are laid out in a grid pattern that is neatly oriented with name streets running due north-south and number streets running east-west. Interstate 35 runs along the western portion of Overland Park, with numerous exits to the community. Metcalf Avenue is a primary artery within Overland Park itself; the street, which runs north and south, makes a handy reference point as it drives right through the heart of the municipality.

Johnson County Transit (The JO) operates a large number of buses, vans and smaller vehicles to support public transportation in the area. Passengers can take advantage of park-and-ride services, and special programs exist for seniors or disabled riders. Johnson County Transit also organizes shared rides to sporting events and festivals at points in both Kansas City, Kansas, and Kansas City, Missouri. A fleet of taxi companies further bolster transportation services within the city and beyond. Bike commuters into Downtown Overland Park can navigate the street system or utilize the Indian Creek Trail system.

## ■ Communications

### Newspapers and Magazines

Since 1880 *The Kansas City Star* has been delivering the news to eastern Kansas, with coverage of local, regional, national, and world events. *The Star* publishes three editions daily, including one edition specific to Johnson County. Business news, sports and entertainment are featured daily in the paper. *The Olathe News* has a distribution throughout Johnson County. *The Overland Park Sun* is published on Thursdays. The weekly *Kansas City Jewish Chronicle* is published in Overland Park and distributed on Fridays.

## Television and Radio

Overland Park tends to rely on Kansas City, Missouri, for its radio and television services. The local airwaves carry a variety of news, talk radio, sports and Christian programming on the AM frequency. FM radio locally offers alternative rock, National Public Radio, oldies, classical, country, Christian, and much more. Television stations broadcast from Kansas City, Missouri, and available in Overland Park include the networks of CBS, NBC, and ABC, along with Fox and CW. Public television, University of Kansas, and Christian channels are also offered.

*Media Information:* *The Kansas City Star*, 1729 Grand Blvd., Kansas City, MO 64108; telephone (816) 234-4926; www.kansascity.com

## Overland Park Online

City of Overland Park. Available www.opkansas.org

Overland Park Chamber of Commerce. Available www.opks.org

Overland Park Convention and Visitors Bureau. Available www.opcvb.org

Overland Park Economic Development Council. Available www.opedc.org

Johnson County Government. Available www.jocogov.org

Johnson County Library System. Available www.jocolibrary.org

BIBLIOGRAPHY

Davis, Kenneth S., *Kansas: A History* (New York, NY, 1984)

# Topeka

## ■ The City in Brief

**Founded:** 1854 (incorporated 1857)

**Head Official:** Mayor William W. Bunten (since 2005)

**City Population**

    1980: 118,690
    1990: 119,883
    2000: 122,377
    2006 estimate: 122,113
    Percent change, 1990–2000: 1.3%
    U.S. rank in 1980: 136th
    U.S. rank in 1990: 149th
    U.S. rank in 2000: 197th

**Metropolitan Area Population**

    1980: 154,916
    1990: 160,976
    2000: 169,871
    2006 estimate: 228,894
    Percent change, 1990–2000: 5.5%
    U.S. rank in 1980: Not available
    U.S. rank in 1990: Not available
    U.S. rank in 2000: 319th

**Area:** 56 square miles (2000)

**Elevation:** Ranges from 876 feet to 971 feet above sea level

**Average Annual Temperatures:** January, 27.2° F; July, 78.4° F; annual average, 54.3° F

**Average Annual Precipitation:** 35.64 inches of rain; 20.7 inches of snow

**Major Economic Sectors:** Services, government, trade, manufacturing

**Unemployment Rate:** 5.0% (June 2007)

**Per Capita Income:** $21,992 (2005)

**2005 FBI Crime Index Property:** 9,662

**2005 FBI Crime Index Violent:** 682

**Major Colleges and Universities:** Washburn University

**Daily Newspaper:** *The Topeka Capital-Journal*

## ■ Introduction

Topeka is the seat of Shawnee County, the capital of Kansas, and center of a metropolitan statistical area that covers five counties. Throughout its history, Topeka has been at the forefront of progress; created as a principal link in the westward expansion of the railroad and settled by New England antislavery supporters in the nineteenth century, the city was in the twentieth century a world leader in the treatment of mental illness. In the last two decades Topeka has experienced business growth with a number of *Fortune* 1000 companies relocating or expanding in the area.

## ■ Geography and Climate

Topeka lies on both banks of the Kansas River about 60 miles upriver from the point where the Kansas joins the Missouri River. Two tributaries of the Kansas River, Soldier and Shunganunga Creeks, flow through the city. The valley near Topeka, bordered by rolling prairie uplands of 200 to 300 feet, ranges from two to four miles in width. Seventy percent of the annual precipitation falls from April through September. Heavy rains pose the threat of flooding, but the construction of dams has reduced the problem. Summers are usually hot, with low humidity and southerly winds; periods of high humidity and oppressively warm temperatures are of short duration. Winter cold spells are seldom prolonged; winter precipitation is often in the form of snow, sleet, or glaze. Severe or disruptive storms occur infrequently.

**Area:** 56 square miles (2000)

**Elevation:** Ranges from 876 feet to 971 feet above sea level

**Average Temperatures:** January, 27.2° F; July, 78.4° F; annual average, 54.3° F

**Average Annual Precipitation:** 35.64 inches of rain; 20.7 inches of snow

# ■ History

## Westward Expansion Targets Kaw River Valley

Two historic nineteenth-century movements combined to create the city of Topeka. One was the antislavery issue and the other was the westward expansion made possible by the railroad, which connected the East with the vast unsettled territory in the West. Before the Kansas frontier was opened by the federal government to settlement, the first people of European descent to live on the site of present-day Topeka were the French-Canadian Pappan brothers. They each married a woman from the Kaw tribe in 1842 and opened a ferry service across the Kaw River. The ferry was temporarily replaced in 1857 when bridge builders ignored warnings from the local Native Americans, who insisted that structures built too close to the Kaw would not be secure against flood waters. The bridge was destroyed in a flood the following year.

Colonel Cyrus K. Holliday, a native of Pennsylvania, came to the Kansas Territory in 1854 with funding from Eastern investors to build a railroad. Holliday and a few pioneers had walked 45 miles from Kansas City to Lawrence, where Holliday approached Dr. Charles Robinson, agent of the New England Emigrant Aid Company, an antislavery organization, about his plan. Then Holliday and Robinson traveled 21 miles to Tecumseh, but businessmen there wanted too much money for their land. Holliday located a spot 5 miles from Tecumseh along the river and purchased land from Enoch Chase, who had previously bought it from the Kaws.

Holliday formed a company, naming himself as president and the Lawrence contingent and Chase as stockholders. Holliday wanted to name the town Webster after Daniel Webster, but the others preferred a name whose meaning was local. They chose Topeka, a Native American word meaning "smokey hill," according to one version, or "a good place to dig potatoes," according to another. The City of Topeka was incorporated February 14, 1857 with Holliday as mayor. Dr. Robinson attracted antislavery New Englanders to settle in Topeka, thus

counteracting the influence of a proslavery group in Tecumseh. A Free State constitutional convention was held in Topeka but federal troops arrested the new legislators when they tried to meet on July 4, 1855.

## Kansas Statehood Brings Capital to Topeka

The Kansas constitution was framed at Wyandotte (later named Kansas City), and Kansas was admitted to the Union in 1861. The constitution specified that the state capital would be selected by election. Dr. Robinson ran for governor, favoring Topeka over Lawrence as the site for the capital; he also supported the Atchison, Topeka & Santa Fe Railway system, which began laying its westward track in 1869. Holliday served as the company's first president, with general offices and machine shops located in Topeka. Topeka's population increased from 700 people in 1862 to 5,000 people in 1870; it then made another dramatic population jump in the late 1880s.

## Foundation in Topeka Gains International Fame

During the 20th century Topeka was known internationally as the home of Menninger, a nonprofit organization dedicated to the study of mental illness and founded by Dr. Karl Menninger and his father, Dr. Charles F. Menninger. In 1920 the Menningers opened a group psychiatric practice that they named the Menninger Clinic; they were joined in 1925 by William, Charles's younger son. The Menningers opened the Topeka Institute of Psychoanalysis in 1938 after the brothers had studied formally in Chicago. The family is credited with introducing psychiatry to America. Karl Menninger's *The Human Mind* was the first book on psychiatry to become a bestseller. The Menningers opened the nonprofit Menninger Foundation, the world's largest psychiatric training center, in 1941. The Menninger Clinic moved to Houston, Texas in 2003.

With the beginning of World War II the city's railroad, meat packing, and agricultural base shifted to manufacturing and government/military services. Forbes Air Force Base was established during the war and the Goodyear Tire and Rubber Company opened a plant in 1944. When the Air Force Base closed in 1974, over 10,000 people left Topeka. However, the air field was passed into local hands through the creation of the Metropolitan Topeka Airport Authority. In the 1980s county voters approved a bond issue that allowed for the redevelopment and expansion of the airport and the surrounding area into the Topeka Air Industrial Park, which now serves the city as a Foreign Trade Zone.

With an eye toward increased development, during the 1990s county voters passed a series of bond issue that allowed for public school improvements, expansion of the public library, a new law enforcement center, and the East Topeka Interchange project. In 2004 county voters

©James Blank.

approved a 12-year half-cent sales tax increase that would generate funds designated for economic development, roads, and bridges.

Today, Topeka is recognized for its strong economic development efforts and high quality of life. In 2003 *Business Facilities* magazine wrote, "While the national economy lags, relocations and expansions are happening all over Kansas, with Topeka leading the way." *Expansion Management* magazine gave the city its highest rating in the Annual Quality of Life Quotient survey.

***Historical Information:*** Kansas State Historical Society, 6425 SW Sixth Avenue, Topeka, KS 66615; telephone (785)272-8681; www.kshs.org

# ■ Population Profile

## Metropolitan Area Residents

1980: 154,916
1990: 160,976
2000: 169,871
2006 estimate: 228,894
Percent change, 1990–2000: 5.5%
U.S. rank in 1980: Not available

U.S. rank in 1990: Not available
U.S. rank in 2000: 319th

## City Residents

1980: 118,690
1990: 119,883
2000: 122,377
2006 estimate: 122,113
Percent change, 1990–2000: 1.3%
U.S. rank in 1980: 136th
U.S. rank in 1990: 149th
U.S. rank in 2000: 197th

**Density:** 2,185 people per square mile (2000)

## Racial and ethnic characteristics (2005)

White: 89,722
Black: 12,953
American Indian and Alaska Native: 2,022
Asian: 1,569
Native Hawaiian and Pacific Islander: 185
Hispanic or Latino (may be of any race): 11,653
Other: 7,264

**Percent of residents born in state:** 67.9% (2000)

## Age characteristics (2005)

Population under 5 years old: 9,647
Population 5 to 9 years old: 7,979
Population 10 to 14 years old: 6,499
Population 15 to 19 years old: 6,199
Population 20 to 24 years old: 8,388
Population 25 to 34 years old: 18,582
Population 35 to 44 years old: 14,778
Population 45 to 54 years old: 16,352
Population 55 to 59 years old: 6,299
Population 60 to 64 years old: 5,464
Population 65 to 74 years old: 8,998
Population 75 to 84 years old: 5,968
Population 85 years and older: 2,173
Median age: 36 years

## Births (2006, MSA)

Total number: 3,147

## Deaths (2006, MSA)

Total number: 2,156

## Money income (2005)

Per capita income: $21,992
Median household income: $35,726
Total households: 53,763

## Number of households with income of…

less than $10,000: 4,995
$10,000 to $14,999: 4,870
$15,000 to $24,999: 8,360
$25,000 to $34,999: 8,035
$35,000 to $49,999: 8,202
$50,000 to $74,999: 9,451
$75,000 to $99,999: 4,217
$100,000 to $149,999: 3,694
$150,000 to $199,999: 983
$200,000 or more: 956

**Percent of families below poverty level:** 11% (2005)

**2005 FBI Crime Index Property:** 9,662

**2005 FBI Crime Index Violent:** 682

# ■ Municipal Government

Topeka adopted a city manager form of government in 2005. Council members from each of nine districts are elected to staggered four-year terms; the mayor is elected at large and sets the council's agenda (but does not vote). A city manager handles daily operations.

**Head Official:** Mayor William W. Bunten (since 2005; current term expires 2009)

**Total Number of City Employees:** 1,400 (2007)

***City Information:*** City Hall, 215 SE 7th Street, Topeka, KS 66603-3914; telephone (785)368-3710; fax (785)368-3958; www.topeka.org

# ■ Economy

## Major Industries and Commercial Activity

The Topeka MSA includes the five counties of Shawnee (of which Topeka is the seat), Jackson, Jefferson, Osage, and Wabaunsee. Government, including federal, state, county, and local entities, accounts for about 25.5 percent of employment in the Topeka MSA. The service sector, including educational, health care, professional, business, and insurance and financial services, accounts for about 29 percent of employment in the Topeka MSA. Four local public school districts and Washburn University are major employers in education. Major health care employers include Stormont-Vail HealthCare, St. Francis Health Center, Colmery-O'Neil VA Hospital, and the Kansas Neurological Institute. Blue Cross and Blue Shield of Kansas and Security Benefit Group are headquartered in Topeka.

Trade, transportation, and utilities make up the next largest sector accounting for nearly 18 percent of employment. Major employers in this sector include Burlington Northern Santa Fe, Westar Energy, and AT&T. Major retail employers in the city include Wal-Mart and Dilon's Grocery Stores. Westar Energy is a *Fortune* 1000 company based in Topeka.

Manufacturing accounts for nearly 8 percent of employment. The *Fortune* 1000 company Payless ShoeSource has manufacturing and distribution headquarters in the city and is one of the major employers. Other major employers in this sector include Goodyear Tire and Rubber Co., Jostens Printing and Publishing, Frito-Lay Inc., Hill's Pet Nutrition, and Hallmark Cards.

**Items and goods produced:** pet foods, tires, greeting cards, commercial publications, snack foods, specialty frozen foods, yearbooks, cellulose films, stationery and envelopes, printed business materials

## Incentive Programs—New and Existing Companies

*Local programs:* Shawnee County has implemented a quarter-cent sales tax that will support local economic development activities. The anticipated revenue will be earmarked for job creation and investment incentives. The city or county may grant up to 10 years of property tax exemptions to companies that promote employment growth or private investment in the area. GO Topeka offers loans to small businesses and startups owned by women or minorities, as well as job training and counseling.

Topeka's One-Stop Business Development Office provides advice, funding and training in affiliation with the Washburn University Small Business Development Center, SCORE, GO Connection Microloan Program, and Wakarusa Certified Development Inc. Downtown Topeka Inc. provides grants to businesses in the downtown area.

*State programs:* The entire state of Kansas is designated as an Enterprise Zone. Businesses located in an Enterprise Zone are eligible for special credits such as an investment tax credit (1 percent), a building and materials sales tax exemption, and inventory tax exemption, and certain property tax exemptions and credits. A job creation tax credit of $1,500 per new job is also available for jobs created in the zone for certified dislocated or economically disadvantaged workers. A research tax credit of 6.5 percent is also available for qualified research and development investments. Businesses that are not eligible for the Enterprise Zone programs may apply for job expansion and investment tax credits. Forbes Field Airport and the Topeka Air Industrial Park are part of a federal-designated Foreign Trade Zone (FTZ). Goods entering FTZs are not subject to customs tariffs until the goods leave the zone and are formally entered into U.S. customs territory. The High Performance Incentive Program offers a 10 percent corporate income tax credit on qualified capital investments for eligible companies. There is no state income tax for either personal or corporate income.

The Kansas Department of Commerce is the state's leading economic development agency. Its Business Development Division offers customized proposals for prospective companies to outline available incentives and financing programs. Financing programs include the Kansas economic Opportunity Initiatives Fund, the Partnership Fund, and Industrial Revenue Bonds. The Kansas Bioscience Authority offers several incentive programs for relocating, expanding, and start-up companies in the bioscience industry.

*Job training programs:* Kansas 1st is a statewide program through which local colleges and universities provide job-related training through individual courses of study and businesses training programs. Through Kansas 1st, companies may create specialized programs for their employees. Companies creating new jobs may qualify for training funds through Investments in Major Projects and Comprehensive Training (IMPACT), Kansas Industrial Training (KIT), and Kansas Industrial Retraining (KIR). Programs are custom designed to meet a company's specific training needs and can involve pre-employment or on-the-job training. Job training programs are available through agencies such as KAW Area Technical School.

## Development Projects

The Kansas State Capitol is undergoing a nine-year restoration at a projected cost of $138 million. Components of this massive effort include restoring the historical integrity of the limestone exterior and the marble and wood interior; transforming the virtually unused basement into office space, a cafeteria and a visitor's center; updating mechanical and electrical systems; and conserving murals and decorative painting. Work is likely to continue until 2009.

In 2007 Alorica Inc., a leading customer service management firm, announced plans to open an in-bound customer service call center in Topeka. The company anticipates a long-term potential of 850 to 1,000 full-time positions. Also in 2007, LB Steel, LLC, headquartered in Chicago, IL, announced that it had obtained ownership of Topeka Metal Specialties Inc. Officials from LB Steel assured city officials that the Topeka facility will retain the Topeka Metal Specialties name and become a division of LB Steel, Inc. The company will gradually add 130 positions over the next year or two for a total of 200 jobs at the site.

The grand opening of the Coca-Cola Enterprises Bottling Company of Kansas took place in summer of 2007. This new 45,000-square-foot sales and distribution center is expected to attract a minimum of 70 full-time jobs. The state-of-the-art Cotton-O'Neil Cancer Center, affiliated with Stormont-Vail HealthCare, opened in December 2006. The 31,500-square-foot facility is located west of the Cotton-O'Neil Digestive Health Center. The continued expansion of Stormont-Vail HealthCare services has helped the system remain one of the largest employers in the city for several years.

In 2007 Hy-Vee Inc. broke ground for its new 75,100-square-foot store located in Topeka. This latest site for the national supermarket chain will include a food court with an eat-in dining area, a Starbuck's, consumer services such as dry cleaning and photo processing, and a Club Room for meetings and parties.

In 2007 Go Topeka (the Greater Topeka Chamber of Commerce) outlined a global marketing strategy featuring five target areas for economic growth. These targets, building upon the already proven strengths of the city's economy, include warehousing and distribution, shared services, value-added food manufacturing, business and professional organizations, and animal and pet food manufacturing and research.

*Economic Development Information:* Greater Topeka Chamber of Commerce, 120 SE Sixth Street, Suite 110, Topeka, KS 66603-3515; telephone (785) 234-2644; www.topekachamber.org

## Commercial Shipping

The largest airport in the city is Forbes Field, which is located within a Foreign Trade Zone. Air cargo and package express is provided by widely recognized national firms. Kansas City International Airport in Missouri, about 75 miles away, has 4 all-cargo carriers and 11-passenger combination carriers.

Burlington Northern Santa Fe Railway and Union Pacific provide commercial rail service to the Topeka area; piggyback service is available within a 60-mile radius. More than 300 motor carriers serve the Topeka region. Two air carriers operate parcel and freight facilities at Forbes Field.

## Labor Force and Employment Outlook

Shawnee County, of which Topeka is the seat, is considered to have one of the highest job/residents ratios in the state, but is also a magnet for commuters. Nearly 20 percent of employment within the county is held by out-of-county commuters. In 2006 about 86.6 percent of residents 25 years and older had a high school diploma or higher. A little over 27 percent had obtained a bachelor's degree or higher. Statewide, more than half of Kansas employees have taken advantage of on-the-job training opportunities.

The highest number of jobs within the city proper have been in government and services. According to state reports on regional occupational trends, office and administrative support, management, and sales and related occupations should see the greatest growth in employment into 2012. If economic development plans within the city are successful, the job market will continue to expand in the service industries, particularly in business and professional services, and in manufacturing, particularly in the value-added foods and pet foot industries. Warehousing and distribution jobs should see some growth as well.

The following is a summary of data regarding the Topeka metropolitan area labor force, 2006 annual averages.

**Size of nonagricultural labor force:** 109,200

**Number of workers employed in ...**

construction and mining: 5,900
manufacturing: 7,600
trade, transportation and utilities: 20,300
information: 2,600
financial activities: 7,500
professional and business services: 8,500
educational and health services: 16,700
leisure and hospitality: 7,600
other services: 5,100
government: 27,600

**Average hourly earnings of production workers employed in manufacturing:** Not available

**Unemployment rate:** 5.0% (June 2007)

| *Largest employers (2007)* | *Number of employees* |
| --- | --- |
| State of Kansas | 8,402 |
| Stormont Vail Health Care Center | 3,100 |
| Topeka USD No. 501 | 2,538 |
| Blue Cross and Blue Shield of Kansas | 1,817 |
| St. Francis Health Center | 1,800 |
| Washburn University | 1,651 |
| Goodyear Tire & Rubber Co. | 1,600 |
| Payless ShoeSource | 1,600 |
| City of Topeka | 1,400 |
| U.S. Government | 1,256 |
| Shawnee County | 1,100 |

## Cost of Living

According to the Greater Topeka Chamber of Commerce, Topeka offers a "quality living experience at a below average cost."

The following is a summary of data regarding several key cost of living factors in the Topeka area.

**2007 (1st quarter) ACCRA Average House Price:** $248,954

**2007 (1st quarter) ACCRA Cost of Living Index:** 90.7

**State income tax rate:** 3.50% to 6.45%

**State sales tax rate:** 5.3%

**Local income tax rate:** None

**Local sales tax rate:** city, 1.0%; county, 1.15%

**Property tax rate:** 141.24 mills per $1,000 of assessed value (2004)

***Economic Information:*** Greater Topeka Chamber of Commerce, 120 SE Sixth Street, Suite 110, Topeka, KS 66603-3515; telephone (785)234-2644; www.topekachamber.org. Kansas Department of Labor, 401 SW Topeka Blvd., Topeka, KS 66603; telephone (785)296-5000; www.dol.ks.gov

## ■ Education and Research

### Elementary and Secondary Schools

There are three public school districts with administrative offices in Topeka. The largest is the Topeka Public Schools (TPS) Unified School District 501. The school superintendent is appointed by a nonpartisan, seven-member board of education.

TPS features two state-of-the-art elementary magnet schools—one emphasizing computer technology and the other with a science and fine arts theme. The district has an extensive special education program, a business partnership program, a school volunteer program, full-day kindergarten in several schools, preschool programs, out-of-district enrollment options, and alternative education programs. The Kaw Area Technical School offers programs in basic adult education and business and industry training.

The two high schools (one traditional, one alternative) and one middle school of the Auburn-Washburn Unified School District 437 are located in Topeka. The district also has four elementary schools and administrative offices in Topeka. Seaman Unified School District 345 serves students in northern part of the city with Seaman High School, two junior high schools, and eight elementary schools.

The following is a summary of data regarding the Topeka Public Schools as of the 2005–2006 school year.

**Total enrollment:** 13,387

**Number of facilities**

>  elementary schools: 21
>  junior high/middle schools: 6
>  senior high schools: 3
>  other: 8

**Student/teacher ratio:** 13:1

**Teacher salaries (2005–06)**

>  elementary median: $35,160
>  junior high/middle median: $35,580
>  secondary median: $37,270

**Funding per pupil:** $8,662

Educational alternatives are offered by several private and parochial private schools in Topeka. The Catholic School System in Topeka is part of the Kansas City, Kansas Archdiocese. Special schools include the Capper Foundation and TARC (the Topeka Association for Retarded Children).

*Public Schools Information:* Topeka Public Schools, USD 501, 624 W 24th Street, Topeka, KS 66611; telephone (785)575-6100; www.topeka.k12.ks.us

## Colleges and Universities

Washburn University, a public institution enrolling over 7,000, offers more than 100 programs in its College of Arts and Sciences and its faculties of law, business, nursing, and applied and continuing education. Washburn's law school counts nationally recognized lawyers, judges and politicians among its alumni. Washburn University was rated sixth in the Midwest among public master's level universities in the 2007 America's Best Colleges rankings by *U.S. News & World Report*.

The Friends University Topeka Educational Center offers bachelor's degrees in business management, human resources, marketing, and organizational management and learning. Master's degrees are available in business

administration, organizational development, teaching, and health care leadership. The main campus of Friends University is in Wichita.

The University of Kansas in Lawrence, Kansas State University in Manhattan, and Emporia State University are within 50 miles of Topeka. Among the ten occupational/technical schools located in Topeka are Kaw Area Technical School and Wichita Technical Institute–Topeka.

## Libraries and Research Centers

Topeka is home to several major libraries. The Topeka and Shawnee County Public Library was reopened in 2002 after a 100,000-square-foot expansion designed by renowned architect Michael Graves. The library holds over 538,000 items, including books, periodicals, microfilms, compact discs, slides, audiotapes and videotapes. Its Alice C. Sabatini Gallery houses the oldest public art collection in the city. The library also offers an outreach program with two bookmobiles and an Adventure Mobile for children.

The Kansas State Library maintains an extensive collection of books, documents and videos with a focus on government and public affairs. The library also operates a free talking book program for patrons with visual impairments, physical impairments or reading disabilities in Emporia. The Kansas State Historical Society Library contains a state archival collection as well as archaeological and genealogical materials, manuscripts, maps, photographs and federal documents.

Washburn University's Mabee Library contains the William I. Koch Art History Collection of over 12,000 items. The Washburn University School of Law Library is part of the national and state depository programs. This library has maintained the published opinions of the Kansas Supreme and Appeals Courts since October 25, 1996 and the opinions of the United States Tenth Circuit Court of Appeals from October 1, 1997. The library also has a special collection on microform of Native American legal materials.

The Kansas Supreme Court Law Library holds over 185,000 volumes and 600 periodical titles. The Topeka Genealogical Society Library offers research services for a fee.

*Public Library Information:* Topeka & Shawnee County Public Library, 1515 SW Tenth Avenue, Topeka, KS 66604; telephone (785)580-4400; www.tscpl.org

# ■ Health Care

The Topeka medical community has expanded with renovation and new construction at the city's major facilities. St. Francis Hospital, affiliated with the Sisters of Charity of Leavenworth Health System, offers 378 patient beds and the premier St. Francis Comprehensive

Cancer Care Center, including the only PET image scanner in the Topeka area. The system also supports the St. Francis Diabetes Center and the St. Francis NewLife Center (maternity and infant care). Other specialty clinics within the hospital include the Midwest Heartburn Clinic, the Stock Eye Institute, the Pain Medicine Center, and the Sleep Disorders Clinic. The Recovery Center at St. Francis North Health Center offers inpatient and outpatient treatments for chemical addictions. St. Francis North Center offers a wide range of testing and diagnostic services as well. Nortonville Medical Clinic, Oskaloosa Medical Clinic, St. Francis Family Medicine, and Valley Falls Medical Center offer primary care services. The Select Specialty Hospital–Topeka, located at St. Francis Medical Center, is an acute care facility for patients requiring care for extended periods of time; the average stay is 25 days.

Stormont-Vail Regional Health Center is a 586-bed acute care facility providing a range of inpatient and outpatient services. It operates the only Level III Neonatal Intensive Care Unit in the county and recently completed a new $35 million surgical center. The hospital is part of the Stormont-Vail HealthCare integrated system, which serves 12 counties in northeast Kansas. Stormont-Vail sponsors several specialty clinics including Cotton-O'Neil Digestive Health Center, the Cotton-O'Neil Cancer Center, the Diabetes and Endocrinology Center, and PediatriCare. Stormont-Vail West provides inpatient and outpatient behavioral health services.

The Colmery-O'Neil Medical Center is part of the VA Eastern Kansas Health Care System and provides a range of services for veterans, including medical, surgical, psychiatric, and nursing home care. The facility has 135 inpatient beds and 96 skilled nursing beds. The Kansas Neurological Institute, affiliated with the Kansas Department of Social and Rehabilitation Services, is recognized for its programs for persons with developmental disabilities. The Kansas Rehabilitation Hospital is a 79-bed facility that provides inpatient and outpatient care in all areas of physical rehabilitation. Specialized programs are available in speech therapy and for patients with Parkinson's disease.

Tallgrass Surgical Center is a physician-owned center providing specialized surgical services in ophthalmology, general and vascular, gynecology, oral and maxillofacial, plastics, and orthopedic surgeries. The center also offers family medicine and immediate care services and a special Balance and Hearing Center.

Valeo Community Residence Program is a private, not-for-profit facility offering residential behavioral health care and support for adults. The nonprofit Capper Foundation provides education and assistive technology for physically handicapped children. It also offers preschool and childcare services.

There are 36 adult care homes in the Topeka area.

# ■ Recreation

## Sightseeing

Historic Ward-Meade Park overlooks the Kansas River valley from its position on a bluff. At the center of the park is the ancestral home of the Anthony Ward family, a Victorian mansion built in 1870. Also on the grounds are the Ward frontier log cabin, a country schoolhouse, botanical gardens, and a restored 1900s Kansas village called Old Prairie Town.

Gage Park includes the 160-acre Topeka Zoo, featuring a gorilla encounter habitat, providing for close observation of great apes through a glass partition; a Lion's Pride exhibit; Black Bear Woods; and a Tropical Rain Forest. Also at Gage Park are the Reinisch Rose Garden and Carousel in the Park.

Topeka's copper-domed state Capitol building is well known for its frescoes and woodworking, but it is the Kansas Murals that give the Capitol its artistic focal point; these murals by John Steuart Curry capture dramatic events in the state's history that proved so controversial at the time they were executed that the project was not finished. The Brown v. Board of Education National Historic Site opened in 2004 at the former Monroe School, marking the 1954 Supreme Court decision that ended segregation in public schools. Topeka High School displays the mast spar from *Old Ironsides* on its lawn.

Great Overland Station is a museum and education center commemorating Topeka's railroad heritage. Future redevelopment of the adjacent Kansas Riverfront Park and Historic North Topeka Business District will turn the area into a rich cultural destination for locals and tourists. Potwin Place is an exclusive section of Topeka with Italianate, Victorian, and nineteenth-century farmhouse-style homes. Cedar Crest Governor's Residence, built by Topeka State Journal publisher Frank P. MacLennan in 1928, has been the home of Kansas Governors since 1962. First Presbyterian Church is one of a handful of churches in the nation decorated with Tiffany windows.

## Arts and Culture

Musical entertainment in Topeka is provided by the Topeka Symphony Orchestra, the Topeka Community Concert Association, the Topeka Opera Society, the Fine Arts Society, and the Topeka Jazz Workshop. Performances take place at the Kansas Expocentre, the Topeka Performing Arts Center, and elsewhere. The Leavenworth Players Group at China Inn offers an interactive murder mystery for entertainment while dining on a seven-course Chinese meal.

The Topeka Performing Arts Center hosts touring Broadway musicals, dance companies, major symphonies, and other entertainment. The Topeka Civic Theater and Academy offers one of the nation's oldest and most highly regarded dinner theaters. Acting classes are available at the academy for students of all ages. Other Topeka theater companies include Helen Hocker Theatre at the Helen Hocker Center for the Performing Arts in Gage Park and the Andrew J. and Georgia Neese Gray Theatre at Washburn University. Musical programs are offered at Washburn University at the Elliott White Concert Hall, which serves as a venue for the Topeka Symphony Orchestra.

More than 20 art galleries as well as public buildings, businesses, and corporations in Topeka display an array of art. Among the more outstanding pieces are John Steuart Curry's *John Brown* in the State Capitol and Peter Felton's *Amelia Earhart* in the rotunda of the State Capitol. The Mulvane Art Museum on the campus of Washburn University exhibits works by Duerer, Goya, Picasso, and Dali in its permanent collection. The Phoenix Gallery Topeka represents over 150 painters, potters, and sculptures from a five-state area who specialize in art of the prairies and Midwest. The Kansas Museum of History chronicles the history of Kansas from the earliest native cultures to the present, using interactive exhibits, programs and videos. The Combat Air Museum at Forbes Field displays airplanes, missiles, military vehicles and aircraft memorabilia dating back to 1917.

*Arts and Culture Information:* Topeka Convention and Visitors Bureau, 1275 SW Topeka Blvd, Topeka, KS 66612-1852; telephone (785)234-1030 or (800)235-1030; www. visittopeka.travel. Mid-America Arts Alliance, 2018 Baltimore Avenue, Kansas City, MO 64108; telephone (816)421-1388; www.maaa.org

## Festivals and Holidays

Kansas Day Celebration in late January commemorates Kansas's admission into the Union. The featured attraction in March is the St. Patrick's Day Parade and Street Fair. Washburn University hosts the Sunflower Music Festival and the Mountain Plains Art Fair in June. The Spirit of Kansas Celebration, Mexican Fiesta, and Shawnee County Fair make for an active July. The Huff 'N' Puff Balloon Rally is a popular September event, as well as Cider Days and the Kansas River Valley Art Festival. Apple Festival, held at Historic Ward-Meade Park in October, celebrates Kansas's folk life. Festival of Trees and Miracle on Kansas Avenue take place during December.

## Sports for the Spectator

The North American Hockey League's Topeka Road-Runners play at the Kansas Expocentre. Washburn University fields teams in intercollegiate competition in a number of sports. The Great Plains Rowing Championship takes place in April on Lake Shawnee. The Kansas State High School Rodeo Championships are held at the Kansas Expocentre Livestock Arena in early June. Drag racing action takes place at Heartland Park in Topeka, while sprint car racing happens at Thunder Hill Speedway.

## Sports for the Participant

The Topeka Parks and Recreation Department maintains parks with 7 community centers, 69 public tennis courts, 5 public swimming pools, 26 baseball or softball diamonds, and a number of playgrounds, picnic facilities and soccer fields. Nine public golf courses are located in the area. East of Topeka is Lake Shawnee, providing opportunities for swimming, fishing, camping, and sailing. Gage Park, in addition to being the home of the Topeka Zoo, features recreational facilities including swimming, volleyball, and tennis. A number of hiking, jogging and nature trails can be found in Topeka. The Topeka Tinman Triathlon takes place at Lake Shawnee in June. Indoor ice skating is offered at the Kansas Expocentre.

## Shopping and Dining

The 1.1 million-square-foot WestRidge Mall is Topeka's main shopping venue. The Flaming Place outdoor mall has unique shops and art galleries as well as some well-known chain stores. Brookwood Shopping Center offers a variety of unique shops and restaurants. There are several smaller local shopping centers serving neighborhood shoppers. There are at least a dozen antique shops in the city.

Steakhouses serving Kansas beef are the main attraction in Topeka. Other dining choices include French, Mexican, Oriental, and Cajun Creole. Topeka's most popular family restaurants specialize in traditional American fare such as Kansas steaks, Southern fried chicken, country fried steaks, barbecued ribs, and homemade pies and pastries. Fine dining is also available at Chez Yasu (French), fritz Company Grille, Kiku Steakhouse of Japan, and the New City Café.

*Visitor Information:* Topeka Convention and Visitors Bureau, 1275 SW Topeka Blvd, Topeka, KS 66612-1852; telephone (785)234-1030 or (800)235-1030; www. visittopeka.travel

# ■ Convention Facilities

The Kansas Expocentre, a multipurpose complex which houses an arena, concert hall, and a convention center, accommodates meetings, conventions, trade shows, and entertainment events. The arena seats up to 10,000 people and contains 210,000 square feet of unobstructed space. Parking is provided on-site and catering service is available. The Ramada Inn Downtown is the largest hotel in Topeka with 34,000 square feet of meeting space. Thirty additional hotels and motels, several of which include complete meeting facilities, offer nearly 3,000 rooms for lodgings.

***Convention Information:*** Kansas Expocentre, One Expocentre Drive, Topeka, KS 66612; telephone (785) 235-1986; www.ksexpo.com. Topeka Convention and Visitors Bureau, 1275 SW Topeka Blvd, Topeka, KS 66612-1852; telephone (785)234-1030 or (800)235-1030; www.visittopeka.travel

## ■ Transportation

### Approaching the City

Commercial airlines fly into Forbes Field, which is about seven miles south of downtown Topeka. The destination for general and business aviation traffic is Phillip Billard Airport, about three miles northeast of the city. Visitors might also arrive first at Kansas City International Airport, about 75 miles from Topeka. Its 13 major commercial airlines offer about 230 daily departures with nonstop service to 70 destinations.

Passenger rail service to Topeka is provided by Amtrak. Greyhound Bus service is also available.

An efficient highway network facilitates access into Topeka. Three interstate and three U.S. highways converge in Topeka: I-70, I-470, and I-335; and U.S. 24, U.S. 40, and U.S. 75.

### Traveling in the City

Topeka is laid out on a grid pattern. Streets running east to west are numbered; streets running north to south are named. Topeka Transit schedules 17 public bus routes in the city Monday through Saturday; evening and Sunday service is available by advance reservation. Topeka Transit's Lift Service provides door-to-door service for persons with disabilities. During weekday mornings and afternoons, Topeka Transit operates the Topeka Trolleys, a downtown shuttle and lunchtime circulator service.

## ■ Communications

### Newspapers and Magazines

Topeka's major daily newspaper is *The Topeka Capital-Journal.* The city is also a center for magazine publishing. Ogden Publications, based in Topeka, publishes several magazines, including *Capper's, Brave Hearts, Grit,* and *Good Things to Eat,* all of which focus on rural living, and *Natural Home, Mother Earth News, Utne Reader,* and *EarthMoment,* all of which focus on sustainable living. They also publish *Gas Engine Magazine, Motorcycle Classics, Farm Collector,* and *Steam Traction. Kansas!* magazine is a quarterly publication published by the Kansas Department of Commerce.

### Television and Radio

Topeka television viewers select programming from four stations based in the city—three commercial network affiliates and one public station. Ten AM and FM radio stations schedule a variety of formats such as educational, talk, adult contemporary, and news and sports. Washburn University is home to KTWU, the first public television station in Kansas.

***Media Information:*** *The Topeka Capital-Journal,* 616 SE Jefferson Street, Topeka, KS 66607; telephone (785)295-1111 or (800)777-7171; www.cjonline.com

### Topeka Online

City of Topeka home page. Available www.topeka.org

Greater Topeka Chamber of Commerce. Available www.topekachamber.org

*The Topeka Capital-Journal* online. Available www.cjonline.com

Topeka Convention and Visitors Bureau. Available www.visittopeka.travel

Topeka Public Schools. Available www.topeka.k12.ks.us

Topeka & Shawnee County Public Library. Available www.tscpl.org

BIBLIOGRAPHY

Cox, Thomas C., *Blacks in Topeka, Kansas: 1865-1915, a Social History* (Louisiana State University Press, 1982)

# Wichita

## ■ The City in Brief

**Founded:** 1868 (incorporated 1871)

**Head Official:** Mayor Carl Brewer (since 2007)

**City Population**

    1980: 279,838
    1990: 304,017
    2000: 344,284
    2006 estimate: 357,698
    Percent change, 1990–2000: 13.2%
    U.S. rank in 1980: 51st
    U.S. rank in 1990: 51st (State rank: 1st)
    U.S. rank in 2000: 59th (State rank: 1st)

**Metropolitan Area Population**

    1980: 442,000
    1990: 485,270
    2000: 545,220
    2006 estimate: 592,126
    Percent change, 1990–2000: 12.4%
    U.S. rank in 1980: 75th
    U.S. rank in 1990: Not available
    U.S. rank in 2000: 77th

**Area:** 138.93 square miles (2000)

**Elevation:** 1,300 feet above sea level

**Average Annual Temperatures:** January, 30.2° F; July, 81.0° F; annual average, 56.4° F

**Average Annual Precipitation:** 30.38 inches of rain; 15.7 inches of snow

**Major Economic Sectors:** Services, manufacturing, trade

**Unemployment Rate:** 4.7% (June 2007)

**Per Capita Income:** $22,379 (2005)

**2005 FBI Crime Index Property:** Not available

**2005 FBI Crime Index Violent:** Not available

**Major Colleges and Universities:** Wichita State University; Friends University; Newman University; University of Kansas School of Medicine-Wichita; Wichita Area Technical College

**Daily Newspaper:** *The Wichita Eagle*

## ■ Introduction

Wichita, the largest city in Kansas and the seat of Sedgwick County, is the focus of a metropolitan statistical area that includes Butler, Sumner, Harvey, and Sedgwick counties. The city's history reflects the major stages of western U.S. development. The primary stop on the Chisholm Trail, Wichita flourished first as a cattle town, then as a rail link and milling center for Kansas grain. Prosperity continued with the discovery of oil near the city limits. Today, Wichita, a three-time winner of the National Civic League's All-America City Award, is an important technology center, particularly in the aviation industry.

## ■ Geography and Climate

Wichita is located on the Arkansas River in the Central Great Plains. The collision of moist air from the Gulf of Mexico with cold air from the Arctic produces a wide range of weather in the Wichita area. Summers, which are generally warm and humid, can often be hot and dry; winters are mild, though cold periods are not infrequent. Temperature variations are extreme, reaching above 110 degrees in the summer and below negative 20 degrees in the winter. Spring and summer thunderstorms can be severe, accompanied by heavy rain, hail, strong winds, and tornadoes. Protection against floods is provided by the Wichita-Valley Center Flood Control Project.

**Area:** 138.93 square miles (2000)

**Elevation:** 1,300 feet above sea level

**Average Temperatures:** January, 30.2° F; July, 81.0° F; annual average, 56.4° F

**Average Annual Precipitation:** 30.38 inches of rain, 15.7 inches of snow

# ■ History

## A Cow Capital

The city of Wichita is named after the Wichita tribe, who settled on the site of the present-day city along the banks of the Arkansas River during the U.S. Civil War to avoid conflict with pro-Southern tribes in Oklahoma. James R. Mead and Jesse Chisholm, who was part Cherokee, opened a trading post next to the tribe's village. Chisholm, on a return trip from the Southwest where he had ventured on a trading expedition, was traveling through a rain storm, and the wheels of his wagon carved deep tracks into the prairie soil. Thus the famous Chisholm Trail was blazed, and the route was used in subsequent years by cattlemen driving cattle to their eventual market destinations.

After the forced relocation of the Wichita tribe to Oklahoma in 1867, the Mead trading post became a center of commerce. As Texas cattlemen drove their longhorn steer up the Chisholm Trail to Abilene, the settlement around the trading post provided a stop on the way. The "first and last chance saloon" was opened there for thirsty cowboys. The settlement named Wichita was platted in 1870 and incorporated in 1871. When rail transport reached the town in 1872 and 350,000 cattle were driven in from the grazing ranges, Wichita became the "cow capital" of eastern Kansas. Wichita was a rough place despite signs posted at the corporation limits that warned visitors to check their guns before entering town.

## Exit Cattle; Enter Wheat, Oil, and Airplanes

Boom times lasted until 1880, when the Chisholm Trail was blocked by barbed-wire fences protecting land planted with wheat, barring drivers from bringing their cattle to Wichita. Businessmen who made their livelihood from cattle relocated to Dodge City, and Wichita land values temporarily tumbled. But revenues from grain quickly outdistanced cattle when farmers brought their harvest to Wichita, transforming the city into a trading and milling center. Whereas the cattle business had supported dance halls and gambling houses, the wheat industry brought the civilizing forces of churches and schools.

Wichita's population steadily increased in the twentieth century, and new forms of wealth and business opportunity emerged. A major oil deposit discovered in Butler County in 1915 earned the nickname "door-step pool" because of its proximity to the city limits. Wichita's first airplane was manufactured the following year, and during the 1920s the city became known as the "Air Capital of America" in recognition of the number of airplane factories located there. By 1929 Wichita produced a quarter of all commercial aircraft in the United States. The aviation industry played an increased role in the city during World War II, and even more so after the establishment of McConnell Air Force Base in 1951. Beech Aircraft Corp. and Learjet Inc. were founded in Wichita and such heavy-weights as the Boeing Co., Bombardier Inc., Cessna Aircraft Co., and Raytheon Co. established major facilities in the city. The population explosion that grew from the aviation industry attracted other types of companies. Two big names in the fast-food industry—Pizza Hut Inc. and White Castle System Inc.—were both founded in Wichita. By the turn of the century the city was headquarters for the Coleman Co. and Koch Industries Inc.

## An All-American City

Three-time winner (since 1961) of the All American City award, Wichita's residents value the small-town atmosphere with modern-city amenities afforded them. A low crime rate, a nationally-recognized school system, low cost of living, ample opportunities for culture and recreation, and revitalized downtown are part of Wichita's success.

*Historical Information:* Wichita-Sedgwick County Historical Museum, 204 S. Main, Wichita, KS 67202; telephone (316)265-9314; www.wichitahistory.org

# ■ Population Profile

**Metropolitan Area Residents**

    1980: 442,000
    1990: 485,270
    2000: 545,220
    2006 estimate: 592,126
    Percent change, 1990–2000: 12.4%
    U.S. rank in 1980: 75th
    U.S. rank in 1990: Not available
    U.S. rank in 2000: 77th

**City Residents**

    1980: 279,838
    1990: 304,017
    2000: 344,284
    2006 estimate: 357,698
    Percent change, 1990–2000: 13.2%

*Courtesy of Greater Wichita CVB/Darren Decker*

U.S. rank in 1980: 51st
U.S. rank in 1990: 51st (State rank: 1st)
U.S. rank in 2000: 59th (State rank: 1st)

**Density:** 2,536.1 people per square mile (2000)

**Racial and ethnic characteristics (2005)**

White: 261,634
Black: 39,470
American Indian and Alaska Native: 5,314
Asian: 15,673
Native Hawaiian and Pacific Islander: 52
Hispanic or Latino (may be of any race): 42,928
Other: 22,209

**Percent of residents born in state:** 59.9% (2000)

**Age characteristics (2005)**

Population under 5 years old: 29,202
Population 5 to 9 years old: 25,162
Population 10 to 14 years old: 25,598
Population 15 to 19 years old: 22,749
Population 20 to 24 years old: 26,221
Population 25 to 34 years old: 52,426
Population 35 to 44 years old: 50,327

Population 45 to 54 years old: 49,647
Population 55 to 59 years old: 19,169
Population 60 to 64 years old: 13,532
Population 65 to 74 years old: 21,314
Population 75 to 84 years old: 14,902
Population 85 years and older: 4,333
Median age: 34.2 years

**Births (2006, MSA)**

Total number: 9,224

**Deaths (2006, MSA)**

Total number: 5,000

**Money income (2005)**

Per capita income: $22,379
Median household income: $40,115
Total households: 144,378

**Number of households with income of . . .**

less than $10,000: 15,926
$10,000 to $14,999: 8,486
$15,000 to $24,999: 20,456
$25,000 to $34,999: 18,509
$35,000 to $49,999: 25,332

$50,000 to $74,999: 26,510
$75,000 to $99,999: 13,321
$100,000 to $149,999: 10,751
$150,000 to $199,999: 2,437
$200,000 or more: 2,650

**Percent of families below poverty level:** 12.4% (2005)

**2005 FBI Crime Index Property:** Not available

**2005 FBI Crime Index Violent:** Not available

# ■ Municipal Government

The city of Wichita operates under a council-manager form of government, with a council comprised of six members and a mayor elected to four-year terms. Council members are elected by district and the mayor is elected at-large.

**Head Official:** Mayor Carl Brewer (since 2007; term expires 2011)

**Total Number of City Employees:** 3,200 (2007)

*City Information:* City Hall, 455 N. Main, Wichita, KS 67202; telephone (316)268-4331; fax (316)268-4333; www.wichita.gov

# ■ Economy

## Major Industries and Commercial Activity

Wichita's principal industrial sector is manufacturing, which accounted for nearly 22 percent of area employment in 2007. Nearly 60 percent of manufacturing is in the aerospace industry. In the early 2000s a national and international recession combined with the after effects of the terrorist attacks on September 11th to depress the aviation sub-sector in and around Wichita. Orders for new aircraft plummeted, prompting Wichita's four largest aircraft manufacturers—Boeing Co., Cessna Aircraft Co., Bombardier Aerospace Learjet, and Raytheon Aircraft Co.—to slash a combined 15,000 jobs between 2001 and 2004. In response, these companies began developing small- and mid-sized airplanes to appeal to business and corporate users. All four of these major companies are still in operation in the city. Another major employer in aerospace is Spirit AeroSystems Inc. Several Wichita companies are leaders in their respective fields. Vulcan Chemicals, which operates a manufacturing plant in Wichita, ranks among the country's top producers of chlorinated solvents used to make such products as plastics, film, soft drinks, and electronic circuitry. Cargill Inc., one of the nation's major agribusiness corporations, has made Wichita the corporate headquarters for its Cargill Meat Solution division. The Coleman Company,

a pioneer in the production of outdoor recreational gear, was founded in the city in the early twentieth century and remains headquartered there. Other manufacturing companies in the city include York International (HVAC equipment), Love Box (packaging), and CNH America LLC (construction equipment).

The services industries combined make up the largest sector of the economy. Health care is Wichita's second-largest sub-sector industry (after aerospace), followed by education. Educational and health services account for about 14 percent of employment. The local leaders are Via Christ Health System, Wesley Medical Center, the Wichita Public School System, and Wichita State University. The professional, business, information, and financial services sub-sectors have been gaining in job creation over the past few years. A few local employers include Bank of America, Cox Communications, T-Mobile USA, Protection One, and CCH Inc.

The government sector, which includes employees at the county, state, and federal level, accounts for about 13 percent of employment.

**Items and goods produced:** aircraft, outdoor recreational equipment and supplies, industrial chemicals and chemical handling equipment, meat products, household appliances, HVAC equipment, balloons, construction equipment, data storage systems, business software

## Incentive Programs—New and Existing Companies

*Local programs:* The City of Wichita offers a number of incentive programs, including Industrial Revenue Bonds and a Neighborhood Revitalization Area Tax Rebate Program, which offers a 75- to 95-percent rebate on increased taxes due to new construction or refurbishment of property in certain areas within the city. The Wichita Business Loan Program has a loan pool of $9 million for existing and new small businesses within Revitalization Strategy Areas. The City of Wichita and the County of Sedgwick may extend tax exemptions for property used for manufacturing, research and development, or storing goods or commodities. Incentives offered by the Wichita Downtown Development Corp. include a Tenant Improvement Grant Fund, Housing and Pilot Landscaping grant programs, Douglas Street Facade Improvement Program, and Historic Preservation Tax Credits. The Wichita Technology Corporation works to encourage new and expanding technology-based businesses through a seed capital fund.

*State programs:* The entire state of Kansas is designated as an Enterprise Zone. Businesses located in an Enterprise Zone are eligible for special credits such as an investment tax credit (1 percent), a building and materials sales tax exemption, an inventory tax exemption, and certain property tax exemptions and credits. A job creation tax credit of $1,500 per new job is also available for jobs created in the zone for certified dislocated or economically disadvantaged workers. A research tax credit of 6.5 percent is also available for qualified research and development investments. Businesses that are not eligible for the Enterprise Zone programs may apply for job expansion and investment tax credits. Foreign Trade Zone (FTZ) incentives are available to Wichita companies under the Sedgwick County FTZ. Goods entering FTZs are not subject to customs tariffs until the goods leave the zone and are formally entered into U.S. customs territory. The High Performance Incentive Program offers a 10 percent corporate income tax credit on qualified capital investments for eligible companies. There is no state income tax for either personal or corporate income.

The Kansas Department of Commerce is the state's leading economic development agency. Its Business Development Division offers customized proposals for prospective companies to outline available incentives and financing programs. Financing programs include the Kansas Economic Opportunity Initiatives Fund, the Partnership Fund, and Industrial Revenue Bonds. The Kansas Bioscience Authority offers several incentive programs for relocating, expanding, and start-up companies in the bioscience industry.

*Job training programs:* Kansas 1st is a statewide program through which local colleges and universities provide job-related training through individual courses of study and businesses training programs. Through Kansas 1st, companies may create specialized programs for their employees. Companies creating new jobs may qualify for training funds through Investments in Major Projects and Comprehensive Training (IMPACT), Kansas Industrial Training (KIT), and Kansas Industrial Retraining (KIR). Programs are custom designed to meet a company's specific training needs and can involve pre-employment or on-the-job training. Wichita Technical Institute offers hands-on training programs in specialized industries. Programs are primarily available in computer electronics and networking technology; electronics technology; heating, air conditioning, and refrigeration technology; and medical assisting. Wichita Area Technical College also offers several training programs.

## Development Projects

Downtown Wichita has attracted over $250 million in investment since 1997. In addition to several residential developments, downtown now features the Old Town Square, a $25 million complex encompassing a six-screen movie theater, retail space, and office space. The City Arts buildings opened in 2004 and the Kansas Sports Hall of Fame held its grand opening in April 2005.

One of the largest projects under construction as of 2007 was the Wichita WaterWalk. Scheduled for completion in 2008, the $138 million development will house

office, retail, restaurant, and residential space. WaterWalk will also include a 2,000-seat amphitheater for concerts and other public events. Also under construction in 2007 was the $201 million Sedgwick County Arena. Located near Old Town Square, the arena will be a multipurpose venue, seating about 15,000 for basketball games and 17,000 for concerts.

In 2007 Universal Lubricants announced that it would expand its manufacturing site in Wichita to include a new facility for lubricant recycling projects. A capital investment of $15.2 million is expected for construction on the five-acre site. Construction is expected to be completed in 2009. Diversified Services, Inc. has also committed to a second site expansion project in Wichita. The company, which works with composite materials, is expected to make a capital investment of $2.1 million for its new location, which will attract about 68 jobs at an average annual payroll of $2.7 million.

*Economic Development Information:* Greater Wichita Economic Development Coalition, 350 W. Douglas, Wichita, KS 67202; telephone (316)268-1133; www.gwedc.org. Wichita Metro Chamber of Commerce, 350 W. Douglas Ave., Wichita, KS 67202; telephone (316)265-7771; www.wichitakansas.org

## Commercial Shipping

Wichita Mid-Continent Airport is the state's largest commercial and general aviation complex. In addition to transporting passengers, the airport handled over 39,000 tons of cargo in 2006. Its major overnight carriers are DHL, FedEx, and UPS. Wichita lies on Interstate 35, the only interstate highway that connects the United States with both Canada and Mexico. This has become a crucial trading route under NAFTA. The city is served by several national and regional interstate common carriers. Three major railroads—Union Pacific, Burlington Northern Santa Fe, and Kansas & Oklahoma Railroad—link the city to most major continental markets. Wichita has access to the U.S. Inland Waterway System from two ports located within 200 miles: the Port of Kansas City and the Tulsa Port of Catoosa provide access to the Missouri and Arkansas rivers, respectively. Wichita is home to the Sedgwick County Foreign Trade Zone 161, an area where foreign goods bound for international destinations can be temporarily stored without incurring an import duty.

## Labor Force and Employment Outlook

Sedgwick County ranks second in the nation for concentration of manufacturing jobs and skilled labor and first for employment in aircraft and parts manufacturing. The concentration of manufacturing firms utilizing high technology design is partially responsible for the highly-skilled workforce. While the number of available manufacturing jobs has fluctuated within the past decade, the industry has begun to stabilize again and new jobs are being created. Investment in training is also a contributor, as Kansas ranks second in the nation for workforce development spending per capita. The regional forecast into 2012 indicates that the service sector should see the greatest increase in job growth, particularly in office and administrative support, health care, and education. Sales and related occupations are also anticipated to see new job growth. Manufacturing (production) is expected to show a small increase.

The following is a summary of data regarding the Wichita metropolitan area labor force, 2006 annual averages.

**Size of nonagricultural labor force:** 293,000

**Number of workers employed in ...**

construction and mining: 16,200
manufacturing: 63,000
trade, transportation and utilities: 49,800
information: 5,800
financial activities: 11,200
professional and business services: 28,200
educational and health services: 40,600
leisure and hospitality: 26,900
other services: 11,100
government: 40,100

**Average hourly earnings of production workers employed in manufacturing:** $18.95

**Unemployment rate:** 4.7% (June 2007)

| *Largest employers (2007)* | *Number of employees* |
|---|---|
| Cessna Aircraft Co. | 8,000 |
| Spirit Aerosystems Inc. | 7,400 |
| Raytheon Aircraft Co. | 7,000 |
| U.S. Government | 5,186 |
| USD 259 Wichita Public School System | 4,955 |
| State of Kansas | 4,800 |
| Via Christi Health System | 4,795 |
| Boeing Integrated Defense Systems Wichita | 3,300 |
| City of Wichita | 3,200 |
| Sedgwick County | 2,695 |

## Cost of Living

The following is a summary of data regarding several key cost of living factors in the Wichita area.

**2007 (1st quarter) ACCRA Average House Price:** $220,772

**2007 (1st quarter) ACCRA Cost of Living Index:** 93.7

**State income tax rate:** 3.50% to 6.45%

**State sales tax rate:** 5.3%

**Local income tax rate:** None

**Local sales tax rate:** 2.0% county tax

**Property tax rate:** $113.387 per $1,000 assessed valuation (most areas; 2004)

**Economic Information:** Greater Wichita Economic Development Coalition, 350 W. Douglas, Wichita, KS 67202; telephone (316)268-1133; www.gwedc.org. Kansas Department of Labor, 401 SW Topeka Blvd., Topeka, KS 66603; telephone (785)296-5000; www.dol.ks.gov

# ■ Education and Research

## Elementary and Secondary Schools

Wichita Public Schools USD 259 is the state's largest school district, accounting for about 11 percent of all public school students in the state. It is administered by a nonpartisan, seven-member board elected to four-year staggered terms. Board members contract a superintendent.

Eleven high schools in the district offer career and technical programs in a wide variety of subjects, including marketing, business, computer technology, automotive technician training, woodworking, print media, culinary arts, and early childhood development. While most children are assigned to a school based on where they live, students may apply to one of many choice schools in the district. In 2007 the district had 19 elementary magnet schools. Five middle schools offered magnet programs and Northeast Magnet High School offered specialized programs in law, science, and visual arts. East High School offers an International Baccalaureate program. One middle school and three high schools offer alternative educational programs. Wichita e-School offers an online curriculum for homeschoolers.

The following is a summary of data regarding the Wichita Public Schools as of the 2005–2006 school year.

**Total enrollment:** 48,770

**Number of facilities**

elementary schools: 57
junior high/middle schools: 17
senior high schools: 11
other: 0

**Student/teacher ratio:** 15.1:1

**Teacher salaries (2005–06)**

elementary median: $39,510
junior high/middle median: Not available
secondary median: $39,870

**Funding per pupil: $8,092**

Wichita offers alternatives to the public school system through a strong parochial school system administered through the Catholic Schools of the Diocese of Wichita, which has won numerous national awards from the National Catholic Educational Association. Non-denominational education is offered by Wichita Collegiate School, serving a pre-school through a college-preparatory curriculum, and the Independent School, which provides the liberal arts education to gifted students of the same age groups. There are 32 private schools in the city that are full members of the Kansas Association of Independent and Religious Schools.

*Public Schools Information:* Wichita Public Schools, 201 N. Water, Wichita, KS 67202; telephone (316)973-4000; www.usd259.com

## Colleges and Universities

Wichita State University is a public four-year college with about 14,298 students. Six undergraduate colleges (arts and sciences, engineering, fine arts, education, business, and health professions) offer 60 degree programs in more than 200 areas of study. The graduate school offers 44 masters degrees, 11 doctoral programs, and 26 graduate certificate programs.

Friends University, a four-year liberal arts school founded by Quakers in 1898, is one of the fastest-growing private universities in Kansas. With about 2,800 students, it offers associate's and bachelor's degrees in a variety of fields and 13 master's programs. Degree completion programs with evening classes are available for working adults. Newman University was founded in 1933 as a Catholic two-year teacher's academy. It is now a four-year liberal arts college with an enrollment of about 2,200 students. The university offers more than 40 undergraduate and graduate degree programs.

The University of Kansas School of Medicine–Wichita, at one time affiliated with Wichita State University and now a separate facility, provides medical education in most fields of specialization. The university, which ranks among the top 10 medical schools in the country whose focus is primary care, maintains cooperative programs with area hospitals and operates its own care center on campus and at clinics throughout the city.

Wichita Area Technical College has several locations in Wichita. Associate's degrees and certificate programs are available in the fields of aviation, business office technology, health sciences, manufacturing and engineering technologies, and automotive service technologies. Other Wichita institutions of higher learning include Wichita Technical Institute, as well as branches of Baker University, Butler, and Cowley County Community Colleges, and Tabor College of Hillsboro.

## Libraries and Research Centers

The Wichita Public Library has a Central Library and nine branches throughout the city, the newest of which is the Lionel Alford Regional Branch Library, opened in April 2003. The collection contains more than 900,000 items including books, videos, music CDs, magazines, motor manuals, art prints, CD-ROMs, maps, and books on cassette. Among special collections are the Driscoll Piracy Collection, Kansas and local history, genealogy, motor manuals, music scores, and state documents. The Central Library houses the Wichita Subregional Library for the Blind and Physically Handicapped.

Wichita State University Libraries include the main Ablah Library, the Thurlow Lieurance Memorial Music Library, and the McKinley Chemistry Library. The Ablah Library has been a federal depository library since 1901 and a Patent and Trademark Depository Library since 1991. It is also a state depository library. The university libraries hold over one million volumes and more than 4,000 periodical subscriptions. Special collections focus on a range of subjects pertaining primarily to Kansas and American history.

The Edmund Stanley Library at Friends University has more than 100,000 volumes and includes a special collection of Quaker archives. Among other libraries and research centers in the city are those affiliated with the Wichita Art Museum, the *Wichita Eagle*, the Midwest Historical and Genealogical Society, the Wichita Sedgwick County Historical Society, and the Boeing Co.

The National Institute for Aviation Research, located at Wichita State University (WSU), is home to 15 laboratories for conducting research in such areas as aerodynamics, aging aircraft, crash dynamics, composites and advanced materials, aircraft icing, structural components, virtual reality, and computational mechanics. WSU's College of Engineering is active in a variety of research programs. The Center for the Improvement of Human Functioning conducts research at the far thresholds of disease management and the John C. Pair Horticulture Research Center conducts turfgrass research.

*Public Library Information:* Wichita Public Library, 223 S. Main, Wichita, KS 67202; telephone (316)261-8500; www.wichita.lib.ks.us

## ■ Health Care

Wichita is a regional center for medical treatment and referral as well as training and research in health care fields. Wesley Medical Center is a 760-bed acute care center affiliated with the Hospital Corporation of America (HCA). The center includes a freestanding family Medicine Center and a freestanding BirthCare Center.

The emergency department is the largest in the state and features a Level I trauma center. Other specialized services include a Gamma Knife Center, neurodiagnositc and stroke care, cancer care, neonatal and pediatric intensive care units, and the area's only hyperbaric oxygen chambers.

The Via Christi Health System supports the Via Christi Regional Medical Center, which has two acute-care campuses in Wichita: Via Christi–St. Francis and Via Christi–St. Joseph. Via Christi is the largest Catholic, not-for-profit medical center in the state. Also in Wichita are Good Shepherd Behavioral Health and Via Christi Rehabilitation Center. The Via Christi Cancer Center is located at the St. Francis campus. The Family Medicine and Sports Medicine Clinics are located at the St. Joseph site. Via Christi Health System is a teaching institution affiliated with the University of Kansas School of Medicine-Wichita.

The Robert J. Dole VA Medical Center and Regional Office, one of the largest in the nation, treats more than 80,000 outpatients each year. Other Wichita hospitals include Galichia Heart Hospital, Kansas Heart Hospital, Kansas Surgery & Recovery Center, Select Specialty Hospital of Wichita, Wesley Rehabilitation Hospital, and Kansas Spine Hospital.

The Kansas Health Foundation is based in Wichita.

# ■ Recreation

## Sightseeing

Wichita has retained its frontier roots while developing a cosmopolitan ambiance. The Old Cowtown Museum capitalizes on Wichita's past as a stop on the Chisholm Trail with 44 original, restored, or replica buildings and displays depicting life between 1865 and 1880, along with programs celebrating Wichita's cattle-driving beginnings. Wichita turned the Arkansas River into a cultural asset by redesigning the riverside for public recreation and for popular events such as River Festival. Wichita's sophistication is evident in the city's outdoor sculptures, which number more than 125 and include such works as the large Joan Miro mosaic mural at Wichita State University. Price Woodward Park is located between Century II and the Arkansas River; on the park grounds are several sculptures.

The Botanica, or Wichita Gardens, is located near the banks of the Arkansas River and is the state's only such garden. Lake Afton Public Observatory, with its 16-inch telescope, is open on weekends for astronomy enthusiasts. At the Sedgwick County Zoo, more than 2,500 animals roam an imitation veldt, a tropical rain forest, and a herpetarium that switches night for day. The Great Plains Nature Center features the Koch Habitat Hall, two miles of hiking trails, and the Coleman Auditorium. Tanganyika Wildlife Park, located three miles west of Wichita in Goddard, allows humans to interact with such animals as giraffes, lemurs, and Bengal tigers. Children enjoy the rides and entertainment offered by Joyland, the largest amusement park in Kansas.

## Arts and Culture

Wichita supports many organizations in the fine, performing, and visual arts. Century II, the city's center for cultural activities, houses the major performance organizations. The Wichita Symphony Orchestra plays a season of classical, chamber, and pops concerts at the Century II Performing Arts and Convention Center; a highlight of the symphony orchestra season is the performance of P.I. Tchaikovsky's *1812 Overture* that concludes the River Festival. The Wichita Pops series features the performances on the "mighty" Wurlitzer organ, which was housed in the New York Paramount Theater. The Metropolitan Ballet's season of concerts always includes a staging of Tchaikovsky's popular *Nutcracker Ballet* during the Christmas season.

Live theater is popular in Wichita. Music Theatre of Wichita features Broadway guest artists performing with a resident company at Century II; the summer season includes five productions in all. The Crown Uptown Dinner Theatre, one of the nation's ten largest dinner theaters, hosts professional performances of Broadway shows. Wichita Children's Theatre & Dance sponsors shows performed by children for children. Wichita Grand Opera offers a professional opera season at Century II, and Wichita Chorus Sweet Adelines International features female barbershop singers.

Museums in the Wichita area are plentiful. The Kansas Sports Hall of Fame opened in Old Town in April 2005 with 126 inductees from Kansas sports. The Wichita Art Museum, the largest museum in Kansas, houses a nationally renowned American Art collection. The Wichita Sedgwick County Historical Museum depicts historical life in the area through unique and informative exhibits. The Museum of World Treasures has an eclectic collection that includes dinosaurs, Egyptian mummies, armor and crown jewels of European royalty, the Hall of American Presidents, and Civil War and World War II artifacts. Exploration Place features interactive science exhibits that stimulate curiosity and creativity. The Kansas Underground Salt Museum, located in nearby Hutchinson, is the Western Hemisphere's only museum to exist in a working salt mine. Other Wichita museums include the Frank Lloyd Wright–Allen Lambe House Museum, the Great Plains Transportation Museum, the Kansas African American Museum, the Kansas Aviation Museum, the Kansas Firefighters Museum, the Lowell D. Holmes Museum of Anthropology, the Mid-America All-Indian Center, the Museum of the Antique Fan Collectors Association, Ulrich Museum of Art at Wichita State University, and Wings Over Wichita.

## Festivals and Holidays

The Wichita River Festival, the city's major festival, draws more than 350,000 people for 10 days each May in a celebration centered on the Arkansas River. Held in conjunction with the festival are several other events, including an art and book fair, trolley tours, and a garden party at Botanica. Also held in May is the three-day Kansas Polkatennial. The Old Cowtown Museum presents music and 1870s saloon shows on the weekends from June to Labor Day; the museum also sponsors the Traditional 1870s Independence Days event over the Fourth of July weekend. More than 10,000 people attend the Old Town Concert Series each summer.

Wichita celebrates its jazz heritage with two festivals: the Wichita Jazz Festival in April and a jazz festival hosted by Friends University in February. The Midwest Winefest is held over three days in April, and the Taste of Wichita takes place in downtown Wichita in early July. The Wichita Flight Festival, founded in 2003 as the Wichita Aviation Festival, features three days of air shows, aircraft displays, and concerts at the Colonel James Jabara Airport in August. September brings the Chili & BBQ Cook-Off. At the Old Cowtown Museum in October the Old-Time County Fair recreates a 1870s Wichita fair.

A number of diversity-based celebrations take place in Wichita throughout the year. Spring brings Multi-Cultural Celebration Week, which features a variety of events celebrating the ethnicity of residents. Traditional Native American dancing is featured at the Intertribal Pow-Wow in July. The Martin Luther King Jr. Celebration is held in January, and an Asian Festival takes place each October. For three days in September, the Wichita Black Arts Festival showcases the artistic heritage of the African American culture. Other multi-cultural events include Cinco de Mayo and the Juneteenth celebration.

## Sports for the Spectator

The Wichita Wranglers of the Double-A minor league Texas League play their home baseball games at the Lawrence Dumont Stadium. They are affiliated with the Kansas City Royals. Each August, this stadium is also the venue for the nation's largest amateur baseball tournament, the National Baseball Congress World Series, which has been held in Wichita since 1931. The Wichita Thunder competes in the Central Hockey League at Kansas Coliseum from October through April.

The Wichita State University baseball team, the Shockers, consistently earns national ranking and holds the record for most victories in a season. Wichita State also fields winning basketball teams in National Collegiate Athletic Association play. Friends University teams, nicknamed the Falcons, play baseball and softball, football, men's golf, women's volleyball, and men's and women's basketball, cross country, soccer, tennis, and track and field. The Jets of Newman University compete in baseball and softball, wrestling, and men's and women's basketball, bowling, cross country, golf, soccer, tennis, and volleyball.

The Wichita International Raceway sponsors drag racing on Saturdays during the summer, while 81 Speedway features dirt track auto races each week between March and October. Parimutuel greyhound racing action takes place year-round at Wichita Greyhound Park.

## Sports for the Participant

Wichita maintains 107 municipal parks on nearly 3,000 acres for such activities as volleyball, croquet, softball, and soccer. Eighty-three public tennis courts are augmented by two private clubs; Riverside Tennis Center has been named one of the best public complexes in the country by the U.S. Tennis Association. For golfers, nine public and nine private courses are located in the area. Fishing and boating are permitted in authorized areas (El Dorado Lake is said to be the spot for prime bass fishing), and water skiing is allowed at Nims Bridge, North Riverside Park. A free fitness trail with 20 exercise stations is maintained in Sim Park. Five city parks feature special model airplane flying areas. O.J. Watson Park has a pony riding corral for children, a miniature train ride, a miniature golf course, and a pedal boat dock. Cycling and rollerskating can be enjoyed in designated areas along the Arkansas River. The Soccer Club operates a regulation size indoor field for practice and league play. W.B. Harrison Park features the city's only rugby field.

## Shopping and Dining

The Wichita area's shopping centers and malls include the state's two largest malls—Towne East Square and Towne West Square—with more than 270 stores and restaurants combined. Wichita is an antiques center; a number of antique stores and shops are located in historic houses and in the downtown district. Wichita Old Town, a historic warehouse district, has been restored and offers shops and restaurants. Old Town Underground near the railroad yards has blossomed into an area of unusual shops. Upscale shopping is the attraction on Rock Road and shoppers also enjoy the Downtown Farm and Art Market. The Newton Factory Outlet Stores lie 20 minutes north of the city.

Wichita restaurants are famous for steaks, prime rib, and barbecue beef, but dining choices also include international cuisine such as Italian, French, Chinese, Mexican, and Indian.

***Visitor Information:*** Greater Wichita Convention and Visitors Bureau, 100 S. Main, Ste. 100, Wichita, KS 67202; telephone (316)265-2800; toll-free (800)288-9424; www.visitwichita.com

# ■ Convention Facilities

The principal meeting and convention facility in Wichita is the Century II Performing Arts and Convention Center. With 19 meeting rooms and 3 performance halls, this complex offers 198,000 square feet of exhibit space. The Brown Exposition Hall at Century II encompasses 93,000 square feet of exhibition space. The Charles Koch Arena at Wichita State University is a multi-purpose facility with meeting rooms and exhibit space. The Kansas Coliseum, the Cotillion, and the Wichita Scottish Rite Center provide alternatives for corporate events. Many of Wichita's hotels also have meeting space available. The Grand Eagle Ballroom at the Hyatt Regency has 10,164 square feet of meeting space, and the Kansas Grand Ballroom of the Wichita Marriott features more than 7,000 square feet. Two of the exhibit halls at the Radisson Broadview exceed 8,700 square feet of space.

*Convention Information:* Greater Wichita Convention and Visitors Bureau, 100 S. Main, Ste. 100, Wichita, KS 67202; telephone (316)265-2800; toll-free (800) 288-9424; www.visitwichita.com

# ■ Transportation

## Approaching the City

Wichita Mid-Continent Airport, a 12-minute drive from downtown, is the destination for most air travelers to Wichita. Twelve commercial carriers provide 52 daily flights from most cities throughout the United States. Mid-Continent served 1.46 million passengers in 2006. Colonel James Jabara Airport is a general aviation facility in northeast Wichita accommodating jets and light planes. Amtrak provides passenger rail service 25 miles north of Wichita at Newton and Greyhound Trailways brings buses into Wichita.

A network of interstate, federal, and state highways links Wichita with the East and West Coasts as well as the Canadian and Mexican borders. Interstate I-35, also known as the Kansas Turnpike, runs north-south around the city. I-135 (Canal Route) passes directly through downtown Wichita, connecting the city with I-40, I-44, and I-70. I-235 passes north-south to the west of Wichita.

## Traveling in the City

The streets of Central Wichita are set up in a general grid pattern. Main Street runs north to south and serves as the dividing line between east and west addresses. Douglas Avenue runs east to west and serves as the dividing line between north and south addresses.

Public bus transportation on a fleet of modern, chairlift-equipped buses is operated by Wichita Transit. Nineteenth-century-style streetcars on the Discover

Historic Wichita Trolley Tour connect major downtown hotels, Lawrence-Dumont Stadium, Century II Convention Center, and the Old Town area.

# ■ Communications

## Newspapers and Magazines

Wichita's daily newspaper is the morning *The Wichita Eagle.* The *Wichita Business Journal* is the city's weekly business newspaper. Feist Publications, publisher of Yellow Book directories, maintains an office in Wichita, and ASR Philanthropic Publishing, producer of books, newsletters, and brochures for fundraising and philanthropic organizations is headquartered there. Other publications produced in the city include *Wichita Family Magazine* and *Wichita Kids Newspaper.*

## Television and Radio

Nine television stations are based in Wichita; cable service is available. Sixteen AM and FM radio stations serve the Wichita metropolitan area with music, news, information, and public interest features.

*Media Information:* The Wichita Eagle, 825 E. Douglas, Wichita, KS 67201; telephone (316)268-6000; www.kansas.com

## Wichita Online

City of Wichita home page. Available www .wichitagov.org
Greater Wichita Convention and Visitors Bureau. Available www.visitwichita.com
Greater Wichita Economic Development Coalition. Available www.gwedc.org
Wichita Area Chamber of Commerce. Available www.wichitakansas.org
*Wichita Eagle* Available www.kansas.com
Wichita Public Library. Available www.wichita.lib .ks.us
Wichita Public Schools. Available www.usd259.com

BIBLIOGRAPHY

Beattie, Robert, *Nightmare in Wichita: The Hunt for the BTK Strangler* (New York, NY: New American Library, 2005)

Price, Jay M., *Wichita's Legacy of Flight* (Chicago, IL: Arcadia Publishing, 2003)

Tanner, Beccy, *Bear Grease, Builders and Bandits: The Men and Women of Wichita's Past* (Wichita, KS: Wichita Eagle & Beacon Publishing, 1991)

# Michigan

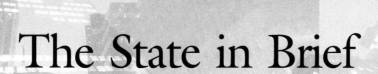

# The State in Brief

**Nickname:** Wolverine State; Great Lakes State

**Motto:** Si quaeris peninsulam amoenam circumspice (If you seek a pleasant peninsula, look about you)

**Flower:** Apple blossom

**Bird:** Robin

**Area:** 96,716 square miles (2000; U.S. rank 11th)

**Elevation:** 572 feet to 1,980 feet above sea level

**Climate:** Temperate with well-defined seasons, tempered by surrounding water; colder in upper peninsula

**Admitted to Union:** January 26, 1837

**Capital:** Lansing

**Head Official:** Governor Jennifer M. Granholm (D) (until 2010)

**Population**

    **1980:** 9,262,000
    **1990:** 9,368,000
    **2000:** 9,938,480
    **2006 estimate:** 10,095,643
    **Percent change, 1990–2000:** 6.9%
    **U.S. rank in 2006:** 8th
    **Percent of residents born in state:** 75.66% (2006)
    **Density:** 178.2 people per square mile (2006)
    **2006 FBI Crime Index Total:** 381,129

**Racial and Ethnic Characteristics (2006)**

    **White:** 8,026,545
    **Black or African American:** 1,426,809
    **American Indian and Alaska Native:** 50,474
    **Asian:** 236,972
    **Native Hawaiian and Pacific Islander:** 1,423
    **Hispanic or Latino (may be of any race):** 392,770
    **Other:** 174,476

**Age Characteristics (2006)**

    **Population under 5 years old:** 639,239
    **Population 5 to 19 years old:** 2,131,276
    **Percent of population 65 years and over:** 12.5%
    **Median age:** 37.3

**Vital Statistics**

    **Total number of births (2006):** 125,014
    **Total number of deaths (2006):** 88,987
    **AIDS cases reported through 2005:** 14,386

**Economy**

    **Major industries:** Manufacturing; trade; agriculture; finance, insurance, and real estate; services
    **Unemployment rate (2006):** 9.5%
    **Per capita income (2006):** $24,097
    **Median household income (2006):** $47,182
    **Percentage of persons below poverty level (2006):** 13.5%
    **Income tax rate:** 3.9%
    **Sales tax rate:** 6.0%

# Ann Arbor

## ■ The City in Brief

**Founded:** 1824 (incorporated 1833)

**Head Official:** Mayor John Hieftje (D) (since 2000)

**City Population**

1980: 107,966
1990: 109,608
2000: 114,024
2006 estimate: 113,206
Percent change, 1990–2000: 3.5%
U.S. rank in 1980: 146th
U.S. rank in 1990: 170th
U.S. rank in 2000: 195th

**Metropolitan Area Population**

1980: 264,740
1990: 282,937
2000: 322,895
2006 estimate: 344,047
Percent change, 1990–2000: 14.1%
U.S. rank in 1980: Not available
U.S. rank in 1990: 173rd
U.S. rank in 2000: 179th

**Area:** 27.0 square miles (2000)

**Elevation:** 802 feet above sea level

**Average Annual Temperature:** 49.2° F

**Average Annual Precipitation:** 30.67 inches

**Major Economic Sectors:** Government, services, manufacturing, trade, information technology

**Unemployment Rate:** 5.2% (June 2007)

**Per Capita Income:** $30,894 (2005)

**2005 FBI Crime Index Property:** 3,379

**2005 FBI Crime Index Violent:** 358

**Major Colleges and Universities:** University of Michigan; Concordia University; Washtenaw Community College

**Daily Newspaper:** *The Ann Arbor News*

## ■ Introduction

The seat of Washtenaw County, Ann Arbor is part of a metropolitan statistical area that includes Detroit. Ann Arbor is the home of the University of Michigan, nationally recognized for a tradition of excellence in education. Having gained prominence as a center for high-technology research and development firms, Ann Arbor consistently ranks high on lists of America's best places to live. Frequently noted are its thriving economy, low crime rate, excellent air and water quality, and cultural attractions befitting a much larger city.

## ■ Geography and Climate

Ann Arbor is located on the Huron River approximately 40 miles west of Detroit in the heart of southeastern Michigan. It is surrounded by rivers, lakes, forests, and farmland. The continental climate is characterized by four distinct seasons.

**Area:** 27.0 square miles (2000)

**Elevation:** 802 feet above sea level

**Average Temperature:** 49.2° F

**Average Annual Precipitation:** 30.67 inches

# ■ History

## Easterners Found Settlement; Industry Attracts Immigrants

By some accounts, Virginians John and Ann Allen and New Yorkers Elisha and Ana Rumsey arrived in the southeastern Michigan Territory in 1824 at a place named Allen's Creek. The men built an arbor for the wild grapevines they found there and named their settlement Anns' Arbor in honor of their wives. According to an unsubstantiated story, however, the settlement was named after a mysterious young woman guide named Ann DA'rbeur who led parties from Detroit westward into the wilderness as early as 1813. Local Native Americans called the settlement "Kaw-goosh-kaw-nick" after the sound of John Allen's gristmill. Settlers from Virginia and New York and immigrants from Ireland and Germany soon arrived as other mills, a tannery, and a general store were opened. Ann Arbor was made the seat of Washtenaw County in 1827; it was incorporated as a village in 1833 and chartered as a city in 1851. Ann Arbor's strategic location on the Huron River, the Territorial Road, and the Michigan Central Railroad contributed to its development as a trading center.

## City Becomes Site of Major American University

The most significant event in the city's history was the relocation of the University of Michigan from Detroit to Ann Arbor in 1841 by the new state legislature after Ann Arbor citizens effectively lobbied for the move. But it was not until 1852 that the university's first president, Henry Philip Tappan, was appointed. President Tappan broke from academia's traditional classical curriculum and introduced a scientific program and elective courses. Erastus Otis Haven, the university's second president, secured an annual state subsidy to bring the institution's finances under control, and President James Burrill Angell's administration added new buildings and programs during a 38-year tenure. Today the University of Michigan is regarded as one of the nation's top public universities, noted for its undergraduate education, research and graduate programs, and athletic teams that compete in the Big Ten Conference.

The university has been the site of historically significant political announcements. Senator John F. Kennedy introduced his plan for a Peace Corps on the steps of the university's Student Union during his 1960 presidential campaign, and President Lyndon Baines Johnson unveiled his Great Society program at commencement exercises there in 1964. A high proportion of Michigan graduates have become astronauts; in fact, during the *Apollo 15* flight a flag was planted on the moon in recognition of University of Michigan alumni astronauts. The influence of the University of Michigan is such that

Ann Arbor is the highest-ranked community in the United States for the educational and medical facilities available to its residents.

High-technology research and development has contributed to the growth in Ann Arbor's population, which also includes an increasing number of residents who commute to work in the Detroit area. Ann Arbor combines big-city amenities with a small-town atmosphere to produce a desirable quality of life. Multicultural influences can be seen in the city's shops, restaurants and arts offerings. The arts are a flourishing and integral part of the community, in part fueled by the university.

***Historical Information:*** Kempf House Center for Local History, 312 S. Division, Ann Arbor, MI; telephone (734)994-4898. University of Michigan Bentley Historical Library, 1150 Beal Ave., Ann Arbor, MI; telephone (734)764-3482

# ■ Population Profile

**Metropolitan Area Residents**

    1980: 264,740
    1990: 282,937
    2000: 322,895
    2006 estimate: 344,047
    Percent change, 1990–2000: 14.1%
    U.S. rank in 1980: Not available
    U.S. rank in 1990: 173rd
    U.S. rank in 2000: 179th

**City Residents**

    1980: 107,966
    1990: 109,608
    2000: 114,024
    2006 estimate: 113,206
    Percent change, 1990–2000: 3.5%
    U.S. rank in 1980: 146th
    U.S. rank in 1990: 170th
    U.S. rank in 2000: 195th

**Density:** 4,223 people per square mile (2000)

**Racial and ethnic characteristics (2005)**

    White: 73,568
    Black: 6,907
    American Indian and Alaska Native: 48
    Asian: 14,699
    Native Hawaiian and Pacific Islander: 34
    Hispanic or Latino (may be of any race): 3,283
    Other: 1,586

**Percent of residents born in state:** Not available

**Age characteristics (2005)**

    Population under 5 years old: 4,848

Airphoto-Jim Wark

Population 5 to 9 years old: 4,316
Population 10 to 14 years old: 5,125
Population 15 to 19 years old: 5,258
Population 20 to 24 years old: 17,939
Population 25 to 34 years old: 19,942
Population 35 to 44 years old: 13,750
Population 45 to 54 years old: 11,343
Population 55 to 59 years old: 4,875
Population 60 to 64 years old: 3,316
Population 65 to 74 years old: 4,409
Population 75 to 84 years old: 2,371
Population 85 years and older: 1,251
Median age: 30.2 years

**Births (2006, MSA)**

Total number: 4,023

**Deaths (2006, MSA)**

Total number: 1,944

**Money income (2005)**

Per capita income: $30,894
Median household income: $45,798
Total households: 44,651

**Number of households with income of...**

less than $10,000: 6,843
$10,000 to $14,999: 2,913
$15,000 to $24,999: 5,015
$25,000 to $34,999: 3,849
$35,000 to $49,999: 5,472
$50,000 to $74,999: 6,779
$75,000 to $99,999: 4,163
$100,000 to $149,999: 4,662
$150,000 to $199,999: 2,428
$200,000 or more: 2,527

**Percent of families below poverty level:** 13.9% (2005)

**2005 FBI Crime Index Property:** 3,379

**2005 FBI Crime Index Violent:** 358

## ■ Municipal Government

The City of Ann Arbor operates under a mayor-city manager form of government. Half of the ten council members are elected annually by ward (two per ward) to two-year terms. The mayor is elected in a city-wide election to a two-year term every even year.

**Head Official:** Mayor John Hieftje (D) (since 2000; current term expires 2008)

**Total Number of City Employees:** 823 full-time (2006)

*City Information:* City Hall, Guy C. Larcom, Jr. Municipal Building, 100 N. Fifth Ave., Ann Arbor, MI 48104; telephone (734)994-2700

# ■ Economy

## Major Industries and Commercial Activity

The University of Michigan is Ann Arbor's largest employer, accounting for nearly 10 percent of the work force. The majority of remaining jobs are split between manufacturing, health care, automotive industry, information technology, and biomedical research fields.

Ann Arbor is now the western anchor of high-technology corridors extending from Detroit along I-94 and M-14. Aiding the increase in firms involved in research, development, or testing is the proximity of the University of Michigan and Eastern Michigan University in Ypsilanti, which provide technical resources and an educated workforce. In 2003 the Ann Arbor/Ypsilanti region of Washtenaw County was named a SmartZone by the State of Michigan as one of ten high technology centers with the potential to create jobs of the future. This builds upon the 1999 designation of the Ann Arbor IT Zone. Together these organizations support the area's historically strong industries of information technology, networking and high-speed Internet services, life sciences, nanotechnologies, and MEMS. Other high-technology industries include business services, computer and data processing, and instrument development. The designation of Ann Arbor as a SmartZone has led to the creation of the organization Ann Arbor SPARK. Ann Arbor SPARK is a public-private partnership with the mission to stimulate economic development in the Ann Arbor area by supporting innovation and entrepreneurship, especially in the technology sector. Members of SPARK are leaders from the local universities, business, government, and the Ann Arbor community.

Trade and information publishing are also strong industries in the region. The Borders Group began as a campus bookstore owned by two University of Michigan graduates and is now a worldwide chain and Fortune 500 company with its headquarters in Ann Arbor. The region is also strong in book printing and manufacturing.

**Items and goods produced:** books, software, computer technology and precision instruments, ball bearings, springs, baling presses, drill heads, tapping and reaming machinery, awnings

## Incentive Programs—New and Existing Companies

*Local programs:* The Washtenaw Development Council (WDC) is a centralized, free information source for expanding industrial, technological, and major commercial businesses. A public and private partnership, the WDC provides a one-stop source of information and services for new, existing, and relocating businesses in Washtenaw County. The WDC also works with several industry groups in the county, such as the Washtenaw County Manufacturers Council, the Ann Arbor IT Zone, the FastTrack Awards Program, and the Washtenaw Work/Life Consortium. Other areas of service include foreign initiatives, the Business Services Directory and the existing business call program. The WDC also provides community tours and introductions to key business leaders; listings of key resources for start-ups and expanding businesses; tax and financial incentives counseling; access to business, educational and community resources; and provision of business cost, demographic, and other statistical data.

*State programs:* Incentives on the state level include tax abatements, tax-exempt revenue bonds, public loans, and grants. The Michigan Economic Development Corporation provides a one-stop business assistance resource for any company already in Michigan or considering a location in the state. Professional account managers work with consultants, utilities, associations and local economic development agencies to match businesses with the best opportunities in Michigan. Free services include new business recruitment, business retention, information on the state and its industries, site location and selection, business incentives and financial assistance, employee recruitment and training, permit assistance, and other resources and services.

*Job training programs:* Michigan offers a coordinated job training system using federal, state, and local resources to provide a highly productive and trained workforce. Grants can provide funding for activities that increase worker productivity. The training itself is done through the institution of the company's choice. Free recruitment and screening services are available for new and expanding employers through the Michigan Employment Security Administration's job service and also through several local school districts. State-sponsored job training programs offered through the Michigan Adult Education Training Initiative include the Job Training Partnership Act, summer youth employment programs, and pre-college programs in engineering and sciences. The Michigan Economic Development Corp. administers a $1.2-million Training Incentive Fund, which provides assistance to employers wishing to upgrade the skills of their current work force. Other programs include Targeted Jobs Tax Credits, and adult and vocational education.

*Economic Development Information:* Washtenaw Development Council, 3135 South State Street, Ste. 205, Ann Arbor, MI 48108; telephone (734)761-9317; fax (734)761-9062

## Development Projects

While high-paying automotive manufacturing jobs seem to be disappearing from Ann Arbor as they are throughout the region and, to a lesser extent, the United States, several automakers continue to invest heavily in new research and development facilities in the area. In 2004 Korean automaker Hyundai broke ground on a new 190,000-square-foot Hyundai America Technical Center in nearby Superior Township. The facility opened in October 2005. In 2004 Pro Quest, an information publisher, announced plans to sign a 15-year, $35 million lease with a southern Ann Arbor office complex, with plans to build an additional 110,000-square-foot facility on the same site. The firm employs 900 workers in the Ann Arbor area. In 2006 the Internet search engine Google Inc. announced that it would be opening an office in Ann Arbor. The company chose Ann Arbor in part because one of the company founders attended the University of Michigan and also because of the wealth of highly educated and skilled workers in the city.

## Commercial Shipping

Air cargo service is available locally at Willow Run Airport, the nation's largest on-demand air charter freight airport. As of 2007 more than 400 million pounds of cargo were being transferred through the airport each year. Detroit Metropolitan Airport is a 15-minute drive to the east off I-94. Conrail and three other railroads provide rail freight shipping, and the city is served by six trucking companies. Within a 50-minute drive are the international port facilities of Detroit and Monroe.

## Labor Force and Employment Outlook

Ann Arbor employers draw on a pool of well-educated, highly skilled workers. These workers include University of Michigan graduates reluctant to leave the city after graduation and willing to work for less money in exchange for the high quality of life in a small-town setting.

Still, the number one problem faced by Ann Arbor businesses is the inability to find qualified employees. The city's unemployment rate is below the national and state averages, limiting the extent to which businesses may expand. This problem is coupled with a shortage of land for business. Manufacturing jobs have been on a steady decline that is expected to continue. Additionally, Ann Arbor businesses must increasingly compete with firms located in Detroit and its western suburbs, which have become attractive to Ann Arbor residents willing to commute for higher-paying jobs. The city has responded

to the employment problem through the creation of the Ann Arbor SPARK program.

The following is a summary of data regarding the Ann Arbor metropolitan area labor force, 2006 annual averages.

**Size of nonagricultural labor force:** 202,300

**Number of workers employed in . . .**

construction and mining: 5,900
manufacturing: 20,300
trade, transportation and utilities: 27,700
information: 3,700
financial activities: 6,000
professional and business services: 27,500
educational and health services: 23,500
leisure and hospitality: 14,300
other services: 6,500
government: 67,000

**Average hourly earnings of production workers employed in manufacturing:** Not available

**Unemployment rate:** 5.2% (June 2007)

| *Largest employers (2005)* | *Number of employees* |
|---|---|
| University of Michigan | 30,574 |
| University of Michigan Health Centers | 11,865 |
| Visteon | 5,581 |
| St. Joseph Mercy Hospital | 4,362 |
| General Motors Corp./ Powertrain Division | 3,200 |
| Pfizer Global Research & Development | 2,700 |
| Eastern Michigan University | 2,200 |
| Washtenaw County | 1,300 |
| Veterans Hospital | 1,235 |
| Borders Group, Inc. | 980 |

## Cost of Living

Ann Arbor residents enjoy the relative quiet and sophistication of a college town while being afforded tremendous cultural amenities (both in town and within an hour's drive of Detroit)—but all of that does come at a price. A 2004 study placed Ann Arbor housing at $40,000 above the national average. With little available land left within the city limits, homebuyers are increasingly looking to the nearby communities of Chelsea, Dexter, Pinckney, and Superior Township, where construction of new homes boomed throughout the late 1990s and early 2000s. Health care costs in Ann Arbor are above the national norm, a reflection of the high-cost, high-technology care available at the University of Michigan Medical Center.

The following is a summary of data regarding several key cost of living factors in the Ann Arbor area.

**2007 (1st quarter) ACCRA Average House Price:** Not available

**2007 (1st quarter) ACCRA Cost of Living Index:** Not available

**State income tax rate:** 3.9% of taxable income

**State sales tax rate:** 6.0%

**Local income tax rate:** None

**Local sales tax rate:** None

**Property tax rate:** $47.36 per $1,000 of assessed value (2004)

*Economic Information:* Washtenaw Development Council, 3135 South State Street, Ste. 205, Ann Arbor, MI 48108; telephone (734)761-9317; fax (734)761-9062

## ■ Education and Research

### Elementary and Secondary Schools

The Ann Arbor School District serves the city of Ann Arbor and parts of eight surrounding townships covering an area of 125 square miles. The district's two conventional high schools, Pioneer and Huron, are among the highest-rated in the state of Michigan. In 2004 the district formulated a plan to build a third high school, Skyline, an $85-million project. The school was scheduled to open in fall 2008. Ann Arbor's two alternative high schools are Roberto Clemente and Stone. The magnet high school, Community High, near the University of Michigan campus, enjoys tremendous popularity and places students through a lottery program. The Ann Arbor School District is administered by a nine-member nonpartisan board that appoints a superintendent. The major emphasis of the system is on early childhood education, mathematics, science, and technology.

The following is a summary of data regarding the Ann Arbor Public Schools as of the 2005–2006 school year.

**Total enrollment:** 16,680

**Number of facilities**

elementary schools: 21
junior high/middle schools: 6
senior high schools: 5
other: 1

**Student/teacher ratio:** 17.2:1

**Teacher salaries (2005–06)**

elementary median: $69,220
junior high/middle median: $61,030
secondary median: Not available

**Funding per pupil:** $10,764

The Ann Arbor area is also served by several private and religiously affiliated schools.

*Public Schools Information:* Ann Arbor Public Schools, 2555 South State St., Ann Arbor, MI 48104; telephone (734)994-2200

### Colleges and Universities

In Ann Arbor education extends to all facets of life: social, cultural, and economic. The city is home to the University of Michigan, Washtenaw Community College, Concordia College, and Cleary College; located in neighboring Ypsilanti is Eastern Michigan University.

At the heart of the Ann Arbor community is the University of Michigan, recognized as one of the nation's foremost public institutions of higher learning. According to a 2007 survey by *U.S. News & World Report,* the University of Michigan tied for 25th among all national universities with the University of California Los Angeles. As of the 2007–08 academic year the university enrolled about 41,000 students and offered a complete range of programs leading to associate's, baccalaureate, master's, and doctoral degrees in 17 schools and colleges. Primary areas of study include liberal arts, architecture and planning, art, business administration, education, engineering, music, natural resources, nursing, pharmacy, dentistry, law, medicine, information and library studies, public health, and social work. Rankings vary from year to year, but several schools, namely law, medicine, business administration, and engineering, routinely rank among the top programs in the nation. *U.S. News & World Report* ranked the UM Medical School as 10th among the nation's top research-oriented medical schools in 2007. The school also placed highly in five specialties: family medicine (4th), geriatrics (5th), women's health (6th), internal medicine (8th), and pediatrics (12th). The school graduates about 170 physicians each year. A 2000 theme issue of the *Journal of the American Medical Association,* devoted entirely to the UM Medical School on its 150th anniversary, described how a university team pioneered extracorporeal membrane oxygenation (ECMO), a device that keeps gravely ill patients alive long enough to allow their bodies to build up their own defenses.

Concordia University, affiliated with the Lutheran Church-Missouri Synod, provides associate's and undergraduate programs through four schools (Liberal Arts and Sciences, Education, Haab School of Business and Management, and Adult and Continuing Education). Eastern Michigan University in Ypsilanti is a full-scale state university with a total enrollment of 24,000 students, 18,000 of whom are undergraduates. The school is known for its education program, as well as the colleges of technology and business. Washtenaw Community College specializes in vocational and technical training and is the site of a robotics repair program. The school enrolls more than 20,000 students annually and has transfer programs with the University of Michigan, Eastern Michigan University, and University of Michigan Dearborn.

**Libraries and Research Centers**

Approximately 25 libraries and research centers, maintained by a variety of organizations and agencies, are located in Ann Arbor. The Ann Arbor District Library maintains holdings of more than 425,000 materials, including more than 394,000 books and 28,000 CDs, cassette tapes, and books on tapes. In addition to the main downtown library, as of 2007 the system operated four branches (Malletts Creek, Northeast, West, and Pittsfield), plus a bookmobile. In 2005 wireless Internet access was added to the Downtown branch; by 2007 wireless Internet access had been added to all branches.

The Washtenaw County Library is the headquarters of the Huron Valley Library System. The library operates as a traditional public-use facility, and also, through its Library Learning Resource Center, as a center for organizational development to be used for training sessions, meetings, workshops, and special events for county government and affiliated organizations. With holdings of more than 40,000 volumes, the library houses a facility for the blind and the physically handicapped; special services include a low-vision center, various aids for the handicapped, homebound service, and a video library.

The Gerald R. Ford Library contains materials pertaining to the life and career of Gerald R. Ford, former president of the United States. Ford was a University of Michigan alumnus and grew up in Grand Rapids, Michigan, where the library's affiliated Gerald R. Ford Museum is located. The non-circulating collection, which is open to the public, includes 9,000 books, 21 million pages of memos, meeting notes, and other documents, plus papers relating to the war in Vietnam, Cambodia, and Laos, which were released to the public in April 2000.

The University of Michigan library system is consistently ranked among the top research libraries in the country. The library system has facilities for all colleges within the university as well as for individual academic departments. Holdings of the 19 university libraries total more than 7 million volumes; nearly 40 special collections include such subjects as American, British, and European literature, radical protest and reform literature, manuscripts, theater materials, and United States and Canadian government documents. In 2005 the library's Shoah Foundation's Visual History Archive was launched, making available 52,000 digitized copies of videotaped testimonies from nine worldwide Holocaust survivor

groups. The University of Michigan School of Business Administration maintains the Kresge Library; among the nine facilities within the Kresge Library system are the Law Library, the Bentley Historical Library, and the Transportation Institute Library.

Other libraries in Ann Arbor are affiliated with Washtenaw Community College and corporations, hospitals, and churches.

Research centers are associated primarily with state and federal government agencies. Among the major research centers are the Environmental Research Institute of Michigan, the Institute for Social Research Library, the Michigan Department of Natural Resources Institute for Fisheries Research Library, the National Oceanic and Atmospheric Administration Great Lakes Environmental Research Laboratory, and the Van Oosten Library of the United States Fish and Wildlife Service.

*Public Library Information:* Ann Arbor Public Library, 343 South Fifth Ave., Ann Arbor, MI 48104-2293; telephone (734)327-4200; fax (734)327-8309

# ■ Health Care

A vital part of the metropolitan Ann Arbor health care community is the University of Michigan Medical Center, ranked in a 2007 *U.S. News & World Report* article as the nation's 14th best hospital. It was the only hospital in Michigan to be ranked. It is a treatment, referral, and teaching complex that houses several facilities: University Hospital, Women's Hospital, Mott Children's Hospital, Holden Perinatal Hospital, Taubman Health Center, and the UM Medical School as well as emergency services, an adult psychiatric hospital, an anatomical donations program, a burn center, an outpatient psychiatric unit, and an eye care center. The University of Michigan Medical Center staff includes more than 800 physicians; about 1,400 more physicians practice within the metropolitan area.

Offering general care are Catherine McAuley Health Center, which operates the Hospice of Washtenaw, home health services, and an Alzheimer's Care and Treatment Center; and St. Joseph Mercy Hospital, which maintains branch clinics in the city and in nearby Saline and the adjacent county of Livingston. St. Joseph's completed work on a new surgery pavilion in 2007 and made plans to complete new patient towers by 2011. Public and private chemical dependency, mental health, urgent care, physical therapy, and fitness programs are also available in Ann Arbor.

# ■ Recreation

## Sightseeing

A number of museums and buildings of architectural significance are located on the University of Michigan campus. The Rackham Building, which covers two city blocks, is made of Indiana limestone, with bronze window and door frames, a copper-sheathed roof, and Art Deco interior. The University of Michigan Exhibit Museum of Natural History is devoted to Michigan's prehistoric past; it houses the state's largest collection of dinosaur bones, including a 15-foot-tall dinosaur that was the forerunner of the Tyrannosaurus and more than 200 species of birds native to Michigan. There are also exhibits on minerals and biology, Native American life, culture, and artifacts, a planetarium, and a hall of evolution. The most popular exhibit is the Michigan Mastodon, an elephant-like creature that became extinct more than 6,000 years ago. In 2005 the museum added an additional gallery for temporary exhibits.

The Kelsey Museum of Archaeology in Newberry Hall exhibits artifacts, statues, and glass discovered on university excavations in Egypt and Iraq. In 2004 the museum received an $8-million donation to build a new wing. The museum closed in August 2007 to begin work on the Upjohn Wing and was scheduled to reopen in 2009. The Museum of Art in Alumni Memorial Hall is the state's second-largest fine arts collection and exhibits a diverse permanent collection that includes a number of works by James Abbott McNeill Whistler. As of 2007 the museum was undergoing a $35.4-million restoration project intended to double the size of the museum. The Burton Memorial Tower is the world's third-largest carillon and presents weekly concerts during the summer. On the steps of the Michigan Union building, in the heart of the campus, a plaque records the place where in 1960 then-Senator John F. Kennedy announced the formation of the Peace Corps.

The Ann Arbor Hands-On Museum displays more than 250 participatory exhibits on the sciences and arts; it is housed in a century-old former fire house. In 2007 the museum celebrated its 25th anniversary. Matthaei Botanical Garden, the university's conservatory and outdoor garden, is a favorite winter oasis. The garden celebrated its 100th anniversary in 2007.

Domino's Farms is the world headquarters of Domino's Pizza, among several other corporations on a sprawling 217-acre campus in eastern Ann Arbor. The Prairie House headquarters building was based on a design by architect Frank Lloyd Wright. The site also maintains a petting farm and a herd of American bison. Cobblestone Farm and Kempf House are among the area's other historical tourist attractions. Ann Arbor is rich in architectural history; among some of the city's distinctive buildings are St. Andrew's Church and several homes dating from the early to mid-nineteenth century.

## Arts and Culture

The city of Ann Arbor and the University of Michigan offer a broad selection of music, dance, theater, and cinema. The university's Hill Auditorium is considered to rank with the Kennedy Center in Washington, D.C., and Carnegie Hall in New York City as one of the nation's premier performing arts facilities. Built in 1913 and designed by renowned architect Albert Kahn, the venue underwent a massive $40-million renovation before reopening in 2004. Renovation included interior restorations and improved seating access but also important infrastructure upgrades to the heating system and the addition, for the first time in its history, of air conditioning. Featuring excellent acoustics, Hill Auditorium houses the Henry Freize Pipe Organ, which was originally unveiled at the 1883 Chicago World's Fair. The University Musical Society, founded in 1879, has hosted many of the world's great performers, conductors, and orchestras throughout its more than 100-year history. The Society schedules dozens of music and dance concerts each year at Hill and other local venues featuring international artists and performing groups.

The Ann Arbor Symphony Orchestra plays a season of concerts at the renovated Michigan Theater; as of 2007 the symphony was conducted by Arie Lipinsky. The Comic Opera Guild is a local semi-professional theater company that is the only one of its kind to tour nationally. It draws members from the community as well as from the students and staff at the University of Michigan. The university's Gilbert and Sullivan Society presents light opera productions in the spring and winter.

The university's drama and music departments stage several large and smaller productions at campus theaters throughout the year. The Ann Arbor Civic Theater, drawing on experienced local artists, stages 11 dramatic productions a season. The Young People's Theater, recruiting young people from across the country, is an outlet for students to write and perform their own works. Since 1954 the Ann Arbor Civic Ballet has programmed dance performances. The Performance Network is a local studio and theater space for original work by local artists creating theater, film, video, music, and dance. Ann Arbor supports several local art galleries and film theaters, including the Michigan Theater, which shows classic and contemporary films. In addition, several film societies are active in the city—virtually every night of the week there are a variety of classic films held in small theaters and university lecture halls throughout the city and campus area.

National touring musical acts stage concerts at Hill Auditorium and the university's 13,000-seat Crisler Arena. Smaller acts play any of a number of local clubs, including the Blind Pig and Bird of Paradise for jazz. The Ark is an internationally-recognized venue on the folk music circuit and also features acoustic blues, rock, and bluegrass.

## Festivals and Holidays

The Ann Arbor Folk Festival is one of the largest and most renowned events of its kind, held each January and in 2008 celebrating its 31st year of existence. The Ann

Arbor Film Festival (46 years running in 2008) is a week-long event held in March. The juried Spring Art Fair brings together hundreds of artists in all media at the University of Michigan Track and Tennis Building on an early April weekend; a Winter Art Fair is held in October/November. More than 300 dealers gather at the Ann Arbor Antiques Market to sell antiques and collectibles every Sunday from April through November.

"Taste of Ann Arbor" on Main Street on a Sunday in June offers specialties from participating Ann Arbor restaurants. The Summer Festival, taking place over several weeks in June and July, presents mime, dance, music, and theater. The Ann Arbor Summer Art Fairs, which comprise one of the oldest and largest street art fairs in the country, bring artists from around the country to Ann Arbor to exhibit and sell their work in three separate fairs spread throughout the entire city and run simultaneously for four days in July; more than a million people attend the Art Fairs. Edgefest, a three-day celebration of jazz and improvised music featuring world-class acts, is held in early October. One hundred fifty artists participate in the Christmas Art Fair at the University of Michigan Coliseum on Thanksgiving weekend.

## Sports for the Spectator

The University of Michigan fields some of the country's finest college sports teams, which compete in the Big Ten athletic conference. The Michigan Wolverines football team is among the most storied and recognizable athletic traditions in the nation. Football Saturdays are like a statewide holiday and near-obsession in Ann Arbor during home games; more than 100,000 fans pack Michigan Stadium, the largest college-owned stadium in the country. The Wolverines strongly compete each season for the Big Ten championship and a berth in the Rose Bowl. The Michigan basketball program (home games at Crisler Arena) likewise has a long and celebrated tradition, and the Michigan hockey team (Yost Arena) has won more NCAA championships than any other institution. Other University of Michigan team sports include men's and women's teams competing in gymnastics, wrestling, softball, soccer, baseball, swimming, and golf. Professional sporting events in nearby Detroit feature the Tigers (baseball), Pistons (basketball), Lions (football), and Red Wings (hockey).

## Sports for the Participant

Among the popular participatory sports that can be enjoyed in Ann Arbor are cycling, running, ice skating, racquetball, paddleball, handball, roller skating, downhill and cross-country skiing, swimming, and tennis. Cycling lanes exist on many of Ann Arbor's main streets; paved paths for walking, running, cycling, or skating run along the Huron River. The Ann Arbor Department of Parks and Recreation maintains the city's nearly 150 parks and sponsors programs for all age groups. The Nichols

Arboretum on the university campus is a 123-acre natural area that serves as a research area for the university and is open to the public for picnicking and hiking. There are more than 50 lakes in Washtenaw County offering water sports and fishing. The Dexter-Ann Arbor Half-Marathon and 10-K Run is sponsored by the Ann Arbor Track Club and held on a Saturday in May. Ann Arbor was ranked the third best cycling city in North America by *Bicycling* magazine, and the Ann Arbor Bicycle Touring Society is the state's largest group for cyclists. The nearby Pinckney-Waterloo Recreation Area has several lakes and miles of trails for hiking and mountain biking. The Huron River can be fished and canoed, and golf is played at city, university-owned, and private courses.

## Shopping and Dining

Ann Arbor's Main Street area, consisting of several blocks of specialty shops, brew pubs, nightspots, and restaurants, forms the central commercial district. State Street, the city's major business district, consists of a cluster of retail stores, restaurants, coffee shops, and several record and book shops that include Shaman Drum, one of the nation's best independent book stores, and the original Borders Book Shop. Nickels Arcade, built in 1915 and modeled after a European arcade, houses shops and galleries. South University is a collection of shops and eateries anchoring the other end of central campus. Kerrytown and the Farmers' Market consist of three restored historic buildings in the Kerrytown district, just east of the Main Street downtown area, that contain more than 30 semi-enclosed shops and other stores offering farm-fresh produce, baked goods, and craft items. Briarwood Mall is anchored by the JCPenney and Marshall Field's department stores and has more than 130 stores. Ann Arbor and nearby Saline are considered antiques centers.

The presence of a major state university in Ann Arbor helps explain the city's many fine restaurants and varied cuisines. Hundreds of Ann Arbor restaurants, far more than what is offered in comparably-sized cities, make this a dining destination city. New American cuisine, traditional American fare, Northern Italian, French, Greek, Korean, Ethiopian, Indian, Japanese, Caribbean, Thai, Turkish, and other cuisines are represented here. A number of restaurants are located in historic or unusual buildings, such as a train depot. Café, deli, and pub settings are also popular choices. Zingerman's Delicatessen, near Kerrytown, is an Ann Arbor institution and recognized as one of the top delicatessens in the country. The small shop and its attendant bakery, mail-order business, and catering operations earned it the distinction as *Inc.* magazine's "Coolest Small Company in America."

***Visitor Information:*** Ann Arbor Convention and Visitors Bureau, 120 West Huron, Ann Arbor, MI 48104; telephone (734)995-7281; toll-free (800)888-9487; email info@annarbor.org

# ■ Convention Facilities

The major convention and meeting facilities in metropolitan Ann Arbor are situated on the University of Michigan campus. The ballroom of the Michigan Union, containing 6,325 square feet of space, can accommodate 30 exhibit booths and seat 420 people for a banquet and 600 people in a theater setting. The union provides 21 meeting rooms that can be used as break-out rooms. The Rackham Auditorium and Amphitheater seat 1,129 people and 240 people, respectively; galleries totaling nearly 4,000 square feet of space hold 25 exhibit booths; and the Assembly Hall hosts receptions for up to 300 participants. The Michigan League offers 5,238 square feet of exhibition space, banquet space for 350, 50 booths, 500 theater seats, and 16 break outs. The Towsley Center for Continuing Medical Education in the medical complex offers two auditoriums, four meeting rooms, a reception area, and a dining room. The Chrysler Center for Continuing Education houses a 225-seat auditorium and four meeting rooms. Among other campus meeting sites for large and small groups are Crisler Arena, Hill Auditorium, Power Center for the Performing Arts, and the Track and Tennis Building.

Washtenaw Community College on Huron River Drive has up to 9,200 feet of space, 8 meeting rooms, and an auditorium. Groups of 30 to 500 can be accommodated. The Convocation Center at Eastern Michigan University can easily accommodate large groups of up to 9,780 people; floor space in the arena with the seats retracted measures 20,000 square feet or 10,000 with the seats pulled out. The atrium area is 7,000 square feet and is ideal for dinners and receptions; the Convocation Center offers 8 luxury suites and parking for 1,053 cars. Additional meeting facilities are available at the Corporate Training Center on the campus of Eastern Michigan University, Concordia University on Geddes Road, Domino's Farms, the Ypsilanti Marriott (10,000 square feet of function space), the Sheraton (with 2 ballrooms of 6,000 square feet each), Webber's Inn, and the North Campus Holiday Inn. Nearly 3,000 hotel and motel rooms are available.

*Convention Information:*   Ann Arbor Convention and Visitors Bureau, 120 West Huron, Ann Arbor, MI 48104; telephone (734)995-7281; toll-free (800)888-9487; email info@annarbor.org

# ■ Transportation

## Approaching the City

The destination of the air traveler to Ann Arbor is most likely Detroit Metropolitan Airport, which is only 15 minutes east of the city. The airport is served by 14 major commercial airlines. Approximately 18,000 people are employed at the facility, which also moves more than 500 million pounds of freight each year. Local general aviation facilities include Ann Arbor City Airport and Willow Run Airport. Passenger rail transportation is available from the east and Detroit as well as from the west and Chicago via Amtrak.

Principal highways leading into Ann Arbor are east-west I-94 and M-14 and north-south U.S. 23.

## Traveling in the City

Ann Arbor Transit Authority buses link all parts of the city. The University of Michigan also provides free bus service to all campus areas. Downtown, Main Street, and the University of Michigan campus are easily explored on foot.

# ■ Communications

## Newspapers and Magazines

*The Ann Arbor News,* which appears evenings Monday through Friday and on Saturday and Sunday mornings, is Ann Arbor's daily newspaper. The student newspaper is *The Michigan Daily,* published daily during the academic year. The *Ann Arbor Observer* is a monthly magazine offering features, profiles, historical articles, business items, restaurant reviews, and a listing of events and exhibits; it also publishes an annual City Guide.

*Automobile Magazine,* a popular magazine for automobile enthusiasts, is published monthly in Ann Arbor. Other special-interest magazines and scholarly journals cover such subjects as health care, Michigan history, religion, and Asian studies.

## Television and Radio

Ann Arbor receives local affiliate television channels, including their national network feeds, broadcasting from surrounding cities such as Lansing and Detroit, plus PBS and three independent channels. In addition, local access television is available from CTN on Channels 16–19 via Comcast Cable.

Six AM and FM radio stations based in Ann Arbor furnish diverse programming choices; National Public Radio broadcasting is available via the Michigan Radio network. Listeners also choose from stations in Detroit; Windsor, Ontario; and other cities.

*Media Information:*   *The Ann Arbor News,* 340 E. Huron Street, Ann Arbor, MI 48106; telephone (734) 994-6989. *Ann Arbor Observer,* 201 Catherine, Ann Arbor, MI 48104; telephone (313)769-3175

## Ann Arbor Online

Ann Arbor Area Convention and Visitors Bureau. Available www.annarbor.org

Ann Arbor District Library home page. Available www.annarbor.lib.mi.us

*The Ann Arbor News.* Available www.mlive.com

Ann Arbor Public Schools. Available www.aps.k12.mi.us

City of Ann Arbor. Available www.ci.ann-arbor.mi.us

Gerald R. Ford Library. Available www.ford.utexas.edu

Historical Society of Michigan. Available www.hsmichigan.org

*The Michigan Daily.* Available www.pub.umich.edu/daily

The University of Michigan home page. Available www.umich.edu

BIBLIOGRAPHY

*Along the Huron: The Natural Communities of the Huron River Corridor in Ann Arbor, Michigan* (Ann Arbor, MI: University of Michigan Press, 1999)

University of Michigan Museum of Art, et al., *From Ansel Adams to Andy Warhol: Portraits and Self-Portraits from the University of Michigan Museum of Art* (Ann Arbor, MI: University of Michigan Press, 1994)

# Detroit

## ■ The City in Brief

**Founded:** 1701 (incorporated 1815)

**Head Official:** Mayor Kwame Kilpatrick (D) (since 2001)

**City Population**

1980: 1,203,339
1990: 1,027,974
2000: 951,270
2006 estimate: 871,121
Percent change, 1990–2000: −7.4%
U.S. rank in 1980: 6th
U.S. rank in 1990: 7th
U.S. rank in 2000: 14th

**Metropolitan Area Population**

1980: Not available
1990: 4,266,654
2000: 4,456,428
2006 estimate: 4,468,966
Percent change, 1990–2000: 5.2%
U.S. rank in 1980: Not available
U.S. rank in 1990: Not available
U.S. rank in 2000: 7th (CMSA)

**Area:** 138.7 square miles (2000)

**Elevation:** 581 feet above sea level at Detroit River

**Average Annual Temperatures:** January, 24.5° F; July, 73.5° F; annual average, 49.7° F

**Average Annual Precipitation:** 32.89 inches of rain; 41.1 inches of snow

**Major Economic Sectors:** Services; trade; manufacturing; finance, insurance, and real estate

**Unemployment Rate:** 8.1% (June 2007)

**Per Capita Income:** $15,042 (2005)

**2005 FBI Crime Index Property:** 53,972

**2005 FBI Crime Index Violent:** 21,240

**Major Colleges and Universities:** Wayne State University; University of Detroit-Mercy

**Daily Newspaper:** *Detroit Free Press; The Detroit News*

## ■ Introduction

Detroit is the seat of Michigan's Wayne County, the center of a consolidated metropolitan statistical area that includes Ann Arbor and Flint, and the center of a metropolitan area that includes Warren and Livonia. One of the oldest settlements in the Midwest, Detroit played an instrumental role in the development of the Northwest Territory. During the War of 1812 Detroit became the only major American city ever to surrender to a foreign power; in 1847 the city lost its status as state capital when the legislature moved the state headquarters to Lansing. Detroit was a leading regional economic power in the nineteenth century. The invention of the automobile and its mass production by Henry Ford changed American and world culture. As more and more manufacturing jobs moved to lower-wage areas of the U.S. and, increasingly, overseas, Detroit's population declined and the economy struggled. In the early 1990s Detroit's position as the automobile capital of the world was being challenged by foreign competition. Throughout, though, the city's metropolitan area has grown and the regional economy diversified, making metropolitan Detroit still one of the largest and most prosperous areas of the country. Detroit has a long history of producing groundbreaking and influential musical talent, such as the Motown greats Iggy Pop, Bob Seger, and the White Stripes, known throughout the world. City sports franchises such as the Detroit Tigers, Red Wings, and Pistons are among the most storied in American history.

# ■ Geography and Climate

Detroit is set on the Detroit River; the metropolitan area includes the St. Clair River, Lake St. Clair, and the west end of Lake Erie. The land is nearly flat, rising gently northwestward from the waterways, then becoming rolling terrain. The climate is influenced by the city's location near the Great Lakes and its position in a major storm track; climatic variations also arise from the urban heat island, the effect becoming most apparent at night, when temperatures downtown will remain significantly higher than those in suburban locations. The city enjoys four distinct seasons. Winters are generally long and cold, and storms can bring combinations of rain, snow, freezing rain, and sleet with heavy snowfall possible at times. Annual snowfalls average around 45 inches. During the summer, storms pass to the north, allowing for intervals of warm, humid weather with occasional thunderstorms that are followed by days of mild, dry weather. Autumn colors can be spectacular, particularly to the north of the city. Air pollution coming from heavy industry in the area is said to have been minimized with state-of-the-art pollution control efforts.

**Area:** 138.7 square miles (2000)

**Elevation:** 581 feet above sea level at Detroit River

**Average Temperatures:** January, 24.5° F; July, 73.5° F; annual average, 49.7° F

**Average Annual Precipitation:** 32.89 inches of rain; 41.1 inches of snow

# ■ History

## Riverside Stronghold Established by French

In July 1701 Antoine de la Mothe Cadillac and his party landed at a riverbank site chosen because the narrow strait there seemed strategically situated for protecting French fur trading interests in the Great Lakes. The river was called d'Etroit, a French word meaning "strait." Cadillac and his men built Fort Pontchartrain on the site, naming the fort after Comte de Pontchartrain, French King Louis XIV's minister of state; soon a palisaded riverfront village developed nearby. Cadillac named the settlement "ville d'etroit," or city of the strait. Eventually the name was simplified to Detroit.

The control of Detroit changed hands three times during the eighteenth century. At the conclusion of the French and Indian War, the resulting treaty specified the surrender of Detroit to Great Britain. Under Henry Hamilton, the settlement's British governor, armies of Native Americans were encouraged to scalp frontier settlers for rewards, earning Hamilton the sobriquet, "Hair

Buyer of Detroit." France's tribal allies, led by Ottawa chief Pontiac, plotted to capture Detroit; when the plot failed, they continued their siege of the fort.

At the end of the American Revolution, the United States claimed lands west of the Alleghenies by treaty, but the British refused to leave Detroit and other western forts, encouraging allied tribes to attack settlers. It was not until two years after General Anthony Wayne defeated the Native Americans at the Battle of Fallen Timbers in 1796 that the British finally left Detroit. During the War of 1812, General William Hull turned Detroit's fort over to the British without a fight, thus making Detroit the only major American city ever to be occupied by a foreign power. The United States regained control of the settlement in 1813 following Oliver H. Perry's victory in the Battle of Lake Erie.

## Manufacturing Center Becomes Automobile Capital

Detroit was incorporated as a town in 1802 and as a city in 1815. In 1805 Detroit was selected the capital of the newly created Michigan territory. On June 11, 1805, a fire totally destroyed the city, and while all residents survived, 200 wood structures were reduced to ashes. Local Catholic leader Father Gabriel Richard observed at the time, "Speramus meliora; resurget cineribus (We hope for better things; it will arise from the ashes)." His statement became the city's motto. Augustus B. Woodward, one of the new territory's judges, awarded a larger piece of land to each citizen who had lost his home. To create a street design for Detroit, Woodward selected Pierre Charles L'Enfant's plan for Washington, D.C.: a hexagon with a park in the middle and wide streets radiating outward in a hub-and-spoke pattern. As Detroit grew, additional hexagons could be added parallel to the original one. This idea was adopted then eventually abandoned and a grid street pattern was superimposed over the hexagonal design. Michigan gained statehood in 1837; ten years later, fearing Detroit's vulnerability to foreign invasion, the young legislature relocated Michigan's capital from Detroit to Lansing.

Detroit's early economic development was spurred by a combination of factors: the opening of the Erie Canal in 1826, the city's Great Lakes location, the increasing use of rail transport, the growing lumber and flour-milling industries, and the availability of a skilled labor force. The Detroit Anti-Slavery Society was organized in 1837 and the city was a station on the Underground Railroad. Abolitionist John Brown brought slaves to Detroit in 1859 and there purportedly planned with Frederick Douglass the notorious raid on Harpers Ferry, Virginia. During the Civil War Detroit provided supplies and provisions to the Union cause. By the end of the century Detroit had emerged as an important industrial and manufacturing center.

In 1896 Charles B. King determined Detroit's destiny when he drove a horseless carriage on the city streets. Soon Henry Ford introduced his own version of the conveyance, and Detroit was on its way to becoming the automobile capital of the world. Along with Ford, such automotive pioneers as W.C. Durant, Walter P. Chrysler, Ransom Olds, Henry Leland, and the Dodge brothers laid the foundation for the companies that emerged as the Big Three auto makers—Ford, General Motors, and Chrysler—by the latter half of the twentieth century.

## Development Brings New Challenges

The automotive industry brought thousands of immigrants into Detroit during the 1920s. Then during the Great Depression the industry was severely shaken, leaving one-third of the workforce out of jobs in 1933. The rise of the union movement under the leadership of Walter Reuther led to sit-down strikes in Detroit and Flint in 1937, resulting in anti-union violence. Federal legislation helped the United Automobile Workers win collective bargaining rights with General Motors and Chrysler in 1937 and with Ford Motor Company in 1941. During World War II, Detroit turned its energies to the war effort as Ford opened a bomber factory and Chrysler a tank plant, leading to a new nickname for Detroit—"the arsenal of democracy."

Detroit's racial tension, traceable to a race riot in 1863, erupted in 1943 when violence resulted in the deaths of 35 people and injury to more than 1,000 others. Much progress was made in solving Detroit's race problems after the 1943 outbreak. Like many urban areas in the late 1960s, however, the city was forced to confront the issue once again when civil disturbances exploded in July 1967; 43 people were killed, hundreds injured, and entire city blocks burned to the ground. The organization New Detroit was founded as an urban coalition to resolve issues of education, employment, housing, and economic development, which were seen as the root causes of race problems.

## A Modern Detroit Emerges

In 1970 a group of business leaders formed Detroit Renaissance to address questions of Detroit's future. The following year the group, restructured under chairman Henry Ford II, announced plans for construction of the Renaissance Center, the world's largest privately financed project, as a symbol of the new Detroit. In 1996 General Motors Corporation purchased the Renaissance Center for its new global headquarters.

In 1974 Detroit elected its first African American mayor, Coleman A. Young. In common with mayors of other large "rust belt cities," Mayor Young oversaw a city in which white residents fled to the suburbs, and Detroit went into a severe economic decline. In 1993 Mayor Young announced that he would not seek a sixth term. The following year Dennis W. Archer assumed the mayorship of Detroit. Highly regarded by citizens and business leaders, Archer won national recognition for himself and his city. By the mid-1990s, after many years of headlines that linked the city with words like "crime," "decay," and "arson," Detroit was being described as "the comeback city," where, according to the *Chicago Tribune,* "a new day may be dawning on this most maligned of America's big cities."

The early years of the twenty-first century saw mixed results in Detroit's resurgence. The new mayor, Kwame Kilpatrick, a charismatic, young politician born and bred in the city, took over the reins at City Hall in 2001. While several large-scale development projects, including three new casinos, continued downtown's transformation, the neighborhoods continued to struggle with problems of blight, poor city services, and declining population.

***Historical Information:*** Detroit Public Library, Burton Historical Collection, 5201 Woodward Ave., Detroit, MI 48202-4007; telephone (313)833-1000; www.detroit.lib.mi.us. Detroit Historical Museum, 5401 Woodward Ave., Detroit, MI 48202; telephone (313) 833-1805; www.detroithistorical.org

# ■ Population Profile

## Metropolitan Area Residents

1980: Not available
1990: 4,266,654
2000: 4,456,428
2006 estimate: 4,468,966
Percent change, 1990–2000: 5.2%
U.S. rank in 1980: Not available
U.S. rank in 1990: Not available
U.S. rank in 2000: 7th (CMSA)

## City Residents

1980: 1,203,339
1990: 1,027,974
2000: 951,270
2006 estimate: 871,121
Percent change, 1990–2000: −7.4%
U.S. rank in 1980: 6th
U.S. rank in 1990: 7th
U.S. rank in 2000: 14th

**Density:** 6,858 people per square mile (2000)

## Racial and ethnic characteristics (2005)

White: 92,796
Black: 686,241
American Indian and Alaska Native: 3,223
Asian: 9,577
Native Hawaiian and Pacific Islander: 271
Hispanic or Latino (may be of any race): 46,993
Other: 31,212

*Image copyright Ivan Cholakov, 2007. Used under license from Shutterstock.com.*

**Percent of residents born in state:** 70.6% (2000)

**Age characteristics (2005)**

Population under 5 years old: 62,231
Population 5 to 9 years old: 66,353
Population 10 to 14 years old: 82,767
Population 15 to 19 years old: 71,192
Population 20 to 24 years old: 56,050
Population 25 to 34 years old: 110,579
Population 35 to 44 years old: 115,762
Population 45 to 54 years old: 110,497
Population 55 to 59 years old: 44,075
Population 60 to 64 years old: 32,116
Population 65 to 74 years old: 42,048
Population 75 to 84 years old: 32,050
Population 85 years and older: 10,336
Median age: 32.5 years

**Births (2006, Metropolitan Division)**

Total number: 27,622

**Deaths (2006, Metropolitan Division)**

Total number: 19,826

**Money income (2005)**

Per capita income: $15,042
Median household income: $28,069
Total households: 311,234

**Number of households with income of...**

less than $10,000: 65,210
$10,000 to $14,999: 26,657
$15,000 to $24,999: 49,851
$25,000 to $34,999: 41,802
$35,000 to $49,999: 43,036
$50,000 to $74,999: 48,429
$75,000 to $99,999: 20,687
$100,000 to $149,999: 11,812
$150,000 to $199,999: 2,340
$200,000 or more: 1,410

**Percent of families below poverty level:** 19.5% (2005)

**2005 FBI Crime Index Property:** 53,972

**2005 FBI Crime Index Violent:** 21,240

# ■ Municipal Government

The government of the city of Detroit is administered by a mayor and a nine-member council. The mayor, who is not a member of council, and councilpersons are elected to four-year terms. Council members are elected in city-wide elections, as opposed to a ward system.

**Head Official:** Mayor Kwame Kilpatrick (D) (since 2001; term expires 2009)

**Total Number of City Employees:** 13,468 (2004)

*City Information:* City of Detroit, Executive Office, Coleman A. Young Municipal Center, 2 Woodward Ave., Detroit, MI 48226; telephone (313)224-3400; www .detroitmi.gov

# ■ Economy

## Major Industries and Commercial Activity

Into the 2000s the regional economy has seen a shift from its solid reliance on manufacturing employment to a more diverse base in services, particularly in business services, health care, and engineering. In 2005 the service sector accounted for about 80 percent of all jobs in the Detroit area, while manufacturing accounted for about 14 percent.

However, within the city automobile manufacturing continues to be a primary force in the economy. General Motors, ranked third on the *Fortune* 500 list in 2007, has its headquarters in Detroit and is the largest employer in the city. Ford Motor Co., with headquarters in Dearborn, was ranked as seventh on the *Fortune* 500 in 2007 and is the second-largest employer in the region. While manufacturing of vehicles and auto parts is still the primary focus, there are a growing number of automotive-related professional and technical services, research and development, and testing facilities moving into the area, making the region a major center for the development of automotive technology as well as manufacturing. Over 100 companies in the Detroit area are focused on research and development in alternative energy sources and power generation.

The shift toward high-tech industry research and development is seen in other sectors of the economy as well. The Woodward Technology Corridor in Detroit is one of four Michigan SmartZones in the region. The zone is supported as a collaborative effort between the city, Wayne State University, Henry Ford Health Systems, General Motors, and others to encourage the growth of high-tech industry in the city. Tenants of the site, called TechTown, include Asterand (a human tissue bank), IC Datacommunications, Neocutis (biopharmaceuticals), and SenSound. The health care industry is encouraged in the city largely by the presence of St. John Health System, Henry Ford Health System, and Detroit Medical Center, all of which are major employers in the city.

Transportation and logistics is important to the Detroit area, which serves as a leading U.S. freight gateway with one of the busiest border crossings in North America. Detroit's Foreign Trade Zone and its port are among the largest in the country. Food services, hospitality, and recreational sectors have grown in the last decade or so as attractions such as the Motor City Casino in Detroit and the Henry Ford Museum and Greenfield Village in Dearborn draw large crowds of tourists.

**Items and goods produced:** automobiles, automotive parts, transportation equipment, robotics equipment and technology, food products, furniture, fabricated metals, paper and printed materials, plastics, rubber, electrical equipment

## Incentive Programs—New and Existing Companies

*Local programs:* Revitalization of Detroit's downtown and neighborhoods is a top priority for city leaders. The Mayor's Office of Neighborhood Commercial Revitalization offers help via grants to community organizations operating or opening shops in city neighborhoods. The Detroit Regional Economic Partnership, representing 10 counties in southeast Michigan, assists companies in relocation and expansion efforts within the city and the surrounding area.

*State and federal programs:* The creation of new jobs that feed into a prosperous economy is the purpose behind the Michigan Economic Growth Authority. Fiscally-responsible companies in the fields of manufacturing, research and development, wholesale trade, or office operations can make use of Small Business Tax credits. Parts of Detroit are designated Michigan Renaissance Zones, which are virtually tax free for any business or resident presently in or moving there. Detroit is one of only five cities nationwide designated a federal empowerment zone. Businesses in the 18.35-square-mile zone are eligible for federal incentives. Woodward Technology Corridor in Detroit is a Michigan SmartZone. Services available through the statewide SmartZone program include access to business feasibility studies and business planning, venture capital preparation, market analysis, incubator space, and coordination of research and development with universities and industry. Detroit is part of a federally designated Foreign Trade Zone (FTZ). Goods entering the zone are not subject to customs tariffs until the goods leave the zone and are formally entered into U.S. customs territory.

Michigan communities can abate up to 50 percent of local property taxes for up to 12 years. Other incentives on the state level include tax abatements, tax-exempt revenue bonds, public loans and grants. The state administers an award-winning brownfield redevelopment program, community development block grants, long-term fixed rated financing for small- and medium-sized businesses, and more.

Michigan has created a system of financial institutions called BIDCOs (Business and Industrial Development Corporations). These semiprivate, independent operations are chartered and partially capitalized by the state and are designed to provide mezzanine-level financing. This is for capital of higher risk than traditional banks will consider and of lower return than venture-capital companies demand.

*Job training programs:* Michigan offers a coordinated job training system called Michigan Works! using federal, state, and local resources to provide a highly productive and trained workforce. The federal Workforce Investment Act and the Michigan Department of Labor and Economic Growth provide funding for the grants that assist in increasing worker productivity. The training itself is done through the institution of the company's choice. Free recruitment and screening services are available for new and expanding employers through the Michigan Employment Security Administration's job service and also through several local school districts. In 2003 mayor Kwame Kilpatrick created the Detroit Economic Development Organization, which has an Employment and Training Department. Several outstanding nonprofit organizations also maintain job training facilities, including Goodwill Detroit and Focus: HOPE, a now-legendary Detroit organization founded by a Catholic priest and other community leaders in the aftermath of the devastating 1967 riots. The center provides training in everything from basic reading to high-technology machining and computer-aided design.

## Development Projects

While Detroit continues to experience population loss similar to that in other large industrial cities, significant incentives such as the availability of inexpensive land and federal empowerment zone money have led to a development boom over the last decade. Among the new projects in Detroit completed in the early 2000s are Campus Martius, a giant office, retail, and hotel development considered the most important downtown project in decades, and the 1.6 acre Campus Martius Park, which includes fountains, gardens, monuments, and a stage for public events.

Two stadiums have been built in the city. The $450-million Ford Field, a domed multi-use stadium, was built in part from the massive Hudson's warehouse building, and the $285-million Comerica Park opened in 2000 as the new home of the Major League Baseball's Detroit Tigers. Three casinos have been built and continue to expand. Greektown Casino will complete an expansion project in 2008 that will result in 100,000 square feet of

gaming space and a 1,500-seat entertainment theater. The Greektown complex will also support a 400-room hotel with 25,000 square feet of convention space. MotorCity Casino completed its own expansion projects in 2007 and now features a 400-room hotel, a 1,200-seat theater, 100,000 square feet of gaming space (with 3,000 slot machines and 106 table games), restaurants, and a full-service spa. The MGM Grand Detroit Casino also features a 400-room hotel and 100,000 square feet of gaming space, plus a full-service spa, a fitness center, a restaurant designed by renowned chef Wolfgang Puck. The casinos generate hundreds of millions of dollars in much-needed tax revenue and provide hundreds of jobs.

Further south, in April 2004 Wayne State University unveiled "TechOne," the first building in TechTown, a planned research and technology park amid an evolving residential and office district. The Detroit Symphony Orchestra also got into the action, with a privately funded renovation of Orchestra Hall on Woodward, along with construction of the adjacent Max M. Fisher Music Center, a 450-seat recital hall that opened in 2003. With a $6 million gift from Bernard and Marilyn Pincus in 1999, the Detroit Symphony Orchestra was able to add the Jacob Bernard Pincus Music Education Center to Orchestra Place. The Pincus Education Center includes a 2,500-square-foot rehearsal hall, practice studios, and a music library. In 2004 the Charles H. Wright Museum of African American History added a $12 million permanent exhibit in 20 galleries that chronicles a journey of 3.5 million years from Africa to modern day Detroit. The Detroit Institute of Art completed a major renovation in 2007, which added 57,650 square feet of exhibit space to the museum.

In 2007 the Northwest Airlines WorldGateway Terminal at Detroit's Metro Airport was completed. The new terminal has nearly 100 gates and dozens of new restaurants and shops. Also in 2007 the Detroit International Riverfront project opened for residents and visitors alike. The $500-million development includes the two-mile East Riverfront RiverWalk and tri-Centennial Park.

*Economic Development Information:* Detroit Regional Chamber of Commerce, One Woodward Ave., Suite 1900, PO Box 33840, Detroit, Michigan 48232-0840; telephone (866)MBR-LINE; www.detroitchamber.com

## Commercial Shipping

Detroit is a major international market. The Greater Detroit Foreign Trade Zone, the largest zone in the country, processes over $2 billion in goods annually. The passage in 1989 of the United States/Canada Free Trade Agreement established the largest free trading block in the world, further expanding the parameters of the Detroit market. Detroit is adjacent to Windsor, Ontario, Canada, and more foreign trade passes through the port than any other in the United States.

The Port of Detroit has direct access to world markets via the Great Lakes/St. Lawrence Seaway System. The Port has two full-service terminals, a liquid-bulk terminal, a bulk facility, and a single-dock facility that can handle up to 10 ocean-going vessels at one time. All types of cargo can be processed through port facilities. Service is provided by four tug and barge lines as well as two auxiliary companies, one of which operates a mail boat that is the only boat in the United States with its own zip code.

The tremendous amount of goods produced in Detroit requires a vast distribution system relying not just on the waterways but also rail and truck carriers. More than 700 motor freight carriers use Greater Detroit's extensive highway system to transport goods to points throughout the United States and Canada. Trucking service is coordinated with that provided by the four rail lines maintaining facilities in Detroit.

The Detroit Metropolitan Airport has scheduled cargo flights through Federal Express and UPS. Air cargo services are also provided by Bishop International Airport in Flint, Willow Run Airport in Ypsilanti, and Detroit City Airport.

## Labor Force and Employment Outlook

Despite the efforts of Governor Jennifer Granholm to maintain the state's manufacturing base and recruit new companies to Michigan, Michigan's unemployment rate of 7.2 percent in 2005 was among the highest in the U.S. in the early 2000s. Reflecting a nationwide trend, the biggest loss of jobs was in the generally high-paying manufacturing sector. In addition, the nation's deep recession following the 2001 World Trade Center attack brought deep job cuts and layoffs in the automotive industry. Not surprisingly, Detroit fared even worse, and in 2005 the jobless rate in the city was at 8.2 percent. The city seems to be turning toward the professional and business services, health care, and engineering sectors for future growth. Occupational forecasts suggest that between 2005 and 2012 the highest percentage of job growth will be seen in professional and business services, education and health services, and construction. The local workforce is considered to be highly skilled.

The following is a summary of data regarding the Detroit-Warren-Livonia metropolitan area labor force, 2006 annual averages.

**Size of nonagricultural labor force:** 2,007,100

**Number of workers employed in...**

construction and mining: 77,300
manufacturing: 268,800
trade, transportation and utilities: 372,400
information: 34,300
financial activities: 115,000
professional and business services: 361,000
educational and health services: 274,200
leisure and hospitality: 183,700
other services: 90,400
government: 230,000

**Average hourly earnings of production workers employed in manufacturing:** Not available

**Unemployment rate:** 8.1% (June 2007)

| *Largest employers (2005)* | *Number of employees* |
|---|---|
| General Motors Corp. | 81,075 |
| Ford Motor Co. | 61,320 |
| DaimlerChrysler Corp. | 43,124 |
| Visteon Corp. | 22,232 |
| SBC | 15,000 |
| St. John Health System | 14,162 |
| Trinity Health | 12,750 |
| Henry Ford Health System | 12,700 |
| Beaumont Hospitals | 11,745 |
| Meijer Inc. | 11,250 |

## Cost of Living

The following is a summary of data regarding several key cost of living factors in the Detroit area.

**2007 (1st quarter) ACCRA Average House Price:** $297,808

**2007 (1st quarter) ACCRA Cost of Living Index:** 102.9

**State income tax rate:** 3.9% of taxable income

**State sales tax rate:** 6.0%

**Local income tax rate:** 3.0% residential; 1.5% non-residential

**Local sales tax rate:** None

**Property tax rate:** $67.97 per $1,000 assessed valuation (2003 millage)

*Economic Information:* Detroit Regional Chamber of Commerce, One Woodward Ave., Suite 1900, PO Box 33840, Detroit, Michigan 48232-0840; telephone (866) MBR-LINE; www.detroitchamber.com

# ■ Education and Research

## Elementary and Secondary Schools

Like many large urban school districts, the Detroit Public School District (DPS) has struggled mightily to maintain a quality level of education in the face of such daunting problems as loss of population, budget shortfalls due to a dwindling local tax base and state-supplied resources, political infighting, and the enormous social implications of a largely impoverished city population.

A large number of state-mandated charter schools have provided some relief to the district, giving parents more options in placing children in smaller schools, many of which stress discipline, fundamental education in reading and mathematics, and even institute a dress code or school uniform policy.

The special education program of DPS includes the Oakman Elementary–Orthopedic School. This school follows the same curriculum as other general elementary schools in the district but offers a barrier free environment for those with physical challenges. The Detroit Day School for the Deaf is staffed by both hearing and deaf teachers with all students and staff using American Sign Language for instruction. The Ferguson Academy for Young Women (grades 7-12) offers advanced studies for gifted and talented girls who are selected for the school by examination. The Detroit International Academy (grades 9-12) offers honors classes and college preparatory studies as part of an African-centered school. DPS has five career and technical schools for high school students, including the Davis Aerospace High School.

The following is a summary of data regarding the Detroit Public Schools as of the 2005–2006 school year.

**Total enrollment: 783,118**

**Number of facilities**

elementary schools: 178
junior high/middle schools: 141
senior high schools: 39
other: 0

**Student/teacher ratio: 18.8:1**

**Teacher salaries (2005–06)**

elementary median: $61,640
junior high/middle median: $63,890
secondary median: $64,560

**Funding per pupil: $10,757**

Several private and parochial school systems offer educational alternatives at preschool, elementary, and secondary levels, including the highly regarded University of Detroit Jesuit High School. In 2004 the Roman Catholic Archdiocese was forced to close several of its schools within the city limits and suburbs due mainly to declining populations in some parishes. Specialized curricula have been designed by the Japanese Society of Detroit Hashuko-Saturday School, Burton International School, Liggett and Waldorf schools, Friends School, and W.E.B. DuBois Preparatory School.

***Public Schools Information:*** Detroit Public Schools, 3031 W. Grand Blvd., Detroit, MI 48202; telephone (313)873-3111; www.detroitk12.org

## Colleges and Universities

Wayne State University is Detroit's largest institution of higher learning and Michigan's only urban research university. Approximately 33,000 students are enrolled in 11 schools and colleges, including the colleges of medicine, nursing, and pharmacy and allied health, and the law school. More than 350 major courses of study are offered including 126 bachelor's degree programs, 139 master's degree programs, 60 doctoral programs, and 32 certificate programs. Particularly strong programs are offered in the college of engineering and the school of fine and performing arts, which includes a nationally recognized drama program. Wayne State is one of 98 universities nationwide to be designated a Carnegie One Research University. The university's 203-acre campus forms part of downtown Detroit's cultural center along the Woodward Avenue corridor; nearby are the Detroit Institute of Arts, the main branch of the Detroit Public Library, and the Museum of African American History.

The University of Detroit–Mercy, a Roman Catholic institution run by the Jesuit order of priests for more than 125 years, enrolls about 5,600 students in 100 baccalaureate, master's, and doctorate programs available through seven schools and colleges. Approximately one-third of its students are minorities. The university has three campuses in Detroit. The Corktown Campus hosts the School of Dentistry and the Riverfront Campus hosts the School of Law. The McNichols Campus is the main center. In 2008 University of Detroit–Mercy was ranked among the top tier of Midwestern Master's Universities by *U.S. News & World Report.*

Marygrove College, located adjacent to the University of Detroit campus, is also affiliated with the Catholic Church. It has an enrollment of about 2,000 undergraduate and graduate students and over 5,800 general continuing education students. Associate's, bachelor's, and master's degrees are offered in several fields.

The College for Creative Studies in Detroit's Cultural Center is a private, four-year college that offers bachelor of fine arts degrees in 11 majors, including animation and digital media, crafts, communication design, fine arts, industrial design, interior design, and photography. The school offers numerous programs and classes for the community as well, for students of all ages.

Colleges located in neighboring suburbs include Detroit College of Business in Dearborn, Lawrence Technological University in Southfield, the Dearborn campus of the University of Michigan, Cranbrook Academy of Art in Bloomfield Hills, and Oakland University in Rochester.

Greater Detroit has a wide selection of community colleges. Wayne County Community College District has three campus locations in Detroit. Central Michigan University maintains centers throughout metropolitan Detroit. Additionally, Eastern Michigan University and the University of Michigan are within a 40-minute drive to the west of the city; Michigan State University in East Lansing is about a 90-minute drive northwest.

### Libraries and Research Centers

The Detroit Public Library, founded in 1865, is not only the city's largest library, it is the largest municipal library system in the state, maintaining 23 branches. The main facility houses more than 3 million book volumes and bound periodicals in addition to 7,200 periodical subscriptions, more than 738,000 microfiche and microfilms, and recordings and videos. Special collections include materials pertaining to national automotive history, Michigan, the Great Lakes, the Northwest Territory, and African Americans in the performing arts.

The Wayne State University Libraries system ranks among the top 60 libraries in the Association for Research Libraries. It is comprised of a central facility with about 3 million volumes and five departmental libraries with separate holdings, including law and medical libraries. In addition, the university offers a nationally ranked American Library Association-accredited Library and Information Science Program. A United States documents depository, the library has special collections in oral history, children and young people, labor and urban affairs, photography, social studies, chemistry, and women and the law.

The University of Detroit–Mercy Library system maintains four separate libraries—the McNichols Campus Library, the Outer Drive Urban Health Education and Dental Library, the Instructional Design Studio/Outer Drive, and the Kresge Law Library. Together they house more than one-half million volumes; 5,000 leading literary, health, scientific and professional print and electronic journals; 11,000 audiovisual titles; and a collection of over 90,000 U.S. Federal and State government documents.

Research centers affiliated with Wayne State University conduct activity in a wide variety of fields. University centers and institutes include the Cohn-Haddow Center for Judaic Studies, the Developmental Disabilities Institute, the Barbara Ann Karmanos Cancer Institute, the Center to Advance Palliative-Care Excellence, the Institute of Environmental Health Science, the Center for Automotive Research, and the Institute for Manufacturing Research.

At centers affiliated with the University of Detroit–Mercy, research is conducted in aging and polymer technologies. The Budd Company, an engineering and manufacturing resource specializing in automotive design, recently opened four research and development centers in southeastern Michigan.

***Public Library Information:*** Detroit Public Library, 5201 Woodward Ave., Detroit, MI 48202-4007; telephone (313)833-1000; www.detroit.lib.mi.us

## ■ Health Care

Detroit is the primary medical treatment and referral center for southeastern Michigan. Vital factors in the health care industry are the education, training, and research programs conducted by the city's institutions of higher learning. The Wayne State University and University of Michigan schools of medicine, nursing, and pharmacy and allied health services provide area hospitals and clinics with medical professionals and support staff. The University of Detroit–Mercy offers programs in dentistry, nursing, and medical technology, and Madonna University in Livonia provides a baccalaureate program in nursing.

The Detroit-area health care network is dominated by six health care providers. Those based in Detroit are the Detroit Medical Center and Henry Ford Health System. The Detroit Medical Center (DMC) is affiliated with Wayne State University; the complex includes Children's Hospital of Michigan, Detroit Receiving Hospital, Harper University Hospital, Hutzel Women's Hospital, Sinai-Grace Hospital, Kresge Eye Institute, Barbara Ann Karmanos Cancer Center, and the Rehabilitation Institute of Michigan. The medical center is also home to the Wayne State University School of Medicine. DMC also sponsors a special International Services Center to accommodate international patients and their families.

Henry Ford Health System operates 32 centers and clinics, with more than 2,800 physicians serving 2.5 million patients throughout Southeastern Michigan each year. Among them are the Center for Chemical Dependency and the new Hermelin Brain Tumor Center, one of only a handful of such facilities in the country. The flagship 903-bed Henry Ford Hospital near Detroit's New Center is consistently ranked among the nation's best hospitals. In 2007 Henry Ford Hospital was ranked among the top 50 heart specialty hospitals in the nation by *U.S. News & World Report*. The organ transplant center at the hospital is one of the largest in the Midwest. The Henry Ford Health System has a generalist training program in affiliation with the medical school of Case Western Reserve University of Cleveland.

Other large hospitals in the metro region include the Renaissance Hospital and Medical Centers, one of Michigan's few minority-owned health systems; St. John Hospital on the city's east side; William Beaumont Hospital in suburban Royal Oak; and the University of Michigan Medical Center in Ann Arbor.

## ■ Recreation

### Sightseeing

Signs of Detroit's revitalization are particularly apparent in the downtown district. The People Mover, an elevated computerized rail transit system, features 13 stations with some of the most impressive publicly commissioned works of art in the country, all viewable from the train cars. Hart Plaza, named in honor of the late Senator Philip A. Hart, stands adjacent to Detroit's most visible symbol of renewal—the recently renovated Renaissance Center, headquarters of General Motors. Hart Plaza is the center of many downtown festivals, parades, and the Freedom Festival fireworks, and includes the Dodge Memorial Fountain, designed by sculptor Isamu Noguchi. Nearby, at the foot of Woodward Avenue, sits Robert Graham's sculpture "The Fist," commemorating fighter Joe Louis and considered the city's most controversial piece of art. Another more conventional statue of Joe Louis stands inside the Cobo Hall Convention Center, where a museum dedicated to the boxer's life is open to the public on weekends.

During its heyday in the post-World War I 1920s, Detroit saw the construction of several high-rises built in ornate Art Deco style. Not all of those buildings are still standing, but those that are include the Penobscot, Guardian, and Buhl buildings downtown, as well as the original General Motors and Fisher buildings further uptown, and several magnificent theaters, including the Fox, the Fisher, the Masonic Temple, and Orchestra Hall. Just west of downtown, the Ambassador Bridge, built in 1929 and the world's longest international suspension bridge, spans the Detroit River and connects Detroit to Windsor, Ontario, a small Canadian city with a casino and charming Italian and Chinese neighborhoods.

The Detroit Zoo in Royal Oak was the first zoo in the United States to make extensive use of barless exhibits; the zoo is home to more than 1,300 animals representing 286 different species. The new "Arctic Ring of Life" exhibit displays several polar bears, arctic foxes, seals, and sea lions in a massive simulated arctic tundra environment. In 2004 the zoo opened the National Amphibian Conservation Center to educate and provide research facilities on amphibians. The "Chimps of Harambee" exhibit covers four acres of naturalistic habitat. Other popular exhibits are the penguinarium, reptile house, free-flying aviary, butterfly garden, and giraffe house.

Belle Isle, located in the Detroit River two miles from downtown, was purchased from the Chippewa and Ottawa native Americans and was landscaped as a 1,000-acre city park in 1879 by Frederick Law Olmsted. Belle Isle is the home of the Anna Scripps Whitcomb Conservatory, a nature center, the nation's oldest fresh water aquarium, the Dossin Great Lakes Museum, the Scott Fountain, and the Floral Clock.

The Cranbrook Institute of Science is a natural history museum and planetarium located north of the city in Bloomfield Hills.

The Detroit area is graced by a number of mansions built by automobile industrialists that are now open to the public. Meadow Brook Hall, a 100-room mansion on a 1,400-acre estate on the campus of Oakland University in Rochester, was built by auto baron John Dodge in 1926. Henry Ford's final home, the 56-room Fairlane, is located on the University of Michigan's Dearborn campus. The Edsel and Eleanor Ford House, overlooking Lake St. Clair in Grosse Pointe Shores on a 90-acre estate, is built with an authentic Cotswold stone roof and leaded glass windows with heraldic inserts. The Fisher mansion on the Detroit River features original Eastern art works, Italian Renaissance and vintage Hollywood architecture, and more than 200 ounces of pure gold and silver leaf on the ceilings and moldings.

Other historic structures in Detroit include Moross House, Old Mariners Church, Sibley House, and Pewabic Pottery, where ceramic Pewabic tiles were first developed. The International Institute of Metropolitan Detroit is an agency for the foreign-born founded by the Young Women's Christian Association (YWCA) in 1919, with a "gallery of nations" featuring the arts and crafts of 43 nations.

## Arts and Culture

The Detroit Symphony, one of the country's few orchestras with international stature, plays a September-to-May season of classical and pops concerts at Orchestra Hall as well as a summer season at Meadow Brook, an outdoor amphitheater in Rochester. Michigan Opera Theatre produces classical grand opera in seasons at the magnificently restored 1922 Detroit Opera House, with two productions each fall and three more each spring. In 2005 the Opera premiered one of the most anticipated new American operas in decades when "Margaret Garner" was performed with a cast of international stars, including Denyce Graves. The opera was based on author Toni Morrison's classic novel "Beloved," with the author also penning the libretto.

Detroit supports an active theater community; performances are staged in some of the finest restored facilities in the country. The Attic Theatre presents the best of the new and the offbeat. The intimate Gem and Century theaters offer Broadway-style shows, comedy acts, and other productions in cabaret style seating. The Fox Theatre, the largest movie theater in the United States, was designed by movie palace architect C. Howard Crane in 1928; it has undergone renovation to preserve its "Siamese Byzantine" interior featuring Far Eastern, Egyptian, Babylonian, and Indian themes and is the site of performing arts events. Another opulent theater facility is the Fisher Theatre, designed by Albert Kahn; it sponsors Broadway shows.

The Music Hall Center for the Performing Arts and Masonic Temple Theatre bring professional touring theater and dance companies to Detroit audiences. Meadow Brook Theatre at Oakland University presents an eight-play season of musicals, classic plays, and new works. Wayne State University's Hilberry Theatre produces classic drama performed by graduate student actors; undergraduate productions are staged at the Bonstelle Theatre. The Cranbrook Performing Arts Theatre in Bloomfield Hills offers orchestra, band, and vocal concerts, in addition to dance and drama, by high school students at the Cranbrook Educational Community. Other venues for the performing arts are the Riverfront Music Theatre in Chene Park, Joe Louis and Cobo arenas, the outdoor amphitheaters DTE Energy Music Theater in Clarkston and Meadow Brook Music Theater in Rochester, and the Palace of Auburn Hills, frequently named Arena of the Year by *Performance Magazine*.

The Detroit Institute of Arts, established in 1885, is the nation's fifth-largest fine arts museum. Art treasures from throughout the world and covering a historical period of 5,000 years are housed in 100 galleries. Among the institute's most prized holdings is the four-wall mural *Detroit Industry* by Diego Rivera. Also known worldwide is the Henry Ford Museum and Greenfield Village in Dearborn, which Henry Ford founded in 1929 to document America's growth from a rural to an industrial society by exhibiting objects from the nation's material culture. Henry Ford Museum is a fourteen-acre complex housing major collections in transportation, industry, agriculture, and the domestic arts; the museum features one of the world's most comprehensive car collections, including the vehicle President John F. Kennedy was traveling in when he was assassinated. A state-of-the-art IMAX Theatre was part of a $125-million makeover that started in 1999. Greenfield Village, a 240-acre outdoor museum, gathers on a single site one of the largest collections of historic American homes, workplaces, and communities; among them are Thomas Edison's Menlo Park laboratory, the Wright brothers' bicycle shop, and Noah Webster's Connecticut home.

The Detroit Historical Museum in the Detroit Cultural Center was founded in 1928 as an archive of the history and customs of Detroiters. The museum's collection of more than 250,000 urban historical artifacts is one of the largest such collections in the country. An educational unit of the Detroit Public Schools, the Children's Museum displays collections that focus on African musical instruments, the Inuit, and American folk crafts and toys. The Charles H. Wright Museum of African American History is dedicated to the contributions of African Americans in the humanities and creative arts. One of its most innovative permanent exhibits is And Still We Rise: Our Journey Through African American History and Culture, which documents a 3.5-million year journey from Africa to modern day Detroit. The Motown Historical Museum, a Michigan Historic Site, is quartered in the former home of Berry Gordy, Jr., Motown's founder, and preserves the music studio and recording equipment used in pioneering the Motown Sound. The

Graystone International Jazz Museum preserves the city's jazz history. Fort Wayne is home to the National Museum of the Tuskegee Airmen, an all-African American unit of World War II fighter pilots.

***Arts and Culture Information:*** Detroit Department of Culture, Arts and Tourism, 2 Woodward Ave., Detroit, MI 48226; telephone (313)224-3470; www.ci .detroit.mi.us/culturalaffair

## Festivals and Holidays

From April until Labor Day, Detroit's downtown riverfront is the scene of a program of ethnic festivals (the largest is the African World Festival in August) and the Downtown Hoedown. June events include the Annual Heritage Fair at the Dearborn Historical Museum; Art on the Pointe, a juried art show at the Ford Estate; and the Muzzle Loaders Festival at Greenfield Village. The International Freedom Festival, begun in 1959, is a summer celebration of the friendship between Canada and the United States; it attracts more than 3 million people and culminates in a large fireworks display on the Detroit River.

On the Fourth of July weekend the Colonial Music and Military Muster at Greenfield Village features uniformed American and British troops in simulated encampment activities. Also in July at Greenfield Village is the Fire Engine Muster with hand-pulled rigs and horse-drawn pumpers in a re-creation of early fire-fighting techniques. The Blues Festival of Detroit, the Henry Ford Day at the Fairlane Mansion, and the Wyandotte Street Art Fair conclude July activities. The Michigan State Fair at the State Fairgrounds, the nation's oldest state fair, takes place in August, as does the Spirit of Detroit Car Show and the Swap Meets at Historic Fort Wayne. The Montreux Detroit Jazz Festival over Labor Day weekend brings together over 100 international artists and local jazz musicians in the nation's largest free jazz festival. The Autumn Harvest Festival in Dearborn, the Detroit Festival of the Arts, the Hamtramck Polish Festival, and the Old Car Festival at Greenfield Village are popular activities in September.

A major event in November is America's Thanksgiving Day Parade, which presents 20 floats, 15 helium balloons, 25 marching bands, more than 1,000 costumed marchers, and Santa Claus in one of the nation's largest Thanksgiving Day parades; televised coverage of the parade is broadcast around the country. Other November events include Detroit Aglow and the Festival of Trees and Christmas Carnival at Cobo Conference Center. Christmas at Greenfield Village in December features Christmases past and present at more than two dozen historic village sites, with yuletide meals cooked at open hearths. Other seasonal shows are Noel Night at the Detroit Cultural Center, the Wassail Feast at the Detroit Institute of Arts, and the Christmas dinner at the Fairlane Manor.

Detroit's automotive era is evoked at numerous local events. The North American International Auto Show is among the most important auto shows in the world and is held each January. Autorama comes to Michigan each March and features classic and custom hot rods. The Concours d'Elegance, an exhibition of the world's finest classic cars, is held at Meadow Brook Hall in the summer. And the Woodward Dream Cruise bills itself as the world's largest one-day celebration of car culture, attracting over 1.7 million visitors from around the U.S. and even foreign countries, and more than 40,000 muscle cars, street rods, custom, collector, and special interest vehicles. Cruisers travel a 16-mile, spectator-lined section of Woodward Avenue through nine communities on the third Saturday in August, though cruising often begins several days before the official event.

## Sports for the Spectator

A tough, gritty, blue-collar town throughout much of its history, Detroit identifies itself through nothing else—except perhaps its rich musical legacy—as it does its passion for the local sports franchises. Detroit supports professional franchises in all the major sports, and each team has a rich tradition of all-time great players, oddball characters, and world championships. The Detroit Red Wings of the National Hockey League host visiting competitors at Joe Louis Arena, located downtown on the riverfront. The Red Wings have won hockey's fabled Stanley Cup 10 times, including three times between the years 1997–2002. The Detroit Tigers, the city's oldest team, began play in the American League of Major League Baseball in 1901; a few years later the club acquired Ty Cobb, who played 22 years in a Detroit uniform and became one of the most legendary players in the history of the game. The club has won four World Series titles, the latest in 1984. In 2000 the Tigers moved to the new Comerica Park, across from the Fox Theater. The Detroit Lions compete in the National Football Conference of the National Football League. In 2002 the team moved its home field to downtown Detroit, adjacent to Comerica Park. The $450-million enclosed Ford Field was privately financed and hosted Super Bowl XL in 2006. The Detroit Pistons of the National Basketball Association play their home games at the Palace of Auburn Hills, a 22,000-seat arena north of the city. The Detroit Shock of the Women's National Basketball Association also plays at the Palace. The University of Detroit-Mercy plays NCAA Division I basketball and other sports in the Horizon League. Both the University of Michigan Wolverines and the Michigan State Spartans compete in Big Ten athletics within an hour's drive of the city.

The Spirit of Detroit Thunderfest brings super-power hydroplanes to race on the Detroit River in June. Harness Racing is on view at the Hazel Park Harness Raceway and at Northville Downs.

## Sports for the Participant

The Detroit Department of Parks and Recreation oversees 6,000 acres of park land. More than 350 city parks contain a total of 318 baseball diamonds, 257 tennis courses, 6 golf courses, and 2 marinas. Detroit has developed four smaller downtown riverfront parks, and there are miles of paved walkways for walking, running, and biking on Belle Isle. The city also sponsors 18 recreation centers. Outdoor sports such as swimming, boating, hiking, fishing, and skating are available at metropolitan parks.

In the greater Detroit region, there are 228 public golf courses, 73 private courses, and 36 driving ranges. The state has the second-highest number of registered boaters in the country, with most residents in the state living within six miles of a lake or stream.

Runners of the *Detroit Free Press* International Marathon cross borders twice—taking in stunning views on the Ambassador Bridge on the way to Windsor and then hoofing it through the underwater tunnel on the way back to Detroit—as they tour both Detroit and Windsor's downtowns over 26.2 miles.

## Shopping and Dining

Detroit offers unique shopping venues like Eastern Market, the largest flower-bedding market in the world and an outlet for fresh meats and produce from neighboring states and Canada. Adjacent to Eastern Market are specialty stores selling fresh meat, poultry, gourmet foods, and wines. Pewabic Pottery, founded in 1903, continues to produce handcrafted vessels and architectural tiles for public and private installations from its East Jefferson factory and gallery. There are numerous shops and restaurants throughout the sprawling Renaissance Center complex, and at the Millender Center directly across Jefferson.

Greektown and International Center, a popular Detroit tourist spot, features bakeries, restaurants, bars, and coffeehouses. Bricktown, located in a refurbished sector of downtown, is anchored by an art gallery selling Oriental vases, Persian rugs, and antique furniture.

Metropolitan Detroit offers about 150 shopping centers of at least 100,000 square feet. Vibrant downtown shopping areas can be found in communities like Birmingham, Grosse Pointe, and Royal Oak. The Somerset Collection and Somerset Collection North in suburban Troy rival the nation's finest shopping areas; the twin centers are anchored by Neiman Marcus, Saks Fifth Avenue, Nordstrom, and Marshall Field's.

Detroit offers elegant dining experiences downtown at Opus One, the Rattlesnake Club, and Sweet Georgia Brown. The Coach Insignia, situated 70 floors atop the Renaissance Center, has dining and panoramic views of Detroit, the river, the Ambassador and Belle Isle bridges, and Windsor, Ontario. Also in the Renaissance Center, Seldom Blues has fine dining, riverfront views, and a lively late-night club scene with some of the best jazz in the city. At the corner of Michigan and Lafayette, the side-by-side Lafayette Coney Island and American Coney Island have been Detroit legends for decades, especially for late-night after-hours crowds, serving up their unique hot dogs on steamed buns with chili, onions, and mustard, plus chili fries, and even a cold beer. Heading north from downtown diners will find sushi at Oslo, the Whitney in a restored Victorian mansion, Agave, Atlas Bistro, and Union Street. West of downtown, near the Ambassador Bridge, Mexican Village has several Mexican restaurants, as well as Spanish and Guatemalan fare. To the east of the city, Grosse Pointe has several excellent restaurants, including The Hill; in the northern suburbs the Lark in West Bloomfield and Tribute in Farmington Hills are consistently given five-star ratings by international publications. Detroit is home to the largest Arab population outside of the Middle East, and many of those immigrants live in Dearborn where a number of authentic Lebanese and Syrian restaurants thrive. Detroit is home to some outstanding Italian restaurants; Creole, Japanese, Chinese, Ethiopian, Thai, Indian, and Turkish cuisine are included among the other ethnic choices. Detroit's culinary history includes the nation's first soda—Vernors—which was created in Detroit by pharmacist James Vernor in 1862. Detroit is also home to Sanders hot fudge, Better Made Potato Chips, Faygo soda pop, and Stroh's Ice Cream.

***Visitor Information:*** Detroit Metropolitan Convention and Visitors Bureau, 211 W. Fort St., Ste. 1000, Detroit, MI 48226; telephone (313)202-1800; toll-free (800)DETROIT; www.visitdetroit.com

# ■ Convention Facilities

Detroit's principal meeting facilities are clustered in the Detroit Civic Center, which stands at the edge of the Detroit River on the approximate site where the city's founder landed in 1701. The Civic Center consists of five complexes: Cobo Conference/Exhibition Center, Cobo Arena, Joe Louis Arena, Hart Plaza, and the Veterans Memorial Building.

Cobo Conference/Exhibition Center contains a total of 2.4 million square feet of meeting space and 85 meeting rooms in five halls. The largest single space is 700,000 square feet. The hall hosts the North American International Auto Show each January and a huge boat show every March, but by 2004 city officials began discussions to expand the Cobo complex even further so the city could attract even larger conventions. The adjacent Cobo Arena, with a seating capacity of over 12,000 people, is used for conventions and shows as well as large functions such as concerts and sports events. Joe Louis Arena, named for the heavyweight boxing champion, was the site of the 1980 Republican National Convention and

hosts major events. The Veterans Memorial Building, the original Civic Center structure built in 1950, houses a ballroom and meeting rooms.

Convention and meeting facilities are also available at the Detroit Historical Museum, the Detroit Institute of Arts, the Detroit Fox Theatre, Orchestra Hall, the Michigan Exposition and Fairgrounds, and Ford Field, as well as at Henry Ford Museum, the Detroit Zoo, restored estates and historic sites, suburban civic centers, college and university campuses, and on yachts and riverboats. All major downtown and suburban hotels and motels offer meeting accommodations for both large and small functions.

***Convention Information:*** Detroit Metropolitan Convention and Visitors Bureau, 211 W. Fort St., Ste. 1000, Detroit, MI 48226; telephone (313)202-1800; toll-free (800)DETROIT; www.visitdetroit.com

# ■ Transportation

## Approaching the City

Served by 18 major commercial airlines, 7 commuter airlines, and 3 charter lines, Detroit Metropolitan Airport serviced more than 35 million passengers in 2006, making it one of the busiest terminals in North America and the world. Metro has more than 100 national and 20 international nonstop flights daily. Destinations for charter and private air traffic are Willow Run Airport and Oakland-Pontiac Airport. Amtrak provides passenger rail transportation to Detroit from Chicago. Detroiters have easy access from Windsor via train to Toronto and virtually all of Canada through that country's excellent Via Rail system.

Detroit was built around the automobile. Hence, the freeways are many and excellent, as they must be in order to get commuters around the sprawling city. Six interstate highways and several limited-access expressways serve the Greater Detroit area. Interstate-75, with its northern terminus in Michigan's Upper Peninsula, extends through the city from north to southwest; north of downtown it is called the Chrysler Freeway, and southwest of downtown it is the Fisher Freeway. I-75 extends all the way to southern Florida. East-west I-94, known as the Ford Freeway, is the primary connection from Detroit Metropolitan Airport and heads across southern lower Michigan to Chicago and Minneapolis. West-northwest I-96, the Jeffries Freeway, approaches Detroit from Muskegon, Grand Rapids, and Lansing. Interstate-696, the Walter Reuther Freeway, is the main east-west route across the northern suburbs in Macomb and Oakland counties. Interstate-275 is a north-south bypass on the city's west side, linking I-75 and I-96. Other major routes leading into Detroit are north to west U.S. 10 (Lodge Freeway) and north-south S.R. 39 (Southfield Freeway). Canadian Highway 401 enters Detroit from Windsor via the Detroit/Windsor International Tunnel and the Ambassador Bridge.

## Traveling in the City

Most Detroit streets conform to a grid system. East-west streets are labeled "mile road" in ascending order northward. The northern boundary of the city is Eight Mile Road. Superimposed on the downtown grid are hubs and squares, the focal point being Kennedy Square and Cadillac Square in the center of the business district. Radiating from this hub are east-west Michigan Avenue, northeast Monroe Street, and east-west Fort Street. The largest hub is Grand Circus Park, which is bisected by Woodward Avenue, a main north-south thoroughfare. Jefferson Avenue follows the curve of the Detroit River and Lake St. Clair past Belle Isle, through the Grosse Pointes into Harrison Township, and downriver past Wyandotte to Grosse Ile.

Detroit is served by two public transportation systems: the Detroit Department of Transportation (D-DOT) and the Suburban Mobility Authority for Regional Transport (SMART). D-DOT offers over 50 fixed routes throughout the city. SMART has about 55 routes serving Wayne, Oakland, and Macomb counties. The People Mover, a 2.9-mile elevated rail circuit, provides travel to major downtown sites from 13 stations.

# ■ Communications

## Newspapers and Magazines

*The Detroit News* and the *Detroit Free Press* are the city's two major daily newspapers. *Hour Detroit* is a monthly glossy metropolitan lifestyle and interview magazine that aims "to feature Detroit in its finest hour." *Real Detroit* and *Metro Times* provide weekly entertainment schedules as well as reviews, humor, and commentary. The monthly newspaper *Latino Press* aims to help Detroit's growing Hispanic community. The *Michigan Chronicle* and *Michigan Citizen* are geared toward African American readers. The *Michigan Catholic* is a weekly publication of the Archdiocese of Detroit.

A number of nationally circulated periodicals originate in Detroit. Among them are *Solidarity*, a monthly publication of the United Automobile Workers; *Better Investing; Manufacturing Engineering; Autoweek*, a weekly magazine for car enthusiasts; and *Automotive News, Ward's Automotive Report* and *Auto World*, auto industry magazines. *Football News* publishes 20 issues during the football season.

## Television and Radio

Detroit television viewers receive broadcasts from seven local stations and several stations from the surrounding area. Pay and cable television services are available in the Detroit metropolitan area. About 23 AM and FM radio

stations schedule a full range of formats. The most popular is adult contemporary music; other formats include adult-oriented rock, African American and African American contemporary, Motown, classic rock, easy listening, jazz, middle of the road, modern country, news and news-talk, pop, oldies, solid gold, and urban contemporary rhythm and blues. Two of the AM stations with 50,000-watt capacity enjoy a longstanding popularity throughout the Midwest; one FM station was the first in the country to offer a full-time news-talk format. Detroit's public radio station originates from Wayne State University, but other National Public Radio programming can be picked up from Ypsilanti, Ann Arbor, and Lansing stations.

*Media Information:* The *Detroit News*, 615 W. Lafayette Blvd., Detroit, Michigan 48226; telephone (313)222-2300; www.detnews.com. *Detroit Free Press*, 600 W. Fort, Detroit, MI. 48226; telephone(313)222-6400; www.freep.com

## Detroit Online

City of Detroit home page. Available www .detroitmi.gov

*Detroit Free Press*. Available www.freep.com

Detroit Institute of Arts. Available www.dia.org

Detroit Metropolitan Convention and Visitors Bureau. Available www.visitdetroit.com

*The Detroit News*. Available www.detnews.com

Detroit Regional Chamber of Commerce. Available www.detroitchamber.com

Detroit Riverfront Conservancy. Available www .detroitriverfront.org

Greater Downtown Partnership. Available www .downtownpartnership.org

Wayne County Economic Development. Available www.waynecounty.com

BIBLIOGRAPHY

Chafets, Ze'Ev, *Devil's Night And Other True Tales of Detroit* (New York: Random House, 1990)

Georgakas, Dan Georgakas, et al., *Detroit, I Do Mind Dying: A Study in Urban Revolution* (South End Press, 1998)

Henrickson, Wilma Wood, ed., *Detroit Perspectives: Crossroads and Turning Points* (Detroit, MI: Wayne State University Press, 1991)

Leonard, Elmore, *Out of Sight* (New York: Delacorte, 1996)

Lichtenstein, Nelson, *The Most Dangerous Man in Detroit: Walter Reuther and the Fate of American Labor* (New York: Basic Books, 1996)

Lindsay, Paul, *Witness to the Truth: A Novel of the FBI* (New York: Random House, 1992)

# Grand Rapids

## ■ The City in Brief

**Founded:** 1831 (incorporated 1850)

**Head Official:** City Manager Kurt Kimball (since 1987)

**City Population**
    1980: 181,843
    1990: 189,126
    2000: 197,800
    2006 estimate: 193,083
    Percent change, 1990–2000: 4.3%
    U.S. rank in 1980: 75th
    U.S. rank in 1990: 83rd
    U.S. rank in 2000: 107th (State rank: 2nd)

**Metropolitan Area Population**
    1980: 602,000
    1990: 937,891
    2000: 1,088,514
    2006 estimate: 774,084
    Percent change, 1990–2000: 16.1%
    U.S. rank in 1980: 56th
    U.S. rank in 1990: Not available
    U.S. rank in 2000: 48th

**Area:** 45 square miles (2000)

**Elevation:** Ranges from 785 to 1,075 feet above sea level

**Average Annual Temperatures:** January, 22.4° F; July, 71.4° F; annual average, 47.6° F

**Average Annual Precipitation:** 37.13 inches of rain; 73.2 inches of snow

**Major Economic Sectors:** Manufacturing, services, retail trade

**Unemployment Rate:** 6.3% (June 2007)

**Per Capita Income:** $18,608 (2005)

**2005 FBI Crime Index Property:** 9,766

**2005 FBI Crime Index Violent:** 1,962

**Major Colleges and Universities:** Grand Valley State University, Calvin College

**Daily Newspaper:** *The Grand Rapids Press*

## ■ Introduction

The seat of Kent County, Michigan, Grand Rapids is the center of a metropolitan statistical area that includes Kent, Ottawa, Muskegon, and Allegan counties. The Grand River, on which the city is located, shaped the future of Grand Rapids first as a leader in the logging industry, then as one of the world's primary furniture manufacturing centers, and now as the office furniture capital. The city's identity also was determined by thousands of Dutch immigrants who settled in Grand Rapids to work in the furniture factories. In 2000 the Grand Rapids metropolitan area had more than one million inhabitants, but as of 2008 the population had dropped to less than 800,000. The city offers innovative cultural institutions, a revitalized downtown core, a diverse economy, and high marks for quality of life factors.

## ■ Geography and Climate

Bisected by the Grand River, Michigan's longest river, Grand Rapids is located in the Grand River valley approximately 30 miles east of Lake Michigan. The region's climate is influenced by the lake, which tempers cold waves from the west and northwest during the winter and produces a regulating effect on both frost and vegetation during the growing season. Consequently, seasonal extremes are infrequent, although hot, humid weather can be expected for about three weeks during the summer and drought occasionally occurs for a short duration; snow cover sometimes remains throughout the winter.

**Area:** 45 square miles (2000)

**Elevation:** Ranges from 785 to 1,075 feet above sea level

**Average Temperatures:** January, 22.4° F; July, 71.4° F; annual average, 47.6° F

**Average Annual Precipitation:** 37.13 inches of rain; 73.2 inches of snow

# ■ History

## Grand River Valley Site of Land Feud

About 2,000 years ago, the Hopewell Indians planted roots at the rapids near the Grand River. Their presence is still seen in the preserved burial mounds southwest of the city. By the late 17th century, the Ottawa tribe had set up villages on the west bank of the Grand River at the site of present day Grand Rapids. Several Baptist mission buildings were completed in the vicinity in 1826. That same year Louis Campau, a French fur trader, settled in the region, establishing a trading post on the east river bank. Local Native Americans nicknamed him "The Fox" for his shrewd trading skills. Campau purchased 72 acres for $90 in 1831 in what is now the downtown area and named it the Village of Grand Rapids. A land surveyor named Lucius Lyon acquired the plotted land to the north and named it the Village of Kent, causing a raging land feud with Campau. By 1838 the Michigan legislature combined both tracts of land to form the Village of Grand Rapids. The area incorporated as a city in 1850.

Inexpensive, fertile land and abundant timber and mineral resources attracted settlers to the area, and by 1860 the population numbered 8,000, more than tripling in 10 years. By then, rail and telegraph had come to Grand Rapids, connecting the community to all parts of the country with travel from the eastern seaboard taking only two days.

## Logging Fuels Grand Rapids Development

Grand Rapids began a period of rapid development in the 1850s when logs from Michigan's rich pine and oak forests floated down the Grand River to the city's new mills. After the Civil War, many soldiers found jobs as lumberjacks, cutting logs and guiding them down the river with pike poles, peaveys, and cant hooks. The men wore bright red flannel, felt clothes, and spiked boots to hold them onto the floating logs; these boots chewed up the wooden sidewalks and flooring of the local bars, leading one hotel owner to supply carpet slippers to all river drivers who entered his hotel. The "jacks" earned $1 to $3 per day and all the "vittles" they could eat, which was usually a considerable amount.

Upstream mill owners often stole the logs headed for Grand Rapids in a practice called "hogging." To prevent hogging, the mills hired men called river drivers, who rode the logs downstream to their rightful destination. In addition, like cattle, all logs were stamped with the brands of their owners so they could be sorted at the log booms and sent to a specific sawmill. From 1865 to the 1880s the logging industry dominated the local economy. The river also harnessed energy. One of the first hydro-electric plants in the United States was built in Grand Rapids.

River ice and log jams proved to be a continual problem for Grand Rapids. A series of floods and heavy rains that launched runaway logs caused repeated damage to the town, notably in 1838, 1852, and 1883. In 1883, so much rain fell one summer's day that an estimated 80 million board feet of logs broke free and jammed against a railroad bridge, creating what some called the biggest log jam in the nation's history. The bridge swayed, bent, groaned, and finally broke away as part of it was carried steadily down the river. Called the Great Log Jam of 1883, the event was spectacular but also marked the beginning of the end for logging on the Grand River.

## Furniture Craftsmanship Gains World Attention

Because of the plentiful supply of fine wood, furniture had been manufactured in Grand Rapids as early as 1838, but it was not until the Philadelphia Centennial Exposition in 1876 that the city gained national recognition for its furniture craftsmanship. Bedroom, dining room, library, and hall furniture made of oak, ash, and maple gained mass popularity. Two years later Grand Rapids held its first furniture mart, attracting buyers worldwide who appreciated the fresh styles and quality work. One of the innovations Grand Rapids manufacturers brought to the furniture industry was catalogs of photographs and color drawings that were distributed throughout the nation.

By 1890, Grand Rapids was home to the nation's largest furniture companies; they set the tone for creative designs, new manufacturing processes and equipment, retailing networks, and inventive marketing schemes. The city ranked third, behind only New York and Chicago, in the amount of furniture its factories produced. Nearly one-third of all city laborers worked in the industry. The high paying and plentiful jobs attracted a large number of immigrants—Dutch, German, Polish, and other northern Europeans. Grand Rapids grew from slightly more than 10,000 residents at the end of the Civil War to nearly 90,000 by 1900. One-third of the city's population had been born in another country by that time.

In Europe, Grand Rapids was best known as the home of Tanglefoot rather than producer of fine furniture. Flies were a nuisance, then as now. An ordinary druggist named Otto Thum developed a sticky paper that not only caught and held flies, but even attracted them. The company is still in existence along with its century old "secret formula."

Another long lived, prosperous Grand Rapids company is Bissell, founded in 1876 and considered the pioneer in the carpet sweeper industry. With the death of company head Melville Bissell in 1889, his wife Anna assumed leadership and became America's first female corporate CEO. She was light-years ahead of her time as an aggressive and innovative manager. Under her guidance, the company developed many new products and expanded the business internationally. Still privately owned, Bissell continues to be an industry pioneer, bringing innovative home- and floor-care products to the international marketplace.

### Turn of the Century Brings Changes to Grand Rapids

Depletion of Michigan's forests put an end to the logging industry, requiring furniture companies to import lumber, as they still do today. Due to a nationwide industry slump between 1905 and 1910, furniture workers received only minimal raises or none at all. This, combined with extremely long hours and poor working conditions, led to 3,000 workers striking in 1911 demanding a 9-hour day, a 10 percent wage increase, and the abolition of pay based on piecework. After four months, the strike ended, but later management granted most of the laborer's requests.

The Grand Rapids residential furniture industry never fully recovered after that strike. World War I, the Great Depression, and World War II led to lessening demand for residential furniture and the Grand Rapids furniture companies did not make the transition well during the war economies. Many companies went under or moved south to be closer to a larger lumber supply.

With the end of World War II, a two-decades long construction boom began and countless new office buildings were erected throughout the nation and worldwide. Some Grand Rapids companies had begun making fine wood and metal furniture for offices in the early 1900s; they now saw tremendous demand. Steelcase grew from 34 employees in 1912 to become the largest office furniture company worldwide with more than 19,000 people. Because of the many office furniture companies in close proximity, Grand Rapids is now known as the nation's office furniture capital. Experience with wood and metal and a traditional entrepreneurial spirit led to a diversifying economy. No one industry dominates the metropolitan area manufacturers, but furniture, industrial machinery, metals, plastics, food processing, and printing are core industrial clusters.

As with other cities after World War II, many Grand Rapids-based families fled to the suburbs and the city's population began to decline along with the downtown area. In the mid 1990s, Grand Rapids began experiencing a renaissance, with more than $200 million in new cultural, recreational, and sports facilities. Downtown revitalization included the 12,000-seat Van Andel Arena for sports, concerts, and entertainment events; the Van Andel Institute, an independent medical research center; and the refurbishing of many warehouses into retail space and loft apartments. The new millennium has seen even more new projects and expansions. The $210-million DeVos Place project incorporates DeVos Hall and the old Grand Center convention space in a new one-million-square-foot facility, which was completed in 2005. Millennium Park is a 10-year restoration of 1,500 acres of industrial land that includes a new beach. New parks, residences, shopping venues, restaurants, and other revitalization projects that mark a new beginning for Grand Rapids abound.

***Historical Information:*** Grand Rapids Public Library, Michigan and Family History Collection, 111 Library St., NE, Grand Rapids, MI 49503; telephone (616) 456-3640

## ■ Population Profile

**Metropolitan Area Residents**
> 1980: 602,000
> 1990: 937,891
> 2000: 1,088,514
> 2006 estimate: 774,084
> Percent change, 1990–2000: 16.1%
> U.S. rank in 1980: 56th
> U.S. rank in 1990: Not available
> U.S. rank in 2000: 48th

**City Residents**
> 1980: 181,843
> 1990: 189,126
> 2000: 197,800
> 2006 estimate: 193,083
> Percent change, 1990–2000: 4.3%
> U.S. rank in 1980: 75th
> U.S. rank in 1990: 83rd
> U.S. rank in 2000: 107th (State rank: 2nd)

**Density:** 4,431.2 people per square mile (2000)

**Racial and ethnic characteristics (2005)**
> White: 130,745
> Black: 40,743
> American Indian and Alaska Native: 1,105
> Asian: 2,997
> Native Hawaiian and Pacific Islander: 0
> Hispanic or Latino (may be of any race): 32,368
> Other: 12,414

Airphoto-Jim Wark

**Percent of residents born in state:** 69.6% (2000)

**Age characteristics (2005)**

Population under 5 years old: 17,111
Population 5 to 9 years old: 14,214
Population 10 to 14 years old: 14,286
Population 15 to 19 years old: 12,443
Population 20 to 24 years old: 17,732
Population 25 to 34 years old: 35,287
Population 35 to 44 years old: 25,267
Population 45 to 54 years old: 23,376
Population 55 to 59 years old: 9,014
Population 60 to 64 years old: 5,279
Population 65 to 74 years old: 8,391
Population 75 to 84 years old: 8,141
Population 85 years and older: 3,027
Median age: 30.8 years

**Births (2006, MSA)**

Total number: 11,233

**Deaths (2006, MSA)**

Total number: 5,742

**Money income (2005)**

Per capita income: $18,608

Median household income: $38,229
Total households: 75,239

**Number of households with income of...**

less than $10,000: 7,730
$10,000 to $14,999: 5,615
$15,000 to $24,999: 10,824
$25,000 to $34,999: 10,462
$35,000 to $49,999: 12,750
$50,000 to $74,999: 14,745
$75,000 to $99,999: 6,938
$100,000 to $149,999: 4,870
$150,000 to $199,999: 824
$200,000 or more: 481

**Percent of families below poverty level:** 11.9% (2005)

**2005 FBI Crime Index Property:** 9,766

**2005 FBI Crime Index Violent:** 1,962

## ■ Municipal Government

Grand Rapids operates under a "weak mayor," commission-manager form of government, in which the seven council members—one of whom serves as mayor—are elected to four-year terms. The city manager, who runs the government, is appointed.

The Grand Valley Metro Council is a voluntary co-alition of 31 units of government assigned to coordinate the region's services and investments that have environmental, economic and social impacts.

**Head Official:** City Manager Kurt Kimball (since 1987)

**Total Number of City Employees:** 1,700 (2008)

*City Information:* City Hall, 300 Monroe NW, Grand Rapids, MI 49503; telephone (616)456-3000

# ■ Economy

## Major Industries and Commercial Activity

The furniture industry has been a mainstay of the Grand Rapids economy since the late 1800s. Today the metropolitan area is home to five of the world's leading office furniture companies: Steelcase, Herman Miller, Haworth, Knoll, and American Seating. Several firms also produce residential furniture. The Grand Rapids metropolitan manufacturing base is among the largest county employers. Steelcase and Amway, manufacturer of home care products, along with Meijer, a supermarket chain, are the largest private companies in the county. In 2007 Steelcase launched its Greenbuild campaign, a campaign to manufacture environment-friendly furniture.

Grand Rapids has always thrived because of its entrepreneurial, family-owned businesses. Among the national firms that began as family operations are Meijer; Bissell, carpet sweeper makers; Wolverine World Wide, makers of Hush Puppies; and Howard Miller, the world's largest manufacturer of grandfather clocks. In 2006 Wolverine World Wide acquired the global license to design Patagonia footwear; Patagonia, Inc., is a leader in outdoor apparel that also sponsors many important projects in global and environmental awareness.

Automotive parts, industrial machinery, printing, graphic arts, plastics and chemicals, grocery wholesalers, and food processors comprise a substantial portion of the economic base. International businesses also play an important role, with more than 50 foreign-owned firms in the county and many metropolitan area firms involved in international trade. Tourism is an emerging industry as West Michigan increasingly becomes a popular vacation and convention destination.

**Items and goods produced:** office furniture and hardware, home furniture, automobile parts, plastics, industrial machinery, tool and dies, home-care products, home appliances, commercial printing, electronic equipment, scientific instruments, food, leather

## Incentive Programs—New and Existing Companies

In 2004 the Michigan Economic Development Corporation approved a total of more than $10.3 million in Single Business Tax credits for the expansion and consolidation of Steelcase and the redevelopment of two contaminated brownfield sites in the city's downtown. Gaines Township will support the Steelcase expansion with a tax abatement valued at approximately $96,000 over four years.

*Local programs:* The city of Grand Rapids and its downtown development authority have committed approximately $6.3 million in local incentives toward the brownfield projects through tax abatements and tax increment financing incentives. The Right Place Program (RPP) is a regional non-profit organization headed by business and government leaders to encourage economic growth through expansion and retention of area businesses and attraction of national and international companies.

*State programs:* More than 800 properties within 10 areas of the city are designated Renaissance Zones, where Michigan Single Business Tax, the state education tax, Michigan personal and real property taxes, and city income taxes are waived. Tax credits and exemptions are also available in the city's SmartZone, an area adjacent to downtown where the city is seeking to locate high tech and life sciences companies. The Grand Rapids Smart-Zone project takes advantage of the many biotech and life science resources available throughout Grand Rapids. The area is known as the "medical mile," and the Grand Rapids SmartZone program has enabled some exciting progess in the medical and biotech fields. In 2007 a lab in Grand Rapids began designing a smaller, more efficient machine to pump oxygen into the blood and help with circulation.

*Job training programs:* Through the Michigan Economic Development Corporation, employees have the opportunity to improve their skills through three Michigan Technical Education Centers (M-TEC) operated through Grand Rapids Community College.

## Development Projects

Rosa Parks Circle, a small, downtown park, opened in 2002. It was designed by architect Maya Lin, who also designed the Vietnam Memorial in Washington, D.C. Millennium Park is a $25-million, 10-year restoration of 1,500 acres of industrial land. A 200-acre section of the park, including Millennium Park Beach, opened in 2003. The $210-million DeVos Place project incorporates DeVos Hall and the old Grand Center convention space in a new one-million-square-foot facility, which was completed in 2005. In 2007 local businesses and civic leaders drew up plans to create an electric streetcar system throughout the greater Grand Rapids area.

***Economic Development Information:*** The Right Place Program, The Waters Building, 111 Pearl Street NW, Grand Rapids, MI 49503; telephone (616)771-0325; fax (616)771-0329

## Commercial Shipping

Because of its strategic location, Grand Rapids is no more than two delivery days away from all Midwest, East Coast, mid-south, and eastern Canadian markets. Ground transportation is available through more than 40 motor carriers, several of which operate terminals in Grand Rapids, and three rail freight systems provide a range of services, such as piggyback shipments, bulk handling, and refrigeration. The South Beltline Corridor connecting I-96 on the east with I-196 on the west and with U.S. 131 in the center was completed in 2005. Seven air cargo carriers and a deep-water port on Lake Michigan, 35 miles away in Muskegon, link Grand Rapids with world markets.

## Labor Force and Employment Outlook

Employers in the Grand Rapids area have access to a young and growing population with a Midwestern work ethic. Employer relations are said to be excellent and work stoppages rare.

The city and region enjoy a high rate of employment overall. With a designated foreign trade zone, Grand Rapids importers and exporters expect to continue to expand markets internationally.

The following is a summary of data regarding the Grand Rapids-Wyoming metropolitan area labor force, 2006 annual averages.

**Size of nonagricultural labor force:** 392,400

**Number of workers employed in** . . .

> construction and mining: 18,200
> manufacturing: 73,500
> trade, transportation and utilities: 74,100
> information: 5,600
> financial activities: 22,500
> professional and business services: 55,700
> educational and health services: 56,100
> leisure and hospitality: 32,900
> other services: 16,500
> government: 37,300

**Average hourly earnings of production workers employed in manufacturing:** $17.86

**Unemployment rate:** 6.3% (June 2007)

| Largest employers (2007) | Number of employees |
|---|---|
| Spectrum Health | 13,000 |
| Meijer, Inc. | 7,000 |
| Herman Miller, Inc. | 5,920 |
| Steelcase, Inc. | 5,000 |
| Alticor, Inc. | 3,900 |
| Axios Incorporated | 3,886 |
| Wal-Mart Stores, Inc. | 3,432 |
| Johnson Controls, Inc. | 3,250 |
| Spartan Stores, Inc. | 2,989 |
| Grand Rapids Public Schools | 2,885 |

## Cost of Living

Grand Rapids is noted for its quality of life and affordable health care costs.

The following is a summary of data regarding several key cost of living factors in the Grand Rapids area.

**2007 (1st quarter) ACCRA Average House Price:** $330,520

**2007 (1st quarter) ACCRA Cost of Living Index:** 105.0

**State income tax rate:** 3.9% of taxable income

**State sales tax rate:** 6.0%

**Local income tax rate:** 1.3% for residents; 0.65% for non-residents

**Local sales tax rate:** None

**Property tax rate:** Property tax rate average: varies from 22.1515 to 29.0215 mills per $1,000 of assessed home value (2004)

***Economic Information:*** The Right Place Program, The Waters Building, 111 Pearl Street NW, Grand Rapids, MI 49503; telephone (616)771-0325; fax (616) 771-0329

# ■ Education and Research

## Elementary and Secondary Schools

Grand Rapids Public School District is the largest in the area. The distict's goal is that by 2008 all students will be at or above grade level in reading, writing, and math, and that 80 percent of incoming ninth graders will graduate.

On August 23, 2007, Madison Middle School was dedicated and renamed Gerald R. Ford Middle School in honor of the former president from Grand Rapids. The school is on the site of the elementary school attended by Ford. In October 2007 the Grand Rapids Board of Education announced the launch of the "Centers of Innovation," a new model of schooling designed to bridge racial achievement gaps.

The following is a summary of data regarding the Grand Rapids Public Schools as of the 2005–2006 school year.

**Total enrollment:** 21,462

**Number of facilities**

elementary schools: 32
junior high/middle schools: 8
senior high schools: 6
other: 4

**Student/teacher ratio:** 17.6:1

**Teacher salaries (2005–06)**

elementary median: $45,310
junior high/middle median: $51,530
secondary median: $52,270

**Funding per pupil:** $10,334

More than 120 parochial, private, church-affiliated, alternative, and specialty schools offer educational curricula from preschool through grade 12 in the Grand Rapids area.

***Public Schools Information:*** Grand Rapids Public Schools, 1331 Franklin SE, P.O. Box 117, Grand Rapids, MI 49501; telephone (616)771-2182. Kent County Intermediate School District, 2930 Knapp NE, Grand Rapids, MI 49525; telephone (616)364-1333

### Colleges and Universities

Grand Valley State University is located in Grand Rapids; undergraduate enrollment in 2007 was more than 19,000. Other institutions of higher learning offering undergraduate and graduate degrees in the Kent County area include: Aquinas College, Calvin College, Central Michigan University, Cornerstone University, Davenport College, Ferris State University, Kendall College of Art and Design (of Ferris State University), Michigan State University, Spring Arbor College, University of Phoenix, and Western Michigan University. Two-year programs are available at Grand Rapids Community College and ITT Technical Institute. Colleges and seminaries providing religious training are Calvin Theological Seminary, Grace Bible College, Grand Rapids Baptist Seminary, and Reformed Bible College.

### Libraries and Research Centers

The Grand Rapids Public Library is the second largest public library system in Michigan; it operates seven branches in addition to its main facility, which is a depository for federal and state documents. Library holdings consist of 660,000 books, tapes, films, maps, and compact discs; periodicals; and special collections covering several fields, such as furniture, foundations, and Michigan history. In 2007 the library created a site for posting commercials and public service announcements on YouTube, the video sharing website.

Kent District Library maintains 19 branches and houses about 774,000 books plus magazines, videos, and compact discs. The library system also provides additional services to blind and handicapped customers. Lakeland Library Cooperative serves one million people in the area. Several libraries have in-depth collections in fields such as law, personal finance, business, art and architecture, and antiques and collectibles.

Research is conducted at Grand Valley State University in water resources, aquatic conservation, land use change, air quality, and waste management. At Steelcase, Inc.'s $111-million Pyramid Research Center, behavioral scientists, designers, and engineers study emerging trends such as ergonomics and translate them into office products. The Van Andel Research Institute (VARI) opened its $60-million, 162,000-square-foot building in 2000. Its board of scientific advisors includes four Nobel Laureates; cancer research is the primary focus.

***Public Library Information:*** Grand Rapids Public Library, 111 Library St. NE, Grand Rapids, MI 49503-3268; telephone (616)588-5400; fax (616)588-5420

## ■ Health Care

Spectrum Health celebrated its tenth anniversary in 2007. It serves as the western Michigan regional center for cancer, diabetes, poisons, sleep disorders, and burn treatment. It has a nationally recognized children's hospital. The $137-million Fred and Lena Meijer Heart Center opened on the hospital's Butterworth Campus in 2004.

St. Mary's Health Care is an integrated health care system that has specialists in kidney transplantation, cardiac care, bloodless medicine, psychiatric medicine, neonatology, gastroenterology, and endocrinology. St. Mary's opened the $42-million, 180,000-square-foot, five-story Lacks Cancer Center in January 2005. The Wege Institute offers traditional services, such as family practice, internal medicine and general surgery, side by side with complementary therapies, including massage, acupuncture, biofeedback, manipulation, and Feldenkrais. In 2006 St. Mary's began work on the Hauenstein Center, a neurological medical center where both inpatient and outpatient neurological care will be provided under the same roof. Scheduled to open in 2008, the center is the first of its kind in the country.

## ■ Recreation

### Sightseeing

The Gerald R. Ford Museum in Grand Rapids honors the 38th President of the United States; permanent exhibits, including a replica of the Oval Office, highlight the significant events of the Ford presidency, such as the Bicentennial celebration, President Nixon's resignation, and the Cambodian conflict. The contributions of Betty Ford as First Lady are also represented.

The Public Museum of Grand Rapids concentrates on the furniture industry, Michigan mammals, archeology, costumes, a 1890s gaslight village, and Native American artifacts.

Heritage Hill is one of the largest urban historic districts in the country. Located near downtown, it contains more than 1,300 structures built in 60 different architectural styles, including Frank Lloyd Wright's Meyer May house.

A Grand Rapids highlight is Alexander Calder's *La Grande Vitesse* (The Grand Rapids), a large-scale outdoor sculpture located in the center of the city. Another Calder work, an abstract painting, has been installed atop the County Building adjacent to the sculpture. Joseph Kinnebrew's *Fish Ladder* sculpture has been placed on the Sixth Street dam. Noted architect and artist Maya Lin (designer of the Vietnam Memorial in Washington, D.C.) designed Rosa Parks Circle, a park and amphitheater located in the downtown Monroe Center.

The 150-passenger sternwheeler *Grand Lady* offers a narrated river cruise pointing out the river landings and town sites of the 1800s.

The John Ball Zoo features more than 237 species and 1,183 specimens. Recent additions include a komodo dragon and a chimpanzee exhibit.

## Arts and Culture

The Arts Council coordinates the Festival of the Arts, the largest volunteer-run festival in the nation and a showcase of the arts. The arts in Grand Rapids are celebrated for three days each June with more than one-half million attendees. During the regular season, the Grand Rapids Symphony, an award-winning orchestra recognized for its innovative programming, presents a program of classical, pops, and family concerts. In 2007 the Symphony received a grant to promote diversity both within the organization as well as within the community. Opera Grand Rapids is the oldest opera theater in Michigan and stages both classical operas and musical theater productions. The Opera celebrated its 40th anniversary in 2007. The Grand Rapids Ballet presents *The Nutcracker* in December plus several other productions each year. In 2006 the Grand Rapids Ballet announced the creation of the Meijer-Royce Center for Dance, a $6.2-million project. Founded in 1883 and designated as a Landmark of American Music, Royce Auditorium is where the St. Cecilia Music Society presents public programs and educational opportunities for youth and adults. Other organizations perform at DeVos Hall and the Van Andel Arena.

Grand Rapids Civic Theatre, the second largest community theater in the country and Michigan's oldest community theater, presents six main stage productions and two children's plays annually. The Civic Theater has 3,000 ticket holders each year. Its School of Theater Arts

offers a complete range of theatrical training courses as well as one-day workshops and summer programs. Circle Theatre, one of the country's largest summer community theaters, is housed at Aquinas College and features children's theater and a cabaret series in addition to its standard summer offerings. Spectrum Theatre, located downtown at Grand Rapids Community College, features innovative and local plays and is the performance home for Actors' Theatre, GRCC Players, the Jewish Theatre Grand Rapids, and Heritage Theatre Group.

The Grand Rapids Art Museum, opened in 1913 and renovated in 1981, houses a permanent collection of paintings, sculpture, and graphic and decorative arts in ten galleries and hosts traveling art exhibits. The furniture design wing features period furniture from the Renaissance to the present. In 2007 the museum opened new galleries to exhibit permanent collections. The Urban Institute for Contemporary Arts provides exhibition and performance space for concerts, performance art, lectures, and readings. The 125-acre Frederik Meijer Gardens and Sculpture Park hosts the largest tropical conservatory in Michigan, in addition to indoor and outdoor plant and butterfly gardens, nature trails, a boardwalk, three indoor art galleries, and the three-story-tall Leonardo da Vinci's Horse, plus 100 other world-class sculptures from classical and contemporary artists.

***Arts and Culture Information:*** Arts Council of Greater Grand Rapids, 532 Ottawa NW, PO Box 2265, Grand Rapids, MI 49503 telephone (616)459-2787; fax (616)459-7160

## Festivals and Holidays

The major festival in Grand Rapids is a three-day arts celebration in June that initiates the summer season. Ethnic festivals take place nearly every summer weekend: Irish, Italian, Polish, German, Native American, Mexican, Latino, and African American celebrations of cultural heritage feature song, food, art, and costumes. The Covered Bridge Bike Tour lets cyclists explore Kent County by bicycle in mid-July. The summer season concludes with the Celebration on the Grand during the second weekend in September. Pulaski Days celebrate Polish heritage in October. One of the state's original nighttime parades starts off the Christmas festivities in early December in nearby downtown Coopersville.

## Sports for the Spectator

The Grand Rapids Hoops team competes in the semi-professional Continental Basketball League. The Grand Rapids Griffins belong to the International Hockey League, and the Grand Rapids Rampage to the Arena Football League. All three teams play at Van Andel Arena. The West Michigan Whitecaps, a Class A minor affiliate of the Detroit Tigers baseball team, play at Fifth Third Park. Berlin Raceway features stock car racing, and

Gratton Raceway presents auto, motorcycle, and go-cart races.

## Sports for the Participant

Sports enthusiasts are provided numerous opportunities to enjoy the outdoors in Grand Rapids and the vicinity. Cross-county ski trails wind through scenic apple orchards and across golf courses. The Winter Sports Complex in nearby Muskegon provides the longest lighted ski trail in the Midwest; the center also maintains a 600-meter chute for luge, one of only four in the nation. Three local resorts feature downhill skiing. Year-round fishing is another popular sport, especially trout and perch fishing.

Charter boats on Lake Michigan are available for salmon and lake trout fishing. Swimmers and sunbathers populate the miles of sandy beaches of Lake Michigan and the many inland lakes during the summer. Rowers are often seen on the Grand River, as are salmon fishers in October and November. The Fifth Third River Bank Run, a 25K event, attracts runners from around the country. In 2007 Fifth Third bank offered $9,000 each to the first place male and female race winners. The Gus Macker three-on-three basketball tournament began in Kent County and happens each summer in downtown Grand Rapids.

Recreational facilities within a 60-mile drive include 11 public and several private golf courses, 21 inland lakes, and dozens of tennis courts and baseball fields. Also under development is Millennium Park, a 10-year project that will return approximately 1,500 acres of industrial land along the Grand River to publicly-owned green space. Once completed, the park will be nearly two and a half times larger than New York's Central Park, making it one of the largest urban parks in the country. Millennium Park currently features a beach house, playground, picnic areas, and fishing ponds. The Grand Rapids recreation department sponsors hundreds of softball teams in league competition, as well as programs in swimming, soccer, baseball, basketball, tennis, golf, scuba diving, and social dancing.

## Shopping and Dining

While Grand Rapids doesn't have a true downtown shopping district, it does offer several smaller neighborhood shopping areas, in addition to several malls and a strip on 28th Street off of I-96, with many restaurants, larger shops, and strip malls. Woodland Mall offers three major department stores and 120 smaller shops. Breton Village Shopping Center features 40 stores, many locally-owned. RiverTown Crossings contains 120 stores, including six anchor stores, as well as a movie theater. Small shopping districts located throughout the city and surrounding towns include the quaint Squire Street Square in Rockford and the Gaslight Village district in East Grand Rapids, a residential district where fine shops are located in period homes.

The city's best restaurants are clustered downtown. The 1913 Room in the Amway Grand Plaza Hotel is Michigan's only AAA five-diamond restaurant. The award-winning Sierra Room serves Southwestern cuisine in an old warehouse. The B.O.B. features five restaurants, a micro-brewery, night club, comedy club, 2,500 bottle cellar, and billiards.

*Visitor Information:* Grand Rapids/Kent County Convention and Visitors Bureau, 171 Monroe Ave NW, Suite 700, Grand Rapids, MI 49503; telephone (616) 459-8287; toll-free (800)678-9859; fax (616)459-7291. Grand Rapids Area Chamber of Commerce, Chamber of Commerce Building, 111 Peal St. NW, Grand Rapids, MI 49503; telephone (616)771-0300; fax (616)771-0318

# ■ Convention Facilities

Grand Rapids was one of the first cities in the country to build a convention center. The 1933 Art Deco-style Civic Auditorium, renamed Welsh Auditorium, was demolished in 2004 to make way for expansion around DeVos Hall, a performing arts venue, which reopened as part of DeVos Place in 2005. DeVos Place features one million square feet of new and renovated space, including a 160,000-square-foot exhibit hall and 21 meeting rooms. During the demolition the Steelcase ballroom was also added to the Welsh Auditorium. The Steelcase ballroom can accommodate up to 3,500 guests and is one of the largest ballrooms in the country. Additional convention facilities include the Amway Grand Plaza Hotel, the Courtyard by Marriott Downtown, and Van Andel Arena. The convention centers are all located within a five block area and are connected by a skyway.

Kent County offers 6,600 hotel rooms, with 1,071 of those in Grand Rapids; many hotels also provide meeting and convention accommodations.

*Convention Information:* DeVos Place, 303 Monroe St., Grand Rapids, MI 49503; telephone (616)742-6500; fax (616)742-6590

# ■ Transportation

## Approaching the City

Michigan's second-largest airport, Gerald R. Ford International Airport, is located 30 minutes from downtown Grand Rapids. Eight airlines provide direct service to and from 15 major cities. In 2007 more than 2 million passengers traveled through Gerald R. Ford International Airport.

A network of interstate, federal, and state highways provides access into Grand Rapids from surrounding communities as well as points throughout the United States and Canada. Interstate highways serving the metropolitan area are I-96, I-196, and I-296. U.S. highways extending through the city are 16 and 131; state routes include 11, 44, 50, 21, and 37. Daily rail passenger transportation from Chicago is provided by Amtrak.

## Traveling in the City

The Interurban Transit Partnership, also known as The Rapid, is the authority that provides a variety of public transportation services for the Grand Rapids metropolitan area. The Rapid operates 19 fixed routes, demand-response services for people with disabilities and those living outside the fixed-route service area, car and vanpooling programs, and the Air Porter shuttle among other services. Go!Bus provides door-to-door transportation for the elderly and disabled. DASH—Downtown Area Shuttle—allows commuters to park in safe city lots by taking the free DASH bus to stops near their downtown destinations.

# ■ Communications

## Newspapers and Magazines

*The Grand Rapids Press* is the city's daily newspaper, appearing in the evening. In 2007 it was estimated that 309,590 people in Michigan read *The Grand Rapids Press*. Other newspapers circulating in the community include *The Grand Rapids Times,* targeted to African American community interests, and *Grand Rapids Business Journal. Grand Rapids Magazine* is a monthly publication that features articles of regional interest. Several special-interest magazines are also published in Grand Rapids; a number of them focus on religious topics.

## Television and Radio

Six television stations broadcast in Grand Rapids—affiliates of PBS, NBC, ABC, Fox, CW, and PAX. Twenty-three AM and FM radio stations are based in the city; several of them broadcast Christian inspirational programming while others broadcast sports, music, news, and information.

***Media Information:*** *The Grand Rapids Press,* Booth Newspapers, Inc., 155 Michigan Street NW, Grand Rapids, MI 49503; telephone (616)459-1567. *Grand Rapids Magazine,* Gemini Publications, 549 Ottawa Ave. NW, Ste. 201, Grand Rapids, MI 49503; telephone (616)459-4545

## Grand Rapids Online

DeVos Place. Available www.devosplace.org
Grand Rapids Area Chamber of Commerce. Available www.grandrapids.org
Grand Rapids/Kent County Convention and Visitors Bureau. Available www.grcvb.org
*The Grand Rapids Press.* Available www.mlive.com/grpress
Grand Rapids Public Library. Available atwww.grpl.org

BIBLIOGRAPHY

Bratt, James D., et al., *Gathered at the River: Grand Rapids, Michigan, and Its People of Faith* (Wm. B. Eerdmans Publishing Co, 1993)

Ford, Gerald R., et al., *Greater Grand Rapids: City that Works* (Towery Publishing, 1998)

# Kalamazoo

## The City in Brief

**Founded:** 1829 (incorporated 1883)

**Head Official:** Mayor Bobby J. Hopewell (since 2007)

**City Population**
1980: 79,722
1990: 80,277
2000: 77,145
2006 estimate: 72,161
Percent change, 1990–2000: −3.9%
U.S. rank in 1980: 271st
U.S. rank in 1990: 322nd
U.S. rank in 2000: 390th

**Metropolitan Area Population**
1980: 279,192 (SMSA)
1990: 429,453 (MSA)
2000: 452,851 (MSA)
2006 estimate: 319,738
Percent change, 1990–2000: 5.4%
U.S. rank in 1980: Not available
U.S. rank in 1990: 82nd (MSA)
U.S. rank in 2000: 91st (MSA)

**Area:** 25.18 square miles (2000)

**Elevation:** Ranges from 700 to 1,000 feet above sea level

**Average Annual Temperatures:** January, 24.7° F; July, 72.9° F

**Average Annual Precipitation:** 36.4 inches of rain; 70 inches of snow

**Major Economic Sectors:** Services, manufacturing, trade, government

**Unemployment Rate:** 6.0% (June 2007)

**Per Capita Income:** $20,088 (2005)

**2005 FBI Crime Index Property:** 4,541

**2005 FBI Crime Index Violent:** 596

**Major Colleges and Universities:** Western Michigan University, Kalamazoo College, Davenport University, Kalamazoo Valley Community College

**Daily Newspaper:** *Kalamazoo Gazette*

## Introduction

The name of this city has inspired songs and poems by Carl Sandburg, Glenn Miller, and others. Kalamazoo is a small Midwestern town with several colleges, a symphony orchestra, and an arts institute that lend it sophistication not usually found in a town its size. The seat of Kalamazoo County, Kalamazoo is an industrial and commercial center in a fertile farm area that produces fruit, celery, and peppermint. The addition of a substantial research and development park, along with community leaders willing to collaborate to overcome economic challenges, has created a positive business climate; the area's 83 lakes offer fantastic tourist appeal, especially for water sports enthusiasts.

## Geography and Climate

Kalamazoo lies on the lower reaches of the Kalamazoo River at its confluence with Portage Creek, 35 miles east of Lake Michigan, 107 miles west of Ann Arbor, and 70 miles west of Lansing. The city also represents the halfway point between Chicago and Detroit. The mucky marshland between the river and the creek once supported vast celery fields; today the fertile soil supports large bedding-plant fields.

Nearby Lake Michigan and the prevailing westerly winds produce a lake effect, which increases cloudiness and snowfall during the fall and winter months.

Kalamazoo rarely experiences prolonged periods of hot, humid weather in summer or extreme cold during the winter. Precipitation is generally well distributed throughout the year, but the wettest month is usually June. Average seasonal snowfall is nearly 70 inches annually.

**Area:** 25.18 square miles (2000)

**Elevation:** Ranges from 700 to 1,000 feet above sea level

**Average Temperatures:** January, 24.7° F; July, 72.9° F

**Average Annual Precipitation:** 36.4 inches of rain; 70 inches of snow

# ■ History

## Early Days as "Celery City"

Sometime before the early seventeenth century, the Potawatomi Indians moved from the east coast of the United States and established settlements in southern Michigan, where they fished and hunted for wild game. They called the river that flows through present-day Kalamazoo "Kikalamazoo," which means "boiling water," because of the hundreds of bubbling springs in it. In 1823 a trading post called Kikalamazoo was established on the banks of the river.

In 1827 the Potawatomi ceded their Michigan lands to the United States, and permanent settlers began to arrive in 1829. They were led by Titus Bronson, who called the town Bronson. But Titus Bronson was an outspoken man who voiced strong political opinions, and some critics say he was overly fond of alcohol. Historians say his crankiness and restless, erratic behavior, symptomatic of what is today called Tourette's syndrome, did not endear him to settlers who came after.

In 1833, with a population of about 100 people, Kalamazoo demonstrated its commitment to higher education by establishing Kalamazoo College. During the winter of 1835 a movement began to officially change the name of the town from Bronson back to its Indian name in the shortened form "Kalamazoo." This was finalized before the state of Michigan was entered into the Union in January 1837.

The years 1834 to 1837 were a time of prosperity in the United States, and the greatest land sales in American history took place. In 1835, the land office at Kalamazoo sold more acres than any other land office in the history of the country. More than 1.6 million acres were sold, accounting for more than $2 million in receipts. According to the *Detroit Democratic Free Press* newspaper, "We are informed that the village of Kalamazoo is literally thronged with purchasers. The public and private houses are full and...in some instances, they are compelled to retire to the barns for...lodging."

In 1847 a group of religious refugees from The Netherlands settled in Kalamazoo at the same time a Scotsman named James Taylor was experimenting with celery seeds imported from England. Taylor could not convince the townsfolk of the joys of eating celery, since they thought it was poisonous. His experiment languished for 10 years until a Dutchman named Cornelius De Bruin began to cultivate celery in the rich black muck along the Kalamazoo River. The De Bruin children sold the celery door to door. Before long the celery fields of "Celery City" were flourishing, and it was not uncommon to see Kalamazoo peddlers selling celery on the streets of the little town.

## Transition to "Paper and Rice City"

With their marshes proving so profitable, civic leaders turned their attention to advertising the city's water resources to potential investors in a paper mill. In 1874 Kalamazoo Paper was established, just the first of many companies that would make Kalamazoo a paper mill center. Soon other industries were attracted to the town, which was strategically located between Detroit and Chicago.

One early entrepreneur was William Erastus Upjohn, who graduated from the University of Michigan Medical School in 1875 and opened up a private practice and a pharmaceutical laboratory in Kalamazoo. He developed a process for making pills and granules that resulted in 1885 in the Upjohn Pill and Granule Company. Upjohn's experiment became Pharmacia & Upjohn Company then Pharmacia Corp. More industries followed at the end of the nineteenth century, and Kalamazoo was turning out stoves, essential oils, and iron and allied products.

## Growth as Educational Center

Kalamazoo was incorporated as a city in 1883 and began a rapid modernization, installing a horse-car line that year and following two years later with an electric light and power plant. The city's educational system also experienced steady growth with the opening of the all-women's Nazareth College in 1871, then Western Michigan University's founding in 1903.

In 1918 Kalamazoo was one of the first cities in Michigan to adopt the commission-manager form of government, led by Dr. Upjohn as the inaugural mayor. Many fine buildings were constructed, including city hall in 1931, the five-story county building in 1937, and fine homes representing several architectural styles, including a number of Frank Lloyd Wright's "Usonian" homes constructed during the 1940s.

By 1937 Kalamazoo boasted 151 industrial establishments manufacturing goods valued at more than $70 million. Thirteen paper mills dominated the industrial scene; other industries included cultivated peppermint and the manufacture of taxicabs, furnaces, auto bodies, transmissions, caskets, clothing, fishing rods and reels, playing cards, and musical instruments. Kalamazoo has nurtured cultural activities as well as industry. The Kalamazoo Symphony Orchestra was established in 1921; the city also boasts the Kalamazoo Institute of Arts, founded in 1924, and numerous performing arts groups.

Kalamazoo opened the country's first permanent outdoor pedestrian shopping mall in 1959. Despite economic turbulence in the early 2000s, the city remains a prosperous center of diverse industries and agricultural products. City planners have worked actively to overcome the loss of major area businesses. The area appeals to workers for its small-town charm coupled with a wide variety of cultural activities. A variety of tax incentives make it enticing to high-growth businesses as well.

*Historical Information:* Western Michigan University Archives & Regional History Collection, Rm. 111, East Hall, Western Michigan University, Kalamazoo, MI 49008; telephone (269)387-8490; www.wmich.edu/library/archives

# ■ Population Profile

## Metropolitan Area Residents

1980: 279,192 (SMSA)
1990: 429,453 (MSA)
2000: 452,851 (MSA)
2006 estimate: 319,738
Percent change, 1990–2000: 5.4%
U.S. rank in 1980: Not available
U.S. rank in 1990: 82nd (MSA)
U.S. rank in 2000: 91st (MSA)

## City Residents

1980: 79,722
1990: 80,277
2000: 77,145
2006 estimate: 72,161
Percent change, 1990–2000: −3.9%
U.S. rank in 1980: 271st
U.S. rank in 1990: 322nd
U.S. rank in 2000: 390th

**Density:** 3,125.4 people per square mile (2000)

## Racial and ethnic characteristics (2000)

White: 54,593
Black: 15,924
American Indian and Alaska Native: 445
Asian: 1,847
Native Hawaiian and Pacific Islander: 50
Hispanic or Latino (may be of any race): 3,304
Other: 1,836

**Percent of residents born in state:** 69.2% (2000)

## Age characteristics (2005)

Population under 5 years old: 4,335
Population 5 to 9 years old: 2,661
Population 10 to 14 years old: 3,399
Population 15 to 19 years old: 3,583
Population 20 to 24 years old: 10,816
Population 25 to 34 years old: 10,637
Population 35 to 44 years old: 7,753
Population 45 to 54 years old: 6,942
Population 55 to 59 years old: 3,099
Population 60 to 64 years old: 1,792
Population 65 to 74 years old: 3,069
Population 75 to 84 years old: 2,876
Population 85 years and older: 588
Median age: 30.5 years

## Births (2006, MSA)

Total number: 3,954

## Deaths (2006, MSA)

Total number: 2,698

## Money income (2005)

Per capita income: $20,088
Median household income: $31,152
Total households: 28,533

## Number of households with income of...

less than $10,000: 4,372
$10,000 to $14,999: 1,697
$15,000 to $24,999: 5,290
$25,000 to $34,999: 4,326
$35,000 to $49,999: 3,908
$50,000 to $74,999: 4,869
$75,000 to $99,999: 1,813
$100,000 to $149,999: 1,443
$150,000 to $199,999: 601
$200,000 or more: 214

**Percent of families below poverty level:** 16% (2005)

**2005 FBI Crime Index Property:** 4,541

**2005 FBI Crime Index Violent:** 596

# ■ Municipal Government

Kalamazoo, seat of Kalamazoo County, has a commission-manager form of government. The city commissioners are elected on an at-large basis every two years (during odd-numbered calendar years). The commissioner who receives the largest number of votes is named as the mayor and is responsible for representing the city at

Courtesy of the Kalamazoo County Convention and Visitors Bureau.

ceremonial functions and signing contracts. The city commission appoints a city manager who is in charge of the city's daily business affairs.

**Head Official:** Mayor Bobby J. Hopewell (since 2007; current term expires 2009)

**Total Number of City Employees:** 786 (2007)

***City Information:*** City of Kalamazoo, 241 W. South St., Kalamazoo, MI 49007-4796; telephone (269)337-8046; www.kalamazoocity.org

## ■ Economy

### Major Industries and Commercial Activity

Kalamazoo County has a diverse economic base with manufacturing, health care and education, and trade and transportation being the strongest industry sectors.

There are over 400 industrial and manufacturing employers in the area. One of the largest is Stryker Medical Technology, a *Fortune* 500 company that produces surgical and hospital equipment and serves as one of the largest employers in the city of Kalamazoo.

However, like many Midwestern cities, Kalamazoo has struggled against the loss of manufacturing jobs in the early 2000s.

For several years downtown Kalamazoo was the site of Pfizer's offices, manufacturing facilities, and research labs, following its 2002 buyout of the homegrown Pharmacia & Upjohn Company (whose presence in the community dated back more than a century). Nearly 1,200 jobs were lost due to the Pfizer acquisition, but Kalamazoo city officials encouraged scientists and mid-level professionals who had been laid off to remain in Kalamazoo to help develop the business incubator Southwest Michigan Innovation Center (SMIC). However, in 2007 Pfizer announced that it would eliminate about 2,400 jobs in Michigan. The Pfizer research facility in Kalamazoo was slated to close by 2008, resulting in a loss of 250 local jobs.

Once a giant paper production area, Kalamazoo's importance in the industry has greatly diminished. However, several paper manufacturing firms, such as the James River Corporation, continue to manufacture paper items locally.

In health care, top employers for the county include the Borgess Medical Center and Bronson Methodist Hospital. In education, Western Michigan University, which employs more than 4,500 people, makes a significant contribution to the local economy. Trade and transportation companies, including distribution and warehouse companies, have a solid base in the local economy as well. Eaton Corporation is a major distributor of automotive parts. Total Logistics Control, a freight and trucking company, maintains two distribution centers within the city area.

Agriculture still plays a minor role in the local economy, especially in Comstock Township, which is east of Kalamazoo. Financial services is a growing industry, with National City Bank as a major employer.

**Items and goods produced:** paper and pulp, surgical equipment, household products, injection molded thermoplastics, recycled paperboard, fluid sealing systems, aircraft engine components, office furniture, plastics, corrugated shipping containers

## Incentive Programs—New and Existing Companies

*Local programs:* Kalamazoo's Community Planning and Development Department assists local businesses and industries by providing technical assistance with site selection for expansion or relocation, tax abatements, and help with permits and other paperwork. The Brownfield Redevelopment Financing Act is operated by the city and provides many tax relief benefits to redevelopers. Southwest Michigan First is an organization dedicated to developing and implementing a successful long-term economic strategy for the area. Kalamazoo College's Stryker Center provides small businesses with information in obtaining commercial loans. The Small Business Revolving Fund can supply up to $40,000 in funding.

*State and federal programs:* The creation of new jobs that feed into a prosperous economy is the purpose behind the Michigan Economic Growth Authority. Fiscally-responsible companies in the fields of manufacturing, research and development, wholesale trade, or office operations can make use of Small Business Tax credits. Parts of Kalamazoo are designated Michigan Renaissance Zones, which are virtually tax free for any business or resident presently in or moving there. The Business Technology and Research Park in Kalamazoo is one of the 11 state-designated SmartZones. Services available through the statewide SmartZone program include access to business feasibility studies and business planning, venture capital preparation, market analysis, incubator space, and coordination of research and development with universities and industry.

Michigan communities can abate up to 50 percent of local property taxes for up to 12 years. Other incentives on the state level include tax abatements, tax-exempt revenue bonds, public loans and grants. The state administers an award-winning brownfield redevelopment program, community development block grants, long-term fixed rated financing for small and medium-sized businesses, and more.

Michigan has created a system of financial institutions called BIDCOs (Business and Industrial Development Corporations). These semiprivate, independent operations are chartered and partially capitalized by the state and are designed to provide mezzanine-level financing. This is for capital of higher risk than traditional banks will consider and of lower return than venture-capital companies demand.

*Job training programs:* Michigan offers a coordinated job training system called Michigan Works! using federal, state, and local resources to provide a highly productive and trained workforce. The federal Workforce Investment Act and the Michigan Department of Labor and Economic Growth provide funding for the grants that assist in increasing worker productivity. The training itself is done through the institution of the company's choice. Free recruitment and screening services are available for new and expanding employers through the Michigan Employment Security Administration's job service and also through several local school districts.

## Development Projects

Kalamazoo's Neighborhood and Economic Development office helps in identifying and promoting properties that are prime for building. A $2.83-million grant from the Clean Michigan Initiative Waterfront Redevelopment is playing a part in the "Riverfront Redevelopment Plan" that strives to utilize the land for a mix of business and residential purposes.

Business Technology and Research Park (BTR), a partnership development between the city and Western Michigan University, continues to expand its Southwest Michigan Innovation Center (SMIC), which has become a major economic catalyst for the area. Southwest Michigan First is the main local organization promoting the growth of high-tech industries in the city. When Pfizer acquired Pharmacia & Upjohn Company in 2002, the Southwest Michigan First organization played a vital role in retaining scientists with its "Stick Around" campaign. This effort has allowed for nearly two dozen companies to move into the research park, including VDDI Pharmaceuticals in 2003 and TEKNA Solutions, Inc., which completed construction on a 24,000-square-foot facility in 2006.

In a continued effort for a new justice center in the downtown area to centralize Kalamazoo's public safety and court facilities, a bond proposal was put into action in April 2005 by the Kalamazoo County Board of Commissioners. A new $32-million wing terminal was proposed in order to increase the Kalamazoo/Battle Creek International Airport to 93,000 square feet; as of late 2007 the expansion project had not yet begun construction.

In 2007 a new Michigan Space & Science Center opened at the Air Zoo. It hosts a $30-million space artifact collection, the fourth largest collection of Smithsonian Institution/National Air and Space Museum artifacts in the United States. The facility is located on 30,000 square feet of land and includes a 120-seat theater. Nearby Gilmore Car Museum expanded their facilities by 50 percent with the addition of three exhibit buildings in 2004.

*Economic Development Information:* Southwest Michigan First, 241 East Michigan Ave., Kalamazoo, MI 49007; telephone (269)553-9588; www.southwest michiganfirst.com

## Commercial Shipping

Situated midway between Chicago and Detroit, Kalamazoo is within a two day truck-drive from about 78 percent of the U.S. population. The Gerald Ford International Airport in Grand Rapids (about 53 miles from Kalamazoo) hosts four cargo airlines. Kalamazoo County has over 20 motor freight carriers; Norfolk Southern provides freight rail service through the area.

## Labor Force and Employment Outlook

Kalamazoo is said to have a diverse labor force with a wide range of skills. Local colleges assist job seekers via training and placement programs in conjunction with area businesses. The economic recession in the early 2000s took a toll on area employment opportunities, though, with dramatic declines in the manufacturing sector. According to the W. E. Upjohn Institute, as of September 2007 the manufacturing industry had failed to progress at a similar rate to national levels, resulting in a 3.0 percent drop in employment. The healthcare and private education sectors both experienced 1 percent growth in employment, and the hospitality industry experienced a 0.6 percent increase in employment between 2006 and 2007.

In October 2007, the unemployment rate for greater Kalamazoo stood at 5.3 percent, slightly above the national average but below its ten-year high of 7 percent in 2003. Between 1997 and 2007 the labor force in metropolitan Kalamazoo grew from 158,819 workers to 175,010 workers.

The following is a summary of data regarding the Kalamazoo-Portage metropolitan area labor force, 2006 annual averages.

**Size of nonagricultural labor force:** 145,800

**Number of workers employed in . . .**

    construction and mining: 6,300
    manufacturing: 23,400
    trade, transportation and utilities: 1,500
    information: 1,500
    financial activities: 7,800
    professional and business services: 15,600

    educational and health services: 21,300
    leisure and hospitality: 15,500
    other services: 6,600
    government: 23,400

**Average hourly earnings of production workers employed in manufacturing:** $14.93

**Unemployment rate:** 6.0% (June 2007)

| *Largest employers (2007)* | *Number of employees* |
|---|---|
| Western Michigan University | 4,606 |
| Borgess Medical Center | 4,475 |
| Pfizer | 4,000 |
| Bronson Methodist Hospital | 3,573 |
| Stryker Corp. | 2,500 |
| Kalamazoo Public Schools | 2,300 |
| National City Bank | 1,600 |
| Meijer, Inc. | 1,594 |
| Portage Public Schools | 1,100 |
| Summit Polymers Inc. | 1,097 |
| County of Kalamazoo | 1,065 |

## Cost of Living

The following is a summary of data regarding several key cost of living factors for the Kalamazoo area.

**2007 (1st quarter) ACCRA Average House Price:** $274,263

**2007 (1st quarter) ACCRA Cost of Living Index:** 97.4

**State income tax rate:** 3.9% of taxable income

**State sales tax rate:** 6.0%

**Local income tax rate:** None

**Local sales tax rate:** None

**Property tax rate:** up to 25 mills per $1,000 (2005)

*Economic Information:* Kalamazoo Regional Chamber of Commerce, 346 W. Michigan Ave., Kalamazoo, MI 49007; telephone (269)381-4000; www .kazoochamber.com

# ■ Education and Research

## Elementary and Secondary Schools

The students in Kalamazoo's schools have access to the Education for Employment (EFE) program, which helps them in planning for their future careers, as well as the

Education for the Arts (EFA) program, which enhances their art education with dance, literary arts, media arts, music, theater, and visual arts classes. The Kalamazoo Area Mathematics & Science Center offers accelerated programs in math, science, and technology to public and private high school students. Kalamazoo Public Schools take pride in a low student to teacher ratio of about 15 to 1 and a wide variety of programs in art, music, drama, and sports.

The Kalamazoo Promise Program offers scholarships to high school graduates who are admitted to any public State of Michigan university or community college. Students must have attended the Kalamazoo public schools for four years or more in order to be eligible for benefits. Those who attend district schools from kindergarten through graduation may receive a scholarship of 100 percent of the cost of tuition and mandatory fees at qualifying schools for up to four years.

The following is a summary of data regarding the Kalamazoo Public Schools as of the 2005–2006 school year.

**Total enrollment:** 10,500

**Number of facilities**

elementary schools: 16
junior high/middle schools: 3
senior high schools: 2
other: 8

**Student/teacher ratio:** 16.6:1

**Teacher salaries (2005–06)**

elementary median: $50,500
junior high/middle median: $52,390
secondary median: $50,380

**Funding per pupil:** $9,438

Private schools in Kalamazoo are primarily affiliated with Christian churches.

***Public Schools Information:*** Kalamazoo Public Schools, 1220 Howard St., Kalamazoo, MI 49008; telephone (269)337-0100; www.kalamazoopublic-schools.com

## Colleges and Universities

Western Michigan University (WMU), one of the top public research universities in the country, offers 141 degree and certificate programs to its nearly 20,000 undergraduates. Its wide array of centers and institutes conduct research and share knowledge gained with business, government, and other organizations.

Kalamazoo College, Michigan's oldest college (founded in 1833), is located in Kalamazoo's historic district and offers its 1,234 students bachelor of arts degree programs in 25 majors and 9 areas of concentration,

such as international and area studies, environmental studies, public policy and urban affairs, and others. The University has a unique curriculum design known as the K-Plan, which emphasizes experiential learning through internships, study abroad and research projects. *U.S. News & World Report* ranked Kalamazoo College as 69th among liberal arts colleges in the United States in 2008. Among its 19 buildings and facilities are the Dow Science Center and the Stryker Center, which offers seminars in business and management.

Davenport University, the largest independent university system in the state, is based in Grand Rapids but has more than 1,000 students on its Kalamazoo campus. The Kalamazoo campus offers associate's and bachelor's degrees as well as certificate programs in a variety of areas in business, health care, and legal studies.

Kalamazoo Valley Community College offers its 9,300 students associate in arts, associate in science, and associate in applied science degrees, as well as certificates. It prides itself on its flexible scheduling and provides areas of study that include liberal arts, health and sciences, business, and the technologies. In September 2007 the college launched its Automotive Academy, an associate's degree program designed to train students to become automotive technicians. The program offers students the opportunity to work with the many automotive facilities located in the southwest Michigan area.

## Libraries and Research Centers

With a stunning granite and limestone exterior, the Kalamazoo Public Library has a four-level rotunda that admits natural light through a skylight via a 79-foot dome. The library's five buildings feature holographic materials and light sculptures that result in an ever-changing rainbow of colors. In addition to the central branch, the library maintains four branches and one bookmobile, contains roughly 275,000 fiction and non-fiction works, and maintains special collections in history, culture, African American studies, and Kalamazoo history. The Raymond W. Fox Law Library, a cooperative effort between the Kalamazoo Public Library and the County of Kalamazoo, serves as an important resource for local attorneys, as well as the general public.

Davenport University, Kalamazoo College, Kalamazoo Valley Community College, and Western Michigan University all have libraries. The W. E. Upjohn Institute for Employment Research Library has titles focusing on labor market issues and state and local economic development, among other topics. Borgess Health Information Library has a special community health information section and Bronson Methodist Hospital Library focuses on allied and consumer health issues.

Two research centers in Kalamazoo are the Kalamazoo Nature Center and the W. E. Upjohn Institute for Employment Research. Western Michigan University is the site of several research centers and institutes, including the Center for Autism, the Institute for Cistercian Studies, the Biological Imaging Center, Environmental Research Center, the Michigan Basin Core Research Laboratory, and the Walker Institute for the Study of Race and Ethnic Relations, to name a few. The university is also a primary sponsor of the Business Technology and Research Park development, which is designed to serve as a central location for the growth and development of high-tech industry in the city.

***Public Library Information:*** Kalamazoo Public Library, 315 S. Rose St., Kalamazoo, MI 49007; telephone (269)342-9837; www.kpl.gov

# ■ Health Care

The health care sector is one of the largest employment industries in the Kalamazoo area. The Borgess Medical Center and the Bronson Methodist Hospital are two of the largest employers in Kalamazoo. Borgess Medical Center, with 424 beds, has special units in coronary, cardiac surgery, intensive, and neurointensive care. It also hosts a Sleep Disorders Clinic, a Women's Heart Program, and the Borgess Wound Care Clinic. The BMC Trauma Center is a Level 1 trauma care site.

Bronson Methodist Hospital, the flagship hospital of Bronson Healthcare Group, has 343 beds and is home to a Level 1 trauma center, the designated Children's Hospital, the Bronson Center for Women, and the Heart Hospital at Bronson. The hospital also has special care units for burn patients, neonatal intensive care, pediatric intensive care, trauma care, and a hyperbaric unit.

Kalamazoo Regional Psychiatric Hospital, established in 1859, provides inpatient services for approximately 100 patients.

# ■ Recreation

### Sightseeing

Kalamazoo's Bronson Park is the centerpiece of the city's downtown and features sculptures, war monuments, and historical markers and hosts various festivals and cultural events. Maps for self-directed walking and driving tours of three historic districts throughout Kalamazoo are available from the Convention Bureau and at City Hall. The Village of Schoolcraft offers tours by appointment of the 1835 Underground Railroad Home where a local physician once hid escaped slaves.

Kalamazoo Valley Museum, in the city's downtown, features the Stryker Theater, a planetarium, a creative preschool activity area, and the Challenger Learning Center, in which children can take off on a simulated space mission. It also houses a 2,300-year-old mummy and hands-on science and history exhibits. The Kalamazoo Institute of Arts includes an interactive gallery called

ARTworks, a new community auditorium, and a museum store, with more than 50,000 items in its various collections.

The Kalamazoo Nature Center has an exhibit hall where visitors can perform experiments, learn about plants and animals, and view natural objects magnified ten-fold. Its Parfet Butterfly House provides an indoor tropical sun-rain room, an outdoor garden, and a barn that houses farm animals. Also on site are an 11-acre arboretum and nature trails that are wheelchair and stroller accessible. In nearby Augusta is the Kellogg Bird Sanctuary where year-round visitors can walk a self-guided trail and observe the native waterfowl and birds of prey along Wintergreen Lake. Also in Augusta is the Fort Custer National Cemetery, an official burial ground for U.S. veterans, which contains the graves of 26 German soldiers held as American prisoners during World War II.

The Kalamazoo Air Zoo presents a display of over 60 vintage aircraft and an area that allows visitors to climb into mock cockpits and pretend to fly. Rides include a virtual reality simulator and a four-dimensional theater that puts visitors in the middle of a World War II bombing mission. In 2007 the Air Zoo opened its Space & Science exhibit, a collection of artifacts from the Smithsonian Air and Space Museum. In nearby Hickory Corners, auto buffs can visit Gilmore Car Museum, rated one of the ten best such museums in the country. The museum outlines the development of the American car in a six-barn, 90-acred, landscaped setting and features over 240 vehicles from the past century. In 2004 the museum began a large expansion project intended to expand the museum by almost 50 percent, making more room for the large number of vehicles. The first phase of this expansion, which included the addition of a new diner for museum patrons, was unveiled in 2007.

Visitors to what was once known as "Celery City" can experience what life was like during the city's past in nearby Portage, were the Celery Flats Interpretive Center features exhibits of the age of celery production. Music lovers can visit the Gibson Heritage Guitar building, a factory where Gibson Guitars were built in the early 1900s.

The Wolf Lake State Fish Hatchery, eight miles west of Kalamazoo, has hourly tours, a slide show, and a display pond. The Kellogg Dairy Center in Hickory Corners provides various tours where visitors can learn about the dairy cycle and observe a computerized milking parlor.

### Arts and Culture

The Epic Center Complex is the primary center for the arts in Kalamazoo. It is home to the Arts Council of Greater Kalamazoo, the Black Arts and Cultural Center, the Crescendo Academy of Music, Fontana Chamber Arts, and the Kalamazoo Symphony Orchestra. The Gilmore International Keyboard Festival and the Stulberg String Competition are based at the Epic Center as well.

Kalamazoo Symphony Orchestra (KSO) presents a full concert series, as well as chamber and family concerts year-round. KSO also offers free summer concerts at local parks. During the 2005-06 season the orchestra performed more than 30 concerts, reaching over 100,000 people in eight counties of southwest Michigan, and made 300 educational and community engagement appearances. Fontana Chamber Arts presents chamber music concerts at various sites throughout the city. In late 2006 Fontana Chamber Arts received an award from the Chamber Music Association for its adventurous programming. The Kalamazoo Concert Band, made up of adult musicians and founded in 1961, presents a series of concerts at several local venues. An array of dance performances, from ballet and folk to highland flings, are presented by the Kalamazoo Ballet Company at the Comstock Community Auditorium and other sites throughout the city.

Miller Auditorium at the Western Michigan University campus made its debut in 1968 and now is the site of touring Broadway shows, conventions, and jazz, rock, and symphonic concerts. Wings Stadium hosts arena-style concerts of popular music acts for audiences of about 8,000. In 2007 the stadium hosted 70 different events over 181 days. The 1,569-seat State Theatre, built in 1927, features music and comedy performers under a star-spangled sky projected on the ceiling. Chenery Auditorium hosts concerts and travel-film series in its handsome 1,900-seat public facility. The intimate 200-seat Suzanne D. Parish Theatre carries several plays throughout the year, while the Carver Center hosts the Civic Arena Theatre, Civic Black Theatre, and Kalamazoo Civic Youth Theatre, among others.

Several area theaters offer a variety of performances, such as WMU's Irving S. Gilmore Theatre Complex, which also hosts a biennial music festival, the Actors & Playwrights' Initiative (API) Theatre, and the Whole Art Theater Company. The New Vic Theatre presents both experimental and traditional fare, including an annual holiday schedule of *A Christmas Carol*. As of 2007 the theatre had presented 325 productions. During its 16-week summer-stock season, the Barn Theatre in nearby Augusta draws about 50,000 patrons.

## Festivals and Holidays

Autumn in Kalamazoo offers the National Street Rod Association race at the Kalamazoo County Fairgrounds. In October Union Pine Wine Sellers holds an annual wine festival with wine tasings, while the annual Festival of Trees takes place at the Radisson Plaza Hotel in November. The Kalamazoo holiday parade takes place in November with floats, marching bands and elves passing out candy and prizes along the parade route in downtown Kalamazoo. December brings the New Year's Fest at Bronson Park and surrounding buildings.

The cold winter weather is perfect for January's Great Winter Adventure, featuring ice sculpting, and at nearby Timber Ridge visitors can enjoy a variety of snow-related activities at the Winter Fest Fun event. Kalamazoo also hosts the Snow Cross Conquest in January, when snowboarders and downhill skiers compete for awards and prizes on Kalamazoo slopes. March turns downtown green for the St. Patrick's Day parade; the Kalamazoo Nature Center is sticky sweet with the Maple Sugar Festival.

The Gold Company hosts an annual jazz competition at Miller Auditorium in early spring. The Annual Spring Conference on Wind and Percussion takes place at WMU/Miller Auditorium in early April and proud canines are the focus of the West Michigan Apple Blossom Cluster A.K.C. Dog Show at the Kalamazoo County Fairgrounds in May.

Among June's activities are the Mayfair celebration at Bronson Park, the Dionysos Greekfest, and the Island Fest at Arcadia Festival Site. Also in June are the Kalamazoo Institute of Arts's Art Fair at Bronson Park, the Do-Dah Parade downtown, and the Parade of Homes, which takes place throughout the Kalamazoo area. The actors of the Michigan Shakespeare Festival take the stage at the Celery Flats Amphitheater at the end of the month.

In July, the Great Lakes Folk Festival is at Celery Flats and the Team U.S. National Hot-Air Balloon championship takes flight at Kellogg Airfield in Battle Creek. Other July events include the Blues Festival, a Taste of Kalamazoo at the Arcadia Festival Place, the New Orleans festival celebrating cajun culture and food, Warbirds Over Kalamazoo at the Kalamazoo Aviation History Museum, and the Silver Leaf Renaissance Faire, which is presented on certain weekends at the River Oaks County Park.

The Kalamazoo County Fair at the Fairgrounds brings food and fun to the citizenry in August, which is also the month for the Ribfest at the Arcadia Festival Site, the weeklong Black Arts Festival that can be seen at various downtown locations, the two-day Red Barns Spectacular at the Gilmore Car Museum, and the Scottish Fest at the Kalamazoo County Fairgrounds.

Arcadia Creek in downtown Kalamazoo is a popular festival area that features a natural river encased underground and surrounded by a park. On the first Friday of the month, starting at 5:00 p.m., Kalamazoo's art galleries and businesses open up for the Kalamazoo Art Hop, which highlights a wide variety of different artists. Every other spring, Kalamazoo is the site of the Gilmore International Keyboard Festival, which involves more than 100 keyboard-related events that take place throughout western Michigan. Kalamazoo also hosts the Kalamazoo Animation Festival International on alternate years. The festival attracts the world's best animatiors and artists together for competition, seminars, retrospectives and screenings.

## Sports for the Spectator

Kalamazoo's professional hockey team, the Michigan K-Wings, is in the International Hockey League (IHL) and plays at Wings Stadium. The Kalamazoo area is also home to the men's Kalamazoo Kingdom of the United Soccer Leagues (USL) and the women's Kalamazoo Quest of the United Systems of Independent Soccer League (USIS). Stowe Stadium at Kalamazoo College hosts the U.S. Tennis Association Boys' 18 and 16 National Tennis Championship in Kalamazoo. Famous tennis players, such as Pete Sampras, Andre Agassi, and John McEnroe all played in Kalamazoo during their junior careers. Since 1980 the Little League Girls' Softball Senior and Big League World Series is held at Vanderberg Park. NASCAR racing has a weekly series at the Kalamazoo Speedway. The Kalamazoo Xplosion, a minor league team of the Continental Indoor Football League, plays at Wings Stadium.

Fans of college sports have many events from which to choose. Western Michigan University has men's baseball, basketball, football, ice hockey, soccer, tennis, and track/cross country, while women compete in basketball, gymnastics, indoor and outdoor track, soccer, softball, tennis, volleyball, golf, precision ice skating, and track/cross country. Many of the competitions are open to spectators.

Kalamazoo College has varsity men's teams competing in baseball, basketball, cross-country, football, golf, soccer, swimming, and tennis. Women's teams compete in basketball, cross country, softball, soccer, swimming, tennis, volleyball, and golf. The Cougars of Kalamazoo Valley Community College have intercollegiate competitions in volleyball, basketball, softball, and tennis for women, and basketball, baseball, tennis, and golf for men.

## Sports for the Participant

The city of Kalamazoo has 36 parks and nine golf courses. Bronson Park is one of the most popular in the city and serves as a site for several festivals and events throughout the year. VerSluis/Dickinson Park features 17 municipal softball and baseball fields, sand volleyball courts, and a cricket field. Wood's Lake is the only public swimming beach in the city. Knollwood Park features an 18-hole disc golf course and lighted soccer fields. Kalamazoo County offers more than 100 public outdoor tennis courts, including Kalamazoo College's Stowe Stadium, and boating opportunities on nearby Gull Lake and Lake Michigan. The Kal-Haven Trail, which runs from the city to South Haven, Michigan, is a multiuse trail for biking, hiking, snowmobiling, and cross country skiing that runs for 34 miles. Water sports are readily accessed via the area's 83 public-access lakes.

## Shopping and Dining

Kalamazoo has four major shopping malls. Kalamazoo Mall, once famous as the first outdoor pedestrian shopping mall in the country, features a variety of shops, galleries, and dining establishments. Four large department stores anchor the Crossroads regional shopping mall, which has more than 100 specialty stores and restaurants. Maple Hill Mall, home to a major office store and discount and specialty stores, underwent renovations in 2001, expanding to 642,000 square feet. Southland Mall features office, book, and clothing shops, as well as other retail stores.

Southwestern Michigan is known for its wineries and microbreweries, whose products can be enjoyed at the wide selection of restaurants in Kalamazoo. Dining choices run from ethnic restaurants featuring Mexican, Italian, Greek, Australian, and Chinese cuisine to local and chain establishments that serve hearty American fare, such as St. Louis-style ribs, seafood, fresh fish, prime rib, and other favorites. The Black Swan provides gourmet continental cuisine with choices like leg of lamb or Beef Wellington for two in its attractive location on Willow Lake. The Black Swan is part of the Millenium Restaurant Group, a professional restaurant company with five restaurant properties and a catering service in the Southwest Michigan area. Webster's Restaurant at the Radisson Plaza hotel is western Michigan's only AAA Four Diamond Award-winning restaurant and features seafood, chops, pasta, and fresh desserts. In 2007, Webster's restaurant offered over 200 wines as part of seasonal menues.

***Visitor Information:*** Kalamazoo County Convention & Visitors Bureau, 141 E. Michigan St., Kalamazoo, MI 49007-3783; telephone (269)488-9000; toll-free (800)888-0509; www.discoverkalamazoo.com

# ■ Convention Facilities

Among Kalamazoo's major conference facilities is the Bernhard Center at Western Michigan University, which has 25 meeting rooms with a maximum capacity of 1,700 people in meeting-style and 1,250 in banquet-style rooms. The Bernhard Canter also has a mall located on its lower level with a food court and several shops and businesses. The John E. Fetzer Center on the Western Michigan University campus has 13 meeting rooms, including a 280-seat banquet area, a 90-seat lecture hall, and a 250-seat auditorium.

The County Center Building furnishes five meeting rooms, the largest of which can accommodate a banquet of 1,300 people. The James W. Miller Auditorium, on Western Michigan University's campus, has two meeting rooms that support 3,485 meeting-style or classroom-style. The auditorium is the third largest theater in Michigan. The Wings Stadium Complex has three meeting rooms. About 8,032 can be seated in the stadium, 2,850 in "The Annex," and 350 in "The Cube." The largest exhibit space is 17,000 square feet and seats 5,113 arena-style.

Dr. William E. Upjohn's former home, Brook Lodge, provides 12,000 square feet of meeting space on an exquisite 637-acre estate. The Yarrow Golf & Conference Center has 12 meeting rooms for up to 300 guests with an 18-hole championship course as the backdrop.

Other meeting or event locations include the Kalamazoo Civic Center, the Kalamazoo State Theater, the Epic Center Complex, and the Cityscape Event Center.

The Clarion Hotel offers 13 meeting rooms and features a 400-seat ballroom along with several banquet-style and classroom-style options in 5,000 square feet of meeting space. The Radisson Plaza Hotel & Suites has 44,000 square feet of meeting space, including 21 meeting rooms with a capacity of 1,000 people, 850 for a banquet, or 544 in classrooms. Holiday Inn West has six meeting rooms including a 400-seat ballroom for receptions.

***Convention Information:*** Kalamazoo County Convention & Visitors Bureau, 141 E. Michigan St., Kalamazoo, MI 49007-3783; telephone (269)488-9000; toll-free (800)888-0509; www.discoverkalamazoo.com

## ■ Transportation

### Approaching the City

The Kalamazoo/Battle Creek International Airport is located on Portage Road in Kalamazoo, just south of Interstate 94. The airport serves over 500,000 passengers annually on four commercial airlines. There are over 50 flights each day. Major highways leading to Kalamazoo include Interstate-94 (running east-west) and U.S. highway 131 (running north-south). Amtrak provides daily rail service to the downtown Internodal Transportation Center, which also receives passengers from Greyhound and Indian Trail buslines.

### Traveling in the City

Local bus service is provided by Kalamazoo Metro Transit, which also operates Metro Van service, a demand-response service for people with disabilities. Two charter bus lines along with several cab services are available.

## ■ Communications

### Newspapers and Magazines

Kalamazoo's daily paper is the *Kalamazoo Gazette*. Western Michigan University's *The Western Herald* student newspaper is published Monday-Thursday throughout the academic year. *Flashes Shopping Guide* appears weekly.

Local magazines include *Bloodlines, Coonhound Bloodlines,* and *Hunting Retriever*, all of which are published by the United Kennel Club. *Business Outlook for West Michigan* is a quarterly publication of the Upjohn Institute. *Third Coast* is a literary magazine published by the Western Michigan University English Department.

A number of journals are associated with WMU and cover business, accounting, drama, Medieval studies, and sociology. Fetzer Institute publishes *Advances in Mind Body Medicine,* a journal on mind-body health.

### Television and Radio

Kalamazoo has one network, one independent, and one cable television station. The city has 13 AM and FM radio stations with a variety of music, news, and talk formats available.

***Media Information:*** *Kalamazoo Gazette*, 401 S. Burdick St., Kalamazoo, MI 49007; telephone (269)345-3511

### Kalamazoo Online

City of Kalamazoo home page. Available www .kalamazoocity.org

Kalamazoo County Convention & Visitors Bureau. Available www.discoverkalamazoo.com

*Kalamazoo Gazette.* Available www.mlive.com/ kzgazette

Kalamazoo Public Library. Available www.kpl.gov

Kalamazoo Public Schools. Available www .kalamazoopublicschools.com

Kalamazoo Regional County Chamber of Commerce. Available www.kazoochamber.com

BIBLIOGRAPHY

Durant, Samuel W., and Ruth Marian Robbins Monteith, *History of Kalamazoo County, Michigan: With Illustrations and Biographical Sketches of its Prominent Men and Pioneers* (Evansville, IN: Unigraphic, 1976)

Lane, Kit, *Built on the Banks of the Kalamazoo* (Douglas, MI: Pavilion Press, 1993)

Massie, Larry B., and Peter J. Schmitt, *Kalamazoo: The Place Behind the Products* (Sun Valley, CA: American Historical Press, 1998)

# Lansing

## ■ The City in Brief

**Founded:** 1837 (incorporated 1849)

**Head Official:** Mayor Virg Bernero (since 2006)

**City Population**

> 1980: 130,414
> 1990: 127,321
> 2000: 119,128
> 2006 estimate: 114,276
> Percent change, 1990–2000: −6.4%
> U.S. rank in 1980: 122nd
> U.S. rank in 1990: 142nd
> U.S. rank in 2000: 204th

**Metropolitan Area Population**

> 1980: 420,000
> 1990: 432,684
> 2000: 447,728
> 2006 estimate: 454,044
> Percent change, 1990–2000: 3.5%
> U.S. rank in 1980: 81st
> U.S. rank in 1990: Not available
> U.S. rank in 2000: 92nd

**Area:** 35.24 square miles (2000)

**Elevation:** 880 feet above sea level

**Average Annual Temperatures:** January, 21.6° F; July, 70.3° F; annual average, 46.8° F

**Average Annual Precipitation:** 31.53 inches of rain; 48.8 inches of snow

**Major Economic Sectors:** Government, trade, services, manufacturing

**Unemployment Rate:** 6.2% (June 2007)

**Per Capita Income:** $17,888 (2005)

**2005 FBI Crime Index Property:** 4,745

**2005 FBI Crime Index Violent:** 1,407

**Major Colleges and Universities:** Michigan State University, Lansing Community College

**Daily Newspaper:** *Lansing State Journal*

## ■ Introduction

Lansing is the capital of Michigan and the focus of a metropolitan statistical area that includes the city of East Lansing and Clinton, Eaton, and Ingham counties. Virtually a wilderness when the site was designated for the building of the state capital, Lansing was slow to develop until the arrival of the railroad. The nation's first land grant college was founded in Lansing, and the city became a world leader in the automotive industry through the pioneering work of the Olds Motor Vehicle Company. Today Lansing's status as the state capital, its industrial base including General Motors, its stable economy, and the presence of Michigan State University in East Lansing contribute to the city's overall strength. These attributes also led *Expansion Management* magazine to name Lansing as Michigan's only "Five Star" city for "Quality of Life Quotient" in 2003 and 2004.

## ■ Geography and Climate

Lansing is located on the Grand River at its junction with the Red Cedar River. The area climate alternates between continental and semi-marine. When little or no wind is present, the weather becomes continental, producing pronounced fluctuations in temperature. The weather turns semi-marine with a strong wind from the Great

Lakes. Snowfall averages about 49 inches annually. Tornadoes occur occasionally, as do thunder and wind storms. Flooding is likely one year out of three; floods cause extensive damage one year out of ten.

**Area:** 35.24 square miles (2000)

**Elevation:** 880 feet above sea level

**Average Temperatures:** January, 21.6° F; July, 70.3° F; annual average, 46.8° F

**Average Annual Precipitation:** 31.53 inches of rain; 48.8 inches of snow

# ■ History

## Wilderness Site Chosen for State Capital

The original settlers of Lansing arrived at the junction of the Grand and Red Cedar rivers expecting to find New Settlement, a city that turned out to exist only on paper. Most of the pioneers were from the village of Lansing, New York, and some decided to settle the area, deciding to call it Lansing Township in honor of their former home. James Seymour, another resident of New York State, migrated to Detroit in the mid-1830s and acquired land holdings in the Michigan interior for purposes of speculation. Seymour was aware that the Michigan constitution of 1835 specified that a permanent site be found by 1847 for the state capital, which was then temporarily located in Detroit. The legislators feared Detroit's proximity to Canada would make it susceptible to foreign invasion, as had been the case in the War of 1812 when it fell under British rule. Since no mutually agreed-upon township could be found, Seymour pressed the idea of Lansing as the site, but his suggestion initially evoked laughter from the legislators. Seymour's persistence finally prevailed and Lansing, a wilderness spot with one log house and a sawmill, became the new center of Michigan's government.

By December 1847, a frame capitol building had been built, and the creation of a business district had begun at the point where Main Street and Washington Avenue now meet. Lansing was incorporated with a population of 1,500 inhabitants in 1849. Five years later a new brick capitol was constructed. Small agricultural implement industries began to introduce mechanical farming techniques to combat the manpower shortage caused by the Civil War. Development, however, was slowed by lack of transportation and the uncertainty of retaining the state capital at Lansing. But the arrival of the railroad boosted the economy by linking Lansing with the rest of the state. The legislature appropriated funding for a new capitol, which was completed in 1878 on a 10-acre park near the Grand River in the center of the city at a cost of more than $1.4 million.

## Industry and Education Join Government

Automotive innovator Ransom E. Olds, who used gasoline power instead of steam, founded the Olds Motor Vehicle Company in 1897. Olds is credited with building the first practical automobile, and by the turn of the century his company was the world's largest car manufacturer and had earned a reputation for high quality. Olds's company lived on as the Oldsmobile Division of General Motors until its discontinuation in 2004. By 1904 Lansing was the base of more than 200 manufacturing businesses and a world leader in the production of agricultural implements, automobiles, and gasoline engines.

Farmers had created the Michigan Agricultural Society in 1850 as a means to be heard in the state legislature. Many of the settlers from the East placed high value on education and culture; they petitioned the state legislature through the Agricultural Society for a college of agriculture to be founded separately from the University of Michigan in Ann Arbor. The nation's oldest land-grant institution, created as part of Michigan's state constitution of 1850, was thus granted authorization in 1855. The Michigan Agricultural College was founded on 676 acres in the woods three miles east of Lansing in present-day East Lansing, which was granted a city charter in 1907. The name of the college was changed to Michigan State College of Agriculture and Applied Sciences in 1923, and became a university upon its centennial celebration in 1955. Finally, in 1964, the name was shortened to Michigan State University.

Today, Lansing is a community where government, industry, education, and culture thrive. Although the city itself has witnessed a population decrease, the metropolitan area increased its population in the early 2000s. Residents enjoy the area for its economic stability and variety of activities. The business climate is active and was recognized by *Entrepreneur* magazine in 2003 as number seven on its list of "Best Cities for Entrepreneurs: Top Midsize Cities in the Midwest." The nearby residence of Michigan State University fosters an academia-minded atmosphere that contributed to the area's seventh place ranking in Richard Florida's bestselling book "Rise of the Creative Class" in 2002 as one of the "Top Ten Most Creative Small Cities."

***Historical Information:*** Library of Michigan, 702 W. Kalamazoo St., Lansing, MI 48909-7507; telephone (517)373-1580; fax (517)373-4480

# ■ Population Profile

## Metropolitan Area Residents

1980: 420,000
1990: 432,684
2000: 447,728

2006 estimate: 454,044
Percent change, 1990–2000: 3.5%
U.S. rank in 1980: 81st
U.S. rank in 1990: Not available
U.S. rank in 2000: 92nd

**City Residents**

1980: 130,414
1990: 127,321
2000: 119,128
2006 estimate: 114,276
Percent change, 1990–2000: −6.4%
U.S. rank in 1980: 122nd
U.S. rank in 1990: 142nd
U.S. rank in 2000: 204th

**Density:** 3,399.0 people per square mile (2000)

**Racial and ethnic characteristics (2005)**

White: 80,686
Black: 28,016
American Indian and Alaska Native: 520
Asian: 4,164
Native Hawaiian and Pacific Islander: 85
Hispanic or Latino (may be of any race): 12,175
Other: 3,497

**Percent of residents born in state:** 72.8% (2000)

**Age characteristics (2005)**

Population under 5 years old: 10,480
Population 5 to 9 years old: 8,181
Population 10 to 14 years old: 8,556
Population 15 to 19 years old: 7,254
Population 20 to 24 years old: 12,162
Population 25 to 34 years old: 19,259
Population 35 to 44 years old: 16,346
Population 45 to 54 years old: 16,034
Population 55 to 59 years old: 5,924
Population 60 to 64 years old: 4,380
Population 65 to 74 years old: 5,467
Population 75 to 84 years old: 4,224
Population 85 years and older: 1,408
Median age: 30.8 years

**Births (2006, MSA)**

Total number: 5,558

**Deaths (2006, MSA)**

Total number: 3,454

**Money income (2005)**

Per capita income: $17,888
Median household income: $34,367
Total households: 49,552

**Number of households with income of...**

less than $10,000: 5,880
$10,000 to $14,999: 3,944
$15,000 to $24,999: 9,238
$25,000 to $34,999: 6,129
$35,000 to $49,999: 8,142
$50,000 to $74,999: 9,157
$75,000 to $99,999: 4,914
$100,000 to $149,999: 1,852
$150,000 to $199,999: 148
$200,000 or more: 148

**Percent of families below poverty level:** 15.4% (2005)

**2005 FBI Crime Index Property:** 4,745

**2005 FBI Crime Index Violent:** 1,407

## ■ Municipal Government

Lansing city government is administered by an eight-member council and a mayor, who does not serve as a member of council; all are elected to four-year terms.

**Head Official:** Mayor Virg Bernaro (D) (since 2006; current term expires 2010)

**Total Number of City Employees:** 1,100 (2007)

*City Information:*   City Hall, 124 W. Michigan Ave., Lansing, MI 48933; telephone (517)483-4000

## ■ Economy

### Major Industries and Commercial Activity

The state government is naturally the most significant employer within the city. Services, wholesale and retail trade, education, and manufacturing (primarily of transportation products) comprise the economic base of the Lansing metropolitan area. Health care accounts for the largest share of the services sector, followed by business services and trade associations. Many insurance companies have corporate or regional offices in Lansing; several are headquartered there. Other important sectors are education—with nearby Michigan State University having annual revenues of about $1.6 billion—along with transportation and public utilities.

The Lansing region is an important notch in the Midwest manufacturing belt. Despite the 2004 departure of the historic Oldsmobile plant, the city received a huge boost by the 2001 opening of a new General Motors (GM) plant. Although the company shut down operations in its Lansing assembly plant in 2005, the company opened a new facility in 2006 in nearby Delta Township, transferring many of its Lansing employees. Industrial leaders such as GM adapt progressive manufacturing processes and new technology. Many firms are following GM's lead to institute advanced materials-handling techniques and to encourage participatory management, with the goal of improving product quality and increasing competitiveness. However, between 2005 and 2006 manufacturing employment dipped by five percent in Lansing. A variety of high-technology firms spawned at Michigan State University have pushed for rapid growth in that industry. Wholesale trade and construction were among the fastest-growing area industries in the mid-2000s.

Major employers include Michigan State University, General Motors, Sparrow Health Systems, and Meijer, a grocery company.

## Incentive Programs—New and Existing Companies

*Local programs:* Promoting the local economy and providing assistance to businesses is the Lansing Economic Development Corporation. The Lansing Brownfield Redevelopment Authority (LBRA) is operated by the city and provides many tax relief benefits to redevelopers. Partnering with the Michigan Economic Development Corporation (MEDC), the LBRA assists in finding sites for businesses to locate and has also received two grants from the U.S. Environmental Protection Agency that it in turn awards. Technology-based business growth in the area is encouraged by the MEDC and the Lansing Regional SmartZone program.

*State programs:* The creation of new jobs that feed into a prosperous economy is the purpose behind the Michigan Economic Growth Authority. Fiscally-responsible companies in the fields of manufacturing, research and development, wholesale trade, or office operations can make use of Small Business Tax credits. The Lansing area has two designated Renaissance Zones that, if a business locates inside one of them, allow for waiving a variety of taxes such as the single business tax, local real property tax, and utility users tax. Lansing's Rensaissance Zones were scheduled to retain their designation until December 2008.

Michigan communities can abate up to 50 percent of local property taxes for up to 12 years. State law also exempts inventory, pollution control equipment, and certain tools, dies, jigs, and fixtures from local property taxes. State law also allows the city of Lansing to abate all new personal property taxes in certain geographic areas to spur economic development. Abatements include all millage, state and local taxes. Eligible projects include manufacturing, mining, research and development, wholesale and trade, and office operations, but not retail businesses.

Michigan has created a system of financial institutions called BIDCOs (Business and Industrial Development Corporations). These semiprivate, independent operations are chartered and partially capitalized by the state and are designed to provide mezzanine-level financing. This is for capital of higher risk than traditional banks will consider and of lower return than venture-capital companies demand.

*Job training programs:* Michigan offers a coordinated job training system called Michigan Works! using federal, state, and local resources to provide a highly productive and trained workforce. The federal Workforce Investment Act and the Michigan Department of Labor and Economic Growth provide funding for the grants that assist in increasing worker productivity. The training itself is done through the institution of the company's choice. Free recruitment and screening services are available for new and expanding employers through the Michigan Employment Security Administration's job service and also through several local school districts.

## Development Projects

Lansing's downtown area continues to undergo a facelift that began in the late 1990s. Loft development is bolstered by grant monies if certain criteria are met.

Although General Motors shut down its Lansing assembly plant in 2005, another GM assembly plant in Delta Township began operations in 2006, producing the Saturn Outlook, Buick Enclave and the GMC Acadia.

In 2007 the Accident Fund announced a revitilization of the historic Ottawa Power Station, which was to be converted into the Accident Fund's national headquarters. Although no completion date had been announced, the project was expected to retain nearly 700 jobs in downtown Lansing, create an additional 500 jobs and reopen the riverfront to public access. Also in 2007 private developers announced a prospective $30-million high-rise luxury condominium development on the site of the former City Club of Lansing on the Grand River in downtown Lansing. The project was pending voter-approval, and no completion date had been announced as of December 2007.

*Economic Development Information:* Lansing Regional Chamber of Commerce, 300 E. Michigan Ave., Ste. 300, PO Box 14030, Lansing, MI 48901; telephone (517)487-6340; fax (517)484-6910

## Commercial Shipping

The CN North America, CSX, and Norfolk Southern rail freight lines serve Lansing. More than 30 motor freight carriers transport goods from the city to markets throughout the country. Air cargo shipments through Capital City Airport increased by more than 10% in 2006 over the previous year, due largely to expanded UPS service. Four interstate highways connect the area to all major North American markets, including Canada.

*Image copyright David M. Converse/Lumigraphic, 2007. Used under license from Shutterstock.com.*

## Labor Force and Employment Outlook

Lansing area employers draw from a large, stable pool of highly skilled, educated, professional workers. Michigan State University's thousands of graduates add to the pool; approximately 30 percent of the labor force that is 25 years old and older has at least an undergraduate degree; nearly 40 percent has a graduate or professional degree.

The forecast for occupational categories in the Lansing/East Lansing area by the Michigan Department of Labor & Economic Growth projected a 10 percent increase in all occupations by 2012. The occupation sector projected to have the fastest growth in the Lansing MSA between 2000 and 2010 was the computer support field, a sector that was expected to grow by more than two-thirds. Five of the eight fastest-growing fields were expected to be in the computer industry.

In October 2007 the unemployment rate in Lansing/East Lansing stood at 5.4 percent, above the national average but down from 10-year highs of 7.2 percent, reached in July of that same year, as well as 2006.

Between 1997 and the end of 2006, the labor force in the metropolitan Lansing area grew from 237,229 workers to 252,124 workers.

The following is a summary of data regarding the Lansing-East Lansing metropolitan area labor force, 2006 annual averages.

**Size of nonagricultural labor force: 227,400**

**Number of workers employed in . . .**

  construction and mining: 8,400
  manufacturing: 21,800
  trade, transportation and utilities: 36,400
  information: 2,900
  financial activities: 15,300
  professional and business services: 20,500
  educational and health services: 28,000
  leisure and hospitality: 19,300
  other services: 11,000
  government: 63,800

**Average hourly earnings of production workers employed in manufacturing:** $23.97

**Unemployment rate:** 6.2% (June 2007)

| Largest employers (2006) | Number of employees |
|---|---|
| State of Michigan | 14,355 |
| Michigan State University | 10,500 |
| General Motors | 6,300 |
| Sparrow Health System | 6,000 |
| Lansing Community College | 3,180 |
| Ingham Regional Medical Center | 2,500 |
| Lansing School District | 2,106 |
| Meijer | 2000 |
| Auto Owners Insurance | 1,500 |
| Peckham, Inc. | 1,400 |

## Cost of Living

The following is a summary of data regarding several key cost of living factors in the Lansing area.

**2007 (1st quarter) ACCRA Average House Price:** Not available

**2007 (1st quarter) ACCRA Cost of Living Index:** Not available

**State income tax rate:** 3.9% of taxable income

**State sales tax rate:** 6.0%

**Local income tax rate:** 1.0% resident; 0.5% non-resident

**Local sales tax rate:** None

**Property tax rate:** Varies widely from 34.7 to 52.7 mills per $1,000 assessed value

*Economic Information:* Lansing Regional Chamber of Commerce, 300 E. Michigan Ave., Ste. 300, PO Box 14030, Lansing, MI 48901; telephone (517)487-6340; fax (517)484-6910

## ■ Education and Research

### Elementary and Secondary Schools

The Lansing School District, one of the largest in the state of Michigan, is administered by an elected nine-member, nonpartisan board of education that appoints a superintendent. Board members serve six-year terms and receive no salary for their positions. The district sponsors nine magnet schools as well as an Early Childhood Education Center and offers school choice to parents.

In 2007 the district drew up a four-year progress plan, "Protocols Of Progress 2008 - 2012," which created ten strategic committees to design and implement yearly academic acheivement goals, to be evaluated on an annual basis.

The following is a summary of data regarding the Lansing School District as of the 2005–2006 school year.

**Total enrollment:** 16,000

**Number of facilities**

elementary schools: 27
junior high/middle schools: 4
senior high schools: 3
other: 1

**Student/teacher ratio:** 17.6:1

**Teacher salaries (2005–06)**

elementary median: $53,940
junior high/middle median: $57,610
secondary median: $58,200

**Funding per pupil:** $10,666

In addition to the public system, church-affiliated schools provide K-12 education, and independent private schools and charter schools offer elementary education. Ingham, Eaton, and Clinton counties have more than 30 private and parochial schools; denominations include Roman Catholic, Lutheran, Baptist, and Seventh Day Adventist. Charter schools enroll about 1,700 students.

*Public Schools Information:* Lansing School District, 519 W. Kalamazoo St., Lansing, MI 48933; telephone (517)325-6200

### Colleges and Universities

Michigan State University (MSU) in East Lansing is the largest institution of higher learning in the area, with an enrollment of more than 45,000 students as of the fall of 2007. It maintains 660 buildings on about 5,200 acres of land for its diverse curriculum of more than 200 programs. According to the 2008 "Best Colleges" edition of *U.S. News & World Report,* MSU ranks 71st among the nation's top schools. The university has gained an international reputation for research and its sponsored funding topped $300 million in the 2003–2004 school year. The school boasts more than 200 programs of study offered by 17 degree-granting colleges and enrolls students from all 83 counties in Michigan, all 50 states in the United States, and approximately 130 other countries.

Thomas M. Cooley Law School in Lansing serves working professionals with a program leading to a Juris Law degree. Great Lakes Christian College offers undergraduate programs in theology, fine arts, and interdisciplinary studies. Lansing Community College in downtown Lansing provides vocational and technical curricula as well as training programs in more than 300 areas of study for its 32,000 annual students, more than 400 of whom are from countries other than the United States. Other schools in the three-county region are Olivet College, Davenport University, and the Capital Area Career Center.

## Libraries and Research Centers

About 25 libraries located in Lansing are maintained by educational institutions, government agencies, and hospitals. The Lansing Public Library is part of the Capital Area District Library, which was formed in 1998. The Lansing branch houses about 400,000 items for patron usage including books, periodical titles, microfilm, audio and video tapes, maps, and art reproductions; South Lansing residents enjoy their own branch. Materials pertaining to local history are among the special collections. The district library operates 13 branches and a bookmobile. Michigan State University maintains a main library and nine branches on campus with a collection that includes more than 4,500,000 volumes, 33,000 magazine and journal subscriptions, 200,000 maps, 40,000 sound recordings, and hundreds of electronic resources. Special collections include fine arts and map libraries.

Established in 1928, the Library of Michigan maintains holdings of well over 5.6 million volumes and special collections in such fields as Michigan local and family history and eighteenth- and nineteenth-century periodicals. Its total holding take up more than 27 miles of shelf space. The library includes the state law library, as well as one of the 10 largest genealogy collections in the country. The Library of Michigan also provides Braille and large-type books and serves as a depository for federal and state documents. Thomas M. Cooley Law School, Lansing Community College, and Great Lakes Christian College also maintain campus libraries.

World-class research is conducted at Michigan State University (MSU) in diverse disciplines related to communications, packaging, food science, and environmental engineering. MSU is home to the National Superconducting Cyclotron Laboratory (NSCL), the Composite Materials and Structures Center, the Crop and Food Bioprocessing Center, the Digital Learning Center for Microbial Ecology, and WKAR, a top public broadcasting center. Adjacent to MSU, the University Corporate Research Park is comprised of building sites on four to 40 acres. Resident companies enjoy access to MSU's scientific and technical facilities (laboratories, libraries, computerized data and research networks, closed circuit TV, and satellite systems).

The Composite Materials and Structure Center is a research partner with the Michigan Molecular Institute, the National Science Foundation, the Ford Motor Company, and the U.S. Department of Defense. The Pesticide Research Center works with pesticides and pest

control. The Michigan Biotechnology Institute (also known as MBI International), a non-profit corporation, applies recombinant deoxyribonucleic acid, plant tissue culture, and immobilized enzymes to the commercialization of biotechnology in the state of Michigan.

***Public Library Information:*** Lansing Public Library, 401 S. Capitol Ave., PO Box 40719, Lansing, MI 48901-7919; telephone (517)367-7919; fax (517)367-6363

## ■ Health Care

Six hospitals serve metropolitan Lansing. Ingham Regional Medical Center (formerly the Michigan Capital Medical Center) is a general acute care, nonprofit hospital with 338 beds. Ingham is affiliated with the Great Lakes Cancer Institute and has 30 additional affiliated practices and teaching clinics. Sparrow Health System, with 710 beds, maintains a wound center, a dialysis unit, a regional cancer center, and a family practice center. St. Lawrence Hospital, part of the Sparrow Health System, operates a poison control center, a health service for persons without physicians, and an alcohol detoxification and counseling unit. Sparrow, which is mid-Michigan's largest health care system, also includes Clinton Memorial Hospital. All major facilities in the city offer 24-hour emergency care and maintain maternity units. Michigan State University provides medical education and training through the College of Human Medicine (with 200 paid and more than 3,200 volunteer staff) and the College of Osteopathic Medicine; it also operates an outpatient clinic open to the public.

## ■ Recreation

### Sightseeing

Completed in 1879, Lansing's Capitol was one of the first state edifices built to emulate the nation's Capitol, and this National Historic Landmark is the center of attraction in Lansing's downtown sector. Two blocks southwest of the Capitol is the Michigan Library and Historical Center, a modern facility with an outdoor courtyard. The museum traces the history of Michigan from its remote past to the twenty-first century, including the evolution of the state's economy in agriculture, timber, mining, and manufacturing to the rise and dominance of the automobile. Impression 5 Science Museum stimulates the senses with interactive displays including a "Bubble Room" that was remodeled in 2005. Next to Impression 5 is the R. E. Olds Transportation Museum, a major transportation museum recognizing the contribution of Ransom E. Olds to the automotive industry and the evolution of transportation in Lansing.

Michigan State University (MSU) in neighboring East Lansing provides many sightseeing opportunities beginning with the W.J. Beal Botanical Gardens, the oldest, continuously operated garden of its type in the country, with 5,000 different types of plants. The university's horticultural demonstration gardens cover seven-and-a-half acres. Abrams Planetarium presents programs on space science topics in the 150-seat Digistar sky theater along with an exhibition area and the astronomy-related paintings at the "Blacklight Gallery." The MSU Museum houses displays on cultural and scientific developments, and the MSU Dairy Plant and Dairy Store offers daily tours at milking time.

Potter Park Zoo places its 100 species of animals in natural settings, with a special display on Michigan animals. The zoo includes an education center, and an animal clinic with the zoo's first full-time veterinarian; it was officially accredited in 2007.

At the Rose Lake Wildlife Research Station, 3,000 acres of woods and marsh are accessible via hiking trails; Woldumar Nature Center stresses environmental education, and its five miles of trails are open to the public for hiking or cross country skiing. Fenner Arboretum maintains self-guided trails leading to a prairie scene with live bison. Nature trails associated with Red Cedar River, Sanford Natural Area, and Baker Woodlot are islands of wilderness on the Michigan State University campus. The Ledges in Grand Ledge, 10 miles west of Lansing, is named for its rock formations, which rise along the Grand River and are over 300 million years old.

## Arts and Culture

Many of Lansing's cultural events take place at the Wharton Center for Performing Arts' two theaters on the campus of Michigan State University. Cobb Great Hall seats 2,500 guests and hosts Broadway and variety shows, while the Pasant Theatre has 600 seats for family presentations. Founded in 1929, the Greater Lansing Symphony Orchestra presents a season of classical and pops concerts with an annual attendance of 15,000 for about one dozen performances. Volunteer singers selected via auditions make up the Greater Lansing Arts Chorale, which presents three concerts per year.

Lansing is particularly strong in theater. The nationally known BoarsHead Theater, a residential professional company based at the Wharton Center, presents a season of modern and classical drama and comedy. Community theater companies are: the Lansing Civic Players Guild, the oldest group in the area, dating back to 1929; Lansing Community College's LCC Theater Program at Dart Auditorium; MSU's Department of Theatre, which features student productions; Riverwalk Theatre, the home to the Community Circle Players; and Spotlight Theatre in nearby Grand Ledge, with several American dramas running from May through early September.

The Greater Lansing Ballet Company is a semi-professional organization that presents classical and contemporary ballets and offers two international exchange programs with companies in Poland and Russia. The Children's Ballet Theatre of Michigan at the Wharton Center puts on holiday and spring shows.

The Lansing Arts Gallery, established in 1964, has two exhibition spaces with different exhibitions every month. At Michigan State University, the Department of Art and Art History displays student art throughout the year at the Kresge Art Museum.

***Arts and Culture Information:*** Arts Council of Greater Lansing, 425 S. Grand Ave., Lansing, MI 48933; telephone (517)372-4636; fax (517)484-2564; email info@lansingarts.org

## Festivals and Holidays

Greater Lansing hosts dozens of festivals and special events year-round. In late winter and early spring, the East Lansing Film Festival previews over 30 independently-made films worldwide but also challenges local talent (Michigan, Illinois, and Wisconsin) to a competition. The East Lansing Art Fair is held the third weekend in May, followed by the Lansing Festival of Art in the Park the last weekend in June at Ferris Park. Also in May, the Fiesta celebrates the Hispanic community with music, folklore performances, and a "Mexican Marketplace." The Lansing Concert Band gives a performance in Riverfront Park for the Fourth of July holiday with fireworks at dusk. Early August brings the Lansing Jazz Fest for two days of live jazz and music clinics; later in the month, the Great Lakes Folk Festival is three days of various activities including music, dance, and storytelling along with ethnic foods. The holiday season is celebrated in three major events: the MSU (Michigan State University) Holiday Arts & Crafts Show, held at the MSU Union for two days to present the works of about 200 regional artisans and crafters; Silver Bells in the City, which draws 80,000 to its parade and fireworks celebrating the lighting of Michigan's official holiday tree; and Wonderland of Lights at Potter Park, where thousands of lights adorn holiday displays and carolers and other musical performances come together.

## Sports for the Spectator

The Michigan State Spartans compete in the Big Ten athletic conference and field nationally competitive teams. The football team plays its home games in the 76,000-seat Spartan Stadium that was expanded in 2005 to accommodate 24 new suites and 862 club seats with access to an 18,500-square-foot club. Munn Ice Arena seats 6,470 fans and is the home of the Spartan hockey team. The Jack Breslin Student Events Center has been the home of the MSU basketball program since 1989; it seats more than 15,000 people.

Lansing's professional minor-league baseball team, the Lugnuts, play an April through September season at Oldsmobile Park. Playing in the western division of the Midwest League, the Lugnuts were previously affiliated with major league's Chicago Cubs but the 2005 season brought a switch to the Toronto Blue Jays. The Spartan Speedway attracts super and hobby stock car racing on Friday nights from mid-May through mid-September. Jackson Harness Raceway features seasonal parimutuel racing at night in nearby Jackson.

## Sports for the Participant

Golf is particularly popular at about three dozen public and private courses of varying difficulty in the area, and many golf tournaments are held in the summer. East Lansing's Timber Ridge was rated one of just twelve public courses in America to earn the top rating by *Golf Digest* magazine.

Nearly 200 city, county, and state parks, campgrounds, and recreation areas offer several thousand acres of green space and leisure opportunities in the Lansing region. River Trail features a canoeing route that follows the banks of the Grand and Red Cedar rivers through urban and natural environments and the campus of Michigan State University. The Brenke Fish Ladder is stocked with salmon and steelhead for urban fishing. Well supplied with bowling centers and ball fields, the Lansing area also has riding stables, about 300 indoor and outdoor tennis courts, and seven public access sites for boating.

The Summit at The Capital Centre is a modern, 180,000-square-foot facility that offers a wide array of sporting activities including ice hockey, soccer, dodge ball, and lacrosse. It also hosts one of the region's top gymnastics clubs, Geddert's Twisters. Other public ice skating facilities are available at Washington Park and Munn Arena at Michigan State University.

The region is noted for the variety of fish in rivers and lakes full of largemouth bass, northern pike, muskie, bluegill, crappie, and perch. Streams contain smallmouth bass, northern pike, walleye, and panfish. In addition, there are spawning runs of steelhead and Chinook salmon in several locations. Throughout the vicinity, state game lands and wooded areas offer rabbit, squirrel, pheasant, deer, and other game.

## Shopping and Dining

The largest shopping center in the region is the Lansing Mall, with over 125 stores and restaurants. An antiques and collectibles store called Pennyless in Paradise opened in 2004. However, one of the state's biggest antiques shops is The Mega Mall with over 300 booths on 40,000 square feet of space. In East Lansing, near the Michigan State University campus, specialty shops that cater to students are clustered among small restaurants, bookstores, and record shops.

The Lansing City Market, at the corner of Cedar Street and Shiawassee since 1909, offers a large selection of fresh fruits and vegetables. The Nokomis Learning Center, next door to Meridian Historic Village, sells beaded jewelry and other items handcrafted by local Native American artists. Several upscale restaurants are located near the university.

***Visitor Information:*** Greater Lansing Convention and Visitors Bureau, 1223 Turner St., Ste. 200, Lansing, MI 48906; telephone (517)487-6800

# ■ Convention Facilities

Meeting and convention planners can choose among several facilities in the Lansing area. The Lansing Center is situated downtown on the Grand River and Riverwalk near the Capitol Complex. It adjoins the Radisson Hotel and a 1,600-car parking area via an enclosed walkway. Accommodating up to 5,600 people and 71,000 square feet of exhibition space, the exhibit halls and meeting rooms function as separate units or in multiple combinations. In downtown Lansing, the Center for the Arts adjoins an art gallery and provides barrier-free space for functions with up to 240 participants.

The Breslin Center on the campus of Michigan State University (MSU) is a 254,000-square-foot facility offering 17,500 square feet of exhibition space, 30,000 maximum square feet of concourse area for product display, and state-of-the-art sound and lighting systems. MSU's Pavilion Agriculture and Livestock Education Center offers over 77,000 square feet in its facilities for trade shows, exhibitions, demonstrations, and livestock auctions.

Lansing-area hotels and motels, containing about 4,000 rooms for lodgings, also offer banquet and meeting rooms. One example is the Sheraton Lansing Hotel, with 212 guest rooms and 14,000 square feet of exhibit space.

***Convention Information:*** Greater Lansing Convention and Visitors Bureau, 1223 Turner St., Ste. 200, Lansing, MI 48906; telephone (517)487-6800

# ■ Transportation

## Approaching the City

Seven commercial airlines schedule regular daily flights into Capital City Airport, located 15 minutes from downtown Lansing. In 2006 there were 557,447 travellers who passed through Capital City Airport, a drop of approximately 8 percent from the previous year. Daily rail service to East Lansing from Chicago and Toronto is provided by Amtrak; Greyhound Bus Lines has terminals in Lansing and East Lansing.

An efficient highway system facilitates access to Lansing and its environs. Part of a beltway circling the southern half of the city, I-96 is intersected by several major and secondary routes; east-west I-69 completes the beltway around the northern sector. I-496 bisects the downtown area westward from north-south U.S. 127 in East Lansing. Other principal highways are U.S. 27 and M 99, both running north-south, and east-west M 43.

### Traveling in the City

Downtown Lansing streets are laid out on a strict grid system with the Capitol Complex as the center of orientation; the web of one-way streets can be confusing. Public bus transportation is provided by Capital Area Transportation Authority (CATA), which operates seven days a week in Lansing and East Lansing as well as to points throughout the metropolitan region. CATA's shuttle service to downtown Lansing and the Capital Loop reduces rush-hour traffic and parking congestion in central city areas. Special service for elderly, handicapped, commuting, and rural patrons is available.

## ■ Communications

### Newspapers and Magazines

The major daily newspaper in Lansing is the morning *Lansing State Journal.* A number of trade publications originate in Lansing, aimed at farmers, florists, grocers, and small business owners. Other Lansing publications include *Michigan History Magazine* and *The State News,* a daily published by Michigan State University.

### Television and Radio

Two commercial television stations are based in Lansing, where cable television service is also available. Lansing radio listeners receive broadcasts from approximately eight AM and FM radio stations in the city and several additional stations in neighboring communities. Musical programming includes country, classical, rock and roll, religious, top 40, and easy listening.

***Media Information:*** *Lansing State Journal,* 120 E. Lenawee, Lansing, MI 48919; telephone (517)377-1000

### Lansing Online

Arts Council of Greater Lansing. Available www.lansingarts.org

City of Lansing home page. Available www.cityoflansingmi.com

Greater Lansing Convention & Visitors Bureau. Available www.lansing.org

Lansing Regional Chamber of Commerce. Available www.lansingchamber.org

Lansing School District. Available www.lansingschools.net

*Lansing State Journal.* Available www.lansingstatejournal.com

Library of Michigan. Available www.michigan.gov/hal

Michigan Historical Center. Available www.michigan.gov/hal

BIBLIOGRAPHY

Celizic, Mike, *The Biggest Game of Them All: Notre Dame, Michigan State, and the Fall of '66* (New York: Simon & Schuster, 1992)

Seale, William, *Michigan's Capitol: Construction & Restoration* (Ann Arbor, MI: University of Michigan Press, 1995)

# Minnesota

# The State in Brief

**Nickname:** North Star State

**Motto:** L'etoile du nord (Star of the north)

**Flower:** Pink and white lady's slipper

**Bird:** Common loon

**Area:** 86,938 square miles (2000; U.S. rank 12th)

**Elevation:** Ranges from 600 feet to 2,301 feet above sea level

**Climate:** North part of state lies in the moist Great Lakes storm belt; western border is at the edge of the semi-arid Great Plains; spring is brief; summer is short, hot, and humid; winter is long and severe with heavy snowfall

**Admitted to Union:** May 11, 1858

**Capital:** Saint Paul

**Head Official:** Governor Tim Pawlenty (R) (until 2010)

**Population**

    **1980:** 4,076,000
    **1990:** 4,432,000
    **2000:** 4,919,492
    **2006 estimate:** 5,167,101
    **Percent change, 1990–2000:** 12.4%
    **U.S. rank in 2006:** 21st
    **Percent of residents born in state:** 69.10% (2006)
    **Density:** 64.5 people per square mile (2006)
    **2006 FBI Crime Index Total:** 175,242

**Racial and Ethnic Characteristics (2006)**

    **White:** 4,538,957
    **Black or African American:** 228,354
    **American Indian and Alaska Native:** 51,922
    **Asian:** 179,295
    **Native Hawaiian and Pacific Islander:** 919
    **Hispanic or Latino (may be of any race):** 195,138
    **Other:** 83,293

**Age Characteristics (2006)**

    **Population under 5 years old:** 347,404
    **Population 5 to 19 years old:** 1,060,840
    **Percent of population 65 years and over:** 12.2%
    **Median age:** 36.8

**Vital Statistics**

    **Total number of births (2006):** 69,727
    **Total number of deaths (2006):** 38,254
    **AIDS cases reported through 2005:** 4,632

**Economy**

    **Major industries:** Manufacturing; trade; finance, insurance, and real estate; agriculture; services
    **Unemployment rate (2006):** 5.2%
    **Per capita income (2006):** $27,591
    **Median household income (2006):** $54,023
    **Percentage of persons below poverty level (2006):** 9.8%
    **Income tax rate:** 5.35% to 7.85%
    **Sales tax rate:** 6.5%

# Duluth

## ■ The City in Brief

**Founded:** 1852 (chartered 1870)

**Head Official:** Mayor Don Ness (since 2007)

**City Population**

    1980: 92,811
    1990: 85,493
    2000: 86,918
    2006 estimate: 84,167
    Percent change, 1990–2000: 1.01%
    U.S. rank in 1980: 184th
    U.S. rank in 1990: 243rd
    U.S. rank in 2000: 321st (State rank: 4th)

**Metropolitan Area Population**

    1980: 266,650
    1990: 239,971
    2000: 243,815
    2006 estimate: 274,244
    Percent change, 1990–2000: 1.02%
    U.S. rank in 1980: Not available
    U.S. rank in 1990: Not available
    U.S. rank in 2000: 146th

**Area:** 87.32 square miles (2000)

**Elevation:** Ranges from 605 to 1,485 feet above sea level

**Average Annual Temperatures:** January, 8.4° F; July, 65.5° F; annual average, 39.1° F

**Average Annual Precipitation:** 31.0 inches of rain; 80.7 inches of snow

**Major Economic Sectors:** Services, trade, government

**Unemployment Rate:** 5.7% (June 2007)

**Per Capita Income:** $22,627 (2005)

**2005 FBI Crime Index Property:** Not available

**2005 FBI Crime Index Violent:** Not available

**Major Colleges and Universities:** University of Minnesota–Duluth; College of St. Scholastica

**Daily Newspaper:** *Duluth News-Tribune*

## ■ Introduction

The seat of St. Louis County in Minnesota, Duluth is the focus of a metropolitan statistical area comprising both St. Louis County and Wisconsin's Douglas County. The city has developed into the second-largest port on the Great Lakes and is the commercial, industrial, and cultural center of northern Minnesota. Duluth is noted for its dramatic geographic setting. Steep inclines, dotted with buildings that seem to pop out of hillsides, provide the backdrop for Duluth's famous 30-mile-long Skyline Parkway, which winds above the city.

## ■ Geography and Climate

Duluth is located on a natural harbor at the western tip of Lake Superior and at the base of a range of hills overlooking the St. Louis River. This position below high terrain and along the lake permits easterly winds to cool the area automatically, thus earning Duluth the nickname of the "Air-Conditioned City." During the summer a westerly wind flow abates at night, and the cool lake air moves back in toward the city. High and low pressure systems and proximity to Lake Superior, the coldest of the Great Lakes, have an important influence on the climate, which is predominantly continental. Summer temperatures are thus cooler and winter temperatures warmer; the frequency of severe storms—wind, hail, tornadoes, freezing rain, and blizzards—is also low in comparison to other areas at a distance from the lake. Fall is an especially pleasant season in Duluth, as the changing leaves produce a striking combination of reds, yellows, and browns.

**Area:** 87.32 square miles (2000)

**Elevation:** Ranges from 605 to 1,485 feet above sea level

**Average Temperatures:** January, 8.4° F; July, 65.5° F; annual average, 39.1° F

**Average Annual Precipitation:** 31.0 inches of rain; 80.7 inches of snow

# ■ History

## Harbor, Timber, and Ore Attract Development

The western Lake Superior area was originally occupied by members of the Sioux and Chippewa tribes. One of the first explorers of European descent to arrive in the area now occupied by Duluth was Frenchman Pierre Esprit Radisson, who explored the region in the 1650s or 1660s. The city was ultimately named, however, for Daniel Greysolon, Sieur du Lhut (variously spelled Dulhut, Derhaut, and du Luth), who visited the southern shore of Lake Superior in 1679 in an attempt to make peace between the Ojibway and Sioux tribes and to secure trading and trapping rights. A fur trading outlet remained in the area until 1847. The site's first permanent resident was George P. Stuntz, who was attracted by the beautiful wilderness landscape surrounding Lake Superior and settled there in 1852.

In 1854 and 1855 settlers flocked to the unnamed town hoping to discover copper deposits, although the Grand Portage and Fon du Lac people had not yet signed the Treaty of La Pointe that relinquished their mineral rights. In 1856 the village was named Duluth and designated the seat of St. Louis County. Almost immediately Duluth was beset by troubles. The panic of 1857 devastated the economy, and in 1859 a scarlet fever epidemic caused a further setback to the community. By the end of the Civil War, only two houses remained occupied in Duluth.

The town's fortunes were quickly reversed when geologists found iron ore and gold-bearing quartz at nearby Lake Vermillion. Then the Eastern financier Jay Cooke selected Duluth as the northern terminus of the Lake Superior & Mississippi Railroad. Adding to the boom, Maine woodsmen relocated to the region to establish a lumber industry. By 1869 the population of Duluth had grown to 3,500 residents, and the city received its first charter a year later.

## Growth Includes New Immigrants

The new prosperity was short-lived, however, as bank and real estate failures hurt the economy and plunged the city government into debt. Duluth was forced to revert to

village status. The city's topsy-turvy early history reversed itself once again, however, when the lumbering industry was revitalized and grain business fueled the economy. By 1887 Duluth's population reached 26,000 residents, and the state legislature granted permission for reclassification as a city. Six lakeshore communities were absorbed into the city by the end of the nineteenth century.

Among the settlers who had made Duluth home were immigrants from the Scandinavian countries and Finland, who settled in the city's West End. These people possessed a commitment to cooperative undertakings, a strong sense of individualism, and a respect for organizational arrangements—qualities that have shaped the city's character. In addition to its residents, Duluth is defined by its topography. The natural harbor is the base of the economy and the source of the city's scenic beauty. Duluth, home to institutions of higher learning, a symphony orchestra, a community theater, ballet, and museums, is highly rated among small Midwestern cities for its livability.

*Historical Information:* Northeast Minnesota Historical Center Archives, University of Minnesota, 10 University Dr., Duluth, MN 55812; telephone (218) 726-8526. Minnesota Historical Society, 345 Kellogg Blvd. W., Saint Paul, MN 55102-1906; telephone (651) 296-6126

# ■ Population Profile

## Metropolitan Area Residents

1980: 266,650
1990: 239,971
2000: 243,815
2006 estimate: 274,244
Percent change, 1990–2000: 1.02%
U.S. rank in 1980: Not available
U.S. rank in 1990: Not available
U.S. rank in 2000: 146th

## City Residents

1980: 92,811
1990: 85,493
2000: 86,918
2006 estimate: 84,167
Percent change, 1990–2000: 1.01%
U.S. rank in 1980: 184th
U.S. rank in 1990: 243rd
U.S. rank in 2000: 321st (State rank: 4th)

**Density:** 1,278.1.6 people per square mile (2000)

## Racial and ethnic characteristics (2000)

White: 80,532
Black: 1,415
American Indian and Alaska Native: 2,122

Walter Bibikow/The Image Bank/Getty Images

Asian: 993
Native Hawaiian and Pacific Islander: 25
Hispanic or Latino (may be of any race): 921
Other: 251

**Percent of residents born in state:** 75.1% (2000)

**Age characteristics (2005)**

Population under 5 years old: 3,960
Population 5 to 9 years old: 4,486
Population 10 to 14 years old: 4,119
Population 15 to 19 years old: 4,663
Population 20 to 24 years old: 9,323
Population 25 to 34 years old: 9,311
Population 35 to 44 years old: 10,444
Population 45 to 54 years old: 11,123
Population 55 to 59 years old: 4,104
Population 60 to 64 years old: 3,876
Population 65 to 74 years old: 4,750
Population 75 to 84 years old: 4,959
Population 85 years and older: 1,800
Median age: 37.5 years

**Births (2006, MSA)**

Total number: 2,873

**Deaths (2006, MSA)**

Total number: 2,947

**Money income (2005)**

Per capita income: $22,627
Median household income: $37,083
Total households: 36,116

**Number of households with income of...**

less than $10,000: 4,144
$10,000 to $14,999: 3,454
$15,000 to $24,999: 4,123
$25,000 to $34,999: 5,454
$35,000 to $49,999: 5,516
$50,000 to $74,999: 6,948
$75,000 to $99,999: 3,095
$100,000 to $149,999: 2,207
$150,000 to $199,999: 471
$200,000 or more: 704

**Percent of families below poverty level:** 12.3% (2005)

**2005 FBI Crime Index Property:** Not available

**2005 FBI Crime Index Violent:** Not available

# ■ Municipal Government

The city of Duluth operates under a mayor-council form of government. The mayor and nine council members are elected to four-year terms. The city's program requiring mandatory arrests in domestic violence cases is a national model.

**Head Official:** Mayor Don Ness (since 2007; current term expires January 2011)

**Total Number of City Employees:** 850 (2007)

*City Information:*   City Hall, Mayor's Office, 411 W. 1st St., Ste. 403, Duluth, MN 55802; telephone (218) 730-5230

# ■ Economy

## Major Industries and Commercial Activity

Principal manufacturing firms in Duluth include heavy and light manufacturing plants, food processing plants, woolen mills, lumber and paper mills, cold storage plants, fisheries, grain elevators, and oil refineries. The city is also a regional center for banking, retailing, and medical care for northern Minnesota, northern Wisconsin, northern Michigan, and northwestern Ontario, Canada. More than 12,000 jobs in Duluth are directly related to the hospital industry; approximately one of every seven residents is employed in healthcare. Area universities and local schools also provide significant employment in education. Arts and entertainment offerings as well as year-round recreation in a natural environment have contributed to expansion of the tourist industry in Duluth. Some 3.5 million visitors each year contribute $400 million to the local economy. Other growing sectors in the Arrowhead Region include aviation, electronics, plastics, precision machining, technology and back office operations.

**Items and goods produced:** steel, cement, metal and wood products, electrical equipment, textiles, prepared foods

## Incentive Programs—New and Existing Companies

*Local programs:*   The Duluth Department of Planning and Development is responsible for overseeing Duluth's growth and is the focus of the city's efforts to attract new businesses to Duluth and retain existing firms. It promotes overall development in Duluth through agencies such as the Duluth Economic Development Authority, The 1200 Fund, Inc., the Duluth Airport Authority, The Seaway Port Authority of Duluth, Team Duluth, and others. It also coordinates economic development with the State of Minnesota and the U.S. Department of Commerce. The Arrowhead Regional Development Commission (ARDC) offers a business loan program, which provides below market rate financing for eligible businesses.

*State programs:*   The Tax Increment Financing Program, a state authorized financing mechanism, is offered to assist basic businesses in financing their local expansion or relocation. Funds may be used to purchase land and make public improvements that support business development projects. Minnesota also offers programs to provide a mechanism for businesses to sell bonds at tax-exempt interest rates, allowing firms to receive long-term, low interest financing for fixed assets.

*Job training programs:*   The Minnesota Department of Employment and Economic Development operates a network of workforce centers throughout the state. This WorkForce Center System, which has an office in Duluth, partners with local businesses to provide customized job training and other workforce development services. Both the College of St. Scholastica and Lake Superior College also provide customized training.

## Development Projects

As the new century progresses, expansion and retention of existing businesses continues to be Duluth's major focus. In 2007 plans were underway for the construction of Lakewalk, a path alongside Lake Superior between Canal Park and 20th Avenue East.

Proposed buildings in 2007 included a $15.3-million new business school building at the University of Minnesota-Duluth. In 2005 the Duluth Downtown Waterfront District was established in order to enhance economic development and push for capital improvements in the downtown district, which covers over 90 blocks. The DDWD also seeks to establish standards of cleanliness and safety, in order to attract and retain businesses, nightclubs, and restaurants.

*Economic Development Information:*   Duluth Area Chamber of Commerce, 5 W. 1st St., Ste. 101, Duluth, MN 55802; telephone (218)722-5501; fax (218)722-3223; email commerce@chamber.duluth.mn.us

## Commercial Shipping

A vital part of the Duluth economy is the Port of Duluth-Superior, which is designated a Foreign Trade Zone and ranks among the top ports in the country in total volume of international and domestic cargo shipped in a 10-month season. An average of 45 million tons of cargo (or $2 billion worth) is handled at Duluth-Superior each year. The impact on the local economy is $200 million annually, and some 2,000 jobs are dependent on the port. Duluth-Superior operates one of the largest grain-handling facilities in the world. Grain is the primary export product; domestic shipments consist mainly of iron ore and taconite, in addition to metal products, twine, machinery, coal, cement, salt, newsprint, lumber, and general cargo.

Connecting the port and the city of Duluth with inland markets are several railroads and over 25 common motor freight carriers. Air cargo carriers serving Duluth International Airport with daily flights are Federal Express, United Parcel Service, and Northwest Airlines.

## Labor Force and Employment Outlook

Duluth boasts an abundant, quality workforce, as well as a commitment to bringing new and expanded job opportunities into the community. Minnesota has the highest high school graduation rate in the nation; more than 70 percent of Duluth students go on to college or post-secondary education.

In September 2007 the unemployment rate was 5.4 percent, down from ten-year highs above 7 percent in 2005. Between 1997 and 2007, the labor force in the Duluth metropolitan statistical area grew only slightly, from 140,483 to 144,325.

The following is a summary of data regarding the Duluth MN-WI metropolitan area labor force, 2006 annual averages.

**Size of nonagricultural labor force:** 131,900

**Number of workers employed in** . . .

构 construction and mining: 8,700
manufacturing: 8,700
trade, transportation and utilities: 25,700
information: 2,400
financial activities: 5,900
professional and business services: 7,100
educational and health services: 26,700
leisure and hospitality: 13,700
other services: 5,900
government: 27,100

**Average hourly earnings of production workers employed in manufacturing:** Not available

**Unemployment rate:** 5.7% (June 2007)

| Largest employers | Number of employees |
|---|---|
| St. Mary's/Duluth Clinic | 3,800 |
| Duluth Public Schools-ISD No. 709 | 1,700 |
| St. Louis County | 1,640 |
| University of Minnesota-Duluth | 1,571 |
| City of Duluth | 1,060 |
| St. Luke's Hospital | 1,143 |

## Cost of Living

The median sale price of a home in Duluth during the first quarter of 2007 was $118,680, up from $116,900 in the first quarter of 2003.

The following is a summary of data regarding several key cost of living factors in the Duluth area.

**2007 (1st quarter) ACCRA Average House Price:** Not available

**2007 (1st quarter) ACCRA Cost of Living Index:** Not available

**State income tax rate:** 5.35% to 7.85%

**State sales tax rate:** 6.5%

**Local income tax rate:** None

**Local sales tax rate:** 1.0%

**Property tax rate:** Single family homestead property— 1.0% times the first $72,000 of estimated market value (EMV) plus 2.0% times the excess over $72,000

***Economic Information:*** Duluth Area Chamber of Commerce, 5 W. 1st St., Ste. 101, Duluth, MN 55802; telephone (218)722-5501; fax (218)722-3223; email commerce@chamber.duluth.mn.us. Minnesota Department of Employment and Economic Development, 332 Minnesota St., Ste. E200, St. Paul, MN 55101; telephone (612)297-1291; toll-free (800)657-3858

# ■ Education and Research

## Elementary and Secondary Schools

The Duluth School District (ISD No. 709) covers 337 square miles, including Duluth. It offers K-12 education, special services for students with handicaps and special needs, an Early Childhood Family Education program, Head Start, alternative schools, and community education.

In 2007 the school district began taking steps toward a long-range capital improvement plan, dubbed the "Red" plan, which called for the construction of two new schools in addition to major improvements of existing facilities. In an effort to better the district's "Continuous Improvement" ranking, The Quality Initiative was created, a cooperative endeavor between the Duluth Federation of Teachers, Duluth School Board, Duluth Principal's Association and district administration. Initiatives have included a "Wellness Task Force" and steering committees for grade-specific issues. In 2007 Duluth outperformed the statewide average on acheivement tests.

The following is a summary of data regarding the Duluth Public Schools as of the 2005–2006 school year.

**Total enrollment:** 10,000

**Number of facilities**

elementary schools: 10

junior high/middle schools: 3
senior high schools: 4
other: 4

**Student/teacher ratio:** 16.7:1

**Teacher salaries (2005–06)**

elementary median: $48,520
junior high/middle median: $44,330
secondary median: $46,720

**Funding per pupil:** $8,818

The Marshall School, an independent, coeducational day school, offers college preparatory classes for students in grades 5–12. Holy Rosary offers Catholic education for grades K–8. Lakeview Christian Academy, an interdenominational, Christian school, serves students from preschool through grade 12 with a Bible-centered curriculum. Summit School is an independent school for children from kindergarten through grade four.

***Public Schools Information:*** Independent School District No. 709, 215 N. 1st Ave. E., Duluth, MN 55802; telephone (218)723-4150

### Colleges and Universities

The University of Minnesota–Duluth enrolls 11,184 students and offers thirteen bachelor's degrees in 77 majors, graduate programs in 22 fields, and the first two years of a medical program. Nearly eighty percent of the student body is from Minnesota. The school was ranked fiftieth among Midwestern master's level universities in the 2008 edition of *U.S News and World Report's* "Best Colleges." The College of St. Scholastica, a private four-year institution enrolling about 2,800 students, has gained recognition in the areas of nursing, management, exercise physiology, health information management, occupational therapy, physical therapy, and education. The school is also affiliated with St. Scholastica Monastery, home of the Benedictine Sisters, and the Benedictine Health Center. Lake Superior College offers more than 70 majors to its 8,500 students and operates an Aircraft Rescue and Fire Fighting Center and a Computer Flex Lab. Business and medical training and college-level general education is available at Duluth Business University. Fond du Lac Tribal and Community College in Cloquet is a joint effort between the Fond du Lac Reservation and the state of Minnesota.

### Libraries and Research Centers

The Duluth Public Library houses more than 618,000 volumes, magazines, maps, charts, video and audio recordings, and framed prints; special collections relate to Duluth, the Great Lakes region, and Minnesota. The library, a depository for federal documents, operates two branches. In 2006 the library had circulation numbers amounting to 969,972. The University of Minnesota–Duluth and the College of St. Scholastica maintain substantial campus libraries. Duluth is home to the Saint Louis County Law Library, the Environmental Protection Agency library, the Karpeles Manuscript Library, and the Northeast Minnesota Historical Center Archives, in addition to the libraries of health service and religious organizations.

The Natural Resources Research Institute, affiliated with UMD and staffed by scientists, engineers, and business consultants, conducts research and development projects on subjects such as forest products and the environment.

***Public Library Information:*** Duluth Public Library, 520 W. Superior St., Duluth, MN 55802; telephone (218)723-3800

## ■ Health Care

Duluth is a regional health care center for the northern sections of Minnesota, Wisconsin, and Michigan and for northwestern Ontario, Canada. The St. Mary's/Duluth Clinic (SMDC) Health System is comprised of Duluth Clinic, St. Mary's Medical Center, St. Mary's Hospital of Superior, Miller-Dwan Medical Center, Polinsky Rehabilitation Center, Pine Medical Center, and Duluth Children's Hospital.

St. Mary's Medical Center offers 24-hour emergency treatment and maintains a Level II trauma center in addition to outpatient services, home care, and community education programs. It also operates the Regional Heart Center and Regional Neuroscience Center, which provides cardiac surgery, cancer care, orthopedic surgery, intensive care, and Level III prenatal care. It has 580 physicians, dentists and podiatrists on staff.

Miller-Dwan administers the largest mental health program in the region and operates a burn clinic along with hemodialysis, medical rehabilitation, rheumatic disease, and radiation therapy units. The Duluth Clinic boasts one of just fifty community clinical oncology programs in the nation and was ranked one of the "Top One Hundred Orthopedic Hospitals" by Solucient in 2006. Polinsky Medical Rehabilitation Center treats adults and children with disabilities. Duluth Children's Hospital is home to over thirty pediatric specialty physicians.

St. Luke's Hospital, which was the first hospital in Duluth, has been federally designated as a Level II Regional Trauma Center; it houses the Regional Vascular Institute, Poison Control Center, and Mental Health Services and has 393 physicians on its staff. A full range of general services is supplemented by such specialties as psychiatry, oncology, physical medicine, hospice care, high cholesterol treatment, occupational health services, lithotripsy, and magnetic resonance imaging. The hospital had 12,438 admissions in 2006.

# ■ Recreation

## Sightseeing

The St. Louis County Heritage and Arts Center is housed in the 1892 Union Depot, a renovated railroad depot with four levels of history and arts exhibits. On display are antique doll and toy collections, a Victorian parlor, Indian crafts, and Depot Square, a recreation of 1910 Duluth that contains 24 old-time stores, a silent movie theater, and an ice-cream parlor. The old immigration room that once processed newcomers to the United States is preserved in its original condition. Railroad cars and locomotives, including the first locomotive in Minnesota and one of the largest steam locomotives ever built, are on exhibit.

The Canal Park Marine Museum houses exhibits on the history of Lake Superior Shipping, while the Lake Superior Museum of Transportation maintains one of the nation's finest collections of historical railroad equipment. At the Lake Superior Zoo, animals from around the world can be viewed in facilities that include a nocturnal house and a children's zoo. Located on the shore of Lake Superior, Glensheen is a Jacobean-style mansion featuring original furnishings and a collection of carriages and sleighs.

The Skyline Parkway, a 30-mile boulevard above Duluth, provides a dramatic view of the city, the harbor, and Lake Superior. Lake Shore Drive parallels Lake Superior from Duluth to Thunder Bay and is considered one of the most scenic coastal highways in the nation. The Aerial Lift Bridge, which connects Minnesota Point with the mainland and spans Duluth harbor, is one of Duluth's most popular tourist attractions. The present bridge, built in 1930, is the world's largest and fastest lift bridge.

## Arts and Culture

The Depot houses eight of Duluth's major arts and cultural institutions. The Duluth Art Institute sponsors major exhibitions in addition to its instructional programs. Rooted in classical ballet with contemporary dance influences, Minnesota Ballet stages three major performance series annually. The Duluth Playhouse, founded in 1914 and one of the nation's oldest community theaters, produces a variety of theatrical presentations. Organized in 1932, the Duluth-Superior Symphony Orchestra presents seven concerts each season, as well as three Pops performances and an annual holiday concert. The Matinee Musicale, Duluth's oldest cultural organization, promotes promising young musicians. The Tweed Museum of Art at the University of Minnesota–Duluth presents historical and contemporary exhibitions in a number of local galleries and is home to the Sax Sculpture Conservatory.

## Festivals and Holidays

The summer season in Duluth features Grandma's Marathon, a run along Lake Superior, and the Park Point Art Fair in June, the Fourth Fest in July, and Bayfront Blues Festival in August. The Festival of Cultures presents music, ethnic foods, and dance at Leif Erikson Park in August.

## Sports for the Spectator

The University of Minnesota–Duluth competes nationally in Division I hockey, playing 20 home games at the Duluth Entertainment Convention Center (DECC). The Beargrease Sled Dog Marathon, the premier dog race of the lower 48 states, is a 400-mile wilderness race held every winter. The race's route, from Duluth to Grand Portage and back, includes 14 checkpoints along Lake Superior's North Shore. The Duluth Yacht Club sailboat races from Duluth and Port Wing take place on Labor Day weekend.

## Sports for the Participant

Spirit Mountain Recreation Area offers downhill skiing, cross-country trails, tennis, camping, and hiking. Duluth maintains, on 11,862 acres of land, 129 municipal parks and playgrounds, two 27-hole golf courses, 41 tennis courts, 20 baseball and softball fields, and 22 community recreation centers. Athletic leagues are available for softball, basketball, no-check hockey, volleyball, touch football, broomball, and bocce. In addition 45 miles of snowmobile trails, 7 hiking trails, and 44 kilometers of groomed cross-country ski trails are maintained by the city. Residents and visitors can compete in Grandma's Marathon, which is run along the North Shore the third weekend in June. The Fond-Du-Luth Gaming Casino, located in downtown Duluth, is another popular attraction.

## Shopping and Dining

The development of Duluth's historic waterfront downtown and the conversion of a local brewery into a hotel, restaurant, and shopping complex on the shore of Lake Superior have modernized Duluth's shopping milieu. The Skywalk system, which covers most of the downtown area, offers protected access to area shops and restaurants. Duluth restaurants offer freshwater fish from Lake Superior. Ethnic cuisine consists principally of Greek, Italian, and Chinese dishes. There are more than fifty restaurants in the city.

***Visitor Information:*** Duluth Convention and Visitors Bureau, 21 W. Superior St., Ste. 100, Duluth, MN 55802; telephone (218)722-4011; toll-free (800)4-DULUTH; email cvb@visitduluth.com

# ■ Convention Facilities

The Duluth Entertainment Convention Center is the principal site for conventions and a wide range of other functions. Attracting more than one million visitors each year, the complex houses 200,000 square feet of meeting and exhibit space along with an 8,000-seat arena and a 2,400-seat auditorium. The facility includes a 26,000-square-foot ballroom and 15 meeting rooms. Numerous hotels and motels, several of them with meeting facilities, provide more than 4,200 rooms for lodging in the Duluth area.

*Convention Information:* Duluth Convention and Visitors Bureau, 21 W. Superior St., Ste. 100, Duluth, MN 55802; telephone (218)722-4011; toll-free (800)4-DULUTH; email cvb@visitduluth.com

# ■ Transportation

## Approaching the City

The Duluth International Airport, located six miles from downtown, is the destination for most air traffic into the city. There are three commercial airlines flying out of the airport: Northwest, Mesaba and Pinnacle Airlines.

Duluth is the terminus point for Interstate 35, which extends from the United States-Mexico border into northern Minnesota; federal highways providing easy access into the city include U.S. 53, 61, and 2. State routes running through Duluth are 23, 39, and 194.

## Traveling in the City

Duluth Transit Authority (DTA) provides public bus transportation throughout the metropolitan area. The DTA operates 41 buses during peak hours on 27 routes. Among the DTA's special services are A Special Transit Ride (STRIDE) for handicapped passengers and carpool and rideshare programs. The DTA operates the Port Town Trolley, a downtown circulator, during the summer months. Visitors may also explore the city on horse-drawn carriages or via the Canal Park waterfront tram.

# ■ Communications

## Newspapers and Magazines

Duluth's major daily newspaper is the morning *Duluth News-Tribune*. Several suburban newspapers and shopping guides circulate weekly. *Labor World*, a labor newspaper established in 1895, appears biweekly on Wednesdays. *The Duluthian*, a bimonthly, is published by the Chamber of Commerce with a business and community orientation. *Lake Superior Magazine*, also

published bimonthly, features articles and photography about the region. A number of special-interest magazines are published in the city on such subjects as mining and mineral processing, the restaurant industry, and the dental profession.

## Television and Radio

More than a dozen television stations, representing the major networks and PBS, broadcast in Duluth, which also receives programming from Hibbing; cable programming is available by subscription. Some 30 AM and FM radio stations offer a variety of formats, including classical, contemporary, and country music, religious programming, news, and public interest features.

*Media Information:* *Duluth News-Tribune*, 424 W. 1st St., Duluth, MN 55802; telephone (218)723-5313. *The Duluthian*, Duluth Area Chamber of Commerce, 5 W. 1st St., Ste. 101, Duluth, MN 55802; telephone (218)722-5501

### Duluth Online

City of Duluth home page. Available www.ci.duluth.mn.us

Duluth Area Chamber of Commerce. Available www.duluthchamber.com

Duluth Convention & Visitors Bureau. Available www.visitduluth.com

Duluth Entertainment Convention Center. Available www.duluthconventioncenter.comwww.decc.org

*Duluth News-Tribune*. Available www.duluthsuperior.com

Duluth Public Library. Available www.duluth.lib.mn.us

Duluth Public Schools. Available www.duluth.k12.mn.us

Minnesota Historical Society. Available www.mnhs.org

BIBLIOGRAPHY

Hertzel, Laurie, ed., *Boomtown Landmarks* (Pfeifer-Hamilton Publishing, 1993)

Sutter, Barton, *Cold Comfort: Life at the Top of the Map* (University of Minnesota Press, 1998)

# Minneapolis

## ■ The City in Brief

**Founded:** 1849 (incorporated 1866)

**Head Official:** Mayor R. T. Rybak (D) (since 2002)

**City Population**

    1980: 370,951
    1990: 368,383
    2000: 382,618
    2006 estimate: 372,833
    Percent change, 1990–2000: 3.9%
    U.S. rank in 1980: 34th
    U.S. rank in 1990: 42nd
    U.S. rank in 2000: 45th

**Metropolitan Area Population**

    1980: 2,137,133
    1990: 2,538,776
    2000: 2,968,806
    2006 estimate: 3,175,041
    Percent change, 1990–2000: 16.9%
    U.S. rank in 1980: 17th
    U.S. rank in 1990: 16th
    U.S. rank in 2000: Not available

**Area:** 54.9 square miles (2000)

**Elevation:** Ranges from 687 feet to 1,060 feet above sea level

**Average Annual Temperatures:** January, 13.1° F; July, 73.2° F; annual average, 45.4° F

**Average Annual Precipitation:** 29.41 inches of rain; 49.9 inches of snow

**Major Economic Sectors:** Services, trade, manufacturing, government

**Unemployment Rate:** 4.4% (June 2007)

**Per Capita Income:** $26,886 (2005)

**2005 FBI Crime Index Property:** 22,417

**2005 FBI Crime Index Violent:** 5,472

**Major Colleges and Universities:** University of Minnesota–Twin Cities; University of St. Thomas-Minneapolis

**Daily Newspaper:** *Star Tribune*

## ■ Introduction

The largest city in Minnesota, Minneapolis is the seat of Hennepin County and the sister city of Saint Paul, with which it forms the 15-county Minneapolis-Saint Paul metropolitan statistical area. Strategically located on the navigable head of the Mississippi River, Minneapolis traces its history to the early exploration of the Northwest Territory. The city encompasses within its boundaries 16 lakes (said to have been formed by Paul Bunyan's footprints) and is noted for its natural beauty and parklands. First a milling and lumbering center, Minneapolis today has one of the largest concentrations of high-technology firms in the nation. The combined cities of Minneapolis and Saint Paul are highly rated for their livability and rank among the country's best places for growing a business.

## ■ Geography and Climate

Minneapolis is part of a 15-county metropolitan statistical area. Minneapolis, which shares geographic and climatic characteristics with Saint Paul, is situated at the point where the Minnesota River joins the Mississippi River on flat or gently rolling terrain. Sixteen lakes are located within the city limits. Most of the lakes are small and shallow, covered by ice in the winter. The city's climate is continental, with large seasonal temperature variations and a favorable growing season of 166 days. Severe weather conditions, such as blizzards, freezing rain, tornadoes, and wind and hail storms are fairly common; winter recreational weather is excellent, however, because of the dry snow, which reaches average depths of 6 to 10 inches.

**Area:** 54.9 square miles (2000)

**Elevation:** Ranges from 687 feet to 1,060 feet above sea level

**Average Temperatures:** January, 13.1° F; July, 73.2° F; annual average, 45.4° F

**Average Annual Precipitation:** 29.41 inches of rain; 49.9 inches of snow

# ■ History

## Falls Provide Townsite and Waterpower

The area where Minneapolis is now located was farmed and hunted by the Sioux tribe before the arrival of Father Louis Hennepin, a French Franciscan missionary who explored the Mississippi River in 1680. Father Hennepin discovered the future site of Minneapolis at a waterfall on the navigable head of the Mississippi River; the falls, which he named after St. Anthony, have since played a crucial role in the city's development. Permanent settlement came in 1820, when Federal troops under the command of Colonel Josiah Snelling built Fort St. Anthony on a bluff overlooking the confluence of the Minnesota and Mississippi rivers. Renamed Fort Snelling in 1825, it safeguarded fur traders from the warring Sioux and Chippewa and served as a trading center and outpost to the Upper Midwest.

The St. Anthony Falls provided the source of power for lumber and flour milling, the two industries that fueled the city's rapid growth. Soldiers built the first flour mill in 1823, and the first commercial sawmill was in operation in 1841. Attracting settlers from New England, particularly lumbermen from Maine, the rich land was ready for settlement. A geographical fault discovered at the falls in 1869 nearly led to economic disaster and the demise of these industries, but an apron built with federal funding secured the source of waterpower and helped the city to grow in wealth and prosperity.

In 1849 the village of All Saints was founded on the west side of the falls and nine years later settlers who squatted on U.S. military reservation land were awarded land rights. Also, in 1855, the village of St. Anthony on the east side of the falls was incorporated. In 1856 the name of All Saints was changed to Minneapolis, which was derived from the Sioux "minne" for water and the Greek "polis" for city. St. Anthony was chartered as a city in 1860 and Minneapolis six years later. Then in 1872 the

two cities become one, spanning both sides of the Mississippi River, with the name of the larger being retained.

## Flour, Lumber Industries Attract New Residents

Immigrants from Northern Europe, particularly Sweden but also Norway, Denmark, and Finland, flocked to Minneapolis to work in the new industries. A shoemaker named Nils Nyberg is credited as being the first Swede to settle, having arrived in St. Anthony in 1851. The wave of Scandinavian immigration after the Civil War was felt in every aspect of life in Minneapolis.

In one short generation Minneapolis emerged as a great American city. The original New England settlers platted the streets to reflect order and prosperity, with the boulevards lined with oak and elm trees. The Mississippi River divided the city and served as the focal point of the street grid. The city's rapid population growth and booming economy were attributable in part to the perfection of the Purifer, a flour-sifting device, that made possible the production of high-quality flour from inexpensive spring wheat and led to the construction of large flour mills.

A mill explosion in 1878 that destroyed half the flour mill district prompted residents to research methods to reduce mill dust. Minnesota emerged as the world's leading flour-milling center by 1882. Steam-powered machinery propelled the lumber industry, and during the period from 1899 to 1905, Minneapolis was the world's foremost producer of lumber. Production was so high that logs actually jammed the river from the timberlands of the north in 1899. Minneapolis became a rail transportation center during this period, further contributing to economic prosperity.

## Progressive Programs Revitalize City

The lumber industry in Minneapolis declined once the great forest lands of the north were exhausted, and the large milling companies were forced to relocate some of their plants in other cities to combat the high cost of transportation, which further hurt the economy. After World War II Minneapolis rebounded and became a national leader in the manufacture of computers, electronics equipment, and farm machinery. It established a reputation as a progressive city, undertaking an ambitious urban development project that improved the downtown core and revitalized the economic base. The innovative Nicollet Mall, with a skywalk system, was one of the first of its kind in a major city. Minneapolis and its twin city, Saint Paul, emerged to form one of the nation's fastest-growing metropolitan areas in the 1960s and 1970s. By the end of the century, the area continued its growth, ranking as the eighth fastest growing area in the country.

Minneapolis embraces continued growth and beautification in the twenty-first century. Leveraging its early roots in the flour milling and lumber industries the city

*Image copyright Jim Parkin, 2007. Used under license from Shutterstock.com.*

has become the home of such major corporations as General Mills, International MultiFoods, and Anderson Windows, while also attracting growth in the technology and healthcare services fields. Development of sporting venues and cleanup of the brownfields add to the appeal of living in the Twin Cities area; Minneapolis's successful transformation has inspired other cities to find solutions to the problems of urban decay.

***Historical Information:*** Hennepin History Museum Library, 2303 Third Avenue South, Minneapolis, MN 55404; telephone (612)870-1329. Minnesota Historical Society, 345 Kellogg Blvd. West, Saint Paul, MN 55102-1906; telephone (651)296-6126

# ■ Population Profile

### Metropolitan Area Residents

1980: 2,137,133
1990: 2,538,776
2000: 2,968,806
2006 estimate: 3,175,041
Percent change, 1990–2000: 16.9%
U.S. rank in 1980: 17th
U.S. rank in 1990: 16th
U.S. rank in 2000: Not available

### City Residents

1980: 370,951
1990: 368,383
2000: 382,618
2006 estimate: 372,833
Percent change, 1990–2000: 3.9%
U.S. rank in 1980: 34th
U.S. rank in 1990: 42nd
U.S. rank in 2000: 45th

**Density:** 6,970.3 people per square mile (2000)

### Racial and ethnic characteristics (2005)

White: 228,305
Black: 58,260
American Indian and Alaska Native: 4,510
Asian: 20,306
Native Hawaiian and Pacific Islander: 196
Hispanic or Latino (may be of any race): 37,017
Other: 28,122

**Percent of residents born in state:** 52% (2000)

**Age characteristics (2005)**

Population under 5 years old: 27,659
Population 5 to 9 years old: 22,072
Population 10 to 14 years old: 15,723
Population 15 to 19 years old: 20,275
Population 20 to 24 years old: 35,079
Population 25 to 34 years old: 74,208
Population 35 to 44 years old: 54,312
Population 45 to 54 years old: 45,425
Population 55 to 59 years old: 17,317
Population 60 to 64 years old: 11,514
Population 65 to 74 years old: 13,010
Population 75 to 84 years old: 9,906
Population 85 years and older: 3,760
Median age: 32.1 years

**Births (2006, MSA)**

Total number: 45,553

**Deaths (2006, MSA)**

Total number: 19,278

**Money income (2005)**

Per capita income: $26,886
Median household income: $41,829
Total households: 156,970

**Number of households with income of . . .**

less than $10,000: 17,744
$10,000 to $14,999: 11,072
$15,000 to $24,999: 20,910
$25,000 to $34,999: 16,629
$35,000 to $49,999: 23,548
$50,000 to $74,999: 28,972
$75,000 to $99,999: 15,301
$100,000 to $149,999: 13,808
$150,000 to $199,999: 5,489
$200,000 or more: 3,497

**Percent of families below poverty level:** 8.3% (2005)

**2005 FBI Crime Index Property:** 22,417

**2005 FBI Crime Index Violent:** 5,472

# ■ Municipal Government

Minneapolis, the seat of Hennepin County, is governed by a mayor and a 13-member council, all of whom are elected to four-year terms. The mayor, who is not a member of the council, shares equally-distributed powers with council members.

**Head Official:** Mayor R.T. Rybak (D) (since 2002; current term expires January 2010)

**Total Number of City Employees:** approximately 7,000 (2007)

*City Information:* City Hall, 350 South Fifth Street, Minneapolis, MN 55415; telephone (612)673-3000

# ■ Economy

## Major Industries and Commercial Activity

Manufacturing is the primary industry in Minneapolis's diversified economic base. Principal manufacturing areas are electronics, milling, machinery, medical products, food processing, and graphic arts. Nineteen of the *Fortune* 500 largest U.S. corporations are headquartered in the Twin Cities, which is among the largest commercial centers between Chicago and the West Coast. The area is home to several of the world's largest private companies, and in 2004 had the fourteenth-largest Gross Metro Product in the nation.

Also integral to the local economy are high-technology industries. With the University of Minnesota and other colleges and technical schools providing applied research and well-trained scientists and engineers, one of the largest concentrations of high-technology firms in the nation—more than 1,300—developed in metropolitan Minneapolis-Saint Paul. In 2005, Minneapolis was ranked the top U.S. city for technology by *Popular Science* magazine.

The headquarters of the Ninth Federal Reserve District Bank is located in the city. Local banks, savings and loan companies, venture capital concerns, and insurance companies play a major role in the economic development of the region.

**Items and goods produced:** electronics, food and dairy products, super computers, structural steel, thermostatic controls, conveyor systems, medical electronics equipment, farm machinery, ball bearings, tools, construction machinery, boilers, tanks, burglar alarms, underwear and hosiery, packaging, garden tools, lawn mowers, sprinklers

## Incentive Programs—New and Existing Companies

The Twin Cities area offers a variety of programs for new and expanding businesses.

*Local programs:* The Minneapolis Community Development Agency (MCDA), the development arm of the City of Minneapolis, provides a host of affordable financing packages and site-search assistance for businesses expanding in or relocating to Minneapolis. As an authorized agent for the federal Small Business Administration, the MCDA can combine federal small business financing with Minneapolis' own unique finance tools to help companies grow. MCDA business experts help businesses realize their goals from preliminary negotiations to closing. BusinessLink is a one-stop business service center located at the MCDA.

*State programs:* The Tax Increment Financing Program, a state authorized financing mechanism, is offered to assist basic businesses in financing their local expansion or relocation. Funds may be used to purchase land and make public improvements that support business development projects. Minnesota also offers programs to provide a mechanism for businesses to sell bonds at tax-exempt interest rates, allowing firms to receive long-term, low interest financing for fixed assets.

*Job training programs:* The Minneapolis Employment and Training Program (METP), a service of the City of Minneapolis, offers a variety of training and job placement services for youth, adult, and mature workers as well as dislocated and welfare workers.

## Development Projects

Fueling the local economy is the redevelopment of downtown Minneapolis. Since the expansion of the now-famous Nicollet Mall in the 1980s and the initiation of the innovative skyway system, billions of dollars have been invested in construction projects. The Franklin-Portland Gateway is a phased multi-use development in an economically troubled urban area; the first phase was completed in April 2004 and included rental and ownership residential units as well as the four-story community and education Children's Village Center. Phase II was completed in 2006, with 41 mixed-income housing units. Phase III began construction in 2007, and Phase IV was slated to begin construction in 2008. Both phases call for more mixed-income housing development.

Economic expansion and construction activity have placed a strain on the city's transportation infrastructure; to address that issue, more than $1 billion in road improvement projects will take place over several years. The Hiawatha Light Rail opened to travelers in 2004; future expansion will make it into a 13-mile line that will connect downtown Minneapolis with Minneapolis-Saint Paul International Airport and the Mall of America in Bloomington. Planning is complete for a regional rail route, the Northstar Corridor, which will connect St. Cloud with Minneapolis using an existing 40-mile freight corridor. The $265-million project is projected to be in service in late 2008. By 2020 the city hopes to develop six bus and train "transitways" in heavily-trafficked regions.

In summer 2007 tragedy struck Minneapolis when the Interstate 35 bridge collapsed over the Missisippi River; by November work was underway on the massive rebuilding project and was expected to be complete by 2008.

In 2007 a new stadium for the Minnesota Twins was in the early construction stage in downtown Minneapolis on the site of a former parking lot; the final design is an outdoor stadium with 40,000 seats and was expected to cost around $390 million by its completion in 2010. In 2006 work was completed on the new Central Library, which has 353,000 square feet, a 18,560-square-foot "green" roof planted with ground cover, and 140,000 square feet of underground parking. The total cost of the project was around $110 million.

*Economic Development Information:* Minneapolis Regional Chamber of Commerce, Young Quinlan Building, 81 South Ninth Street, Suite 200, Minneapolis, MN 55402; telephone (612)370-9100; fax (612)370-9195; email info@minneapolischamber.org.

## Commercial Shipping

An important factor in the Minneapolis economy is the Minneapolis-Saint Paul International Airport, which is served by 17 cargo carriers and air-freight forwarders. The Twin Cities area is also linked with major United States and Canadian markets via a network of four railroad companies.

Considered one of the largest trucking centers in the nation, Minneapolis-Saint Paul is served by approximately 150 motor freight companies that provide overnight and four- to five-day delivery in the Midwest and major markets in the continental United States. Vital to the Twin Cities' role as a primary transportation hub is the port of Minneapolis, which, together with the port of Saint Paul, processes annually more than 11 million tons of cargo to and from domestic and foreign markets.

## Labor Force and Employment Outlook

The Twin Cities boasts an educated work force; approximately a quarter of people 25 years old or older have four or more years of college. Unemployment in the Twin Cities remained low in the early 2000s, but by 2007 it had caught up with national averages. Companies are expanding rapidly, and there is considerable competition for skilled workers, especially in the areas of healthcare and technical positions, social services, personal care, construction, and computer professions.

The suburban Mall of America, one of the most popular tourist destinations in the United States, has a significant economic impact. The Twin Cities' economy is keeping pace with and in some cases surging ahead of the national economy. Some of the leading industries are medical instrument and supplies manufacturing, printing and publishing, transportation equipment, computer and data processing services, finance, and engineering and management services. In 2005, BestJobsUSA.com selected Minneapolis as one of the "Top 20 Best Places to Live & Work in America."

In September 2007 the unemployment rate in the Minneapolis-St. Paul-Bloomington metropolitan statistical area stood at 4.7 percent, on the rise but still slightly lower than ten year highs above five percent in 2004.

Between 1997 and 2007 the area labor force rose from 1,645,537 to 1,858,316.

The following is a summary of data regarding the Minneapolis-St. Paul-Bloomington MN-WI metropolitan area labor force, 2006 annual averages.

**Size of nonagricultural labor force:** 1,788,000

**Number of workers employed in...**

construction and mining: 83,400
manufacturing: 204,700
trade, transportation and utilities: 340,900
information: 40,900
financial activities: 143,100
professional and business services: 259,800
educational and health services: 235,700
leisure and hospitality: 161,600
other services: 76,200
government: 241,700

**Average hourly earnings of production workers employed in manufacturing:** $18.31

**Unemployment rate:** 4.4% (June 2007)

| *Largest employers (2007)* | *Number of employees* |
|---|---|
| University of Minnesota | 25,000 |
| Fairview University Medical Center | 8,000 |
| Target Corp. | 7,848 |
| Methodist Hospital | 7,000 |
| Wells Fargo | 6,398 |
| Ameriprise Financial | 5,500 |
| UPS | 5,400 |
| Fairview Southdale Hospital Services | 5,000 |
| Regions Hospital | 5,000 |

### Cost of Living

The Twin Cities region has one of the lowest costs of living among the 25 largest cities in the United States. The median home sale price in 2007 was $203,000 according to the real estate web site Homescape; the U.S. Census Bureau reported the average home sale price in 2000 as $170,722.

The following is a summary of data regarding several key cost of living factors in the Minneapolis area.

**2007 (1st quarter) ACCRA Average House Price:** Not available

**2007 (1st quarter) ACCRA Cost of Living Index:** Not available

**State income tax rate:** 5.35% to 7.85%

**State sales tax rate:** 6.5%

**Local income tax rate:** None

**Local sales tax rate:** 0.5%

**Property tax rate:** $118.42 per $1,000 assessed value (2005)

***Economic Information:*** Minneapolis Regional Chamber of Commerce, Young Quinlan Building, 81 South Ninth Street, Suite 200, Minneapolis, MN 55402; telephone (612)370-9100

## ■ Education and Research

### Elementary and Secondary Schools

The Minneapolis Public Schools district, the largest school district in Minnesota, provides students with a truly international education that will prepare them for life in a global community. Students in the districts who are currently learning English also speak one of 90 other languages in their homes. Families may choose from 19 contract alternative schools and five charter schools. Ninety-eight percent of incoming kindergarten families receive their first choice. The district introduced all-day kindergarten in 2001 and was the first district in the state to do so. Since the mid-nineties, a $608-million investment in school renovation and construction has resulted in 16 new schools.

While many districts are cutting funding for arts programs, 35 Minneapolis Public Schools received a $10 million Annenberg Challenge Grant to integrate the arts throughout the curriculum, a strategy that has been shown to improve academic achievement. Elementary school students benefited from a $650,000 grant from the Medtronic Foundation to revitalize the kindergarten through fifth grade science program. Nearly $10 million from the Walling family makes college scholarships available for Minneapolis Public School seniors to further their education. Other special programs include Achieve! Minneapolis, Girls in Engineering, Mathematics & Science, and the Arts for Academic Achievement.

The following is a summary of data regarding the Minneapolis Public Schools as of the 2005–2006 school year.

**Total enrollment:** 36,370

**Number of facilities**

elementary schools: 45
junior high/middle schools: 7
senior high schools: 7
other: 40

**Student/teacher ratio:** 17.7:1

**Teacher salaries (2005–06)**

elementary median: $46,260

junior high/middle median: $45,470
secondary median: $46,410

**Funding per pupil:** $11,558

Hennepin County is served by more than forty private schools offering alternative educational curricula.

***Public Schools Information:*** Minneapolis Public Schools, 807 Northeast Broadway, Minneapolis, MN 55413-2398; telephone (612)668-0000.

### Colleges and Universities

The University of Minnesota—Twin Cities, a state institution with an enrollment of 28,645 in fall 2006, is located in Minneapolis. The university ranks among the nation's top ten public research universities; in the 2008 edition of the *U.S. News and World Report* college rankings, UMTC was ranked 71st among national universities. Five degree levels—baccalaureate, first-professional, master's, intermediate, and doctorate—are available in 250 fields in the University of Minnesota system, including architecture, medicine, engineering, journalism, management, teacher education, public health, and music. Former students and faculty members have been awarded 12 Nobel Prizes in physics, medicine, chemistry, economics, and peace.

Augsburg College and North Central University, private religious institutions, award associate's, baccalaureate, and master's degrees. Augsburg, which is Lutheran, offers master's degree programs in business, education, leadership, nursing, physician assistant studies, and social work. North Central has an enrollment of about 1,200 students. The Minneapolis College of Art and Design offers four-year programs in fine and applied arts. Community and technical colleges in the metropolitan area include Minneapolis Community and Technical College, and Hennepin Technical College.

### Libraries and Research Centers

The Minneapolis Public Library operates a central library and 14 branches. The central library has the largest collection of any public library in Minnesota. In 2000 a $140-million referendum was passed for the building of a new central library and improvements to all 14 branches over a 10- or 11-year period. The new central library, which opened in 2006, totals 353,000 square feet, and has a 18,560-square-foot "green" roof planted with ground cover and 140,000 square feet of underground parking. The central library boasts the third largest per capita public library collection of any major city in America. Its collection has more than 3 million items, and nearly all of its holdings are accesible in the new building. In 2007 there was a measure under consideration that would merge the Minneapolis Public Library with the suburban Hennepin County Library system.

The University of Minnesota Libraries—Twin Cities, also located in Minneapolis, have total holdings of more than 6 million volumes in major academic departments. Special collections include literature on ballooning, the Hess Dime Novel Collection, the Charles Babbage Institute, and the Performing Arts Archives, which were undergoing a major digitization project in 2007. The library is a depository for federal and state documents. The Immigration History Research Center at the university houses one of the nation's most comprehensive collections of the immigrant past.

More than 70 special libraries and research centers serve the city. Most are affiliated with state and county government agencies, businesses and corporations, hospitals, churches and synagogues, and arts organizations.

***Public Library Information:*** Minneapolis Public Library, 300 Nicollet Mall, Minneapolis, MN 55401; telephone (612)630-6000

## ■ Health Care

A vital force in the Minneapolis medical community is the University of Minnesota Medical Center, Fairview, where the first open heart surgery was performed in 1954. The hospital is also known as a leading organ transplant center. In the 2008 *U.S. News and World Report* list of "America's Best Hospitals," the U of M Medical Center ranked among the top 50 hospitals in the country in nine medical specialties, including digestive disorders, endocrinology, and kidney diseases. Among the other major hospitals in Minneapolis are the University of Minnesota Children's Hospital, which operates six affiliated clinics, Shriner's Hospital, the Veteran's Administration Medical Center, the Hennepin County Medical Center (with 422 beds and ranked in the *2007 U.S. News and World Report* list for its kidney care), and the Sister Kenny Rehabilitation Institute. The Mayo Clinic is located 75 miles southeast of Minneapolis, in Rochester.

## ■ Recreation

### Sightseeing

Sightseeing in Minneapolis might begin with the Chain of Lakes—Lake of the Isles, Lake Calhoun, and Lake Harriet—just a few miles west of downtown; in all, 16 lakes are located within the city limits and more than 1,000 are in close proximity. Minnehaha Falls, the point at which Minnehaha Creek plunges into the Mississippi River, was made famous by Henry Wadsworth Longfellow in his poem *The Song of Hiawatha*. A life-size statue of Hiawatha holding his wife Minnehaha is located on an island just above the falls.

For those with an interest in Minneapolis's historical roots, the American Swedish Institute maintains a turn-of-the-century 33-room mansion that displays Swedish immigrant artifacts as well as traveling exhibits. The Ard Godrey House, built in 1849 and the oldest existing frame house in the city, features authentic period furnishings. Minneapolis's early history and development are captured at the Hennepin History Museum.

Fort Snelling, a historic landmark dating from 1820 overlooking Fort Snelling State Park, has been restored to its frontier-era appearance and is open six months a year. At the Minnesota Zoo, seven trails lead to exhibits in natural settings. The Minneapolis Planetarium, with a 40-foot dome, projects over 2,000 stars. More than 1,000 acres cultivated with numerous varieties of trees, flowers, and shrubs make up the Minnesota Landscape Arboretum.

## Arts and Culture

In both Minneapolis and Saint Paul, business and the arts go hand-in-hand. The Five Percent Club consists of local businesses and corporations that donate five percent of their pre-tax earnings to the arts, education, or human services. This investment results in such high-quality institutions as the Guthrie Theater, named for Sir Tyrone Guthrie, which ranks as one of the best regional and repertory theater companies in the United States. The Walker Art Center exhibits progressive modern art in an award-winning building designed by Edward Larrabee Barnes, which has been judged among the best art exhibition facilities in the world. The center, housing a permanent collection that represents major twentieth-century movements, also sponsors programs of music, dance, film, theater, and educational activities.

The Minnesota Orchestra, performing at Orchestra Hall on Nicollet Mall and at Ordway Music Theater in Saint Paul, presents a season of concerts that includes a great performers series, the weekender series, a pop series, and a summer festival. Family holiday concerts are performed at Christmas time. The Minnesota Opera performs traditional and new works at the Opera Center in Minneapolis. Touring Broadway musicals and musical stars perform at the restored Orpheum Theater. The Children's Theater Company offers a world-class theater education program for young people. International theater professionals work with student actors and technicians to present productions of the highest quality.

The Minneapolis Sculpture Garden, adjacent to the Walker Art Center, was designed by landscape architect Peter Rothschild; it consists of four symmetrical square plazas that display more than 55 works by Henry Moore, George Segal, and Deborah Butterfield, among others. The Minneapolis Institute of Arts showcases world art in a collection of more than 100,000 objects from every period and culture.

## Festivals and Holidays

Minneapolis celebrates March with a St. Patrick's Day Parade and a Spring Flower Show. The Minneapolis Aquatennial, established in 1940, is a 10-day extravaganza held in late July with a special theme each year; the Aquatennial Association programs over 250 free events that focus on the city's proximity to water. Many Minneapolis festivals honor the city's Scandinavian heritage. Other festivals celebrate ethnic cultures with music, dance, food, arts, and crafts. Uptown Art Fair, one of the largest such events in the country, is held on a weekend in early August.

## Sports for the Spectator

The Hubert H. Humphrey Metrodome is home to two of the city's major sports franchises: the Minnesota Twins of the western division of baseball's American League and the Minnesota Vikings of the central division of the National Football League play their home games in this domed stadium, conveniently located downtown. In 2007 work was underway on a new Twins Ballpark. The National Basketball Association's Timberwolves play at the Target Center. The Women's National Basketball Association team, the Minnesota Lynx, came to the Twin Cities in 2000. Sports fans can also attend major and minor sporting events at the University of Minnesota–Twin Cities, which fields Big Ten teams like the Gophers, who play to sellout crowds.

## Sports for the Participant

Minneapolis is one of the country's most naturally beautiful cities, enhanced by over 6,400 acres of city parks, with 17 lakes and ponds, 49 recreation centers, two water parks, 396 sports fields, 181 tennis courts, and six skate parks. The abundance of easily accessible water makes possible a full range of water sports and activities in both summer and winter. Four thousand acres of city park land are available for swimming, canoeing, sailing, windsurfing, waterskiing, roller-skating, and biking along with playing softball, tennis, and golf. About 136,900 acres of land are set aside in the Twin Cities region for parks, trails, and wildlife management areas. Winter sports include skating, skiing, snowshoeing, and ice fishing. The city was named the "Most Athletic City" by *Men's Fitness Magazine* in 2005.

## Shopping and Dining

Minneapolis is the originator on a grand scale of the "second floor city" concept, integrating essentially two downtowns—a sidewalk-level traditional downtown and a second city joined by an elaborate skywalk system. Nicollet Mall, completed in 1967, redefined the urban downtown and eliminated the element of weather as a deterrent to the shopper. This all-weather skywalk system connects an indoor shopping center whose four major department stores and hundreds of specialty shops cover over 30 city blocks. Shopping activity is also a part of the City Center mall, which underwent renovations in 2005. St. Anthony Main, along the historic Mississippi riverfront, consists of old warehouses and office buildings converted to a shopping center. Suburban Bloomington is home to the largest mall in North America, the Mall of America.

Elegant dining is possible at The 510 Restaurant, Goodfellow's, and Rosewood Room, named by *Food and Wine* magazine as Distinguished Restaurants of North America. Dinner cruises on the Mississippi River are offered during the summer.

*Visitor Information:* The Greater Minneapolis Convention & Visitors Center, 250 Marquette South, Ste. 1300, Minneapolis, MN 55402; telephone (612) 767-8000

## ■ Convention Facilities

The primary meeting and convention site in Minneapolis is the Minneapolis Convention Center, which opened in 1990 and underwent major renovations in 2002. The facility offers 480,000 square feet of trade show space, 87 conference meeting rooms, a 28,000-square-foot ballroom, and an auditorium. More than 5,000 guest rooms are located downtown, nearly 3,000 of which are connected to the Minneapolis Convention Center via the skyway system.

*Convention Information:* Minneapolis Convention Center, 1301 Second Ave. South, Minneapolis, MN 55403; telephone (612)335-6000

## ■ Transportation

### Approaching the City

Located southeast of downtown Minneapolis, the Minneapolis-Saint Paul International Airport underwent a major expansion between 1996 and 2005. The resulting facility boasts 2.8 million square feet in its main terminal, with an additional 398,000 square feet in a secondary terminal. In 2004, Minneapolis-St. Paul International Airport was named Best Airport in the Americas and Best Domestic Airport by the International Air Transport Association and Airports Council International. Airlines serve 131 non-stop markets, and in 2006 there were 35,612,133 passengers served. Several reliever airports are also located in the metropolitan area. Amtrak runs a major east-west line from Chicago and the East into Saint Paul.

Two major interstate highways serve Minneapolis: I-94 (east-west) and I-35W (north-south). Two belt-line freeways, I-494 and I-694, facilitate travel around the Twin-City suburbs. Seven federal and 13 state highways also link the city with points throughout the United States and Canada.

### Traveling in the City

Minneapolis is laid out on a grid pattern, with streets south of Grant Street intersecting on a north-south axis and those north of Grant running diagonally northeast-southwest. Residents think of their hometown as made up of five major parts: North Side, South Side, Northeast, Southeast, and downtown, each with its own distinct character and attractions. The Minneapolis Skyway System connects major downtown public buildings and retail establishments with elevated, covered walkways. There are also smaller communities such as Uptown on the South Side and Dinkytown on the edge of the University of Minnesota's Minneapolis campus.

Serving Minneapolis, Saint Paul, and the surrounding suburbs is the Metropolitan Council Transit Operations (MCTO), the second-largest bus system in the United States. Additional bus service is provided by five private operators, including Gray Line, which conducts sightseeing tours, stopping at Nicollet Mall and at various hotels in Minneapolis and Saint Paul. The city is noted for efficiency of commuting time: the freeway system, moderate population density, and two central business districts contribute to high levels of mobility during peak and non-peak hours.

In 2004 the first route of the Hiawatha Light Rail Transit (LRT) was opened to the public; the light rail has 17 stations between downtown Minneapolis and the airport, as well as the Mall of America.

## ■ Communications

### Newspapers and Magazines

The major daily newspaper in Minneapolis is the *Star Tribune.* Several neighborhood and suburban newspapers are distributed weekly in the city.

*Mpls. St.Paul* is a magazine focusing on metropolitan life in the Twin Cites. A popular publication with a national distribution is *The Utne Reader.* Other special interest magazines based in Minneapolis pertain to such subjects as religion, aviation, business, entertainment, hunting and conservation, minority issues, medicine, politics, and computers.

### Television and Radio

Four television stations broadcast out of Minneapolis, as do two cable stations. Radio listeners can choose from nearly twenty AM and FM stations. Programming includes ethnic music, jazz, gospel, classical music, easy listening, and news and public affairs.

***Media Information:*** *Star Tribune,* 425 Portland Avenue, Minneapolis, MN 55415; telephone (612)673-4000; toll-free (800)827-8742

**Minneapolis Online**

BusinessLink, Minneapolis Community Development Agency home page. Available www .mcda.net

City of Minneapolis home page. Available www.ci .minneapolis.mn.us

Greater Minneapolis Chamber of Commerce home page. Available www.minneapolischamber.org

Greater Minneapolis Convention and Visitors Association home page. Available www .minneapolis.org

Mall of America home page. Available www .mallofamerica.com

Minneapolis Public Library home page. Available www.mpls.lib.mn.us

Minneapolis Public Schools home page. Available www.mpls.k12.mn.us

Minnesota Historical Society home page. Available www.mnhs.org

*Star Tribune home page.* Available www.startribune .com

BIBLIOGRAPHY

Weiner, Jay, *Stadium Games: Fifty Years of Big League Greed and Bush League Boondoggles* (University of Minnesota Press, 2000)

# Rochester

## ■ The City in Brief

**Founded:** 1854 (incorporated 1858)

**Head Official:** Mayor Ardell F. Brede (NP) (since 2003)

**City Population**
1980: 57,906
1990: 70,729
2000: 85,806
2006 estimate: 96,975
Percent change, 1990–2000: 12.9%
U.S. rank in 1980: 349th
U.S. rank in 1990: 319th (State rank: 5th)
U.S. rank in 2000: 329th (State rank: 3rd)

**Metropolitan Area Population**
1980: 92,006
1990: 106,470
2000: 124,277
2006 estimate: 179,573
Percent change, 1990–2000: 11.7%
U.S. rank in 1980: 292nd
U.S. rank in 1990: 238th
U.S. rank in 2000: 231st

**Area:** 39.61 square miles (2000)

**Elevation:** 1,320 feet above sea level

**Average Annual Temperatures:** January, 11.8° F; July, 70.1° F; annual average, 43.4° F

**Average Annual Precipitation:** 31.40 inches of rain; 48.9 inches of snow

**Major Economic Sectors:** Services, trade, manufacturing

**Unemployment Rate:** 3.9% (June 2007)

**Per Capita Income:** $31,142 (2005)

**2005 FBI Crime Index Property:** 2,465

**2005 FBI Crime Index Violent:** 261

**Major Colleges and Universities:** Mayo Foundation, Minnesota Bible College, Rochester Community and Technical College, Saint Mary's University of Minnesota–Rochester, Winona State University–Rochester Center

**Daily Newspaper:** *Post-Bulletin*

## ■ Introduction

Rochester, the seat of Olmsted County, is known worldwide as the home of the famed Mayo Clinic. The city is the business and cultural hub for southeastern Minnesota, and its local health care facilities are among the finest in the world. Clean air, low crime, and a strong sense of community, as well as attractive offerings in the arts and recreational areas, contribute to the city's appeal as a place to settle. Rochester was rated one of the nation's 100 best cities in which to live in 2006 by *Money* magazine and snagged the top ranking in 2000 for the best small city. In its review, *Money* praised Rochester's good schools, high-tech job growth, easy commuting, and the Mayo Clinic.

## ■ Geography and Climate

Rochester is located 76 miles southeast of Minneapolis/ Saint Paul, 41 miles north of the Iowa border, and 36 miles west of the Wisconsin border. The Zumbro River flows through the city, which is set on rolling farmland. There are also three creeks within the city limits.

Rochester enjoys a four-season climate. Spring is usually brief, and summer is pleasant and occasionally very hot, with approximately seven days exceeding 90 degrees. In July the relative humidity ranges between a high of 90 percent and a low of 62 percent. Summer brings prevailing winds from the south and southwest, and the winds shift during the winter months to come from the northwest. Autumn offers beautiful sunny days. Winter is cold, with snowfall averaging 48.9 inches annually. Severe storms including blizzards, freezing rain, or tornadoes are not uncommon. There are occasional flash floods of the Zumbro River.

**Area:** 39.61 square miles (2000)

**Elevation:** 1,320 feet above sea level

**Average Temperatures:** January, 11.8° F; July, 70.1° F; annual average, 43.4° F

**Average Annual Precipitation:** 31.40 inches of rain; 48.9 inches of snow

# ■ History

Long before the coming of Europeans, members of the Chippewa and Sioux nations lived in the area of the Minnesota Territory. Rochester was founded in 1854 when a group of U.S. surveyors staked claims on the banks of the Zumbro River. George Head began a pioneer settlement there, and by 1888, the settlement, which Head named in honor of his hometown in New York, had grown to 1,500 people. Many of those drawn to the area came because of the fertile farmland. In 1863 William Worall Mayo, examining surgeon for the Union Army Enrollment Board, settled in the town and, along with his sons, founded a medical practice. The Mayo Medical Center, which started out in a five-story brick building, now occupies about 10 million square feet.

The coming of the east-west railroad in the 1880s, which provided an excellent distribution system for the local farmers' products, added to the growth of the community, and agriculture has continued to be an important part of the local economy. A terrible tornado struck the city in 1883, and doctors were forced to treat its many victims under inadequate, makeshift conditions. Mother Alfred Moes, founder of the Sisters of St. Francis, proposed the building and staffing of a hospital, in which W.W. Mayo would provide the care. In 1889 St. Mary's Hospital opened with 27 beds.

Beginning in 1892, new staff members were added to the Mayo Clinic team. Dr. Henry Plummer, from a nearby small town, joined the Mayos in 1892 and designed many group practice systems that are the basis for those used today. They include the use of a common medical record, X-rays, conveyors for moving records, a registration system, and one of the first telephone paging systems. In 1907 the first patient registration number was assigned.

As physicians from around the world came to observe how the Mayo Clinic was operated, the clinic in 1915 initiated one of the world's first graduate training programs for doctors, called the Mayo Graduate School of Medicine. In 1919 the Mayos turned over all their profits and established the nonprofit Mayo Properties Association. Both of the Mayo brothers died within months of one another in 1939, but their work continued.

The local economy developed in a new direction with the establishment of an International Business Machines (IBM) plant in the 1950s. In 1990 that plant earned the prestigious Malcolm Baldrige National Quality Award.

The Mayo Medical School opened in 1972. The integration of Mayo Clinic Rochester, Saint Mary's Hospital, and Rochester Methodist Hospital took place in 1986, and that same year the clinic expanded with the opening of Mayo Clinic Jacksonville (Florida). In 1987 Mayo Clinic Scottsdale (Arizona) opened, and St. Luke's Hospital in Jacksonville became part of Mayo.

In 1992 a merger took place between Mayo Clinic and Luther Hospital and Midelfort Clinic in Eau Claire, Wisconsin. That same year Mayo affiliated with Decorah Medical Associates in Decorah, Iowa, and Community Clinics in Wabasha, Minnesota. Today, the Mayo Clinic, along with a symphony orchestra, museums, and other amenities, contributes to Rochester's livability. Since the turn of the century, Rochester has become the new home for more than 2,000 citizens each year. As a result, the city's mayor adopted a "smart growth" program to accommodate these newcomers into Rochester's existing population. In 2004, the city celebrated its 150th birthday.

***Historical Information:*** History Center of Olmstead County, 1195 W. Circle Dr. SW, Rochester, MN 55902; telephone (507)282-9447

# ■ Population Profile

**Metropolitan Area Residents**

  1980: 92,006
  1990: 106,470
  2000: 124,277
  2006 estimate: 179,573
  Percent change, 1990–2000: 11.7%
  U.S. rank in 1980: 292nd
  U.S. rank in 1990: 238th
  U.S. rank in 2000: 231st

**City Residents**

  1980: 57,906
  1990: 70,729
  2000: 85,806

Mayo Civic Center at Mayo Park. *Andre Jenny/Mira.com/drr.net*

2006 estimate: 96,975
Percent change, 1990–2000: 12.9%
U.S. rank in 1980: 349th
U.S. rank in 1990: 319th (State rank: 5th)
U.S. rank in 2000: 329th (State rank: 3rd)

**Density:** 2,166.3 people per square mile (2000)

**Racial and ethnic characteristics (2000)**

White: 75,088
Black: 3,064
American Indian and Alaska Native: 258
Asian: 4,830
Native Hawaiian and Pacific Islander: 33
Hispanic or Latino (may be of any race): 2,565
Other: 996

**Percent of residents born in state:** 55.4% (2000)

**Age characteristics (2005)**

Population under 5 years old: 5,897
Population 5 to 9 years old: 4,299
Population 10 to 14 years old: 6,741
Population 15 to 19 years old: 5,259

Population 20 to 24 years old: 5,245
Population 25 to 34 years old: 14,704
Population 35 to 44 years old: 14,276
Population 45 to 54 years old: 13,027
Population 55 to 59 years old: 5,075
Population 60 to 64 years old: 3,189
Population 65 to 74 years old: 5,511
Population 75 to 84 years old: 3,199
Population 85 years and older: 1,916
Median age: 36.3 years

**Births (2006, MSA)**

Total number: 2,741

**Deaths (2006, MSA)**

Total number: 1,165

**Money income (2005)**

Per capita income: $31,142
Median household income: $54,000
Total households: 37,710

**Number of households with income of . . .**

less than $10,000: 1,196

$10,000 to $14,999: 2,091
$15,000 to $24,999: 3,752
$25,000 to $34,999: 4,443
$35,000 to $49,999: 5,800
$50,000 to $74,999: 7,739
$75,000 to $99,999: 5,574
$100,000 to $149,999: 4,839
$150,000 to $199,999: 834
$200,000 or more: 1,442

**Percent of families below poverty level:** 5.9% (2005)

**2005 FBI Crime Index Property:** 2,465

**2005 FBI Crime Index Violent:** 261

# ■ Municipal Government

Rochester has a strong council-weak mayor form of government with an executive city administrator. The city council is comprised of seven council persons, the mayor, and the city administrator, each of whom serve a four-year term.

**Head Official:** Mayor Ardell F. Brede (NP) (since 2003; current term expires 2011)

**Total Number of City Employees:** 800 (2007)

*City Information:* Rochester City Hall, 201 4th St. SE, Rochester, MN 55904; telephone (507)285-8086

# ■ Economy

## Major Industries and Commercial Activity

The health care industry dominates Rochester's economy, thanks to the world-famous Mayo Clinic, which treats more than 500,000 patients annually and employs over 28,000 people at its Rochester location. Many of the city's 1.5-million annual visitors come for treatment at the Mayo Clinic. Mayo Medical Ventures licenses medical products and treatments worldwide that are developed at Mayo.

Wholesale and retail trade is the second-largest employment sector in the county. Many local industries sell their goods to the local International Business Machines (IBM) plant and to Mayo Medical Center. The Blue Gene/L computer, being developed at the Rochester IBM facility, was named No. 1 on the TOP 500 super computers list in fall 2006.

Rochester has been rated by *Inc.* magazine as one of the top entrepreneurial cities in the country. Production at the more than 150 area manufacturing firms includes food and dairy processing, computer and computer components, electronics, and precision machining.

Strong areas of growth in the economy are agricultural, metal fabrication, and distribution companies. Other businesses having a major impact on the local economy are construction, printing, packaging, hotels, restaurants, communications, and entertainment facilities. The service industry accounts for more than eighty percent of the local economy. The continuing growth of the economy is evidenced by the addition of some 20 firms over the past several years.

Agriculture still plays an important role in Rochester's economy, along with food processing and dairy production. Area farms produce annual crops of soybeans, corn, and a variety of fruits and vegetables. The area has 1,400 working farms, a cannery and three dairy processors. Rochester is the home of Marigold Foods, which produces the well-known Kemps brand of ice cream.

**Items and goods produced:** hospital/surgical equipment, electronics, metal fabrication, food processing, agricultural-related products, home pasteurizers, silos, beverages, toilet preparations, computer equipment, grain, poultry

## Incentive Programs—New and Existing Companies

*Local programs:* It is the mission of the Rochester Area Economic Development, Inc. (RAEDI) to assist new and existing companies with expansion, location, or research efforts. RAEDI has a corporation to provide better access to the U.S. Small Business Administration's 504 Loan Program, which finances long-term assets for 10- or 20-year terms. The program normally leverages a bank loan with a 504 loan to finance up to 90 percent of the project costs. RAEDI also administers the MicroEnterprise Loan Fund, which aids eligible businesses that are located in the city and have five or fewer employees, a written business plan, and an owner or 51 percent of employees who are at low or moderate income levels. The maximum loan amount is $7,500.

*State programs:* The Tax Increment Financing Program, a state authorized financing mechanism, is offered to assist basic businesses in financing their local expansion or relocation. Funds may be used to purchase land and make public improvements that support business development projects. Minnesota also offers programs to provide a mechanism for businesses to sell bonds at tax-exempt interest rates, allowing firms to receive long-term, low interest financing for fixed assets.

*Job training programs:* The Minnesota Department of Employment and Economic Development operates a network of workforce centers throughout the state. This WorkForce Center System, which has an office in Rochester, partners with local businesses to provide customized job training and other workforce development services.

## Development Projects

The creation of Cascade Lake Park, nearing completion in fall 2007, was intended to support a lake with the best possible water quality and provide residents and visitors with a variety of recreational and educational opportunities. Also in 2007, a yearlong project was underway to expand the downtown Peace Plaza; a 150,000-square-foot BioBusiness Center was being built near the Mayo Clinic; and University of Minnesota Rochester was in the planning stages of a new downtown facility, to include a student center and bookstore.

Rochester Area Economic Development, Inc. (RAEDI), Rochester's one-stop shop for businesses seeking economic assistance, has as its goal the development of a varied economy. It reports that Rochester and environs have the highest concentration of high-tech industries among all U.S. metropolitan areas. Rochester' technology base has continued to grow over the past decade with the addition of more than 20 new technology firms.

*Economic Development Information:* Rochester Area Economic Development, 220 S. Broadway, Ste. 100, Rochester, MN 55904; telephone (507)288-0208

## Commercial Shipping

Daily freight rail service is offered by the Dakota Minnesota & Eastern Railroad. Rochester has more than 20 motor freight carriers. Cargo carriers flying out of Rochester International Airport include FedEx and DHL.

## Labor Force and Employment Outlook

In September 2007 the unemployment rate in Rochester stood at 4 percent, down slightly from ten-year highs of 5 percent in 2005. Between 1997 and 2007 the metropolitan area work force increased from 87,478 to 106,305. With the health care industry booming nationally in 2007, the Mayo Clinic was expected to continue to bring moderate but steady growth to the area in the years ahead.

The following is a summary of data regarding the Rochester metropolitan area labor force, 2006 annual averages.

**Size of nonagricultural labor force:** 106,600

**Number of workers employed in ...**

    construction and mining: 4,700
    manufacturing: 13,200
    trade, transportation and utilities: 16,200
    information: 2,000
    financial activities: 2,800
    professional and business services: 5,500
    educational and health services: 39,000

    leisure and hospitality: 8,800
    other services: 3,600
    government: 10,800

**Average hourly earnings of production workers employed in manufacturing:** Not available

**Unemployment rate:** 3.9% (June 2007)

| *Largest employers (2007)* | *Number of employees* |
|---|---|
| Mayo Clinic | 28,000 |
| International Business Machines (IBM) | 4,400 |
| Rochester School District 535 | 2,150 |
| Olmstead County | 1,135 |
| Hyvee | 775 |
| Olmsted Medical Center | 998 |
| Wal-Mart | 981 |
| City of Rochester | 800 |
| Crenlo, Inc. | 755 |
| Sunstone Hotel Properties | 680 |

## Cost of Living

The cost of living in the Rochester area is slightly below the national average, except for housing prices, which tend to be slightly above the median. Nevertheless, Rochester residents can be assured that real estate is a good investment; Rochester's home appreciation rate is in the top quarter of all metropolitan areas.

The following is a summary of data regarding several key cost of living factors for the Rochester metropolitan area.

**2007 (1st quarter) ACCRA Average House Price:** $273,900

**2007 (1st quarter) ACCRA Cost of Living Index:** 97.4

**State income tax rate:** 5.35% to 7.85%

**State sales tax rate:** 6.5%

**Local income tax rate:** 1.0% of first $72,000; 2.0% over $72,000

**Local sales tax rate:** 0.5%

**Property tax rate:** tax capacity (1.0 to 1.25%) multiplied by 118.794%

*Economic Information:* Rochester Area Chamber of Commerce, 220 S. Broadway, Ste. 100, Rochester, MN 55904; telephone (507)288-1122; fax (507)282-8960

# ■ Education and Research

## Elementary and Secondary Schools

Independent School District 535 covers 205 square miles and has the seventh-largest enrollment in the state. The district is governed by a seven-member school board and employs more than 1,100 teachers. Rochester students consistently rank higher than average on standardized test scores, and in 2006 the district boasted nineteen National Merit Finalists. There are seven "choice" schools within the district, including a Montessori; other programs include alternative learning centers and the "Transition to Adulthood" program.

The following is a summary of data regarding the Rochester Public Schools (Independent School District 535) as of the 2005–2006 school year.

**Total enrollment:** 16,300

**Number of facilities**

    elementary schools: 16
    junior high/middle schools: 4
    senior high schools: 3
    other: 0

**Student/teacher ratio:** 16.7:1

**Teacher salaries (2005–06)**

    elementary median: $44,590
    junior high/middle median: Not available
    secondary median: $42,830

**Funding per pupil:** $7,595

***Public Schools Information:*** Rochester Public Schools, 615 7th St. SW, Rochester, MN 55902; telephone (507)285-8551

## Colleges and Universities

Rochester is the home of an impressive number of quality educational institutions. The Mayo Foundation conducts formal education in several areas: Mayo Graduate School of Medical Education and Research, Mayo Graduate School, Mayo Medical School, and the Mayo School of Health-Related Sciences, in addition to the residencies and fellowships the Foundation offers. The Mayo Medical School enrolls 42 students per year.

The University of Minnesota–Rochester is the newest school in the University of Minnesota system. It was formally established as a separate entity in December 2006 and offers 35 academic programs at the undergraduate, graduate, and doctoral levels. Winona State University–Rochester Center, with about 1,500 students at the location, offers a variety of undergraduate programs, and participates in the "2 plus 2" program, whereby students can complete an undergraduate degree in Rochester by transferring credits from other

institutions. The school has 40 resident faculty. Rochester Community and Technical College provides its 7,534 students with technical and transfer programs in a wide variety of majors, including business, trade/industry, allied health, human services, science, and social science. Its largest programs are in the liberal arts, nursing, business, digital arts, and law enforcement.

Other colleges are Crossroads College, formerly Minnesota Bible College, which enrolls nearly 100 students in courses that fulfill associate of arts, bachelor of arts, and bachelor of science degree requirements for the professional ministry and related areas, and Saint Mary's University of Minnesota-Rochester.

## Libraries and Research Centers

The Rochester Public Library houses a material collection of 418,917. These include films, multimedia resources, in-house CD-ROMs, and magazines. The library is a document depository for the City of Rochester.

Special libraries are maintained by the Mayo Foundation, Mayo Clinic, Crossroads College, the History Center of Olmsted County, the *Post Bulletin*, and International Business Machines (IBM).

The Mayo Clinic research funding exceeds $185 million annually, with about $40 million coming from external sources. Research is performed at several institutes associated with the Mayo Clinic, including the Mayo Biomedical Imaging Resource, Mayo Cancer Center, a $15-million broad-based cancer research institute, and Mayo Clinic and Foundation, which studies allergic diseases. Other research institutes in Rochester are the Center for Basic Research in Digestive Diseases and the North Central Cancer Treatment Group, which received a $34.4-million grant from the National Cancer Institute in 2007.

***Public Library Information:*** Rochester Public Library, 101 2nd St. SE, Rochester, MN 55904; telephone (507)285-8011; fax (507)287-1910

# ■ Health Care

The world famous Mayo Clinic can diagnose and treat just about any medical problem. Across its three locations (the flagship clinic in Rochester and two others in Florida and Arizona) Mayo has a staff of 3,300 physicians, scientists and researchers, and 46,000 health staff. The clinic has the largest association of physicians in the private practice of medicine in the world. Combined, the three clinics treat over half a million patients a year. The Mayo Clinic was ranked second overall on the 2007 *U.S. News and World Report* list of "America's Best Hospitals." The Clinic also was ranked among the best hospitals in fifteen specialties.

Staffed by Mayo Clinic physicians, Rochester Methodist and Saint Mary's Hospital are also world-renowned. Rochester Methodist is a 794-bed acute-care facility. The hospital provides care in such areas as organ transplantation, human fertility, oncology/hematology, and bone marrow transplantation. Its nursing units have been uniquely designed to allow research personnel to study the methods that serve patients most efficiently.

Saint Mary's Hospital, one of the largest private not-for-profit hospitals in the world, implements some of the most current advances in medical science. These include computer-assisted laser neurosurgery, kidney stone and gallstone dissolution without surgery, and magnetic resonance imaging. The hospital has 1,157 beds, 53 operating rooms, and eight intensive care units. The buildings that make up Saint Mary's Hospital are named in honor of Saint Marys' foundress, Mother Alfred, and its administrators—Sisters Joseph, Domitilla, Mary Brigh, and Generose. Mayo Eugenio Litta Children's Hospital is an 85-bed hospital within Saint Mary's. Research centers that are part of Saint Mary's include the General Clinical Research Center, Gastrointestinal Research Unit, and the Endocrine Research Unit and Diabetes Research Unit.

The Federal Medical Center, a federal correctional facility, provides medical, psychiatry, and chemical dependency services for inmates.

## ■ Recreation

### Sightseeing

Mayo Clinic, Rochester's most famous institution, offers general tours Monday through Friday. Self-guided tours of St. Mary's Hospital and Rochester Methodist Hospital are also available. Mayowood Mansion is the former home of doctors Charles H. and Charles W. Mayo. The 50-room mansion is full of many beautiful objects collected by the Mayos throughout their lifetime. It is open for viewing throughout the year, and is especially popular during the holiday season, when Christmas at Historic Mayowood is presented. Two local residences, the 1856 Heritage House in Town Square and the Plummer House of the Arts, are open to the public. The 49-room Tudor-style Plummer House is set on an 11-acre site with beautiful gardens.

### Arts and Culture

The major setting for arts activities in Rochester is the Mayo Civic Center, with its 7,200-seat arena. Throughout the year the center presents artistic performances of all sorts, as well as sports, exhibitions, and conventions. Rochester Civic Theater offers nine performances yearly, including comedies, dramas, and musicals. The Rochester Repertory Theatre presents contemporary and classic productions. Hill Theatre, at the University Center Rochester, offers theatrical programs and productions in conjunction with classes. Children's plays are the focus of the Masque Youth Theatre.

Music thrives in Rochester, and the Rochester Civic Music–Riverside Concerts presents live concerts, featuring local, national, and international acts in rock, pop, R&B, and many other genres. Riverside Live! is a series of outdoor concerts held from May to September in the Mayo Civic Center. Talented young musicians participate in the Southern Minnesota Youth Orchestra. Recently privatized, the Rochester Orchestra and Chorale offers six concerts of chamber, symphonic, and pops programs featuring local talent.

The Mayo Clinic Collection displays throughout its facilities works of art that were donated by benefactors and former patients. Traveling exhibits of arts and crafts are on view at the Rochester Art Center, which opened a new facility in May 2004. The center also offers classes for adults and children, as well as films and other special events. Famed Rochester sculptor Charles Eugene Gagnon has more than 40 bronze sculptures on display at his studio and galleries. The Southeastern Minnesota Visual Artists Gallery presents a rotating display of works by more than 80 artists, including basketry, paintings, sculpture, pottery, wearable art, and jewelry. The Museum of the Olmstead County Historical Society contains more than 600,000 items, including photos, books, and maps related to Rochester and the county.

### Festivals and Holidays

Rochester salutes spring with its annual Daffodil Days, sponsored by the American Cancer Society, and the Rochester World Festival, a celebration of the cultures of the world. April brings the Gingerbread Craft Show at Mayo Civic Center. The Covered Bridge Music & Arts Festival and Rochesterfest, with its food, street dances, parade, music, and crafts displays, enliven the summer.

July brings the Independence Day celebration at Silver Lake; the two-day threshing show, with hayrides, food, and demonstrations of early crafts; and the Olmsted County Fair at Rochester Fairgrounds, which continues into August and features a midway, grandstand shows, livestock competitions, and the largest county draft horse show in the country.

The Fall Festival is held at Mayowood and features an open-air market of Minnesota produce, a flower show, and woodworking exhibits and demonstrations. During Thanksgiving weekend the Festival of Trees spotlights special displays and holiday foods.

### Sports for the Spectator

The Minnesota Ice Hawks Junior B U.S. Hockey league plays its games at the Rochester–Olmstead Recreation Center from November through May. Rochester Honkers collegiate baseball league takes place at Mayo Field downtown from June through August. The Rochester Giants semi-professional football team plays at Soldiers Field.

## Sports for the Participant

Rochester has approximately 3,500 acres of park land, more than 60 miles of trails, 56 playgrounds, 42 tennis courts, and 14 picnic shelters. There are also two outdoor pools within the city limits, a beach, 35 horseshoe courts, 46 ball diamonds, 28 soccer fields, 11 basketball courts, two dog parks, 18 sand volleyball courts, an archery range, and two Frisbee golf courses. The Quarry Hill Nature Center offers hiking and biking trails on more than 290 acres of parkland, including a pond, stream, quarry, cave and restored prairies, as well as deciduous pine forests. Every year, more than 30,000 Canadian geese make their home at Silver Lake Park, which is the summertime site of canoeing and paddle boat rentals, walking paths, and picnicking. Whitewater State Park offers camping, trout fishing, picnic grounds, and hiking trails.

The Rochester Amateur Sports Commission spotlights the many amateur sporting events that take place in the area throughout the year. From May through September patrons enjoy activities at the Skyline Raceway & Waterslide, while bowling is offered year-round at Colonial Lanes and Recreation Lanes.

## Shopping and Dining

Apache Mall, with 100 specialty shops, is the city's premier shopping site. The Kahler Plaza, located beneath the Kahler Grand and Marriott hotels, offers shops, businesses, and restaurants. Small, unique shops are the focus of Rochester's Historic Mercantile District, and the Centerplace Galleria Mall is at the center of the skyway system. Other popular shopping centers include Crossroads, Maplewood, and Silver Lake. Contemporary fine art is offered at Callaway Galleries, and Wild Wings Gallery features the work of local wildlife artists.

Rochester has restaurants to appeal to every taste—from informal bar and grills to more formal dining rooms. Ethnic cuisine runs the gamut from American barbecue to Greek and Mexican, and just about everything in between. At the Lord Essex Fine Dining and Pub in the Kahler Hotel, patrons can enjoy fine dining in a pub atmosphere. The Henry Wellington is another popular restaurant.

*Visitor Information:* Rochester Convention and Visitors Bureau, 30 Civic Center Drive SE, Suite 200, Rochester, MN 55904; telephone (507)288-4331; fax (507)288-9144

## ■ Convention Facilities

Rochester's primary meeting place is the Mayo Civic Center, which houses the 11,000-square-foot Grand Lobby and the 25,000-square-foot Taylor Arena, accommodating 4,500 theater-style and 1,000 classroom-style. The civic center's 11,800-square-foot auditorium

can seat 3,400 festival-style, while its theater can handle 1,340 theater-style and provides up to 17 breakout rooms. The facility also has many patios and a 3,000-square-foot outdoor stage. Graham Arena One and Graham Arena Two are at the Olmsted County Fairgrounds. Graham Arena One provides a total exhibit area of 28,000 square feet with seating for 2,500. Graham Arena Two has 22,000 square feet of exhibit space. In 2007 Graham Arena Three had recently opened and Graham Arena Four was under construction.

Rochester has about 4,600 hotel rooms, with more than 1,500 of them linked by climate-controlled skyways and subways to dining, shopping, services, the Mayo Clinic, and the Mayo Civic Center. There are 51 hotels and motels in the Rochester area.

*Convention Information:* Rochester Convention and Visitors Bureau, 150 S. Broadway, Ste. A, Rochester, MN 55904; telephone (507)288-4331; toll-free 800-634-8277; fax (507)288-9144

## ■ Transportation

### Approaching the City

U.S. Highway 14 and State Highway 30 run east and west through Rochester, while U.S. Highway 52 and U.S. Highway 63 run north and south. Interstate 35 is 35 miles west of the city. Rochester International Airport, located south of the city just off U.S. Highway 63, averaged 164 aircraft operations per day in 2006. The airport is served by American Airlines, which has daily flights to Chicago, and Northwest Airlines, with daily flights to Minneapolis and Detroit. Local van service is also available to Minneapolis Airport. Intercity bus lines include Greyhound and Rochester City Lines Commuter Services. Daily bus service is offered to Winona, Minnesota, 45 miles east, where the closest Amtrak depot is located.

### Traveling in the City

In Rochester, streets generally run east and west, and avenues run north and south. The city is divided into quadrants designated NW, NE, SW and SE. Broadway is the east/west divider street, and Center Street is the north/south divider street. Local bus service is provided by Rochester City Lines.

## ■ Communications

### Newspapers and Magazines

The *Post-Bulletin*, Rochester's daily, is an evening newspaper. The *Agri-News* is a farm newspaper that appears weekly. Monthly journals published in Rochester are *Fertility and Sterility,* a journal on reproductive medicine, and the *Mayo Clinic Proceedings.*

## Television and Radio

Television stations available in Rochester include NBC and FOX affiliates. The city is served by almost 30 AM and FM stations with diverse formats, including news/talk, country, and public radio.

*Media Information:*    *Post-Bulletin,* 18 1st Ave. SE, PO Box 6118, Rochester, MN 55903; telephone (507) 285-7600

## Rochester Online

City of Rochester home page. Available www.ci.rochester.mn.us

Mayo Clinic Health Oasis. Available www.mayoclinic.com

Mayo Clinic Rochester. Available www.mayo.edu

Minnesota Historical Society. Available www.mnhs.org

Rochester Convention & Visitors Bureau. Available www.rochestercvb.org

Rochester *Post-Bulletin.* Available www.postbulletin.com

Rochester Public Library. Available www.rochesterpubliclibrary.org

Rochester Public Schools. Available www.rochester.k12.mn.us

BIBLIOGRAPHY

Hodgson, Harriet W., *Rochester: City of the Prairies* (Northridge, CA: Windsor Publications, 1989)

Leonard, Joseph A., *History of Olmsted County Minnesota* (Chicago, IL: Goodspeed History Association, 1910)

Severson, Harold R., *Rochester: Mecca for Millions* (Rochester, MN: Marquette Bank & Trust, 1979)

# Saint Paul

## ■ The City in Brief

**Founded:** 1846 (incorporated 1849)

**Head Official:** Mayor Chris Coleman (since 2006)

**City Population**
   1980: 270,230
   1990: 272,235
   2000: 287,151
   2006 estimate: 273,535
   Percent change, 1990–2000: 5.5%
   U.S. rank in 1980: 54th
   U.S. rank in 1990: 57th (State rank: 2nd)
   U.S. rank in 2000: 59th (State rank: 2nd)

**Metropolitan Area Population**
   1980: 2,137,133
   1990: 2,538,776
   2000: 2,968,806
   2006 estimate: Not available
   Percent change, 1990–2000: 19.6%
   U.S. rank in 1980: 17th
   U.S. rank in 1990: Not available
   U.S. rank in 2000: 16th

**Area:** 53 square miles (2000)

**Elevation:** 834 feet above sea level

**Average Annual Temperature:** 44.7° F

**Average Annual Precipitation:** 26.41 inches of rain; 49.9 inches of snow

**Major Economic Sectors:** Services, trade, manufacturing, government

**Unemployment Rate:** 4.4% (June 2007)

**Per Capita Income:** $23,541 (2005)

**2005 FBI Crime Index Property:** 13,693

**2005 FBI Crime Index Violent:** 2,443

**Major Colleges and Universities:** University of Minnesota–Twin Cities, Metropolitan State University, Macalester College, University of St. Thomas, College of St. Catherine, Hamline University, William Mitchell College of Law

**Daily Newspaper:** *Saint Paul Pioneer Press*

## ■ Introduction

Saint Paul is the capital of Minnesota and the seat of Ramsey County. Along with Minneapolis, it occupies the center of the fifteen-county Twin Cities metropolitan statistical area. The city developed in the late nineteenth century through the efforts of railroad baron James Hill and religious leader Archbishop John Ireland. In addition to being a primary transportation and distribution hub, Saint Paul has gained a national reputation for its effective local government, attractive architecture, rich cultural environment, and quality of life. The combined cities of Minneapolis and Saint Paul are highly rated for their livability and rank among the country's best places for growing a business.

## ■ Geography and Climate

Saint Paul occupies with Minneapolis the center of the 15-county Twin Cities metropolitan statistical area. Saint Paul is located with Minneapolis at the confluence of the Mississippi and Minnesota Rivers over the heart of an artesian water basin. The surrounding terrain is flat or rolling and dotted with lakes. The climate is predominantly continental with wide seasonal temperature variations, ranging from minus 30 degrees to 100 degrees and above.

**Area:** 53 square miles (2000)

**Elevation:** 834 feet above sea level

**Average Temperature:** 44.7° F

**Average Annual Precipitation:** 26.41 inches of rain;
49.9 inches of snow

# ■ History

## River Fort Draws Traders, Settlers

Jonathan Carver, a New Englander, was attempting to find a northwest passage to the Pacific Ocean in the winter of 1766 when he stopped near the future site of Saint Paul, where he discovered a Native American burial ground (now known as Indian Mound Park). When the Louisiana Purchase became part of United States territory in 1803, federally-financed expeditions explored the new territory, which included present-day Saint Paul. In 1805 Lieutenant Zebulon M. Pike camped on an island later named Pike Island and entered into an unofficial agreement with the Sioux tribe for land at the confluence of the Mississippi and Minnesota rivers; also included in the pact was land that became the site of Fort Snelling.

In 1819, Colonel Henry Leavenworth built an army post on the Minnesota River on a spot named Mendota south of present-day Saint Paul; the next year the fortress was moved across the river where Colonel Josiah Snelling constructed Fort Anthony, which was later renamed Fort Snelling. The presence of the fort allowed an Indian agency, fur trading post, missionaries, and white settlers to gain a foothold there. Settlers living on federal land were eventually expelled, and Pierre "Pig's Eye" Parrant, a French Canadian, joined others in building a settlement named after Parrant's colorful nickname near Fort Snelling. In 1841, Father Lucian Galtier named a log chapel in Pig's Eye after his patron saint, Saint Paul, and persuaded others to accept the name for their emerging community, as well.

Saint Paul was platted in 1847; two years later it was named the capital of the Minnesota Territory and incorporated as a town. Saint Paul received its city charter in 1854 and when Minnesota became a state in 1858, the city retained its status as state capital. By the start of the Civil War, 10,000 people lived in Saint Paul.

## Rail Transport and New Residents Shape City

Two men had major roles in the development of Saint Paul in the post-Civil War period. The railroad magnate James J. Hill used the city and the Great Northern Railroad to accumulate great individual wealth and to wield immense political power. Hill envisioned his adopted city of Saint Paul as the base for an empire in the northwest, built on his railroad holdings. The other major influence on Saint Paul's development was Catholic Archbishop John Ireland, a native of Ireland who settled in Saint Paul at the age of fourteen and, as an adult, established a religious base for community endeavors. He brought thousands of destitute Irish families to Saint Paul, where they relocated in colonies and started a new life. The Catholic influence in the shaping of Saint Paul can be traced to the pioneering efforts of Archbishop Ireland. Another notable figure who called Saint Paul home is F. Scott Fitzgerald.

In the nineteenth century a number of distinct population groups contributed to the character of Saint Paul. One was from the New England states and New York; these transplanted Easterners brought their educational values and business experiences to the prairie community. Another consisted of immigrants from Germany and Ireland who flocked to the United States by the tens of thousands. Among the professional groups were German physicians and Irish politicians and lawyers. German musical traditions and beer-making practices found a new home in Saint Paul. Scandinavians also immigrated to the city, but in fewer numbers than those who settled in neighboring Minneapolis.

In the twentieth century, Saint Paul erected fine buildings like the state capitol and developed many cultural institutions, including theaters; a notable peace monument in the concourse of the city hall; the state historical society building, containing a museum and library; and the Saint Paul Arts and Science Center. Saint Paul is also home to many educational institutions. Although its Twin City, Minneapolis, surpassed Saint Paul shortly before the turn of the twentieth century as the larger, wealthier, industrially more powerful of the two cities, Saint Paulites believe their city possesses more character and charm. Contributing to that charm are a good symphony orchestra and the stately mansions of former railroad and timber barons along Summit Avenue. The city is also known as environmentally friendly, ranking fourth on a list of top 10 green cities in the U.S. by "The Green Guide."

***Historical Information:*** Minnesota History Center, 345 Kellogg Blvd W., Saint Paul, MN 55102; telephone (651)296-6126

# ■ Population Profile

### Metropolitan Area Residents

1980: 2,137,133
1990: 2,538,776
2000: 2,968,806
2006 estimate: Not available
Percent change, 1990–2000: 19.6%
U.S. rank in 1980: 17th
U.S. rank in 1990: Not available
U.S. rank in 2000: 16th

©James Blank.

### City Residents

 1980: 270,230
 1990: 272,235
 2000: 287,151
 2006 estimate: 273,535
 Percent change, 1990–2000: 5.5%
 U.S. rank in 1980: 54th
 U.S. rank in 1990: 57th (State rank: 2nd)
 U.S. rank in 2000: 59th (State rank: 2nd)

**Density:** 5,441.7 people per square mile (1999)

### Racial and ethnic characteristics (2005)

 White: 172,922
 Black: 35,836
 American Indian and Alaska Native: 1,897
 Asian: 35,324
 Native Hawaiian and Pacific Islander: 87
 Hispanic or Latino (may be of any race): 22,402
 Other: 9,065

**Percent of residents born in state:** 59.6% (2000)

### Age characteristics (2005)

 Population under 5 years old: 22,204

 Population 5 to 9 years old: 18,982
 Population 10 to 14 years old: 20,329
 Population 15 to 19 years old: 17,780
 Population 20 to 24 years old: 19,367
 Population 25 to 34 years old: 39,676
 Population 35 to 44 years old: 42,042
 Population 45 to 54 years old: 37,823
 Population 55 to 59 years old: 13,379
 Population 60 to 64 years old: 8,289
 Population 65 to 74 years old: 10,078
 Population 75 to 84 years old: 8,056
 Population 85 years and older: 3,554
 Median age: 33.4 years

### Births (2006, MSA)

 Total number: 45,553

### Deaths (2006, MSA)

 Total number: 19,278

### Money income (2005)

 Per capita income: $23,541
 Median household income: $44,103
 Total households: 107,979

**Number of households with income of...**

less than $10,000: 12,380
$10,000 to $14,999: 5,778
$15,000 to $24,999: 11,087
$25,000 to $34,999: 13,375
$35,000 to $49,999: 17,699
$50,000 to $74,999: 21,158
$75,000 to $99,999: 11,826
$100,000 to $149,999: 9,172
$150,000 to $199,999: 2,971
$200,000 or more: 2,533

**Percent of families below poverty level:** 8.3% (2005)

**2005 FBI Crime Index Property:** 13,693

**2005 FBI Crime Index Violent:** 2,443

## ■ Municipal Government

Saint Paul, the seat of Ramsey County, operates under a mayor-council form of government, with strong power being delegated to the mayor, who serves for four years. The seven council members are elected by ward to two-year terms.

**Head Official:** Mayor Chris Coleman (since 2006; current term expires January 2010)

**Total Number of City Employees:** 3,495 (2007)

*City Information:* City Hall, 400 City Hall Annex Saint Paul, MN 55102; telephone (651)266-8510

## ■ Economy

### Major Industries and Commercial Activity

The principal economic sectors in Saint Paul are services, wholesale and retail trade, manufacturing, and government. Along with Minneapolis, Saint Paul is the site of one of the largest concentrations of high-technology firms in the United States. Statewide, there are more than 8,000 high-tech firms employing nearly 270,000 skilled workers. The city is also among the largest livestock and meatpacking centers in the nation. Nineteen of the *Fortune* 500 largest U.S. corporations are headquartered in the Twin Cities area, which is among the largest commercial centers between Chicago and the West Coast. The area is home to several of the world's largest private companies, and in 2004 had the fourteenth-largest Gross Metro Product in the nation. Local companies are involved in the manufacturing of super computers, electronics, and medical instruments, as well as milling, machine production, food processing, and graphic arts. There are approximatey 31,000 total companies in the Saint Paul region.

Approximately 24 percent of area workers are employed in education, health, and social services. Thirteen percent work in manufacturing and twelve percent in professional/administrative/management services.

The city was selected as the site of the 2008 Republican National Convention, which was expected to generate significant tourism revenue for the Twin Cities.

**Items and goods produced:** hoists and derricks, rugs, computers, food products, medical products, machinery, electronic materials, automobiles, appliances, chemicals, abrasives, beer, printed products

### Incentive Programs—New and Existing Companies

Various programs are available for small business incentive and expansion; among them are the Small Business Development Loan Program, offering fixed-rate low-interest direct loans, and tax credits for corporations that assist small businesses.

*Local programs:* The City of Saint Paul's Department of Planning and Economic Development offers a variety of services to assist new or expanding businesses; services include small business financing and loan guarantees/direct loans. Specific financial assistance programs include the city's Capital City Business Development Program, Strategic Investment Program, Minority Business and Development Retention Program (MBDR), and the Socially Responsible Investment Fund (SRIF). In 2007 the city instituted the "Sustainable Saint Paul Awards" to reward green building projects.

*State programs:* The Tax Increment Financing Program, a state authorized financing mechanism, is offered to assist basic businesses in financing their local expansion or relocation. Funds may be used to purchase land and make public improvements that support business development projects. Minnesota also offers programs to provide a mechanism for businesses to sell bonds at tax-exempt interest rates, allowing firms to receive long-term, low interest financing for fixed assets.

*Job training programs:* The City of Saint Paul's Business Resource Center offers a variety of services including information, technical assistance, financing, site searches, and job training. Other programs are available through area colleges and universities, including the Saint Paul Technical College and Vocational Institute.

### Development Projects

Saint Paul continues to profit from the Neighborhood Development Program, a unique redevelopment initiative that has gained the city national recognition. Since 1997, the Saint Paul Port Authority has partnered with neighborhood organizations to select brownfield sites for redevelopment. Through creative use of public and private funding, it has completed several projects, replacing brownfields with light industrial manufacturing facilities and donating land for designated open spaces. Saint Paul funds its brownfield projects with a combination of general obligation bonds, tax increment financing, local sales tax revenues, municipal grants, loan guarantees, Economic Development Administration grants, Community Development Block Grants, Enterprise Community grants, and EPA Brownfields Pilot grants. The city was the recipient of the 2005 Phoenix Award Grand Prize for "Excellence in Brownfield Redevelopment" for its Phalen Corridor initiative.

In 2007 planning was in the early stages for a large-scale economic initiative to develop a vision and development strategy for University Avenue and the Capitol/Downtown area, called the "Central Corridor Plan." Key tenets of the plan included stringent requirements for the design of new development, new housing for all incomes, minority business development and apprenticeship programs, increased pedestrian and bicycle connections, revamped streetscape design, and new parks, open space, and public art. No completion date had been set for the initiative.

In 2007 a major building project was underway in nearby Minneapolis; a new stadium for the Minnesota Twins was in the early construction stage downtown on the site of a former parking lot. The final design is an outdoor stadium with 40,000 seats and was expected to cost around $390 million by its completion in 2010.

***Economic Development Information:*** Saint Paul Port Authority, Suite 1900 Landmark Towers, 345 St. Peter St., Saint Paul, MN 55102

## Commercial Shipping

Saint Paul is a Foreign Trade Zone with duty free facilities. The ports of Saint Paul and Minneapolis are served by nine barge lines operating on the Mississippi, Minnesota, and St. Croix rivers; together the ports handle more than 11 million tons of cargo annually. Air transportation is available at the Minneapolis-Saint Paul International Airport, which is served by 17 cargo carriers and air-freight forwarders. The Twin Cities area is also linked with major United States and Canadian markets via a network of four railroad companies.

Considered one of the largest trucking centers in the nation, Minneapolis-Saint Paul is served by approximately 150 motor freight companies that provide overnight and four- to five-day delivery in the Midwest and major markets in the continental United States.

## Labor Force and Employment Outlook

Local educational institutions assure employers of well-trained workers, particularly in high-technology areas, where engineers, scientists, researchers, and technicians are in demand. The Twin Cities boasts an educated work force; approximately a quarter of people 25 years old or older have four or more years of college. Unemployment in the Twin Cities remained low in the early 2000s, but by 2007 it had caught up with national averages. The highest growth was expected in the areas of healthcare, technical and social services, personal care, construction, and computer professional occupations. Projections in 2007 indicated that a diversified economy and low cost of living would help growth in the Twin Cities remain fairly steady.

The suburban Mall of America, one of the most popular tourist destinations in the United States, has a significant economic impact. The Twin Cities' economy is keeping pace with, and in some cases surging ahead of, the national economy. In September 2007 the unemployment rate in the Minneapolis-Saint Paul-Bloomington metropolitan statistical area stood at 4.7 percent, on the rise but still slightly lower than ten year highs above five percent in 2004. Between 1997 and 2007 the area labor force rose from 1,645,537 to 1,858,316.

The following is a summary of data regarding the Saint Paul city metropolitan area labor force, 2005 annual averages.

**Size of nonagricultural labor force:** 128,011

**Number of workers employed in ...**

    construction and mining: 4,058
    manufacturing: 14,664
    trade, transportation and utilities: 22,267
    information: 5,539
    financial activities: 10,448
    professional and business services: 14,050
    educational and health services: 29,473
    leisure and hospitality: 11,903
    other services: 8,705
    government: 18,570

**Average hourly earnings of production workers employed in manufacturing:** Not available

**Unemployment rate:** 4.4% (June 2007)

| *Largest employers (2007)* | *Number of employees* |
| --- | --- |
| Northwest Airlines | 16,900 |
| State of Minnesota | 13,298 |
| West Group | 4,500 |
| Anderson Corp. | 4,000 |
| U.S. Bank | 3,636 |
| Regions Hospital | 3,425 |
| Wells Fargo | 3,379 |
| Deluxe Corp. | 3,100 |
| United Hospitals | 2,400 |
| St. Paul Travelers | 2,300 |

## Cost of Living

The Twin Cities' region has one of the lowest costs of living among the 25 largest cities in the United States. The cost of living is reported as being near the national average; the cost of housing and food is below the national average. The average home price in 2007 was listed as $187,453 by HomeScape, a web site for realtors. The U.S. Census Bureau reported that the average home sale price in 2000 was $175,515.

The following is a summary of data regarding several key cost of living factors in the Saint Paul area.

**2007 (1st quarter) ACCRA Average House Price:** Not available

**2007 (1st quarter) ACCRA Cost of Living Index:** Not available

**State income tax rate:** 5.35% to 7.85%

**State sales tax rate:** 6.5%

**Local income tax rate:** None

**Local sales tax rate:** 0.5%

**Property tax rate:** 17.0% of first $68,000 of market value; 27.0% over $68,000

*Economic Information:* Saint Paul Area Chamber of Commerce, 401 North Robert Street, Suite 150, Saint Paul, Minnesota 55101; telephone (651)223-5000; fax (651)223-5119

# ■ Education and Research

## Elementary and Secondary Schools

Public schools in Saint Paul are administered by Independent School District 625, the second-largest school system in Minnesota. A superintendent is chosen by a seven-member, nonpartisan board of education. Students in the district speak more than 70 dialects and languages, and the district offers educational collaboratives with the Office of the Mayor, the Children's Museum, and local businesses. Alternative learning programs include an international academy, a creative arts high school, and a lifelong learning center.

The following is a summary of data regarding the Saint Paul Public Schools as of the 2005–2006 school year.

**Total enrollment:** 42,000

**Number of facilities**

  elementary schools: 53
  junior high/middle schools: 11
  senior high schools: 10
  other: 0

**Student/teacher ratio:** 17.7:1

**Teacher salaries (2005–06)**

  elementary median: $46,260
  junior high/middle median: $45,470
  secondary median: $46,410

**Funding per pupil:** $10,928

A variety of private schools in Saint Paul enroll more than 12,000 students.

*Public Schools Information:* Saint Paul Public Schools, 360 Colborne Street, Saint Paul, MN 55102; telephone (651)293-5100

## Colleges and Universities

Saint Paul is home to several colleges and universities. The University of Minnesota–Twin Cities operates a main campus in Saint Paul as well as in Minneapolis. The state institution had an enrollment of 28,645 in fall 2006. The university ranks among the nation's top ten public research universities; in the 2008 edition of the *U.S. News and World Report* college rankings, UMTC was ranked 71st among national universities. Five degree levels—baccalaureate, first-professional, master's, intermediate, and doctorate—are available in 250 fields in the University of Minnesota system, including architecture, medicine, engineering, journalism, management, teacher education, public health, and music. Former students and faculty members have been awarded 12 Nobel Prizes in physics, medicine, chemistry, economics, and peace.

Metropolitan State University, part of the Minnesota State University system, offers undergraduate and graduate programs in liberal arts, nursing, and management; the administrative offices of Minnesota State University are located in Saint Paul. The William Mitchell College of Law is a privately operated professional school devoted solely to the study of law.

Macalester College, affiliated with the Presbyterian church and founded in 1874, enrolled 1,920 students in 2007. Twelve percent of its enrollment consists of international students. Macalester was ranked 26th on the 2008 *U.S. News and World Report* list of top liberal arts colleges. Between 1997 and 2007 Macalester students received four Rhodes Scholarships, 28 Fulbrights, 23 National Science Foundation Fellowships, three Truman Scholarships, ten Watson Fellowships, two Mellon Fellowships and three Goldwater Scholarships.

Hamline University, affiliated with the United Methodist Church, provides undergraduate and graduate programs in such areas as chemistry, law, music, and teacher education. It enrolled 1,902 students in 2006. Bethel University is a four-year institution associated with the Baptist General Conference. The four-year Concordia College is operated by the Lutheran Church-Missouri Synod. Lutheran Northwestern Seminary is the divinity school for the American Lutheran Church and the

Lutheran Church in America. Other church-related colleges include Northwestern College, which is associated with the Presbyterian Church. The College of St. Catherine, the University of St. Thomas, and the Saint Paul Seminary School of Divinity are Roman Catholic institutions.

Vocational and technical training is available at community colleges and specialized schools in Saint Paul and Minneapolis; among them is Saint Paul Technical College and Vocational Institute.

### Libraries and Research Centers

Nearly 70 public and private libraries are based in Saint Paul. The Saint Paul Public Library system includes a main facility, 12 branches, and a bookmobile. The library, which is a depository for federal and city documents, houses more than 1 million volumes as well as 2,000 periodicals, and CDs, maps, and other items. Special collections include oral history and the history of the city of Saint Paul. Adjacent to the Saint Paul Public Library is the James J. Hill Reference Library; its business and economic collection is open to the public. The Minnesota Historical Society maintains an extensive reference library with subject interests in genealogy, Minnesota history, and Scandinavians in the United States, among other areas. Most colleges and universities in Saint Paul operate campus libraries, the largest being the University of Minnesota system, which consists of a main facility and four department libraries; its collection numbers more than four million catalogued volumes.

Among the larger state agency libraries in the city are the Minnesota State Law Library and the Minnesota Legislative Reference Library. Other specialized libraries are associated primarily with corporations, churches, and hospitals.

Research centers in the Twin Cities affiliated with the University of Minnesota include the Hubert H. Humphrey Institute of Public Affairs; the Industrial Relations Center; the Metropolitan Design Center; the Northern Tier Technology Corridor; the Underground Space Center; the Immigration History Research Center; and the Minnesota Center for Twin and Adoption Research.

*Public Library Information:* Saint Paul Public Library, 90 West Fourth Street, Saint Paul, MN 55102; telephone (651)266-7000

## ■ Health Care

Minneapolis-Saint Paul is a regional health care center. Six hospitals are based in Saint Paul. The largest facility is Regions Medical Center, a teaching and research hospital that specializes in heart care, women's services, cancer, digestive care, seniors' services, burns, emergency, and trauma. Regions also houses an ambulatory care clinic and provides general medical, surgical, pediatric,

psychiatric, and chemical dependency services. The hospital has 427 beds. Gillette Children's Specialty Healthcare is a center specializing in children's health issues; it is located in Regions Hospital.

Children's Hospital, a teaching and referral center for infants and children with pediatric disorders, includes among its specialties open heart surgery and cardiac catheterization, and infant apnea diagnosis. Other hospitals in Saint Paul include St. John's, St. Joseph's, United Hospital, and Bethesda Healtheast.

Nearby Minneapolis is also home to a number of hospitals, including the University of Minnesota Medical Center, Fairview, where the first open heart surgery was performed in 1954. The hospital is also known as a leading organ transplant center. In the 2008 *U.S. News and World Report* list of "America's Best Hospitals," the U of M Medical Center ranked among the top 50 hospitals in the country in nine medical specialties, including digestive disorders, endocrinology, and kidney diseases. Among the other major hospitals in Minneapolis are the University of Minnesota Children's Hospital, which operates six affiliated clinics, Shriner's Hospital, the Veteran's Administration Medical Center, the Hennepin County Medical Center (with 422 beds and ranked in the *2007 U.S. News and World Report* list for its kidney care), and the Sister Kenny Rehabilitation Institute.

## ■ Recreation

### Sightseeing

Landmark architectural structures provide unique space for Saint Paul's arts institutions. The state Capitol was designed by Cass Gilbert in 1904 and blends Minnesota stones with imported marble; paintings, murals, and sculptures represent the state's history. A trip to Saint Paul might include a visit to Saint Paul Cathedral, which is modeled after St. Peter's in Rome. Landmark Center, once a Federal Courts Building, is now the city's arts center and winner of a national restoration award.

Historic Fort Snelling has been restored to its original state; costumed guides tell about the fort's early history as the first non-Native American settlement in the Saint Paul area. The Alexander Ramsey House was the home of Minnesota's first territorial governor; tours of the home are available year round. Reflecting the opulence of Saint Paul's most famous nineteenth-century railroad baron, the 32-room James J. Hill House was at one time the largest home in the Midwest. A 5-mile stretch of Summit Avenue is lined with Victorian homes. A few blocks away, at 481 Laurel, is writer F. Scott Fitzgerald's birthplace (not open to the public).

Como Zoo and Marjorie McNeely Conservatory feature a children's zoo, a large cats house, an aquatic house, and a new visitor's center. The Children's Museum features hands-on exhibits.

## Arts and Culture

Like Minneapolis, Saint Paul enjoys a national reputation in the performing arts. The Ordway Center for the Performing Arts is the home of the Saint Paul Chamber Orchestra and the Minnesota Opera Company. The Landmark Center is a Romanesque Revival building whose south tower is modeled after Boston's Trinity Church. The Schubert Piano Club and Keyboard Instruments Museum is located in the center. The American Museum of Art recently opened its Riverfront Gallery on Kellogg Boulevard; the museum houses contemporary and Asian art as well as sculpture, paintings, photography, and drawings.

The Science Museum of Minnesota features the Dinosaurs and Fossils Gallery, Omnitheater and a 3D cinema representing the latest in high-tech entertainment. At the Mississipi River Gallery, visitors can unlock the secrets of locks and dams, explore an authentic Mississippi River towboat, and view the river from the museum's balcony. At the Human Body Gallery, visitors can view their own cells through a microscope; in the Experiment Gallery, visitors can make a tornado and create waves in the wave tank. The Minnesota History Center presents interpretations of the state's history through exhibits and material objects.

Saint Paul's theater companies include the Park Square Theater, which concentrates on classic plays; the Great North American History Theater, which presents local historical drama; and Penumbra Theater, a professional African American theater company.

***Arts and Culture Information:*** Metropolitan Regional Arts Council, 2324 University Ave. W., Saint Paul, MN 55114; telephone (651)645-0402

## Festivals and Holidays

The Saint Paul Winter Carnival is the largest winter celebration in the nation. This annual festival, held the last weekend in January through the first weekend in February, features parades, ice and snow sculpture, fine arts performances, a ball, unusual winter sporting events, and a re-enactment of the legend of King Boreas. Saint Paul hosts the largest celebration of St. Patrick's Day outside of New York City. The Festival of Nations in late April celebrates the food and cultures of more than 50 countries. Grand Old Day on an early June Sunday begins with a parade on a one-mile stretch of Grand Avenue and includes entertainment, food, and crafts; the celebration is the largest one-day street fair in the Midwest. Taste of Minnesota on the Fourth of July weekend is held on the Minnesota State Capitol Mall and concludes with a fireworks display on Independence Day. The Minnesota State Fair, one of the largest state fairs in the country, runs for 10 days ending on Labor Day at the Minnesota State Fairgrounds.

## Sports for the Spectator

The Twin Cities are home to five professional sports teams. The Minnesota Vikings compete in the National Football Conference in the North Division. The Minnesota Twins are in the Central Division of baseball's American League. The Minnesota Timberwolves are in the National Basketball Association. The baseball and football teams play home games in the Hubert H. Humphrey Metrodome in downtown Minneapolis. The Timberwolves compete at the Target Center in downtown Minneapolis. The Minnesota Wild of the National Hockey League play in the 650,000-square-foot Xcel Energy Center. The Women's National Basketball Association team, the Minnesota Lynx, came to the Twin Cities in 2000.

University of Minnesota teams compete in the Big Ten in football, baseball, hockey, and basketball. Thoroughbred horses run at Canterbury Downs Racetrack in Shakopee in a mid-May to mid-August season.

## Sports for the Participant

The Rice & Arlington Sports Dome hosts softball, soccer, and baseball leagues. In addition, the dome is used for private lessons, clinics, parties, and batting practice. The playing area of the dome features a full-size softball field with a 330-foot, straight-away center and two soccer fields that are 50 yards wide by 60 yards long. The soccer fields can also be played on lengthwise, creating a field 100 yards long by 60 yards wide.

Outdoor sports in the Saint Paul area include fishing, swimming, boating, and water skiing in the summer and ice fishing, ice skating, cross-country skiing, and hockey in the winter. The Twin Cities Marathon is an annual event that attracts as many as 10,000 runners and is usually held the first or second Sunday in October.

## Shopping and Dining

Saint Paul boasts one of the world's longest public skyway systems; it consists of 5 miles of second-level walkways that link downtown hotels, restaurants, stores, and businesses. At the center of four square blocks of more than 100 retail and dining establishments is the Town Square Park, which is an enclosed, year-round park. The Farmers Market is an old-world open market selling home-grown foods and crafts on weekends. Historic Grand Avenue is lined with private homes, retail shops, boutiques, and antique stores. A local shopping square is housed in a turn-of-the-century railroad building. There are antique stores as well as specialty stores promoting Minnesota goods located throughout the Twin Cities.

Saint Paul restaurants stress American home cooking and Midwest cuisine; ethnic choices range from Afghan and Vietnamese menus to continental and French restaurants. Fresh fish, prime rib, and 16-ounce steaks are local favorites. Dinner cruises on the Mississippi River are offered. The quaint river town of Stillwater, 25 miles east of Saint Paul, also offers dining and shopping opportunities.

***Visitor Information:*** Saint Paul Convention and Visitors Bureau, 175 West Kellogg Boulevard, Suite 502, Saint Paul, MN 55102; telephone (651)265-4900. Explore Minnesota Tourism, 100 Metro Square, 121 7th Place East, Saint Paul, MN 55101; telephone (651)296-5029

# ■ Convention Facilities

River Centre Convention and Entertainment complex accommodates events such as seminars, banquets, and conventions. The facility has a total of 902,819 square feet of space, with 162,299 in the Saint Paul's RiverCentre and 90,520 in the Roy Wilkins auditorium; the adjacent arena has 650,000 square feet. Saint Paul's skyway system connects the facility to more than 700 downtown hotel rooms. The Radison Riverfront Hotel offers 55,000 square feet of flexible meeting space, 25 meeting rooms, and a glass ballroom overlooking the Mississippi River and Kellogg Square Park. The Fitzgerald Theatre, the city's oldest standing theater, provides seating for more than 900 people for meetings and various kinds of presentations in a two-balcony hall. The Minnesota State Fair Grounds maintains 13 indoor facilities, ranging from 2,000 to 100,000 square feet, for use outside of the fair season. Four conference sites, accommodating from 100 to 4,000 people, and lodging rooms for 1,000 people are available on the Macalester College campus.

Several hotels and motels offer meeting and banquet facilities for both large and small groups. Approximately 5,000 lodging rooms can be found in Saint Paul.

***Convention Information:*** Saint Paul Convention and Visitors Bureau, 175 West Kellogg Boulevard, Suite 502, Saint Paul, MN 55102; telephone (651)265-4900

# ■ Transportation

## Approaching the City

The principal destination of most air travelers bound for Saint Paul is the Minneapolis-Saint Paul International Airport, 15 minutes from downtown Saint Paul. The Minneapolis-Saint Paul International Airport underwent a major expansion between 1996 and 2005. The resulting facility boasts 2.8 million square feet in its main terminal, with an additional 398,000 square feet in a secondary terminal. In 2004, Minneapolis-St. Paul International Airport was named Best Airport in the Americas and Best Domestic Airport by the International Air Transport Association and Airports Council International. Airlines serve 131 non-stop markets, and in 2006 there were

35,612,133 passengers served. Several reliever airports are also located in the metropolitan area.

An efficient highway system permits easy access into Saint Paul. Interstate-94 intersects the city from east to west and I-35E from north to south. I-494 and I-694 form a beltway circling the north, south, east, and west perimeters. Serving metropolitan Minneapolis-Saint Paul are seven federal and 13 state routes.

Passenger rail service to Saint Paul from Chicago and Seattle is provided by Amtrak. Bus service is provided by Greyhound.

## Traveling in the City

Saint Paul proper has an East Side roughly east of downtown, but its West Side actually lies south of the central business district. The West Side should not be confused with West Saint Paul, which is a suburb on the south edge of town (on the west edge of South Saint Paul, another suburb). Other Saint Paul communities include Frogtown, the Historic Hill District, the Midway, Macalester-Groveland, and Highland Park.

Saint Paul's freeway system, moderate population density, and two business districts facilitate high levels of traffic mobility throughout Minneapolis-Saint Paul during both peak and non-peak hours. The Twin Cities' Metropolitan Council Transit Operations (MCTO), one of the largest bus transportation systems in the country, operates regularly scheduled routes in Saint Paul as well as Minneapolis and the surrounding suburbs.

# ■ Communications

## Newspapers and Magazines

Saint Paul's major daily newspaper is the *Saint Paul Pioneer Press.* Other newspapers appearing daily in the Twin Cities area are the *Minneapolis Star Tribune, Minnesota Daily,* and *Finance and Commerce. Minnesota Monthly* is a magazine focusing on topics of state and regional interest.

Approximately 60 magazines, journals, and newsletters originate in the metropolitan area, covering topics such as law, furniture, religion, feminist issues, and agriculture. Member or special interest publications for professional associations, religious organizations, trade groups, and fraternal societies are also based in the city.

## Television and Radio

Two commercial and two public television stations broadcast from Saint Paul; cable service is also available. AM and FM stations furnish music, news, and information programming. The headquarters of the Minnesota Public Radio Network, an affiliate of National Public Radio, is located in Saint Paul. American Public Media produces "Saint Paul Sunday," a popular program that is broadcast live nationally from Saint Paul, as well as "A

Prairie Home Companion," which broadcasts from the Fitzgerald Theater.

***Media Information:*** *Saint Paul Pioneer Press,* 345 Cedar Street, Saint Paul, MN 55101; telephone (651) 222-1111. *Minnesota Monthly,* Minnesota Monthly Publications, Inc., 730 Second Ave., Minneapolis, MN 55402; telephone (612)371-5800

### Saint Paul Online

City of Saint Paul home page. Available www.ci .stpaul.mn.us

Mall of America home page. Available www .mallofamerica.com

Minnesota Department of Trade and Economic Development home page. Available www.deed .state.mn.us

Minnesota Historical Society home page. Available www.mnhs.org

Saint Paul Area Chamber of Commerce home page. Available www.saintpaulchamber.com

Saint Paul city guide online. Available www.saint-paul.com

Saint Paul Convention and Visitors Bureau home page. Available www.stpaulcvb.org

*Saint Paul Pioneer Press* home page. Available www .twincities.com

Saint Paul Public Library home page. Available www .stpaul.lib.mn.us

BIBLIOGRAPHY

Brin, Ruth F., *Bittersweet Berries: Growing Up Jewish in Minnesota* (Holy Cow Press, 1998)

Fitzgerald, F. Scott, *Taps at Reveille* (New York: C. Scribner's Sons, 1935)

Valdes, Dionicio Nodin, *Barrios Nortenos: St. Paul and Midwestern Mexican Communities in the Twentieth Century* (University of Texas Press, 2000)

# Missouri

# The State in Brief

**Nickname:** Show Me State

**Motto:** Salus populi suprema lex esto (The welfare of the people shall be the supreme law)

**Flower:** Hawthorn

**Bird:** Bluebird

**Area:** 69,704 square miles (2000; U.S. rank 21st)

**Elevation:** Ranges from 230 feet to 1,772 feet above sea level

**Climate:** Continental, with seasonal extremes; affected by cold air from Canada, warm moist air from the Gulf of Mexico, and dry air from the Southwest

**Admitted to Union:** August 10, 1821

**Capital:** Jefferson City

**Head Official:** Governor Matt Blunt (R) (until 2008)

**Population**

    1980: 4,917,000
    1990: 5,117,073
    2000: 5,595,211
    2006 estimate: 5,842,713
    Percent change, 1990–2000: 9.3%
    U.S. rank in 2006: 18th
    Percent of residents born in state: 66.33% (2006)
    Density: 84.2 people per square mile (2006)
    **2006 FBI Crime Index Total:** 255,450

**Racial and Ethnic Characteristics (2006)**

    White: 4,905,832
    Black or African American: 661,535
    American Indian and Alaska Native: 21,082
    Asian: 86,010
    Native Hawaiian and Pacific Islander: 3,333
    Hispanic or Latino (may be of any race): 160,898
    Other: 62,026

**Age Characteristics (2006)**

    Population under 5 years old: 390,715
    Population 5 to 19 years old: 1,197,335
    Percent of population 65 years and over: 13.3%
    Median age: 37.2

**Vital Statistics**

    Total number of births (2006): 78,815
    Total number of deaths (2006): 55,620
    AIDS cases reported through 2005: 10,630

**Economy**

    Major industries: Manufacturing; trade; finance, insurance, and real estate; retail trade; services
    Unemployment rate (2006): 6.3%
    Per capita income (2006): $22,916
    Median household income (2006): $42,841
    Percentage of persons below poverty level (2006): 13.6%
    Income tax rate: 1.5% to 6.0%
    Sales tax rate: 4.225%

# Columbia

## ■ The City in Brief

**Founded:** 1818 (incorporated 1826)

**Head Official:** Mayor Darwin Hindman (NP) (since 1995)

**City Population**

1980: 62,061
1990: 69,101
2000: 84,531
2006 estimate: 94,428
Percent change, 1990–2000: 18.25%
U.S. rank in 1980: 324th
U.S. rank in 1990: 331st (State rank: 6th)
U.S. rank in 2000: 339th (State rank: 6th)

**Metropolitan Area Population**

1980: 100,376
1990: 112,379
2000: 135,454
2006 estimate: 155,997
Percent change, 1990–2000: 20.5%
U.S. rank in 1980: 282nd
U.S. rank in 1990: 288th
U.S. rank in 2000: 221st

**Area:** 58 square miles (2005)

**Elevation:** 889 feet above sea level

**Average Annual Temperatures:** January, 27.8° F; July, 77.4° F; annual average, 54.0° F

**Average Annual Precipitation:** 40.28 inches of rain; 22.8 inches of snow

**Major Economic Sectors:** Education, government, insurance, trade, services

**Unemployment Rate:** 4.0% (June 2007)

**Per Capita Income:** $24,535 (2005)

**2005 FBI Crime Index Property:** 3,065

**2005 FBI Crime Index Violent:** 477

**Major Colleges and Universities:** University of Missouri-Columbia, Stephens College, Columbia College

**Daily Newspaper:** *Columbia Daily Tribune, Columbia Missourian*

## ■ Introduction

Known locally as "College Town U.S.A.," Columbia is the seat of Boone County in central Missouri, about midway between Kansas City and St. Louis. This fast-growing city offers a top rate school system, fine health care facilities, cultural opportunities, a low cost of living, and a clean environment. Columbia, with its highly educated populace, consistently ranks among the best places to live in the United States. In 2006 *Money* magazine ranked the city as one of the "Top 100 Best Places to Live" and *Expansion Management* magazine gave the city five stars on its "Quality of Life Quotient."

## ■ Geography and Climate

Columbia is located halfway between St. Louis to the east and Kansas City to the west, with the state capital, Jefferson City, about 25 miles directly south. It is also halfway between Des Moines and Memphis. The city is set on gently rolling terrain where prairie meets forest. It has cold winters and warm, often humid summers. In winter the cold periods are often interrupted by a warm spell, and the temperature only drops below zero for a few days. Snows rarely last longer than a week, most commonly appearing in March. Freezing temperatures usually end after April first, and the first frost is generally in late October. Late spring and early summer are the rainiest seasons, and summertime temperatures sometimes reach above 100° F.

**Area:** 58 square miles (2005)

**Elevation:** 889 feet above sea level

**Average Temperatures:** January, 27.8° F; July, 77.4° F; annual average, 54.0° F

**Average Annual Precipitation:** 40.28 inches of rain; 22.8 inches of snow

# ■ History

Before the coming of Europeans, Osage and Missouri tribes roamed the area of Columbia and Boone County. The "Missouri," meaning "people with dugout canoes," were originally from the Ohio River Valley, prehistoric evidence shows. The fierce Osage were the predominant tribe of the area. They were a pierced and tattooed, jewelry bedecked, tall, robust, warlike people who dominated other tribes in the region. The men shaved their heads but for a strip at the crown, and wore loincloths and buckskin leggings; the women wore deerskin dresses, and leggings and moccasins as well. They were primarily migrating hunters and gatherers, although they also farmed corn, beans, and pumpkins. The Osage are considered a fringe Plains tribe even though they dwelled mostly in forested areas, because they spoke a Sioux branch of language and went on buffalo hunting excursions on the Great Plains twice annually.

The first Europeans to encounter the Osage were the French, led by Marquette's exploration down the Mississippi for New France in the 1670s. The French and the Osage soon became partners in the fur trade, and with guns and horses gained from this union, the Osage dominated other tribes even more than before. They helped the French defeat the British in 1755 but stayed out of the colonial war. More Europeans came to the area; the Spanish influence grew as that of the French waned. The Osage were pushed to reservations in Kansas and finally what is now Oklahoma by a series of treaties made through the 1800s.

The United States gained the Missouri Territory from France in 1803. The Lewis and Clark expedition passed nearby in that same year, and Daniel Boone and his sons started a settlement in 1806. They also established the Booneslick Trail, which led all the way from Kentucky to the Columbia area. In 1818 the town of Smithton, named for its purchaser, the Smithton Land Company, was established. However, in need of a better water supply, the entire town of 20 residents was moved to its present site in 1821. The settlement of mud-daubed log huts, which was surrounded by wilderness, was renamed Columbia, a popular name at the time, and became the seat of Boone County. Although Columbia is in the Midwest, it had a very Southern feel in the early days, as many of its settlers were from below the Mason-Dixon Line.

From its beginnings, the economy of Columbia has rested on education. It also benefited from being a stagecoach stop of the Santa Fe and Oregon trails, and later from the Missouri Kansas Texas Railroad (nicknamed Katy). Columbia was incorporated in 1826, five years after Missouri became the 24th state. The city's progress can be traced through the development of its institutions. In 1824 Columbia was the site of a new courthouse; in 1830 its first newspaper began; in 1832 the first theater in the state was opened; and in 1834 a school system began to serve its by then 700 citizens. The state's first agricultural fair was held in Columbia in 1835. A school for girls was opened in 1833 and an institution called Columbia College (unrelated to the present school) was opened in 1834. Also in 1834, one of the country's finest portrait artists, George Caleb Bingham, opened a studio in Columbia. In 1841 the University of Missouri was built in Columbia after Boone County won out over several competing counties in raising money and setting aside land. In 1851 Christian Female College was established; it went coed in the 1970s and changed its name to Columbia College. In 1855 Baptist Female College was established; still a women's-only school, it is now known as Stephens College. By 1839 the population and wealth of Boone County, with 13,000 citizens, was exceeded in Missouri only by that of St. Louis County.

Slavery was a largely accepted practice in Columbia in its early days, and the slave population had reached more than 5,000 by the beginning of the Civil War. In fact, the sale of slaves continued until 1864. Before the Civil War many Columbians were very nationalistic and supported the Missouri Compromise, which would admit Missouri into the Union as a slave state, but would placate northerners with the admission of Maine as a free state and the establishment of the rest of the Louisiana Purchase, north and west of Missouri's southern border, as free territory. Early in the Civil War, Union forces secured the area and enforced mandatory draft into the local militia; however, although the state was officially Union, people were in reality sharply divided, and supported both sides with supplies and men.

Since the turmoil of the Civil War and Reconstruction, Columbia's history was marked by steady and quiet growth and prosperity, based largely on its roots in education and the growth and development of the University of Missouri–Columbia. The University of Missouri School of Medicine opened in 1872 and the Parker Memorial Hospital was built in 1901 as the first training hospital. The Medical Center was built in 1960 and was later renamed University Hospitals. In the early 2000s, Columbia was among the top cities in the nation for

Photo courtesy of Jason Swindle, Columbia, MO.

medical facilities per capita with both the University Hospitals and clinics (sponsored by University of Missouri HealthCare) and the Boone Hospital Center serving as major employers for the city.

In 1908 the Missouri School of Journalism opened as the first of its kind in the world. The university's student-run newspaper, *University Missourian*, widened its scope of reporting to include local and national news and was renamed the *Columbia Missourian*, which has become a major daily newspaper for the city.

The University of Missouri has continued to grow by leaps and bounds and has had a major impact on the growth and development of the city into the early 2000s. In 2006 it was estimated that research programs at the university supported over 9,000 jobs and had an annual economic impact of $440 million. In 2007 the university was working with local development organizations in the construction of Discovery Ridge Research Park. Located at the site of the former South Farm Agriculture Experiment Station of the university, the new development is expected to attract high-tech business and research organizations to the city.

***Historical Information:*** State Historical Society of Missouri, Lowry Mall, University of Missouri, Columbia campus; telephone (573)882-7083. Boone County Historical Society, 3801 Ponderosa Street, Columbia, MO; telephone (573)443-8936; http://shs.umsystem.edu

## ■ Population Profile

### Metropolitan Area Residents

1980: 100,376
1990: 112,379
2000: 135,454
2006 estimate: 155,997

Percent change, 1990–2000: 20.5%
U.S. rank in 1980: 282nd
U.S. rank in 1990: 288th
U.S. rank in 2000: 221st

### City Residents

1980: 62,061
1990: 69,101
2000: 84,531
2006 estimate: 94,428
Percent change, 1990–2000: 18.25%
U.S. rank in 1980: 324th
U.S. rank in 1990: 331st (State rank: 6th)
U.S. rank in 2000: 339th (State rank: 6th)

**Density:** 1,592.8 people per square mile (2000)

### Racial and ethnic characteristics (2005)

White: 68,397
Black: 7,376
American Indian and Alaska Native: 280
Asian: 2,959
Native Hawaiian and Pacific Islander: 81
Hispanic or Latino (may be of any race): 2,417
Other: 1,334

**Percent of residents born in state:** 62.5% (2000)

### Age characteristics (2005)

Population under 5 years old: 6,150
Population 5 to 9 years old: 3,756
Population 10 to 14 years old: 3,833
Population 15 to 19 years old: 4,544
Population 20 to 24 years old: 14,292
Population 25 to 34 years old: 15,815
Population 35 to 44 years old: 10,997

Population 45 to 54 years old: 10,228
Population 55 to 59 years old: 3,303
Population 60 to 64 years old: 2,062
Population 65 to 74 years old: 3,607
Population 75 to 84 years old: 2,189
Population 85 years and older: 1,327
Median age: 29.7 years

**Births (2006, MSA)**

Total number: 2,160

**Deaths (2006, MSA)**

Total number: 923

**Money income (2005)**

Per capita income: $24,535
Median household income: $37,051
Total households: 39,624

**Number of households with income of...**

less than $10,000: 5,473
$10,000 to $14,999: 2,637
$15,000 to $24,999: 5,506
$25,000 to $34,999: 5,510
$35,000 to $49,999: 5,372
$50,000 to $74,999: 6,489
$75,000 to $99,999: 3,208
$100,000 to $149,999: 3,973
$150,000 to $199,999: 573
$200,000 or more: 883

**Percent of families below poverty level:** 19.4% (2005)

**2005 FBI Crime Index Property:** 3,065

**2005 FBI Crime Index Violent:** 477

# ■ Municipal Government

Columbia has a council-manager form of government, with a mayor and six council members. The council members are elected by ward and serve three-year terms. The mayor is also elected every three years as a council member at-large. This unpaid elected body directly supervises a city manager, city clerk, and three municipal judges.

**Head Official:** Mayor Darwin Hindman (NP) (since 1995; current term expires 2010)

**Total Number of City Employees:** 1,220 (2007)

***City Information:*** City of Columbia, Daniel Boone Building, 701 East Broadway, Columbia, MO 65205; telephone (573)874-7111; www.gocolumbiamo.com

# ■ Economy

## Major Industries and Commercial Activities

Columbia's thriving economy is primarily based on the education, health care, and insurance industries. Major employers in these sectors include the University of Missouri–Columbia, Columbia Public Schools, University of Missouri HealthCare (hospitals and clinics), Boone Hospital Center, State Farm Insurance Companies, and Shelter Insurance Companies. The government sector, including city, county, and state organizations, accounts for a large number of jobs for the region as well.

Columbia's manufacturers make and sell a wide variety of products. 3M is a major employer, producing projection lenses, optical equipment, electronic products, and interconnect systems. MBS Textbook Exchange is a textbook distribution center. Columbia Foods, a division of Oscar Mayer, employs about 620 workers at its food processing plant. Watlow-Columbia, Inc. manufactures electrical heating elements; Square D Corporation makes circuit breakers; and Hubbell Power Systems produces electric utility equipment.

The city is consistently named as a top place in the nation to live, retire, and do business in publications such as *Money, Entrepreneur, Kiplinger's Personal Finance,* and *Expansion Management. Forbes* listed Columbia as one of the "Best Small Metros for Business and Careers" in 2006.

**Items and goods produced:** electric utility equipment, processed foods, optical equipment, circuit breakers, automotive parts, newspapers, snack foods, HVAC equipment, plastic pipes, foam products

## Incentive Programs—New and Existing Companies

***Local programs:*** The Columbia and Boone County area's main economic development contact is the Regional Economic Development, Inc. (REDI). REDI is a public/private entity created to promote economic expansion while maintaining quality of life. REDI provides services, financing, tax credits and exemptions, job training, and other local perks for businesses, such as no local income tax, moderate property taxes and low sales tax. Community Development Block Grants are available outside the city limits for public infrastructure. Financing takes the form of Industrial Revenue Bonds for qualifying projects, and other low-interest loans and incentive financing for large development projects. Tax exemptions include no sales taxes on manufacturing equipment or on materials used to install such equipment, no sales taxes on air or water pollution control devices, and a property tax exemption on business and industrial inventories.

***State programs:*** Tax credit programs offered by the state of Missouri include a Business Modernization and Technology Credit, Small Business Incubator Credit,

Neighborhood Assistance Program, Historic Preservation Credit, New Markets Tax Credit and a Community Bank Investment Credit. Tax credits through these programs range from 45 percent to 70 percent for qualified programs. A Research Expense Tax Credit program offers a credit of 6.5 percent for qualified expenses. The BUILD Missouri Program provides incentives for the relocation or expansion of large business projects (generally in excess of 100 jobs). The program provides Missouri state income tax credits to the business in the amount of debt service payments for bonds related to a portion of project costs. The tax credits may be sold if not used by the recipient. A number of loan financing programs are also available.

*Job training programs:* The New Jobs Training Program (NJTP) provides education and training to workers employed in newly created jobs in Missouri. The new jobs may result from a new industry locating in Missouri or an existing industry expanding its workforce in the state. The Missouri Customized Training Program (MCTP) helps Missouri employers with funding to offset the costs of employee training and retraining. It assists new and expanding businesses in recruiting, screening, and training workers, and it helps existing employers retain their current workforce when faced with needed upgrading and retraining. The Missouri Job Retention Training Program offers retraining assistance to employers who have retained a minimum of 100 employers for at least two consecutive years and have made a capital investment of at least $1 million.

The Columbia Area Career Center offers business seminars, computer classes, and skilled trade and industry training for adults. Occupational programs are available in fields such as practical nursing and EMT/paramedic training.

## Development Projects

Growing somewhat naturally out of Columbia's strength in the education and health care industries is the biological sciences research business. There are three key organizations in the area that promote expansion into this growing field: the Mid-MO BIO, the MU Life Science Business Incubator at Monsanto Place, and Scientific Partnership and Resource Connection, or SPARC. SPARC works with Regional Economic Development, Inc. (REDI) and University of Missouri's College of Agriculture, Food, and Natural Resources to procure funding for research and the building of related facilities. This has resulted in a new, $60-million Life Sciences Center, which opened in 2004 on the University of Missouri-Columbia's campus.

The University of Missouri–Columbia maintains its own Foundation for Economic Development department, which has had an enormous impact on the local economic growth and development as well. One of the major projects under development in 2007 was Discovery Ridge, formerly the South Farm agriculture experiment station of the University of Missouri. As of 2007, only two tenants were located on the site: Analytical Bio-Chemistry Laboratories and the Research Animal Diagnostic Laboratory, the latter of which is the second-largest lab animal diagnostic and pathology lab in the world. However, once development is complete, the site is expected to serve as a major attraction for high-tech companies that would work in collaboration with both the University and private businesses. In 2006 the MIZZOU Business Development Extension assisted in business start-ups valued at over $19 million, resulting in the creation of over 1,115 new jobs.

In 2007 the Missouri Life Science Research Board announced plans to locate a statewide Center of Excellence in Columbia. This center will be designed to focus on agricultural research, specifically in the areas of bioenergy, plant science, and animal health and nutrition. The University of Missouri–Columbia will also be involved in this project, along with a number of state agricultural associations.

In November 2007 the city opened its first landfill-gas-to-energy project at the Columbia landfill. The project will generate 2.1 megawatts of renewable energy from gases created through landfill waste decomposition. This is the amount of energy needed to power about 1,500 homes in the city. The $2.85-million project was partially funded through an electric bond issue passed by voters in 2006. The plant has been designed for possible expansion.

*Economic Development Information:* Regional Economic Development, Inc., 302 Campusview Dr., Ste. 208, Columbia, MO 65201; telephone (573)442-8303; www.columbiaredi.com. Missouri Department of Economic Development, 301 W. High Street, Jefferson City, MO 65102; telephone (573)751-4962; www.ded.mo.gov

## Commercial Shipping

Boone County has over a dozen major motor freight lines serving the area. Railroads serving the area's freight needs include Norfolk Southern, Gateway Western, and COLT (Columbia Terminal), a short-line railroad owned by the city. Air cargo travels through Columbia Regional Airport, primarily through Airborne Express and the U.S. Postal Service.

## Labor Force and Employment Outlook

The Columbia workforce is very well-educated in comparison to national averages. According to 2006 estimates, nearly 92 percent of the population age 25 years and over had obtained a high school diploma or higher. Nearly 55 percent of this population had obtained a bachelor's degree or higher. In 2006 *Expansion Management* magazine ranked Columbia as a five-star city in their annual Knowledge Worker Quotient, based on the apparent ability of the workforce to support technological industries. In 2007 the largest employment sectors were government and retail, followed by manufacturing, and finance, insurance, and real estate. Employment projections into 2014 suggest that the greatest number of new jobs will be added in health services and marketing, sales, and services. Local development projects are underway to attract new business and research jobs in life sciences.

The following is a summary of data regarding the Columbia metropolitan area labor force, 2006 annual averages.

**Size of nonagricultural labor force:** 91,400

**Number of workers employed in . . .**

> construction and mining: Not available
> manufacturing: Not available
> trade, transportation and utilities: 15,100
> information: Not available
> financial activities: Not available
> professional and business services: Not available
> educational and health services: Not available
> leisure and hospitality: Not available
> other services: Not available
> government: 29,700

**Average hourly earnings of production workers employed in manufacturing:** Not available

**Unemployment rate:** 4.0% (June 2007)

| Largest employers (2006) | Number of employees |
|---|---|
| University of Missouri-Columbia | 8,002 |
| University Hospital & Clinics | 4,520 |
| Columbia Public Schools | 2,150 |
| Boone Hospital Center | 1,769 |
| City of Columbia | 1,220 |
| State Farm Insurance Companies | 1,151 |
| Shelter Insurance Companies | 1,040 |
| MBS Textbook Exchange | 947 |
| Hubbell Power Systems, Inc. | 910 |
| US Department of Veterans Affairs | 910 |

## Cost of Living

Columbia consistently ranks below the national average for cost of living. The following is a summary of data regarding several key cost of living factors for the Columbia metropolitan area.

**2007 (1st quarter) ACCRA Average House Price:** $257,325

**2007 (1st quarter) ACCRA Cost of Living Index:** 91.5

**State income tax rate:** 1.5% to 6.0%

**State sales tax rate:** 4.225%

**Local income tax rate:** None

**Local sales tax rate:** 3.125%

**Property tax rate:** $6.32 per $100 of assessed value (2004)

***Economic Information:*** Missouri Department of Economic Development, 301 W. High Street, P.O. Box 1157, Jefferson City, MO 65102; telephone (573)751-4962; http://ded.mo.gov. Regional Economic Development, Inc., 302 Campusview Dr., Ste. 208, Columbia, MO 65201; telephone (573)442-8303; www.columbiaredi.com

# ■ Education and Research

## Elementary and Secondary Schools

The Columbia Public School District is one of the largest districts in the state of Missouri. Within the district, proficiency scores through the Missouri Assessment Program are generally higher than the state average. In 2007 nearly 55 percent of all teachers in the district held a master's degree or higher. Special assessment efforts, reading-intensive activities and summer school programs are directed at students at risk of dropping out. At the other end of the achievement spectrum is the A+ program, in which students with superior attendance, grades, and citizenship records can earn free tuition to a two-year community college, vocational-technical schools, or the Columbia Area Career Center (run by the public school district). The free Summer Enrichment program offers core academic studies in the morning and enrichment activities in the afternoon. There is a Parents As Teachers program, a family literacy program in which adults can work on GED certification or other educational goals such as learning English while their children attend preschool, and other volunteer programs that encourage adult volunteers from the community to join in a partnership for mentoring or service skills education.

The following is a summary of data regarding the Columbia Public Schools as of the 2005–2006 school year.

**Total enrollment:** 23,150

**Number of facilities**

> elementary schools: 20

junior high/middle schools: 6
senior high schools: 4
other: 0

**Student/teacher ratio:** 13.2:1

**Teacher salaries (2005–06)**
  elementary median: $36,810
  junior high/middle median: Not available
  secondary median: $41,480

**Funding per pupil:** $7,319

Columbia also has over a dozen private schools, including Catholic, Lutheran, Seventh-day Adventist, and Islamic schools.

*Public Schools Information:* Columbia Public Schools, 1818 W. Worley St., Columbia, MO 65203; telephone (573)886-2100; www.columbia.k12.mo.us

## Colleges and Universities

The University of Missouri–Columbia (MU), with more than 28,250 students, offers 274 degree programs, including 86 bachelor's degrees, 93 master's degrees, and 67 doctorates. MU, founded in 1839, was the first public university west of the Mississippi. MU is considered to be one of the most prestigious research universities in the nation. For 2008 the university was listed among the top 100 "Best National Universities" by *U.S. News & World Report.*

Columbia College, a private, coeducational institution, was originally called Christian Female College when it was founded in 1851. It was the first women's college west of the Mississippi to be chartered by a state legislature. It changed its name in 1970 when it went coed and offered bachelor's and post-graduate degrees in addition to associate's degrees. The school maintains a covenant affiliation with the Christian Church (Disciples of Christ). The school offers master's degrees in teaching, business administration, and criminal justice and bachelor's and associate's degrees in a wide variety of fields. Columbia College now has almost 1,000 students at its day campus and over 3,000 working adults at its evening campus, both of which are located in Columbia. There are 32 extended campuses around the nation, including one at Guantanamo Bay, and an impressive online college.

Stephens College, founded in 1833, is the nation's second oldest women's college. Stephens offers a liberal arts curriculum and pre-professional programs, with over 50 majors and minors in three schools of study. There is also a program available for student-designed majors. Stephens is the only four-year women's college in Missouri and remains dedicated to women's education in the new millennium. The division of Graduate and Continuing studies offers programs for both men and women. Stephens College was listed as one of the "Best Midwestern Colleges" for 2008 in the *Princeton Review.*

The Columbia Area Career Center offers business seminars, computer classes, and skilled trade and industry training for adults. Occupational programs are available in fields such as practical nursing and EMT/paramedic training.

## Libraries and Research

The Columbia Public Library is the headquarters of the Daniel Boone Regional Library system, which serves Boone and Callaway counties as well as the city of Columbia through three branches and two bookmobile services. The $22-million Columbia Public Library was completed in 2002. The design of the new building features curves and cylindrical shapes and a carefully planned system of signs that allow patrons to find things easily. The system maintains a collection of over 518,000 materials.

The University of Missouri–Columbia libraries maintain the largest library collection in the state and one of the largest collections in the Midwest. The university library system includes the main Ellis Library and seven specialized libraries (law, veterinary medicine, geological sciences, health sciences, engineering, journalism, and mathematical sciences). Holdings include over 3.2 million volumes, 6.8 million microforms, 1.6 million government documents, and over 26,000 journal subscriptions. Its online catalog of resources, called MERLIN for Missouri Education and Research Libraries Information Network, makes materials available from the University of Missouri's four campuses and St. Louis University. MU's special collections include an extensive historical and contemporary collection of government documents, Microform Collection, Rare Book Collection, Newspaper Collections, and the Comic Art Collection with originals and reprints of classic comic strips, underground comics, and graphic novels.

Columbia College's Stafford Library maintains a general collection of over 80,000 volumes and 600 periodical subscriptions. Its special Library of American Civilization contains materials on all aspects of American life from pre-colonial times through World War I. The Stafford Library also maintains special collections in biography, history, and costumes. The Arthur catalog links the library collections of the Stafford Library and four other central Missouri college libraries, plus the collection of the Missouri State Library.

The State Historical Society of Missouri Library has special collections on church histories, literature, Midwestern history, and Missouri newspapers. The Midwest Science Center Library features a collection on wildlife research. Stephens College has special libraries that encompass women's studies, educational resources, and children's literature.

The University of Missouri–Columbia spends an estimated $211 million each year on research activates. MU is one of 34 public universities in the nation to be designated as Doctoral Research Extensive by the Carnegie Foundation for Advancement of Teaching. This designation marks the school as one of the most prestigious research institutions in the country. Research centers and institutes maintained at the university include the Agricultural Experiment Station Research Farms, Ellis Fischel Cancer Research Center, the Missouri Center for Mathematics and Science Teacher Education, the National Center for Explosion Resistant Design, the National Center for Gender Physiology, the National Center for Soybean Biotechnology, and the Health and Behavior Risk Research Center, to name a few.

A number of institutions have research facilities in Columbia. These include the Mid-Missouri Mental Health Center, which conducts research along with providing psychiatric inpatient treatment; the Missouri Coop Fish and Wildlife Research Unit; a division of the U.S. Geological Survey of the Department of the Interior; Missouri Lions Eye Research Foundation, which holds an eye tissue bank and does research into glaucoma treatment and all things involving preserving and restoring eyesight; the Rehabilitation Research Foundation, part of MU's Health Psychology Department; and the U.S.D.A. Biological Control of Insects Research Laboratory.

*Public Library Information:* Columbia Public Library, PO Box 1267, 100 W. Broadway, Columbia, MO 65205; telephone (573)443-3161; www.dbrl.org

# ■ Health Care

Columbia's hospitals provide quality health care for Central Missourians, comparable to that of cities many times its size.

University of Missouri HealthCare (UMHC) sponsors the 189-bed Columbia Regional Hospital and the 274-bed University Hospital, both in Columbia. University Hospital (UH) features the only Level I trauma center and helicopter service in the region. The UH critical care center includes cardiac, medical, neurological and surgical intensive care units as well as mid-Missouri's only burn intensive care unit. It also boasts of the most comprehensive center for wound care and hyperbaric medicine in the region. Other specialized services through UH include the region's only cochlear implant center, a diabetes center, an ophthalmology institute, a sleep disorders center, and an endoscopy center. The Children's Hospital at UH is a 115-bed unit providing specialized pediatric care services.

UMHC also sponsors the Ellis Fischel Cancer Center, which is the only hospital in the state dedicated to cancer care and research. The Howard A. Rusk Rehabilitation Center is managed jointly through UMHC and HealthSouth, a rehabilitative care organization based in Alabama. The Rusk Center features specialized programs for spinal cord injuries, brain injuries, stroke recovery,

amputee rehabilitation, and multiple sclerosis patients, to name a few. The UMHC Missouri Rehabilitation Center is a 124-bed long-term care facility. This center houses the largest traumatic brain injury program in the state. It is also considered to be a leading center for pulmonary rehabilitation. UMHC also sponsors several primary care clinics in the city and the Sinclair Home Care network.

The Boone Hospital Center (BHC) is a 388-bed hospital with specialties in cardiology, neurology, oncology, and obstetrics. The hospital has a Level III Neonatal Intensive Care Unit and a Neuroscience Intensive Care Unit, as well as general surgical and medical intensive care units. BHC sponsors the Advanced Wound Care Clinic, the Harris Breast Center, a Pain Management Clinic, and the Joint Replacement Center. The hospital also sponsors several outpatient primary care clinics and community wellness programs.

Mid-Missouri Mental Health Center offers short term intensive psychiatric help for children and adults. Eligible veterans are served by the 54-bed Harry S. Truman Memorial Veteran's Hospital.

# ■ Recreation

## Sightseeing

Downtown Columbia itself is a stunning sight to see, where four massive columns stand in front of the stately Boone County Courthouse. The Firestone Baars Chapel, which was designed by architect Eero Saarinen of the St. Louis Arch fame, is also in the heart of downtown Columbia. Tours of the Victorian-era Maplewood Home, built in 1877 and beautifully restored, are available to give the public a glimpse into 19th century country estate life. The Columbia Audubon Trailside Museum has exhibits on birds and other creatures and offers workshops on nature. A genealogy center, a photo collection, an art collection and works of local artists are among many historical artifacts on display at the State Historical Society housed in the Ellis Library on the MU campus. More than 1,500 types of flowers and 300 trees can be seen at Shelter Insurance Gardens, which also features a one-room red brick school house, a "sensory garden" designed for the visually impaired, and many other attractions such as a giant sundial. It also hosts free summer concerts on its five acres. The writings of Dr. Martin Luther King, Jr., as part of a sculptured amphitheater at King Memorial Gardens, are another must-see in Columbia. The gardens' landscaping, with benches and walkways, provides a placid setting for cultural events.

Historic Rocheport, just 12 miles west of the city, began as an early trading post on the Missouri River in 1825 and prospered due to the building of the railroad. Now on the National Register of Historic Places, this charming town offers top-rate antique and craft shops, excellent restaurants, a local winery, and an annual RiverFest in early June.

## Arts and Culture

The Missouri Theatre is central Missouri's only pre-Depression-era movie palace and vaudeville stage. It presents a variety of programs throughout the year. The Rhynsberger Theater, on the University of Missouri's campus, is the site for dramatic performances by visiting actors as well as faculty and students. The Repertory Theatre performs there in the summertime. Both professional and student productions can be enjoyed at Stephens College's Macklanburg Playhouse and Warehouse Theatre. Columbia's primary community theater group is the Maplewood Barn Community Theater, located in Nifong Park, which performs outdoors in summer months. The Columbia Entertainment Company is a dynamic theatrical troupe that gives rousing musical and dramatic performances throughout the year, in addition to offering a drama school for adults and children. Columbia can also boast of Arrow Rock Lyceum Theater and two acting groups that focus on children: PACE, or Performing Arts in Children's Education, and TRYPS, or Theater Reaching Young People and Schools.

The Missouri Symphony makes its home in the historic Missouri Theatre Center for the Arts and holds its summer festival every June and July. The University Concert Series brings opera, ballet, orchestra, chamber music, jazz, dance, and theatrical performances. Other musical groups in the city are the Columbia Community Choir and the Columbia Chorale Ensemble.

Columbia's museums offer a variety of lectures, classes, and exhibits. More than 13,000 artifacts and works of art from prehistoric times to the present are housed at the University of Missouri-Columbia's Museum of Art and Archaeology. Also on campus, the Museum of Anthropology displays Native American materials and archaeology from the Midwest and the Rogers Gallery highlights exhibits on architecture and interior design, as well as student art works. Rotating exhibits of professional and amateur artists are showcased at the Columbia Art League Gallery, while the work of students and faculty is shown at the Columbia College Art Gallery.

African American intellectual culture is the focus of the Black Culture Center, which offers various programs and conducts research. The story of Boone County over the decades is the subject of the Walters-Boone County Historical Museum and Visitor's Center, set in a wood-hewn family farmhouse with weathered boards and wide porches. This 16,000-square-foot house features exhibits on westward expansion along the Booneslick Trail and portrays the pioneers who settled in the region.

## Festivals and Holidays

Columbia ushers in spring in April with the annual Earth Day celebration. With May comes the Salute to Veterans Air Show and Parade, the largest free air show in the United States. June is the time for the annual Art in the Park Fair and the weekly Twilight Festivals. June also features the J.W. Boone Ragtime Festival, where folks can enjoy the sounds of early jazz and ragtime of the Roaring '20s. The Fourth of July celebration, called Fire in the Sky, kicks off the month, and the Boone County Fair and Horse Show keeps the excitement going. The International Buckskin Horse World Championship and the Lion's Antique show are held in August. In September the Twilight Festivals restart, but the highlight of the month must be the Heritage Festival at Maplewood Farm in Nifong Park, which celebrates the work of local artists and performers. The September Columbia Festival of the Arts at Courthouse Square combines the celebration of visual, performing, and literary arts in a two-day event sponsored by the city's Office of Cultural Affairs and local businesses. October sees the annual Missouri Fall Festival, in which Courthouse Square is transformed into a showcase of regional arts and crafts. November events include the Annual Fall Craft Show and the Downtown Holiday Parade. The downtown Holiday Festival and the Christmas Past 1865 at the Maplewood Home celebrate the December holiday season, which is capped by the First Night Celebration and Midway Invitational Rodeo and Dance on December 31st and January 1st.

## Sports for the Spectator

Big 12 conference basketball, football, NCI Division baseball, wrestling, volleyball, softball, gymnastics, and track and field are all available for sports fan to watch. The city is close enough to both St. Louis and Kansas City to enjoy their major league baseball, football, and basketball teams.

## Sports for the Participant

Columbia enjoys 50 parks, with such basic facilities as swimming pools, tennis courts, softball fields, volleyball courts, fishing lakes, hiking and wheelchair-accessible trails, golf courses, and even horseshoe pits. The city maintains two golf courses, Lake of the Woods and L.A. Nickell. There is a skate park at the Columbia Cosmopolitan Recreation Area. The Show-Me State Games, an annual Olympic-style athletic competition, welcomes amateur competitors. Bikers and runners enjoy the MKT Nature & Fitness Trail, an 8.9-mile path that connects with the 225-mile Katy Trail, the nation's longest rails-to-trails conversion. In 2005 the University of Missouri–Columbia Student Recreation Complex was named as the best student rec center in the nation by *Sports Illustrated*.

## Shopping and Dining

Columbia provides a variety of shopping experiences with 16 shopping centers in addition to its major downtown shopping district. The largest mall is the 140-store Columbia Mall, which features major national chain stores. Forum Shopping Center has a big indoor entertainment center for children. The District, located downtown and bordered on three sides by college campuses, features 110 specialty shops and retail stores, including an abundance of antique shops, such as the 6,000-square-foot Grandma's Treasures, which features antique jewelry, glass collectibles, and furniture. The District also has about 70 bars and restaurants and several venues offering live entertainment each week.

Dining establishments come in all forms in the city; there are more than 300 restaurants, from American bistros, haute cuisine establishments, ethnic eateries, and one of central Missouri's only brewpubs, the Flat Branch Pub & Brewery, located near the courthouse. Les Bourgeois Vineyard in Rocheport offers an elegant menu and variety of award-winning wines.

## ■ Convention Facilities

There are 34 hotels and motels in and around Columbia with more than 3,500 rooms. The largest facilities for conventions and exhibitions are at Boone County Fairgrounds, with 107,300 square feet; the Hearnes Center, with 70,000 square feet; the Midway Expo Center, with 66,000 square feet; and the Holiday Inn Executive Center, with 20,000 square feet. The Columbia EXPO Center has about 18,600 square feet of meeting space available. Smaller groups can be accommodated at many local hotels.

## ■ Transportation

### Approaching the City

Columbia is located on Interstate 70, which runs east and west, and U. S. Highway 63, which runs north and south. It is twenty minutes away from U.S. 54 to the east and the Missouri River to the west. Columbia Regional Airport offers four daily flights to Kansas City and St. Louis through U.S. Airways Express. Amtrak rail service is available to nearby Jefferson City and Greyhound has daily bus service to St. Louis and Kansas City, all with connections to many other places.

### Traveling in the City

Columbia's relatively flat streets are arranged in an easy grid pattern, with numbered streets running north and south. Columbia Area Transit (CAT) provides bus service in the city through six fixed routes. Paratransit service is available. The University of Missouri has its own shuttle, as does Columbia Regional Airport.

## ■ Communications

### Newspapers and Magazines

Columbia's two daily newspapers are the *Columbia Daily Tribune,* which appears every evening, and the *Columbia Missourian,* which is the morning daily paper. The

*Columbia Missourian* is staffed primarily by students and faculty of the Missouri School of Journalism (University of Missouri). The same staff works on the publication of *Adelante!,* a Spanish-English publication, and the weekly entertainment paper, *Vox. The Columbia Business Times* is published every other Saturday.

People in the area also read the *Boone County Journal, Columbia Senior Times,* and the *Centralia Fireside Guard.*

Publications affiliated with the University of Missouri include the monthly *Journal of Chemical Crystallography,* semi-annuals *Journal of Dispute Resolution* and *Theatre Topics,* and the quarterlies *Missouri Historical Review* and *Missouri Law Review. MIZZOU Magazine* is an MU alumni quarterly and *The Missouri Review* is a quarterly literary journal.

*Columbia Home and Lifestyle* magazine and *Inside Columbia* are monthly publications.

### Television and Radio

The city has six television network affiliates and two cable television networks. The formats of the 13 FM and AM radio stations available to Columbia listeners cover the gamut of musical tastes along with news, talk, and public broadcasting

***Media Information:*** *Columbia Daily Tribune,* 101 N. Fourth St., PO Box 798, Columbia, MO 65205; telephone (573)815-1700; www.columbiatribune.com. *Columbia Missourian,* 221 S 8th St., Columbia, MO 65211; telephone (573)882-5720; www.columbia-missourian.com

### Columbia Online

City of Columbia, Missouri. Available www .gocolumbiamo.com

Columbia Chamber of Commerce. Available www .chamber.columbia.mo.us

Columbia Convention and Visitors Bureau. Available www.visitcolumbiamo.com

*Columbia Daily Tribune.* Available www .columbiatribune.com

Columbia Public Schools. Available www.columbia .k12.mo.us

Regional Economic Development, Inc. Available www.columbiaredi.com

BIBLIOGRAPHY

Batterson, Paulina Ann, *The First Fifty Years* (Columbia Public Relations Committee, Columbia Chamber of Commerce, 1965)

# Jefferson City

## ■ The City in Brief

**Founded:** 1823 (incorporated 1825)

**Head Official:** Mayor John Landwehr (since 2003)

**City Population**

    1980: 33,619
    1990: 35,481
    2000: 39,636
    2006 estimate: 39,274
    Percent change, 1990–2000: 10.8%
    U.S. rank in 1980: Not available
    U.S. rank in 1990: Not available
    U.S. rank in 2000: (State rank: 15th)

**Metropolitan Area Population**

    1980: 56,663
    1990: 63,579
    2000: 71,397
    2006 estimate: 73,296
    Percent change, 1990–2000: 12.3%
    U.S. rank in 1980: Not available
    U.S. rank in 1990: Not available
    U.S. rank in 2000: 693rd

**Area:** 27.3 square miles (2000)

**Elevation:** 702 feet above sea level

**Average Annual Temperature:** 54.4° F

**Average Annual Precipitation:** 38.43 inches of rain; 23.5 inches of snow

**Major Economic Sectors:** Government, trade, services

**Unemployment Rate:** 4.5% (June 2007)

**Per Capita Income:** $21,268 (1999)

**2005 FBI Crime Index Property:** 1,733

**2005 FBI Crime Index Violent:** 312

**Major Colleges and Universities:** Lincoln University, Columbia College-Jefferson City

**Daily Newspapers:** *Daily Capital News, Jefferson City News Tribune*

## ■ Introduction

Jefferson City, the seat of Cole County, is named after the esteemed third president of the United States. It is a genteel, conservative city full of charming and refurbished old homes. The Missouri State Capitol building, reminiscent of the U.S. Capitol, stands grandly at the center of this planned city, which serves as a center for Midwestern trade. Visitors view its many historic structures while enjoying the friendly, easygoing family atmosphere the city offers.

## ■ Geography and Climate

Jefferson City lies in the geographical center of Missouri, extending east, south, and westward from a bluff on the Missouri River. The city spreads inland across finger-like ridges and valleys paralleling the river.

    Like the rest of the state, Jefferson City is affected by cold air blowing down from Canada; warm, moist air from the Gulf of Mexico; and dry southwestern air. Spring is the rainy season. Snowfall averages 23.5 inches per year and snow is most prevalent from December through February. Like all of Missouri, Jefferson City lies in a region where tornadoes are a danger. Summers can be hot with temperatures sometimes reaching more than 100° F.

**Area:** 27.3 square miles (2000)

**Elevation:** 702 feet above sea level

**Average Temperature:** 54.4° F

**Average Annual Precipitation:** 38.43 inches of rain; 23.5 inches of snow

# ■ History

## Missouri's Early Development

Before the coming of white settlers, the region surrounding Jefferson City was home to an ancient group known as the Mound People. In fact, America's largest prehistoric city was located only 160 miles away at what is now Cahokia, Illinois. Why this civilization disappeared remains a mystery.

At the time Europeans arrived in the area in the seventeenth century, the Osage Indians inhabited the region. In 1673 the French explorers Joliet and Marquette explored the region. In 1682 the explorer LaSalle sailed down the Mississippi River and claimed the area of Jefferson City for France. In 1715 Antoine de la Mothe Cadillac opened a lead mine nearby, where until 1744 white men used slaves to work the mines. During the mid-1700s, settlements were begun at Ste. Genevieve and at St. Louis. Soon many new settlers began arriving from Kentucky and Tennessee by way of the Ohio River and its tributaries.

In the 1780s the Spanish built a road northward from New Madrid, Missouri to St. Louis, which today is known as U.S. Route 51. The area was explored by members of the Lewis and Clark expedition in 1804. In the early 1800s frontiersman Daniel Boone carved out the Boone's Lick Trail, which is now Interstate Highway 70. It ran westward from St. Charles to the Missouri River at Franklin. In time the Santa Fe Trail was developed, running from Franklin westward to Independence, then southward. The Oregon Trail branched westward from Independence.

## Created to Serve as Capital

Jefferson City holds the distinction of having been created specifically to serve as the state capital by a commission appointed by the Missouri state legislature in 1821. But until government buildings could be constructed, the town of St. Charles served as the capital.

Jefferson City was laid out by Daniel Morgan Boone, the son of the frontiersman. It was named for U.S. President Thomas Jefferson, who served from 1801-1809. The town was incorporated in 1825, and the general assembly moved there in 1826. At that time, the town had thirty-one families, a general store, a hotel, and a few other buildings.

For several years, other towns attempted to have the capital city changed, and in 1832 Governor John Miller suggested that a state penitentiary be built in Jefferson City to strengthen the town's position as capital. The prison was completed in 1836.

The next year, the Capitol burned and all the state records went up in flames. Five years later, a new statehouse was completed at the site of the present Capitol building. At that time, modern steamboats regularly visited the city and stage coach routes brought travelers. This encouraged the growth of local industries, including grist mills, flour mills, tanneries, and distilleries. The 1830s saw the influx of German immigrants, who were mostly farmers.

## Civil War Brings Strife and Division

In 1839 Jefferson City was incorporated as a city and in 1840 the population stood at 1,174 people, including 262 slaves. A frightening incident took place in 1849, when a ship carrying Mormon church members, some of whom had cholera, landed at the city dock. For two years the plague infected residents in the area, paralyzing the local trade.

In 1855 the Pacific Railroad line was completed between St. Louis and Jefferson City. However, the first trip between the two cities was a disaster. As residents waited for the president of the railroad and other dignitaries to arrive, a pier collapsed on a bridge that crossed the Gasconade River, and the resulting train accident killed 28 people and injured 30 others. Regular train service did not begin until the next year.

The coming of the Civil War (1860–1865) brought to a head the question of whether slavery would continue in Missouri. While President Abraham Lincoln encouraged an end to slavery, Missouri Governor Claiborne F. Jackson favored the retention of slavery and the secession of the southern states, including Missouri.

## Decades Pass Before Wounds Heal

Soon after, a convention was held in Missouri to decide which position the state assembly would embrace. The convention voted to remain in the Union. But Governor Jackson refused to recognize federal authority and also refused to send troops to fight for the Union Army.

Instead, he rallied 50,000 volunteers for the state militia and marched from the capital to join Confederate forces at Booneville. But two days later, Union troops overran Jefferson City and pitched camp on Capitol Hill. In 1864 the Confederate general and former Missouri governor Sterling Price and his men marched to within four miles of the city and announced they would attack. Troops exchanged fire, but in the end Price withdrew and fled westward toward Kansas City, and Jefferson City remained in Union hands.

Decades passed before the city recovered from the rifts occasioned by the Civil War. But the Missouri constitution of 1875 restored peace of mind to the citizens and a period of expansion began. Such industries as printing and shoe manufacturing developed in the city, and within ten years a bridge was built across the Missouri River, uniting the pro-South Jefferson City with its pro-

North neighbors in Kansas. In 1896, the town of Sedalia tried to wrest the capital from Jefferson City, but the attempt failed when Jefferson City triumphed in a popular vote among Missouri citizens.

## The City in the Twentieth Century

After 1900 the local economy began to grow again with the expansion of the state government. In 1904 the Supreme Court Building was constructed with funds from the St. Louis World's Fair. The next year St. Mary's Hospital was built. In 1911 street car service began in the city and a dramatic fire brought the destruction of the old State House. A new one was completed in 1917 and the present Capitol building was dedicated in 1924.

For the next forty years the business of state government business continued to dominate the local scene, throughout the periods of two world wars and the Great Depression. The city slowly continued to grow, as more people left the local farms and gravitated to the city.

In 1951 Still Hospital was built and in 1954 a major prison riot took place at the state prison in Jefferson City. The 1960s saw the construction of Memorial Hospital, the opening of Rex M. Whitten Expressway, and Jefferson City's development as a manufacturing center. In 1983 the John G. Christy Municipal Building opened. A major flood in 1993 caused extensive damage, but by the end of the 1990s the city had fully recovered. Jefferson City, notable for its livability, relatively low cost of living, and high per capita income, entered the 2000s with vitality.

*Historical Information:* Cole County Historical Society, 109 Madison St., Jefferson City, MO, 65101; telephone (573)635-1850; www.colecohistsoc.org

# ■ Population Profile

## Metropolitan Area Residents

1980: 56,663
1990: 63,579
2000: 71,397
2006 estimate: 73,296
Percent change, 1990–2000: 12.3%
U.S. rank in 1980: Not available
U.S. rank in 1990: Not available
U.S. rank in 2000: 693rd

## City Residents

1980: 33,619
1990: 35,481
2000: 39,636
2006 estimate: 39,274
Percent change, 1990–2000: 10.8%
U.S. rank in 1980: Not available
U.S. rank in 1990: Not available
U.S. rank in 2000: (State rank: 15th)

**Density:** 1,454.4 people per square mile (2000)

**Racial and ethnic characteristics (2000)**

White: 32,303
Black: 5,828
American Indian and Alaska Native: 150
Asian: 488
Native Hawaiian and Pacific Islander: 20
Hispanic or Latino (may be of any race): 616
Other: 847

**Percent of residents born in state:** 71.7% (2000)

**Age characteristics (2000)**

Population under 5 years old: 2,314
Population 5 to 9 years old: 2,210
Population 10 to 14 years old: 2,295
Population 15 to 19 years old: 2,705
Population 20 to 24 years old: 3,133
Population 25 to 34 years old: 6,202
Population 35 to 44 years old: 6,518
Population 45 to 54 years old: 5,613
Population 55 to 59 years old: 1,766
Population 60 to 64 years old: 1,337
Population 65 to 74 years old: 2,646
Population 75 to 84 years old: 2,023
Population 85 years and older: 874
Median age: 36.5 years

**Births (2006, MSA)**

Total number: 2,007

**Deaths (2006, MSA)**

Total number: 1,243

**Money income (1999)**

Per capita income: $21,268
Median household income: $39,628
Total households: 15,870

**Number of households with income of . . .**

less than $10,000: 1,488
$10,000 to $14,999: 1,034
$15,000 to $24,999: 2,329
$25,000 to $34,999: 2,189
$35,000 to $49,999: 2,628
$50,000 to $74,999: 3,212
$75,000 to $99,999: 1,725
$100,000 to $149,999: 839
$150,000 to $199,999: 142
$200,000 or more: 284

**Percent of families below poverty level:** 8.1% (1999)

**2005 FBI Crime Index Property:** 1,733

**2005 FBI Crime Index Violent:** 312

Airphoto-Jim Wark

## ■ Municipal Government

Jefferson City is the capital of Missouri and the seat of Cole County. The city itself has a mayor-council form of government; there are ten council members, each of whom serves a two-year term and may be elected to serve a total of up to eight years. Two council members are elected from each of five wards. The mayor serves for four years and may be re-elected for a second term.

**Head Official:** Mayor John Landwehr (since 2003; term expires 2011)

**Total Number of City Employees:** 776, full- and part-time (2007)

*City Information:* Mayor's Office, City of Jefferson City, 231 Madison Street, Jefferson City, MO 65101; telephone (573)634-6304; www.jeffcitymo.org

## ■ Economy

### Major Industries and Commercial Activity

The major business in Jefferson City is government, which provides more than 28,000 local jobs through state, county, and city entities. Much of the state government business is carried on in the city, home of the Missouri Legislature, Missouri Supreme Court, and many offices that house the different state departments.

Jefferson City also serves as a trading center for the agricultural produce grown in the area. The main cash crops raised are corn, wheat, and soybeans. Between 1997 and 2002, the number of farms in the county decreased by 6 percent, from 1,162 farms to 1,098; however, the size of farms increased by 4 percent, from 162 acres to 169 acres. Retail trade is one of top employing industries in the city.

Health care has become an important part of the local economy with Capital Region Medical Center and St. Mary's Health Center both serving as major employers for the city. Two major educational publishing companies, Scholastic, Inc. and Von Hoffman Press, Inc, have facilities in Jefferson City.

**Items and goods produced:** structural steel products, heat transfer equipment, books, educational materials, cosmetics, automotive seating, radiators, washer parts

### Incentive Programs—New and Existing Companies

Business incentives and economic programs are administered at the state level to Jefferson City businesses.

*State programs:* Tax credit programs offered by the state of Missouri include a Business Modernization and Technology Credit, Small Business Incubator Credit, Neighborhood Assistance Program, Historic Preservation Credit, New Markets Tax Credit and a Community Bank Investment Credit. Tax credits through these programs range from 45 percent to 70 percent for qualified programs. A Research Expense Tax Credit program offers a credit of 6.5 percent for qualified expenses. The BUILD Missouri Program provides incentives for the location or expansion of large business projects (generally in excess of 100 jobs). The program provides Missouri state income tax credits to the business in the amount of debt service payments for bonds related to a portion of project costs. The tax credits may be sold if not used by the recipient. A number of loan financing programs are also available.

*Job training programs:* The New Jobs Training Program (NJTP) provides education and training to workers employed in newly created jobs in Missouri. The new jobs may result from a new industry locating in Missouri or an existing industry expanding its workforce in the state. The Missouri Customized Training Program (MCTP) helps Missouri employers with funding to offset the costs of employee training and retraining. It assists new and expanding businesses in recruiting, screening, and training workers, and it helps existing employers retain their current workforce when faced with needed upgrading and retraining. The Missouri Job Retention Training Program offers retraining assistance to employers who have retained a minimum of 100 employers for at least two consecutive years and have made a capital investment of at least $1 million.

## Development Projects

In September 2007 the city approved a resolution of intent to annex 309.52 acres of unincorporated land to an area southwest of the city known as the Route C/Capital Hills area. The resolution states that annexation is reasonable and necessary for the growth and development of the city. As of late 2007 plans were underway to build a new federal courthouse in Jefferson City. Site selection and design had been completed at that time; however, final approval for costs (about $60 million) had not yet been considered by the U.S. Congress. Local officials believe that the presence of the federal courthouse will boost the economic growth and development of the city. City officials were also beginning a series of meetings and a feasibility study concerning the possible development of a new conference center for the city.

*Economic Development Information:* Jefferson City Chamber of Commerce, 213 Adams St., Jefferson City, MO 65101; telephone (573)634-3616; fax (573)634-3805; www.jcchamber.org. Missouri Department of Economic Development, 301 W. High Street, Jefferson City, MO 65102; telephone (573)751-4962; www.ded.mo.gov

## Commercial Shipping

The Union Pacific Railroad provides rail freight service. Several motor freight carriers serve the city. Barge lines ship cargo through Jefferson City via the Missouri River.

## Labor Force and Employment Outlook

The education levels of Jefferson City residents are generally higher than the national average. About 85 percent of the population age 25 years and over has obtained a high school diploma or higher. Nearly 31 percent of this population has achieved a bachelor's degree or higher. A 2004 study shows that job prospects in Cole County and surrounding counties are the best in the state; prospects are especially strong in the categories of durable goods manufacturing, transportation/public utilities, and services. Occupation projections into the year 2014 suggest that, within the region, the most new job growth will be in health services and marketing, sales, and service sectors.

The following is a summary of data regarding the Jefferson City metropolitan area labor force, 2006 annual averages.

**Size of nonagricultural labor force:** 78,200

**Number of workers employed in...**

construction and mining: Not available
manufacturing: Not available
trade, transportation and utilities: 13,800
information: Not available
financial activities: Not available
professional and business services: Not available
educational and health services: Not available
leisure and hospitality: Not available
other services: Not available
government: 28,000

**Average hourly earnings of production workers employed in manufacturing:** Not available

**Unemployment rate:** 4.5% (June 2007)

| *Largest employers (2007)* | *Number of employees* |
|---|---|
| State of Missouri | 16,423 |
| Scholastic, Inc. | 1,920 |
| Capital Region Medical Center | 1,268 |
| St. Mary's Health Center | 1,254 |
| Jefferson City Public Schools | 1,150 |
| ABB Power T & D Company | 875 |
| Von Hoffmann Press | 700 |
| Central Bank | 650 |

| Largest employers (2007) | Number of employees |
|---|---|
| Wal-Mart Supercenter | 585 |
| Jefferson City Medical Group | 559 |

## Cost of Living

The following is a summary of data regarding several key cost of living factors for the Jefferson City area.

**2007 (1st quarter) ACCRA Average House Price:** $225,800

**2007 (1st quarter) ACCRA Cost of Living Index:** 90.7

**State income tax rate:** 1.5% to 6.0%

**State sales tax rate:** 4.225%

**Local income tax rate:** None

**Local sales tax rate:** 2.0% (1.5% city; 0.5% county)

**Property tax rate:** $.72 per $100 assessed valuation

***Economic Information:*** Jefferson City Chamber of Commerce, 213 Adams St., Jefferson City, MO 65101; telephone (573)634-3616; Missouri Department of Economic Development, 301 W. High Street, P.O. Box 1157, Jefferson City, MO 65102; telephone (573)751-4962; http://ded.mo.gov

# ■ Education and Research

## Elementary and Secondary Schools

Jefferson City Public School System's elementary schools offer instruction in language arts, social studies, science, math, fine arts, and physical education. Two middle schools, identical in physical design, feature innovative curriculums for grades 6-8. All ninth graders attend the Simonsen Center. In tenth grade, the students transfer to Jefferson City High School. The Simonsen Center and the high school operate on a 4x4 block schedule through which students take four 90-minute courses each day for 18 weeks (or one semester). High school students may also opt to enroll in classes offered by Nichols Career Center, which offers classes in a variety of vocational areas as well as basic adult education courses. The Exploration, Enrichment and Research program is offered for gifted students in grades three through eight. The Jefferson City Academic Center is an alternative high school for students who do not perform well in the traditional setting.

The following is a summary of data regarding the Jefferson City Public Schools as of the 2005–2006 school year.

**Total enrollment:** 8,243

**Number of facilities**

elementary schools: 11
junior high/middle schools: 2
senior high schools: 1
other: 3

**Student/teacher ratio:** 11.8:1

**Teacher salaries (2005–06)**

elementary median: $32,690
junior high/middle median: $40,110
secondary median: $37,670

**Funding per pupil:** $6,939

Jefferson City is home to several private schools. The largest of these is Helias Interparish High School, which enrolls about 900 students from three local Catholic parishes. Emphasis at Helias is placed on a four-year program in math, science, English, social studies, and foreign language. Courses are taught in computer applications with computer assisted instruction in other courses.

***Public Schools Information:*** Jefferson City Public Schools, 315 E. Dunklin St., Jefferson City, MO 65101; telephone (573)659-3000; www.jcps.k12.mo.us

## Colleges and Universities

Lincoln University, founded in 1866 by African American Civil War veterans, has changed over time from an African American university to a major coeducational state university with a multi-ethnic student body. The university offers undergraduate degrees in arts and sciences, as well as accounting, business administration, public administration, marketing, business education, economics, computer science, technology, military science, and agribusiness. Graduate programs are available in business, education, and social science. Enrollment is about 3,159 students.

Columbia College–Jefferson City is a private liberal arts and sciences college that offers associate's and bachelor's degrees in several fields of study. Courses are available both onsite and online. The Jefferson City campus is one of 32 Columbia College extensions nationwide. The main campus is in Columbia, Missouri.

The Jefferson City campus of William Woods University (WWU) offers graduate and undergraduate degree completion studies through its Graduate and Adult Studies Program. The main campus of WWU is in Fulton, Missouri. Metro Business College is a private career college offering associate's degrees and certificates in the fields of business, healthcare, and information technology. The Jefferson campus is one of four throughout the state.

## Libraries and Research Centers

Jefferson City is served by the Missouri River Regional Library, which consists of a main library in Jefferson City and an Osage County branch in Linn. The library has nearly 200,000 volumes and approximately 400 periodical subscriptions; it maintains special collections on local and state history. The system also has two bookmobiles.

The Missouri State Library has special collections on health and education policy issues, human service, legislative reference, public finance, and state government. The Wolfner Library for the Blind and Physically Handicapped, featuring Braille and large-type books, has holdings of over 360,000 volumes and over 70 periodical subscriptions. Other state libraries located in the city include the library maintained by the Missouri Committee on Legislative Research, with 5,200 volumes and 125 periodical subscriptions; the Missouri Department of Corrections Libraries, with more than 100,000 book titles; the Missouri Supreme Court Library, which has more than 110,000 volumes; and the Office of the Secretary of State, Missouri State Archives, which has 12,500 volumes.

Other local libraries include Lincoln University's Inman E. Page Library, which has over 204,948 volumes and over 358 periodical titles. The library is part of the MOBIUS Consortium that links the libraries of 55 colleges and universities in the state of Missouri and special collections on ethnic studies. The library of the Cole County Historical Society has special collections on oral history.

Lincoln University's Cooperative Research and Extension Program conducts studies in agricultural science, nutrition, and environmental science.

***Public Library Information:*** Missouri River Regional Library, 214 Adams St., Jefferson City, MO 65102; telephone (573)634-2464; www.mrrl.org

# ■ Health Care

Capital Region Medical Center is a 100-bed facility affiliated with the University of Missouri Health Sciences System. The affiliation combines the strengths of an academic medical center with the strengths of a community-based hospital. Capital Region offers prenatal and maternity services, an inpatient rehabilitation center, advanced cardiac and oncology services, and ambulance service. In addition to being a full-service hospital, the center operates six clinics in the area offering urgent care services and specialty physician practices.

St. Mary's Health Center is a faith-based, full-service hospital, with 167 beds, extensive cardiology and open-heart surgery, a maternal and child care center, an oncology center, and a network of primary care clinics. The Heart Center at St. Mary's is one of the leading cardiac care centers in the region. St. Mary's also has one of the first Wound Healing Centers in the region offering hyperbaric oxygen technology. Also at St. Mary's is Villa Marie Skilled Nursing Facility, a 120-bed facility offering intermediary and skilled nursing care as well as a complete rehabilitation program.

# ■ Recreation

## Sightseeing

The State Capitol, which houses the Missouri State Museum, is the third state Capitol building, the first two having been destroyed by fires in 1837 and 1911. The stone building, built between 1913-1917, sits on a limestone bluff on the south bank of the Missouri River. A 1936 mural within the Capitol building's House Lounge, painted by Missouri artist Thomas Hart Benton, is entitled *A Social History of the State of Missouri.* The mural, which depicts average citizens involved in their daily activities, was at first criticized for showing a lack of refinement, but has since become a beloved visual record. Free guided tours of the building are available daily. Located adjacent to the Capitol Rotunda, the Missouri State Museum houses a History Hall and a Resource Hall. The latter tells the story of Missouri from its earliest history to modern times. Located on the Capitol grounds is the large Fountain of Centaurs that was designed by sculptor Adolph A. Weinman.

The Missouri Governor's Mansion is perched on a bluff within walking distance of the State Capitol. An outstanding example of Renaissance Revival style architecture, the mansion has been beautifully restored. The three-story red brick building is trimmed in stone and has an imposing portico with four stately pink granite columns, and its mansard roof is crowned by iron grillwork. The work of Missouri painters Thomas Hart Benton and George Caleb Bingham adorns the walls. The mansion is decked out as a haunted house at Halloween, and is ornately decorated at holiday time.

The Jefferson Landing State Historic Site is a complex of three historic buildings—the Christopher Maus House, the Lohman Building, and the Union Hotel—located just one block from the Capitol. They form the state's oldest remaining Missouri River commercial district. The buildings were restored in 1976 and serve as the Capitol complex's visitors center. The 1854 Christopher Maus House typifies the small, red brick residences of its time. The Union Hotel, built in 1865, houses a gallery with historical exhibits. The Lohman Building, which serves as the visitor center for the Missouri State Museum, was once a store that supplied boat merchandise and general items to the local citizenry. Across the street, the Cole County Historical Society displays artifacts of the city's earlier days, including a collection of inaugural ball gowns of former Missouri first ladies.

The Runge Conservation Nature Center has a 3,000-square-foot exhibit hall that provides hands-on exhibits of Missouri wildlife habitats and features a 2,400-gallon fish aquarium holding indigenous fish. Adjacent to the Runge Conservation Nature Center are five hiking trails with self-guided exhibits. More than 3,500 veterinary artifacts and instruments, some more than a century old, can be viewed at the Missouri Veterinary Medical Foundation Museum, along with old diaries and sample drug cases.

The Missouri State Information Center, which houses the State Records and Archives Division of the Secretary of State's office, is a must for genealogy buffs. Visitors to the Missouri State Highway Patrol Safety Education Center and Law Enforcement Museum can view old patrol cars; gun, drug, alcohol, and seat belt displays; and various law enforcement antiques.

## Arts and Culture

The Little Theatre of Jefferson City, based at Lincoln University's Richardson Auditorium, stages musicals, drama, and comedy. Four major productions are presented annually. The Stained Glass Theatre Mid-Missouri, a non-denominational Christian theatre, stages seven shows per year. The Capitol City Players presents dinner theater entertainment ranging from traditional Broadway musicals to more contemporary fare.

The Jefferson City Symphony offers three annual concerts at Richardson Auditorium, in cooperation with the Community Concert Association. In addition, Lincoln University Vocal Ensemble, Dance Group, and "Share in the Arts" series invites members of the community to enjoy its theatre, music, dance, and poetry events. The Jefferson City Cantorum offers annual concerts in the spring and at Christmas.

## Festivals and Holidays

Jefferson City keeps things lively with a number of annual events. January is highlighted by a bridal show and a boat show. In mid-March the Annual Ice Show provides a colorful extravaganza at the covered Washington Park Ice Arena. May brings the Collectibles and Antique Show and Antique Fair. The city welcomes Independence Day with the Salute to America, featuring musical entertainment, a parade, historical reenactments, arts and crafts, and fireworks. In September, the town celebrates the colors of fall with the Cole County Fall Festival, an arts and crafts fair; the Jefferson City Multicultural Fall Festival, focusing on the city's diversity; Art inside the Park, where contemporary artists create installations in Memorial Park; and the Annual JazzFest on the Capitol grounds. Oktoberfest celebrates residents' German heritage with a festival featuring a beer garden, wine, carriage rides, food, and home tours.

December is filled with holiday activities that begin during the first weekend with the Living Christmas Showcase downtown. It features music, carriage rides, hayrides, tours of historic buildings, and living window displays. Candlelight tours of the Governor's Mansion, decorated for the holiday season, are available. The Annual Christmas Parade takes place on the first Saturday of the month.

## Sports for the Spectator

Both students and community members like to watch the Blue Devils in action during athletic activities that take place at Lincoln University. These events include women's basketball, softball, cross-country/track and field, and tennis, as well as men's basketball, baseball, cross-country/track and field, soccer, and golf. In 2005 the women's cross-country/track and field team won their third straight NCAA Division II Track and Field Championship.

## Sports for the Participant

Ellis Porter Riverside Park offers 60 acres on a bluff overlooking the Missouri river. The park includes a 9,500-square-foot swimming pool, ball playing areas including a basketball court and three lighted handball/racquetball courts, trails, and an outdoor amphitheater. Binder Park, with 650 acres, is the city's largest park. It provides a 150-acre lake for fishing, a boat launch ramp, a campground, lighted softball fields, and two sand volleyball courts. Washington Park features a skating and ice arena, tennis courts, ball fields, and a skate park. Oak Hills Golf Center/Hough Park complex has an eight-acre lake with a boat launching area and an 18-hole golf course. The Tinker Creek Golf Center has a nine-hole par three course and a miniature golf course. Other parks in the city offer a variety of facilities including trails, horse-shoe pits, ball fields, and an ice arena. Public and private golf courses in the area include Eagle Knoll (public), Railwood Golf Club (public), Turkey Creek Golf Center (public); and Jefferson City Country Club and Meadow Lake Acres Country Club (private). The Greenway is a multi-use 6.5-mile trail for walking, jogging, biking, and skating.

South of Jefferson City, the Lake of the Ozarks State park offers more than 17,000 acres of camping, hiking, swimming, and boating facilities.

## Shopping and Dining

High Street is the focal point of downtown shopping, with restaurants and galleries tucked among the brick-fronted shops. Shoppers may also browse at the Capital Mall, which offers dozens of stores, three department stores—Dillard's, Sears, and JCPenney—and a multi-screen cinema. Other local shopping areas include the Southside area, the Eastside with its many quaint shops, and the Westside/Wildwood Crossings area, which has more than 30 restaurants concentrated along Missouri Boulevard.

Local restaurants offer many opportunities to sample the cuisines of various cultures. Menus feature big Midwestern steaks and local catfish, as well as Greek, Asian, Mexican, Italian, and German offerings. There are two wineries in the area: Native Stone Winery and Summit Lake Winery.

*Visitor Information:* Jefferson City Convention and Visitors Bureau, 100 East High St., Jefferson City, MO 65101; telephone (573)632-2820 or (800)769-4183; www.visitjeffersoncity.com

## ■ Convention Facilities

The Truman Hotel and Conference Center has three large halls, each of which may be partitioned into smaller rooms, and 14 meeting rooms that encompass about 22,000 square feet of meeting space. The hotel features 233 guest rooms and suites and a full-service restaurant with catering service available.

*Convention Information:* The Truman Hotel and Conference Center, 1510 Jefferson Street, Jefferson City, MO 65101; telephone (573)635-7171; www.trumanjeffersoncity.com

## ■ Transportation

### Approaching the City

Jefferson City is located at the crossroads of U.S. Highways 54 and 63, which run north and south, and U.S. Highway 50, which runs east and west. Columbia Regional Airport (COU), about twelve miles north of downtown, has commuter air carrier service through Air Midwest (U.S. Airways Express). COU has daily flights to and from Kansas City and St. Louis. The airport shuttle offers trips downtown and taxi service is also available. The Jefferson City Memorial Airport is a flight base for military, corporate, and general aviation aircraft. Amtrak offers train transportation to the city and bus service is provided by Show-Me Coach Lines. USA Express provides bus service eight times a day between Jefferson City and the St. Louis airports.

### Traveling in the City

Highway 50/63 runs east and west through the city just two blocks south of the State Capitol Building; in town it is known as the Whitton Expressway. Highway 54, known as Christy Lane, runs north to Fulton and south to the Lake of the Ozarks State Park. Downtown, West Main Street and East Capitol Avenue run directly to the Missouri Capitol Building. Jefferson City is served by Jefferson City Transit Authority (JEFFTRAN) bus line.

## ■ Communications

### Newspapers and Magazines

The *Jefferson City News Tribune* is published weekday afternoons; the *Daily Capital News* is published Tuesday through Saturday mornings; and the *Sunday News Tribune* is a combination of both publications.

*The Catholic Missourian* is the official weekly newspaper of the Diocese of Jefferson City, while *Word and Way* is a religious tabloid published by the Missouri Baptist Convention. *Jefferson City Home & Lifestyle* is published six times a year.

Locally published trade journals include *Journal of the Missouri Bar, Rural Missouri, Missouri Municipal Review, Missouri Conservationist, The Missouri Nurse, Focus MDA,* and *Missouri Pharmacist.*

### Television and Radio

There are 10 AM and FM radio stations broadcasting a variety of formats, including talk, news, Christian music, and top 40. While there are no major network stations broadcasting directly from the city, city residents receive broadcasts from other locations.

*Media Information:* Jefferson City News Tribune, PO Box 420, Jefferson City, MO 65102; telephone (573) 636-3131; www.newstribune.com

### Jefferson City Online

City of Jefferson City home page. Available www .jeffcitymo.org

Jefferson City Chamber of Commerce. Available www.jcchamber.org

Jefferson City Convention and Visitors Bureau. Available www.visitjeffersoncity.com

*Jefferson City News Tribune.* Available www .newstribune.com

Jefferson City Public Schools. Available www.jcps .k12.mo.us

Missouri River Regional Library. Available www .mrrl.org

BIBLIOGRAPHY

Digges, Deborah, *Fugitive Spring: A Memoir* (New York: Vintage Books, 1993)

Ford, James E., *History of Jefferson City, Missouri's State Capital, and of Cole County* (Salem, MA: Higginson Book Company, 1994)

Young, Robert Emmett, *Pioneers of High, Water, and Main: Reflections of Jefferson City* (Jefferson City, MO: Twelfth State, 1997)

# Kansas City

## ■ The City in Brief

**Founded:** 1821 (incorporated 1853)

**Head Official:** Mayor Mark Funkhouser (since 2007)

**City Population**
- 1980: 448,028
- 1990: 431,236
- 2000: 441,545
- 2006 estimate: 447,306
- Percent change, 1990–2000: 1.5%
- U.S. rank in 1980: 27th
- U.S. rank in 1990: 31st
- U.S. rank in 2000: 45th

**Metropolitan Area Population**
- 1980: 1,433,000
- 1990: 1,587,875
- 2000: 1,776,062
- 2006 estimate: 1,967,405
- Percent change, 1990–2000: 12.2%
- U.S. rank in 1980: 25th
- U.S. rank in 1990: Not available
- U.S. rank in 2000: 26th

**Area:** 314 square miles (2000)

**Elevation:** 742 feet above sea level

**Average Annual Temperatures:** January, 26.9° F; July, 78.5° F; annual average, 54.2° F

**Average Annual Precipitation:** 37.98 inches of rain; 19.9 inches of snow

**Major Economic Sectors:** Trade, transportation, and utilities; government; professional and business services; educational and health services

**Unemployment Rate:** 5.3% (June 2007)

**Per Capita Income:** $24,567 (2005)

**2005 FBI Crime Index Property:** 34,822

**2005 FBI Crime Index Violent:** 6,536

**Major Colleges and Universities:** University of Missouri at Kansas City, Metropolitan Community Colleges

**Daily Newspaper:** *The Kansas City Star*

## ■ Introduction

Kansas City is a thriving cultural and economic center at the heart of the United States. The largest city in Missouri, Kansas City is the center of a bi-state Metropolitan Statistical Area that covers several counties in both Missouri and Kansas. First a trading post and river port settlement, the city developed after the Civil War as a link in the intercontinental railroad network, which led to prosperous grain, livestock, and meat-packing industries. During the twentieth century Kansas City garnered a national reputation for its distinctive architecture, boulevard system, and innovations in urban redevelopment. This redevelopment has continued into the twenty-first century, prompting *Entrepreneur* magazine to name Kansas City as the best city in the Midwest in 2006.

## ■ Geography and Climate

Surrounded by gently rolling terrain, Kansas City is located near the geographical center of the United States. It is situated on the south bank of the Missouri River at the Missouri-Kansas state line. The climate is modified continental, with frequent and rapid fluctuations in weather during early spring. Summer is characterized by warm days and mild nights; fall days are mild and the nights cool. Winter is cold with the heaviest snowfall coming late in the season.

**Area:** 314 square miles (2000)

**Elevation:** 742 feet above sea level

**Average Temperatures:** January, 26.9° F; July, 78.5° F; annual average, 54.2° F

**Average Annual Precipitation:** 37.98 inches of rain; 19.9 inches of snow

# ■ History

### River Site Aids Westward Expansion

The area along the Missouri River now occupied by Kansas City was originally territory within the domain of the Kansa (Kaw) Native Americans. The first persons of European descent to enter the region were Meriwether Lewis and William Clark, who camped at the confluence of the Kansas and Missouri rivers in 1804 during their Louisiana Purchase expedition. Several years later, in 1821, Francois Chouteau opened a depot for the American Fur Company on the site; after a flood destroyed his warehouse in 1826, he relocated to the site of a ferry boat service, where the town of Kansas soon developed.

In 1832 John Calvin McCoy settled nearby and built a store; the following year he platted the town of Westport in Missouri, offering lots for new business development. Westport was soon competing with neighboring Independence, the seat of Jackson County, to be chosen as the eastern terminus of the Santa Fe Trail. Meanwhile Chouteau's settlement, Kansas, developed more slowly; in 1838 the Kansas Town Company was formed to sell property near Chouteau's warehouse. Both Westport and Kansas Town prospered under westward migration until the height of the Gold Rush in 1849, when an epidemic of Asiatic cholera reduced the local population by one-half and drove business elsewhere.

The Kansas Town settlement remained substantial enough, however, to be incorporated in 1850 as the Town of Kansas and then as the City of Kansas in 1853. By 1855 overland trade had returned and the city began to prosper once again, just in time to be disrupted by the nation's conflict over the issue of slavery, during which Southern and Northern forces vied for dominance in the Kansas Territory. Kansas border ruffians invaded Wyandotte County, Kansas, creating havoc in the City of Kansas, which fell into disrepair and economic difficulty with the outbreak of the Civil War. In a pivotal conflict, the Union Army resisted a Confederate Army attack at the Battle of Westport (Missouri) in October of 1864.

### Rail Center Develops Architectural Refinement

When the Missouri Pacific Railroad arrived in 1865, the City of Kansas at the confluence of the Kansas and Missouri rivers was found to be the perfect location for a railroad distributing center. The first stockyards opened in 1870 and, after weathering the grasshopper plagues of 1874, the City of Kansas emerged as a wheat and grain exchange center. The economy was further stimulated when the Kansas River was bridged in 1866, followed by the construction of the Hannibal Bridge across the Missouri River in 1869. Kansas City adopted its current name in 1889 and annexed Westport in 1897.

The figure who exercised the greatest impact in transforming Kansas City into a beautiful metropolis was William Rockhill Nelson, an Indiana native who settled in Kansas City in 1880 to become owner and editor of the *Kansas City Star*. Nelson persuaded the community's elite to commit themselves to civic betterment. Through Nelson's constant nudging, a residential development project was begun, turning a rundown neighborhood into the exclusive Country Club district that contained the internationally acclaimed business section, Country Club Plaza. Carefully landscaped with parks, fountains, and European statuary, this enclave remains Kansas City's most popular tourist attraction. At Nelson's encouragement, George E. Kessler planned Kansas City's much-admired boulevard system, which helps define its distinctive character. The city still contains a number of architecturally significant buildings, especially in the Art Deco style, which credit their existence to Nelson's ability to convince people to express their civic pride through architecture, landscaping, and city planning.

In the 1920s Democrat Thomas J. Pendergast introduced machine politics to Kansas City, with mixed blessings. Although civic improvements were initiated, Kansas City developed a reputation for a corrupt government that functioned under "boss rule," a reputation that continued until 1940 when reformers were voted into office. Since then, Kansas City has prospered through urban redevelopment projects. Crown Center, Hallmark Cards' "city within a city," is credited by some with halting the drain of business into the suburbs. Major development projects completed in the early 2000s included major renovations and expansion of the Kansas City Convention Center and the construction of the Sprint Center arena development. The Kansas City Power and Light District was completed in 2007 to serve as the cornerstone of a major urban renaissance for the city. The development covers nine city blocks and includes retail, entertainment, office, and retail space. It is considered to be the largest entertainment district in the Midwest.

Through these and other developments, Kansas City has become a sophisticated community offering many attractions, from a lyric opera company to five professional sports teams, and from world-class shopping to its famous Kansas City barbeque. Famous natives include pioneering pilot Amelia Earhart; director Robert Altman; actors Edward Asner, Noah and Wallace Beery, and Jean

Harlow; composers Virgil Thompson and Burt Bacharach; rocker Melissa Etheridge; professional golfer Tom Watson; and baseball player Casey Stengel.

***Historical Information:*** Kansas City Museum, 3218 Gladstone Boulevard, Kansas City, MO 64123; telephone (816)483-8300; www.unionstation.org/kcmuseum.cfm. University of Missouri, Western Historical Manuscript Collection, 302 Newcomb Hall, 5100 Rockhill Road, Kansas City, MO 64110; telephone (816) 235-1543; www.umr.edu/~whmcinfo.

# ■ Population Profile

## Metropolitan Area Residents

1980: 1,433,000
1990: 1,587,875
2000: 1,776,062
2006 estimate: 1,967,405
Percent change, 1990–2000: 12.2%
U.S. rank in 1980: 25th
U.S. rank in 1990: Not available
U.S. rank in 2000: 26th

## City Residents

1980: 448,028
1990: 431,236
2000: 441,545
2006 estimate: 447,306
Percent change, 1990–2000: 1.5%
U.S. rank in 1980: 27th
U.S. rank in 1990: 31st
U.S. rank in 2000: 45th

**Density:** 1,408.2 persons per square mile (2000)

## Racial and ethnic characteristics (2005)

White: 271,210
Black: 132,187
American Indian and Alaska Native: 1,988
Asian: 10,878
Native Hawaiian and Pacific Islander: 1,054
Hispanic or Latino (may be of any race): 35,995
Other: 13,387

**Percent of residents born in state:** 57% (2000)

## Age characteristics (2005)

Population under 5 years old: 32,120
Population 5 to 9 years old: 28,167
Population 10 to 14 years old: 29,358
Population 15 to 19 years old: 30,553
Population 20 to 24 years old: 31,572
Population 25 to 34 years old: 68,060
Population 35 to 44 years old: 67,071
Population 45 to 54 years old: 61,877
Population 55 to 59 years old: 26,402
Population 60 to 64 years old: 19,167
Population 65 to 74 years old: 24,852
Population 75 to 84 years old: 17,290
Population 85 years and older: 4,396
Median age: 35.1 years

## Births (2006, MSA)

Total number: 29,175

## Deaths (2006, MSA)

Total number: 15,721

## Money income (2005)

Per capita income: $24,567
Median household income: $41,069
Total households: 187,448

## Number of households with income of...

less than $10,000: 21,358
$10,000 to $14,999: 11,561
$15,000 to $24,999: 21,820
$25,000 to $34,999: 24,982
$35,000 to $49,999: 29,546
$50,000 to $74,999: 33,488
$75,000 to $99,999: 20,976
$100,000 to $149,999: 16,910
$150,000 to $199,999: 2,935
$200,000 or more: 3,872

**Percent of families below poverty level:** 10.4% (2005)

**2005 FBI Crime Index Property:** 34,822

**2005 FBI Crime Index Violent:** 6,536

# ■ Municipal Government

Kansas City operates under a council-manager form of government, with the mayor and 12 council members all elected to four-year terms. The mayor and six council members are elected at-large with one at-large council member representing each district. The remaining six council members are elected only by voters within their district. All council members and the mayor are limited to two consecutive terms. The city manager serves and advises the mayor and council.

**Head Official:** Mayor Mark Funkhouser (since 2007; term expires in 2011)

**Total Number of City Employees:** approximately 4,400 (2007)

***City Information:*** City Hall, 414 East 12th St, Kansas City, MO 64106; telephone (816)513-3500; www.kcmo.org

# ■ Economy

## Major Industries and Commercial Activity

As defined by the Kansas City Area Development Council, the Kansas City KS-MO Metropolitan Statistical Area (KC MSA) includes Kansas City KS-MO; the Lawrence, KS, and St. Joseph, MO MSAs; and the Atchison, KS, Chillicothe, MO, Ottawa, KS, and Warrensburg, MO areas. This KC MSA supports a major trade and transportation center for the nation. It is one of the largest rail centers in the nation based on the amount of freight carried through the area. Along the Missouri River there are 41 docks and terminal facilities in the KC MSA with 7 barge lines operating from the area. The Kansas City International Airport serves as a major hub for Kansas, Missouri, Iowa, and Nebraska with 15 airlines handling cargo. Air, rail, and river transportation is all supplemented by the presence of over 300 motor freight carriers in the area.

In the Missouri portion of the MSA the professional, scientific, and technical services industries accounted for one of the top employing sectors. Education and health care services have a strong role in the local economy as well, with the public school districts, HCA Midwest Health Systems, St. Luke's Health System, and Truman Medical Centers serving as major employers in the city. DST Systems, which offers information processing and business computer software services, also maintains a headquarters in the city and is one of the major employers.

While the number of manufacturing jobs in the area has declined over the last decade, there are still a significant number of jobs available in the sector. The Ford Motor Company in nearby Claycomo, MO, is a major employer for the area. The headquarters of two major greeting card companies—Attic Salt Greetings, Inc. and Hallmark Cards, Inc.—are in Kansas City, MO. American Italian Pasta, the largest producer of pasta in North America, has corporate offices in the city.

Federal, state, and local government all serve as major employers in the city and the vicinity. Hospitality services (food service and accommodations) are also important to the city economy.

In 2006 Kansas City, MO ranked first on the list of best cities in the Midwest in a survey by *Entrepreneur* magazine. The KC MSA ranked 11th on the national list for large cities in the same survey.

**Items and goods produced:** automobiles, food products, greeting cards, commercial printing and publishing, computer software, information systems, telecommunications equipment, personal care items, railroad signal and traffic control systems

## Incentive Programs—New and Existing Companies

***Local programs:*** One of the main development assistance organizations in the city is the Economic Development Corporation of Kansas City (EDCKC). This organization oversees a Tax Increment Financing (TIF) Program through which developers may be eligible to recover construction costs by recapturing part of the increased property, sales, and utilities taxes generated by the project. Redirection of property and economic activity taxes may occur for up to 23 years. Through the Rebuilding Communities Tax Program, existing, new, or relocating businesses may choose between a 40 percent income credit or a 40 percent specialized equipment credit, plus obtain a 1.5 percent employee credit.

The Kansas City Area Development Council is a bi-state, regional coalition of business, government, economic development, and chambers of commerce leaders. The council works with community partners to attract business and industry to the bi-state metropolitan area. Businesses locating within the Kansas City area are eligible for several incentive programs that, at the time of initial investment, offer direct cost reductions. The Greater Kansas City Chamber of Commerce's Business Resource Center provides information for the research and business planning stage.

***State programs:*** Kansas City is part of a state designated Enhanced Enterprise Zone through which eligible businesses may receive tax credits for up to 10 years for new development. The business must create at least two new jobs and offer $100,000 in new investment for each year in order to be eligible for tax credits. A job creation tax credit of $400 per eligible employee is available against state income taxes for up to 10 years. Other tax credits include up to $1,200 for hiring Enterprise Zone residents or "special employees." Local Enterprise Zone incentives include a 50 percent property tax abatement for real estate improvements. Foreign Trade Zone (FTZ) incentives are available in several zones throughout the KC MSA. Goods entering FTZs are not subject to customs tariffs until the goods leave the zone and are formally entered into U.S. customs territory. Other tax credit programs offered by the state of Missouri include a Business Modernization and Technology Credit, Small Business Incubator Credit, Neighborhood Assistance Program, Historic Preservation Credit, New Markets Tax Credit and a Community Bank Investment Credit. Tax credits through these programs range from 45 percent to 70 percent for qualified programs. A Research Expense Tax Credit program offers a credit of 6.5 percent for qualified expenses. The BUILD Missouri Program provides incentives for the location or expansion of large business projects (generally in excess of 100 jobs). The program provides Missouri state income tax credits

to the business in the amount of debt service payments for bonds related to a portion of project costs. The tax credits may be sold if not used by the recipient. A number of loan financing programs are also available.

***Job training programs:*** The New Jobs Training Program (NJTP) provides education and training to workers employed in newly created jobs in Missouri. The new jobs may result from a new industry locating in Missouri or an existing industry expanding its workforce in the state. In greater Kansas City, NJTP services are provided by the Metropolitan Community Colleges system. The Missouri Customized Training Program (MCTP) helps Missouri employers with funding to offset the costs of employee training and retraining. It assists new and expanding businesses in recruiting, screening, and training workers, and it helps existing employers retain their current workforce when faced with needed upgrading and retraining. The Missouri Job Retention Training Program offers retraining assistance to employers who have retained a minimum of 100 employers for at least two consecutive years and have made a capital investment of at least $1 million.

## Development Projects

The Kansas City Power and Light District was completed in 2007 and serves as the cornerstone of a major urban renaissance for the city. The development covers nine city blocks and includes retail, entertainment, office, and retail space. The $850 million project was developed in partnership with the city and state governments and has created one of the largest entertainment districts in the Midwest. The new Sprint Center was completed in 2007 as well. This $276 million development serves as the home for the National Association of Basketball Coaches Hall of Fame. The center also serves as a venue for major entertainment events. The city hopes that the center will attract a new professional basketball and/or hockey franchise. The Kansas City Convention Center completed a $135 million expansion and renovation project in 2007, which included major technology upgrades for the facility and a new 50,000-square-foot ballroom.

A plan for redevelopment of East Village was underway in 2007 with an expected completion date of 2009. The $357 million project is anchored by the new headquarters of JE Dunn Construction Group and will include 1,200 residential units and 85,000 square feet of retail space. Another major downtown project is the Kauffman Center for the Performing Arts. This $326 million development will include a 1,800-seat new theater home for the Kansas City Ballet and the Lyric Opera. The theater will also host national and international touring artists. A 1,600-seat Concert Hall will be the new home for the Kansas City Symphony. There will also be a multi-purpose Celebration Hall for performances, banquets, and educational programs.

The $200 million Federal Reserve Bank of Kansas City building project is expected to be completed in 2008. The 600,000-square-foot tower will include 12 floors above a two-story base and will house a coin museum. Children's Mercy Hospital has added a new Pediatric Research Center and Primary Care Clinics to its facility and has plans for new outpatient clinics, classrooms, and educational building to be completed in 2010. The total investment for these projects will be about $120 million.

***Economic Development Information:*** Kansas City Area Development Council, 2600 Commerce Tower, 911 Main Street, Kansas City, MO 64105; telephone (816)842-2865 or (800)99KCADC; www.thinkkc.com. Economic Development Corporation of Kansas City, Missouri, 1100 Walnut, Ste. 1700, Kansas City, MO 64106; telephone (816)221-0636 or (800)889-0636; www.edckc.com

## Commercial Shipping

Located at the juncture of three interstate highways, four interstate linkages, and 10 federal highways, Kansas City is served by more than 300 motor freight carriers, including Yellow Corp., the nation's largest less-than-truckload carrier, which is headquartered in Kansas City. Kansas City is the third largest truck terminal in the United States. The second-largest rail center in the United States, Greater Kansas City is served by four Class I rail carriers: Burlington Northern Santa Fe, Kansas City Southern, Norfolk Southern, and Union Pacific. Regional rail service is provided through the Iowa, Chicago, & Eastern line and Missouri & Northern Arkansas.

Seven barge lines offer shipping from the Kansas City area of the Missouri River. There are 41 docks and terminals in the metropolitan area. The shipping season runs from March through November. As an important inland port, Kansas City ranks first in the country in Foreign Trade Zones space. Kansas City International Airport has 4 all-cargo carriers and 11-passenger combination carriers. The Downtown Airport supports small charter air cargo flights.

## Labor Force and Employment Outlook

The Kansas City area labor force is said to be well-educated, motivated, and highly productive. In 2006 an estimated 86 percent of the adult population had earned

a high school diploma or higher level of education. About 29 percent of the adult population had achieved a bachelor's degree or higher. About 27 percent of those employed in the city are also residents.

In 2007 the largest employment sectors were professional, technical, and scientific services; health care and social assistance; and accommodation and food services. Projections for 2004–2014 suggest that the greatest number of new jobs will be created in health care, financial services, business management and administration, and marketing, sales and services.

The following is a summary of data regarding the Kansas City MO-KS Metropolitan Statistical Area metropolitan area labor force, 2006 annual averages.

**Size of nonagricultural labor force:** 994,000

**Number of workers employed in ...**

   construction and mining: 54,600
   manufacturing: 82,900
   trade, transportation and utilities: 205,200
   information: 41,400
   financial activities: 73,500
   professional and business services: 141,400
   educational and health services: 114,100
   leisure and hospitality: 95,200
   other services: 40,200
   government: 145,700

**Average hourly earnings of production workers employed in manufacturing:** Not available

**Unemployment rate:** 5.3% (June 2007)

| *Largest employers (2007)* | *Number of employees* |
|---|---|
| Federal Government | 25,004 |
| Sprint Nextel Corp. | 16,403 |
| HCA - Midwest Division | 7,320 |
| McDonald's USA LLC | 7,111 |
| State of Missouri | 6,078 |
| Ford Motor Company KC Assembly Plant | 5,453 |
| DST Systems | 5,200 |
| Saint Luke's Health System | 4,808 |
| Hallmark Cards Inc. | 4,500 |
| City of Kansas City, MO | 4,400 |

## Cost of Living

Kansas City's cost of living has consistently been at or below the national average. A major component of the overall low cost of living is the affordability of housing in the area.

The following is a summary of data regarding several key cost of living factors in the Kansas City area.

**2007 (1st quarter) ACCRA Average House Price:** $271,279

**2007 (1st quarter) ACCRA Cost of Living Index:** 94.9

**State income tax rate:** 1.5% to 6.0%

**State sales tax rate:** 4.225%

**Local income tax rate:** 1.0% of earnings

**Local sales tax rate:** 2.875%

**Property tax rate:** 1.32 per $100 of assessed value of improved and unimproved land, personal property, and footage on or abutting boulevards, parkways, and trafficways

*Economic Information:* Kansas City Area Development Council, 2600 Commerce Tower, 911 Main Street, Kansas City, MO 64105; telephone (816)842-2865 or (800)99KCADC; www.thinkkc.com. Economic Development Corporation of Kansas City, Missouri, 1100 Walnut, Ste. 1700, Kansas City, MO 64106; telephone (816)221-0636 or (800)889-0636; www.edckc.com

# ■ Education and Research

## Elementary and Secondary Schools

There are 15 public school districts serving students from Kansas City. Of those there are five with administrative offices within the city proper. The largest in terms of number of student residents served is the Kansas City, Missouri School District. In 2007 the district had 17 magnet schools, including the Longan French Magnet School and the Crispus Attucks Communication and Writing Magnet School. Several schools have focused arts programs, including the Kansas City Middle School of the Arts and Paseo Academy. The Afrikan Centered Education (ACE) Collegium Campus serves students from kindergarten through ninth grade with a program of study that features high academic standards and a focus on social responsibility and leadership in a culturally relevant approach. The school expects to add a full high school curriculum by 2010. The Clark ACE Middle School offers similar programming. Gladstone Academy has special programs for students who are deaf or hard of hearing, and offers the ARENA Gifted Program. Lincoln College Preparatory Academy is open to high school students. Technical and occupational programs are also available throughout the system for older youth and young adults.

The following is a summary of data regarding the Kansas City, Missouri School District as of the 2005–2006 school year.

**Total enrollment:** 26,980

**Number of facilities**

elementary schools: 47
junior high/middle schools: 9
senior high schools: 7
other: 8

**Student/teacher ratio:** 14.5:1

**Teacher salaries (2005–06)**

elementary median: $39,490
junior high/middle median: $39,580
secondary median: $39,190

**Funding per pupil:** $9,237

More than 150 private and parochial schools operate in the metropolitan area.

*Public Schools Information:* Kansas City, Missouri School District, 1211 McGee, Kansas City, MO 64106; telephone (816)418-7000; www2.kcmsd.net

## Colleges and Universities

The largest institution in the city is the University of Missouri–Kansas City, with an enrollment of about 14,200 students. Granting baccalaureate, master's, and doctorate degrees, the university operates a College of Arts and Sciences, a conservatory of music and dance, and schools of business and public administration, computing and engineering, education, law, pharmacy, dentistry, nursing, medicine, and biological sciences. Several undergraduate and graduate certificate programs are also available.

Avila University is a four-year Catholic liberal arts college founded in 1916. The school offers 60 undergraduate majors, 5 graduate programs, and 3 certificate programs. The most popular majors are business, education, nursing, communications, radiologic science, psychology, and art. Enrollment is about 2,000 students. Rockhurst University is a Catholic Jesuit liberal arts university with an enrollment of about 3,000 students. The school offers bachelor's degrees in a wide variety of fields and master's degrees in nursing, business administration, education, and physical and occupational therapy.

The Kansas City Art Institute, which began as a sketch club in 1885, offers a four-year fine and applied arts curriculum with 12 areas of emphasis, including animation, digital filmmaking, fibers, and art history.

Metropolitan Community Colleges supports seven campuses in the Kansas City area, with four located within the city proper. A wide variety of two-year associate's degree and certificate programs are available.

Credits are easily transferred to other local and state colleges and universities.

## Libraries and Research Centers

The Kansas City Public Library, with holdings of over 2 million volumes and more than 34,000 periodical subscriptions, operates 10 branches, including the new $50 million Central Library Branch unveiled in 2004 and the Plaza Branch opened in April 2005. Special collections include African American history, Missouri Valley history and genealogy, oral history, and federal and state government documents. The Kansas City Library Consortium is a network of the public library and seven local college and university libraries through which each organization shares resources.

The Black Archives of Mid-America is a collaborative effort with the Kansas City Public Library and the Missouri State Library. The archive is the largest depository of artifacts and documents of the African American experience in the four-state region. The collection contains written histories, personal documents, newspapers, diaries, and documents from churches, clubs, and other social and business establishments. An oral archive has been developed through the Kansas City Association of Trust and Foundations.

The University of Missouri–Kansas City Libraries feature a wide variety of special collections and research materials in numerous fields of study. The system holds over 1.1 million volumes and over 6,000 periodical subscriptions. The Miller Nichols Library is a general library that also houses the Special Collections Department, which includes the Marr Sound Archives of American social and cultural history recordings, the Snyder Collection of Americana, and a collection of the Midwest Center for American Music. Miller Nichols Library is also a federal depository library for the Fifth U.S. Congressional District. Other libraries within the system include the Leon E. Bloch Law Library, the Health Sciences Library, and the Dental Library. Students and researchers have access to all libraries in the University of Missouri system.

The Linda Hall Library of Science, Engineering & Technology is one of the largest privately endowed libraries of its kind in the country, holding more than 1 million volumes and more than 15,000 periodicals. Special collections include National Aeronautics and Space Administration (NASA) and Department of Energy technical reports, Soviet and European scientific and technical publications, and United States patent specifications. The Kansas City Branch of the National Archives and Records Administration holds records of various federal government agencies.

A wide variety of research projects take place among the students and faculty of the University of Missouri–Kansas City. Facilities include the Shock Trauma Research Center, the Oral Biology Research Lab, the Transgenic Lab, and the Neurophysiology/Pharmacology Lab.

The 600,000-square-foot Stowers Institute for Medical Research boasts one of the nation's finest laboratory complexes dedicated to conducting basic research into complex genetic systems to unlock the mysteries of disease and find the key to their causes, treatment, and prevention. In 2007 the institute sponsored 24 research programs.

***Public Library Information:*** Kansas City Public Library, 14 West 10th St., Kansas City, MO 64105; telephone (816)701-3400; www.kclibrary.org

# ■ Health Care

HCA Midwest Health System is one of the largest health systems in the region. The 545-bed Research Medical Center, founded in 1896, offers general and specialized care in such areas as arthritis, cardiac, and pulmonary rehabilitation, pain management, and speech and hearing disorders. The hospital sponsors a Certified Stroke Center, Transplant Institute, and specialized cardiovascular and oncology departments. In 2005 the Research Cancer Center unveiled a new genetic counseling/screening program. The Research Psychiatric Center provides a complete range of psychiatric treatment for adults and adolescents.

St. Luke's Health System is also one of the largest health care systems in the region. St. Luke's Hospital in Kansas City is a 629-bed tertiary care institution. In 2007 the hospital was ranked within the top 40 best hospitals for heart care, neurology and neurosurgery, and gynecology by *U.S. News & World Report*. The emergency department includes a Level I Trauma Center and a specialized sexual assault treatment center. Other specialty centers within the hospital include the Kidney Dialysis and Transplant Center, the Center for Surgical Weight Loss, Cancer Institute, the Mid-American Heart Institute, the Brain and Stroke Institute, The Children's SPOT (speech, physical and occupational therapy), the Regional Arthritis Center, and a Pain Management program. The Crittenton Children's Center, also affiliated with the St. Luke's Health System, offers inpatient and outpatient psychiatric care and sponsors school- and home- based programs as well.

Truman Medical Centers (TMC) is a two-hospital system that also serves as a primary teaching center for the University of Missouri-Kansas City schools of medicine, dentistry, pharmacy, and nursing. The TMC Hospital Hill campus features a Level I Trauma Center and has specialized programs in care of asthma, diabetes, obstetrics, ophthalmology, weight management, and women's health.

Children's Mercy Hospitals and Clinics sponsors the Children's Mercy Hospital and Hall Family Outpatient Center and Children's Mercy Northland, both in Kansas

City, Missouri, and Children's Mercy South in Overland Park, Kansas. Each location features a wide variety of specialty clinics and urgent care services.

# ■ Recreation

## Sightseeing

Kansas City is regarded as one of the most cosmopolitan cities of its size in the United States. Second only to Rome, Italy, in the number of its fountains (more than 200), Kansas City also has more miles of boulevards than Paris, France. Country Club Plaza, the nation's first planned community, boasts Spanish-style architecture, beautiful landscaping, and a plethora of shops, restaurants, hotels, and apartments. More than 1,000 of the city's structures are included on the National Register of Historic Places; among them are the Scarritt Building and Arcade, the *Kansas City Star* Building, Union Station, and the Kansas City Power and Light Building. The Mutual Musicians Foundation, a hot-pink bungalow acquired by the Black Musicians Union Local 627 in 1928, received a National Historic Landmark designation.

A unique feature of the city is a system of underground limestone caves that were formerly quarries. This 20-million-square-foot "subtropolis" is now a commercial complex used for offices and warehouses. The Hallmark Visitors Center showcases the history and most recent developments of the Hallmark Greeting Card Company. The Harry S. Truman Library and Museum in Independence, Missouri, captures Truman's political career and years as 33rd President of the United States. The nation's second largest urban park, Swope Park, includes the Kansas City Zoo and a Braille trail.

One of the city's most popular attractions is Worlds of Fun, a 175-acre theme park featuring MAMBA, one of the tallest, longest, fastest steel coasters in the world. Oceans of Fun, located on the grounds of Worlds of Fun, is a tropically-themed water park featuring a million-gallon wave pool and giant water slides.

The towns around Kansas City are full of historic homes and sites, including the home and presidential library of Harry S. Truman in Independence. One of the more unusual sites is the Jesse James Bank Museum in Liberty, the site of the first daylight bank robbery in the United States. History aficionados can still see ruts created by covered wagons along the Santa Fe Trail, established in 1821, and the Quindaro Ruins in Kansas City, Kansas, represent the largest underground-railroad archeological site in the nation.

The Negro Leagues Baseball Museum in Kansas City's 18th and Vine District honors the history of African American baseball before 1947, when Kansas City Monarchs shortstop Jackie Robinson broke the color barrier by joining major league baseball. Sports fans will also enjoy a tour of the National Collegiate Athletic Association Hall of Champions in Overland Park, Kansas, to commemorate great moments in intercollegiate athletics through multi-image and video presentations, displays, and exhibits.

## Arts and Culture

Kansas City's Nelson-Atkins Museum of Art, one of the largest museums in the United States and ranked in the top 15, maintains a permanent collection that represents art from all civilizations and periods, from Sumeria to the present. Opened in 1933, the museum covers 20 landscaped acres and is home to the only Henry Moore Sculpture Garden outside the artist's native England. A new 165,000-square-foot expansion designed by internationally acclaimed architect Steven Holl is slated to open in 2007.

The Kemper Museum of Contemporary Art, built in 1994, presents rotating contemporary exhibits free of charge to the public. The Liberty Memorial Museum, conceived as a "monument to peace," is the nation's only public museum devoted solely to World War I and America's involvement in that conflict. Its dedication in 1921 brought together five Allied commanders who met for the first and only time in their lives. The Toy and Miniature Museum of Kansas City is one of only three museums of its kind in the country. The Kansas City Museum features hands-on science and history exhibits; its "If I Had a Hammer" program gives fourth through twelfth graders hands-on experience assembling a house. The museum's Science City at Union Station combines the best of a museum, science center, theme park, and theater. Other museums in the city include the Black Archives of Mid-America, the Federal Reserve Bank Visitors Center, and the home and studio of the late painter, Thomas Hart Benton.

Kansas City, "the mother of swing and the nurturer of bebop," is noted for a distinctive jazz musical style, which consists of a two-four beat, predominance of saxophones, and background riffs. It has been played by musicians in local clubs since the early 1900s. The late Count Basie and Charlie "Bird" Parker, regarded as two of the greatest practitioners of the genre, began their careers in Kansas City. The Museums at 18th and Vine celebrate this heritage. The American Jazz Museum section is the first museum in the country devoted exclusively to this art form. The museum's interactive exhibits tell the story of "America's classical music" in an entertaining and educational format. In addition to in-depth exhibits on such greats as Count Basie, Ella Fitzgerald, and Charlie Parker, the museum includes artifacts such as a Charlie Parker saxophone and a discovery room where visitors can listen to jazz performances. In the evenings, visitors can swing into the Blue Room, a jazz club recognized by *Downbeat Magazine* in 2004 as one of the 100 greatest jazz clubs in the world.

Kansas City ranks third in the nation for professional theaters per capita, boasting more than 20 equity and community theater companies. The Gem Theater Cultural and Performing Arts Center, one of the Museums at 18th and Vine, is a historic structure. With its neon marquee, it has been transformed into a 500-seat state-of-the-art facility for musical and theatrical performances. The center also hosts dance theaters and multimedia events for the public.

The Missouri Repertory Theatre performs a seven-show season, hosting nationally known actors and performing a stage adaptation of Charles Dickens's *A Christmas Carol* each holiday season. Among the other theater companies in Kansas City are the Coterie Family Theatre, American Heartland Theatre, Quality Hill Playhouse, Unicorn Theatre, and Kansas City Repertory Theatre.

Folly Theatre, a former burlesque house refurbished in 1981, is the first theater to appear on the National Historic Register; it hosts professional theater productions. The Midland Center for the Performing Arts, also on the National Historic Register, is a 1920s movie palace that was refurbished and reopened in 1981. Touring Broadway shows are presented in this ornate structure, which is decorated with gold leaf overlays, Tiffany glass, and bronze chandeliers.

The Lyric Theater is the home of the Kansas City Ballet, and the Kansas City Symphony and Lyric Opera, which presents all of its performances in English, as well as the headquarters of the State Ballet of Missouri. The Heart of America Shakespeare Festival presents professional productions of Shakespeare's plays in Southmoreland Park in June and July. One of the nation's largest outdoor amphitheaters, the 7,795-seat Starlight Theatre is located in Swope Park and presents musicals and concerts in the summer.

## Festivals and Holidays

Kansas City offers entertaining, educational, and flavorful festivals and events year-round. The culture and unique foods of many different countries are celebrated at the Northland Ethnic Festival in April, the Taiwanese Festival in May, the Annual Greek Festival in June, the Sugar Creek Slavic Festival in June, the Ethnic Enrichment Festival in August, and the Kansas City Irish Festival in September. The "Rhythm & Ribs" Jazz Festival in June combines two of Kansas City's favorite things—barbeque and jazz. Food is also the theme of the Platte City BBQ Fest in June and the Kansas City Chocolate Festival in October.

Other events that celebrate Kansas City's Midwestern heritage include the Prairie Village Art Show in June, the Heart of America Quilt Festival in October, and the Missouri Town 1855 Festival of Arts, Crafts, and Music in October. There are fairs aplenty, including the Platte County Fair in July, the oldest continuously running fair west of the Mississippi. The more arts-minded

visitor will appreciate the Women' Playwriting Festival and the Kansas City Comedy Arts Fest in March, the Filmmakers Jubilee Film Festival in April, and the variety of music and theater festivals throughout the summer.

Autumn brings a full calendar of harvest festivals and horse racing. In November the 100-foot-tall Mayor's Christmas Tree is illuminated by 7,200 white lights, with 47,500 more strung throughout Crown Center Square. After Christmas the tree is made into ornaments for the next year, which are sold with proceeds going to the Mayor's Christmas Tree Fund. Christmas in Kansas City would not be the same without the annual production of "A Christmas Carol" by the Kansas City Repertory Theatre or the "Festival of Lights" at Country Club Plaza.

## Sports for the Spectator

Kansas City athletes compete in three of the most modern sports facilities in the United States. The Harry S. Truman Sports Complex consists of the 40,000-seat Kauffman Stadium and 79,000-seat Arrowhead Stadium. Arrowhead is the home of the Kansas City Chiefs in the Western Division of the American Conference of the National Football League. Kauffman Stadium is the home of the Kansas City Royals of the Western Division of baseball's American League. Kemper Arena, close to downtown Kansas City, features an award-winning circular and pillar-less structure that allows unobstructed and intimate viewing from all locations. The Kansas City Comets play indoor soccer and the Kansas City Knights play ABA basketball, both at Kemper Arena. The Kansas City Brigade plays in Kemper Arena as part of the Arena Football League. Professional golfer Tom Watson, a Kansas City native, is affectionately known as the city's "fourth sports franchise."

Sprint Center, the 20,000-seat arena opened in 2007, houses the National Collegiate Basketball Hall of Fame. Kansas City is also headquarters of the National Association of Intercollegiate Athletics (NAIA) and the Fellowship of Christian Athletes (FCA). Since the Kansas Speedway (in Kansas) was inaugurated in 2001, racing fans have enjoyed NASCAR, Indy Racing, and Truck series events at the 1.5 mile tri-oval track.

The American Royal, the world's largest combined livestock show, horse show, and rodeo, takes place in autumn at the American Royal Complex in the stockyard district.

## Sports for the Participant

The beautiful and popular Kansas City parks offer an outlet for sports enthusiasts who enjoy fishing, golf, hiking, jogging, swimming, boating, ice skating, or tennis. Swope Park, the second largest city park in the nation, provides two 18-hole golf courses, a nature center, athletic fields, a swimming pool, the Kansas City Zoo, and a Braille trail. The 250-acre Shawnee Mission Park is one of the best spots for sailing and canoeing. Fishing and sailing are available at nine public access lakes within an hour's drive. The area has facilities for amateur auto racing as well as horse- and dog-race tracks. In total Kansas City Parks and Recreation sponsors 212 parks with 5 public golf courses and 150 athletic fields.

Those who enjoy gambling spend time on the Missouri River just north of downtown, where four riverboats offer a number of opportunities to court Lady Luck. There is no admission charge to board the boats, most of which have cruise times every two hours from 8 a.m. to 3 a.m. and offer numerous dining choices and virtually nonstop entertainment.

## Shopping and Dining

The City Market, at the north end of Main Street, offers shopping in a bazaar-like atmosphere. A Saturday morning trip to City Market for produce is a local tradition. Further south on Main Street, the Country Club Plaza, developed by Jessie Clyde Nichols in 1922, enjoys the distinctions of being "America's Original Shopping Center" and Kansas City's most popular tourist attraction, welcoming 10 million visitors each year. Located five miles south of downtown, the Plaza covers 55 acres and houses almost 200 retail and service businesses, including 40 restaurants. The Plaza, with its tile-roofed, pastel-colored buildings and imported filigree ironwork, borrows heavily from Hispanic architecture in honor of Seville, Spain, Kansas City's sister city. The European ambiance is enhanced with a number of towers, fountains, and horse-drawn carriages. The Plaza inaugurated America's outdoor Christmas lighting tradition in 1926.

Hallmark Cards's Crown Center, described as a city within a city, is a one-half billion-dollar downtown complex of shops, restaurants, hotels, offices, apartments, and condominiums over 85 acres. The Crown Center Shops occupy three levels topped by Halls Crown Center, a 100,000-square-foot specialty store. Crown Center revitalized the inner city by creating a downtown suburb where families can live and work. Town Pavilion, a trilevel shopping complex at the base of a major office building downtown, is connected by walkways to other office complexes. Just a couple miles from downtown lies Westport, Kansas City's historic district, featuring boutiques, restaurants, and nightly entertainment. In nearby Olathe, Kansas, shoppers converge at the 130 outlet stores of the Olathe Great Mall of the Great Plains.

Kansas City barbecue is one of America's most savory contributions to world cuisine. Since 1908, when Henry Perry first started selling 25-cent slabs of barbecued meat cooked on an outdoor pit and wrapped in newspaper, Kansas City barbecue has held its own alongside traditional Texas and Carolina versions. The process requires that the meat be dry rub-spiced, cooked slowly over wood—preferably hickory—for as long as 18 hours, and slathered with rich, sweet-tangy sauce. More than 90 Kansas City barbecue establishments serve ribs, pork, ham, mutton, sausage, and even fish. Each establishment prides itself on its own unique recipe for sauce; the most famous sauce, KC Masterpiece, was developed in the 1980s by Rich Davis. The barbecue restaurant owned by the legendary Arthur Bryant has been described by food critic Calvin Trillin as "the single, best restaurant in the world."

Kansas City ranks number three in the United States for sheer number of restaurants. Elegant dining is possible at establishments like the Savoy Grill, Le Fou Frog, Fedora Café & Bar, and the Peppercorn Duck Club, famous for its rotisserie duck and ultra chocolatta bar.

***Visitor Information:*** Kansas City Convention and Visitors Association, 1100 Main St., Ste. 2200, Kansas City, MO 64105; telephone (816)221-5242; toll-free (800)767-7700; www.visitkc

## ■ Convention Facilities

Kansas City is a popular convention destination, ranking among the top meeting centers in the nation. The Kansas City Convention and Entertainment Centers is the site of most major functions in the city. Covering eight city blocks in downtown Kansas City, the Convention Center includes nearly 400,000 square feet of column-free space and 29 meeting rooms. The attached Conference Center is a three-story complex with up to 19 additional meeting rooms, a 33,000-square-foot lobby, and a 24,000-square-foot ballroom. The Municipal Auditorium is an art deco landmark with self-contained venues, including the Music Hall, Arena, Little Theatre, and Exhibition Hall; located directly across the street, Barney Allis Plaza is an outdoor park concealing underground parking facilities for 1,000 vehicles.

Located near the convention center is the American Royal Center, a 14-acre complex that includes Kemper Arena, the American Royal Arena, Hale Arena, and American Royal Museum. The newly expanded Kemper Arena is the site of large functions such as political conventions.

Additional convention facilities for both large and small groups can be found at metropolitan area hotels and motels, where more than 17,000 rooms are available.

***Convention Information:*** Kansas City Convention and Visitors Association, 1100 Main St., Ste. 2200, Kansas City, MO 64105; telephone (816)221-5242; toll-free (800)767-7700; www.visitkc

## ■ Transportation

### Approaching the City

Kansas City International Airport, located about 22 miles from the downtown area, is the primary entry point for air travelers. Its 13 major commercial airlines offer about 230 daily departures with nonstop service to 70 destinations.

The Charles B. Wheeler Downtown Airport (sometimes referred to simply as the Kansas City Downtown Airport), serves charter, corporate, and other fixed-based operator flights.

Primary highway routes into Kansas City are north-south I-35 and I-29, which join U.S. 71 leading into the city. The I-435 bypass links with east-west I-70 from the south. Amtrak provides passenger rail service to two stops in the metropolitan area. Greyhound and Jefferson bus lines serve destinations in Kansas City and around the country.

### Traveling in the City

Kansas City's streets are laid out in a basic grid pattern except in areas contiguous with the Kansas and Missouri rivers, where one-way streets predominate. The principal downtown thoroughfare is Main Street, which runs north to south. Beginning at the Missouri River, east-west streets are numbered in ascending order southward through the city. State Line Road separates Kansas City, Missouri, from Kansas City, Kansas; the two cities are connected via I-70.

Public bus transportation is operated by the Kansas City Area Transit Authority, which provides service throughout the entire metropolitan area. The new MAX (Metro Area Express) connects the River Market, downtown Kansas City, Crown Center, and Country Club Plaza, carrying travelers along exclusive lanes through coordinated traffic signals. Dial-A-Ride offers public transit service for persons with disabilities. Senior Group Transportation is also available. Johnson County Transit (The JO), operates bus services throughout Johnson County Kansas and to points in both Kansas City, Kansas, and Kansas City, Missouri.

# ■ Communications

### Newspapers and Magazines

The major daily newspaper in Kansas City is the morning *The Kansas City Star*. *The Daily Record* is a legal newspaper serving Kansas City and Independence. Several community newspapers also circulate weekly, including *The Call*, which serves the African American community; *The Pitch*, an alternative press publication; and the *Kansas City Business Journal*. *Dos Mundos* is a weekly bilingual newspaper (Spanish).

The National Catholic Reporter Publishing Company is based in Kansas City. The company publishes the news-weekly *National Catholic Reporter* and the monthly

*Celebration*, a resource magazine primarily for priests and church workers. *Ingram's* is a monthly business and lifestyle magazine. *Jam* (Jazz Ambassadors Magazine) is published six times a year to keep visitors and residents up-to-date on the local music scene.

### Television and Radio

Six television stations—major network affiliates and one PBS—are based in Kansas City. Broadcasts are also received from stations in neighboring Fairway, Kansas, and Shawnee Mission, Kansas. Seventeen AM and FM radio stations in Kansas City broadcast a range of program formats, including music, news, and information; many more are available from nearby cities.

*Media Information:* The Kansas City Star, 1729 Grand Blvd., Kansas City, MO 64108; telephone (816) 234-4926; www.kansascity.com

### Kansas City Online

City of Kansas City home page. Available www .kcmo.org

Economic Development Corporation of Kansas City, Missouri. Available www.edckc.com

Experience Kansas City. Available www .experiencekc.com

Greater Kansas City Chamber of Commerce. Available www.kcchamber.com

Kansas City Area Development Council. Available www.smartkc.com

Kansas City Convention and Visitors Association. Available www.visitkc.com

*The Kansas City Star.*Available www.kansascity.com

Missouri Department of Economic Development. Available www.ded.mo.gov

Missouri Department of Elementary and Secondary Education. Available www.dese.mo.gov

BIBLIOGRAPHY

DeAngelo, Dory, *Kansas City, A Historical Handbook* (Kansas City, MO: Two Lane Press, 1995)

Hemingway, Ernest, *Ernest Hemingway, Cub Reporter; Kansas City Star Stories* (Pittsburgh, PA: University of Pittsburgh Press, 1970)

Pearson, Nathan W., Jr., *Goin' to Kansas City (Music in American Life)* (University of Illinois Press, 1988)

# St. Louis

## ■ The City in Brief

**Founded:** 1763 (incorporated 1822)

**Head Official:** Mayor Francis G. Slay (D) (since 2001)

**City Population**

    1980: 453,085
    1990: 396,685
    2000: 348,189
    2006 estimate: 347,181
    Percent change, 1990–2000: −12.2%
    U.S. rank in 1980: 26th
    U.S. rank in 1990: 34th
    U.S. rank in 2000: 53rd

**Metropolitan Area Population**

    1980: 2,377,000
    1990: 2,492,348
    2000: 2,698,687
    2006 estimate: 2,796,368
    Percent change, 1990–2000: 4.6%
    U.S. rank in 1980: 14th
    U.S. rank in 1990: Not available
    U.S. rank in 2000: 18th

**Area:** 62 square miles (2000)

**Elevation:** 535 feet above sea level

**Average Annual Temperatures:** January, 29.6° F; July, 80.2° F; annual average, 56.3° F

**Average Annual Precipitation:** 38.75 inches of rain; 19.6 inches snow

**Major Economic Sectors:** Services, wholesale and retail trade, manufacturing, government

**Unemployment Rate:** 5.4% (June 2007)

**Per Capita Income:** $19,153 (2005)

**2005 FBI Crime Index Property:** 38,245

**2005 FBI Crime Index Violent:** 8,323

**Major Colleges and Universities:** Washington University; Saint Louis University; University of Missouri-St. Louis; St. Louis Community College

**Daily Newspaper:** *St. Louis Post-Dispatch*

## ■ Introduction

St. Louis, the second largest city in Missouri, is the center of the metropolitan statistical area comprised of Franklin, Jefferson, Lincoln, St. Charles, St. Louis, Washington, and Warren counties in Missouri and Bond, Calhoun, Clinton, Jersey, Macoupin, Madison, Monroe, and St. Clair counties in Illinois. Since its founding St. Louis has undergone several significant stages of development, which parallel the nation's westward expansion, symbolized by the city's famous Gateway Arch. St. Louis enjoys a rich and culturally diverse life and a revitalized downtown commercial district. As one of the first regions in the country to confront defense cutbacks in the 1990s and develop plans for dealing with them, the St. Louis area has emerged as a national laboratory for the post-Cold-War economy.

## ■ Geography and Climate

Located at the confluence of the Mississippi and Missouri rivers, St. Louis is near the geographic center of the United States. Its modified continental climate is characterized by four seasons without prolonged periods of extreme heat or high humidity. Alternate invasions of moist air from the Gulf of Mexico and cold air masses from Canada produce a variety of weather conditions. Winters are brisk and seldom severe; annual snowfall averages about 19 inches. Hot days with temperatures of

100 degrees or higher occur on the average of five days per year. Severe storms are often accompanied by hail and damaging winds, and tornadoes have caused destruction and loss of life.

**Area:** 62 square miles (2000)

**Elevation:** 535 feet above sea level

**Average Temperatures:** January, 29.6° F; July, 80.2° F; annual average, 56.3° F

**Average Annual Precipitation:** 38.75 inches of rain; 19.6 inches snow

# ■ History

## Fur Trade Establishes St. Louis Townsite

The first known attempted settlement near present-day St. Louis was the Jesuit Mission of St. Francis Xavier, established in 1700 at the mouth of the Riviere des Peres (River of the Fathers). Two Native American bands settled at the site with the Jesuit party, but within three years the mission was abandoned and no permanent settlement was attempted again in that area for more than 60 years.

Around 1760 the New Orleans firm of Maxent, Laclede & Company secured exclusive rights from France to trade with Native Americans in the Missouri River Valley and the territory west of the Mississippi River as far north as the St. Peter River. Pierre Laclede Liguest selected the present site of St. Louis for a trading post in December 1763. Laclede said his intent was to establish "one of the finest cities in America." The village was named for the patron saint of France's King Louis XV. North of the village were Native American ceremonial mounds; these mounds stood outside the original village boundary but were eventually leveled as the city expanded. The largest, known as Big Mound, was located at the present-day St. Louis intersection of Mound and Broadway streets.

In its early years St. Louis was nicknamed *Pain Court* because of the absence of local agriculture to supply such staples as bread flour. Laclede's fur business prospered but in time France lost control of the territory and the ruling Hispanic government withdrew Laclede's exclusive fur-trading rights. This opened the city to new settlers and new businesses. During the American Revolutionary War, the Mississippi-Ohio River route was protected when soldiers and townsmen successfully rebuffed an attack by British General Haldimand's troops; this victory secured the strategic importance of St. Louis. After the Revolution Mississippi River pirates disrupted trade on the river but in 1788 boats carrying fighting crews from New Orleans defeated the pirates. St. Louis quickly emerged as a trading center as the village grew into an oasis of wealth, culture, and privilege.

## American Influence Brings Westward Expeditions

This early period of splendor ended in 1803 when France, which had regained control of the surrounding territory, sold the vast tract of land to the new government of the United States in a land deal known as the Louisiana Purchase. American migrants soon brought gambling, violence, and mayhem into the community. Nearby Bloody Island gained a national reputation as a place of infamous duels, such as the one in 1817 when Thomas Hart Benton shot and killed a man. The rough-and-tumble village life eventually stabilized itself; the *Missouri Gazette,* St. Louis's first newspaper, and the opening of the first English school helped to improve the local environs.

St. Louis-based fur trappers and traders were the source of great local wealth; the Missouri Fur Company was founded in 1809 and dominated the Missouri Valley for the next 40 years. The city became a logical point of departure for explorers setting off on westward journeys. The most famous of these undertakings is the Lewis and Clark expedition of 1804 to 1806. Eventually as many as 50 wagons a day crossed the Mississippi River at St. Louis on the trek westward, and the arrival of the first steamboat from New Orleans in 1817 was the first sign of the city's importance as a river trading center.

St. Louis was incorporated as a village in 1808 and as a city in 1822. The city asserted its political dominance early in Missouri's public life, but tension between businessmen and farmers in outlying areas resulted in the election of Alexander McNair as the state's first governor and the eventual establishment of the state government in Jefferson City.

## Industry and Immigration Prompt Development

St. Louis's first manufacturing enterprises were operated by craftsmen in small shops, but by mid-century the city was an industrial center as the development of flour mills, ironworks, and factories for the production of foodstuffs and manufactured goods fueled the economy. Between 1832 and 1850, more than 30,000 German immigrants started new lives in St. Louis. As industry brought another wave of new wealth, many of the city's existing civic, educational, and cultural institutions were established. During this period, credit for introduction of the highball, Southern Comfort, and Planter's Punch was attributed to local bartenders.

Serious damage to the city's downtown resulted when a fire on the steamboat *White Cloud* in 1849 spread to the wharf district and destroyed 15 blocks in the commercial district; estimates of property damage ran as high as $6 million. St. Louis rebuilt by replacing log and wood buildings with masonry; public health issues such as sewage disposal and contaminated water were also addressed.

At the outset of the Civil War, St. Louis was divided in its sympathies. The city's role was decided when General Nathaniel Lyon led the Union Army action, surrounding Missouri state troops at Camp Jackson. St. Louis became a base of Federal operations, and the city benefited from the purchase of manufactured goods by the Chief Quartermaster that totaled $180 million. St. Louis's industrial capability increased by almost 300 percent in the decade between 1860 and 1870.

## Prosperity, Culture Draw World Notice

In the post-Civil War period railroads replaced steamboats as the primary transportation mode, and a new route to the east was opened. The Eads Bridge, the world's first arched steel truss bridge, was completed in 1874 and the city's first Union Station was built in 1878. The new prosperity was diverted in part to cultural enrichments such as the Missouri Botanical Gardens and Tower Grove Park. The St. Louis Symphony Orchestra, the nation's second oldest, was founded in 1880. The Mercantile Library Association, which opened in 1846, began purchasing and commissioning original art works. Joseph Pulitzer's *Globe-Democrat* and Carl Schurz's *Westliche Post* were two of many newspapers that reported on the political and social issues of the day. St. Louis was, in 1876, the first city west of the Mississippi River to host a national political convention. In 1877 St. Louis's city charter separated it from the county and freed the city from state government control except for general laws.

By the turn of the century St. Louis had a population of 575,000 residents. In 1904 the city hosted the Louisiana Purchase Exposition, which focused national and world attention on St. Louis. Many European nations were represented in yearlong festivities that were considered a success. The first Olympiad to be held in the United States took place in St. Louis in 1904. The ice cream cone, the hot dog, and iced tea mark their beginnings at this world's fair. In 1926 an $87 million bond issue improved the city's infrastructure and financed the construction of new public buildings. A second bond issue in 1934 continued the improvements. New industrial initiatives in the late 1930s helped St. Louis pull out of the Great Depression.

In 1965 the Gateway Arch became a part of the St. Louis skyline, marking the spot where Laclede first established St. Louis. After failing to solve public housing problems in the 1950s, 1960s, and 1970s, the city emerged in the 1980s as a model for urban housing renewal, with stable neighborhoods of rehabilitated structures. A renovated warehouse district near the Gateway Arch called Laclede's Landing attracts tourists to the historic roots of modern St. Louis.

## St. Louis approaches the Millennium

In the summer of 1993 St. Louis suffered extensive damage from flooding when the Missouri and Mississippi rivers joined forces just north of the city and swept down over its protective levees in some of the worst flooding in the country's history. Damage in the flood region was estimated at more than $10 billion.

Also in 1993, Democrat Freeman Bosley, Jr. was elected St. Louis's first African American mayor. Four years later African American police chief Clarence Harmon became mayor after an acrimonious campaign in which the vast majority of white voters preferred Mr. Harmon, while Mr. Bosley claimed the support of African American ministers and civil-rights activists. Race relations remain a thorny issue in St. Louis, but city leaders continue to address the problem.

## St. Louis in the New Millennium

St. Louis entered the twenty-first century recognizing itself as a big city without some of the major big city problems. Looking past a downturn in population and instead focusing on a vibrant future, St. Louis has attracted major companies, revitalized the downtown area, and improved the educational system. Renovations, remodels, and additions to St. Louis arts and history establishments, parks, buildings, infrastructure, and athletic venues have modernized the city, while traditional values continue to reign supreme in this mid-America city. Mayor Francis Slay, in one of his Neighborhood Newsletters, stated it well: "... the people of St. Louis embody the values that make America a great country. We applaud hard work, dedication and effort. We judge players by their performance on the field—not where they came from. We demand integrity, selflessness, and teamwork. We never give up, no matter how hard the task."

***Historical Information:*** Missouri Historical Society, PO Box 11940, St. Louis, MO 63112-0040; telephone (314)454-3150; www.mohistory.org

# ■ Population Profile

## Metropolitan Area Residents

1980: 2,377,000
1990: 2,492,348
2000: 2,698,687
2006 estimate: 2,796,368
Percent change, 1990–2000: 4.6%
U.S. rank in 1980: 14th
U.S. rank in 1990: Not available
U.S. rank in 2000: 18th

## City Residents

1980: 453,085
1990: 396,685
2000: 348,189
2006 estimate: 347,181
Percent change, 1990–2000: −12.2%

*Image copyright Mike Liu, 2007. Used under license from Shutterstock.com.*

U.S. rank in 1980: 26th
U.S. rank in 1990: 34th
U.S. rank in 2000: 53rd

**Density:** 5,622.9 people per square mile (2000)

**Racial and ethnic characteristics (2005)**

White: 147,955
Black: 168,909
American Indian and Alaska Native: 1,603
Asian: 7,199
Native Hawaiian and Pacific Islander: 0
Hispanic or Latino (may be of any race): 8,268
Other: 3,403

**Percent of residents born in state:** 70.3% (2000)

**Age characteristics (2005)**

Population under 5 years old: 26,160
Population 5 to 9 years old: 20,745
Population 10 to 14 years old: 25,131
Population 15 to 19 years old: 21,911
Population 20 to 24 years old: 22,705
Population 25 to 34 years old: 48,137
Population 35 to 44 years old: 50,829
Population 45 to 54 years old: 48,707

Population 55 to 59 years old: 16,828
Population 60 to 64 years old: 13,409
Population 65 to 74 years old: 18,758
Population 75 to 84 years old: 15,661
Population 85 years and older: 4,749
Median age: 35.4 years

**Births (2006, County)**

Total number: 5,231

**Deaths (2006, County)**

Total number: 3,790

**Money income (2005)**

Per capita income: $19,153
Median household income: $30,874
Total households: 141,408

**Number of households with income of . . .**

less than $10,000: 22,967
$10,000 to $14,999: 13,969
$15,000 to $24,999: 21,618
$25,000 to $34,999: 21,240
$35,000 to $49,999: 22,413
$50,000 to $74,999: 20,423

$75,000 to $99,999: 9,344
$100,000 to $149,999: 6,858
$150,000 to $199,999: 1,267
$200,000 or more: 1,309

**Percent of families below poverty level:** 10.9% (2005)

**2005 FBI Crime Index Property:** 38,245

**2005 FBI Crime Index Violent:** 8,323

# ■ Municipal Government

St. Louis functions with a mayor-council form of government; the mayor and 28 aldermen are elected to four-year terms. Voters choose a mayor in April of odd-numbered years; half the number of aldermen, each from a single ward, are selected every two years. Established as both a city and a county, the city of St. Louis operates under home rule, but St. Louis County, without home rule, conforms to Missouri's state requirements for county government.

**Head Official:** Mayor Francis G. Slay (D) (since 2001; term expires April 2009)

**Total Number of City Employees:** 7,070 (2007)

*City Information:* City of St. Louis, Office of the Mayor, 200 City Hall, 1200 Market Streets, St. Louis, MO 63103; telephone (314)622-3201; http://stlouis.missouri.org

# ■ Economy

## Major Industries and Commercial Activity

The economy of St. Louis and the surrounding metropolitan area is quite diverse. In 2007 St. Louis was the world headquarters of 17 *Fortune* 1000 companies, including Emerson Electric, Anheuser-Busch Companies, Inc., Monsanto, Ameren, Charter Communications, Peabody Energy, and Graybar Electric, which were all in the *Fortune* 500 that year.

St. Louis supports a strong manufacturing sector that accounts for about 15 percent of the region's gross product and about 11 percent of regional employment. The General Motors and Chrysler assembly plants in the area have been ranked as the most productive automotive assembly plants in the country by the *Harbour Report*. The city is also home to over 90 companies that produce automotive parts, including HBPO Group and Kelsey-Hayes. Aerospace and defense manufacturing has become a major growth sector as St. Louis is the headquarters for Boeing's Integrated Defense Systems unit. Other companies in this subsector include GKN Aerospace and DRS Engineered Air Systems. Food and beverage

manufacturing is also important, with companies such as Anheuser-Busch, Sara Lee Bakery group, and Bunge International taking the lead in this subsector.

The transportation and distribution sector of the economy also has a solid base in the local economy. Served by several major motor freight carriers, 14 active river ports, and 2 Foreign Trade Zones, St. Louis is the second-largest inland port in the United States by tonnage. There are over 125 distribution companies operating large facilities in the Greater St. Louis area, including Hershey Foods, Proctor and Gamble, Whirlpool, Aldi's Foods, and US Food Service.

St. Louis is the base for the Eighth Federal Reserve District Bank and several national investment firms, such as A.G. Edwards (a *Fortune* 1000 company), Edward Jones, Scottrade, and Stifel-Niclaus. There are also several mid-sized investment and venture capital firms in the Greater St. Louis area, such as Advantage Capital, Ascension Health Ventures, and RiverVest Venture Partners. Several banks have regional headquarters in St. Louis, including Bank of America, National City, and U.S. Bancorp. St. Louis is also the headquarters for Citi-Mortgage.

Into the 2000s, the city is emerging as a center for major new economy industries. World class research and development in plant and life sciences is conducted by industry giants such as Pfizer and Monsanto; St. Louis is becoming known as the heart of the bio-belt for progress in this arena. The city also boasts of a high concentration of information technology jobs with companies such as World Wide Technology, the Newberry Group, and Reuters.

**Items and goods produced:** vans and minivans, automotive parts, animal feed and pet foods, cooking oils, baked goods, electrical equipment and electronics, appliances, primary metals

## Incentive Programs—New and Existing Companies

*Local programs:* The St. Louis Regional Chamber and Growth Association (RCGA) is the economic development organization for the Greater St. Louis region. Developers may receive assistance with renovations and new construction projects through the St. Louis Real Estate Tax Abatement program.

*State programs:* Portions of the city have been designated by the state as an Enhanced Enterprise Zone through which eligible businesses may receive tax credits for up to 10 years for new development. The business must create at least two new jobs and offer $100,000 in new investment for each year in order to be eligible for tax credits. A job creation tax credit of $400 per eligible employee is available against state income taxes for up to 10 years. Other tax credits include up to $1,200 for hiring Enterprise Zone residents or "special employees." Some parts of the city have also been designated by the federal government as Empowerment Zones, which offer special financing incentives. Foreign Trade Zone (FTZ) incentives are available in two areas of Greater St. Louis. Goods entering FTZs are not subject to customs tariffs until the goods leave the zone and are formally entered into U.S. customs territory. Other tax credit programs offered by the state of Missouri include a Business Modernization and Technology Credit, Small Business Incubator Credit, Neighborhood Assistance Program, Historic Preservation Credit, New Markets Tax Credit and a Community Bank Investment Credit. Tax credits through these programs range from 45 percent to 70 percent for qualified programs. A Research Expense Tax Credit program offers a credit of 6.5 percent for qualified expenses. The BUILD Missouri Program provides incentives for the location or expansion of large business projects (generally in excess of 100 jobs). The program provides Missouri state income tax credits to the business in the amount of debt service payments for bonds related to a portion of project costs. The tax credits may be sold if not used by the recipient. A number of loan financing programs are also available.

*Job training programs:* The New Jobs Training Program (NJTP) provides education and training to workers employed in newly created jobs in Missouri. The new jobs may result from a new industry locating in Missouri or an existing industry expanding its workforce in the state. The Missouri Customized Training Program (MCTP) helps Missouri employers with funding to offset the costs of employee training and retraining. It assists new and expanding businesses in recruiting, screening, and training workers, and it helps existing employers retain their current workforce when faced with needed upgrading and retraining. The Missouri Job Retention Training Program offers retraining assistance to employers who have retained a minimum of 100 employers for at least two consecutive years and have made a capital investment of at least $1 million. Career development and professional training programs are available locally through several schools, including the St. Louis Community College and Rankin Technical College.

## Development Projects

Several new and continuing development projects were underway in the city as of 2007. AT&T announced that it has chosen St. Louis for the national corporate headquarters of its Yellow Pages. The project will involve a $1.6 million investment in the city. Jambo Kenya Coffee and Tea International moved into the city, opening a 12,000-square-foot roasting, packaging, and distribution facility for specialty coffees in the downtown area. The capital investment was estimated at $1.1 million. Central Transport International expanded its facility in St. Louis with the promise of creating about 115 new jobs at an aver-

age annual wage of $36,400. Centene Corporation announced plans to build a new headquarters in the Ballpark Village area of downtown St. Louis. The first phase of the project, which will include offices and street-level retail establishments, is expected to cost about $250 million and to create about 1,000 new jobs. Steel Warehouse Co. announced plans to open a new steel processing plant on land leased from the St. Louis Port Authority. The new facility will employ about 100 people.

The massive Forest Park, site of the 1904 World's Fair and the home to St. Louis's main cultural institutions, has undergone a $100 million transformation. Once stagnant ponds and lakes are now connected by a river that greatly improves park aesthetics. More than 7,500 new trees were planted, historic areas and buildings were preserved, and recreational facilities and park facilities were upgraded.

In 2006 the Lambert–St. Louis Airport completed construction of a new $1 billion, 9,000-foot runway project and began a $105 million renovation project on the main airport terminal.

In 2007 the Missouri Life Science Research Board announced that it would sponsor a new Center of Excellence in St. Louis to focus on research and development activities in the areas of bioenergy, plant science, and animal health and nutrition. The St. Louis Center for Excellence will represent a partnership between the Danforth Plant Science Center, the Missouri Botanical Gardens, St. Louis University, University of Missouri–St. Louis, and Washington University. This project is one of many regional and statewide development projects designed to encourage the growth of life science business and industry in the area.

***Economic Development Information:*** St. Louis Regional Chamber and Growth Association, One Metropolitan Square, Suite 1300, St. Louis, MO 63102; telephone (314)231-5555; www.stlrcga.org

## Commercial Shipping

St. Louis is a prime location for air, land, and water transportation networks. Among the commodities shipped through the city are coal, grain, cement, petroleum products, and chemicals. One of the nation's leading rail centers, St. Louis is served by six Class I, one regional, and three switching railroad lines. Four interstate highways converge in St. Louis, affording trucking companies overnight to third-morning access to markets throughout the country. Many of these firms maintain terminals within the Commercial Truck Zone, which covers all or portions of a seven-county area. St. Louis is one of the nation's largest inland ports, as well as the country's northernmost port with ice-free access year round; the port connects St. Louis via the Mississippi, Illinois, and Missouri river system with New Orleans and international waterways. St. Louis waterways offer more than 100 docks and terminal facilities. Air freight service is available at Lambert-St. Louis International Airport through five air cargo carriers. MidAmerica Airport in St. Clair County in Illinois provides state-of-the-art facilities for cargo as well. The St. Louis area has two Foreign Trade Zones (No. 31 and No. 102).

## Labor Force and Employment Outlook

During the 1990s thousands of jobs were lost as major employers downsized, moved out, or merged. In response to the state and nation-wide economic downturn of the early 2000s, the Missouri state legislature has passed several legislative bills to stimulate economic growth and decrease unemployment. The state as a whole continues to experience stability and growth, recognizing four times the national growth rate in the manufacturing sector. In the northern metro St. Louis region, several areas show strong momentum with St. Charles, Warren, and Franklin counties ranked as top performers.

The St. Louis area has a fairly high concentration of scientists and engineers, accounting for about 4 percent of the workforce. The percentage of adults age 25 and over who have obtained a bachelor's degree or higher tends to be higher than the national average, and with several educational facilities within the area there are several opportunities for specialized employee training. Occupational forecasts into the year 2014 suggests job growth in several sectors, including health sciences; business, management, and administration; education and training; architecture and construction; and information technology.

The following is a summary of data regarding the St. Louis MO-IL metropolitan area labor force, 2006 annual averages.

**Size of nonagricultural labor force:** 1,349,400

**Number of workers employed in** . . .

   construction and mining: 83,100
   manufacturing: 139,100
   trade, transportation and utilities: 255,100
   information: 30,100
   financial activities: 79,000
   professional and business services: 192,200
   educational and health services: 203,300
   leisure and hospitality: 142,200
   other services: 57,800
   government: 167,500

**Average hourly earnings of production workers employed in manufacturing:** $20.74

**Unemployment rate:** 5.4% (June 2007)

| *Largest employers (2006)* | *Number of employees* |
|---|---|
| BJC HealthCare | 21, 814 |
| Boeing Integrated Defense Systems | 16,259 |
| Scott Air Force Base | 13,065 |
| Washington University in St. Louis | 12,505 |
| Wal-Mart Stores Inc. | 11,921 |
| SSM Health Care | 11,905 |
| Schnuck Markets Inc. | 10,700 |
| SBC Communications Inc. | 9,920 |
| St. John's Mercy Health Care | 8,699 |
| McDonald's | 8,000 |

## Cost of Living

Among the nation's top 20 metro areas, St. Louis housing is among the most affordable. The following is a summary of data regarding several key cost of living factors in the St. Louis area.

**2007 (1st quarter) ACCRA Average House Price:** $266,620

**2007 (1st quarter) ACCRA Cost of Living Index:** 97.1

**State income tax rate:** 1.5% to 6.0%

**State sales tax rate:** 4.225%

**Local income tax rate:** 1.0%

**Local sales tax rate:** 3.291%

**Property tax rate:** personal property is assessed at 33-1/3%; rates vary by tax jurisdiction

***Economic Information:*** St. Louis Regional Chamber and Growth Association, One Metropolitan Square, Suite 1300, St. Louis, MO 63102; telephone (314)231-5555; www.stlrcga.org. Missouri Department of Economic Development, 301 W. High Street, Jefferson City, MO 65102; telephone (573)751-4962; www.ded.mo.gov

# ■ Education and Research

## Elementary and Secondary Schools

The St. Louis Public Schools district is the largest district in the state. As of 2006 St. Louis students were performing below the state average on the Missouri Assessment Program tests. That year, 22 percent of fifth-graders and 13 percent of tenth graders scored as proficient or advanced in mathematics, compared to the statewide average of 44 percent of fifth-graders and 42 percent of tenth graders. In communication arts, only 18 percent of St. Louis eleventh-graders scored as proficient and advanced, compared to an average 43 percent statewide. The annual dropout rate for 2006 was about 18 percent. However, there are a few high points for the district. In

2007, Metro Academic and Classical High School was included on the list of "Best Public High Schools in the Nation" by *Newsweek*. There were 24 schools in the St. Louis Magnet Schools Program in 2007. Over 1,400 students were enrolled in technical and career education programs in 2006.

The St. Louis Special School District provides educational alternatives for nearly 30,000 area students with special needs. Schools in this district include the Missouri School for the Blind, Central Institute for the Deaf, and the Moog Center for Deaf Education, all of which are in St. Louis.

The following is a summary of data regarding the St. Louis Public Schools as of the 2005–2006 school year.

**Total enrollment:** 39,500

**Number of facilities**

    elementary schools: 55
    junior high/middle schools: 19
    senior high schools: 16
    other: 5

**Student/teacher ratio:** 15.1:1

**Teacher salaries (2005–06)**

    elementary median: $43,780
    junior high/middle median: $43,860
    secondary median: $44,950

**Funding per pupil:** $10,492

In 2007 there were over 400 private schools in the St. Louis MSA. One of the largest is the Christian Brothers College High School, an all-boys Catholic College Preparatory school. About 42 schools in the St. Louis Area are associated with the Independent Schools of St. Louis; these include the Chaminade College Preparatory School, a Catholic boarding school for boys in grades 6-12, and Brehm Preparatory School, a coed boarding school for students with learning disabilities (grades 6-12). There are several schools with religious affiliations. The Saul Mirowitz Days School–Reform Jewish Academy serves students from K-5.

## Colleges and Universities

Washington University, a private independent institution, offers 90 programs and 1,500 courses in such fields as business, architecture, engineering, social work, and teacher education; the university operates schools of medicine, dentistry, and law. More than 13,500 students attend this research university. In 2008 Washington University was ranked as 12th in the nation for best national universities by *U.S. News & World Report*.

Saint Louis University, established in 1818, is a Jesuit, Catholic university that offers over 50 graduate and 85 undergraduate programs in its 13 colleges/schools. Enrollment is over 11,000 students. The university main-

tains a campus in Madrid, Spain. In 2008 Saint Louis University was ranked in the top 100 (82nd) best national universities by *U.S. News & World Report*.

Webster University awards baccalaureate and master's degrees in 13 bachelor's and 9 graduate programs. While the main campus is located in suburban Webster Groves, there are 107 worldwide campuses, including one in downtown St. Louis.

The University of Missouri–St. Louis is both a graduate and undergraduate institution and part of the state university system. More than 15,500 students attend classes on the 300-acre campus. The University of Missouri–St. Louis is the third largest university in Missouri. Degrees are offered in 30 fields of study in 10 colleges and schools.

Missouri Baptist University is a liberal arts institution that offers professional certificates as well as undergraduate and graduate degrees in seven academic divisions: business, education, fine arts, health and sport sciences, humanities, natural sciences, and social and behavioral sciences. Enrollment at the main campus in St. Louis is about 1,700 students. Saint Louis Christian College offers three bachelor's degree programs and two associate's degree programs.

Concordia Seminary in St. Louis is affiliated with the Lutheran Church–Missouri Synod and offers master's degrees and doctorates in a variety of religious studies. Covenant Theological Seminary, affiliated with the Presbyterian Church, and Eden Theological Seminary, affiliated with the United Church of Christ, also offer graduate programs in religious studies.

St. Louis Community College is the largest community college in Missouri and one of the largest in the United States. The college's four campuses offer college transfers, career and developmental programs, and non-credit courses. Rankin Technical College offers associate's degrees in 13 fields and bachelor's degrees in 2 fields (applied management and architectural technology).

Southern Illinois University at Edwardsville, also a state university, is in neighboring Edwardsville, Illinois. Fontbonne College, Harris-Stowe State College, and Maryville University are four-year institutions located in the St. Louis area.

## Libraries and Research Centers

The St. Louis Public Library operates a central library, a bookmobile, and 15 branches with holdings of over 4.6 million book volumes and bound periodicals, periodical titles, and CDs, microfiches, films, audio- and videotapes, slides, maps, and art reproductions. Special collections include African American history, genealogy, architecture, and federal and state documents.

The St. Louis County Library, with 19 locations and 10 bookmobiles, has more than 2.3 million books and over 209,000 federal, state, and county documents. The library also offers a special collection in genealogy. The

Missouri Historical Society holds a reference collection of over 80,000 items on topics pertaining to regional and state history.

Most area colleges and universities maintain substantial campus libraries; among the most extensive is the Washington University Libraries system, which maintains 14 libraries on three campuses. In the entire system there are holdings of over 3.8 million volumes and 41,339 journal titles. Special collections include the Black Film Promotional Material Collection, Islamic Studies, Jewish Studies, the Mozart and Beethoven Collection, and the Dred Scott Case collection. The Olin Library on the main campus is a depository for European Union publications and select U.S. government documents.

In 2006 Washington University received about $546.3 million in total research support, including $451.8 million in federal obligations. Topics for research cover a wide spectrum of social and scientific fields. Centers and institutes affiliated with the university include the Aerospace Research and Education Center, the Center for Advanced Renewable Energy Committee, the Center for the Study of Human Values, the Center for Research in Economics and Strategy, the Center for Joint Studies, and the Center for Mental Health Services Research.

The University of Missouri–St. Louis also supports a wide variety of research activities. Centers and institutes affiliated with this university include the Center for Eye Care and Vision Research, the Public Policy Research Center, the Center for Character and Citizenship, the Center for Transportation Studies, and the Center for Trauma Recovery.

The city is fast becoming a center for the bio-tech industry; the industry is supported by several research facilities in this area. Monsanto's multimillion-dollar agricultural headquarters and Life Science Research Center are both based in St. Louis, comprising one of the world's largest and most sophisticated facilities searching for ways to improve agriculture through biotechnology and genetic engineering. The Donald Danforth Plant Science Center is another major component in the area's biotech development, along with the 40,000-square-foot plant and life sciences incubator, the Nidus Center.

The Sigma-Aldrich Corp. Life Science Technology Center is a $57 million, four-story research and technology center near its headquarters in mid-town St. Louis. The center is home to 220 life science chemists and also serves as a corporate learning center. The 150,000-square-foot building makes possible continuing technical discovery that builds on Sigma-Aldrich's half-century of success in the development of life science and high-tech products.

***Public Library Information:*** St. Louis Public Library, 1301 Olive Street, St. Louis, MO 63103; telephone (314)241-2288; www.slpl.org. St. Louis County Library, 1640 S. Lindbergh Blvd., St. Louis, MO 63131; telephone (314)994-3300; www.sicl.org

# ■ Health Care

As one of the country's leading medical care centers, St. Louis is served by more than 50 hospitals, two of which—the Washington University Medical Center and the St. Louis University Hospital—are top-rated teaching facilities.

The Washington University Medical Center consists of Washington University School of Medicine, Barnes-Jewish Hospital, St. Louis Children's Hospital, the Center for Advanced Medicine, Siteman Cancer Center, Central Institute for the Deaf, St. Louis College of Pharmacy, the Schools of Occupational and Physical Therapy, and Barnard Hospital. In 2007 Barnes-Jewish Hospital was ranked ninth on the national honor roll of best hospitals by *U.S. News & World Report.* The hospital ranked within the top ten in the nation for care of respiratory disorders, neurology and neuroscience, endocrinology, kidney disease, heart health, ophthalmology, and ear, nose and throat. It is the only hospital in the region offering comprehensive transplant services, including heart, heart and lung, double lung, kidney, liver, pancreas, islet cell, and bone marrow transplants. St. Louis Children's Hospital was ranked as the seventh best children's hospital in the nation in *U.S. News & World Report* for 2007.

St. Louis University Hospital is a 356-bed academic teaching hospital with specialties that include geriatrics, orthopedics, rheumatology, urology, heart care and digestive diseases. The hospital is also a certified Level I Trauma Center in both Missouri and Illinois. The 582-bed St. Mary's Health Center was ranked as one of the top 50 hospitals in the nation for care in neurology and neuroscience by *U.S. News & World Report.* St. Mary's also has specialty clinics for women's health and cardiology. St. Anthony's Medical Center operates a 767-bed tertiary care facility with specialized care in cardiology, women's services, oncology/cancer care, orthopedics, neurology and emergency medicine.

# ■ Recreation

### Sightseeing

The Gateway Arch, which rises 630 feet above the banks of the Mississippi River, is the starting point of a tour of St. Louis. Designed by Eero Saarinen and commemorating the nineteenth-century westward movement and St. Louis's role in settling the frontier, the Gateway Arch is the nation's tallest memorial. Beneath the Arch is the Old Courthouse, where the Dred Scott case was heard. A proud Greek revival structure, its dome was a forerunner of the style in public architecture that would sweep the country. The building holds displays relating to the Scott case and is home to the Museum of Westward Expansion, which documents the westward movement and life in St. Louis in the 1800s.

An attraction popular with kids of all ages, Six Flags St. Louis is an amusement park offering thrilling rides and attractions. The St. Louis Zoo in Forest Park houses more than 11,400 animals in naturalistic settings. The Fragile Forest at the zoo features chimpanzees, orangutans and lowland gorillas in an outdoor habitat. The zoo also features an insectarium, Children's Zoo, and Big Cat Country, a habitat for feline predators. Opposite from the zoo is the Missouri History Museum. The Museum's featured exhibit celebrates St. Louis's history-making 1904 World's Fair with documents, sights and sounds that bring the century-old event alive. Also featured are exhibits on slave trade and the American presidency.

A Digistar computerized planetarium projector, OMNIMAX Theater, hands-on science and computer exhibits, and outdoor science exhibits are featured at the St. Louis Science Center in Forest Park. The center's Discovery Room is currently under renovation; when complete, children will enjoy dressing as a surgeon, exploring fossils, and playing with robots as well as other participative activities. The 79-acre Missouri Botanical Garden, founded in 1859, is one of the oldest botanical gardens in the country and is considered one of the most beautiful; unique features include a 14-acre Japanese strolling garden and the Climatron conservatory, a domed greenhouse featuring tropical plants and birds. Sightseers can view one of the nation's few contemporary sculpture parks at the Laumeier Sculpture Park. The St. Louis Carousel provides a rare opportunity to ride an authentic carousel at its Faust County Park location. Operated by Anheuser-Busch and ranked seventh best family attraction in the nation by U.S. Family Travel Guide, Grant's Farm features a cabin built by General Grant in 1856; the farm's miniature zoo features a Clydesdale stallion barn and bird and elephant shows. Jefferson Barracks Historical Park combines military history and recreation with two museums and a number of sports fields; Robert E. Lee and Ulysses S. Grant are two of the many famous American military leaders whose service included a stay at Jefferson Barracks.

St. Louis museums include the National Museum of Transport, which highlights rail, road, air, and water modes of transportation; the AKC Museum of the Dog, which presents exhibits on the dog through history; the recently expanded Magic House, St. Louis Children's Museum; and the Soldiers' Memorial Military Museum.

The Missouri Chapter of the American Institute of Architects is located in St. Louis and provides complete information about this architecturally rich city. Among some of the significant structures are the Cathedral of St. Louis (New Cathedral), which houses 41.5 million pieces of glass tessarae, one of the largest collections of mosaic art in the West; Christ Church Cathedral, the first

Episcopal church west of the Mississippi; and Old Cathedral, the city's first church.

## Arts and Culture

St. Louis is a major cultural center for the Midwest. The award-winning St. Louis Symphony Orchestra, winner of six Grammies and 36 nominations, presents a season of classical music concerts with internationally known guest artists at Powell Symphony Hall. In the summer the orchestra plays a series of pops concerts at Greensfelder Recreation Center. Theater is presented year round in St. Louis by a diverse range of organizations. The Repertory Theatre of St. Louis performs a season of plays on two stages, including modern drama, musicals, and comedies at the recently-expanded Loretto Hilton Center. The Opera Theatre of St. Louis performs its four dramatic productions of classical and new opera in English during a month-long season beginning in late May. The Fox Theatre was restored in 1982 and now sponsors a Broadway series, ballet, and pop music concerts as well pre-event buffet dining. The Muny in Forest Park is a 12,000-seat outdoor amphitheater that stages Broadway musical theater during the summer. History is re-lived in words and music in four shows per year by the Historyonics Theatre Company.

The Black Repertory Company performs at the 450-seat Grandel Square Theater, a handsome 1883 structure that was once a church. Stages St. Louis, a musical theater group, also performs in St. Louis.

Dance St. Louis sponsors performances with local, national, and international companies, and offers a dance education program. The First Street Forum is a multipurpose arts center that sponsors exhibitions, performances, lectures, and symposia.

The St. Louis Art Museum in Forest Park was the Fine Arts Palace of the 1904 World's Fair and today offers contemporary and audio/video art in additional to traditional pieces. Washington University's Gallery of Art was the first museum west of the Mississippi River. At the Missouri Historical Society Museum, the major events and individuals in St. Louis history from the first settlers to Charles Lindbergh are recaptured. The Concordia Historical Institute maintains an authentic collection of American Lutheran historical documents as well as Protestant Reformation artifacts. Among St. Louis's other museums are the newly restored Campbell House Museum, which features a Victorian era home and furnishings; the Holocaust Museum and Learning Center, which is dedicated to educating and preserving the Holocaust's history and consequences; and the Eugene Field House and Toy Museum, which presents an extensive collection of antique toys and dolls.

## Festivals and Holidays

Major venues for celebrations in St. Louis are the Missouri Botanical Gardens and Jefferson Barracks Historical Park. At the Botanical Gardens, an orchid show in

January features more than 800 plants. The Spring Floral Display begins in March. November brings the St. Louis International Film Festival, the African Arts Festival, and a Festival of Trees. The city rings in the new year with a community celebration called First Night St. Louis & Riverfront Fireworks Festival.

Jefferson Barracks Historical Park presents a World War II Reenactment in April and American Indian Days in May. May is also the month for arts and crafts displays at Laumeier Sculpture Park and Tilles County Park. Parades and other events at various locales mark St. Patrick's Day, Independence Day, Veterans' Day, and Christmas.

## Sports for the Spectator

The St. Louis Cardinals compete in the Western Division of the Major League Baseball Association's National League and play their home games in Busch Stadium. The St. Louis Cardinals Hall of Fame, which is located inside the International Bowling Museum and Hall of Fame, houses displays and movies on baseball, football, basketball, hockey, golf, bowling, and soccer. The St. Louis Rams of the National Football League play home games at the Edward Jones Dome at America's Center downtown.

The St. Louis Blues compete in the National Hockey League and play home games at the Scottrade Center, which is also home to Saint Louis University Billikens basketball team. The St. Louis Aces play professional tennis at the Dwight Davis Tennis Center. The River City Rage of the National Indoor Professional Football League play at the Family Arena in St. Charles. The St. Louis Stunners play for the American Basketball Association.

Sixteen NCAA Division I athletics teams including baseball, basketball, swimming, and cross country compete for St. Louis University. Teams from Washington University–St. Louis are also popular for sports fans.

Balloonists compete in the Great Forest Park Balloon Race scheduled in September; the balloon race is one of the largest sporting events in Missouri with 70 balloons and 130,000 spectators. For two weeks in September horse owners and trainers from around the country participate in the St. Louis National Charity Horse Show at Queen County Park.

## Sports for the Participant

A city of parks and sports enthusiasts, St. Louis offers attractive outdoor facilities and a selection of major and minor sports for the individual, including golf, tennis, bicycling, softball, and water sports such as swimming, water skiing, and boating. There are over 100 city parks. Forest Park, the showcase of the 1904 World's Fair, offers recreational opportunities that include skating, jogging, and tennis, on nearly 1,300 acres; the park is 500 acres larger than New York City's Central Park. Forest Park is also the site of the St. Louis Zoo, the St. Louis Art Museum, the St. Louis Science Center, and two golf courses. The city has 18 spray pools and 10 recreation centers with indoor swimming pools. There are also 43 cricket and rugby fields.

Riverboat gambling on the Mississippi River is a popular activity, with boats departing from East St. Louis and St. Charles.

## Shopping and Dining

Downtown St. Louis offers boutique shopping in the Union Station complex, the city's major train terminal and inspiration for the classic *Meet Me in St. Louis*. Featuring vaulted ceilings and stained glass windows, Union Station is a historical, architectural, shopping, and dining landmark. St. Louis Centre is anchored by Famous-Barr department store and is located near Metro Link, the Arch, and the Edward Jones Dome. Plaza Frontenac is anchored by Missouri's only Neiman-Marcus and Saks Fifth Avenue. Crestwood Plaza offers more than 100 upscale stores and restaurants. Cherokee Street Antique Row offers restaurants, cafes, antiques, collectibles, and specialty shops in a six-block historic area.

The Saint Louis Galleria in Richmond Heights consists of 3 levels, 165 stores, an Italian marble interior, and a 100-foot-high atrium; Lord & Taylor, Mark Shale, and Dillard's anchor the Galleria.

Diners in St. Louis can choose from among hundreds of fine restaurants, including Cafe de France, Giovanni's, and Tony's. The city boasts an Italian district, known as "the Hill," which offers a number of fine moderately priced Italian eateries; a popular appetizer is fried ravioli. Chinese, German, and other ethnic restaurants are located throughout the city. Regional specialties available in St. Louis include barbecued lamb, ribs, pork, ham, and sausage; pecan pie; and sweet potato pie.

*Visitor Information:* St. Louis Convention and Visitors Commission, 701 Convention Plaza, Ste. 300, St. Louis, MO 63101; telephone (314)421-1023; toll-free (800)916-8938; www.explorestlouis.com

# ■ Convention Facilities

The major convention facility in St. Louis is the America's Center convention complex. The America's Center offers 502,000 square feet of contiguous, one-level exhibit space that can be broken down into six separate exhibition halls, including the 162,000-square-foot domed stadium/exhibit hall, the Edward Jones Dome. Other amenities offered by America's Center are 83 flexible meeting rooms, a 28,000-square-foot grand ballroom, a 1,411 fixed-seat lecture hall, and the St. Louis Executive Conference Center, which serves as a site for smaller meetings.

Ample hotel space is available in the metropolitan area. More than 35,000 hotel rooms are available area-wide; several luxury hotels have been built in recent years, and thousands of first-class hotel rooms are located near America's Center.

***Convention Information:*** St. Louis Convention and Visitors Commission, One Metropolitan Square, Suite 1100, St. Louis, MO 63102; telephone (314)421-1023; toll-free (800)916-8938; fax (314)421-0394; email vis-info@explorestlouis.com

# ■ Transportation

## Approaching the City

Lambert-St. Louis International Airport, one of the busiest airports in the country, provides non-stop service to 81 cities through 10 major airlines. There are also 15 commuter airlines and 2 major charter companies. Daily, more than 780 flights arrive and depart Lambert for destinations in North America and Europe. MidAmerica Airport, about 24 miles away in St. Clair County, Illinois, offers commercial airline services at a slightly less crowded site.

St. Louis, with a geographically central location, is easily accessible from points throughout the United States via four interstate highways that converge in the city: I-44, I-55, I-64, and I-70. State Route 61 enters the city as well. Rail transportation to St. Louis is provided by Amtrak and bus transportation is by Greyhound.

## Traveling in the City

The city streets form a basic block grid pattern. Market Street downtown is the dividing point for north and south addresses. St. Louis Metro operates the city's 22-mile light rail MetroLink system, offering light rail shuttle service from the airport to America's Center as well as to other area attractions. Metro also features a fleet of 395 MetroBuses with over 50 fixed routes. Call-a-Ride service is available only for persons with disabilities who have registered to use the service.

# ■ Communications

## Newspapers and Magazines

The city's major daily newspaper is the morning *St. Louis Post-Dispatch*, which is owned by Lee Enterprises. Lee Enterprises is also the publisher of the *Suburban Journals*, which come out in 31 separate weekly editions that are distributed free to nearly 660,000 households in the greater St. Louis area. These include the *South City Journal*, the *South County Journal*, and the *SouthWest City Journal*. The *St. Louis Business Journal* is a business weekly. *The Riverfront Times* is a weekly alternative press publication. The *St. Louis American* and the *St. Louis Argus* are weeklies serving the African American community. *St. Louis Jewish Light* is also a weekly paper. There are several local interest and hobby magazines published in the area, including *St. Louis Homes and Lifestyle* and *Sauce* magazine (a local restaurant guide). *St. Louis Commerce* magazine is published by the Greater St. Louis Chamber of Commerce.

The Associated Press and United Press International operate offices in St. Louis. Several specialized magazines and journals are based in St. Louis; the majority are journals published for medical professionals by the Elsevier Health Sciences Publishing Company and other firms.

## Television and Radio

Television viewers in metropolitan St. Louis tune in broadcasts from six stations and cable is available. A complete range of radio programming—including classical, jazz, classic rock, "oldies," Christian, and gospel music, as well as news and public interest features—is offered by 19 AM and FM radio stations.

***Media Information:*** *St. Louis Post-Dispatch*, 900 North Tucker Boulevard, St. Louis, MO 63101-9990; telephone (314)340-8000; toll-free (800)365-0820; www.stltoday.com

## St. Louis Online

City of St. Louis. Available www.stlouis.missouri.org
Missouri Department of Economic Development. Available www.ded.mo.gov
*St. Louis Commerce* magazine. Available www.stlcommercemagazine.com
St. Louis Convention and Visitors Commission. Available www.explorestlouis.com
*St. Louis Post-Dispatch.* Available www.stltoday.com
St. Louis Public Library. Available www.slpl.org
St. Louis Regional Chamber and Growth Association. Available www.stlrcga.org

BIBLIOGRAPHY

Clamorgan, Cyprian, *The Colored Aristocracy of St. Louis* (University of Missouri Press, 1999)

Peters, Frank, et al., *A Guide to the Architecture of St. Louis* (University of Missouri Press, 1990)

Twain, Mark, *The Adventures of Huckleberry Finn* (New York: Puffin, 1988, 1953)

Twain, Mark, *The Adventures of Tom Sawyer* (Hartford, CT: The American Publishing Co., 1876)

# Springfield

## ■ The City in Brief

**Founded:** 1830 (incorporated 1838)

**Head Official:** City Manager Bob Cumley (since 2006)

**City Population**

    1980: 133,116
    1990: 140,494
    2000: 151,580
    2006 estimate: 150,797
    Percent change, 1990–2000: 7.4%
    U.S. rank in 1980: 126th
    U.S. rank in 1990: 151st
    U.S. rank in 2000: Not available

**Metropolitan Area Population**

    1980: 207,704
    1990: 264,346
    2000: 325,721
    2006 estimate: Not available
    Percent change, 1990–2000: 23%
    U.S. rank in 1980: Not available
    U.S. rank in 1990: Not available
    U.S. rank in 2000: 122nd

**Area:** 73.16 square miles (2000)

**Elevation:** 1,268 feet above sea level

**Average Annual Temperatures:** January, 31.7° F; July, 78.5° F; annual average, 56.2° F

**Average Annual Precipitation:** 44.97 inches of rain; 17.8 inches of snow

**Major Economic Sectors:** Services, wholesale and retail trade, manufacturing, government

**Unemployment Rate:** 4.2% (June 2007)

**Per Capita Income:** $17,711 (1999)

**2005 FBI Crime Index Property:** 12,723

**2005 FBI Crime Index Violent:** 892

**Major Colleges and Universities:** Missouri State University, Drury University

**Daily Newspaper:** *The News-Leader*

## ■ Introduction

Springfield is the seat of Missouri's Greene County and the center of a metropolitan statistical area that includes Christian, Greene, Webster, Polk, and Dallas counties. Called the Gateway to the Ozark Mountains, Springfield is part of a resort area whose primary attractions are the largest cave in North America, an outdoor exotic animal park, and Bass Pro Shops Outdoor World, one of the most-visited tourist attractions in the state. The Battle of Wilson's Creek was fought in the first year of the American Civil War near Springfield and the site is now a national battlefield monument. Today the city is a regional agribusiness center and a dairy-product shipping center. In 2007 *Expansion Management* magazine gave Springfield a five-star rating in its annual "Quality of Life Quotient" survey.

## ■ Geography and Climate

Surrounded by flat or gently rolling tableland, Springfield is set atop the crest of the Missouri Ozark Mountain plateau. The climate is characterized as a plateau climate, with a milder winter and a cooler summer than in the upland plain or prairie. Springfield occupies a unique location for natural water drainage—the line separating two major water sheds crosses the north-central part of the city, causing drainage north of this line to flow into the Gasconade and Missouri Rivers; drainage to the south flows into the White and Mississippi Rivers.

**Area:** 73.16 square miles (2000)

**Elevation:** 1,268 feet above sea level

**Average Temperatures:** January, 31.7° F; July, 78.5° F; annual average, 56.2° F

**Average Annual Precipitation:** 44.97 inches of rain; 17.8 inches of snow

# ■ History

### Removal of Delaware Tribe Opens Farmland

In 1821 Pioneer Thomas Patterson attempted to make the first permanent settlement on the site of present-day Springfield; however, the Delaware people arrived the following year to claim the land as a federal Indian reservation. James Wilson was the lone settler to remain, and after the further relocation of the Delaware in 1830 he farmed land in the area. New settlers followed immediately. Among them was John Polk Campbell, who staked a claim in 1829 on a site that was then called Kickapoo Prairie; he carved his initials in an ash tree where four springs unite to form Wilson's Creek. This location was well situated, and a settlement soon grew up around the Campbell homestead.

Campbell was made county clerk when Missouri's Greene County was organized in 1833 and two years later he and his wife deeded land for a townsite. Springfield's name comes from a spring that creates Jordan Valley Creek downtown. Springfield was incorporated in 1838 and chartered in 1847.

Springfield's location and commercial base made it a military target during the Civil War. Sentiments regarding the war were split in the town, with the professional classes descended from Tennessee slaveholders supporting the Southern cause and rural settlers favoring the North. The Battle of Wilson's Creek was fought on August 10, 1861, resulting in a victory for the Confederate army; Union forces won the next battle in February, 1862, however, and held the area until the end of the war. Among the soldiers based at the Union Army's Springfield headquarters was James Butler Hickok, nicknamed Wild Bill, who served as a scout and spy. During a gun fight in July 1865 on the city square with his former friend, gambler Dave Tutt, Hickok shot Tutt through the heart. Hickok was acquitted in a trial in which he was defended by John S. Phelps, a future Missouri governor.

### Railroad Brings Expansion, New Business

In 1870 land speculators persuaded the Atlantic & Pacific Railroad to build a railroad through a new town north of Springfield despite the protests of Springfield citizens, who claimed that the new route violated the original charter. Nonetheless, the Ozark Land Company was organized and

the new town was deeded to the company. As both communities grew, they were consolidated in 1887.

During the first half of the twentieth century, Springfield became an agricultural and distribution center; after World War II, the population grew rapidly as the result of the expansion of Eastern manufacturing companies into the West. The city's proximity to the Ozark Mountains makes it a popular tourist destination.

A vital economy, low cost of living, commitment to education, scenic location, and commitment to downtown revitalization are ensuring the city's steady growth in population.

***Historical Information:*** Springfield-Greene County Library, 4653 South Campbell, Springfield, MO 65810; telephone (417)882-0714; http://thelibrary.springfield.missouri.org

# ■ Population Profile

### Metropolitan Area Residents

1980: 207,704
1990: 264,346
2000: 325,721
2006 estimate: Not available
Percent change, 1990–2000: 23%
U.S. rank in 1980: Not available
U.S. rank in 1990: Not available
U.S. rank in 2000: 122nd

### City Residents

1980: 133,116
1990: 140,494
2000: 151,580
2006 estimate: 150,797
Percent change, 1990–2000: 7.4%
U.S. rank in 1980: 126th
U.S. rank in 1990: 151st
U.S. rank in 2000: Not available

**Density:** 2,072 people per square mile (2000)

### Racial and ethnic characteristics (2005)

White: 129,115
Black: 4,151
American Indian and Alaska Native: 755
Asian: 2,108
Native Hawaiian and Pacific Islander: 107
Hispanic or Latino (may be of any race): 593
Other: 3,174

**Percent of residents born in state:** 60.1% (2000)

### Age characteristics (2000)

Population under 5 years old: 8,635

©Andre Jenny/Alamy

Population 5 to 9 years old: 8,439
Population 10 to 14 years old: 7,987
Population 15 to 19 years old: 12,155
Population 20 to 24 years old: 19,064
Population 25 to 34 years old: 22,032
Population 35 to 44 years old: 20,438
Population 45 to 54 years old: 17,912
Population 55 to 59 years old: 6,563
Population 60 to 64 years old: 5,469
Population 65 to 74 years old: 10,572
Population 75 to 84 years old: 8,545
Population 85 years and older: 3,469
Median age: 33.5 years

**Births (2006, MSA)**

Total number: 5,516

**Deaths (2006, MSA)**

Total number: 3,636

**Money income (1999)**

Per capita income: $17,711
Median household income: $29,563
Total households: 64,779

**Number of households with income of . . .**

less than $10,000: 2,267
$10,000 to $14,999: 2,105
$15,000 to $24,999: 5,499
$25,000 to $34,999: 6,199
$35,000 to $49,999: 7,882
$50,000 to $74,999: 6,411
$75,000 to $99,999: 2,681
$100,000 to $149,999: 1,739
$150,000 to $199,999: 468
$200,000 or more: 680

**Percent of families below poverty level:** 13.1% (1999)

**2005 FBI Crime Index Property:** 12,723

**2005 FBI Crime Index Violent:** 892

## ■ Municipal Government

The city of Springfield, which is also the seat of Greene County, is administered by a council-manager form of government. Eight council members are elected to four-year terms (with staggered elections) on a non-partisan basis and a mayor is elected for a two-year term. Four council members are elected to represent particular wards and four are elected at large. The city manager is appointed by the council to be the chief executive and administrative officer of the city.

**Head Official:** City Manager Bob Cumley (since 2006)

**Total Number of City Employees:** 1,825 (2007)

*City Information:* City of Springfield, 840 Boonville Avenue, PO Box 8368, Springfield, MO 65801-8368; telephone (417)864-1000; www.springfieldmo.gov

# ■ Economy

## Major Industries and Commercial Activity

The manufacturing and logistics sector is a major force in Springfield MSA, which includes Greene, Christian, Webster, Polk, and Dallas Counties. A 2006 report showed that manufacturers contributed about $18.6 billion annually to the regional economy, with logistics accounting for another $14.3 billion. Manufacturing and logistics together accounted for about 16 percent of employment the same year. O'Reilly Automotive, a *Fortune* 1000 company, has its headquarters in the city. Other manufacturers in Springfield include Kraft Foods, Paul Mueller Company, Willow Brook Foods, Solo Cup, and 3M. Springfield Iron and Metal, one of the newest manufacturers in the city, has been built on the site of the closed Springfield Southwest Regional Stockyards.

Food processing and distribution companies have developed in the city, not only for the resources of agriculture and livestock, but for the unique location of the Springfield Underground. Springfield Underground maintains an active limestone mining operation. Over 75 million cubic feet of underground caverns created by mining have been developed for lease, primarily by food manufacturing and distribution companies, such as Kraft, Dairy Farmers of America, and Willow Brook Foods. As mining operations continue, so does development of what Springfield Underground calls its "Food Technology Park."

Health care and education have also grown to have an enormous impact on the local economy. The health care industry employs about 15 percent of the workforce and is estimated to have an annual impact of about $4.5 billion. St. John's Health System and CoxHealth, two of the largest employers in the city, sponsor major hospitals and numerous clinics throughout Springfield. Higher education has an impact of about $900 million, with Missouri State University being the largest university employer in Springfield.

The third-largest retail market in Missouri—sales total more than $3 billion annually—Springfield ranks in the top 170 markets in the nation. The retail total for the metropolitan area is over $6 billion. Wal-Mart, Lowe's Stores, Meeks Building Centers, and Dillons Food Stores are a few of the largest retailers in the area.

Professional and business services and financial activities have begun to take root in the city. BKD, LLP, one of the 10 largest certified public accountant and advisory firms in the country, has its headquarters in Springfield. T-Mobile and Bell Industries have customer service call stations in the city.

In 2007 *Inc. Magazine* ranked Springfield number 20 on its list of the "Hottest Mid-Sized Cities in the Nation for Entrepreneurs."

**Items and goods produced:** dairy products, paper cups and containers, food and chemical processing equipment, auto parts, food products, iron and steel, engines and engine components, electronic parts

## Incentive Programs—New and Existing Businesses

*Local programs:* The Springfield Business Development Corporation is the economic development subsidiary of the Springfield Area Chamber of Commerce. It offers competitive rates and reliable service through City Utilities of Springfield, and administers enterprise zone tax credits and abatements through the Missouri Department of Economic Development.

*State programs:* A large portion of the city has been designated by the state as an Enhanced Enterprise Zone through which eligible businesses may receive tax credits for up to 10 years for new development. The business must create at least two new jobs and offer $100,000 in new investment for each year in order to be eligible for tax credits. A job creation tax credit of $400 per eligible employee is available against state income taxes for up to 10 years. Other tax credits include up to $1,200 for hiring Enterprise Zone residents or "special employees." Foreign Trade Zone (FTZ) incentives are available in Springfield, which has a U.S. Customs office at the Springfield-Branson Regional Airport. Goods entering FTZs are not subject to customs tariffs until the goods leave the zone and are formally entered into U.S. customs territory. Other tax credit programs offered by the state of Missouri include a Business Modernization and Technology Credit, Small Business Incubator Credit, Neighborhood Assistance Program, Historic Preservation Credit, New Markets Tax Credit and a Community Bank Investment Credit. Tax credits through these programs range from 45 percent to 70 percent for qualified programs. A Research Expense Tax Credit program offers a credit of 6.5 percent for qualified expenses. The BUILD Missouri Program provides incentives for the location or expansion of large business projects (generally in excess of 100 jobs). The program provides Missouri state income tax credits to the business in the amount of debt service payments for bonds related to a portion of project costs. The tax credits may be sold if not used by the recipient. A number of loan financing programs are also available.

***Job training programs:*** The New Jobs Training Program (NJTP) provides education and training to workers employed in newly created jobs in Missouri. The new jobs may result from a new industry locating in Missouri or an existing industry expanding its workforce in the state. The Missouri Customized Training Program (MCTP) helps Missouri employers with funding to offset the costs of employee training and retraining. It assists new and expanding businesses in recruiting, screening, and training workers, and it helps existing employers retain their current workforce when faced with needed upgrading and retraining. The Missouri Job Retention Training Program offers retraining assistance to employers who have retained a minimum of 100 employers for at least two consecutive years and have made a capital investment of at least $1 million. The Springfield Business Development Corporation coordinates customized training programs through Ozarks Technical Community College.

## Development Projects

The Partnership Industrial Center (PIC), which broke ground in 1993, is part of the economic development public/private partnership between the City of Springfield, city utilities, the Springfield Area Chamber of Commerce, and the Springfield Business and Development Corporation. The partnership was formed in 1991 to promote and encourage the retention and creation of quality manufacturing and industrial jobs in the Springfield area. In 2006 the PIC reached build-out capacity with 21 companies. Partnership Industrial Center West, the second site for the group, was still under development in 2007, with four tenants at the site that year.

Downtown Springfield continues to be a focus for developers. Plans were announced in 2005 for a retail, entertainment, and parking complex for the Market Avenue Redevelopment Area in downtown Springfield. In 2006 developers broke ground for College Station, which will include a 14-screen movie theater within a 75,000-square-foot urban entertainment complex that will also house restaurants and retail space. The entire project is expected to cost $20 million with a completion date of early 2008.

In 2007 the city welcomed a new customer service call center for T-Mobile Central and T-Mobile USA. The new center was expected to involve an investment of $17.5 million and create 650 new jobs at an average annual wage of $18,720. Also in 2007, the Missouri Life Science Research Board announced that it would locate one of its Centers of Excellence in Springfield. The Springfield center, which will focus on agricultural research in the areas of bioenergy, plant science, and animal health and nutrition, will be built as a collaborative effort with Missouri State University, St. John's Health System, Drury University,

Cox Health Systems, the Springfield Business and Development Corporation, and other private and non-profit organizations. Local officials hope that the center will draw new life sciences businesses and organizations.

In December 2007 the new scrap metal processing plant for Springfield Iron and Metal was still under construction, with an expected completion date by mid-2008. The facility is being built on the site of the old Southwest Regional Stockyards, which was sold to Springfield Iron and Metal in January 2007. The new processing plant represents an investment of about $20 million and is expected to employ about 45 people.

Also in December 2007, the city opened its newest park. Rutledge-Wilson Farm Park is a 207-acre site that features an animal barn, milking barn, farmhouse, fishing pond, playground, classrooms, gift shop and book store, and forty acres of land to support demonstration crops. The $2.6 million park was funded in part by the voter approved quarter-cent Sales Tax for Parks, which took effect in 2001. A second phase of development for the park will include a farm museum to be placed in the farm house. The park is designed for both recreational and educational purposes.

***Economic Development Information:*** Springfield Area Chamber of Commerce, 202 S. John Q. Hammons Parkway, Springfield, MO 65806; telephone (417)862-5567; www.springfieldchamber.com

## Commercial Shipping

Springfield is linked with national and international markets by a network of air, rail, and motor freight carriers. Exporting has become an integral part of the local economy; Springfield-Branson Regional Airport is the site of a Foreign Trade Zone and Port of Entry operated by the United States Customs Service. National companies provide customs house and freight forwarding services. Air cargo services are provided by a few airlines. FedEx, UPS, and Airborne Express all operate at the airport as well. Rail transportation is provided by Missouri-North Arkansas and Burlington Northern and Santa Fe Railway, which maintains an intermodal hub for piggyback trailer shipping in the city. There are more than 30 trucking terminals in Springfield, representing all major national carriers.

## Labor Force and Employment Outlook

In 2006 about 85 percent of the population age 25 and over had obtained a high school diploma or higher, with about 26 percent of this population achieving bachelor's degrees or higher. While education and health services, retail trade, government, and manufacturing were the largest employment industries in 2006, the largest growth industries in terms of employment were professional and business services and construction and mining. Projections to 2014 suggest that health sciences will still see the greatest growth in new jobs, particularly in jobs for registered nurses. Jobs in marketing, sales, and service are also expected to increase.

In 2007 *Expansion Magazine* ranked Springfield as 12th among the top mid-sized metros for recruitment and attraction of new business and jobs.

The following is a summary of data regarding the Springfield metropolitan area labor force, 2006 annual averages.

**Size of nonagricultural labor force:** 195,600

**Number of workers employed in...**

construction and mining: 10,400
manufacturing: 17,700
trade, transportation and utilities: 46,300
information: 4,300
financial activities: 12,100
professional and business services: 34,300
educational and health services: 18,200
leisure and hospitality: 18,800
other services: 8,500
government: 24,900

**Average hourly earnings of production workers employed in manufacturing:** Not available

**Unemployment rate:** 4.2% (June 2007)

| *Largest employers (2007)* | *Number of employees* |
|---|---|
| St. John's Health System | 7,610 |
| CoxHealth | 6,759 |
| Wal-Mart Stores | 4,100 |
| Springfield Public Schools | 2,995 |
| Missouri State University | 2,840 |
| United States Government | 2,540 |
| State of Missouri | 2,465 |
| Bass Pro Shops/ Tracker Marine | 2,375 |
| City of Springfield | 1,825 |
| Chase Card Services | 1,650 |

### Cost of Living

The following is a summary of data regarding several key cost of living factors in the Springfield area.

**2007 (1st quarter) ACCRA Average House Price:** $231,572

**2007 (1st quarter) ACCRA Cost of Living Index:** 92.5

**State income tax rate:** 1.5% to 6.0%

**State sales tax rate:** 4.225%

**Local income tax rate:** None

**Local sales tax rate:** city, 1.875%; county, 0.5%

**Property tax rate:** $4.5262 per $100 assessed valuation. Assessed valuation is 33 1/3%

***Economic Information:*** Springfield Area Chamber of Commerce, 202 S. John Q. Hammons Parkway, Springfield, MO 65806; telephone (417)862-5567; www.springfieldchamber.com. Missouri Department of Economic Development, 301 W. High Street, Jefferson City, MO 65102; telephone (573)751-4962; www.ded. mo.gov

# ■ Education and Research

### Elementary and Secondary Schools

Public school education began in Springfield in 1867; today, Central High and Lincoln School are on the National Register of Historic Places. Public elementary and secondary schools in Springfield are part of the School District of Springfield R-XII, the third largest public school system in Missouri. An elected seven-member, nonpartisan board of education selects the superintendent. In 2006 the system had a 78 percent graduation rate.

Special courses for high school students are available through Ozarks Technical Community College. High schools students may also choose to participate in the International Baccalaureate Program at Central High. The system sponsors the Bailey Alternative School, for students who may achieve more in a non-traditional school setting, and the Phelps Center for Gifted Education, which offers programs for gifted students of all ages.

The following is a summary of data regarding the Springfield Public Schools as of the 2005–2006 school year.

**Total enrollment:** 24,000

**Number of facilities**

elementary schools: 36
junior high/middle schools: 9
senior high schools: 5
other: 8

**Student/teacher ratio:** 14.9:1

**Teacher salaries (2005–06)**

elementary median: $34,360
junior high/middle median: $34,980
secondary median: $42,390

**Funding per pupil:** $6,448

There are about 15 private elementary and secondary schools in the city, serving about 2,550 students. The Greenwood Laboratory School is affiliated with Missouri State University and has an enrollment of about 365 students from kindergarten through 12th grade. The faculty members of Greenwood are master's degree students at Missouri State.

*Public Schools Information:* Springfield Public Schools, 940 N. Jefferson Ave., Springfield, MO 65802; telephone (417)523-0000; http://springfieldpublic schoolsmo.org

## Colleges and Universities

Missouri State University (MSU) is Springfield's largest institution of higher learning and the second largest university in the state. The Springfield campus is the main campus of MSU, with two additional branch campuses at West Plains and Mountain Grove. The Springfield campus enrolls about 19,000 students and awards baccalaureate degrees in 88 disciplines and master's degrees in 40 disciplines There are seven colleges, which include the colleges of business administration, education, natural and applied sciences, health and human services, arts and letters, and humanities and public affairs. The first doctoral program to be offered by the university was recently initiated in audiology. Pre-professional programs are also available for fields such as engineering, journalism, law, medicine, theology, and dentistry.

Drury University has over 5,000 students in undergraduate and graduate programs. The school offers 63 undergraduate majors and special programs. Master's degrees are available in education, criminology, criminal justice, communication, and business administration. Graduate certificates are offered in instructional mathematics K-8, instructional technology, terrorism issues and analysis, and web design.

Ozarks Technical Community College was founded in 1990 to offer associate's degrees and other technical education programs and certificates for adults and high school students in the area. Customized training programs are also available to local businesses for employee training. Associate's degrees are available in the fields of mathematics, English and communication, life and physical science, social sciences and humanities, business, computer services, construction, human services, industrial, and transportation. Allied health programs are also available.

Southwest Baptist University (SBU), which is based in Bolivar, maintains a branch campus in Springfield that offers baccalaureate and master's degrees in business administration. This Springfield campus is also home to the SBU College of Nursing and Health Sciences, which offers associate's and bachelor's degrees in nursing.

Cox College of Nursing and Health Sciences is a private college with an enrollment of about 600 students. The college offers associate's and bachelor's degrees in nursing and certificates in medical transcription and medical coding. The Forest Institute of Professional Psychology offers postgraduate certificates in specialized counseling fields, master's degrees in counseling and clinical psychology, and a doctorate in clinical psychology.

Evangel University, Central Bible College, and Assemblies of God Theological Seminary are all private colleges affiliated with the Assemblies of God. Vattertot College offers vocational and technical programs in business, medical fields, trades, court reporting, and culinary arts. There is a branch of Everest College in Springfield that also offers a variety of career training programs.

## Libraries and Research Centers

The Springfield-Greene County Library system's main facility is Library Center, a newer facility that occupies an 82,000-square-foot former home improvement store and features a café, gift shop, and other amenities. The system has seven full-service branch locations, including Library Station, which also features a gift shop and café. A state-of-the-art bookmobile serves the system's outreach program. The system has also established a Book Stop within a local grocery store where library patrons can return books borrowed from any library location or pick-up books that have been ordered for reserve. The system has holdings of well over half a million volumes in addition to periodicals and special collections in such areas as genealogy, Missouri history, and Ozarks folklore.

Missouri State University maintains the Duane G. Meyer Library, which houses a collection of more than 835,000 volumes and current subscriptions to 3,600 periodicals and newspapers. The Music Library, established at MSU in 1986, has a collection of over 5,000 books, scores, and recordings and over 100 periodical subscriptions. The Haseltine Library at Greenwood Laboratory School is designed for the students of that K-12 school.

Specialized libraries located in the city are operated by the Missouri State Court of Appeals and the Springfield Art Museum, among other organizations.

Missouri State University sponsors a number of research programs and centers, including the Center for Biomedical and Life Sciences, the Center for Archaeological Research, The Center for Grapevine Biotechnology, the Ozarks Environmental and Water Resources Institute, and the Ozarks Public Health Institute.

*Public Library Information:* Springfield-Greene County Library, 4653 South Campbell, Springfield, MO 65810; telephone (417)882-0714; http://thelibrary .springfield.missouri.org

# ■ Health Care

The city's major hospitals are St. John's Hospital, Cox Medical Center South/Cox Walnut Lawn, Cox Medical Center North, Lakeland Regional Hospital, and Doctors Hospital of Springfield.

St. John's Hospital is affiliated with the Sisters of Mercy Health System–St. Louis, which is one of the largest Catholic health systems in the nation. St. John's Hospital in Springfield has the only Level I Trauma Center (for both adults and children) and Burn Center in the region. The full-service hospital offers specialized services in women's health, sports medicine, neurosciences, cancer treatment, senior health, and cardiology. The Children's Hospital is a department of St. John's that offers specialized pediatric care. St John's Clinic is a physician-led multi-specialty group practice that sponsors over 70 specialized clinic site locations throughout Springfield, with services ranging from primary care in family medicine to specialized care in allergies and immunology, behavioral health, dermatology, and ophthalmology.

CoxHealth sponsors three facilities in Springfield. Cox Medical Center South is a 563-bed full-service care facility. The 102-bed Cox Walnut Lawn is part of the Cox South campus, serving patients in need of rehabilitative services, wound care, and urgent care. Cox North is a 72-bed facility. CoxHealth also supports several primary care and specialized clinics in the city.

Doctors Hospital of Springfield is a 45-bed acute care facility with specialties that include family practice, internal medicine, gynecology, ophthalmology, orthopedic surgery, plastic surgery, general surgery, oral surgery, ENT, podiatry, and psychiatry.

Lakeland Regional Hospital is owned by Youth and Family Centered Services, Inc., based in Austin, Texas. The facility provides comprehensive residential and outpatient psychiatric care services and includes recreational and fitness facilities that are open to the community.

# ■ Recreation

## Sightseeing

One of Springfield's major sightseeing attractions is Wilson's Creek National Civil War Battlefield, the site of the first battle between Union and Confederate armies in Missouri and west of the Mississippi. An automobile tour of nearly five miles encompasses all the major points with historic markers and exhibits. Springfield National Cemetery is the only cemetery where soldiers from both the North and South are buried side by side. The Wonders of Wildlife American National Fish and Wildlife Museum entertains and educates visitors about the need to preserve the environment and protect fish and wildlife. This new museum facility is adjacent to the Bass Pro Shops

Outdoor World. The Close Park Botanical Gardens and Arboretum and the Mizumoto Japanese Garden at Nathanael Greene Park may be the place to go for a quiet, relaxing afternoon walk.

Fantastic Caverns, a natural wonder, is the only cave in North America and one of three in the world that is so large visitors must tour it in motorized vehicles. Exotic Animal Paradise, 12 miles east of Springfield in Stratford, is a 400-acre park that is home to more than 3,000 wild and exotic animals and birds. Springfield's Dickerson Park Zoo, nationally known for its elephant herd, offers elephant rides to children. The zoo also breeds cheetahs and bald eagles.

## Arts and Culture

The Springfield Regional Arts Council, established in 1978, sponsors numerous arts organizations and events through the city. The council has offices and meeting spaces at the Creamery Arts Center, which also serves as a community center and the home offices for the Springfield Ballet, the Springfield Regional Opera, and the Springfield Symphony.

A principal venue for the performing arts in Springfield is the Juanita K. Hammons Hall for the Performing Arts. A variety of cultural events are staged there, including touring Broadway productions and performances by the symphony. The Springfield Symphony Orchestra and the Little Theater are the city's two oldest cultural organizations. Among the city's other performance arts institutions are the Springfield Regional Opera (performing at the 1909 Landers Theater, a historic landmark) and the Springfield Ballet. Missouri State University offers a summer series at its Tent Theater. Within the area, more than 20 music theaters like the Roy Clark Celebrity Theater and the Ray Price Show entertain country-music lovers. The Shepherd of the Hills is an outdoor theater in Branson that attracts a large audience each season with its stories on Ozark mountain families. Numerous local museums and other historic points of interest increase cultural awareness in the Springfield area. The Air and Military Museum of the Ozarks houses more than 5,000 pieces of military history. Nearby Mansfield is home to the Laura Ingalls Wilder Museum.

## Festivals and Holidays

Bass Pro Shops, "the world's greatest sporting goods store," presents a Spring Fishing Classic in Springfield in March. Historic Walnut Street is the site of a May Artsfest. A balloon race and Firefall—a fireworks display accompanied by the Springfield Symphony—are popular Fourth of July events. The Ozark Empire Fair in August also attracts large crowds. The Springfield Art Museum hosts a national "Watercolor USA" show each summer. In nearby Silver Dollar City, the Mountain Folks Music Festival is held the third week of June. Ozark Empire Fair, Missouri's second largest and one of the top-rated fairs in the country, is held in late July. Wilson's Creek National Battlefield sponsors special programs each year on Memorial Day, Independence Day, August 10, and Labor Day. The Ozark Auto Show, a collector car auction, draws vintage automobile buffs to nearby Branson on the last weekend of October.

*Arts and Culture Information:* Springfield Regional Arts Council, 411 N. Sherman Parkway, Springfield, MO 65802; telephone (417)862-2787; www.springfieldarts.org

## Sports for the Spectator

The Springfield Cardinals, a minor league baseball team, play in Hammons Field, a multimillion dollar baseball park that opened in 2004. Six local colleges and universities field a variety of teams in intercollegiate sports competition. The Drury Panthers and the Missouri State University Bears basketball teams frequently compete in national tournament play, as do the Lady Bears. The Springfield Lasers, a professional team, compete at the Cooper Tennis Complex.

## Sports for the Participant

Over 50 city parks are located throughout Springfield. Nearby is the Mark Twain National Forest and Mincy Wildlife area. A number of freshwater lakes close to Springfield provide opportunities for fishing, swimming, boating, and water skiing. For the golfer Springfield offers three municipal courses. The city maintains more than 50 tennis courts and 8 city pools. A variety of sports programs are sponsored by the city. Skiing in the Ozark Mountains is possible year-round.

*Recreation Information:* Springfield–Greene County Parks and Recreation, 1923 North Welter, Springfield, MO 65803; telephone (417)864-1049; www.parkboard.org. For hunting and fishing information, Missouri Department of Conservation, 2901 West Truman Boulevard, Jefferson City, MO 65102; telephone (573)751-4115; http://mdc.mo.gov

## Shopping and Dining

Battlefield Mall, one of the state's largest shopping malls, with 170 shops and 4 anchor department stores, is located in Springfield. A popular shopping district is a nineteenth-century village consisting of renovated buildings with shops offering quilts, crafts, and folk art. An antique mall and flea market houses more than 70 dealers in a three-story building, the largest such enterprise in the Ozarks. This antique mart sells everything from comic books and baseball cards to antique coins, dolls, toys, jewelry, furniture, and furnishings. A large reproduction shop is also on the premises. Nearby Silver Dollar City features products made by resident craftsmen using nineteenth-century skills. Bass Pro Shops, billing itself as the world's largest sporting goods store, is located in Springfield and specializes in equipment for anglers, hunters, and others. This unusual shop sports a two-story log cabin with water wheel, a four-story waterfall, fresh water and salt water aquariums, and daily fish feedings by divers, as well as a 300,000-square-foot showroom and a NASCAR shop.

The more than 600 restaurants in Springfield specialize in a variety of cuisines that include authentic ethnic foods and Southern cooking. One of the more popular dining establishments serves fish one night and prime rib the next, in addition to an eclectic menu that offers Ozark dishes.

*Visitor Information:* Springfield, Missouri Convention and Visitors Bureau, 3315 East Battlefield Road, Springfield, MO 65804; telephone (417)881-5300; toll-free (800)678-8767; www.springfieldmo.org

# ■ Convention Facilities

Several meeting sites in Springfield cater to a full range of meeting needs, from small parties to merchandise shows. The Springfield Exposition Center at Jordan Valley Park and improvements to an existing trade center were completed in September 2003. The center offers 112,000 square feet of convention and exhibit space that can accommodate 543 booths. A theater seats 4,500 people. There is also a 977-space parking garage. The center is across the street from the University Plaza Hotel and Convention Center, which offers 39,000 square feet of meeting space and 271 guest rooms.

The Shrine Mosque features a 6,900-square-foot auditorium with variable capacity that includes up to 40 exhibit booths and seating for 3,289 people in a theater setting and 650 people for banquets. A lower-level, 12,650-square-foot exhibit area can contain 40 additional booths and accommodate up to 800 people for a reception.

The Missouri Entertainment and Event Center (formerly known as the Ozark Empire Fairgrounds) is a multi-purpose complex that sponsors indoor and outdoor trade shows, seminars, auctions, and other consumer shows as well as a variety of entertainment events, such as horse shows, fairs, and paintball tournaments. A main arena seats ups to 3,000 people.

Pythian Castle offers a variety of meeting, reception, or exhibition spaces, as well as a small theater to accommodate about 217 people. Hammons Student Center and McDonald Arena on the MSU campus, designed principally for university use, are also available for special events. Several Springfield area hotels and motels offer meeting accommodations; more than 5,000 lodging rooms are available in metropolitan Springfield.

*Convention Information:* Springfield, Missouri, Convention and Visitors Bureau, 3315 East Battlefield Road, Springfield, MO 65804; telephone (417)881-5300; toll-free (800)678-8767; www.springfieldmo.org

# Transportation

## Approaching the City

Commercial air service at Springfield-Branson Regional Airport is offered by 5 airlines with over 30 daily flights to 13 U.S. cities. Interstate 44 is the primary route into Springfield. U.S. 60 and U.S. 65 wrap around the city and connect to I-44. State Route 13 passes through the city from north to south. Greyhound provides bus transportation into the city.

## Traveling in the City

The downtown Springfield area is set up in a basic grid street pattern. The public transit system is operated by City Utilities Transit System, usually referred to as The Bus. The Bus has 15 fixed routes with frequent service on Mondays through Saturday from 6am to 6pm. Modified schedules and routes apply for Sundays, evenings, and holidays. Paratransit service is available. A system of bike routes, lanes, and multipurpose paths crisscross the city and are maintained by the city, Ozark Greenways Trails, and Missouri State University. All city buses feature bike racks through the Bike and Bus program.

# Communications

## Newspapers and Magazines

Springfield's daily newspaper is *The News-Leader,* which appears in daily and Sunday morning editions. The *Springfield Business Journal* is a weekly publication. The monthly *Springfield! Magazine* features articles on topics of local and community interest; *417 Magazine* caters to the area's upscale residents with lifestyle, decorating, travel, and entertainment articles. *The Mirror* is a weekly religious newspaper published by the Catholic Church of Southern Missouri.

Gospel Publishing House of the General Council of the Assemblies of God is based in Springfield. The company publishes religious resources and curriculums for churches and pastors.

## Television and Radio

Five television stations, including four major network affiliates and one public network outlet, plus cable, broadcast in Springfield. Sixteen AM and FM radio stations schedule music, religious, and news and information programming.

***Media Information:*** *The News-Leader,* 651 Boonville Ave., Springfield, MO 65806; telephone (417)836-1100 or (800)695-1969; www.news-leader.com

## Springfield Online

City of Springfield home page. Available www .springfieldmo.gov

Missouri State University. Available www .missouristate.edu

*The News-Leader.*Available www.springfieldnews-leader.com

Springfield Business Development Corporation. Available www.business4springfield.com

Springfield, Missouri Convention and Visitors Bureau. Available www.springfieldmo.org

Springfield Museum. Available www .wondersofwildlife.org

Springfield Regional Arts Council. Available www .springfieldarts.org

BIBLIOGRAPHY

Boyle, Shanna, et al., eds., *Crossroads at the Spring: A Pictorial History of Springfield, Missouri* (Donning Marketing Company, 1997)

# Nebraska

# The State in Brief

**Nickname:** Cornhusker State

**Motto:** Equality before the law

**Flower:** Goldenrod

**Bird:** Western meadowlark

**Area:** 77,353 square miles (2000; U.S. rank 16th)

**Elevation:** Ranges from 840 feet to 5,426 feet above sea level

**Climate:** Continental, with wide variations of temperature

**Admitted to Union:** March 1, 1867

**Capital:** Lincoln

**Head Official:** Governor Dave Heineman (R) (until 2010)

## Population

**1980:** 1,570,000
**1990:** 1,578,385
**2000:** 1,711,263
**2006 estimate:** 1,768,331
**Percent change, 1990–2000:** 8.4%
**U.S. rank in 2006:** 38th
**Percent of residents born in state:** 65.53% (2006)
**Density:** 22.9 people per square mile (2006)
**2006 FBI Crime Index Total:** 64,058

## Racial and Ethnic Characteristics (2006)

**White:** 1,566,980
**Black or African American:** 72,095
**American Indian and Alaska Native:** 16,112
**Asian:** 29,815
**Native Hawaiian and Pacific Islander:** 785
**Hispanic or Latino (may be of any race):** 130,230
**Other:** 56,014

## Age Characteristics (2006)

**Population under 5 years old:** 128,307
**Population 5 to 19 years old:** 372,131
**Percent of population 65 years and over:** 13.2%
**Median age:** 36

## Vital Statistics

**Total number of births (2006):** 26,291
**Total number of deaths (2006):** 14,998
**AIDS cases reported through 2005:** 1,377

## Economy

**Major industries:** Finance, insurance, and real estate; trade; agriculture; manufacturing; services
**Unemployment rate (2006):** 4.8%
**Per capita income (2006):** $23,248
**Median household income (2006):** $45,474
**Percentage of persons below poverty level (2006):** 11.5%
**Income tax rate:** 2.56% to 6.84%
**Sales tax rate:** 5.5%

# Lincoln

## ■ The City in Brief

**Founded:** 1864 (incorporated 1869)

**Head Official:** Mayor Chris Beutler (D) (since 2007)

**City Population**
1980: 171,932
1990: 191,972
2000: 225,581
2006 estimate: 241,167
Percent change, 1990–2000: 17.5%
U.S. rank in 1980: 81st
U.S. rank in 1990: 81st
U.S. rank in 2000: 87th

**Metropolitan Area Population**
1980: 192,864
1990: 213,641
2000: 250,291
2006 estimate: 283,970
Percent change, 1990–2000: 17.2%
U.S. rank in 1980: Not available
U.S. rank in 1990: Not available
U.S. rank in 2000: 144th

**Area:** 75.38 square miles (2000)

**Elevation:** 1,167 feet above sea level

**Average Annual Temperatures:** January, 22.4° F; July, 77.8° F; annual average, 51.1° F

**Average Annual Precipitation:** 28.37 inches of rain; 27.8 inches of snow

**Major Economic Sectors:** Government, services, wholesale and retail trade, manufacturing

**Unemployment Rate:** 3.1% (June 2007)

**Per Capita Income:** $23,803 (2005)

**2005 FBI Crime Index Property:** 12,703

**2005 FBI Crime Index Violent:** 1,364

**Major Colleges and Universities:** University of Nebraska–Lincoln, Nebraska Wesleyan University, Union College

**Daily Newspaper:** *Lincoln Journal Star*

## ■ Introduction

Lincoln is the capital of Nebraska and the seat of Lancaster County. Lincoln and Lancaster County form a metropolitan statistical area, which serves as a commercial, educational, and government center for a grain and livestock producing region. Named after President Abraham Lincoln, the city was an important railroad junction for major western routes during the nineteenth century. William Jennings Bryan dominated the political life of Lincoln when he ran for president three times. The Nebraska state Capitol building, completed in 1932, rises 400 feet above the prairie and was designed to symbolize the spirit of the Plains. Voted by *Expansion Management* magazine in 2003 as a "Five Star Community," Lincoln is appealing for its small-town feel yet offers a wide array of cultural attractions and business development opportunities.

## ■ Geography and Climate

Set near the center of Lancaster County in southeastern Nebraska, Lincoln is surrounded by gently rolling prairie. The western edge of the city lies in the valley of Salt Creek, which flows northeastward to the lower Platte River. The upward slope of the terrain to the west causes instability in moist easterly winds. Humidity remains at moderate to low levels except during short summer periods when moist tropical air reaches the area. The summer sun shines an average of two-thirds of possible duration; high winds combined with hot temperatures occasionally cause crop damage. A chinook or foehn effect often produces rapid temperature rises in the winter. Although annual snowfall is approximately 28 inches, it has sometimes exceeded 59 inches.

**Area:** 75.38 square miles (2000)

**Elevation:** 1,167 feet above sea level

**Average Temperatures:** January, 22.4° F; July, 77.8° F; annual average, 51.1° F

**Average Annual Precipitation:** 28.37 inches of rain; 27.8 inches of snow

# ■ History

## Saline Deposits Attract First Settlers

As early as 1853, salt companies were sending men to study the possibility of salt manufacture in the salt flats northwest of the present city of Lincoln. Actual processing by any salt company did not start until the early 1860s, but it was never commercially successful, and efforts to manufacture salt were abandoned around 1887. However, Captain W. T. Donovan, representing the Crescent Salt Company, settled on the west bank of Salt Creek near the intersection of Oak Creek in 1856. He named his claim Lancaster. By 1859 the area had sufficient population to be considered for organization of a county. Donovan participated in the committee that was to determine the site and name of the county seat. It was named after Donovan's home town of Lancaster, Pennsylvania.

As a state capital, Lancaster was a compromise choice between North Platters—who favored Omaha, the territorial capital since 1854—and South Platters—who vied for a capital site south of the Platte River. Ultimately Lancaster was chosen and a new name proposed: "Capital City." Lancaster was finally renamed Lincoln, after President Abraham Lincoln. August F. Harvey, a state surveyor, replatted Lincoln in 1867, setting up a grid system of streets lettered from A to Z, with O as the division point, and north and south blocks numbered. In the heart of downtown were four square blocks for the state Capitol and a proposed university. The city plan also called for the planting of more than two million trees, mostly oak, which would line boulevards and parks. The attention to the natural landscaping of the city is a civic responsibility each generation of Lincolnites since has taken seriously.

In December 1868, the state government moved its property in covered wagons to hide the transfer of power from armed Omahans upset with the relocation. Local investors feared that Lincoln would not remain the state capital long since it numbered just 30 inhabitants in 1867, but within a year 500 people lived there, and new businesses started to develop. One event in Lincoln's history at this time symbolized the early difficulties. A herd of 1,000 Texas longhorns collapsed the wooden bridge over Salt Creek at O Street, but the wild herd blocked local officials from locating the cattle's owner and monetary restitution for the bridge's reconstruction was never obtained.

## State Capital Weathers Troubled Times

At the first meeting of the Nebraska legislature in Lincoln in 1869, immediate action was taken to authorize land grants for railroad construction and a bill was passed to establish the University of Nebraska. The Burlington & Missouri River railroad line reached Lincoln in 1870, the same year the population reached 2,500 people. One popular rumor of the time was that Lincoln was built over an underground ocean that would provide a source of saline springs with commercial potential, but nothing of this sort materialized.

In the 1870s Lincoln suffered a difficult period. The state's first governor was impeached, a depression hit the local economy, and the legality of transferring the capital was questioned. Grasshoppers infested the area for more than three years. Saloons, gambling, and prostitution flourished, prompting the formation of the Women's Christian Temperance Union, which set a moral tone that dominated local politics until Prohibition. Lincoln reversed its fortunes in the 1880s, as public services were introduced, businesses prospered, and a reform party was victorious in 1887. But as the new mayor and city council began cleaning up the local government, a crooked judge had them arrested and convicted in a circuit court case that was eventually reversed by the U.S. Supreme Court.

## Twentieth Century Brings New Challenges

At the turn of the century William Jennings Bryan dominated the political life of Lincoln, running unsuccessfully for president as the Democratic candidate in 1896, 1900, and 1908. Bryan published *The Commoner,* a weekly newspaper with a circulation of more than 100,000 after his defeat in 1900. Bryan was an oddity—a radical Democrat in conservative Lincoln. During World War I, segments of Lincoln's German population openly supported the Central Powers. A misplaced sense of American patriotism gripped the Lincoln populace and local German culture was shunned. The University Board of Regents conducted a hearing in which 80 professors faced charges of "lack of aggressive loyalty" and three were asked to resign.

The Capitol structure built in Lincoln in the 1880s began to settle into the ground, and one corner had sunk eight inches by 1908. Serious concern for the condition of the Capitol prompted a contest to select the best new cost-effective design. All the entries except two involved the traditional federal dome style. The winning design featured a 400-foot tower that could be built around the old Capitol, saving Nebraska nearly $1 million in office rental and making it possible to defray the costs of construction by the time the new capitol was completed in 1932. Its design revolutionized public and government buildings by ushering in a modernist style.

Lincoln today is a typical "All-American" city, boasting clean, healthy air and safe streets. Answering a question about where he sees Lincoln by the year 2006, former Mayor Mike Johanns declared: "Lincoln will continue to be a vibrant and healthy community with a unique sense of place. Growth will continue to occur at locations carefully chosen in the 1990s, maintaining Lincoln's interface with its agricultural hinterland. Lincoln in 2006 will still be one of the best cities in which to live in the United States."

### Planning for Lincoln's Future

Current community planners have continued this vision by actively working to develop the downtown area. In 2004, a comprehensive plan was drafted by the Downtown Lincoln Association that included a civic center, hotels, and additional parking. Residents enjoy cultural amenities along with outdoor and professional sports. Meanwhile, Lincoln has been cited by Population Connection's *Kid-Friendly Cities Report Card* as number 17 of 80 on its "Kid-Friendly Cities" 2004 list and was ranked twentieth on *Child* magazine's "Best Cities for Families." Further, it was featured as an economical travel destination by AAA in 2005. And with a diversified business climate, population growth, and increase in the area's workforce, it follows that Lincoln ranked on a 2006 *Expansion Management* list as a "5-Star Business Opportunity Metro."

*Historical Information:* Nebraska State Historical Society, 1500 R St., PO Box 82554, Lincoln, NE 68501; telephone (402)471-3270. American Historical Society of Germans from Russia (AHSGR), 631 D St., Lincoln, NE 68502-1199; telephone (402)474-3363; fax (402) 474-7229; email ahsgr@ahsgr.com

## ■ Population Profile

**Metropolitan Area Residents**

> 1980: 192,864
> 1990: 213,641
> 2000: 250,291
> 2006 estimate: 283,970
> Percent change, 1990–2000: 17.2%
> U.S. rank in 1980: Not available
> U.S. rank in 1990: Not available
> U.S. rank in 2000: 144th

**City Residents**

> 1980: 171,932

> 1990: 191,972
> 2000: 225,581
> 2006 estimate: 241,167
> Percent change, 1990–2000: 17.5%
> U.S. rank in 1980: 81st
> U.S. rank in 1990: 81st
> U.S. rank in 2000: 87th

**Density:** 3,370.7 people per square mile (2000)

**Racial and ethnic characteristics (2005)**

> White: 202,867
> Black: 7,184
> American Indian and Alaska Native: 1,668
> Asian: 7,572
> Native Hawaiian and Pacific Islander: 0
> Hispanic or Latino (may be of any race): 9,672
> Other: 3,627

**Percent of residents born in state:** 66.6% (2000)

**Age characteristics (2005)**

> Population under 5 years old: 16,457
> Population 5 to 9 years old: 14,566
> Population 10 to 14 years old: 12,333
> Population 15 to 19 years old: 12,583
> Population 20 to 24 years old: 24,280
> Population 25 to 34 years old: 38,893
> Population 35 to 44 years old: 30,069
> Population 45 to 54 years old: 32,019
> Population 55 to 59 years old: 12,192
> Population 60 to 64 years old: 9,058
> Population 65 to 74 years old: 11,442
> Population 75 to 84 years old: 8,691
> Population 85 years and older: 3,479
> Median age: 33.3 years

**Births (2006, MSA)**

> Total number: 4,343

**Deaths (2006, MSA)**

> Total number: 1,875

**Money income (2005)**

> Per capita income: $23,803
> Median household income: $45,790
> Total households: 97,128

**Number of households with income of . . .**

> less than $10,000: 8,797
> $10,000 to $14,999: 6,014
> $15,000 to $24,999: 12,257
> $25,000 to $34,999: 10,747

©2007 PRANGE Aerial Photography

$35,000 to $49,999: 14,280
$50,000 to $74,999: 22,947
$75,000 to $99,999: 10,923
$100,000 to $149,999: 7,992
$150,000 to $199,999: 1,336
$200,000 or more: 1,835

**Percent of families below poverty level:** 11.1%
(2005)

**2005 FBI Crime Index Property:** 12,703

**2005 FBI Crime Index Violent:** 1,364

## ■ Municipal Government

The city of Lincoln is governed by a mayor and seven-member council, all of whom are elected to four-year terms on a nonpartisan ballot.

**Head Official:** Mayor Chris Beutler (D) (since 2007; current term expires 2011)

**Total Number of City Employees:** 2,746 (2003)

*City Information:* City of Lincoln, 555 S 10th St., Lincoln, NE 68508; telephone (402)441-7511; fax (402)441-7120

## ■ Economy

### Major Industries and Commercial Activity

In May 2005, *Forbes* chose Lincoln as the seventh "Best Smaller Metro" area for business and careers with a third place ranking for income growth. Located in a grain and livestock producing region, Lincoln has, since its founding, been a communications, distribution, and wholesaling hub, thanks to its central location. Important industries include the manufacture and repair of locomotives, flour and feed milling, grain storage, and diversified manufacturing. In 2006 the government sector accounted for 21 percent of Lincoln's jobs; education and health services represented 14 percent; retail, 12 percent; professional services, 11 percent; and manufacturing, 9 percent. State government and the University of Nebraska constitute approximately a quarter of the city's economy, but about 90 percent of Lincoln's some 8,000 employers are companies with 20 or fewer employees.

Lincoln is also the corporate headquarters of several insurance companies.

During the 1980s and 1990s Lincoln experienced sustained growth that brought economic expansion, with the employment base increasing 2.5 percent annually. Despite the recession in the early 2000s, retail trade, for example, continued to grow at a higher rate than other metropolitan areas in the state. In 2007 Lincoln's overall economy was stronger than the national economy, and its cost of living was lower than that of metropolitan averages nationwide.

A number of Lincoln's local companies conduct business throughout the United States and in foreign countries. Among them are Ameritas Financial Services, Lester Electrical, and Cook Family Foods. Sandhills Publishing (formerly Peed Corporation), publisher of national trade magazines, has maintained its facilities in Lincoln since 1985. Biotechnology is a fast-growing industry in Lincoln, especially for firms specializing in agriculture and animal science. MDS Harris Laboratories, a pharmaceutical testing and research firm that serves all 50 states and dozens of nations abroad, has an office in Beijing, China. It expanded its medical testing business into the development of a biological warfare vaccine for the U.S. Army, which was the first such test conducted under Food and Drug Administration standards. In addition to its traditional strength of testing medicines on "well normal" people to confirm safety standards, the company tests how people with illnesses react to new medicines. Pfizer Laboratories supplies veterinary products in the United States and dozens of foreign countries. Novartis Consumer Health, Inc., expanded its Lincoln facilities and now makes products such as No-Doz and Excedrin in Lincoln.

**Items and goods produced:** creamery products, farm machinery, farm belts, veterinary supplies, radiator hoses, telephone equipment, biological products, pharmaceutical supplies, plumbing supplies, pumps, motors, motor scooters, wax, filing equipment and office supplies, and printing, lithographic, engraving, metal, stone, and concrete products

## Incentive Programs—New and Existing Businesses

*Local programs:* The Lincoln Independent Business Association, the Chamber of Commerce, Southeast Community College, the University of Nebraska-Lincoln, and the city of Lincoln operate a small business resource center that helps businesses secure financing, permits, and information about other resources. Several major established industrial parks cover more than 1,000 acres and are designed for both heavy industry and multiple use. The City of Lincoln Research and Development Department, with assistance from the Nebraska Research and Development Authority, provides block grant funds to aid

startup businesses. The Lincoln Partnership for Economic Development (LPED) began formal operations in 1996. LPED is a community-based, public-private, permanent venture to provide strategic, focused direction for Lincoln's economic development activities. Community Development Resources (CDR) provides loans and capital with a focus on assisting low-income, minority groups, microentrepreneurs, and women.

*State programs:* Qualified Lincoln businesses can take advantage of state programs such as the Nebraska Business and Development Center and the Procurement Technical Assistance Center, which provide technical and research assistance. Invest Nebraska partners with the state of Nebraska along with other donors to introduce entrepreneurs to individual investors and venture capital firms. Federal and state programs include the Nebraska Investment Finance Authority (NIFA), various Small Business Administration loans, the Nebraska Research and Development Authority, the Small Business Innovation Research Program (SBIR), and the Urban Development Action Grant. Nebraska Advantage is a five-tiered program designed to create new jobs and increase statewide investment.

The state of Nebraska has emphasized its commitment to revitalized economic growth in all parts of the state with a series of laws designed to make the state an even better place to do business. Firms can now earn a series of tax credits and refunds for investment and new job creation through the provisions of the Employment and Investment Growth Act (LB 775), as well as the Employment Expansion and Investment Incentive Act (LB 270), the Enterprise Zone Act (LB 725), the Quality Jobs Act (LB 829), Incentive Electric Rates (LB 828), and the Nebraska Redevelopment Act (LB 830).

*Job training programs:* Community Development Resources (CDR) offers a variety of training and workshops for both profit and nonprofit businesses. For manufacturing firms, the Nebraska Department of Economic Development facilitates a Customized Job Training Program for eligible companies and disperses job training grants. The Nebraska Worker Training Program works to update the skills of existing employees and awards grants quarterly.

## Development Projects

Lincoln's downtown business district continues to thrive and its growth is a critical focus for city planners. They implemented a "Downtown Master Plan," begun in 2004, intended to ensure new construction and renovation while maintaining the natural beauty of the area. Proposals included a civic square with 100,000 square feet of office space and 5,000 square feet of retail space, along with new hotels, conversion of a power station to condominiums, and additional parking structures. Several projects had been completed as of 2007, including a new movie theater and renovation of the Cornhusker Hotel. No completion date had yet been set for the entire project.

2015 Vision is a private organization that seeks to provide a framework and funding for improvements to downtown Lincoln. As of July 2007 the group had received more than $25 million in philanthropic donations to encourage private development; projects were planned on a number of "pillars for Lincoln's future," including the creation of a West Haymarket Arena, the expansion of Haymarket Park, the creation of a "Nebraska Sports Triangle," the development of a Humanities and Art Center near the university, and a retail corridor along P and Q streets.

***Economic Development Information:*** Lincoln Partnership for Economic Development, 1135 M St., Ste. 200, Lincoln, NE 68508; telephone (402)436-2350; Fax (402)436-2360

## Commercial Shipping

Lincoln is connected with national and world markets via the Burlington Northern/Santa Fe railroad; more than thirty motor freight companies; and several national and local air express and freight carriers, including United States Postal Service, UPS, FedEx, Airborne Express, American Courier Corp, and Greyhound Package Express. In total, Nebraska has more than 8,000 licensed motor freight carriers with global connections. Next to the Lincoln Municipal Airport lies a 372-acre Foreign Trade Zone (FTZ) that helps in facilitating imported goods. The city is also conveniently situated within 50 miles of water transportation at Mississippi River terminals.

## Labor Force and Employment Outlook

Lincoln's labor force is described as dependable, productive, and highly skilled and educated. Employers may draw from a large student population. Work stoppages are rare, with unionization estimated around 25 percent. As agriculture declines, more rural laborers are seeking jobs in the city.

A diversified economy has enabled employment in Lincoln to remain resilient since the nationwide recession during the early 2000s. Among non-manufacturing categories, Lincoln has been strong in construction, wholesale and retail trade, and services.

In September 2007 the unemployment rate in Lincoln was 2.7 percent, well below the national average and down from its ten-year high above 4 percent in 2005. Between 1997 and 2007 the Lincoln labor force grew from 151,605 to 167,179.

The following is a summary of data regarding the Lincoln metropolitan area labor force, 2006 annual averages.

**Size of nonagricultural labor force:** 171,000

**Number of workers employed in...**

construction and mining: 8,400
manufacturing: 15,300
trade, transportation and utilities: 29,300
information: 2,700
financial activities: 12,400
professional and business services: 18,500
educational and health services: 23,900
leisure and hospitality: 15,800
other services: 7,400
government: 37,400

**Average hourly earnings of production workers employed in manufacturing:** $15.55

**Unemployment rate:** 3.1% (June 2007)

| *Largest employers (2007)* | *Number of employees* |
|---|---|
| University of Nebraska | 5,100 |
| State of Nebraska | 5,000 |
| Lincoln Public Schools | 5,000 |
| BryanLGH Medical Center | 3,500 |
| Saint Elizabeth Health Systems | 2,800 |
| Kawasaki Motors Manufacturing USA | 1,800 |
| BNSF Railway | 1,600 |
| Madonna Rehabilitation Hospital | 1,300 |
| State Farm Insurance | 1,265 |
| Duncan Aviation | 1,250 |

## Cost of Living

The city of Lincoln boasts a low tax burden with a high quality of services. The following is a summary of data regarding several key cost of living factors in the Lincoln area.

**2007 (1st quarter) ACCRA Average House Price:** Not available

**2007 (1st quarter) ACCRA Cost of Living Index:** Not available

**State income tax rate:** 2.56% to 6.84%

**State sales tax rate:** 5.5%

**Local income tax rate:** None

**Local sales tax rate:** 1.5%

**Property tax rate:** $2.051 per $100 of actual value (consolidated, 2004)

*Economic Information:* Lincoln Partnership for Economic Development, 1135 M St., Ste. 200, Lincoln, NE 68508; telephone (402)436-2350; fax (402)436-2360

# ■ Education and Research

## Elementary and Secondary Schools

The Lincoln Public Schools system is the second largest district in the state of Nebraska. A seven-member, nonpartisan board of education selects a superintendent. Lincoln's students consistently score above the national average on standardized tests, and the system's high school graduation rate is one of the highest in the country at about 80 percent. In 2007 Lincoln High School was named one of the country's "25 Healthiest Schools" by School Nutrition Association and the President's Council on Physical Fitness and Sports. The district is a growing one, reaching record-high enrollments in 2007.

The following is a summary of data regarding the Lincoln Public Schools as of the 2005–2006 school year.

**Total enrollment:** 39,818

**Number of facilities**

    elementary schools: 36
    junior high/middle schools: 11
    senior high schools: 13
    other: 0

**Student/teacher ratio:** 14:1

**Teacher salaries (2005–06)**

    elementary median: $41,260
    junior high/middle median: $39,300
    secondary median: $41,010

**Funding per pupil:** $7,715

The city is served by approximately 30 private and parochial schools.

*Public Schools Information:* Lincoln Public Schools, 5901 O St., Lincoln, NE 68510; telephone (402)436-1000

## Colleges and Universities

The University of Nebraska–Lincoln (UNL), which enrolls approximately 22,000 students (with 18,000 of those being undergraduates), maintains two campuses in Lincoln. Selected as fourth place overall by *The Scientist* on its list of "2004 Best Places to Work in Academia," UNL offers 140 undergraduate (with 275 programs of study) and 112 graduate programs, along with operating a law school and a dental college. The school also boasts the second-highest per capita enrollment of National Merit Scholars in the United States. Two liberal arts colleges, Nebraska Wesleyan University and Union College, schedule courses leading to the baccalaureate degree. Union, which is affiliated with the Seventh-day Adventist church, enrolled 982 students in 2006, who hailed from 46 states and 30 countries; the functioning one-room George Stone School on campus permits education majors to acquire small-class teaching experience. Union offers more than fifty majors in seven academic divisions. Founded in 1887 by Nebraskan Methodists, Wesleyan is comprised of 1,600 students and was chosen in 2005 by *U.S. News and World Report* as the leading liberal arts college in the state of Nebraska. The school has a student-faculty ratio of about 13:1 and an average class size of nineteen.

Technical and vocational schools located in the Lincoln area include Southeast Community College–Lincoln Campus and Hamilton College-Lincoln (formerly The Lincoln School of Commerce). Of historical interest, Charles Lindbergh learned to fly at the Lincoln Airplane and Flying School, though it is no longer in business.

## Libraries and Research Centers

The Lincoln City Libraries system, headquartered downtown, operates seven branches and a bookmobile; it maintains holdings of about 800,000 volumes, more than 2,000 periodical titles, plus microfiche, books on tape, videos, CDs, DVDs, and CD-ROMs. Special collections feature Nebraska authors and sheet music; the library is a depository for state documents. Free Internet access is available. The library also sponsors a literacy program, called Prime Time Family Reading Time.

Union College and Southeast Community College–Lincoln Campus operate campus libraries. The Nebraska Wesleyan University Library has over 135,000 holdings and is also home to a collection of university archives and the United Methodist Heritage Center. Several federal and state agencies maintain libraries in Lincoln; among them are the the Nebraska Game and Parks Commission, the Nebraska Legislative Council, the Nebraska Library Commission, and the Nebraska State Historical Society. The American Historical Society of Germans from Russia, as well as hospitals, churches and synagogues, and corporations, also operate libraries in the city.

The University of Nebraska–Lincoln maintains extensive holdings in eight academic libraries, including a collection of Great Plains art. It is also a center for specialized research; facilities include the Barkley Memorial Center for speech therapy and hearing impaired study, the Engine Technology Center, the Food Processing Center, and the UNL Center for Mass Spectrometry. The Nebraska Technology Development Corporation and the Nebraska Research and Development Authority provide links between research and commercial product development.

***Public Library Information:*** Lincoln City Libraries, 136 S 14th St., Lincoln, NE 68508; telephone (402)441-8500

# ■ Health Care

Bryan LGH Medical Center, with 529 beds and over 4,000 staff members, specializes in cardiac and pulmonary care and rheumatology, oncology, dialysis, and ophthalmology services and operates the BryanLGH College of Health Sciences. Bryan LGH received an Orthopedic Care Award from HealthGrades in 2006, and has also been recognized as the state's only five-time recipient of the Solucient "100 Top Hospitals Award" for excellence in cardiovascular care. Saint Elizabeth Regional Medical Center, with 475 physicians, operates a regional burn care unit and a neonatal care center. The 242-bed non-profit facility was founded Sisters of St. Francis of Perpetual Adoration in 1889. Lincoln is also home to Veterans Administration Medical Center, Madonna Rehabilitation Hospital, nursing homes, nationally recognized substance-abuse services, and several in-home care agencies.

# ■ Recreation

## Sightseeing

The Nebraska State Capitol Building was designed to reflect the spirit of the state of Nebraska; its large square base represents the Plains and its 400-foot tower is meant to convey the dreams of the pioneers. Described as the nation's first state Capitol to be designed to depict the state's cultural heritage and development, the building features an interior enhanced with mosaics, paintings, and murals portraying the history of Nebraska. On the Capitol grounds is Daniel Chester French's sculpture of the seated Abraham Lincoln.

Folsom Children's Zoo and Botanical Gardens presents more than 300 exotic animals from around the world on 19 acres that are lined with 7,000 annual flowers and more than 30 varieties of trees. Antelope Park stretches throughout the city and contains the Sunken Gardens with thousands of flowers, lily pools, and a waterfall. Pioneers Park Nature Center focuses on animals and prairie grasses native to 1850s Nebraska; animal exhibits include deer, elk, red foxes, wild turkeys, and wild buffalo.

Historic houses on view in Lincoln include Kennard House, home of Nebraska's first U.S. secretary of state Thomas P. Kennard; Fairview, residence of William Jennings Bryan; and the governor's mansion, which features a collection of dolls depicting Nebraska's first ladies in their inaugural gowns.

## Arts and Culture

Lincoln is highly rated for the quality of the cultural activities in a city its size. The Lincoln Symphony Orchestra opens its season with a pops concert followed by a subscription series of classical music at Lied Center for Performing Arts, which also hosts performances by Lincoln Midwest Ballet Company. Other local music offerings include the Nebraska Symphony Chamber Orchestra and Abendmusik. Lincoln's Zoo Bar is one of the nation's oldest blues clubs booking touring blues bands and rock artists.

Designed by Phillip Johnson, the Sheldon Memorial Art Gallery is located on the campus of the University of Nebraska and exhibits American art from the eighteenth through the twentieth centuries with an emphasis on the realist tradition and abstract expressionism.

The Museum of Nebraska History exhibits depict Nebraska from prehistoric times through the days of the Native American tribes of the Great Plains and on to pioneer days. The world's largest articulated fossil elephant is on display at the University of Nebraska State Museum's Elephant Hall, which is also home to Mueller Planetarium. The American Historical Society of Germans from Russia Museum traces the history and culture of this ethnic group that settled in Lincoln in the nineteenth century. Lincoln is also home to the National Museum of Roller Skating, Great Plains Art Museum, and the Lincoln Children's Museum.

***Arts and Culture Information:*** Lincoln Arts Council, 920 O St., Lincoln, NE 68508; telephone (402) 434-2787; fax (402)434-2788; email info@artscene.org

## Festivals and Holidays

Held the third weekend in June is Haymarket Heydays, a celebration of the state's railroad heritage that features a street fair, Farmers Market Craft Fair, musical events, and activities for children. July starts off with the bang of Independence Day fireworks at Oak Lake Park after a day of food and fun; later in the month, the July Jamm brings jazz, fine artists, and restaurateurs from around the state for a three-day event. In August, the largest downtown event is the RibFest, sponsored by the Nebraska Pork Producers, which features four days of barbecuing and live music. The Nebraska State Fair draws about 600,000 visitors for 10 days, ending on Labor Day; the fair features national performers of country and rock music, midway rides, livestock shows, and agricultural and industrial exhibits. The Christmas season begins with the parade of the Star City Holiday Festival, a colorful event with floats, giant balloon characters, and costumed participants, held on the first Saturday in December; meanwhile the downtown area is aglow with holiday lights and decorations.

## Sports for the Spectator

When the University of Nebraska Cornhuskers football team plays home games at Lincoln's Memorial Stadium on fall Saturday afternoons, the crowd of nearly 74,000 fans becomes the state's third-largest "city." Nicknamed

Big Red because of its bright red uniforms, the team competes in the Big Twelve conference and had won nine or more games each season and played in a bowl game each season since 1972 until the streak ended with the 2004 season. The University of Nebraska also fields competitive teams in wrestling, volleyball, track and field, and men's and women's basketball.

The Lincoln Capitols of the National Indoor Football League is a minor league team in the Pacific Conference. Playing 13 regular-season games from March through July with home games at the Pershing Center, the team fields players from most of the state colleges and draws talent from across the country. Lincoln is also home to the Lincoln Stars in the western division of the United States Hockey League (USHL) who play at the State Fair Park Coliseum (the "Ice Box"). After winning the championship in the debut season in 1996–1997, they remained one of the league's top teams despite not capturing the Clark Cup again until 2002–2003.

Lincoln is the site of the high school state championships in basketball, wrestling, volleyball, gymnastics, and swimming and diving. Thoroughbred horse racing, with parimutuel betting permitted, takes place at the State Fair Park.

### Sports for the Participant

For sports enthusiasts in Lincoln there are 106 parks on about 6,000 acres, more than 80 miles of bike paths and trails (most are paved), 11 golf courses, 11 outdoor pools, 8 recreation centers, about 65 tennis courts, and surrounding recreation areas totaling 15,000 acres with 10 lakes. Team and league sports for all age levels are also available. The Lincoln Track Club sponsors the Lincoln Marathon and Half Marathon each May. The Cornhusker State Games, attracting nearly 10,000 competitors, features sports such as badminton, biathlon, fencing, tae kwon do, archery, and wrestling. Wilderness Park, Lincoln's largest park, maintains bridle trails, jogging and exercise trails, and cross country ski trails. Holmes Lake and Park is available for non-motorized boating on its large lake; it also features the Hyde Memorial Observatory. The Pioneers Park Nature Center includes five miles of trails. Lincoln is surrounded by the seven Salt Valley Lakes with recreational areas providing opportunities for such pursuits as fishing, camping, and boating.

### Shopping and Dining

The nation's longest straight main street is Lincoln's O Street, which runs all the way through the city; a number of retail centers are located along the route. Antiques, art galleries, and specialty shops are the focus in the Central Business District and Historic Haymarket District, which feature more than 100 restaurants and clubs. Westfield S Gateway Mall is the area's largest enclosed shopping center with several department stores and a children's "Playtown." SouthPointe Pavilions claims 50 stores in its outdoor mall and presents free concerts on Friday nights throughout the summer. Local dining specialties include succulent Nebraska beef, barbecue ribs, and chicken, served at Skeeter Barnes among others, as well as other traditional American fare and ethnic favorites. Many of the national chain restaurants are represented, such as Olive Garden and Red Lobster.

*Visitor Information:* Lincoln Convention & Visitors Bureau, 1135 M St., Ste. 300, Lincoln, NE 68501; telephone (402)434-5335; toll-free (800)423-8212; fax (402)436-2360; email info@lincoln.org

## ■ Convention Facilities

Meeting and convention planners may choose from several major facilities that accommodate a full range of group functions. Pershing Center, located downtown on Centennial Mall, houses an arena with more than 28,000 square feet of exhibit space and a capacity for 200 booths. The arena has eight different floor arrangements with a seating capacity of up to 7,500 guests. Other amenities include concession facilities, catering services, and sound and lighting systems. Devaney Sports Center and Nebraska State Fair Park host trade shows, exhibitions, and athletic events as well as banquets and meetings; ample parking is provided at both sites.

The Burnham Yates Conference Center in Lincoln offers 46,000-plus square feet of meeting room space, and reception, exhibit, and banquet space designed to accommodate up to 1,500 people. It features the latest in meeting space design and a state-of-the-art acoustic system. The center is decorated in the grand style and tradition of The Cornhusker, a Marriott hotel.

Lodging for meeting-goers is available at downtown and metropolitan area hotels and motels offering a total of about 3,000 rooms; several also provide meeting facilities.

*Convention Information:* Lincoln Convention & Visitors Bureau, 1135 M St., Ste. 300, Lincoln, NE 68501; telephone (402)434-5335; toll-free (800)423-8212; fax (402)436-2360; email info@lincoln.org

## ■ Transportation

### Approaching the City

Lincoln Municipal Airport is served by three commercial air carriers with regularly scheduled daily direct and connecting flights from major United States cities as well as points throughout the world. Commuter service is also provided from cities in central and western Nebraska. The airport averages 74 departing flights per week. Amtrak provides railway transportation into Lincoln, and Greyhound provides bus transportation.

An efficient highway system permits easy access into Lincoln. I-80 approaches from the northeast and exits due west; U.S. 6 also bisects the city from northeast to west. U.S. 34 runs northwest to south, in the center of downtown joining U.S. 77, which extends from the south, and joining Nebraska Highway 2, which approaches from the southeast.

## Traveling in the City

Lincoln's streets are laid out on a grid pattern, with lettered streets running east and west and numbered streets running north and south. The main east-west thoroughfare is O Street. Public bus service is provided by StarTran with 60 full-size coaches and 9 vans.

# ■ Communications

## Newspapers and Magazines

Lincoln's daily newspaper is the *Lincoln Journal Star*. Several neighborhood newspapers and shopping guides are distributed weekly.

A number of special-interest magazines are based in Lincoln. The Sandhills Publishing Company publishes four national trade magazines plus *Smart Computing*. The Christian Record Services publishes magazines for blind adults and children and has a lending library as well. *Letras Femeninas* is a journal of contemporary Hispanic literature by women published two times a year in Lincoln; *Prairie Schooner* is a quarterly literary magazine published by the University of Nebraska. Other publications pertain to such subjects as agriculture, medicine, education, college engineering students, outdoor recreation and conservation, Nebraska history, and literature.

## Television and Radio

Several television channels, including a PBS affiliate, a CBS affiliate, and an ABC affiliate, broadcast in the city, which also has cable and receives channels from nearby communities. Over a dozen Lincoln AM and FM radio stations schedule a complete range of musical programming such as rock and roll, classical, country, big band, jazz, blues, and gospel. Lincoln radio listeners can also tune into several Omaha stations.

***Media Information:*** *Lincoln Journal Star*, 926 P St., Lincoln, NE 68508; telephone (402)475-4200; email feedback@journalstar.com

## Lincoln Online

American Historical Society of Germans from Russia. Available www.ahsgr.org

City of Lincoln Home Page. Available www.lincoln.ne.gov

Lincoln Arts Council. Available www.artscene.org

Lincoln Chamber of Commerce. Available www.lcoc.com

Lincoln City Libraries. Available www.lcl.lib.ne.us

Lincoln Convention and Visitors Bureau. Available www.lincoln.org

*Lincoln Journal Star*. Available www.journalstar.com

Lincoln Partnership for Economic Development. Available www.lincolnecdev.com

Lincoln Specialty Care Home Page. Available www.lincoln.specialtycare.org

Nebraska Economic Development Information. Available www.sites.nppd.com

Nebraska State Historical Society. Available www.nebraskahistory.org

State of Nebraska. Available www.nebraska.gov

BIBLIOGRAPHY

Cather, Willa, *The Song of the Lark* (Boston, New York: Houghton Mifflin, 1915)

Keteyian, Armen, *Big Red Confidential: Inside Nebraska Football* (Chicago, IL: Contemporary Books, 1989)

Neihardt, John Gneisenau, *The End of the Dream and Other Stories* (Lincoln, NE: University of Nebraska Press, 1991)

Osborne, Tom, *More Than Winning* (Nashville, TN: T. Nelson, 1985)

# Omaha

## ■ The City in Brief

**Founded:** 1854 (incorporated 1857)

**Head Official:** Mayor Mike Fahey (D) (since 2001)

**City Population**

    1980: 314,255
    1990: 344,463
    2000: 390,007
    2006 estimate: 419,545
    Percent change, 1990–2000: 13.2%
    U.S. rank in 1980: 48th
    U.S. rank in 1990: 48th
    U.S. rank in 2000: 53rd

**Metropolitan Area Population**

    1980: 585,122
    1990: 618,262
    2000: 716,998
    2006 estimate: 822,549
    Percent change, 1990–2000: 16.0%
    U.S. rank in 1980: 57th
    U.S. rank in 1990: Not available
    U.S. rank in 2000: 60th

**Area:** 118.88 square miles (2000)

**Elevation:** ranges from 965 to 1,300 feet above sea level

**Average Annual Temperatures:** January, 22.4° F; July, 75.6° F; annual average, 50.9° F

**Average Annual Precipitation:** 30.08 inches; 31.2 inches of snow

**Major Economic Sectors:** Services, wholesale and retail trade, government, manufacturing

**Unemployment Rate:** 3.6% (June 2007)

**Per Capita Income:** $23,500 (2005)

**2005 FBI Crime Index Property:** 22,056

**2005 FBI Crime Index Violent:** 2,327

**Major Colleges and Universities:** University of Nebraska at Omaha, Creighton University, University of Nebraska Medical Center

**Daily Newspaper:** *The Omaha World-Herald*

## ■ Introduction

Omaha, the seat of Douglas County, is the focus of a metropolitan statistical area that includes Douglas, Sarpy, Cass, and Washington counties in Nebraska and Pottawattamie County in Iowa. The city's development as a railroad center was augmented by the Union Stockyards and the meat-packing industry. Throughout its history Omaha has benefited from the civic commitment of its citizens. Father Edward J. Flanagan's establishment of Boys Town in the Omaha area brought national recognition to the plight of homeless children. Today, Omaha is an insurance and telecommunications center, home to the U.S. Air Force Strategic Command, and notable for its inexpensive housing, good schools, and relatively few social and environmental problems. The downtown is vibrant and growing and the business climate is thriving, as recognized by *Forbes* magazine's nineteenth-place ranking in its "Best City for Business and Careers" list in 2007.

## ■ Geography and Climate

Omaha is located on the bank of the Missouri River and is surrounded by rolling hills. The area's continental climate, which produces warm summers and cold, dry winters, is influenced by its position between two zones: the humid east and the dry west. Low pressure systems crossing the country also affect the weather in Omaha, causing periodic and rapid changes, especially in the winter. An annual average of 31 inches of snow falls during Omaha's winters, which are relatively cold. Sunshine occurs 50 percent of the possible time in the winter and 75 percent in the summer.

**Area:** 118.88 square miles (2000)

**Elevation:** ranges from 965 to 1,300 feet above sea level

**Average Temperatures:** January, 22.4° F; July, 75.6° F; annual average, 50.9° F

**Average Annual Precipitation:** 30.08 inches of rain; 31.2 inches of snow

# ■ History

## Omaha Furthers Westward Expansion

The first people to live in the area surrounding present-day Omaha were the Otoe, Missouri, and Omaha tribes, who roamed and hunted along the Missouri River, which divides Iowa and Nebraska. The Mahas, a Nebraska plains tribe, lived where Omaha now stands. Meriwether Lewis and William Clark, on their mission to chart the Louisiana Purchase, reached the future site of Omaha in the summer of 1804, and held council with Otoe and Missouri Native Americans. As early as the War of 1812, Manuel Lisa established a fur-trading post in the area.

Mormon pioneers set up camp in Florence, a small settlement north of Omaha, in the winter of 1846 to 1847. Six hundred residents died during that harsh winter, and the Mormon Pioneer Cemetery today contains a monument by sculptor Avard Fairbanks that marks the tragedy. Florence, later annexed by Omaha, served for years as a Mormon way station in the westward journey to Utah. Omaha served as the eastern terminus and outfitting center for pioneers headed to the west to find their fortune in the California gold fields or to settle available, inexpensive land.

A rush for land officially began in the area on June 24, 1854, when a treaty with the Omaha Native Americans was concluded. The Council Bluffs & Nebraska Ferry Company, the town's founders, named the new town Omaha, from the Maha word meaning "above all others upon a stream" or "up-river people." When it seemed likely that a Pacific Railroad line was to be constructed out of Omaha, the new town was proposed as the site of the future state capital. The first territorial legislature did meet in Omaha on January 16, 1855. Omaha was incorporated in 1857, but Lincoln was designated the capital when Nebraska was admitted to the Union in 1867.

## Rail Transport Establishes Omaha's Future

The city's early years were full of incidents that prompted the administering of so-called frontier justice, including lynchings, fist and gun fights, and an arbitration body calling itself the Claim Club. Ignoring Federal land laws in favor of local interpretations, the Claim Club went so far as to construct a house on wheels that could be used to protect the claims of people in need of a home to retain possession of the land. The U.S. Supreme Court in later rulings decided not to go against land title disputes made during this colorful but lawless time.

The fortunes of Omaha took a positive turn when President Abraham Lincoln selected Council Bluffs, Iowa, for the terminus of the Pacific Railroad, which was subsequently relocated on Omaha's side of the Missouri River. Actual construction began in 1863, the first step in Omaha's development into one of the nation's largest railroad centers.

The historic trial that gave Native Americans their citizenship took place in Omaha and was decided by Judge Elmer Dundy of the U.S. District Court for Nebraska on May 12, 1879; the case is known as *Standing Bear* v. *Crook*. The Poncas, after accepting a reservation in southeastern South Dakota, decided to return to their homeland. Led by Chief Standing Bear, they were arrested by a detachment of guards sent by Brigadier General George Crook, commander of the Department of the Platte, who was based at Ft. Omaha. General Crook, a veteran fighter in the Indian campaigns, was nonetheless an advocate of fair treatment of Indians. He cooperated fully in the trial, and some evidence indicates he even instigated the suit. Thomas Henry Tibbles, an editor of the *Omaha Daily Herald*, publicized the case nationwide, focusing attention on Omaha and on the humanitarian sentiments of General Crook and himself, an abolitionist-turned-journalist.

## Meatpacking Industry Spurs New Growth

The establishment of the Union Stockyards and the great packing houses in the 1880s invigorated the Omaha economy and drew to the city immigrants from Southern Europe and an assortment of colorful individuals who figured prominently in the city's growth. After a flood in 1881, residents relocated to the other side of the Missouri River, triggering another real estate boom. Fifty-two brickyards were by that time in operation, producing more than 150 million bricks each year. Omaha's first skyscraper, the New York Life Insurance Building (renamed the Omaha Building in 1909), dates from this era.

The Knights of Ak-Sar-Ben (Nebraska spelled backwards), Omaha's leading civic organization, was created in 1895 to promote the city; they organized the Trans-Mississippi and International Exposition in 1898, bringing more than one million people to a city of less than 100,000 in a year-long event. The Omaha Grain Exchange was established at the turn of the century, helping the city develop as a grain market. Agriculture has proved to be the city's economic base, augmented by insurance.

Father Edward J. Flanagan founded Boys Town in the Omaha area in 1917 with 90 dollars he borrowed and with the philosophy that "there is no such thing as a bad boy." This internationally famous boys' home, which was incorporated as a village in 1936, is located west of the city and now provides a home for boys and girls alike. After World War II, Omaha native and aviation pioneer Arthur C. Storz, son of brewing giant Gottlieb Storz, lobbied to have Omaha designated the headquarters of the U.S. Air Force. Today, Omaha's Offutt Air Force Base serves as headquarters of the Strategic Command, or USSTRATCOM.

## Telecommunications Replaces Meatpacking

During the 1980s, while other cities were trying to attract industries, Omaha began a highly successful campaign to attract telecommunications companies. Promoting advantages like cheap real estate, comparatively low wage and cost of living, and its educated and reliable work force, Omaha succeeded to the point that by 1991 its number of telecommunications jobs was more than twice the number of meatpacking jobs. Omaha is also home to several of the nation's largest telemarketers.

## Downtown Growth in the 2000s

Omaha's community leaders have addressed the need for growth within the city by implementing a $2 billion downtown development plan including condominiums and townhouses along with considerable business growth. A new Hilton Hotel accompanies the expansive Qwest Center Omaha that opened in 2003. The commitment to Omaha's healthy business environment is reflected in several recognitions, such as its inclusion on *Entrepreneur* magazine's list of 20 best cities for small business.

***Historical Information:*** Douglas County Historical Society Library/Archives Center, 5730 N. 30 St., #11B, Omaha, NE 68111-1657; telephone (402)451-1013; fax (402)453-9448; email archivist@omahahistory.org

# ■ Population Profile

## Metropolitan Area Residents

1980: 585,122
1990: 618,262
2000: 716,998
2006 estimate: 822,549
Percent change, 1990–2000: 16.0%
U.S. rank in 1980: 57th
U.S. rank in 1990: Not available
U.S. rank in 2000: 60th

## City Residents

1980: 314,255

1990: 344,463
2000: 390,007
2006 estimate: 419,545
Percent change, 1990–2000: 13.2%
U.S. rank in 1980: 48th
U.S. rank in 1990: 48th
U.S. rank in 2000: 53rd

**Density:** 3,370.7 people per square mile (2000)

**Racial and ethnic characteristics (2005)**

White: 288,708
Black: 50,452
American Indian and Alaska Native: 1,944
Asian: 6,971
Native Hawaiian and Pacific Islander: 125
Hispanic or Latino (may be of any race): 39,674
Other: 17,352

**Percent of residents born in state:** 60.1% (2000)

**Age characteristics (2005)**

Population under 5 years old: 27,502
Population 5 to 9 years old: 24,853
Population 10 to 14 years old: 26,202
Population 15 to 19 years old: 24,097
Population 20 to 24 years old: 30,393
Population 25 to 34 years old: 56,428
Population 35 to 44 years old: 52,361
Population 45 to 54 years old: 52,828
Population 55 to 59 years old: 20,781
Population 60 to 64 years old: 16,141
Population 65 to 74 years old: 20,935
Population 75 to 84 years old: 15,416
Population 85 years and older: 5,278
Median age: 34.1 years

**Births (2006, MSA)**

Total number: 13,121

**Deaths (2006, MSA)**

Total number: 5,979

**Money income (2005)**

Per capita income: $23,500
Median household income: $40,484
Total households: 156,292

**Number of households with income of . . .**

less than $10,000: 17,160
$10,000 to $14,999: 9,882
$15,000 to $24,999: 20,932
$25,000 to $34,999: 19,979
$35,000 to $49,999: 25,793
$50,000 to $74,999: 29,380

*©Royalty-Free/Corbis.*

$75,000 to $99,999: 15,782
$100,000 to $149,999: 11,391
$150,000 to $199,999: 2,950
$200,000 or more: 3,043

**Percent of families below poverty level:** 10.3% (2005)

**2005 FBI Crime Index Property:** 22,056

**2005 FBI Crime Index Violent:** 2,327

# ■ Municipal Government

The city of Omaha operates under a mayor-council form of government. The mayor, who does not serve on the council, and seven council members are all elected to four-year terms.

**Head Official:** Mayor Mike Fahey (D) (since 2001; current term expires 2009)

**Total Number of City Employees:** 4,000 (2007)

***City Information:*** Mayor's Office, 1819 Farnam St., Ste. 300, Omaha, NE 68183; telephone (402)444-5000; email mfahey@ci.omaha.ne.us

# ■ Economy

## Major Industries and Commercial Activity

In 2005 Omaha was listed among "America's 50 Hottest Cities" for business expansion by *Expansion Management* magazine. There are more than 20,900 business establishments in the metro area. Omaha is home to five Fortune 500 companies: ConAgra, Peter Kiewit Sons, Berkshire Hathaway, Union Pacific, and Mutual of Omaha. More than 30 other Fortune 500 companies have manufacturing plants in the metropolitan area.

Omaha is an important center for the insurance industry, with a number of companies headquartered in the area. More than half of the approximately two dozen telemarketing/direct response/reservation centers operating in Omaha also have their corporate headquarters located in the metropolitan area. Many other large firms have their headquarters in Omaha, including Lozier Corporation, First Data Corp., ITI Marketing Services, Omaha Steaks International, Pamida, Oriental Trading Company, Valmont Industries, Inc., and Godfather's Pizza, Inc.

The Omaha economy is well diversified, with no industry sector accounting for more than a third of total employment. Omaha's highest concentration of employment is in trade, transportation, and utilities (at nearly 22 percent) with strong showings in education and health services as well as professional and business services. This is offset by a relatively smaller share of total employment in the manufacturing, construction and mining, and information sectors.

**Items and goods produced:** a variety of food items from raw products like meat and flour to finished consumer goods like frozen dinners and cereal; irrigation equipment; phone apparatus; store fixtures; hydraulic motors and pumps; paper boxes and packaging materials; furniture; computer components

## Incentive Programs—New and Existing Companies

*Local programs:* Assisting in the expansion of new and existing businesses at the local level are the Small Business Council, the Omaha Small Business Network, Inc., and the Omaha Regional Minority Purchasing Council. Among other finance programs are community development block grants, improvement financing, industrial development revenue bonds, and a range of local and state tax credits.

*State programs:* Qualified Omaha businesses can take advantage of state and local programs such as the Nebraska Business and Development Center and the Procurement Technical Assistance Center, which provide technical and research assistance. Invest Nebraska partners with the state of Nebraska along with other donors to introduce entrepreneurs to individual investors and venture capital firms. Federal and state programs include the Nebraska Investment Finance Authority (NIFA), various Small Business Administration loans, the Nebraska Research and Development Authority, the Small Business Innovation Research Program (SBIR), and the Urban Development Action Grant. Nebraska Advantage is a five-tiered program designed to create new jobs and increase statewide investment.

The state of Nebraska has emphasized its commitment to revitalized economic growth in all parts of the state with a series of laws designed to make the state an even better place to do business. Firms can now earn a series of tax credits and refunds for investment and new job creation through the provisions of the Employment and Investment Growth Act (LB 775), as well as the Employment Expansion and Investment Incentive Act (LB 270), the Enterprise Zone Act (LB 725), the Quality Jobs Act (LB 829), Incentive Electric Rates (LB 828), and the Nebraska Redevelopment Act (LB 830).

*Job training programs:* Community Development Resources (CDR) offers a variety of training and workshops for both profit and nonprofit businesses. For manufacturing firms, the Nebraska Department of Economic Development facilitates a Customized Job Training Program for eligible

companies and disperses job training grants. The Nebraska Worker Training Program works to update the skills of existing employees and awards grants quarterly.

## Development Projects

As of 2007 over $2 billion dollars had been invested in downtown Omaha for the ongoing Riverfront Development project. Work began in 1999 on the 33-block redevelopment area. The spring of 2004 saw the debut of the $66 million, 450-room Hilton Hotel that is attached to the Qwest Center Omaha by an elevated walkway. Work began in 2006 on the $22 million Missouri River pedestrian bridge. Upon its scheduled completion in late 2008, the bridge was expected to be one of the largest of its kind in the world. In 2007 a new baseball stadium, intended to host the College World Series, was awaiting taxpayer approval.

The North Omaha Development Project, begun in 2006, is a plan for the economic development of the area, with a focus on attracting private investors. In 2007 more than $750,000 dollars of philanthropic donations had been committed to the project. Destination Midtown, a similar project, was begun in 2003 to help encourage private investment and commercial development. Proposed changes in the 3.6-mile area included transportation improvements/traffic flow management.

*Economic Development Information:* Economic Development Council, Greater Omaha Chamber of Commerce, 1301 Harney St., Omaha, NE 68102; telephone (402)346-5905; toll-free (800)852-2622

## Commercial Shipping

More than 135 million pounds of cargo passed through Eppley Airfield in 2006. An international point of entry with access to a Foreign Trade Zone, it is served by eight air freight carriers. The Union Pacific and several other major railroads provide freight service that is coordinated with many of the trucking companies serving the metropolitan area.

## Labor Force and Employment Outlook

The Omaha labor force is described as highly productive, possessing an old-fashioned work ethic, and lacking a regional accent, so workers are considered excellent for the phone operations and high-technology jobs proliferating there. In 2005 Omaha was ranked among the top 25 cities for "Best Educated Workforce" by *Business Facilities*. However, the workforce does suffer from wage rates that are well below the national average.

In September 2007 the unemployment rate stood at 3.1 percent, below the national average and down from ten year highs topping 5 percent in 2005. Between 1997 and 2007 the labor force in the Omaha metropolitan statistical area grew from 409,771 to 450,944.

The following is a summary of data regarding the Omaha-Council Bluffs NE-IA metropolitan area labor force, 2006 annual averages.

**Size of nonagricultural labor force: 458,600**

**Number of workers employed in ...**

construction and mining: 26,900
manufacturing: 32,900
trade, transportation and utilities: 99,300
information: 12,900
financial activities: 37,900
professional and business services: 62,900
educational and health services: 65,300
leisure and hospitality: 43,200
other services: 16,500
government: 60,800

**Average hourly earnings of production workers employed in manufacturing: $17.05**

**Unemployment rate: 3.6% (June 2007)**

| *Largest employers (2007)* | *Number of employees* |
| --- | --- |
| Offutt Air Force Base | Not available |
| Alegent Health | Not available |
| Omaha Public Schools | Not available |
| Methodist Health System | Not available |
| First Data Corp. | Not available |
| First National Bank | Not available |
| Union Pacific Corporation | Not available |
| University of Nebraska Medical Center | Not available |
| Mutual of Omaha Insurance | Not available |
| The Nebraska Medical Center | Not available |

## Cost of Living

The following is a summary of data regarding several key cost of living factors in the Omaha area.

**2007 (1st quarter) ACCRA Average House Price: $255,321**

**2007 (1st quarter) ACCRA Cost of Living Index: 89.1**

**State income tax rate: 2.56% to 6.84%**

**State sales tax rate: 5.5%**

**Local income tax rate: None**

**Local sales tax rate: 1.5%**

**Property tax rate:** $1.85460 to $2.39067 per $100 of assessed valuation (2004)

**Economic Information:** Greater Omaha Chamber of Commerce, 1301 Harney St., Omaha, NE 68102; telephone (402)346-5000; fax (402)346-7050; email info@omahachamber.org

# ■ Education and Research

## Elementary and Secondary Schools

Omaha Public Schools district is the largest elementary and secondary public education system in Nebraska. A nonpartisan, twelve-member board of education appoints a superintendent. Approximately sixty percent of high-school graduates in the district pursue post-secondary education. District teachers boast an average of 11.7 years of experience and 43 percent hold advanced degrees. The district offers a "school choice" program. There are magnet schools options at the elementary, junior, and high school levels, for students interested in mathematics, technology, the arts, and international studies. Several magnet schools also offer programs in Spanish.

The following is a summary of data regarding the Omaha Public Schools as of the 2005–2006 school year.

**Total enrollment: 136,081**

**Number of facilities**

elementary schools: 60
junior high/middle schools: 11
senior high schools: 8
other: 5

**Student/teacher ratio: 14.8:1**

**Teacher salaries (2005–06)**

elementary median: $44,460
junior high/middle median: $44,880
secondary median: $42,040

**Funding per pupil: $7,486**

An extensive parochial school system as well as a number of private schools provide complete curricula, including religious instruction, for students in kindergarten through twelfth grade. The most notable private institution is Boys Town, a residential facility founded in 1917 as the "city of little men" by Father Edward J. Flanagan.

**Public Schools Information:** Omaha Public Schools, 3215 Cuming St., Omaha, NE 68131-2024; telephone (402)557-2222

## Colleges and Universities

The University of Nebraska at Omaha, with an enrollment of 15,000 students, awards graduate and undergraduate degrees in nearly 200 fields, including business, chemistry, engineering, social work, criminal justice, elementary education, and fine and dramatic arts. Affiliated with the university is the University of Nebraska Medical Center, which offers programs at all degree levels from associate to doctorate in areas that include dental hygiene, dentistry, medical technology, medicine, nuclear medicine technology, nursing, pharmacy, physical therapy, physician's assistant, radiation technology, and radiological technology.

Awarding associate through doctorate degrees, Creighton University is one of 28 Jesuit institutions nationwide. The private institution has colleges of arts and sciences and business administration and schools of law, nursing, pharmacy and allied health, dentistry, medicine, and graduate study and an annual enrollment of more than 6,500 students. Creighton was ranked first among master's-level institutions in the Midwest by *U.S. News and World Report* in 2008. Opened in 1943, Grace University is a private school with some 500 enrollees. Among the colleges located in the Omaha area are the College of Saint Mary (a Catholic women's college with approximately 1,000 attendees) and Metropolitan Community College (with 27,179 credit students and 17,333 non-credit students). Area vocational schools offer specialized and technical training.

### Libraries and Research Centers

The Omaha Public Library operates a main downtown facility, the W. Dale Clark Library (built in 1976), and ten branches while also providing services for the hearing- and visually-impaired. With holdings of approximately 800,000 volumes, plus videos, music cassette tapes, and compact discs, the library is also a depository for federal and state documents. The library maintains several special digital collections, including "TransMiss Expo of 1898," "Nebraska Memories," and "Early Omaha." Extensive main and departmental libraries are located on the campuses of all colleges and universities in the city. The University Library at the University of Nebraska at Omaha consists of 700,000 print volumes, over 2,300 print subscriptions, music recordings, videos, and extensive electronic holdings. Special collections include the Arthur Paul Afghanistan collection. Other libraries in Omaha are associated with government agencies, corporations, hospitals, religious groups, arts organizations, and the local newspaper.

Research centers affiliated with Omaha-area colleges and universities conduct studies in such fields as cancer, allergies, gerontology, human genetics, and neonatology. Founded in 1960, the Eppley Institute for Research in Cancer and Allied Diseases is funded by the National Cancer Institute and housed at the University of Nebraska Medical Center. It conducts research programs in biochemistry, biology, chemistry, immunology, nutrition, pathology, pharmacology, and virology.

***Public Library Information:*** Omaha Public Library, 215 S 15th St., Omaha, NE 68102; telephone (402)444-4800; email webdesk@omaha.lib.ne.us

## ■ Health Care

The health care industry is one of Omaha's largest employers. The city is a center for medical education and research, with medical schools at Creighton University and the University of Nebraska Medical Center, a dental school, and a number of schools of nursing.

St. Joseph Hospital is the teaching hospital for the Creighton University School of Medicine, specializing in renal dialysis, metabolic research, cardiac diagnosis and treatment, and cancer care. Adjacent to St. Joseph is the Boys Town National Research Hospital, a national diagnostic, treatment, and research facility for children with hearing, speech, or learning disorders. Boys Town serves about 36,000 patients each year. The University of Nebraska Medical Center, the teaching hospital for the University of Nebraska School of Medicine, operates units for pediatric cardiology, cancer therapy, and high-risk newborn care, and a pain rehabilitation institute. The Medical Center also includes centers for women's health and genetics. Alegent Health's Lakeside Hospital opened in fall 2004 and is a 45-bed acute care facility. The facility has been dubbed a "smart hospital," which means that it has all wireless technology, a filmless/paperless environment and a cutting edge all-digital diagnostic center.

## ■ Recreation

### Sightseeing

Omaha received national attention when the Hollywood movie "Boys Town," starring Spencer Tracy and Mickey Rooney, was released in 1938. Today Tracy's Academy Award Oscar is on display in the Hall of History Museum on the Boys Town campus. The Hall traces the history of the country's most famous institution for the care of home-less children, presenting exhibits on the history of juvenile delinquency and of social programs designed to address it.

The PhilaMatic Museum exhibits stamp, coin, and currency collections for the hobbyist. General Crook House, a restored Victorian house on the grounds of Ft. Omaha, was the home of General George Crook, head of the Army of the Platte, who gained fame for his testimony in the trial of Chief Standing Bear. The Gerald Ford Birthplace, an outdoor park and rose garden, contains a replica of the home where former President Ford was born as well as memorabilia from his White House years and is often used for weddings.

The U.S. Air Force Strategic Air Command Museum, located in nearby Ashland, charts the history of the United States Air Force in indoor and outdoor exhibits; the $29.5-million museum displays more than thirty vintage and modern airplanes year round, in addition to four missiles. The Henry Doorly Zoo attracts about 1.6 million visitors annually. Species include rare white Siberian tigers. The zoo's aviary is the second largest in the world with 500 exotic species, and its indoor rain forest is the world's largest. The Lied Jungle at the zoo, winner of *Time* magazine's 1992 design award, was described by the magazine as "architecturally stupendous...and zoologically thrilling." It features a half-mile maze of trails offering views of exotica such as Malayan tapirs and pygmy hippos in an authentic rain forest atmosphere. In 2002 an indoor desert, the world's largest, was constructed and features plant and animal life from deserts in Africa, Australia, and the United States. The Mutual of Omaha Wild Kingdom wildlife pavilion presents the theme of animal adaptation for survival. Ak-Sar-Ben Aquarium, the only aquarium between Chicago and the West Coast, is open year-round and exhibits 50 species of fresh-water fish.

The Mutual of Omaha Dome exhibits memorabilia from the Mutual of Omaha's "Wild Kingdom" television program; the Dome is an underground facility topped by a large glass dome. Completely redesigned, the Union Pacific Railroad Museum at the Union Pacific Railroad's headquarters building traces the history of the company's railroad.

Twenty-five miles north of Omaha, the 7,800-acre DeSoto Bend National Wildlife Refuge offers opportunities in the spring and fall to view thousands of migrating birds that use the Missouri Valley flyway for their seasonal migration. Fontenelle Forest in North Bellevue is a 1,300-acre sylvan area within the city. Peony Park, Nebraska's largest amusement park, combines amusement park rides, shows in an outdoor amphitheater, and the state's largest swimming pool.

## Arts and Culture

Omaha Community Playhouse, founded in 1924, is one of the nation's largest and most recognized community theaters—whose alumni include Henry Fonda and Dorothy McGuire—and schedules year-round productions. Main-stage productions as well as studio and experimental theater are presented in what is physically the largest amateur theater facility in the country. Omaha Theater Company for Young People is a professional company offering original adaptations of classic children's literature.

The Omaha Symphony plays a season of classical, pop, and chamber music; and Opera Omaha sponsors three productions annually. Incorporated in 2000, the Omaha Chamber Music Society performs a summer concert series along with monthly "Music at Midday"

concerts. The Tuesday Musical Concert Series brings internationally-known classical musicians to the Holland Performing Arts Center.

The Joslyn Art Museum, built in 1931 in honor of business leader George Joslyn, is an Art Deco facility on three levels that houses a permanent collection emphasizing European, American, and Western art. The Durham Western Heritage Museum is housed in the restored Union Station depot. The museum charts the city's history from pioneer days to the 1950s and features a vintage soda fountain manned by volunteer soda jerks. The Great Plains Black History Museum chronicles the contributions and achievements of African Americans in the Midwest. Designed for children to interact with the exhibits, the Omaha Children's Museum features art projects that complement the displays. John Raimondi's *Dance of the Cranes* at Eppley Airfield, the largest bronze sculpture in North America, is a five-story, 15-ton sculpture depicting sandhill cranes in a ritual dance.

## Festivals and Holidays

Omaha sponsors festivals and special indoor and outdoor events year round. The major cultural institutions of the city host many of these festivals in honor of the city's heritage. During the second weekend in February a softball tournament held throughout the city raises money for the March of Dimes. In mid-March Triumph of Agriculture Exposition, one of the largest farm equipment shows in the world, draws participants to the Qwest Convention Center.

Nearly 200 artists and crafters are featured at the Summer Arts Festival, held at the Gene Leahy Mall for three days in late June. The Nebraska Shakespeare Festival is presented outdoors in Elmwood Park on weekends through June and July. In August the Offutt Air Force Base open house and air show enjoys the participation of the 55th Strategic Reconnaissance Wing. The Omaha Federation of Labor sponsors Septemberfest in honor of Omaha's working men and women over Labor Day weekend at the Qwest Center. This is also when La Festa Italiana brings music, dance, and food to a celebration at Roncalli High School.

Ak-Sar-Ben Rodeo and Livestock Exposition in October is the world's largest 4-H livestock show; the rodeo attracts the nation's top rodeo competitors. Dickens in the Market takes place the first weekend in December at Old Market and features costumed entertainers performing holiday music and vignettes of Charles Dickens' novels.

## Sports for the Spectator

Omaha hosts the National Collegiate Athletic Association (NCAA) college baseball World Series each June at Rosenblatt Stadium. The Omaha Royals, the Triple-A farm team of professional baseball's American League Kansas City Royals, play their home season at Rosenblatt Stadium. Bluffs Run in Council Bluffs offers greyhound dog racing with individual televisions in the clubhouse for viewing each race.

Late-model stock car racing takes place at Little Sunset Speedway at the I-80 Speedway from May through October. College sports are played by the Creighton Bluejays and the University of Nebraska at Omaha Mavericks; the Mavericks rank high among the nation's most competitive wrestling teams. In 2008 the city is scheduled to play host to the U.S. Olympic Trials in swimming.

### Sports for the Participant

The Omaha Parks and Recreation Department administers more than 200 city parks on 8,300 acres of land, two ice arenas, 14 neighborhood recreation centers, and various recreational leagues. The most popular is the summer softball program; Omaha claims the title of "Softball Capital of the World" with approximately 2,500 teams and 60 fields. The metropolitan area boasts around 50 golf courses and nearly 20 public pools along with several private pools, outdoor and indoor tennis courts, and facilities for hockey and ice skating. One downhill skiing facility operates in nearby Crescent, Iowa, though the area's relative flatness lends well to cross-country skiing trails at Elmwood Park and N.P. Dodge Park.

### Shopping and Dining

Omaha's Old Market in its earliest days was a warehouse district where pioneers purchased the goods they needed for the journey to the West. In 1968 Old Market began renovation, first converting to an artists' colony; today it is a thriving shopping and restaurant district as well as a fruit and vegetable marketplace. A number of downtown locations have been renovated into malls as part of the revitalization of Omaha's downtown commercial district. The Crossroads Mall and Oak View Mall both house around 100 stores. Omaha claims the largest independent jewelry store in the United States. Possibly the city's most visited store is the Nebraska Furniture Mart, which records the nation's largest volume of furniture sales.

Some of the best beefsteaks in the world are served in Omaha restaurants; the city is also noted for catfish caught in the Missouri River, and for Continental, French, East Indian, and Creole cuisine. *Food and Wine* magazine named Omaha's Le Cafe de Paris a "Distinguished Restaurant of North America." "Runza," a dough pocket filled with ground beef and cabbage, is a local specialty served at Runza Hut. Godfather's Pizza, one of the largest pizza chains in the country, originated in Omaha.

***Visitor Information:*** Greater Omaha Convention & Visitors Bureau, 1001 Farnam-on-the-Mall., Ste. 200, Omaha, NE 68102; telephone (402)444-4660; toll-free (866)937-6624; fax (402)444-4511

## ■ Convention Facilities

Centrally located downtown, within easy access of sightseeing, entertainment, shopping, dining, and lodging, the Omaha Civic Auditorium is a popular site for regional events as well as national conventions, trade shows, and meetings. The main exhibition hall, with 43,400 square feet of space, can be partitioned into separate meeting rooms. The Omaha Civic Auditorium seats up to 9,300 for sporting events and 10,960 for concerts. The multipurpose, 25,000-square-foot convention hall, providing space for 176 booths, hosts banquets and large meetings.

In 2003 the Qwest Center Omaha debuted with its 194,000-square-foot exhibition hall (that can be divided into three separate spaces) and 17,000-seat arena. Set on 422 acres and highlighted by a 31,000-square-foot ballroom, the center also has 12 meeting rooms with seating ranging from 71 to 503 guests. The Qwest Center connects to the 450-room Hilton Omaha.

The Peter Kiewit Conference Center, located in the new mall area, is operated by the College of Continuing Studies of the University of Nebraska at Omaha. Accommodations at the 192,000-square-foot facility include an auditorium with a seating capacity of more than 500 people, 18 meeting rooms for groups of 5 to 500 people, dining and catering service, and teleconferencing and computer access. Additional convention and meeting facilities are available at two clusters of hotels at 72nd and Grover streets and 108th and L streets; some of these, including the Holiday Inn Convention Center, offer a selection of meeting rooms for functions involving from 35 to 1,800 participants. There are over 10,000 hotel rooms in Omaha.

***Convention Information:*** Greater Omaha Convention & Visitors Bureau, 1001 Farnam St., Ste. 200, Omaha, NE 68102; telephone (402)444-4660; toll-free (866)937-6624; fax (402)444-4511

## ■ Transportation

### Approaching the City

The terminal at Eppley Airfield, four miles northeast of downtown Omaha, is served by twenty-two jet service air carriers and one commuter air carrier with direct flights to twenty cities and connecting flights to points throughout the world. Located on 2,650 square feet of land, it served 4.2 million passengers in 2006. Several general aviation airports in the metropolitan area are open to the public.

Principal highway routes providing access to the Omaha metropolitan area are I-80 and I-29; U.S. 6, 30, 75, and 275; and Nebraska 36, 38, 50, 64, 85, 92, 131, 133, and 370.

## Traveling in the City

Omaha's streets are arranged in a grid pattern, with Dodge Street dividing the city into north and south sectors. Streets running north-south are numbered; east-west streets are named. Public bus transportation is provided by Metro Area Transit (MAT), which operates routes in Omaha, Council Bluffs, Bellevue, Papillion, Ralston, Boys Town, Carter Lake, La Vista, and Northeast Sarpy County. MAT schedules morning and evening express service; reduced fares for students and senior and handicapped passengers are available.

# ■ Communications

## Newspapers and Magazines

Omaha's daily newspaper is *The Omaha World-Herald,* published daily. Several special-interest newspapers and magazines are also published in Omaha. Among them are *The Catholic Voice* and *Jewish Press.* The weekly *Midlands Business Journal* presents local business information on a weekly basis.

## Television and Radio

Television stations broadcasting from Omaha include affiliates of CBS, Fox, PBS, ABC, and NBC; two additional channels are received from Lincoln. Several companies supply cable television service to the metropolitan area. Radio programming that includes a range of musical formats such as rock, classical, jazz, and religious, as well as educational, information, and news features, is provided by the more than thirty AM and FM stations available in Omaha.

*Media Information:* *Omaha World-Herald,* 1334 Dodge St., Omaha, NE 68102; telephone (402)444-1000

## Omaha Online

City of Omaha Home Page. Available www.ci .omaha.ne.us

Greater Omaha Chamber of Commerce. Available www.accessomaha.com

Omaha Convention and Visitors Bureau. Available www.visitomaha.com

Omaha by Design community development home page. Available www.livelyomaha.org

Omaha Public Library. Available www.omaha.lib .ne.us

Omaha Public Schools. Available www.ops.org

*Omaha World-Herald.* Available www.omaha.com

BIBLIOGRAPHY

Crary, Margaret, *Susette La Flesche: Voice of the Omaha Indians* (New York: Hawthorn Books, 1973)

Larsen, Lawrence H., and Barbara J. Cottrell, *The Gate City: A History of Omaha* (Lincoln, NE: University of Nebraska Press, 1997)

Menard, Orville D., *Political Bossism in Mid America: Tom Dennison's Omaha, 1900–1933* (Lanham, MD: University Press of America, 1989)

# North Dakota

# The State in Brief

**Nickname:** Flickertail State; Sioux State; Peace Garden State

**Motto:** Liberty and Union, now and forever, one and inseparable

**Flower:** Wild prairie rose

**Bird:** Western meadowlark

**Area:** 70,699 square miles (2000; U.S. rank 19th)

**Elevation:** Ranges from 750 feet to 3,506 feet above sea level

**Climate:** Continental, with a wide variety of temperatures; brief, hot summers; winter blizzards; semi-arid in the west and 22 inches average rainfall in the east

**Admitted to Union:** November 2, 1889

**Capital:** Bismarck

**Head Official:** Governor John Hoeven (R) (until 2008)

## Population

1980: 653,000
1990: 638,800
2000: 642,200
2006 estimate: 635,867
Percent change, 1990–2000: 0.5%
U.S. rank in 2006: 48th
Percent of residents born in state: 71.05% (2006)
Density: 9.2 people per square mile (2006)
2006 FBI Crime Index Total: 13,532

## Racial and Ethnic Characteristics (2006)

White: 578,919
Black or African American: 5,999
American Indian and Alaska Native: 33,219
Asian: 4,348
Native Hawaiian and Pacific Islander: 241
Hispanic or Latino (may be of any race): 9,332
Other: 4,775

## Age Characteristics (2006)

Population under 5 years old: 39,094
Population 5 to 19 years old: 129,629
Percent of population 65 years and over: 14.6%
Median age: 37.1

## Vital Statistics

Total number of births (2006): 8,380
Total number of deaths (2006): 5,886
AIDS cases reported through 2005: 140

## Economy

Major industries: Agriculture, manufacturing, mining
Unemployment rate (2006): 3.3%
Per capita income (2006): $22,619
Median household income (2006): $41,919
Percentage of persons below poverty level (2006): 11.4%
Income tax rate: 2.1% to 5.54%
Sales tax rate: 5.0%

# Bismarck

## ■ The City in Brief

**Founded:** 1871 (incorporated 1875)

**Head Official:** Mayor John Warford (since 2002)

**City Population**

    1980: 44,485
    1990: 49,256
    2000: 55,532
    2006 estimate: 58,333
    Percent change, 1990–2000: 11.1%
    U.S. rank in 1980: Not available
    U.S. rank in 1990: 527th
    U.S. rank in 2000: 620th

**Metropolitan Area Population**

    1980: 54,811 (Burleigh County)
    1990: 83,831 (MSA)
    2000: 94,719 (MSA)
    2006 estimate: 101,138
    Percent change, 1990–2000: 13.0%
    U.S. rank in 1980: Not available
    U.S. rank in 1990: Not available
    U.S. rank in 2000: 260th

**Area:** 27.0 square miles (2000)

**Elevation:** 1,700 feet above sea level

**Average Annual Temperatures:** January, 10.2° F; July, 70.4° F; annual average, 42.3° F

**Average Annual Precipitation:** 16.84 inches of rain; 44.3 inches of snow

**Major Economic Sectors:** Services, trade, transportation, energy, government

**Unemployment Rate:** 3.2% (June 2007)

**Per Capita Income:** $20,789 (1999)

**2005 FBI Crime Index Property:** 1,488

**2005 FBI Crime Index Violent:** 51

**Major Colleges and Universities:** Bismarck State College, University of Mary, University of North Dakota School of Medicine, United Tribes Training College

**Daily Newspaper:** *The Bismarck Tribune*

## ■ Introduction

Bismarck, the capital of North Dakota, seat of Burleigh County, and part of the metropolitan statistical area that also includes Mandan, is known as the hub city for the Lewis and Clark Trail. Since the time that Meriwether Lewis and William Clark explored the region's rolling plains in 1804–1805, the Bismarck region has remained a center for outdoor adventures, from hiking and canoeing to mountain biking and boating, offering some of the finest fishing and hunting opportunities in the country. It is also recognized as the region's business, cultural, and financial center.

## ■ Geography and Climate

Bismarck is located on the east bank of the Missouri River in south-central North Dakota. It is situated on butte-like hills overlooking the river, and lies within one of the country's leading wheat-producing areas. North Dakota's climate is continental and fairly uniform throughout; the Bismarck region is temperate with moderate rainfall. Winters are long and severe; summers are short but favorable for agriculture because of the long hours of sunshine.

**Area:** 27.0 square miles (2000)

**Elevation:** 1,700 feet above sea level

**Average Temperatures:** January, 10.2° F; July, 70.4° F; annual average, 42.3° F

**Average Annual Precipitation:** 16.84 inches of rain; 44.3 inches of snow

# ■ History

## Crossing on the Missouri Exploited by Indians, Whites

Long before white settlement of the Northern Plains began, a natural ford on the site of present-day Bismarck was known to Plains Indian tribes as one of the narrowest and least dangerous crossings on the Missouri River. Stone tools and weapons found in the vicinity indicate that the area was used thousands of years ago by prehistoric big-game hunting tribes. By the time white explorers arrived in the 1700s, those tribes had been displaced by the Mandan and Hidatsa peoples. Unlike nomadic Plains tribes, the Mandan and Hidatsa built fortified towns, raised cultivated plants in settled communities in and around present-day Bismarck, and developed a thriving Northern Plains trading hub.

The Mandan were among the first people on the Plains to be contacted by whites, and relations between them were generally friendly. The first recorded visitor was French explorer Pierre Gaultier de Varennes, Lord de La Verendrye, who discovered Mandan earthen lodges in present-day Bismarck in 1738 while searching for a water route to the Pacific Ocean. Most subsequent contact was with Canadian fur traders, until Lewis and Clark camped with the Mandan in 1804–1805. In the 1820s and 1830s, American traders out of St. Louis, Missouri, began to ply the Missouri River in steamboats and an outpost of the American Fur Company was established near Bismarck. Contact with white traders and white diseases proved nearly fatal to the Mandan; in 1837, the tribe was virtually destroyed by smallpox. By that time, a small white settlement had been established at present-day Bismarck called Crossing on the Missouri, and it thrived in a small way as a port for steamboats carrying military troops and supplies to forts and Indian agencies in the Missouri River basin.

## Dakota Territory Opened; Railroad and Gold Spur Settlement

The U.S. Congress organized the Dakota Territory in 1861 (originally consisting of the two present-day Dakotas plus parts of Montana and Wyoming), but white settlement did not begin in earnest until the indigenous tribes had been expelled. In 1871-1872, squatters who anticipated the arrival of Northern Pacific Railway tracks settled at the Crossing on the Missouri. In 1872, Camp Greeley (later Camp Hancock), a military post, was established nearby to protect the railroad crews, and in June 1873, the railroad reached the crossing. It carried

printing presses for the *Bismarck Tribune,* which published its first edition in July 1873; today it is North Dakota's oldest newspaper still publishing. The paper scored its greatest scoop when it was first to publish the story of Custer's last stand at the Little Big Horn in Montana in 1876. Bismarck mourned the loss of Custer and his men, who often left their post at nearby Fort Abraham Lincoln to join in the social life of the town. In 1881 Mandan, Bismarck's sister city, was established across the Missouri River just north of Fort Lincoln.

In 1873, the settlement was renamed Bismarck in honor of the first chancellor of the German Empire. Germans had previously invested in American railroads, and it was hoped that Germany would invest in the financially ailing Northern Pacific. Bismarck's first church service was organized in 1873 by distinguished citizen, author, and suffragette Mrs. Linda Warfel Slaughter, who also started the first school, became the first county school superintendent, and organized the Ladies Historical Society. Bismarck was incorporated in 1875 and began to grow as a steamboat port and, until 1879, as the western terminus of the Northern Pacific Railway. The town attracted rivermen and wood choppers, who supplied personnel and fuel needs for riverboats.

Life in the little town was rugged. River traffic closed in the winter because of low water, and the railroad discontinued operating out of Fargo, North Dakota, into Bismarck until spring, when Bismarck residents might look forward to the flooding of the river. Fires were frequent, thanks to poorly constructed, flimsy homes, tents, and rough wooden buildings lit by kerosene lamps.

In 1874, gold was discovered in the Black Hills of South Dakota. Bismarck experienced its first boom as gold seekers poured in to outfit themselves for the 200-mile trip to Deadwood, South Dakota. Some stayed to take advantage of new business opportunities.

As railroad tracks were laid across America, word spread to the East and to Europe of the rich land of the Plains, suitable for growing wheat and grazing livestock. Men and women came to break the virgin soil and to build sod houses, barns, frame houses, and windmills. Those who settled around Bismarck suffered considerably when the Missouri River flooded in 1881; livestock drowned, homes were destroyed, and wildlife were carried down the river on ice floes. Bismarck residents who lived on higher ground were more fortunate. In 1882, Northern Pacific built a bridge across the Missouri River at Bismarck. While the trains would no longer have to cross the river on barges in the summer and on tracks laid over the ice in the winter, the event marked the end of Bismarck's prominent position as a center for railroad freight transfers.

## City Becomes Center for Dakota Government

In 1882 Bismarck replaced Yankton, South Dakota, as the capital of the Dakota Territory, and a second boom began. The price of land skyrocketed, and everyone believed that Bismarck was on its way to becoming a major population center. It was with high hopes that the cornerstone of the capitol building was laid in 1883 in a gala ceremony that included many prominent figures of the day. Some attendees, such as ex-President U.S. Grant, were members of the Golden Spike Excursion, on their way west to mark the completion of the Northern Pacific Railway. Others present at the ceremony included U.S. congressmen, foreign noblemen, and the Sioux chief Sitting Bull. Despite high hopes for rapid change, Bismarck grew steadily but slowly. Federal and state government offices emerged and it became a center for shipping wheat to Minneapolis. Other businesses flourished, including flour mills, creameries, grain elevators, and the innovative Oscar H. Will Company, specialists in seed corn like that used by the Mandan Indians, as well as several varieties of hardy, drought-resistant plants.

When the Dakota Territory was divided and North and South Dakota entered the Union in 1889, Bismarck became the capitol of North Dakota. As the town developed politically, new buildings went up, including schools, churches, and frame houses to replace sod shanties. By 1890, 43 percent of the population was foreign-born, and mostly comprised of Russians, Germans, Norwegians, Canadians, English, Irish, and Swedes. In 1898 the Northern Pacific freight depot caught fire; the fire spread and destroyed most of downtown Bismarck. However, citizens rallied and the town was quickly rebuilt.

The population around Bismarck swelled in 1903 when thousands of German farmers moved from Wisconsin and began producing dairy products, wool, honey, and corn, all of which were shipped out of Bismarck. In 1909 the Bureau of Indian Affairs opened an Indian boarding school in Bismarck. By 1910 the population had risen to 4,913 people; by 1920 the population was 7,122; and by 1930 it reached 11,090. The population increase was mostly due to farmers moving into town to retire or to look for schools for their children. A drought and an invasion of hordes of grasshoppers in the 1930s destroyed wheat crops and intensified the need to diversify farming in the region.

In December 1930, with the Great Depression and the drought under way, the old capitol building burned down and talk turned to moving the capitol elsewhere. By a popular statewide vote in 1932, it was decided to keep Bismarck as the capital. On October 8, 1932, the cornerstone was laid for a new statehouse.

## Manmade Changes Usher in the Modern Era

Bismarck farmers and ranchers benefited from the 1947 construction of the Garrison Dam, 75 miles up the Missouri River. It lessoned spring flood danger, but the project remains controversial. Local Indian tribes claim that land was taken from them for the massive project, and environmentalists decry the loss of the natural shortgrass land and the flooding of countless acres of bottomland. The project was headquartered at Fort Lincoln, and attracted new residents to Bismarck. Sister projects like the Heart Butte Dam and the Dickinson Dam opened up new recreational opportunities to Bismarckers. By 1950, over 18,540 people called Bismarck home.

In 1951, oil was discovered near Tioga, North Dakota. Although it was flowing from wells 200 miles away, it led to the formation of state agencies and oil company offices in Bismarck, and the city became a center for oil leasing activities. Bismarck continued to cope with floods and droughts, but farms thrived because of improved farming methods. Bismarck's population soared to 27,670 people in 1960. During that decade, attention turned to soil and wildlife preservation and water conservation, and new office buildings, a junior college, a conservatory of music, and highways were constructed. Construction continued into the 1970s, when shopping centers and homes were built, and prospects for Bismarck's growth and prosperity looked bright.

Today Bismarck is the center of North Dakota state government and home to an impressive historical museum as well as several colleges, including a unique intertribal college owned and operated by five Native American tribes. A thriving medical, transportation and trade center, Bismarck boasts amenities typically found in much larger cities.

Famous or notorious former residents of Bismarck include poet James W. Foley, author of the official state song and several books including *Prairie Breezes*; Alexander McKenzie, politician, friend of the railroads, and the man credited with moving the Dakota Territory capital to Bismarck; the French-born Marquis de Mores, who hoped to establish a huge meat packing industry in the Badlands, was tried three times in a sensational murder case and found not guilty, and founded the town of Medora, North Dakota, named in honor of his wife; former President Theodore Roosevelt, who owned a cabin in town from 1883 to 1885 when he was a rancher in the Badlands; and General E.A. Williams, first representative from Burleigh County to the Territorial Assembly.

***Historical Information:*** State Historical Society of North Dakota, State Archives & Historical Research Library, Heritage Center, Capitol Grounds, 612 East Boulevard Avenue, Bismarck, ND 58505-0830; telephone(701)328-2666; fax (701)328-3710

# ■ Population Profile

## Metropolitan Area Residents

  1980: 54,811 (Burleigh County)
  1990: 83,831 (MSA)
  2000: 94,719 (MSA)

The North Dakota State Capitol building in Bismarck. ©*iStockPhoto.com*

2006 estimate: 101,138
Percent change, 1990–2000: 13.0%
U.S. rank in 1980: Not available
U.S. rank in 1990: Not available
U.S. rank in 2000: 260th

## City Residents

1980: 44,485
1990: 49,256
2000: 55,532
2006 estimate: 58,333
Percent change, 1990–2000: 11.1%
U.S. rank in 1980: Not available
U.S. rank in 1990: 527th
U.S. rank in 2000: 620th

**Density:** 2,065.2 people per square mile (2000)

## Racial and ethnic characteristics (2000)

White: 52,634
Black: 156
American Indian and Alaska Native: 1,884
Asian: 251
Native Hawaiian and Pacific Islander: 15
Hispanic or Latino (may be of any race): 415
Other: 95

**Percent of residents born in state:** 77.4% (2000)

## Age characteristics (2000)

Population under 5 years old: 3,356
Population 5 to 9 years old: 3,431
Population 10 to 14 years old: 3,790
Population 15 to 19 years old: 4,308
Population 20 to 24 years old: 4,380
Population 25 to 34 years old: 7,339
Population 35 to 44 years old: 8,842
Population 45 to 54 years old: 7,815
Population 55 to 59 years old: 2,545
Population 60 to 64 years old: 2,084
Population 65 to 74 years old: 3,888
Population 75 to 84 years old: 2,631
Population 85 years and older: 1,123
Median age: 36.5 years

## Births (2006, MSA)

Total number: 1,267

## Deaths (2006, MSA)

Total number: 680

## Money income (1999)

Per capita income: $20,789

Median household income: $39,422
Total households: 23,163

**Number of households with income of . . .**

less than $10,000: 2,065
$10,000 to $14,999: 1,682
$15,000 to $24,999: 3,255
$25,000 to $34,999: 3,337
$35,000 to $49,999: 4,102
$50,000 to $74,999: 4,910
$75,000 to $99,999: 2,129
$100,000 to $149,999: 1,102
$150,000 to $199,999: 286
$200,000 or more: 295

**Percent of families below poverty level:** 9.4% (1999)

**2005 FBI Crime Index Property:** 1,488

**2005 FBI Crime Index Violent:** 51

# ■ Municipal Government

The city of Bismarck operates under the commission form of government. Four commissioners and a president (who also serves as mayor) are elected at large to four-year terms. The commission meets regularly on the second and fourth Tuesday of each month.

**Head Official:** Mayor John Warford (since 2002; current term expires 2010)

**Total Number of City Employees:** 490 (full-time; 2007)

*City Information:* City/County Office Building, 221 N. 5th Street, P.O. Box 5503, Bismarck, ND 58506-5503; telephone (701)222-6471; fax (701)222-6470

# ■ Economy

## Major Industries and Commercial Activity

Bismarck has a strong, diversified economy that has been continually expanding since the 1980s. As the capital city of North Dakota, it serves as a major hub for government, business and finance; it is also a major distribution center for the agricultural industry. Services and retail trade continue to dominate the local market, together employing more than 50 percent of the non-agricultural workforce.

The state government is Bismarck's largest employer with more than 4,300 workers as of 2007. The health care industry is the second largest industry; MedCenter One and St. Alexius hospitals and their related clinics employ more than 4,200 people. Bismarck Public Schools and the North Dakota federal offices each employ more than 1,000 people.

**Items and goods produced:** energy (coal, natural gas), food and food products, heavy equipment

## Incentive Programs—New and Existing Companies

*Local programs:* Interest buydowns, reduced interest loans, grants, exemptions, and other financial incentives are available through the Bismarck Vision Fund. Other local sources of funding include micro-loan programs that provide short-term loans of $15,000 to $25,000 with a bank turndown at standard bank rates; the Bismarck Loan Pool, a group of local lending institutions and utilities; Bismarck Industries, Inc., which offers supporting participation in construction or leasing of buildings and equipment purchase; and the Small Business Investment Company, a private investment firm that uses its own funds plus money backed by federal Small Business Administration guarantees to make capital investments in small businesses. The Bismarck-Mandan Development Association can help new and expanding companies negotiate preferred terms or grants from local service providers.

*State programs:* North Dakota is the only state in the nation to control its own development bank. The Bank of North Dakota (BND) arranges financing for the MATCH program, aimed at attracting financially strong companies to North Dakota via loans and low interest rates. The BND also administers the Business Development Loan Program, for new and existing business with higher risk levels; and the PACE fund, which targets community job development. The North Dakota Development Fund provides "gap financing" to primary sector businesses. The SBA 504 Loan Program offers long-term, fixed asset financing in partnership with private lenders; the borrower provides 10 percent in cash equity. The SBA 7(a) Loan Program is available to small businesses unable to obtain financing in the private credit marketplace.

*Job training programs:* Job Service North Dakota administers state- and federally-funded workforce training programs including customized training, on-the-job training, occupational upgrading and Workforce 2000 employee training. The North Dakota New Jobs Training Program provides incentives to businesses that create new employment opportunities in the state. Bismarck State College and the University of Mary are both recognized for meeting the needs of Bismarck-area business and industry; both institutions offer scholarships and grants for expanding businesses requiring employee training.

## Development Projects

The Capital Area Transit fixed-route public bus system was launched in May 2004. In 2005 the city of Bismarck opened a $25 million airport terminal; the state-of-the-art facility incorporates high ceilings and glass walls in an "open spaces" concept designed to complement its prairie setting. In 2007 the city of Bismarck announced plans to develop an intermodal rail service for the Northern Plains Commerce Center.

***Economic Development Information:*** Bismarck/Mandan Chamber of Commerce, 2000 Schafer Street, Bismarck, ND 58501; telephone (701)223-5660; fax (701)255-6125

## Commercial Shipping

The city of Bismarck lies at the intersection of Interstate 94 and U.S. Highway 83. Bismarck is served by Burlington Northern Santa Fe Railroad Company and Dakota, Missouri Valley, and Western Rail. Air freight service is available at the Bismarck Airport.

## Labor Force and Employment Outlook

Employment in Bismarck is provided by state and federal government, energy companies, trade, transportation, and health services. Growing fields include data processing and customer service. Statewide, agriculture and tourism are top industries.

The 2007 Bismarck-Mandan Labor Study reported high workforce productivity and credited a well-educated population combined with a Midwest work ethic. The local workforce is also considered loyal and dependable; 89 percent of employers report daily absenteeism below 6 percent and the average length of employment is 8.75 years.

The following is a summary of data regarding the Bismarck metropolitan area labor force, 2006 annual averages.

**Size of nonagricultural labor force:** 58,700

**Number of workers employed in ...**

   construction and mining: 3,500
   manufacturing: 3,000
   trade, transportation and utilities: 12,200
   information: 1,200
   financial activities: 3,100
   professional and business services: 5,900
   educational and health services: 10,100
   leisure and hospitality: 5,300
   other services: 2,800
   government: 11,600

**Average hourly earnings of production workers employed in manufacturing:** Not available

**Unemployment rate:** 3.2% (June 2007)

| Largest employers | Number of employees |
|---|---|
| State of North Dakota | 4,309 |
| Medcenter One Health Systems | 2,500 |
| St. Alexius Medical Center | 2,129 |
| Bismarck Public School District | 1,658 |
| ND Federal Offices | 1,198 |
| BOBCAT/Ingersoll-Rand | 1,130 |
| City of Bismarck | 790 |
| MDU Resources Group | 748 |
| Aetna | 570 |
| University of Mary | 520 |
| Dan's Supermarkets | 517 |

## Cost of Living

Bismarck-Mandan ranks consistently high in quality of life surveys. Bismarck ranked second in a Harvard University study of "community attitudes and civic engagement." North Dakota consistently has the lowest crime rate in the nation in most categories of crime.

The following is a summary of data regarding several key cost of living factors for the Bismarck area.

**2007 (1st quarter) ACCRA Average House Price:** Not available

**2007 (1st quarter) ACCRA Cost of Living Index:** 93.8

**State income tax rate:** 2.1% to 5.54%

**State sales tax rate:** 5.0%

**Local income tax rate:** None

**Local sales tax rate:** 1.0%

**Property tax rate:** 483.72 mills per $1,000 (2003)

***Economic Information:*** Bismarck-Mandan Chamber of Commerce, 2000 Schafer Street, P.O. Box 1675, Bismarck, ND 58502-1675; telephone (701)223-5660; fax (701)255-6125

# ■ Education and Research

## Elementary and Secondary Schools

The Bismarck Public School system is the largest school district in the state. In the 2006–07 school year the dropout rate was only 1.95 percent and average daily attendance was 96.7 percent. Special education and early learning opportunities are offered in both private and public schools. Several local schools have earned the national honor of being designated "Blue Ribbon Schools." Bismarck Public School District has been recognized year after year for meeting the needs of families in the national "What Parents Want" competition; the annual survey honored just 16 percent of public school districts in the country in 2005.

The following is a summary of data regarding the Bismarck Public Schools as of the 2005–2006 school year.

**Total enrollment:** 15,206

**Number of facilities**

elementary schools: 15
junior high/middle schools: 3
senior high schools: 2
other: 3

**Student/teacher ratio:** 14.6:1

**Teacher salaries (2005–06)**

elementary median: $40,280
junior high/middle median: Not available
secondary median: $36,910

**Funding per pupil:** $7,013

Nearly 2,000 students in the greater Bismarck area are served by the region's secular and religious private schools.

***Public Schools Information:*** Bismarck Public Schools, 806 North Washington, Bismarck, ND 58501; telephone (701)355-3000; fax (701)355-3001

## Colleges and Universities

Bismarck State College (BSC) is a two-year college offering more than 30 vocational and technical programs. Bismarck State College students may also take their first two years towards a bachelor's degree in arts or sciences. Medcenter One College of Nursing accepts students in their junior year for a two-year bachelor's degree focusing on general nursing science, clinical practice and research. Minot State University offers four-year degree programs in its three schools: the College of Arts and Sciences, the College of Business and the College of Education and Health Sciences. The University of North Dakota (UND) is North Dakota's most comprehensive research university. As of 2006 there were 12,834 students enrolled in both undergraduate and graduate levels. The University of North Dakota (UND) Graduate Center offers master's programs in such fields as education, business administration, social work, and public administration; students can enroll in online, evening, and weekend classes. The UND School of Medicine offers a four-year doctor of medicine degree. As of 2006, approximately 20 percent of the working American Indian doctors in the United States trained at UND through the Indians Into Medicine (INMED) program.

The University of Mary is a private Christian school offering four-year degrees in 34 programs, as well as graduate degrees in nursing, management, education,

and physical therapy. In 2007 the University added a new graduate program for a professional degree in occupational therapy. St. Alexius Medical Center is home of the North Dakota School of Respiratory Care and St. Alexius School of Radiologic Technology. Both programs are part of collaboration between the medical center and the University of Mary. The United Tribes Technical College is a unique intertribal college, owned and operated by five Native American tribes. The college offers 10 associate degree programs and certificates in 10 other areas, as well as adult education and on-site daycare. In 2007 the United Tribes Medical Center agreed to be an outlet for a new Nike shoe named the "Air Native," which was to be marketed specifically to Native Americans.

## Libraries and Research Centers

As of 2007, the Bismarck Veterans Memorial Public Library had 195,421 books, 684 magazine subscriptions, 6,607 audiotapes and compact discs, 6,608 videotapes and DVDs, and 262 miscellaneous items ranging from artwork to fishing poles. Approximately 16,450 of these items were added to the library in 2006 when the collection was updated. The library building is 70,000 square feet in size and underwent construction from 1988–1998, which cost $5.1 million dollars. Its bookmobile collection includes over 2,000 fiction and nonfiction works and travels approximately 7,000 miles each year throughout the county. A U.S. government document depository, the library has special collections on Northern Missouri River history and the Lewis and Clark Expedition.

The North Dakota State Library on the Capitol grounds specializes in state government publications. The State Historical Society of North Dakota Library houses the official state archives. It has special collections on anthropology and the history of the Northern Great Plains, as well as archaeological artifacts. In 2007 the Historical Society opened a Public Death Index through the department of Health website, which allows individuals to find and order copies of death certificates.

Other major libraries in Bismarck are the Bismarck State College Library, which has 55,000 book titles and specializes in North Dakota history; the University of Mary's Welder Library, which holds 70,000 volumes; and the Q & R MedCenter One Health Sciences Library, which specializes in clinical medicine and nursing.

***Public Library Information:*** Bismarck Public Library, 515 N. Fifth St., Bismarck, ND 58501; telephone (701)222-6410

## ■ Health Care

St. Alexius Medical Center was opened in 1885 by a group of Benedictine Sisters and was the first hospital in Dakota Territory. The 289-bed facility serves the

Bismarck area as well as central and western North Dakota, northern South Dakota and eastern Montana. In 2007 the Alexian brothers Hospital Network, the hospital system to which St. Alexius belongs, teamed with the Institute of Healthcare Improvement in a campaign to save 100,000 lives through the implementation of enhanced patient safety measures. Medcenter One Health Systems offers a range of services, including 9 primary care clinics, a home health agency, 3 long-term care facilities, and a 238-bed hospital. The two institutions have combined resources to offer state-of-the-art cancer care at the Bismarck Cancer Center. The health system received the Distinguished Service Award in 2007 form the North Dakota Healthcare Association for supporting the Smith Gate Clinic, the only pediatric burn clinic in Iraq.

# ■ Recreation

## Sightseeing

Visitors to the grounds of the North Dakota State Capitol, also known as the "Skyscraper on the Prairie," can tour the building and also enjoy the arboretum trail that winds among various state buildings and features 75 species of trees, shrubs, and blooming flowers. Also on site is a statue of Sacajawea, the Indian woman who accompanied Lewis and Clark on their expedition through Bismarck. The statue of the guide was erected by the North Dakota Federation of Women's Clubs in 1910. Nearby, the North Dakota Heritage Center, the most comprehensive of the state's museums, houses one of the largest collections of Plains Indian artifacts in the United States. Also open for tours is the Historic Governor's Mansion that served as the governor's residence from 1893 to 1960.

Docked at the historic Port of Bismarck, the *Lewis & Clark* riverboat offers paddlewheel cruises of the Missouri River. Open daily from April through October (and only weekends in the winter season), the Dakota Zoo is home to more than 125 species of birds, reptiles, and mammals. As of 2007 there were over 600 individual animals in residence at the North Dakota Zoo. Camp Hancock State Historic Site includes an interpretive museum of military life and local history in its original log building, an early Northern Pacific Railroad locomotive, and Bismarck's first Episcopal church. Double Ditch Indian Village State Historic Site displays the ruins of a Mandan Indian earthlodge village inhabited from years A.D. 1500–1781. The restored Fort Lincoln Trolley offers a unique scenic rail trip from Bismarck to Fort Abraham Lincoln State Park.

Fort Abraham Lincoln houses the reconstructed home of General George Custer. Visitors can view a staff performance set in Custer's time, visit the soldiers' central barracks, and shop at the commissary store. In 2004 the Fort Abraham Lincoln Foundation, which manages the fort, built a 7th cavalry stable. The hill above the fort provides panoramic views of the Missouri Valley. On-a-Slant Indian Village displays replicas of Indian earth lodges on the site of an ancient Mandan village. An on-site museum contains Native American and military artifacts. Visitors to Fort Abraham Lincoln State Park can experience the Custer Trail Ride and explore the panoramic views from bluffs overlooking the Missouri River.

The Lewis & Clark Interpretive Center, 35 miles north of Bismarck in Washburn, provides a view of what life was like on the trail for the explorers, and features the world-famous artwork of Karl Bodmer, who chronicled Plains Indian life and local river landscapes. The center is managed by the USDA Forest Service and the 25,000-square-foot building includes the permanent exhibit hall, 158-seat theater, an education room for hands-on curriculum-based activities, and a retail store.

North Bismarck's Gateway to Science offers hands-on exhibits that provide learning opportunities for visitors of all ages. The museum hosts an annual Environmental Festival which invites fifth grade classes from across the state to learn about environmental issues. The Railroad Museum, north of nearby Mandan, has on view hand-made models, photographs, and uniforms, and offers miniature train rides. Located just a few miles east of Bismarck, Buckstop Junction contains reconstructed buildings that date back to the 1800s and early 1900s. Visitors can tour a mining camp complete with a coal mine, gas shovel, scale house, and mine buildings.

Bismarck is about 130 miles east of the South Unit of Theodore Roosevelt National Park and is a stopping-off point for visitors to that monument to the 26th President of the United States.

## Arts and Culture

A primary venue for the performing arts in Bismarck is the Belle Mehus Auditorium, which is on the National Register of Historic Places. Built in 1914, the auditorium hosts performances of the Bismarck-Mandan Symphony Orchestra and the Northern Plains Ballet, one of the state's fastest growing performing arts organizations. In 2007 the Northern Plains Ballet was named the official host of the Nickelodeon Worldwide Day of Play, a joint venture between the American Heart Association and the William J. Clinton Foundation to encourage children to exercise.

Sleepy Hollow Summer Theatre offers live performances and classes. The Shade Tree Players is a children's theater group offering summer productions. The Bismarck/Mandan area is also home to the North Dakota Association of Dance and Drill and to the Dakota West Arts Council, the area's arts umbrella agency.

***Arts and Culture Information:*** Bismarck-Mandan Symphony Orchestra, P.O. Box 2031, Bismarck, ND 58502; telephone (701)258-8345

## Festivals and Holidays

September is a festive month in Bismarck. The city hosts one of the nation's largest Native American cultural events—the annual United Tribes International Pow Wow. More than 70 tribes are represented at this award-winning festival, which features 1,500 dancers and drummers and draws 30,000 spectators. Also in September is the Annual International Indian Art Expo, which highlights Native American artists and provides traditional song, music, dance, and storytelling. The Folkfest Celebration takes place over four days in September, with a parade, carnival, street fair, book festival, tractor pull, walking and running events, and plenty of food. Bismarck Marathon, North Dakota's only major marathon, is also held in September and attracts runners from around North America.

The highlight of October is the Edge of the West PRCA Rodeo, featuring the nation's toughest rough stock and champion cowboys. Month's end brings the Children's All-City Halloween Party. December begins with the annual Fantasy of Lights Parade, featuring lighted holiday floats. Sertoma Park is the site of the Christmas In The Park display of lighted trees. Fort Abraham Lincoln State Park hosts Custer Christmas; guests can tour General Custer's home decorated for the holidays and celebrate the season with sleigh rides and a buffalo burger buffet.

July events include Frontier Army Days at Fort Abraham Lincoln State Park, featuring a look at the lives of the ladies of the frontier army, as re-enactors cook and launder and hold cavalry and artillery drills. The annual Mandan Rodeo Days celebration also takes place in July, with more than 100 artist booths, ethnic food, music, a carnival, and a petting zoo.

August is the month for the Bismarck Art & Galleries Association annual art fair on the State Capitol Grounds. Also in August, the Fur Trader Rendezvous at Fort Abraham Lincoln features demonstrations of fire starting, toolmaking, rifle marksmanship, and dancing.

The Bismarck Civic Center hosts a number of annual events, including the Bismarck Tribune Sport Show in February, the Spring Blossoms Craft Fair in May, the Missouri River Festival in June, and the Monaco International Motorcoach Event in August.

The Bismarck-Mandan Symphony League, a volunteer organization, schedules festive fundraisers throughout the year, such as Holiday Home Walk and Wild n' Wooly Wing Ding, which has received two national awards from the American Symphony Orchestra League as one of the six most unique and effective fundraisers in the nation.

## Sports for the Spectator

The Bismarck Bobcats bring exciting North American Hockey League action to the VFW Sports Center. The Dakota Wizards, a team in the NBA Development League, play basketball at the Bismarck Civic Center.

## Sports for the Participant

Bismarck has an outstanding parks and recreations system that includes bicycle and skate parks, an archery range, baseball diamonds, boat ramps, jogging and exercise tracks, hockey and figure skating rinks, all-season arenas, racquetball courts, swimming pools, tennis courts, and soccer fields. There are seven golf courses in the area.

With its location on the Missouri River in the North Central Flyway, the Bismarck-Mandan area offers some of the best fishing and hunting opportunities available in North America. Nineteen of North Dakota's 23 game fish species are found in the Missouri River. Some of the best natural areas of the relatively unaltered habitat left on the Missouri River system are just upstream and downstream from Bismarck-Mandan. The habitat is home to abundant upland and big game. Pheasant, grouse, partridge, dove, white-tailed deer and many other non-game species of birds and animals are available for picture taking, observing, and hunting. Other activities enjoyed in the Bismarck area include camping, curling, gymnastics, horseshoes, cross-country skiing, go-cart racing, and downhill skiing.

## Shopping and Dining

Bismarck-Mandan is the retail hub for south-central North Dakota, a retail trade area that includes nearly 170,000 people. Downtown Bismarck offers more than 70 stores, as well as art galleries and antique shops. Kirkwood Mall features more than 100 specialty stores and 5 major department stores. Other malls include Arrowhead Plaza, Northbrook Shopping Center, Gateway Mall, and Upfront Plaza.

The historic Burlington Northern Railroad Depot on Main Street in Mandan is home to Native American arts and crafts. Works of more than 200 North Dakota American Indian artists are available for purchase.

A variety of dining establishments can be found in Bismarck, from the Captains Table Restaurant, boasting one of the largest menus in the upper Midwest, to Space Aliens restaurant, which promises "out of this world food," to the Fiesta Villa, where south-of-the-border food is served in Bismarck's historic Spanish mission-style depot. Other restaurants feature hot buffets, Italian food, regional beef and prime rib, and seafood.

***Visitor Information:*** Bismarck-Mandan Convention and Visitors Bureau, 1600 Burnt Boat Drive, Bismarck, ND 58503; toll-free (800)767-3555

# ■ Convention Facilities

The Bismarck Civic Center features 16 meeting rooms, 84,000 square feet of exhibit space, and arena seating for 10,000 in two separate but connected buildings. The Pavilion at Prairie Knights Casino and Resort seats 2,000 and offers 34,000 square feet of meeting and exhibit space. The Mandan Community Center is a full-service recreation and convention center. Bismarck-Mandan also has more than 2,600 rooms in 30 hotels and motels.

***Convention Information:*** Bismarck-Mandan Convention and Visitors Bureau, 1600 Burnt Boat Drive, Bismarck, ND 58503; telephone (800)767-3555

# ■ Transportation

## Approaching the City

The Bismarck Airport has daily commercial service via Northwest, United Express, Big Sky, and Allegiant airlines to Minneapolis, Denver, and Las Vegas. The airport is served by three major national auto rental chains. Rimrock Stages provides bus service in the area.

## Traveling in the City

The Capital Area Transit System, known as the CAT, serves the Bismarck-Mandan area. The Bis-Man Transit Board offers Greyhound bus service, a Taxi 9000 on-demand service, and an elderly and handicapped transit system. A restored trolley car that once ran in Bismarck now offers a unique trip to Fort Abraham Lincoln State Park.

# ■ Communications

## Newspapers and Magazines

*The Bismarck Tribune,* North Dakota's oldest newspaper still publishing, appears every morning. Other newspapers published in Bismarck are the biweekly *Farm and Ranch Guide,* and the monthly *Dakota Catholic Action.*

Magazines published in Bismarck include the monthlies *Enterprise Connection,* a business publication; *Dakota Country,* which promotes hunting and fishing; *North Dakota Stockman;* and *Vintage Guitar,* which focuses on the hobby of guitar playing. *North Dakota Outdoors,* a natural resources magazine, is issued ten times per year. *The Sunflower,* a magazine for sunflower producers, is issued six times per year. Locally published quarterlies include *North Dakota Horizons,* a consumer magazine of North Dakota lifestyles and *North Dakota*

*History,* which focuses on the history and culture of North Dakota and the Great Plains.

## Television and Radio

Bismarck has six television stations—four network stations, one public station, and one community access station. The city is also served by three AM radio stations and six FM stations.

***Media Information:*** *Bismarck Tribune,* P.O. Box 5516, Bismarck, ND 58506; telephone (701)223-2500; fax (701) 223-2063

## Bismarck Online

Bismarck-Mandan Chamber of Commerce. Available www.chmbr.org

Bismarck-Mandan Convention & Visitors Bureau. Available www.bismarckmandancvb.com

Bismarck-Mandan Development Association. Available www.bmda.org

Bismarck Public Schools. Available www.bismarck .k12.nd.us

*The Bismarck Tribune.* Available www .bismarcktribune.com

City of Bismarck Home Page. Available www .bismarck.org

North Dakota State Library. Available www.ndsl.lib .state.nd.us

State Historical Society of North Dakota. Available www.state.nd.us/hist

Theodore Roosevelt National Park. Available www .nps.gov/thro

BIBLIOGRAPHY

Bird, George F., and Edwin J. Taylor, Jr., *History of the City of Bismarck North Dakota: The First 100 Years 1872-1972,* (Bismarck, ND: Bismarck Centennial Association, 1972)

Rogers, Ken, Allison Hawes Bundy, Laura Seibel, eds., *Bismarck by the River* (Bismarck, ND: The *Bismarck Tribune,* 1997)

# Fargo

## ■ The City in Brief

**Founded:** 1871 (incorporated 1875)

**Head Official:** Mayor Dennis Walaker (since 2006)

**City Population**
> 1980: 61,383
> 1990: 74,084
> 2000: 90,599
> 2006 estimate: 90,056
> Percent change, 1990–2000: 22.3%
> U.S. rank in 1980: 329th
> U.S. rank in 1990: 297th
> U.S. rank in 2000: 302nd

**Metropolitan Area Population**
> 1980: 137,574
> 1990: 153,296
> 2000: 174,367
> 2006 estimate: 187,001
> Percent change, 1990–2000: 13.7%
> U.S. rank in 1980: Not available
> U.S. rank in 1990: Not available
> U.S. rank in 2000: 179th

**Area:** 38 square miles (2000)

**Elevation:** 900 feet above sea level

**Average Annual Temperatures:** January, 6.8° F; July, 70.6° F; annual average, 41.5° F

**Average Annual Precipitation:** 21.19 inches of rain; 40.8 inches of snow

**Major Economic Sectors:** Wholesale and retail trade, services, government

**Unemployment Rate:** 3.2% (June 2007)

**Per Capita Income:** $26,596 (2005)

**2005 FBI Crime Index Property:** 2,348

**2005 FBI Crime Index Violent:** 104

**Major Colleges and Universities:** North Dakota State University

**Daily Newspaper:** *The Forum*

## ■ Introduction

Fargo is the largest city in North Dakota and the seat of Cass County. It is the focus of a metropolitan statistical area that extends over Cass County, North Dakota, and Clay County, Minnesota, where Fargo's sister city, Moorhead, is located. Founded by the Northern Pacific Railway, the city was an important transportation and marketing point for the surrounding fertile wheat-growing region. Today it is an agribusiness and agricultural research center. *Money* magazine consistently ranks Fargo among the nation's most livable small cities, noting that it is a safe city and a "booming regional center for health care and financial services." The city has been declared a "Great Plains success story, with locally grown high-tech firms and a state university" by *Kiplinger's Personal Finance* magazine.

## ■ Geography and Climate

Flat and open terrain surrounds Fargo, which is situated on the eastern boundary of North Dakota opposite Moorhead, Minnesota, in the Red River Valley of the North. The Red River, part of the Hudson Bay drainage area, flows north between the two cities. Precipitation is generally Fargo's most significant climatic feature. The Red River Valley lies in an area where lighter amounts of precipitation fall to the west and heavier amounts to the east. Seventy-five percent of the precipitation, accompanied by electrical storms and heavy rainfall, occurs during the growing season, April to September. Summers are comfortable, with low humidity, warm days, and cool nights. Winters are cold and dry, the temperatures remaining at zero or below approximately half of the time; snowfall is generally light. The legendary Dakota blizzards result from drifting of even minimal snowfall, caused by strong winds that blow unimpeded across the flat terrain.

**Area:** 38 square miles (2000)

**Elevation:** 900 feet above sea level

**Average Temperatures:** January, 6.8° F; July, 70.6° F; annual average, 41.5° F

**Average Annual Precipitation:** 21.19 inches of rain; 40.8 inches of snow

# ■ History

### Railroad Route Creates Townsite

The city of Fargo was founded by the Northern Pacific Railway in 1871 in expectation of the railroad track to be built across the Red River of the North. This particular location was selected as a safeguard against flooding because it represented the highest point on the river. The city was named for William G. Fargo, founder of the Wells-Fargo Express Company and a director of the Northern Pacific Railway. When the railroad announced in 1871 that a track would be laid from Lake Superior to the Pacific Ocean, land speculators sought to capitalize on the opportunity. Attempts ensued on the part of both the railroad and the speculators to outwit one another and gain first possession of the land. For a time the railroad staked a claim but after much litigation decided to withdraw.

During the winter of 1871 to 1872, the settlement was divided into two distinct communities. The first, "Fargo on the Prairie," became the headquarters of the Northern Pacific engineers and their families. Although they lived in tents, the accommodations were the best available given the conditions. The other, "Fargo in the Timber," was much cruder and more primitive, consisting of huts, log houses, dugouts, and riverbank caves. The Timber community became known for its hard-drinking, gun-carrying men who had a rough sense of humor and enjoyed practical jokes. A delivery of potatoes to the Prairie community was once sabotaged by the Timber men, who loosened the wagon endgates and shot their guns to scare the horses. The potatoes that spilled onto the ground turned out to be the only supply available for the winter.

Fargo was located in what was still legally Native American territory, and the railroad company claimed the Timber residents were illegal squatters on Native

American land and were selling illegal liquor. In February of 1872, federal troops surrounded the Timber settlement, issuing warrants for the arrest of those accused of selling liquor and ordering the others to leave under threat of destruction of their crude homes. The settlers appealed to the government, claiming their land rights had been violated. A treaty was negotiated with the native tribes that opened the land to settlement, and those who had not broken the law were able to retain their land.

### Agricultural Prosperity Survives Disasters

Law and order followed with the arrival of new settlers on the first train of the Northern Pacific to cross the Red River in June of 1872. Residents were surprised to learn that Fargo was situated on rich wheat land. With the reduction of freight rates in 1873, farming became economically profitable and the town prospered. Two decades later Fargo suffered a severe fire, which began on one of the main streets and consumed the entire business district as well as the northwestern sector. This tragedy led to many civic improvements and put an end to wood construction.

Near disaster struck again four years later, when the Red River, dammed by ice north of Fargo, began to rise. It continued rising for a week; in order to save the railroad bridges, locomotive and threshing machines were placed on them. Citizens were forced to evacuate through second-story windows, and the flood carried away 18 blocks of sidewalk and 20 blocks of wooden street paving.

During the first 30 years of the twentieth century, Fargo prospered from an influx of Norwegian immigrants who were attracted by the promise of a better life and a free farm. Fleeing economic depression in their own country, they introduced their customs to the upper Red River Valley, thus helping to shape the character of present-day Fargo. The city remains an important agricultural center as well as a regional distribution and transportation hub.

Due to its affordable housing, workforce availability, high standards of living and education, and low unemployment rate, in 2004 *Expansion Management* magazine awarded Fargo a "Five Star Community" rating in its annual "Quality of Life Quotient."

***Historical Information:*** North Dakota State University Library, North Dakota Historical Manuscript, Photograph, and Book Collection, 1301 12th Ave. North, PO Box 5599, Fargo, ND 58105; telephone (710)231-8886

# ■ Population Profile

### Metropolitan Area Residents

1980: 137,574
1990: 153,296

*Photo courtesy of the Fargo-Moorhead Convention and Visitors Bureau.*

2000: 174,367
2006 estimate: 187,001
Percent change, 1990–2000: 13.7%
U.S. rank in 1980: Not available
U.S. rank in 1990: Not available
U.S. rank in 2000: 179th

**City Residents**

1980: 61,383
1990: 74,084
2000: 90,599
2006 estimate: 90,056
Percent change, 1990–2000: 22.3%
U.S. rank in 1980: 329th
U.S. rank in 1990: 297th
U.S. rank in 2000: 302nd

**Density:** 2,388.2 people per square mile (2000)

**Racial and ethnic characteristics (2005)**

White: 83,542

Black: 1,306
American Indian and Alaska Native: 1,326
Asian: 1,133
Native Hawaiian and Pacific Islander: 178
Hispanic or Latino (may be of any race): 1,473
Other: 332

**Percent of residents born in state:** 59.0% (2006)

**Age characteristics (2005)**

Population under 5 years old: 5,181
Population 5 to 9 years old: 4,079
Population 10 to 14 years old: 6,028
Population 15 to 19 years old: 4,533
Population 20 to 24 years old: 11,469
Population 25 to 34 years old: 17,359
Population 35 to 44 years old: 11,536
Population 45 to 54 years old: 12,953
Population 55 to 59 years old: 5,533
Population 60 to 64 years old: 1,920
Population 65 to 74 years old: 3,914

Population 75 to 84 years old: 2,963
Population 85 years and older: 1,341
Median age: 31.3 years

**Births (2006, MSA)**

Total number: 2,424

**Deaths (2006, MSA)**

Total number: 1,108

**Money income (2005)**

Per capita income: $26,596
Median household income: $39,886
Total households: 42,619

**Number of households with income of . . .**

less than $10,000: 3,590
$10,000 to $14,999: 2,547
$15,000 to $24,999: 5,993
$25,000 to $34,999: 6,347
$35,000 to $49,999: 7,322
$50,000 to $74,999: 7,799
$75,000 to $99,999: 3,501
$100,000 to $149,999: 3,828
$150,000 to $199,999: 735
$200,000 or more: 957

**Percent of families below poverty level:** 12.1% (2005)

**2005 FBI Crime Index Property:** 2,348

**2005 FBI Crime Index Violent:** 104

# ■ Municipal Government

Fargo, the seat of Cass County, is governed by a city commission comprised of five at-large members, one of whom serves as mayor. Commissioners are elected to four-year terms. All commissioners, including the mayor, are subject to a limit of three consecutive terms.

**Head Official:** Mayor Dennis Walaker (since 2006; current term expires June 2010)

**Total Number of City Employees:** 730 (2007)

*City Information:* City Commission, 200 North Third Street, Fargo, ND 58102; telephone (701)241-1310

# ■ Economy

## Major Industries and Commercial Activity

The Fargo economy is based on education, the medical industry, agricultural equipment manufacturing, retailing, and services. The city is a retail magnet for the entire

Upper Plains; its per capita retail spending is usually among the nation's highest because so many people from the region go to Fargo to do their shopping. Because of its central location, the city is a transportation hub for the northern Midwest region. Agriculture has long been of primary importance to Fargo, as the Red River Valley area contains some of the richest farmland in the world; related industries include agribusiness and agricultural research. However, in recent years, software companies have brought a touch of Silicon Valley to the area. As of 2007 Microsoft was the largest employer in the city of Fargo.

The principal manufacturing employer is Case New Holland, makers of agricultural and construction equipment. Terminals for two oil pipeline systems—Standard Oil Company of Indiana and Great Lakes Pipeline Company of Oklahoma—are located in Fargo-Moorhead. The Standard Oil pipeline is connected with the company's refinery in Whiting, Indiana, which as of 2007 processed approximately 405,000 barrels of crude oil per day. In late 2007 the Canadian government attempted to run a petroleum pipeline under the city of Fargo, but the mayor disallowed it because of the potential damage to the city's water supply.

Fargo has received many accolades for its economy and pro-business environment. In 2004 *Business Development Outlook* magazine ranked the Fargo-Moorhead area fifth on its list of "Best Places for a Thriving Economy." In 2007 *Forbes* magazine ranked it fourth on a list of "Best Metro Areas in the Country for Business and Careers." That same year Fargo was named one of the "10 Most Affordable Places to Live and Work" by MSN Real Estate.

**Items and goods produced:** food, concrete, dairy and meat products, fur coats, jewelry, luggage, neon signs, electrical apparatus, sweet clover and sunflower seeds

## Incentive Programs—New and Existing Companies

*Local programs:* Several incentive programs are available to businesses that locate or expand in Cass County; among them are property tax and income tax exemptions, an interest rate subsidy program, and loans of up to $8,000 at U.S. treasury rates. The Chamber of Commerce of Fargo Moorhead offers business services to its members, including an employee assistance program, group medical insurance, and seminars.

*State programs:* North Dakota's Economic Development & Finance Division assists businesses with start-up, expansion, and recruitment. The Dakota Certified Development Company (CDC) administers the Small Business Administration 504 Loan Program. The program creates and retains jobs via the financing of real estate and equipment. The North Dakota Development fund provides secondary sources of funding to businesses through loans and equity investments.

*Job training programs:* Several state and federal programs assist in training or retraining workers. Workforce 2000 aids North Dakota employers in implementing new technologies and work methods. Under the Workforce 2000 program, the cost of employee training may be reimbursed. New Jobs Training provides financial assistance to businesses filling hourly job positions.

*Economic Development Information:* Fargo-Cass County Economic Development Corporation, 51 Broadway, Suite 500, Fargo, ND 58102; telephone (701)364-1900

## Development Projects

In 1999, the North Dakota legislature established the Renaissance Zone program to encourage private sector investment in neglected areas. Fargo's Renaissance Zone, which encompasses 35 blocks of the downtown area, saw more than $200 million worth of development projects each year between 1999 and 2004. The downtown revitalization has included storefront rehabilitation, beautification, and the conversion of unused buildings into commercial and residential space. The city was featured in *The Wall Street Journal* in 2006 for its revitalization of the downtown area as well as for its economic growth over the previous 15 years.

In 2002 MeritCare Health System began a five-year, $55 million renovation to the downtown MeritCare Medical Center campus. This project was the first major renovation to the facility since the 1970s. In 2005 a new MeritCare facility, which included a cutting-edge heart center, opened. Other scheduled renovations underway in 2007 included the expansion and renovation of the children's hospital, the conversion of most patient hospital rooms into private rooms, and the construction of a two-tier parking facility.

## Commercial Shipping

Fargo is served by the Burlington Northern/Santa Fe Railroad, which has its Dakota Division headquarters in Fargo. More than 120 regional, national, and international truck lines serve Cass County, transporting products, machinery, and bulk commodities to and from Fargo.

## Labor Force and Employment Outlook

Fargo has become a resettling point for Bosnians, Somalis, Sudanese, and others who have joined Fargo's labor force. Fargo boasts a well-educated labor force that has been shown to be 20 percent more productive than the national average. A strong Midwestern work ethic contributes to a low absentee rate, and over half of Cass County businesses have a turnover rate of 5 percent or less. In 2007 more than 80 percent of Fargo's workforce

held high school diplomas. North Dakota is a right-to-work state. In September 2007 Fargo's unemployment rate was just under 3 percent; an unemployment rate of 3 percent or less is considered full employment.

The following is a summary of data regarding the Fargo ND-MN metropolitan area labor force, 2006 annual averages.

**Size of nonagricultural labor force:** 115,900

**Number of workers employed in** ...

   construction and mining: 7,100
   manufacturing: 9,200
   trade, transportation and utilities: 26,000
   information: 3,200
   financial activities: 8,400
   professional and business services: 12,500
   educational and health services: 16,500
   leisure and hospitality: 11,600
   other services: 4,800
   government: 16,500

**Average hourly earnings of production workers employed in manufacturing:** $13.70

**Unemployment rate:** 3.2% (June 2007)

| *Largest primary sector employers (2007)* | *Number of employees* |
|---|---|
| Microsoft | 946 |
| US Bank Service Center | 770 |
| Noridian | 719 |
| Case New Holland Corp. | 672 |
| Phoenix International Corp. | 597 |
| Integrity Windows by Marvin | 557 |
| American Crystal Sugar | 485 |
| DMS Health Group | 411 |
| SEI Information Technology | 378 |
| Swanson Health Products | 358 |

## Cost of Living

The cost of living in Fargo is well below the national average.

The following is a summary of data regarding several key cost of living factors in the Fargo area.

**2007 (1st quarter) ACCRA Average House Price:** $259,382

**2007 (1st quarter) ACCRA Cost of Living Index:** 95.3

**State income tax rate:** 2.1% to 5.54%

**State sales tax rate:** 5.0%

**Local income tax rate:** None

**Local sales tax rate:** 1.5%

**Property tax rate:** 484.06 mills for School District #1; 418.53 mills for School District #6 (2004)

***Economic Information:*** Fargo-Cass County Economic Development Corporation, 51 Broadway, Suite 500, Fargo, ND 58102; telephone (701)364-1900

# ■ Education and Research

## Elementary and Secondary Schools

Public elementary and secondary schools in Fargo are part of Fargo Public School District #1. A superintendent is appointed by a nine-member, nonpartisan school board. The district offers special education classes to students with special needs. Advanced placement classes are available to high-performing high school students. Career and technical education classes at the high school level allow students to receive instruction in fields that pertain to specific careers or interests.

The following is a summary of data regarding the Fargo Public Schools as of the 2005–2006 school year.

**Total enrollment:** 27,719

**Number of facilities**

    elementary schools: 15
    junior high/middle schools: 3
    senior high schools: 2
    other: 2

**Student/teacher ratio:** 15.4:1

**Teacher salaries (2005–06)**

    elementary median: $37,290
    junior high/middle median: Not available
    secondary median: $44,580

**Funding per pupil:** $7,751

Six parochial schools are operated by the Catholic and Lutheran churches in Fargo.

***Public Schools Information:*** Fargo Public Schools, 415 Fourth Street North, Fargo, ND 58102; telephone (701)446-1000

## Colleges and Universities

The Fargo-Moorhead community is served by three universities as well as several vocational schools. North Dakota State University in Fargo, with an enrollment of more than 12,500 students, awards baccalaureate, master's, and doctorate degrees in a wide range of disciplines; colleges within the university are humanities and social sciences, agriculture, engineering and architecture, home economics, pharmacy, science and mathematics, and teacher education. Located on the North Dakota State University campus is Tri-College University, a consortium of area colleges and universities that allows students to take classes at North Dakota State University, Concordia College, and Minnesota State University Moorhead at no extra charge. In 2007 the Tri-College University consortium launched a grant program, awarding its students and faculty small amounts of money to promote collaborative projects between the different campuses. Cardinal Meunch Seminary (CMS) trains young men for the priesthood. In 2006 Pope Benedict XVI bestowed five alumni from CMS with the honorary title of "Monsigneur." In 2007 Aakers College merged with Webster College to form Rasmussen College, a private university offering two- and four-year degrees. Concordia College, Moorhead State University, and Moorhead Technical College are located in Moorhead.

## Libraries and Research Centers

The Fargo Public Library maintains holdings of more than 133,000 volumes, more than 250 magazine and newspaper subscriptions, compact discs, films, DVDs, audiotapes, and videotapes. The library maintains computers with Internet access and various software applications that are available to the public. Children's services include story time and a summer reading program. The library operates one branch library and a bookmobile in addition to the main branch. Online research databases may be accessed through the library's Internet website. In late 2007 the city of Fargo broke ground on the site of its new main library. The library was expected to open in fall of 2008. As of 2007 the North Dakota State University Library housed about 655,472 books, 8,646 periodical and subscription titles, CD-ROMs, audiotapes, videotapes, and maps. Special collections include bonanza farming, the North Dakota Biography Index, North Dakota Pioneer Reminiscences, and the North Dakota Historical Manuscript, Photograph and Book Collection; the library is also a depository for federal and state documents. In 2000, severe flooding in North Dakota caused damage to the library's collection of government microfiche and many older journal subscriptions. The library launched a local restoration project, in which it purchases replacements of damaged items from community members. Specialized libraries in the city are affiliated with hospitals, fraternal societies, and religious organizations.

The Northern Crop Science Laboratory on the North Dakota State University campus is a division of the Agricultural Research Service of the U.S. Department of Agriculture. Government and university scientists conduct cooperative research on barley, hard red spring wheat, durum wheat, flax, sunflowers, and sugar beets; the goal is to expand and retain profitable production of these crops through the use of the most advanced equipment and research techniques.

*Public Library Information:* Fargo Public Library, 102 North Third Street, Fargo, ND 58102; telephone (701)241-1472

# ■ Health Care

Fargo is the primary health care center for the region between Minnesota and the West Coast. The major health system is MeritCare Health System, which is the largest group practice and largest hospital in the state. Nearly 400 physicians specialize in 74 areas of medicine, including internal medicine, prenatal care, cancer care, and eating disorders. Two hospital locations provide 583 patient beds and 32 surgical suites. In 2005 MeritCare opened its new facility, part of a large $55 million renovation project. In 2006, MeritCare was rated one of Solucient's "Top 100 Heart Hospitals." As of 2007 MeritCare Heart Center had been named one of nation's "Top 100 Heart Hospitals" eight times in nine years by the Thomson 100 Top Hospitals "Cardiovascular Benchmarks for Success" study, which compares success rates at 1,000 heart centers nationwide.

# ■ Recreation

## Sightseeing

A visit to Fargo might begin with a stop at the Fargo-Moorhead Convention & Visitors Bureau Visitors Center, where the Walk of Fame has been providing a little bit of Hollywood in the Midwest since 1989 with hand prints or footprints of more than 80 musicians, athletes, movie stars, and dignitaries, including Neil Diamond, Bob Costas, Garth Brooks, President George W. Bush, and the Eagles.

One of downtown Fargo's more recent attractions is the Plains Art Museum; it offers regional art, guided tours, and facilities for receptions. Included in the museum's permanent collection are pieces by Mary Cassatt, Luis Jimenez, and William Wegman. In 2006 more than 53,000 people attended programs offered at, or through, the Plains Museum. Bonanzaville USA is a recreated pioneer village of 40 restored buildings on a 15-acre site; the structures were relocated from a number of small North Dakota towns and represent various types of architecture. Included among them are a drugstore, general store, sod and farm houses, district courtroom, and barber shop. Vintage automobiles, farm machinery, and airplanes are also on exhibit. The main attraction at Moorhead's Heritage Hjemkomst Interpretive Center is the sailing ship the late Robert Asp of Moorhead

modeled after ancient Viking vessels. Housed in an architecturally distinctive building that also includes the Clay County Historical Museum, the ship made a journey from Duluth, Minnesota, to Bergen, Norway, in 1982.

The Solomon G. Comstock Historic House in Moorhead is the former home of this prominent Fargo-Moorhead figure who was a financier and a political and cultural force in the community. The authentically restored Victorian house contains its original furnishings. The Roger Maris Museum in the West Acres Shopping Center pays tribute to the city's most famous athlete, who broke Babe Ruth's single-season home run record in 1961 when he hit 61 home runs. Maris donated all of his trophies and sports memorabilia to the museum as a tribute to the city in which he grew up. In 2003 the museum was completely rebuilt with better lighting and ventilation to help preserve the artifacts. The Children's Museum at Yunker Farm, a century-old farm house, presents participatory learning exhibits in the physical, natural, and social sciences.

## Arts and Culture

The Fargo Theatre, a landmark movie theater built in 1926, was fully restored in 1999 and is the site of film showings as well as live theater, music, and dance performances. On weekends, the Mighty Wurlitzer organ performs intermission music during each show at the theater. The Fargo Theater is the only theater in the Eastern Dakota area with capabilities of showing 16-mm, 35-mm, and 70-mm film presentations. The Fargo-Moorhead Community Theatre group stages 12 annual productions at the Fargo-Moorhead Community Theatre. Other local performing groups are the Fargo-Moorhead Symphony Orchestra (which celebrated its 75th season in 2006), the Fargo-Moorhead Opera, and the Red River Dance and Performing Company. The Trollwood Performing Arts School provides arts education, entertainment, and activities for children.

## Festivals and Holidays

The Fargo Film Festival, in March, screens the best in independent filmmaking at the Fargo Theatre and other downtown locations. In July, the Downtown Street Fair features craft booths, food, and entertainment. Bonanzaville USA holds Pioneer Days in August, when more than 100 demonstrators revive the skills and crafts of the past. The Fargo Blues Festival, in August, is a two-day event that features world class bands; more than 20 Grammy winners or nominees have performed at the event, which has been called one of "America's Best" by actor Dan Aykroyd. The Big Iron Farm Show fills the Red River Valley Fairgrounds on the second weekend in September, bringing the latest farm products and services from 400 agribusiness exhibitors. The holiday season brings Christmas on the Prairie at Bonanzaville USA and the annual Santa Village at Rheault Farm, with opportunities to feed deer, meet Santa, and enjoy a sleigh ride. A Winter Blues Fest is held in February.

## Sports for the Spectator

Although Fargo does not field any major league sports teams, it is home to other professional and collegiate teams. The Fargo-Moorhead Redhawks of the Northern League play baseball at Newman Outdoor Field. In 2007 average attendance for the season was 3,620 people. The Fargo-Moorhead Jets are a Junior A developmental league hockey team for 17- to 20-year-olds making the transition from high school to college; they play a 54-game season from September through March at the John E. Carson Coliseum.

The North Dakota State University Bisons have won 20 National Collegiate Athletic Association (NCAA) Division II national championships, including the 2002 women's indoor track and field championship. In 2004 North Dakota State University was reclassified as a Division I team in all sports other than football. The university fields men's and women's teams in 10 sports, including football, basketball, baseball, and softball. In 2006 the university was accepted into the Summit League, and played in the league conference for the first time in 2007. The Moorhead State University Dragons and the Concordia College Cobbers also present a complete schedule of men's and women's major and minor sports. The Red River Valley Speedway presents stock car racing.

## Sports for the Participant

The Fargo Park District sponsors an extensive sports program for all age groups. Recreational facilities include 73 public parks, 12 public golf courses, 38 public tennis courts, and 4 public swimming pools. Winter sports are particularly popular with ice skating, figure skating, and youth and adult hockey available at both indoor and outdoor facilities; outdoor rinks are equipped with warming houses. Other recreational pursuits include volleyball, basketball, track, soccer, walking, cross-country skiing, ballroom dancing, table tennis, and broom ball. The Fargo Park District also sponsors a number of adaptive recreational activities, or sports for developmentally disabled adults and children. The Scheels and Adidas Fargo Marathon is held in May. In 2007 some 1,190 people completed the marathon.

Charitable and cultural organizations sponsor gaming operations at 39 casinos in Fargo-Moorhead's public establishments. Profits benefit the programs of the sponsoring organizations, and fraternal groups allocate profits to public causes. Games include blackjack, paper slot machines, bingo, and tri-wheel.

## Shopping and Dining

The Fargo shopping scene is a mix of unique local establishments and national retailers. The Crafters Mall, open year round, has more than 250 display areas featuring crafts from around the country. The Fargo Antique Mall is one of the largest in the state, with more than 7,000 square feet of antiques, books, and collectibles. Gordmans is a local department store selling name brand clothing and shoes, fragrances, furniture, and home accessories. West Acres Shopping Center, the largest mall in the region with more than 120 stores and restaurants, is anchored by Marshall Field's, JCPenney, Sears, and Herberger's.

Fargo offers a range of culinary choices, with over 250 restaurants in the city. Ethnic options include Asian, Indian, Italian, Mediterranean, and Mexican. Dining in historic settings is offered at Runck Chateau Ranch, a working cattle ranch, and at The White House, District 31, Victoria's, and The Conservatory.

***Visitor Information:*** Fargo-Moorhead Convention & Visitors Bureau, 2001 44th Street SW, Fargo, ND 58103; telephone (701)282-3653; toll-free (800)235-7654

## ■ Convention Facilities

Fargo's main convention/multipurpose facility, the $48 million Fargodome, opened in 1992. It is the largest multipurpose facility of its kind between Minneapolis and Spokane. Fargodome's seven meeting rooms total more than 13,500 square feet; the 80,000-square-foot arena seats more than 26,000 guests.

Constructed in 1960, the Fargo Civic Center hosts a variety of events, including state political conventions, concerts, trade exhibitions, sporting events, and business gatherings. The 11,000-square-foot arena accommodates over 3,000 persons for sports events and concerts and 1,200 people in a banquet setting. The exhibition hall, measuring 40 feet by 150 feet, seats 600 people for both theater-style and banquet functions; the hall can be divided into four rooms for private meetings.

The Red River Valley Fairgrounds offers facilities for agricultural expositions, trade shows, conventions, and entertainment.

***Convention Information:*** Fargo-Moorhead Convention & Visitors Bureau, 2001 44th Street SW, Fargo, ND 58103; telephone (701)235-7654; toll-free (800) 235-7654. Fargodome, 1800 North University Drive, Fargo, ND 58102; telephone (701)241-9100

## ■ Transportation

### Approaching the City

Hector International Airport is situated 10 minutes northwest of downtown Fargo. United Express and Northwest Airlines offer daily flights to Minneapolis, Chicago, and Denver. The year 2006 was the busiest in terms of total passengers for the airport; more than

609,000 passengers either enplaned or deplaned at Hector International Airport. Also, in 2006, the Municipal Airport Authority initiated a terminal expansion project to meet the needs of the passenger terminal for the next 20 years. Amtrak provides two daily trains, one eastbound and one westbound. Bus service by Greyhound is also available.

Highways serving metropolitan Fargo include I-94, extending east to west through the south sector of the city, and I-29, which runs north to south and provides links to I-70, I-80, and I-90, all east-west connections. U.S. 10 and 52 are east-west routes, and U.S. 81 extends through the city from north to south. State routes serving Fargo are 20 and 294, both running east to west.

### Traveling in the City

Except for streets following the configuration of the Red River, Fargo is laid out on a grid pattern. The city is divided into quadrants; roadways running north to south are designated "street," while those running east to west are labeled "avenue." First Avenue and Main Avenue are major thoroughfares crossing the river to connect Fargo with Moorhead, Minnesota.

Public bus transportation in Fargo is provided by Fargo Metropolitan Area Transit (MAT). MAT operates 10 bus routes in Fargo and one in West Fargo; the system is coordinated with the Moorhead Transit System for a combined total of 18 bus routes. Passengers with disabilities who are unable to ride without assistance may use the MAT Paratransit service. As of 2007 there were 35 buses in the MAT fleet and drivers covered over 600,000 miles on the Fargo fixed route.

## ■ Communications

### Newspapers and Magazines

Fargo's daily newspaper is *The Forum*. The paper's Internet website also provides daily coverage as well as archives of previous stories. Other newspapers include

*New Earth,* a Catholic Diocese publication, and *Spectrum,* the bi-weekly North Dakota State University student newspaper. *The Area Woman* is a free quarterly magazine. *The Fargo-Moorhead Magazine* is a free local-interest magazine published every other month. *Prairie Business,* a regional business magazine targeted toward readers in North Dakota, South Dakota, and western Minnesota, is published monthly.

### Television and Radio

Six television stations—five commercial and one public—broadcast in Fargo; cable service is available. Sixteen AM and FM radio stations schedule a variety of programming.

*Media Information:* *The Forum,* 105 Fifth Street North, Fargo, ND 58102-4826; telephone (701)235-7311

### Fargo Online

City of Fargo. Available www.ci.fargo.nd.us

Fargo-Cass County Economic Development Corporation. Available www.fedc.com

Fargo-Moorhead Chamber of Commerce. Available www.fmchamber.com

Fargo-Moorhead Convention & Visitors Bureau. Available www.fargomoorhead.org

Fargo Public Library. Available www.ci.fargo.nd.us/library

*The Forum.* Available www.in-forum.com

North Dakota State University. Available www.ndsu.nodak.edu

BIBLIOGRAPHY

Gudmundson, Wayne, *Crossings: A Photographic Document of Fargo, North Dakota* (Fargo, ND: North Dakota Institute for Regional Studies, 1995)

# Grand Forks

## ■ The City in Brief

**Founded:** 1875

**Head Official:** Mayor Michael R. Brown (since 2000)

**City Population**

    1980: 43,765
    1990: 49,417
    2000: 49,321
    2006 estimate: 50,372
    Percent change, 1990–2000: −0.2%
    U.S. rank in 1980: Not available
    U.S. rank in 1990: 511th (State rank: 2nd)
    U.S. rank in 2000: 404th (Grand Forks, ND and East Grand Forks, MN combined; State rank: 2nd)

**Metropolitan Area Population**

    1980: 66,100
    1990: 103,272
    2000: 97,478
    2006 estimate: 96,523
    Percent change, 1990–2000: −5.6%
    U.S. rank in 1980: 280th
    U.S. rank in 1990: Not available
    U.S. rank in 2000: 258th

**Area:** 19.2 square miles (2000)

**Elevation:** 834 feet above sea level

**Average Annual Temperatures:** January, 5.3° F; July, 69.4° F; annual average, 40.3° F

**Average Annual Precipitation:** 19.60 inches of rain; 44.3 inches of snow

**Major Economic Sectors:** Trade, government, services

**Unemployment Rate:** 3.9% (June 2007)

**Per Capita Income:** $18,395 (1999)

**2005 FBI Crime Index Property:** 2,074

**2005 FBI Crime Index Violent:** 65

**Major Colleges and Universities:** University of North Dakota

**Daily Newspaper:** *Grand Forks Herald*

## ■ Introduction

Since the 1870s when the juncture of the Red River of the North and the Red Lake River became a crossroads for people and their river-oriented business, the cities of Grand Forks and East Grand Forks have been a focal point of trade and services between the plains of North Dakota and the pine forests of northern Minnesota. Located 75 miles south of the Canadian border, the city is centered in one of the world's richest agricultural regions. The business community is deeply rooted in agriculture and its related enterprises. Today more than 300,000 people in an 18-county area come to Greater Grand Forks for the commercial, recreational, and cultural services it has to offer, which include nearly 40 arts organizations. The city is headquarters for a major university and boasts a key military installation that has an important economic impact on the local community.

## ■ Geography and Climate

Flat and open terrain surrounds Grand Forks, which is just 75 miles south of the Canadian border, and situated on the western boundary of the Red River Valley of the North. Seventy-five percent of precipitation accompanied by electrical storms and heavy rainfall occurs during the growing season, April through September. Summers are comfortable with low humidity, warm days and cool nights. Winters are cold and dry with temperatures remaining at zero or below approximately half the time. Snowfall is generally light. The legendary Dakota blizzards result from drifting of even minimal snowfall caused by strong winds that blow unimpeded across the flat terrain.

**Area:** 19.2 square miles (2000)

**Elevation:** 834 feet above sea level

**Average Temperatures:** January, 5.3° F; July, 69.4° F; annual average, 40.3° F

**Average Annual Precipitation:** 19.60 inches of rain; 44.3 inches of snow

# ■ History

## Railroads Stimulate Growth of City

Located at the junction of the Red Lake River and the Red River of the North, the area of Grand Forks served as a camping and trading site for Native Americans for centuries. French, British, and American fur traders peddled their wares in and around "La Grand Fourches," as the French named it, meaning "the great forks."

In the 1850s, furs and trade goods passed through the Forks on oxcarts enroute between Winnipeg, Canada, and St. Paul, Minnesota. Steamboats replaced oxcarts in 1859. The shallow-draft steamboats could operate in less than three feet of water as they negotiated the Red River from Fargo to Winnipeg. Alexander Griggs, an experienced Mississippi River steamboat captain, established the town site of Grand Forks in 1870. Griggs teamed up with James J. Hill in the Red River Transportation Line of steamboats in the 1870s.

Grand Forks really began to grow after James J. Hill's Great Northern Railroad came to town in 1880. The Northern Pacific Railroad also built tracks to the city in 1882 and business boomed. Early arrivals who stayed in the region were mostly of northern European background including Scandinavian, German, and Polish immigrants.

## Wheat and Lumber Anchor Economy

Wheat farming served as the basis of the Red River Valley's prosperity. In 1893 Frank Amidon, chief miller at the Diamond Mills in Grand Forks, invented "Cream of Wheat." George Clifford, George Bull, and Emery Mapes financed the new breakfast porridge venture, and the city became a part of a national breakfast legend.

From the 1880s to 1910, pine logs were floated down the Red River or brought in by rail to sawmills in the city. Many houses in Grand Forks were built of the majestic white pines from the vast forests of northern Minnesota. The University of North Dakota, founded in 1883, became the premier liberal arts institution in the state. The city grew from the river toward the college campus to the west. The Metropolitan Theatre opened in 1890 and for the next 25 years it presented quality productions of music and drama. During the period of the "Gilded Age" at the end of the last century, spacious and elegant houses were built along historic Reeves Drive and South Sixth Street for the local elite.

By 1900, Grand Forks had a population of almost 10,000 people. The wealth from the lumber companies, wheat farms, and railroads enabled the community to take its place as a leading city of the "Great Northwest." After his arrival in the early 1880s, local architect Jon W. Ross designed many of the area's most beautiful buildings. In 1902, Joseph Bell Deremer, trained at Columbia University, began to make his mark upon the community through the new buildings he designed.

The North Dakota Mill and Elevator, the only state-owned flour mill in the country, opened in 1923. The mill allowed North Dakota farmers to bypass Minneapolis-based railroads and milling monopolies. The mill distributed free flour to needy people during the Great Depression of the 1930s. Even today, the mill sends its trademark flour "Dakota Maid" around the world.

## Twentieth Century Ends in Disaster; City Rebuilds

Grand Forks grew as a regional trade center in the twentieth century. In recent times Grand Forks residents have endured several hardships. The winter of 1995–1996 brought record snowfall (more than 100 inches in many areas) and eight blizzards. In April 1997, Grand Forks was devastated by a flood that saw the Red River rise to more than 53 feet, 25 feet above the flood stage. With 60 percent of the city covered with water, most residents were forced to abandon the city, and the state was declared a disaster area. Damage from the flood totaled around $1.3 billion. Many residents pledged to return and rebuild, although Mayor Patricia Owens acknowledged that some residents would probably never return. She declared: "The lesson we've learned is that material things don't mean a thing. Pretty soon we'll be back, bigger and better."

Analysts estimated that Grand Forks lost about 2,000 residents, nearly 4 percent of its population, because of destroyed homes and lost job opportunities from the great flood. But, with the initiative of then-Mayor Patricia Owens, the city began to rebuild. She secured $171.6 million in Community Development Block Grant money to help Grand Forks rebuild. She also got the federal government to earmark more than $1 billion for buyouts and relocations of homes, businesses, and schools; money for farmers who lost livestock; and money for infrastructure repair (including the town's sewer system, which was hit particularly hard). Today, under the leadership of Mayor Brown, the city continues to grow.

Photo by Bordner Aerials

Grand Forks has become known as a "Destination City" for its pro-business practices, affordable housing, and community events.

***Historical Information:*** University of North Dakota, Elwyn B. Robinson Department of Special Collections, Chester Fritz Library, Box 9000, Grand Forks, ND 58202-9000; telephone (701)777-2617

## ■ Population Profile

**Metropolitan Area Residents**

   1980: 66,100
   1990: 103,272
   2000: 97,478
   2006 estimate: 96,523
   Percent change, 1990–2000: −5.6%
   U.S. rank in 1980: 280th
   U.S. rank in 1990: Not available
   U.S. rank in 2000: 258th

**City Residents**

   1980: 43,765
   1990: 49,417

   2000: 49,321
   2006 estimate: 50,372
   Percent change, 1990–2000: −0.2%
   U.S. rank in 1980: Not available
   U.S. rank in 1990: 511th (State rank: 2nd)
   U.S. rank in 2000: 404th (Grand Forks, ND and
      East Grand Forks, MN combined; State rank:
      2nd)

**Density:** 2,563 people per square mile (2000)

**Racial and ethnic characteristics (2000)**

   White: 46,040
   Black: 426
   American Indian and Alaska Native: 1,357
   Asian: 472
   Native Hawaiian and Pacific Islander: 28
   Hispanic or Latino (may be of any race): 921
   Other: 288

**Percent of residents born in state:** 63.0% (2000)

**Age characteristics (2000)**

   Population under 5 years old: 2,910
   Population 5 to 9 years old: 2,819

Population 10 to 14 years old: 2,924
Population 15 to 19 years old: 5,012
Population 20 to 24 years old: 8,174
Population 25 to 34 years old: 6,981
Population 35 to 44 years old: 6,657
Population 45 to 54 years old: 5,867
Population 55 to 59 years old: 1,747
Population 60 to 64 years old: 1,394
Population 65 to 74 years old: 2,317
Population 75 to 84 years old: 1,768
Population 85 years and older: 751
Median age: 28.3 years

**Births (2006, MSA)**

Total number: 1,267

**Deaths (2006, MSA)**

Total number: 754

**Money income (1999)**

Per capita income: $18,395
Median household income: $34,194
Total households: 19,658

**Number of households with income of...**

less than $10,000: 2,390
$10,000 to $14,999: 1,438
$15,000 to $24,999: 3,055
$25,000 to $34,999: 3,153
$35,000 to $49,999: 3,436
$50,000 to $74,999: 3,463
$75,000 to $99,999: 1,564
$100,000 to $149,999: 706
$150,000 to $199,999: 230
$200,000 or more: 223

**Percent of families below poverty level:** 12.3% (1999)

**2005 FBI Crime Index Property:** 2,074

**2005 FBI Crime Index Violent:** 65

# ■ Municipal Government

Grand Forks has been a home rule city since 1970; it was the first city in the state to adopt home rule. Grand Forks has a mayor-council form of government. The mayor and 14 councilpersons representing 7 wards or districts in the city are elected to four-year terms. The formal powers of the mayor of Grand Forks are limited. The mayor presides over city council meetings but can vote only if there is a tie. The mayor can veto actions of the council.

**Head Official:** Mayor Michael R. Brown (since 2000; current term expires June 2008)

**Total Number of City Employees:** 500 (2007)

***City Information:*** City Hall, 255 North 4th St., PO Box 5200, Grand Forks, ND 58206-5200; telephone (701)746-4636; fax (701)787-3725; email info@grand forksgov.com

# ■ Economy

## Major Industries and Commercial Activity

Grand Forks has a stable, agriculturally-based economy that has been expanding and diversifying since the early 1980s. More than 2,500 businesses are located in the area. Abundant moisture assists the growth of the hard spring wheat, corn, oats, sunflowers, durum, barley, potatoes, sugar beets, dry edible beans, soybeans, and flax that represent its major crops. Cattle, sheep and hogs also contribute to the local farm economy. Plants operate for the processing of potatoes, for the conversion of locally grown mustard seed for table and commercial use, for the refining of beets into sugar, and for the pearling of barley. The counties surrounding Grand Forks include 2,000 farming operations with a value of nearly $250 million in production. Much of the area's durum wheat is marketed through the North Dakota State Mill and Elevator.

While in the early 1980s almost all businesses were agriculturally based, other enterprises such as high-technology firms, a wood products company, and concrete firms now play an important role in the local economy. Some important local firms include: J. R. Simplot, which processes potatoes and other foods; American Woods, which produces outdoor lawn furniture; Strata Corporation, which produces ready-mix concrete and handles asphalt and masonry; the American Crystal Sugar refinery; Young Manufacturing, which custom designs, engineers, and manufactures metal products; Energy Research Center, which conducts research on energy-related products; and R. D. O., which deals in processed foods. In 2001 and 2002, after its 1999 acquisition of Acme Tool Crib of the North, Internet retailer Amazon.com expanded and located a portion of its customer service operations in Grand Forks. Amazon.com is now one of the region's top employers. Retail is one of the fastest growing sectors in the Grand Forks economy, with much of its growth coming from "big box" stores like Target, Walmart, and Sam's Club.

The University of North Dakota (UND) is a major contributor to the city's economic life as well as its cultural and entertainment life. UND contributes nearly $1 billion annually to the state and local economy.

Grand Forks U.S. Air Force Base is one of the bases in the Air Mobility Command, headquartered at Scott AFB, Illinois. The base is home to the 319th Air Refueling Wing and is the second-largest employer in the city.

**Items and goods produced:** farm crops, fertilizer, chemicals, seeds, wood products, metal products, concrete, computer software

## Incentive Programs—New and Existing Companies

*Local programs:* The Urban Development Department is responsible for the administration and management of a variety of economic development programs. These activities are performed under the guidance and supervision of the Grand Forks City Council, Grand Forks Housing Authority, and miscellaneous advisory bodies. For example, the Urban Development Department works with the Grand Forks Region Economic Development Corporation to assist businesses and industries wishing to expand or locate in Grand Forks by helping secure funding through various local, state, and federal resources.

*State programs:* North Dakota is the only state in the nation to control its own development bank. The Bank of North Dakota (BND) arranges financing for the MATCH program, aimed at attracting financially strong companies to North Dakota via loans and low interest rates. The BND also administers the Business Development Loan Program, for new and existing business with higher risk levels; and the PACE fund, which targets community job development. The North Dakota Development Fund provides "gap financing" to primary sector businesses. The SBA 504 Loan Program offers long-term, fixed asset financing in partnership with private lenders; the borrower provides 10 percent in cash equity. The SBA 7(a) Loan Program is available to small businesses unable to obtain financing in the private credit marketplace

*Job training programs:* Job Service North Dakota administers state- and federally-funded workforce training programs including customized training, on-the-job training, occupational upgrading and Workforce 2000 employee training. The North Dakota New Jobs Training Program provides incentives to businesses that create new employment opportunities in the state.

## Development Projects

Slowly but surely downtown Grand Forks has rebuilt itself. To prevent another flood disaster, the city, along with East Grand Forks, Minnesota and the St. Paul District of the U.S. Army Corps of Engineers, undertook an estimated $386 million flood protection project, which reached functional completion in 2007. The city secured $40 million of the U.S. President's 2006 budget to assist with construction, which included a 100,000-gallon-per-minute pump station to divert runoff that would otherwise flow into the community. Other major features include 12.3 miles of levees, 1.1 miles of floodwall, bike paths, and a new pedestrian bridge spanning the Red River and joining Grand Forks and East Grand Forks.

The floodwall was the first of its kind to be built in the United States. The city also increased its efforts to redevelop its industrial park, where more than 1,000 new jobs were added between 1997 and 2007.

In 2005 Canadian developers broke ground on a $50-million hotel and entertainment complex next to the Alerus; as of 2007 no completion date had been announced. The Wellness Center at the University of North Dakota, begun in 2004 and completed in 2006, will provide for the wellness needs of the university community. The $19.3 million building offers fitness oriented programs such as group exercise and personal training, fitness assessments, weight and cardio machines, and massage therapy.

*Economic Development Information:* Grand Forks Region Economic Development Corp., 600 DeMers Avenue, Suite 501, Grand Forks, ND 58201; telephone (701)746-2720.

## Commercial Shipping

Burlington Northern-Santa Fe schedules 200 freight trains peer week through the region. Seventy motor carriers and several package service carriers are located in the city.

## Labor Force and Employment Outlook

Post-flood, Grand Forks civic leaders are looking for ways to make Grand Forks more appealing to professionals and young people.

The following is a summary of data regarding the Grand Forks ND-MN metropolitan area labor force, 2006 annual averages.

**Size of nonagricultural labor force:** 53,100

**Number of workers employed in . . .**

    construction and mining: 2,700
    manufacturing: 4,100
    trade, transportation and utilities: 11,200
    information: 700
    financial activities: 1,700
    professional and business services: 3,600
    educational and health services: 8,400
    leisure and hospitality: 5,500
    other services: 2,000
    government: 13,300

**Average hourly earnings of production workers employed in manufacturing:** Not available

**Unemployment rate:** 3.9% (June 2007)

| *Largest employers* | *Number of employees* |
| --- | --- |
| University of North Dakota | 4,945 |

| *Largest employers* | *Number of employees* |
|---|---|
| Grand Forks Air Force Base | 4,265 |
| Altru Health System | 3,550 |
| Grand Forks Public Schools | 1,310 |
| Hugo's Stores | 775 |
| Simplot | 539 |
| City of Grand Forks | 517 |
| Valley Memorial Homes | 500 |
| Amazon.com | 400 |

## Cost of Living

The following is a summary of data regarding several key cost of living factors in the Grand Forks area.

**2007 (1st quarter) ACCRA Average House Price:** Not available

**2007 (1st quarter) ACCRA Cost of Living Index:** 91.1

**State income tax rate:** 2.1% to 5.54%

**State sales tax rate:** 5.0%

**Local income tax rate:** None

**Local sales tax rate:** 1.75%

**Property tax rate:** 2.25% of appraised value (2005)

*Economic Information:* Grand Forks Chamber of Commerce, 203 Third Street North, Grand Forks, ND 58203; telephone (701)772-7271

## ■ Education and Research

### Elementary and Secondary Schools

The Grand Forks Public School District is a progressive school district, with both standard and non-traditional subjects covered in the curriculum. Students routinely use computers and other technologies in the classroom, and all students receive some foreign language instruction prior to high school. The district's special education department is recognized as one of the best in the state; it provides services to disabled persons ages 3 through 21. Gifted students are provided with enrichment opportunities, including Advanced Placement courses at the high school level. Extracurricular opportunities in sports and the arts are offered to students in all grades. The Grand Forks Foundation for Education is a private organization that provides private donations, scholarships, and endowments to the district's schools and its students.

The following is a summary of data regarding the Grand Forks Public School District #1 as of the 2005–2006 school year.

**Total enrollment:** 14,618

**Number of facilities**

elementary schools: 12
junior high/middle schools: 4
senior high schools: 3
other: 3

**Student/teacher ratio:** 12.9:1

**Teacher salaries (2005–06)**

elementary median: $43,870
junior high/middle median: Not available
secondary median: $42,790

**Funding per pupil:** $7,061

Five parochial and private schools provide an alternative to the public school curriculum. Two schools at Grand Forks Air Force Base provide education for students in grades kindergarten through eighth grades; high school students on the base are bused to Central High School.

*Public Schools Information:* Grand Forks Public Schools, 2400 47th Avenue South, Grand Forks, ND 58201; telephone (701)746-2200

## Colleges and Universities

The University of North Dakota (UND), with nearly 13,000 students, is one of the largest institutions of higher learning in the Upper Midwest. Founded in 1883, the university has a strong liberal arts course and a constellation of 10 professional and specialized colleges and schools. The school has an economic impact on the region of nearly $1 billion annually, and just over half of its students hail from North Dakota. Academic programs are offered in 193 fields, and the curriculum spans arts and sciences, aviation, business, fine arts, engineering, human resources, education, nursing, law, medicine, and graduate studies. It is one of just 47 public universities with accredited programs in both law and medicine. UND's school of medicine is recognized as a national leader in training rural health care providers.

## Libraries and Research Centers

The Grand Forks Public Library houses more than 300,000 volumes and subscribes to approximately 400 periodicals. Its Grand Forks Collection includes books, pictures, and oral history of the local area. The library hosts story hours for young children and has meeting facilities available to the public for a small fee. The library's computer facilities offer free word processing and Internet access. Patrons can access the library's catalog via its Internet website. Greater Grand Forks's libraries hold more than 3 million volumes as well as periodicals, reports, microfilms, and documents.

The University of North Dakota has an international reputation for research. Among its research centers and service units are the Energy and Environmental Research Center, the Bureau of Governmental Affairs, the Bureau of Educational Services and Applied Research, the Center for Rural Health, and the Upper Midwest Aerospace Consortium. Special collections at the University of North Dakota Chester Fritz library include rare books, North Dakota history, and books on the geography and history of the Great Plains.

The Research Center at Altru Hospital participates in research and clinical trials in specialties that include cardiology, oncology, infectious diseases, pain management, and surgery. The Center collaborates with other healthcare providers and academic institutions in a 17-county region of northeastern North Dakota and northwestern Minnesota.

***Public Library Information:***   Grand Forks Public Library, 2110 Library Circle, Grand Forks, ND 58201; telephone (701)772-8116

# ■ Health Care

Altru Health System of Grand Forks serves the more than 200,000 residents of northeast North Dakota and northwest Minnesota. Altru is an integrated health system with headquarters on a 90-acre medical campus. It was created July 1, 1997 when the Grand Forks Clinic and United Health Services integrated following the Red River Flood. Facilities include a 261-bed acute care hospital, a 34-bed rehabilitation facility, a free-standing cancer center, and a 172-unit retirement living community. There are more than 3,000 staff, including 180 physicians, nurses, and health care professionals. Specialized services include a surgical center; women's services; heart services; and cancer, diabetes, rehabilitation, and vascular centers. The Altru Cancer Center was the first in the state to provide High-Dose Rate Brachytherapy. Altru provides care from 8 locations in Grand Forks and 12 regional clinics in northeast North Dakota and northwest Minnesota. Additionally, the University of North Dakota sponsors the Grand Forks Family Medicine Residency, and East Grand Forks is home to Meritcare East Grand Forks.

# ■ Recreation

## Sightseeing

The Grand Forks County Historical Society grounds feature the Myra Museum, which displays the heritage of the Grand Forks area. Exhibits and displays include the Quiet Room, which contains furnishings from the 1700s; the Chapel, with its stained glass windows and objects from historic local churches; and the Lake Agasssiz

display, which offers a history lesson in the ancient lake that produced the rich Red River Valley soil. The 1879 Campbell House displays furnishings of family life including a working loom, toys, and a summer kitchen. A 1917 school house and the 1870s post office are some of the first buildings constructed in the town. The grounds are open for tours May 15 through September 15, with guided tours available every day of the week.

## Arts and Culture

Grand Forks has a thriving cultural scene, with performing arts venues that include the Fire Hall Theatre, which offers a season of musicals, dramas, classics, and comedies in an intimate 114-seat setting, and the restored 1919 Empire Arts Center. The Chester Fritz Auditorium on the University of North Dakota (UND) campus presents a diversity of national, regional, and local theatrical productions and is home of the Greater Grand Forks Symphony Orchestra. The campus's Burtness Theatre is the site of excellent college dramatic productions. Community performing arts groups include the Greater Grand Forks Symphony and Youth Symphony, Grand Forks Master Chorale, Grand Forks City Band, and North Dakota Ballet Company.

The North Dakota Museum of Art, located on the UND campus, is the state's official art gallery and serves as the center of cultural life for a five-state region. The museum exhibits national and international contemporary art with shows changing every six to eight weeks. During the winter, the Museum Concert Series presents classical music concerts. The Hughes Fine Arts Center Gallery on the UND campus exhibits the works of national and regional artists as well as students. The UND Witmer Art Center displays quality works by professional artists.

## Festivals and Holidays

Guest writers and poets from across the nation come to Grand Forks in March for the Writer's Conference. April's Time Out/Wacipi, sponsored by the Native American Studies Department at UND, offers a variety of activities and entertainment focused on Native American life. During three weekends in June, July, and August, Summerthing presents Music in the Park, Kids Days, and Artfest. In June, the Greater Grand Forks Fair and Exhibition offers carnival rides, concerts, 4-H entries, and races. From June through September, an outdoor farmers market with free entertainment and concessions is held on the town square. A popular summer U.S. Air Force Base event, Friends and Neighbors Day, brings thousands of people to watch aerial demonstrations and to peer into cockpits. Crazy Days offers bargain shopping at many local marketplaces in August, and later in the month the two-day Heritage Days Festival includes old time threshing demonstrations and antique machinery. The Potato Bowl in September features football games, a queen pageant, and a golf tournament, among other activities. Christmas in the Park, held from late November through early January, is a driving tour of holiday light displays.

## Sports for the Spectator

The University of North Dakota is the home of the Fighting Sioux, with historically excellent Division I ice hockey and Division II men's and women's basketball, football, and swimming programs.

## Sports for the Participant

The Grand Forks Park District maintains 43 parks and facilities on more than 850 acres of land. Facilities include biking and jogging lanes and paths, two golf courses (including an Arnold Palmer signature golf course), one public swimming pool, eleven outdoor skating rinks, four indoor ice arenas, and tennis and racquetball courts. The Park District's Center Court Fitness Club houses indoor tennis courts, aerobics studios, and a weight room. Two rivers provide outstanding fishing opportunities; the Red River is internationally known for its trophy-sized channel catfish. Winter offers opportunities for snowmobiling, ice fishing, and cross-country skiing.

## Shopping and Dining

The largest indoor mall in the region is Columbia Mall, whose 70 stores are anchored by JCPenney, Marshall Field's, and Sears. The Grand Cities Mall, anchored by Big K-Mart, includes stores such as Grand Cities Antiques and Collectibles and Zimmerman's Furniture. The Grand Forks Marketplace, located off of Interstate 29 and opened in 2001, is home to national retailers such as Target and Lowe's. The Riverwalk Centre, in East Grand Forks, offers unique shopping opportunities in a scenic setting along the Red River. Barnes and Noble University Bookstore is the anchor for the "University Village" on the UND campus, which opened in 2000.

East Grand Forks, Minnesota, is home to Cabela's, featuring an extensive collection of hunting, fishing, and outdoor gear in a five-story-high store with a 35-foot high mountain with game mounts, a gigantic aquarium, and indoor firearm testing areas.

The Grand Forks area has more than 85 restaurants serving fast food to gourmet meals, including Chinese, Mexican, Bavarian, and Italian fare as well as the Midwest staple steak-and-potatoes dinner.

***Visitor Information:*** Greater Grand Forks Convention & Visitors Bureau, 4251 Gateway Drive, Grand Forks, ND 58203; telephone (701)746-0444; toll-free (800)866-4566. Grand Forks Parks District, 1210 7th Avenue South, Grand Forks, ND 58208; telephone (701)746-2750

## ■ Convention Facilities

Grand Forks is the largest sports, convention, and entertainment center between Minneapolis and Seattle. Its Alerus Center is the largest sports, entertainment, and convention facility in the upper Midwest. The facility includes more than 145,000 square feet of banquet, meeting, and exhibit space; adjustable concert seating for up to 22,000 people; 12 conference rooms; and a 26,000-square-foot ballroom. Several local banquet halls, hotels, and restaurants also provide meeting facilities.

***Convention Information:*** Alerus Center, 1200 42nd Street South, Grand Forks, ND 58203; telephone (701) 792-1200. Greater Grand Forks Convention & Visitors Bureau, 4251 Gateway Drive, Grand Forks, ND 58203; telephone (701)746-0444; toll-free (800)866-4566

## ■ Transportation

### Approaching the City

Grand Forks is accessible by two major highways: Interstate 29, which runs north and south, and U.S. Highway 2, which runs east and west. Grand Forks International Airport, located 4.5 miles west of the city, is North Dakota's busiest commercial airport. Northwest Airlines and Northwest Airlinks (Mesaba Airlines and Pinnacle Airlines) operate daily flights with a traffic total of almost 40,000 flights per month. Amtrak operates daily passenger trains. Interstate bus service is provided by Greyhound and Triangle bus lines.

### Traveling in the City

The Cities Area Transit (CAT) provides bus service to both Grand Forks and East Grand Forks Monday through Saturday. CAT offers a door-to-door senior ride service for adults 55 and older. Dial-a-Ride service is available for the physically handicapped.

## ■ Communications

### Newspapers and Magazines

The city's daily newspaper is the *Grand Forks Herald*; although its building burned to the ground in April 1997 during the great flood, the newspaper managed to win a Pulitzer Prize for its coverage of the flood. The paper maintains an Internet website with daily news, a week's worth of archived news, local classified ads, and "online extras." The *Dakota Student*, the student-published campus newspaper of UND, is published twice weekly during the fall and spring semesters. The paper is free to students and community members. The University of North Dakota publishes scholarly journals, including *North Dakota Quarterly*, a literary review.

## Television and Radio

Residents of Grand Forks receive programming from one public and one commercial television station and from AM and FM radio stations that include religious and classic rock formats, as well as a University of North Dakota station. Grand Forks also receives programming from Fargo. Cable service is available.

***Media Information:*** *Grand Forks Herald,* Knight-Ridder, Inc., 375 2nd Ave. N., PO Box 6008, Grand Forks, ND 58206-6008; telephone (701)780-1100; toll-free (800)477-6572

### Grand Forks Online

City of Grand Forks. Available www.grandforksgov .com

Grand Forks Air Force Base. Available public .grandforks.amc.af.mil

Grand Forks Chamber of Commerce. Available www.gfchamber.com

Grand Forks Convention and Visitors Bureau. Available www.visitgrandforks.com

Grand Forks County Historical Society. Available www.grandforkshistory.com

*Grand Forks Herald.* Available www .grandforksherald.com

Grand Forks Park District. Available www.gfparks .org

Grand Forks Public Library. Available www .grandforksgov.com/library

Grand Forks Public Schools. Available www .gfschools.org

Grand Forks Region Economic Development Corporation. Available www.grandforks.org

Office of Urban Development. Available www. grandforksgov.com/gfgov/home.nsf/Pages/ Urban+Development

University of North Dakota. Available www.und.edu

BIBLIOGRAPHY

Hanson, Nancy Edmonds, *Bread Basket of the World: Fargo, Grand Forks, and the Red River Valley* (Fargo, ND: Dakota Graphic Society, 1987)

Smith, Janet Elaine, *The Flood of the Millennium: The Real Story: The Survivors* (East Grand Forks, MN: VanJan Publishing, 1997)

# Ohio

# The State in Brief

**Nickname:** Buckeye State

**Motto:** With God, all things are possible

**Flower:** Scarlet carnation

**Bird:** Cardinal

**Area:** 44,825 square miles (2000; U.S. rank 35th)

**Elevation:** Ranges from 455 feet to 1,550 feet above sea level

**Climate:** Temperate and continental; humid with wide seasonal variation

**Admitted to Union:** March, 1, 1803

**Capital:** Columbus

**Head Official:** Governor Ted Strickland (D) (until 2010)

**Population**

1980: 10,798,000
1990: 10,847,115
2000: 11,353,140
2006 estimate: 11,478,006
Percent change, 1990–2000: 4.7%
U.S. rank in 2006: 7th
Percent of residents born in state: 75.12% (2006)
Density: 280.0 people per square mile (2006)
2006 FBI Crime Index Total: 462,444

**Racial and Ethnic Characteristics (2006)**

White: 9,645,844
Black or African American: 1,357,343
American Indian and Alaska Native: 21,570
Asian: 175,000
Native Hawaiian and Pacific Islander: 2,447
Hispanic or Latino (may be of any race): 265,762
Other: 104,589

**Age Characteristics (2006)**

Population under 5 years old: 736,175
Population 5 to 19 years old: 2,364,272
Percent of population 65 years and over: 13.3%
Median age: 37.6

**Vital Statistics**

Total number of births (2006): 147,791
Total number of deaths (2006): 107,614
AIDS cases reported through 2005: 14,381

**Economy**

Major industries: Trade; finance, insurance, and real estate; manufacturing; agriculture; tourism; services
Unemployment rate (2006): 7.1%
Per capita income (2006): $23,543
Median household income (2006): $44,532
Percentage of persons below poverty level (2006): 13.3%
Income tax rate: 0.649% to 6.555%
Sales tax rate: 5.5%

# Akron

## ■ The City in Brief

**Founded:** 1825 (incorporated 1836)

**Head Official:** Mayor Donald L. Plusquellic (D) (since 1987)

**City Population**

    1980: 237,177
    1990: 223,019
    2000: 217,074
    2006 estimate: 209,704
    Percent change, 1990–2000: −2.7%
    U.S. rank in 1980: Not available
    U.S. rank in 1990: 71st (State rank: 5th)
    U.S. rank in 2000: 82nd (State rank: 5th)

**Metropolitan Area Population**

    1980: 2,938,277
    1990: 2,859,644
    2000: 2,945,831
    2006 estimate: 2,917,801
    Percent change, 1990–2000: 3.0%
    U.S. rank in 1980: Not available
    U.S. rank in 1990: Not available
    U.S. rank in 2000: 16th

**Area:** 62.41 square miles

**Elevation:** 1,050 feet above sea level

**Average Annual Temperatures:** January, 25.2° F; July, 71.8° F; annual average, 49.5° F

**Average Annual Precipitation:** 38.47 inches of rain; 47.1 inches of snow

**Major Economic Sectors:** Research and development, manufacturing, healthcare, education

**Unemployment Rate:** 5.9% (June 2007)

**Per Capita Income:** $19,497 (2005)

**2005 FBI Crime Index Property:** 12,040

**2005 FBI Crime Index Violent:** 1,265

**Major Colleges and Universities:** University of Akron

**Daily Newspaper:** *The Akron Beacon Journal*

## ■ Introduction

Akron is the cradle of the rubber industry in the United States, home of the National Inventors Hall of Fame, birthplace of Alcoholics Anonymous and current site of the leading edge of polymer engineering and research. Akron's history has been one of adaptation, of seeing opportunity and developing a response, all of which has led to the community becoming an industrial power. The city balances a long tradition of manufacturing and transportation businesses with fine cultural tastes. Akron has given the United States automotive tires, plastics, oatmeal, basketballer LeBron James, rocker Chrissie Hynde of the Pretenders, New Wave band Devo, and the All–American Soap Box Derby—a true show of the city's diversity.

## ■ Geography and Climate

Akron's natural surroundings provide a little of everything—to the south and east lie the gently rolling Appalachian Foothills; to the north is the glacial legacy of Lake Erie; and Akron itself sits on the Cuyahoga River in the Great Lakes Plains region. The Plains are renowned for their fertility, while the Appalachian Plateau is not only beautiful but a concentrated repository of minerals.

Akron experiences four distinct seasons throughout the year. A consistently high level of humidity makes for cold winters and hot summers. The winter season can be quite snowy, although Akron's relative distance from Lake Erie protects it from the full barrage of lake effect precipitation experienced by Cleveland. Year-round moisture generates an excellent growing climate.

**Area:** 62.41 square miles

**Elevation:** 1,050 feet above sea level

**Average Temperatures:** January, 25.2° F; July, 71.8° F; annual average, 49.5° F

**Average Annual Precipitation:** 38.47 inches of rain; 47.1 inches of snow

# ■ History

## Great Lake, Good Spot to Settle

The last Ice Age left northern Ohio a priceless gift—a mammoth body of water to support fish, game and agriculture, along with rich soil and mineral deposits. Lake Erie was named for a tribe of native people who lived on its shores; other early inhabitants attracted by the bountiful flora and fauna included Iroquois, Miami, Shawnee, Wyandot, Delaware, and Ottawa Indian tribes. The first residents left little mark on the land, aside from a well-worn trail that became known as the Portage Path used to transport canoes between large bodies of water. The native tribes also left a linguistic heads-up—their words for the concepts of "hunger" and "cold" were soon understood by subsequent European explorers.

Northern Ohio's riches of fish and furs couldn't be ignored by adventurers from across the pond. French trappers set up outposts to protect their fur trade and subsequently fought the British for the area in what came to be known as the French and Indian War. As part of a treaty, France ceded Ohio and the Great Lakes to Great Britain, which forbade U.S. settlers to occupy the area. Not known for obedience to the Queen, pioneers from the eastern U.S. colonies continued to traverse the area; following the American Revolution, Great Britain ceded Ohio and the Northwest Territories to the United States. However, the British continued to occupy fortifications that they had agreed to leave. Tensions had continued to run high between the U.S. and Great Britain after the war of American independence, and a new generation of "warhawks" on the east coast fed the unrest with reports that the Brits were inciting native tribes to perpetrate violence on U.S. pioneers and explorers along the Great Lakes. War was declared in 1812, with British and Canadian troops taking on an under-prepared U.S. military. Native American tribes picked a side and fought for reasons ranging from survival to revenge, although the tribes's alliance with the British was effectively ended when the Shawnee Chief Tecumseh was killed shortly after the Battle of Lake Erie.

The War of 1812 ultimately ended in a stalemate but with lasting effects on both Canada and the U.S.—national identity was cemented in both countries, and a firm border was established along the Great Lakes. Ohio had been a state since 1803, and the U.S. had just spent a great deal of effort to ensure that the productive, fertile area remained part of the Union. But how to bring those riches to the rest of the country?

## The Ohio-Erie Canal

Ever since humans first cast eyes on the ocean-like expanse of Lake Erie, the creation of a navigable route between the lake and other major water systems nearby was a primary objective. The Appalachian and Adirondack Mountains created obstacles to ground transportation methods of the time, and water was viewed as an easy route. Plans for a canal system had been percolating for decades before the War of 1812 ; after the war, construction commenced on the Erie Canal that would connect the northeast end of the lake with the Hudson River, allowing for transportation of goods and people on to the Atlantic Ocean. A parallel canal was begun from the south shore of Lake Erie with a plan to join the Ohio River at Portsmouth, then proceed east through Pennsylvania to the wealthy eastern communities hungry for Ohio wheat, furs, and minerals.

Communities sprang up along the canal construction route and its attendant industries. An hour south of Lake Erie, at the high point of the Ohio-Erie canal, the town of Akron (Greek for "high") was platted in 1811 and founded in 1825. The canal required 17 locks to be passed in the vicinity of Akron, necessitating that passengers spend a number of hours in the burgeoning town. Businesses were developed to meet the needs and desires of the pass-through traffic as well as to facilitate the freight trade—barrels and pottery containers were manufactured in Akron amid taverns, general stores and boat building enterprises. Hard-working immigrants came to Akron to labor on the canal and stayed to prosper in canal-related businesses after the waterway was completed. Akron was established as a true crossroads, and then found itself at the figurative crossroads of the U.S. Civil War.

## "Farmers of Rich and Joyous Ohio ..."

In the mid-1800s, Ohio was a microcosm of the nation. The northern counties, including Summit, were home to some of the most passionate abolitionists in the country. The southern counties, abutting pro-slavery states Kentucky and Virginia, were equally passionate in support of states' rights. In this atmosphere of division, the pro-abolition family of John Brown moved to northern Ohio in search of a politically supportive community. Brown and his family lived a somewhat chaotic existence, as he struggled to provide for his wife and children as a tanner, sheep farmer and wool merchant. In 1844, Brown moved to Akron and partnered with city founder Simon Perkins in a wool business; the partnership was dissolved in 1851 for financial reasons and Brown moved his family out of Ohio as he became increasingly troubled by slavery in the United States. Events in "bleeding Kansas" inspired Brown and several of his sons to travel to the free state to take part in raids on pro-slavery factions. Brown gained a national platform for his views and actions, which culminated in his band's raid on Harper's Ferry, Virginia (now West Virginia). Brown was apprehended by Robert E. Lee and was hanged in 1859—arguably, the raid on Harper's Ferry pushed the country into Civil War and ultimately gained Brown's goal of ending slavery in the United States.

With Brown's fierce beliefs in its memory and Sojourner Truth's Akron speech ringing in its ears, Ohio joined the Union and contributed more than its conscripted quota of volunteers to the army during the Civil War. During and after the war, life in Akron and northern Ohio underwent a shift from the agrarian to the industrial, as entrepreneurs adapted to meet the demands of a nation doing battle. Railroads began to crisscross the country, and Akron was not immune—train transport of goods eventually led to the demise of the Ohio-Erie Canal in 1913. However, in the late 1800s, Akron needed all the freight transport systems available: B.F. Goodrich had come to town.

## Akron's Beginnings in Rubber

Dr. Benjamin Franklin Goodrich grew up on the east coast and received his medical education in Cleveland, Ohio. After serving as a surgeon during the Civil War, Goodrich could see the potential in vulcanized rubber products as developed by Charles Goodyear and decided in 1870 to locate a company in Akron. A couple of decades later, the Goodyear Tire and Rubber Company, named in honor of Charles Goodyear, based its headquarters in Akron and provided competition for Goodrich. Firestone Rubber followed in 1900 and General Tire in 1915, establishing Akron as the "Rubber Capital of the World." Rubber production at that time consisted mainly of bicycle and carriage tires and rubber pads for horseshoes. The industry pulled in workers not only from other states but from other countries, making for a motivated and diverse population.

Akron's fortunes were boosted by rubber demand during World War I; the ensuing Great Depression had an economic impact on the industry and the city as a whole, but the American love affair with the automobile came to the rescue. In the early 1900s, the Model T had been outfitted with Goodyear tires; by 1926, Goodyear had become the world's largest rubber company as it sprinted to keep ahead of its competitors in Akron. World War II again increased the need for fighter plane tires and other equipment, bringing more growth and wealth to the Rubber Capital. With many men serving in the military, women entered the industrial workforce in droves; the local rubber manufacturers used women in advertising to both promote the war effort and their products.

After the war, change was in the air. In the 1950s and 1960s, radial tires became the industry standard and Akron's factories weren't equipped for the switch. Some companies attempted a hybrid tire with poor results, and B.F. Goodrich converted its machinery over to radial production equipment at great expense to the company. These costs, coupled with industry strikes and factory shutdowns in the 1970s and 1980s, decimated the rubber business in Akron. Today, Firestone maintains a technical research center in Akron and Goodyear continues to produce racing tires while researching new tire technology, but most of the other rubber companies have left.

## Post-Rubber Akron

Akron has rebounded from the tough days in the rubber industry, again demonstrating its ingenuity and resourcefulness in the field of polymer research and engineering. More than 400 polymer-related companies operate in the area, and the University of Akron has created both a degree program in polymer engineering and a research facility that supports local efforts. In addition, aerospace design is taking flight in local industry.

The city of Akron is redefining itself and rediscovering itself as it celebrates its contributions to American inventiveness, music, and sports. The downtown area is undergoing a renaissance, and the Ohio & Erie Canal National Heritage Corridor has been preserved in recognition of the history of the waterway. Akron is facing forward, but it remembers how it got where it is today.

***Historical Information:*** Summit County Historical Society, 465 South Portage Path, Akron, OH 44320; telephone (330) 535-1120; fax (330) 535-0250

## ■ Population Profile

### Metropolitan Area Residents

1980: 2,938,277
1990: 2,859,644
2000: 2,945,831
2006 estimate: 2,917,801
Percent change, 1990–2000: 3.0%
U.S. rank in 1980: Not available
U.S. rank in 1990: Not available
U.S. rank in 2000: 16th

### City Residents

1980: 237,177
1990: 223,019
2000: 217,074
2006 estimate: 209,704

*Eric M. Miller 2008.*

Percent change, 1990–2000: −2.7%
U.S. rank in 1980: Not available
U.S. rank in 1990: 71st (State rank: 5th)
U.S. rank in 2000: 82nd (State rank: 5th)

**Density:** 3,497.3 people per square mile (2000)

**Racial and ethnic characteristics (2005)**

> White: 131,244
> Black: 60,590
> American Indian and Alaska Native: 369
> Asian: 3,497
> Native Hawaiian and Pacific Islander: 61
> Hispanic or Latino (may be of any race): 3,485
> Other: 1,447

**Percent of residents born in state:** 75.6% (2006)

**Age characteristics (2005)**

> Population under 5 years old: 13,894
> Population 5 to 9 years old: 15,159

Population 10 to 14 years old: 12,886
Population 15 to 19 years old: 12,529
Population 20 to 24 years old: 16,138
Population 25 to 34 years old: 30,436
Population 35 to 44 years old: 28,297
Population 45 to 54 years old: 26,764
Population 55 to 59 years old: 11,303
Population 60 to 64 years old: 8,540
Population 65 to 74 years old: 11,636
Population 75 to 84 years old: 9,913
Population 85 years and older: 2,686
Median age: 34.7 years

**Births (2006, MSA)**

> Total number: 8,195

**Deaths (2006, MSA)**

> Total number: 6,806

**Money income (2005)**

> Per capita income: $19,497

Median household income: $32,937
Total households: 85,558

**Number of households with income of...**

less than $10,000: 11,644
$10,000 to $14,999: 7,565
$15,000 to $24,999: 13,030
$25,000 to $34,999: 12,619
$35,000 to $49,999: 15,287
$50,000 to $74,999: 12,901
$75,000 to $99,999: 5,936
$100,000 to $149,999: 4,842
$150,000 to $199,999: 1,091
$200,000 or more: 643

**Percent of families below poverty level:** 11.3% (2005)

**2005 FBI Crime Index Property:** 12,040

**2005 FBI Crime Index Violent:** 1,265

# ■ Municipal Government

The City of Akron operates under the council-mayor form of government, with the 13-member council and the mayor working together to establish administrative departments and to oversee the city finances. The city is divided into 10 wards, each of which elect a council member for a two-year term of service. The other three council members are elected by the city populace at-large and serve four-year terms in office. The mayor is also elected by the general populace of Akron and serves a four-year term. The mayor selects a cabinet composed of the Deputy Mayors of Economic Development, Planning, Public Service, Safety, Labor Relations, Intergovernmental Relations, Finance, and Law.

**Head Official:** Mayor Donald L. Plusquellic (D) (since 1987; current term expires 2012)

**Total Number of City Employees:** 2,585 (2007)
*City Information:* City of Akron, Municipal Building, Ste. 200, 166 South High Street, Akron, OH 44308; telephone (330)375-2345; fax (330) 375-2468

# ■ Economy

## Major Industries and Commercial Activity

From its former honor as the "Rubber Capital of the World," Akron has moved forward into the world of liquid crystal and polymer research, development, and technology. More than 400 companies in the area are at work on one aspect or another of polymers, creating what is now referred to as "The Polymer Valley." The area is the leading site nationwide for the manufacture of plastic

processing equipment; more than 16,000 polymer industry employees live in greater Akron. The University of Akron supports the industry with both a College of Polymer Engineering and a specialized laboratory and research facility accessible by Akron area business partners. The greater Akron area is home to more than 21,000 businesses, approximatly 150 of which are *Fortune* 500 companies.

As a transportation hub between the east coast of the United States and parts west, Akron has built an industry around motor vehicle production, movement of freight, and aeronautics. In 2003 the local branch of Lockheed-Martin was awarded a $2 million Department of Defense contract to develop a new high altitude airship capable of carrying a variety of payloads. Local researchers in the aeronautics field have been studying "lighter than air" technology for aircraft since the days of the Goodyear Blimp being docked in Akron.

**Items and goods produced:** plastic products, polymers, chemicals, metals, motor vehicles and related equipment, biomedical products, aeronautical instruments, and controls

## Incentive Programs—New and Existing Companies

*Local programs:* Through Tax Increment Financing, the City of Akron offers businesses the opportunity to apply real property taxes to a public infrastructure improvement that will directly benefit the business. In addition, businesses that locate or expand into an Akron Enterprise Community Zone are eligible for a tax abatement program that allows for up to 100 percent of tangible personal property taxes to be in abatement for up to 10 years.

*State programs:* The state of Ohio offers a number of incentives designed to encourage new companies and retain existing businesses. Tax credit programs include those for job creation, machinery and equipment investment, export, research and development franchise, and technology investment. Ohio also offers a property tax abatement for areas identified as enterprise zones and sales tax exemptions for research and development.

*Job training programs:* The state of Ohio has created the Enterprise Ohio Network of public community colleges and universities that work with businesses and organizations to provide continuing education for employees. The Ohio Investment in Training Program offers reduced-cost training and materials to new or expanding businesses, with an emphasis on employment sectors in which training costs are comparatively high.

Summit County's Employment Resource Center assists employers with recruitment and skills testing for prospective employees, customizes on-the-job training for new or reallocated workers, and can advise employers and employees during layoff situations.

## Development Projects

In an effort to counter the outflow of businesses and residents to malls and suburbs, downtown Akron became a Special Improvement District in the mid-1990s. This designation as a private nonprofit entity has enabled the enhancement of parking and transit services, marketing of the downtown area, business recruitment and retention, and the physical presentation and security of the area. The restoration project has included adaptive reuse of large, unoccupied businesses in the district; examples include the Roetzel & Andress Office Center (bringing 85,000 square feet of retail space and 100,000 square feet of office space to the downtown area) and Advanced Elastomer Systems (now located in buildings 40 and 41 of the B.F. Goodrich complex and continuing the trend of innovation in a most appropriate setting). As of 2007, more than $2.5 billion dollars in private capital had been invested in new plants and plant expansions in Summit, Portage and Medina Counties. In 2004 alone, 42 projects contributed to nearly $150 million in private capital investment.

In 2007 the City of Akron had a number of business and industrial parks under development or open for new enterprises. The Ascot Business Park was being cultivated for light industrial and manufacturing businesses, with 52 of the 228 total acres remaining for development in 2007. Tenants included companies that produce plastics, chemicals, aluminum, glass, and graphic art rubber products. The Airport Development Area encourages location of businesses that fit within the existing aviation, commercial, and industrial themes. In 2006 a $10 million grant was made to the University of Akron in order to support the University Park Alliance's economic development plan to revitalize the downtown district. Developers hoped to bring 500 new housing units, create 1,000 new jobs, attract new businesses and mixed-use developments, and draw additional investments of $500 million to $1 billion.

In 2003 the Akron Public Schools District embarked on an ambitious 15-year plan to renovate existing school structures into state-of-the-art community learning centers. The updated facilities were intended to serve as modern school buildings for Akron Public School students during the day, and in the evening will be available for community programs, adult education, recreation, and after-school enrichment activities. The total project budget was $800 million, and as of 2007 three community centers had been opened, including the Helen E. Arnold Community Learning Center in October 2007. Three more community centers were planned or under construction.

The Akron Art Museum underwent extensive renovations that were unveiled in 2007. The museum expanded to 65,000 square feet of soaring architecture with tripled gallery space and increased outdoor exhibit areas with the opening of the new John S. and James L. Knight Building.

## Commercial Shipping

Akron is ideally situated within a 500-mile radius of 42 major U.S. cities that comprise 55 percent of U.S. manufacturing plants, 57 percent of the U.S. population and 60 percent of its buying power. Akron businesses have a variety of choices when it comes to shipping, considering the city's proximity to major waterways, airports, roadways, and rail systems. The Akron Fulton Airport, located in the southeast corner of the municipality, was home to the original Goodyear Airdock and site of the first lighter-than-air craft. The airport has four paved runways and can accommodate all types of private, single- and multi-engine aircraft. The Akron-Canton Airport offers a range of commercial flight and cargo shipping options. Carriers include AirTran, Delta, Frontier, Northwest, United and US Airways Express. Further air cargo options are available up the road 40 miles in Cleveland, where Cleveland Hopkins International Airport hosts eight carriers that include UPS, FedEx and the United States Postal Service.

A multitude of interstate, U.S. and state highways intersect in Akron, providing ready access to and from all points in the country. Interstates 71, 76 and 77 all pass through the city; bypasses have been created to encourage smooth traffic flow. Local trucking and transport firm Roadway Express, a subsidiary of Yellow Roadway Corporation, leads the ground transport field with a network of shipping options extending to Canada, Alaska, Hawaii, Puerto Rico and across the globe. Akron's industrial history has made the city a magnet for many other companies that specialize in handling and transport of a range of freight. Several rail systems pass through Akron as well, including CSX and Norfolk Southern Railroads.

The Great Lakes Seaway from the Port of Cleveland and the St. Lawrence Seaway link the Akron area to the Atlantic Ocean, providing access to Europe, Africa, South America, Australia and Asia. The Port of Cleveland, the largest overseas general cargo port on Lake Erie and third largest port on the Great Lakes, serves more than 50 countries, shipping cargo to and receiving cargo from 120 ports around the world.

## Labor Force and Employment Outlook

Developments in the early 2000s portended that the manufacturing sector was likely to see more layoffs and lost jobs in the future. Analysts believed that the manufacture of durables might rebound somewhat, but the employment sectors that were expected to demonstrate significant growth included health care and social assistance, science and technology professions, administration and support services, leisure and hospitality, wholesale trade, transportation and warehousing, construction, retail trade, services, and recreation, arts and entertainment. Adaptation and retraining were considered critical for workers to make the shift from production to a more service-oriented job market.

The following is a summary of data regarding the Akron metropolitan area labor force, 2006 annual averages.

**Size of nonagricultural labor force:** 339,700

**Number of workers employed in ...**

construction and mining: 14,900
manufacturing: 47,700
trade, transportation and utilities: 67,400
information: 4,600
financial activities: 14,400
professional and business services: 51,200
educational and health services: 45,100
leisure and hospitality: 31,400
other services: 13,800
government: 49,300

**Average hourly earnings of production workers employed in manufacturing:** $16.07

**Unemployment rate:** 5.9% (June 2007)

| *Largest metropolitan area employers (2007)* | *Number of employees* |
|---|---|
| Summa Health System | 6,102 |
| Akron General Health System | 4,267 |
| Goodyear Tire & Rubber Co. | 4,000 |
| Akron School District | 3,500 |
| Kent State University | 3,500 |
| The University of Akron | 2,845 |
| Akron General Medical Center | 2,820 |
| City of Akron | 2,585 |
| Akron Children's Hospital | 2,360 |
| FirstEnergy Corp. | 2,300 |

## Cost of Living

The following is a summary of data regarding several key cost of living factors in the Akron area.

**2007 (1st quarter) ACCRA Average House Price:** $251,053

**2007 (1st quarter) ACCRA Cost of Living Index:** 95.7

**State income tax rate:** 0.68% to 6.87%

**State sales tax rate:** 5.5%

**Local income tax rate:** 2.25% (Akron)

**Local sales tax rate:** 0.75% (Summit County)

**Property tax rate:** $89.270 per $1,000 assessed value

*Economic Information:* Greater Akron Chamber, One Cascade Plaza, 17th Floor, Akron, OH 44308-1192; telephone (303)376-5550; toll-free (800)621-8001.

# ■ Education and Research

## Elementary and Secondary Schools

In 2001 Akron Public Schools committed to a ten-point contract with the community, vowing to heighten academic standards, raise test scores and graduation rates, keep schools safe, cut costs and limit growth, execute and enforce contracts with parents of students, move students into alternative school programs as necessary, provide continuing education for teachers and administrators, work closely with community partners, monitor the budget closely, and delay requests for more operational monies until the ten points of the contract were met (which happened as of the 2004-2005 school year). Akron Public Schools is a large district that boasts a student body that is approximately half African American and half Anglo-American, along with representation from Asian, Pacific Islander, Latino, and American Indian cultural and ethnic groups. The district's diverse language program is a source of pride.

A plethora of specialized programs and studies are offered in classes that meet all state standards for education. Team and individual sports, music, and art offerings have been supported in Akron Public Schools, demonstrating the district's commitment to individualized learning; classes in French, Spanish, Latin and Chinese are all offered, and Firestone High School participates in the prestigious International Bacalaureate Program. The district has incorporated alternative school facilities that serve students who are at risk of dropping out of the general school population or who pose a discipline problem. Project GRAD (Graduation Really Acheives Dreams) is a district-wide program to encourage students to stay in school; it targets achievement levels among low-income students.

In 2003 the district embarked on an ambitious 15-year plan to renovate existing school structures into state-of-the-art community learning centers. The updated facilities were intended to serve as modern school buildings for Akron Public School students during the day, and in the evening will be available for community programs, adult education, recreation, and after-school enrichment activities. The total project budget was $800 million, and as of 2007 three community centers had been opened, including the Helen E. Arnold Community Learning Center in October 2007.

In 2007 two Akron public schools, Firestone and Ellet High Schools, were chosen as two of eight Ohio sites and two of nineteen for the national "High Schools

That Work" awards and designated as "Gold Improvement" Award schools.

The following is a summary of data regarding the Akron Public Schools as of the 2005–2006 school year.

**Total enrollment: 26,385**

**Number of facilities**

> elementary schools: 36
> junior high/middle schools: 10
> senior high schools: 7
> other: 0

**Student/teacher ratio: 15.4:1**

**Teacher salaries (2005–06)**

> elementary median: $52,360
> junior high/middle median: $53,130
> secondary median: $52,860

**Funding per pupil: $9,845**

The city of Akron is also home to a number of private middle and high school programs, most of which are operated under the auspices of religious institutions, such as Walsh Jesuit, a Catholic high school. A Waldorf school is located in nearby Copley, Ohio, and several Montessori schools are located in Akron and surrounding communities.

***Public Schools Information:*** Akron Public Schools, Administration Building, 70 N. Broadway, Akron, OH 44308-1911; telephone (330)761-1661

## Colleges and Universities

With the unlikeliest of mascots (Zippy the Kangaroo), the University of Akron has a student body 24,704 students representing 44 U.S. states and 79 foreign countries. The university functions on the semester system and offers more than 200 undergraduate majors, more than 110 master's and doctoral degrees, and 4 law degree tracks. The university has adapted to economic trends in the Akron area by instituting a College of Polymer Science and Engineering; other degree programs prepare students for careers in nursing, education, the fine arts, the social sciences and more. There are more than 735 instructors, over 85 percent of whom hold a doctoral degree in their field.

Adult vocational education is available at several institutions in the Akron area, including the Ohio College of Massotherapy (OCM). Enrolling approximately 250 full-time students, OCM combines classroom and experiential work in pursuit of an associate's degree in Applied Science or a diploma in Massage Therapy. Specialized healthcare programs in X-ray technology or nursing can be studied through the local hospitals organized under the Summa Health System, including St. Thomas Medical Center and Akron City Hospital.

Other institutions for post-secondary education include the Academy of Court Reporting, Akron Barber College, Stafford Flight Academy, and the Akron Machining Institute.

Akron is a mere hour south of Cleveland and within easy reach of the main campuses and branches of several post-secondary education programs, including Case Western Reserve University and Cleveland State University. Kent State University is located about 24 miles to the northeast of Akron.

## Libraries and Research Centers

Akron and its surrounding communities are served by the Akron-Summit County Public Library system, which is comprised of a main library facility in Akron, 17 branch libraries, and a bookmobile. The library system provides access to more than 1.2 million books, approximately 250,000 audio-visual materials, and 1,800 periodicals. The main library houses a number of special collections centered around local history; one of the newer collections has preserved musical contributions of local Summit County performers from the past to present day. Photographs, books, articles, and other materials chronicle the history of the rubber industry, the World Series of Golf, and the Soap Box Derby in Akron. Each branch of the library system offers a variety of reading and education programs for children, teens, and adults throughout the year. Book delivery is available for homebound readers.

Located on the fourth floor of the Summit County Courthouse, the Akron Law Library promotes the study of law and legal research to its membership of attorneys, judges, magistrates, and other court personnel. More than 81,500 volumes are on hand for browsing, along with an increasing number of audio-visual formats. Library members can also utilize online legal research resources, and three professional law librarians are onsite to assist with research questions and access to materials.

Future legal eagles conduct research in the Law Library associated with the law school at the University of Akron. The library maintains a comprehensive selection of books, audio-visual materials and periodicals related to the legal profession, supporting the academic work of students and the pedagogical efforts of faculty members. The university also provides a general library service for students in other degree programs, with materials including electronic books, government documents, maps, periodicals, and printed books.

The University of Akron is the site of breakthrough research efforts such as an examination of the D.A.R.E. (Drug Abuse Resistance Education) program, with procedural revisions expected as an outcome, and applied polymer research taking place in the Institute of Polymer Engineering. The institute works with a variety of businesses in the polymer industry, providing lab equipment and personnel trained in research and testing techniques.

The University of Akron Research Foundation has total assets of over $3 million to be allocated through various university programs.

***Public Library Information:*** Akron-Summit County Public Library, 60 South High Street, Akron, OH 44326; telephone (330)643-9000

# ■ Health Care

One of the Akron area's largest employers, Summa Health System operates more than 1,200 licensed, inpatient beds throughout Akron City, St. Thomas and Cuyahoga Falls General Hospital campuses. Summa also offers outpatient care in four health centers in surrounding communities. There are more than 900 physicians employed by the Summa Health Network, and in 2006 there were 38,374 patient admissions. Akron City Hospital specializes in diagnosis, treatment and ongoing care in the areas of orthopedics, oncology, cardiovascular issues, geriatrics, and obesity. The facility was named a "Leapfrog Top Hospital" for 2007, one of just 33 nationwide. In 2007, for the tenth year in a row, Summa was selected as one of "America's Best Hospitals" by *U.S. News and World Report*. St. Thomas Hospital offers wound care, eye surgery, orthopedics and behavioral health treatment. Cuyahoga Falls General Hospital is a 257-bed acute care facility.

Akron General Medical Center was founded in 1914 and has evolved into a tertiary care, nonprofit teaching hospital with 537 licensed beds. The facility provides emergency and trauma care, critical care, and services in a wide variety of specialties such as sleep disorder diagnosis and treatment, pain management, heart and vascular treatment, endocrinology and diabetes care. Akron General is equipped to respond to many conditions, disorders and diseases; as a full-service medical facility, it provides its students with opportunities to research, observe and intervene with a broad spectrum of health concerns. Its staff includes 1,000 physicians and 3,400 healthcare professionals.

The Children's Hospital Medical Center of Akron is the largest pediatric care provider in northeast Ohio. The design of the structure and the approach of the staff are intended to promote calm and healing in the hospital's young patients, who visit the hospital for treatment of conditions such as trauma, cystic fibrosis, speech and hearing issues, and cancer. The hospital houses a regional burn trauma center for the treatment of both adults and children, and a Ronald McDonald House is located across from the facility for the convenience and comfort of families whose children have been admitted.

Edwin Shaw Rehabilitation Hospital provides therapeutic treatment for patients recovering from disorders that have disrupted physical or mental function. The hospital employs traditional methods along with fun and innovative approaches such as the Challenge Golf Course designed to improve the skills of players with identified disabilities.

Private practices in general and specialized medicine are available in Akron, as are walk-in and urgent care clinics. Practitioners of massage therapy, chiropractic care, acupuncture and hypnotherapy also exist in the metro area.

# ■ Recreation

## Sightseeing

Sightseeing in Akron might start where the city itself started—with the Ohio & Erie Canal. The original canal route has been transformed into a recreational and historical education zone called the CanalWay, which was designated as a National Heritage site in 1996. The 110-mile area can be explored by biking or walking all or part of the 60 miles of Towpath Trail along the route where mules once towed barges, or by driving the CanalWay Ohio National Scenic Byway that stretches from Canton to Cleveland, or by riding the Cuyahoga Valley Scenic Railroad. Both the byway and the railroad pass near destinations such as Inventure Place (the National Inventors Hall of Fame), Akron's Northside, the Visitors Center for the Canal, Rockside Road, and Quaker Square. The original Quaker Oats Company building has been converted into a unique center for entertainment, shopping, and dining; the silos of the old factory can be rented as lodging in one of Akron's most memorable hotels.

The CanalWay transports visitors to downtown Akron by way of the Northside District, a collection of restored buildings, outdoor sculptures, unique cafés, galleries, and restaurants in the city's reborn city center. Northside makes a good jumping-off point for a tour of Akron history; just north of the train station in Northside are the nine locks that allowed barges to climb the canal from Little Cuyahoga River to the Portage Summit. The restored Mustill Store reflects the 19th century canal-era design and houses a visitors center with exhibits on local industry related to the canal.

The Glendale Cemetery was established in 1839 and reveals much of the history of Akron in its engravings and epitaphs. A restored 1876 Gothic chapel remains on the grounds, and mausoleums exhibiting Egyptian, Greek, Roman, Gothic, and Art Moderne influences line Cypress Avenue as it runs through the grounds.

At the Goodyear World of Rubber Museum on East Market Street, visitors can retrace the beginnings of vulcanization, observe modern rubber production processes, and check out an Indy 500 race car with Goodyear tires.

Heading south and east through downtown, visitors will come upon the National Inventors Hall of Fame, which honors the creative and brave individuals who have advanced technology and the sciences over the course of the country's existence. The Inventors Workshop onsite stimulates innovation and problem-solving in visitors who participate in interactive and fun exhibits, demonstrations, and experiments. Camp Invention provides a week-long immersion experience during the summer for children in grades two through six, and older students can compete in the Collegiate Inventors Competition sponsored by the museum.

The Akron Zoological Park is home to more than 400 animals in exhibits such as the Tiger Valley habitat, the Bald Eagle exhibit, the Otter exhibit, and the Penguin Point exhibit. The aviary and Lemur Island are perennially popular attractions. As an accredited world conservation zoo, the Akron Zoo coordinates breeding programs to conserve endangered species. The zoo offers seasonal and special events throughout the year, including Senior Safari, Boo at the Zoo, and Snack with Santa.

The home of Dr. Bob, co-founder of Alcoholics Anonymous in 1935, is open to tourists. It all started in a tidy house on Ardmore Avenue when Bill Wilson helped Dr. Robert Smith kick his alcohol addiction. The two opened the house to other alcoholics, creating a grassroots addiction treatment program that is thriving today.

Other must-see attractions include Stan Hywet Hall and Gardens (former home of Goodyear co-founder Frank Seiberling), St. Bernard Church, the American Marble and Toy Museum, and the Pan African Culture and Research Center on the grounds of the University of Akron.

## Arts and Culture

The Akron Art Museum underwent extensive renovations that were unveiled in 2007. The museum expanded to 65,000 square feet of soaring architecture with tripled gallery space and increased outdoor exhibit areas with the opening of the new John S. and James L. Knight Building. The museum's collections include works of Warhol, Stella, Bourke-White, and Callahan.

The Akron Symphony is the headliner for local performing arts; it is comprised of a symphony orchestra, a youth symphony and a symphony chorus. The professional orchestra offers free Picnic Pops concerts in local parks, chamber music during Sundays at the Elms, three Family Series concerts, seven Classic Series concerts, a Gospel Meets Symphony performance, and educational outreach programs and concerts for the public schools.

The E.J. Thomas Performing Arts Hall at the University of Akron hosts musical performances (both national and local), plays and musicals. The performance hall has joined forces with Broadway Across America, one of the largest live theater production companies in the U.S., and now offers a Broadway in Akron series. The Civic Theatre in Akron participates in the Broadway in Akron series production and provides an elegant venue for musical, dramatic and comedic performances.

Nationally-recognized musical performers are often booked at the Blossom Music Center in Cuyahoga Falls.

The Ohio Ballet, a professional company in residence at the University of Akron, performs classical and more contemporary ballet pieces. The Children's Ballet Theatre in Akron was founded in 1993 to provide a pre-professional performance opportunity for select young dancers from 10 to 18 years of age. The Children's Ballet Theatre annually performs "The Nutcracker" and has become recognized for productions of "Coppelia" and "Cinderella."

The Weathervane Playhouse is a community theater that produces a year-round schedule of family theater, musicals, and contemporary comedies and dramas. The 2004-2005 season offered an eclectic mix, ranging from "Winnie the Pooh" and "Forever Plaid" to "The Rocky Horror Picture Show." The Playhouse holds classes in Hands-On Theater, audition tactics, and musical theater techniques in addition to summer camps for younger performers.

Akron is home to the largest professional dinner theater in the world—in its 51,000 square feet of space, the Carousel Dinner Theatre can entertain up to 1,000 guests with dinner and a show.

***Arts and Culture Information:*** Akron-Summit Convention and Visitors Bureau, 77 E. Mill Street, Akron, OH 44308; telephone (330)374-7560

## Festivals and Holidays

The cold of the Ohio winter means festivities are either inside or on the ski slopes in January. Early in the month, the One Act Play Festival takes place at the Miller South School for the Visual and Performing Arts, while a number of races and demo events are occurring at nearby Boston Mills and Brandywine ski resorts. Ski and snowboard events continue throughout February. The Akron/Canton Home and Flower Show in February awakens thoughts of spring, with gardening seminars held in the John S. Knight Center. March is a month of festival as well as weather extremes, with the Annual Spring Needlework Show and the Fists Against Hunger Martial Arts Tournament. March also brings an Akron tradition of wintry night hikes in anticipation of spring.

Earth Day activities and resumption of baseball season herald the arrival of spring in April. Akron's newest extravaganza is the National Hamburger Festival, held each Memorial Day weekend in celebration of an all-American culinary creation. The first festival was held in May of 2006 in downtown Akron.

Father's Day in Akron is observed with the high-flying antics of the Aero Expo air show at the Akron Fulton Airport. Throughout the weekend, aerobatic performances are staged by modern military aircraft and the Tuskegee Airmen. Toward the end of June, Boston Mills Ski Resort hosts its annual Artfest, with juried fine arts and crafts shows featuring more than 160 artists.

The Fourth of July weekend sets off musical and culinary fireworks with the Akron Family Barbecue at Lock 3 on the Canal. Rib vendors, carnival rides and games, street entertainers, and children's activities light up the July nights. At the end of the month, the annual Akron Arts Expo coordinates a juried art show with more than 165 exhibitors, plus food and live entertainment. July winds up with the All-American Soap Box Derby World Championships at Derby Downs. In the heat of August, folks from around the region dress up in Civil War garb for the Annual Civil War Encampment and Reenactment held at Hale Farm and Village.

During the entire month of September, locals take advantage of cooler temperatures by indulging in Metro Parks' Fall Hiking Spree, following any of the 13 trails that wander through prime fall foliage. Two festivals at the end of the month say goodbye to summer (the Annual Barberton Mum Fest at Lake Anna Park) and hello to fall (the Annual Loyal Oak Cider Fest at Crawford Knecht Cider Mill). In October, the Annual Wonderful World of Ohio Mart is held at Stan Hywet Hall and Gardens, while the Akron Zoo celebrates Halloween with Boo at the Zoo. The month of November ushers in the Annual Holiday Mart at the Summit County Fairgrounds Arena, followed by the Holiday Tree Festival at the John S. Knight Center later in the month. The annual Christmas Music Spectacular in mid-December has become a beloved tradition, and FirstNight Akron is catching on as a family-friendly, alcohol-free way to see in the New Year.

## Sports for the Spectator

The big event in Akron is the All-American Soap Box Derby World Championship Finals, held each August at Derby Downs. Since 1934, the Soap Box Derby has been encouraging youth to build and race their own non-motorized vehicles. The race has become increasingly sophisticated and now has three divisions ranging from beginners in the Derby to more advanced participants to a Masters Division. The festivities last for a week and are attended by locals, celebrities, and sports personalities from across the country.

From April to September, hardball fans enjoy Akron Aeros games at beautiful Canal Park Stadium. The Aeros are the AA farm team affiliate of the Cleveland Indians, drawing half a million fans each season. The Akron Racers are one of six national pro fast-pitch women's softball teams; games are played at Firestone Stadium.

The University of Akron Zips play a number of sports in Division I of the National Collegiate Athletic Association, providing college sports fans with football, baseball, basketball, softball, volleyball, and track events. Nearby Cleveland is also home to several professional teams, including the Indians baseball franchise, the Browns football team, and the Cavaliers basketball organization.

## Sports for the Participant

The City of Akron organizes year-round individual and team sports through its recreation bureau, including basketball, wrestling, baseball, softball, volleyball, and weight training at local community centers operated by the city. Akron also maintains a championship golf course; Good Park Golf Course is located on the west side of the city and offers watered tees, greens, and fairways during golf season. A snack bar and pro shop are onsite as well. Riverwoods Golf Course provides nine holes for public use, and Turkeyfoot Lake Golf Links has an 18-hole course located in the Portage Lakes area. Valley View Golf Club has 27 holes. Mud Run has a nine-hole course and a driving range.

The Metro Parks system, which serves Akron and the greater Summit County community, maintains more than 8,700 acres of recreational and educational space. A 33-mile Bike and Hike Trail provides safe workout areas for cyclists and walkers, and the extensive trail systems throughout Metro Parks are appropriate for light hiking and mountain biking in the warmer seasons and cross-country skiing in the winter.

Camping, boating, swimming, and fishing can be enjoyed within the bounds of Portage Lakes State Park in Akron. The Portage Lakes formed when chunks of glacier settled in depressions in the ground; the resulting plants in the area are unique and consist of tamarack trees, skunk cabbage, and cranberry. A wide variety of animals and birds can be observed near the lakes, and anglers can fish for largemouth bass, walleye, bullhead, carp, pickerel, pan fish, and channel catfish.

Great fishing can also be experienced on Lake Erie, otherwise known as the "Walleye Capital of the World." Besides walleye, anglers can hook smallmouth bass, yellow perch, salmon, and silver bullet steelhead. For a fish-eye view of the lake, it's possible to scuba dive into the depths of Lake Erie to explore a number of shipwreck sites.

Cuyahoga Valley National Park contains more than 125 miles of hiking trails that cross a variety of habitats and ecosystems. Some trails are accessible to all visitors; others are more challenging, though elevation change on the trails is relatively minimal. When winter hits, sledding and cross-country skiing fun can be had at the Kendall Lake Winter Sports Center in the Park. All trails can be accessed by snowshoe, and Kendall Lake often reaches sufficient thickness for ice skating.

The Road Runner Akron Marathon has gained a reputation as one of the best marathons in the U.S., based on the organization of the race and the quality of the course. Participants can choose to run the full marathon or be part of a marathon relay team. The event kicks off with inspirational speakers and a pasta party, followed by a celebration at Canal Park Stadium after the race has ended. A Kids Fun Run is also available.

In the winter months, the Brandywine and Boston Mills Ski Resorts are the scene of downhill skiing, snowboarding, and sledding galore.

## Shopping and Dining

The former Quaker Oats Factory has been given new life as the Quaker Square Complex, home of unique specialty stores, a hotel, galleries, and restaurants. The complex was purchased by the University of Akron in 2007. The shopping experience continues in local shops throughout the downtown area. The Summit Mall on West Market Street houses more than 120 vendors beneath its roof. The Plaza at Chapel Hill incorporates a collection of 45 stores and an 8-screen theater. Don Drumm Studios and Gallery in Akron features works by more than 500 artists in a gallery that spans two buildings. Foodies will appreciate the West Point Market, a 25,000-square-foot buffet of gourmet foods such as Belgian chocolates, premium wines, imported caviar, homemade breads and a convenient café.

Akron's dining scene is continental, in reflection of its immigrant past; Italian and Chinese eateries abound, as do Mexican restaurants. Many culinary tastes are represented, however, including Cajun, Thai, Korean, Indian, French, Greek, Japanese, and Irish. Establishments range from homey cafés to fine dining bistros. The Menches Brothers Restaurant experience commemorates the invention of two American favorites by the local Menches Brothers of Akron: hamburgers and the cornucopia ice cream cone. After-dinner coffee can be found at a small selection of local coffee houses.

## ■ Convention Facilities

The John S. Knight Center has served downtown Akron since 1994, greeting conventioneers and meeting participants with its dramatic glass rotunda and spiral staircase in the 22,000-square-foot lobby. The facility offers a 30,000-square-foot exhibition hall, 12,000 square feet of banquet space, and another 12,600 square feet for meetings. Meeting areas are flexible and can be customized in a variety of configurations; all spaces meet specifications of the Americans with Disabilities Act.

The Arena Complex at the Summit County Fairgrounds contributes 68,000 square feet of exhibition space capable of accommodating 296 booths and seating for up to 2,500 people. The complex adds 3,000 square feet of meeting space and 2,500 square feet for banquet functions.

Greystone Hall in Akron contains 10,000 square feet of exhibition space, with seating for 400; 120 square feet of meeting space and 400 square feet of banquet area are also available. Two local theaters can also be utilized for meetings and conventions: the Carousel Dinner Theatre can be converted into 14,000 square feet of exhibition area with seating for 1,000 and the Akron Civic Theatre has seating for 2,700 in the performance hall.

## ■ Transportation

### Approaching the City

The Akron-Canton Airport is located just south of Akron proper and is accessed by Interstate 77. The airport offers a range of commercial flight options, with carriers such as AirTran, Delta, Frontier, Northwest, United, and US Airways Express. Akron-Canton had 1,434,233 total passengers in 2005. The Cleveland Hopkins International Airport 40 miles north of Akron provides another air option, with flights serving all regions of the U.S. and the globe. Amtrak supplies passenger train service to the area.

A number of interstate, U.S. and state highways intersect in Akron, making the city easily accessible by road. Interstates 71, 76, and 77 all pass near or through the city, and U.S. Highway 224 cuts a north-south swath through its heart. State highways 18, 21, and 8 aid travelers entering Akron. Greyhound bus service provides ground transportation to supplement personal vehicle travel.

### Traveling in the City

Market Street runs from the northwest to the southeast through the center of Akron, where it is intersected at almost a 90-degree angle by Main Street as it runs from the northeast to the southwest edge of the city. These streets make good navigational reference points in a city where several of the arterials are not constructed on a grid but rather radiate out from the city center like spokes in a wheel. Interstate 76 and State Highway 8 also can guide travelers within Akron.

Bus service within the city is provided by the Metro Regional Transit Authority, with an extensive route system and customized transportation options for senior or disabled riders. Taxi companies supplement the mass transit services. The CanalWay offers safe bike passage to portions of Akron, and the city is in the process of implementing a 20-year strategic plan that will allow for creation of more bike lanes and increased options for alternative transportation.

## ■ Communications

### Newspapers and Magazines

The mainstream daily paper in the area is the *Akron Beacon Journal*, which is available in both home delivery and digital versions. The newspaper covers international, national, and local news, along with sports, entertainment and business happenings. Special sections are published periodically to address seasonal interests in gardening, sports, and travel. Community news is the focus of Akron's *West Side Leader* periodical. Several other local newspapers address specific groups or interest areas, including the legal community, seniors, the rubber and plastics industry, and women's issues.

The City of Akron publishes *Akron City Magazine* three times a year to keep the community abreast of developments and events. Several industry-specific publications are produced locally and distributed nationally.

## Television and Radio

No television stations broadcast from Akron; most programming is relayed from the Cleveland area. A governmental channel for City of Akron issues exists, and the region receives network channels ABC, FOX, CBS and NBC in addition to the CW, PBS and PAX. Cable service is available.

Akron's nearly ten AM and FM radio stations offer oldies, adult contemporary, talk, news, and alternative programming. Other radio station options are received via Cleveland and other nearby cities.

***Media Information:*** Akron-Summit Convention and Visitors Bureau, 77 E. Mill Street, Akron, OH 44308; telephone (330)374-7560

### Akron Online

Akron Public Schools. Available www.akronschools .com

Akron-Summit Convention & Visitors Bureau. Available www.visitakron-summit.org

Akron-Summit County Public Library. Available www.akronlibrary.org

City of Akron. Available www.ci.akron.oh.us

Greater Akron Chamber. Available www .greaterakronchamber.org

Summit County Historical Society. Available summithistory.org

BIBLIOGRAPHY

Endres, Kathleen L., *Rosie the Rubber Worker: Women Workers in Akron's Rubber Factories During World War II* (Kent, OH: Kent State University Press, 2000)

Havighurst, Walter, *Ohio: A History* (New York: Norton, 1976)

# Cincinnati

## ■ The City in Brief

**Founded:** 1789 (incorporated 1819)

**Head Official:** Mayor Mark Mallory (D) (since 2005)

**City Population**

    1980: 385,457
    1990: 364,040
    2000: 331,285
    2006 estimate: 332,252
    Percent change, 1990–2000: −9.1%
    U.S. rank in 1980: 32nd
    U.S. rank in 1990: 45th
    U.S. rank in 2000: 63rd

**Metropolitan Area Population**

    1980: 1,660,000
    1990: 1,525,090
    2000: 1,646,395
    2006 estimate: 2,104,218
    Percent change, 1990–2000: 8.9%
    U.S. rank in 1980: 20th
    U.S. rank in 1990: 23rd
    U.S. rank in 2000: 23rd

**Area:** 78 square miles (2000)

**Elevation:** 869 feet above sea level

**Average Annual Temperature:** 53.3° F

**Average Annual Precipitation:** 42.6 inches of rain; 23.4 inches of snow

**Major Economic Sectors:** Services, wholesale and retail trade, manufacturing, government

**Unemployment Rate:** 5.6% (June 2007)

**Per Capita Income:** $20,593 (2005)

**2005 FBI Crime Index Property:** 22,411

**2005 FBI Crime Index Violent:** 3,723

**Major Colleges and Universities:** University of Cincinnati, Xavier University

**Daily Newspaper:** *The Cincinnati Enquirer, The Cincinnati Post*

## ■ Introduction

Cincinnati, the seat of Hamilton County, is Ohio's third largest city and the center of a metropolitan statistical area comprised of Clermont, Hamilton, and Warren counties in Ohio, Kenton County in Kentucky, and Dearborn County in Indiana. Praised by Charles Dickens and Winston Churchill among others, Cincinnati is noted for its attractive hillside setting overlooking the Ohio River. The city enjoys a rich cultural history, particularly in choral and orchestral music, dating from German settlement in the nineteenth century. Once the nation's pork capital and the country's largest city, Cincinnati today is home to several leading national corporations.

## ■ Geography and Climate

Cincinnati is set on the north bank of the Ohio River in a narrow, steep-sided valley on the Ohio-Kentucky border in southwestern Ohio. The city is spread out on hills that afford beautiful vistas of downtown and give the city a picturesque landscape. The area's continental climate produces a wide range of temperatures from winter to summer. Winters are moderately cold with frequent periods of extensive cloudiness; summers are warm and humid with temperatures reaching 90 degrees about 19 days each year.

**Area:** 78 square miles (2000)

**Elevation:** 869 feet above sea level

**Average Temperature:** 53.3° F

**Average Annual Precipitation:** 42.6 inches of rain; 23.4 inches of snow

# ■ History

## Ohio River Crossing Part of Northwest Territory

The Ohio River basin first served as a crossing point for Native Americans traveling south. It is believed that Robert Cavelier, sieur de La Salle, was the first explorer to reach this spot on the Ohio River as early as 1669. Part of the Northwest Territory that the newly formed United States government received from England at the conclusion of the Revolutionary War, Cincinnati became a strategic debarkation point for settlers forging a new life in the wilderness.

Congressman John Cleves Symmes of New Jersey purchased from the Continental Congress one million acres of land between the two Miami rivers, and three settlements were platted. In February 1789, John Filson named one of the settlements Losantiville, meaning "the place opposite the Licking [River]." The next year, General Arthur St. Clair, governor of the Northwest Territory, renamed the village Cincinnati in honor of the Roman citizen-soldier Lucius Quinctius Cincinnatus and after the Society of the Cincinnati, an organization of American Revolutionary army officers. He made Cincinnati the seat of Hamilton County, which he named after Alexander Hamilton, then president general of the Society of Cincinnati.

## River Traffic Swells City's Population

Fort Washington was built in the area in 1789 as a fortification from which action was mounted against warriors of the Ohio tribe, but the military efforts proved unsuccessful until General Anthony Wayne trained an army that defeated the Ohio at Fallen Timbers in 1794, securing the area for settlement. Cincinnati was chartered as a town in 1802 and as a city in 1819. The introduction of the river paddle-wheeler on the Ohio River after the War of 1812 turned Cincinnati into a center of river commerce and trade. The opening of the Miami Canal in 1827 added to the town's economic growth. William Holmes McGuffey published his Eclectic Readers in Cincinnati in 1836, and eventually 122 million copies were sold. The first mass migration of Germans in 1830 and Irish a decade later swelled Cincinnati's population to 46,338 people.

The economy continued to boom as the South paid cash for foodstuffs produced in the city, and by 1850 Cincinnati was the pork-packing capital of the world. More than 8,000 steamboats docked at Cincinnati in

1852. Cincinnati merchants protested the cutoff of Southern trade at the outbreak of the Civil War, but federal government contracts and the city's role as a recruiting and outfitting center for Union soldiers righted the economy. Cincinnati was a major stop on the Underground Railroad, a secret network of cooperation aiding fugitive slaves in reaching sanctuary in the free states or Canada prior to 1861. Cincinnati also served as a center of Copperhead political activity during the Civil War; Copperheads were Northerners sympathetic to the Southern cause. The city's proximity to the South spread fear of invasion by the Confederate Army, and martial law was decreed in 1862 when raiders led by Edmund Kirby-Smith, a Confederate commander, threatened invasion.

Cincinnati residents played an important role in the Abolitionist cause. James G. Birney, who published the abolitionist newspaper *The Philanthropist,* and Dr. Lyman Beecher of the Lane Theological Seminary were leading Northern antislavery activists. Dr. Beecher's daughter, Harriet Beecher Stowe, lived in Cincinnati from 1832 to 1850 and wrote much of her best seller, *Uncle Tom's Cabin,* there. African Americans have in fact been prominent in Cincinnati's history since its founding. The city's first African American church was built in 1809 and the first school in 1825. African Americans voted locally in 1852, 18 years before the passage of the Fifteenth Amendment. The first African American to serve on city council was elected in 1931, and two African Americans have served as mayor.

## Prosperity Follows End of Civil War

A suspension bridge designed by John R. Roebling connected Ohio and Kentucky upon its completion in 1867. Cincinnati prospered after the Civil War and, with a population that grew to 200,000 people, became the country's largest city before annexing land to develop communities outside the basin. Cincinnati's most revered public monument, the Tyler Davidson Fountain, was unveiled in 1871 in the heart of downtown. During this period Cincinnati's major cultural institutions were founded, including the art museum and art academy, the conservatory of music, the public library, the zoo, and Music Hall. Two of the city's most cherished traditions also date from this time: the May Festival of choral music at Music Hall and the first professional baseball team, the Cincinnati Red Stockings.

In reaction to the decline of riverboat trade in the 1870s, the city of Cincinnati built its own southern rail line—it was the first and only city to do so—at a cost of $20 million, rushing to complete the project in 1880. The era of boss-rule in the municipal government was introduced in 1884 when newly elected Governor Joseph B. Foraker appointed George Barnsdale Cox, a tavern keeper, to head the Board of Public Affairs. With control of more than 2,000 jobs, Cox and his machine ruled Cincinnati through a bleak period of graft and corruption, which finally came to an end with a nonpartisan reform movement that won election in 1924. The city's new charter corrected the abuses of the Cox regime.

On the national scene, a political dynasty was established when Cincinnatian William Howard Taft was elected President and then became the only President to be appointed Chief Justice of the U.S. Supreme Court. Taft's son, Robert A. Taft, was elected to three Senate terms; and his grandson, Robert Taft, Jr., was elected to the U.S. House of Representatives.

## City Retains Vitality in Twentieth Century

Cincinnati weathered the Great Depression better than most American cities of its size, largely because of a resurgence of inexpensive river trade. The rejuvenation of downtown began in the 1920s and continued into the next decade with the construction of Union Terminal, the post office, and a large Bell Telephone building. The flood of 1937 was one of the worst in the nation's history, resulting in the building of protective flood walls. After World War II, Cincinnati unveiled a master plan for urban renewal that resulted in modernization of the inner city. Riverfront Stadium and the Coliseum were completed in the 1970s, as the Cincinnati Reds baseball team emerged as one of the dominant teams of the decade. Tragedy struck the Coliseum in December 1981 when eleven people were killed in a mass panic prior to The Who rock and roll concert. In 1989, the two-hundredth anniversary of the city's founding, much attention was focused on the city's Year 2000 plan, which involved further revitalization.

The completion of several major new development projects enhanced the city as it entered the early years of the new millennium. Cincinnati's beloved Bengals and Reds teams both have new, state-of-the-art homes: Paul Brown Stadium opened in 2000 and the Great American Ball Park opened in 2003. Two new museums have opened: the Rosenthal Center for Contemporary Art in 2003 and the National Underground Railroad Freedom Center in 2004. The Banks is a developing 24-hour urban neighborhood of restaurants, clubs, offices, and homes with sweeping skyline views, along the city's riverfront. Cincinnati has received such accolades as "Most Liveable City," by Partners for Livable Communities in April 2004.

*Historical Information:* Cincinnati Historical Society, Museum Center, Cincinnati Union Terminal, 1301 Western Avenue, Cincinnati, OH 45203; telephone (513)287-7030

# ■ Population Profile

## Metropolitan Area Residents

1980: 1,660,000
1990: 1,525,090
2000: 1,646,395
2006 estimate: 2,104,218
Percent change, 1990–2000: 8.9%
U.S. rank in 1980: 20th
U.S. rank in 1990: 23rd
U.S. rank in 2000: 23rd

## City Residents

1980: 385,457
1990: 364,040
2000: 331,285
2006 estimate: 332,252
Percent change, 1990–2000: –9.1%
U.S. rank in 1980: 32nd
U.S. rank in 1990: 45th
U.S. rank in 2000: 63rd

**Density:** 4,249.0 people per square mile (2000)

## Racial and ethnic characteristics (2005)

White: 140,285
Black: 132,152
American Indian and Alaska Native: 188
Asian: 6,874
Native Hawaiian and Pacific Islander: 0
Hispanic or Latino (may be of any race): 3,855
Other: 2,400

**Percent of residents born in state:** 73.0% (2006)

## Age characteristics (2005)

Population under 5 years old: 22,870
Population 5 to 9 years old: 20,301
Population 10 to 14 years old: 18,488
Population 15 to 19 years old: 19,238
Population 20 to 24 years old: 24,594
Population 25 to 34 years old: 44,945
Population 35 to 44 years old: 37,189
Population 45 to 54 years old: 41,437
Population 55 to 59 years old: 15,472
Population 60 to 64 years old: 10,531
Population 65 to 74 years old: 14,453
Population 75 to 84 years old: 14,164
Population 85 years and older: 3,858
Median age: 33.3 years

## Births (2006, MSA)

Total number: 29,408

## Deaths (2006, MSA)

Total number: 17,537

## Money income (2005)

Per capita income: $20,593
Median household income: $29,554
Total households: 136,949

*Image copyright Bryan Busovicki, 2007. Used under license from Shutterstock.com.*

**Number of households with income of . . .**

less than $10,000: 25,344
$10,000 to $14,999: 11,550
$15,000 to $24,999: 22,915
$25,000 to $34,999: 18,366
$35,000 to $49,999: 19,972
$50,000 to $74,999: 18,114
$75,000 to $99,999: 10,191
$100,000 to $149,999: 6,542
$150,000 to $199,999: 2,065
$200,000 or more: 1,890

**Percent of families below poverty level:** 11.6% (2005)

**2005 FBI Crime Index Property:** 22,411

**2005 FBI Crime Index Violent:** 3,723

# ■ Municipal Government

Since 1926, the top vote-getter of city council automatically became mayor, but as of 2001, the mayor is elected independently. A city manager is appointed by the mayor and the city's nine-member council. Council members are elected to two-year terms; the city manager serves for an indefinite period.

**Head Official:** Mayor Mark Mallory (D) (since 2005; current term expires 2009)

**Total Number of City Employees:** approximately 1,000 (2007)

*City Information:* City Hall, 801 Plum Street, Cincinnati, OH 45202; telephone (513)591-6000

# ■ Economy

## Major Industries and Commercial Activity

Cincinnati's diversified economic base includes manufacturing, wholesale and retail trade, insurance and finance, education and health services, government, and transportation. Known worldwide for Procter & Gamble soap products and U.S. Playing Cards, the city ranks high nationally in the value of manufacturing shipments. Ten *Fortune* 500 companies have established headquarters in the Cincinnati area: AK Steel (steel manufacturer), American Financial (financial services), Ashland Inc. (chemicals), Cinergy Corp. (public utilities), Federated Department Stores (retail stores), Fifth Third

Bancorp (financial services), The Kroger Co. (grocery stores), Omnicare (pharmacy services), Procter & Gamble Co. (consumer goods), and Western & Southern Financial (financial services).

More than one thousand area firms have contributed to Cincinnati's position as an international trade center, generating approximately $6.7 billion in sales to markets outside the United States each year. Foreign investment in the local economy is substantial; more than 300 Cincinnati-area firms are presently owned by companies in Asia (especially Japan), Europe (especially France, Germany, and the United Kingdom), Canada, South America, and Africa. Among these companies are: AEG, Bayer, Faurecia, Krupp-Hoesch, Mitsubishi Electric, Siemens, Snecma, Sumitomo Electric, Toyota Motor Mfg.-North American Headquarters, and Valeo. Toyota, one of Cincinnati's largest employers, chose the greater Cincinnati area for its North American manufacturing plant because, in the words of its Senior Vice President of Corporate Affairs, Dennis C. Cuneo, "The area has an excellent transportation system, a world-class airport, an excellent quality of life and a positive business climate." The fastest-growing business sectors in Cincinnati are management, business and financial, professional, and service occupations. In 2007 the city of Cincinnati was continuing efforts to attract more biotechnology, biomedical manufacturing, and software firms; there are over 200 biotechnology-related firms in the area.

Federal agencies with regional centers located in the city are the United States Postal Service, the U.S. Internal Revenue Service, the U.S. Environmental Protection Agency, and the National Institute for Occupational Safety and Health.

**Items and goods produced:** aircraft engines, auto parts, motor vehicles, chemicals, valves, alcoholic beverages and soft drinks, food and kindred products, playing cards, drugs, cosmetics, toiletries, detergents, building materials, cans, metalworking and general industrial machinery, toys, apparel, mattresses, electric motors, robotics, electronic equipment, housewares, shoes, printing and publishing

## Incentive Programs—New and Existing Companies

Greater Cincinnati offers a wide range of economic development assistance programs to businesses planning to expand or locate new operations within the 13-county region.

*Local programs:* Local organizations offer assistance for small businesses, women, and minority business owners. One such organization, the Cincinnati Business Incubator (CBI), specializes in assisting woman- and minority-owned small businesses operating—or seeking to start a business—in designated Empowerment Zones. CBI offers training and workshops that focus on business skills and profit building.

*State programs:* The state of Ohio offers a number of incentives designed to encourage new companies and retain existing businesses. Tax credit programs include those for job creation, machinery and equipment investment, export, research and development franchise, and technology investment. Ohio also offers a property tax abatement for areas identified as enterprise zones, and sales tax exemptions for research and development.

*Job training programs:* The City of Cincinnati Employment and Training Division oversees vocational, life, and pre-employment skills training and job placement employment initiatives. Cincinnati Works focuses on four service areas: job readiness, job search, retention, and advancement. Great Oaks Center for Employment Resources offers customized training and services to meet the needs of companies. Services and programs include comprehensive vocational assessment, employee assessment, employment services, professional development, job profiling, return to work services, workplace programs, and customized training. TechSolve, a non-profit organization for manufacturers, offers help with change in manufacturing operations; its training programs aim to maintain a high performance workforce.

## Development Projects

The Dr. Albert B. Sabin Cincinnati Convention Center expansion, which opened in 2006, was projected to have an economic impact of $417 million and boasts over 750,000 square feet of exhibit, meeting, and entertainment space. The main hall comprises over 200,000 square feet; there is also a 40,000-square-foot ballroom and space for 37 individual meeting rooms.

The University of Cincinnati has been a hotbed of building activity since it undertook a strategic architectural plan in 1989. Among its most recent additions are a Central Utility Plant (2004); Marge Schott Stadium (2004); Gettler Stadium (2004); Veterinary Technology Center (2005); and the Campus Recreation Center (2006), a $112 million undertaking that includes an athletic core, six electronic classrooms, housing, restaurants and dining, and stadium grandstands.

In 2007 the Cincinnati Public Schools opened three new schools: Roberts Paideia Academy, the Douglass School on Park Avenue in Walnut Hills, and George W. Hays School on Cutter Street in the West End. Also in 2007 work was underway on a renovation of the downtown library, scheduled to be completed by February 2008.

*Economic Development Information:* Ohio Department of Development, PO Box 1001, Columbus, OH 43216; telephone (800)848-1300

## Commercial Shipping

The Cincinnati/Northern Kentucky Airport pumps approximately $4 billion into the local economy; contributing significantly to the region's transportation system, it is considered a major inducement in attracting new industry. The airport is the primary U.S. hub for DHL Worldwide Express. The area has two foreign trade zones, one in Hamilton County and the other in Boone County, Kentucky near the international airport. Greater Cincinnati has one of the largest inland U.S. ports for domestic loads, with more than fifty million tons of cargo transported annually through Cincinnati on the Ohio River system.

All major markets are easily reached from Greater Cincinnati via interstate. Three interstates (I-71, I-74 and I-75) link Cincinnati with the nation, while I-70, 55 miles to the north, links the east and west coasts. Twenty major metropolitan areas are served by one day's trucking service and another 30 metropolitan areas are within two days. Three major railroad systems—CSX Transportation, Norfolk Southern Corp., and Conrail—serve the region.

## Labor Force and Employment Outlook

Graduates from the colleges and universities within a 200-mile radius add more than 100,000 young professionals to the workforce each year. The region is noted for its strong work ethic, which translates into a workforce that is productive, responsible, and dedicated. The city has been successful in attracting new business including company headquarters in recent years. Among the rapidly growing sectors of the area's economy are high-tech manufacturing, aerospace (in 2003, the Cincinnati-Dayton corridor was awarded $2.5 billion in defense spending and $1.4 billion in U.S. defense projects), automotive manufacturing, and life sciences.

In September 2007 the unemployment rate in Cincinnati stood at 5.1 percent, close to the national average and below ten-year highs above 6 percent in 2005. Between 1997 and 2007 the labor force in the metropolitan Cincinnati area grew from 1,004,438 to 1,124,365. Growth in Cincinnati is comparable to that of the nation as a whole, and in 2007 analysts predicted upward growth in the years ahead would be slower but fairly consistent. A chamber of commerce economic outlook report stated in 2007 that "there is a clear need for more opportunities for young, educated entrepreneurs as well as members of the creative class."

The following is a summary of data regarding the Cincinnati-Middletown OH-KY-IN metropolitan area labor force, 2006 annual averages.

**Size of nonagricultural labor force:** 1,038,400

**Number of workers employed in ...**

　　construction and mining: 52,600
　　manufacturing: 121,700
　　trade, transportation and utilities: 209,600
　　information: 15,700
　　financial activities: 65,300
　　professional and business services: 156,000

　　educational and health services: 137,400
　　leisure and hospitality: 105,200
　　other services: 42,500
　　government: 132,500

**Average hourly earnings of production workers employed in manufacturing:** $19.58

**Unemployment rate:** 5.6% (June 2007)

| *Largest regional employers (2007)* | *Number of employees* |
|---|---|
| Wright Patterson Air Base | 24,000 |
| University of Cincinnati | 15,400 |
| Kroger Co. | 14,000 |
| Health Alliance | 13,141 |
| Procter & Gamble | 12,000 |
| Wal-Mart | 11,307 |
| Premier Health Partners | 10,023 |
| Fifth Third Bank | 8,964 |
| Children's Hospital | 8,102 |
| GE Aircraft Engines | 7,400 |

## Cost of Living

The following is a summary of data regarding several key cost of living factors in the Cincinnati area.

**2007 (1st quarter) ACCRA Average House Price:** $249,811

**2007 (1st quarter) ACCRA Cost of Living Index:** 93.5

**State income tax rate:** 0.68% to 6.87%

**State sales tax rate:** 5.5%

**Local income tax rate:** 2.1%

**Local sales tax rate:** 1.0%

**Property tax rate:** ranges from $61.66 to $133.45 per $1,000 of assessed valuation; assessed at 35% of market value (Hamilton County)

*Economic Information:* Greater Cincinnati Chamber of Commerce, 441 Vine Street, Suite 300, Cincinnati, OH 45202; telephone (513)579-3100; fax (513)579-3101

# ■ Education and Research

## Elementary and Secondary Schools

The Cincinnati Public School (CPS) district is spread across the city plus Amberley Village, Cheviot, Golf Manor, most of the city of Silverton, parts of Fairfax and

Wyoming, and parts of Anderson, Columbia, Delhi, Green, and Springfield townships, with a total area of 92 square miles. It is the third-largest public school district in the state. CPS opened the first public Montessori elementary school in the country in 1975. Magnet school offerings include quadrants in Spanish, French, and Arabic; there are six different magnet programs offered at twenty different elementary schools. The district's $985 million Facilities Master Plan, launched in 2002, is financing the building or renovation of more than a dozen schools; the first new school resulting from this plan—Rockdale Academy—was completed in January 2005. The beginning of the 2007-2008 school year also marked the opening of three new schools: Roberts Paideia Academy, the Douglass School on Park Avenue in Walnut Hillls, and George W. Hays School on Cutter Street in the West End.

In 2006-2007 CPS was recognized on the State Report Card for "steady academic achievement."

The following is a summary of data regarding the Cincinnati Public Schools as of the 2005–2006 school year.

**Total enrollment:** 35,508

**Number of facilities**

    elementary schools: 46
    junior high/middle schools: 0
    senior high schools: 16
    other: 0

**Student/teacher ratio:** 16.9:1

**Teacher salaries (2005–06)**

    elementary median: $47,560
    junior high/middle median: $50,320
    secondary median: $51,170

**Funding per pupil:** $11,019

A parochial school system operated by the Catholic Diocese as well as a variety of private schools throughout the area provide instruction from kindergarten through twelfth grade. Cincinnati is home to more than 130 private schools. Its Catholic school system is the ninth largest in the nation. There are 42 charter schools within the Cincinnati school district.

***Public Schools Information:*** Cincinnati Public Schools, PO Box 5381, Cincinnati, OH 45201; telephone (513)363-0000

## Colleges and Universities

The University of Cincinnati (UC), part of Ohio's state higher education system, was founded in 1819. The university has an enrollment of more than 35,000 students and grants degrees at all levels, from associate through doctorate, in a complete range of fields. The university includes a main academic campus, a medical campus, a branch campus in suburban Blue Ash, and a rural branch campus in Clermont County, east of Cincinnati. The university is a nationally recognized research institution known for its professional schools, notably the colleges of medicine, engineering, law, business, applied science, and design, architecture, art, and planning. UC offers 98 doctoral degrees, 170 at the master's level, 167 bachelor's, and 139 associate's degrees. Cooperative education originated at the University of Cincinnati in 1906; other UC firsts include the development of the oral polio vaccine and the first antihistamine. Both its physiology and criminal and justice studies programs were ranked sixth in the nation by *Faculty Scholarly Productivity Index* in 2005.

Cincinnati is also home to Xavier University, a Jesuit institution founded in 1831, which offers undergraduate and graduate programs in such areas as theology, criminal justice, psychology, business, education, English, health services administration, nursing, and occupational therapy. According to the *U.S. News & World Report* 2008 edition of "America's Best Colleges," among Midwestern universities Xavier was ranked second overall.

Hebrew Union College-Jewish Institute of Religion, a graduate rabbinical seminary, was founded in 1875 and is the nation's oldest institution of higher Jewish education. In addition to its Rabbinical School, the College-Institute includes Schools of Graduate Studies, Education, Jewish Communal Service, Sacred Music, and Biblical Archaeology. Branch campuses are located in Los Angeles, New York, and Jerusalem.

The Athenaeum of Ohio is an accredited center of ministry education and formation within the Roman Catholic tradition. Other colleges in Cincinnati are the Art Academy of Cincinnati, a small independent college of art and design; The Union Institute, designed for adults who have the desire to assume a significant measure of personal responsibility for planning and executing their degree programs; and Cincinnati Christian University.

Colleges and universities in the metropolitan area include Miami University in Oxford, offering specialized studies in more than 100 academic majors and pre-professional programs, and particularly known for its business school; Northern Kentucky University; Thomas More College; and College of Mount St. Joseph.

Vocational and technical education is available at a variety of institutions such as Cincinnati State Technical and Community College, and Gateway Community and Technical College.

## Libraries and Research Centers

The Public Library of Cincinnati and Hamilton County is the third-oldest library in the nation, and loaned 14,783,307 items in 2006. The library system is comprised of a downtown facility and 40 branches. The 542,527 square-foot main library includes a library for the blind. Special collections cover a range of topics, including inland rivers, sacred music, patents from 1790 to the present, nineteenth and twentieth century illustrators, and Bibles and English language dictionaries; the library is also a depository for federal documents. In 2007 work was underway on a renovation of the downtown library, scheduled to be completed by February 2008. Changes are to include a 100-computer technology center, a popular library, genealogy and local history center, and a teen center.

Cincinnati-area colleges and universities also maintain campus libraries. The largest is the University of Cincinnati Libraries, which include a central facility with 3,209,337 volumes and 42,265 periodicals; the law school and the University of Cincinnati Medical Center operate separate library systems. The Hebrew Union College-Jewish Institute of Religion Klau Library, with holdings of approximately 425,000 volumes and 2,340 periodical subscriptions, is an important center for such subject interests as Hebraica, Judaica, ancient and near-Eastern studies, and rabbinical studies. Several cultural and scientific organizations operate libraries, including the Art Museum, the Cincinnati Museum Center, the Taft Museum, and the Zoological Society. The Cincinnati Historical Society Library holds more than 90,000 books relating to the history of the United States, Ohio, and the Old Northwest Territory, especially metropolitan Cincinnati.

The U.S. Department of Health and Human Services has a library in Cincinnati that is open to the public. Collections are maintained by the Cincinnati Law Library Association and the Young Men's Mercantile Library Association. Other specialized libraries are affiliated with hospitals, churches, and synagogues.

The University of Cincinnati (UC) is a major research center, and its research funding continues to increase steadily. In 2006, UC earned more than $330 million in research grants and contracts and was home to ten Ohio "Eminent Scholars." Research is conducted in a wide variety of fields, including sociology, biology, aeronautics, health, psychology, and archaeology. The university's Medical Center campus features such research facilities as the Genome Research Institute, and is home to BIO/START, a biomedical business incubator.

*Public Library Information:* Public Library of Cincinnati and Hamilton County, 800 Vine Street, Cincinnati, OH 45202-2009; telephone (513)369-6900

# ■ Health Care

The Cincinnati medical community, a regional health care center, has gained prominence for education, treatment, and research. The University of Cincinnati maintains the oldest teaching hospital/medical center in the country and is the place where Albert Sabin developed the first polio vaccine and Leon Goldman performed the first laser surgery for the removal of cataracts. In 1994, University Hospital joined with The Christ Hospital to form the Health Alliance, which consists of eight hospitals—University Hospital; Drake Center; Jewish Hospital, where Henry Heimlich developed his famous maneuver; Fort Hamilton Hospital; West Chester; The Lindner Center of Hope; The Neuroscience Insitute; and University Pointe Surgical Institute—in Cincinnati and northern Kentucky. University Hospital consistently ranks among *U.S News and World Report*'s "Best Hospitals," and is especially well-known for its Endocrinology and Urology programs. Drake Center is a specialized rehabilitation facility set on 42 acres. The Linder Center of Hope, established by a 2005 charitable donation, is a behavioral health center expected to open in 2008. Children's Hospital Medical Center, one of the nation's largest and most respected pediatric hospitals, also operates the largest pediatric residency program and developed the first heart-lung machine.

More than 30 hospitals serve the Cincinnati area. Among the general care and specialized facilities are the Shriners Hospital, St. Elizabeth Medical Center, Good Samaritan Hospital, Bethesda North Hospital, and Deaconess hospitals.

# ■ Recreation

### Sightseeing

A tour of Cincinnati can begin downtown at Fountain Square, the site of the Tyler Davidson Fountain, one of the city's most revered landmarks, which was made in Munich, Germany, and erected in 1871. Several historic monuments, including statues in honor of three United States presidents—James A. Garfield, William Henry Harrison, and Abraham Lincoln—are also located in the downtown area.

Eden Park in Mt. Adams, one of Cincinnati's oldest hillside neighborhoods and named after President John Quincy Adams, provides a panoramic view of the city and of northern Kentucky across the Ohio River. In Eden Park the Irwin M. Krohn Conservatory maintains several large public greenhouses showcasing more than 3,500 plant species: the Palm House features palm, rubber, and banana trees in a rainforest setting with a 20-foot waterfall; the Tropical House has ferns, bromeliads, begonias, chocolate and papaya trees, and vanilla vine; the Floral House has seasonal floral displays among its permanent collection of orange, kumquat, lemon, and grapefruit trees; the Desert Garden is home to yuccas, agaves, cacti, and aloes; and the Orchid House displays 17 genera of orchids.

The Cincinnati Zoo & Botanical Garden, opened in 1872, is the second oldest zoo in the United States. Set on 75 acres, the zoo is home to 510 animal species as well as 3,000 plant varieties. The zoo is recognized worldwide for the breeding of animals in captivity; the zoo introduced the nation's first insect world exhibit. It also features such rare animals as the white Bengal tiger, Sumatran rhinoceros, and lowland gorilla, as well as manatees, alligators and crocodiles, orangutans, elephants, giraffes, and polar bears. At Wolf Woods, which opened in May 2005, visitors can view the rare Mexican gray wolf and other North American animals, including river otters, gray fox, wild turkey, striped skunk, and thickbilled parrots.

Historic houses open for public viewing include the former homes of Harriet Beecher Stowe, author of *Uncle Tom's Cabin*; and William Howard Taft, 27th President of the United States. The Harriet Beecher Stowe House displays artifacts of African American history, featuring documents from the Beecher family. The William Howard Taft National Historic Site was Taft's birthplace and boyhood home; several rooms have been restored to reflect Taft's family life. Dayton Street on Cincinnati's West End features restored nineteenth-century architecture. The Spring Grove Cemetery and Arboretum, a national historic landmark, contains 1,000 labeled trees on 733 landscaped acres lined with statuary and sculpture.

Kings Island Theme Park, 20 minutes north of Cincinnati, features more than 80 amusement attractions and is known nationally for its daring rollercoasters and water rides, among them The Beast, the world's longest wooden rollercoaster. The nearby Beach Waterpark has nearly 50 waterslides and rides. Meier's Wine Cellar, Ohio's oldest and largest winery, offers tours.

## Arts and Culture

Many of Cincinnati's cultural institutions date from the mid-nineteenth century, and the city takes particular pride in their longevity and quality. The primary venues for the performing arts are Music Hall which, built in 1878, retains its nineteenth-century elegance and is affectionately known as the city's Grand Dame; and the Aronoff Center for the Arts, opened in 1995, which features three performance spaces as well as the Weston Art Gallery, and presents thousands of exhibits and performances each year. Cincinnati is home to the Cincinnati Symphony Orchestra, Cincinnati Ballet, and Cincinnati Opera. The symphony, established in 1895, performs classical and pops concert series. The ballet company, based at the Aronoff Center, offers more than 30 performances annually, presenting both classical and contemporary dance. The opera company, the second oldest in the United States, presents four productions during a summer season. Based at Music Hall, The Corbett Opera Center, a four-story opera headquarters, opened in October 2005.

Riverbend Music Center, an open-air amphitheater designed by noted architect Michael Graves, is the summer performance quarters for the Cincinnati Pops Orchestra and Symphony Orchestra, as well as the site for concerts by visiting artists. Popular music traditions in Cincinnati include the Matinee Musicale, founded in 1911; the Linton Chamber Music Series; and the Taft Chamber Concerts.

Music in Cincinnati is not limited to the classical tradition. Cincinnati and nearby Covington, Kentucky, support an active jazz club scene. The Blue Wisp Jazz Club features local and national talent.

Cincinnati Playhouse in the Park, a professional regional theater, is housed in a modern facility in Eden Park. Recipient of the 2004 Regional Theatre Tony Award, the Playhouse presents a September-June season of comedies, dramas, classics, and musicals on a main stage and in a smaller theater. The University of Cincinnati's College-Conservatory of Music presents nearly 1,000 events per year and is most noted for its philharmonic orchestra concerts, operas, and musical theater productions; many performances are free. The Showboat Majestic, a restored nineteenth-century showboat on the Ohio River Public Landing, is one of the last original floating theaters still in operation. Performances on the showboat include dramas, comedies, old-fashioned melodramas, and musicals. The Ensemble Theatre of Cincinnati presents regional, world, and off-Broadway premiere productions at its theater downtown.

In addition to music and performing arts, the visual arts are an integral part of the city's cultural heritage. The Women's Art Museum Association was responsible for the construction of the Cincinnati Art Museum in 1871; the museum, which has undergone an extensive renovation, houses nearly 100 galleries and offers 60,000 works spanning 6,000 years. Its permanent collection features an outstanding collection of Asian art and musical instruments, and a Cincinnati Wing with local artworks dating from 1788 through the present. Downtown's Taft Museum, housed in an 1820 mansion and formerly the home of art patrons Charles and Anna Taft, was presented as a gift to the city in 1932. The museum holds paintings, decorative arts, sculpture, furniture, and more. The Rosenthal Center for Contemporary Art, also located downtown, opened in 2003 and presents changing exhibitions of modernist art in a variety of forms; its "UnMuseum" is designed for children. A number of art galleries occupy converted warehouses near the shopping district.

Union Terminal, a former train station declared a masterpiece of Art Deco construction when it opened in 1933, has been restored and is home to the Cincinnati Museum Center at Union Terminal. The center includes the Cincinnati History Museum, featuring recreations of historical settings showcasing the city's past; the Museum of Natural History and Science, where visitors can walk through glaciers, explore caves, and learn about the human body; the Cinergy Children's Museum, where kids can climb, crawl, explore, and learn about the world in educational exhibits; and an Omnimax theater. The National Underground Railroad Freedom Center, opened in 2004, is a 158,000-square-foot facility tracing the 300-year history of slavery in America and highlighting the role of the Underground Railroad. The Cincinnati Fire Museum, located in a 1907 firehouse, exhibits the history of fire fighting in Cincinnati.

## Festivals and Holidays

Each year Cincinnati presents a number of festivals that celebrate the city's heritage and institutions. The Celtic Lands Culture Fest in March includes storytelling, dancing, food, music and crafts. The nation's professional baseball season opens in April with the Cincinnati Reds game at Riverfront Stadium. Preceding the game is an Opening Day Parade originating at historic Findlay Market. The Appalachian Festival, held in May, has mountain crafts, live music, dancing, and storytellers; it is said to be the largest craft show in the country. May Festival, a tradition begun in 1873, is the oldest continuing festival of choral and orchestral music in the country. The Taste of Cincinnati celebration held over Memorial Day weekend downtown affords the city's best restaurants an opportunity to feature some of their favorite menu items. Summerfair brings an arts and crafts show to the city's riverfront the second weekend in June. Juneteenth Festival is a celebration of African-American freedom, featuring diverse music and food. The day-long Riverfest celebration on Labor Day honors the area's river heritage and is the city's largest celebration. The festival features water skiing, sky diving and air shows, and riverboat cruises, and is capped by a spectacular fireworks display. The Harvest Home Fair, held the following weekend in nearby Cheviot, features horse, art, and flower shows, a parade, 4-H auction, petting zoo, and more. The Harvest Home Fair, also in September, features wine, tours, food, music, camping, arts, crafts and activities. Oktoberfest Zinzinnati features German food, customs, dancing, and beer; downtown streets are blocked off for the festivities. Early December brings Balluminaria at Eden Park, where hot air balloons are lit up at dusk near Mirror Lake.

Popular Christmas-holiday events in Cincinnati include the annual tree-lighting on Fountain Square, the Festival of Lights at the Cincinnati Zoo, and the Boar's Head and Yule Log Festival at Christ Church Cathedral downtown, a Cincinnati tradition since 1940.

Events are held throughout the year in nearby Sharon Woods Village and in the MainStrasse Village in Covington, Kentucky, across the Ohio River.

## Sports for the Spectator

The Cincinnati Reds, World Series winners in 1975, 1976, and 1990, is America's oldest professional baseball team; they play their home games at the new Great American Ball Park. Opened in 2003, the park has a seating capacity of 42,059 and is praised for its innovative features, breathtaking views, and tributes to the Reds' rich history. The Cincinnati Bengals, who captured the American Football Championship in 1981 and 1988, play home games at Paul Brown Stadium, opened in 2000. The stadium has a seating capacity of 65,535, on three levels; its open-ended design allows for stunning views of the downtown skyline and the riverfront.

The Cincinnati Cyclones are in the International Hockey League and play at the U.S. Bank Arena. The University of Cincinnati and Xavier University provide a schedule of college sports teams and cross-town rivalry in basketball, in which both schools enjoy strong traditions and some national prominence.

Thoroughbred racing takes place at River Downs Racetrack in late April through Labor Day, and at Turfway Park in Florence, Kentucky, from September through mid-October, and Thanksgiving through mid-April. The Association of Tennis Professionals compete in tournament play each August in nearby Mason.

## Sports for the Participant

Cincinnati maintains more than 100 parks on 5,000 acres of land in attractive urban settings. The city manages 5 regional parks, 70 neighborhood parks, 34 natural areas, 5 neighborhood nature centers, 16 scenic overlooks and 65 miles of hiking and bridle trails. Alms Park and Eden Park offer dramatic views of the Ohio River and northern Kentucky, and these parks, as well as others, attract joggers because of their natural beauty and challenge for runners. The Cincinnati Nature Center-Rowe Woods is comprised of 1,025 acres with nature trails covering more than 17 miles, and a nature center featuring a bird-viewing area, library, and displays. The 1,466 acres of Mount Airy Forest feature hiking and picnic areas. The city's recreation department sponsors an array of sports from softball to soccer for all age groups and manages neighborhood swimming pools and tennis courts throughout the summer. Sawyer Point on the Ohio River provides facilities for pier fishing, rowboating, skating, tennis, and volleyball.

## Shopping and Dining

Cincinnati consists of distinct neighborhoods where shopping districts provide an atmosphere not found in many cities today. The city's revitalization is most evident downtown in the area known as Over-the-Rhine, the old German neighborhood around Vine and Main Streets. There, art galleries, restaurants, and breweries flourish in restored nineteenth-century buildings. Cincinnati's skywalk system connects downtown stores, hotels, and restaurants, allowing visitors to explore the shopping district free of traffic and weather concerns. The downtown Tower Place mixes local and nationally known stores with specialty shops in a compact area. Other downtown Cincinnati shopping highlights include Macy's and Saks

Fifth Avenue department stores. Neighborhood and suburban shopping districts and malls abound on both sides of the river, and the region offers endless antique shops, boutiques, arts and crafts shops, and ethnic and fashion collections. Other shopping opportunities include large regional malls, factory outlets, discount houses, and museum stores. The Findlay Market, an open-air marketplace that has been in operation since 1852, offers ethnic foods in an old-world atmosphere.

Cincinnati restaurants have been rated highly by critics and travel guides. The city is home to several restaurants that have received critical acclaim nationally, including Maisonette, a French restaurant that has received Five Stars from Mobil for 40 consecutive years; it moved to the suburbs from its downtown location in 2005. One of Cincinnati's specialties is moderately priced German cuisine. Cincinnati restaurateurs have been successful in opening establishments in architecturally interesting buildings, such as firehouses, police precincts, or riverboat paddle-wheelers. A locally made ice cream, Graeter's, is widely popular, as is a downtown New York-style deli, Izzy's, known for its corned beef. The city's oldest tavern, opened in 1861, is still in business as a bar and grill. Cincinnati chili, Greek in origin, is flavored with cinnamon and chocolate as the "secret" ingredients and served over spaghetti; 3-way, 4-way, or 5-way chili choices consist of various combinations of grated cheese, onions, beans, and oyster crackers.

*Visitor Information:* Greater Cincinnati Convention and Visitors Bureau, 300 West Sixth Street, Cincinnati, OH 45202; telephone (513)621-2142

# ■ Convention Facilities

Duke Energy Center, formerly the Dr. Albert B. Sabin Cincinnati Convention Center, is conveniently situated downtown and connected via the 20-block Skywalk system with shops and stores, restaurants, entertainment and cultural activities, and hotels. The center underwent a $160 million renovation and expansion, completed in 2006, that resulted in over 750,000 square feet of exhibit, meeting, and entertainment space. The main hall comprises over 200,000 square feet; there is also a 40,000-square-foot ballroom, and space for 37 individual meeting rooms. Technological upgrades include increased security and optic networking throughout the building.

Meeting and convention accommodations can also be found at several luxury hotels clustered downtown near the Convention Center and at other hotels and motels throughout the Greater Cincinnati area. More than 22,500 lodging rooms are available citywide.

*Convention Information:* Greater Cincinnati Convention and Visitors Bureau, 300 West Sixth Street, Cincinnati, OH 45202; telephone (513)621-2142

# ■ Transportation

## Approaching the City

Cincinnati/Northern Kentucky International Airport served 1,229,332 passengers in 2006. Located only 15 minutes from downtown Cincinnati, it is one of the fastest growing airports in the world. It is the second largest hub for Delta Air Lines, and is served by 7 other commerical airlines. The airport offers non-stop air service from the region to approximately 120 cities, including international service to Frankfurt, London, Paris, Rome, Amsterdam, Montreal and Toronto.

Metropolitan Cincinnati is linked to other areas via I-75, a major north/south route running between the Canadian border through Florida; I-71, running between Louisville and northeast Ohio; and I-74, the area's principal link from the west. I-70, a major transcontinental route, runs east/west approximately 55 miles north of the city. Other highways providing access to downtown and the metropolitan region are Interstates 275, which circles the metropolitan area, and 471, which runs in to downtown; U.S. 50 and 52; and several state and county routes.

Passenger rail service into renovated Union Terminal is available by Amtrak. Bus transportation is provided by Greyhound.

## Traveling in the City

Downtown streets are in a grid pattern, making travel within the city relatively easy. Streets running east/west are numbered, beginning with 2nd Street near the Ohio River. The public transit bus system is operated by Metro, which schedules regular routes in the city and the suburbs.

# ■ Communications

## Newspapers and Magazines

Cincinnati's major daily newspapers are *The Cincinnati Enquirer,* circulated every morning, and the afternoon *The Cincinnati Post.* The *Cincinnati Herald,* an African American oriented newspaper, appears weekly. Both the Associated Press and United Press International maintain offices in Cincinnati. *Cincinnati Magazine* is a monthly publication focusing on topics of community interest.

A number of nationally circulated magazines are published in Cincinnati; among them are *Writer's Digest,* a professional magazine for writers; *Dramatics Magazine,* for students interested in theatre as a career; and *St. Anthony Messenger,* a family-oriented Catholic magazine. Specialized publications originating in the city are directed toward readers with interests in business, medicine, pharmacy, engineering, the arts, crafts, and other fields.

## Television and Radio

Cincinnati is the broadcast media center for southwestern Ohio, northern Kentucky, and southeastern Indiana. Seven commercial, public, and independent television stations are received in the city; cable service is available. Approximately thirty-five AM and FM radio stations broadcast educational, cultural, and religious programming as well as rock and roll, contemporary, classical, gospel, blues, jazz, and country music.

***Media Information:*** *The Cincinnati Enquirer,* Gannet Co., 312 Elm Street, Cincinnati, OH; telephone (513)721-2700. *The Cincinnati Post,* E.W. Scripps Co., 125 E. Court, Cincinnati, OH 45202; telephone (513) 352-2000

## Cincinnati Online

*The Cincinnati Enquirer.* Available enquirer.com

Cincinnati Museum Center. Available www .cincymuseum.org

Cincinnati Public Schools. Available www.cpsboe .k12.oh.us

Cincinnati Regional Links. Available www.rcc.org/ reglinks.html

City of Cincinnati home page. Available www.ci .cincinnati.oh.us

Greater Cincinnati Chamber of Commerce. Available www.cincinnatichamber.com

Greater Cincinnati Convention and Visitors Bureau. Available www.cincyusa.com

Public Library of Cincinnati and Hamilton County. Available www.cincinnatilibrary.org

University of Cincinnati Medical Center. Available medcenter.uc.edu

BIBLIOGRAPHY

Howells, William Dean, *A Boy's Town: Described for "Harper's Young People"* (New York: Harper & Brothers, Franklin Square, 1890)

Howells, William Dean, *My Year in a Log Cabin* (New York, Harper & Brothers, 1893)

Miller, Zane L., and Bruce Tucker, *Changing Plans for America's Inner Cities: Cincinnati's Over-The-Rhine and Twentieth-Century Urbanism* (Ohio State University Press, 1998)

Walker, Robert Harris, *Cincinnati and the Big Red Machine* (Indiana University Press, 1988)

# Cleveland

## ■ The City in Brief

**Founded:** 1796 (incorporated 1836)

**Head Official:** Mayor Frank Jackson (D) (since 2006)

**City Population**

    1980: 573,822
    1990: 505,616
    2000: 478,403
    2006 estimate: 444,313
    Percent change, 1990–2000: −5.4%
    U.S. rank in 1980: 18th
    U.S. rank in 1990: 23rd
    U.S. rank in 2000: 40th (State rank: 2nd)

**Metropolitan Area Population**

    1980: Not available
    1990: 2,202,069
    2000: 2,250,871
    2006 estimate: 2,114,155
    Percent change, 1990–2000: 0.2%
    U.S. rank in 1980: 11th
    U.S. rank in 1990: Not available
    U.S. rank in 2000: 16th (PMSA)

**Area:** 82.42 square miles (2000)

**Elevation:** most of the city is on a level plain 60 to 80 feet above Lake Erie

**Average Annual Temperatures:** January, 25.7° F; July, 71.9° F; annual average, 49.6° F

**Average Annual Precipitation:** 38.71 inches of rain; 56.9 inches of snow

**Major Economic Sectors:** Services, wholesale and retail trade, manufacturing, government

**Unemployment Rate:** 6.3% (June 2007)

**Per Capita Income:** $14,825 (2005)

**2005 FBI Crime Index Property:** 28,543

**2005 FBI Crime Index Violent:** 6,416

**Major Colleges and Universities:** Case Western Reserve University; Cleveland State University

**Daily Newspaper:** *Plain Dealer*

## ■ Introduction

The seat of Cuyahoga County, Cleveland is Ohio's second largest city and is at the center of a metropolitan statistical area that encompasses Cuyahoga, Geauga, Lake, and Medina counties. The city's location on Lake Erie accounts for its success as a transportation, industrial, and commercial center. Cleveland contributed a number of industrial discoveries that benefited national growth and prosperity in the nineteenth century. In the early twentieth century, the local political system set a standard for reform that contributed to the general welfare of its citizens. Today Cleveland's revitalized central business and commercial districts complement its cultural institutions and major professional sports teams.

## ■ Geography and Climate

Extending 31 miles along the south shore of Lake Erie, Cleveland is surrounded by generally level terrain except for an abrupt ridge that rises 500 feet above the shore on the eastern edge of the city. Cleveland is bisected from north to south by the Cuyahoga River. The continental climate is modified by west to northerly winds off Lake Erie, which lower summer temperatures and raise winter temperatures. Summers are moderately warm and humid, winters relatively cold and cloudy. Snowfall fluctuates widely, ranging from 45 inches in west Cuyahoga County to 90 inches in the east. Thunderstorms often bring damaging winds of 50 miles per hour or greater; tornadoes occur frequently.

**Area:** 82.42 square miles (2000)

**Elevation:** most of the city is on a level plain 60 to 80 feet above Lake Erie

**Average Temperatures:** January, 25.7° F; July, 71.9° F; annual average, 49.6° F

**Average Annual Precipitation:** 38.71 inches of rain; 56.9 inches of snow

# ■ History

## Lake Erie Port Attracts Development

U.S. General Moses Cleaveland was sent in 1796 by the Connecticut Land Company to survey the Western Reserve, a one-half million acre tract of land in northeastern Ohio, which was at that time called "New Connecticut." General Cleaveland platted a townsite on Lake Erie at the mouth of the Cuyahoga River, named from a Native American term for crooked river because of the unusual U shape that causes it to flow both north and south. Cleaveland copied the New England style of town square layout. The settlement was abandoned, however, when dysentery and insects drove Cleaveland and his company back to New England. The eventual taming of the Western Reserve wilderness has been credited to Lorenzo Carter, who arrived at General Cleaveland's original townsite in 1799. Carter, a man of impressive ability and stature, brought stability to the primitive setting and established friendly relations with the Native Americans in the area. The revived settlement was named for its initial founder; the current spelling of the name can be traced to a newspaper compositor who dropped the first "a" from Cleaveland in order to fit the name on the newspaper masthead. Cleveland's geographic position as a Lake Erie port made it ideally situated for development in transportation, industry, and commerce.

By 1813 the port was receiving shipments from the cities in the East. Cleveland was chosen as the northern terminus of a canal system connecting the Ohio River and Lake Erie; it was completed in 1832. Cleveland was incorporated in 1836 as its population increased dramatically. Telegraph lines were installed in 1847, and shortly thereafter Western Union telegraph service was founded in Cleveland by Jeptha H. Wade. The opening of the Soo Canal in 1855 and the arrival of the railroad soon thereafter strengthened Cleveland's position as a transportation center.

The city played a significant role in the Civil War. Clevelanders generally opposed slavery, and a prominent local lawyer defended abolitionist John Brown. As a principal stop along the Oberlin-Wellington Trail,

Cleveland was active in the Underground Railroad. While the city sent its share of volunteers to fight for the Union cause, during the Civil War the ironworks industry grew, aided by the discovery of soft coal in canal beds. After the war the iron industry continued to expand in Cleveland, and local fortunes were made in steel and shipping; those who benefited created the Cleveland residential district known as "Millionaires Row."

## Industry and Reform Spell Progress

John D. Rockefeller's Standard Oil Company, organized in 1870, put Cleveland on the map as the nation's first oil capital. A rise in trade unionism paralleled Cleveland's industrialization. The Brotherhood of Locomotive Engineers established headquarters in the city, which was the site of national labor meetings that eventually led to walkouts and brought about better conditions for workers. Inventors found a hospitable environment in Cleveland. Charles F. Brush, originator of the carbon arc lamp, founded the Brush Electric Light and Power Company and installed arc lamps throughout the city. He also invented and manufactured the first practical storage battery. Worcester R. Warner and Ambrose Swasey perfected automotive gear improvements and designed astronomy instruments, bringing about innovations in both industries.

Cleveland gained a reputation as a reform city during the five-term administration of Thomas Loftin Johnson, a captain of the steel and transportation industries. Johnson was influenced by the American social philosopher Henry George, and his administration won high praise from muckraking journalist Lincoln Steffens, who called Johnson the nation's "best mayor" and Cleveland "the best governed city in the United States." First elected to office on the "three-cent fare program," Johnson fought to overcome the entrenched political interests of his nemesis, Mark Hanna, who used his power to work against Johnson's reforms. Johnson, a mentor to a generation of young politicians, improved life in Cleveland by building new streets and parks, creating a municipal electric company to curb the abuses of private utilities, and introducing city-owned garbage and refuse collection. He also set standards for meat and dairy products, and even took down "keep off the grass" signs in city parks.

Like other Rust Belt cities, Cleveland suffered in the 1950s and 1960s, becoming the subject of national attention and ridicule when the polluted Cuyahoga River burst into flames in 1969. The event, a low point in Cleveland history, became a rallying point in the passage of the Clean Water Act of 1972.

Cleveland's renaissance began in the early 1980s. From grass roots efforts initiated by neighborhood groups, to the city's top brass—business, civic, and political leaders—citizens have worked hard to mold Cleveland into a model city for America. The result: $7 billion in capital investment, including new hotels and world-class attractions. The city has also gained

©James Blank.

international and national attention as a model city for urban progress. Cleveland has been awarded the coveted "All America City" distinction five times.

The sheen from that title was growing tarnished by the mid-2000s, however. With a high school graduation rate among the lowest in the nation, along with taxes among the highest, Cleveland faced challenges in many arenas. Community leaders and businesses united to tackle these problems by stimulating innovation and entrepreneurship, attracting new businesses while retaining existing ones, and encouraging education and workforce development.

*Historical Information:* Western Reserve Historical Society, 10825 East Boulevard, Cleveland, OH 44106; telephone (216)721-5722. Great Lakes Historical Society, Clarence Metcalf Research Library, 480 Main St., PO Box 435, Vermillion, OH 44089; telephone (216)967-3467; email glhs1@inlandseas.org.

# ■ Population Profile

### Metropolitan Area Residents

1980: Not available
1990: 2,202,069

2000: 2,250,871
2006 estimate: 2,114,155
Percent change, 1990–2000: 0.2%
U.S. rank in 1980: 11th
U.S. rank in 1990: Not available
U.S. rank in 2000: 16th (PMSA)

### City Residents

1980: 573,822
1990: 505,616
2000: 478,403
2006 estimate: 444,313
Percent change, 1990–2000: −5.4%
U.S. rank in 1980: 18th
U.S. rank in 1990: 23rd
U.S. rank in 2000: 40th (State rank: 2nd)

**Density:** 6,166.5 people per square mile (2000)

### Racial and ethnic characteristics (2005)

White: 160,254
Black: 222,837
American Indian and Alaska Native: 2,312
Asian: 6,289
Native Hawaiian and Pacific Islander: 188

Hispanic or Latino (may be of any race): 32,085
Other: 16,626

**Percent of residents born in state:** 71.2% (2000)

**Age characteristics (2005)**

Population under 5 years old: 31,522
Population 5 to 9 years old: 32,416
Population 10 to 14 years old: 31,866
Population 15 to 19 years old: 30,472
Population 20 to 24 years old: 28,015
Population 25 to 34 years old: 50,558
Population 35 to 44 years old: 63,804
Population 45 to 54 years old: 62,057
Population 55 to 59 years old: 19,977
Population 60 to 64 years old: 17,701
Population 65 to 74 years old: 23,286
Population 75 to 84 years old: 16,830
Population 85 years and older: 6,030
Median age: 35.3 years

**Births (2006, MSA)**

Total number: 25,788

**Deaths (2006, MSA)**

Total number: 21,358

**Money income (2005)**

Per capita income: $14,825
Median household income: $24,105
Total households: 177,817

**Number of households with income of** . . .

less than $10,000: 41,066
$10,000 to $14,999: 17,422
$15,000 to $24,999: 32,697
$25,000 to $34,999: 24,620
$35,000 to $49,999: 23,477
$50,000 to $74,999: 21,919
$75,000 to $99,999: 9,263
$100,000 to $149,999: 5,977
$150,000 to $199,999: 811
$200,000 or more: 565

**Percent of families below poverty level:** 13.8% (2005)

**2005 FBI Crime Index Property:** 28,543

**2005 FBI Crime Index Violent:** 6,416

# ■ Municipal Government

Cleveland city government is administered by a mayor and a 21-member council. Councilpersons and the mayor, who is not a member of council, are elected to four-year terms.

**Head Official:** Mayor Frank Jackson (D) (since 2006; current term expires January 2010)

**Total Number of City Employees:** 8,136 (2007)

*City Information:* Cleveland City Hall, 601 Lakeside Ave., Cleveland, OH 44114; telephone (216)664-2000

# ■ Economy

## Major Industries and Commercial Activity

Diversified manufacturing is a primary economic sector, resting on a traditional base of heavy industry in particular. Consistent with a nationwide trend, the services industry—transportation, health, insurance, retailing, utilities, commercial banking, and finance—is emerging as a dominant sector. Cleveland serves as headquarters to 5 companies on the *Fortune* 500 list, both industrial and non-industrial. These firms are, in order of their *Fortune* 500 rank: National City Corp., Eaton Corp., Parker Hannifin Corp., Sherwin-Williams Co., and KeyCorp. Cleveland is also home to approximately 150 international companies from 25 different countries.

Manufacturing has traditionally been the primary industry of northeast Ohio. It remains so today, although the local economy has suffered along with the rest of the nation during the recession of the late 1990s and early 2000s, and the service industry has become crucial to the region as well. Dubbed "Polymer Valley," the metropolitan Cleveland area has the largest concentration of polymer companies in the United States; Goodyear Tire & Rubber Co., the world's largest tire company, is headquartered in nearby Akron. The area's other manufacturing companies are engaged in such fields as the automotive industry, fabricated metals, electrical/electronic equipment, and instruments and controls.

Supported by the manufacturing industry is the science and engineering field. More than 160 engineering companies are located in the Cleveland metro area. These firms engage in civil engineering, construction, and the burgeoning field of information technology. Among the local institutions of science and engineering are the Cleveland Engineering Society, the Cleveland Society of Professional Engineers, the Great Lakes Science Center, the NASA John H. Glenn Research Center, ASM (American Society for Metals) International, and the engineering schools of Case Western Reserve University, Cleveland State University, and the University of Akron.

Cleveland's research base for the biotechnology and biomedical industry has grown exponentially in recent years. More than 100 biotechnology firms are located in northeast Ohio, along with more than 100 research laboratories. The Cleveland Clinic Foundation has the nation's largest hospital-based department of biomedical engineering. Area colleges offer training in biomedical or bioscience technology; among them are Case Western Reserve University, Cleveland State University, Kent State University, Lakeland Community College, and the University of Akron.

**Items and goods produced:** automobile parts, bolts and nuts, machine tools, paints and lacquers, rubber and oil products, chemicals, rayon, foundry and machine shop products, electrical machinery and appliances, men's and women's clothing, iron and steel

## Incentive Programs—New and Existing Businesses

*Local programs:* The Greater Cleveland Partnership (GCP) was formed in 2003 through the merger of the Greater Cleveland Roundtable, the Greater Cleveland Growth Association, and Cleveland Tomorrow. GCP provides access to local and state business incentives and job training programs. It can link businesses with a variety of assistance including international trade, business financing, tax credits and abatement programs, technology transfer, labor force recruitment, and training and market data. GCP is also affiliated with Growth Capital Corp., which provides financing assistance to businesses in northeast Ohio to facilitate business expansion, new facility construction, and equipment purchases. Neighborhood Progress Inc. is a non-profit organization that offers up to $5 million per year in low-interest funds to develop Cleveland's neighborhoods.

*State programs:* The state of Ohio offers a number of incentives designed to encourage new companies and retain existing businesses. Tax credit programs include those for job creation, machinery and equipment investment, export, research and development franchise, and technology investment. Ohio also offers a property tax abatement for areas identified as enterprise zones, and sales tax exemptions for research and development.

*Job training programs:* The Ohio Investment Training Program (OITP) provides financial assistance and technical resources for customized training involving employees of new and expanding Ohio businesses. OITP may assist a company up to a maximum of one-half of the project's total eligible training costs. The Ohio Job Training Tax Credit is offered to businesses engaged in manufacturing and other specified service industries. Career Service Centers offer customized training programs designed to meet the needs of a specific business, as well as other ongoing skill training for current or new employees; these Career Service Centers are operated by Case Western Reserve University, Cleveland Institute of Art, Cleveland State University, Cuyahoga Community College, and David N. Myers College.

## Development Projects

In March 2004 *Site Selection* magazine ranked the Cleveland area, with 96 projects, the tenth in the nation for number of new and expanded corporate facility projects. Among these corporate projects were the expansion of Minolta's Cleveland facility, which added 25,000 square feet; the $4.5 million expansion of U.S. Cotton's facility; and a new, 5,000-square-foot distribution center for Netflix Inc.

Groundbreaking began in September 2005 on a six-year, $258-million expansion and renovation of the Cleveland Museum of Art, expected to be completed by 2011. In 2007 Euclid Avenue was undergoing a $168 million renovation between the downtown Public Square and the Playhouse Square Center to create the "Euclid Transportation Corridor"; construction was scheduled for completion in 2008. The corridor was intended to connect the downtown business district (the region's largest employment center) with the University Circle area (the second largest employment center) and major cultural, medical and educational districts. In 2007 plans were announced by the Regional Transit Authority to build a new Rapid Transit stop in the University Circle/Little Italy area; the plans were in the design stage and no completion date had yet been finalized.

*Economic Development Information:* Greater Cleveland Partnership; The Higbee Building, 100 Public Square, Suite 210, Cleveland, OH 44113-2291; telephone (216)621-3300; fax (216)621-4617

## Commercial Shipping

Cleveland is at the center of the nation's largest concentration of industrial and consumer markets. The city of Cleveland is home to more than 100 offices of motor freight carrier companies and there are many others located throughout the metropolitan area. Three railroads—Norfolk Southern, CSX Transportation, Wheeling & Lake Erie Railroad—serve the region. More than 1,200 miles of highways connect the region with other U.S. markets, and the World Trade Center Cleveland assists companies with international business ventures. Cleveland-Hopkins International Airport is served by 8 cargo carriers.

The Port of Cleveland, the largest overseas general cargo port on Lake Erie and third largest port on the Great Lakes, serves more than 50 countries, shipping cargo to and receiving cargo from 120 ports around the world. The Port is also the site of Foreign Trade Zone #40, an area where foreign goods bound for international destinations can be temporarily stored without incurring an import duty. Every service for shippers—banking, insurance, customs, stevedoring, and storage—is available from experienced firms. Each year the port handles over 12 million tons of cargo, primarily semi-finished products, machinery, and such bulk cargo as iron ore, stone, cement, and salt.

## Labor Force and Employment Outlook

In September 2007 the unemployment rate in Greater Cleveland stood at 5.9 percent, above the national average and down only slightly from ten-year highs of 6.8 percent in 2003. Between 1997 and 2007 the metropolitan labor force experienced a slight net gain, from 1,057,207 to 1,097,211 workers. However, the city of Cleveland itself experienced a loss of population; between 1980 and 2000, Cleveland lost fully one-sixth of its population.

In 2007 analysts were not optimistic about the Cleveland economy; the employment situation showed little signs of improvement throughout the mid 2000s, and the region was particularly hard-hit by summer 2007's subprime mortgage crisis. The health care industry and increased efforts to make the city a center of "green" manufacturing were the major bright spots for the area as it looked into the 2010s and beyond.

The following is a summary of data regarding the Cleveland-Elyria-Mentor metropolitan area labor force, 2006 annual averages.

**Size of nonagricultural labor force:** 1,076,100

**Number of workers employed in** . . .

    construction and mining: 41,600
    manufacturing: 147,600
    trade, transportation and utilities: 199,600
    information: 18,900
    financial activities: 77,600
    professional and business services: 140,600
    educational and health services: 171,500
    leisure and hospitality: 95,000
    other services: 44,100
    government: 139,400

**Average hourly earnings of production workers employed in manufacturing:** $19.10

**Unemployment rate:** 6.3% (June 2007)

| *Largest Cuyahoga County employers (2007)* | *Number of employees* |
|---|---|
| Cleveland Clinic | 27,755 |
| University Hospitals Health System | 16,611 |
| Cuyahoga County | 9,142 |
| Progressive Corporation | 9,017 |
| City of Cleveland | 8,136 |
| Cleveland Municipal School District | 7,472 |
| KeyCorp | 6,397 |
| National City Corp. | 6,051 |
| Metrohealth | 5,503 |

## Cost of Living

The following is a summary of data regarding several key cost of living factors in the Cleveland area.

**2007 (1st quarter) ACCRA Average House Price:** $255,228

**2007 (1st quarter) ACCRA Cost of Living Index:** 99.7

**State income tax rate:** 0.68% to 6.87%

**State sales tax rate:** 5.5%

**Local income tax rate:** 2.0%

**Local sales tax rate:** 7.5%

**Property tax rate:** Ranges from 96.5 to 183.40 mills per $1,000 of assessed value

***Economic Information:*** Greater Cleveland Partnership, Tower City Center, Ste. 200, 50 Public Sq., Cleveland, OH 44113; telephone (216)621-3300; toll-free (888)304-GROW; fax (216)621-4617; email customer service@clevegrowth.com

# ■ Education and Research

## Elementary and Secondary Schools

The Cleveland Municipal School District, administered by a mayor-appointed school board that appoints a superintendent, enrolls the largest student population of any Ohio school system. More than 300 businesses and other organizations have joined in a partnership with the city's schools; one of these is NASA John H. Glenn Research Center.

Cleveland's schools experienced academic, financial, and structural crises in the mid-2000s. In 2004 the high school graduation rate was only 40.8 percent, while only 11.3 percent of residents achieved a college degree. Worsening the situation, the Cleveland Municipal School District had a $36 million operating deficit; in order to rectify the shortfall, the board of education closed a number of schools and laid off part of the workforce for the 2005–2006 school year. In June 2002, prompted by the collapse of a school gym roof, a $1.5 billion Facilities Plan was approved to replace or renovate each school in the district within 10-12 years. The 2007-2012 phase of the school district's plan called for the institution of a "Zero Tolerance" disciplinary policy, a mentoring program with 700 local legal professionals, and the opening of an academy to help former dropouts obtain a high school diploma.

The 2007-2008 school year was one of important changes for the District; it marked the opening of the Ginn Academy for at-risk boys, named after famous area football coach Ted Ginn, Sr. That same year four single-sex academies were opened throughout the city and a strict dress code was instituted.

The following is a summary of data regarding the Cleveland Metropolitan School District as of the 2005–2006 school year.

**Total enrollment:** 319,901 (includes all districts)

**Number of facilities**

elementary schools: 81
junior high/middle schools: 2
senior high schools: 20
other: 0

**Student/teacher ratio:** 16.5:1

**Teacher salaries (2005–06)**

elementary median: $58,920
junior high/middle median: $60,590
secondary median: $58,970

**Funding per pupil:** $10,420

More than 30 parochial and private schools offer a range of educational alternatives at the pre-school, kindergarten, elementary, and secondary levels in the Cleveland metropolitan area. Among them is the University School, a more than 100-year-old independent day school for boys; St. Ignatius High School; Gilmour Academy; Hathaway Brown School; the Laurel School; and Magnificat High School.

*Public Schools Information:* Cleveland Municipal School District, 1380 E. 6th St., Cleveland, OH 44114; telephone (216)574-8000; email info@cmsdnet.net

## Colleges and Universities

Cleveland State University (CSU), predominantly a commuter institution, enrolls more than 16,000 students. The university offers 1,000 courses supporting 200 major fields of study at the bachelor, master, doctoral, and law degree levels, including doctoral programs in regulatory biology, chemistry, engineering, urban studies, and urban education. CSU's Cleveland-Marshall College of Law is the largest law school in Ohio. Case Western Reserve University offers undergraduate, graduate, and professional education in more than 60 areas of study, such as medicine, dentistry, nursing, law, management, and applied social sciences; it is a major research institution ranking among the best in undergraduate engineering and business programs. In the 2008 *U.S. News and World Report* list of "America's Best Colleges," Case Western was ranked 41st among national universities, 21st among medical schools for research, and 53rd among law schools. The Laura and Alvin Siegal College of Jewish Studies is one of only a handful of colleges in North America to be accredited as an institution of higher Jewish learning.

The Cleveland Institute of Art offers a five-year bachelor of fine arts program. The Cleveland Institute of Music grants baccalaureate, master's, and doctoral degrees in various music fields in conjunction with Case Western Reserve University, which provides the academic curriculum. Other colleges in Cleveland include David N. Myers University and Cuyahoga Community College (CCC, or Tri-C), which is the city's largest college and the fourth largest in the state. Offering career education leading to an associate's degree and enrolling more than 55,000 credit and non-credit students at its Metropolitan, Eastern, and Western campuses, Tri-C's programs include allied health, business technologies, engineering technologies, early childhood education, law enforcement, and mental health.

Among the colleges and universities enrolling more than 1,000 students and located in the surrounding area or within commuting distance of Cleveland are Baldwin-Wallace College, John Carroll University, Kent State University, Lakeland Community College, Lorain County Community College, Oberlin College, University of Akron, and Ursuline College, which is the oldest Catholic women's college in the nation.

## Libraries and Research Centers

Approximately 90 libraries are operated in Cleveland by a diverse range of public agencies, private corporations, and other organizations. The Cleveland Public Library maintains a main facility set on 529,204 square feet, 28 branches, a Library for the Blind and Physically Handicapped, and a Public Administration Library in City Hall. The Cleveland Public Library, the third largest public research library in the United States, has nearly 10 million items and is also the largest repository worldwide for chess-related items. The library is a depository for federal, state, international, local, and United Nations documents. The Library for the Blind and Physically Handicapped offers 11,000 Braille titles, 150,000 cassettes, and 48,000 discs; the library also includes material on visual and physical disabilities in their collection.

In 2003 the Ohio Center for the Book was dedicated at the main Cleveland Public Library, enabling it to serve the entire state. That year the library system became the first in the nation to offer eBooks to patrons. The Langston Hughes branch was the recipient of an Ohio Historical Marker in December 2003 in honor of its namesake, the Cleveland poet James Mercer Langston Hughes.

The Cuyahoga County Public Library, which houses nearly 3 million books, operates 27 full-service branches throughout the county, all with free Wi-Fi access. The Western Reserve Historical Society, the Cleveland Museum of Art, and the Cleveland Museum of Natural History maintain reference libraries. As a major research institution, Case Western Reserve University maintains holdings of more than 1.5 million books, nearly 14,000 periodical subscriptions, and approximately 35 special collections in such fields as literature, history, philosophy, urban studies, psychology, and the sciences; six departmental libraries are also located on campus. The Cleveland Health Sciences Library is operated by Case Western Reserve University and the Cleveland Medical Library Association. Other colleges and universities, as well as several corporations, hospitals, and religious organizations, maintain libraries in the city.

More than 400 public and private research centers are based in the Cleveland metropolitan area. Among them are the John H. Glenn Research Center of the National Aeronautics and Space Administration (NASA), the Cleveland Clinic Educational Foundation, and the Cleveland Psychoanalytic Center. In 2003 Case Western Reserve University was awarded an $18 million grant to create the Wright Center of Innovation to focus on fuel cell research. University Hospitals represents the largest concentration of biomedical research in Ohio. Greater Cleveland's medical community as a whole receives more than $100 million in research dollars from the National Institutes of Health each year, making Cleveland a leading center nationwide for biomedical research and spending. In 2006 the Cleveland Clinic alone spent $144.3 million on medical and scientific research.

***Public Library Information:*** Cleveland Public Library, 325 Superior Ave. NE, Cleveland, OH 44114; telephone (216)623-2800; fax (216)623-7015; email info@library.cpl.org

# ■ Health Care

Cleveland is home to a number of the nation's top institutions providing health care, medical education, and medical research and technology. The Cleveland metropolitan area is served by approximately 50 hospitals; more than 20 are affiliated with medical schools, including Case Western Reserve University School of Medicine. The region employs more than 9,000 physicians and 23,000 health care professionals.

Cleveland Clinic and University Hospital Health Systems control 90-plus percent of the area's hospital beds. The Cleveland Clinic Foundation, which pioneered kidney transplants and open-heart surgery, occupies 140 acres and 37 buildings on its main campus, and serves patients throughout the United States and the world. It consistently ranks among the best hospitals in the country in *U.S. News & World Report* surveys. In 2007 the hospital was ranked the 4th best overall and was ranked in the top ten for twelve of its specialties. The Cleveland Clinic rates highly for care in cardiology, gastroenterology, neurology, orthopedics, and urology. The Clinic also has facilities in Florida, Canada, and Abu Dhabi. Rainbow Babies and Children's Hospital is one of the country's best for pediatric and neonatal intensive care. University Hospitals (UH), nationally recognized for cancer research and treatment, receives excellent rankings in three specialties.

UH has more than 150 locations throughout the Greater Cleveland area. In 2006 it was ranked among the top fifty hospitals in thirteen specialties by *U.S. News and World Report.* Among other Cleveland facilities is St. Vincent Charity Hospital, which participated in the development of the first heart-lung machines.

***Health Care Information:*** Cleveland Health Education Museum, 8911 Euclid Ave., Cleveland, OH; telephone (216)231-5010

# ■ Recreation

## Sightseeing

One of Cleveland's most popular attractions is the Rock and Roll Hall of Fame and Museum. Situated on the shores of Lake Erie, the museum houses six floors of costumes, interactive exhibits, and original films, along with the most extensive collection of rock and roll artifacts and memorabilia in the world. Adjacent to the Rock and Roll Hall on North Coast Harbor is the Great Lakes Science Center. Visitors can explore the wonders of science, the environment, and technology via more than 400 interactive exhibits. Located inside the center is the six-story OMNIMAX theater, with supersized images and digital sound that allows viewers to feel as though they were actually in the film.

North America's largest collection of primate species is housed at the Cleveland Metroparks Zoo and RainForest, located five miles south of downtown. The zoo has more than 3,300 animals from around the world, including 84 endangered species, and occupies 168 rolling, wooded acres. The two-acre RainForest is home to more than 600 animals and 10,000 plants from the jungles of the world, and features a 25-foot waterfall and simulated tropical storm.

The NASA John H. Glenn Research Center is the only NASA facility north of the Mason-Dixon line. Named after the Ohio astronaut, it presents programs on space exploration, aircraft propulsion, satellites, and alternative energy sources. Two of Cleveland's best-known monuments are the Garfield Monument in Lakeview Cemetery and the National Shrine of Our Lady of Lourdes, which resembles the original shrine in France and is located 10 miles east of the city.

Seasonal amusement parks located in Greater Cleveland include Geauga Lake & Wildwater Kingdom and Cedar Point (located 63 miles from Cleveland, in Sandusky, Ohio), known for its world-record-breaking collection of roller coasters and rides. Sandusky is also home to Kalahari Resort, the largest indoor waterpark in Ohio.

## Arts and Culture

University Circle, located four miles east of downtown, boasts the largest concentration of cultural institutions and museums in the country. Within one square mile, visitors will find more than 40 non-profit institutions including the Cleveland Museum of Art (undergoing major renovations in 2007), Cleveland Museum of Natural History (which merged with HealthSpace Cleveland in January 2007), Cleveland Botanical Garden, Children's Museum of Cleveland, Crawford Auto-Aviation Museum, and Museum of Contemporary Art Cleveland (MOCA).

Museums located outside of University Circle include the Hungarian Heritage Society, the Shaker Historical Society and Museum, the Steamship William G. *Mather* Museum, and the Dunham Tavern Museum, the oldest Cleveland museum building on its original site. The Milton & Tamar Maltz Museum of Jewish Heritage opened in the fall of 2005. The Christmas Story House, a museum dedicated to the movie of the same name, opened in November 2006.

The Cleveland Orchestra, considered one of the nation's top orchestras, plays a season of concerts at Severance Hall from September to May; the summer season is scheduled at the open-air Blossom Music Center from June to August. Blossom also hosts opera, classical, pop, jazz, rock, and folk concerts during the summer months. The Cleveland Chamber Music Society and the Cleveland Chamber Symphony offer a schedule of chamber music each year. The Cleveland Institute of Music presents hundreds of concerts by faculty, students, and visiting artists, and the Cleveland Pops Orchestra performs music from motion pictures and Broadway shows. The internationally acclaimed Cleveland Quartet gives performances throughout the world. The nation added its eighth House of Blues with the 2004 opening of Cleveland's concert club.

Two dance companies perform in Cleveland: Dance Cleveland and Akron's Ohio Ballet. Cleveland's opera companies—Opera Cleveland (which merged with the city's Lyric Opera in spring 2007) and Cleveland Institute of Music—stage operatic presentations.

Cleveland supports a number of theater companies. Cleveland Play House, the country's first professional resident company, presents a season of classical drama and new works. Playhouse Square Center, with its five beautifully restored circa 1920 theaters, is the nation's second largest performing arts center. The Ohio Theatre is home to the Great Lakes Theater Festival; the others host touring Broadway shows, musicals, concerts, opera, and ballets. Karamu House, from the Swahili for "a center of enjoyment, a place to be entertained," has earned a national reputation as a center of African American culture.

## Festivals and Holidays

Cleveland schedules a full calendar of annual events. Each January, Cleveland organizes a Martin Luther King Jr. celebration, followed two months later by a festive St. Patrick's Day Parade through downtown. The Cleveland International Film Festival also takes place in March with nearly 200 film screenings. The state's largest environmental event is EarthFest, held in April at the Cleveland

Metroparks Zoo. The Cleveland Botanical Garden Flower Show, the largest outdoor flower show in North America, takes place in May at the Cleveland Botanical Gardens.

June brings the Parade the Circle Celebration, featuring an art parade and free admission to University Circle facilities. Visitors can join in Cleveland's annual July birthday bash in the Flats with riverfront festivities and performances as well as an amazing fireworks and laser light show. Samples of savory ribs, live entertainment, and family fun are on the menu at the Great American Rib Cookoff in late May. Cleveland showcases its diversity at summer festivities such as the Irish Cultural Festival, the Annual Polish Heritage Festival, and the Cleveland Pride Parade & Festival, celebrating the lesbian-gay-bi-transsexual community.

The week-long Cuyahoga County Fair in August features rides, exhibits, and shows. An unforgettable Labor Day weekend event is the Cleveland National Air Show at Burke Lakefront Airport. Art meets technology at the Ingenuity Festival, taking place at various downtown locations in early September; running nearly simultaneously with this event is Taste of Cleveland, at which food from more than 30 local restaurants can be sampled. The Johnny Appleseed Festival at Mapleside Farms and the Midwest Oktoberfest are among the area's many fall festivals. The Christmas season marks its start with the annual Holiday Lighting ceremony on downtown's Public Square the day after Thanksgiving.

## Sports for the Spectator

Cleveland is a major-league sports city with major-league sports facilities. Gund Arena hosts NBA Cleveland Cavaliers basketball and the American Hockey League's Lake Erie Monsters (an affiliate of the Colorado Avalanche), as well as more than 200 family events and concerts each year. State-of-the-art Jacobs Field is home to Major League Baseball's Cleveland Indians. The Cleveland Browns professional football team, named for their first coach, the legendary Paul Brown, is part of the National Football League's American Conference and play home games at the lakefront Cleveland Browns Stadium. The Cleveland Junior Lumberjacks play youth hockey at the Metroplex. The Grand Prix of Cleveland is held over three June days at the Burke Lakefront Airport. Thistledown Race Track offers thoroughbred racing and Northfield Park schedules harness races.

## Sports for the Participant

Cleveland's Metroparks system, consisting of more than 20,000 acres on 16 reservations that surround the city's core, represents one of the nation's largest concentrations of park land per capita. Facilities are available for hiking, cycling, tennis, swimming, golf, boating, and horseback riding. Winter activities include cross-country skiing, tobogganing, ice skating, and ice fishing. Downhill skiing is available at three nearby resorts. Greater Cleveland encompasses more than 70 public and private golf courses. One hundred miles of Lake Erie shoreline, as well as inland lakes, reservoirs, rivers, and streams, make fishing a favorite pastime; the annual catch in Lake Erie equals that of the other four Great Lakes combined. Cuyahoga Valley National Park, Cleveland Lakefront State Park, Huntington Beach, and Mentor Headlands State Park are popular summer spots for water sports enthusiasts. The Cleveland Marathon and 10K is held downtown in May.

### Shopping and Dining

More than 600 retail businesses are located in downtown Cleveland. The elegant Tower City Center offers shopping and dining at more than 100 establishments. Eton Collections, situated on Chagrin Boulevard, houses retail and dining establishments amid fountains, gardens, and sculptures, and recently underwent a $50 million expansion and renovation. Just west of downtown Cleveland is the new Crocker Park, a $450 million shopping center that encompasses 12 city blocks in Westlake. To the east of the city is Beachwood Place, a large indoor mall, and Legacy Village, a village-style, upscale shopping center. Unique shopping opportunities can be found throughout the city: Antique Row on Lorain Avenue, which attracts antique buyers; the Arcade, a nineteenth-century marketplace; the Larchmere area, well known for its antiques; and the West Side Market in nearby Ohio City which sells fresh fish and meats, vegetables and fruits, baked goods, cheeses, and ethnic foods.

*Visitor Information:* Convention & Visitors Bureau of Greater Cleveland, Higbee Building 100 Public Square, Suite 100, Cleveland, OH 44113; telephone (216)875-6600

## ■ Convention Facilities

The International Exposition & Conference Center is one of the largest facilities nationwide for exhibition space. Situated on a 175-acre site next to Cleveland-Hopkins International Airport, the center contains over a million square feet of exhibit space, 800,000 of which is contained in a single room. It also offers a renovated 85,000-square-foot carpeted conference center with 26 meeting rooms.The Cleveland Convention Center, located downtown, contains 375,000 square feet of flexible exhibit space that can be divided into four separate meeting halls; 37 meetings rooms are available to accommodate up to 10,000 attendees. The largest room in the Cleveland Masonic Temple & Auditorium is 15,000 square feet, and the largest in the Cleveland State University's Wolstein Center is 23,520 square feet.

Other convention and meeting facilities are located throughout the Greater Cleveland area; among them are the Forum, Grays Armory, Play House Square Center,

and the Spitzer Conference Center, located in Elyria approximately 20 minutes from the Cleveland-Hopkins International Airport.

*Convention Information:* Convention & Visitors Bureau of Greater Cleveland, Higbee Building 100 Public Square, Suite 100, Cleveland, OH 44113; telephone (216)875-6600

## ■ Transportation

### Approaching the City

Cleveland-Hopkins International Airport, the Midwestern hub for Continental Airlines, was the 37th busiest airport in the nation in 2006, with 249,967 operations that year. There are approximately 320 daily nonstop flights from 9 commercial airlines to over 80 destinations. The Rapid Transit system connects the airport to downtown. Commuter air service to regional cities is available at Burke Lakefront Airport; business and general aviation traffic is handled at Cuyahoga County Airport. Twenty-one other general aviation facilities are located in the metropolitan area.

Three major interstates intersect downtown Cleveland: I-77 and I-71, which run north and south, and I-90, which runs east and west. In addition, I-480 connects the eastern and western Cleveland suburbs and runs south of the city, bypassing the downtown area; I-490 does the same by connecting I-90 and I-71 to I-77. Amtrak provides rail transportation service into Cleveland, and Greyhound operates a bus terminal downtown.

### Traveling in the City

The Regional Transit Authority (RTA) operates Cleveland's extensive rapid transit system. RTA has a direct link from downtown Public Square to Hopkins International Airport. The Waterfront Line, a light rail transportation system, connects Cleveland's downtown attractions. Other lines extend to the University Circle area and the eastern suburbs. Visitors can conveniently and economically travel from Public Square and Tower City Center's hotels and shopping venues to the Flats Entertainment District and North Coast Harbor attractions like the Rock and Roll Hall of Fame, Great Lakes Science Center, and Cleveland Browns Stadium. Trolley tours and riverboat cruises offer unique and informative views of the city.

## ■ Communications

### Newspapers and Magazines

Cleveland's major daily newspaper is the *Plain Dealer*, which is also Ohio's largest daily newspaper. Numerous community newspapers, including the *Call & Post*, an

African American community newspaper, also circulate in the city. *Cleveland Magazine,* for readers in the Cleveland metropolitan area, features articles on politics and urban and suburban contemporary living and events. *Northern Ohio LIVE,* a monthly magazine describing entertainment opportunities, and *Crain's Cleveland Business* are also published there. The award-winning *Cleveland Scene* is an alternative magazine published weekly; the *Free Times* is another alternative newsweekly.

About 80 specialized magazines and trade, professional, and scholarly journals are published in Cleveland on such subjects as explosives engineering, local history, fraternal organizations, lawn care, ethnic culture, business and economics, religion, medicine, welding and metal production, food service, and building trades.

## Television and Radio

Cleveland is the broadcast media center for northeastern Ohio. Greater Cleveland television viewers tune in to programming scheduled by seven stations based there. More than a dozen AM and FM radio stations broadcast a wide range of listening choices, from religious and inspirational features, to news and talk shows, to all major musical genres.

*Media Information:* *Plain Dealer,* 1801 Superior Ave., Cleveland, OH 44114; telephone (216)999-6000. *Cleveland Magazine,* 1422 Euclid Ave., Ste. 730, Cleveland, OH 44115; telephone (216)771-2833; fax (216) 781-6318. *Northern Ohio LIVE,* 11320 Juniper Rd., Cleveland, OH 44106; telephone (216)721-2525; email info@livepub.com

## Cleveland Online

City of Cleveland Home Page. Available www.city .cleveland.oh.us

Cleveland Municipal School District. Available www .cmsdnet.net

Cleveland Public Library. Available www.cpl.org

Convention & Visitors Bureau of Greater Cleveland. Available www.travelcleveland.com

Greater Cleveland Partnership. Available www .gcpartnership.com

*Plain Dealer.*Available www.plaindealer.comwww .cleveland.com

Rock and Roll Hall of Fame. Available www .rockhall.com

BIBLIOGRAPHY

Chapman, Edmund H., *Cleveland, Village to Metropolis: A Case Study of Problems of Urban Development in Nineteenth-Century America* (Cleveland, OH: Western Reserve Historical Society, 1964)

Grubb, Davis, *The Night of the Hunter* (New York: Harper & Row, 1953)

Grubb, Davis, *Oh Beulah Land: A Novel* (New York: Viking, 1956)

Miller, Carl H., *Breweries of Cleveland* (Schnitzelbank Press, 1998)

Phillips, Kimberley L., *Alabama North: African-American Migrants, Community, and Working-Class Activism in Cleveland, 1915-45 (The Working Class in American History)* (University of Illinois Press, 2000)

Schneider, Russell, *The Boys of the Summer of '48* (Sports Publishing Inc., 1998)

# Columbus

## ■ The City in Brief

**Founded:** 1797 (incorporated 1834)

**Head Official:** Mayor Michael B. Coleman (D) (since 2003)

**City Population**

> 1980: 564,871
> 1990: 632,945
> 2000: 711,470
> 2006 estimate: 733,203
> Percent change, 1990–2000: 12.4%
> U.S. rank in 1980: 19th
> U.S. rank in 1990: 16th
> U.S. rank in 2000: 15th

**Metropolitan Area Population**

> 1980: 1,244,000
> 1990: 1,345,450
> 2000: 1,540,157
> 2006 estimate: 1,725,570
> Percent change, 1990–2000: 14.5%
> U.S. rank in 1980: 28th
> U.S. rank in 1990: Not available
> U.S. rank in 2000: 32nd

**Area:** 225.9 square miles (2000)

**Elevation:** Ranges from 685 to 893 feet above sea level

**Average Annual Temperatures:** January, 28.3° F; July, 75.1° F; annual average, 52.9° F

**Average Annual Precipitation:** 38.52 inches of rain; 27.7 inches of snow

**Major Economic Sectors:** Services, wholesale and retail trade, government, manufacturing, education

**Unemployment Rate:** 5.4% (June 2007)

**Per Capita Income:** $22,134 (2005)

**2005 FBI Crime Index Property:** 54,141

**2005 FBI Crime Index Violent:** 6,111

**Major Colleges and Universities:** The Ohio State University, Capital University, Ohio Dominican University

**Daily Newspaper:** *The Columbus Dispatch*

## ■ Introduction

Columbus, the capital of Ohio and the state's largest city, is the seat of Franklin County. The focus of an urban complex comprised of Grandview Heights, Upper Arlington, Worthington, Bexley, and Whitehall, Columbus is the center of the metropolitan statistical area that includes Delaware, Fairfield, Franklin, Licking, Madison, Pickaway, and Union counties. Chosen by the Ohio General Assembly as the state capital because of its central location, Columbus developed in the nineteenth century as an important stop on the National Highway and as a link in the nation's canal system. Today, the city is a leader in research, education, technology, and insurance. *Inc.* magazine describes Columbus as "clean, with good schools, reasonably priced housing, and a college-town atmosphere that helps attract and retain young people."

## ■ Geography and Climate

Situated in central Ohio in the drainage area of the Ohio River, Columbus is located on the Scioto and Olentangy rivers; two minor streams running through the city are Alum Creek and Big Walnut Creek. Columbus's weather is changeable, influenced by air masses from central and southwest Canada; air from the Gulf of Mexico reaches the region during the summer and to a lesser extent in the fall and winter. The moderate climate is characterized by four distinct seasons. Snowfall averages around 27 inches annually.

**Area:** 225.9 square miles (2000)

**Elevation:** Ranges from 685 to 893 feet above sea level

**Average Temperatures:** January, 28.3° F; July, 75.1° F; annual average, 52.9° F

**Average Annual Precipitation:** 38.52 inches of rain; 27.7 inches of snow

# ■ History

## Central Location Makes Columbus Ohio's Capital

After Ohio gained statehood in 1803, the General Assembly set out to find a geographically centralized location for the capital. Congress had enacted the Ordinance for the Northwest Territory in 1787 to settle claims from the American Revolution and a grant was given to Virginia for lands west of the Scioto River. Lucas Sullivant, a Virginia surveyor, established in 1797 the village of Franklinton, which quickly turned into a profitable trading center. In 1812 plans for a state Capitol building and a penitentiary at Franklinton were drawn up and approved by the legislature, which also agreed to rename the settlement Columbus. Construction of the state buildings was delayed for four years by the War of 1812.

During its early history the major threat to Columbus was a series of fever and cholera epidemics that did not subside until swamps close to the center of town were drained. With the opening in 1831 of the Ohio & Erie Canal, which was connected to Columbus by a smaller canal, and then the National Highway in 1833, Columbus was in a position to emerge as a trade and transportation center. Then, on February 22, 1850, a steam engine pulling flat cars made its maiden run from Columbus to Xenia, 54 miles away, and Columbus entered the railroad age. Five locally financed railroads were in operation by 1872.

Columbus, with a population of 20,000 people in 1860, became a military center during the Civil War. Camp Jackson was an assembly center for recruits and Columbus Barracks—renamed Fort Hayes in 1922—served as an arsenal. Camp Chase, also in the area, was the Union's largest facility for Confederate prisoners, and the Federal Government maintained a cemetery for the more than 2,000 soldiers who died there.

## Academic Prominence Precedes High-Technology Growth

Columbus prospered economically after the Civil War, as new banks and railroad lines opened and horse-and-buggy companies manufactured 20,000 carriages and

wagons a year. The city's first waterworks system and an extended streetcar service were built during this period. In 1870 the Ohio General Assembly created, through the Morrill Land Grant Act, the Ohio Agricultural and Mechanical College, which became a vital part of the city's life and identity. This coeducational institution, renamed The Ohio State University in 1878, is now one of the country's major state universities. The Columbus campus consists of nearly 400 permanent buildings on 1,644 acres of land. Today, the university's technological research facilities, coupled with the Battelle Memorial Institute, comprise one of the largest private research organizations of its kind in the world.

Two events prior to World War I shook Columbus's stability. The streetcar strike of 1910 lasted through the summer and into the fall, resulting in riots and destruction of street cars and even one death. The National Guard was called out to maintain order, and when the strike finally ended, few concessions were made by the railway company. Three years later, the Scioto River flood killed 100 people and left 20,000 people homeless; property damages totaled $9 million.

Traditionally a center for political, economic, and cultural activity as the state capital, Columbus is today one of the fastest-growing cities in the east central United States. The downtown area underwent a complete transformation in the 1990s, and the economy surged as high-technology development and research companies moved into the metropolitan area. Franklin County saw its population top 1,000,000 for the first time in the 2000 census and celebrated its bicentennial in 2003.

***Historical Information:*** Ohio Historical Society, 1985 Velma Avenue, Columbus, OH 43211; telephone (614)297-2510

# ■ Population Profile

**Metropolitan Area Residents**

    1980: 1,244,000
    1990: 1,345,450
    2000: 1,540,157
    2006 estimate: 1,725,570
    Percent change, 1990–2000: 14.5%
    U.S. rank in 1980: 28th
    U.S. rank in 1990: Not available
    U.S. rank in 2000: 32nd

**City Residents**

    1980: 564,871
    1990: 632,945
    2000: 711,470
    2006 estimate: 733,203
    Percent change, 1990–2000: 12.4%
    U.S. rank in 1980: 19th

*Image copyright Bryan Busovicki, 2007. Used under license from Shutterstock.com.*

U.S. rank in 1990: 16th
U.S. rank in 2000: 15th

**Density:** 3,225 people per square mile (2000)

**Racial and ethnic characteristics (2005)**

White: 454,368
Black: 181,977
American Indian and Alaska Native: 1,674
Asian: 27,125
Native Hawaiian and Pacific Islander: 75
Hispanic or Latino (may be of any race): 24,607
Other: 10,661

**Percent of residents born in state:** 66.1% (2006)

**Age characteristics (2005)**

Population under 5 years old: 60,740
Population 5 to 9 years old: 44,050
Population 10 to 14 years old: 43,489
Population 15 to 19 years old: 39,725
Population 20 to 24 years old: 62,170
Population 25 to 34 years old: 131,641
Population 35 to 44 years old: 106,624
Population 45 to 54 years old: 88,634

Population 55 to 59 years old: 32,186
Population 60 to 64 years old: 24,541
Population 65 to 74 years old: 31,627
Population 75 to 84 years old: 21,435
Population 85 years and older: 7,121
Median age: 32.1 years

**Births (2006, MSA)**

Total number: 25,687

**Deaths (2006, MSA)**

Total number: 12,973

**Money income (2005)**

Per capita income: $22,134
Median household income: $40,405
Total households: 301,325

**Number of households with income of . . .**

less than $10,000: 33,463
$10,000 to $14,999: 18,842
$15,000 to $24,999: 38,332
$25,000 to $34,999: 38,717
$35,000 to $49,999: 54,669
$50,000 to $74,999: 56,151

$75,000 to $99,999: 32,116
$100,000 to $149,999: 21,985
$150,000 to $199,999: 3,930
$200,000 or more: 3,120

**Percent of families below poverty level:** 12.1% (2005)

**2005 FBI Crime Index Property:** 54,141

**2005 FBI Crime Index Violent:** 6,111

# ■ Municipal Government

The city of Columbus is governed by a mayor and a council comprised of seven members who are elected at large to four-year terms.

**Head Official:** Mayor Michael B. Coleman (D) (since 2003; current term expires 2011)

**Total Number of City Employees:** 8,106 (2006)

*City Information:* City Hall, 90 W. Broad St., Rm. 247, Columbus, OH 43215

# ■ Economy

## Major Industries and Commercial Activity

Columbus has been nationally recognized for its strong business climate. The city was ranked 88 of 200 among the "Best Places for Business and Careers" by *Forbes* in 2007. Columbus's diversified economy is balanced among the services, trade, government, and manufacturing sectors. State government, education, banking, research, insurance, and data processing in particular have helped the city to resist recession. Telecommunications, retailing, health care, and the military are other strong employment areas. Home to more than 70 insurance companies, Columbus ranks among the insurance capitals of the United States. There are four *Fortune* 500 firms in the Columbus area, and the city is the corporate headquarters for nationwide firms such as Nationwide Insurance Enterprise, Big Lots, Limited Brands, American Electric Power, Wendy's International, Huntington Bancshares, Inc., Abercrombie and Fitch, Borden Inc., Ashland Chemical, Battelle Memorial Institute, and Bob Evans Foods Inc. Approximately twenty of Columbus's largest financial institutions operate more than 400 offices throughout the metropolitan region. J.P. Morgan, a nationwide financial services institution, maintains a significant presence in Columbus.

The U.S. government is among the city's largest employers; it operates the Defense Supply Center, whose 3,000 employees operate a massive central storehouse that ships up to 10,000 items a day to military posts around the world. Manufacturing comprises about 10 percent of the metropolitan Columbus economic base;

the main production categories are machinery, fabricated metal, printing and publishing, and food processing. Local industry profits from proximity to coal and natural gas resources. Limestone and sandstone quarries operate in the area.

**Items and goods produced:** airplanes, auto parts, appliances, telephone components, computer equipment, glass, coated fabrics, shoes, food products

## Incentive Programs—New and Existing Companies

Several city and state programs are available to assist existing companies and proposed startups in the Columbus metro area.

*Local programs:* The Columbus Development Department incentive programs focus on small business lending and inner-city revitalization, including the Office of Financial Assistance, to help create and sustain jobs and companies; among their specialties are infrastructure assistance and urban brownfields redevelopment. The Greater Columbus Chamber of Commerce oversees very successful public and private partnerships and small business programs to ensure the success of the region's businesses. Training programs are available through the Small Business Administration.

*State programs:* The state of Ohio offers a number of incentives designed to encourage new companies and retain existing businesses. Tax credit programs include those for job creation, machinery and equipment investment, export, research and development franchise, and technology investment. Ohio also offers a property tax abatement for areas identified as enterprise zones, and sales tax exemptions for research and development.

*Job training programs:* The Ohio Investment Training Program (OITP) provides financial assistance and technical resources for customized training involving employees of new and expanding Ohio businesses. OITP may assist a company up to a maximum of one-half of the project's total eligible training costs. The Ohio Job Training Tax Credit is offered to businesses engaged in manufacturing and other specified service industries.

## Development Projects

Columbus is one of the nation's fastest-growing cities, and saw $2.18 billion in public and private investment from 2000 to 2007. The city's focus is on downtown development; in 2001 the city commenced a Strategic Business Plan to revitalize downtown Columbus and bring jobs and investment to the city center. The city sought input from businesses and from the community with a "Tell Us Your Great Idea" campaign, and the Columbus Downtown Development Corporation was formed to bring the ideas to fruition. Public and private entities invested $1.72 billion in the downtown area between 2001 and 2004. The plan was slated for completion by the city's bicentennial in 2012. The goals of the project were fivefold: to build more downtown housing (a goal of 10,000 units by 2012), add jobs and stabilize the downtown office market, create new downtown neighborhoods on Gay Street and in RiverSouth District, develop a riverfront park system called the Scioto Mile, and improve parking and city transit.

In 2007 work was completed on Phase One of the all-"green" rehabilitation of the Lazarus Building downtown. With a budget of over $60 million, the project included construction of the Galleria and the renovation of office space for the Ohio Department of Job and Family Services (ODJFS) and the Ohio Environmental (EPA) Protection Agency.

Work was nearing completion on a new 130,000-square-foot nuclear engineering building at Ohio State in 2007; the $72.5 million project was expected to be open for spring semester 2008. A major renovation of Ohio State's Thompson Library began in 2006, with completion slated for 2009.

*Economic Development Information:* Greater Columbus Chamber of Commerce, 37 N. High St. Columbus, OH 43215; telephone (614)221-1321; fax (614)221-1408

## Commercial Shipping

Strategically located between the Northeast and Midwest regions and served by an excellent transportation system, Columbus is a marketing, distribution, and warehouse center. An important link in the import/export shipping network is Rickenbacker Air/Industrial Park, which has been designated a free trade zone. In 2005 the shipping firm DHL, one of 31 air cargo carriers at Rickenbacker, committed $4 million dollars to a long-term expansion of its operations at Rickenbacker. Several major railroads operate routes through Columbus; all provide piggyback and rail car shipping. Completing the ground transportation system are more than 100 motor freight companies. One of three inland ports in the United States, Columbus receives and ships U.S. Customs-sealed containers to the Pacific Rim.

## Labor Force and Employment Outlook

Among Ohio's 10 largest cities, Columbus is the only one whose population increased in the 1990s, and this trend continued in the 2000s. Greater Columbus is the third fastest growing major metropolitan area in the Midwest. More than 80 percent of the population over age 25 are high school graduates and nearly 30 percent have college degrees; around 70 percent of the population over the age of 16 is in the labor force. While the region has a more desirable workforce than most of the nation, the increase in average age is causing some concern. The Chamber of Commerce has launched

several projects to give businesses the tools to compete in such a market.

Traditional economic mainstays such as government, The Ohio State University, corporate headquarters, and large financial institutions continue to lend stability to the local economy. The Columbus area lost manufacturing jobs in the late 1990s and early 2000s, but has added positions in services to create a net gain in jobs overall.

In October 2007 the unemployment rate in metropolitan Columbus stood at 5.0 percent, slightly below ten-year highs of 6 percent that occurred in 2003. The metropolitan Columbus labor force grew from 815,641 to 956,339 between 1997 and 2007.

The following is a summary of data regarding the Columbus metropolitan area labor force, 2006 annual averages.

**Size of nonagricultural labor force: 932,200**

**Number of workers employed in** ...

construction and mining: 39,900
manufacturing: 78,100
trade, transportation and utilities: 187,900
information: 18,900
financial activities: 73,500
professional and business services: 142,600
educational and health services: 107,800
leisure and hospitality: 89,200
other services: 37,700
government: 156,600

**Average hourly earnings of production workers employed in manufacturing: $18.85**

**Unemployment rate:** 5.4% (June 2007)

| *Largest employers (2006)* | *Number of employees* |
|---|---|
| The State of Ohio | 26,613 |
| The Ohio State University | 19,919 |
| JP Morgan Chase & Co | 14,276 |
| United States Government | 12,800 |
| Nationwide | 11,834 |
| OhioHealth | 9,413 |
| City of Columbus | 8,106 |
| Columbus Public Schools | 7,432 |
| Limited Brands | 7,200 |
| Honda of America Manufacturing Inc. | 6,900 |

## Cost of Living

The following is a summary of data regarding several key cost of living factors in the Columbus area.

**2007 (1st quarter) ACCRA Average House Price:** $313,567

**2007 (1st quarter) ACCRA Cost of Living Index:** 102.1

**State income tax rate:** 0.68% to 6.87%

**State sales tax rate:** 5.5%

**Local income tax rate:** 2.0%

**Local sales tax rate:** 6.75% (total)

**Property tax rate:** Taxes on real property are assessed on 35 percent of the property's total market value. Businesses with personal property valued at $10,001 or more must also pay personal property tax in the state of Ohio.

*Economic Information:* Greater Columbus Chamber of Commerce, 37 N. High St. Columbus, OH 43215; telephone (614)221-1321; fax (614)221-1408

# ■ Education and Research

## Elementary and Secondary Schools

The Columbus Public Schools (CPS) are administered by a seven-member board of education that supports a superintendent. The system's Alexander Graham Bell Elementary School for the hearing impaired is considered one of the nation's finest. Alternative/magnet schools; a high school for the performing arts; a virtual high school; and the International Baccalaureate diploma program, giving qualified graduates access to the world's leading universities, are also among the system's offerings.

In 2002–2003 CPS met 5 of 18 state standards on proficiency tests and graduation and attendance rates; by 2003–2004 the rate remained at 5 of 18 standards, and the district maintained or improved performance in 16 of 18 standards. In 2005 the district met 41 of 42 standards for Adequate Yearly Progress (AYP) and in 2004, CPS had more teachers achieve National Board Certified Status than any other school district in Ohio. Approximately 72 percent of the class of 2007 graduated and earned a combined $45.8 million in grant and scholarship awards. In 2007-2008 the district opened the DeVry Advantage Academy, which incorporates dual enrollment in DeVry University for high school juniors and seniors. The Africentric Early College High School (also opened in 2007) is a similar program, sponsoring dual enrollment with Columbus State Community College.

The following is a summary of data regarding the Columbus Public Schools as of the 2005–2006 school year.

**Total enrollment:** 290,930

**Number of facilities**

elementary schools: 76
junior high/middle schools: 23
senior high schools: 17
other: 12

**Student/teacher ratio:** 17:1

**Teacher salaries (2005–06)**

elementary median: $52,080
junior high/middle median: $53,040
secondary median: $51,280

**Funding per pupil:** $10,444

Columbus is also served by more than two dozen charter, private and parochial schools that offer a range of curricula, including special education programs.

## Colleges and Universities

The Ohio State University, a major institution of higher learning at both the state and national levels, had an enrollment of 52,568 students as of October 2007, making it the largest student body in the country. The school awards undergraduate through doctorate degrees. In addition to its Columbus campus, the university maintains four regional campuses and a two-year branch facility. The Ohio State system includes 8 schools and 18 colleges that administer 12,000 courses, 174 undergraduate majors, and 204 graduate programs. The school was ranked 19th among the nation's top 50 public universities in the *U.S. News & World Report* 2007 edition of "America's Best Colleges."

Capital University schedules courses leading to undergraduate and graduate degrees in such fields as arts and sciences, music, nursing, business administration, and law; the university also operates an adult education division. The school enrolled 3,825 undergraduate and graduate students in 2006 and employed 201 full-time and 198 part-time faculty. Other four-year institutions located in the Columbus area include the Columbus College of Art and Design, DeVry University, and Franklin University. Columbus State Community College, enrolling more than 23,000 students, grants two-year associate degrees in business, health, public service, and engineering technologies.

## Libraries and Research Centers

Columbus is home to more than 60 libraries that are maintained by a range of institutions, corporations, government agencies, and organizations. The Columbus Metropolitan Library (CML) operates 20 branches in Columbus and throughout Franklin County in addition to the Main Library. CML also jointly operates the Northwest Library with the Worthington Public Library. The collections of several Central Ohio library systems, including CML, are linked electronically in the Discovery

Place Libraries consortium. CML's collection contains more than 3 million items, including books, periodicals, videotapes, DVDs, CD-ROMs, films, audiocassettes, compact discs, circulating visuals, maps, charts, microfilm/microfiche, sheet music, and photos. In addition, the Library maintains special collections on local and state history and federal and state documents. CML is also part of the Ohio Public Library Information Network (OHIOLINK), a statewide on-line resource. OHIOLINK was created to help guarantee that all Ohio citizens continue to have access to information regardless of location or format. In 2006 CML patrons checked out 16 million items, made 8.2 million visits to the library and asked 1.2 million reference questions, making it one of the most heavily utilized libraries in the country.

The Ohio State University Libraries hold about 5.8 million volumes and receive approximately 35,000 serial titles. The University Libraries, which include Moritz Law Library and the Prior Health Sciences Library, operate numerous department libraries and five campus facilities. Included in the more than 25 special collections are the American Association of Editorial Cartoonist Archives, including a long term loan of more than 3,000 original "Calvin and Hobbes" cartoons by Bill Watterson; American playwrights' theater records; film scripts; Ohio News Photographers Association Archives; and various author collections featuring the works of such writers as Miguel de Cervantes, Emily Dickinson, Nathaniel Hawthorne, Edith Wharton, James Thurber, and Samuel Beckett. The library is a depository for federal, state, and European Economic Community documents.

As the state capital, Columbus is the site of libraries associated with state governmental divisions, including the Supreme Court of Ohio, the Ohio Department of Transportation, the Ohio Environmental Protection Agency, the Ohio Legislative Service Commission, and the Public Utilities Commission of Ohio. The *Columbus Dispatch,* all local colleges and universities, most major hospitals, several churches and synagogues, and cultural organizations maintain libraries in the city. Private corporations and law firms provide library facilities for both employee and public use. Among the research institutions that house libraries are Battelle Columbus Laboratories, Chemical Abstracts Service, and the National Center for Research in Vocational Education.

Columbus is home to the headquarters of Battelle Memorial Institute, among the world's largest independent research organizations, which conducts research, analysis, testing, design, and consultation in fields that include energy, environmental quality, health sciences, engineering and manufacturing technology, and national security. Battelle has 20,000 staff members and conducts $3.9 billion in annual research and development The American Ceramic Society performs educational, technical, scientific, and information services for the international ceramic community. The Online Computer Library Center (OCLC) maintains an automated information and cataloging system for more than 6,000 libraries in the United States.

More than 60 research centers at The Ohio State University provide research, testing, analysis, design, and consultation services. Other research facilities located in Columbus are Chemical Abstracts Service of the American Chemical Society, Edison Welding Institute, and several engineering, pharmaceutical, and chemical firms.

***Public Library Information:*** Columbus Metropolitan Library, 96 South Grant Avenue, Columbus, OH 43215; telephone (614)849-1265

# ■ Health Care

The Columbus and Franklin County metropolitan region is served by 15 hospitals and 3 nationally recognized medical research facilities including The Ohio State University's Arthur G. James Cancer Hospital and Research Institute, which was ranked the 15th best specialty cancer hospital by *U.S. News and World Report* in 2007. The Ohio State University Hospital was ranked 10th best for rehabilitation in the same report.

Children's Hospital, the country's fifth-largest children's health care institution, conducts research on childhood illnesses and specializes in burn treatment. In 2006 the hospital, with a staff of 5,822, conducted 16,527 total surgeries. Among the other hospitals in Columbus are Columbus Community Hospital, Riverside Methodist Hospital, Grant Medical Center, and Doctors Hospital, the largest osteopathic teaching facility in the nation.

# ■ Recreation

### Sightseeing

At the center of Columbus's downtown is the State Capitol Building, an example of Greek Doric architecture. Several blocks south of the Capitol, German Village, one of the city's major attractions, is a restored community in a 230-acre area settled by German immigrants in the mid-1800s. The largest privately funded restoration in the United States, the district features German bakeries, outdoor beer gardens, restaurants, and homes.

The Center of Science and Industry (COSI) maintains hands-on exhibits in health, history, science, and technology for all ages. COSI's 300,000-square-foot building consists of a modern style element joined to the existing historic building. The facility features a curved facade, a large atrium, a host of Learning Worlds, and two unique theaters. The Space Theater boasts DIGISTAR 3-D technology while the IWERKS Theater, a six-story, multimillion-dollar theater, seats 400 people and presents nationally known films.

The Columbus Zoo displays animals in natural habitats and has gained a reputation for successfully breeding endangered species, including gorillas, cheetahs, snow leopards, polar bears, and eagles. The zoo houses the world's largest reptile collection and is the home of four generations of gorillas. The first phase of the zoo specializes in North American wildlife and features the Manatee Coast Exhibit; this is modeled after the 10,000 Island wildlife area in southwestern Florida, one of the few remaining untouched natural places in the United States. The zoo's second phase, the African Forest project, opened in June 2000. The African Forest outdoor gorilla exhibit features two large glass viewing areas and landscaping. Creative exhibits and a holding building reflect simple African forest architecture and offer indoor viewing of colobus monkeys and Congo gray parrots, as well as a mixed species aviary. The next phase, Asia Quest, began construction in March 2005 and opened in summer 2006.

Franklin Park Conservatory and Garden Center cultivates tropical, subtropical, and desert plants. Columbus's Park of Roses, among the world's largest municipal rose gardens, displays 450 varieties of roses. Located seven minutes from downtown, the Ohio Historical Center and Ohio Village recreate a nineteenth-century Ohio town, where period dishes are served at the Colonel Crawford Inn. Costumed craftspeople add to the authenticity of the exhibits. The Mid-Ohio Historical Museum displays antique dolls and toys. Hanby House, a station on the Underground Railroad, is now a memorial to Ben Hanby, who composed "Darling Nelly Gray."

## Arts and Culture

Columbus is a national leader in local government support of the arts. The Greater Columbus Arts Council distributes approximately $2 million annually to support a more than $52 million cultural industry. One focus of cultural activities is the Martin Luther King, Jr. Arts Complex, which showcases African American cultural events, while the Cultural Arts Center, located in a renovated arsenal, hosts visual and performing arts events classes.

Three elegant theaters are also the scene of cultural activity in Columbus. The Palace Theatre, opened in 1926, has been completely renovated and now houses Opera Columbus and presents Broadway touring musicals and plays, concerts, and films. The Ohio Theatre, a restored 1928 movie palace and the official theater for the state of Ohio, is the home of the Columbus Symphony Orchestra, BalletMet, the new Broadway series, and presentations sponsored by the Columbus Association for Performing Arts. The 102-year-old Southern Theatre closed between 1979 and 1998 and then reopened after a $10 million restoration project.

The Reality Theatre, Contemporary American Theatre Company, Gallery Players, and the theater department at The Ohio State University stage live theater performances ranging from world premieres to revivals of classic plays.

The Columbus Museum of Art houses a sculpture garden and a permanent collection of European and American art works. The restored Thurber House, the home of James Thurber during his years as a student at Ohio State, is now a writers' center that displays Thurber memorabilia.

## Festivals and Holidays

The first weekend of March marks the annual Arnold Sports Festival, a health and fitness convention headed by actor Arnold Schwarzenegger at which bodybuilders and other athletes come together to socialize and compete. The Open Garden Tour, featuring both parks and private homes, is held in April. Music in the Air, sponsored by the city Recreation and Parks Department, is the country's largest free outdoor concert series; 200 concerts are presented at Columbus parks beginning in late May and concluding on Labor Day weekend. The Columbus Arts Festival, which draws 500,000 people to the city, begins the summer festival season in early June. The city's Red, White & Boom! Parade in early July is followed by one of the largest fireworks displays in the Midwest. The Columbus Jazz and Rib Fest draws participants to downtown locations the last weekend in July. A major event in Columbus is the Ohio State Fair; held in August, the fair features livestock shows, agricultural and arts exhibitions, horse shows, rides, and concessions. Columbus observes First Night Columbus on December 31 to bring family-friendly New Year's celebrations to the area.

## Sports for the Spectator

Columbus is home to a Major League Soccer team, the Columbus Crew, who play in Columbus Crew Stadium. The stadium, opened in 1999, is the first specifically built for professional soccer in the United States and combines European soccer atmosphere with traditional American amenities to make it one of the premier soccer venues in the country. The Columbus Blue Jackets, a National Hockey League team, first played in 2000 at Nationwide Arena, a 20,000-seat, 685,000-square-foot, $150 million venue.

The Big Ten conference Ohio State Buckeyes, one of the nation's top college football teams, play a home schedule to sold-out crowds on fall Saturday afternoons in the 90,000-seat Ohio Stadium. The Buckeyes also field men's and women's basketball teams that play home games at Jerome Schottenstein Center, a 20,000-seat arena that opened in October 1998. The Columbus Clippers, a Triple-A affiliate of baseball's professional New York Yankees, play a 70-game home schedule at 15,000-seat Cooper Stadium, and the city is finalizing funding to build a larger, newer stadium near the Nationwide Arena to replace the 1932 Cooper Stadium.

The Columbus Marathon, held each October, attracted 10,000 runners in 2007, and the Capital City Half Marathon, first run in April 2004, is an annual event. Harness racing is on view at Scioto Downs, where more than a dozen world records have been set in a season that runs from early May to mid-September. The Little Brown Jug, the year's biggest harness race, is held at the Delaware County Fairgrounds. Columbus's most important golf event, the Memorial Golf Tournament, is sometimes referred to as the "fifth major"; competitors tee-off in nearby Dublin at the Muirfield Village course that Jack Nicklaus designed.

## Sports for the Participant

Columbus city parks cover 14,000 acres (9,000 acres of land and 5,000 acres of water) and include parks, golf courses, conservation areas, reservoirs, 28 recreation centers, 11 swimming pools, and the Columbus Zoo. Water sports can be enjoyed on two major rivers and three lakes in the city; among the area's popular activities are fishing, boating, sailing, water skiing, and paddleboating. The city maintains municipal tennis courts; indoor tennis and racquetball courts are available at private clubs. The city's scenic commuter routes are popular among joggers and cyclists. Year-round recreational programs for all age groups are available at the city parks.

## Shopping and Dining

One of the largest shopping showcases in Columbus is the innovative outdoor shopping and entertainment district called Easton. Easton features nearly 120 shops, a luxury Hilton Hotel and Easton Town Center, anchored by the world's first Planet Movies by AMC, a 6,200-seat, 30-screen megaplex movie theater complex. In addition, Easton includes a mall with a Nordstrom's and other national retailers.

Columbus City Center downtown offers approximately 130 upscale stores and restaurants. Among the distinctive shopping districts in Columbus is German Village, where small shops and stores offer specialty items. Short North exhibits and sells the works of Columbus and national artists as well as clothing and home furnishings. High Street, the Main Street of the university district, offers eclectic shopping and dining options.

Diners in Columbus can choose from among a number of restaurants serving contemporary American, European, and ethnic cuisine. In 2005 *Food and Wine* magazine named Kahiki one of the world's five coolest bars. Several restaurants are housed in architecturally interesting buildings such as churches and firehouses. The renovated North Market features local produce and German, Middle Eastern, Indian, and Italian delicatessens. Columbus is also home base to both Wendy's and Bob Evans national restaurant chains.

*Visitor Information:* Greater Columbus Convention and Visitors Bureau; telephone (614)221-6623; toll-free (800)354-2657

# ■ Convention Facilities

Convention and meeting planners are offered a wide range of facilities in the metropolitan Columbus area. The Greater Columbus Convention Center, which opened in 1993 and underwent expansion in 2001, hosted more than 2,500,000 attendees and delegates that year. The Convention Center features 1.7 million square feet of exhibition space and 100,000 square feet of retail space. The nearby Ohio Center Mall is an added attraction to the convention center. Other meeting facilities include Franklin County Veterans Memorial, Ohio Expo Center (site of the Ohio State Fair), and the Palace and Ohio theaters.

First-class downtown hotels, including the Hyatt Regency, the Westin, the Courtyard by Marriott, and the Doubletree Guest Suites, maintain a complete range of meeting and banquet facilities. There are more than 3,000 hotel rooms within walking distance of the Convention Center.

*Convention Information:* Greater Columbus Convention Center; telephone (614) 827-2500; toll-free (800)626-0241

# ■ Transportation

## Approaching the City

Twenty-one commercial domestic and international airlines schedule daily flights into Port Columbus International Airport, which underwent a $92 million improvement to celebrate its 75th anniversary in 2005. Port Columbus, just eight minutes from downtown, is serviced by ten major commercial airlines and served 568,339 passengers in 2006. Rickenbacker International Airport also services the Columbus area. General aviation facilities are provided at Bolton Field.

Two interstate highways—north-south I-71 and east-west I-70—intersect in the city; I-270 serves as a bypass, and I-670 is a downtown innerbelt. Several other major highways provide convenient access into and out of Columbus.

## Traveling in the City

Columbus streets conform to a grid pattern, the principal thoroughfares being Broad Street (U.S. 40/62) and High Street (U.S. 23 south of I-70), which form the main downtown intersection and divide north-south streets and east-west avenues. Efficient traffic flow into the center city permits commuting time of no more than 45 minutes from outlying areas.

The public bus system is operated by Central Ohio Transit Authority (COTA).

# ■ Communications

## Newspapers and Magazines

The principal daily newspaper in Columbus is *The Columbus Dispatch* (morning). *Business First,* a business weekly, presents current news as well as analyses of local commerce. Several suburban newspapers also have a wide circulation in the metropolitan area.

Columbus is the publishing base for magazines and journals with extensive state and national distribution. Especially popular with Ohio readers is *Ohio Magazine,* which contains articles on local and state topics. A number of professional organizations publish their official journals in the city; among them are the Ohio Academy of Science, the Ohio State Bar Association, the Ohio Historical Society, and the Ohio Education Association. Other specialized publications are directed toward Ohio readers with interests in such fields as agriculture, religion, education, library science and communications, banking, business and industry, and sports.

Columbus is also home to membership publications of several national organizations, including Business Professionals of America and the American Society for Nondestructive Testing. The Ohio State University Press publishes several scholarly journals in such fields as theoretical geography, higher education, banking, and urban planning; several academic departments and colleges also issue publications.

## Television and Radio

Columbus is the broadcast media center for central Ohio. Three commercial network affiliates and one public station—all locally based—provide television programming for viewers in the city and surrounding communities. Cable service is also available. Radio listeners tune in to music, news, special features, and public-interest programs scheduled by more than a dozen locally-based AM and FM radio stations.

***Media Information:*** *The Columbus Dispatch,* 34 South Third Street, Columbus, OH 43215; telephone (614)461-5000. *Columbus Monthly,* PO Box 29913, Columbus, OH 43229; telephone (614)888-4567

## Columbus Online

City of Columbus home page. Available ci .columbus.oh.us

*The Columbus Dispatch.* Available www.dispatch .com

Columbus Metropolitan Library. Available www .cml.lib.oh.us

Columbus Public Schools. Available www.columbus .k12.oh.us

The Greater Columbus Convention & Visitors Bureau. Available www.columbuscvb.org

Greater Columbus Super Site. Available www .columbus.org

Ohio Historical Society Archives/Library. Available www.ohiohistory.org/resource/archlib

Ohio State University Extension Data Center. Available www.osuedc.org/current

BIBLIOGRAPHY

Conway, W. Fred, *The Most Incredible Prison Escape of the Civil War* (Fire Buff House, 1991)

Howells, William Dean, *Years of My Youth* (New York and London: Harper & Brothers, 1916)

Jacobs, Gregory S., *Getting Around Brown: Desegregation, Development, and the Columbus Public Schools* (Ohio State University Press, 1998)

# Dayton

## ■ The City in Brief

**Founded:** 1795 (incorporated 1805)

**Head Official:** Mayor Rhine D. McLin (D) (since 2002)

**City Population**

    1980: 203,371
    1990: 182,011
    2000: 166,179
    2006 estimate: 156,771
    Percent change, 1990–2000: −8.7%
    U.S. rank in 1980: 70th
    U.S. rank in 1990: 89th
    U.S. rank in 2000: 141st

**Metropolitan Area Population**

    1980: 942,000
    1990: 951,270
    2000: 950,558
    2006 estimate: 838,940
    Percent change, 1990–2000: −0.1%
    U.S. rank in 1980: 39th
    U.S. rank in 1990: 51th
    U.S. rank in 2000: 52nd

**Area:** 56.63 square miles (2000)

**Elevation:** 750 feet above sea level

**Average Annual Temperatures:** January, 26.3° F; July, 74.3° F; annual average, 51.5° F

**Average Annual Precipitation:** 39.58 inches of rain; 27.3 inches of snow

**Major Economic Sectors:** Wholesale and retail trade, manufacturing, services, government, transportation

**Unemployment Rate:** 6.5% (June 2007)

**Per Capita Income:** $16,191 (2005)

**2005 FBI Crime Index Property:** 11,471

**2005 FBI Crime Index Violent:** 1,533

**Major Colleges and Universities:** University of Dayton; Wright State University

**Daily Newspaper:** *Dayton Daily News*

## ■ Introduction

Dayton, the seat of Ohio's Montgomery County, is the focus of a four-county metropolitan statistical area that includes Montgomery, Miami, Clark, and Greene counties and the cities of Kettering, Miamisburg, Xenia, Fairborn, Oakwood, and Vandalia. World-famous through the pioneering efforts of the Wright brothers, today Dayton is an aviation center and home of Wright-Patterson Air Force Base, headquarters of the United States Air Force bomber program. Dayton, once vulnerable to severe flooding, was the site of the first comprehensive flood control project of its kind. Today the city is at the center of industrial and high-technology development, serving traditional and new markets.

## ■ Geography and Climate

Surrounded by a nearly flat plain that is 50 to 100 feet below the elevation of the adjacent rolling countryside, Dayton is situated near the center of the Miami River Valley. The Mad River, the Stillwater River, and Wolf Creek, all tributaries of the Miami River, join the master stream within the city limits. The Miami Valley is a fertile agricultural region because of evenly distributed precipitation and moderate temperatures. High relative humidity throughout the year can cause discomfort to people with allergies. Winter temperatures are moderated by the downward slope of the Miami River; cold polar air from the Great Lakes produces extensive cloudiness and frequent snow flurries.

**Area:** 56.63 square miles (2000)

**Elevation:** 750 feet above sea level

**Average Temperatures:** January, 26.3° F; July, 74.3° F; annual average, 51.5° F

**Average Annual Precipitation:** 39.58 inches of rain; 27.3 inches of snow

# ■ History

## Town Planned Despite Flood Danger

The point where the Mad River flows into the Great Miami was a thoroughfare for native tribes on their way from Lake Erie to Kentucky and for frontier heroes such as George Rogers Clark, Simon Kenton, Daniel Boone, and Anthony Wayne. Revolutionary War veterans General Arthur St. Clair, General James Wilkinson, Colonel Israel Ludlow, and Jonathan Dayton of New Jersey, for whom Dayton is named, purchased 60,000 acres in the area from John Cleves Symmes. Ludlow surveyed the town plot in the fall of 1795, and the first settlers arrived on April 1, 1796. In spite of well-founded Native American warnings against the danger of floods, settlers occupied the area where Dayton now stands at the confluence of four rivers and creeks.

Ohio gained statehood in 1803, and two years later Dayton was incorporated as a town and became the seat of Montgomery County. The opening of the Miami & Erie Canal in 1828 brought booming cannons and cheering crowds in celebration of future economic prosperity. That year 100,000 people descended upon Dayton, whose population then numbered 6,000 people, to hear William Henry Harrison, Whig presidential candidate. A year later Dayton was incorporated as a city. In 1851 the Mad River & Lake Erie Railroad reached Dayton, motivating Daytonians to establish new industries that were expanded during the Civil War boom years. Local Congressman Clement L. Vallandigham was head of the anti-Lincoln Copperhead faction in the North, which brought riots, murder, and the destruction of the Republican *Dayton Journal* newspaper office. Vallandigham was banished from the Union for treason.

## Industrial Innovation Characterizes Dayton

Dayton entered its golden age of invention and business acumen when John Patterson bought James Ritty's cash register company and his "mechanical money drawer" in 1884. Two years later, Patterson introduced the "daylight factory," a new work environment in which 80 percent of the walls were glass. National Cash Register soon set the standard for this indispensable business device.

Dayton-based inventors Wilbur and Orville Wright taught themselves aerodynamics by reading every book on the subject in the Dayton public library. They experimented with kites and gliders and built the world's first wind tunnel to test their ideas. Then on December 17, 1903, the Wright brothers made aviation history at Kitty Hawk, North Carolina, when their flying machine made its first successful flight. The Wrights' common-sensical approach to solving the centuries-old problem of heavier-than-air flight is considered one of the great engineering achievements in history.

The next inventor and engineer to make his mark in Dayton was Charles "Boss" Kettering, who began his career at National Cash Register by inventing an electric cash register. Kettering and a partner founded the Dayton Engineering Laboratories Company (Delco), which became a subsidiary of General Motors in 1920 when Kettering was appointed a vice president and director of research at General Motors. Kettering repeatedly revolutionized the automobile industry; he designed the motor for the first practical electric starter, developed tetraethyl lead that eliminated engine knock and led to ethyl gasoline, and, with chemists, discovered quick-drying lacquer finishes for automobile bodies. Kettering is considered to have demonstrated the value of industrial research and development.

## Reform, Cooperation Meet City's Challenges

Newspaper publisher James Cox bought the *Dayton News* in 1898 and then purchased other newspapers in Ohio, Florida, and Atlanta, Georgia. Cox turned to politics in 1909, serving as Dayton's congressman, then as Ohio governor, and running for the presidency in 1920 on the Democratic ticket but losing to Warren G. Harding. As governor, Cox initiated a number of reforms, including the initiative and referendum, minimum wage, and worker's compensation.

Destructive floods had frequently plagued Dayton during the city's first 100 years. Total devastation came on March 25, 1913, when the Great Miami River, swollen by a five-day downpour that brought ten inches of rain, burst through protective levees and flooded the city. So powerful was the flood that houses were literally wrenched from their foundations and sent down the Great Miami. The water level did not recede until March 28, by which time 361 people had died and property damage had reached $100 million.

The flood forced citizens to find a solution to this perennial threat; they responded by raising $2 million in 60 days. Arthur E. Morgan, a self-taught engineer who was then head of the Tennessee Valley Authority—and later became the president of Antioch College in nearby Yellow Springs—was charged with the responsibility of finding solutions. A systematic plan of flood protection consisting of five huge dams and retaining basins was proposed. The Miami Conservancy District, the first comprehensive flood-control project of its kind in the United States, was

©W. Cody/Corbis.

established by the state legislature on June 18, 1915. Construction was completed in 1922. In another response to the flood crisis, Dayton turned to the nonpartisan, democratically controlled commission-manager form of government, becoming the first major American city to do so and inspiring other cities to follow suit.

During both World Wars, Dayton's manufacturing facilities produced planes, tanks, guns, and other war materials that were vital to successful military efforts. In the post-war years, the focus of Dayton's industry shifted to consumer products. Household appliances, automobiles, and early components of the computer industry were manufactured in Dayton from mid-century on.

In 2005 the city celebrated its bicentennial anniversary of incorporation. Today, Dayton is home to fine educational institutions, an art institute, a symphony orchestra, a natural history museum, and Wright-Patterson Air Force Base. Dayton blends metropolitan amenities with the feel of an All-American city.

## ■ Population Profile

### Metropolitan Area Residents

1980: 942,000

1990: 951,270
2000: 950,558
2006 estimate: 838,940
Percent change, 1990–2000: −0.1%
U.S. rank in 1980: 39th
U.S. rank in 1990: 51th
U.S. rank in 2000: 52nd

### City Residents

1980: 203,371
1990: 182,011
2000: 166,179
2006 estimate: 156,771
Percent change, 1990–2000: −8.7%
U.S. rank in 1980: 70th
U.S. rank in 1990: 89th
U.S. rank in 2000: 141st

**Density:** 2,979.4 people per square mile (in 2000)

**Racial and ethnic characteristics (2005)**

White: 68,151
Black: 60,290
American Indian and Alaska Native: 151
Asian: 1,827

Native Hawaiian and Pacific Islander: 0
Hispanic or Latino (may be of any race): 1,693
Other: 979

**Percent of residents born in state:** 72.6% (2006)

**Age characteristics (2005)**

Population under 5 years old: 9,827
Population 5 to 9 years old: 8,953
Population 10 to 14 years old: 8,670
Population 15 to 19 years old: 8,578
Population 20 to 24 years old: 10,907
Population 25 to 34 years old: 18,591
Population 35 to 44 years old: 18,277
Population 45 to 54 years old: 19,341
Population 55 to 59 years old: 8,707
Population 60 to 64 years old: 5,382
Population 65 to 74 years old: 7,196
Population 75 to 84 years old: 5,545
Population 85 years and older: 2,705
Median age: 35.4 years

**Births (2006, MSA)**

Total number: 10,525

**Deaths (2006, MSA)**

Total number: 7,836

**Money income (2005)**

Per capita income: $16,191
Median household income: $25,928
Total households: 59,914

**Number of households with income of...**

less than $10,000: 11,188
$10,000 to $14,999: 7,033
$15,000 to $24,999: 10,749
$25,000 to $34,999: 8,214
$35,000 to $49,999: 9,181
$50,000 to $74,999: 7,419
$75,000 to $99,999: 3,747
$100,000 to $149,999: 2,008
$150,000 to $199,999: 171
$200,000 or more: 204

**Percent of families below poverty level:** 12.7% (2005)

**2005 FBI Crime Index Property:** 11,471

**2005 FBI Crime Index Violent:** 1,533

# ■ Municipal Government

The Dayton City Commission is comprised of the mayor and four commissioners, who serve part-time. They are elected at large on a non-partisan basis for four-year overlapping terms. Each member of the commission has equal voting power.

**Head Official:** Mayor Rhine D. McLin (D) (since 2002; current term expires January 2010)

**Total Number of City Employees:** 4,637 (2007)

*City Information:* City of Dayton, 101 W. Third St., Dayton, OH 45402; telephone (937)333-3333

# ■ Economy

## Major Industries and Commercial Activity

Dayton's balanced economy is supported principally by manufacturing, wholesale and retail trade, and services. In recent years, Dayton has suffered from many of the ills plaguing the national economy. Most major industries charted reductions in jobs in the early 2000s, and those industries related to the automotive industry were the hardest hit. Dayton businesses are working toward a resurgence by focusing on increased business investment and diversifying into the manufacturing of technical products and services. Dayton employers are also concerned about the constraints of a stagnant and aging population; employers are working to recruit highly skilled employees to the region, particularly in the high-tech fields. The most important factor in determining Dayton's economic future, however, is the fate of the area's major manufacturing employers such as Delphi Automotive, General Motors, and Behr, whose presence is so vital to the area's continued prosperity.

In the past ten years, employment in education and health services has grown steadily in Dayton. More than 30 institutions of higher learning in the metropolitan area provide a significant number of jobs. Area health care facilities have been steadily expanding both their physical facilities and the services offered. Technological advances in health care have been readily adopted in Dayton area hospitals, making this economic sector one of the most promising for the region.

More than 1,500 other firms in the Dayton area manufacture accounting systems, bicycles, castings and forgings, compressors, concrete products, washing machines, generators, hoists and jacks, industrial belts, machine tools, name plates, paints and varnishes, paper and paper-making machinery, plastics, precision gauges, tools and dies, and meat products.

Wright-Patterson Air Force Base, the research and development arm of the U.S. Air Force, is the fifth largest employer in the state of Ohio and the largest employer at a single location. Wright-Patterson employs almost one of every twelve people working in the greater Dayton area, approximately 22,000 total, with sixty base units. Wright-Patterson is the headquarters of the Air Force Logistics Command, Air Force Material Command, and the

Aeronautical Systems Division (ASD), in addition to more than 100 other Department of Defense divisions. The U.S. Defense Department Joint Logistics Systems Center, affiliated with Wright-Patterson, oversees the installation of new computer systems for all military services; the center generates many private sector jobs. The ASD at Wright-Patterson manages the U.S. Air Force bomber program; also housed at the base is the Center for Artificial Intelligence Applications (CAIA). Wright-Patterson also houses the Air Force Institute for Technology, which trains thousands of students each year. In addition, Wright-Patterson is credited with bringing to Dayton one of the highest concentrations of aerospace/high-technology firms in the nation. These firms employ scientists, engineers, technicians, and specialists actively involved in development and application in both the private and public sectors.

Another vital factor in the metropolitan area economy is the Miami Valley Research Park, supported by the Miami Valley Research Foundation, a private, nonprofit corporation; the 1,500-acre park is a university-related research facility that is the site of corporate, academic and government research firms. Approximately 4,500 workers are employed at the park. The Research Park's goal is to promote research, technology, and science in the region, while helping to create and preserve employment opportunities. Dayton is the seventh-largest information technology center and is second in the nation (behind Silicon Valley) for the highest concentration of science and engineering Ph.Ds.

## Incentive Programs—New and Existing Companies

*Local programs:* The CityWide Direct Loan program offers assistance for the acquisition of real estate, facility renovation and construction, and equipment purchasing. Dayton has a Foreign Trade Zone; companies that operate there pay no duties or quota charges on reexports. The West Dayton Development Trust Fund provides funding for community and economic development projects that benefit designated areas within the City of Dayton.

*State programs:* The State of Ohio grants direct low interest loans, industrial revenue bonds, and financial assistance for research and development to companies creating or retaining jobs in Ohio. Additionally, the Ohio Job Creation Tax Credit provides tax credits for Ohio companies that expand as well as companies relocating to Ohio. Enterprise zones provide significant tax reductions on property investments made by businesses expanding in or relocating to specific areas of Ohio.

*Job training programs:* The Ohio Investment in Training program provides financial assistance and technical resources for assisting Ohio businesses in the training of employees. Additionally, area colleges and universities offer many options for training.

## Development Projects

The Dayton Downtown Partnership has been committed to the development of Dayton's urban space for more than a decade; between 1998 and 2007, more than $585 million was invested in the downtown Dayton area. The Dayton Downtown Partnership's "Vision 2013" plan called for the addition of 750 new downtown housing units by 2013, in addition to a proposed Interactive Innovation/Invention Science Center.

In 2006 plans were approved for the construction of Ballpark Village, a 24-hour city center slated to include entertainment, retail, office and housing located north of Fifth Third Field in an area bounded by Monument Avenue, Webster Street and Riverside Drive.

In 2007 plans were underway for the third phase of the Five Rivers MetroParks RiverScape improvement project; an entertainment pavilion and other amenities were planned, while feasability studies were underway for a proposed downtown waterpark in RiverScape Park. In 2006 CareSource Management Group announced plans to build a $55 million headquarters at the corner of Main Street and Monument Avenue, with a completion date slated for 2008.

*Economic Development Information:* Dayton Area Chamber of Commerce, 1 Chamber Plaza, Dayton, OH 45402-2400; telephone (937)226-1444

## Commercial Shipping

Dayton International Airport, ranking among the nation's busiest air-freight facilities, is home to several cargo carriers, including Aviation Facilities Company, Inc; FedEx; FedEx Trade Networks; Exel Global; and UPS Supply Chain. Dayton's central location means that the Dayton International Airport is within 90 minutes by air from 55 percent of the nation's population. Passengers can find nonstop flights from Dayton International to 22 major cities, including Detroit, Chicago, New York, Atlanta, and Houston. Approximately thirty trucking companies maintain terminals in the metropolitan area. Just north of the city, the intersection of interstates 70 and 75 creates a hub that is a focal point of the nation's transportation network and has lured transportation companies to the Dayton area.

Three Class I rail systems furnish rail cargo transportation, including trailer on flat car service; both CSX and Conrail operate switching yards in the city. Because of its transportation system, which affords direct access to major markets, Dayton has become an important warehouse and distribution center.

## Labor Force and Employment Outlook

Dayton educational institutions provide employers with skilled workers. In particular, the region abounds with employees highly educated in the fields of science and engineering. Dayton area businesses have increasingly been attempting to retain area-educated employees to their workforces. In the early 2000s, jobs were lost in Dayton's traditional manufacturing sectors, which are highly dependent on the fortunes of the automobile industry.

In September 2007 the unemployment rate in the greater Dayton area stood at 5.9 percent; ten-year highs of 7 percent unemployment occurred in January 2007 and in 2005.

The following is a summary of data regarding the Dayton metropolitan area labor force, 2006 annual averages.

**Size of nonagricultural labor force:** 408,200

**Number of workers employed in . . .**

construction and mining: 15,200
manufacturing: 56,500
trade, transportation and utilities: 70,000
information: 10,600
financial activities: 20,100
professional and business services: 52,300
educational and health services: 64,700
leisure and hospitality: 37,800
other services: 16,400
government: 64,800

**Average hourly earnings of production workers employed in manufacturing:** $20.28

**Unemployment rate:** 6.5% (June 2007)

| *Largest regional employers* (2007) | *Number of employees* |
|---|---|
| Wright-Patterson Air Force Base | 22,000 |
| Premiere Health Partners | 11,500 |
| Delphi | 6,680 |
| DHL | 6,000 |
| Kroger | 5,959 |
| Montgomery County | 5,293 |
| Meijer, Inc. | 4,967 |
| City of Dayton | 4,637 |
| Kettering Medical Network | 4,460 |
| United States Postal Service | 4,450 |

## Cost of Living

The following is a summary of data regarding several key cost of living factors in the Dayton area.

**2007 (1st quarter) ACCRA Average House Price:** $262,877

**2007 (1st quarter) ACCRA Cost of Living Index:** 94.2

**State income tax rate:** 0.68% to 6.87%

**State sales tax rate:** 5.5%

**Local income tax rate:** 2.25%

**Local sales tax rate:** 1.5%

**Property tax rate:** $61.55 per $1,000 assessed valuation (2005)

***Economic Information:*** Dayton Area Chamber of Commerce, 1 Chamber Plaza, Dayton, OH 45402-2400; telephone (937)226-1444

# ■ Education and Research

## Elementary and Secondary Schools

The Dayton City Schools system, the sixth largest district in the state of Ohio, is administered by a seven-member, nonpartisan board of education that appoints a superintendent. The system supports a Montessori school, single-sex schools, an International Baccalaureate program, an advanced placement program, an early college program, career technology programs, and the specialized Dayton Design Technology High School.

Between 2001 and 2006 the graduation rate in DPS grew from approximately fifty percent to nearly eighty percent. The Dayton Early College Academy was one of five programs nationally named "most innovative" in a study by WestEd for the Bill and Melinda Gates Foundation.

The following is a summary of data regarding the Dayton Public Schools as of the 2005–2006 school year.

**Total enrollment:** 130,087

**Number of facilities**

elementary schools: 25
junior high/middle schools: 4
senior high schools: 6
other: 0

**Student/teacher ratio:** 17.1:1

**Teacher salaries (2005–06)**

elementary median: $49,830
junior high/middle median: $48,910
secondary median: $52,200

**Funding per pupil:** $9,327

Catholic, Jewish, Baptist, Seventh Day Adventist, Church of God, and nondenominational groups also operate schools in the region. Approximately fifty charter schools operate within Dayton.

## Colleges and Universities

A wide range of higher learning resources are available within driving distance of Dayton. Located in the area are more than 25 colleges and universities, and approximately 10 vocational and technical schools that offer curricula for traditional as well as nontraditional students. The largest state-funded institution is Wright State University, with an enrollment of nearly 17,000 students in more than 100 undergraduate and 50 doctorate, graduate, and professional degree programs; Wright State operates schools of law, medicine, pharmacy, and nursing.

The University of Dayton, founded in 1850, is the state's largest independent university and grants associate, baccalaureate, master's, and doctorate degrees in 120 fields of study. The university operates professional schools in education, business administration, engineering, and law. The United Theological Seminary, affiliated with the United Methodist Church, offers graduate programs in theology. Based near Dayton in Yellow Springs is Antioch University. Founded by Horace Mann in 1852, Antioch has long been respected for its innovative role in alternative and cooperative education; in 2007 the Antioch board of directors considered suspending the operations of the university, but national media coverage and an outcry from alumni prompted the board to reverse their decision. Central State University, in neighboring Wilberforce, is Ohio's only public university with a traditionally African American student enrollment.

Sinclair Community College, located in downtown Dayton, awards two-year associate degrees in such areas as allied health, business, engineering technologies, and fine and applied arts. With an enrollment of 24,000 students, Sinclair is one of the largest community colleges in the nation. The school is known for its robotics program, operated in association with General Motors Fanacu. The Air Force Institute of Technology (AFIT) at Wright-Patterson Air Force Base is operated by the Air Force for military personnel. Designed primarily as a graduate school, AFIT also offers upper-level baccalaureate study as well as continuing education for civilians. Included among AFIT graduates are 25 U.S. astronauts.

## Libraries and Research Centers

Dayton is home to approximately 30 libraries operated by a variety of institutions, businesses, and organizations. The Dayton Metro Library is the largest facility in the Miami Valley. Containing about 1.7 million books in addition to periodicals, compact discs, microfiche, audio- and videotapes, and films, the library operates a main library and 21 branches; special collections include local history and federal and state documents. All of the colleges and universities in the area maintain substantial campus libraries with holdings in a wide range of fields. Most specialized libraries are affiliated with hospitals, law firms, major corporations, and government agencies.

Dayton's higher education community is involved in technological research of national scope. The University of Dayton Research Institute works in association with Wright-Patterson Air Force Base, the foremost aeronautical research and development center in the Air Force; about 10,000 scientists and engineers are employed at the base. Human-computer interaction is studied at the university's Information System Laboratory. The engineering department at Central State University conducts projects for the National Aeronautics and Space Administration and for high-technology firms. Wright State University School of Medicine's Cox Heart Institute has received recognition for the development of diagnostic and surgical treatment of heart disease. Wright State receives annual research grants of more than $60 million; in 2007 the university received a grant of $4.8 million for neuroscience-related research. Also located in Dayton is the Cancer Prevention Institute, one of several independent cancer research facilities in the country.

***Public Library Information:*** Dayton Metro Public Library, 215 East Third Street, Dayton, OH 45402-2103; telephone (937)227-9500; fax (937)227-9524

# ■ Health Care

With a medical community that comprises the third-largest employment sector in the Miami Valley region, Dayton is a primary health care center for southwestern Ohio. The Upper Valley Medical Centers, comprised of three hospitals, is the region's largest health care provider, with 836 beds.

Miami Valley Hospital, providing 811 beds, is the city's largest medical single facility; Miami Valley operates an air ambulance service and maintains a Level 1 regional trauma center as well as units specializing in kidney dialysis, burn treatment, maternity services, and women's health programs. In 2006 it was selected as one of the nation's 100 Top Hospitals for Cardiovascular Care by Solucient.

In addition to furnishing in-patient and out-patient care, 560-bed Good Samaritan Hospital houses the Family Birthing Center, the Marie-Joseph Living Care Center, and a substance abuse treatment center. St. Elizabeth Medical Center, founded in 1878 near downtown Dayton, provides 631 beds and specializes in family medicine, physical therapy, sports medicine, women's health programs, and senior health care. In suburban Kettering, the Kettering Memorial Hospital/Sycamore Hospital provides 470 beds, and in 2007 was named a "Top 50 Hospital" for Neurology and Neurosurgery by *US News & World Report*. Grandview/Southview Hospitals has 452 beds and in 2005 was selected by *U.S News & World Report* as a "Top 50 Hospital" in both Neurology and Neurosurgery and the treatment of

Respiratory Disorders. Among other medical facilities in Dayton are Children's Medical Center, Dartmouth Hospital, and Veterans Affairs Medical Center.

# ■ Recreation

## Sightseeing

The Boonshoft Museum of Discovery maintains a planetarium and observatory, and operates SunWatch, a twelfth-century Native American village restoration south of the city, which is considered the most complete prehistoric settlement of any culture east of the Mississippi. The National Museum of the United States Air Force is the world's largest military aviation museum. Historic Dayton buildings and collections of artifacts from the city's golden age of invention are presented at the Kettering Moraine Museum. The Oregon Historic District, Dayton's oldest neighborhood, is a center of shopping, dining, and nightlife amidst nearly 200-year-old architecture. In downtown Dayton on Thursdays, Fridays, and Saturdays, the "market district," centered around the National City 2nd Street Public Market and the Webster Street Market, showcases home-baked bread, fresh produce, and other foods and crafts. The National Afro-American Museum and Cultural Center, located in Wilberforce, a stop on the Underground Railroad, consists of the museum and renovated Carnegie Library.

At Carillon Historical Park, on 65 acres next to the Great Miami River, the carillon bells that are a Dayton landmark are among the featured displays, which also include the Wright Flyer III and the Barney & Smith railroad car. RiverScape provides facilities for paddleboating on the river and a venue for live music as well as serving as the setting for displays relating to Dayton's history and the many inventions born in the city. Festival Plaza, the focal point of Riverscape, features gardens, fountains, and pools in the summer and a skating rink during winter months. The Cox Arboretum is a 160-acre public garden set in native woodlands. Five miles of trails wind through woods and meadows containing more than 150 indigenous Ohio plant species at Aullwood Audubon Center, a 200-acre nature sanctuary. Other nature preserves in the Dayton area include Wegerzyn Horticultural Center and Bergamo/Mt. St. John.

The Paul Laurence Dunbar House, the restored home of one of the country's great African American poets, is open to the public. The Wright Memorial commemorates the spot where the Wright brothers tested their airplane during its invention; the Wright Brothers Bicycle Shop is a National Historic Landmark. At the center of Dayton's downtown district, the Montgomery County Historical Society is housed in the Old Courthouse, which was built in 1850 and is considered one of the nation's finest examples of Greek Revival architecture.

## Arts and Culture

Dayton supports an active cultural community. The Arts Center Foundation was created in 1986 to plan and fund new facilities to house Dayton's major arts institutions. The restoration and renovation of Victoria Theatre, listed on the National Register of Historic Places, transformed the theatre into a modern performing arts complex. The Victoria Theatre is home to the JP Morgan Chase Broadway Series, a summer film series, the Dayton Ballet, and the Dayton Contemporary Dance Company. The Dayton Art Institute, founded in 1919, sponsors exhibition programs, Sunday afternoon musicales, twilight concerts, gallery talks, and studio classes. Artworks by the members of the Dayton Society of Painters and Sculptors, Inc., are exhibited in two galleries at the society's Victorian mansion quarters in the historic St. Anne's Hill district. Permanent collections include Oceanic, Native American, and African art, as well as a sizeable glass collection.

The Dayton Philharmonic Orchestra, founded as a chamber orchestra in 1933, is now an 85-member orchestra performing classical, pops, chamber, and a summer band concert series at Memorial Hall and other Dayton locations. Dayton Opera, founded in 1960, presents four fully staged operas at the Benjamin and Marian Schuster Performing Arts Center. The Center, which opened in 2003, includes a 2,300-seat performance hall as well as a rehearsal hall, a Wintergarden and glass atrium, and an 18-story tower with first-class office and condominium space. Dayton Ballet's season of four productions includes traditional and new ballet works. Dayton Contemporary Dance Company, nationally acclaimed for innovative work, presents three performances a year in addition to national tours.

The Dayton Music Club celebrated its centennial in 1988; it sponsors free music programs at various city locations with performances by local and national artists. Other regularly scheduled musical events include the chamber concert Vanguard Series, the Bach Society choral productions, the CityFolk ethnic and folk music series, and concerts at area churches.

Theater companies offering full seasons of traditional and experimental works include the Dayton Playhouse, the Human Race, and the Dayton Theatre Guild. The Victoria Theatre, which opened in 1865 as Dayton's first theatrical house for live entertainment, sponsors touring companies' productions as well as a season of children's drama. Wright State University, the University of Dayton, and Sinclair Community College stage theater performances for the general public. The Muse Machine, a Dayton organization designed to inform young people about the arts and culture, each year stages a theatrical production showcasing student performers. *Blue Jacket,* an outdoor drama about the white Shawnee war chief, is presented each summer at a facility six miles southeast of neighboring Xenia.

## Festivals and Holidays

Art in the Park in May attracts artists from around the nation for an outdoor fine arts and crafts show. At A World A'Fair, held in May at the Convention Center, 35 countries share their native culture, cuisine, and costumes. Dave Hall Plaza Park hosts music festivals in the summer.

The Vectren Dayton Air Show, one of the largest of its kind in the world, draws more than 200,000 spectators to the Dayton International Airport in July. Aerobatic displays, military jet demonstrations, and entertainment for the whole family make the Air Show one of the most important events on Dayton's calendar. Arts and crafts, ethnic foods, music and dancing, and special children's activities are featured at Oktoberfest, held in early October on the grounds of the Dayton Art Institute. Each year the Dayton Holiday Festival begins the day after Thanksgiving with a tree-lighting ceremony at Courthouse Square. Ohio Renaissance Festival is held on weekends in August and September near Waynesville. In May, the Dayton Amateur Radio Association hosts Hamvention, a convention that draws ham radio enthusiasts from across the country.

## Sports for the Spectator

Dayton is home to the Dayton Dragons, a Midwest League baseball Class A club in the Cincinnati Reds' farm system; they play at Fifth Third Field. Dayton also boasts a Class AA ECHL ice hockey team, the Dayton Bombers. The Bombers play at the Nutter Center, which also hosts Wright State University athletic events and various regional and state high school tournaments. Dayton sports fans support both the Cincinnati Reds baseball team and the Cincinnati Bengals football team. The University of Dayton Flyers field a football team in National Collegiate Athletic Association (NCAA) Division III, as does Wittenberg University in nearby Springfield. The Flyers' basketball team has a record of successful competition on the national level.

## Sports for the Participant

The Dayton Recreation and Parks Department sponsors sports programs for preschoolers to senior citizens at nearly 80 parks and 10 recreation centers. Programs include soccer and tennis camps, summer day camps for children, and softball leagues. Swimming, canoeing, golf, tennis, basketball, volleyball, boating, sailing, fishing, and winter sports are also available. Among the facilities managed by the department are the Jack Nicklaus Sports Center, the Wesleyan Nature Center, and the Horace M. Huffman River Corridor Bikeway, a 24-mile path along the Great Miami River. Golfing opportunities in Dayton include Kittyhawk Golf Center, the largest public golf facility in Ohio, and the Madden Golf Center, designed by notable course architect Alex Campbell. The Urban

Krag Climbing Center features an 8,000-square-foot vertical climbing wall in a beautifully restored church.

## Shopping and Dining

Downtown, the Merchants Row District offers jewelry, antiques, books, and more. The Oregon Historic District is a 12-block area near downtown that features shops, restaurants, and clubs among restored turn-of-the-century homes. The National City Second Street Public Market features the wares of local farmers and food and gift vendors, including fresh flowers and produce, gourmet coffee, and homemade baked goods. The Webster Street Market, housed in a restored nineteenth-century railroad freight depot, also provides a unique market-style shopping experience. The public markets are open Thursday through Sunday. There are nearly 30 shopping centers in the region, the largest being Dayton Mall and Fairfield Commons Mall.

Dining choices in Dayton include Japanese, Chinese, Mexican, Italian, Indian, and American cuisine. One critically acclaimed restaurant, which specializes in French and continental cuisine, is known for its rack of lamb, duck, and fresh seafood. Another serves authentic German dishes. One of the city's most popular eateries is a traditional steak and chop house that does not take reservations or serve desserts.

***Visitor Information:*** Dayton/Montgomery County Convention and Visitors Bureau, 1 Chamber Plaza, Suite A, Dayton, OH 45402; toll-free (800)221-8235

# ■ Convention Facilities

Situated in the central business district, the Dayton Convention Center is within walking distance of hotels, restaurants, shopping, and entertainment. The Convention Center offers two exhibit halls, with capacities of 47,000 square feet and 21,300 square feet, which can be combined to accommodate from 3,600 to 9,970 people in a variety of settings. Also part of the complex are 22 meeting rooms, a 674-seat theater, a fully equipped kitchen, and teleconferencing, sound, and lighting systems. Hara Arena Conference and Exhibition Center, the second-largest facility of it kind in the state of Ohio, contains a total of 165,575 square feet of space, which includes an 8,000-seat arena. On the Wright State University campus is the multipurpose Ervin J. Nutter Center, which can hold up to 12,500 people at full capacity, with conference rooms seating 400.

Dayton area hotels and motels offer meeting and banquet accommodations for large and small groups; more than 7,500 lodging rooms can be found in the Dayton-Montgomery County area.

***Convention Information:*** Dayton/Montgomery County Convention and Visitors Bureau, 1 Chamber Plaza, Suite A, Dayton, OH 45402; telephone (800)221-

8235. Dayton Convention Center; telephone (937)333-4707

# ■ Transportation

## Approaching the City

The destination for the majority of air traffic into Dayton is the Dayton International Airport, near the junction of I-70 and I-75 north of the city. Dayton International is served by ten airlines with non-stop service to more than twenty cities. It is the 81st busiest airport in North America. Seven general aviation airports are located throughout the Miami Valley.

Highways into metropolitan Dayton include two major interstate freeways—east-west I-70 and north-south I-75. I-675, a bypass, connects these highways and provides direct access to the city from Columbus and Cincinnati. U.S. 35 extends from east to west through the southern sector of Dayton. State routes leading into Dayton from points throughout the state and the immediate vicinity are 4, 202, 48, 49—all with a general north-south orientation.

## Traveling in the City

Regional Transit Authority (RTA) provides regularly scheduled mass transit bus service throughout Montgomery County and in parts of Greene County; RTA operates special routes to Wright-Patterson Air Force Base and Wright State and Central State Universities. Dayton is one of the few U.S. cities to have retained an electric trolleybus system.

# ■ Communications

## Newspapers and Magazines

Established in 1808 and merged with the *Journal Herald* in 1988, the *Dayton Daily News* is the city's daily morning newspaper. More than 20 suburban newspapers plus local college and university publications circulate weekly, including *Dayton Business Journal*, the *Oakwood Register*, and the *WSU Guardian*. Special-interest magazines published in Dayton cover such subjects as religion, African American culture, and management.

## Television and Radio

Dayton is the primary center for television and radio north of Cincinnati in southwestern Ohio. Five television stations—four commercial affiliates and one public—broadcast from Dayton; cable service is available. More than fifteen AM and FM radio stations schedule a variety of programs such as jazz, gospel, Celtic and folk, African American, contemporary, and classical music, educational features, and news.

*Media Information:* *Dayton Daily News*, Dayton Newspapers Inc., 45 South Ludlow Street, Dayton, OH 45402; telephone (937)222-5700

## Dayton Online

City of Dayton Home Page. Available www.ci.dayton.oh.us

Dayton Area Chamber of Commerce. Available www.daytonchamber.org

Dayton/Montgomery County Convention & Visitors Bureau. Available daytoncvb.com

Dayton Public Schools. Available www.dps.k12.oh.us

BIBLIOGRAPHY

Bernstein, Mark, *Grand Eccentrics: Turning the Century: Dayton and the Inventing of America* (Orange Frazer Press, 1996)

Huffman, Dale, Andy Snow, et al., *Dayton: The Cradle of Creativity* (Towery, 1998)

# Toledo

## ■ The City in Brief

**Founded:** 1817 (incorporated 1837)

**Head Official:** Mayor Carty S. Finkbeiner (D) (since 2005)

**City Population**

> 1980: 354,635
> 1990: 332,943
> 2000: 313,619
> 2006 estimate: 298,446
> Percent change, 1990–2000: −5.8%
> U.S. rank in 1980: 40th
> U.S. rank in 1990: Not available
> U.S. rank in 2000: 66th

**Metropolitan Area Population**

> 1980: 617,000
> 1990: 614,128
> 2000: 618,203
> 2006 estimate: 653,695
> Percent change, 1990–2000: .65%
> U.S. rank in 1980: 55th
> U.S. rank in 1990: Not available
> U.S. rank in 2000: 69th

**Area:** 81 square miles (2000)

**Elevation:** 615 feet above sea level

**Average Annual Temperatures:** January, 23.9° F; July, 73.0° F; annual average, 49.5° F

**Average Annual Precipitation:** 33.21 inches of rain; 37.1 inches of snow

**Major Economic Sectors:** Services, wholesale and retail trade, manufacturing, government

**Unemployment Rate:** 6.6% (June 2007)

**Per Capita Income:** $17,953 (2005)

**2005 FBI Crime Index Property:** 23,630

**2005 FBI Crime Index Violent:** 3,725

**Major Colleges and Universities:** University of Toledo; Davis College; Stautzenberger College; Medical College of Ohio; Owens Community College

**Daily Newspaper:** *The Toledo Blade*

## ■ Introduction

Toledo, the seat of Ohio's Lucas County, is the focus of a metropolitan complex comprised of Ottawa Hills Maumee, Oregon, Sylvania, Perrysburg, and Rossford. The city played a strategic role in the War of 1812, after which the victorious Americans enjoyed unimpeded settlement of the Northwest Territory. The site of pioneer advancements in the glass-making industry, today Toledo continues to be headquarters of international glass companies. The Port of Toledo is a major Great Lakes shipping point. Toledo's commitment to arts, culture, education, and citywide revitalization has residents and city leaders looking toward a bright future.

## ■ Geography and Climate

Toledo is located on the western end of Lake Erie at the mouth of the Maumee River, surrounded by generally level terrain. The soil is quite fertile, particularly along the Maumee Valley toward the Indiana state line. The proximity of Lake Erie moderates temperatures. Snowfall in Toledo is normally light.

**Area:** 81 square miles (2000)

**Elevation:** 615 feet above sea level

**Average Temperatures:** January, 23.9° F; July, 73.0° F; annual average, 49.5° F

**Average Annual Precipitation:** 33.21 inches of rain; 37.1 inches of snow

# ■ History

### French, British Settle Maumee Valley

As early as 1615 Etienne Brule, Samuel de Champlain's French-Canadian scout, discovered the Erie tribe of Native Americans living at the mouth of the Maumee River, the largest river that flows into the Great Lakes. Robert Cavelier, sieur de La Salle, claimed the territory in the name of France's King Louis XIV in 1689, and French trading posts were subsequently established in the Maumee Valley. A century later the British built Fort Miami there. Following the French and Indian War in 1763, France ceded all claims in the territory to Britain, who annexed the region to the Canadian Province of Quebec in 1774. At the end of the American Revolution, the region became part of the United States and was designated as part of the Northwest Territory in 1787. Renegade agents incited Native American warriors to attack settlers in the area; when American military forces were sent there in 1790, the native tribes prevailed. Four years later, General Anthony Wayne defeated 2,000 Native Americans at the Battle of Fallen Timbers southwest of present-day Toledo. General Wayne then directed the building of several forts, of which one was Fort Industry, constructed at the present site of Toledo.

At the outbreak of the War of 1812 the few settlers in the vicinity fled. In January 1813, General William Henry Harrison, later President of the United States, erected Fort Meigs, a massive fortification enclosing nine acres, which became known as the "Gibraltar of the Northwest." In the Battle of Lake Erie, off Put-In-Bay, the U. S. Navy's young Commodore Perry defeated the British naval force, followed by Harrison's defeat of General Proctor at the Battle of the Thames. These victories re-secured the Northwest Territory for the United States. After the war, a permanent settlement was formed on the northwest side of the Maumee River near the mouth of Swan Creek. In 1817 an Indian treaty conveyed most of the remaining land in the area to the federal government. The village of Port Lawrence near Fort Industry was formed by a Cincinnati syndicate in 1817, but it failed in 1820 and was then revived. Port Lawrence voted in 1835 to consolidate with the settlement of Vistula, one mile away, and the two were incorporated as Toledo in 1837.

The choice of the name of Toledo for the new city is shrouded in local legend. Popular versions give credit to a merchant who suggested Toledo because it "is easy to pronounce, is pleasant in sound, and there is no other city of that name on the American continent." Whatever the

source, friendly relations with the city of Toledo, Spain, have resulted. The Hispanic government awarded *The Blade*, the city's oldest newspaper, the royal coat of arms, and the University of Toledo has permission to use the arms of Spain's Ferdinand and Isabella as its motif.

### Border Dispute Precedes Industrial Growth

The "Toledo War" of 1835-36 between Ohio and Michigan over their common boundary did not involve bloodshed but it did result in federal intervention to resolve the dispute. Governor Robert Lucas of Ohio led a force of 1,000 soldiers to Perrysburg in March 1835, with the intent of driving Michigan militia from Toledo, but emissaries sent by President Andrew Jackson arranged a truce. Governor Lucas held a special session of the legislature in June, creating Lucas County out of the land in Wood County involved in the dispute. The new county held court in Toledo on the first Monday of September, which proved it had exercised jurisdiction over the disputed territory by holding a Court of Common Pleas in due form of law. Finally, Congress settled the issue by stipulating that the condition of Michigan's entrance into the Union would award Ohio the contested land and Michigan, in compensation, would receive what is now the state's Upper Peninsula.

Toledo in the mid-nineteenth century benefitted from the opening of new canals, the establishment of businesses along the river bank to accommodate trade and new shipping industries, and the arrival of the railroad. Prosperity continued during the Civil War, and by the end of the century the city became a major rail center in the United States. During the 1880s Toledo's industrial base, spurred by the discovery of inexpensive fuel, attracted glass-making entrepreneurs. Edward Libbey established a glassworks in Toledo, and then hired Michael Owens to supervise the new plant. The two pioneers revolutionized the glass business with inventions that eliminated child labor and streamlined production. Edward Ford arrived in the Toledo region in 1896 to found the model industrial town of Rossford and one of the largest plate-glass operations of its time.

Two politicians stand out in the history of Toledo. Samuel M. "Gold Rule" Jones was elected mayor on a nonpartisan ticket and emerged as a national figure. His reform efforts in city government introduced one of the first municipal utilities, the eight-hour workday for city employees, and the first free kindergartens, public playgrounds, and band concerts. Mayor Brand Whitlock continued Jones's reforms by securing a state law for the nonpartisan election of judges and Ohio's initiative and referendum law in 1912.

John Willys moved his Overland automobile factory from Indianapolis to Toledo in 1908, and, in time, automotive-parts manufacture flourished in the area; the industry was firmly established by such firms as Champion Spark Plug and Warner Manufacturing Company, maker

©James Blank.

of automobile gears. A strike by Auto-Lite workers in 1934 was marred by violence and prompted the intervention of U.S. troops and the Federal Department of Labor; the resolution of this strike, which received national attention, helped contribute to the unionization of the automotive industries. The Toledo Industrial Peace Board, set up in 1935 to resolve labor disputes by round-table discussion, served as a model for similar entities in other cities.

## An All-American City

Toledo today boasts amenities and points of interest including the University of Toledo; the Medical College of Ohio at Toledo; a symphony, ballet and opera company; the Toledo Museum of Art; the Toledo Zoo; and the Anthony Wayne suspension bridge (1931). The site of the battle of Fallen Timbers, a national historic landmark, is in a nearby state park. Toledo's commitment to arts and culture is evident, as is its focus on neighborhood revitalization. A renewed vitality, even in the face of diminishing central-city residents, has city planners looking toward the future.

***Historical Information:*** Toledo-Lucas County Public Library, History-Travel-Biography Department, 325 Michigan Street, Toledo, OH 43624; telephone (419)259-5207

## ■ Population Profile

### Metropolitan Area Residents

    1980: 617,000
    1990: 614,128
    2000: 618,203
    2006 estimate: 653,695
    Percent change, 1990–2000: .65%
    U.S. rank in 1980: 55th
    U.S. rank in 1990: Not available
    U.S. rank in 2000: 69th

### City Residents

    1980: 354,635
    1990: 332,943
    2000: 313,619
    2006 estimate: 298,446
    Percent change, 1990–2000: −5.8%
    U.S. rank in 1980: 40th
    U.S. rank in 1990: Not available
    U.S. rank in 2000: 66th

**Density:** 3,890 people per square mile (2000)

**Racial and ethnic characteristics (2005)**

> White: 189,641
> Black: 72,657
> American Indian and Alaska Native: 546
> Asian: 4,150
> Native Hawaiian and Pacific Islander: 0
> Hispanic or Latino (may be of any race): 18,404
> Other: 10,789

**Percent of residents born in state:** 77.4 % (2000)

**Age characteristics (2005)**

> Population under 5 years old: 21,308
> Population 5 to 9 years old: 20,374
> Population 10 to 14 years old: 19,790
> Population 15 to 19 years old: 19,276
> Population 20 to 24 years old: 21,892
> Population 25 to 34 years old: 43,134
> Population 35 to 44 years old: 38,344
> Population 45 to 54 years old: 40,552
> Population 55 to 59 years old: 16,848
> Population 60 to 64 years old: 9,988
> Population 65 to 74 years old: 16,198
> Population 75 to 84 years old: 13,754
> Population 85 years and older: 4,479
> Median age: 34.2 years

**Births (2006, MSA)**

> Total number: 8,515

**Deaths (2006, MSA)**

> Total number: 6,004

**Money income (2005)**

> Per capita income: $17,953
> Median household income: $33,044
> Total households: 120,970

**Number of households with income of . . .**

> less than $10,000: 19,654
> $10,000 to $14,999: 10,438
> $15,000 to $24,999: 17,144
> $25,000 to $34,999: 16,354
> $35,000 to $49,999: 18,632
> $50,000 to $74,999: 21,220
> $75,000 to $99,999: 9,844
> $100,000 to $149,999: 6,598
> $150,000 to $199,999: 734
> $200,000 or more: 352

**Percent of families below poverty level:** 15.2% (2005)

**2005 FBI Crime Index Property:** 23,630

**2005 FBI Crime Index Violent:** 3,725

# ■ Municipal Government

The city of Toledo is administered by a strong-mayor form of government. The mayor and 12 council members are elected to four-year terms.

**Head Official:** Mayor Carty S. Finkbeiner (D) (since 2005; current term expires 2009)

**Total Number of City Employees:** approximately 2,950 (2005)

***City Information:*** Toledo City Hall, One Government Center, 640 Jackson, Ste. 2200, Toledo, OH 43604; telephone (419)936-2020

# ■ Economy

## Major Industries and Commercial Activity

Manufacturing comprises about one-fifth of Toledo's economic base. Nearly 1,000 manufacturing facilities are located in the metropolitan area. Such manufacturing facilities include automotive assembly and parts production (notably, the Jeep vehicle is manufactured in Toledo), glass, plastic, and metal parts. Toledo is home to the headquarters of such corporations as The Andersons, Dana Corporation, Libbey, Inc., Owens Corning, and Owens-Illinois. Major employers include Chrysler, General Motors/Powertrain, ProMedica Health Systems, and Toledo Public Schools; more than forty *Fortune* 500 companies maintain a presence in northwestern Ohio. Toledo is also a banking and finance center for northwestern Ohio.

Medical and technologically-oriented businesses are a major force in the local economy; Lucas County ranks among the 50 counties in the United States that account for 50 percent of medical industry production. Several private testing laboratories and manufacturers of medical instruments and allied products are located in the Toledo area. In addition, more than 400 plastics, metalworking, and electronics companies adapt engineering and production capabilities to the medical device and instrument industries. With its many nearby universities and large public school system, education is also an economic pillar. The Medical College of Ohio is among the largest employers in Toledo and contributes approximately $500 million to the economy per year. Since the turn of the 21st century, the service industry has been the fastest growing sector of Toledo's economy.

**Items and goods produced:** automotive and truck components, health care products, glass products, fiberglass, packaged foods, plastic and paper products, building materials, furniture, metal products

## Incentive Programs—New and Existing Companies

*Local programs:* The Regional Growth Partnership, Inc. (RGP) is the principal agency for facilitating business expansion and location in the Toledo metropolitan area. Created as a non-profit public/private partnership, the RGP is charged with the mission of creating employment and capital investment needed to generate economic growth in greater Toledo and northwest Ohio. The RGP works closely with all public and private economic development organizations. The RGP provides customized services to fit the individual needs of each business client. Services include customized location proposals and sales presentations, comprehensive site and facility searches, project financial and incentive packaging, labor market information, other market and community data, regional evaluation tours, and leadership networking.

*State programs:* The State of Ohio grants direct low interest loans, industrial revenue bonds, and financial assistance for research and development to companies creating or retaining jobs in Ohio. Additionally, the Ohio Job Creation Tax Credit provides tax credits for Ohio companies that expand as well as companies relocating to Ohio. Enterprise zones provide significant tax reductions on property investments made by businesses expanding in or relocating to specific areas of Ohio.

*Job training programs:* The Ohio Investment in Training program provides financial assistance and technical resources for assisting Ohio businesses in the training of employees. Additionally, area colleges and universities offer many options for training.

*Economic Development Information:* Regional Growth Partnership, 300 Madison Avenue, Suite 270, Toledo, OH 43604; telephone (419)252-2700; fax (419)252-2724

## Development Projects

The economy continues to thrive in Toledo. Major university projects include the Toledo Science and Technology Center, a program to stimulate economic development by creating jobs and assisting local businesses. Downtown Toledo, Inc. is an ongoing public-private partnership made up of local business leaders, property owners, and citizens. It was created to enhance the quality of life and economy of the downtown Toledo area.

In 2007 master plans were unveiled for a large-scale renovation of the Toledo Botanical Gardens, with groundbreaking to begin in 2008; additions will include a conference center and banquet facilities, a new children's garden, a greenhouse-like conservatory, and a new visitor's center. The Toledo Public Schools "Build For Success" initiative, begun in 2003, had built or renovated 17 schools by 2007, with a total of 29 slated for the project. Also in 2007 work was underway on a new multipurpose sports arena, to be completed by 2009 and intended to house a minor league hockey team and perhaps an arena football team.

## Commercial Shipping

Toledo is situated at the center of a major market area; located within 500 miles of the city are approximately 43 percent and 47 percent, respectively, of U.S. and Canadian industrial markets. A commercial transportation network, consisting of a Great Lakes port, railroads, interstate highways, and two international airports, provides access to this market area as well as points throughout the nation and the world.

Toledo is served by both Toledo Express in Toledo and Detroit Metropolitan Airport in nearby Detroit, Michigan. Toledo Express, served by five airlines, carries passengers and is a major air freight center. Named one of the five best small airports in the Midwest, Toledo Express has four air cargo carriers. Detroit Metropolitan Airport is within a 50-minute drive.

The Port of Toledo, on the Maumee River, is a 150-acre domestic and international shipping facility that includes a general cargo center, mobile cargo handling gear, and covered storage space. The port handles over 15 million tons of cargo annually, including coal, iron ore, and grain. Designated as a Foreign Trade Zone, the complex affords shippers deferred duty payments and tax savings on foreign goods.

Toledo is served by several railroad systems, which provide direct and interline shipping; Norfolk/Southern maintains piggyback terminal facilities in the city. More than 90 truck firms link Toledo with all major metropolitan areas in the United States and points throughout Canada.

## Labor Force and Employment Outlook

Businesses in Toledo have access to graduates from at least 20 higher educational institutions within a one-hour drive of the city. Farming, industrial production, and agriculture contribute to the area's growing economy. Manufacturing accounts for nearly one-fifth of the jobs in metropolitan Toledo. The Toledo area has a strong automotive industry base and is one of the top three machine tooling centers in the United States. The area has experienced strong growth in the steel, metals, and plastic industries. Retail and service businesses continue to expand; however, declining growth in the automotive and manufacturing industries nationwide in the early 2000s were an area of major concern for the Toledo economy.

In October 2007 the unemployment rate in Toledo stood at 7 percent, down slightly from 7.8 percent earlier that year, but trending upwards. Ten-year unemployment highs topping out at 8 percent occurred in 2004.

The following is a summary of data regarding the Toledo metropolitan area labor force, 2006 annual averages.

**Size of nonagricultural labor force:** 332,900

**Number of workers employed in . . .**

construction and mining: 15,400
manufacturing: 50,400
trade, transportation and utilities: 65,100
information: 4,100
financial activities: 13,100
professional and business services: 34,400
educational and health services: 51,300
leisure and hospitality: 33,300
other services: 15,100
government: 50,800

**Average hourly earnings of production workers employed in manufacturing:** $21.18

**Unemployment rate:** 6.6% (June 2007)

| *Largest metropolitan area employers (2007)* | *Number of employees* |
| --- | --- |
| ProMedica Health Systems | 11,500 |
| Mercy Health Partners Hospitals | 6,799 |
| Bowling Green State University | 5,400 |
| Chrysler Corporation | 5,256 |
| The University of Toledo | 5,079 |
| Toledo Public Schools | 4,730 |
| Lucas County Government | 4,168 |
| Toledo Jeep Assembly Plant | 4,000 |
| Kroger, Inc. | 3,900 |
| General Motors | 3,425 |
| Medical University of Ohio | 3,400 |
| Sauder (HQ) | 3,050 |

### Cost of Living

The following is a summary of data regarding several key cost of living factors in the Toledo area.

**2007 (1st quarter) ACCRA Average House Price:** Not available

**2007 (1st quarter) ACCRA Cost of Living Index:** 98.6

**State income tax rate:** 0.68% to 6.87%

**State sales tax rate:** 5.5%

**Local income tax rate:** 2.25%

**Local sales tax rate:** 1.25% (county)

**Property tax rate:** $91.80 per $1,000 assessed value (2008)

***Economic Information:*** Regional Growth Partnership, 300 Madison Avenue, Suite 270, Toledo, OH 43604; telephone (419)252-2700

## ■ Education and Research

### Elementary and Secondary Schools

Public elementary and secondary schools in Toledo are administered by the Toledo Public Schools system, the fourth largest public school system in the state of Ohio. Five partisan board of education members select a superintendent. "Small school" academies for high schoolers focus on subject matter such as business, the arts, or the humanities. A new program in 2007, funded by a grant from the state of Ohio, focuses on closing the acheivement gap for at-risk, low income high school males. The school system also houses an aviation center, one of only a dozen such programs nationwide. "Building For Success," an $800 million dollar district capital improvement plan undertaken in 2003, was projected to take 10-12 years for completion.

Washington Local Schools serve much of the northwest area of the city.

The following is a summary of data regarding the Toledo Public Schools as of the 2005–2006 school year.

**Total enrollment:** 107,660

**Number of facilities**

elementary schools: 38
junior high/middle schools: 7
senior high schools: 9
other: 0

**Student/teacher ratio:** 17.1:1

**Teacher salaries (2005–06)**

elementary median: $47,460
junior high/middle median: $48,810
secondary median: $47,660

**Funding per pupil:** $10,083

The Catholic Diocese of Toledo operates an extensive parochial school system in the city and surrounding area. Other private and church-related schools also offer educational alternatives, including Toledo Christian School.

*Public Schools Information:* Toledo Public Schools, 420 East Manhattan, Toledo, OH 43608; telephone (419)729-8200

## Colleges and Universities

The University of Toledo's eleven colleges offer degrees in undergraduate and graduate fields, including engineering and pharmacy. Its honors program is one of the oldest of its kind in the nation, and Centennial Mall, a lawn in the middle of campus, is one of the "100 most beautifully landscaped places in the country," according to the American Society of Landscape Architects. The Medical College of Ohio (MCO) grants a medical degree as well as graduate degrees in medical science and industrial hygiene; MCO conducts joint educational programs and collaborative research with area businesses and educational institutions. Owens Community College offers two-year programs in biomedical equipment, computer-integrated manufacturing, and glass engineering, among others. The school has campuses in Toledo and Findlay and boasts over 130 academic programs, with more than 45,000 credit and non-credit students.

Within commuting distance of Toledo are Bowling Green State University and the University of Michigan.

## Libraries and Research Centers

Toledo is home to about two dozen libraries operated by public agencies, private organizations, and corporations. The Toledo-Lucas County Public Library houses more than 2.3 million books and has an annual circulation of over 6 million; the library system includes 18 branches and 2 bookmobiles located throughout the city and the county. Special collections include the Art Tatum African American Resource Center, which houses a collection of more then 84,750 circulating and reference materials. The University of Toledo, the Medical College of Ohio at Toledo, and Owens Community College maintain campus libraries. Other libraries are associated with the Toledo Museum of Art, law firms, hospitals, and churches and synagogues.

The Medical College of Ohio (MCO) in Toledo is active in medical research and development. MCO has created the Advanced Technology Park to house college facilities and provide facilities for the growing biotechnology research sector.

Research and development is also conducted at the University of Toledo's Polymer and Thin Films Institute and Eitel Institute for Silicate Research. The federally-funded National Center for Tooling and Precision Products Research is housed at the University of Toledo. The National Drosophilia Species Resource Center, affiliated with nearby Bowling Green State University, is internationally known for fruit-fly research.

*Public Library Information:* Toledo-Lucas County Public Library, 325 N. Michigan Street, Toledo, OH 43624-1332; telephone (419)259-5207; fax (419)255-1332

# ■ Health Care

A number of major hospitals serve the metropolitan Toledo area with complete general, specialized, and surgical care. The largest facilities are Toledo Hospital, with 774 beds, 1,110 physicians and more than 4,000 staff members, and St. Vincent Mercy Medical Center, which sees over 60,000 emergency center visits annually and has more than 750 physicians on staff. Toledo Hospital was a recipient of HealthGrades' 2007 "Distinguished Hospital Award for Clinical Excellence." Toledo Children's Hospital, part of Toledo Hospital, offers 60 newborn intensive care unit beds, 56 general pediatric beds, 18 pediatric intensive care unit beds, 10 psychiatric beds and 7 pediatric hematology/oncology beds. Flower Hospital, in nearby Sylvania, is a 279-bed facility with a Level III Trauma Center. Other hospitals include St. Anne Mercy Hospital, St. Charles Mercy Hospital, Wood County Hospital, and St. Luke's. A valuable resource in the community is the Medical College of Ohio, which operates three hospitals and provides training for health care professionals. In 2000 the Medical College of Ohio Cancer Institute opened to provide patients with cutting-edge treatment while conducting cancer research at the molecular, cellular, and physiological levels. The Center also offers a specialty center for the treatment of breast cancer.

# ■ Recreation

## Sightseeing

Fort Meigs, located near Toledo along the southern bank of the Maumee River west of Perrysburg, was the largest walled fortification in North America. Built in 1813 under the direction of General William Henry Harrison (who later became president of the United States), Fort Meigs is an impressive structure of earthworks and timber. Toledo's Old West End, covering 25 blocks, is one of the largest collections of late-Victorian architecture in the country; Frank Lloyd Wright studied the Old West End in preparing his plans for Oak Park, Illinois.

The freighter SS *Willis B. Boyer* was first launched in 1911 and served for many years on the Great Lakes as the largest ship of its type. Now restored, it is docked at International Park and open for tours. The Sauder Farm and Craft Village, a living-history museum in nearby Archbold, recaptures life in northwest Ohio in the 1830s. Wolcott House Museum in Maumee depicts life in the Maumee Valley from 1840 to 1860.

The Toledo Zoo, one of the nation's highest rated zoological parks, offers state-of-the-art exhibits, together with historical architecture, fully integrated to provide more than 4,000 animals with the best possible environment and offer visitors an exciting experience. An innovative exhibition called Africa! opened in May of 2004.

Located in a firehouse that dates from around 1920, the Toledo Firefighters Museum preserves 150 years of fire fighting in the city. Thousands of items are on exhibit, including many large pieces of vintage fire fighting equipment.

The Toledo Botanical Garden cultivates herbs, roses, azalea, rhododendron, and wildflowers; artists' studios and galleries are maintained on the grounds. Toledo boasts over 140 parks covering more than 2,300 acres. The Metroparks of the Toledo Area preserves 8,000 acres of parks in Lucas County. The nine metroparks of the Toledo area preserve sand dunes, tall grass prairies, upland woody swamp forests, and oak savannahs. The parks offer elevated views of the Maumee River Valley. From May through October, the Miami and Erie Canal Restoration at Providence Metropark features a mule-drawn canal boat that carries passengers along a one and one-fourth mile stretch of the original canal, through a working canal lock, and past the Isaac Ludwig Mill, which features heritage crafts and water-powered milling demonstrations. Oak Openings Preserve protects threatened and endangered plant species, while Pearson Preserve protects one of the few remnants of the Great Black Swamp. The metroparks present many free nature and history programs and capture a sense of the natural beauty of the area at the time it was first settled.

## Arts and Culture

The Toledo Museum of Art was founded in 1912 when Edward Libbey made a contribution of money and land to help initiate the museum's first stage of construction. The museum's permanent collection represents holdings from diverse cultures and periods, including ancient Egyptian tombs, a medieval cloister, a French chateau, glass, furniture, silver, tapestries, and paintings by world masters.

Without a doubt, the cultural highlight of Toledo's downtown revitalization efforts is the Valentine Theatre. When it originally opened in 1895, the Valentine was the finest theatrical venue between New York and Chicago. The Valentine Theatre is also home of the Toledo Symphony and the Toledo Ballet. The intimate and acoustically superior 901-seat, $28 million theater allows for excellent viewing of the stage and projected English titles when necessary.

The Toledo Symphony Orchestra presents a full season of concerts in Peristyle Hall at the Toledo Museum of Art. Stranahan Theater hosts performances by the Toledo Opera Association and touring Broadway shows. Two community theater groups, Toledo Repertoire Theatre and the Village Players, stage several productions annually. The Toledo Ballet Association presents local and guest performers, sometimes in collaboration with the opera and symphony. Both the University of Toledo and Bowling Green State University schedule plays and other cultural events, many featuring well-known performing artists and speakers.

## Festivals and Holidays

Many festivals celebrate Toledo's history and its ethnic diversity. In June, the Toledo Jazz Society sponsors the Art Tatum Jazz Heritage Festival. Through the summer, Rallies by the River offers music and refreshments at Promenade Park on Friday evenings. In June, the Old West End Festival opens restored Victorian homes to the public. The Crosby Festival of the Arts is held in late June at the Toledo Botanical Garden. The annual fireworks display takes place downtown on the river. Also in July, the Lucas County Fair is held at the fairgrounds. The Northwest Ohio Rib-Off takes place in August at Promenade Park.

## Sports for the Spectator

The Toledo Mud Hens, the Triple A farm team for professional baseball's Detroit Tigers, compete in the International League with home games at Fifth Third Field. The Toledo Storm, East Coast Hockey League affiliates for the National Hockey League's Detroit Red Wings, suspended operations in 2006 while a new stadium was under construction, expected to be completed by 2009. Raceway Park presents harness racing on a spiral-banked five-eighths mile track from March to December. Stock car racing is on view at Toledo Speedway. The University of Toledo Rockets and the Bowling Green State University Falcons field teams in Mid-American Conference sports.

## Sports for the Participant

Toledo, the largest port on Lake Erie, offers some of the best fishing in the world. Walleye season runs from May to August, followed by perch in the fall; white and smallmouth bass are other popular catches. Ice fishing is available in January and February. Toledo maintains one of Ohio's best park systems, with more than 140 areas for sports and relaxation. The Lucas County Recreation Department provides facilities for swimming, tennis, track, handball, and softball. Toledo Area Metroparks offer boating, cycling, hiking, jogging, water and field sports, and fitness trails on over 8,000 acres. Toledo boasts some of the finest golf courses in the country. The Toledo Roadrunners Club has been holding the Glass City Marathon for more than 30 years; runners race along country roads and through neighboring communities and downtown Toledo. The race pays tribute to the memory of Sy Mah, a Toledo runner who once held the Guinness

World Book record for running 524 marathons in his lifetime.

## Shopping and Dining

Unique shopping opportunities in Toledo and environs include glass factory outlet stores, featuring all types and styles of glassware; flea markets; the Erie Street Market; and art galleries. Four major shopping centers are located in the area.

Among Toledo's hundreds of restaurants is Tony Packo's Cafe, celebrated by Corporal Klinger, a character on the television program "M*A*S*H." Featuring an extensive Tiffany lamp collection, the restaurant serves a distinctive hot dog, Hungarian hamburgers, and a vegetable soup with Hungarian dumplings. The Docks on the Maumee River offer a variety of interesting restaurants; these include Gumbo's, Real Seafood Co., Zia's Italian Restaurant, Tango's Mexican Cantina, and Cousino's Navy Bistro.

*Visitor Information:*   The Greater Toledo Convention and Visitors Bureau, 401 Jefferson Avenue, Toledo, OH 43604; telephone (419)321-6404; toll-free (800) 243-4667

## ■ Convention Facilities

The principal meeting and convention site in Toledo is the SeaGate Convention Centre, situated downtown one block from the Maumee River; connected to the convention center is the University of Toledo at SeaGate Center facility. When combined, the three-level complex features 75,000 square feet of multipurpose space, which can be divided into 3 separate halls and 25 meeting rooms. Hotels and motels provide additional meeting space, accommodating groups ranging from 12 to 800 participants; more than 7,000 guest rooms are available in the greater Toledo area.

*Convention Information:*   The Greater Toledo Convention and Visitors Bureau, 401 Jefferson Avenue, Toledo, OH 43604; telephone (419)321-6404; toll-free (800)243-4667. SeaGate Convention Center, 401 Jefferson Avenue, Toledo, OH 43604; telephone (419) 255-3300

## ■ Transportation

### Approaching the City

Toledo Express Airport is served by five commercial airlines providing direct and connecting flights to major cities throughout the United States. The airport also handles corporate and private aircraft. Additional general aviation services are available at Metcalf Field, operated by the Port Authority and located south of the city.

Detroit Metropolitan Airport, less than an hour's drive from Toledo, is served by international as well as domestic flights.

A network of interstate, federal, and state highways facilitates access into and around the city and links Toledo to points in all sectors of the nation. Interstate 75 extends north through Michigan and south through Florida; the Ohio Turnpike (I-80 and I-90) connects Toledo with the East and West Coasts. Other highways include U.S. 24, 25, 20, and 23.

Amtrak provides east-west rail service to Toledo plus daily service from Detroit. Greyhound and Trailways buses travel into the city.

### Traveling in the City

Streets in the city of Toledo are laid out on a grid pattern; downtown streets are tilted on a northwest-southeast axis to conform to the Maumee River. Toledo's bus-based public transportation system, the Toledo Area Regional Transit Authority (TARTA), schedules routes throughout the city and suburban areas. Boat, train, trolley, and horse-drawn carriage tours are available.

## ■ Communications

### Newspapers and Magazines

The major daily newspaper in Toledo is *The Blade*. *The Toledo Journal* is a weekly African American newspaper. Several neighborhood newspapers as well as scholarly, academic, and religious journals, and special-interest tabloids and magazines are also published in the city.

### Television and Radio

Toledo is the broadcast media center for northwestern Ohio and parts of southeastern Michigan. Television viewers receive programs from six stations—one public and five commercial—based in the city. More than a dozen AM and FM radio stations schedule a complete range of music, news, information, and public interest features; one broadcasts performances by local cultural groups.

*Media Information:*   The Toledo Blade Company, 541 N. Superior Street, Toledo, OH 43660; toll-free (800)724-6000

### Toledo Online

The Blade. Available www.toledoblade.com

City of Toledo Home Page. Available www.ci .toledo.oh.us

Greater Toledo Convention and Visitors Bureau. Available www.toledocvb.com

Regional Growth Partnership. Available www .rgp.org

Toledo Area Chamber of Commerce. Available www.toledochamber.com

Toledo-Lucas County Public Library. Available www.library.toledo.oh.us

BIBLIOGRAPHY

Geha, Joseph, *Through and Through: Toledo Stories* (Graywolf Press, 1990)

Jones, Marnie, *Holy Toledo: Religion and Politics in the Life of 'Golden Rule' Jones* (University Press of Kentucky, 1998)

Toledo Museum of Art et al., *Toledo Treasures: Selections from the Toledo Museum of Art* (Hudson Hills Press, 1995)

# South Dakota

# The State in Brief

**Nickname:** Coyote State; Mount Rushmore State

**Motto:** Under God the people rule

**Flower:** Pasque flower

**Bird:** Ringnecked pheasant

**Area:** 77,116 square miles (2000; U.S. rank 17th)

**Elevation:** 966 feet to 7,242 feet above sea level

**Climate:** Continental, characterized by seasonal extremes of temperature as well as persistent winds, low humidity, and scant rainfall

**Admitted to Union:** November 2, 1889

**Capital:** Pierre

**Head Official:** Governor Mike Rounds (R) (until 2010)

**Population**

> 1980: 691,000
> 1990: 696,004
> 2000: 754,844
> 2006 estimate: 781,919
> Percent change, 1990–2000: 8.5%
> U.S. rank in 2006: 46th
> Percent of residents born in state: 65.21% (2006)
> Density: 10.2 people per square mile (2006)
> 2006 FBI Crime Index Total: 14,004

**Racial and Ethnic Characteristics (2006)**

> White: 681,785
> Black or African American: 5,262
> American Indian and Alaska Native: 67,614
> Asian: 7,064
> Native Hawaiian and Pacific Islander: 56
> Hispanic or Latino (may be of any race): 15,544
> Other: 7,767

**Age Characteristics (2006)**

> Population under 5 years old: 53,701
> Population 5 to 19 years old: 163,504
> Percent of population 65 years and over: 14.3%
> Median age: 37.3

**Vital Statistics**

> Total number of births (2006): 11,590
> Total number of deaths (2006): 7,386
> AIDS cases reported through 2005: 244

**Economy**

> **Major industries:** Finance, insurance, and real estate; agriculture; tourism; wholesale and retail trade; services
> **Unemployment rate (2006):** 4.3%
> **Per capita income (2006):** $22,066
> **Median household income (2006):** $42,791
> **Percentage of persons below poverty level (2006):** 13.6%
> **Income tax rate:** None
> **Sales tax rate:** 4.0%

# Aberdeen

## ■ The City in Brief

**Founded:** 1880 (incorporated 1882)

**Head Official:** Mayor Mike Levsen (since 2004)

**City Population**

    1980: Not available
    1990: 24,927
    2000: 24,658
    2006 estimate: 24,071
    Percent change, 1990–2000: −1%
    U.S. rank in 1980: Not available
    U.S. rank in 1990: Not available
    U.S. rank in 2000: Not available

**Metropolitan Area Population**

    1980: Not available
    1990: Not available
    2000: Not available
    2006 estimate: 38,707
    Percent change, 1990–2000: Not available
    U.S. rank in 1980: Not available
    U.S. rank in 1990: Not available
    U.S. rank in 2000: Not available

**Area:** 13 square miles (2000)

**Elevation:** 1,302 feet above sea level

**Average Annual Temperatures:** January, 11.0° F; July, 72.2° F; annual average, 43.8° F

**Average Annual Precipitation:** 20.22 inches of rain; 37.0 inches of snow

**Major Economic Sectors:** Trade, transportation, utilities

**Unemployment Rate:** 2.5% (2005)

**Per Capita Income:** $17,923 (1999)

**2005 FBI Crime Index Property:** Not available

**2005 FBI Crime Index Violent:** Not available

**Major Colleges and Universities:** Northern State University, Presentation College

**Daily Newspaper:** *The Aberdeen American News*

## ■ Introduction

Aberdeen, the county seat of Brown County, emerged with the coming of the railroads, flourished into a strong agricultural economy, and has diversified into a manufacturing and service center. A city of Midwestern hospitality combined with metropolitan progressiveness, Aberdeen offers an excellent quality of life. Aberdeen fancies itself the "land of Oohs and Oz," due to the fact that L. Frank Baum, resident of Aberdeen from 1888 to 1891, wrote the children's classic *The Wizard of Oz*. The theme, settings, and characters from the Wizard of Oz provided the inspiration for Aberdeen's theme parks, Storybook Land and Land of Oz.

## ■ Geography and Climate

Aberdeen is located in the northeastern part of the state, in the James River valley, approximately 11 miles west of the river. The city is situated directly west of Moccasin Creek, which flows south and then northeast to the James River. Aberdeen is approximately 125 miles northeast of Pierre, South Dakota's capital. Aberdeen is also three hours from Fargo, North Dakota, and Sioux Falls, South Dakota, and approximately five hours from Minneapolis-St. Paul, Minnesota.

    Like the rest of the state, Aberdeen has cold winters, warm to hot summers, light moisture in the winter, and moderate moisture in the summer. The city survived severe flooding in May 2007.

**Area:** 13 square miles (2000)

**Elevation:** 1,302 feet above sea level

**Average Temperatures:** January, 11.0° F; July, 72.2° F; annual average, 43.8° F

**Average Annual Precipitation:** 20.22 inches of rain; 37.0 inches of snow

# ■ History

The Aberdeen area was long inhabited by the Sioux Indians. The arrival of whites to the area came with the founding of fur trading posts during the 1820s.

Aberdeen's history is directly linked to the development of the railroads. Aberdeen was settled in 1880, mapped out on January 3, 1881, and incorporated in 1882. Alexander Mitchell, a railroad agent and president of the Chicago, Milwaukee, and St. Paul Railroad, named the city after his birthplace of Aberdeen, Scotland. The city prospered; by 1886, Aberdeen had three different railroad companies operating in town, and Aberdeen earned the nickname "Hub City" due to the fact that the railroad tracks radiated out of the city like the spokes of a wheel. Today, only one of these railroads, the Burlington Northern Santa Fe, is still operating in Aberdeen.

The city has a strong agricultural base but has developed as a center for manufacturing and service industries as well. Aberdeen is a regional center for shopping, health and social services, higher education, library services, and cultural and recreational activities, for a 100-mile radius. In recent years, Aberdeen has developed as a telecommunications hub, providing technical services to a worldwide market.

Aberdeen was the site of severe flooding in May 2007. For two days beginning on May 4, Aberdeen received 9.12 inches of rain. The rain flooded city streets, making many of them impassable, and caused water damage to many homes. More than 300 families requested assistance from disaster response agencies, more than 100 houses were condemned, and some 50 were declared unlivable. Brown County was declared a disaster area.

***Historical Information:*** The South Dakota State Historical Society, 900 Governors Drive, Pierre, SD 57501; telephone (605)773-3458; fax (605)773-6041

# ■ Population Profile

**Metropolitan Area Residents**

1980: Not available
1990: Not available
2000: Not available
2006 estimate: 38,707
Percent change, 1990–2000: Not available

U.S. rank in 1980: Not available
U.S. rank in 1990: Not available
U.S. rank in 2000: Not available

**City Residents**

1980: Not available
1990: 24,927
2000: 24,658
2006 estimate: 24,071
Percent change, 1990–2000: −1%
U.S. rank in 1980: Not available
U.S. rank in 1990: Not available
U.S. rank in 2000: Not available

**Density:** 1,902.1 people per square mile (2000)

**Racial and ethnic characteristics (2000)**

White: 23,328
Black: 92
American Indian and Alaska Native: 782
Asian: 133
Native Hawaiian and Pacific Islander: 31
Hispanic or Latino (may be of any race): 196
Other: 48

**Percent of residents born in state:** 73.3% (2000)

**Age characteristics (2000)**

Population under 5 years old: 1,543
Population 5 to 9 years old: 1,382
Population 10 to 14 years old: 1,489
Population 15 to 19 years old: 2,061
Population 20 to 24 years old: 2,389
Population 25 to 34 years old: 2,993
Population 35 to 44 years old: 3,521
Population 45 to 54 years old: 3,042
Population 55 to 59 years old: 1,052
Population 60 to 64 years old: 935
Population 65 to 74 years old: 1,859
Population 75 to 84 years old: 1,685
Population 85 years and older: 707
Median age: 36.5 years

**Births (2006, Micropolitan Statistical Area)**

Total number: 511

**Deaths (2006, Micropolitan Statistical Area)**

Total number: 481

**Money income (1999)**

Per capita income: $17,923
Median household income: $33,276
Total households: 10,514

**Number of households with income of...**

less than $10,000: 1,263

Dakota Aerials, Yankton, SD

$10,000 to $14,999: 918
$15,000 to $24,999: 1,743
$25,000 to $34,999: 1,575
$35,000 to $49,999: 1,957
$50,000 to $74,999: 1,978
$75,000 to $99,999: 579
$100,000 to $149,999: 323
$150,000 to $199,999: 95
$200,000 or more: 83

**Percent of families below poverty level:** 16.6% (1999)

**2005 FBI Crime Index Property:** Not available

**2005 FBI Crime Index Violent:** Not available

# ■ Municipal Government

The powers of the city, under its home rule charter of 2004, are vested in the city council. City council is composed of the mayor and eight council members. Council members are elected to staggered five-year terms. The mayor, who also acts as city manager, is elected to a five-year term.

**Head Official:** Mayor Mike Levsen (since 2004; current term expires 2009)

**Total Number of City Employees:** 246 (2006)

*City Information:* Aberdeen City Hall, 123 S. Lincoln St., Aberdeen, SD 57401; telephone (605)626-7025; fax (605)626-7042

# ■ Economy

## Major Industries and Commercial Activity

Trade/transportation/utilities made up the largest percentage of Brown County's salaried employees in 2005 (21.92%), followed by education/health services (16.48%), government (14.62%), manufacturing (10.63%), leisure/hospitality services (10.35%), professional/business services (9.64%), financial activities (5.57%), construction (4.83%), other services (3.45%), information (1.76%), and mining/natural resources (0.76%).

Aberdeen's major employers include Avera St. Luke's Hospital, Aberdeen Public Schools, the 3M Co., Cendant Corp., Hub City Inc., South Dakota Wheat Growers,

Northern State University, Kessler's Grocery Store, Midstates Printing/Quality Quick Print, EAC Educational Services, Wells Fargo Financial, Aman Collection Service Inc., and Wyndham Worldwide. As of 2007, the following major companies had set up operations in Aberdeen in the previous ten years: Mutual of Omaha; Four Star Plastics; APA; Menards; Quantum Plastics; Verifications; and Progen.

**Items and goods produced:** wheat, respiratory protection products, printed items, gear drives, electric motors, power transmission components, plastics, precision optics

## Incentive Programs—New and Existing Companies

*Local programs:* The Northeast Council of Governments (NECOG), which serves Northeast South Dakota and is based in Aberdeen, offers a Revolving Loan Fund to fund small businesses, to expand existing businesses, and to create new jobs. One job must be created for each $10,000 loaned. Interest rates are comparable to regional lending institutions. NECOG also helps businesses prepare grant applications for the following: Community Development Block Grants; Consolidated Water Facilities Construction Grants; USDA Rural Development grants and loans; Environmental Protection Agency grants and loans; Economic Development Administration grants and loans; and the Revolving Economic Development and Initiative (REDI) Fund. The Tom & Danielle Aman Business Resource Center (TDABRC) is located in the NECOG offices and provides business information, education, and assistance designed to help entrepreneurs start, operate, and grow their businesses in South Dakota.

*State programs:* The South Dakota MicroLOAN program offers funds of up to $20,000 to qualifying businesses for working capital, equipment, real estate, or other fixed costs. The USDA Business & Industry Guaranteed Loans make funds available for working capital, equipment, buildings, and debt refinancing.

*Job training programs:* The Workforce Development Program provides companies with the money needed to train new and existing employees. Job Service of South Dakota provides training in leadership, customer service, and business. The Aberdeen Area Career Planning Center is designed to assist individuals who have become unemployed and are in need of assistance getting back into the job market. In addition, the Center helps people who are employed but want to make a career change. The Center also provides a variety of services to area employers in an effort to meet their staffing needs with qualified, dependable employees.

## Development Projects

In 2006 manufacturer 3M announced plans to invest $34 million in its Aberdeen facility, in addition to the $12 million invested in 2005. The 3M Aberdeen operation is a world leader in the manufacture of respiratory protection products that are used in homes and workplaces.

As of 2007 the preservation and restoration of the Milwaukee Railroad Depot was taking place. The depot, built in 1881, is a reminder of Aberdeen's history and heritage. Although rebuilt in 1911 after the original structure suffered severe fire damage, the Milwaukee Railroad Depot today has almost all its original architectural features present. The depot was listed on the National Register of Historic Places in 1977 and is the largest brick passenger depot still standing in South Dakota. The depot restoration project is being combined with the creation of a Native American Cultural Center to enhance Aberdeen's downtown area.

*Economic Development Information:* Governor's Office of Economic Development, 711 E. Wells Ave., Pierre, SD 57501; telephone (800)872-6190; email goedinfo@state.sd.us. Aberdeen Development Corporation, 416 Production St. N., Aberdeen, SD 57401; telephone (605)229-5335; toll-free (800)874-9198; fax (605)229-6839; email adc@midco.net

## Commercial Shipping

The Burlington Northern Santa Fe Railway conveys freight and grain through Aberdeen. There are 15 motor carriers operating in Aberdeen.

## Labor Force and Employment Outlook

The following is a summary of data regarding the Aberdeen City metropolitan area labor force, 2006 annual averages.

**Size of nonagricultural labor force:** 13,244

**Number of workers employed in ...**

construction and mining: 1,108
manufacturing: 1,452
trade, transportation and utilities: 368
information: 311
financial activities: 752
professional and business services: 1,020
educational and health services: 3,099
leisure and hospitality: 1,438
other services: 666
government: 2,253

**Average hourly earnings of production workers employed in manufacturing:** Not available

**Unemployment rate:** 2.5% (2005)

| Largest employers (2006) | Number of employees |
|---|---|
| Avera St. Luke's Hospital | 1,272 |
| Aberdeen Public School | 615 |
| 3-M Company | 569 |
| Hub City, Inc. | 405 |
| Cendant Corp. | 375 |
| Northern State University | 310 |
| Midstates/QQP | 275 |
| Wells Fargo Financial | 265 |
| Kessler's Grocery Store | 260 |
| South Dakota Wheat Growers | 250 |
| EAC Educational Services | 110 |

## Cost of Living

The following is a summary of data regarding key cost of living factors for the Aberdeen area.

**2007 (1st quarter) ACCRA Average House Price:** Not available

**2007 (1st quarter) ACCRA Cost of Living Index:** Not available

**State income tax rate:** None

**State sales tax rate:** 4.0%

**Local income tax rate:** None

**Local sales tax rate:** 2.0%

**Property tax rate:** 1.8%

*Economic Information:* Aberdeen Area Chamber of Commerce, 516 S. Main St., Aberdeen, SD 57401; telephone (605)225-2860. Aberdeen Development Corporation, 416 Production St. N., Aberdeen, SD 57401; telephone (605)229-5335; toll-free (800)874-9198; fax (605)229-6839; email adc@midco.net

## ■ Education and Research

### Elementary and Secondary Schools

The Aberdeen School District 6-1 had its founding in 1890. Hub Area Technical School, supported by Aberdeen Central High School, Frederick High School, Northwestern High School, Roncalli High School, and Warner High School, offers the following programs: Automotive Technology, Building Trades, CISCO Academy, Computer Technician Fundamentals, Electronics, Graphic Communications, Health Occupations, Machine Tool Technology, and Radio/TV Production.

The following is a summary of data regarding the Aberdeen Public Schools as of the 2005–2006 school year.

**Total enrollment:** 5,547

**Number of facilities**
elementary schools: 5
junior high/middle schools: 2
senior high schools: 1
other: 1 (technical school)

**Student/teacher ratio:** 13.9:1

**Teacher salaries (2005–06)**
elementary median: $26,000 (base for all levels)
junior high/middle median: Not available
secondary median: Not available

**Funding per pupil:** $6,000

There are a number of private and parochial schools in Aberdeen, including the Roncalli Catholic schools, Aberdeen Christian High School, First Baptist Christian School, Trinity Lutheran School, Dakota School House, and Children House of Montessori.

*Public Schools Information:* Aberdeen School District 6-1, 314 South Main Street, Aberdeen, SD 57401; telephone (605)725-7100; fax (605)725-7199

## Colleges and Universities

Aberdeen is home to Northern State University. Northern State University enrolls nearly 3,000 students from 36 states and 20 foreign countries. NSU offers 38 majors and 42 minors, as well as six associate, eight pre-professional, and nine graduate degree areas.

Presentation College, a Catholic-Christian college sponsored by the Sisters of the Presentation of the Blessed Virgin Mary (PVBM), is a specialty Health Science Baccalaureate institution with a campus in Aberdeen. Presentation College offers 26 different programs through campuses in Aberdeen, Fairmont, and Eagle Butte, as well as virtual programs. Enrollment is approximately 770 students at all campuses and in the virtual programs.

## Libraries and Research Centers

Alexander Mitchell Library, Aberdeen's public library, has in its holdings more than 100,000 books, 2,500 audio materials, nearly 2,500 video materials, and more than 350 serial subscriptions. Andrew Carnegie gave $15,000 to construct the first library building in Aberdeen. Carnegie asked that the library be named for his friend Alexander Mitchell, president of the Chicago, Milwaukee and St. Paul Railroad, who named Aberdeen after his hometown in Scotland.

*Public Library Information:* Alexander Mitchell Library, 519 S. Kline St., Aberdeen, SD 57401; telephone (605)626-7097; email library@aberdeen.sd.us

# ■ Health Care

Avera St. Luke's Hospital was established in 1901 as a 15-bed hospital by the Presentation and Benedictine Sisters. Avera St. Luke's is now a regional medical center offering comprehensive medical and health services to people residing in the ten counties surrounding Aberdeen. In addition to its 137-bed hospital, Avera St. Luke's provides services through Avera Mother Joseph Manor Retirement Community, Avera Eureka Health Care Center, and through its clinic division. Avera St. Luke's employs more than 1,300 people in the hospital, long-term care, and clinic divisions. A medical/dental staff of some 85 local physicians represents 34 different specialties.

Dakota Plains Surgical Center LLP is a short-term hospital with eight beds. Its specialties are hip and knee replacement and back and neck surgery.

*Health Care Information:* Avera St. Luke's Hospital, 305 S. State St., Aberdeen, SD 57401; telephone (605)622-5000; toll-free (800)22-LUKES

# ■ Recreation

## Sightseeing

The Milwaukee Railroad Depot, a downtown landmark of Aberdeen's founding and history, was listed on the National Register of Historic Places in 1977 and is the largest brick passenger depot still standing in South Dakota. It was being restored in 2007.

Aberdeen's claim to fame comes in the person of L. Frank Baum, noted author and resident of Aberdeen from 1888 to 1891, who wrote the timeless children's classic *The Wizard of Oz.* Aberdeen paid homage to Baum by creating Storybook Land, a theme park. Dorothy, Toto, the Scarecrow, Tin Man, and Cowardly Lion greet visitors on a journey down the Yellow Brick Road. There are more than 60 exhibits at Storybook Land, including Captain Hook's Ship, animals at Old MacDonald's Farm, and the Storybook Land Express train. Aberdeen's newest theme park is called the Land of Oz; it is a ten-acre park located just northwest of Storybook Land, featuring a farmstead area with Dorothy's house, a children's petting zoo, Munchkin Land, Scarecrow's house, Tin Man's house, Wicked Witch Castle, and Emerald City. Movies are shown on select summer evenings in Sleeping Beauty's Castle and children's theater productions also are held.

## Arts and Culture

Although Aberdeen is small, it offers a number of interesting artistic and cultural venues and events. The Granary is a cultural center that includes art galleries housed in a renovated granary, a large gazebo, a relocated historic town hall, and park-like grounds. The Aberdeen Community Theater stages ambitious productions throughout the year. There are many theatrical opportunities for children through community theater, touring children's troupes, and outdoor performances at Storybook Land Theater. Aberdeen's Community Concert Association brings nationally recognized musicians to the city. Northern State University offers performances by its faculty and students and sponsors special appearances by well-known musicians. Christmas music lovers look forward to the annual "Living Christmas Tree" concerts. Weekly performances by the community band are held during the summer in Melgaard Park. The Dacotah Prairie Museum features several excellent galleries hosting touring exhibits and artist presentations.

## Festivals and Holidays

Arts in the Park takes place in June in Melgaard Park—it is a weekend of entertainment and artists selling their work in outdoor booths. The Oz festival is also held in June. The Fourth of July is celebrated in Wylie Park. Also in July the Great Aberdeen Pig Out features food vendors, eating contests, musicians, cooking contests, a beer garden, dunk tank, and children's events. The Brown County Fair is held each August. In October, the Pheasant Season Opener takes place and a Haunted Forest is held in Wylie Park and Storybook Land for Halloween. Winterfest is an indoor arts festival that takes place in November. The Downtown Parade of Lights happens right after Thanksgiving and holiday lighting displays are held at Wylie Park through December. Children can visit Santa at the Lakewood Mall throughout the holiday season.

## Sports for the Spectator

Sports fans pack the Brown County Speedway to watch auto racing or wager on Thoroughbred horses. Northern State University fans cheer on the Wolves in NCAA Division II sporting events in the Barnett Center. As of 2007 Presentation College was building its own competitive sports programs in a brand new field house.

## Sports for the Participant

Aberdonians are kept active hunting, fishing, camping, boating, cross-country skiing, bird-watching, biking, snowmobiling, and engaging in many organized team sports. There are excellent public and private golf courses. Sand Lake National Wildlife Refuge, a short drive from the city, is a nationally recognized wildlife sanctuary. Pheasant, duck, and goose hunting draws outdoorsmen from across the country each fall. Some of the finest walleye fishing in the nation is found 90 miles away on the Missouri River's Lake Oahe. There are also many scenic and sizable lakes in the Aberdeen area, including the Mina and Richmond Lakes. The Glacier Lakes region is an hour-long drive away in the rolling hills to the northeast. Aberdeen has an excellent park system, highlighted by Wylie Park, with its swimming lake, water slide, go-carts, mini-golf, campsites, and bike trails.

### Shopping and Dining

Shopping takes place in the Lakewood Mall and in dozens of new shops that have sprung up around the mall in recent years. The mall itself is home to 2 large department stores, a major discount store, and over 40 specialty shops. Downtown Aberdeen is designated as a historic district, with interesting shops and a lively collection of nightspots and restaurants. Along 6th Avenue there are convenience stores, retail chains, grocery stores, and service industries. Throughout the city restaurants offer diverse cuisine in many different settings. From fine dining and impressive wine lists to fast food, deli sandwiches, and family-style fare, all tastes are satisfied.

*Visitor Information:* Aberdeen Convention and Visitors Bureau, 10 Railroad Ave. SW, PO Box 78, Aberdeen, SD 57402-0078; telephone (605)225-2414; toll-free (800)645-3851; fax (605)225-3573; email info@aberdeencvb.com

## ■ Convention Facilities

The Best Western Ramkota Hotel & Convention Center includes a boardroom, lecture hall (with 212 permanent theater-style seats), and indoor courtyard and concourse area for vendor displays. The 10,000-square-foot convention hall seats 1,500 participants or services 1,200 for meals. In addition there are five Dakota Rooms of approximately 5,000 square feet. The Ramada Inn Executive Conference & Convention Center has 7,600 square feet that can comfortably seat up to 1,000 visitors. The center breaks into eight separate meeting rooms along with two executive boardrooms for smaller meetings. The AmericInn Lodge & Suites Event Center can accommodate meetings of up to 250 people. A 40-person board room and a breakfast area are also available and can be reserved for smaller functions. The Joseph H. Barnett Center, an athletic-education complex on the campus of Northern State University, is available for large functions, offering seating for several thousand. The Holum Expo building, located at the Brown County Fairgrounds, is a popular location for trade shows. There are also several other buildings,

stock barns, and a grandstand at the fairgrounds that can be used for events.

*Convention Information:* Aberdeen Convention and Visitors Bureau, 10 Railroad Ave. SW, PO Box 78, Aberdeen, SD 57402-0078; telephone (605)225-2414; toll-free (800)645-3851; fax (605)225-3573; email info@aberdeencvb.com

## ■ Transportation

### Approaching the City

Aberdeen Regional Airport is served by Mesaba Airlines, operating as a Northwest Airlink affiliate under agreement with Northwest Airlines. Service is offered to Denver International Airport and Minneapolis-St. Paul International Airport.

US Route 281 runs north-south and US Route 12 runs east-west. US-12 becomes 6th Avenue in Aberdeen.

### Traveling in the City

Aberdeen is laid out in a grid pattern. Jefferson Lines offers bus service from Aberdeen to Fargo, North Dakota, and Minneapolis, Minnesota.

## ■ Communications

### Newspapers and Magazines

*The Aberdeen American News* is Aberdeen's daily newspaper. The Farm Forum Online is affiliated with the newspaper.

### Television and Radio

KDSD TV 16 is Aberdeen's PBS television station. Three AM and three FM radio stations provide news, talk radio, country, rock, and adult contemporary music.

*Media Information:* *The Aberdeen American News*, 124 S. 2nd St., PO Box 4430, Aberdeen, SD 57402; telephone (605)225-4100; toll-free (800)925-4100; email americannews@aberdeennews.com

### Aberdeen Online

*The Aberdeen American News.* Available www .aberdeennews.com

Aberdeen Area Chamber of Commerce. Available www.aberdeen-chamber.com

Aberdeen Convention and Visitors Bureau. Available www.aberdeencvb.com

Aberdeen Downtown Association. Available www .aberdeendowntown.org

Aberdeen Public Schools. Available www.aberdeen
.k12.sd.us
Alexander Mitchell Public Library. Available www
.ampl.sdln.net
City of Aberdeen. Available www.aberdeen.sd.us
Northeast Council of Governments. Available www
.abe.midco.net/necog

BIBLIOGRAPHY

Hoover, Herbert T., and Larry J. Zimmerman, *South Dakota Leaders: From Pierre Choteau, Jr. to Oscar Howe* (Vermillion, SD: University of South Dakota Press, 1989)

# Pierre

## ■ The City in Brief

**Founded:** 1880 (incorporated 1883)

**Head Official:** Mayor Dennis Eisnach (since 2002)

**City Population**
- 1980: 11,973
- 1990: 12,906
- 2000: 13,876
- 2006 estimate: 14,095
- Percent change, 1990–2000: 2.7%
- U.S. rank in 1980: Not available
- U.S. rank in 1990: 1,963rd
- U.S. rank in 2000: Not available (State rank: 7th)

**Metropolitan Area Population**
- 1980: 14,244
- 1990: 14,814
- 2000: 16,416
- 2006 estimate: 19,761
- Percent change, 1990–2000: 9%
- U.S. rank in 1980: Not available
- U.S. rank in 1990: Not available
- U.S. rank in 2000: Not available

**Area:** 13.01 square miles (2000)

**Elevation:** 1,484 feet above sea level

**Average Annual Temperature:** 44° F

**Average Annual Precipitation:** 16.8 inches of rain; 40 inches of snow

**Major Economic Sectors:** Finance, insurance, real estate, trade

**Unemployment Rate:** 3.7% (March 2005, South Dakota)

**Per Capita Income:** $20,462 (1999)

**2005 FBI Crime Index Property:** Not available

**2005 FBI Crime Index Violent:** Not available

**Major Colleges and Universities:** Capital University Center

**Daily Newspaper:** *Capital Journal*

## ■ Introduction

Pierre (pronounced peer) is the seat of Hughes County and the second smallest capital city in the United States. Pierre is located on the east bank of the Missouri River in central South Dakota. Pierre is the administrative center of South Dakota and a major distribution point for the area's agricultural concerns. Except for the winter months each year, when the legislature is in session, Pierre remains a sleepy small town with a beautifully restored state capitol building.

## ■ Geography and Climate

Pierre is located in the center of South Dakota on the Missouri River, 105 miles west of Huron, South Dakota, and 2 miles from the geographical center of the United States.

Seventy percent of the time, the skies over Pierre are clear and visibility is more than forty-five miles. Like the rest of the state, Pierre has cold winters, warm to hot summers, light moisture in the winter, and moderate moisture in the summer.

**Area:** 13.01 square miles (2000)

**Elevation:** 1,484 feet above sea level

**Average Annual Temperature:** 44° F

**Average Annual Precipitation:** 16.8 inches of rain; 40 inches of snow

# ■ History

## Early History and Exploration by Whites

The first white men to see the Pierre area were the two LaVerendrye brothers. They were the sons of the French explorer who first claimed the region for France in 1743, Pierre Gaultier de Varennes. At the site above present-day Fort Pierre, South Dakota, at one of the bluffs above the Missouri River, the brothers left an inscribed lead plate, which thereafter lay covered until found by a group of children in 1913. The plate is now on display at the South Dakota Cultural Heritage Center in Pierre.

In the mid-eighteenth century, the Sioux Indians, who had been pushed out of Minnesota by the Chippewa, arrived at the Missouri River. Their arrival challenged the claim of the Arikara, the native people who lived in palisaded forts around present-day Pierre. In 1794, the battle for control of central South Dakota finally came to an end when the Sioux drove the Arikara from the area.

In 1803, the United States completed the Louisiana Purchase from France, which included the area that would later be named South Dakota. In September 1804, Meriwether Lewis and William Clark anchored their canoe at the site of present-day Pierre. During that time, Lewis and Clark met with 50 or more chiefs and warriors, including the Teton Sioux. They named the nearby river Teton, in honor of the tribe, but it is now called the Bad River.

The meeting started out badly but negotiations soon improved when the explorers and the Indians shared a feast of buffalo meat, corn, pemmican, and a potato dish. After all present smoked a peace pipe, the explorers continued their journey upriver. During their visit to the Pierre area, Lewis and Clark raised the United States flag there.

## City is Established

When the explorers returned to St. Louis in 1806, they described the streams full of beaver and grasslands full of buffalo, and they noted the lack of trading forts in the Pierre area. Their report soon attracted people interested in exploiting the riches of the region.

In 1817, Joseph LaFramboise built a fur trading post across the river from where Pierre now sits. In 1831, a representative of the American Fur Company, Pierre Chouteau, Jr., built Fort Pierre to replace the old LaFramboise trading post. In 1855, the U.S. Army bought Fort Pierre for use as a military post, but abandoned it two years later in favor of nearby Fort Randall. Even after the army departed, people continued to live at the site of Fort Pierre.

In 1861, the Dakota Territory was formally established. Once the railroad line made South Dakota more accessible, settlers began to pour in, causing the Great Dakota Boom of 1878-1887. During that period, in 1880, the new town of Pierre began as a ferry landing at the site of a railroad terminal, across the river from Fort Pierre on what was formerly Arikara Indian tribal grounds. Rapid growth ceased when droughts struck throughout South Dakota, bringing the period of prosperity to a quick end. On February 22, 1889, South Dakota entered the union as the 40th state.

## Pierre Chosen as Capital

The period from 1889 to 1897 saw development slowed by a depressed national economy, a time known in South Dakota as the Great Dakota Bust. The number of new settlers greatly declined and some who had moved to Pierre and the rest of the state departed. But by the late 1890s, the state and the nation began to recover.

In 1890 Pierre was made the capitol of South Dakota after a drawn-out political battle between its supporters and supporters of the town of Mitchell, which was situated further east and nearer to the bulk of the state's population. In the end, however, Pierre won a statewide vote by a large margin.

In 1908 the cornerstone for the new capitol was set down, and the Capitol Building in Pierre opened its doors in 1910. As state government grew, the building expanded and separate office buildings were constructed. The original structure still stands today as part of the capitol complex.

## Pierre in the Twentieth Century

During the 1930s, South Dakotans faced not only the Great Depression but severe problems caused by drought and dust. Many jobs were created for Pierre citizens by the Civilian Conservation Corps and other government agencies.

In 1944, the U.S. Congress passed legislation that resulted in the construction of the Oahe Dam near Pierre, which still serves the region. In 1949 a terrible blizzard struck the area, and the railroad line from Pierre to Rapid City, South Dakota, was blocked for weeks. A 1952 flood of the Missouri River caused severe damage to the town of Pierre but it was not destroyed, making clear to the citizens of Pierre the wisdom of the Oahe Dam building project. The project remains controversial among the Cheyenne River Sioux, who believe land was taken from them illegally for the dam construction.

The dam, the largest of six Missouri River dams and one of the largest dams in the world, has a generating capacity of 700,000 kilowatts. Along with the other dams on the Missouri River in South Dakota, it generates more than 2 million kilowatts of electricity. Other benefits of the dam include expanded recreation areas, irrigation,

The State Capitol building in Pierre. ©*James Blank.*

increased public water supplies, and fish and wildlife development.

During the wintertime, Pierre is abuzz with activity, as legislators from various parts of the state meet for three months to decide issues of state government. The rest of the year, Pierre is a quiet tourist town and farming center. In recent years, Pierre has invested millions of dollars in projects that benefit businesses and the community.

***Historical Information:*** The South Dakota State Historical Society, 900 Governors Drive, Pierre, SD 57501; telephone (605)773-3458; fax (605)773-6041

# ■ Population Profile

## Metropolitan Area Residents

1980: 14,244
1990: 14,814
2000: 16,416
2006 estimate: 19,761
Percent change, 1990–2000: 9%
U.S. rank in 1980: Not available
U.S. rank in 1990: Not available
U.S. rank in 2000: Not available

## City Residents

1980: 11,973
1990: 12,906
2000: 13,876
2006 estimate: 14,095
Percent change, 1990–2000: 2.7%
U.S. rank in 1980: Not available
U.S. rank in 1990: 1,963rd
U.S. rank in 2000: Not available (State rank: 7th)

**Density:** 9.9 people per square mile (2000, South Dakota state figure)

## Racial and ethnic characteristics (2000)

White: 12,337
Black: 28
American Indian and Alaska Native: 1,188
Asian: 64
Native Hawaiian and Pacific Islander: 3
Hispanic or Latino (may be of any race): 173
Other: 40

**Percent of residents born in state:** 74.8% (2000)

## Age characteristics (2000)

Population under 5 years old: 909

Population 5 to 9 years old: 954
Population 10 to 14 years old: 1,208
Population 15 to 19 years old: 1,023
Population 20 to 24 years old: 583
Population 25 to 34 years old: 1,716
Population 35 to 44 years old: 2,248
Population 45 to 54 years old: 2,076
Population 55 to 59 years old: 699
Population 60 to 64 years old: 505
Population 65 to 74 years old: 913
Population 75 to 84 years old: 680
Population 85 years and older: 362
Median age: 37.6 years

**Births (2006, Micropolitan Statistical Area)**

Total number: 243

**Deaths (2006, Micropolitan Statistical Area)**

Total number: 134

**Money income (1999)**

Per capita income: $20,462
Median household income: $42,962
Total households: 5,949

**Number of households with income of...**

less than $10,000: 431
$10,000 to $14,999: 301
$15,000 to $24,999: 745
$25,000 to $34,999: 835
$35,000 to $49,999: 1,070
$50,000 to $74,999: 1,276
$75,000 to $99,999: 522
$100,000 to $149,999: 249
$150,000 to $199,999: 96
$200,000 or more: 79

**Percent of families below poverty level:** 5.5% (1999)

**2005 FBI Crime Index Property:** Not available

**2005 FBI Crime Index Violent:** Not available

# ■ Municipal Government

Pierre is the seat of Hughes County and the state capital of South Dakota. The city has a mayor-commission form of government. Its five commissioners, including the mayor, serve three-year terms.

**Head Official:** Mayor Dennis Eisnach (since 2002; current term expires 2008)

**Total Number of City Employees:** 140 (2007)

*City Information:* Mayor's Office, 222 E. Dakota Ave., Pierre, SD 57501; telephone (605)773-7341; fax (605)773-7406

# ■ Economy

## Major Industries and Commercial Activity

Pierre serves as the major trading center for central South Dakota. Its economy is supported by government, agriculture, and recreational activities tied in with the Missouri River reservoirs. Pierre's retail area has a radius of 100 miles and comprises approximately 100,000 people. Nearby lakes Oahe and Sharpe, both reservoirs on the Missouri River, make it possible for Pierre businesses to enjoy low electric rates and abundant water for production processes.

Pierre's economy depends largely on the state government, which has its operations in the city and is the largest local employer. The largest private employer is St. Mary's Hospital, with 452 employees. Small businesses and tourism are the remaining sources of jobs and income. Tourism was spurred by the lakes created by the Missouri Basin Development Plan.

Agriculture remains an important part of the economy of Hughes County, home to 215 farms with farmhouses and 168 farms with no dwelling for a total of 415,151 taxable acres. The principal crops in the area are wheat, rye, oats, wild hay, flax, corn, barley, mint, soy beans, and alfalfa. Farmers raise cattle, chickens, hogs, buffalo, and horses, and produce eggs and milk.

**Items and goods produced:** assembly metal works, water conditioners, helicopters, dairy products, bottled beverages, wheat, corn, barley, processed furs

## Incentive Programs—New and Existing Companies

*Local programs:* Development assistance and financing programs are offered by the Pierre Economic Development Corporation (PEDCO) and the Economic Development Administration. Free business consultation and a local revolving loan fund have helped dozens of new businesses get started and older ones to expand. PEDCO also works with business owners contemplating selling their businesses, and offers a free office and manufacturing space database to help in finding locations for businesses. E-commerce is well supported through seminars and other programs. The Small Business Administration Development Center helps with business plan development, market surveys, cash flow projections, and financing options.

*State programs:* The South Dakota MicroLOAN program offers funds of up to $20,000 to qualifying businesses for working capital, equipment, real estate, or other fixed costs. The USDA Business & Industry Guaranteed Loans make funds available for working capital, equipment, buildings, and debt refinancing.

*Job training programs:* The Workforce Development Program provides companies with the money needed to train new and existing employees. Job Service of South Dakota and Capital University Center provide training in leadership, customer service, and business. The Capital University Center offers short-term training and certificate programs to meet the needs of businesses in central South Dakota. The Right Turn, a career learning center, offers programs to help individuals train for employment; programs include GED preparation and testing, the Alternative High School program, medical transcription, clerical/computer skills, a basic skills brush-up class, career/education counseling, and job search assistance.

## Development Projects

Building projects that have been completed since the beginning of the new century include dedication of the $3.9-million Aquatic Center, the opening of a 72,000-square-foot distribution center for Running Supply Inc., and a $2-million city golf course renovation. On top of the recent $11-million addition to Saint Mary's Healthcare Center, a $12 million-expansion to include a new area for transitional care, kidney dialysis and rehabilitation was completed in 2004. Futher development was taking place at Saint Mary's in 2007, with completion scheduled for 2009. The four-lane Pierre-to-Interstate connection has been expanded. A new soccer complex also held its first statewide tournaments in 2007.

*Economic Development Information:* Pierre Economic Development Corporation (PEDCO), 800 W. Dakota Ave., Pierre, SD 57501; telephone (605)224-6610; toll-free (800)962-2034

## Commercial Shipping

In addition to the Pierre Municipal Airport, the city is served by numerous trucking companies and package service is provided by Federal Express, United Parcel Service, DHL, and Airborne Express. The Dakota, Minnesota & Eastern Railroad also serves the city.

## Labor Force and Employment Outlook

Well-known for its superb labor force, the Greater Pierre area has a labor force of approximately 14,000 people, and they have among the highest educational level in the state. The area has a good balance of skilled, semi-skilled, technical, and entry-level workers.

The South Dakota Department of Labor affirms that the fastest growing industries in the state are health care and social assistance, followed by accommodation and food services, finance and insurance, and construction. Industries that are declining on a statewide basis include

local government positions, manufacturing, agriculture, forestry, fishing and hunting.

The following is a summary of data regarding the Pierre metropolitan area labor force, 2005 annual averages.

**Size of nonagricultural labor force:** 13,430

**Number of workers employed in . . .**

construction and mining: 750
manufacturing: 100
trade, transportation and utilities: 2,575
information: 185
financial activities: 680
professional and business services: 535
educational and health services: 1,360
leisure and hospitality: 1,590
other services: 725
government: 4,930

**Average hourly earnings of production workers employed in manufacturing:** Not available

**Unemployment rate:** 3.7% (March 2005, South Dakota)

| *Largest employers (2006)* | *Number of employees* |
|---|---|
| State Government | 2,300 |
| St. Mary's Hospital | 452 |
| Wal-Mart | 350 |
| Pierre School District | 350 |
| Federal Government | 240 |
| Morris Inc. | 170 |
| City of Pierre | 135 |
| Medical Associates Clinic | 135 |
| BankWest | 131 |
| Pierre Indian Learning Center | 112 |
| Lynn's Dakotamart | 82 |

## Cost of Living

The following is a summary of data regarding several key cost of living factors for the Pierre area.

**2007 (1st quarter) ACCRA Average House Price:** Not available

**2007 (1st quarter) ACCRA Cost of Living Index:** Not available

**State income tax rate:** None

**State sales tax rate:** 4.0%

**Local income tax rate:** None

**Local sales tax rate:** 2.0% (plus 1.0% on hotel/motel, restaurant, and liquor establishments; food and drugs are exempt)

**Property tax rate:** $3.71 per $1,000 of assessed valuation, city of Pierre, plus $23.53 per $1,000, Hughes County and schools (2001)

*Economic Information:* Pierre Area Chamber of Commerce, PO Box 548, 800 West Dakota Ave., Pierre, SD 57501; telephone (605)224-7361; fax (605)224-6485; toll-free (800)962-2034; email contactchamber@pierre.org

# ■ Education and Research

## Elementary and Secondary Schools

The Pierre School District has always held itself to high academic standards and the community has long been a source of support for its schools. The school district has a computer education program that has become a model for the state and region, and features networked computer labs in all buildings. Increased communication through the use of the Oahe Cable Channel by airing drama, chorus, band performances, and activities and lessons is a current focus of the district. Riggs High School hosts adult education classes and is home to the Community Concert Series and the Short Grass Arts Council. Pierre Public Schools currently partners with the Capital University Center providing classrooms and technology. The Pierre Education Foundation provides financial support via grants for innovative Pierre educators. A cooperative spirit with the community of Pierre flourishes through several programs including: Right Turn, Advanced High, Character Education, Youth to Youth, Junior Achievement, Reading Buddies, the Mentorship Program for Students at Risk, Fine Arts and Athletic Booster Clubs, and Native American Liaison.

The following is a summary of data regarding the Pierre School District as of the 2005–2006 school year.

**Total enrollment:** 3,147

**Number of facilities**

elementary schools: 4
junior high/middle schools: 1
senior high schools: 1
other: 0

**Student/teacher ratio:** 15:1

**Teacher salaries (2005–06)**

elementary median: $32,414 (all levels)
junior high/middle median: Not available
secondary median: Not available

**Funding per pupil:** $6,081

Pierre also has a Catholic elementary school, an Indian Learning Center, and an alternative education program operated in conjunction with The Right Turn, a career learning center.

*Public Schools Information:* Pierre Public Schools, 211 South Poplar Ave., Pierre, SD 57501; telephone (605)773-7300; fax (605)773-7304

## Colleges and Universities

While Pierre is not the site of any colleges or universities, it does boast the Capital University Center. This nonprofit institution helps students earn university degrees through Northern State University, South Dakota State University, the University of South Dakota, and South Dakota School of Mines & Technology. The center offers courses that enable students to obtain associate's degrees in business and master's degrees in business administration, industrial management, and technology management.

## Libraries and Research Centers

The R.E. Rawlins Municipal Library, which celebrated 100 years in 2003, contains over 43,000 books and has special collections on the history of South Dakota. The library has complete collections of periodicals and records, talking books, large print books, cassettes, compact discs, videos, and artwork. A story hour and other programs are offered for children. Meeting rooms and computers are available for public use. The South Dakota State Library houses more than 170,000 volumes, with special collections on Native American and South Dakota history.

Other libraries in the city include those of the South Dakota State Historical Society, the South Dakota Supreme Court, St. Mary's Healthcare Center, the South Dakota Braille & Talking Book Library, and the South Dakota Department of Game, Fish & Parks Wildlife Division Library.

*Public Library Information:* Rawlins Municipal Library, 1000 E. Church St., Pierre, SD 57501; telephone (605)773-7421; fax (605)773-7423

# ■ Health Care

Pierre is served by Saint Mary's Healthcare Center, a 60-bed acute care facility. The center's north building facility includes a laboratory, expanded radiology lab, and an obstetrics unit with home-like labor, delivery, and recovery rooms. Services at St. Mary's include medical, surgical, pediatrics, obstetrics, ambulatory care, home health care, and Countryside Hospice, as well as a variety of specialties.

*Health Care Information:* Saint Mary's Healthcare Center, 801 E. Sioux Ave, Pierre, SD 57501; telephone (605)224-3100

# ■ Recreation

## Sightseeing

A must-see for Pierre visitors is the beautiful 1910 State Capitol, one of the most fully restored in the nation. Its rotunda reaches 96 feet and features a brightly colored Victorian glass top. Pillars flank the marble staircase and the terrazzo tile floor includes 66 blue tiles, each representing one of the artisans who worked on laying it by hand. Finishing touches are provided by marble water fountains and brass door fixtures, art murals and sculptures. Out on the capitol grounds is a fountain fed by an artesian well with a natural gas content so high it can be lit. The glowing fountain serves as a memorial to war veterans.

At the Cultural Heritage Center, South Dakota history is brought to life through museum exhibits and publications, educational programming and research services. High-tech exhibits feature early Native American cultures, an early history of white settlement, the river boat era, and the railroad period. Among the Native American exhibits are a teepee visitors can walk through, a rare Sioux horse effigy, and a full headdress. The Verendrye Museum in Fort Pierre, across the river from the city, provides an eclectic display of exhibits and items of historical interest.

The Discovery Center and Aquarium is a hands-on display of 50 self-guided science activities in the areas of sound, vision, light, electricity, and motion. Its Aquatic Education wing has three aquariums featuring Missouri River fish. The planetarium provides a look at the skies overhead.

The South Dakota National Guard Museum displays a wide range of military weapons and other items such as an A-7D jet fighter plane, a Sherman tank and several artillery pieces, military uniforms, small arms, and helicopter and jet engines.

Six miles north of Pierre, tours of the Oahe Dam are available. The dam is the second largest rolled-earth dam in the world. A visit to the Oahe Dam and Powerhouse and Oahe Visitor Center, dedicated in 1962, tells the story of the dam and has displays on such topics as the Lewis and Clark Expedition and the dam itself. On this site is the Oahe Chapel, removed from its original site at the old Arikara Indian Village, which was flooded when the dam was built.

## Arts and Culture

Pierre Players, the longest running community theater group in South Dakota, offers productions throughout the year. The Pierre Concert Series presents a variety of musical and dance productions by professional touring troupes. Canvasbacks is a local group of artists. Nightwriters, a group of writers and poets, and many other talented local artists live in the Pierre area.

## Festivals and Holidays

September activities in Pierre center on statewide softball tournaments held in the city and Goosefest, an outdoor festival that features a South Dakota Arts Showcase, craft and Native American pottery and food booths, and Lewis and Clark reenactments. October brings the Native American Day festival and the Annual Governor's Hunt. The holidays are heralded by the Pierre Players' Christmas Pageant and the Capitol Christmas Tree display. June's many events include the Oahe Days and Arts Festival, softball tournaments, band concerts, and concerts in the parks. July is highlighted by the Independence Day celebration, including a rodeo and parade, baseball and softball tournaments, concerts, summer theater, and the Governor's Cup Walleye Tournament. August is enlivened by the 4-H Rodeo and the three-day Riverfest Festival, which features music; water ski, car, and air shows; water events; and a kids' carnival.

## Sports for the Spectator

Pierre's Expo Center features indoor hockey and skating events. In nearby Fort Pierre, pari-mutuel horse racing is offered in the springtime; rodeos and stock shows are also held there.

## Sports for the Participant

Farm Island and the La Framboise Island offer such activities as biking, hiking, camping, and wildlife observation. Pierre maintains 285.5 acres of attractive parkland for residents and visitors. Pierre's city parks system boasts 11 tennis courts, 8 softball fields, 3 baseball fields, a beach volleyball court, a Frisbee course, a soccer complex, a hockey arena, ice skating rink, basketball courts, football stadium, horseshoe pits, 2 swimming beaches, indoor and outdoor swimming pools, a band concert shell, an assortment of playground equipment, fishing piers, pony league field, and 20 miles of walking, biking, and hiking trails. Griffin Park, the major park area with 32 acres, is located in a riverside setting and has a swimming pool, tennis courts, boating, fishing, playground equipment, and newly renovated camping facilities. Pierre also owns an 18-hole, 72-par municipal golf course located one mile east of the city.

Five miles upstream from Pierre, Lake Oahe's 2,250-mile shoreline offers swimming, boating, water skiing, scuba diving, snorkeling, camping and picnicking. Anglers come to Lake Oahe in search of a variety of sport fish, including walleye, northern pike, Chinook salmon, channel catfish, small mouth bass, white bass, sauger, bluegill, and crappies. Public hunting grounds offer excellent waterfowl and upland game hunting, featuring

Canada geese, mallards, pheasants, and grouse. Whitetail and mule deer and antelope also abound, offering challenges to the big game hunter. Knowledgeable guides and game lodges are available to provide enjoyable and successful hunting experiences.

## Shopping and Dining

The city's main shopping center is the 34-store Pierre Mall, which is anchored by JCPenney, Sears, and Kmart. There is also a Wal-Mart in the city.

Pierre's variety of restaurants primarily offer American cuisine and include Mad Mary's Steakhouse, McClelland's Restaurant, Pier 347, the Longbranch Restaurant and Lounge, and Jake's Good Times Place.

*Visitor Information:* Pierre Convention & Visitors Bureau, 800 West Dakota Ave., Pierre, SD 57501; telephone (605)224-7361

## ■ Convention Facilities

Pierre is the meeting headquarters for many South Dakota organizations. The King's Inn Hotel and Conference Center and the Rivercenter Best Western Ramkota Convention Center are two hotels with the largest meeting facilities. In total Pierre has 30 meeting rooms in 6 facilities that can accommodate any size group from 20 to 1,900. Pierre completed a $3.4-million convention center located on the waterfront in 1987. This 30,000-square-foot development includes a banquet hall, meeting rooms, two "state of the art" amphitheaters, and exhibit space. Fifteen motels with 974 rooms are available to serve the visiting tourist, sportsman, or businessperson.

*Convention Information:* Pierre Convention & Visitors Bureau, 800 West Dakota Ave., Pierre, SD 57501; telephone (605)224-7361; toll-free (800)962-2034

## ■ Transportation

### Approaching the City

The Pierre Regional Airport, located three miles from central Pierre, includes offices and boarding and baggage terminals. It is served by Mesaba (a Northwest Airlink), Capital Air Carrier, and Great Lakes Aviation. Greyhound offers bus transportation.

### Traveling in the City

U.S. Highway 148 runs north and south through Pierre, connecting State Highway 34 that runs east and west and U.S. Highway 14/83 that extends eastward to Pierre from Ft. Pierre and turns north, then northeast as it runs through the city of Pierre. Other main streets are Missouri, Dakota, and Sioux avenues, which run east and west, and Capitol, Nicolett, and Broadway avenues, which surround the State Capitol Building.

## ■ Communications

### Newspapers and Magazines

The *Capital Journal* is Pierre's daily paper; *The Times* appears weekly, and there are two weekly trade papers: *The Farmer & Rancher Exchange* and the *Reminder Plus.* Local magazines include *Dakota Outdoors* and the *South Dakota High Liner.* The journal *South Dakota History* covers the history of the Northern Great Plains.

### Television and Radio

Pierre is served by some 20 radio stations. Pierre also has a local PBS television station.

*Media Information:* *Capital Journal,* 333 W. Dakota, PO Box 878, Pierre, SD 57501; telephone (605) 224-7301; fax (605)224-9210

### Pierre Online

*Capitol Journal.* Available www.capjournal.com

Pierre Area Chamber of Commerce. Available www .pierre.org

Pierre Convention & Visitors Bureau. Available www.pierre.org

Pierre Economic Development Corporation. Available www.pedco.biz

Rawlins Municipal Library. Available www.rpllib .sdln.net

BIBLIOGRAPHY

Hoover, Herbert T., and Larry J. Zimmerman, *South Dakota Leaders: From Pierre Choteau, Jr. to Oscar Howe* (Vermillion, SD: University of South Dakota Press, 1989)

Jensen, Delwin, *Fort Pierre-Deadwood Trail* (Pierre, SD: State Publishing Company, 1989)

# Rapid City

## ■ The City in Brief

**Founded:** 1876 (incorporated 1882)

**Head Official:** Mayor Alan Hanks (since 2007)

**City Population**

> 1980: 46,492
> 1990: 54,523
> 2000: 59,607
> 2006 estimate: 62,715
> Percent change, 1990–2000: 8.1%
> U.S. rank in 1980: Not available
> U.S. rank in 1990: 445th
> U.S. rank in 2000: 472nd

**Metropolitan Area Population**

> 1980: 70,361
> 1990: 81,343
> 2000: 88,565
> 2006 estimate: 118,763
> Percent change, 1990–2000: 8.9%
> U.S. rank in 1980: 276th
> U.S. rank in 1990: Not available
> U.S. rank in 2000: 222nd

**Area:** 45 square miles (2000)

**Elevation:** 3,200 feet above sea level

**Average Annual Temperatures:** January, 22.4° F; July, 71.7° F; annual average, 46.6° F

**Average Annual Precipitation:** 16.64 inches of rain; 39.7 inches of snow

**Major Economic Sectors:** Agriculture, wholesale and retail trade, services, government

**Unemployment Rate:** 2.6% (June 2007)

**Per Capita Income:** $19,445 (1999)

**2005 FBI Crime Index Property:** 2,551

**2005 FBI Crime Index Violent:** 257

**Major Colleges and Universities:** South Dakota School of Mines and Technology, Western Dakota Technical Institute, National American University

**Daily Newspaper:** *Rapid City Journal*

## ■ Introduction

Rapid City, the seat of Pennington County, is a diverse and thriving small Midwestern city that refers to itself as "The Star of the West." Tourists are drawn to the area, which was celebrated in the 1990 award-winning film *Dances With Wolves,* to see the presidents' busts carved into Mount Rushmore and to visit the Black Hills. The city enjoys a thriving economy based on the farmers who have been raising beans, wheat, and alfalfa since the turn of the last century. A regional center for retail shopping and medical facilities, the city is home to the South Dakota School of Mines and Technology as well as Ellsworth Air Force Base. Seven percent of Rapid City's population is made up of Native Americans whose arts and crafts abound in the city's shops. Locals like to say that the city has the quality of life of a small town with the business and cultural benefits of a city.

## ■ Geography and Climate

Rapid City, the natural eastern gateway to the great growing empire known as the West River Region, is surrounded by contrasting land forms. The forested Black Hills rise immediately west of the city, while the other three edges of the city look out on the prairie. Protected by the 6,000- to 7,000-foot peaks of the Black Hills, Rapid City enjoys an enviable climate, free of the icy blizzards and scorching summers typical of much of the rest of the Dakotas. Summers are warm but dry and autumn is noted for its delightful "Indian summer" weather. Mild, sunny days are common throughout the winter and occasional "chinook" or warm winds frequently follow a stint of snowy weather. Spring is characterized by wide variations in temperature and occasionally some wet snowfall. Low humidity levels, infrequent precipitation, and northwesterly winds prevail in the city.

**Area:** 45 square miles (2000)

**Elevation:** 3,200 feet above sea level

**Average Temperatures:** January, 22.4° F; July, 71.7° F; annual average, 46.6° F

**Average Annual Precipitation:** 16.64 inches of rain; 39.7 inches of snow

# ■ History

## New City Becomes Regional Trade Center

The discovery of gold in 1874 brought an influx of settlers into the Black Hills region of South Dakota. Rapid City was founded in 1876 by a group of disappointed miners, who promoted their new city as the "Gateway to the Black Hills." John Brennan and Samuel Scott, with a small group of men, laid out the site of the present Rapid City, which was named for the spring-fed Rapid Creek that flows through it. A square mile was measured off and the six blocks in the center were designated as a business section. Committees were appointed to bring in prospective merchants and their families to locate in the new settlement. Although it began as a hay camp, the city soon began selling supplies to miners and pioneers. By 1900 Rapid City had survived a boom and bust and was establishing itself as an important regional trade center.

## Tourism and the Military Spur Economy

The invention of the automobile brought tourists to the Black Hills. Gutzon Borglum, the famous sculptor, began work on Mount Rushmore in 1927, and his son, Lincoln Borglum continued the carving of the presidents' faces in rock following his father's death. The massive sculpture was completed in 1938. Although tourism sustained the city throughout the Great Depression of the 1930s, the gas rationing of World War II had a devastating effect on the tourist industry in the town.

The city benefited greatly from the opening of Ellsworth Air Force Base, an Army Air Corps base. As a result, the population of the area nearly doubled between 1940 and 1948, from almost 14,000 to nearly 27,000 people. Military families and civilian personnel soon took every available living space in town, and mobile parks

proliferated. Rapid City businesses profited from the military payroll.

## Rapid City Since Mid-Century

In 1949 city officials envisioned the city as a retail and wholesale trade center for the region and designed a plan for growth that focused on a civic center, more downtown parking places, new schools, and paved streets. A construction boom continued into the 1950s. Growth slowed in the 1960s, but the worst natural disaster in Rapid City's history led to another building boom a decade later. On June 9, 1972, heavy rains caused massive flooding of the Rapid Creek. More than 200 people lost their lives and more than $100 million in property was destroyed.

The devastation of the flood and the outpouring of private donations and millions of dollars in federal aid led to the completion of one big part of the 1949 plan—clearing the area along the Rapid Creek and making it a public park. New homes and businesses were constructed to replace those that had been destroyed. Rushmore Plaza Civic Center and a new Central High School were built in part of the area that had been cleared. In 1978, Rushmore Mall was built, adding to the city's position as a retail shopping center.

In recent times, Rapid City has been highly rated for its manufacturing climate. A hardworking labor force and a governmental structure deeply rooted in the concept of being a partner in the success of its business community remain major assets. The city offers an extraordinary quality of life with abundant recreational activities, culture, and short workplace commutes. Recent city development efforts show a continued vision for improvement and growth in the area.

# ■ Population Profile

## Metropolitan Area Residents

1980: 70,361
1990: 81,343
2000: 88,565
2006 estimate: 118,763
Percent change, 1990–2000: 8.9%
U.S. rank in 1980: 276th
U.S. rank in 1990: Not available
U.S. rank in 2000: 222nd

## City Residents

1980: 46,492
1990: 54,523
2000: 59,607
2006 estimate: 62,715
Percent change, 1990–2000: 8.1%
U.S. rank in 1980: Not available

©Roger Bickel/Mira.com/drr.net

U.S. rank in 1990: 445th
U.S. rank in 2000: 472nd

**Density:** 1,336.7 people per square mile (2000)

**Racial and ethnic characteristics (2000)**

White: 50,266
Black: 579
American Indian and Alaska Native: 6,046
Asian: 594
Native Hawaiian and Pacific Islander: 35
Hispanic or Latino (may be of any race): 1,650
Other: 434

**Percent of residents born in state:** 58% (2000)

**Age characteristics (2000)**

Population under 5 years old: 4,169
Population 5 to 9 years old: 3,973
Population 10 to 14 years old: 4,309
Population 15 to 19 years old: 4,654
Population 20 to 24 years old: 5,009
Population 25 to 34 years old: 7,866
Population 35 to 44 years old: 9,259
Population 45 to 54 years old: 7,768

Population 55 to 59 years old: 2,533
Population 60 to 64 years old: 2,179
Population 65 to 74 years old: 4,017
Population 75 to 84 years old: 2,781
Population 85 years and older: 1,090
Median age: 34.8 years

**Births (2006, MSA)**

Total number: 1,863

**Deaths (2006, MSA)**

Total number: 914

**Money income (1999)**

Per capita income: $19,445
Median household income: $35,978
Total households: 23,969

**Number of households with income of . . .**

less than $10,000: 2,291
$10,000 to $14,999: 1,625
$15,000 to $24,999: 4,080
$25,000 to $34,999: 3,765
$35,000 to $49,999: 4,537
$50,000 to $74,999: 4,263

$75,000 to $99,999: 1,782
$100,000 to $149,999: 1,057
$150,000 to $199,999: 266
$200,000 or more: 366

**Percent of families below poverty level:** 14.1% (1999)

**2005 FBI Crime Index Property:** 2,551

**2005 FBI Crime Index Violent:** 257

# ■ Municipal Government

Rapid City has a mayor-council form of government with an elected, full-time mayor and two part-time council members from each of the city's five wards, who are elected to staggered two-year terms. All positions are non-partisan.

**Head Official:** Mayor Alan Hanks (since 2007; current term expires 2009)

**Total Number of City Employees:** approximately 700 (2007)

*City Information:* City of Rapid City, 300 Sixth Street, Rapid City, SD 57701; telephone (605)394-4110; fax (605) 394-6793

# ■ Economy

## Major Industries and Commercial Activity

Agriculture, tourism, mining, logging, professional services/retail, and Ellsworth Air Force Base are the major factors in Rapid City's economy. The area is also known for the manufacture of high-value, low-bulk items that can be swiftly shipped to market or assembly centers in other parts of the nation.

Agriculture is a major industry in South Dakota, and Rapid City is the regional trade center for farm-ranch activity in the southwest part of the state and neighboring counties in Montana, Wyoming, and Nebraska. Cattle and sheep production dominate the agricultural scene, as well as processing and packing of meat and meat byproducts, but the cultivation of small grains is also important. Services offered to area farmers and ranchers include selling of new and used farm equipment, spare parts and repairs, and flour milling.

The health care sector is strong, employing more than 8,000 people in the Black Hills region at major health care organizations such as Rapid City Regional Hospital. Other important industrial and employment institutions include several large construction companies, rock quarries, steel fabrication firms, and trucking firms. Several light industries and services located in the city include manufacturing of computer parts, printing, Native American crafts, and

headquarters for insurance companies and other businesses. Regional or headquarters facilities of many state and federal offices also operate in the city.

Centrally located in the beautiful Black Hills region, Rapid City benefits from a large annual tourist trade. Within half a day's drive of Rapid City are five of the country's most famous national park areas: Mount Rushmore National Memorial, Devil's Tower National Monument, Badlands National Park, Jewel Cave National Monument, and Wind Cave National Park. The area further boasts of a variety of restaurants, several large annual events and attractions, more than 4,400 hotel/motel rooms and many modern campgrounds.

Each year the multimillion-dollar payroll for workers at Ellsworth Air Force Base, the largest employer in the state, boosts the local economy. The top of the Base Operations building at Ellsworth Air Force Base was removed during demolitions in October 2007. This facility was replaced by an $8.8 million U.S. Army Corps of Engineers construction project.

**Items and goods produced:** computer components, jewelry, cement, processed foods, steel products, printing, wood products

## Incentive Programs—New and Existing Companies

The city of Rapid City, along with Pennington County and the Governor's Office of Economic Development, offers a number of financial incentives to aid industry looking to establish operations in the area.

*Local programs:* Black Hills Vision is a regional economic development initiative that encourages tech-based employment and seeks to develop a high-tech corridor in the Rapid City area. A small business incubator called the Black Hills Business Development Center is a cornerstone of the Black Hills Vision; it offers technical support and collaboration opportunities for emerging businesses. Having opened in 2006, the center is located on the South Dakota School of Mines & Technology Campus. The Rapid City Economic Development Partnership oversees the incubator jointly with West River Foundation. Rapid City rebates the tax increment created by investments in real property for up to 15 years. The Rapid City Economic Development Loan Fund (Rapid Fund) is a low-interest loan program that is focused on the development of primary jobs in the manufacturing sector. A portfolio of 14 different loans are available for business expansion, relocation, or start-up. Pennington County has a real estate tax incentive offered to new industrial or commercial structures, or new non-residential agricultural structures.

*State programs:* The South Dakota REDI Fund lends money at three percent interest to companies creating new jobs in the state. Designed and administered by a board of

13 business leaders, the program is known to be efficient, flexible, and responsible. The money can be used for almost any capital purchase or operating financing for which a company qualifies under standard banking guidelines. The MicroLOAN South Dakota Loan Program makes loans to small businesses, including main street and retail operations, for working capital, equipment, real estate or other fixed asset project costs. The state offers a variety of other loans, subfunds and training assistance. Federal Small Business Administration (SBA) participation loans and SBA Direct loans are also available.

*Job training programs:* Career counseling and customized job training are offered at the Career Learning Center. The South Dakota Workforce Development Program extends training opportunities in conjunction with approved educational institutions; new employee skills, retraining, and advancement/promotion assistance is offered.

## Development Projects

In 1992, gathering energy and tax dollars after redevelopment efforts following the 1972 flood, Rapid City formed Vision 2012, a program of long-term planning for the community. Projects include the Meadowbrook Golf Course, Canyon Lake Restoration, the Journey Museum, and the Rapid City Boys Club.

Among recent development projects is the $10.8-million Dahl Arts Center building, which includes a 457-seat theater, 3 multi-purpose spaces, 3 gallery spaces, 3 art education classrooms, a gift shop, kitchen, administration wing, and art reference library. The Dahl Education Complex opened in December 2007. Other important projects include a Children's Care Rehab and Development Center, to service youth on an outpatient basis; Rushmore Civic Plaza Addition, a $14.5-million project to add seating for sporting events; and an Emergency Response Training Center. In July 2007 the Western Dakota Technical Institute and Rapid City officials unveiled a new burn building to be used for a variety of emergency and fire-training exercises. The burn building will be the centerpiece for the Emergency Response Training Center when it is complete.

*Economic Development Information:* Rapid City Area Economic Development Partnership, 525 University Loop, Suite 101, Rapid City, SD 57701; telephone (605)343-1880; toll-free (800)956-0377; fax (605)343-1916; email info@rapiddevelopment.com

## Commercial Shipping

The Rapid City Regional Airport handles cargo aircraft. Rapid City is served by the Dakota, Minnesota, & Eastern Railroad and offers piggyback service with daily switching service. Nearly 30 motor freight carriers, as well as terminals, are located in Rapid City. Parcel service is provided by United Parcel Service.

## Labor Force and Employment Outlook

Rapid City boasts of a young and eager workforce that is well educated. Ninety-six percent of residents have a high school diploma; 20 percent have a bachelor's degree. In September 2007 the civilian labor force numbered 66,500 people. Approximatley 1,800 workers were unemployed, for an unemployment rate of 2.8 percent, well below the national average of 4.7 percent.

The following is a summary of data regarding the Rapid City metropolitan area labor force, 2006 annual averages.

**Size of nonagricultural labor force:** 60,300

**Number of workers employed in ...**

construction and mining: 4,900
manufacturing: 3,700
trade, transportation and utilities: 12,800
information: 1,100
financial activities: 3,600
professional and business services: 4,400
educational and health services: 8,900
leisure and hospitality: 8,400
other services: 2,600
government: 9,900

**Average hourly earnings of production workers employed in manufacturing:** Not available

**Unemployment rate:** 2.6% (June 2007)

| *Largest employers (2007)* | *Number of employees* |
|---|---|
| SD National Guard | |
| Army | 5,450 |
| Ellsworth AFB | |
| (military) | 3,916 |
| R.C. Regional Hospital | 2,824 |
| R.C. School District | 1,619 |
| City of Rapid City | 1,515 |
| Federal Government | 1,307 |
| State of SD | 983 |
| Black Hills Corporation | 750 |
| Sanmina-SCI | 660 |
| Ellsworth AFB (civilian) | 609 |

## Cost of Living

Low utility costs and no personal income taxes are factors that help Rapid City offer a reasonable cost of living. In August 2007 the median asking price for a single family home was $182,500, according to the the Rapid City Realtors multiple listing service.

The following is a summary of data regarding several key cost of living factors in the Rapid City area.

**2007 (1st quarter) ACCRA Average House Price:** Not available

**2007 (1st quarter) ACCRA Cost of Living Index:** Not available

**State income tax rate:** None

**State sales tax rate:** 4.0%

**Local income tax rate:** None

**Local sales tax rate:** 2.0%

**Property tax rate:** $30.1323 per $1,000; assessed at 85% (2000)

*Economic Information:*   Rapid City Area Economic Development Partnership, 444 Mt. Rushmore Road N., PO Box 747, Rapid City, SD 57701; telephone (605) 343-1880; toll-free (800)956-0377; fax (605)343-1916; email info@rapiddevelopment.com

# ■ Education and Research

## Elementary and Secondary Schools

The Rapid City School District, second largest in the state, covers 419 square miles. The district offers services to special education and academically gifted children as well as technology staff development and Native American education programs. Serving Ellsworth Air Force Base and the surrounding area, the Douglas School District has 2,400 students, one preschool, three elementary schools, one middle school, and one high school.

The following is a summary of data regarding the Rapid City Area Schools as of the 2005–2006 school year.

**Total enrollment:** 12,708

**Number of facilities**

elementary schools: 15
junior high/middle schools: 5
senior high schools: 3
other: 0

**Student/teacher ratio:** 14.8:1

**Teacher salaries (2005–06)**

elementary median: $37,240
junior high/middle median: Not available
secondary median: Not available

**Funding per pupil:** $6,529

Rapid City also has several alternative academies— Jefferson Academy and Odyssey Academy—and several Christian high schools, including Saint Thomas More and Rapid City Christian High School.

## Colleges and Universities

South Dakota School of Mines and Technology (SDSM&T) has long been recognized as one of the best science and engineering colleges in the county. SDSM&T, which enrolls about 2,400 students, is known for its technological expertise and innovation, as well as for its world-famous Museum of Geology. The school offers 31 bachelor's, master's, doctoral, and co-curricular degrees. More than 85 percent of all School of Mines students have gained work experience through internships and co-ops before graduating. Over 90 percent of graduates have indicated they would return to the Black Hills if positions were available. Western Dakota Technical Institute provides diplomas and Associate in Applied Science degrees in 25 career fields to more than 4,000 students; fields of study include business and construction trades, agriculture, electronics, human services, computer-aided drafting, and mechanical career fields. Western Dakota Tech works closely with the local business community to provide student training programs. National American University offers a wide variety of bachelor's and associate's degrees in business to more than 2,300 students.

## Libraries and Research Centers

The Rapid City Public Library, with more than 147,000 volumes, has strong collections in business and audio-visual materials, and operates one bookmobile, a homebound service and homework help. Its South Dakota collection includes many items for historical research. The library subscribes to several hundred magazines and newspapers and houses the collection of the Rapid City Society for Genealogical Research Inc. South Dakota School of Mines and Technology (SDSM&T), National American University, and Rapid City Regional Hospital also have libraries.

SDSM&T has been involved in providing research services for government, industry, and business for at least a century, with a primary emphasis on energy, the environment, and mineral development. They are also a regional Patent and Trademark Depository and house a large computer lab.

*Public Library Information:*   Rapid City Public Library, 610 Quincy Street, Rapid City, SD 57701; telephone (605)394-4171; fax (605)394-4064

# ■ Health Care

Rapid City Regional Hospital provides comprehensive acute care services to South Dakota and portions of North Dakota, Nebraska, Wyoming, and Montana. The hospital is the main health care center between Minneapolis and Denver with 42 specialties including radiation, cardiology, and emerging medicine. The hospital is licensed for 310 acute-care and 56 psychiatric beds.

Employing more than 3,000 people, the hospital system offers care at Black Hills Rehabilitation Hospital, the John T. Vucurevich Cancer Care Center and the Regional Behavioral Health Center as well as clinics and out-patient care.

The Black Hills Regional Eye Institute is a not-for-profit corporation dedicated to providing the most modern and complex eye care for children and adults of the region. More than 2,000 eye surgeries are performed each year in one of the four surgical rooms at the Eye Surgery Center. The Institute physicians and staff travel to 12 satellite clinics throughout a five-state area to provide treatment of eye problems within the local communities.

Health care is also available at Rapid City Community Health Center, Sioux San Hospital, and the Black Hills Surgery Center.

# ■ Recreation

## Sightseeing

The Black Hills Visitor Information Center has maps and brochures and is a good first stop on a trip to Rapid City. Visitors may wish to begin with a trip to Storybook Island, an 11-acre park with free attractions for youngsters. It is filled with dozens of larger-than-life sets that depict children's nursery rhymes and tales, including Yogi Bear's picnic basket and the Crooked Man's house. The unique Stavkirk Chapel, an exact replica of the famous 830-year-old Borgund Church in Norway, features intricate woodcarvings, strange dragon heads, and ingenious pegged construction. Fossil skeletons of giant, prehistoric marine reptiles command attention at the Museum of Geology at the South Dakota Schools of Mines and Technology. The museum also houses the world's finest exhibits of Badlands fossils and an extensive collection of rare and beautiful rocks, gems, and minerals from the Black Hills; more than 250,000 vertebrate fossils and 6,000 minerals are housed at the museum. Seven life-size concrete replicas of monstrous prehistoric reptiles are located in the outdoor park-like setting at Dinosaur Park.

With four different major collections, the Journey Museum tells the story of the Great Plains. Displays of rock formations, fossilized remains and documentation of significant scientific discoveries are found at the Museum of Geology. Collections from thousands of archeological sites can be examined at the Archeological Research Center. The Black Hills region's frontier past can be relived at the Minnilusa Pioneer Museum, which focuses on historic events and people. The Sioux Indian Museum celebrates Native Americans of the present and past through their artistry and achievements.

Twenty-five miles southwest of Rapid City, Mt. Rushmore National Memorial was carved from a mountainside of solid granite and features the busts of four American presidents: Washington, Jefferson, Theodore Roosevelt, and Lincoln. Mt. Rushmore is host to almost three million visitors a year from across the country and around the world. Discovered in 1900, Jewel Cave, a national monument, contains more than 132 miles of surveyed passageways in an underground labyrinth that offers rare and unusual calcite crystal formations. Wind Cave, the first cave designated as part of the National Parks system, provides more than 125 miles of mapped corridors and halls, making it the fourth-longest cave in the world. With its jagged cliffs, deep canyons, flat-topped buttes, and rich fossils, Badlands National Park is one of the most stunning geological displays on earth. Crazy Horse Memorial is a mountain carving of the great Indian hero. Reptile Gardens, founded in 1937, gives spectators the opportunity to observe colorful birds and reptiles surrounded by thousands of orchids and other tropical and desert plants in its Skydome. The gardens also feature miniature horses and donkeys; the Bird Program, featuring hawks, owls, eagles, parrots, and other birds; an alligator and crocodile show; Bewitched Village, featuring trained animals; and the Snake Program. Bear Country U.S.A., a 250-acre drive-through wildlife park, features the world's largest collection of black bears plus a large and varied collection of North American wildlife including grizzly bears, timber wolves, mountain lions, buffalo, moose, elk, and more. Visitors are treated to the recently expanded visitor center, which allows visitors to step out of their vehicles and see young and smaller animals up close. The Air and Space Museum at the entrance of Ellsworth Air Force Base features more than 25 vintage aircraft. Several tour companies offer guided tours to some of the memorable sites featured in the award-winning film *Dances With Wolves*.

## Arts and Culture

Dahl Fine Arts Center features exhibits of paintings and sculptures by local artists, especially local Native American artists. A 180-foot-long oil-on-canvas mural depicts 200 years of American History. The museum, which will move into a new facility in 2008, offers tours and family events. The Black Hills Community Theatre, Inc., the city's only community theater, is based in the Dahl Center's 170-seat auditorium. The nearby Black Hills Playhouse at Custer State Park is a professional theater and training center. Two puppet theaters entertain the community. Black Hills Dance Theatre, Inc. engages a variety of regionally and nationally recognized dance companies. The Black Hills Symphony Orchestra's 90 members offer educational outreach programs in the community and perform a variety of concerts. Other community arts attractions include the Blacks Hills Chamber Music Society, Rapid City Municipal Band, and the Dakota Choral Union.

## Festivals and Holidays

More than 25 years of music and family entertainment is the focus of the Black Hills Bluegrass Music Festival, which is held in June. The Black Hills Heritage Festival celebrates the cultural heritage of the Black Hills at the end of June. The Sturgis Motorcycle Rally in nearby Sturgis attracts more than 500,000 visitors each August for concerts, food, vendors and demo and scenic motorcycle rides. The Central States Fair, a week-long extravaganza that entertains crowds from all over the region, also occurs in August. The Dakota Celtic Festival is held at the end of August/beginning of September. September brings fall color to the hills and a treat to the tastebuds at the nearby Taste of Spearfish celebration. October's Buffalo Roundup, where the visitor is invited to feel the thunder of 1,500 herded buffalo, is held annually at nearby Custer State Park. The annual Festival of Lights is held on Thanksgiving weekend. Rodeo fun is the attraction at January's Black Hills Stock Show and Rodeo. There are Mardi Gras and Chinese New Year celebrations in February. In addition, Indian pow wows are scheduled at various times throughout the state.

## Sports for the Spectator

The Don Barnett Arena plays host to the Rapid City Flying Aces, an indoor football team. Rapid City's Annual Black Hills Stock Show & Rodeo in late January-early February, draws large crowds.

## Sports for the Participant

Rapid City has more than 25 parks, playgrounds and special outdoor public facilities spanning 1,500 acres of park land inside the city limits. The largest, Sioux Park, offers 210 acres. A 13.5-mile bicycle path spans the town, which boasts a large number of golf courses, tennis courts, horseshoe courts, racquetball courts, outdoor swimming pools, an indoor aquatic facility, ball field complexes, soccer facilities, an ice arena, a hockey rink, and frisbee golf courses.

Outdoor lovers enjoy two ski areas, 400 miles of trails and nature walks, 14 mountain lakes and 300 miles of streams and reservoirs; blue ribbon trout fishing and many types of hunting are also available.

## Shopping and Dining

Since its inception, Rapid City has been a commercial center for miners, ranchers, the military, and tourists. Downtown Rapid City, with more than 400 businesses, is a diverse mix of retail stores, financial institutions, service businesses, and lodging. Anchored by JCPenney, Sears, Herbergers and Target, the Rushmore Mall has a total of 120 retail stores. Other local shopping areas include Baken Park, the city's first shopping center; Prairie Market; Northgate Shopping Center; Haines Station; and the Sturgis Road shopping area. A number of Rapid City shops specialize in fine hand-crafted paintings, pottery, jewelry, and museum quality reproductions created by the Sioux who live in the region. Manufacturers and retailers of the area's famous Black Hills Gold abound; many offer tours as well as retail stores.

Many fine restaurants are located throughout the city, featuring sizzling steaks cut from prime South Dakota beef. Fine dining can be enjoyed at the Corn Exchange Restaurant Bistro, Enigma Restaurant at the Radisson Hotel, Firehouse Brewing Company, Fireside Inn, Khoury's Mediterranean Cuisine, and Minerva's Restaurant and Bar.

***Visitor Information:*** Rapid City Convention and Visitors Bureau, PO Box 747, Rapid City, SD 57709; telephone (605)718-8484; toll-free (800)487-3223; fax (605)348-9217; email tourist@rapidcitycvb.com. South Dakota Department of Tourism, 711 East Wells Avenue, Pierre, SD 57501; telephone (605)773-3301; toll-free (800)732-5682; fax (605)773-3256; email sdinfo@state.sd.us.

# ■ Convention Facilities

The Rushmore Plaza Civic Center, located near the heart of downtown Rapid City, provides a 10,000-seat arena, 150,000 square feet of exhibit space, a luxurious 1,752-seat theater, meeting rooms, and catering facilities. Seventy-five motels/hotels provide some 4,400 rooms. Alongside a flowing creek, greenway, and bike path is the Central States Fairgrounds convention facilities, which can accommodate groups of 25 to 6,000. It offers services such as a 224-unit campground, 6,000-seat grandstand, 8,000 vehicle parking spaces, and food service locations.

***Convention Information:*** Rapid City Convention and Visitors Bureau, PO Box 747, Rapid City, SD 57709; telephone (605)718-8484; toll-free (800)487-3223; fax (605)348-9217; email tourist@rapidcitycvb.com

# ■ Transportation

## Approaching the City

The Rapid City Regional Airport, 9 miles east of the city, is the third most active airport in the Northern Rockies. It offers flights to and from six major U.S. cities on five airlines: Northwest, Allegiant Air, SkyWest/Delta, United Express, and Frontier Airlines. Two fixed-base operators provide charter service. Charter bus service is provided by Black Hills Touring, Dakota Bus Service, Jack Rabbit Lines, Stagecoach West, and Gray Line of the Black Hills. Dakota Minnesota and Eastern Railroad offers transport to the east, south and west.

Several wide, modern highways intersect in the city. Interstate 90 runs east and west. State Highway 79, which runs north and south, is being expanded to a four-lane highway. U.S. Highway 14, which cuts through the city on an angle, runs northwest to southeast. U.S. Highway 16 approaches the city center from the south. Six highways lead from the north, west, and south into the canyons and mountains.

## Traveling in the City

The city is divided into three main areas named by locals according to compass direction: South Robbinsdale, North Rapid City, and West Rapid. Two inter-city bus lines serve Rapid City. City bus service is offered by the Rapid Transit System. Dial A Ride offers curb to curb service for transport of ADA certified passengers. Rapid Ride, a fixed-route bus system, takes passengers to more than 200 stops along five city and two connector routes.

# ■ Communications

## Newspapers and Magazines

The city's daily newspaper is the *Rapid City Journal.* Other local newspapers include the weeklies *The Plainsman* and *Indian Country Today. The Visitor* is a quarterly magazine; *Investment Report* is a monthly magazine published in Rapid City.

## Television and Radio

Rapid City is served by four network television stations and two cable companies. The city has 12 AM and FM radio stations.

***Media Information:*** *Rapid City Journal,* 507 Main Street, PO Box 450, Rapid City, SD 57701; telephone (605)394-8400

## Rapid City Online

City of Rapid City. Available www.rcgov.org

Ellsworth Air Force Base. Available www.ellsworth .af.mil

Rapid City Area Economic Development Partnership. Available www.rapiddevelopment .com

Rapid City Convention & Visitors Bureau. Available www.rapidcitycvb.com

Rapid City Public Library. Available www .rapidcitylibrary.org

South Dakota Arts Council. Available www .sdarts.org

BIBLIOGRAPHY

Riney, Scott, *The Rapid City Indian School, 1898-1933* (University of Oklahoma Press, 1999)

# Sioux Falls

## ■ The City in Brief

**Founded:** 1856 (incorporated 1889)

**Head Official:** Mayor Dave Munson (since 2002)

**City Population**

    1980: Not available
    1990: 100,836
    2000: 123,975
    2006 estimate: 142,396
    Percent change, 1990–2000: 22.9%
    U.S. rank in 1980: 223rd
    U.S. rank in 1990: 194th
    U.S. rank in 2000: 195th

**Metropolitan Area Population**

    1980: 109,435
    1990: 139,236
    2000: 172,412
    2006 estimate: 212,911
    Percent change, 1990–2000: 23.8%
    U.S. rank in 1980: 270th
    U.S. rank in 1990: Not available
    U.S. rank in 2000: 180th

**Area:** 56.34 square miles (2000)

**Elevation:** 1,421 feet above sea level

**Average Annual Temperatures:** January, 14.0° F; July, 73.0° F; annual average, 45.1° F

**Average Annual Precipitation:** 24.69 inches of rain; 41.1 inches of snow

**Major Economic Sectors:** Wholesale and retail trade, services, manufacturing

**Unemployment Rate:** 2.3% (June 2007)

**Per Capita Income:** $25,345 (2005)

**2005 FBI Crime Index Property:** 4,264

**2005 FBI Crime Index Violent:** 473

**Major Colleges and Universities:** Augustana College; University of Sioux Falls

**Daily Newspaper:** *Argus Leader*

## ■ Introduction

Sioux Falls, seat of South Dakota's Minnehaha County, is the largest city in the state and the center of the metropolitan statistical area that includes Sioux Falls as well as Lincoln and Minnehaha counties. The city first grew during the Dakota boom years of the late nineteenth century as the arrival of the railroad made possible the nationwide transportation of granite quarried in Sioux Falls. Sioux Falls has grown in many ways since then, and consistently tops the rankings by *Forbes* and *Inc.* magazines of top cities for business.

## ■ Geography and Climate

Located in the Big Sioux River Valley in southeast South Dakota, Sioux Falls is surrounded by gently rolling terrain that slopes to higher elevations approximately 100 miles to the north-northeast and to the south. The city's climate is continental, exhibiting frequent weather changes from day to day and from week to week as differing air masses move into the area. During the late fall and winter, strong winds cause abrupt drops in temperature, but cold spells are usually of short duration. Snowfall and sleet average 41.1 inches yearly, and one or two heavy snows fall each winter, with blizzard conditions sometimes resulting. Thunderstorms are common in late spring and summer; tornadoes can occur from spring through summer. Flooding from melting snow runoff in the spring along the Big Sioux River and Skunk Creek is reduced by a diversion canal around the city.

**Area:** 56.34 square miles (2000)

**Elevation:** 1,421 feet above sea level

**Average Temperatures:** January, 14.0° F; July, 73.0° F; annual average, 45.1° F

**Average Annual Precipitation:** 24.69 inches of rain; 41.1 inches of snow

# ■ History

## Falls on Big Sioux River Attract Settlers

Attracted by the economic potential of the Sioux Falls on the Big Sioux River, Dr. George M. Staples of Dubuque, Iowa, organized Western Town near the falls in 1856. Staples and his group hoped that the settlement would become the capital of the Territory of Dakota, but it was not chosen. Instead, in the winter of 1856, the Legislature of Minnesota Territory chartered the Dakota Land Company and established the town of Sioux Falls.

In August 1862 the settlers, fearing violence from the local Native Americans, abandoned the village. Raiders burned the buildings and destroyed everything, including an old Smith printing press used by the *Sioux Falls Democrat* that was dumped in the Big Sioux River after it was stripped of decorative items. Fort Dakota, a military post, was established in the area in May 1865, to help assure the resettlement of Sioux Falls. Another incentive came when the water power of the falls was harnessed in 1873. A scourge of grasshoppers in 1874 hurt resettlement, but by 1876 Sioux Falls claimed a population of 600 people. Sioux Falls was incorporated as a town in 1877 and as a city in 1889.

In the last decades of the nineteenth century, Northern European immigrants were attracted to the Territory of Dakota, which resembled their homeland. The establishment of rail transport in the area in 1878 enabled locals to begin shipping "Sioux Falls granite," a pink quartzite bedrock second only to diamond in hardness. The city's two church-affiliated private schools date to this period; Augustana College, a Lutheran school, was founded in 1860, and the University of Sioux Falls, a Baptist school, opened in 1883.

## Agriculture Provides Economic Base

Life on the Plains was a test of endurance. Snow began falling in October 1880 and continued until the following spring, isolating residents and forcing them to burn corn, wheat, hay, and railroad ties for heat sources. In spite of hardship, Sioux Falls gained in economic importance. South Dakota's lenient divorce law brought outsiders into Sioux Falls until the law was changed in 1908. One memorable case unfolded when the wife of heavyweight boxing champion Bob Fitzsimmons sought a divorce in Sioux Falls. Her distraught husband followed her and managed to change her mind. To celebrate their reunion, Fitzsimmons forged horseshoes and passed them out to admirers; in the process, the local blacksmith shop's floor gave way, injuring a young boy. Fitzsimmons then organized a benefit performance and gave the proceeds to the boy's family.

In 1942 the U.S. War Department leased Sioux Falls land for the construction of the Air Force Technical Radio School, invigorating the local economy and social life. Sioux Falls native Joe Foss won the Congressional Medal of Honor for shooting down 31 enemy airplanes in the Pacific campaign of World War II; after the war, Foss returned to Sioux Falls to become a successful businessman and commander of the South Dakota Air National Guard.

## A Leader in Financial Services and Retail

Today Sioux Falls, through the processing of agricultural products, serves as a distribution center for farms in Iowa, Minnesota, and South Dakota. Ushered in by Citicorp, financial services has emerged as a primary industry, with healthcare close behind. The city is also a retail hot spot—the largest retail center between Denver and Minneapolis-St. Paul, Sioux Falls attracts more than 14 million shoppers each year. Spurred in part by a statewide initiative, the city is focusing on becoming a driving force in research and technology. Sioux Falls offers amenities and points of interest including the University of Sioux Falls and Augustana College, a Baptist seminary, a school for the deaf, and its namesake, the Falls of the Big Sioux River.

***Historical Information:*** Pettigrew Home & Museum, 8th and Duluth, Sioux Falls, SD 57102; telephone (605)367-7097

# ■ Population Profile

**Metropolitan Area Residents**

  1980: 109,435
  1990: 139,236
  2000: 172,412
  2006 estimate: 212,911
  Percent change, 1990–2000: 23.8%
  U.S. rank in 1980: 270th
  U.S. rank in 1990: Not available
  U.S. rank in 2000: 180th

**City Residents**

  1980: Not available
  1990: 100,836
  2000: 123,975

*Photograph by Rich Murphy. Provided by the Sioux Falls Convention and Visitors Bureau.*

2006 estimate: 142,396
Percent change, 1990–2000: 22.9%
U.S. rank in 1980: 223rd
U.S. rank in 1990: 194th
U.S. rank in 2000: 195th

**Density:** 2,201.4 people per square mile (in 2000)

**Racial and ethnic characteristics (2000)**

White: 113,938
Black: 2,226
American Indian and Alaska Native: 2,627
Asian: 1,479
Native Hawaiian and Pacific Islander: 68
Hispanic or Latino (may be of any race): 3,087
Other: 1,521

**Percent of residents born in state:** 57.5% (2006)

**Age characteristics (2005)**

Population under 5 years old: 10,825
Population 5 to 9 years old: 8,196
Population 10 to 14 years old: 7,889
Population 15 to 19 years old: 8,116
Population 20 to 24 years old: 11,128

Population 25 to 34 years old: 21,491
Population 35 to 44 years old: 19,234
Population 45 to 54 years old: 18,588
Population 55 to 59 years old: 7,495
Population 60 to 64 years old: 4,683
Population 65 to 74 years old: 7,417
Population 75 to 84 years old: 5,692
Population 85 years and older: 1,604
Median age: 34.4 years

**Births (2006, MSA)**

Total number: 3,308

**Deaths (2006, MSA)**

Total number: 1,539

**Money income (2005)**

Per capita income: $25,345
Median household income: $44,341
Total households: 57,108

**Number of households with income of...**

less than $10,000: 4,124
$10,000 to $14,999: 3,405
$15,000 to $24,999: 7,983

$25,000 to $34,999: 7,609
$35,000 to $49,999: 9,159
$50,000 to $74,999: 12,072
$75,000 to $99,999: 6,001
$100,000 to $149,999: 4,305
$150,000 to $199,999: 882
$200,000 or more: 1,568

**Percent of families below poverty level:** 10% (2005)

**2005 FBI Crime Index Property:** 4,264

**2005 FBI Crime Index Violent:** 473

# ■ Municipal Government

Sioux Falls is governed by a full-time mayor and eight part-time council persons. Three of the council members are elected at-large and five are elected from council districts. Voters elect the mayor and council persons to staggered four-year terms.

**Head Official:** Mayor Dave Munson (since 2002; current term expires 2010)

**Total Number of City Employees:** approximately 1,100 (2007)

*City Information:*  City of Sioux Falls, 224 W. 9th St., Sioux Falls, SD 57117; telephone (605)367-8000

# ■ Economy

## Major Industries and Commercial Activity

In 2007 for the fifth consecutive year, *Forbes* magazine named Sioux Falls the best small city for business and careers, a ranking based on employment, job and income growth, cost of doing business, labor pool, crime rate, housing costs, and net migration. The Sioux Falls economy is comprised of a diversity of sectors, including finance, healthcare, retailing, agriculture, tourism, and distribution and trade.

Set in a fertile agricultural region and the site of one of the world's largest stockyards, Sioux Falls has traditionally been a center for the agricultural industry. Crops grown include corn and soybeans. Hogs, cattle, poultry, and eggs are also raised in the region. John Morrell & Company, a meat packer, is the city's fourth largest employer. Among other agriculture-related activities are meat processing, the production of dairy and bakery items, livestock feed milling, and the manufacture of farm implements and equipment.

When Citicorp moved its credit card operations to Sioux Falls in 1980, it launched the city to new heights in financial services. In the two decades since that time, other financial companies followed, as did those in such related sectors as insurance and real estate. The main offices of state and regional banks, as well as brokerage and insurance firms with nationwide connections, are based in the downtown financial district.

The healthcare industry figures significantly in the city's economic stability. Sioux Falls has emerged as a regional health care center, with the two major hospitals ranking as the top employers in the city, employing more than 9,500 combined. Private physician clinics employ more than 1,000 workers.

Sioux Falls is the largest retail center between Denver and Minneapolis-St. Paul. As such, it attracts more than 14 million shoppers annually from throughout the state as well as from Iowa, Minnesota, and Nebraska. Approximately 3,500 retail outlets employ 20 percent of Sioux Falls' labor force.

Other economic sectors important to the city are tourism, which is South Dakota's second largest industry, and distribution and trade, which take advantage of the interstate highway network and the Sioux Falls Regional Airport.

**Items and goods produced:** meat and meat products, fabricated steel, concrete blocks and prestressed concrete, millwork, sewn items, electronic test equipment, corrugated boxes, computer components

## Incentive Programs—New and Existing Companies

*Local programs:*  To encourage economic expansion, the Sioux Falls Development Foundation and the Chamber of Commerce jointly undertook a long-range marketing program titled "Forward Sioux Falls." The program goals include diversification of the local and state economies, creation of new enterprises, expansion of existing businesses, growth of the tax base through capital investment, and continued development of medical services, food processing, and retailing.

The Sioux Falls Development Foundation offers a number of incentives to attract new companies and retain existing businesses. The Property Tax Abatement allows new structures to be taxed at a lower rate. The Rural Electric Economic Development Fund, available in the eastern part of the state, offers financing for business development. The Minnehaha County Economic Development Association offers a Revolving Loan Fund for projects that result in significant capital investment and/or the creation of quality jobs.

*State programs:*  The business climate of South Dakota is the first big plus for new and expanding businesses. Company owners pay no corporate or personal state income tax, no business inventory tax, and very low workers compensation rates. Additionally, the Micro-LOAN South Dakota Program offers loans to small businesses in amounts up to $50,000 for use as working capital or for equipment, real estate, or other project costs. The state also offers the Revolving Economic Development & Initiative Fund to provide financing for new or existing businesses, and Economic Development Finance Authority Bonds to finance up to 80 percent of new construction and 75 percent of new equipment expenditures.

*Job training programs:* The state's Workforce Development Program provides businesses with partial funding to train new employees, retrain existing workers, or upgrade the training of current employees. Kilian Community College meets the educational demands of the local labor force by providing continuing education and customized training programs.

## Development Projects

By the early 2000s, the population of Sioux Falls was growing at a rate of more than 3,000 residents each year, putting a strain on indoor public facilities. In response, the city established the Public Facilities Task Force in early 2004 to examine alternatives for accommodating this growth while still attracting visitors and new residents. One problem in particular needed to be addressed—the 40-year-old Sioux Falls Arena was typically booked with sporting events, rendering it unavailable for conventions and meetings. The task force arrived at a three-pronged solution. An Event Center would be constructed to accommodate stage productions and professional, college, and high school sports, as well as such events as rodeos, circuses, and rallies. A Recreation Center would offer indoor features including swimming pools, hockey rinks, soccer fields, a walking/jogging track, adventure gym, playground area, and conditioning area. Finally, the existing Sioux Falls Arena would be redesigned as a convention center complex. The Event Center would be located downtown and the Recreation Center would be built at Nelson Park. Remodeling of the Sioux Falls Arena was scheduled to begin in 2008.

The "Phillips to the Falls" project was underway in the mid-2000s. This expansion project will connect Falls Park, the city's natural beauty centerpiece, to downtown via Phillips Avenue, enabling people to walk from the park through the city's showcase of restored twentieth-century commercial architecture. By acquiring additional land, the city was also pursuing expansion of Falls Park to the north.

South Dakota has adopted the "2010 Initiative," a state-wide program to increase economic growth and visitor spending by the year 2010. Among the goals of the initiative are to double visitor spending from $600 million to $1.2 billion; to increase the gross state product by $10 billion; and to become a recognized leader in research and technology. By 2005 Sioux Falls was already experiencing success in these areas. In 2003 Hematech LLC, a biotechnology firm, announced plans to construct a $15 million headquarters and plant in the city. As of

2007 Hematech occupied nearly 20,000 square feet of laboratory space in the Sioux Falls Technology Park.

*Economic Development Information:* Sioux Falls Development Foundation, 200 N. Phillips Ave., Ste. 101, Sioux Falls, SD 57101; telephone (605)339-0103; toll-free (800)658-3373; fax (605)339-0055; email info@siouxfalls.com

## Commercial Shipping

Sioux Falls, known as one of the "Crossroads of the Nation," is situated at the intersection of I-90, an east-west highway connecting Boston, MA, with Seattle, WA, and I-29, which runs north-south between Kansas City, Kansas, and Winnipeg, Manitoba, Canada. So situated, the city has long been a hub for the distribution of automobiles, trucks, food, fuel, oil, gasoline, machinery, plastics, and paper products. More than 50 truck lines provide over-the-road transportation through Sioux Falls to markets throughout the nation. Rail service is provided by Burlington Northern Santa Fe and the Ellis & Eastern railroads. Air cargo services at Sioux Falls Regional Airport, the largest regional airport in South Dakota, are provided by FedEx, United Parcel Service, and DHL Worldwide. Additionally, the airport serves as the state's only Foreign Trade Zone, an area where foreign goods bound for international destinations can be temporarily stored without incurring an import duty.

## Labor Force and Employment Outlook

Sioux Falls is consistently listed among the top metropolitan areas for economic strength and an expanding business community. Companies moving to Sioux Falls routinely report an increase in productivity and a decrease in overhead costs. In September 2007 the total civilian labor force was approximately 125,400; 3,000 workers were unemployed, for an unemployment rate of 2.4 percent, well below the national average of 4.7 percent.

The following is a summary of data regarding the Sioux Falls metropolitan area labor force, 2006 annual averages.

**Size of nonagricultural labor force:** 129,400

**Number of workers employed in...**

construction and mining: 7,800
manufacturing: 13,100
trade, transportation and utilities: 27,900
information: 3,000
financial activities: 15,800
professional and business services: 10,000
educational and health services: 22,900
leisure and hospitality: 12,600
other services: 4,600
government: 11,700

**Average hourly earnings of production workers employed in manufacturing:** Not available

**Unemployment rate:** 2.3% (June 2007)

| Largest employers (2007) | Number of employees |
|---|---|
| Sanford Health | 5,000 |
| Avera McKennan Hospital and University Medical Center | 4,600 |
| Citibank South Dakota | 3,200 |
| John Morrell and Co. | 3,000 |
| Women's Center | 2,000 |
| U.S Air National Guard | 1,100 |
| HSBC Card SVC | 1,000 |
| Wells Fargo Bank | 1,000 |
| Hutchinson Technology Co. | 750 |

## Cost of Living

The following is a summary of data regarding several key cost of living factors in the Sioux Falls area.

**2007 (1st quarter) ACCRA Average House Price:** Not available

**2007 (1st quarter) ACCRA Cost of Living Index:** 92.0

**State income tax rate:** None

**State sales tax rate:** 4.0%

**Local income tax rate:** None

**Local sales tax rate:** 1.92%

**Property tax rate:** $24.546 per $1,000 of assessed valuation (2003)

***Economic Information:*** Sioux Falls Development Foundation, 200 N. Phillips Ave., Ste. 101, Sioux Falls, SD 57101; telephone (605)339-0103; toll-free (800) 658-3373; fax (605)339-0055; email info@siouxfalls.com

# ■ Education and Research

## Elementary and Secondary Schools

South Dakota boasts one of the highest graduation rates in the country. Public elementary and secondary schools in Sioux Falls are in Sioux Falls School District, which enrolls the highest number of students in the state. A five-member, nonpartisan school board appoints a superintendent. Teachers in the district have an average of 15 years of experience, and more than 45 percent hold advanced degrees.

The following is a summary of data regarding the Sioux Falls School District as of the 2005–2006 school year.

**Total enrollment:** 18,181

**Number of facilities**

elementary schools: 23
junior high/middle schools: 5
senior high schools: 3
other: 0

**Student/teacher ratio:** 15.1:1

**Teacher salaries (2005–06)**

elementary median: $37,728 (all levels)
junior high/middle median: Not available
secondary median: Not available

**Funding per pupil:** $6,464

Some 20 parochial and private elementary and secondary schools provide alternative educational curricula to about 4,000 students. Special schools in the city include a vocational school for the handicapped, a school and hospital for disabled children, and a school for the deaf.

***Public Schools Information:*** Sioux Falls School District, 201 E. 38th St., Sioux Falls, SD 57105; telephone (605)367-7900

## Colleges and Universities

Sioux Falls is home to Augustana College, the largest private college in the state. Affiliated with the Evangelical Lutheran Church and enrolling 1,650 full-time students each year, the college awards Bachelor of Arts degrees in more than 40 areas of study and Masters of Arts in nursing and secondary/special education. The University of Sioux Falls, affiliated with the American Baptist Churches USA, enrolls 1,670 students pursuing degrees in such areas as business administration, elementary education, exercise science, biology, and theology/philosophy. University Center is a partnership of five universities—the University of South Dakota, South Dakota State University, Dakota State University, Northern State University, and Black Hills State University. The University Center caters to adult students by offering evening and once-per-week classes; each year more than 1,900 students pursue degrees at the certificate, associate's, bachelor's, master's, and doctoral levels.

In 2001 the Southeast Technical Institute, which serves 3,500 full- and part-time students, opened the newest building on its 168-acre campus. The Sioux Falls campus of Colorado Technical University offers associate, bachelors, and masters degrees in such areas as technology, business, criminal justice, and health sciences. Sioux Falls serves as the primary clinical campus of the Sanford

School of Medicine of the University of South Dakota, as well as the site for the nurse anesthesia graduate program of Mount Marty College. Kilian Community College, located in downtown Sioux Falls, offers studies in such areas as accounting, business management, computers, chemical dependency, medical office professional, and word processing. Other institutions of higher learning include National American University, Sioux Falls Seminary, and the Sanford School of Radiologic Technology.

### Libraries and Research Centers

The Siouxland Libraries System maintains holdings of about 387,000 items including periodical titles, tapes, videos, and art prints. It consists of the main library, 11 branches, a bookmobile, and an outreach service van. The library, a depository for federal and state documents, houses special collections in South Dakota history and oral history.

The Mikkelsen Library and Learning Resources Center at Augustana College holds more than 200,000 volumes; the Center for Western Studies, a special collection within the library system, brings together 30,000 volumes pertaining to the Upper Great Plains and oral history.

A dozen or so other libraries and research centers are operated by colleges, hospitals, Siouxland Heritage Museums, and such government agencies as the Sioux Falls Police Department, the South Dakota State Penitentiary, and the United States Geological Survey.

*Public Library Information:* Siouxland Libraries, PO Box 7403, Sioux Falls, SD 57117-7403; telephone (605)367-8720; fax (605)367-4312

## ■ Health Care

Sioux Falls has emerged as a major center for health care in a four-state region of the Upper Midwest. Central to the health care community is the University of South Dakota School of Medicine; several of the city's practicing physicians serve on the faculty of the School of Medicine, which maintains an association with five hospitals in the area. Sanford Health, previously known as Sioux Valley Hospitals and Health System, is a network of more than 150 healthcare facilities with more than 350 physicians. In February 2007 the system announced its name change to Sanford Health to commemorate a $400 million gift from businessman and philanthropist T. Denny Sanford. Sanford was named "One of America's Best" by *US News & World Report* in 2006, and ranked as one of the "Nation's Top Hospitals for 2006" by the National Research Corporation. The largest hospital in the system in Sanford USD Medical Center, and the Sanford Clinic is the largest and most comprehensive in the region. In 2002 Sanford opened the NORTH Center, specializing in orthopedic and neurosciences. The

Avera Heart Hospital of South Dakota is the area's only hospital specializing in cardiovascular disease: the hospital is a cooperative venture between Avera McKennan Hospital and University Health Center, North Central Heart Institute, and MedCath, Inc. The 490-bed Avera McKennan Hospital offers the region's only burn unit, bone marrow transplant program, and kidney transport program. Other facilities include the Sioux Falls Veterans Affairs Medical Center, the Children's Care Hospital and School, and Select Specialty Hospital, providing long-term acute care to patients with such health problems as traumatic brain injuries, ventilator dependence, and postsurgical complications.

## ■ Recreation

### Sightseeing

Local sightseeing revolves around the natural beauty and history of Sioux Falls. A good place to begin a sightseeing tour is at the Visitor Information Center and 50-foot observation tower at Falls Park. This park is located where the Big Sioux River forms the Falls, a natural phenomenon from which the city takes its name. Falls Park is home to two buildings listed on the National Register of Historic Places—the 1907 Sioux Falls Light & Power Hydroelectric Plant, known as the "NSP Building," and the Queen Bee Mill, a flour mill built in the nineteenth century that proved to be too large for the river's typical water flow. The Memorial to the Pioneers at the junction of North Drive and North Cliff Avenue marks the spot where pioneers from Iowa first saw the Falls of the Sioux. The Monarch of the Plains Sculpture is a 12-ton piece of mahogany granite, and the Horse Barn Arts Center features the works of local artists. Falls Park also offers Sound and Light shows, self-guided historic walking tours, and a farmers market. St. Joseph Cathedral is a 1918 Romanesque and French Renaissance cathedral and is one of the city's finest and most recognizable landmarks. Also on the grounds is a Mothers Garden, including a grotto of Our Lady of Lourdes.

The 45-acre Great Plains Zoo is home to more than 100 species represented by more than 400 live reptiles, birds, and mammals from around the world. The adjoining Delbridge Museum of Natural History features an extensive display of mounted animals. Sertoma Park, situated aside the Big Sioux River, features picnic shelters, the Outdoor Campus park, and the Sertoma Butterfly House, a facility housing nearly 1,000 butterflies that opened in 2002. Created between 1928 and 1936, the Shoto-teien Japanese Gardens near Covell Lake have been restored. The Pettigrew Home and Museum is the renovated home of one of South Dakota's first two United States Senators. The USS *South Dakota* Battleship Memorial honors the most decorated battleship of World War II. At EROS Data Center, a United States

Department of Interior research and development facility near Sioux Falls, millions of satellite and aircraft photos of the earth are on display together with a pictorial history of Sioux Falls from 1937 to the present. Located five miles west of Sioux Falls is Buffalo Ridge, a cowboy ghost town featuring more than 50 exhibits, a buffalo herd, and the region's largest souvenir and fireworks store.

## Arts and Culture

The Sioux Falls Community Playhouse stages a season of theater productions at the Orpheum Theatre; these range from drama to musicals and children's shows and draw casts from local performers. The Olde Towne Dinner Theatre in Worthing presents live theater and dinner. The drama departments at Augustana College and the University of Sioux Falls mount productions during the school year. Local cultural groups sponsor touring dance, musical, and Broadway performances at the University of Sioux Falls' Jeschke Fine Arts Center.

The Washington Pavilion of Arts & Science is the region's leading entertainment, cultural, and educational facility, comprised of several distinct components. The Husby Performing Arts Center is home to the South Dakota Symphony, which presents classical and pops concerts featuring guest artists and soloists during a September-through-May season. The Kirby Science Discovery Center features interactive exhibits and the Wells Fargo CineDome Theater presents IMAX motion pictures in a 60-foot domed theater. Six art galleries comprise the Visual Arts Center. The Washington Pavilion also houses an educational and gift shop, as well as a café.

Exhibits at the Siouxland Heritage Museums and Center for Western Studies capture the culture of the area's Plains tribes and the city's early settlers. The Old Courthouse Museum features a restored 1890s courtroom and law library. Art from the nation's top western artists, including work by the late Jim Savage, and Sioux culture items are on display at the Center for Western Studies. Minnehaha County's historic rural churches offer a chance to examine nineteenth-century church architecture and religious customs imported to the western frontier from Norway, Sweden, and other Scandinavian countries. Sioux Falls also has a wealth of galleries for art lovers to discover.

## Festivals and Holidays

More than 30,000 visitors attend the Sioux Falls and Sioux Empire farm shows at the W.H. Lyon Fairgrounds over four days in January. St. Patrick's Day is celebrated with a parade downtown. A major spring event is the Festival of Choirs at Augustana College. June brings RibFest, known as "South Dakota's Biggest Backyard BBQ." Also taking place that month are the Siouxland Renaissance Festival, the Sioux Falls Festival of Cultures, Artfalls Fine Arts Festival, Automania, and Nordland

Fest, Augustana College's tribute to Scandinavia. Free jazz and blues music can be heard for two days in July at JazzFest. Hot Harley Nights, which includes a motorcycle parade through downtown, and Hot Summer Nites, offering rock and roll music and a display of hundreds of Corvettes and Harleys, both take place in July as well.

The Sidewalk Arts Festival, the region's largest one-day outdoor festival, draws 50,000 people each September with 350 fine art, folk art, craft, and food booths. German Fest, the Downtown Harvest Festival, and Spirit of the West, a tribute to the area's western heritage, are also held in September. High school marching bands participate in competitions and a parade in October's Festival of Bands. Also in October is Autumn Fest, an arts and crafts fair with more than 500 artists and crafts people from 30 states exhibiting one-of-a-kind handcrafted gifts. The holiday season begins in November with the Parade of Lights, Festival of Trees, and Winter Wonderland at Falls Park. The year comes to a close with First Night, an alcohol-free family celebration taking place throughout Sioux Falls during the day and evening of December 31st.

## Sports for the Spectator

The Sioux Falls Arena hosts home games of the Continental Basketball Association's Sioux Falls Skyforce, the U.S. Hockey League's Sioux Falls Stampede, and the Indoor Football League's Sioux Falls Storm, which had its inaugural season in 2001. The Sioux Falls Stampede won the U.S. Hockey League's Clark Cup during the 2006-07 season. The Sioux Falls Storm won three consecutive championships in 2005, 2006, and 2007, and by November 16, 2007 had won 38 straight games, the longest winning streak in professional sports history. The Sioux Falls Canaries play baseball at Sioux Falls Stadium. O'Gorman High School hosts the minor league football competitions of the Dakota Lawdawgs. On September 26, 2007 the Sioux Falls Spitfire soccer team suspended operations.

Augustana College and the University of Sioux Falls both have successful football college teams that compete in most collegiate sports. State high school basketball tournament competition takes place at Sioux Falls Arena in March. Sioux Falls softball and baseball fields and the Sioux Falls Stadium host local, regional, and national competition throughout the season. The acclaimed Howard Wood Field hosts track and football events.

## Sports for the Participant

*Golf* magazine has raved about Sioux Falls's golf courses and the opportunities they offer for "prairie golf." The magazine praised the area's "gently rolling topography with an ambiance close to the links courses of Scotland, minus the heather and ocean spray." The city of Sioux Falls maintains some 70 parks and outdoor recreation centers totaling more than 2,800 acres. In addition to the usual park facilities there are swimming pools, soccer fields, lighted skating areas, sand volleyball courts, a disc golf course, and cross-country ski trails. The 16-mile Greenway system of bicycle and hiking trails is a popular attraction. The city is the gateway to the glacial lakes region and the Missouri River, where the walleye fishing is said to be the best in the country. Hundreds of thousands of hunters come to South Dakota each fall for ring-neck pheasant and waterfowl hunting. Winter sports enthusiasts gather at Great Bear Recreation Park for downhill skiing, snowboarding, and tubing.

### Shopping and Dining

Shopping malls and a redeveloped downtown retail district in Sioux Falls offer shoppers more than 3,200 options ranging from small specialty shops to major retail outlets. The Empire Mall and Empire East contain 180 retail establishments. Park Ridge Galleria, the oldest enclosed shopping center in Sioux Falls, is an upscale specialty mall located downtown. Sioux Falls is a central trading center for Native American crafts. Buyers travel to state reservations, including Rosebud and Pine Ridge, to supply local outlets such as Prairie Star Gallery with star quilts, painted hides, sculpture, and jewelry, designed and made by tribal crafters. Shopping is also available at the Old Courthouse Museum downtown. The Downtown Farmer's Market is open every Saturday from the beginning of May to the end of October. Vendors offer a large variety of farm fresh fruits and vegetables, honey, meats, poultry, eggs, plants, flowers, baked goods, and herbs.

More than 500 restaurants present menu choices that include Japanese, Chinese, French, Mexican, and Greek dishes. The local specialty is beefsteak; venison is also popular.

***Visitor Information:*** Sioux Falls Convention & Visitors Bureau, 200 N. Phillips Ave., Ste. 102, Sioux Falls, SD 57104; telephone (605)336-1620; toll-free (800)333-2072; fax (605)336-6499; email sfcvb@sioux-falls.com

## ■ Convention Facilities

With more than 50,000 square feet of column-free exhibit space on the main floor and an additional 11,000 square feet in meeting rooms, the Sioux Falls Convention Center is the largest in the state. It hosts major national and regional conventions, meetings, and trade shows. The convention center is physically attached to the Sioux Falls Arena, which adds seating for 8,000 people and brings the total amount of exhibit space to more than 100,000 square feet; the Sioux Falls Arena will undergo a transformation into an exclusive convention and meeting facility in 2008. Meeting facilities are also offered by hotels and motels that provide more than 3,800 guest rooms in metropolitan Sioux Falls.

***Convention Information:*** Sioux Falls Convention & Visitors Bureau, 200 N. Phillips Ave., Ste. 102, Sioux Falls, SD 57104; telephone (605)336-1620; toll-free (800)333-2072; fax (605)336-6499; email sfcvb@sioux-falls.com

## ■ Transportation

### Approaching the City

The largest air facility in South Dakota, Sioux Falls Regional Airport at Joe Foss Field is the destination for air traffic into Sioux Falls. Northwest Airlines and Northwest Airlink, Delta Connection, United Express, and Allegiant Air offer connections to over 200 domestic cities as well as many international destinations.

East-west I-90, joining Boston and Seattle, and north-south I-29, connecting metropolitan Kansas City with Winnipeg, Canada, intersect northwest of Sioux Falls. I-229, a beltway around the eastern sector of the city, links I-90 and I-29. U.S. highways 18 and 81 also serve the area.

### Traveling in the City

Sioux Falls Transit provides bus transportation and a trolley available for special tours, and Sioux Falls Para-transit provides service to the elderly and disabled. The Sioux Falls Trolley offers free transport to Falls Park and downtown attractions on weekdays and Saturdays throughout the summer.

## ■ Communications

### Newspapers and Magazines

The Sioux Falls daily newspaper is the *Argus Leader,* which is distributed every morning. Other newspapers, including a farm tabloid and college publications, appear weekly and bimonthly. Several magazines are published in Sioux Falls on such subjects as education, wool growing, trucking, knitting and weaving, and poetry.

### Television and Radio

Six television stations are received in Sioux Falls: ABC, CBS, NBC, FOX, PBS, and an independent station. Cable channels are available by subscription. Radio listeners tune in programs on nearly two dozen AM and FM radio stations in the city, which also receives radio broadcasts from Florence and Reliance, South Dakota.

***Media Information:*** *Argus Leader,* 200 S. Minnesota Ave., PO Box 5034, Sioux Falls, SD 57117-5034; telephone (605)331-2300; fax (605)331-2294; email argusnews@argusleader.com

## Sioux Falls Online

*Argus Leader.* Available www.argusleader.com

City of Sioux Falls home page. Available www
.siouxfalls.org

Sioux Falls Area Chamber of Commerce. Available
www.siouxfallschamber.com

Sioux Falls Convention & Visitors Bureau. Available
www.siouxfallscvb.com

Sioux Falls Development Foundation. Available
www.siouxfallsdevelopment.com

Sioux Falls School District. Available www.sf.k12
.sd.us

Siouxland Libraries. Available www.siouxlandlib.org

**BIBLIOGRAPHY**

Landau, Elaine, *The Sioux* (New York: F. Watts, 1989)

LaPointe, Frank, *The Sioux Today* (New York: Crowell-
Collier Press, 1972)

Turner, Ann Warren, *Grasshopper Summer* (New York:
MacMillan, 1989)

Wilder, Laura Ingalls, *By the Shores of Silver Lake* (New
York: Harper & Row, 1971)

Wood, Ted, *A Boy Becomes a Man at Wounded Knee: Ted
Wood with Wanbli Numpa Afraid of Hawk* (New
York: Walker, 1992)

# Wisconsin

# The State in Brief

**Nickname:** Badger State

**Motto:** Forward

**Flower:** Wood violet

**Bird:** Robin

**Area:** 65,498 square miles (2000; U.S. rank 23rd)

**Elevation:** Ranges from 579 feet to 1,951 feet above sea level

**Climate:** Tempered by the Great Lakes, with winters more severe in the north and summers warmer in the south

**Admitted to Union:** May 29, 1848

**Capital:** Madison

**Head Official:** Governor Jim Doyle (D) (until 2010)

**Population**

    **1980:** 4,706,000
    **1990:** 4,891,769
    **2000:** 5,363,675
    **2006 estimate:** 5,556,506
    **Percent change, 1990–2000:** 9.6%
    **U.S. rank in 2006:** 20th
    **Percent of residents born in state:** 72.13% (2006)
    **Density:** 101.9 people per square mile (2006)
    **2006 FBI Crime Index Total:** 172,354

**Racial and Ethnic Characteristics (2006)**

    **White:** 4,859,689
    **Black or African American:** 328,376
    **American Indian and Alaska Native:** 47,727
    **Asian:** 110,778
    **Native Hawaiian and Pacific Islander:** 1,622
    **Hispanic or Latino (may be of any race):** 256,304
    **Other:** 136,736

**Age Characteristics (2006)**

    **Population under 5 years old:** 351,702
    **Population 5 to 19 years old:** 1,122,393
    **Percent of population 65 years and over:** 13.0%
    **Median age:** 37.6

**Vital Statistics**

    **Total number of births (2006):** 69,650
    **Total number of deaths (2006):** 46,922
    **AIDS cases reported through 2005:** 4,332

**Economy**

    **Major industries:** Manufacturing; agriculture; finance, insurance, and real estate; wholesale and retail trade; services
    **Unemployment rate (2006):** 5.5%
    **Per capita income (2006):** $24,875
    **Median household income (2006):** $48,772
    **Percentage of persons below poverty level (2006):** 11.0%
    **Income tax rate:** 4.6% to 6.75%
    **Sales tax rate:** 5.0%

# Appleton

## ■ The City in Brief

**Founded:** 1835 (incorporated 1853)

**Head Official:** Mayor Timothy M. Hanna (NP) (since 1996)

### City Population

1980: 58,913
1990: 65,695
2000: 70,087
2006 estimate: 70,191
Percent change, 1990–2000: 6.6%
U.S. rank in 1980: 340th
U.S. rank in 1990: 352nd
U.S. rank in 2000: 435th

### Metropolitan Area Population

1980: 291,369
1990: 315,121 (MSA)
2000: 358,365
2006 estimate: 217,313
Percent change, 1990–2000: 13.7%
U.S. rank in 1980: 131st
U.S. rank in 1990: Not available
U.S. rank in 2000: 115th

**Area:** 20.88 square miles (2000)

**Elevation:** 780 feet above sea level

**Average Annual Temperature:** 43.6° F

**Average Annual Precipitation:** 30 inches of rain; 47 inches of snow

**Major Economic Sectors:** Manufacturing, services, trade

**Unemployment Rate:** 5.1% (June 2007)

**Per Capita Income:** $26,044 (2005)

**2005 FBI Crime Index Property:** 2,083

**2005 FBI Crime Index Violent:** 173

**Major Colleges and Universities:** Lawrence University, Fox Valley Technical College

**Daily Newspaper:** *The Post-Crescent*

## ■ Introduction

Appleton, once known as the "woodland city" and later "the Lowell of the West" (after the city in Massachusetts) grew up along the Fox River, which provided water power and transportation for the paper manufacturing industry that still dominates the area. Today, fourteen Wisconsin communities including Appleton refer to themselves as Fox Cities. Appleton's history is strongly tied to that of Lawrence University, which grew up with the town after it was chartered in 1847. Lawrence University's 84-acre campus, which includes 32 instructional, recreational and administrative buildings, lies east of the city's downtown. Students and faculty members supply the community with a variety of music, drama, and sports activities.

Appleton is the seat of Outagamie County, but parts of Appleton are also located in Calumet and Winnebago counties. The many trees, city parks, a river lined with old mansions, and interesting shops provide the community with a lively downtown. The once-polluted river, unique in that it is one of the few American rivers flowing northward for its entire course, has been largely restored and is a popular site for swimming, fishing, and boating. Appleton consistently scores high on lists of the best places to live in the United States; it is safe, affordable, and offers a variety of cultural and artistic events.

# ■ Geography and Climate

Appleton is located on rolling terrain that was carved out by glaciers. The city has a continental climate and experiences four distinct seasons, with cold winters and warm summers. It has an average annual snowfall of 47 inches. The ground usually remains snow-covered from late November through late March. April is the most common time for flooding to occur.

**Area:** 20.88 square miles (2000)

**Elevation:** 780 feet above sea level

**Average Temperature:** 43.6° F

**Average Annual Precipitation:** 30 inches (average annual snowfall, 47 inches)

# ■ History

Long before the coming of the Europeans, the area that is now Appleton was inhabited by the Menominee Indians. The Outagamie Indians, also known as the Fox, lived nearby, as did the Winnebago. Early French explorers such as Duluth, Hennepin, and LaSalle floated up the northerly-flowing Fox River into the Indian lands. In the mid-1600s French trappers and traders traveled the waterway of the Fox River in search of furs, particularly beaver pelts. They were followed by Catholic missionaries, including Pere Marquette and Louis Joliet, who passed by in 1673 on their search for the Mississippi River. Later, soldiers crossed the area as they made their way to the three forts that were built on the Fox-Wisconsin waterway, and settlers followed in 1835. That year, Hyppolyte Grignon and his family opened the White Heron trading post just above the Grand Chute. They were followed soon after by John and Jeanette Johnson, whose house became the first hotel, trading post, church, and hospital.

After the building of a canal around the river rapids, steamboats bearing travelers and cargo became a common sight. Wheat farming in the surrounding area gave way to the dairy farms, for which the region is now famous.

However, Appleton itself was first established as the site for a university. At that time it was one of three villages clustered together, the others being Grand Chute (site of the treacherous river rapids) and White Heron. When Amos Lawrence, a Boston Methodist, donated money for a "university in the wilderness" to be constructed in 1847, he decided to honor his wife's family, the Appletons, in naming the new site.

Outagamie County was founded in 1851, and Grand Chute was named the county seat. As neighboring settlements developed, they decided to incorporate under the single name Appleton in 1853. By the next year the new village included a paper mill, two sawmills, several flour mills, and a newspaper. As the center grew, it was incorporated as a city on May 2, 1857.

The power of the Fox River was harnessed in 1882 with the establishment of the world's first hydro-electric plant. The paper mills that developed along the river, and the support industries that grew along with them, played a major role in the economy of the "Paper Valley" that continues into the present day.

New Englanders were the first settlers of the region, but Dutch, German, and Polish settlers had become part of the city by the early twentieth century. More recent immigrants, the Hmong-Laotian refugees from the period of the Vietnam War, have made their mark on the area's culture since the late 1970s.

Appleton today is a prosperous community founded in an appreciation for education, maintaining a certain "small-town charm" in the midst of economic prosperity and downtown revitalization.

***Historical Information:*** Outagamie County Historical Society and Museum, 330 E. College Avenue, Appleton, WI 54911; telephone (920) 733-8445

# ■ Population Profile

**Metropolitan Area Residents**
    1980: 291,369
    1990: 315,121 (MSA)
    2000: 358,365
    2006 estimate: 217,313
    Percent change, 1990–2000: 13.7%
    U.S. rank in 1980: 131st
    U.S. rank in 1990: Not available
    U.S. rank in 2000: 115th

**City Residents**
    1980: 58,913
    1990: 65,695
    2000: 70,087
    2006 estimate: 70,191
    Percent change, 1990–2000: 6.6%
    U.S. rank in 1980: 340th
    U.S. rank in 1990: 352nd
    U.S. rank in 2000: 435th

**Density:** 3,356 people per square mile (2000)

**Racial and ethnic characteristics (2000)**
    White: 64,116
    Black: 695
    American Indian and Alaska Native: 401

©Aero-Fotografik/Chris Wawro

Asian: 3,231
Native Hawaiian and Pacific Islander: 21
Hispanic or Latino (may be of any race): 1,775
Other: 733

**Percent of residents born in state:** 73.3% (2000)

**Age characteristics (2005)**

Population under 5 years old: 4,237
Population 5 to 9 years old: 4,316
Population 10 to 14 years old: 4,278
Population 15 to 19 years old: 6,326
Population 20 to 24 years old: 5,217
Population 25 to 34 years old: 9,325
Population 35 to 44 years old: 10,424
Population 45 to 54 years old: 11,824
Population 55 to 59 years old: 3,669
Population 60 to 64 years old: 2,832
Population 65 to 74 years old: 3,635
Population 75 to 84 years old: 2,582
Population 85 years and older: 824
Median age: 36.0 years

**Births (2006, MSA)**

Total number: 2,888

**Deaths (2006, MSA)**

Total number: 1,447

**Money income (2005)**

Per capita income: $26,044
Median household income: $52,468
Total households: 28,753

**Number of households with income of . . .**

less than $10,000: 1,320
$10,000 to $14,999: 1,596
$15,000 to $24,999: 2,802
$25,000 to $34,999: 3,300
$35,000 to $49,999: 4,480
$50,000 to $74,999: 6,666
$75,000 to $99,999: 4,884
$100,000 to $149,999: 2,197
$150,000 to $199,999: 846
$200,000 or more: 662

**Percent of families below poverty level:** 6.5% (2005)

**2005 FBI Crime Index Property:** 2,083

**2005 FBI Crime Index Violent:** 173

## ■ Municipal Government

Appleton has a mayor-council form of government, made up of 16 city council members plus the mayor. Each term, council members elect a Council President. Council members serve two-year terms and the mayor serves for four years.

**Head Official:** Mayor Timothy M. Hanna (NP) (since 1996; current term expires 2008)

**Total Number of City Employees:** 670 (2007)

*City Information:* City of Appleton, 100 N. Appleton St., Appleton, WI 54911; telephone (920)832-6173

## ■ Economy

### Major Industries and Commercial Activity

Since the mid-nineteenth century the paper industry and its allied industries have been the foundation for Appleton's economy. In fact, the Fox River Valley is home to the highest concentration of paper-making facilities in the world, and accounts for more than 10 percent of the area's total employment and one-third of all manufacturing employment. With approximately 80 paper manufacturing facilities and around 90 publishing companies, the Fox Cities (a cluster of 16 small cities along the region's Fox River) has the highest concentration of paper-related companies in the world. Of nearly as great importance is the metals-machinery industry, which produces fire and utility trucks, crushing and screening equipment, farm machinery, and iron and brass castings. The local economy is also diversifying; several insurance companies are headquartered in the Fox Valley, as well as a growing network of thriving financial institutions. The Fox Cities region is also an important center for regional trade and services. In 2006, manufacturing accounted for 23 percent of all employment in the Fox Cities region, the largest single sector; trade, transportation and utilities were 18 percent; and education/health services as well as business and professional services each accounted for 11 percent.

**Items and goods produced:** paper, paper products, books, metals and machine products, farm machinery, knit, wire, canned goods

### Incentive Programs—New and Existing Companies

*Local programs:* The city of Appleton has several tax incremental financing programs, which it uses to finance public costs like infrastructure and land assembly and sometimes to assist in development costs of a project. The city also has a gap financing program—a community development loan pool resulting from a partnership between the city and some of Appleton's financial institutions. It provides funds to fill the gap between what a bank will lend and the full cost of a project, and can be used for capital expansion, procuring new business locations, and capital equipment. Appleton participates in the Northeast Wisconsin Regional Economic Partnership Technology Tax Credit Program, which provides income tax credits for high-tech business development.

*State programs:* Wisconsin corporate taxes remain among the lowest in the nation due to property tax exemptions on manufacturing machinery and equipment, inventory exemptions, and lack of franchise and unitary taxes.

The Wisconsin Economic Development Association (WEDA) and the Wisconsin Economic Development Institute (WEDI) are two nonprofit agencies that provide information and financial services, legal and legislative assistance, and networking opportunities for their member businesses. On the government side, the Division of Business Development of the Wisconsin Department of Commerce provides technical assistance and financial incentives to businesses in the areas of business planning, site selection, capitalization, permits, training and recruitment, and research and development. On April 28, 2000, Governor Tommy G. Thompson signed into law a bill that created the Wisconsin Technology Council, a nonprofit, nonpartisan board that serves to create, develop and retain science and technology-based business in Wisconsin, and to serve as an advisor to the Governor and the Legislature. The Council also serves as the key link between the state's colleges and universities and the business expertise and capital offered by the financial service industry; the firm published its "Vision 2020: A Model Wisconsin Economy" as a blueprint for its efforts.

*Job training programs:* A local Chamber of Commerce study found that partnerships between social service providers and employers in the Fox Cities have led to successful workforce development, particularly in creating entry-level employment. The State of Wisconsin has programs available to provide grants to businesses training workers in new technologies. The Fox Valley Technical College is an award-winning vocational and technical training institute that has formed long-standing relationships with several area companies to provide top-quality customized training programs.

### Development Projects

Since its inception in 1996, Appleton's Neighborhood Revitalization Program has won national awards, by 2005 having helped four neighborhoods improve both residentially and commercially, with a fifth well underway. In addition, residents have access to the HOME Rental Rehabilitation Loan Program and the

Housing Rehabilitation Loan Program for access to low-interest loans for improving their homes or rental units. In 2006 there were a total of 4,389 new building permits issued.

Construction on the first phase of Appleton's RiverHealth project was expected to begin in summer 2008 and be completed by 2010. The $25 million project is a 15-acre mixed used development designed to meet rigorous environmental standards. In 2005 the Fox Cities Children's Museum received a $1.7 million loan from the state to purchase a new building for expansion and increased promotion.

***Economic Development Information:*** Fox Cities Chamber of Commerce & Industry, 227 S. Walnut Street, PO Box 1855, Appleton, WI 54913-1855; telephone (920)734-7101. City of Appleton Department of Development, 100 North Appleton Street, Appleton, WI 54911; telephone (920)832-6468; fax (920)832-5994

## Commercial Shipping

Outagamie County Regional Airport ships 10 million pounds of freight and mail annually. Rail freight is provided by Canadian National, while more than 60 trucking and warehouse firms service the greater Fox Cities area. The Port of Green Bay, 30 miles north of Appleton, and the Port of Milwaukee, 100 miles south, provide access to the Great Lakes shipping corridor.

## Labor Force and Employment Outlook

The Fox Valley Technical College is an award-winning vocational and technical training institute that has formed long-standing relationships with several area companies to provide top-quality customized training programs. In an effort to increase the strength of the manufacturing labor force, the Fox Cities Chamber of Commerce led a fund drive (the "Brain Train") to bring four-year college degree programs in engineering to the University of Wisconsin-Fox Valley campus.

The following is a summary of data regarding the Appleton metropolitan area labor force, 2006 annual averages.

**Size of nonagricultural labor force:** 118,500

**Number of workers employed in . . .**

   construction and mining: 8,600
   manufacturing: 23,700
   trade, transportation and utilities: 22,300
   information: 2,000
   financial activities: 7,500
   professional and business services: 13,000
   educational and health services: 12,500
   leisure and hospitality: 11,000
   other services: 6,200
   government: 11,800

**Average hourly earnings of production workers employed in manufacturing:** Not available

**Unemployment rate:** 5.1% (June 2007)

| *Largest county employers (2005)* | *Number of employees* |
|---|---|
| Thedacare Inc. | 999+ |
| Appleton Area School District | 999+ |
| Thrivent Financial for Lutherans | 999+ |
| Appleton Papers Inc. | 999+ |
| Wal-Mart | 999+ |
| Sara Lee Corp. (Hillshire Farms) | 999+ |
| Outagamie County | 999+ |
| Fox Valley Technical College | 999+ |
| Miller Electric Manufacturing | 999+ |
| St. Elizabeth Hospital | 500-999 |

## Cost of Living

The following is a summary of data regarding several key cost of living factors for the Appleton metropolitan area.

**2007 (1st quarter) ACCRA Average House Price:** $241,567

**2007 (1st quarter) ACCRA Cost of Living Index:** 96.7

**State income tax rate:** 4.6% to 6.75%

**State sales tax rate:** 5.0%

**Local income tax rate:** None

**Local sales tax rate:** None

**Property tax rate:** $23.56 per $1,000 of full market value (2003, Outagamie County assessment)

***Economic Information:*** Fox Cities Chamber of Commerce and Industry, 227 South Walnut Street, P.O. Box 1855, Appleton, WI 54912-1855; telephone (920) 734-7101; toll-free (800)999-3224; email econ@foxcitieschamber.com

# ■ Education and Research

## Elementary and Secondary Schools

The Appleton Area School District (AASD) is Wisconsin's sixth largest school district and is one of its fastest growing. The district encompasses the city of Appleton and the towns of Grand Chute, Buchanan, Harrison, and a small part of Menasha. Wisconsin traditionally leads the nation in test scores, and Appleton area students consistently exceed state and national test score averages. Special programs in the district include a Montessori school, e-learning programs, a school for the arts, and several charter schools. Since 1997 the Appleton Education Foundation, an independent organization of concerned citizens and business leaders, has awarded grants to Appleton schools totaling more than $1 million to fund educational programs not funded by public sources. The Fox Cities Alliance for Education helps local school districts collaborate with area businesses on school-to-work initiatives.

The following is a summary of data regarding the Appleton Area School District as of the 2005–2006 school year.

**Total enrollment:** 39,352

**Number of facilities**

    elementary schools: 16
    junior high/middle schools: 4
    senior high schools: 3
    other: 14

**Student/teacher ratio:** 15.2:1

**Teacher salaries (2005–06)**

    elementary median: $44,240
    junior high/middle median: $43,460
    secondary median: $41,180

**Funding per pupil:** $8,527

The Appleton Catholic Education System (ACES) consists of four elementary schools and a middle school. The city's ACES schools strive to foster higher level thinking skills. There is also a Catholic High School, Xavier. Appleton also has non-denominational and Lutheran private schools.

### Colleges and Universities

Lawrence University has been a coeducational institution since its founding in 1847 and is the second oldest co-ed college in the country. In 1964 the college merged with Milwaukee's Downer College, a well-regarded women's college. Lawrence, ranked among the nation's top liberal arts colleges in 2008 by *U.S. News & World Report,* enrolls 1,400 undergraduate students. B.A. programs are offered in more than 30 areas, and the school boasts a retention rate of nearly ninety percent. The school is well-known for its Conservatory of Music. The Fox Valley Technical College, with an enrollment of nearly 9,000 students, offers a diverse curriculum and is regarded as one of the most progressive technical institutions in the country. The college has more than 70 associate degree programs, apprenticeship training, continuing education, and customized training. Also located in the Fox Cities

are the University of Wisconsin-Oshkosh, the University of Wisconsin-Fox Valley, and a branch of the Milwaukee School of Engineering (Appleton).

### Libraries and Research Centers

Appleton Public Library has 300,000 volumes and 500 periodical subscriptions as well as a CD collection and audio- and videotapes. The library is a state document depository and has a special area on local history. An expansion in the late 1990s resulted in more space for children's programs and added shelf space for books. More than 1,500 people visit the 85,000-square-foot facility daily, and the library website is accessed 75,000 times per month. The special subject interests of the Fox Valley Technical College, which has more than 61,000 volumes, include agriculture, business and management, environmental studies, medicine, and science and technology. Lawrence University Library, with its nearly 400,000 volumes, is also a state document depository.

***Public Library Information:*** Appleton Public Library, 225 N. Oneida St., Appleton, WI 54911-4780; telephone (920)832-6170; fax (920)832-6182

## ■ Health Care

The city of Appleton is served by three hospitals with a total of nearly 800 beds—St. Elizabeth Hospital (372 beds), Appleton Medical Center (160 beds), and Theda Clark Medical Center (260 beds). There are more than 900 physicians in the three hospitals and two walk-in emergency clinics. The Fox Cities rank among the least expensive regions in the United States for hospital and physician care. St. Elizabeth offers specialized services in cardiac care, behavioral medicine, a center for women and families, extensive rehabilitation facilities, and the Comprehensive Cancer Center. Appleton Medical Center offers magnetic resonance imaging and a linear accelerator. Theda Clark Medical Center in Neenah is also home to Children's Hospital of Wisconsin.

Additionally, there are approximately 200 dentists in the Fox City area, as well as health maintenance organizations that include Affinity Health System, Inc, Aurora Healthcare, Network Health Plan, Prevea Health Plan, United Healthcare, and Unity Health Plans.

## ■ Recreation

### Sightseeing

Visitors learn about the life of what may be Appleton's most famous citizen, Harry Houdini, by taking the Houdini Walking Tour of the city and observing the collection of his many magic feats. From mid-May through mid-September tours are available to the grand log home of James Doty, Wisconsin's second territorial governor. In nearby Kaukauna, guides dressed in circa-1830s garb escort visitors through the Greek revival mansion of prominent fur trader Charles Grignon, which captures the flavor of the fur trading era. The Children's Farm at Plamann Park gives kids the chance to observe young farm animals in a lovely park setting, and the Memorial Park Arboretum & Gardens displays a variety of native Wisconsin trees and plants. The Paper Discovery Museum has exhibits that educate about one of the region's most important industries. The Fox Cities Children's Museum has hands-on activities for kids. At the Hearthstone Historic House Museum, visitors can observe the world's first home lit by a central hydro-electric power plant, and can try generating hydro-power at the new Hydro Adventure Center. More than 1,000 dolls dating from 1850 to the present are on display at the Amelia Bubolz Doll Collection. The Gordon Bubolz Nature Preserve is an 862-acre park with eight miles of hiking trails. The Tayco Street Bridge Tower Museum, in nearby Menasha, has exhibits concerning the bygone era of river navigation during the time when the Fox River was the main highway for commerce and travel in the area. Menasha's University of Wisconsin Center Fox Valley Planetarium presents various shows explaining the wonders of the stars.

## Arts and Culture

Major performing arts facilities in Appleton include the new Fox Cities Performing Arts Center, which has Broadway shows, concerts by the Fox Valley Symphony and national acts, and other events in its 2,100-seat theater; the 1883 Grand Opera House, which presents more than 200 events annually; the Performing Arts at Lawrence University, which offers an artists series, a jazz series and a variety of concerts; and the Lawrence Conservatory of Music, which schedules more than 130 classical performances each year.

The semi-professional Little Sandwich Theatre in the Mall presents live dinner theater productions of musicals, dramas, and children's plays at the Avenue Mall. Community theater for the Fox Valley is provided by the Attic Theatre, which produces four summer shows and a holiday production.

The Fox Valley Symphony has a more than 30-year history and presents five subscription concerts each year, plus a holiday concert and two concert chamber series. Appleton's citizens enjoy music making and some of the more prominent musical groups include the Appleton MacDowell Male Chorus, the Chaminade Women's Chorus, the Green Apple Folk Music Society, and the White Heron Chorale.

The Bergstrom-Mahler Museum displays the world's foremost collection of glass paperweights and an exhibit of Germanic glass dating back to the 1500s, as well as a variety of traveling exhibits. The Outagamie Museum/(Harry) Houdini Historical Center features Houdini memorabilia, including a fascinating handcuff display and magic shows in the summer. The museum also has paper-

making exhibits and exhibits on subjects of local interest. Works of fine art and student exhibits are on display at the architecturally whimsical Wriston Art Center on the Lawrence University Campus, with its glass walls and turrets, fanciful curves, and recessed amphitheater.

The Fox Cities Children's Museum provides youngsters with 27,000 square feet of opportunities for hands-on exploration. The museum features a giant human heart kids can climb onto and slide out of and interactive displays on electricity, wildlife, rocks, bubbles, fire trucks, other cultures, music and machines, as well as the Science Spectrum, a trip through the world of science.

The city also has some impressive public artworks, including the Appleton Aurora, a unique 10 by 60 foot sculpture atop the Appleton Center, and the Fox River Oracle, a massive sculpture at the north end of Appleton's Skyline Bridge.

***Arts and Culture Information:*** Fox Valley Arts Alliance; telephone (920)734-4860

## Festivals and Holidays

Spring events include the Nature's Image Spring Fair at the 1,000 Islands Environmental Center in Kaukauna; the Antiques Showcase & Sale in April; the Memorial Garden Festival, which takes place at Memorial Park Arboretum & Gardens in May; and the grand finale of the month of May, the Memorial Day Parade downtown. June brings the Flag Day Parade in downtown Appleton and the Great Wisconsin Cheese Festival in Little Chute. Independence Day is saluted at the Civic Celebration held at Memorial Park; also in July is the annual Paperfest in Kimberly. The Fox Cities Marathon is held in September. The enjoyment of German food and culture, including a variety of beer, is the focus of Oktoberfest, held each September. The Harvest Song Fall Festival at Bubolz Nature Preserve, the Crop Walk, and the Romp in the Swamp are the city's highlights for October. Christmas is celebrated with Holiday Candlelight Tours followed by January's Victorian Christmas.

## Sports for the Spectator

The Timber Rattlers, the Class A affiliate of the Seattle Mariners, play baseball in the 3,400-seat Fox Cities Stadium. The thrills and spills of stock-car racing can be enjoyed at nearby Kaukauna's Wisconsin International Raceway. Sports enthusiasts have easy access to the excitement of the Green Bay Packers, the Milwaukee Bucks, and the Milwaukee Brewers; the University of Wisconsin Badgers compete collegiately in the Big Ten conference in Madison, just a 90 minute drive away.

## Sports for the Participant

World class runners congregate in the area each October to trek over seven bridges through seven cities, part of the 26.2-mile route of the Fox Cities Marathon. The Gordon

Bubolz Nature Preserve offers 762 acres of wildlife habitat. Hikers and skiers enjoy eight miles of trails along a trout pond and through a white cedar forest. The city of Appleton's Parks and Recreation System consists of 600 acres and 26 parks, plus an ice arena. Appleton's Talulah and Memorial parks feature bike paths, and Lutz Park has a boat landing. Golfers enjoy the Chaska and Reid public golf courses, and the city has five parks with lighted tennis courts. The USA Youth Sports Complex boasts soccer fields and baseball diamonds. The Appleton Rugby Club holds a spring and a fall season of games, and the Fox Cities Rugby Club offers both adult and youth leagues. Erb and Meade Parks have public swimming pools and Plamann Park offers snowmobile trails and access to the state trail system.

## Shopping and Dining

Appleton's Fox River Mall, with more than 180 retail shops, is one of the largest in Wisconsin. The mall is anchored by large department stores such as Marshall Fields, JCPenney, Sears, and Target. Other major malls include the Avenue Mall, featuring specialty shops and Herberger's Department Store; and the Jansport Outlet. Lamers Dairy in Appleton has tours of its milk-bottling plant as well as a country gift store. Simons Specialty Cheese in Little Chute has 100 varieties of cheese and Wisconsin-themed gifts. The Country Squire Christmas Shoppe in Neenah is locally famous for ornaments and Christmas decorations from around the world. The Frame Workshop in Appleton is an award-winning frame shop and art gallery that also has hand-blown glass ornaments from Germany. Vande Walle's Candy Shop offers self-tours of candy-making and pastry-making. The Abracadabra Magic Shop, owned by a local magician, offers magic trick materials and books. More than 60,000 titles, a coffee bar, and a fine selection of gifts is available at Conkey's Book Store, a 100-year old landmark that was recently expanded.

The city offers a variety of restaurants featuring the cuisines of Greece, Italy, Japan, Mexico, Thailand, China, and France, as well as casual American fare or upscale continental dining. For fine dining, there is Peggy's Café on College Avenue downtown, The Seasons on Nicolet, or George's Steak House, a family-owned institution for more than 50 years. Mark's East Side and Old Bavarian celebrate the area's strong German influences.

***Visitor Information:*** Fox Cities Convention & Visitors Bureau, 3433 W. College Ave., Appleton, WI 54914; telephone (920)734-3358

## ■ Convention Facilities

The Radisson Paper Valley Hotel and Conference Center has 390 guest rooms and 25 meeting rooms, and can fit up to 2,000 people for meetings. Overall the Fox Cities region has more than 30 hotels and motels, over 2,900 guest rooms, and conference facilities that can fit 1,750 people in one room, theater-style and 1,200 people in one room, banquet-style. The renovated Tri-County Arena and Expo Center in nearby Neenah offers more than 35,000 square feet of floor space, plus special use rooms. The facility is available for trade shows and exhibitions from April through September; in the winter months it serves as an ice rink. The Fox Cities Convention and Visitors Bureau offers a variety of site selection and planning services.

***Convention Information:*** Fox Cities Convention & Visitors Bureau, 3433 W. College Ave., Appleton, WI 54914; telephone (920)734-3358

## ■ Transportation

### Approaching the City

Located two miles west of the city, Outagamie County Airport, one of the fastest-growing airports in Wisconsin, offers service by United Express, Comair/Delta Connection, Northwest Airlink, and Midwest/Express/Skyway Airlines. Outgamie served 572,000 passengers in 2006 with over 57,500 aircraft operations. Additional flights can be taken from Green Bay's Austin Straubel Field just 30 minutes away. Inter-regional bus service is provided by Greyhound Bus Lines, with daily trips to Milwaukee, Green Bay and Stevens Point. Lamers Bus Lines offers one daily departure to the Amtrak station in Milwaukee.

### Traveling in the City

Appleton's main thoroughfares include U.S. Highways 10, 41, and 45. Secondary passages are State Highways, 47, 55, 76, 96, 114, 150, and 441. Valley Transit offers local bus service.

## ■ Communications

### Newspapers and Magazines

*The Post-Crescent,* Appleton's daily paper, appears in the evenings. The *Milwaukee Journal Sentinel* also covers news in the city. Magazines published in Appleton include *The New American,* a conservative magazine covering international affairs; *Marketplace Magazine,* a business magazine covering northeastern Wisconsin, and *The Scene,* focusing on what's happening in the Fox Cities.

### Television and Radio

Time Warner Cable offers both digital cable and Roadrunner high-speed internet. Appleton television viewers have broadcast access to network programming that includes ABC, CBS, NBC, and PBS. Approximately 25 radio stations broadcast to the Appleton area, with programming ranging from adult contemporary, to news/talk, public radio, big band, and classic rock.

***Media Information:*** *The Post-Crescent,* 306 West Washington Street, PO Box 59, Appleton, WI 54912-0059; telephone (800)236-6397

### Appleton Online

Appleton Public Library. Available www.apl.org/index.html

City of Appleton. Available www.appleton.org

Fox Cities Chamber of Commerce and Industry. Available www.foxcitieschamber.com

Fox Cities Convention and Visitors Bureau. Available www.foxcities.org

The Heart of the Valley Chamber of Commerce. Available www.heartofthevalleychamber.com

BIBLIOGRAPHY

Bubolz, Gordon, ed., *Land of the Fox, Saga of Outagamie County* (Outagamie County State Centennial Committee, 1949)

Kort, Ellen, *The Fox Heritage* (Woodland Hills, CA: Windsor Publications, 1984)

Ryan, Thomas Henry, *History of Outagamie County, Wisconsin: Being a General Survey Including a History of the Cities, Towns, and Villages* (Chicago, IL: Goodspeed Historical Association, 1911)

# Green Bay

## ■ The City in Brief

**Founded:** 1701 (incorporated 1854)

**Head Official:** Mayor James J. Schmitt
(since 2003)

**City Population**

    1980: 87,899
    1990: 96,466
    2000: 102,213
    2006 estimate: 100,353
    Percent change, 1990–2000: 5.9%
    U.S. rank in 1980: 200th
    U.S. rank in 1990: 205th
    U.S. rank in 2000: 240th

**Metropolitan Area Population**

    1980: 175,280
    1990: 194,594
    2000: 226,178
    2006 estimate: 299,003
    Percent change, 1990–2000: 16.2%
    U.S. rank in 1980: Not available
    U.S. rank in 1990: Not available
    U.S. rank in 2000: 153rd

**Area:** 43.8 square miles (2000)

**Elevation:** 582 feet above sea level

**Average Annual Temperatures:** January, 15.6° F; July,
69.9° F; annual average, 44.4° F

**Average Annual Precipitation:** 29.19 inches of rain;
47.7 inches of snow

**Major Economic Sectors:** Wholesale and retail trade,
services, manufacturing

**Unemployment Rate:** 5.2% (June 2007)

**Per Capita Income:** $22,843 (2005)

**2005 FBI Crime Index Property:** 2,931

**2005 FBI Crime Index Violent:** 495

**Major Colleges and Universities:** University of Wisconsin–Green Bay, St. Norbert College, Northeast
Wisconsin Technical College

**Daily Newspaper:** *Green Bay Press-Gazette*

## ■ Introduction

Green Bay, named for the green-tinted streaks that stripe
its bay in springtime, is the seat of Wisconsin's Brown
County and the center of a metropolitan statistical area
that includes the entire county. The oldest permanent
settlement in Wisconsin, Green Bay began as a French
fur-trading post and mission that was important to the
exploration of the Upper Midwest in the early seventeenth century. Since the nineteenth century the local
economy has been based on the lumbering, meat packing, and paper making industries, with a currently
expanding service sector. Today Green Bay is known as
"the tissue paper capital of America" and is home to the
famous Green Bay Packers professional football team.
Green Bay was recently named an "All-America City" and
consistently ranks high on "best-places" lists.

## ■ Geography and Climate

Green Bay is located at the mouth of the Fox River, one
of the largest northward-flowing rivers in the United
States, which empties into the south end of Lake
Michigan's Green Bay. The surrounding topography—
the bay, Lakes Michigan and Superior, and to a lesser
extent the slightly higher terrain terminating in the Fox
River Valley—modifies the continental climate. The lake

effects and the limited hours of sunshine, caused by cloudiness, produce a narrow temperature range. Three-fifths of the total annual rainfall occurs during the growing season, May through September; the high degree of precipitation, combined with the low temperature range, is conducive to the development of the dairy industry. Long winters with snowstorms are common, though winter extremes are not so severe as would be indicated by Green Bay's northern latitude location. Snowfall averages 47.7 inches each year.

**Area:** 43.8 square miles (2000)

**Elevation:** 582 feet above sea level

**Average Temperatures:** January, 15.6° F; July, 69.9° F; annual average, 44.4° F

**Average Annual Precipitation:** 29.19 inches of rain; 47.7 inches of snow

# ■ History

## Great Lakes-Mississippi Water Link Sought

On a mission for Samuel de Champlain, the governor of New France, Jean Nicolet was charged with finding a route from the Great Lakes to the Mississippi River. In 1634 he arrived at La Baye des Puans, where the Fox River empties into Lake Michigan, and claimed the region for France. But La Baye did not gain importance until 1669 when Jesuit missionary Father Claude Allouez, who established a mission there, traveled the length of the Fox River and discovered a waterway to the Mississippi River, indirectly linking the St. Lawrence and the Gulf of Mexico.

La Baye became a fur-trading center and its future importance was secured when Nicolas Perrot was made commandant of La Baye. Perrot was an effective diplomat who made alliances and trade agreements with Native Americans. The lands of the upper Mississippi became the possession of the French Empire when a formal agreement was signed at Fort St. Antoine in 1689, turning a lucrative fur trading region over to the French. But when Perrot was recalled to France in 1716, his diplomatic policy was replaced by a military regime. The resulting tensions developed into warfare with the Fox Indians that continued until 1740, when fur trading again prospered and permanent housing was constructed.

In 1745 Augustin de Langlade established a trading center on the bank of the Fox River; his relations with Native Americans were built on trust and respect. Langlade's large family controlled the region's trade, owned large parcels of land, married Menominee tribe women, and lived independent of French rule. During the French and Indian War, the Langlades left La Baye to fight against the British in Ohio and Canada. The British

gained control of what was known as the Northwest Territory and captured Fort La Baye, which they rebuilt and renamed Fort Edward August. The British also renamed the area Green Bay, after the green-tinted streaks that stripe the bay in springtime. Trade flourished for both French and English settlers during the period of British rule and continued to prosper after the Northwest Territory was transferred to the U.S. government after the Revolutionary War.

## City Develops With Lumber, Professional Sports

It was not until after the War of 1812 that financier John Jacob Astor's American Fur Company secured control of the fur trade. Fort Howard at Green Bay and Fort Crawford at Prairie du Chine were built to protect U.S. commercial interests. The opening of the Erie Canal, linking the Great Lakes to New England, further advanced Green Bay as a trading center. Daniel Whitney platted one part of present-day Green Bay in 1829 and named it Navarino while Astor platted an opposite section and built the Astor Hotel to attract settlers. Astor priced his land too high and when the hotel burned down in 1857 his company relinquished claims on the land. Farming was soon replaced by lumber as the dominant economic activity in Green Bay and in 1854, the year the city was incorporated, 80 million feet of pine lumber were milled.

Today, Green Bay is known as the smallest city in the United States to sponsor a professional football team. The Green Bay Packers were founded in 1919 by "Curly" Lambeau and George Calhoun, sports editor of the *Green Bay Press-Gazette,* and the team takes its name from the Indian Packing Corporation, which purchased the team's first uniforms. The Packers joined the National Football League in 1919 and have had a distinctive history. Under coach Vince Lombardi in the 1960s the Packers set a standard of team performance and dedication that other teams in the league have come to emulate in the modern football era. The Packers won the first two Super Bowl games in 1967 and 1968, and Lombardi and his players became national heroes. Thirty years later, the team won Super Bowl XXXI, beginning a new era under coach Mike Holmgren and general manager Ron Wolf. In addition to championship sports teams, Green Bay supports colleges, a symphony, community chorus, community theater, and several museums. And unlike many Midwestern cities with lagging economic growth, Green Bay has enjoyed a diverse and growing local economy. Using job growth and economic balance as its measures, in 2004 *Inc.* magazine ranked Green Bay as the country's top medium-sized metropolitan area for doing business. Green Bay is poised to become even more vibrant in the future; in 2005 the Alliance for Youth named it the best community nationwide for young people.

©Aero-Fotografik/Chris Wawro

*Historical Information:* University of Wisconsin-Green Bay Area Research Center, 2420 Nicolet Drive, Green Bay, WI 54311-7001; telephone (920)465-2539

# ■ Population Profile

## Metropolitan Area Residents

1980: 175,280
1990: 194,594
2000: 226,178
2006 estimate: 299,003
Percent change, 1990–2000: 16.2%
U.S. rank in 1980: Not available
U.S. rank in 1990: Not available
U.S. rank in 2000: 153rd

## City Residents

1980: 87,899
1990: 96,466
2000: 102,213
2006 estimate: 100,353
Percent change, 1990–2000: 5.9%
U.S. rank in 1980: 200th

U.S. rank in 1990: 205th
U.S. rank in 2000: 240th

**Density:** 2,333.6 people per square mile (2000)

**Racial and ethnic characteristics (2005)**

White: 76,902
Black: 1,937
American Indian and Alaska Native: 2,255
Asian: 4,577
Native Hawaiian and Pacific Islander: 36
Hispanic or Latino (may be of any race): 8,572
Other: 6,325

**Percent of residents born in state:** 74.4% (2000)

**Age characteristics (2005)**

Population under 5 years old: 5,575
Population 5 to 9 years old: 5,231
Population 10 to 14 years old: 6,697
Population 15 to 19 years old: 5,586
Population 20 to 24 years old: 7,750
Population 25 to 34 years old: 13,226
Population 35 to 44 years old: 14,152
Population 45 to 54 years old: 15,674

Population 55 to 59 years old: 5,844
Population 60 to 64 years old: 3,472
Population 65 to 74 years old: 5,047
Population 75 to 84 years old: 4,302
Population 85 years and older: 1,686
Median age: 37.0 years

**Births (2006, MSA)**

Total number: 3,731

**Deaths (2006, MSA)**

Total number: 2,095

**Money income (2005)**

Per capita income: $22,843
Median household income: $40,477
Total households: 41,823

**Number of households with income of . . .**

less than $10,000: 3,349
$10,000 to $14,999: 3,503
$15,000 to $24,999: 5,928
$25,000 to $34,999: 5,899
$35,000 to $49,999: 7,289
$50,000 to $74,999: 7,971
$75,000 to $99,999: 4,091
$100,000 to $149,999: 2,715
$150,000 to $199,999: 497
$200,000 or more: 581

**Percent of families below poverty level:** 9.5% (2005)

**2005 FBI Crime Index Property:** 2,931

**2005 FBI Crime Index Violent:** 495

# ■ Municipal Government

The Green Bay city government is administered by a mayor and 12 alderpersons. The mayor is elected to a four-year term; the alderpersons are elected to two-year terms.

**Head Official:** Mayor James J. Schmitt (since 2003; current term expires in 2011)

**Total Number of City Employees:** 1,000 (2007)

*City Information:* City of Green Bay, 100 N. Jefferson St., Green Bay, WI 54301; telephone (920)448-3010

# ■ Economy

## Major Industries and Commercial Activity

Green Bay's economy is highly diversified. Approximately one of every five jobs in the county is in manufacturing, many of which are within or directly related to the paper industry. Growing industries in Green Bay are healthcare,

insurance, and transportation. Tourism is growing, as well. A study in the late 1990s found that the Green Bay Packers generated $144 million in total annual spending in Brown County, 1,620 full- and part-time jobs, and $9.6 million in annual tax revenue to local and state government. Other major employers include Schneider National, Inc., a transportation company, and the Georgia Pacific Corp, which manufactures paper products.

Brown County is among the top four jobbing, wholesale, and distribution points in Wisconsin. Green Bay is the site of a petroleum storage terminal. The city ranks as a major retailing center for northeastern Wisconsin and Upper Michigan.

In 2007, the fastest-growing industries in the area included business computer and data processing services, financial services, insurance, real estate, health services, transportation, communication and utilities.

**Items and goods produced:** tissue paper and paper products, cheese, food products, lumber, woodwork, paper mill machinery, paper boxes, clothing, steel furniture, auto parts, dairy products, gloves, fertilizers, foundry products, brick tile, sheet metal, awnings

## Incentive Programs—New and Existing Companies

*Local programs:* The principal economic development organization in Green Bay is the Advance Business Development Center, a publicly and privately supported branch of the Green Bay Area Chamber of Commerce. Advance uses its online database to inform interested business about available sites and buildings. The Business Retention committee assists companies in troubleshooting municipal service problems, job training needs, and other issues. The Chamber's Small Business Council assists and meets regularly to promote the interests of businesses with up to 300 employees. The Advance Business Development Center is one of the most successful incubators in Wisconsin, having graduated more than 100 start-up firms by allowing them to lease increasingly larger amounts of shared light industrial and office space as their firms grow.

*State programs:* Wisconsin corporate taxes remain among the lowest in the nation due to property tax exemptions on manufacturing machinery and equipment, inventory exemptions, and lack of franchise and unitary taxes.

The Wisconsin Economic Development Association (WEDA) and the Wisconsin Economic Development Institute (WEDI) are two nonprofit agencies that provide information and financial services, legal and legislative assistance, and networking opportunities for their member businesses. On the government side, the Division of Business Development of the Wisconsin Department of

Commerce provides technical assistance and financial incentives to businesses in the areas of business planning, site selection, capitalization, permits, training and recruitment, and research and development. On April 28, 2000, Governor Tommy G. Thompson signed into law a bill that created the Wisconsin Technology Council, a nonprofit, nonpartisan board that serves to create, develop and retain science and technology-based business in Wisconsin, and to serve as an advisor to the Governor and the Legislature. The Council also serves as the key link between the state's colleges and universities and the business expertise and capital offered by the financial service industry; the firm published its "Vision 2020: A Model Wisconsin Economy" as a blueprint for its efforts.

*Job training programs:* Partners in Education (PIE), coordinated by the Green Bay Area Chamber of Commerce, works with businesses, educators, and community organizations to provide training that helps students transitioning from school to work.

## Development Projects

Downtown Green Bay, Inc., brings together people, organizations, and funds to implement and facilitate downtown development projects. The organization also gives special grants for façade and sign improvement on existing facilities. As of 2007 the organization had assisted with Baylake Bank's restoration of the old Boston Store property; a $4.5 million, 26,000-square-foot addition to the YWCA; and construction of a $16-million, four-story building for the Nicolet National Bank. They also won approval from the Common Council on a riverfront redevelopment plan that will include an urban beach and boardwalk. Other projects in the works in 2007 included a major hotel/condominium project for the old Younkers Building site on Washington, called River Center. The project includes the Astor Place Condominiums and Riverfront Lofts residential developments, commercial space, and a $12-million boardwalk. Developers hoped that tenants could begin moving in by 2008.

Austin Straubel Airfield unveiled the results of a $26-million renovation in 2006, which included a grand lobby and the addition of four new gates. In November 2007, the University of Wisconsin opened its new $33 million dollar sports complex, the Kress Events Center.

*Economic Development Information:* Green Bay Area Chamber of Commerce, 400 S. Washington St., PO Box 1660, Green Bay, WI 54305-1660; telephone (920) 437-8704; fax (920)437-1024

## Commercial Shipping

The Port of Green Bay is an international and domestic port with a navigation season extending from April through December. More than 200 commercial vessels transport cargo through the channel each year; port tonnage averages more than 2.4 million metric tons annually. Linking the port with inland markets are an interstate highway, air cargo service, around 40 motor freight carriers, and the Soo Line, Union Pacific, and Escanaba & Lake Superior railroads.

## Labor Force and Employment Outlook

A relatively diverse economy and an attractive small-town lifestyle kept Green Bay's job outlook ahead of the curve in the early 2000s, despite a nationwide rise in unemployment in recent years. The local education prospects are excellent on both a secondary and university/technical level, providing a pool of well-trained workers. During years of strong economic growth, however, firms have often found a shortage of qualified workers and recruitment and retention become issues of concern. Partners in Education (PIE), coordinated by the Green Bay Area Chamber of Commerce, provides a link between businesses, educators, and community organizations with an objective to assist students in developing the skills necessary for successful transition from school to an eventual career.

The following is a summary of data regarding the Green Bay metropolitan area labor force, 2006 annual averages.

**Size of nonagricultural labor force:** 169,400

**Number of workers employed in ...**

construction and mining: 8,600
manufacturing: 30,200
trade, transportation and utilities: 35,600
information: 2,400
financial activities: 11,800
professional and business services: 15,700
educational and health services: 21,400
leisure and hospitality: 15,800
other services: 7,200
government: 20,800

**Average hourly earnings of production workers employed in manufacturing:** Not available

**Unemployment rate:** 5.2% (June 2007)

| *Largest employers (2006)* | *Number of employees* |
|---|---|
| Schneider National, Inc. | 3,696 |
| Georgia-Pacific Corp. | 3,181 |
| Oneida Tribe of Indians of Wisconsin | 2,910 |
| Humana | 2,900 |
| Green Bay Public Schools | 2,655 |
| Bellin Health | 1,928 |
| St. Vincent Hospital | 1,750 |
| Shopko Stores, Inc. | 1,728 |
| Aurora Health Care | 1,613 |
| WPS Resources | 1,586 |

## Cost of Living

The cost of living in Green Bay ranks consistently below the national average in health care, utilities, housing, food, and miscellaneous goods and services.

The following is a summary of data regarding several key cost of living factors in the Green Bay area.

**2007 (1st quarter) ACCRA Average House Price:** $266,700

**2007 (1st quarter) ACCRA Cost of Living Index:** 94.4

**State income tax rate:** 4.6% to 6.75%

**State sales tax rate:** 5.0%

**Local income tax rate:** None

**Local sales tax rate:** None

**Property tax rate:** $25.75 per $1,000 of assessed value

*Economic Information:* Advance, Green Bay Area Economic Development, PO Box 1660, Green Bay, WI 54305-1660; telephone (920)437-8704.

# ■ Education and Research

## Elementary and Secondary Schools

The Green Bay Area Public School District, the fourth largest school system in the state of Wisconsin, includes, in addition to the city of Green Bay, the towns of Allouez and Scott and parts of the towns of Bellevue, DePere, Eaton, and Humboldt. A seven-member nonpartisan board hires a superintendent. Special programs include a manufacturing academy, an international business school, and a special high school for students interested in pursuing a career in education.

The following is a summary of data regarding the Green Bay School District as of the 2005–2006 school year.

**Total enrollment:** 49,079

**Number of facilities**

    elementary schools: 25
    junior high/middle schools: 5
    senior high schools: 4
    other: 1

**Student/teacher ratio:** 14.2:1

**Teacher salaries (2005–06)**

    elementary median: $47,410
    junior high/middle median: $46,040
    secondary median: $46,030

**Funding per pupil:** $9,266

Nearly 30 parochial schools, including Catholic and Lutheran, enroll students in kindergarten through twelfth grade curricula.

*Public Schools Information:* Green Bay Area Public Schools, PO Box 23387, Green Bay, WI 54305; telephone (920)448-2000

## Colleges and Universities

Part of the statewide university system, the University of Wisconsin-Green Bay grants associate, undergraduate, and graduate degrees in such areas as arts and sciences, business, and natural and biological sciences. The school enrolls more than 6,000 students per year and boasts a student to faculty ratio of 24-to-1. In 2007, students hailed from approximately 71 Wisconsin counties, 37 other states, and 27 other countries. Top fields of study are business administration, psychology, and human development. St. Norbert College is a four-year liberal arts institution operated by the Norbertine Fathers. St. Norbert enrolls more than 2,000 students annually and has a student to faculty ratio of 14-1. Vocational, technical, and adult education is provided by the Northeast Wisconsin Technical College as well as trade schools specializing in particular skills.

## Libraries and Research Centers

The largest library in Green Bay is the award-winning Brown County Library. In 2006 the library had approximately 1.3 million visits, with 2.4 million items checked out. These resources are available through a central library, a bookmobile, and eight branch libraries. Special collections pertain to Brown County history, genealogy, Wisconsin history, and oral history; the library is a depository for state documents. The Nicolet Federated Library is a regional library, serving a population of more than 330,000 and assisting 42 member public libraries with their operations. The University of Wisconsin-Green Bay Cofrin Library serves the University of Wisconsin system as well as the northeast Wisconsin community. Libraries are also maintained by Northern Wisconsin Technical College, county agencies, health care organizations, churches, and corporations.

*Public Library Information:* Brown County Library, 515 Pine Street, Green Bay, WI 54301; telephone (920)448-4400; fax (920)448-4364

# ■ Health Care

Green Bay is served by several major hospitals, a number of clinics and health care agencies, and approximately 20 nursing homes. St. Vincent Hospital, with 542 beds, is the city's largest hospital and a regional center for cancer treatment, neuroscience, pediatrics, trauma, rehabilitation, perinatal care, and poison information. Operated by Bellin Health, Bellin Memorial Hospital is a 167-bed general care facility that specializes in the treatment of heart disease, mental health and addictive services, obstetrics, and orthopedics. Employing more than 2,300 people, Bellin Health also operates the four-year Bellin School College of Nursing. St. Mary's Hospital, with 158 private rooms, houses one of the state's largest 24-hour emergency wards; other services include an alcohol and drug abuse program and a sick child day care program. It is the only hospital located on the west side of the city. The Prevea Clinic, a joint effort among St. Vincent Hospital, Beaumont-Webster Clinic and the West Side Clinic, has more than 100 physicians trained in 21 specialty care areas who treat patients from throughout northeastern Wisconsin. Aurora Bay Medical Center, the area's newest hospital, has a 24-hour emergency room and is home to the Vince Lombardi Cancer Clinic. In 2007 Aurora Bay announced plans to build a new medical office building, also slated to host the sports medicine and orthopedic programs.

Other area clinics are operated by Oneida Community Health Center, Baycare Health Systems, and Aurora Health Care. Brown County offers a Crisis Center and Mental Health Clinic for its residents.

# ■ Recreation

## Sightseeing

The 25,000-square-foot Green Bay Packer Hall of Fame was moved to the Lambeau Field Atrium as part of a stadium renovation project. One of Green Bay's most popular attractions, the museum has trophies, memorabilia, and mementos of the Green Bay Packers, including the Vince Lombardi collection and displays on the club's league championships and Super Bowl victories; tours of Lambeau Field are also available. The 40-acre Heritage Hill State Historical Park features furnished historical buildings grouped according to four heritage themes: pioneer, small town, military, and agricultural. Among them are a 1762 fur trader's cabin, a reproduction of Wisconsin's first courthouse, Wisconsin's oldest standing house, Fort Howard buildings dating from the 1830s, and a Belgian farmhouse.

Hazelwood, a home built by Morgan L. Martin, president of the second Wisconsin Constitutional Convention, dates from 1837 and contains the table on which Wisconsin's constitution was drafted. The National Railroad Museum is a locomotive museum that exhibits locomotives and cars from the steam and diesel eras, including "Big Boy," one of the world's largest locomotives. Special attractions are U.S. Army General Dwight D. Eisenhower's World War II staff train and British Prime Minister Winston Churchill's traveling car. Other popular attractions are Oneida Bingo and the NEW Zoo,

a life science institute that seeks to enhance visitors' understanding of animal life and its relationship to ecological systems.

Many visitors to Green Bay like to take a side trip to Door County, 90 minutes north; it offers miles of shoreline, state parks, and lighthouses, and is home to many artists and craftspersons.

## Arts and Culture

The Green Bay Symphony performs a six-concert season at the Edward W. Weidner Center for the Performing Arts at the University of Wisconsin-Green Bay. Both classic and modern plays, ballet, musical events, and nationally touring musical acts are featured at the beautifully-restored Meyer Theater, a 1,000-seat member of the League of Historic American Theaters. The Civic Music Association sponsors visiting artists. St. Norbert College hosts a performing arts series and college theater productions, and the Weidner Center also hosts a variety of entertainments, including ballet performances and Broadway musicals. Concerts and ice shows take place at the Resch Center and Brown County Veterans Memorial Complex.

Brown County's Neville Public Museum houses six galleries of art, natural history, and science exhibits; the "On the Edge of the Inland Sea" exhibit traces 13,000 years of northeast Wisconsin history. The Oneida Nation Museum captures the history of the Oneida Utopian community's life after it moved from New York to Wisconsin.

## Festivals and Holidays

Artstreet is Green Bay's annual celebration of the performing and visual arts, held in the downtown district. Other annual celebrations include Arti Gras, Bayfest, Celebrate Americafest, the Oneida Indian Pow Wow, Brown County Fair, the Wet Whistle Wine Festival and Ethnic Festival in September, the Terror on the Fox Haunted House and Train Ride in October, and the Holiday Parade.

## Sports for the Spectator

The Green Bay Packers, the oldest modern professional football team, enjoy one of the most heralded histories in professional sports; the team plays in the National Football Conference of the National Football League. They compete at home at Lambeau Field against perennial rivals that include the Detroit Lions, Chicago Bears, and Minnesota Vikings. Playing in by far the smallest city in the entire NFL, the Packers are the local passion and enjoy a national following; despite the town's size, Packers games are always sold out. In college athletics, St. Norbert College provides small-college football and baseball in nearby DePere. The University of Wisconsin-Green Bay supports a successful soccer program and competes in Division I basketball, making the NCAA basketball tournament and even winning one tournament game in 2005. The national champion Green Bay Gamblers play in the Junior A U.S. Hockey League.

### Sports for the Participant

The Green Bay Parks and Recreation Department oversees numerous city parks large and small, including the Bay Beach Amusement Park and Wildlife Sanctuary, the Metro Boat Launch at the mouth of the Fox River, the SK8 Park for skateboarders and inline skaters, and the Triangle Recreation Area. The department also sponsors sports leagues for all age groups. Facilities include courts for indoor tennis and racquetball, indoor and outdoor public swimming pools, ice skating and hockey rinks, outdoor tennis courts, ski and toboggan hills, and cross-country ski trails. Soccer and rugby teams compete in leagues. Several more boating facilities are available along Green Bay. Green Bay, Fox River, and Lake Michigan provide fishermen with pike, bass, salmon, trout, muskie, and panfish. Hunters can obtain licenses to bag duck, deer, and small game. Children enjoy rides and other activities at Bay Beach Amusement Park. Across the street from the amusement park at Wildlife Sanctuary, a 700-acre urban wildlife refuge, visitors can observe native fauna and hike the nature trails.

### Shopping and Dining

The Green Bay area is the regional shopping center for northeastern Wisconsin. Shoppers may choose from among three major shopping malls with nearly 200 stores, mini-malls, and craft stores. There are quaint shopping districts with unique shops in the Historic Broadway District of Green Bay on Broadway, and on Main Street in nearby DePere. The Flying Pig Gallery and Greenspace in Algoma is a local attraction. Of unique interest is the Green Bay Packer Hall of Fame Store, offering Packer treasures, at the Lambeau Field Atrium.

Green Bay's more than 100 restaurants offer options ranging from gourmet cuisine to ethnic menus, sports bars, and casual dining establishments, and the options continue to expand. A more recent addition to the menu, diners can enjoy a sunset dinner boat that cruises the Green Bay waterways. Patrick's on the Bay offers beautiful waterside views and what many consider to be the best dining in the area.

*Visitor Information:* Green Bay Area Visitor and Convention Bureau, 1901 S. Oneida St., PO Box 10596, Green Bay, WI 54307; telephone (920)494-9507; visitorinfo@packercountry.com

## ■ Convention Facilities

With the opening of the KI Convention Center, Green Bay established itself as a leading regional meeting and convention destination. Offering more than 46,000

square feet of flexible meeting and convention space, the KI is connected to the Regency Suites Hotel and is within walking distance of the downtown business and shopping district. A popular meeting site in Green Bay is the Brown County Memmorial Complex, which offers a combined total of more than 60,000 square feet of exhibition space. Providing modern equipment and facilities, the complex accommodates a variety of functions such as trade and consumer shows, conventions, and banquets, in addition to sports events. Brown County Veterans Memorial Arena features a number of floor layout options, ranging from 185 exhibit booths to portable seating for nearly 3,000 people. The Green Bay Packer Hall of Fame at the new Lambeau Field Atrium hosts breakfast meetings, cocktail receptions, and banquets for groups of 50 to 500 people. Parking for 7,000 automobiles is available on the grounds. Alternative sites for small to mid-sized meetings can be found at the Neville Public Museum, St. Norbert College, and the Weidner Center for the Performing Arts.

More than 70 downtown and suburban hotels and motels provide lodging for visitors and many have complete meeting accommodations, including the Radisson Inn and Conference Center and Kress Inn on the St. Norbert College campus; more than 3,000 guest rooms are available in the Green Bay metropolitan area.

*Convention Information:* Green Bay Area Visitor and Convention Bureau, 1901 S. Oneida St., PO Box 10596, Green Bay, WI 54307; telephone (920)494-9507; visitorinfo@packercountry.com

## ■ Transportation

### Approaching the City

Three commercial airlines schedule daily flights into Austin Straubel Airfield, operated by Brown County and located in Ashwaubenon on the outskirts of the city. The airfield unveiled the results of a $26 million renovation in 2006, which included a grand lobby and the addition of four new gates.

As the transportation hub for northeastern Wisconsin, Green Bay is served by motor routes linked by the state's only complete beltline. Interstate 43, connecting Green Bay with Milwaukee, circles the east side of the city from northwest to southeast and is linked with the north-south U.S. 41 on the west side by Highway 172. Other principal highways are U.S. 141 and State 29, 32, 54, and 57.

### Traveling in the City

Intracity public bus transportation on Green Bay Metro Transit is available Monday through Saturday on regularly scheduled routes throughout Green Bay and the nearby towns of Allouez, Ashwaubenon, Bellevue, De

Pere, and the Oneida Casino. The Titletown Trolley offers rides to and from several local attractions (no service on Mondays).

# ■ Communications

## Newspapers and Magazines

The major daily newspaper in Green Bay is the *Green Bay Press-Gazette*. Several neighborhood and regional newspapers appear weekly. *Musky Hunter,* a magazine for anglers, is published six times a year.

## Television and Radio

There are local network affiliates in Green Bay for ABC, CBS, NBC, Fox, PBS, and the CW; subscription cable service is available. Several FM and AM radio stations broadcast out of Green Bay; from nearby cities, more than 30 FM and approximately 10 AM radio stations are available to Green Bay listeners. Most stations schedule music programming with an emphasis on country, oldies, and light rock; there are several news/talk stations, sports talk, and two public radio outlets.

***Media Information:*** *Green Bay Press-Gazette,* 435 East Walnut, PO Box 23430, Green Bay, WI 54305; telephone (920)435-4411

## Green Bay Online

Brown County Library. Available www.co.brown.wi .us/library

City of Green Bay. Available www.ci.green-bay.wi.us

Green Bay Area Public Schools. Available www .greenbay.k12.wi.us

Green Bay Area Visitors & Convention Bureau. Available www.greenbay.com

Green Bay Packers. Available www.packers.com

BIBLIOGRAPHY

Carlson, Chuck, *Tales from the Packers Sidelines: A Collection of the Greatest Stories Ever Told* (Sports Publishing, 2003)

# Madison

## ■ The City in Brief

**Founded:** 1836 (incorporated 1856)

**Head Official:** Mayor Dave Cieslewicz
(since 2003)

**City Population**

1980: 170,616
1990: 190,766
2000: 208,054
2006 estimate: 223,389
Percent change, 1990–2000: 8.9%
U.S. rank in 1980: 84th
U.S. rank in 1990: 82nd
U.S. rank in 2000: 81st

**Metropolitan Area Population**

1980: 324,000
1990: 367,085
2000: 426,526
2006 estimate: 543,022
Percent change, 1990–2000: 16.2%
U.S. rank in 1980: 100th
U.S. rank in 1990: Not available
U.S. rank in 2000: 97th

**Area:** 68.7 square miles (2000)

**Elevation:** 845.6 feet above sea level (average)

**Average Annual Temperatures:** January, 17.3° F;
July, 71.6° F; annual average, 46.1° F

**Average Annual Precipitation:** 32.95 inches of
rain; 44.1 inches of snow

**Major Economic Sectors:** Government, services,
wholesale and retail trade

**Unemployment Rate:** 4.1% (June 2007)

**Per Capita Income:** $23,498 (1999)

**2005 FBI Crime Index Property:** 7,737

**2005 FBI Crime Index Violent:** 839

**Major Colleges and Universities:** University of Wisconsin–Madison

**Daily Newspaper:** *Wisconsin State Journal; The Capital Times*

## ■ Introduction

The capital of Wisconsin, Madison is also the seat of Dane County and the focus of a metropolitan statistical area that includes the entire county. The city was founded as the state capital, where no other permanent settlement had previously existed, on a unique geographic site, a narrow isthmus of land called Four Lakes Isthmus between two lakes. Since Madison was founded, the natural beauty of its setting has been enhanced by parks and boulevards with an impressive State Capitol Building and plaza at the center of the city. Madison is the base of the University of Wisconsin, a nationally respected research institution known for a tradition of academic excellence.

## ■ Geography and Climate

Set on a narrow isthmus of land between Lake Mendota and Lake Monona, Madison is surrounded by a network of lakes and rivers. The topography is rolling. The continental climate is consistent with the city's location in interior North America; the temperature range is wide, with an extreme winter low of minus 40 degrees and an extreme summer high of 110 degrees. Tornadoes can be prevalent during spring, summer, and fall; moderate temperatures and humidity prevail during a generally pleasant summer. Annual average snowfall is just over 44 inches.

**Area:** 68.7 square miles (2000)

**Elevation:** 845.6 feet above sea level (average)

**Average Temperatures:** January, 17.3° F; July, 71.6° F; annual average, 46.1° F

**Average Annual Precipitation:** 32.95 inches of rain; 44.1 inches of snow

# ■ History

## Land Speculator Prevails in State Capital Bid

The Winnebago tribe were the first inhabitants of the area where the city of Madison now stands; these Native Americans lived off the land's bounty and camped alongside Lake Monona and Lake Mendota. Madison owes its founding to James Doty, a native New Yorker who served as circuit judge of the Western Michigan Territory, which included Wisconsin and points as far west as the Dakotas and Iowa. Doty became a land agent for fur trader and financier John Jacob Astor and in August 1835, he started buying land around the site that was to become Madison; soon he owned more than 1,200 acres on the Four Lakes isthmus.

When the Wisconsin Territorial legislature convened for the first time in October 1836, with the task of selecting the site for the capital, land speculators flocked to the village with "paper" towns for the legislators to consider. In all, 18 townsites were considered, but Doty's vision proved to be the most persuasive. Doty had selected the name Madison in honor of James Madison, the former United States President. The recently deceased Madison had been the last surviving signer of the U.S. Constitution. Doty's design of Madison, with a square in the middle housing the Capitol and streets radiating diagonally from it like spokes in a wheel, was the same as Pierre Charles L'Enfant's street plat of Washington, D.C. The widest street was to be named Washington, and the other streets named after the other signers of the Constitution. When the legislators complained of being cold during their meetings, Doty dispatched a man to Dubuque, Iowa, to purchase Buffalo robes to warm the freezing public officials.

Eben and Rosaline Peck and their son Victor were the first non-Native American family to settle in Madison, arriving in the spring of 1837. They built a crude log inn and named it Madison House, which became the center of early activity and boarded the workmen who had arrived to begin work on the new capitol. Augustus A. Bird supervised a crew of workmen who first built a steam-driven sawmill and then proceeded to try to complete the capitol building before the first legislative session. In November 1838, the legislators arrived to find the statehouse incomplete; when they finally moved into the new statehouse, the conditions were terrible: inkwells were frozen, ice coated the interiors, and hogs squealed in the basement. Legislators threatened to move the capital to Milwaukee but better accommodations could not be guaranteed. The statehouse was not completed until 1848.

## Growth and Development Preserve Natural Setting

Improvements were slow to come to Madison and the living conditions remained crude until the arrival of Leonard J. Farwell in 1849. Farwell, a successful Milwaukee businessman, began developing the land by channeling a canal between Lakes Mendota and Monona, damming one end of Lake Mendota, building a grist and flour mill, and opening streets and laying sidewalks. But even as late as 1850, when Madison's population numbered more than 1,600 people, the isthmus thickets were still dense and impenetrable.

The University of Wisconsin was founded in 1848, the year Wisconsin was admitted to the Union. The first graduating class, in 1854, numbered two men. That year the first railroad service arrived in Madison and during the decade before the Civil War, Madison's business economy began to grow. The Madison Institute sponsored a successful literary lyceum and boasted 1,300 volumes in its library. Streets were gas-illuminated by 1855, when three daily and five weekly newspapers were published in the new capital and the population had increased to more than 6,800 people. The city was incorporated in 1856. The following year Madison's citizens voted to donate $50,000 in city bonds to enable the legislature to enlarge and improve the Capitol building.

The Madison Park and Pleasure Drive Association was organized in 1894 and citizens donated lakeshore and forest-bluff tracts as well as money to create scenic drives, parks, and playgrounds in the city. Four years later, the city council started annual contributions to the park association. By 1916, the park association had spent more than $300,000 on improvements to the shoreline and parks.

In February 1904, a fire destroyed much of the Capitol's interior. A new Capitol was constructed in stages between 1906 and 1917 on the site of the old one, featuring the only granite state Capitol dome in the United States. As both a state capital and home to a major state university, Madison has experienced a stable economic and educational base.

In rankings of U.S. cities, Madison consistently scores very high on seemingly every form of criteria. In recent years Madison has appeared several times on *Money* magazine's list of the best places to live. It has been cited by *Zero Population Growth* as the "#1

*Image copyright Suzanne Tucker, 2007. Used under license from Shutterstock.com.*

healthiest city in the nation to raise children." *Outside* magazine calls Madison a "Dream Town"; *The Utne Reader* calls it one of America's "10 Most Enlightened Towns" and "The Heartland's Progressive Hotbed." In addition, *Sports Illustrated* called Madison "America's #1 College Sports Town," while *Prevention* magazine labeled it one of its "12 Best Walking Towns."

***Historical Information:*** State Historical Society of Wisconsin, 816 State Street, Madison, WI 53706; telephone (608)264-6534

# ■ Population Profile

**Metropolitan Area Residents**

1980: 324,000
1990: 367,085
2000: 426,526
2006 estimate: 543,022
Percent change, 1990–2000: 16.2%
U.S. rank in 1980: 100th
U.S. rank in 1990: Not available
U.S. rank in 2000: 97th

**City Residents**

1980: 170,616
1990: 190,766
2000: 208,054
2006 estimate: 223,389
Percent change, 1990–2000: 8.9%
U.S. rank in 1980: 84th
U.S. rank in 1990: 82nd
U.S. rank in 2000: 81st

**Density:** 3,028.4 people per square mile (2000)

**Racial and ethnic characteristics (2000)**

White: 174,689
Black: 12,155
American Indian and Alaska Native: 759
Asian: 12,065
Native Hawaiian and Pacific Islander: 77
Hispanic or Latino (may be of any race): 8,512
Other: 3,474

**Percent of residents born in state:** 57.1% (2006)

**Age characteristics (2000)**

Population under 5 years old: 10,815

Population 5 to 9 years old: 10,016
Population 10 to 14 years old: 10,332
Population 15 to 19 years old: 18,192
Population 20 to 24 years old: 32,394
Population 25 to 34 years old: 37,054
Population 35 to 44 years old: 29,925
Population 45 to 54 years old: 26,553
Population 55 to 59 years old: 7,941
Population 60 to 64 years old: 5,648
Population 65 to 74 years old: 9,508
Population 75 to 84 years old: 7,025
Population 85 years and older: 2,651
Median age: 30.6 years

**Births (2006, MSA)**

Total number: 6,890

**Deaths (2006, MSA)**

Total number: 3,441

**Money income (1999)**

Per capita income: $23,498
Median household income: $41,941
Total households: 89,267

**Number of households with income of . . .**

less than $10,000: 8,645
$10,000 to $14,999: 5,285
$15,000 to $24,999: 10,696
$25,000 to $34,999: 11,561
$35,000 to $49,999: 15,934
$50,000 to $74,999: 18,338
$75,000 to $99,999: 9,271
$100,000 to $149,999: 6,542
$150,000 to $199,999: 1,631
$200,000 or more: 1,364

**Percent of families below poverty level:** 10.4% (1999)

**2005 FBI Crime Index Property:** 7,737

**2005 FBI Crime Index Violent:** 839

# ■ Municipal Government

The city of Madison operates under a mayor-alderperson form of government. Twenty alders, representing 20 city districts, are chosen for two-year terms in a nonpartisan election. The mayor, who is not a member of council, is chosen for a four-year term in a nonpartisan election.

**Head Official:** Mayor Dave Cieslewicz (since 2003; current term expires 2011)

**Total Number of City Employees:** approximately 3,000 (2007)

*City Information:* City Hall, 215 Martin Luther King Jr. Boulevard, Madison, WI 53703; telephone (608)266-4611

# ■ Economy

## Major Industries and Commercial Activity

The principal economic sectors in Madison are manufacturing, services, and government. Meat packing and the production of agriculture and dairy equipment have long been established industries in the city; among other items produced by area manufacturing firms are hospital equipment, advanced instrumentation, storage batteries, and air circulating fixtures. Diversified farming contributes significantly to the Madison economy; nearly one-sixth of all Wisconsin farms are located within the Greater Madison market region. Dane County ranks among the top ten counties in the nation for agricultural production, the primary products being corn, alfalfa, tobacco, oats, eggs, cattle, hogs, and dairy foods.

The offices of more than 30 insurance companies are located in Madison; included among them are American Family, CUNA Mutual Insurance Group, and General Casualty. The city is also the world headquarters of Promega Corporation and Oscar Mayer. Government and education are major economic sectors; about one third of the area work force is employed in federal, state, and local government jobs, and the University of Wisconsin employs more than 29,000 workers. Madison is a banking and finance center, serving the metropolitan region with more than 120 banks, credit unions, and savings and loan institutions. Other service areas important to the local economy are health care and research and development. The high-tech industry is among the fastest-growing sectors of the local economy.

**Items and goods produced:** agricultural products, food packaging products, dry cell batteries, farm machinery, hospital equipment, optical instruments, lenses, fabricated structural steel

## Incentive Programs—New and Existing Companies

*Local programs:* The city of Madison Office of Business Resources leads start-up, relocating, and expanding businesses through the range of available financial and consultative benefits the local government has to offer. The Small Business Development Center (SBDC) at the University of Wisconsin is an award-winning community resource that aids small businesses by providing practical, customer-focused management education, training, counseling and networking. In addition to counseling, the SBDC conducts workshops and seminars. The city provides below market-rate interest loans for real estate projects in the Downtown Isthmus area and selected other areas of the city. Madison Development Corporation (MDC) provides loans of up to $200,000 to businesses in the City of Madison that show continued job growth.

*State programs:* Wisconsin corporate taxes remain among the lowest in the nation due to property tax exemptions on manufacturing machinery and equipment, inventory exemptions, and lack of franchise and unitary taxes.

The Wisconsin Economic Development Association (WEDA) and the Wisconsin Economic Development Institute (WEDI) are two nonprofit agencies that provide information and financial services, legal and legislative assistance, and networking opportunities for their member businesses. On the government side, the Division of Business Development of the Wisconsin Department of Commerce provides technical assistance and financial incentives to businesses in the areas of business planning, site selection, capitalization, permits, training and recruitment, and research and development. On April 28, 2000, Governor Tommy G. Thompson signed into law a bill that created the Wisconsin Technology Council, a nonprofit, nonpartisan board that serves to create, develop and retain science and technology-based business in Wisconsin, and to serve as an advisor to the Governor and the Legislature. The Council also serves as the key link between the state's colleges and universities and the business expertise and capital offered by the financial service industry; the firm published its "Vision 2020: A Model Wisconsin Economy" as a blueprint for its efforts.

*Job training programs:* The area's universities and technical colleges offer ample education and training programs. The State of Wisconsin has programs available to provide grants to businesses training workers in new technologies.

## Development Projects

In July 1998, Madison businessman W. Jerome Frautschi announced a major civic gift to improve the cultural arts facilities in downtown Madison. Called the Overture Center for the Arts, it is a privately funded initiative to promote excellence in the arts and stimulate a downtown Madison renaissance. Phase One of the Overture project, including the brand new, state-of-the-art Overture Hall, a 2,250-seat theater that houses the Madison Symphony, Madison Opera, and the Madison Ballet, was completed in 2004. Phase Two, which includes a renovation of the old Capitol Theater and a new Madison Museum of Contemporary Art, was completed in 2006. All design comes under the guise of internationally known architect Cesar Pelli and as plans have expanded development costs surpassed $205 million, all of which was funded by Mr. Frautschi.

In 2007 plans were underway for two new buildings at the UW-Madison School of Education: the Education Building and Art Lofts. Construction on the Education Building was expected to be complete by December 2010, and the Art Lofts Project, which was to be the new home of the graduate art program, was expected to be completed by 2009.

*Economic Development Information:* Greater Madison Chamber of Commerce, 615 E. Washington Ave., PO Box 71, Madison, WI 53701-0071; telephone (608)256-8348. City of Madison Department of Planning and Development, 215 Martin Luther King, Jr. Blvd., Madison, WI 53703; telephone (608)266-4635; fax (608)267-8739.

## Commercial Shipping

Madison is served by the Chicago & Northwestern, Soo/Milwaukee, and Wisconsin & Calumet railroads. More than 40 motor freight carriers link the city with markets throughout the nation via an extensive interstate highway system. Air cargo is shipped through Dane County Regional Airport by two companies, Federal Express and Airborne.

## Labor Force and Employment Outlook

Madison enjoys relatively low unemployment and a high percentage of high-paying jobs in the growing high-technology sector of the economy, all of which provide a strong boost to the local economy in many ways. Many of these new businesses are in the high-tech sector of the local economy. In 2005 more than 450 firms in the Madison area were identified as high-tech. Madison Schools are consistently ranked among the best in the nation, and the University of Wisconsin is regarded as one of the nation's finest public universities, turning out thousands of graduates each year and providing a high number of jobs in research and development.

The following is a summary of data regarding the Madison metropolitan area labor force, 2006 annual averages.

**Size of nonagricultural labor force:** 346,600

**Number of workers employed in . . .**

   construction and mining: 17,400
   manufacturing: 32,500
   trade, transportation and utilities: 60,700
   information: 8,900
   financial activities: 27,900
   professional and business services: 36,000
   educational and health services: 34,900
   leisure and hospitality: 29,700
   other services: 17,700
   government: 80,800

**Average hourly earnings of production workers employed in manufacturing:** Not available

**Unemployment rate:** 4.1% (June 2007)

| *Largest employers (2004)* | *Number of employees* |
|---|---|
| State of Wisconsin (includes University of Wisconsin) | 41,151 |
| UW Health Hospitals/ Clinics | 29,253 |
| Madison Metropolitan School District | 5,921 |
| U.S. Government | 4,629 |
| American Family Insurance | 3,700 |
| Wisconsin Physicians Service Group | 3,604 |
| Meriter Health Services | 3,393 |
| Dean Health System | 3,306 |
| City of Madison | 3,071 |
| University of Wisconsin Medical Foundation | 3,064 |

## Cost of Living

The following is a summary of data regarding several key cost of living factors in the Madison area.

**2007 (1st quarter) ACCRA Average House Price:** Not available

**2007 (1st quarter) ACCRA Cost of Living Index:** Not available

**State income tax rate:** 4.6% to 6.75%

**State sales tax rate:** 5.0%

**Local income tax rate:** None

**Local sales tax rate:** 0.5% (Dane County)

**Property tax rate:** Effective tax rate $23.46 per $1,000 of assessed valuation (2004)

*Economic Information:* Greater Madison Chamber of Commerce, 615 E. Washington Ave., PO Box 71, Madison, WI 53701-0071; telephone (608)256-8348.

## ■ Education and Research

### Elementary and Secondary Schools

Public, elementary, and secondary schools in Madison are part of the Madison Metropolitan School District, the third-largest system in the state of Wisconsin, with an annual budget of more than $330 million. The Madison Metropolitan School District has early childhood programs and alternative programs at the secondary level (6-12). Nearly 10 percent of enrolled students speak Spanish as their first language and 15 percent of all students are enrolled in English as a second language program. The district covers approximately 65 square miles, including all or part of the cities of Madison and Fitchburg, the villages of Maple Bluff and Shorewood Hills, and the towns of Blooming Grove, Burke and Madison. A superintendent is appointed by a seven-member, nonpartisan board of education.

A new elementary school was scheduled to be added to the Madison Metropolitan School District in fall 2008.

The following is a summary of data regarding the Madison Metropolitan School District as of the 2005–2006 school year.

**Total enrollment:** 81,118

**Number of facilities**

elementary schools: 31
junior high/middle schools: 11
senior high schools: 4
other: 1

**Student/teacher ratio:** 12.9:1

**Teacher salaries (2005–06)**

elementary median: $43,050
junior high/middle median: $45,020
secondary median: $44,250

**Funding per pupil:** $11,702

Parochial elementary and secondary school systems are operated by the Roman Catholic and Lutheran churches; there are a total of 22 private schools in Dane County.

*Public Schools Information:* Madison Metropolitan School District, 545 West Dayton Street, Madison, WI 53703-1995; telephone (608) 663-1879

## Colleges and Universities

The University of Wisconsin—Madison, chartered in 1848, is one of the country's top 10 public universities. It enrolls more than 41,400 students and grants undergraduate and graduate degrees in more than 100 disciplines, including agriculture, allied health professions, education, environmental studies, law, pharmacy, medicine, veterinary medicine, and nursing. As a major research institution, the university is known for work in a variety of fields such as agriculture, bacteriology, chemistry, engineering, forest products, genetics, land use, medicine, nuclear energy, and physics. Over 60 percent of enrolled students hail from the state of Wisconsin, with all 50 states and more than 100 countries represented in the student body. In the 2008 edition of *U.S. News and World Report*'s "Best Colleges," the school was ranked 38th among national universities.

Edgewood College is a private liberal arts college awarding associate and baccalaureate degrees; a cooperative program in medical technology with area schools and limited cross-registration with the University of Wisconsin-Madison are available. The school offers more than 40 majors to its 2,400 students and boasts a student-faculty ratio of 13:1. Vocational training and/or bachelor's degrees are offered by Madison Area Technical College (which enrolls more than 44,000), Herzing College of Technology, and Madison Media Institute; areas of specialization include aviation, computers, cosmetology, dance, electronics, music, nursing, recreation, and television.

### Libraries and Research Centers

Madison is home to approximately 180 public, governmental, special, and academic libraries. The Madison Public Library, with a centrally located main facility, operates nine branches throughout the city. Holdings include more than 1.2 million volumes, including periodicals, and compact discs, DVD and video recordings, books on tape, maps, charts, and art reproductions; the library is a partial depository for federal and city documents. In 2005 the Library had 2.2 million visitors, another 2.6 million hits on its online databases, and circulated 4.5 million volumes. It is also part of South Central Library System, a network of public libraries in the surrounding seven-county area. The University of Wisconsin-Madison Libraries represent the 11th largest research collection in North America. The libraries house more than 7.3 million printed volumes, 55,000 serial titles, and 6.2 million microforms; UW-Madison's Memorial Library is the largest library in the city. The State Historical Society library specializes in Wisconsin lore and has a special African American History Collection.

As the state capital, Madison is the site for libraries affiliated with governmental agencies; among them are the Wisconsin Department of Justice Law Library, the Wisconsin Legislative Reference Bureau, the Wisconsin Department of Public Instruction, the Public Service Commission of Wisconsin, the Wisconsin Department of Transportation Library, and the Wisconsin State Law Library. Several county agencies also maintain libraries in the city. Other specialized libraries are operated by colleges, public interest groups, labor organizations, churches, hospitals, corporations, museums, and newspapers.

The University of Wisconsin-Madison ranks among the top American research universities. UW-Madison annually spends more than $680 million on research. This represents the third-largest expenditure by a university on research nationwide. U.S. government research laboratories located in Madison include the U.S. Forest Products Lab, the U.S. Fish and Wildlife Laboratory, the Space Science and Engineering Center, the Waisman Center on Mental Retardation and Human Development, the Enzyme Institute, the Sea Grant Institute, Air Pollution Lab, and the U.S. Department of Agriculture Research Service. A number of private research and testing centers, such as Hazelton Laboratories America, Inc., are also based in Madison.

***Public Library Information:*** Madison Public Library, 201 West Mifflin Street, Madison, WI 53703; telephone (608)266-6300

## ■ Health Care

Madison, home to the University of Wisconsin Medical School, is a major center for medical research and testing. The school particularly focuses its research on aging, cancer, cardiovascular and respiratory sciences, neuroscience, population and community health sciences, rural health and women's health. The University of Wisconsin Hospital and Clinics is comprised of approximately 60 clinics throughout the state, including the UW Comprehensive Cancer Center, which has a national reputation for excellence in cancer care and research. The UW system employs more than 1,100 physicians. In the 2006 edition of *U.S. News and World Report*'s "Best Hospitals" list, the University of Wisconsin Hospital and Clinics was ranked among the top 50 hospitals for several specialties: cancer, digestive disorders, kidney disease, urology, and gynecology.

Additional medical service for the region is provided by five Dane County general hospitals (with a total of more than 1,400 beds) and more than 90 general and urgent-care clinics. Among the principal facilities are Meriter Hospital and St. Mary's Hospital.

## ■ Recreation

### Sightseeing

The starting point for sightseeing in Madison is the State Capitol building, located between lakes Mendota and Monona. The dome is topped with Daniel Chester French's gilded bronze statue, *Wisconsin*. The Capitol's interior features 43 varieties of stone and murals, glass mosaics, and hand-carved wood furniture. The State Historical Society on the Capitol Square recaptures the history of Wisconsin with exhibits on Native American tribal life from prehistoric times to the present, pioneer days, paintings and statues. Adjacent is the Wisconsin Veterans Museum, which honors Wisconsin's citizen-soldiers through large-scale exhibits, displays, and presentations.

The architect Frank Lloyd Wright, who resided in nearby Spring Green, designed two buildings that are open to the public in Madison. In 1997, the Monona Terrace Community and Convention Center opened its doors some 60 years after Wright first proposed the project, which marries the capitol with Lake Monona. The Unitarian Meeting House, opened in 1951, still serves as a venue for Unitarian Universalist services. About 45 minutes away is Taliesin, Wright's home and architectural school in Spring Green.

To the north of town visitors will find the Circus World Museum, the Wollersheim Winery in Prairie du Sac (which holds a Grape Stomp Festival each fall at harvest time), and the Wisconsin Dells, a favorite family vacation destination with natural beauty, lakes and rivers, and shopping.

The University of Wisconsin Arboretum, maintained for research and instruction by the institution, consists of 1,200 acres of natural forests, prairie, and orchards inside the city; 250 varieties of lilacs and a number of effigy mounds highlight the Arboretum's park trails. Olbrich Botanical Gardens, a 52-acre park and conservatory, displays gorgeous annuals, perennials, and shrubs outside and a lush tropical paradise inside the 50-foot glass pyramid. The Tenney Park Locks and Dam connect Lakes Mendota and Monona, providing passageway for nearly 20,000 watercraft each season and a popular spot for fishing or feeding ducks. On the other end of Lake Mendota is the University of Wisconsin campus with its rich architectural history and scenic beauty. Along Observatory Drive is the Carillon Tower and Bells, the only carillon to be supported at a university by gifts of senior classes.

The Henry Vilas Park Zoo, bordering the shore of Lake Wingra, is home to hundreds of species of exotic animals.

## Arts and Culture

The new jewel in downtown Madison's restoration and the city's arts scene is the Overture Center for the Arts, anchored by Overture Hall, new home of the Madison Symphony, the Madison Opera, and national touring productions. The intimate Isthmus Playhouse provides the stage for the Madison Repertory Theatre. Summer performances of Shakespeare and other classics by the American Players Theater are held in Spring Green.

Music is a popular pastime, too, as evidenced by the free concerts throughout the year at Monona Terrace Community and Convention Center and the summertime Wisconsin Chamber Orchestra Concerts on the Square. The University of Wisconsin Chazen Museum of Art maintains an eclectic permanent collection ranging from Native American miniatures, Japanese prints, and European medals to Soviet paintings and European and American art. The university's other museums concentrate in the fields of geology and zoology. Exhibits at the Madison Children's Museum involve children in learning about science, culture, and art.

## Festivals and Holidays

*USA Today* said about Madison: "There's always something to do ... an almost constant parade of free events." The Capitol Square is the center of many of Madison's

special events and activities. In June "Cows on the Concourse" celebrates dairy month. The Badger States Games are held in June, attracting from throughout the state thousands of amateur athletes who participate in 18 different sports. Rhythm and Booms is Madison's Independence Day Celebration; it sets spectacular fireworks to music over Lake Mendota. Art Fair on the Square, held the second weekend in July, brings nearly 500 artists to the Capitol Square to exhibit their works. It is accompanied by Art Fair off the Square, highlighting Wisconsin artists. The Maxwell Street Days, a bazaar of bargains along Madison's famous State Street, is another popular event, as is the Paddle 'N Portage Canoe Race and Taste of Madison, held on Labor Day weekend, when area restaurants serve their most exotic and popular dishes. From May to October, the Dane County Farmers' Market is held on Wednesday and Saturday mornings around the picturesque Capitol. Autumn features the Thirsty Troll Brewfest and the Annual Mount Horeb Fall Heritage Festival. The grey days of winter are brightened by the Madison Auto Show and Kites on Ice, a two-day kite-flying event that attracts participants from around the world to Lake Monona in February. There is an annual St. Patrick's Day Parade on Capitol Square.

## Sports for the Spectator

The University of Wisconsin Badgers compete in the Big Ten athletic conference in 12 sports; the football, basketball, and hockey teams consistently draw large crowds. Home football Saturdays in Madison are like a community holiday, with tailgate parties beginning early in the morning and parties lasting well into the night, regardless of how the team fared on the field that day. In 2004 *Sports Illustrated* magazine named Madison "Best College Sports Town" in America for its spirited support of the Badgers. The Madison Mallards is a collection of promising collegiate baseball players that play summer ball in the Northwoods League. The Green Bay Packers of the National Football League are adopted by the entire state of Wisconsin, and in nearby Milwaukee, professional baseball (the Brewers) and basketball (the Bucks) are closely followed by Madison fans.

## Sports for the Participant

Water sports are particularly attractive in Greater Madison, where five lakes provide ideal conditions for swimming, fishing, boating, canoeing, windsurfing, and ice skating in winter. Year-round fishing is popular, with typical catches including muskie, northern pike, walleye, bass, panfish, and cisco. The Madison Parks Department maintains more than 7,200 acres of park land. Around forty parks maintain ice skating ponds, the majority of which are lighted for evening skating; many provide warming houses. Cross country ski trails line city parks. Many of the parks are equipped with outdoor tennis courts. The Dane County Park System offers a spectacular array of scenery and recreational opportunities at more than 30 area metroparks.

In a city where bicycles may outnumber automobiles, approximately 100 miles of bicycle paths are provided for cycling enthusiasts. Favorite routes circle Lake Monona and the University of Wisconsin Arboretum, cutting through Madison's historic residential district, the zoo, and alongside Lake Wingra. Public golf courses, of varying lengths and difficulties for golfers of all ability levels, are located in Madison. The Springs Golf Course and University Ridge are highly-rated 18-hole courses designed by Robert Trent Jones. In 2004 nearby Whistling Straits Golf Course in Kohler hosted the PGA Championship; the public course was designed by legendary golf course architect Pete Dye. The Mad City Marathon in late May brings thousands of runners to test their mettle against 26.2 miles through some of the most scenic spots in town.

## Shopping and Dining

The major shopping malls—East Towne, Hilldale, West Towne, and Westgate—offer comprehensive selection and competitive prices. The Johnson Creek Outlet Center just 30 miles east of Madison has more than 60 brand name stores. The State Capitol district offers a selection of restaurants and stores in a park setting. The pedestrians-only State Street Mall connects the Capitol Square with the University of Wisconsin; the lower section of the Mall is populated by street vendors selling crafts and food. Madison boasts that it has more restaurants per capita than any city in America, with cuisine from around the world appealing to the eclectic tastes of the city's progressive population. Specialty shops and some of the city's finest restaurants are located on State Street. Monroe Street on Madison's near west side also offers charm and unique restaurants and shops. Friday night fish fries are a local custom, and one restaurant caters to specialties native to Wisconsin. The Farmers' Market comes highly recommended for purchasing fresh produce from local growers.

*Visitor Information:*   Greater Madison Convention & Visitors Bureau, 615 East Washington Avenue, Madison, WI 53703; telephone (608)255-2537; toll-free (800)373-6376

## ■ Convention Facilities

In all, the Madison area has more than 8,000 hotel rooms and 400,000 square feet of meeting space, which makes it an annual gathering place for such conventions as the World Dairy Expo. Located on the shore of Lake Monona and inspired by a design created by Frank Lloyd Wright in 1938, Monona Terrace is two blocks from Capitol Square, to which it is linked by a pedestrian promenade. In 2001 the facility added the 240-room Hilton Madison Monona Terrace with direct access to the convention facility by enclosed walkway. The facility offers approximately 250,000 square feet of convention and meeting space, including a ballroom, an exhibit hall, a multimedia auditorium, gift shop, pre-function areas, and a 90-foot extension over the water. The roof features a park and bandshell, and there is parking for about 550 cars.

The Alliant Energy Center of Dane County is a 160-acre multibuilding complex including 100,000 square feet of column-free exhibition space and a 9,500-seat arena. The Overture Center for the Arts has unique meeting space for smaller groups in several spectacular settings. Three downtown hotels providing meeting and convention facilities are The Concourse, with three ballrooms and several meeting rooms; the Best Western Inn on the Park, with a variety of meeting room styles; and The Edgewater, with five meeting rooms.

Additional meeting accommodations are available on the campus of the University of Wisconsin—Madison, as well as at numerous hotels and motels throughout metropolitan Madison.

*Convention Information:*   Greater Madison Convention & Visitors Bureau, 615 East Washington Avenue, Madison, WI 53703; telephone (608)255-2537; toll-free (800)373-63763

## ■ Transportation

### Approaching the City

The Dane County Regional Airport, east of the city, is an international airport with more than 100 regularly scheduled daily flights, serving 1.6 travellers annually. The airport is also a general aviation facility.

I-90 and I-94, two of Wisconsin's interstate highways, pass through Madison, connecting the city with Chicago (2.5 hours), Minneapolis (4.5 hours), and Milwaukee (1.5 hours). The highway system also includes U.S. routes 12, 14, 18, 51, and 151 and state roads 30 and 113. The West Beltline, formed by U.S. 18, 151, 12, and 14, bypasses the city. Three companies provide intercity bus service.

### Traveling in the City

Madison is long and narrow, following a northeast-southwest orientation along the shores of Lakes Mendota and Monona. Within this configuration, downtown streets radiate from the Capitol hub; principal thoroughfares are Washington, Johnson, and Williamson, which run northeast and southwest, and State Street and University Avenue, which extend due east.

Madison is one of the most bicycle-friendly cities in America, with miles of paved bike paths and an extensive map system to help bikers get around. Intracity public bus transportation is operated by Madison Metro Bus Company, which provides Metro Plus service for elderly and handicapped patrons. Unlimited access to the bus system comes for just $3 per day.

# ■ Communications

## Newspapers and Magazines

Daily newspapers in Madison are the morning and Sunday *Wisconsin State Journal* and the evening (Monday through Friday; mornings on Saturday) *The Capital Times*. Several other newspapers also circulate in the city; among them are the alternative weekly *Isthmus*, and University of Wisconsin student dailies.

Madison is the center of extensive magazine and journal publishing activity, including *Madison Magazine* and *In Business*. Magazines with wide circulation focus on such subjects as agriculture, athletics, money management, economic justice, and Wisconsin recreation. Several academic journals are based at the University of Wisconsin and numerous specialized magazines and journals, many affiliated with government agencies, are printed in Madison.

## Television and Radio

Six television channels—four commercial and two public—broadcast from Madison, which also receives programming from Green Bay and Wausau. Cable service is available. Several television production firms are located in the city.

More than a dozen AM and FM radio stations serve Greater Madison with a variety of programming that includes classical music, jazz, easy listening, farm news, and topics of public interest.

***Media Information:*** *The Capital Times,* 1901 Fish Hatchery Road, PO Box 8060, Madison, WI 53708; telephone (608)252-6363. *Wisconsin State Journal,* 1901 Fish Hatchery Road, Madison, WI 53708; telephone (608)252-6363

## Madison Online

City of Madison Home Page. Available www.ci.madison.wi.us

Greater Madison Chamber of Commerce. Available www.greatermadisonchamber.com

Greater Madison Convention and Visitors Bureau. Available www.visitmadison.com

Madison Metropolitan School District. Available www.madison.k12.wi.us

Madison Public Library. Available www.madisonpubliclibrary.org

University of Wisconsin-Madison. Available www.wisc.edu

BIBLIOGRAPHY

Brown, Harriet, *Madison Walks* (Madison, WI: Jones Books, 2003)

# Milwaukee

## ■ The City in Brief

**Founded:** 1839 (incorporated 1846)

**Head Official:** Mayor Tom Barrett (since 2004)

**City Population**

1980: 636,212
1990: 628,088
2000: 596,974
2006 estimate: 573,358
Percent change, 1990–2000: −5.0%
U.S. rank in 1980: 16th
U.S. rank in 1990: 17th
U.S. rank in 2000: 25th (State rank: 1st)

**Metropolitan Area Population**

1980: Not available
1990: 1,607,183
2000: 1,689,572
2006 estimate: 1,509,981
Percent change, 1990–2000: 5.1%
U.S. rank in 1980: Not available
U.S. rank in 1990: Not available
U.S. rank in 2000: 64th (CMSA)

**Area:** 96.1 square miles (2000)

**Elevation:** 581.2 feet above sea level

**Average Annual Temperatures:** January, 20.7° F; July, 72.0° F; annual average, 47.5° F

**Average Annual Precipitation:** 34.81 inches of rain; 47.3 inches of snow

**Major Economic Sectors:** Services, wholesale and retail trade, manufacturing

**Unemployment Rate:** 5.7% (June 2007)

**Per Capita Income:** $17,696 (2005)

**2005 FBI Crime Index Property:** 32,812

**2005 FBI Crime Index Violent:** 6,010

**Major Colleges and Universities:** University of Wisconsin-Milwaukee; Marquette University

**Daily Newspaper:** *Milwaukee Journal Sentinel*

## ■ Introduction

Milwaukee, the seat of Milwaukee County, is the largest city in Wisconsin and the center of a metropolitan statistical area comprised of Milwaukee, Ozaukee, Washington, and Waukesha counties. Mid-nineteenth century German immigration laid the foundation for Milwaukee's "golden age," when cultural and political life flourished, culminating in the election of the country's first socialist mayor in 1912. The city is a major Great Lakes port, traditionally known for manufacturing and breweries. Milwaukee has in recent years reemerged as a primary cultural and entertainment center for the Upper Midwest.

## ■ Geography and Climate

Situated on the western shore of Lake Michigan at the confluence of the Milwaukee, Menomonee, and Kinnickinnic rivers, Milwaukee experiences a continental climate characterized by a wide range of temperatures. The frequently changeable weather is influenced by eastward-moving storms that cross the middle section of the nation. Severe winter storms often produce ten inches of snow, and incursions of arctic air result in several days of bitterly cold weather. The Great Lakes influence the local climate during all seasons, modifying air masses before they reach the city; Lake Michigan, in particular, causes dramatic shifts in temperature. Summer temperatures seldom exceed 100 degrees, although a combination of high temperatures and humidity occasionally develops.

**Area:** 96.1 square miles (2000)

**Elevation:** 581.2 feet above sea level

**Average Temperatures:** January, 20.7° F; July, 72.0° F; annual average, 47.5° F

**Average Annual Precipitation:** 34.81 inches of rain; 47.3 inches of snow

# ■ History

## Tribal Meeting Place Draws Permanent Settlement

Mahn-a-waukee Seepe, a Native American word meaning "gathering place by the river," was the name given to the land next to the natural bay where the Milwaukee, Menomonee, and Kinnickinnic rivers flow into Lake Michigan and where a number of tribes met to hold counsel. The Potawatomi was the largest of the local tribes and they, along with the Menominee, were under French control in the seventeenth century. As white traders moved into the territory, the Native Americans withdrew into the wilderness. The Menominee gave up land east and north of the Milwaukee River in 1831, and the United Nation of Chippewa, Ottawa, and Potawatomi signed a treaty in Chicago in 1833 that relinquished a large section of land south and west of the Milwaukee River.

In 1835 three men bought the first land holdings in Milwaukee at a land auction in Green Bay. French trader Solomon Juneau had operated a trading post near the Milwaukee River since 1818, and he purchased the land between the Milwaukee River and Lake Michigan that he named Juneautown. Byron Kilbourn named his western tract Kilbourntown, and George H. Walker claimed a southern section. Juneau accrued great wealth through his trading business; he also served as an interpreter and peacemaker between the Native Americans and white settlers. Juneau sold some of his land, and he and the new investors established a village that they named Milwaukee. The first population wave took place when Irish and New England settlers and German immigrants arrived. In 1838 the Potawatomi were relocated to Kansas.

A feud called the Bridge War, notorious in Milwaukee history, began in 1840 when the villages of Juneautown and Kilbourntown, which were consolidated in 1839, disputed payments for river bridges required by the legislature. This feuding continued for five years and in 1845 erupted in violence. The Bridge War was finally resolved when the legislature ordered that costs be shared equally between the two founding communities. The next year the city charter was ratified and Solomon Juneau was elected the first mayor of Milwaukee.

By that time the city's population numbered 10,000 people, half of them German and a higher percentage Catholic. John Martin Henni was appointed bishop of the new diocese, becoming the first German Catholic bishop in America. In 1848 the arrival of the "forty-eighters," German intellectuals forced to flee their homeland after their rebellion failed, helped to influence the direction of Milwaukee history. These men wanted to establish a free German republic but settled for improving the cultural and political life of the city by creating theaters and musical societies, and generally upgrading Milwaukee's intellectual life. Between 1850 and 1851 Milwaukee's population more than doubled to 46,000 people. The economy prospered during the Civil War as local industries grew rapidly and filled in the gaps created by the closing of southern markets.

## Progress Continues Despite Setbacks

Several disasters threatened Milwaukee's progress. In 1867, the city's first major labor union, the Knights of St. Crispin, was formed in the shoe industry. As the economy expanded so did the labor movement, which received a setback when state troops fired on labor demonstrators in 1886, killing five. Almost 300 people drowned in 1859 when the *Lady Elgin* collided with the *Augusta*; Milwaukee again mourned when a fire at the Newhall House in 1883 took at least sixty-four lives. Both events were commemorated in popular ballads. In 1892 sixteen residential and business blocks between the Milwaukee River and Lake Michigan were destroyed by fire. Despite this tragedy, the decade of the 1890s in Milwaukee was described as the "golden age," marked by the flourishing of German theater and musical societies.

The rise of Milwaukee's brand of socialism dates from this period, when Socialist leader Victor L. Berger forged an alliance with labor, bringing the Social Democratic party into existence. Emil Seidel was elected the first Socialist mayor in 1910 and Berger became the first Socialist in the U.S. House of Representatives. The "bundle brigade" delivered campaign pamphlets in twelve languages to rally votes. In addition to Seidel, Daniel W. Hoan and Frank P. Zeidler later also served as Socialist mayors. In keeping with anti-German sentiments during World War I, the statue of *Germania* was removed from the Brumder Building and Berger was convicted of conspiracy to violate the Espionage Act. This decision was, however, reversed by the U.S. Supreme Court in 1921.

Milwaukee has been a shipping center and industrial giant in the Midwest, noted in the nineteenth century for wheat and then in the twentieth century for manufacturing, primarily metal trades, meat packing, tanning and leather goods, brewing, and durable goods.

©James Blank.

Milwaukee industry has contributed to national and international progress with steam shovels to dig the Panama Canal, turbines to harness Niagara Falls, and agricultural equipment to farm the world's land. Today Milwaukee maintains its status as a leader in manufacturing technology and practice while it makes the transition to a service-based economy. Milwaukee boasts good schools, a diverse economy, a strong work ethic, a high quality of life, and a beautiful location on the western edge of Lake Michigan in the rolling hills of the Kettle Moraine. The city has also become a cultural leader, with a world-class symphony orchestra, around 20 performing arts groups, a ballet, two opera companies, a zoo, professional sports teams, several major universities, and Summerfest, the world's largest music festival.

***Historical Information:*** Milwaukee County Historical Society, 910 N. Old World 3rd St., Milwaukee, WI 53203; telephone (414)273-8288

## ■ Population Profile

### Metropolitan Area Residents

1980: Not available
1990: 1,607,183
2000: 1,689,572
2006 estimate: 1,509,981
Percent change, 1990–2000: 5.1%
U.S. rank in 1980: Not available
U.S. rank in 1990: Not available
U.S. rank in 2000: 64th (CMSA)

### City Residents

1980: 636,212
1990: 628,088
2000: 596,974
2006 estimate: 573,358
Percent change, 1990–2000: −5.0%
U.S. rank in 1980: 16th
U.S. rank in 1990: 17th
U.S. rank in 2000: 25th
   (State rank: 1st)

**Density:** 6,214.3 people per square mile (2000)

**Racial and ethnic characteristics (2005)**

White: 248,855
Black: 223,775
American Indian and Alaska Native: 4,150
Asian: 19,854

Native Hawaiian and Pacific Islander: 235
Hispanic or Latino (may be of any race): 80,945
Other: 48,514

**Percent of residents born in state:** 65.2% (2000)

**Age characteristics (2005)**

Population under 5 years old: 48,153
Population 5 to 9 years old: 42,313
Population 10 to 14 years old: 45,687
Population 15 to 19 years old: 42,100
Population 20 to 24 years old: 44,102
Population 25 to 34 years old: 82,060
Population 35 to 44 years old: 81,053
Population 45 to 54 years old: 72,754
Population 55 to 59 years old: 29,328
Population 60 to 64 years old: 17,338
Population 65 to 74 years old: 25,234
Population 75 to 84 years old: 20,548
Population 85 years and older: 6,278
Median age: 31.8 years

**Births (2006, MSA)**

Total number: 21,121

**Deaths (2006, MSA)**

Total number: 12,890

**Money income (2005)**

Per capita income: $17,696
Median household income: $32,666
Total households: 228,861

**Number of households with income of...**

less than $10,000: 30,344
$10,000 to $14,999: 20,292
$15,000 to $24,999: 37,924
$25,000 to $34,999: 34,024
$35,000 to $49,999: 36,420
$50,000 to $74,999: 40,195
$75,000 to $99,999: 17,723
$100,000 to $149,999: 8,343
$150,000 to $199,999: 1,810
$200,000 or more: 1,786

**Percent of families below poverty level:** 12.5% (2005)

**2005 FBI Crime Index Property:** 32,812

**2005 FBI Crime Index Violent:** 6,010

# ■ Municipal Government

Milwaukee is governed by a 15-member council and a mayor, who is not a member of council; all are elected to four-year terms. The council holds all policy-making and legislative powers of the city, including the adoption of ordinances and resolutions, the approval of the city's annual budget, and the enactment of appropriation and tax levy ordinances. In addition to their powers as legislators, council members serve as district administrators, responsible to the citizens in their districts for city services.

**Head Official:** Mayor Tom Barrett (since April 2004; current term expires March 2008)

**Total Number of City Employees:** 7,200 (2007)

***City Information:*** City Hall, 200 E. Wells St., Milwaukee, WI 53202; telephone (414)286-2200

# ■ Economy

## Major Industries and Commercial Activity

Milwaukee, a commercial and industrial hub for the Great Lakes region, is home to 14 *Fortune* 1000 companies (including Harley-Davidson Inc., Rockwell Automation, Kohl's Inc., and Johnson Controls), banks, and diversified service companies as well as one of the nation's ten largest insurance firms. An additional 50 *Fortune* 1000 firms maintain facilities in the Milwaukee area. The metropolitan area places among the top manufacturing centers in the United States, ranking second among major metropolitan areas in the percentage of its workforce in manufacturing. Approximately 16 percent of the area's work force is employed in manufacturing, producing more than $31 billion worth of manufactured products annually. The economy is dominated by small- to medium-size firms with representatives in nearly every industrial classification. The city is a regional finance center; area banks and savings associations have deposits of over $38.5 billion.

Metropolitan area firms are engaged primarily in the manufacture of machinery; contrary to Milwaukee's reputation as a brewery capital, less than one percent of the city's industrial output is related to brewing. In recent years, the metro region has earned a reputation as a center for precision manufacturing. It leads the nation in the production of industrial controls, X-ray equipment, steel foundry parts, and mining machinery. The area is also considered a printing and publishing center.

Professional and managerial positions are the fastest-growing occupations in Milwaukee, accounting for more than 110,000 workers. More than 136,000 workers are employed in health care and eduction; the area is home to four major multi-hospital health systems.

Nearly a quarter of the state's high-tech firms, employing more than one-third of Wisconsin's technology industry staff, are located in Milwaukee County. Between 1990 and 2004, Milwaukee added 97,300 jobs in the high tech sector, a 17.2% increase. High tech businesses in the area total more than 2,500 and employ over 78,200 people.

Tourism is also a major contributor to the local economy. Milwaukee hosts many festivals and parades throughout the year, and is home to nationally recognized museums, a zoo, professional sports teams, and entertainment venues. Altogether these attractions bring more than 5 million tourists and generate nearly $2 billion annually.

**Items and goods produced:** automobile frames and parts, heavy pumping machinery, gas engines, heavy lubricating and agricultural equipment, large mining shovels, dredges, saw mill and cement machinery, malt drinks and products, packaged meat, boots, shoes, leather products, knit goods, women's sportswear, gloves, children's clothes, diesel engines, motorcycles, outboard motors, electrical equipment, products of iron and steel foundries, metal fabricators

## Incentive Programs—New and Existing Businesses

Milwaukee is known for its harmonious working relationship with the business community throughout the entire area. Its Milwaukee Economic Development Corporation (MEDC) is a nonprofit corporation offering financial resources to aid in the city's economic growth. Its staff provides financial, technical, training, and ombudsman services to Milwaukee businesses and also assists in securing state of Wisconsin business development funds for Milwaukee firms. MEDC is very supportive of minority-owned businesses. Additionally, the city of Milwaukee's Emerging Business Enterprise Program helps emerging and small businesses with support services, contract opportunities, and financial resources, and helps establish mentor relationships between emerging and established businesses.

*Local programs:* The city's Community Block Grant Administration oversees the use of approximately $30 million of federal funds or programs in 18 targeted central city neighborhoods. The funding is used for housing rehab programs, special job and business development, and public service programs such as crime prevention, job training, housing for homeless, youth recreation programs and community organization programs.

*State programs:* Wisconsin corporate taxes remain among the lowest in the nation due to property tax exemptions on manufacturing machinery and equipment, inventory exemptions, and lack of franchise and unitary taxes. The Wisconsin Economic Development Association (WEDA) and the Wisconsin Economic Development Institute (WEDI) are two nonprofit agencies that provide information and financial services, legal and legislative assistance, and networking opportunities for their member businesses. On the government side, the Division of Business Development of the Wisconsin Department of Commerce provides technical assistance and financial incentives to businesses in the areas of business planning, site selection, capitalization, permits, training and recruitment, and research and development. On April 28, 2000, Governor Tommy G. Thompson signed into law a bill that created the Wisconsin Technology Council, a nonprofit, nonpartisan board that serves to create, develop and retain science and technology-based business in Wisconsin, and to serve as an advisor to the Governor and the Legislature. The Council also serves as the key link between the state's colleges and universities and the business expertise and capital offered by the financial service industry; the firm published its "Vision 2020: A Model Wisconsin Economy" as a blueprint for its efforts.

*Job training programs:* The Milwaukee industrial and business community profits from area educational institutions, which provide technology transfer, research services, and training programs. The state's Customized Labor Training program assists companies that are investing in new technologies or manufacturing processes by providing a grant of up to 50 percent of the cost of training employees on the new technologies. Also available in Milwaukee is the "Small Business School" television program, a series that highlights some of America's most successful small businesses and their owners.

## Development Projects

In 2005, the city of Milwaukee received $20.2 million in federal assistance for continued economic development. This assistance took the form of an $18 million New Market Tax Credit allocation and $2.2 million in brownfield grants from the U.S. Environmental Protection agency. The New Market Tax Credit was allocated to offer low-interest loans to businesses in low-income areas of the city. The brownfield grants were intended to clean up properties contaminated from previous uses, such as former gas station sites.

In 2004, Real Estate Recycling spent $10 million to renovate a former foundry plant, creating the 200,000-square-foot Stadium Business Park, used for light industrial businesses. In 2007 General Capital Group began construction on a $12 million, 51-unit condominium project in Brown Deer, in addition to a 70-unit condominium building called Bradley Village at the site of the former Bradley Village Shopping Center.

*Economic Development Information:* Metro Milwaukee Association of Commerce, 756 N. Milwaukee St., Ste. 400, Milwaukee, WI 53202; telephone (414) 287-4100. Milwaukee Economic Development Corporation, 809 N. Broadway, PO Box 324, Milwaukee, WI 53201; telephone (414)286-5840

## Commercial Shipping

Because of its location near the nation's population center—nearly 66 million people and one-third of U.S. manufacturing output is within 600 miles of the city—Milwaukee is a major commercial shipping hub. Of vital importance to both the local and state economies is the

Port of Milwaukee, a shipping and receiving point for international trade as well as the primary heavy-lift facility on the Great Lakes. The port has 330,000 square feet of covered warehouse space, plus an additional fifty acres for dry dock storage. A protected harbor permits year-round navigation through the port from three rivers in addition to Lake Michigan. With access to the eastern seaboard via the St. Lawrence Seaway and to the Gulf of Mexico through the Mississippi River, the Port of Milwaukee processes three million tons of cargo annually and has helped the state maintain an export growth rate twice the national average. Principal inbound commodities include cement, coal, machinery, steel, salt, limestone, asphalt, and crushed rock.

More than 500 multiservice motor freight carriers are engaged in shipping goods from Milwaukee to markets throughout the country. Two major rail lines serve the greater Milwaukee area: the CP/Soo Line and the Union Pacific Railroad pass through the Port of Milwaukee. Approximately 200 million pounds of cargo and mail are handled annually by air freight carriers at General Mitchell International Airport, Wisconsin's primary terminal for commercial air travel and freight shipments. Air freight carriers include Evergreen, FedEx, and UPS.

## Labor Force and Employment Outlook

Milwaukee is noted for a well-educated workforce with a strong work ethic. Employees call in sick less frequently than those in other major urban areas, and children consistently rank near the top in scholastic achievement tests. Private business drives the city's economy, with less than 11 percent of area employees working in the public sector. Just under 22 percent of Milwaukee's workers are in manufacturing jobs, the second-highest percentage among U.S. metropolitan areas. While manufacturing is a strong component of the city's economy, service jobs have shown the most growth in recent years.

The city's diverse economy and strong work ethic have helped keep area unemployment under the national average in each of the last 30 years. Milwaukee ranks slightly below the national average in pay levels for most occupations.

The following is a summary of data regarding the Milwaukee-Waukesha-West Allis metropolitan area labor force, 2006 annual averages.

**Size of nonagricultural labor force:** 847,500

**Number of workers employed in . . .**

  construction and mining: 34,800
  manufacturing: 132,600
  trade, transportation and utilities: 154,200
  information: 17,900
  financial activities: 57,300
  professional and business services: 110,900
  educational and health services: 136,300
  leisure and hospitality: 70,300
  other services: 41,200
  government: 91,900

**Average hourly earnings of production workers employed in manufacturing:** $18.02

**Unemployment rate:** 5.7% (June 2007)

| *Largest employers (2006)* | *Number of employees* |
|---|---|
| Aurora Health Care | 15,000 |
| Wheaton Franciscan Healthcare | 9,000 |
| Marshall & Ilsley Corp. | 7,000 |
| AT&T Wisconsin | 5,600 |
| Columbia-St. Mary's | 5,600 |
| Quad/Graphics Inc. | 5,100 |
| GE Healthcare Technologies | 5,000 |
| Kohl's Corp. | 5,000 |
| ProHealth Care Inc. | 5,000 |
| Rockwell Automation | 5,000 |

## Cost of Living

Metropolitan Milwaukee's cost of living, at just about equal to the national average, ranks below other major metropolitan areas. The area offers a wide array of homes in a variety of price ranges.

The following is a summary of data regarding several key cost of living factors in the Milwaukee area.

**2007 (1st quarter) ACCRA Average House Price:** $326,029

**2007 (1st quarter) ACCRA Cost of Living Index:** 100.6

**State income tax rate:** 4.6% to 6.75%

**State sales tax rate:** 5.0%

**Local income tax rate:** None

**Local sales tax rate:** 0.6%

**Property tax rate:** Range from $14.79 to $39.45 per $1,000 assessed valuation (2004)

***Economic Information:*** Metro Milwaukee Association of Commerce, 756 N. Milwaukee St., Ste. 4001, Milwaukee, WI 53202; telephone (414)287-4100

# ■ Education and Research

## Elementary and Secondary Schools

The Milwaukee Public Schools system is administered by a nine-member, nonpartisan board of school directors that appoints a superintendent. The system employs more than 8,500 teachers and administrators. In 2004-2005, Milwaukee Public Schools had a 65 percent graduation rate. Overall, students maintained nearly a 90 percent attendance rate in 2005-2006. Milwaukee public schoolteachers are well-educated; in 2004, 46 percent of teachers held a master's degree or higher.

Special programs include year-round schools, bilingual education, the "High/Scope" method for early childhood development, and specially targeted small classrooms (funded by grants from the Bill and Melinda Gates foundation). The district also operates a community center and a truancy abatement program.

The following is a summary of data regarding the Milwaukee Public Schools as of the 2005–2006 school year.

**Total enrollment:** 243,487

**Number of facilities**

elementary schools: 120
junior high/middle schools: 21
senior high schools: 66
other: 11

**Student/teacher ratio:** 16.2:1

**Teacher salaries (2005–06)**

elementary median: $50,640
junior high/middle median: $47,680
secondary median: $53,860

**Funding per pupil:** $10,375

More than 100 private elementary and secondary schools serve metropolitan Milwaukee. Choices include Montessori schools, charter schools, and a number of parochial schools.

***Public Schools Information:*** Milwaukee Public Schools, Administration Building, 5225 W. Vliet St., Milwaukee, WI 53208; telephone (414)475-8393

## Colleges and Universities

Milwaukee is home to many higher education institutions. A 2000 study by McGill University in Montreal ranked Milwaukee 5th in a list of U.S. and Canadian cities with the highest number of college students per 100 residents. One of the largest schools in the area is the University of Wisconsin-Milwaukee. It is one of two doctoral universities in the University of Wisconsin system, and has an enrollment of more than 28,000. The school offers 155 degree programs throughout its 12 schools and colleges.

Marquette University is a Catholic, Jesuit school composed of 6 colleges with professional schools in law, dentistry, and professional studies. The school also sponsors a program for students to spend a semester in Washington D.C. In the 2008 edition of *U.S News and World Report*'s "Best Colleges," Marquette was ranked 82nd among national universities. Its College of Nursing's graduate programs scored 54th and nursing-midwifery was 18th; the biomedical engineering program merited a 37th place ranking.

The Medical College of Wisconsin is part of the Milwaukee Regional Medical Center. It is a private, academic institution that emphasizes education, research, patient care, and local partnerships. The Medical College enrolls more than 1,200 students. Alverno College is a four-year, Catholic women's liberal arts college. Other schools in the area include Cardinal Stritch University, Carroll College, Carthage College, Concordia University Wisconsin, the Milwaukee Institute of Art and Design, Mount Mary College, and Wisconsin Lutheran College.

The area also boasts a number of technical colleges. Milwaukee Area Technical College offers more than 200 associate degrees, technical diplomas, and short-term certificates. At nearby Gateway Technical College, the school has more than 70 career options. Waukesha County Technical College focuses on technical education, occupational training, and enrichment programs.

## Libraries and Research Centers

In addition to its main facility, the Milwaukee Public Library operates 12 branches throughout the city and a bookmobile. Total library holdings include more than 3 million books and other materials such as periodicals, films, CDs, records, art reproductions, sheet music, and art objects. In 2006, there were 2,469,423 visitors to the library, and its computer classes enrolled nearly 5,000 local residents. Special collections are maintained on a wide range of subjects and computer resources are also available. The library was a recipient of the University of Wisconsin-Milwaukee School of Education 2004 Promoting Educational Achievement for Kids Award for its many literacy and education programs. The Golda Meir Library at the University of Wisconsin-Milwaukee maintains holdings of more than 5.2 million catalogued items as well as special collections in many scholarly fields. The library's largest and most distinguished research collection is the American Geographical Society Library. It holds more than one million items dating from 1452 to the present, with items ranging from rare old manuscripts to early printed books of satellite data. The Morris Fromkin Memorial Collection has around 10,000 items relating to American Reform movements from the end of the Civil War to the New Deal Era. Additional resources are found in such specialized collections as the Hebraica and Judaica Collection, the Slichter and Hohlweck Civil War Collections, and the Harry and Dorothy Jagodzinski Franklin Delano Roosevelt Collection.

The James J. Flannery Map Library is another University of Wisconsin-Milwaukee collection that includes U.S. Geological Survey topographical maps, wall maps, air photos, and various other maps; the Map Library is a government depository library for maps and is open to the public. The Medical College of Wisconsin Libraries have three facilities pertaining to basic sciences, clinical medicine, and nursing; the main library is a depository for World Health Organization publications. The Medical College is recognized as a leading center for research in such fields as interferon, obesity, allergies, eye disorders, arthritis, heart disease, childhood cancer, and diagnostic imaging.

The University of Wisconsin-Milwaukee maintains the Office of Industrial Research and Technology Transfer, the International Business Center, and the Femtosecond Laser Laboratory. Marquette University conducts in-house training programs in management development, computer technology, and industrial technology. The Biological and Biomedical Research Institute at Marquette University stimulates collaborative research by scientists in the life sciences. The Milwaukee School of Engineering houses the Applied Technology Center and the nationally known Fluid Power Institute.

***Public Library Information:*** Milwaukee Public Library, 814 W. Wisconsin Ave., Milwaukee, WI 53233; telephone (414)286-3000

# ■ Health Care

The metropolitan Milwaukee area has been a leader in developing managed care programs to control health care costs while providing quality care. One of the city's largest facilities is the Milwaukee Regional Medical Center, a sprawling campus of hospitals, outpatient clinics, health-related educational facilities, and research centers. The center is home to Children's Hospital of Wisconsin, a 222-bed pediatric facility where in 2006, 22,190 infants, children and adolescents were admitted. The Children's Hospital was ranked the 30th best pediatric program nationwide in 2007 by *U.S. News and World Report*. The center also includes the Curative Rehabilitation Center, with 40 specialty clinics; Froedtert Memorial Lutheran Hospital, which operates a Level One Trauma Center; the Blood Center of Southeastern Wisconsin; and the Medical College of Wisconsin. More than 1,200 students are enrolled at the school, including more than 800 medical students and physicians enrolled in the Master's of Public Health degree program. Medical College faculty supervise 700 physicians in residency training and provide continuing medical education to more than 12,000 health professionals annually.

Milwaukee residents also have access to several multi-hospital healthcare delivery systems in a four-county area, including Aurora Health Care, Wheaton Franciscan Health Care, and Horizon Home Care and Hospice. Aurora Health Care operates 13 hospitals, 130 pharmacies, and more than 100 clinics. The organization employs 700 physicians in its medical group; its Milwaukee hospitals are St. Luke's and Aurora Sinai Medical Center.

# ■ Recreation

## Sightseeing

Milwaukee successfully mixes old and new architectural styles that tell the history of the city from its beginning to the present. Kilbourntown House, the 1844 home of one of the city's founding fathers, was built by Benjamin Church and is an example of temple-type Greek Revival architecture. It is open to the public and furnished with mid-nineteenth century furniture and decorative arts. The Jeremiah Curtin House, built in 1846, is an example of Irish cottage architecture, and was the first stone house to be built in the town of Greenfield. Built about the same time, the Lowell Damon House exemplifies the colonial style and is furnished with nineteenth century furniture, décor, and art. Milwaukee's City Hall, completed in 1894, was designed by Henry C. Koch and Company, and cost more than $1 million to build. The building stands more than 350 feet tall and is in Flemish Renaissance style, featuring carved woodwork, black granite, leaded glass, stenciled ceilings, and stained-glass windows. The Pabst Mansion, another example of Flemish Renaissance architecture, was built in 1892 and contains decorative woodwork and ironwork.

Milwaukee is also noted for its church architecture. The St. Joan of Arc Chapel at Marquette University is a fifteenth-century French chapel moved from France to Milwaukee in 1965. Under its dome, modeled after St. Peter's in Rome, the Basilica of St. Josaphat displays stained glass, murals, and a collection of relics and portraits. Designed during a time of revival fantasy architecture, the Tripoli Shrine Temple is one of a few examples of the Indian Saracenic architectural style in the United States. It was modeled after the Taj Mahal in India, and features three domes, two recumbent camel sculptures, ceramic tile, plaster lattice work, and decorative floral designs. The Holy Hill National Shrine of Mary looks out onto one of Wisconsin's national parks and features spires, mosaics, stained glass windows, and a nineteenth-century statue of Mary and Jesus. St. Stephen's Catholic Church is the last remnant of the 1840 German settlement of New Coeln, and the church's wood carvings are said to be world famous.

The Milwaukee County Zoo is home to more than 2,500 mammals, birds, fish, amphibians, and reptiles, representing more than 300 species; the zoo also features workshops, holiday celebrations, concerts, and food festivals. The Mitchell Park Horticultural Conservatory, also known as "the Domes," cultivates tropical, arid, and seasonal plant displays in three beehive-shaped domes. The Boerner Botanical Gardens at Whitnall Park displays perennials, wildflowers, annuals, and herbs, and features a highly praised rose garden. The Wehr Nature Center, also in Whitnall Park, offers self-guided tours, nature programs, live animals, and three formal gardens. The Center also features 200 acres of land with 5 miles of hiking trails.

## Arts and Culture

Milwaukee's cultural heritage dates to the nineteenth century when German immigrants established the city's first music societies and theater groups. Today the Milwaukee Symphony Orchestra—the state's only professional orchestra—performs more than 150 classical and pop concerts each season, with nearly 90 full-time musicians. The Orchestra is attended by more than 300,000 people annually and runs one of the largest state touring programs of any U.S. orchestra. At home, the Orchestra plays at the Marcus Center for the Performing Arts, which is also the home of the Milwaukee Ballet Company, the Milwaukee Youth Symphony, and the Florentine Opera Company. The Skylight Opera Theatre, founded in 1959, presents a season of more than 80 productions ranging from Mozart to Gilbert and Sullivan. The Theatre is located in the Broadway Theatre Center in the city's historic Third Ward.

For more than 50 years, the Milwaukee Repertory Theater's multi-play season has been produced in the Patty and Jay Baker Theater Complex, which includes a Mainstage theater seating 720 patrons, the Stiemke Theatre featuring flexible seating, and the Stackner Cabaret where patrons take advantage of the full-service bar and restaurant. Riverside Theater presents theatrical shows and musical performances. The Milwaukee Chamber Theater has been producing first-class live theater for more than 30 years.

Milwaukee's museums present a variety of choices for the art enthusiast. The Milwaukee Art Museum on Lake Michigan is housed in the War Memorial Center designed by Finnish architect Eero Saarinen, who also designed the St. Louis Arch. The Museum's permanent collection consists of nineteenth- and twentieth-century painting and sculpture, extensive Haitian art holdings, and the Bradley gift of modern art displayed in a wing built in 1975. In 2001, the Museum unveiled the Quadracci Pavilion, designed by Santiago Calatrava. The Charles Allis Art Museum houses its collection of nineteenth-century French and American paintings in a 1911 Edwardian mansion. The collection spans 2,000 years and includes original and antique furnishings. The American Geographical Society Collection at the University of Wisconsin-Milwaukee exhibits material related to geography, exploration, cartography, and the earth and social sciences.

Other Milwaukee museums include the Discovery World Museum, with 150 hands-on exhibits and live theater shows; the Thomas A. Greene Memorial Museum with minerals, crystals, and fossils; the Haggerty Museum of Art at Marquette University, with a wide range of art forms; the Milwaukee County Historical Center; and America's Black Holocaust Museum. With more than 150,000 square feet of exhibit space, the Milwaukee Public Museum features a Costa Rican rainforest, archeological exhibits, and a live butterfly house. The Villa Terrace Decorative Arts Museum, overlooking Lake Michigan, displays its collections in an Italian Renaissance-style villa.

## Festivals and Holidays

Milwaukee, dubbed the "City of Festivals," is the site of a wide variety of ethnic and cultural festivals, many of them held along the city's lakefront. Most events are scheduled in the summer, beginning with RiverSplash in June, which hosts a paddleboat race, canoe rides, fireworks, street vendors, food booths, and live music. In July, Bastille Days celebrates all things French with a myriad of French cuisine, live entertainment, and a 5K run. Summerfest, billed as the world's largest music festival, attracts national headliners for a week-plus celebration. Set on the shore of Lake Michigan, Summerfest takes place in a 23,000-seat amphitheater and offers unique attractions and food from more than 50 restaurants in addition to live music.

For parade fans, Milwaukee hosts a St. Patrick's Day Parade every March, complete with bagpipes, clowns, local politicians and celebrities, floats, and marching bands. The annual Great Circus Parade in July, presented by Baraboo's Circus World Museum, attracts hundreds of thousands of spectators. The event features 75 historical circus wagons, clowns, 750 horses, and elephants, camels, and zebras. On parade day, circus performers and animals follow a three-mile route for an authentic recreation of a turn-of-the century circus parade. Another popular event close to Milwaukee is the Wisconsin State Fair in August; the Fair runs 11 days and features agriculture, food, shopping, and 28 stages of local and national entertainment.

## Sports for the Spectator

Major league baseball's Milwaukee Brewers compete in the National League and play their home games at Miller Park. The Milwaukee Bucks of the National Basketball Association are based at the Bradley Center, a privately funded $94 million sports and concert facility that provides the city with one of the nation's most architecturally significant and functional sports facilities. Bradley Center is also home to the Marquette University Golden Eagles NCAA basketball team and the Milwaukee Admirals of the American Hockey League. From its home at the U.S. Cellular Arena, the Milwaukee Wave became the 2005 Major Indoor Soccer League Champions. The Wave is the oldest continually operating professional soccer team in the United States.

Marquette University and the University of Wisconsin-Milwaukee Panthers field teams in most collegiate sports. Jetrockets, wheelstanders, and funny cars are featured in a season of competition at the Great Lakes Dragway from April through November. The Milwaukee

Mile, the oldest operating motor speedway in the world, attracts nationally known drivers for Indy car, Stock Car, and NASCAR events.

### Sports for the Participant

The Milwaukee County Park System, which celebrated its 100th anniversary in 2007, maintains more than 140 parks on nearly 15,000 acres. Indoor and outdoor recreational activities offered year-round include rugby, soccer, softball, baseball, swimming, tennis, golf, ice skating, tobogganing, and boating. Public skating is available at the Pettit National Ice Center, which contains the country's first U.S. indoor 400-meter racing oval, one of just a few worldwide. The center was the first facility to house speed skating, hockey, and figure skating under one roof, and has hosted events such as the World Sprint Speed Skating Championships and the U.S. Olympic Speed Skating Time Trials. Milwaukee's location on Lake Michigan offers a myriad of water-related recreational opportunities.

### Shopping and Dining

Milwaukee is one of a few Midwestern cities with a skywalk system connecting the downtown commercial district; one section, called Riverspan, bridges the Milwaukee River. The Riverwalk walkway along the Milwaukee River is lined with shops and restaurants. Downtown, the Shops of Grand Avenue is an enclosed multilevel four-block marketplace of 150 shops and restaurants and 5 historic buildings forming the core of the glass skywalk system. The Historic Third Ward is a restored warehouse district featuring art galleries, restaurants, antiques, and the Milwaukee Institute of Art and Design. Old World Third Street gives visitors a taste of Old Milwaukee with cobblestone intersections and ethnic markets and restaurants. Brady Street serves as Milwaukee's Italian neighborhood with authentic restaurants, markets, bakeries, and an artistic, student-oriented crowd. Several neighborhood and regional shopping malls also serve the metropolitan area. Fondy Farmers' Market, the city's largest farmers' market, is open six days a week in season and specializes in locally grown and produced fruits, vegetables, and food products.

Some of the best German restaurants in the country are located in Milwaukee, such as Karl Ratzsch's, Restaurant, Mader's Restaurant, and the Bavarian Wurst Haus. Dining in Milwaukee is not limited to award-winning German cuisine, however; besides Continental, Italian, Mexican, and Chinese restaurants, Milwaukee offers a surprising mix of other ethnic choices, such as African, Irish, Cajun, Polish, Serbian, and Thai. One of the city's most popular food specialties is the fish fry, which can be found at Buck Bradley's, Harry's Bar and Grill, Red Rock Café, and the Potawatomi Bingo Casino.

*Visitor Information:* Greater Milwaukee Convention and Visitors Bureau, Inc., 648 Plankinton Ave., Ste. 425, Milwaukee, WI 53203; toll-free (800)231-0903

## ■ Convention Facilities

The Midwest Airlines Center opened in 1998; the $170 million, 667,475-square-foot center is located in the heart of Milwaukee and features 188,695 square feet of exhibit space, a 37,506-square-foot grand ballroom, and 28 meeting rooms, as well as cutting-edge technology and $1.2 million in public artwork. More than 3,000 hotel rooms, a theater, shopping, nightlife, the RiverWalk, restaurants, and museums are within walking distance of the Midwest Airlines Center. The city has a number of other convention and meeting facilities for groups of any size. Recent area hotel renovations have included an $8 million renovation of the Hyatt Regency Milwaukee and a nearly $4 million renovation at the Wyndham Milwaukee Center.

*Convention Information:* Greater Milwaukee Convention and Visitors Bureau, Inc., 648 Plankinton Ave., Ste. 425, Milwaukee, WI 53203; toll-free (800)231-0903

## ■ Transportation

### Approaching the City

General Mitchell International Airport is the destination for most air traffic into Milwaukee. Situated adjacent to I-94, 8 miles south of downtown, Mitchell Airport is the largest airport in Wisconsin. Mitchell is served by 13 commercial airlines and offers approximately 235 daily departures in addition to 235 daily arrivals. In 2006 there were a total of 7,299,294 combined enplanements and deplanements. The terminal is highly regarded by frequent travelers. Based at General Mitchell International Airport is Midwest Airlines; *Travel+Leisure* magazine recognized Midwest Airlines as "Best Domestic Airline" in 2004, 2003 and 2002, for a total of 5 times in 8 years. The principal general aviation facility for Milwaukee is Timmerman Field.

A 160-mile freeway system permits direct access to central Milwaukee within 20 minutes from points throughout a 10-mile radius, except during the peak rush-hour period. Milwaukee's average commute time of approximately 20 minutes is the eighth shortest among the nation's largest metro areas, according to a 2007 study conducted by American City Business Journals.

Amtrak and Greyhound provide passenger rail and bus services into Milwaukee.

### Traveling in the City

The city of Milwaukee lies along the shore of Lake Michigan and is intersected from north to south by the Milwaukee River. Streets are laid out on a grid pattern; Lincoln Memorial Drive runs along the lakeshore downtown. North-south streets are numbered and east-west streets are named.

The Milwaukee County Transit System, which ranks among the nation's largest all-bus transportation systems, operates bus routes in Milwaukee County. The System has 484 air-conditioned buses that operate frequently from 5 a.m. until after midnight on 57 routes, traveling a total of eighteen million miles per year. Additional services include express routes from park-ride lots and special routes to the university area and the stadium. Taxi and limousine services are also available.

# ■ Communications

## Newspapers and Magazines

The major daily newspaper of the Greater Milwaukee area is the morning *Milwaukee Journal Sentinel.* Several other newspapers, including the *Business Journal of Milwaukee,* circulate biweekly or weekly.

More than 35 trade and special-interest magazines and journals are published in Milwaukee; they cover such subjects as personal improvement, religion, hobbies, the social sciences, business and finance, computers, railroads, construction and building trades, and archaeology.

## Television and Radio

Seven commercial, two public, one university, and two independent television stations broadcast in Milwaukee. More than forty AM and FM radio stations play a wide range of music, news, and talk radio in the county. The Milwaukee Symphony Orchestra produces national radio broadcasts.

***Media Information:*** *Milwaukee Journal Sentinel,* PO Box 661, Milwaukee, WI 53201; telephone (414)224-2000.

## Milwaukee Online

City of Milwaukee home page. Available www.ci.mil.wi.us

Greater Milwaukee Convention and Visitors Bureau. Available www.milwaukee.org

Historic Milwaukee Inc. Available www.historicmilwaukee.org

James J. Flannery Map Library. Available www.uwm.edu/Dept/GML

Metro Milwaukee Association of Commerce. Available www.mmac.org

Metro Milwaukee Guide to Relocation. Available metromilwaukee.org

Milwaukee Economic Development Corporation. Available www.medconline.com

*Milwaukee Journal Sentinel.* Available www.jsonline.com

Milwaukee Public Library. Available www.mpl.org

Wisconsin Department of Commerce. Available www.commerce.state.wi.us

BIBLIOGRAPHY

Buck, Diane M., and Virginia A. Palmer, *Outdoor Sculpture in Milwaukee: A Cultural and Historical Guidebook* (State Historical Society of Wisconsin, 1994)

Derleth, August William, *The Wind Leans West* (New York: Candlelight Press, 1969)

Leavitt, Judith Walzer, *The Healthiest City: Milwaukee and the Politics of Health Reform* (University of Wisconsin Press, 1996)

# Racine

## ■ The City in Brief

**Founded:** 1834 (incorporated 1848)

**Head Official:** Mayor Gary Becker (since April 2003)

**City Population**

    1980: 85,725
    1990: 84,298
    2000: 81,855
    2006 estimate: 79,592
    Percent change, 1990–2000: −3.0%
    U.S. rank in 1980: Not available
    U.S. rank in 1990: 248th
    U.S. rank in 2000: 356th (State rank: 5th)

**Metropolitan Area Population**

    1980: Not available
    1990: 175,034
    2000: 188,831
    2006 estimate: 196,096
    Percent change, 1990–2000: 7.9%
    U.S. rank in 1980: 23rd
    U.S. rank in 1990: Not available
    U.S. rank in 2000: 26th (CMSA)

**Area:** 16 square miles (2000)

**Elevation:** 620 feet above sea level

**Average Annual Temperature:** 47.2° F

**Average Annual Precipitation:** 35.3 inches of rain; 47.3 inches of snow

**Major Economic Sectors:** Manufacturing, services, trade

**Unemployment Rate:** 6.3% (June 2007)

**Per Capita Income:** $19,428 (2005)

**2005 FBI Crime Index Property:** 4,557

**2005 FBI Crime Index Violent:** 391

**Major Colleges and Universities:** University of Wisconsin-Parkside, Gateway Technical College

**Daily Newspaper:** *Journal Times*

## ■ Introduction

Located on Lake Michigan in the corridor between Milwaukee and Chicago, the lakeside city of Racine has been primarily manufacturing-oriented for at least a century. With the construction in the 1980s of the largest recreational boat harbor on Lake Michigan, Racine diversified its economy from one based on durable goods to one that embraces tourism. The marina and its restaurants, the development of bed and breakfast inns, a charming lakefront zoo, and one of the largest and most prestigious furniture galleries in the Midwest add to the city's attractions. Racine County hosts more than a hundred festivals, concerts, carnivals, fairs, parades, sporting events, picnics and celebrations annually, which also boosts tourism to the "Belle City of the Lakes."

## ■ Geography and Climate

Racine is located on the western shore of Lake Michigan in southeastern Wisconsin about 75 miles north of Chicago and 30 miles south of Milwaukee. Racine's weather is influenced to a considerable extent by Lake Michigan, especially when the temperature of the lake differs markedly from the air temperature. During spring and early summer a wind shift from westerly to easterly can cause a 10 to 15 degree drop in temperature. In autumn and winter the relatively warm water of Lake Michigan prevents nighttime temperatures from falling as low as they do a few miles inland from shore.

**Area:** 16 square miles (2000)

**Elevation:** 620 feet above sea level

**Average Annual Temperature:** 47.2° F

**Average Annual Precipitation:** 35.3 inches of rain; 47.3 inches of snow

# ■ History

## City Settled by Yankees

The first known visit by white men to the Root River area, the site of present-day Racine, occurred in 1679 when explorers LaSalle and Tonti stopped there on their search for a route to the Mississippi River. Prior to the 1830s, the area of southeastern Wisconsin was inhabited by the Potawatomi tribe, whose rights to the lands were recognized by the federal government. By 1833 the U.S. government made an agreement with the Potawatomi to purchase five million acres of land, including the area where Racine is located. Soon after, the Potawatomi were moved by the government to areas in the western United States. The first settlers arrived in what came to be Racine County about 1820 and established trading posts along the Root River in the present day cities of Racine and Caledonia.

In 1834 Gilbert Knapp settled at the mouth of the Root River and blazed out a 160-acre claim. From 1834 to 1836 the community was named Root for the river on which the city was settled (Root being the English translation for the name the Potawatomi called the river). After 1836 the name was changed to Racine, the French word for root, but the English word was retained for the name of the river. From the spot at the mouth of the river and spreading westward across the entire county, commercial and industrial enterprises sprang up. In 1834 and 1835 hundreds of settlers migrated west to the newly open lands. Northern Europeans settled along waterways throughout Racine County, utilizing them for transportation and power.

Shortly after Racine's founding, a saw mill was constructed, which proved to be a real convenience to the settlers. By 1840, 337 settlers lived in the area and by 1844 the city had 1,100 people. The government built a lighthouse in 1839, a $10,000 courthouse in 1840, and several bridges and a major hotel. Between 1844 and 1860 the government assisted in the completion of the harbor. A large elevator was built in 1867 to load the ships with wheat that was brought to Racine and stored in dozens of grain warehouses. The elevator was destroyed in a fire in 1882.

## Manufacturing Anchors Local Economy

The young city was supported by a large farming community that came to town for manufactured goods. The city's growth coincided with the invention and development of agriculture machinery and other labor-saving devices. A flour and feed business was Racine's first. Other early industries were boots and shoes, tanneries,

clothing, wagons and carriages, soap and candles, saddles, trucks, harnesses, and blacksmithing. By 1860 boat building and brick making were added.

Racine's first school was built in 1836. During the Civil War, the Camp Utley federal war camp was built in Racine. In 1884 the first ship entered the newly built harbor. That same year, upon the city's fiftieth birthday, a monument that still stands in Monument Square was erected to honor the city's Civil War soldiers.

Over the years, as waterways declined in importance, railroads became the major transport for freight. The first railroad to reach Racine arrived in 1853 and the first steam engine came into use in 1867.

A number of local industries have had a vital relation to the growth and prosperity of the city itself. The J. I. Case Plow Threshing Machine Works was established in 1844. In 1886 S.C. Johnson began a parquet flooring manufacturing operation, which diversified over the years and is now one of the city's largest employers. Gold Metal Camp Furniture was started in 1892, the Racine Rubber Company in 1910, Mitchell Motor Car Company in 1903, and Western Publishing in 1908.

The Great Depression of the 1930s was especially severe in the agricultural sector and the sale of farm machinery drastically declined. By 1937 recovery had begun, and World War II accelerated that recovery. However, from 1945 through 1960 the business community, always sensitive to national business cycles, experienced slow postwar growth. In the 1960s, the voluntary desegregation of the schools became a national model. During the 1960s and 1970s Racine manufacturing entered a growth cycle, and printing, publishing, and chemical production became more predominant.

During the 1970s there was an increased movement of industry from central Racine to the outlying areas. In 1971 the University of Wisconsin-Parkside was founded in a rural setting between Racine and the nearby city of Kenosha.

The construction of the multimillion-dollar Racine Civic Center Festival Park marina complex in the 1980s spurred the growth of tourist visits to the city, particularly from the Chicago and Milwaukee areas. Today, Racine's waterfront community thrives with cultural attractions, sporting activities, festivals, and other tourist attractions. This influx of tourism has boosted many aspects of Racine's economy.

***Historical Information:*** Racine County Historical Society and Museum, 701 S. Main St., PO Box 1527, Racine, WI 53401; telephone (414)637-8585

# ■ Population Profile

## Metropolitan Area Residents

1980: Not available
1990: 175,034

©Aero-Fotografik/Chris Wawro

2000: 188,831
2006 estimate: 196,096
Percent change, 1990–2000: 7.9%
U.S. rank in 1980: 23rd
U.S. rank in 1990: Not available
U.S. rank in 2000: 26th (CMSA)

**City Residents**

1980: 85,725
1990: 84,298
2000: 81,855
2006 estimate: 79,592
Percent change, 1990–2000: −3.0%
U.S. rank in 1980: Not available
U.S. rank in 1990: 248th
U.S. rank in 2000: 356th (State rank: 5th)

**Density:** 5,267.6 people per square mile (2000)

**Racial and ethnic characteristics (2000)**

White: 58,214
Black: 17,692
American Indian and Alaska Native: 736
Asian: 669

Native Hawaiian and Pacific Islander: 74
Hispanic or Latino (may be of any race): 11,422
Other: 6,714

**Percent of residents born in state:** 70.2% (2000)

**Age characteristics (2005)**

Population under 5 years old: 6,052
Population 5 to 9 years old: 6,738
Population 10 to 14 years old: 5,102
Population 15 to 19 years old: 5,842
Population 20 to 24 years old: 5,959
Population 25 to 34 years old: 11,100
Population 35 to 44 years old: 10,856
Population 45 to 54 years old: 11,138
Population 55 to 59 years old: 4,058
Population 60 to 64 years old: 2,637
Population 65 to 74 years old: 3,572
Population 75 to 84 years old: 3,461
Population 85 years and older: 762
Median age: 32.8 years

**Births (2006, MSA)**

Total number: 2,513

**Deaths (2006, MSA)**

Total number: 1,558

**Money income (2005)**

Per capita income: $19,428
Median household income: $38,156
Total households: 31,391

**Number of households with income of...**

less than $10,000: 3,560
$10,000 to $14,999: 2,830
$15,000 to $24,999: 4,108
$25,000 to $34,999: 3,763
$35,000 to $49,999: 5,830
$50,000 to $74,999: 5,830
$75,000 to $99,999: 3,011
$100,000 to $149,999: 1,992
$150,000 to $199,999: 195
$200,000 or more: 272

**Percent of families below poverty level:** 10.5% (2005)

**2005 FBI Crime Index Property:** 4,557

**2005 FBI Crime Index Violent:** 391

## ■ Municipal Government

The city of Racine has a mayor-council form of government. The mayor is elected at-large for a four-year term. The council is made up of 15 members, known as aldermen. Each alderman represents a geographic electoral district. The aldermen serve two-year terms; eight are elected in even years and seven are elected in odd years. In 2004 the city established a city administrator position. The city administrator functions as the chief operating officer; the administrator is appointed by the mayor, subject to approval by a majority of the city council.

**Head Official:** Mayor Gary Becker (since April 2003; current term expires 2010)

**Total Number of City Employees:** 1,000 (2007)

*City Information:* City of Racine, 730 Washington Ave., Racine, WI 53403; telephone (262)636-9111

## ■ Economy

### Major Industries and Commercial Activity

The recent history of the city of Racine is a story of downtown revitalization. During the 1980s Racine County lost an average of 1,000 jobs per year and many downtown retailers closed or moved to new outlying malls or elsewhere. A group of local business leaders marshaled private, county, and city support in their efforts to turn a declining downtown area with a failing commercial harbor into a vital, attractive harbor complex that would attract tourism and convention activity. The project included a 110-acre, 921-slip luxury harbor/marina; a 16-acre county park; and a 6-acre, city-owned festival park that contains both indoor and outdoor facilities designed for year-round use. By the early 1990s, 50 new retailers had moved to the central city and more than 100,000 square feet of first-class office space was added to the downtown. In addition, the revitalized lakefront spurred more than $30 million in private investment, including a 76-unit lakefront condominium.

Racine's small-business, industrial base is an important part of the region's economy. As of 2005, there were more than 300 established manufacturing firms across Racine County, employing 25,000 people; a number of the firms are based in the city of Racine. The 10 largest manufacturers employ about 60 percent of the workers, with the remaining 40 percent working for small companies. Racine is world headquarters of S.C. Johnson Wax, one of the world's leading manufacturers of chemical specialty products for home care, insect control, and personal care. One of the largest privately-held family controlled businesses in the United States, it is among the city's largest employers. Another important local firm is In-Sink-Erator, the world's largest manufacturer of food waste disposers and hot water dispensers. The first food disposer was created in 1927 in Racine by John W. Hammes, founder of the company that began operations in 1937. Today the company also markets water heaters, dishwashers, and trash compactors.

In 1842 Jerome Increase Case began a threshing machine works in Racine, and today CNH (formerly J.I. Case) is known worldwide for its quality agricultural and construction equipment. With origins in the city dating back more than 40 years, Master Appliance Corporation has become one of the world's leading designers, manufacturers and marketers of heat tools for industry. Golden Books (formerly Western Publishing Company), the nation's largest publisher and producer of children's storybooks, was founded in Racine in 1907 as a small printing company. The company is also a major producer of puzzles and youth electronic books and products, and ranks among the largest commercial printers in the United States.

In addition to manufacturing, the largest industries in Racine include the service industry, administrative and support services, education, health care, government, and specialty trade contractors.

**Items and goods produced:** paper products, electric and electronic products, rubber and plastic products, fabricated metal products, wood products, apparel, transportation equipment, printing and publishing

## Incentive Programs—New and Existing Companies

*Local programs:* The Racine County Economic Development Corporation (RCEDC) offers a number of different loans for purposes such as purchase of land, buildings, machinery and equipment, new construction or relocation, working capital, inventory, and fixed assets; some are specific to companies in Racine county, others to companies in the city of Racine. With the Racine Development Group loan fund, businesses and developers that are interested in working in low or moderate income Racine neighborhoods are eligible to apply. Other RCEDC loans benefit businesses that are women- or minority-owned. The Racine Area Manufacturers and Commerce (RAMAC) organizes a number of projects and programs to assist area businesses. RAMAC's Golden Key Awards recognize outstanding businesses in the Racine area; the Business After 5 program offers local networking opportunities; RAMAC's Speakers Bureau provides knowledgeable speakers on a variety of subjects; and the International Outreach Office assists local businesses in accessing world markets.

*State programs:* Wisconsin corporate taxes remain among the lowest in the nation due to property tax exemptions on manufacturing machinery and equipment, inventory exemptions, and lack of franchise and unitary taxes.

The Wisconsin Economic Development Association (WEDA) and the Wisconsin Economic Development Institute (WEDI) are two nonprofit agencies that provide information and financial services, legal and legislative assistance, and networking opportunities for their member businesses. On the government side, the Division of Business Development of the Wisconsin Department of Commerce provides technical assistance and financial incentives to businesses in the areas of business planning, site selection, capitalization, permits, training and recruitment, and research and development. On April 28, 2000, Governor Tommy G. Thompson signed into law a bill that created the Wisconsin Technology Council, a nonprofit, nonpartisan board that serves to create, develop and retain science and technology-based business in Wisconsin, and to serve as an advisor to the Governor and the Legislature. The Council also serves as the key link between the state's colleges and universities and the business expertise and capital offered by the financial service industry; the firm published its "Vision 2020: A Model Wisconsin Economy" as a blueprint for its efforts.

*Job training programs:* Gateway Technical College, in addition to offering both associate and technical degrees in more than 75 different fields, can create customized training programs offered either on campus or at employer sites. The school also provides one-on-one technical assistance in areas such as production and marketing. Gateway's staff consults with local businesses to determine employee retraining needs, and can also give technical assistance to those companies seeking to develop grants for other local, state, or federal training programs. The Wisconsin Department of Development offers Customized Labor Training grants for training or retraining of in-state workers, providing an economic contribution to the area. Through the Job Training Partnership Act, the Southeastern Wisconsin Private Industry Council provides trained employees and customized training to unskilled adults and youths for entry into the labor force. It also offers on-the-job training with 50 percent wage reimbursement offered to employers along with summer youth programs.

## Development Projects

In 2007, the city of Racine opened a 14-acre business park on the site of former Jacobsen Manufacturing complex, which was abandoned in 2001. In 2007, plans continued to move forward with the Kenosha-Racine-Milwaukee (KRM) commuter rail Metra extension, despite budget setbacks in October of that year. Wisconsin government and business community officials formulated development plans that would add a 33-mile extension of the Chicago Metra service that currently ends in Kenosha. The expansion was expected to use existing upgraded rail right-of-way and provide seven round-trip trains per day between Chicago and Milwaukee, with stops planned in Milwaukee, Cudahy-St. Francis, South Milwaukee, Oak Creek, Caledonia, Racine, and Somers.

In 2007, improvement plans under consideration by the city included a Douglas Avenue Revitilization plan and a Downtown Improvement Plan.

*Economic Development Information:* Racine County Economic Development Corporation, 2320 Renaissance Blvd., Sturtevant, WI 53177; telephone (262)898-7400; email rcedc@racinecountyedc.org

## Commercial Shipping

Rail freight service is provided by the Union Pacific Railroad, CP Rail Service, and the Wisconsin & Southern Railroad Co. There are approximately 70 widely distributed trucking and warehousing establishments in Racine County; the area has direct access to Interstate Highway 94 via state trunk highways. The city is located 30 miles south of the Port of Milwaukee, which provides Great Lakes Seaway access and a Foreign Trade Zone. Three Racine County aviation facilities accommodate all business aircraft, with Chicago's O'Hare International Airport and Milwaukee's Mitchell International Airport both less than 60 miles away. Mitchell International Airport has three cargo carriers: Evergreen, UPS, and FedEx.

## Labor Force and Employment Outlook

Together with the labor force from surrounding communities, Racine has an abundant supply of workers. In Wisconsin, absenteeism is below the national average, and the state has the lowest national percentage of employees who leave jobs by choice. On average, Wisconsin's labor hours lost due to work stoppages are only one-fifth that of the nation, which contributes to businesses' increased productivity and reduced manufacturing costs.

The following is a summary of data regarding the Racine metropolitan area labor force, 2006 annual averages.

**Size of nonagricultural labor force:** 80,000

**Number of workers employed in ...**

> construction and mining: 3,300
> manufacturing: 18,800
> trade, transportation and utilities: 15,200
> information: 600
> financial activities: 2,800
> professional and business services: 6,800
> educational and health services: 10,800
> leisure and hospitality: 6,900
> other services: 4,600
> government: 10,100

**Average hourly earnings of production workers employed in manufacturing:** Not available

**Unemployment rate:** 6.3% (June 2007)

| *Largest employers (2007)* | *Number of employees* |
| --- | --- |
| Wheaton Franciscan Healthcare | 3,459 |
| SC Johnson and Sons | 3,400 |
| CNH Global | 1,811 |
| In-Sink-Erator | 1,202 |
| County of Racine | 1,075 |
| City of Racine | 1,000 |
| Modine Manufacturing Co. | 690 |
| Ruud Lightning | 520 |
| Bombardier Recreational Products | 500 |
| Putzmeister, Inc. | 471 |

## Cost of Living

In 2000 the median value of a home in Racine was $83,600 according to the U.S. Census Bureau.

The following is a summary of data regarding several key cost of living factors in the Racine area.

**2007 (1st quarter) ACCRA Average House Price:** Not available

**2007 (1st quarter) ACCRA Cost of Living Index:** Not available

**State income tax rate:** 4.6% to 6.75%

**State sales tax rate:** 5.0%

**Local income tax rate:** None

**Local sales tax rate:** 0.1%

**Property tax rate:** $27.97 per $1,000 of equalized valuation

***Economic Information:*** Wisconsin Department of Commerce, 201 W. Washington Ave., Madison, WI 53708; telephone (608)266-1018

# ■ Education and Research

## Elementary and Secondary Schools

The Racine Unified School District is a composite of city, suburban, and rural areas contained in a 100-square-mile area. Racine County is known for having outstanding schools, and many innovative, state-wide models have been developed in the school districts. The district achieves above national test score averages on standardized tests and on both SAT and ACT tests. More than 70 percent of district high school graduates indicate attending a post-secondary institution. Approximately two-thirds of the district's teachers hold master's degrees and the average teacher has more than fourteen years of experience. Alternative programs include charter and magnet schools.

The following is a summary of data regarding the Racine Unified School District as of the 2005–2006 school year.

**Total enrollment:** 30,802

**Number of facilities**

> elementary schools: 23
> junior high/middle schools: 6
> senior high schools: 3
> other: 0

**Student/teacher ratio:** 15.6:1

**Teacher salaries (2005–06)**

> elementary median: $42,150
> junior high/middle median: $42,360
> secondary median: $44,220

**Funding per pupil:** $9,379

There are dozens of private schools in Racine, including the Prairie School, an independent college preparatory school that teaches nursery through twelfth grade and emphasizes arts education. Racine has approximately thirty parochial schools in the area.

***Public Schools Information:*** Racine Unified School District, 2220 Northwestern Ave., Racine, WI 53404; telephone (262)635-5600

## Colleges and Universities

The University of Wisconsin-Parkside, part of the University of Wisconsin system, serves approximately 5,000 undergraduate and graduate students on its 700-acre campus located between the cities of Racine and Kenosha. The university has schools of liberal arts and science and technology, and offers undergraduate course work in 33 major fields of study. Top majors include business management, criminal justice, sociology/anthropology, communication, and psychology. UW-Parkside has a student-faculty ratio of 19:1. In addition, the school offers a master's degree in business administration and a master's degree in applied molecular biology, the only one of its kind in Wisconsin. Gateway Technical College offers associate degree, diploma, and certificate programs, as well as educational classes offered to specifically meet area employment needs. The school offers programs in 65 fields. Its facilities include three full-service campuses.

In nearby Kenosha County, Carthage College offers liberal arts degrees in more than 45 fields and enrolls more than 2,000 students, with around 100 faculty members. Carthage also offers a Master's in Education. The short commute to Milwaukee allows Racine residents to attend classes at dozens of colleges and universities, including Marquette University, Milwaukee School of Engineering, and the University of Wisconsin-Milwaukee.

## Libraries and Research Centers

The Racine Public Library contains more than a quarter of a million volumes, subscribes to approximately 650 publications, and has more than 5,000 microfilms and films. The library's special collections include works on Racine history and the Early Childhood Resource Collection. In addition to the spacious main library that offers views of Lake Michigan, the library operates a bookmobile and has a number of return box locations. Programs for teens, children, adults, and families are also available.

At the University of Wisconsin-Parkside Center for Survey and Marketing Research, studies on travel and tourism and product and market feasibility are conducted. The university's Bio Medical Institute conducts applied and fundamental research in drug design, evaluation, and electromagnetic field application.

***Public Library Information:*** Racine Public Library, 75 Seventh St., Racine, WI 53403; telephone (262)636-9252; email ref_rac@racinelib.lib.wi.us

# ■ Health Care

Racine's main hospital, All Saints, has locations at Spring Street Campus and 1320 Wisconsin Avenue, and is affiliated with Wheaton Franciscan Services, Inc. Wheaton Franciscan also operates the Racine Family Medicine Center, the Wheaton Franciscan Medical Group, and an extended care facility at Lakeshore Manor. Its organization includes All Saints Medical Group, which consists of more than 120 primary and specialty care physicians who practice at several locations; All Saints Visiting Nurse Association and Hospice; and All Saints Healthcare Foundation. All Saints employs more than 3,500 staff and specialties include cancer care, comprehensive headache care, emergency care and walk-in care, heart care, mental health and addiction care, orthopedics, and rehabilitation services. Both locations offer community education programming and older adult services. All Saints also serves as teaching facility affiliated with the Medical College of Wisconsin, the Racine Family Medicine Residency, and the School of Radiologic Technology. Aurora Health Care also supports a number of health clinics in eastern Wisconsin.

The cost of health care in Racine is among the highest statewide.

# ■ Recreation

## Sightseeing

Racine's Southside Historic District has an impressive collection of more than 14 blocks of homes and buildings on the National Register of Historic Places. The district contains many architectural styles, including Tudor, Victorian, Federal, Italianate, and Queen Anne. Of special interest are the English Gothic-style buildings at the DeKoven Center Retreat/Conference Center. The Henrietta Benstead Hall, built in the Colonial Revival style, incorporates the classical details of the Queen Anne style, and features Tiffany windows and quality furnishings. Across the street is the Italianate style Masonic Temple, built circa 1856. The mansion contains two operable theaters and features a unique Egyptian motif in the style of the 1920s. Both structures are lavishly lighted and decorated during the Christmas season and are open for tours.

A favorite local site for picnic outings and observation of more than 200 resident animals is the 32-acre Racine Zoological Society, located on the shores of Lake Michigan. One of the few free zoos in the country, it is home to popular exhibits such as the recently remodeled primate and large cat building. Each summer, the zoo's amphitheater hosts nationally known jazz musicians and weekly concerts by the Racine Concert Band. The Firehouse 3 Museum, in an authentic fire house, features antique fire fighting equipment including an 1882 steamer, a 1930 pumper, a working Gamewell Telegraphic Alarm System, and a hand-drawn hose cart. A theater shows films and videos on fire prevention. The Modine-Benstead Observatory is open to the public to examine the skies when visibility allows; its facilities include two dome observatories and a main building that houses a telescope, an observation deck, library, and meeting room.

The beautiful grounds of the S.C. Johnson Wax Company, one of the city's largest employers, house the Golden Rondelle Theater, the center for the company's guest relations and public tour program. Originally designed by Lippincott and Margulies as the S.C. Johnson Pavilion at the 1964 World's Fair, it featured the film *To be Alive!*, which summarized the joys of living through sight and sound. After the fair, the theater was relocated to Racine, where the structure was redesigned to complement the Frank Lloyd Wright-designed Administration Building and Research Tower, which is open for tours. The theater, which is also open to the public, features films on flight, ecology, and U.S. history.

West of Racine are rural communities, including Union Grove, Wind Lake, Caledonia, Burlington, and Waterford. These western Racine County towns and cities offer a wide variety of interests including antique shops, parks for picnicking, lakes and rivers for watersports, and farmers markets.

## Arts and Culture

For more than 60 years, the Racine Theatre Guild has produced comedies, suspense thrillers, musicals, and dramas in an 8-play season. The Malt House Theater, in nearby Burlington, is home of the Haylofters, Wisconsin's oldest community theater group. The group presents three productions and a children's play each year in the renovated malt house.

Founded in 1932, the Racine Symphony Orchestra is the only orchestra in the state to perform year-round. The Orchestra performs three distinct concert series annually in addition to a summer Lakeside Pops series. The Racine Choral Arts Society, founded in 1987, performs a varied repertoire ranging from medieval chant to African American gospel. The Chorus schedules solo performances and performs with the Racine and Milwaukee symphony orchestras.

The Racine Art Museum (formerly the Charles A. Wustum Museum of Fine Arts) has, for more than 60 years, provided changing exhibits, classes, tours, and lectures. It features one of the top 10 craft collections in the country and houses a shop with artist-made gifts. The museum is located in a historic Italianate mansion on 13 acres of land, complete with a formal garden. The Racine County Historical Society and Museum, a registered historic landmark, is devoted to the preservation of county artifacts and archives through its exhibits, events, and other educational programs.

## Festivals and Holidays

May's Lakefront Artist Fair features original art and handicrafts by more than 100 artists, and is the Racine Montessori School's major fundraiser. In September the

Racine Antiques Fair at the County Fairgrounds offers one of the Midwest's finest collections of antiques, while later that month Preservation Racine's annual Tour of Historic Homes features tours of houses of historical interest. For more than 16 years, November's Festival of Trees at the Racine on the Lake Festival Hall displays more than 100 professionally decorated Christmas trees, wreaths, and gingerbread houses. Thousands are drawn to May's two-day Chocolate City Festival in nearby Burlington, which features outdoor music, a city bike ride, parade, and many chocolate exhibits—with tasting encouraged.

One of Racine's most popular events is Harbor Fest, held at the Lake Festival Park every June. The festival hosts more than 25 live musical performances on 3 stages, 12 regional restaurants, a children's area, and numerous special events and displays. In July, also along the lakefront, Racine's Big Fish Bash (formerly Salmon-A-Rama) is considered the world's largest freshwater fishing event. The nine-day fishing contest, with prizes totaling $100,000, is accompanied by a festival featuring live music, food vendors, and commercial exhibits.

## Sports for the Spectator

Professional baseball, hockey, soccer, basketball, and football sporting events can be found in Racine and in nearby Kenosha, Milwaukee, and Chicago. The Racine Raiders, part of the North American Football League, stir up semi-pro football excitement at historic Horlick Field.

## Sports for the Participant

The YWCA Riverbend Nature Center, an 80-acre year-round nature and recreation center, offers hiking, bird watching, demonstrations, nature studies, and canoe rental along Racine's Root River. Quarry Lake Park, a former limestone quarry, is a mecca for scuba divers and a great place for swimmers looking for spring-fed waters. The 40-acre park has an expansive sandy beach and an 18-acre lake that varies in depth up to 100 feet. North Beach provides more than a mile of clean, white sandy beach with lifeguards and picnic areas. Sixteen-acre Racine County Harbor Park, which extends out into Lake Michigan, offers fishing, a modern fish-cleaning station, and an observation deck with spectacular views. Visitors can enjoy a peaceful stroll around the Reefpoint Marina. Racine is host to the world's biggest freshwater fishing contest, Big Fish Bash, an annual event that attracts thousands of fishermen to take their shot at landing "the big one."

Racine County is home to a number of 18-hole golf courses and one 27-hole golf course located on rolling green hills. The City of Racine maintains the grounds of more than 85 parks on a total of 1,100 acres that feature baseball diamonds, boat launches, soccer fields, fishing facilities, picnic areas, and tennis courts. The city maintains five community centers. Racine County also offers one of the most complete and varied bicycle trail networks, with a signed 100-mile bicycle route that circles the entire county. Off-road bicycle trails, surfaced with either crushed limestone or blacktop, total more than 17 miles. Lake Michigan provides opportunities for both boating and game fishing.

## Shopping and Dining

The city and county of Racine offer many shops filled with antiques, resale items, and collectibles. A waterfront showplace, downtown Racine, which is linked with the Racine Civic Centre complex and the nearly 1,000-slip Reefpoint Marina, has many beautifully renovated buildings housing fine jewelry shops and unique collections of sportswear, quality clothing, fine furniture, and specialty shops. Porters of Racine, an 80,000 square-foot fine furniture store, is recognized throughout the region and may be the oldest retail establishment in the Midwest. Milaeger's offers a wide variety of flowering plants in more than 70 greenhouses; the company specializes in perennials, and has merchandize pertaining to all facets of gardening and outdoor living. The county is also home to The Seven Mile Fair, Wisconsin's largest flea market. Open every weekend, the market features hundreds of vendors selling clothes, toys, tools, jewelry, electronics, luggage, and more. During the summer months a farmers market is also in operation.

No visit to Racine would be complete without sampling the local delicacy, Danish Kringle, a flaky, oval-shaped coffee cake made of traditional Danish pastry and filled with a variety of fruits or nuts. O&H Danish Bakery, founded in 1949, makes them daily using all-natural ingredients. Kewpee Sandwich Shop, known throughout the Midwest, is one of the oldest hamburger restaurants in the area. Mid-priced family restaurants share the local spotlight with ethnic eateries, including Italian and Chinese, as well as places offering meat and potatoes or the catch of day from the Great Lakes.

*Visitor Information:* Racine County Convention and Visitors Bureau, 14015 Washington Ave., Sturtevant, WI 53177; toll-free (800)C-RACINE

## ■ Convention Facilities

Situated on five acres along the shores of Lake Michigan, Racine Civic Center Festival Park is the city's newest multiuse facility. Opened in 1987, Festival Park can accommodate conventions, trade shows, meetings, art exhibits, and concerts. Facilities include Festival Hall, a 15,700-square-foot area with a theater that can seat 1,500 people, a classroom that can accommodate 1,000, and banquet space for 1,200 people; the Green Room, a 1,050-square-foot space that can handle 75 people in theater-style seating, 50 people classroom-style, and 60 people for banquets; the Colonnade, a free-standing

covered structure measuring nearly 9,000 square feet under its canopy; and a 40-by-80-foot outdoor stage with a 43,000-square-foot concert area.

Overlooking Lake Michigan, the Civic Center's Memorial Hall is the location for many concerts, crafts, and various local functions. It features an 8,400-square-foot main auditorium and the 2,400-square-foot East Hall. Built in 1938 by Frank Lloyd Wright as a private residence, Wingspread, a National Historic Landmark, is a private international conference facility operated by the Johnson Foundation.

*Convention and Meeting Information:* Racine County Convention and Visitors Bureau, 14015 Washington Ave., Sturtevant, WI 53177; toll-free (800) C-RACINE

## ■ Transportation

### Approaching the City

General Mitchell International Airport, located seven miles north of the city in Milwaukee, is the nearest commercial airport. Its 13 airlines offer approximately 235 daily departures and arrivals. Chicago's O'Hare International Airport is 60 miles to the south. Three Racine County general aviation facilities can accommodate all types of business aircraft.

Interstate 94, situated eight miles west of the city, links Racine County with Milwaukee and Chicago. State highways 11, 20, 31, 32, and 38 also serve the city. Passenger service is provided by Amtrak and by Wisconsin Coach Lines, Inc., which provides intercity bus service between Kenosha, Racine, and Milwaukee every day.

### Traveling in the City

The city of Racine owns and operates the Belle Urban System. Downtown Racine Lakefront Trolleys, with clanging bells, shuttle visitors to shops and sites along the lakefront.

## ■ Communications

### Newspapers and Magazines

The daily paper is the morning *Journal Times*. The *Milwaukee Journal Sentinel* publishes a multi-page Racine section that is inserted into the Sunday paper.

### Television and Radio

Racine receives approximately a dozen network, independent, and public television stations from Milwaukee, as well as several Chicago stations. The city has three FM stations and two AM stations and receives many stations from Milwaukee and Chicago.

**Media Information:** *Journal Times,* 212 Fourth St., Racine, WI 53403; telephone (262)634-3322

## Racine Online

City of Racine. Available www.cityofracine.org

Downtown Racine. Available www .downtownracine.com

The Journal Times online. Available www .journaltimes.com

Racine Area Manufacturers and Commerce. Available www.racinechamber.com

Racine County Convention and Visitors Bureau. Available www.visitracine.org

Racine County Economic Development Corporation. Available www.racinecountyedc.org

Racine Public Library. Available www.racinelib.lib .wi.us

Wisconsin Department of Commerce. Available www.commerce.state.wi.us

BIBLIOGRAPHY

Kherdian, David, *I Called It Home* (Blue Crane Books, 1997)

# Cumulative Index

The 199 cities featured in *Cities of the United States,* Volume 1: *The South,* Volume 2: *The West,* Volume 3: *The Midwest,* and Volume 4: *The Northeast,* along with names of individuals, organizations, historical events, etc., are designated in this Cumulative Index by name of the appropriate regional volume, or volumes, followed by the page number(s) on which the term appears in that volume.

## X

## Y

## Z